LANGUAGE, MEMORY, AND COGNITION IN INFANCY AND EARLY CHILDHOOD

LANGUAGE, MEMORY, AND COGNITION IN INFANCY AND EARLY CHILDHOOD

EDITORS-IN-CHIEF

JANETTE B. BENSON
and
MARSHALL M. HAITH
Department of Psychology, University of Denver,
Denver, Colorado, USA

Amsterdam • Boston • Heidelberg • London • New York • Oxford
Paris • San Diego • San Francisco • Singapore • Sydney • Tokyo
Academic Press is an imprint of Elsevier

Academic Press is an imprint of Elsevier
The Boulevard, Langford Lane, Kidlington, Oxford OX5 1GB, UK
525 B Street, Suite 1900, San Diego, CA 92101-4495, USA

First edition 2009

Copyright © 2009 Elsevier Inc. All rights reserved.

The following article is a US Government work in the public domain and is not subject to copyright:
PLAY

No part of this publication may be reproduced, stored in a retrieval system or transmitted in any form or by any means electronic, mechanical, photocopying, recording or otherwise without the prior written permission of the publisher.

Permissions may be sought directly from Elsevier's Science & Technology Rights Department in Oxford, UK: phone (+44) (0) 1865 843830; fax (+44) (0) 1865 853333; email: permissions@elsevier.com. Alternatively, requests may be submitted online by visiting the Elsevier web site at http://elsevier.com/locate/permissions, and selecting *Obtaining permission to use Elsevier material*.

Notice
No responsibility is assumed by the publisher for any injury and/or damage to persons or property as a matter of products liability, negligence or otherwise, or from any use or operation of any methods, products, instructions or ideas contained in the material herein. Because of rapid advances in the medical sciences, in particular, independent verification of diagnoses and drug dosages should be made.

British Library Cataloguing in Publication Data
A catalogue record for this book is available from the British Library

Library of Congress Catalog Number: 2009928182

ISBN: 978-0-12-375069-3

For information on all Elsevier publications
visit our website at books.elsevier.com

PRINTED AND BOUND IN THE USA
09 10 11 12 13   10 9 8 7 6 5 4 3 2 1

Working together to grow libraries in developing countries

www.elsevier.com | www.bookaid.org | www.sabre.org

ELSEVIER   BOOK AID International   Sabre Foundation

CONTENTS

Contents	v–vii
Contributors	ix–xi
Preface	xiii–xiv

A

Amnesia, Infantile	*P J Bauer*	1
Artistic Development	*C Golomb*	12
Attention	*M L Courage and J E Richards*	26

B

Bayley Scales of Infant Development	*E M Lennon, J M Gardner, B Z Karmel, and M J Flory*	37
Bilingualism	*N Sebastián-Gallés, L Bosch, and F Pons*	48
Birth Order	*D L Paulhus*	58
Brain Development	*D Fair and B L Schlaggar*	65
Brain Function	*M de Haan and M Martinos*	79

C

Categorization Skills and Concepts	*L M Oakes*	91
Cognitive Development	*C D Vallotton and K W Fischer*	102
Cognitive Developmental Theories	*G S Halford*	114
Cognitive Neuroscience	*M H Johnson*	125
Critical Periods	*D B Bailey and J-L Gariépy*	134

D

Developmental Disabilities: Cognitive	*S L Pillsbury and R B David*	147

E

Exploration and Curiosity	*A Baxter and H N Switzky*	157

F

Future Orientation   *N Wentworth* — 169

G

Genetics and Inheritance   *A Balasubramanian, J Koontz, and C A Reynolds* — 181

Grammar   *D Matthews and M Tomasello* — 192

H

Habituation and Novelty   *K A Snyder and C M Torrence* — 205

Head Start   *J W Hagen and F G Lamb-Parker* — 217

Humor   *D Bergen* — 227

I

Imagination and Fantasy   *J D Woolley and A Tullos* — 237

Imitation and Modeling   *A N Meltzoff and R A Williamson* — 247

Intellectual Disabilities   *D J Fidler and J S Jameson* — 256

L

Language Acquisition Theories   *S Goldin-Meadow* — 267

Language Development: Overview   *E Lieven* — 277

Learning   *R L Gómez* — 290

Literacy   *C M Connor and S Al'Otaiba* — 301

M

Mathematical Reasoning   *K McCrink and K Wynn* — 315

Memory   *H Hayne and J Richmond* — 325

Milestones: Cognitive   *M W Daehler* — 337

N

Neonativism   *A Needham and K Libertus* — 347

O

Object Concept   *S P Johnson and K C Soska* — 357

P

Perception and Action   *B I Bertenthal* — 369

Piaget's Cognitive-Developmental Theory   *J P Byrnes* — 381

Play	*M Sumaroka and M H Bornstein*	390
Pragmatic Development	*N Akhtar and K Herold*	399
Preverbal Development and Speech Perception	*R Panneton, M McIlreavy, and N Bhullar*	409

R

Reasoning in Early Development	*E K Scholnick*	421

S

School Readiness	*F J Morrison and A H Hindman*	433
Self Knowledge	*A E Bigelow*	445
Semantic Development	*J Bhagwat and M Casasola*	456
Separation and Stranger Anxiety	*A Scher and J Harel*	466
Speech Perception	*G W McRoberts*	476
Symbolic Thought	*S M Carlson and P D Zelazo*	485

T

Theory of Mind	*J W Astington and L A Dack*	495
Twins	*L F DiLalla, P Y Mullineaux, and K K Elam*	508

Index	519

CONTRIBUTORS

N Akhtar
University of California, Santa Cruz, Santa Cruz, CA, USA

S Al'Otaiba
Florida State University, Tallahassee, FL, USA

J W Astington
University of Toronto, Toronto, ON, Canada

D B Bailey
RTI International, Research Triangle Park, NC, USA

A Balasubramanian
University of California, Riverside, Riverside, CA, USA

P J Bauer
Emory University, Atlanta, GA, USA

A Baxter
University of South Alabama, Mobile, AL, USA

D Bergen
Miami University, Oxford, OH, USA

B I Bertenthal
Indiana University, Bloomington, IN, USA

J Bhagwat
Cornell University, Ithaca, NY, USA

N Bhullar
Widener University, Chester, PA, USA

A E Bigelow
St. Francis Xavier University, Antigonish, NS, Canada

M H Bornstein
National Institutes of Health, Bethesda, MD, USA

L Bosch
Universitat de Barcelona, Barcelona, Spain

J P Byrnes
Temple University, Philadelphia, PA, USA

S M Carlson
Institute of Child Development, Minneapolis, MN, USA

M Casasola
Cornell University, Ithaca, NY, USA

C M Connor
Florida State University, Tallahassee, FL, USA

M L Courage
Memorial University, St. John's, NL, Canada

L A Dack
University of Toronto, Toronto, ON, Canada

M W Daehler
University of Massachusetts, Amherst, MA, USA

R B David
St. Mary's Hospital, Richmond, VA, USA

L F DiLalla
Southern Illinois University School of Medicine, Carbondale, IL, USA

K K Elam
Southern Illinois University School of Medicine, Carbondale, IL, USA

D Fair
Washington University School of Medicine, St. Louis, MO, USA

D J Fidler
Colorado State University, Fort Collins, CO, USA

K W Fischer
Harvard Graduate School of Education, Cambridge, MA, USA

M J Flory
New York State Institute for Basic Research, Staten Island, NY, USA

J M Gardner
New York State Institute for Basic Research, Staten Island, NY, USA

J-L Gariépy
The University of North Carolina at Chapel Hill, Chapel Hill, NC, USA

R L Gómez
The University of Arizona, Tucson, AZ, USA

S Goldin-Meadow
University of Chicago, Chicago, IL, USA

C Golomb
University of Massachusetts, Boston, Boston, MA, USA

Contributors

M de Haan
University College London Institute of Child Health, London, UK

J W Hagen
University of Michigan, Ann Arbor, MI, USA

G S Halford
Griffith University, Brisbane, QLD, Australia

J Harel
University of Haifa, Haifa, Israel

H Hayne
University of Otago, Dunedin, New Zealand

K Herold
University of California, Santa Cruz, Santa Cruz, CA, USA

A H Hindman
University of Michigan, Ann Arbor, MI, USA

J S Jameson
Colorado State University, Fort Collins, CO, USA

M H Johnson
University of London, London, UK

S P Johnson
New York University, New York, NY, USA

B Z Karmel
New York State Institute for Basic Research, Staten Island, NY, USA

J Koontz
University of California, Riverside, Riverside, CA, USA

F G Lamb-Parker
Columbia University, New York, NY, USA

E M Lennon
New York State Institute for Basic Research, Staten Island, NY, USA

K Libertus
Duke University, Durham, NC, USA

E Lieven
Max Planck Institute for Evolutionary Anthropology, Leipzig, Germany

M Martinos
University College London Institute of Child Health, London, UK

D Matthews
University of Manchester, Manchester, UK

K McCrink
Yale University, New Haven, CT, USA

M McIlreavy
University of Georgia, Athens, GA, USA

G W McRoberts
Haskins Laboratories, New Haven, CT, USA

A N Meltzoff
University of Washington, Seattle, WA, USA

F J Morrison
University of Michigan, Ann Arbor, MI, USA

P Y Mullineaux
Southern Illinois University School of Medicine, Carbondale, IL, USA

A Needham
Duke University, Durham, NC, USA

L M Oakes
University of California, Davis, Davis, CA, USA

R Panneton
Virginia Tech, Blacksburg, VA, USA

D L Paulhus
University of British Columbia, Vancouver, BC, Canada

S L Pillsbury
Richmond, VA, USA

F Pons
Universitat de Barcelona, Barcelona, Spain

C A Reynolds
University of California, Riverside, Riverside, CA, USA

J E Richards
University of South Carolina, Columbia, SC, USA

J Richmond
Harvard University, Boston, MA, USA

A Scher
University of Haifa, Haifa, Israel

B L Schlaggar
Washington University School of Medicine, St. Louis, MO, USA

E K Scholnick
University of Maryland, College Park, MD, USA

N Sebastián-Gallés
Universitat de Barcelona, Barcelona, Spain

K A Snyder
University of Denver, Denver, CO, USA

K C Soska
New York University, New York, NY, USA

M Sumaroka
National Institutes of Health, Bethesda, MD, USA

H N Switzky
Northern Illinois University, DeKalb, IL, USA

M Tomasello
Max Planck Institute for Evolutionary Anthropology, Leipzig, Germany

C M Torrence
University of Denver, Denver, CO, USA

A Tullos
The University of Texas, Austin, TX, USA

C D Vallotton
Harvard Graduate School of Education, Cambridge, MA, USA

N Wentworth
Lake Forest College, Lake Forest, IL, USA

R A Williamson
University of Washington, Seattle, WA, USA

J D Woolley
The University of Texas, Austin, TX, USA

K Wynn
Yale University, New Haven, CT, USA

P D Zelazo
Institute of Child Development, Minneapolis, MN, USA

PREFACE

In 2008, Elsevier published the three-volume Encyclopedia of Infant and Early Childhood Development, encompassing all aspects of development in the 0–3 age range. Articles were selected on the basis of where there were significant bodies of research and/or significant interest in what constitutes normal development, how it progresses, milestones, and what may adversely or positively affect that development. The original three-volume work was a successful publication for library purchase. It seems a shame, however, to have such succinct, eminently readable research summaries by our most distinguished researchers be limited only to libraries. Hence the birth of this volume, selecting only those articles relating to language, memory, and cognition development, and intended for individual purchase.

Because the articles are only those that were included on this topic in the larger work, we cannot say that the coverage is necessarily soup to nuts on all topics relating to language, memory, and cognition. We were looking for balance in the larger work across all elements of development, and hence we were selective in topic coverage relative to other aspects of development. What this means is that you have larger, more inclusive articles and on those topics with the strongest research base rather than more numerous but narrowly focused topics that could have been largely theoretical.

Contents

Several strands run through this work, and they reflect the current themes inherent in the work of developmental psychologists, including the interaction of genes and environment. Of course, the nature-nurture debate is one strand, but no one seriously stands at one or the other end of this controversy any more. Although advances in genetics and behavior genetics have been breathtaking, even the genetics work has documented the role of environment in development, and researchers acknowledge that experience can change the wiring of the brain as well as how actively the genes are expressed. There is increasing appreciation that the child develops in a transactional context, with the child's effect on the parents and others playing no small role in his or her own development.

There has been increasing interest in brain development, partly fostered by the Decade of the Brain in the 1990s, as we have learned more about the role of early experience in shaping the brain and, consequently, personality, emotion, and intelligence. The "brainy baby" movement has rightly aroused interest in infants' surprising capabilities, but the full picture of how abilities develop is being fleshed out as researchers learn as much about what infants cannot do as well as of what they are able. Parents wait for verifiable information about how advances may promote effective parenting.

The central focus of the articles is on typical development. However, considerable attention is also paid to psychological and medical pathology in our attempt to provide readers with a complete picture of the state of knowledge about early language, memory, and cognition development. We asked authors to tell a complete story in their articles, assuming that readers will come to this work with a particular topic in mind, rather than reading the volume whole or many articles at one time. As a result, there is some overlap between articles at the edges; one can think of partly overlapping circles of content, which was a design principle in as much as nature does not neatly carve topics in human development into discrete slices for our convenience. At the end of each article, readers will find suggestions for further readings that will permit them to take off in one neighboring direction or another, as well as web sites where they can garner additional information of interest.

Coverage in this volume includes articles that span a broad array of topics. For example, there are articles on basic language, memory, and cognition processes (e.g., attention, cognitive milestones, grammar, habituation and novelty, imitation and modeling, language development, memory, object concept, perception and action, preverbal development and speech perception, mathematical reasoning, symbolic thought), factors that influence the development of language, memory, and cognition (e.g., birth order, brain development, brain function, critical periods, genetics and inheritance,

Head Start, school readiness), and theories and frameworks that guide and challenge research (e.g., cognitive developmental theories, cognitive neuroscience, neonativism, Piaget's Cognitive-Developmental Theory).

Interest in and opinion about early human development is woven through human history from as early as the Greek and Roman eras, repeated through the ages to the current day. Even earlier, the Bible provided advice about nutrition during pregnancy and rearing practices. But the science of human development can be traced back little more than 100 years, and one cannot help but be impressed by the advances in methodologies that are documented in this volume for learning about infants and toddlers. Scientific advances lean heavily on methods, and few areas have matched the growth of knowledge about human development over the last few decades. The reader will be introduced not only to current knowledge in this field but also to how that knowledge is acquired and the promise of these methods for future discoveries.

Audience

Articles have been prepared for a broad readership, including advanced undergraduates, graduate students, working professionals in allied fields, parents, and even researchers in their own disciplines. We plan to use several of these articles as readings for our own seminars.

A project of this scale involves many actors. We are very appreciative of the advice and review efforts of our original editorial advisory board, as well as the efforts of our authors, to abide by the guidelines that we set out for them. Nikki Levy, the editor at Elsevier for this work, has been a constant source of wise advice, consolation, and balance. Her vision and encouragement made this project possible. Barbara Makinster, also from Elsevier, provided many valuable suggestions for us, and we thank her, along with the Production team in England. It is difficult to communicate all the complexities of a project this vast; let us just say that we are thankful for the resource base that Elsevier provided. Finally, we thank our families and colleagues for their patience over the past few years.

Janette B. Benson
and
Marshall M. Haith

Amnesia, Infantile

P J Bauer, Emory University, Atlanta, GA, USA

© 2008 Elsevier Inc. All rights reserved.

Glossary

Autobiographical memory – Constituted of memories of specific events from the past that have relevance to the self; also characterized by a sense of reliving at the time of retrieval from memory.

Autonoetic awareness – Conscious or self-knowing awareness; in the case of autobiographical memory, awareness that the source of one's memory is an event that happened at some point in the past.

Childhood amnesia – Synonymous with infantile amnesia; the relative paucity among adults for memories of events from the first 3 years of life and a gradual increase in memories of events from ages 3–7 years, when an adult-like distribution is reached.

Elaborative style – A narrative style adopted by some parents in conversations with their children, marked by more cues to and details about past events, and invitations to the child to co-construct the story of the event.

Hippocampus – Medial temporal structure implicated in the encoding and consolidation of new memories of events and experiences.

Infantile amnesia – Synonymous with childhood amnesia.

Repetitive style – A narrative style adopted by some parents in conversations with their children, marked by repetition of questions seeking specific information, fewer cues and details, and overall fewer contributions to conversations.

Temporal cortical network – Network of neural structures implicated in memory for past events and experiences; includes cortical and medial temporal structures, including the hippocampus.

Introduction

Infantile or childhood amnesia is the relative paucity among adults for autobiographical memories from early childhood. It is virtually universal yet there are individual and group differences in its offset and density. Explanation of the amnesia requires understanding of the development of autobiographical memory in childhood, the course of which is multiply determined, by factors ranging from brain development to culture. These multiple dynamic sources of variance contribute to differences in the rate of formation of memories and the rate at which they are forgotten. The crossover of these complementary functions marks the offset of infantile amnesia.

Infantile Amnesia

Adults have relatively continuous personal histories from about the age of 7 years onward. That is, adults can recall events that took place from age 7 years or older, place them in spatial and temporal context, and attribute to them some degree of personal relevance or significance. Prior to age 7 years, however, most adults suffer from an amnesic syndrome that has two phases. From the first phase – prior to age 3 years – adults have few if any personal or autobiographical memories. From the second phase – between the ages of 3 and 7 years – adults have a smaller number of autobiographical memories than would be expected based on forgetting alone. In the literature, this two-part phenomenon is known as infantile amnesia or childhood amnesia.

For What Is There Amnesia?

Childhood amnesia is a paucity of a certain type of memory known as autobiographical memory. Autobiographical memories relate to events that happened to one's self; events in which one participated; and about which one had emotions, thoughts, reactions, and reflections. From a theoretical standpoint, childhood amnesia is interesting and important because of its implications for one's sense of self. Although we consider ourselves as continuous in space and time, there is a point in development at which that continuity ends. That moment in time is the boundary of childhood amnesia. Childhood amnesia thus presents itself as apparent evidence of discontinuity in development.

In addition to the defining feature of self-relevance, autobiographical memories have a number of characteristic features. They tend to (1) be of unique events that happened at a specific place, at a specific time; (2) entail a sense of conscious, autonoetic, or self-knowing awareness that one is re-experiencing an event that happened at some point in the past; (3) be expressed verbally; (4) be long-lasting; and (5) be veridical. This family resemblance definition of autobiographical memory (i.e., a concept specified by characteristic, as opposed to defining, features) has important implications for how we conceptualize its developmental course (see section entitled 'Explaining autobiographical memory development').

The Phenomenon of Infantile or Childhood Amnesia

Age of Earliest Memory

Research on the phenomenon that would come to be called childhood amnesia dates back to the 1890s when scholars conducted surveys of adults asking them to think about the earliest experience they could remember, and how old they were at the time. The results were consistent, with respondents dating their earliest memories to age 3 years. The phenomenon received its name in 1905, when Sigmund Freud coined the term to describe the early memories of some of his patients. He noticed that few of the adults he saw in his psychoanalytic practice had memories from their early years and that the memories they did have were sketchy and incomplete.

Subsequent to these early investigations, numerous studies of adults' memories of their childhoods have been conducted. They have yielded one of the most robust findings in the memory literature, namely, that in Western cultures, among adults, the average age of earliest autobiographical memory is 3–3.5 years. This age is obtained whether participants are asked to respond to free recall prompts such as those used by the early researchers of the phenomenon, or whether they are asked to remember a specific event the date of which is clearly known, such as the birth of a younger sibling.

Distribution of Early Memories

The age of earliest memory is only one component of the definition of childhood amnesia. The second component is that from the ages of 3 to 7 years, the number of memories that adults are able to retrieve is smaller than the number expected based on forgetting alone. Normal forgetting is a linear function of the time since experience of an event. Among adults, however, there is an under-representation of memories from ages 3 to 7 years. The strongest evidence of this under-representation is from studies employing the cue-word technique: respondents are asked to provide a memory related to each of a number of cue words (e.g., ice cream), and to estimate how old they were at the time of the event. From these data researchers have created distributions of memories over the first decade of life; a sample such distribution is illustrated in **Figure 1**. Both components of childhood amnesia are clearly apparent in the figure. Respondents report few memories from the period before age 3 years. The number of memories reported increases gradually from 3 to 7 years, at which time a steeper, more adult-like distribution is observed. This pattern has proved to

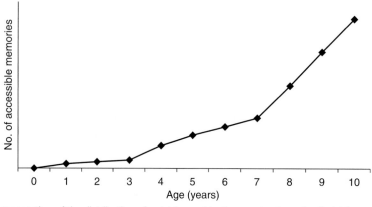

Figure 1 Schematic representation of the distribution of autobiographical memories from the first 10 years of life.

be quite robust. It is observed regardless of the specific method used to elicit the memories and the age of the respondents at the time the memories were cued.

The Universality of Childhood Amnesia

One of the features of childhood amnesia that makes it so compelling is its universality. That is, virtually every adult suffers from it, to one extent or another. That does not mean that its form is identical across individuals, however. There are individual and group differences in the timing of its offset, in its density, and in the content of reports of early memories. The differences are interesting and important in their own right. They also are critical to evaluation of theories as to the sources of childhood amnesia in that an adequate theory must account not only for the normative trend, but for individual and group differences as well.

Individual Differences

Whereas more than a century of research has revealed age 3–3.5 years as the average age of earliest memory, from the beginning of the study of adults' early autobiographical memories, individual differences in the age of earliest memory have been apparent. In virtually all historical and contemporary reports of adults' early autobiographical memories that provide information on variability, there are instances of a small number of memories from the first year of life. Memories from at least some respondents from age 2 years are more the rule than the exception. There are also differences in the latest early memory, with some adults reporting their earliest memory from as old as 6–9 years of age. There are few developmental phenomena for which the age of onset is so variable. In addition to differences in the age of earliest memory, there are individual differences among adults in the density of early memories. That is, some adults are able to recall many memories from their childhood years, whereas others remember only a few.

Group Differences

Table 1 summarizes some of the groups for which differences in the age of earliest memory have been reported, three of which are discussed below.

Gender. Of all the possible sources of group difference in the age of earliest memory one could contemplate, possible gender differences have received the most attention. A consistent finding is that women have memories from earlier in life than do men. In some cases the differences are statistically reliable, whereas in other cases they are not. Regardless of their statistical reliability, differences in the ages of earliest memories for women and men typically are small in magnitude.

Table 1 Group differences in the age of earliest memory

Source of variance in age of earliest memory	Groups reporting earlier and later memories	
	Earlier early memories	Later early memories
Gender	Women	Men
Birth order	First-borns	Later-borns
Culture group	Western cultures	Eastern cultures
Family moved before age 4 years	Yes	No
Attended preschool	Yes	No

There are also some reports of differences in the length of women's and men's reports of early childhood events, in their affective qualities, and in the interpersonal themes represented in them. Specifically (1) women tend to provide longer, more detailed, and more vivid accounts of their early memories, relative to men; (2) women more often refer to anger, shame, and guilt in the earliest memories relative to men; and (3) women's early emotional memories tend to concern attachment issues (i.e., concerns regarding security, approval, separation, and reunion), whereas those of men tend to concern competence issues (i.e., concerns regarding ability, performance, achievement, and identity).

Birth order. Although it has received significantly less research attention, relative to gender, birth order also has been found to be systematically related to age of earliest memory. Children who are first-born have earlier memories than children who are later-born. There also appear to be differences in the age of earliest memory as a function of the number of children in the family, and their spacing. Only-children have earlier autobiographical memories, relative to the oldest children in multichild families. First-borns for whom there is a larger difference in ages between themselves and their oldest siblings report autobiographical memories from earlier in life, relative to first-borns whose oldest siblings are more closely spaced.

Culture. Most of the research on adults' early memories has been conducted with individuals from Western societies, including Canada, the UK, and the US. Studies with individuals from Eastern cultures make clear the limits to generalizability of the findings from Western culture. There are systematic differences in the age of earliest memory with Western samples reporting memories from earlier in life, relative to the Eastern samples. In some cases the differences are pronounced, with American adults reporting memories that are a year or more earlier than adults from Eastern cultures.

There are also cultural differences in the content of adult women's and men's reports of their early experiences. For example, relative to respondents from Eastern cultures, Americans provide longer memory narratives; their memories are more frequently of a single event or specific memory, as opposed to a more general memory; and they more frequently comment on their own experiences and attitudes, including emotions and feeling states.

Explaining Infantile or Childhood Amnesia

Why is it that adults experience amnesia for events from the first 3–3.5 years of life, and have fewer memories from the ages of 3 to 7 years than would be expected based on forgetting alone? There are two major categories of theories to explain childhood amnesia. By one category of accounts, memories for early-life events are formed, but later functionally disappear or become inaccessible. By the other category of accounts, adults lack memories of events from infancy and very early childhood because, in effect, no memories were created. Alternatively, memories were created but lacked an important feature or features that precluded them from being entered into the autobiographical record.

Memories Are Formed but Become Inaccessible

One category of explanation for childhood amnesia suggests that young children and perhaps even infants form memories of the events of their lives, but that over the course of time and development, these early memories become inaccessible.

Freud's explanation in terms of repression and screening. In 1905, Sigmund Freud delivered a lecture in which he gave infantile or childhood amnesia its name. In the lecture he commented on the fact that the first 6–8 years of life are full of accomplishments (e.g., children learn to walk and talk, they accrue a lot of knowledge about the world, and so forth) yet adults remember few of the experiences that led to them. He further commented that the memories that survive seem unreliable. He deemed them unreliable because the early memories that his patients reported were not of the psychic struggles that Freud assumed consumed much of mental life but of bland, unemotional, and often commonplace events and experiences. Freud was also impressed by the observation that his patients often described their memories from the unrealistic third-person perspective. That is, rather than through the eyes of the beholder, the memories were described as from the perspective of a third party. Given that this was an impossible perspective for an autobiographical memory, Freud concluded that these memories were the result of reconstructive processes. Based on these observations, Freud advanced the theory that early memories were blockaded or screened from consciousness. He suggested that the relative paucity of early memories was due to repression of inappropriate or disturbing content of early, often traumatic (due to their sexual nature) experiences. Events that were not repressed were altered to remove the offending content. In effect, he hypothesized that the negative emotion in these memories was screened off, leaving only the bland skeleton of a significant experience.

Freud's explanation for childhood amnesia in terms of repression and affective screening was internally consistent with his larger theoretical framework. External to the theory, however, the explanation has not fared especially well. One issue is that although adults remember fewer early-life events than would be expected based on forgetting alone, they nevertheless have more memories from childhood than would be expected by Freud's model of repression. In addition, contrary to the suggestion that memories of early-life events would be devoid of emotion or overwhelmingly positive, both traumatic and non-traumatic events from childhood are recalled. In some studies, memories of negative episodes actually outnumber positive episodes. A second issue is that although many early memories are from the third-person perspective, there are also many from the first-person perspective. Moreover, many later memories are from the third-person perspective. Some scholars suggest that the perspective adopted has more to do with the event being remembered than age at the time it occurred. Today, Freud's suggestions of repression and screening of early memories generally are not considered adequate explanations for childhood amnesia.

Different cognitive lenses. The second exemplar of an explanation of childhood amnesia in terms of memories that are formed but become inaccessible is actually not itself a unified theory. Instead, it is a category of explanations that has in common the suggestion that there are different cognitive lenses for different times of life. As individuals change lenses over the course of their lives, they lose the ability to access memories created with the old lens type (not unlike the inaccessibility that results from a change in operating systems on a computer). By some accounts, the lenses differ in their reliance on language. Because they lack language, infants and young children encode memories visually or imaginally, but not symbolically. With the advent of language skills, exclusively nonverbal encoding gives way to primarily verbal encoding. As the system becomes more and more verbally saturated, it becomes increasingly difficult to gain access to memories encoded without language.

Other accounts place emphasis not on language but on differences in life periods, each of which has distinct hopes, fears, and challenges, for example. Life periods may correspond to elementary vs. secondary school vs. college, or before vs. after marriage, or before vs. after retirement. Memories from different lifetime periods may differ from those from the current period not only because of the passage of time, but because of the new phase of life, which may herald concomitant changes in thinking or world view.

Models that implicate different cognitive lenses as the explanation for childhood amnesia make two critical predictions, namely, that (1) early memories are not accessible later in life, and (2) memories from within a life period should be more readily accessible than memories across life periods. Though it is negative in nature, there is overwhelming evidence for the first of these predictions. If we allow that infants and children form memories (see section titled 'Explaining autobiographical memory development' for evidence that they do), then the very phenomenon of childhood amnesia is one of later inaccessibility of early memories. Critically, there is no direct evidence that developments in language actually *cause* early memories to become inaccessible. Moreover, although preverbal memories do not readily lend themselves to verbal description, under some circumstances, they can be described with language once it is acquired.

There is evidence that memories from within a life period are more readily accessible than memories across life periods. Some of the most compelling illustrations come from studies in which immigrants are asked to retrieve memories of events that took place before vs. after they emigrated. Memories retrieved from the time before immigration more frequently are in the native language and memories retrieved from the time after immigration more frequently are in the language of the adopted home. Similarly, cue words from the native language elicit memories from before immigration, whereas cue words from the language of the adopted home elicit memories from after immigration. Thus, it seems that memories from within a life period are more accessible in the language of that period. Other reasons why memories might become differentially accessible over time are discussed in 'Explaining autobiographical memory development'.

Autobiographical Memories of Early Life Events Are Lacking

The second category of explanation of childhood amnesia suggests that adults have few autobiographical memories from infancy and very early childhood because during this period no such memories were formed, due to general or more specific cognitive deficits. Similarly, these accounts explain that the number of memories that adults have from the preschool period is smaller than would be expected based on forgetting alone because during this period autobiographical memory competence is under construction and so, consequently, there are relatively fewer memories from this period.

The suggestion that cognitive deficits explain the relative paucity of memories from early in life has had a number of proponents but the name that is most readily associated with the perspective is Jean Piaget. Although Piaget did not advance a specific theory of childhood amnesia, he nonetheless provided a compelling explanation for it. He maintained that for the first 18–24 months of life, infants and children did not have the capacity for symbolic representation. As a result, they could not mentally represent objects and entities in their absence. They thus had no mechanism for recall of past events.

Piaget further suggested that even once children had constructed the capacity to represent past events, they still were without the cognitive structures that would permit them to organize events along coherent dimensions that would make the events memorable. One of the most significant dimensions that Piaget suggested preschool-age children lacked was an understanding of temporal order. Specifically, he suggested that it was not until children were ~5–7 years of age that they developed the ability to sequence events temporally. Without this fundamental organizational device, children were not able to form coherent memories of the events of their lives. The more contemporary, so-called neo-Piagetian perspectives suggest that limits on cognitive capacity (e.g., working memory capacity) either prevent information from being encoded in an accessible format to begin with, or that limitations on retrieval mechanisms prevent it from being recalled at a later time.

There are also suggestions that specific conceptual changes play a role in the explanation of childhood amnesia. By some accounts, adults have few memories from early in life because, for the first 2 years, there is no 'cognitive self' around which memories can be organized. As a consequence, there is no 'auto' in autobiographical. By other accounts, for the first 5–7 years of their lives, children lack autonoetic awareness, rendering it impossible for them to create memories that have this characteristic feature. As a consequence, autobiographical memories are not formed and thus are not available to be retrieved by adults.

The suggestions that infants and very young children lack the symbolic capacity to form memories and that the memories of preschool-age children are disorganized are no longer tenable. As will be seen in the next section, even in the first year of life infants encode and later retrieve memories of past events. Nevertheless, there are pronounced changes in the basic processes of memory, which have implications for the reliability, robustness, and temporal extent of memory through infancy and early childhood. Thus, although infants and very young children are no longer seen as total mnemonically incompetent, neither are their memory systems as effective and efficient as those of adults. The differences have implications for the density of representation of autobiographical memories from the early years of life (see section—entitled 'Explaining autobiographical memory development'). Finally, it is increasingly apparent that no single factor, such as development of a self concept or absence of autonoetic awareness, will provide a sufficient explanation for why autobiographical memory seems to begin when it does or why adults lack autobiographical memories from a period of their lives (respectively). Rather, it is recognized that autobiographical memory is a complex, multifaceted capacity, the development and operation of which are influenced by many factors.

Explaining Autobiographical Memory Development

Autobiographical memory involves a number of capacities and skills. It requires that events and experiences be encoded and stored in an accessible manner, and later retrieved. Once retrieved, the memory must be expressed. The most informative expression is via a narrative that provides the listener with information about the who, what, where, when, why, and how of the event. Moreover, autobiographical memories are of events that happened to the self at a specific place and time. They are accurate, long-lasting, and when they are retrieved, there is a sense of awareness that they are based on past experience. Critically, each of these aspects of the ability has its own developmental course. An adequate explanation of the development of autobiographical memory – and thus of achievement of an adult-like distribution of memories – must recognize this complexity as well as account for the individual and group variability that is apparent in autobiographical records. This is best accomplished by undertaking analysis at multiple levels, ranging from the brain systems that support memory to the cultural influences on verbal expression of memory.

The Neural Substrate of Autobiographical Memory and Its Development

The ability to encode, store, and later retrieve autobiographical memories depends on a multicomponent neural network that includes structures in the medial temporal lobes (including the hippocampus), as well as neocortical structures. The network is schematically represented in **Figure 2**. Specifically, primary, secondary, and association cortices register what we are seeing, smelling, hearing, and so forth, and integrate it all into a coherent experience. For that experience to endure beyond the moment, it must be consolidated into a memory trace. Consolidation depends on neurochemical and neuroanatomical changes that create a physical record of the experience. The processes are carried out by medial temporal structures in general and the hippocampus in particular, in concert with the cortex. Throughout the period of consolidation – which may take weeks to months in the human – memories are vulnerable to disruption and interference. Eventually, however, they become stabilized,

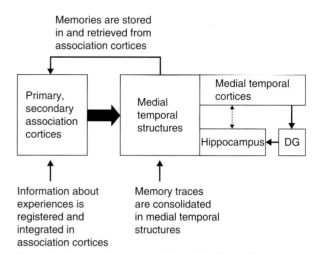

Figure 2 Schematic representation of the flow of information through the temporal cortical network responsible for formation of autobiographical memories. DG, dentate gyrus.

and no longer require the participation of the hippocampus for their survival. Rather, they are maintained in the cortices that gave rise to the original experience. Finally, the prefrontal cortex in particular is implicated in retrieval of memory traces from these long-term stores.

Portions of the medial temporal structures mature relatively early. For instance, the cells that make up most of the hippocampus are formed in the first half of gestation and, by the end of the prenatal period, virtually all have migrated to their adult locations. In some areas of the hippocampus, synapses are present as early as 15 weeks gestational age. By ~6 postnatal months, the number and density of synapses have reached adult levels, as has glucose utilization in the temporal cortex. In contrast, development of the dentate gyrus of the hippocampus is protracted. At birth, the dentate gyrus includes only ~70% of the adult number of cells and it is not until 12–15 postnatal months that the morphology of the structure appears adult-like. Maximum density of synaptic connections in the dentate gyrus is also reached relatively late. The density of synapses increases dramatically (to well above adult levels) beginning at 8–12 postnatal months and reaches its peak at 16–20 months. After a period of relative stability, excess synapses are pruned until adult levels are reached at ~4–5 years of age.

The association areas also develop slowly. For instance, it is not until the seventh prenatal month that all six cortical layers are apparent. The density of synapses in prefrontal cortex increases dramatically beginning at 8 postnatal months and peaks between 15 and 24 months. Pruning to adult levels is delayed until puberty and beyond. Other maturational changes in the prefrontal cortex, such as myelination, continue into adolescence, and adult levels of some neurotransmitters are not seen until the second and third decades of life.

The full temporal cortical network can be expected to function as an integrated whole only once each of its components, as well as the connections between them, has reached a level of functional maturity. This leads to the prediction of emergence of long-term memory by late in the first year of life, with significant development over the course of the second year, and continued (albeit less dramatic) development for years thereafter. The timeframe is based on increases in the formation of new synapses beginning at ~8 months in both the dentate gyrus and prefrontal cortex, with continued synaptogenesis through 20 and 24 months, respectively. The expectation of developmental changes for months and years thereafter stems from the schedule of protracted selective reduction in synapses both in the dentate gyrus (until 4–5 years) and in the prefrontal cortex (throughout adolescence or early adulthood).

Developments in Basic Memory Processes

The relatively late development of aspects of the temporal cortical network has implications for behavior. Because of their involvement in all phases of the life of a memory, protracted development of cortical structures can be expected to impact the encoding, consolidation, and storage, as well as retrieval, of memories. Late development of the dentate gyrus of the hippocampus is critical because, at least in the adult, it is the major means by which information makes its way from the cortex into the hippocampus where new memory traces are consolidated for long-term storage (see **Figure 2**). The immaturity of these structures and connections between them would present challenges to these processes. As they develop, we would expect to see age-related changes in behavior.

The time course of changes in behavior matches what is known about developments in the temporal cortical memory network. Using nonverbal measures of memory (elicited and deferred imitation in which props are used to produce novel sequences of actions that infants are invited to imitate), researchers have demonstrated that between 9 and 20 months of age, the length of time over which recall is apparent increases dramatically, from 1 to 12 months. Over the same period, the robustness of memory increases such that infants remember more, based on fewer experiences of events. In addition, long-term memory is more reliably observed. Whereas at 9 months of age only ~50% of infants show evidence of long-term recall, by 20 months, individual differences in whether or not infants recall are the exception rather than the rule (though there remain individual differences in how much is remembered).

Because the actions and sequences on which infants are tested are novel to them, their behavior provides evidence that they are able to remember unique events. Moreover, because infants recall sequences in the correct temporal order, there is evidence that they remember when events occurred. Infants also demonstrate that they remember specific features of events, in that they reliably select the correct objects from arrays including objects that are different from, yet perceptually similar to, those used to produce event sequences. These behaviors make clear that by the end of the second year of life, children have many of the memory skills necessary to form an autobiography.

Over the course of the preschool years, memory abilities change in at least two important ways that are relevant to developments in autobiographical memory. First, memory processes sharpen to the point that a single experience of an event is sufficient to ensure retention over the long term. Prior to the preschool years, very long retention is seemingly dependent on multiple experiences of an event. In contrast, by the age of 3–4 years, children remember events experienced only once. This age-related change likely is linked to developments in the temporal cortical network supporting memory. Second, children develop the ability to locate events in a particular time and place. This development is apparent in age-related increases in the use of temporal markers such as yesterday and last summer, for example. Such markers serve as a time line along which records of events can be ordered. These and other changes in basic memory abilities mean that more events can be stored with more of the elements of autobiographical memories: unique events, with distinctive features, accurately located in time and place, that are maintained for long periods of time.

Developments in Nonmnemonic Abilities

Developments in nonmemory abilities also contribute to age-related improvements in autobiographical memory. Two of the most prominent have already been mentioned: changes in self-concept and development of autonoetic awareness.

Self-concept. Because autobiographical memories are about one's self, a self-concept is a necessary ingredient for an autobiographical memory. Children's first references to themselves in past events occur at about the same point in developmental time as they begin to recognize themselves in a mirror. In the second half of the second year of life, children who recognize themselves in the mirror have more robust event memories and they make faster progress in independent autobiographical reports, relative to children who do not yet exhibit self-recognition. Over the preschool years, there are further developments in recognition of continuity of self over time, both in physical features and in psychological characteristics. These developments have implications for autobiographical memory: for a past event to be relevant to present self, the rememberer must realize that the self who is remembering is the same as the self who experienced the event in the past. Also over the preschool years children develop a more subjective perspective on experience. This facilitates inclusion of events in an autobiographical record because experiences are not just objective events that play out, but are events that influence the self in one way or another. The personal significance of the events is conveyed, in particular, by references to the emotional and cognitive states of the one who experiences. Such references indicate the sense of personal ownership and unique perspective that is so characteristic of autobiographical memories. Together, these and other developments in the self concept mean that more aspects of more events have relevance to the self thus providing more opportunity for formation of self-relevant memories.

Autonoetic awareness. Retrieval of autobiographical memories is accompanied by autonoetic awareness: an understanding that the recollected event is one that happened in the past. It is not until children are 4–6 years of age that they reliably identify the sources of their knowledge. This ability aids in location of events in space and time, thereby contributing to the specificity of memories (as discussed earlier in this section). Understanding that the source of a current cognition is a past event can also contribute to better event narratives. Children who have this realization can be expected to provide their listeners with orientation to the circumstances of the past; to advise them of the specifics of the event, such as who was there and where it took place; and to provide their own subjective perspective on the event. Consistent with this suggestion, 3.5–4.5-year-olds who perform better on tasks that measure their understanding of knowledge also have more sophisticated conversational skills. Autonoetic awareness may foster autobiographical memory development more directly as well. As children come to appreciate that the sources of their cognitions are representations, and that others too have representations, both of which are unique to the individuals, they can begin to construct personal perspectives on events. Over time, the practice of reflecting on one's evaluation of an event would be expected to foster further development of the self concept, in that children have the opportunity to reflect on the continuities (as well as discontinuities) in their own and others' reactions to events and experiences. In a variety of ways then, both indirectly and directly, conscious appreciation that the source of a representation is a past event contributes to increases in autobiographical memories.

Developments in Language and Narrative Expression

Because autobiographical memories are expressed verbally, developments in language and in narrative expression play a role in autobiographical memory development. In the first years of life, children who have larger vocabularies and more sophisticated syntax make more contributions to memory conversations relative to children with less developed language skills. Over the preschool years, children play increasingly active roles in conversations. For example, they provide (1) more of the elements of a complete narrative (i.e., the who, what, where, when, why, and how of events), (2) more descriptive details, and (3) more evaluative information, thereby adding texture to their narratives. A more complete narrative not only makes for a better story for the listener but also provides the storyteller with a structure for organizing memory representations, for differentiating events from one another, and for creating associative links between events. It thus works to facilitate encoding and consolidation of event memories in a way that simultaneously preserves their uniqueness and integrates them with other memories in long-term stores, thereby strengthening their representation. The organizational frame provided by a complete narrative also may aid memory retrieval.

The Social Context of Remembering

The development of autobiographical memory does not occur in a vacuum. From early in their lives, children participate in the activity of sharing their own and others' memories. At first, much of the work of recollecting past experiences falls to more verbally and narratively accomplished partners, typically the children's parents. Parents tell what happened in an event and children participate by affirming the parents' contributions, and by adding a bit of memory content here and there. Through these conversations, children begin to learn what to include in their memory reports and also how to organize their narratives. As noted earlier, as they internalize the narrative form, it comes to serve important mnemonic functions at encoding as well as retrieval. Through conversations about past events, children also learn the social function of talking about the past, which is to share thoughts, feelings, reactions, and experiences with other people. Families or cultures that place a high premium on talking about the past, and on the child's own experience of events, likely will promote more rapid development of structures for organizing autobiographical memories, relative to families and cultures that place less emphasis on these aspects of experience. These variables will interact with characteristics of the individual child, resulting in individual as well as group variation.

Variability among children. There are numerous individual differences that may affect the development of autobiographical memory. For example, there are individual differences in the most basic element of the self concept, namely, self-recognition. In the middle of the second year, ~50% of children already indicate self-recognition. Whereas another 25% recognize themselves by the end of the second year, the remaining 25% still do not. A similar range is apparent on tasks that assess the temporally extended self. That is, at 3 years of age, 25% of children already show evidence of recognition that the past self and present self are one and the same. A full year later, 75% of children show this evidence but 25% still do not.

Individual differences also are apparent in many of the other domains that relate to developments in autobiographical memory, including (1) the amount that infants and children remember, (2) the accuracy of memories, (3) acquisition of temporal concepts that aid in location of events in time and in relation to one another, and (4) understanding of a variety of cognitive concepts that are hypothesized to relate to autonoetic awareness. Children also differ in their verbal and narrative sophistication and thus in their abilities to express their memories. These sources of variability have direct, indirect, and as described next, even interactive effects on autobiographical memory development.

Variability among families. Individual children bring their individual differences into home environments that themselves are variable. One of the ways that home environments differ is in the narrative style of the parents. For example, some mothers use a large number of evaluative terms in autobiographical memory conversations. Over time, their children come to use a larger number of such terms when they report on events. More broadly, some parents exhibit an elaborative style of talking about the past, providing cues and details about events and inviting their children to join in on the story. Other parents exhibit a more repetitive style, asking children questions for which they seem to have a particular answer in mind. Children exposed to the elaborative style report more about events both concurrently and over time. It seems that they are internalizing a narrative form that helps them organize, remember, and subsequently retrieve stories of previous life events. Importantly, parental style is, to a certain degree, a misnomer, in that characteristics of the child and even of the dyad influence it. For example, parents are more elaborative with children who are more verbal and with daughters relative to sons. The attachment security of the dyad also is related to parental style: mothers in securely attached dyads are more elaborative. Even family demographics may relate to autobiographical memory development. For instance, on tests of understanding of the representational nature of mind, a concept implicated in autobiographical memory, children who are first-born and thus have no older siblings have low rates of success. In sum, there are numerous differences among families that may affect the course of development of autobiographical memory in any given child.

Variability among cultures. Just as important as differences in the child who is doing the remembering and in the familial environment in which memory is being shaped are differences in the larger cultural milieu of experience. Illustrative examples come from research that involves contrasts between children from Eastern and Western culture groups. Briefly, the early autobiographical memory reports of children from Eastern cultures include fewer references to themselves and fewer personal evaluations, relative to reports from children in Western cultures. In addition, the autobiographical memory reports of children from Eastern cultures tend to feature generic as opposed to specific events, and they are shorter and less detailed, relative to those provided by children in the West. Thus, on at least three critical features – significance to the self, specificity in place and time, and verbal expression – the early narratives of children from Eastern cultures may be viewed as less prototypically autobiographical, relative to the narratives of children from Western cultures.

Linking Autobiographical Memory Development and Infantile or Childhood Amnesia

If, over the course of infancy and the preschool years, memories of events appear more and more autobiographical, why then do adults have so few personal memories from this period? Addressing this question requires consideration of the rate at which autobiographical memories are formed and the complementary rate at which they are forgotten. Although the preschool years are marked by an increasing rate of formation of event memories with autobiographical features, they also are marked by a rate of forgetting that is accelerated, relative to the rate of forgetting in later childhood and adulthood. At some point, the rate at which new, more autobiographical memories are formed overtakes the rate at which they are forgotten. From adults' retrospective perspective, that point is the offset of infantile or childhood amnesia.

The Rate at Which Memories Are Formed

There is incontrovertible evidence that over the course of the preschool years, children form memories that are more and more autobiographical. As early as they are able to use past tense markers, children refer to past events of relevance to themselves. As they gain in narrative sophistication, children's stories become more complete and more coherent. Their narratives about past events also take on more and more elements of drama and they contain an increasing amount of evidence of the significance of the event for the child. Stories are told not only about routine events but about unique experiences that happened at a particular place, at a particular time. Some events – though certainly not all – are remembered for months and even years. Although prior to 4–6 years of age children do not pass tasks that permit researchers to say that they are aware of the sources of their representations, children's narratives certainly contain evidence of vivid recollections of events from the past: they include elements that provide a sense of the intensity of experience, elements of suspense, and information about the internal states of the participants, for example. In sum, over the course of the preschool years, children's stories of their lives bear more and more of the marks of typical autobiographical reports. As a result, children exhibit an increasing number of memories that are recognized as autobiographical.

The Rate at Which Memories Are Forgotten

Even infants and young children remember, but they also forget. The younger the infant or the child, the faster the rate of forgetting. Age-related differential forgetting results from a number of sources. One source is the relative immaturity of the neural structures responsible for formation and maintenance of memories over the long term. Because the temporal cortical network is relatively less developed, encoding and consolidation processes are less effective and efficient in younger infants and children than in older children. As a result, they exhibit a faster rate of forgetting.

Differential rates of forgetting also likely result from several nonmnemonic sources. In effect, the memories that the young child is asking her or his immature brain to consolidate and store contain fewer of the features that typify autobiographical memories: (1) the self to which they are referenced is not as stable and coherent a construct as it will be later in development; (2) relative to later memories, early memories tend to contain fewer distinctive features and are less specifically located in space and time; (3) younger children likely encode fewer of the elements that make for a good narrative, relative to older children, thereby denying themselves an effective organizational tool; and (4) early-memory representations contain fewer indications of their origin in events from the past, relative to those encoded with a more mature understanding of the representational nature of the human mind. In short, in early childhood we have less than optimal processes operating on less than optimal raw materials. The quality of the resulting output is simply not as high as it is in later childhood and adulthood, when we have more optimal processes operating on more optimal materials. The net result is a faster rate of forgetting. Importantly, this analysis implies that the rate of forgetting is not accelerated as suggested by the second component of the definition of infantile or childhood amnesia. That is, the analysis implies that the number of memories of events from the ages of 3 to 7 years is not smaller than would be expected based on forgetting alone. That characterization holds only when an adult rate of forgetting is applied. Consideration of a more developmentally appropriate rate of forgetting is expected to yield a more normal distribution.

The Crossover of Two Functions

The net effect of this analysis is a model that suggests that, among adults, we see an increase in autobiographical memories dating from around age 4 to 6 years because, as depicted in **Figure 3**, this is the point at which the functions of memory formation (ascending solid line) and

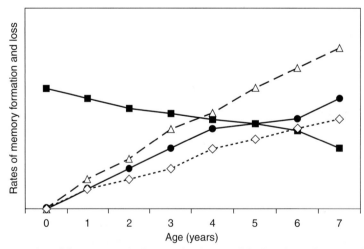

Figure 3 Schematic representation of the crossover in the preschool years of the functions of memory formation (the rate of which increases with age; solid ascending line) and memory loss (the rate of which decreases with age; solid descending line). The period of intersection between ages 4 and 6 years is recognized as the offset of infantile or childhood amnesia. Also illustrated are possible patterns of individual differences in the offset of infantile amnesia as a function of differences in the slope of change of the remembering function. The dashed line represents a steeper increase in the memory function and an earlier crossover with forgetting (at age 4 years). The dotted line represents a more shallow increase in the memory function and a later crossover with forgetting (at age 6 years).

memory loss (descending solid line) cross over. Prior to the age of 4 years, the rate at which memories are lost is faster than the rate at which they are gained; after the age of 6 years, the rate at which memories are formed is faster than the rate at which they are lost. Considering the adult phenomenon of childhood amnesia to be a result of the crossover of two functions provides a ready account of individual and group differences in the age of, and distribution of, autobiographical memories from early in life. Two individuals who as children had the same rate of forgetting may nevertheless have vastly different offsets of childhood amnesia as a function of differences in the slopes of change in the remembering function. Children in a family and cultural environment that places a premium on narrative, and that encourages reflection on the meanings of events and their significance for the child, may have autobiographical memories from earlier in the preschool years (dashed line crossing at age 4 years). In contrast, children in a family and cultural environment that uses a less elaborative style and which does not encourage reflection on the self may have autobiographical memories from later in the preschool years (dotted line crossing at age 6 years).

Individual differences also could result from differences in the slopes of forgetting functions (not shown in **Figure 3**). That is, individuals whose rates of increase in the formation of autobiographical memories are the same could nevertheless experience a different course of development of autobiographical memory because of differences in the rate at which memories are forgotten. Variability in the forgetting function no doubt is associated with a variety of factors, including different rates of maturational change in the temporal cortical network and associated differences in the basic mnemonic processes of encoding, consolidation, storage, and retrieval. As such, the conceptualization provides a ready account of individual and cultural differences: they result from differences in the quality of the autobiographical memories that are formed during the period and from the likelihood of survival of the memories over time.

Summary and Conclusions

Whereas adults have a wealth of memories from later childhood and early adulthood, there is a virtually universal paucity of memories from the first years of life. For over a century, there have been reports that the average age of earliest memory among Western adults is age 3–3.5 years. Adults report a larger and gradually increasing number of memories from the ages of 3 to 7 years. The number of events adults remember from the age of 7 years onward is consistent with what would be expected, based on adult rates of forgetting.

From a theoretical standpoint, this distribution of autobiographical memories is interesting and important because of its implications for the self concept. For much of the lifetime there is a continuous time line of events and experiences. The boundary of childhood amnesia represents a break in the otherwise continuous history and thus a challenge to a fully integrated sense of self. Infantile or childhood amnesia also is interesting and important because of its clinical and forensic implications. Theories of personality and psychopathology look to early experiences as an important source of adult attitudes and behaviors. For these analyses, determination of the nature of the trace that early experiences leave behind is crucial. Forensic concerns also compel research on memory for events during the period obscured by childhood amnesia. The veridicality and accessibility of memories of events from early in life are questions the answers to which can have profound consequences for childhood victims of crimes, as well as their alleged perpetrators.

The fact that the phenomenon of childhood amnesia is almost universal does not mean that there are no individual and group differences in early memory. On the contrary, there is wide variation in the age of earliest memory, and there are differences as a function of gender, birth order, and culture group. Theories that hope to explain the relative lack among adults of memories of specific events from early in life must account not only for the age of earliest memory and distribution of early memories, but for these systematic sources of individual and group variability as well.

Theories to explain infantile or childhood amnesia have suggested either that memories for early life events are formed but then later become inaccessible, or that memories are not accessible later in life because they were never formed. Although these explanations may seem incompatible, it is likely that elements of both figure in the development of autobiographical memory and thus the offset of childhood amnesia. Consideration of age-related developments in the neural substrate of autobiographical memory, in the processes that it subserves, and in a number of nonmnemonic concepts and domains (including language), implies that, in infancy and the preschool years, memories are formed but that they are relatively quickly forgotten. Conversely, developments in all of these domains imply that, over the same period of time, the memories that are formed are increasingly autobiographical. The point at which the two functions – rate of forgetting and rate of remembering – cross over one another is the point that we recognize as the offset of infantile or childhood amnesia. The crossover point varies as a function of individual differences in children, in their families, and even in the culture group in which they are raised. This analysis makes infantile or childhood amnesia less enigmatic. At the same time, it makes additional research on the processes and determinants of remembering and forgetting in infancy, early childhood, and beyond, all the more imperative.

See also: Birth Order; Cognitive Development; Memory.

Suggested Readings

Bauer PJ (2006) Event memory. In: Damon W and Lerner RM (eds.) *Handbook of Child Psychology: Cognition, Perception, and Language,* 6th edn., pp. 373–425. Hoboken, NJ: Wiley.

Bauer PJ (2006) *Remembering the Times of Our Lives: Memory in Infancy and Beyond.* Mahwah, NJ: Erlbaum.

Brewer WF (1996) What is recollective memory? In: Rubin DC (ed.) *Remembering Our Past: Studies in Autobiographical Memory,* pp. 19–66. New York: Cambridge University Press.

Markowitsch HJ (2000) Neuroanatomy of memory. In: Tulving E and Craik FIM (eds.) *The Oxford Handbook of Memory,* pp. 465–484. New York: Oxford University Press.

Mullen MK (1994) Earliest recollections of childhood: A demographic analysis. *Cognition* 52: 55–79.

Nelson CA, Thomas KM, and de Haan M (2006) Neural bases of cognitive development. In: Damon W and Lerner RM (eds.) *Handbook of Child Psychology, Vol. 2: Cognition, Perception, and Language,* 6th edn., pp. 3–57. Hoboken, NJ: Wiley.

Nelson K and Fivush R (2004) The emergence of autobiographical memory: A social cultural developmental theory. *Psychological Review* 111: 486–511.

Rubin DC (2000) The distribution of early childhood memories. *Memory* 8: 265–269.

Wang Q (2003) Infantile amnesia reconsidered: A cross-cultural analysis. *Memory* 11: 65–80.

Wetzler SE and Sweeney JA (1986) Childhood amnesia: An empirical demonstration. In: Rubin DC (ed.) *Autobiographical Memory,* pp. 191–201. New York: Cambridge University Press.

Artistic Development

C Golomb, University of Massachusetts, Boston, Boston, MA, USA

© 2008 Elsevier Inc. All rights reserved.

Glossary

Divergent perspective – Lines that depict the edges of an object by diverging rather than converging on a vanishing point.

Frontal plane – The plane lying perpendicular to the viewer's line of sight.

Globals – A circle or oblong with facial features that represent the human figure.

Intellectual realism – The child draws what he knows, not what he sees.

Linear perspective – Lines that represent the edges of an object in a scene that converge on a single point, called the vanishing point near the back of the center.

Representation – The ability to evoke mentally the image of an absent object and give it form in drawing or modeling.

Synthetic incapacity – The young preschool child's inability to coordinate the parts of a figure into a coherent drawing.

Tadpole figure – The global human sprouts arms and legs.

Viewpoint – The notional position occupied by a monocular viewer in relation to a scene (Willats).

Introduction

Representational development in drawing and sculpture examines the evolution of forms that can stand for the objects in a scene. Representation is a mental activity of symbol formation concerned with creating forms of equivalence in a given medium. Unlike imitation of reality which aims for a one-to-one correspondence to its referent, artistic representation implies finding structural equivalents for the referent. Its development documents the manner in which young children invent simple, economical forms and the processes of differentiation that lead to a more effective depiction. This development is orderly and rule governed, universal in its early phases that encompass phenotypical diversity on basic structural equivalents.

Children's Drawings

For over 100 years, psychologists and educators have shown a fascination with children's drawings, an interest that dates from the latter part of the nineteenth century and coincides with the beginnings of a systematic psychological study of child development. The first publications of children's drawings stem from this period, suggestive of later stage theories of mental development. The topic of child art subsumes drawing, painting, and modeling, but given the easy access to paper, pencils, and magic markers, drawings have been most widely studied.

Child art, which emerges in the early preschool years, is a symbolic activity that is unique to human beings. Non-human primates such as the great apes are able to recognize photographs and line drawings of familiar objects, but despite extensive training in the use of symbols, they do not create the simple representational forms that most 3-year-old children spontaneously draw and name. It is an amazing accomplishment of the human child to create, without training, these first representational shapes for which there are no readily available models (see **Figures 1(a)** and **1(b)**). These early representations comprised of a large circle with facial features and legs are simple but recognizable representations of a human or an animal.

Psychologists who at the end of the nineteenth century set out to study children's drawings were faced with the peculiarities of child art. Young children's drawings appeared bizarre and they were puzzled by the omission of significant features, their frequent displacement, the lack

Figure 1 (a) Global humans. (b) Tadpole figure. (c) Open trunk figures. (d) Figures with a graphically differentiated torso. (e) Tadpole animal.

of proportion and perspective, mixed views, the arbitrary use of colors, the transparencies of features not visible to an observer, and many other faults. Concluding that the drawings of the young were indicative of a conceptually immature mind, they studied the changes in children's drawings as an index of the growth of intelligence. Over the next decades, many extensive cross-sectional and longitudinal studies were undertaken with the intention to chronicle the stages in graphic development and their anticipated progression toward a realistic representation. With Florence Goodenough's Draw-a-Man test published in *Measurement of Intelligence by Drawings* (1926), drawings of the human figure were standardized and scored according to the number of parts depicted and the realism of some of the features that were assumed to correspond to the child's conceptual maturity or intelligence quotient (IQ). This test of intelligence became a widely used instrument that was restandardized by Dale Harris in 1963.

A different conception of child art was held by the modernist artists at the beginning of the twentieth century. Artists and art educators organized the first exhibitions of child art and often displayed their own work along with the drawings and paintings of children. Artists such as Paul Klee, Wassily Kandinsky, Ernst Ludwig Kirchner, Gabriele Münter, and Pablo Picasso appreciated the spontaneity and esthetics of children's drawings and paintings; they considered the language of child art an authentic expression of a creative mind unencumbered by social conventions.

These contrasting approaches to child art and its development have found further elaboration in the writings of Jean Piaget and Rudolf Arnheim both of whom have had a profound impact on research in this field.

Jean Piaget, in his influential book co-authored with Bärbel Inhelder *The Child's Construction of Space* (1956), proposes to view drawing development in distinct stages that correspond to the stages of spatial-mathematical reasoning. The first stage pertains to the preschool years; the child draws closed shapes that differentiate the figure from its background but ignores the true shape and size of the object they represent. These drawings are based on topological relations that distinguish the inside from the outside of a form, and the manner in which they are connected. Only gradually are children able to order the various parts of the figure, and the difficulty in organizing the major parts of a figure into a coherent representation Piaget terms synthetic incapacity. Piaget relates this phase of drawing to the early preoperational period of cognitive development (ages 3–4 years). The next stage sees progress in the differentiation of parts of a figure and the adoption of more varied forms that are also better organized. Following the art historian George Henry Luquet who provided a longitudinal account of his daughter's drawing development, Piaget calls this phase intellectual realism (ages 5–7 years). This term signifies that the drawing child has a better conception of the object he or she is representing although the resemblance to the model remains crude and the perspective of the observer is ignored. This phase is often described as 'the child draws what he knows, not what he sees'. During the concrete operational period of cognitive development (ages 8–11 years), visual realism becomes the dominant form of drawing. Children now consider their viewing point when drawing, and their intuitive understanding of Euclidean concepts of measurement and of projective geometry lead to a more realistic depiction of a scene. New techniques appear for the depiction of depth and volume, experimentation now leads to the use of occlusion of parts hidden from view and to size diminution, and eventually to the use of perspective. By the end of the concrete operational period children are supposed to have made progress toward optical realism in their drawings, a highly valued endpoint in drawing development.

Rudolf Arnheim in his influential book *Art and Visual Perception* published in 1974 provides a new perspective on the psychology of art. On the basis of his extensive reading of the history of art he rejects the notion that realism is a natural endpoint of artistic development. Arnheim points out that in its long history, perspective was invented only once, by the artists of the Renaissance, and that before and since that time there have been multiple forms of artistic expression that do not rely on perspective in their art form. Arnheim contrasts the nature of representation with that of replication. Unlike replication, which aims for a faithful rendition of the elements that comprise an object, representation requires the invention of forms that are structurally or dynamically equivalent to the object. Artists are not motivated to imitate nature, they do not aim for one-to-one correspondence of elements, and all artistic thinking begins with highly abstract and simplified forms. At an early level of development, and that applies to all beginners, simple generalized forms are the only options available to the inexperienced artist. Thus, inexperience not childhood is the true starting point for representational development in the arts, and the experience with the two-dimensional medium, its possibilities and constraints, becomes a major force leading to the differentiation of forms and their composition. Differentiation does not imply a single developmental trajectory, and Arnheim emphasizes that there are multiple solutions to representational problems. The perspective inventions of the artists of the Renaissance are only one among many achievements, and they ought not to be seen as the ideal endpoint of ontogenetic or cultural development.

These contrasting approaches have animated numerous studies of children's drawings and the following sections report on general trends that, in the absence of formal training, characterize the evolution of form, space, color, and composition. Most of the research has been conducted on ordinary, normally developing children, but a brief section on talented children and some information on mentally handicapped children will be included. The impact of sociocultural factors will be reviewed, followed by an account of representational development in a three-dimensional medium that highlights the role of the medium.

Form

Representation is intimately linked to the creation of form or shape that resembles the referent, and thus the true beginning of drawing as a representational activity can be seen in the drawing of simple but recognizable forms that can stand for the object. When preschoolers begin to control their earlier scribble actions and recognizable shapes emerge, they tend to identify them as either humans or animals. The first forms are globals, consisting of a large circular or oblong shape that is endowed with facial features (see **Figure 1(a)**). Fairly soon thereafter, the global figure becomes graphically more differentiated, it sprouts arms and legs and thus a universally seen early figure of a human or animal is created, often called the tadpole figure (see **Figure 1(b)**). As the global circle shrinks in size, the lines that stand for legs increase in length and yield a new figure, the open trunk figure with the trunk implied between the two verticals (see **Figure 1(c)**). Children discover several solutions to graphically differentiate the trunk section: drawing a horizontal line that connects the verticals thus closing the open trunk, drawing of a stick figure composed of a single one-dimensional vertical line that joins head and limbs, and/or drawing a separate circle underneath the head (see **Figure 1(d)**). In the case of animal figures, the generic tadpole sprouts four legs, followed by a horizontally drawn body that marks its distinction from the human figure (see **Figure 1(e)**).

In the beginning, while focused on evolving basic forms, children are most concerned with creating a basic likeness to the human or animal figure, and relative size, proportion, orientation, and color are of minor concern. Once the basic forms and their organization have been mastered to the child's satisfaction, some attention is paid toward those other variables. Relative size now enables the drawer to indicate age differences, for example, between adults and children; detail can convey information on gender, endow the figures with individual characteristics (braids, mustache, earrings, eye glasses), portray emotions (tears, anger, happiness); and orientation is useful when action is portrayed. Although the child artist is yet unconcerned with anatomical fidelity or optical realism, attention to these variables creates a more successful narrative. It is worth noting that throughout the childhood years children prefer the frontal orientation of objects, often called the canonical view that provides the most salient information about the referent. Overall, the young artist attends to the essential characteristics of an object, an object centered view, and generally tends to ignore its momentary and changing view. The latter involves varying degrees of distortion of the true shape of an object, for example, in drawing a rectangular table with converging lines or the foreshortening of the human figure. There is a price for deviating from the real shape of an object and focusing on a specific view as seen in tasks in which the handle of a cup has been turned to occlude it from view. Although the handle is invisible, the younger children, invariably, draw a cup with a handle since this is its distinct feature that differentiates it from a glass or a bowl. The older and more experienced children will consider viewpoint as they go beyond depicting some of the invariable characteristics useful for identifying the referent, to less static and more dynamic forms that call for some of the distortions they avoided earlier on.

Along with greater graphic differentiation of the parts of a figure, we also note changes in the use of lines: from one-dimensional lines for limbs to two-dimensional ones, from right-angular relations of the arms to the body to oblique ones useful for the depiction of action and, somewhat later, to interaction among the figures. By the age of 5 or 6 years, children also experiment with a single contour line that encompasses all the major parts of the figure in one comprehensive outline (see **Figure 2(a)**). Further on, children discover that occluding lines of parts that are hidden from view can be useful for the depiction of volume and depth of a figure (see **Figure 2(b)**).

In this process of graphic differentiation, which is not strictly age dependent, the two-dimensional shapes or regions of the early tadpoles and of figures with a separate trunk (see **Figures 1(b)–1(d)**) represent whole volumes, that is, the totality of the object that is not further specified. With practice and the growing ambition to provide more information about the object, regions become more specified and come to represent the faces or surfaces of objects. With a more advanced understanding of the function of lines, one-dimensional lines come to represent edges or contours of an object.

In general, the developmental trends in the untutored drawings that have been outlined tend to reach a plateau in the middle childhood years that still carry some of the typical features of the child art style. Without specific training programs only highly motivated and talented children are the exception, searching for and discovering new techniques for the depiction of their pictorial world.

Space

The drawing child does not create figures in total isolation, and in addition to mapping out the spatial relations that are internal to a figure, relations among different figures need to be worked out and placed in a common

Figure 2 (a) Figures drawn with a continuous outline. (b) Occlusion of body parts that are hidden from view.

spatial field. This brings us to the question how children organize their figures in the pictorial plane and how they deal with the missing third dimension. Representing a three-dimensional object on a two-dimensional surface presents a formidable challenge for all beginners and the child's earliest organization of pictorial space begins with a principle of proximity, placing items near each other, indicating that they belong together. Soon thereafter, a new directional rule yields side-by-side placements, mostly along the horizontal or vertical axis. The horizontal direction specifies left–right directions, while the vertical represents up–down and near–far dimensions. Only gradually do children come to understand the different demands made upon the vertical axis, by discovering, for example, that the vertically drawn game of hopscotch competes with the sun and the clouds for the same space. From their different trials they learn that diminishing the size of an item, placing it higher on the page, and partially occluding objects can suggest distance, that color gradients can serve to unify the foreground, middle ground, and background of a scene, and that diagonals can be used to depict the sides of an object. In the case of highly motivated children, one notes experimentation with foreshortening (the proportionate contraction of some of the parts of a figure that suggest its depth and volume) and the converging lines of linear perspective. However, only a few children arrive at these technical skills on their own, without explicit training or working from ready-made models.

Color

The order in which representational skills evolve privileges forms over color. Once the drawing of basic shapes has been accomplished, children use bold and contrasting colors for their sheer enjoyment, at first disregarding their realistic function. Thus, children begin with a subjectively determined choice of color and gradually the drawer imposes some restrictions on their use, such as monochromatic outlines for humans and animals, red for strawberries, green for grapes, brown for tree trunks, yellow for the sun and the moon. Although the general trend is toward a more naturalistic use of color, color remains central in the decorative designs that embellish many drawings and paintings, designs that are unaffected by the rules of realism. By the middle childhood years, color no longer is subservient to form, it becomes a dominant force uniting the diverse elements in a drawing or painting as is the case when a light coloring of the background creates the impression of the outdoors and provides some continuity between the different elements of a scene. Above all, color can become the carrier of mood and feelings with bright colors indicating happy events, dark colors sadness and illness. Color is a major factor in children's attraction to art, in the esthetics of child art, and its ornamental tendencies.

Composition

Drawings are meant to tell a story or to express feelings and this requires the organization of all the elements that comprise a work, that is, the use of line, form, space, and color. Two compositional principles seem to underlie children's drawings: a grid-like alignment of figures along the horizontal or vertical axes and centering strategies that organize items around a pictorial center.

Following a very short-lived phase of forms that appear to be distributed arbitrarily across the page, children begin to organize their figures along one or more horizontal axes. At first, these alignments are imprecise and give the impression that the items are floating in an unspecified space. Gradually, alignments tend to become more organized, with attention to the size of the figures and the distance between them, followed by the introduction of a ground or base line that anchors all elements firmly in the common plane. Depending on the theme, subgroupings appear that indicate that the items belong together or that the actors have a special relationship or a common interest (see **Figure 3(a)**). Such groupings are formed on the basis of similarity of size, color, form, or activity, and convey to the viewer what the picture is about. For example, a family picture can be organized according to the age of its members, from the youngest to the oldest, or grouped in terms of relationships among the members. The compositional strategy of creating meaningful subunits and coordinating the parts into a coherent and balanced configuration can yield a successful and pleasing picture based on thematic unity (see **Figure 3(b)**).

The second compositional principle is expressed in the tendency to center figures on a page and the creation of symmetrical arrangements. Symmetry can be defined as the correspondence in size, shape, and relative position of items that are drawn on opposite sides of a dividing line or distributed around a center. Simple forms of centering and symmetry can already be seen in the earliest drawings of 3- and 4-year-olds, and with more experience the complexity of these arrangements increases. These include equal spacing among figures, similar distance from the edges of the page, systematic variation in the size of figures, pair formation, and the repetition of patterns (see **Figure 3(c)**). Compositions based on complex symmetry maintain spatial order and meaning with more varied items whose organization no longer demands strict one-to-one correspondence of items. The more advanced symmetrical arrangements create a more dynamic balancing of the individual elements that enhance the meaning of the work and its esthetic appeal (see **Figure 3(d)**). Visual narratives that tell a story in a series of frames also represent a dynamic form of symmetry (see **Figure 3(e)**).

Overall, compositional development proceeds from multiple local graphic solutions of isolated descriptions, in which each object is an independent unit, to mixed views of varying degrees of interdependence and coordination. A unitary conception that organizes all the elements into a coherent whole is rarely achieved in childhood or adolescence.

Motivation and the Expression of Feelings

Drawings and paintings are expressive statements about what one knows, feels, and wants to understand. But so far we have looked at child art mostly from a cognitive perspective, as a problem-solving enterprise that highlights the representational abilities that underlie the evolution of form and spatial organization. Drawing children are not only inventors of a pictorial vocabulary, they are motivated to tell a story, to give expression to their experiences, to the joys, sorrows, fears, struggles, victories, and defeats of their daily lives. The motivation to create a pictorial world on a previously blank page draws on deeply felt desires, fantasies, and wishes that endow the maker with a sense of power, to make and to unmake, to create and to obliterate at will. Drawings depict events that affect the child, the family, and, beyond it – the wider community. They depict holidays, birthdays, contests, pregnancy, birth and death, earthquakes, and terrorist attacks. In some cases, illness and the fear of dying can lead, even in the drawings of young children, to surprisingly effective pictorial metaphors.

The theme that the child chooses is the main carrier of the affectively charged message. In many cases the subject matter of a drawing and its simple composition convey the intended meaning without ambiguity as seen in a birthday party that features balloons, a cake, and presents or in the drawing of a crying child, tears running down its cheeks, and a broken toy on the floor. In cases that involve complex emotions such as anger at a sibling, feelings of rejection, ambivalence toward a parent, competition, or the desire for recognition, the child may not fully understand the range of emotions that are embedded in a scene he has just created. The following account of the pictorial expression of deeply felt emotions that are not fully understood by the drawing child comes from a retrospective account of an artist who reviewed one of her childhood paintings. Her comments illustrate the complexity of motivational factors

Figure 3 (a) Alignment strategy and the grouping of elements. (b) Picnic: thematic unity of the composition. (c) Symmetry. (d) Complex symmetry. (e) Love: a visual narrative.

that may not reach the level of conscious awareness and verbalization:

> I see myself standing in front of a big white sheet of paper ... and I begin to work. I take a wide brush, dip it into paint, and on the white paper arises the large figure of a black woman. The black woman grows, surrounded by decorative ornaments and symbols of great beauty. Below her feet, at the bottom of the page, I add a little grave of the child who died, over which the black woman weeps. How did she get onto my paper? Over whom did I grieve when I was 10 years old? What feelings were stirred up in me that here appear in my painting?
>
> Gering (1998)

While the theme and composition are intimately linked and able to convey message in a general way, the ability to depict the mood of the protagonist graphically emerges only gradually, with the head or the face singled out as the carrier of affective meaning. Thus, happiness, sadness, and anger are portrayed by changes in the drawing of the mouth, with an upwardly curving line depicting a smiling face, a downward curve sadness, while anger may be shown in a set of prominently displayed teeth, a straight or zigzag line for the mouth, and somewhat later also in the diagonal slashes of the eyebrows.

Changes in posture that are congruent with the experience of contrasting emotions occur infrequently in the drawings of younger children, and are used sparingly by the older ones who may avail themselves of verbal commentary that augments a message, such as 'beat it'. With few exceptions, notably the direction of the arms, body posture remains essentially static, that is, undifferentiated. At times exaggerating the form and size of body parts can be an effective means to convey affect, and the use of energetic brush strokes, choice of primary colors, and an emphasis on symmetry can heighten the expressive power of a drawing or painting.

It is important to note that the depiction of feelings in a child's drawing does not tell us who the referent is. The drawing of a sad child need not indicate that the child artist is sad, and we need to be aware that a drawing is not a simple printout of the child's heart and mind. In the presence of an empathic participant observer the highly personal meaning of a drawing might be elucidated. Indeed, a large literature attests to the desirability of using drawings in a therapeutic context. In such a context, drawing may be a useful technique to help an emotionally distressed child to discover and convey feelings he or she harbors about the self and others and to develop the ability to express them in a meaningful way. For some youngsters, drawing is a substitute for verbal communication, for others it is an additional avenue for discovering and communicating important feelings that can be shared with the therapist. Drawing in the presence of the therapist encourages the child to understand his or her own message and to become more active in one's own behalf. Above all, drawing in the presence of an accepting adult encourages the child to face the inner world of demons as such a confrontation is now less threatening. A drawing, however, does not provide solutions magically, and in most therapeutic encounters drawings are seen as aids in the working through of the child's emotional problems.

Talent or Giftedness in the Arts

Children who at an early age perform at the near-adult levels valued in their culture have generally been identified as gifted and at various times have been apprenticed to an artist's studio. In our Western culture, a child who at an early age masters three-dimensional techniques and represents objects in a naturalistic style is most commonly identified as gifted (see **Figures 4(a)** and **4(b)**). Under the impact of modern art and such influential art educators as Franz Cizek and Viktor Lowenfeld the conception of giftedness has been broadened to include compositions of the child art style that show originality and cohesion, the use of vibrant colors, and the ornamental qualities reminiscent of folk art. One notes a division between researchers working in the Piagetian tradition who consider giftedness mostly in terms of the acquisition of skills of optical realism and educators who bring a broader esthetic to bear on the question of giftedness.

Regarding the developmental progression of talented children, most investigators agree that they do not skip stages or phases but move much faster through them, sometimes in the case of hours or days. While there are dramatic differences in the style of artistically gifted children, they are likely to be endowed with a heightened sensitivity for the appearance of objects, develop an early awareness of the function of lines and planes, and are able to extract the rules that underlie graphic depiction.

Noteworthy are the marked individual differences in the style gifted children develop ranging from realists, to colorists, expressionists, and cartoonists. Some children are enamored of the appearance of objects and strive to represent them with utmost fidelity. These are the youngsters who will teach themselves the major projective drawing systems and other three-dimensional techniques that can portray the objects of their interest with vitality and verisimilitude. **Figures 4(a)–4(d)** provide an example of accelerated development coupled with an unusual graphic talent that captures the excitement and realism of the objects that engaged this child's imagination. Having just turned 2 years, he drew his family as tadpole figures, but within the scope of a few months he mastered, on his own, some of the major projective drawing systems, incorporating different faces into his drawings of cars, trucks, buses, airplanes, tractors, combines, tricycles, and bicycles, and by the age 4 years he began to experiment with

(a)

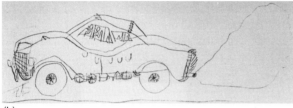
(b)

(c)

(d)

Figure 4 The pull of realism. Drawings of a precociously talented boy. (a) Cement truck, age 2; (b) Car in divergent perspective, age 3; (c) City of Jerusalem, car drawn in convergent perspective, age 4; (d) Construction scene, age 5.

convergent perspective (see **Figure 4(d)**). With uncommon persistence, this preschooler developed his own graphic vocabulary and his daily efforts demonstrate the ongoing processes of problem setting and solving, the kind of visual thinking that enabled him to discover or invent useful representational techniques.

Other gifted young artists are colorists, they tend to use dramatic form rather than realistic ones, they relish expressive and decorative attributes of texture and design (see **Figures 5(a)** and **5(b)**). They may also be more attuned to their internal states unlike the realism-oriented child artist whose attention is focused outward, on the appearance of his world. In contrast to the above-mentioned gifted children, cartoonists create worlds of adventure populated with villains and heroes, based on models that inspire their graphic work.

Altogether, children who are highly talented in the arts pursue their own pathways whether they are colorists, expressionists, or realists. They appear to be driven, in the words of Ellen Winner they experience a 'rage to master', and are determined to teach themselves what they need to know. But, of course, all children, even the talented ones, do not grow up in social isolation, they are influenced by the material made available to them (paper, crayon, charcoal, paints, brushes, ink, etc.), by the images that surround them, by peers, teachers, magazines, etc. This is particularly well illustrated in the case of Yani, a Chinese prodigy, who from an early age painted in her father's studio. Although her work with brush, paint, and rice paper (the traditional tools of Chinese painters) is recognizable child art, one is struck by the impact of Chinese artistic traditions in her work.

Drawing of Mentally Handicapped Children

The great majority of children with mental retardation for whom no organic impairment has been established are most commonly classified as familial or cultural retardates and their IQ scores range from 50 to 70. Early investigators assumed that the drawings of these children deviate from the normal course of drawing development. However, later and more carefully controlled studies documented that familial retarded children draw like normally developing children of matched mental age. Findings that identify mental age as a determining factor seem to support the assumptions underlying the Goodenough–Harris drawing of the human figure as an index of conceptual development or IQ. Indeed, studies on Western populations show a good correlation between the Goodenough–Harris Draw-a-Man test and IQ scores for ages 5–10 years.

However, this linkage between drawing of the human figure and IQ scores has been seriously challenged in the her spectacular drawing ability. With the publication of additional cases the question whether savant talent is an indication of a unique conceptual deficit or a mark of unusual talent moved center stage. The results of a series of studies that matched savants with mental retardation to a group of normally developing talented adolescents indicated that, in terms of their graphic talent, the two groups were indistinguishable, which presents a serious challenge to the commonly assumed relationship between IQ (defined as linguistic and mathematical ability) and artistic talent. The artistic accomplishments of several savant artists, one of whom attended an art academy and successfully completed his studies and others whose paintings have been acquired by individual collectors, attest to their talent. From these studies it appears that talent is a major variable that is somewhat independent of IQ scores.

The Sociocultural Milieu

The developmental trends outlined so far, provide an account of children's drawings in Western industrialized settings. To what extent is this representational development characteristic of all children, regardless of time and place? This raises the question of universals in drawing development and the influence of the social milieu on the form children's drawings take.

An early extensive collection of 60 000 drawings from the non-Western world assembled by Paget in 1932 revealed that unschooled preliterate children can, upon request, create drawings of the human figure that, in their diversity, resemble the drawings of children commonly found in Western settings: stick figures, tiny heads, contourless heads and bodies, triangular, squarish, oval, and scribble trunks. Some of these models can be found in any of the large collections assembled in the beginning of the twentieth century, and also resemble the rock carvings and paintings found in such diverse locations as northern Italy, Utah, Guadeloupe, and Hawaii. More recent cross-cultural studies confirm such findings that are especially striking when one observes how naive subjects, never before exposed to paper and pencil, create the same timeless models of animate figures, humans and animals. They attest to a universal factor in the creation of graphic equivalents, at least in early stages of drawing development. There is an underlying logic based on a principle of structural equivalence that generates the diversity of the early models. Local traditions, peers, availability of graphic models, and teachers affect the particular way in which the underlying structure of child art finds expression. In Japan, a culture with a rich artistic heritage, the tadpole figures and their descendents tend to show large eyes, tiny noses, and broad and somewhat flattened heads, clearly influenced by the prevailing comics literature.

(a)

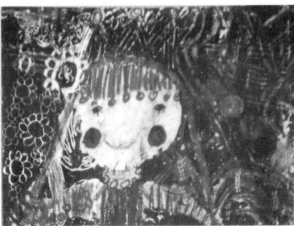
(b)

Figure 5 Expression and love of ornamentation. Drawings of talented children: (a) Warrior, boy, age 6. (b) An imaginary world, girl, age 5.

drawings of children known as savants, mentally retarded children with autism who show an unusual artistic ability. The term savant refers to individuals with serious mental handicaps who have a special island of ability that stands in marked contrast to their handicap of mental retardation and autism. The publication of *Nadia: A Case of Extraordinary Drawing Ability in an Autistic Child* by Lorna Selfe (1977) posed a serious theoretical problem given the absence of a correlation between the child's low IQ and

While it demonstrates the distinct impact of the culture, the similarity to the structural characteristics of early child art is unmistakable.

Divergent Interpretations

The developmental progression outlined so far, especially in regard to the evolution of form and space, finds support among major students of child art. This consensus, however, does not extend to the interpretation of findings. Researchers differ regarding the meaning of the developmental steps, with Piagetian and neo-Piagetian researchers emphasizing the cognitive limitations that underlie the typical childhood drawings, and investigators in the tradition of Arnheim emphasizing the problem-solving intelligence at work and the productivity of visual thinking in a difficult medium. Underlying much of this disagreement is the question of the hypothesized endpoint of drawing development. Researchers in the Piagetian tradition emphasize that the end goal is some degree of optical realism and that the typical childhood drawings are immature and flawed productions that can be attributed to either conceptual deficiencies, production difficulties, and/or limitations on working memory that ought to be overcome by the end of the concrete operational period (ages 10–11 years). Researchers influenced by Arnheim's emphasis on the creation of equivalence of forms rather than imitation as the motivator for art making emphasize the well-established discrepancies between what the child or the inexperienced adult knows and understands about the world he or she wishes to depict, and the specific skills necessary to do so. Many studies indicate significant intra- and interindividual differences depending on the nature of the task and the child's motivation. Above all, the hypothesis of a singular idealized endpoint of optical realism in art whether attained during the concrete or the formal operational period has not been supported. Without training and the high motivation of children talented in the visual arts, there is no evidence of reaching such a state.

The Development of Sculpture

The evolution of children's ability to represent figures in a three-dimensional medium is of interest in its own right while also providing a useful perspective on drawing development. In drawing we observe the difficulties children encounter with the flat two-dimensional medium of paper and their efforts to deal with the missing third dimension. Does the same problem manifest itself in the three-dimensional medium? If so, do children develop their spatial conceptions in analogy to drawing, beginning first with one-dimensional sticks, progressing to two-dimensional flattened slabs arranged in one plane, and only later achieve a three-dimensional conception and production of an object or, alternatively, do they show an early, albeit intuitive, understanding of the three-dimensional nature of representation in this medium? This question has been addressed in a series of studies that closely examine children's modeling strategies on a variety of human and animal tasks. Of particular interest are strategies that might be based on a three-dimensional conception such as modeling multiple faces of an object, emphasizing an upright posture, shaping protrusions and using hollowing out procedures that suggest the inside as well as the outside of a figure, and modeling several distinct layers of an object.

Similar to the earliest scribble actions in drawing, young preschoolers explore clay by squishing, stretching, patting, and rolling it until they discover some likeness in their clay shapes and begin to name them. At first, the three-dimensional medium tends to foster imitative actions, bouncing a piece of clay in imitation of a ball or moving a blob across the table like a train. Between the age of 3 and 4 years children tend to discover the representational possibilities in this medium and make their first attempts to model humans and animals.

Modeling the Human Figure

Early efforts to create a human figure yield three distinct models: a global figure comprised of a sphere with facial features, an erect standing column, and a layout model composed of separately shaped, disconnected parts, mostly facial features and occasionally a tummy and limbs (see **Figures 6(a)–6(c)**). These early models are short lived and soon the one-unit sphere sprouts arms and legs, thus becoming a tadpole figure; the erect standing column undergoes differentiation such that various body parts are either internally represented or the head is modeled separately and placed on top of the erect standing body-column; the layout figure develops into an outline graphic model in clay (see **Figures 7(a)–7(c)**). The columns and their variants are free standing or held upright, while the tadpole and graphic models are placed horizontally on the tabletop. These different models are the simplest structural equivalents for the human figure. From these early and primitive sculpting models one can infer the representational concepts that give rise to them. As in drawing, they are characterized by generality, such that a global form comes to stand for another global entity, in this case a person. Verticality, uprightness, and facial features serve as the defining attributes of these early representations of the human figure.

Progress in modeling can be seen when body parts are differentiated: the upright standing figure modeled from separately formed solid parts, the horizontal figure constructed of rounded or flattened parts, and the graphic outline figure enriched with greater detail. With the

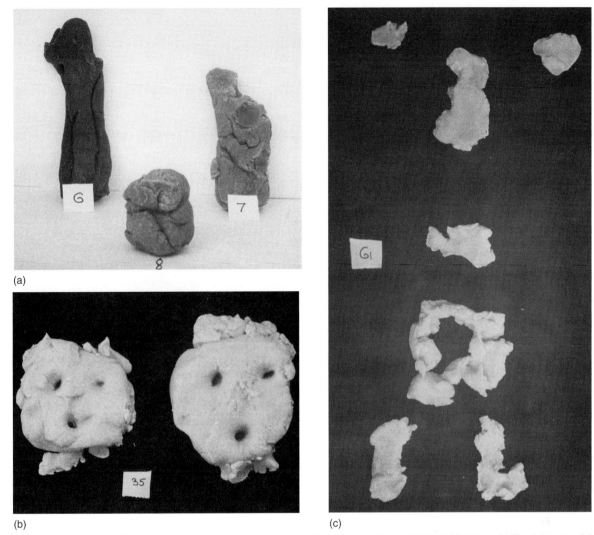

Figure 6 Early models of the human figure in clay. (a) Upright standing column. (b) Ball with facial features. (c) The layout model.

exception of the graphic model, simplicity and economy of form dominate this art form.

Simplicity of form does not imply ignorance on the part of the young artist. Children comment freely on the perceived flaws in their clay figure, with the younger ones providing corrections verbally or reinterpreting the original intention in line with the perceived outcome. What appears as indifference to the correct proportions of a figure is often a function of the child's working style. Thus, when the arms are first endowed with fingers, their size is determined by the enthusiastic action of rolling the clay and the need for symmetry rather than by realistic proportions. Most frequently the sun-radial is adopted for the hand, frequently in the form of three fingers that create a balanced structure (see **Figure 8(a)**).

With age and practice, the figure gains in the number of its modeled parts, in attention to detail, proportion, and measurement. The overall trend is toward increasing complexity of the figure and its subdivision into distinctive parts. These include the distinction between the upper and the lower torso, shoulders, neck, clothing in the form of shirts with sleeves, flaring skirts or pants, and accessories.

With increasing complexity of the modeled parts of the human figure, children face the difficulty of maintaining an upright stance when head and body are joined to two spindly legs. This leads to the somewhat paradoxical finding that with increasing age and the sophistication to model the different parts of the human figure, verticality is often sacrificed out of frustration with the difficulty to maintain the upright posture without the help of an armature.

With age and practice come technical skills and some refinements in the appearance of the sculptures, even though many continue to be modeled quite crudely. Often the technique of some of the older children is not better than that of the younger ones, but their serious reflection

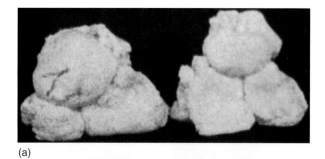

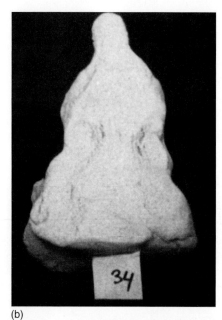

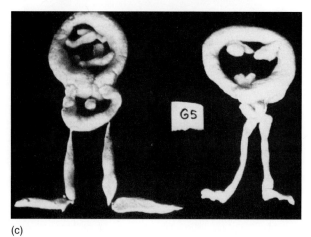

Figure 7 Beginning differentiation of the modeled human figure: (a) tadpole; (b) column with internal differentiation of parts; and (c) graphic model in clay.

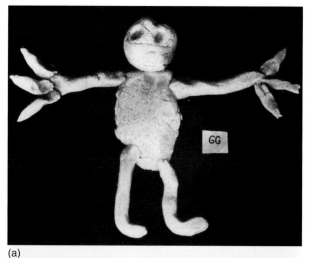

Figure 8 (a) Man with large hands. (b) Cow with udders and bell.

and concentrated work distinguish between them. Along with more planning and increased skill come a more critical awareness and often a negative evaluation of the outcome.

In analogy to drawing, the frontal part of the human figure receives the greatest attention since it carries the most identifying characteristics of the human that indicate gender and individuality. However, unlike the distinctly two-dimensionally drawn figures, in modeling attention is paid to three-dimensional aspects, turning the figure and adding or subtracting clay as children model the back and sides, and comment on their work. It is interesting that unlike drawing, the facial features in the clay figure play a less important role and are altogether omitted in 30% of the human figure sculptures, while the trunk section is represented earlier than in the corresponding drawings.

Modeling Animal Figures

Modeling of four-footed animals (dog, cow, turtle) provides much insight into children's three-dimensional conceptions in clay. Given the basic symmetry of the animal structure with the two major sides near duplicates of each other, and the body resting on four legs, children past the stage of the early globals, modeled their animals, with few exceptions, standing upright with attention paid to more than a single side, with some 4-year-olds modeling up to six sides of the figure. Noteworthy is the strategy of turning figures upside down to attach the front and hind legs, sideways to model the tail, frontally to attach the head and differentiate the orientation of the head from the sides of the body. Again, with age and practice, there is a growing interest in size differences, and attempts are made to enliven the figure by action and gesture and the addition of such defining characteristics as spots on the turtle, a collar on the dog, a bell and udders on the cow. (See **Figure 8(b)**). In general, differentiation of form is mostly age related, with older children being more skillful and able to model better balanced sculptures. However, age per se does not guarantee skill, and for most of the children representational intention exceeds their ability to give it adequate expression.

Although facial features are lacking in 40% of the animal figures, the orientation of head and body is most commonly well differentiated, and ears are modeled to indicate the direction of the head. Mixed views so common in drawing, are infrequent in clay modeling. Most interesting is the observation that children adopt a variety of different models on the human and animal figures tasks, clearly demonstrating that there is no single underlying conceptual template that guides production. Different representational models coexist in the same child.

At the beginning of this section the question whether the dimensional progression established for drawing would also be applicable to the domain of sculpture was raised. The results reported so far do not support such a view and instead suggest that from the beginning of children's intention to model a figure they employ some basic, albeit simple, three-dimensional representational concepts as indicated by their attention to multiple sides, volume, and upright posture. Although the untrained efforts of the preschoolers and of many older children yield mostly crude figures, there is early on some basic intention to model in the round.

Concluding Comments

The comparison between drawing and modeling has provided greater insight into the principles that underlie artistic thinking and problem solving and the diverse routes the search for equivalences can take. Studies on drawing and modeling support the conception of an orderly sequence in the acquisition of representational skills. In both domains there is a rule-governed progression in the problem-solving activity that underlies the child's discovery of a graphic and plastic language. The search for forms of equivalence in drawing and modeling is of a universal nature, it manifests itself in ordinary, talented, and mentally handicapped children, and across diverse cultures. Progress in the differentiation of form and space enables young artists to eliminate ambiguity, to express their thoughts and feelings better, and to articulate their sense of esthetics. With age and practice evolve the ability to attend to multiple variables, to plan, monitor, review critically, and to revise the emerging representation. Artistic development, in the absence of training, is a spontaneous and largely self-regulated process that flourishes during the early childhood years and tends to reach a plateau during the middle childhood years.

During the elementary school years, a gradual decline in spontaneous artistic productions is noted, and the work of most children signals the end of a very creative and productive period in child art. There are likely to be diverse reasons and competing interests that lead to this decline of artistic activity. Above all, alternative outlets for self expression can be found in the widening horizons of middle childhood that afford access to sports, dance, music, chess and computer games, and the opportunities for social activities. For some children, the technical problems associated with more advanced pictorial strategies spell the end of their artistic explorations. In some cases, the arts are taken up again in adulthood as a hobby or even a serious endeavor.

See also: Cognitive Development; Imagination and Fantasy; Symbolic Thought.

Suggested Readings

Arnheim R (1968) *Visual Thinking.* Berkeley: University of California Press.
Fineberg J (1997) *The Innocent Eye.* Princeton, NJ: Princeton University Press.
Freeman N (1980) *Strategies of Representation in Young Children.* London: Academic Press.
Hermelin B (2001) *Bright Splinters of the Mind.* London: Jessica Kingsley.
Willats J (2005) *Making Sense of Children's Drawings.* London: Lawrence Erlbaum Associates.
Winner E (1996) *Gifted Children: Myths and Realities.* New York: Basic Books.

Attention

M L Courage, Memorial University, St. John's, NL, Canada
J E Richards, University of South Carolina, Columbia, SC, USA

© 2008 Elsevier Inc. All rights reserved.

Glossary

Attention – The selective enhancement of some behavior at the expense of other behavior. Several different types of attention exist, including stimulus orienting, sustained attention, and executive attention.

Cognitive neuroscience – Cognition is the study of mental processes, such as attention, learning, discrimination, memory, and decision making. Cognitive neuroscience is a field of research that studies brain areas (neuroscience) that control cognitive processes.

Event-related potential – The electroencephalogram (EEG) can be linked to specific experimental or internal (cognitive) events, and EEG responses linked to such events are labeled event-related potentials (ERPs). ERPs may provide a direct and noninvasive measure of brain functioning controlling cognitive processes. One such ERP, the Nc (negative central) has been shown to index orienting of attention to novel stimuli and may be generated by the anterior cingulate of the brain.

Executive attention – An executive function ability to allocate attention in a way that is consistent with self-established goals and plans. Executive attention show the most extended developmental changes, beginning in the late phases of infancy (12 months) and showing changes throughout early childhood and into the first years of adolescence.

Habituation – Habituation refers to a cognitive process in which the initial stimulus orienting to a stimulus is diminished with repeated presentation. This process has been used profitably in the study of infant attention to show which objects elicit stimulus orienting and how infants learn about the objects through repeated presentation.

Heart rate-defined attention phases – Infants heart rate changes during attention. Heart rate can be used to define several types of attention, including stimulus orienting, sustained attention, and inattention.

Neurotransmitters – Chemicals that are used in the brain for transmitting information in neurons and synapses. The noradrenergic and cholinergic neurotransmitters are controlled by an extended network of neural connections and are important in the control of arousal and attention.

Paired-comparison procedure – A procedure in which two visual stimuli are show side by side, and the infant's preference for one or the other stimulus is measured by the amount of time the infant looks at one stimulus. Infants will show a preference to a novel stimulus, so that novelty preference is an index of the familiarity with the nonpreferred familiar stimulus.

Stimulus orienting – A form of attention in which sensory and perceptual systems are excited and often involves moving sensors (ears, eyes) toward environmental events. This type of attention begins development very early in infancy and is fully developed by 6 months of age.

Sustained attention – An extended engagement of a behavior system that enhances social and cognitive processes. This is very similar to arousal and is controlled by brain systems involved in behavioral state and arousal. Sustained attention shows dramatic developmental changes from 3 to 18 months of age.

Introduction

The study of attention has a long history in both cognitive and brain sciences. One of the founders of experimental psychology in the US, William James, wrote in his 1890 text *The Principles of Psychology* that

> Everyone knows what attention is. It is the taking possession by the mind in clear and vivid form, of one out of what seem several simultaneously possible objects or trains of thought.   James (1980, p. 403)

This statement reflects a certain commonsense view that attention is a ubiquitous psychological process whereby we can select certain elements of the environment for scrutiny and ignore others. It also implies that the selected elements can be external, such as a particular sound or image, or internal, as when one is 'deep in thought'. James went on to discuss the significance of related processes such as alerting, focus, shifting, and distractibility – all key components of the modern study of attention. Notably absent from James's writing was any reference to the underlying neural mechanisms and processes that might mediate these components of attention. Currently, there is a substantial research literature on these underlying substrates and their role in attention. This research has confirmed that attention is not a single process, but rather a complex and multidimensional one. It performs a variety of functions including the self-regulation of emotion and cognition, is tuned to many sources of information in the environment, and depends on a variety of separate neural systems in the brain. Moreover, attention can be shared, as in joint attention with others or divided as when one talks on a cell telephone while driving a car.

Developmental research on attention has a recent history. In its formative years the study of attention was of secondary interest in research where processes such as perception, discrimination, learning, strategy acquisition, planning, or working memory were of primary concern. The study of attention is currently important in its own right as cognitive developmental research has become increasingly integrated with research in cognitive neuroscience. Significant practical issues have also contributed to the growing interest in the development of attention. For example, individual differences in attention observed during infancy are predictive of achievements in language, cognition, and play later in childhood. Moreover, deficits and anomalies in attention processes contribute to or are symptomatic of the learning and behavior difficulties experienced by children with conditions such as attention-deficit hyperactivity disorder (ADHD), fetal alcohol spectrum disorder (FASD), autism, and early exposure to teratogenic agents and environmental contaminants.

This developmental research indicates that attention changes dramatically over the period of infancy and early childhood. Infants who are less than 3 months of age have very poor vision and attend primarily to salient physical characteristics of their environments. Behavioral state control is limited during this period of time, such that very young infants attend with nonspecific orienting only during their limited periods of alertness. Arousal and visuo-spatial orienting are key emergent aspects of attention in this timeframe. Between about 3 and 18 months of age the development of alert, vigilant, sustained attention occurs. Sustained attention allows the focusing of processing resources and thus during this age infants begin to engage in active processing. This alertness not only affects cognitive processes such as remembering, perceiving, and discrimination, but also allows the infant to engage in social interactions and maintain attentive states for social–emotional drives. Beginning at about 12 months of age, an internal executive system of control begins to operate. This system is used to voluntarily guide the deployment of attention. This executive attention system has an extended developmental time course, showing changes throughout early childhood and into the first adolescent years. Many of the early changes in attention are based largely on age-related changes in the brain, whereas later advances are impacted by the child's experience and specific training activities.

The present article has three objectives. First, behavioral changes in the development of visuo-spatial orienting, sustained attention, and endogenous or executive attention in infancy and early childhood will be described. The major brain structures that are involved in the development of attention will be identified. These brain systems include a general arousal system that affects many cognitive functions as well as specific attention systems that are more limited in their effects on cognition and attention. Second, psychophysiological measures that have been useful in the study of brain–attention relations in infants will be discussed. The use of heart rate as a measure of the general arousal system will be emphasized. The usefulness of these psychophysiological methods in research on attention in infants will be described and illustrated with relevant research on recognition memory. Third, the relationship between developments in visual fixation and visual attention will be discussed with illustrative examples from research on individual differences in attention. It should be noted that this article focuses on the development of visual attention as there is a vast literature on this topic. However, comments about visual attention should generalize to other sensory systems as well.

Attention in Infancy and Early Childhood

Newborn infants orient toward and attend selectively to stimuli during the brief periods when they are alert and awake. This occurs in spite of the immaturity in both structure and function of the human visual system. Robert Fantz in pioneering work on infant visual abilities showed that between birth and 2 months of age infants looked longer at patterned than at unpatterned stimuli and that depending on factors such as familiarity, size, and the amount of contrast, they preferred to look (i.e., looked longer) at some stimuli over others. Some of the infants' early abilities are based on visual reflexes (e.g., saccadic and pursuit movements) that are present at birth at least in rudimentary form. However, more general visuo-motor immaturity restricts infants' ability to scan stimuli extensively or to detect stimuli beyond about 30° in the peripheral visual field. Moreover, when infants visually capture an element in the environment, they seem to have trouble disengaging or looking away from it, a phenomenon that has been referred to as obligatory looking or sticky fixation.

The early immaturities in the young infants' visual system do not last long. There is rapid neurological development in the retina and in the visual pathways to the cortex between 2- and 3-months of age. This neurological development coincides with significant improvement in all aspects of visual functioning (e.g., visual acuity, color vision, smooth pursuit), an expansion of the visual field, moderation of inhibitory mechanisms that restricted eye movements, and the onset of more mature perceptual abilities whereby infants come to recognize objects and to determine their spatial layout. Coincident with this shift toward greater cortical control of vision, infants begin to spend more time awake and in an alert state. They also begin to look about the environment in a way that is less reflexive and appears to be more voluntary in nature. This emerging competence in visual attention reflects developments in the specific structures and pathways within the visual system and the brain.

There are changes in behavioral state that are very important for infant attention development. The physiological and psychological state of being awake and alert is called arousal. Arousal acts to energize primary sensory areas in the cortex and to increase the efficiency of responding in those areas. Its effects are generally nonspecific and affect multiple modalities, cognitive systems, and cognitive processes. Newborn infants spend most of their time in sleeping states and have only very short periods of time when they are in such a state of arousal. Both behavioral control of sleep state (i.e., infants sleeping through the night) and increases in alert states of arousal show dramatic changes from 2 to 6 months. The mature form of arousal invigorates, energizes, and regulates cognitive processes leading to increased processing efficiency, shorter reaction times, better detection, and sustaining of cognitive performance for extended periods of time. The infants' increases in its ability to attain and then maintain a state of alertness or arousal is fundamental to the development of effective information processing.

The arousal aspect of attention is controlled by several systems in the brain. These can be seen in **Figure 1**. They include the neuroanatomical connections between the mesencephalic reticular activating system in the brainstem, the thalamus, and the cortex. The thalamus is the major sensory connection area between incoming sensory information and the cortex and its reticular nucleus is enhanced bidirectionally, both by the ascending reticular activity and by feedback mechanisms from the primary sensory cortex. The mesencephalic reticular activating system also stimulates extrinsic neurotransmitters that in turn influence the limbic system areas. The noradrenergic and cholinergic transmitter systems are thought to be the neurochemical systems that are most closely involved in cortical arousal as it is related to attention. The dopaminergic system is thought to affect the motivational and energetic aspects of cognitive processing, and the serotonin system is thought to affect the overall control of state. These four neurochemical systems also show changes over the

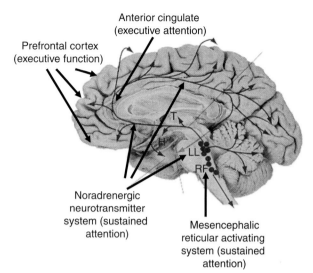

Figure 1 Some areas of the brain involved in attention. Sustained attention is controlled by the noradrenergic and cholinergic neurotransmitter systems. Executive attention is controlled by areas in the prefrontal cortex, including the anterior cingulate cortex.

period of infancy and this implies that the arousal controlled by these systems also develops in that time period.

Orienting

Holly Ruff and Mary Rothbart characterized infant's visual behavior in the first postnatal year of life as dominated by an 'orienting/investigative system' of attention. There are two inter-related components in this system. First, a spatial-orienting network (including the posterior parietal cortex with several subcortical systems such as the superior colliculus, pulvinar, and the locus coeruleus in the brainstem), is alerted by peripheral stimuli and directs attention to potentially important locations (i.e., where) in the environment. This mediates attentional functions such as, engagement, disengagement, shifting, and inhibition of return. Second, an object recognition network (including pathways from the primary visual cortex to the parietal cortex and the inferior temporal cortex) mediates attention to object features and gathers detailed information about form, color, and pattern that enables the identification (i.e., what) of objects. Ruff and Rothbart suggest that there is a marked developmental transition in the structure and function of this system between 3 and 9 months of age. Rapid maturation at all levels of the visual system with increased arousal and alertness enables infants to deploy their attention more flexibly and quickly. They begin to respond to stimulus objects and patterns around them in terms of experiential factors such as the novelty or complexity of objects and events rather than by their salience or intensity alone.

Sustained Attention

A major advance that contributes to this marked developmental transition is the infant's ability to sustain his or her attention. Sustained attention to object features, also called focused attention, is the extended selective engagement of a behavior system that primarily enhances information processing in that system. It is similar to a state of arousal during which cognitive processing is enhanced. Many of the infant's cognitive and social activities occur during episodes of sustained attention. For example, we know that infants prefer to look at relatively novel objects, faces, and sounds. Novel stimuli elicit an initial stimulus orienting, followed by sustained attention; maintenance of sustained attention then leads to the infant being able to learn about and remember aspects of the stimulus as it becomes familiar. Infants as young as 3 months of age will engage in 5–10 s periods of sustained attention. Beginning at about this age and extending into the second year, the duration that an infant can sustain attention increases markedly. As with visuo-spatial orienting, the development of sustained attention during the period of infancy is closely related to the development of brain systems controlling arousal and state. Sustained attention is a manifestation of this global arousal system of the brain that controls responsiveness to events in the environment and affects sensory systems. Thus, sustained attention represents the activation of this arousal system in situations calling for attention.

Executive or Endogenous Attention

At the end of the first year, Ruff and Rothbart suggest that the rudiments of another major attention system, one in which the infant begins to acquire a system of higher level controls over the allocation and deployment of cognitive resources, begins to emerge. This capacity is evident in a wide range of behaviors. For example, infants' look duration to static stimuli and simple objects continues to decline whereas their look duration to complex objects increases. Infants also look more to their caregivers in situations that call for social referencing and joint attention and they begin to show the beginnings of behavioral inhibition on the A-not-B task. Further evidence of emerging intentionality is evident in improvements in deferred imitation, means-end problem solving, and recall memory that occur late in the first year of life. By about 18 months of age, this endogenous control of attention acquires an increasingly executive function. Executive function is a description of psychological activities that control behavior, allocate cognitive resources, evaluate behavior progress, and direct activity with goals and plans. For example, if a toddler decides to stack rings on a dowel he or she must select the relevant rings from a toy box and ignore other irrelevant objects such as blocks that might also be available. Similarly, other activities in the environment that might be of interest to the child must be ignored so as not to disrupt this planful behavior. Executive attention and functioning are closely related to brain activity, in particular to the prefrontal cortex, anterior cingulate, and frontal eye fields. These changes in visual attention and their neural substrates enable (and may be enabled by) coincident changes in language (e.g., comprehension), cognition (e.g., representation), and self-regulation (e.g., behavioral inhibition) that begin in this timeframe and continue to advance across the preschool years. The timing of these developments in attention from birth to early childhood can be seen in summary form in **Figure 2** that has been compiled by John Colombo.

Psychophysiological Measures of Infant Attention

Psychophysiological measures have been useful in the research on infant attention and brain development. Psychophysiology is the study of psychological processes using physiological measures. The physiological measures are noninvasive and can be used with infant participants. The use of heart rate, electroencephalogram (EEG), and event-related potential (ERP) data as psychophysiological measures of attention will be reviewed to illustrate the type of information that this approach provides.

Heart Rate

The most common measure used by psychophysiologists studying young infants is heart rate. The infant's heart rate can be measured in response to psychological manipulations and used as an index of attention. John E. Richards proposed a model in which the phasic changes in infants' heart rates that occur as they look at a stimulus correspond to different levels of attentional engagement. There are four key phases in this model and these are illustrated in **Figure 3**. First, when the stimulus is initially presented there is a brief automatic interrupt phase that reflects the detection of a change in environmental stimulation. A very brief, reflexive, biphasic deceleration–acceleration in heart rate occurs. This automatic interrupt may activate the subsequent attention phases. The second phase is stimulus orienting. Stimulus orienting indicates the beginning of attentional engagement and initiates preliminary processing of the information in the stimulus. A large, rapid deceleration in heart rate from its prestimulus level occurs during this phase. The third phase is sustained attention. Sustained attention reflects the activation of the alertness/arousal system of the brain and involves voluntary, subject-controlled cognitive processing of the stimulus information. The heart rate deceleration that was reached during stimulus orienting

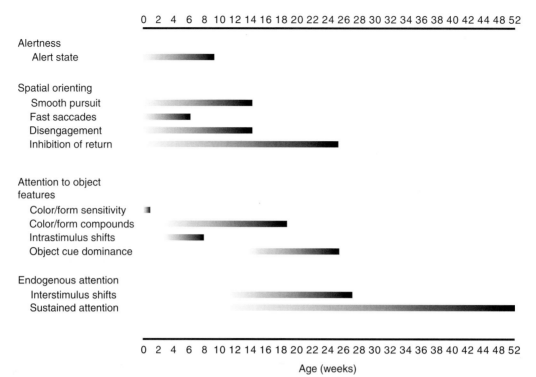

Figure 2 Summary table of the developmental course of visual attentional functions in infancy. The relative darkness of the line indicates the relative degree of maturity at each age. From Colombo J (2001) The development of visual attention in infancy. *Annual Review of Psychology* 52: 337–367.

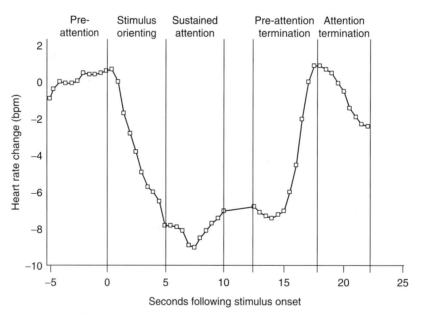

Figure 3 Heart rate changes that define attention. Stimulus orienting is an initial orienting toward a visual pattern or sound. Sustained attention represents engaged arousal. Attention termination represents inattentiveness. bpm, beats per minute. From Richards JE and Casey BJ (1991) Heart rate variability during attention phases in young infants. *Psychophysiology* 28: 43–53.

is maintained during this phase. Heart rate also shows decreased variability and certain other somatic changes that facilitate attentiveness such as reduced body movement and slower respiration may also occur. The fourth phase is attention termination. During this last phase the infant continues to look at the stimulus but is no longer processing its information (i.e., is inattentive). The heart rate begins to return to its prestimulus levels during this phase.

Many research studies validate this model across infancy and early childhood and show that the phases are elicited by a wide range of stimuli and conditions. These include brief exposures to black and white achromatic patterns and faces, extended exposure to audiovisual material (children's television programs), and the visual and manual examination of toys. Moreover, there is evidence that infants' information-processing activity occurs primarily during the heart-rate phase of sustained attention rather than during the other phases. For example, it is in sustained attention that infants (1) encode information and demonstrate later recognition of it, (2) show attenuated localization of a distracter stimulus located in the peripheral visual field, and (3) are more resistant to distraction from competing stimuli during toy play.

The phases of sustained attention and attention termination (inattention) are markers of the nonspecific arousal system of the brain. The neural control of this heart rate change originates from cardioinhibitory centers in the cortex via the vagus (tenth cranial) nerve. This area has reciprocal connections with the limbic system and through these connections is involved in modulating activity within the mesencephalic reticular formation arousal system and the related neurotransmitter systems. The cardioinhibitory centers act through the parasympathetic nervous system to slow heart rate when the arousal system is engaged. The heart rate changes occurring during sustained attention (sustained heart rate slowing) index the onset and continuing presence of this arousal. The heart rate changes during attention termination (return of heart rate to its prestimulus level) index the lack of activation of this arousal system. These two phases of attention therefore reflect the nonspecific arousal that may affect a number of sensory and brain systems.

EEG and ERPs

EEG activity has been used with both adults and infants as a measure of nonspecific arousal. This measure is important because it is a more direct measure of neural activity than is heart rate. Therefore, it is possible that EEG could be used as a noninvasive measure of the neural activity affected by attention. Scalp-recorded ERPs are derived from the EEG recording. The ERPs are derived from EEG by linking the EEG recording to a specific experimental event and then averaging out the varying EEG activity unrelated to the event. The remaining averaged EEG is thus electrical potential change that is related to the event. If the experimental event is known to be associated with a cognitive process controlled by brain activity, the ERP reflects specific cognitive processes that originate from particular brain areas. Therefore they provide a noninvasive and direct measure of functioning in those areas. For example, specific components of the ERP change in response to familiar and unfamiliar visual stimuli. One such ERP change is closely related to attentional responses. This is a negative-going electrical potential change over the central leads on the scalp. This has been labeled the Nc (negative central). The Nc is thought to represent a relatively automatic alerting response to the presence of a visual stimulus (see **Figure 4**).

Attention and Recognition Memory in Infancy

The usefulness of ERP and heart rate measures can be nicely illustrated from research on the development of recognition memory in infants. Behavioral research on infant recognition memory is typically studied with the paired-comparison procedure. In this procedure infants are shown a single stimulus (familiar stimulus) during a brief familiarization phase. Later, during the recognition memory test phase, the familiar stimulus is paired with a novel stimulus that has not been seen previously. Recognition memory for the familiar stimulus is inferred if the infants show a novelty preference (i.e., look longer at) the novel stimulus than at the familiar stimulus during the paired-comparison test. This method has provided a large database in the conditions under which infants encode, store, and retrieve information. John E. Richards used this procedure in conjunction with the heart rate-defined phases of attention. Infants between the ages of 3 and 6 months of age were first presented with a recording of the 'Sesame Street' television program. Then, when the infants were showing sustained attention to the television program, simple geometric patterns were shown for about 5 s. Infants showed recognition of the stimuli only if they were showing sustained attention to the television programs. Interestingly, the demonstration of a novelty preference that is taken as the measure of recognition of the familiar stimulus likely reflects the infant's attempt to acquire new information from the previously unseen stimulus during sustained attention.

Recognition memory has also been examined in a variant of the paired-comparison procedure called the oddball paradigm. Here infants are exposed to repeated presentations of two different stimuli. They are then exposed to one of the familiar stimuli on 60% of the trials (frequent familiar), the other familiar stimulus on 20% of the trials (infrequent familiar), and novel stimulus presentations on the remaining 20% of the trials (infrequent novel). Stimulus presentations are very brief (500 ms) in this procedure. Charles Nelson tested infants in a series of studies using the oddball procedure with ERP and found a large Nc component occurring about 400–800 ms after stimulus onset (see **Figure 4**). He found no differences in the Nc component for any of the stimulus presentation conditions for 4-, 6-, and 8-month-old infants and concluded that the Nc is indicative of a general alerting or orienting response. Other (later) components of the ERP did differ between stimulus presentation conditions for

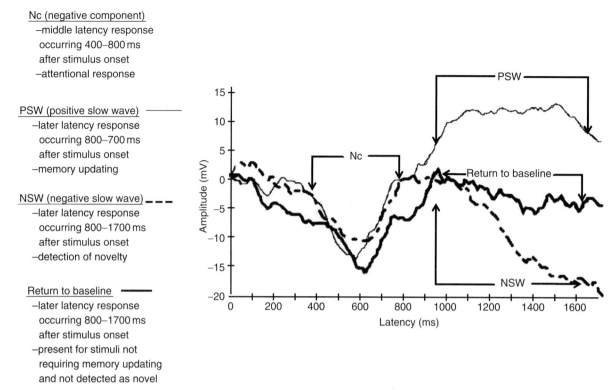

Figure 4 The Nc ERP component. The Nc is the large negative deflection in EEG potential occurring about 600 ms after stimulus onset. It is closely related to attention. Later slow waves in the ERP represent other aspects of visual information processing. From De Haan M and Nelson CA (1997) Recognition of the mother's face: A neurobehavioral study. *Child Development* 68: 187–210.

older infants. They demonstrated a negative slow wave following novel stimulus presentations and a positive slow wave following infrequent familiar stimulus presentations. The positive slow wave is likely a response associated with an updating of working memory following presentation of a familiar yet only partially encoded stimulus, whereas the negative slow wave represents the initial processing of new information provided by a novel stimulus. Thus, it is likely that the late slow wave ERP components reflect processes associated with recognition memory, while the Nc component reflects general orienting and attention.

These findings were refined in a series of reports by John E. Richards in which he showed how the ERP measures of brain activity in the oddball paradigm were affected by infants' phases of attention and inattention as defined by their heart rate changes. Infants were 4.5, 6, and 7.5 months of age. The ERP responses to frequent familiar, infrequent familiar, and novel stimuli were recorded and separated into those that occurred when then infant was in sustained attention or was inattentive. He found that there was a larger Nc during sustained attention than during inattention regardless of the familiarity (familiar, novel) or frequency (frequent, infrequent) of the stimulus (**Figure 5**). There were also age changes

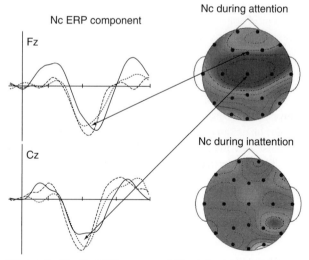

Figure 5 The Nc ERP component. The left graphs show a tracing of the ERP from the onset of a brief visual stimulus. The top left graph is from the Fz electrode and the bottom left graph from the Cz electrode (arrows point to location on scalp). The right graphs are topographical maps reflecting the electrical potential changes across the scalp at the largest negative deflection of the ERP during the Nc. The dark portions on the upper left topographical map shows the enhanced Nc occurring during sustained attention.

in the amplitude of the Nc during sustained attention. The close association of the Nc with attention supports the view that this component reflects a general attention process of orienting to the stimulus. Concerning recognition memory, late slow waves were found at about 1000–2000 ms following stimulus onset. During attention, 4.5-month-olds demonstrated a positive late slow wave that was similar for familiar and novel presentations. The older infants displayed a negative late slow wave following presentations of the novel stimulus, which stood in contrast to the positive slow wave these groups displayed following infrequent familiar stimulus presentations. The age differences suggest that (during sustained attention but not inattention) the older two age groups were sensitive to stimulus novelty and probability, whereas the younger infants were sensitive only to stimulus probability. Finally, although ERPs are voltage changes recorded from the scalp, Greg Reynolds and John E. Richards used high-density EEG recording and specialized analyses to estimate the cortical sources locations of the ERP components. For example, the cortical source of the Nc component appears to be in regions of the prefrontal cortex including the anterior cingulate. The anterior cingulate is part of the cingulate cortex, a region of the brain that shares reciprocal connections with several subcortical, cortical, and limbic regions. Studies have shown that the anterior cingulate is involved in visual target detection and the control or direction of attention.

The general importance of this work is in showing that the arousal component of attention is related to complex infant cognition. Recognition memory involves several brain areas and cognitive functions. It requires the acquisition of stimulus information and memory storage over some period of time as well as demonstration of the existence of the stored memory. It is likely that the arousal aspect of attention invigorates each of these cognitive processes. This enhances familiarization when information acquistion is occurring, may facilitate memory consolidation during the waiting period, and enhances the processes involved in the exhibition of recognition memory. The facilitative effect of attention on infant recognition memory may occur because specific brain areas responsible for information acquisition or recognition are enhanced during attention.

Visual Fixation and Attention: What Does Looking Mean?

The direction and duration of visual fixation (or looking) are core dependent measures in research on infants' attention. Over many years these measures have provided a wealth of information about the development of infants' sensory, perceptual, and cognitive processes. More recently, these measures and the attention processes they imply have become a focus of interest in their own right. In particular, the duration of infants' fixations obtained from research using habituation and selective looking procedures has been informative. A typical and very robust finding is that older infants habituate in less time, at a faster rate, and with shorter look durations than do younger infants. Older infants take less familiarization time than younger infants to show the preferences for novel stimuli indicative of recognition memory. These findings have been attributed to an increase in speed and/or efficiency in information processing with age.

Individual differences in these same look duration measures within age have also been observed. Infants who show brief look durations during visual fixation compared to age mates who show long look durations also encode information more quickly, show better recognition memory, and disengage fixation from a stimulus more readily. In addition, they show higher performance on certain measures of language, representational play, and cognition in later childhood. Longer and less efficient look duration is ostensibly less mature and is typical of very young infants and has also been observed in those who are at risk for developmental delay (e.g., preterm infants, infants with Down syndrome). Although these findings about look duration and the quality of information processing have been widely replicated, much of it has been gathered from infants who were between 3 and 6 months of age when tested initially. In contrast, research from other paradigms that involved object examination or extended media viewing indicated that when infants' attention is actively engaged with complex and/or interactive stimuli (e.g., toys or video clips), look duration actually increases across age. Much of this research was done with older infants in their second year of life.

John Colombo conducted a meta-analysis of look duration data obtained from infants of various ages across the first year of life in order to reconcile these apparently discrepant sets of findings. The results suggested a model in which infant look duration might follow a triphasic course of development over the first year or so of life. In this model, different patterns of looking reflect the maturational state of the different neural mechanisms and processes underlying infants' attention systems. This model is illustrated in **Figure 6**. In the first phase of the model, the early increase in look duration between birth and 2 months indicates the emergence of the alertness or arousal aspect of attention that is elicited most readily by external or exogenous stimuli and events. Advances in alertness over this time likely reflect an increase in subcortical (i.e., brainstem reticular system and the associated ascending pathways and neurotransmitters) influence on higher-order (i.e., neocortical) structures. In the second

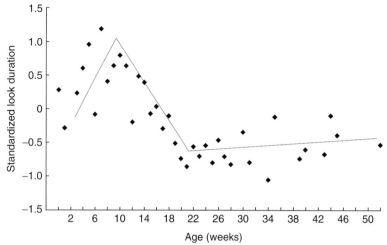

Figure 6 Changes in fixation duration reflecting attention development in infants. The figure shows a systematic decline in fixation from 3 to 6 months to simple stimuli reflecting an increase in processing speed and decline in the amount of time necessary to process simple visual patterns. From Colombo J (2002) Infant attention grows up: The emergence of a developmental cognitive neuroscience perspective. *Current Directions in Psychological Science* 11: 196–200.

phase, there is a decline in look duration from 3 to about 6 months that primarily reflects improvements in the ability to disengage from a stimulus. Disengagement and shifting of attention have been linked to developments in the posterior orienting network that includes the posterior parietal cortex in conjunction with a number of subcortical connections. The decline may also reflect an increase in sustained attention, leading to more efficient cognitive processing, and a decline in the amount of time necessary to process simple visual patterns. Finally, improvements in visual function (e.g., visual acuity, binocularity), object recognition, and speed of information processing emerge in this timeframe as maturation of the visual and inferior temporal areas of the cortex advance. In the third phase, the plateau or increase in look duration reflects the emergence of an endogenous, apparently volitional directing of attention as a function of the task at hand, in particular the inhibition of the tendency to shift attention away from a task that is interesting or demanding. This endogenous aspect of attention and the control of looking are mediated by developments in the frontal cortical areas that occur late in the first postnatal year, though these are still integrally related to the lower level brainstem systems that direct arousal and alertness.

Mary Courage, Greg Reynolds, and John E. Richards examined this model. They presented infants from 3 to 12 months of age with a variety of visual stimuli. These included simple black and white geometric patterns, faces, and clips from the Sesame Street television program. They measured how long the infant looked at the stimulus and the heart rate changes that indicate the occurrence of attention or inattention. **Figure 7** shows the average look durations to clips from the television program Sesame Street, to faces, and to simple black and white geometric patterns. There was a decrease in look duration for all stimuli during the first 6 months of age. After that there was an increase in look duration from 6 to 12 months for the Sesame Street material and to a lesser degree the faces, but no change in the amount of time spent looking at the geometric patterns. The increase in looking time to complex visual patterns indicates that infants will engage in selective enhanced processing if sufficient complexity exists in the stimulus.

The difference in the development of looking at complex and simple stimuli has been shown to continue into the later parts of childhood. John E. Richards has presented children ranging in age from 6 months to 2 years with the Sesame Street movie, 'Follow that Bird', and with simple computer-generated black-and-white geometric forms. The movie was accompanied by the appropriate soundtrack and the geometric forms with computer-generated music. As with the complex stimuli mentioned above, there was an increase in the duration of the look toward the Sesame Street movie from 6 months to 2 years. Alternatively, the 6-month-old infants looked for equal duration at the movie and the computer-generated stimuli. However, there was no change in the amount of time spent looking at the simple forms. In a similar vein, Daniel Anderson has shown that 3–5-year-old children are very sensitive to the comprehensibility of television programs. Young children will show very long and extended looks at programs that are at their comprehension level, but only brief looks at programs that are either too complex or too simple for their cognitive level. These findings indicate that from 6 months to 5 years of age there is an increase in the selective enhanced processing of audio and visual information.

An important implication of these endings is that look duration means different things at different ages. In the

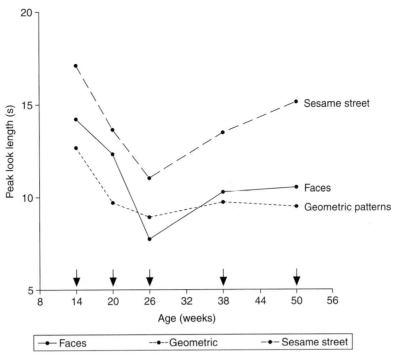

Figure 7 Mean peak look durations for static and dynamic versions on each stimulus type (faces, geometric patterns, Sesame Street) as a function of age. Note the decline over ages in all functions until 6 months, the lack of change after 6 months in look duration for the faces and geometric patterns, and the increase from 6 to 12 months in the looking time toward Sesame Street.

early months of life infants who show short look durations appear to be at an advantage on certain cognitive tests later in childhood. Their brief looks indicate that they process stimulus information quickly and efficiently and that they can readily disengage from a stimulus and shift their attention to another object or location in the environment as needed. However, by the end of the first year, longer look durations are likely more adaptive than short looks, especially in situations where the affordances of the environment are complex and engaging and resistance to distraction during information processing is important. John Colombo suggested that the longer look durations seen at older ages reflect the ability to voluntarily sustain attention to an object or to maintain focus on a short-term goal that signals the operation of endogenous attention. By early childhood, attention is directed to objects or audiovisual information that is meaningful to the infant, and information that is too complex or not meaningful is ignored.

Finally, there is an important caveat to the strict interpretation of the duration of infants' looking as an index of visual attention and information processing. This is clearly evident from John E. Richards' model of the heart rate defined phases of attention and the data that support it. Although many researchers define visual attention in terms of the duration of time that the infant keeps his or her eyes directed toward a stimulus, young infants often will continue to look at a visual pattern even when their heart rate (i.e., sustained attention is not occurring) shows that they are no longer attending to it or presumably processing its information. This may be particularly likely in the first 3 months of life when an infant's looking may be captured by a pattern from which they cannot easily disengage although it is evident later in infancy and early childhood as well. Indeed, even older children and adults can appear to be looking intently at something but are in fact not processing its information at all but have covertly directed their attention elsewhere. An implication of this is that it may be important to provide convergent evidence from both behavioral measures (looking) and physiological measures (cardiac change) of attention when developmental changes in infants' information processing are of interest.

Individual Differences in Attention

There are marked individual differences in several aspects of attention during infancy and toddlerhood that have implications for attention, learning, and memory in later childhood. The precise meaning of these individual differences as well as their developmental trajectory are not entirely clear and will continue to be explored in future research. However, one might speculate that they will have implications for a range of practical developmental issues such as academic performance, the impact of the extensive exposure to television and other screen media that infants and toddlers experience, and in the design of interventions for infants and children who are at risk for attention disorders and difficulties. A good example in which research on attention processes has informed individual differences in attention is attention deficit hyperactivity disorder (ADHD).

Attention Deficit Hyperactivity Disorder

This is one type of attention difficulty seen in young children, particularly as they enter school. ADHD affects from 5% to 10% of school-aged children. It is characterized by inattentiveness, hyperactivity, poor impulse control, and behavior management problems. These children often come to the attention of healthcare professionals when entering school because they do poorly in situations demanding sustained behavior control. ADHD is usually separated into three subtypes: ADHD-inattentive (ADHD-I), ADHD-hyperactive (ADHD-H), and ADHD-combined type (ADHD-C). The children who are diagnosed as ADHD-I have problems in attention control, sustained attention, and are often inattentive. The children diagnosed as ADHD-H show poor impulse control and exhibit high levels of activity. The ADHD-C children show signs of both inattentiveness and hyperactivity. The treatment for ADHD is generally pharmacological (e.g., methylphenidate (Ritalin)).

The subtypes of ADHD may be related to the distinction between sustained attention and executive attention. A common hypothesis about the cause of ADHD-H is a poorly functioning executive attention system. Supporting this, ADHD-H children have been shown to do poorly on tasks requiring plans, the inhibition of reflexive or automatic behavior, and impulse control. Several studies link deficits in the prefrontal cortex to ADHD-H children. Alternatively, children with the diagnosis of ADHD-I perform nearly as well as normal children on executive function tasks. However, they show deficits on tasks requiring sustained attention, covert shifting of attention, and selective attention. The ADHD subtypes are likely due to differences in the brain regions controlling sustained attention and executive attention. Individual differences in sustained attention in the early part of infancy may be related to ADHD-I outcomes, particularly in infants showing extremely low amounts of sustained attention. Deficits in parts of the brain that allow the sustaining of attention over extended time periods may be impaired leading to consistent poor performance for these infants and children. Alternatively, ADHD-H is not predicted by individual differences in attention observer prior to 2 or 3 years of age. This is likely due to the factor that the areas of the frontal cortex controlling executive attention are not yet sufficiently developed. As early identification is critically important to early intervention and potentially better prognosis, information from developmental and brain sciences could possibly serve to ameliorate attention difficulties and to optimize outcomes for these children.

Conclusion

Attention is the selective enhancement of some behavior at the expense of other behavior. Marked developmental changes occur in stimulus orienting and sustained attention during the first 2 years of life. Stimulus orienting involves the general orientation of sensory systems and receptors to important environmental events and sustained attention involves the enhanced and selective processing of information for specific psychological behaviors. Thus, by the end of infancy these aspects of attention are fully developed. The development of attention in the toddler years and into early and middle childhood involves the development of executive attention, which is the ability to carry out tasks with planfulness, allocate attention to self-established goals and plans, and monitor one's progress in complex tasks. Changes in orienting, sustained attention, and executive attention are closely linked to brain development. One of the most recognized childhood disorders, ADHD, is closely related to problems in the executive attention system and may be caused by a deficit in the brain areas involved in the development of executive function and executive attention.

See also: Brain Function; Habituation and Novelty; Memory.

Suggested Readings

Colombo J (2001) The development of visual attention in infancy. *Annual Review of Psychology* 52: 337–367.

Colombo J (2002) Infant attention grows up: The emergence of a developmental cognitive neuroscience perspective. *Current Directions in Psychological Science* 11: 196–200.

Courage ML, Reynolds GD, and Richards JE (2006) Infants' visual attention to patterned stimuli: Developmental change and individual differences from 3- to 12-months of age. *Child Development* 77: 680–695.

De Haan M and Nelson CA (1997) Recognition of the mother's face: A neurobehavioral study. *Child Development* 68: 187–210.

James W (1980) *The Principles of Psychology*. New York: Dover Publications.

Reynolds GD and Richards JE (2007) Infant heart rate: A developmental psychophysiological perspective. In: Schmidt LA and Segalowitz SJ (eds.) *Developmental Psychophysiology: Theory, Systems and Applications*, pp. 173–212. New York: Cambridge Press.

Richards JE (1998) *Cognitive Neuroscience of Attention: A Developmental Perspective*. Mahwa, NJ: Erlbaum.

Richards JE (2001) Attention in young infants: A developmental psychophysiological perspective. In: Nelson CA and Luciana M (eds.) *Handbook of Developmental Cognitive Neuroscience*, pp. 321–338. Cambridge, MA: MIT Press.

Richards JE and Casey BJ (1991) Heart rate variability during attention phases in young infants. *Psychophysiology* 28: 43–53.

Ruff HA and Rothbart MK (1996) *Attention in Early Development: Themes and Variations*. New York: Oxford University Press.

Bayley Scales of Infant Development

E M Lennon, J M Gardner, B Z Karmel, and M J Flory, New York State Institute for Basic Research, Staten Island, NY, USA

© 2008 Elsevier Inc. All rights reserved.

Glossary

Adjusted age – In the assessment of preterm infants, age is usually calculated based on expected date of birth, rather than on actual date of birth, in order to adjust for the preterm infant's neurological immaturity relative to same-age peers born full-term. Standard scores are derived by referring to the norms table appropriate for this adjusted age.

Basal and ceiling rules – In developmental scales covering a wide age range, only a subset of the test items are administered at each age. Basal and ceiling rules determine the specific test items administered. Different tests have different criteria for establishing basal and ceiling levels. For example, on the first edition of the Bayley Scales, the child was required to pass 10 successive items (ordered by degree of difficulty) to establish a basal level and fail 10 successive items to establish a ceiling level on the mental scale before testing was discontinued and a score could be obtained.

Norm-referenced test – A test that has been standardized and tested on a large sample selected to be representative of the larger population, in order to establish a reference group. Standard scores are obtained by comparing an individual's performance to the performance of same-age peers in this reference group.

Standardization – A consistent set of procedures for administering test items and scoring a test, so that all test-takers are assessed under the same standard conditions. Standardized procedures are developed so that children assessed by different examiners and in different locations are all tested under comparable test conditions, and therefore differences in test scores among children are less likely to be due to differences among examiners or test settings. Adhering to standardized procedures is especially important when examiners wish to compare an individual to a particular reference group of others who have taken the same test under standardized conditions.

Introduction

The Bayley Scales of Infant Development are a set of individually administered developmental scales designed to measure current developmental functioning in the areas of cognition, motor skills, and behavior. Nancy Bayley's unique contribution to the field of infant assessment was to create a standardized test for infants and young children with a flexible administration format. Bayley worked with various research editions of her scales for more than 40 years before the first commercially available edition of the Bayley Scales was released in 1969. The second edition was published in 1993, shortly before Bayley's death in 1994. The third and most recent edition, now titled the Bayley Scales of Infant and Toddler Development, was released in 2006. In the first edition, many test items were borrowed or adapted from items on other developmental scales; others were created by Bayley during her work on the Berkeley Growth Project. In the more recent editions, the age ranges were extended, and many items that were based on infant and child development research from a variety of different theoretical perspectives were added. Thus, all three editions of the Bayley Scales are considered theoretically eclectic, because their content and structure were influenced by a variety of different sources rather than being based on a specific developmental theory. Nevertheless, certain underlying assumptions about the nature of cognitive and motor development guided the construction of the original Bayley Scales, although subsequent editions reflected somewhat different theoretical positions.

It is clear that Bayley had her own theoretical perspective, based on an epigenetic developmental approach that integrated seemingly disparate points of view. This is evident in her interactionist position on the structure of intelligence and the factors contributing to intellectual growth. Bayley felt that cognitive growth occurred as a result of an interaction between a process of maturational unfolding and environmental influences. She believed that later intelligence arose out of earlier simpler functions, such as visual perception, that were subsequently integrated into more complex functions such as visually guided reaching for objects. Eventually, higher-level abilities emerge and become differentiated into separate domains such as memory or problem solving. While development of the earlier simpler functions may follow a maturational timetable, emergence of more complex abilities also depends on environmental influences. Thus, Bayley anticipated contemporary perspectives that consider maturational and environmental influences on infant development to be inseparable and dynamically interactive over time.

The first part of this article will focus on the theoretical and historical background relevant to infant assessment, specifically on the extent to which Bayley's theoretical perspective shaped the construction of her scales. Each of the three editions of the Bayley Scales will be described in turn. The final section will describe contemporary research that has addressed some of the same questions that Bayley anticipated at the beginning of her career.

Historical Background

The study of intellectual development and its measurement historically has involved debate about several theoretical issues, all of which have implications for test design. One issue concerned the structure of intelligence, which was described as either a general global intellectual capacity, complex but unified, or a combination of many separate abilities. The determinants of individual differences in intellectual capacity and rate of development also were the subject of much debate when Bayley first started the construction of her scales. For example, proponents of the view that intelligence is predetermined by either the child's genetic heritage or by a maturational timetable argued that intellectual capacity is fixed and unchanging across the lifespan, while others maintained that environmental influences contributed to changes in performance on intelligence tests over time. Finally, an important theoretical issue concerned whether cognitive development can be characterized as qualitative change, involving reorganization and restructuring at each new developmental level, or as a quantitative change involving the steady and incremental accumulation of knowledge with no qualitative change in the nature of intelligence. During the first half of the twentieth century, these issues influenced both the intelligence testing movement and the movement to catalog the course of human growth in large longitudinal studies, as exemplified by the work of Alfred Binet and Arnold Gesell.

In 1905, Binet developed an intelligence test for young children to determine placement in special remedial classes in the French school system. Binet's test contained items selected to assess complex mental processes such as memory, attention, and comprehension. Its structure was based on the concept of general intelligence, which was widely accepted in the early years of the twentieth century. According to this view, intelligence tests could be constructed of a variety of items measuring performance in different domains combined together into a single scale, rather than divided into separate subscales for different abilities, since each individual item presumably tapped into the same underlying level of general intelligence. Binet test scores for individual children were fairly stable over time, leading some to conclude that this general intellectual capacity was constant throughout the lifespan, although Binet himself was opposed to this idea.

Working with a longitudinal sample in the early 1920s, Gesell developed test items designed to measure age-related changes in infant abilities in five areas: postural, presensory, perceptual, adaptive, and language–social behavior, and created a test divided into five corresponding scales. Gesell believed that responses to test items presented in early infancy were precursors to more mature forms of related behaviors observed at later ages. His five separate scales with no overall composite score implied that Gesell believed abilities in these areas developed independently. Gesell's position was that predetermined biological maturation accounted for the development of these separate abilities, which unfolded in a fixed sequence, and that heredity determined the upper limits of an individual's capacity and rate of development.

Even though Bayley's views differed from many of the theoretical positions of Gesell and Binet, both the content and the structure of the Bayley Scales were strongly influenced by their work. For example, much of the content of her early scales consisted of developmentally ordered items taken directly from Gesell's work, and she employed Gesell's method of administering the same test items at different ages in order to elicit a range of different responses. Bayley shared Gesell's interest in motor development, although she emphasized the inseparability of motor and mental skills in early development. She disagreed with Gesell that items measuring infant abilities could be organized into different subscales, believing that mental abilities were not divided into separate factors, particularly in early infancy. Accordingly, the Bayley Scales were structured like the Binet scales, with items testing performance in different domains grouped together by age levels rather than divided into separate subscales for different kinds of mental abilities. Despite the influence of Binet and Gesell, Bayley did not subscribe to most of the underlying assumptions of the intelligence testing movement, particularly the idea of a fixed intelligence.

The notion of intellectual capacity as fixed and unchanging across the lifespan, based on the idea that intelligence was genetically predetermined, had two important implications for infant assessment: it should be possible to predict later intelligence from performance on tests given in infancy, and performance on intelligence tests should not be influenced by environmental factors such as level of parental education or the amount of stimulation in the home. Bayley's early research directly addressed these issues and helped to formulate her own theoretical perspective on the structure of intelligence and the nature of intellectual growth. Evidence from her longitudinal studies demonstrating that performance on infant tests did not predict later outcome led her to conclude that intellectual capacity is not immutable. If intelligence is not fixed, but rather changes over time, consideration of the determinants of intellectual growth necessarily included environmental factors. Thus, Bayley's developmental perspective led her to take an interactionist position on this issue, and her work supported the idea that maturation and environment had different effects on the course of cognitive development at different points in time. For example, she found that in early infancy, individual differences in performance on the mental scale appeared to be a function of different rates of sensorimotor maturation, while environmental influences on mental scores became more evident in the second year. Her earlier finding that correlations between mental and motor scores decreased with age in typically developing infants supported this conclusion. Bayley took a similarly developmental perspective on the question of whether intelligence was best described as a general mental ability or as separate factors, writing that early in development mental abilities consist of the most simple and basic functions, out of which more complex functions gradually emerge and are eventually differentiated into separate abilities in different domains.

Development of the Early Scales

In 1928, Bayley started work on the Berkeley Growth Study, a longitudinal study of 61 children tested at regular and frequent intervals starting at 2 months of age and continuing into adulthood. A primary focus was to examine the normative development of cognitive and motor abilities. To achieve this goal, Bayley developed a series of tests published between 1933 and 1936: The California First-Year Mental Scale, the California Infant Scale of Motor Development, and the California Preschool Mental Scale. These scales were used to test her sample monthly for the first 15 months and every 3 months thereafter until 3 years, after which they were tested at 6-month intervals until 5 years of age.

The original California scales were revised in 1958 and tested on a large nationwide sample of infants from 1 to 15 months. In contrast to the primarily middle-class families in the Berkeley Growth Study, these infants constituted a more diverse sample representative of the US population in terms of level of parental education, which Bayley considered a valid index of socioeconomic status. Bayley found that level of parental education did not predict performance on either the mental or the motor scale at any age between 1 and 15 months, supporting her earlier conclusion that individual differences in performance during the period of rapid development in the first year may be less subject to environmental influences, and more a function of sensorimotor maturation.

This research edition, which also included a version of the Infant Behavior Record, was expanded in 1960 to extend the age range to 30 months. It formed the basis for the first commercially available edition of the Bayley Scales, published in 1969 and considered the most carefully standardized infant test of its time. Bayley used a sample of 1262 children, with 83 to 95 children at each of 14 age groups between 2 and 30 months, selected to be representative of the 1960 US population by gender, race, level of parental education, and geographic location. Children were excluded if they were born more than 1 month prematurely or had severe emotional or behavioral problems. Additionally, children over 12 months from bilingual homes who had difficulty using English were not included in the final standardization sample.

Bayley Scales of Infant Development

The first edition of the Bayley Scales (BSID-I) consisted of three complementary scales designed to assess developmental status of young children between 2 and 30 months of age. The Mental and Motor Scales were composed of tasks directly administered to children in order to elicit a set of behavioral responses. Although it was not constructed as an intelligence test, the Mental Scale was designed to measure cognitive abilities considered to be the foundation for later intelligence. It included tasks measuring responses to visual and auditory stimulation, perceptual discrimination, imitation and social communication, object permanence, memory, eye–hand coordination, problem-solving, classification, vocal ability, and receptive and expressive language skills. The Motor Scale was designed to measure motor control, gross motor coordination, and manipulatory or fine motor skills. The Infant Behavior Record, completed after the administration of the Mental and Motor Scales, allowed the examiner to rate the child on factors such as activity level, attention span, motivation, persistence, and other characteristics displayed during the test session.

Particular care was taken to make the BSID-I as appealing as possible to infants and young children. The original test manual and the manual supplement published in 1984 presented strategies to produce the most reliable and valid test performance in a playful and child-friendly test session. The test materials were items likely to engage the interest of young children, such as rattles, blocks, puzzles, crayons, and picture books. The BSID-I had a very flexible administration format, with order of item administration, as well as the pacing of transitions from one item to the next, based on the child's responsiveness, in order to elicit the child's best performance. The emphasis on flexibility included crediting of incidentally observed behavior and caregiver administration of some items. The re-administration of items initially failed was encouraged, based on the reasoning that the failure may have been the result of inattentiveness, or the child's initial interest in exploring the new item rather than complying with the examiner's instructions. This flexible approach was augmented by specific administration directions to insure a standardized administration of each item.

Each administration of the BSID-I involved a subset of the 163 items on the Mental Scale and the 81 items on the Motor Scale, with the specific items administered dependent on a combination of the child's age and ability level. Although the test items were organized on the record form in order of difficulty, they were not administered in this order. Instead, sequential presentation of items of increasing difficulty using the same materials or testing the same underlying constructs, such as object permanence or language skills, was recommended. This approach allowed the examiner to gain a great deal of information without overtiring the child. In one example cited in the manual it was noted that a total of 13 items, 10 from the Mental Scale and three from the Motor Scale, could be scored from the presentation of three blocks to a young infant.

Items measuring different areas such as language, social skills, problem-solving, and eye–hand coordination were interspersed on the Mental Scale record form, arranged according to the age level assigned to each item, which corresponded to the age that it was passed by 50% of the children in the normative sample. Basal and ceiling criteria required passing and failing a specified number of items consecutively ordered on the record form. On the Mental Scale, the recommended basal criterion was 10 consecutive passes, and the ceiling criterion was 10 consecutive failures, while on the Motor Scale the recommended criterion was six consecutive items passed or failed. There was flexibility even in this, however, and the final decision of when to stop testing was left to the judgment of the examiner. Examiners typically would begin with an item about 1 month below the child's age, ideally an item part of a sequence spanning several age levels. Based on the child's performance the examiner would be able to score several items and determine whether it was necessary to drop back to a younger age level to meet the basal criterion. Following the administration of an adequate number of items in a particular sequence, the examiner would select items from sequences measuring skills in different domains and continue to score for passes and failures until the basal and ceiling criteria were met. Examiners were cautioned that testing should not be discontinued until it was clear that the child would not be able to pass any further items, and it was emphasized that the goal was to capture the child's full range of successful functioning. The basal and ceiling rules insured that the upper and lower limits of behaviors in all domains would contribute to the final score.

Thus, the specific sequences of items presented were determined by the child's overall level of ability across domains. Children who had particular strengths in one area, such as language, would sometimes be close to meeting the ceiling criteria but then would pass an item in their area of strength, and additional items were administered to obtain the ceiling level. A major advantage of this test design was that the child's final score would be based on a range of items measuring skills in different domains such as problem solving, language, and fine motor skills. Following the administration of the Mental and Motor Scales, the raw scores were tabulated and referenced to norms appropriate for the child's age to obtain the standardized score for each scale, the Mental Developmental Index (MDI) and the Psychomotor Developmental Index (PDI). Performance on the Mental and Motor Scales yielded standard scores with a mean of 100 and a standard deviation of 16.

In contrast to the Mental and Motor Scales, which measured the infant's performance of specific skills, the Infant Behavior Record was a record of the examiner's impression of infant behaviors observed during the test session, such as social responsiveness, activity level and attention, emotional tone, cooperation and persistence, orientation to objects, and muscle tone. Most of these behaviors were measured with rating scales. A few additional items consisted of the examiner's judgment of whether the test performance appeared to be an accurate reflection of the child's optimal behavior, as well as more qualitative descriptions of unusual behaviors observed and an overall summary of the child's performance. Although initially there was a great deal of interest in the inclusion of a measure of behavior in a test of infant development, in practice this scale was not used as frequently.

Much of the early research using the Bayley Scales was concerned with the issue of whether mental scores in infancy predicted performance on childhood measures of intelligence, based in part on the concept of a general intelligence that was fixed and stable over time. In general, studies done with typically developing infants replicated Bayley's earlier findings that there was limited evidence for predictive validity based on mental scores in the first year, although toward the end of the second year mental scores were more strongly related to preschool outcome. Better evidence for prediction to later outcome was found for infants with the lowest scores. When it became clear that global scores on tests given to young, typically developing infants did not reliably predict later outcome, the focus shifted to attempts to identify the specific items or sets of items that might predict more effectively, and some limited ability to predict later outcome in related areas was found. In this endeavor, subsets of items measuring skills related to language development emerged as a relatively stronger predictor of later outcome. Moreover, different subsets of items were better predictors of later performance at different ages – for example, visual–motor tasks given in early infancy, and language items in the second year. These latter results were consistent with Bayley's view that there was a discontinuity in the very nature of intelligence itself, such that intelligence takes different forms at different points in development.

Performance on the Bayley Scales was considered an accurate assessment of current level of functioning, however, and soon emphasis shifted from investigation of its predictive validity to the use of the BSID-I as an outcome measure in studies investigating prediction from early risk factors. Consistent with Bayley's early findings with respect to different influences at different points in development for typically developing children, many studies with high-risk infants indicated a greater influence of biomedical risk factors during the first year while environmental effects became more evident in the second year. While group means indicated an association between increased neonatal risk and subsequent lower BSID-I scores, it was not possible to predict outcome for individual children based on early risk factors. Researchers who investigated patterns of performance over time, rather than relying on scores from one point in development, found that individual developmental trajectories based on scores from three or four different points in time were better predictors of later outcome than either single scores or early risk factors, except in extreme cases.

In the 1984 BSID-I manual supplement it was recommended that examiners calculate age based on expected date of birth for premature infants, and refer to the norms table appropriate for this adjusted age. This was based on research suggesting this may provide a better estimate of the developmental level of premature infants. This issue became more important during the 1980s and 1990s when advances in obstetric and perinatal medicine led to new procedures for treating infertility as well as an improved ability to sustain high-risk pregnancies for longer periods. There was a subsequent increase in deliveries of viable high-risk infants, including preterm and multiple gestation infants. Furthermore, innovative techniques in neonatology led to even higher rates of survival for very premature and other medically fragile infants who were being born in greater numbers and at increased risk for poor neurodevelopmental outcome. As follow-up programs were created to monitor the development of these infants, there was an increased need for objective methodologies to assess them. Consequently, the BSID-I was being used increasingly to assess children with atypical development, not just in follow-up programs but also to test for eligibility for early intervention programs for infants and children with developmental disabilities. Although the normative approach Bayley took in developing her test allowed clinicians to determine the extent to which infants with atypical development deviated from the normative sample, the test was not designed to provide diagnostic information about specific patterns of abnormality. For example, many infants with genetic syndromes or significant central nervous system (CNS) injury due to loss of oxygen at birth have lower mental and motor scores relative to their typically developing peers. Statistical deviation from normative performance does not provide differential diagnostic criteria for abnormality, however, and fails in many cases to establish early abnormality unless it is severe.

The question of whether to adjust for degree of prematurity in calculating scores on developmental assessments is related to theoretical issues about the relative influences of maturation and experience. Premature infants, although they have increased extra-uterine experience compared to full-term infants matched for time from conception, actually show behaviors based on neurological maturity rather than experience, particularly on tasks measuring earlier emerging functions such as visual perception. In general, performance of premature infants on the BSID-I was more consistent with full-term infants with the same time from conception than with full-term infants with the same date of birth. Thus, a 9-month-old infant born 3 months prematurely might be considered delayed compared to a full-term 9-month-old, but would most likely perform comparably to a full-term 6-month-old. If this infant earned a raw score of 74 on the BSID-I Mental Scale, this score would be converted to a scaled score of 100 using the 6-month norms table, indicating age-appropriate cognitive skills. This same child would receive a scaled score of 63 based on the 9-month norms table, indicating significantly delayed cognitive development. Adjustment for degree of prematurity was often discontinued at 2 years of age, based on the idea that premature infants should have caught up to their same-age peers by the age of 2 years, and that continued use of adjusted age might mask underlying deficits or developmental delays. While many premature infants may indeed have obtained scores appropriate for chronological age as they got older, these scores may have reflected proportionally smaller differences between adjusted and chronological ages and a correspondingly smaller difference between scores based on adjusted and chronological age. In some cases, improved test performance for preterm infants at older ages also may have reflected environmental influences at home or in early intervention programs, since test items in the upper age ranges on the Mental Scale measured complex skills influenced by environmental differences.

A method for obtaining age-equivalent scores to determine functional levels for children with atypical or delayed development was described in the manual, although in general this practice was discouraged. Because these children may display very different patterns of abilities from typically developing peers with the same raw scores, examiners were advised to study the test protocol carefully to discover the children's specific areas of strength and weakness. The performance of high-risk infants does tend to be more variable across domains, and this variability would contribute to some of the controversy surrounding the changes made in the second edition of the Bayley Scales.

Bayley Scales of Infant Development-II

The second edition of the Bayley Scales (BSID-II) was published in 1993. It maintained the three scales, the Mental Scale and the Motor Scale, which were extensions from the first edition, and the Behavior Rating Scale, which replaced the Infant Behavior Record. One of the goals of the revision was to preserve the basic qualities of the Bayley Scales, thus the BSID-II similarly was designed to assess the infants' current level of functioning through the presentation of a series of items and observation of the infant's behavioral responses. It also combined standardized item administration and scoring procedures with flexibility in the sequence and pacing of the item administration. Some of the changes made in the second edition had the unintended effect of limiting the flexibility that had been a hallmark of the first edition of the Bayley, however.

There were several substantive changes in the second edition. The norms were updated to reflect the US population as of 1988 in terms of race and ethnicity, geographic location, and level of parental education, and the age range was extended to include children between 1 and 42 months. The standardization sample of 1700 consisted of 50 boys and 50 girls at each of 17 age groups. The BSID-II, like its predecessor, was considered to be a carefully standardized infant test. Nevertheless, characteristics of the normative sample may have influenced scores obtained at certain ages or by specific groups of children. For example, children who were born prior to 36 weeks gestation, had significant medical problems, or were receiving services for mental, physical, or behavioral problems were excluded from the normative sample. This latter criterion for exclusion would have disproportionately excluded older children, as full-term infants without medical problems typically are not referred for services in early infancy unless they exhibit global delays. In particular, referrals for services for language delays often do not occur until late in the second year. Therefore, in the upper age ranges the normative sample consisted of children who were increasingly higher functioning relative to the children in the younger age ranges of the sample as well as to the general population. Moreover, the standardization sample contained very few low-scoring children, and, therefore, their performance did not reflect the full range of behavior found among low-scoring children in the larger population. This is especially relevant in light of the increasing use of the Bayley Scales with atypical populations, as will be discussed further below.

Stimulus materials were updated to make them more colorful and more durable, and new items were developed for the extended age ranges. Even more important for developmentalists, items were added to reflect advances in infant and child development research. In addition to the skills measured by the first edition, the BSID-II Mental Scale contained new items designed to improve measurement of cognitive abilities, including visual preference tasks and visual and auditory habituation in younger infants, and problem-solving and categorization skills in older infants. There also was an increase in the percentage of items measuring language skills, especially by the middle of the second year. Tasks intended to assess early school readiness skills, such as number concepts, categorization, and prewriting skills were added in the upper age range of the test. The Motor Scale measured gross and fine motor control and coordination, and also included some new items designed to measure sensory integration and perceptual–motor development. The percentage of fine motor items was increased at the upper ages, as the first edition had been criticized for being weak in this area.

The Behavior Rating Scale consisted of five-point rating scales designed to assess behaviors observed during the test session that yielded scores for the areas of Attention/Arousal, Orientation/Engagement, Emotional Regulation, and Motor Quality, although not all of these factors were assessed at each age.

The original Bayley Scales grew out of the movement to study infant and preschool development in order to establish normative data for the developmental changes that rapidly occur during this period, but in practice the scales were frequently used to evaluate high-risk infants in clinical settings. Reflecting this shift in emphasis, the second edition was described as being appropriate for diagnosing developmental delay and planning intervention strategies, and included suggestions to facilitate the clinician's description of the child's strengths and weaknesses. Information on the performance of children from eight high-risk clinical samples was presented in the BSID-II test manual, intended to provide examiners working with these populations with profiles of children in these different groups. The number of children in each clinical sample was small, however, and these data were not necessarily designed to improve the discriminant validity of the test. Large-scale developmental studies investigating performance over time would provide a better picture of the range of functioning of children in these various high-risk groups.

Other changes were made based on critiques of the first edition. Because previous research found that the BSID-I had limited predictive validity, specific items thought to be predictive of later outcome were added, mostly based on the recommendations of specialists in the field of early childhood assessment working with children with delayed or atypical development. Guidelines were not provided for their interpretation or use in planning intervention strategies, however. Since studies that investigated performance on related sets of items suggested that this approach might predict later outcome better than the global mental and motor scores, facet scores were constructed and added to scoring procedures to facilitate interpretation of the child's performance in the areas of cognitive, language, personal/social, and motor skills. In practice, however, several issues limited the usefulness of these facet scores; for example, the lack of equivalent representation across all facets at each age, most notable in the Personal/Social facet that consisted of only five items above the age of 4 months.

The biggest and most controversial change in the second edition was the introduction of age-based item sets, which were developed in an effort to shorten the administration time of the test and to insure that infants of the same age achieved scores that were based on the same items. Initially, infants were administered a predetermined set of items based on their age level. Social, language, memory, visual–motor, and problem-solving items were intermingled on the Mental Scale item sets, while the Motor Scale item sets consisted of a mixture of gross and fine motor items. On the Mental Scale, the basal criterion was passing at least five items within the item set, and the ceiling criterion was failure of at least four items within the item set. For the Motor Scale, basal and ceiling rules required the child to pass at least three items and fail at least two items within the item set. As long as the child met the basal and ceiling criteria, the index score was based strictly on the child's performance on the items within the item set. All items below the item set were credited as if they were passed, and if the child demonstrated proficiency on any items above the item set, credit for these items was not included in determining the final score. Children who did not meet either the basal or ceiling criteria for the item set based on their age were administered items in the item sets above or below their age level until these criteria were satisfied and a score was obtained.

In both the BSID-I and the BSID-II, the test items were arranged on the record form in order of difficulty, and therefore items from a number of different domains were interspersed. The BSID-I had basal and ceiling rules based on a specified number of consecutive items in the order that they appeared on the record form, insuring that testing would be discontinued only when the lower and upper limits of the child's abilities across domains was determined. In contrast, the basal and ceiling rules in the BSID-II did not require the child to pass and fail a number of consecutive items, instead they were just required to pass and fail a specified number of items within the item set based on their age. This meant that children whose development was uneven across domains were likely to meet their basal criteria on tasks testing skills in one domain, while they met their ceiling criteria on tasks testing skills in another domain. In order to illustrate this problem, we present the example of a hypothetical 12-month-old infant whose language and memory skills are somewhat better developed than her visual–motor skills. This child says several words, follows verbal commands, and has good memory and problem-solving abilities. While she can perform many tasks measuring visual–motor skills appropriately for her age, there were several visual–motor tasks that she did not pass at the upper end of her item set. She satisfied the ceiling criteria by failing four items measuring visual–motor skills within the 12-month item set. There are eight additional items measuring language and memory skills above her item set that she would have been able to pass, however, but performance on these items would not be included in her final score because she met the ceiling criterion for her item set. If this child was tested on the BSID-I, she would have failed the same items measuring visual–motor skills but these items were interspersed on the record form with other items measuring language, memory, and problem-solving skills that she would have passed. The ceiling rule based on failure of 10 consecutive items would have insured that testing would have continued until she had demonstrated the limits of her abilities in all domains.

The use of the item sets was a departure from the BSID-I, which had a structure that seemed to provide a more complete picture of the infant's true range of abilities. The BSID-I basal and ceiling rules virtually insured that an approach of testing the child's limits was incorporated into the standardized administration of the test. As a result, test performance on a wide range of items yielded a profile of the child's strengths and weaknesses across the different domains. In contrast, the item sets and the basal and ceiling rules in the BSID-II meant that scores were based on a restricted range of items, not necessarily reflective of the full range of the child's strengths and weaknesses.

Thus, the structure of the first edition, with items testing different domains combined together in one scale but with basal and ceiling rules designed to insure that abilities in all domains are included in the final score, reflected Bayley's theoretical perspective that mental abilities are initially unified but with development they gradually differentiate into separate areas. Bayley also recognized that development is typically uneven across domains, particularly for high-risk infants. The use of the item set approach in the second edition reflects a somewhat different theoretical perspective, specifically that skills develop at the same rate across domains and that performance on a relatively small number of items is an accurate indication of the range of abilities across multiple domains. Much of the early research on the BSID-II was designed to address the item set problem, and demonstrated that these assumptions were not valid. Studies with both typically developing infants and infants with different risk factors for poor developmental outcome found that performance in both groups can be uneven across domains. As a result, infants frequently satisfied basal and ceiling criteria for multiple item sets, resulting in different scores depending on which item set was used, thereby increasing the likelihood of either underestimating or overestimating the child's true ability level.

This issue was even more complex for premature infants, as selection of item sets typically was based on adjusted age, with scaled scores derived from the corresponding norms table. Recommendations for testing premature infants were not very specific, however, and examiners were encouraged to select the item set that was closest to the their estimation of the child's level of functioning, leading to inconsistencies across testing sites. Children could receive different raw scores depending on which item set was administered. If the item set was selected based on chronological age, the scaled score was derived from the norms table appropriate for the child's chronological age. Unless they had global delays, premature infants tended to have higher scaled scores based on the administration of the item set appropriate for their chronological age than they would have if they were tested based on their corrected age. These scores might have been inflated because infants were being given credit for items below the item set that they might not have passed if the items actually were administered, or conversely the scores may have been more accurate than those based on the corrected age item set because the child received credit for items that they were able to pass above the corrected age item set. In contrast, premature infants tested with the BSID-I would have the same raw score regardless of whether adjusted age or chronological age was used, because the raw score was based on their actual performance rather than on *a priori* assumptions about their level of functioning, as in the BSID-II.

Studies comparing the same child's performance on the first and second editions of the Bayley typically found that scores on the second edition were lower than on the first edition. The BSID-II manual reported a mean difference of 11.8 points on the Mental Scale and 10.1 points on the Motor Scale. Discrepancies between scores on the two tests as large as 30 points have been reported, and it is interesting to note that the largest discrepancies were observed in children who scored in the accelerated range on the BSID-I. Higher scores on the BSID-I compared to the BSID-II have been attributed to the Flynn effect, the finding that performance on psychometrically based scales with outdated norms usually produced inflated scores, whereas scores on subsequent editions of the same test with more recent norms were likely to be lower. An alternative explanation with respect to the BSID-I is that lower scores on the BSID-II may in fact have been due to the item set problem, since the restricted range of items presented during the administration of the BSID-II was less likely to yield scores reflecting the true range of the child's abilities. This argument is supported by a study comparing the BSID-II to the third edition of the Bayley Scales (Bayley-III), which found that in contrast to what would be predicted by the Flynn effect, the more recently normed Bayley-III had mean composite scores that were approximately 7 points higher than BSID-II Mental and Motor Index scores for a group of children administered both versions of the test. The extended range of functioning allowed by the different basal and ceiling rules in both the BSID-I and the Bayley-III may contribute to higher and presumably more accurate scores on both of these scales. The full extent to which the item set problem affected the results of studies using the BSID-II as an outcome measure is unknown, although it is frequently cited as a possible contributing factor to scores that were lower than expected.

Bayley Scales of Infant and Toddler Development

The Bayley-III was developed for the stated purpose of updating the normative data and making the test more appropriate for use in clinical settings, while maintaining the basic qualities of the previous editions. For the first time, the standardization sample included children with various risk conditions, in an attempt to be more representative of the range of functioning in the general population of infants and toddlers. The content and structure of the test were revised, and the item set approach was discontinued. The most significant departure from the previous editions, in direct contrast with Bayley's theoretical positions, was the creation of five distinct scales to measure cognitive, language, motor, social–emotional, and adaptive behavior. The first three scales consist of items that are directly administered to the child, while the latter two scales are caregiver questionnaires. These areas were selected to make the test more appropriate for determining eligibility for early intervention programs, thereby broadening its appeal and increasing its utility to practitioners involved with providing services to the developmentally delayed. Adjustment for prematurity is recommended through 24 months of age.

Many items on the newly constructed Cognitive Scale were taken from the Mental Scale in the previous edition and were chosen to assess abilities such as sensorimotor manipulation and exploration, early memory and problem-solving skills and concept formation, and to differentiate these domains from language skills. Changes in item directions and administration rules were made to reduce the verbal content of the cognitive tasks and to decrease the reliance on motor skills. The newly formed Language Scale is divided into Receptive and Expressive Communication subtests, and the Motor Scale is divided into Gross and Fine Motor subtests. Many items that were part of the Mental Scale in the previous edition now are placed on either the Expressive or Receptive Communication subtests, the Cognitive Scale, or the Fine Motor subtest. New items also were added, increasing the estimated administration time. A Behavior Observation Inventory incorporates examiner observations of behavior during the test session and caregiver ratings of how representative these behaviors were of the child's typical behavior, to assist in the interpretation of the child's scores on these three scales.

The Social–Emotional and Adaptive Behavior Scales consist of questionnaires completed by the child's parent or primary caregiver. The Social–Emotional Scale was designed to measure the acquisition of major social–emotional milestones occurring in infancy and early childhood. The Adaptive Behavior Scale assesses daily functional skills in 10 different areas, and scores from these areas are combined to form a composite score for Adaptive Behavior.

The separate Language and Cognitive Scales on the Bayley-III address the criticism that low scores on the BSID-II Mental Scale might have reflected poor performance on the language items or deficits in fine motor skills or both, but this could not be determined from the global Mental Scale score. A potential disadvantage with the Bayley-III, however, especially for researchers using the Bayley Scales in their longitudinal studies, is that there is no composite mental score, making it difficult to compare performance on the Bayley-III with performance on the previous edition. Based on the reasoning that a global score would not be appropriate for clinicians who use the tests for determination of eligibility for early intervention programs, there are no plans to develop a composite score comparable to the BSID-II MDI. Researchers desiring to use the third edition in longitudinal research may wish to investigate whether it is feasible to construct a composite score for the purpose of comparison with the previous edition.

The Bayley-III discards the often-criticized item-set approach used in the previous edition. Its five subtests all have the same basal and ceiling rules: the infant must pass three consecutive items and fail five consecutive items before testing is discontinued. Separate scales and subtests insure that acceleration in one area will not obscure deficits in another area. Items with the same content area are generally administered as part of a series of related items, although the administration format of the Bayley-III is somewhat less flexible for items within a subtest. There is flexibility in the order of administration of the different scales and subtests, although it is recommended that the Receptive Communication subtest be administered before the Expressive Communication subtest.

The Bayley-III should provide added information from the separate scales and subtests measuring different areas of development, and the removal of the item sets should lead to a better sense of the true range of the infant's abilities. The controversy over the item sets in the BSID-II led to a series of studies that yielded evidence for variability in performance across multiple domains, and made it clear that the structure of the BSID-II did not allow for a complete picture of the infant's true range of abilities across domains. Bayley recognized that development is typically uneven across domains, especially in high-risk children, although she argued against the use of separate subscales in tests measuring infant development. This raises the question of what Bayley would have thought about the Bayley-III. Evidence from subscales derived from the BSID-I indicated that different sets of skills at different points in infancy were predictive of later outcome, however, and this supported Bayley's theoretical perspective that intellectual development consists of a number of qualitative changes that occur particularly rapidly during infancy. Additionally, the Bayley-III appears to be similar to the original BSID-I in that the structure of the test is designed to test the upper and lower limits of the infant's abilities across domains. Therefore, it is likely that Bayley might have approved of the structure of the Bayley-III, although she might have argued for a composite score, in addition to the scale and subtest scores, or perhaps advocated for some other way to capture the complex developmental relationships among skills in different domains.

Contemporary Research using the Bayley Scales

An important theoretical issue during the time that Bayley constructed her scales was the question of whether cognitive and motor development is a process that involves mostly predetermined sensorimotor maturation or whether it is influenced by the environment. Bayley took an interactionist position, anticipating contemporary views, and maintained that there were different influences on performance at different ages. This view is supported by the results from our longitudinal sample of infants born at varying risk for poor neurodevelopmental outcome. These infants were classified into four CNS risk groups: those with no discernable brain injury, those without structural damage but with abnormal auditory brainstem responses (Abnormal ABR only), those with mild-to-moderate CNS involvement, and those with strong-to-severe CNS injury, as measured by cranial ultrasound. As a part of a series of studies investigating attention and arousal in high-risk infants, the BSID-II was administered every 3 months between the ages of 4 and 25 months. Bayley's description of development in the first year reflecting the rate of sensorimotor maturation and in the second year increasingly reflecting the influence of environmental factors was supported by the performance of the children in our sample who had no discernable CNS injury. For these infants, mental and motor scores were correlated in the first year, but the strength of this relationship decreased throughout the second year, and the relationship between level of maternal education and performance on the Mental Scale increased throughout the second year. Different developmental patterns were displayed by children who had different degrees of perinatal risk.

The results presented here are based on analyses conducted especially for this article using all of the available data from our ongoing longitudinal studies, comprising 11 170 tests on 2132 infants tested at ages 4 to 25 months. **Figure 1** shows scores combined across all ages tested for each of the four CNS risk groups. In our overall sample, degree of CNS injury predicts both BSID-II mental and motor scores, and, as expected, scores are the lowest for children with the most severe CNS injury. The group means presented in this figure obscure developmental patterns, however, and when scores are presented by test age, a more complex picture emerges. The importance of using trajectories of performance over time rather than attempting to predict from one point in development or from scores combined across age cannot be overstated. By modeling cognitive and motor development using risk factors such as degree of CNS injury, level of maternal education and gender, evidence for complex relationships among these variables emerged. Interactions of these risk factors with time were not straightforward, and differed between the MDI and the PDI.

Figure 2 presents the MDI and PDI scores across age for children in each CNS risk group. For all four groups, BSID-II mental and motor scores have an inherent downward trend during the second year. The extent to which

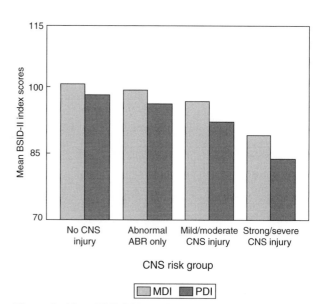

Figure 1 Mean BSID-II Mental Developmental Index (MDI) and Psychomotor Developmental Index (PDI) scores for four central nervous system (CNS) risk groups. (Abnormal ABR only: no structural damage but abnormal auditory brainstem response.)

characteristics of the BSID-II normative sample or the item-set problem contributed to this downward trend even in our low-risk groups cannot be determined. For the MDI, however, this trend may reflect in part the increasingly verbal content of the BSID-II after the middle of the second year. Indeed, there were significant relationships between MDI scores and a parent report measure that indicated delayed language development in over a quarter of our sample. This association was particularly strong for second-year MDI scores. For both the MDI and the PDI, the decline in scores in the second year is the greatest for children with severe CNS injury.

CNS injury was the strongest predictor of MDI scores until about the middle of the second year, when maternal education becomes a stronger predictor. CNS injury was the strongest predictor of PDI scores at all ages, and there was no relationship between maternal education and the PDI. The effect of maternal education on MDI scores was greatest among infants with mild or moderate CNS injury; high maternal education did little to raise the scores of more severely injured infants. **Figure 3** shows the relationship between maternal education and MDI scores for the four CNS risk groups.

The interactions among these factors differ for male and female infants. In general, girls' MDI and PDI scores are higher than those of boys in our sample, and the effects of CNS injury on scores, especially in the second year, are stronger for boys than for girls. Boys with severe CNS injury show a markedly sharper decline in second-year MDI and PDI scores than do girls with severe CNS injury or boys with less severe CNS injury.

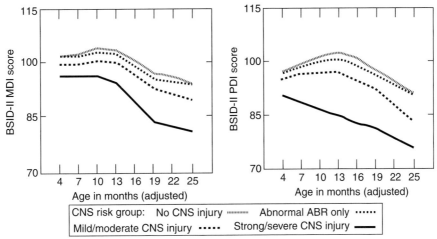

Figure 2 Mean BSID-II Mental Developmental Index (MDI) and Psychomotor Developmental Index (PDI) scores across age for four central nervous system (CNS) risk groups.

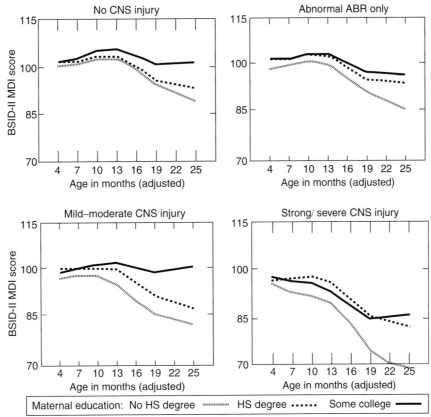

Figure 3 Mean BSID-II Mental Developmental Index (MDI) scores across age by central nervous system (CNS) risk group for three levels of maternal education. (HS: high school).

Summary

Nancy Bayley's developmental perspective, derived from her work with a group of infants growing up in Berkeley, CA in the early years of the twentieth century, continues to have relevance today. The most recent editions of the Bayley Scales are routinely used to assess infants who have much smaller birthweights, earlier gestational ages, and more significant neonatal risk factors than the infants who were assessed with the earliest editions of the Bayley Scales, yet contemporary research with typically developing and high-risk infants supports Bayley's theoretical perspective on the nature of cognitive and motor development in the first few years of life.

See also: Developmental Disabilities: Cognitive; Milestones: Cognitive.

Suggested Readings

Aylward GP (2002) Cognitive and neuropsychological outcomes: More than IQ scores. *Mental Retardation and Developmental Disabilities Research Reviews* 8: 234–240.

Bayley N (1969) *Bayley Scales of Infant Development.* San Antonio, TX: The Psychological Corporation.

Bayley N (1970) Development of mental abilities. In: Mussen J (ed.) *Carmichael's Manual of Child Psychology,* 3rd edn., pp. 1163–1209. New York: Wiley.

Bayley N (1993) *Bayley Scales of Infant Development,* 2nd edn. San Antonio, TX: The Psychological Corporation.

Bayley N (2006) *Bayley Scales of Infant and Toddler Development,* 3rd edn. San Antonio, TX: Harcourt Assessment.

Black MM and Matula K (2000) *Essentials of Bayley Scales of Infant Development-II Assessment.* New York: Wiley.

Brooks-Gunn J and Weinraub M (1983) Origins of infant intelligence testing. In: Lewis M (ed.) *Origins of Intelligence: Infancy and Early Childhood,* 2nd edn., pp. 25–66. New York: Plenum Press.

Gardner JM, Karmel BZ, Freedland RL, *et al.* (2006) Arousal, attention and neurobehavioral assessment in the neonatal period: Implications for intervention and policy. *Journal of Policy and Practice in Intellectual Disabilities* 3: 22–32.

Stott LH and Ball RS (1965) Infant and preschool mental tests: Review and evaluation. *Monographs of the Society for Research in Child Development* 30(3, Serial No. 101).

Bilingualism

N Sebastián-Gallés, L Bosch, and F Pons, Universitat de Barcelona, Barcelona, Spain

© 2008 Elsevier Inc. All rights reserved.

Glossary

Communicative development inventory (CDI) – A tool for gauging the vocabulary of infants and toddlers.

Mutual exclusivity principle – Strategy that children may use for inferring the meaning of a novel noun. It is based on object terms being mutually exclusive, that is, each object should only have one basic level label.

Perceptual reorganization – In the early months of life, infants are able to discriminate both native and non-native contrasts easily. However, by the end of the first year, these perceptual abilities change, involving both decreasing sensitivity to non-native speech contrasts and realignment of initial boundaries.

Rhythmic class – Language rhythms are separated into three major classes reflecting linguistic metrical timing units: stress (English), syllable (Spanish), and a subsyllabic unit termed mora (Japanese). There is also a quantitative analysis of the acoustic characteristics of consonant and vowel units to classify it.

Simultaneous bilingual – When a child becomes bilingual by learning two languages at the same time from birth.

Voice onset time (VOT) – The length of time that passes between when a consonant is released and when voicing, the vibration of the vocal folds, begins.

Introduction

Learning a language is a complex achievement that human beings accomplish with great ease in the first years of life. To learn a language, human infants must discover the fundamental properties of the language of the environment. As discussed elsewhere in this encyclopedia, this is a complex process and to attain it, infants and children must learn multiple properties of the language they hear. If, as adults, we are fascinated by the easiness with which infants learn a language, we are even more astounded when bilingual infants are considered. However, one wonders if such a phenomenal task is out of the reach of young infants; thus, early bilingual exposure might be an undesirable circumstance. It is common that parents and caregivers wonder if infants acquiring two languages at the same time follow a troubled course, marked by delays and confusion.

In this article we describe what is known about very early stages of bilingual language acquisition. We concentrate on infants who are exposed to two languages from the very first day of their lives. These infants are called simultaneous bilinguals, as opposed to successive bilinguals (this type of acquisition has also been referred to as 'bilingual first language acquisition'). For these individuals there is not a first or a second language, in a chronological sense. However, because perfect identical exposure is practically impossible, there is always a language to which infants are more exposed; in this sense, there is a dominant language and a nondominant language in the environment.

As it will be seen, there is no evidence of trouble or confusion; nevertheless, infants learning two languages sometimes follow a developmental path different from that of infants learning just one language. We pay special attention to the perceptual abilities of bilingual infants, in particular, in the preverbal stage. This will lead to focus on the development of phonology and the lexicon, as opposed to the development of morphosyntax, a topic usually addressed in studies analyzing toddlers, and children's production abilities.

Early studies of how young infants and children become bilingual are relatively scarce, in particular when compared with studies with monolingual infants. However, this topic has a long history. The first empirical study on bilingual development dates from 1913. Jules Ronjat, a French linguist, was the first scholar to describe bilingual behavior. Thirty years later, another linguist, Werner Leopold, published a monumental monograph of four volumes describing the acquisition of language in a French–English bilingual child. In fact, still today, most of the studies on early language acquisition rely on observational data of infants' utterances. This type of methodology poses severe limitations if we want to know how language develops from birth. If we exclude babbling, by the time young children start to speak, they have acquired a fairly sophisticated knowledge of the language of the environment. If only studying language production is an important limitation for the study of language development in monolingual infants, as it will be seen below, it is even more important in the case of bilingual children.

Early Differentiation

To be able to learn two languages, infants must realize the existence of two different auditory systems in the speech input. But human beings are already able to make some distinctions at birth. As research on initial language differentiation capacities has shown, newborns can notice the differences between languages belonging to different rhythmic classes, but they cannot if both languages belong to the same rhythmic class. For instance, newborns can detect differences between Japanese and Dutch or French and Russian, but not between English and Dutch or Spanish and Italian. So, even without previous experience with multiple languages, the auditory system is already able to make some language distinctions. Therefore, an infant born in a bilingual family should be able to differentiate between languages if they belong to different rhythmic groups. Two studies carried out with bilingual infants, exposed to English and Tagalog (i.e., to languages belonging to different rhythmic groups) and to Spanish and Catalan (i.e., to languages belonging to the same rhythmic group) have shown converging results in this respect (Spanish and Catalan are, like French, Italian, and Portuguese, Romance languages; Tagalog is one of the major languages spoken in the Philippines and rhythmically very different from English). Two different measures have been obtained to draw this conclusion.

In an auditory preference procedure, infants can control the delivery of sentences by giving high-amplitude sucks (energetic). Every time they make a high-amplitude suck, a new sentence is played. It has been observed that when presented with sentences of their maternal language and of a foreign language, newborns show higher sucking rates for the maternal language than for the unknown one. In the study with newborn infants who were exposed to both English and Tagalog approximately equally throughout gestation, babies were presented with alternated minutes of these two languages. The results showed equivalent sucking rates for English and Tagalog. Importantly, newborn infants who were exposed to only English prenatally showed higher rates for English sentences than for Tagalog ones. Therefore, it is not that English and Tagalog sentences are equally attractive *per se* to newborns, but that bilingual infants are equally attracted to both (unlike English monolinguals).

The other experiment showing equivalent behavior for the two languages of the environment in bilingual infants studied 4.5-month-old infants with a procedure based on a visual orientation latency measure. In this procedure, infants listen to sentences of two languages, presented in a random order. Sentences can be played back from two different loudspeakers located at the right and the left of a central monitor in front of the infants (see **Figure 1**). For every infant, there is no correspondence between a particular loudspeaker and language being heard. At the beginning of each trial, an attractive image is shown in a central monitor. After a short variable time interval, the image disappears and a sentence is played in one of the lateral loudspeakers. Eye movements are recorded and orientation latencies are estimated. It has been observed that infants orient faster to the maternal language, than to unknown ones. When young bilingual infants (born in Spanish and Catalan bilingual families) are confronted with their two first languages, they show equivalent latencies, therefore, indicating that both languages are equally familiar to them (at this age, as described below, Spanish–Catalan bilingual infants when studied in a different paradigm can differentiate both languages).

The results of these experiments indicate that already in the very first months of their life, infants exposed to bilingual environments have been able to extract distinctive acoustic properties of both languages and that they treat them in a special way. However, these results do not answer the question of how early bilingual infants can notice the existence of two systems in their environment. So, do bilingual infants differentiate the languages?

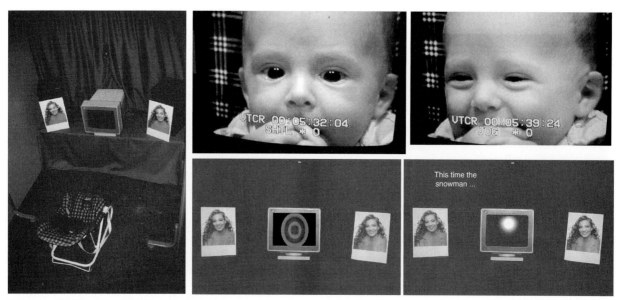

Figure 1 Preference: orientation time procedure.

The first evidence of language differentiation in infants exposed to bilingual environments has been obtained with 4.5-month-old Catalan–Spanish bilinguals. In this study, infants were tested using an adaptation of the familiarization-novelty preference procedure. Infants were familiarized with six different sentences of the language of their mother. After 2 min of familiarization, eight new sentences were presented (test sentences). Half of them were in the same language of the familiarization phase (the language of the mother) and the other half in the other language (the language of the father). Infants raised in bilingual environments increased their visual attention times to test sentences in a language different than that of the familiarization phase, when compared with test sentences in the same language of the familiarization phase. Their results were fully equivalent to those obtained with infants exposed to either Catalan or Spanish monolingual environments.

Taken together, these results indicate that a simultaneous bilingual exposure does not generate specific problems in the processes of language differentiation. Importantly, this precocious differentiation was observed in a perceptually challenging situation, where the two languages of exposure are rhythmically very similar (and cannot be discriminated at birth), as it is the case with Catalan and Spanish.

Nevertheless, bilingual infants do not discriminate languages in the same way as monolingual infants do. Using the visual orientation latency procedure just described, monolingual (Spanish and Catalan) and Catalan–Spanish bilingual infants were also tested presenting the maternal language (Spanish or Catalan) and English as a foreign language. As expected, monolingual infants orient faster to the maternal language than to a foreign one (solid line in **Figure 2**). The opposite pattern is observed with bilingual

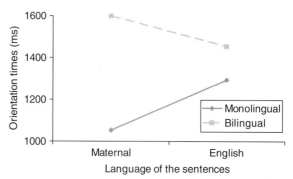

Figure 2 Results of orientation times to familiar and unfamiliar languages. Reproduced from Bosch L and Sebastián-Gallés N (1997) Native-language recognition abilities in four-month-old infants from monolingual and bilingual environments. *Cognition* 65: 33–69, with permission from Elsevier.

infants. Although they also show significant differences between the orientation times to the maternal language and the unknown one, they orient slower to the maternal language (the language of the mother in this particular experiment) than to the unknown one (dashed line in **Figure 2**). Importantly, both monolingual and bilingual infants show equivalent orientation times to the unknown language: the differences are specific to the orientation times to the maternal language. This atypical pattern of orientations has been replicated with different language pairs (Spanish–English, Catalan–English, Spanish–Italian, and Catalan–Italian), as well as different ages (4.5 and 6 months). Although at present no satisfactory explanation to this response pattern can be given, it is a clear index of precocious adaptation of the speech-processing mechanisms in the rich and varied environment bilingual infants are exposed to.

Building Up Phonetic Categories

Research with monolingual infants has shown that starting at 6 months of age infants specialize in the phonetic repertoire of their maternal language. Before this age, infants can distinguish phoneme contrasts they have never heard before and that their parents are unable to discriminate. For instance, monolingual Japanese young infants can differentiate between /r/ and /l/ in a fully equivalent way than their English-learning peers. At 6 months, as a consequence of exposure to the maternal language, a perceptual reorganization takes place and infants start to lose this capacity to discriminate sounds in all languages. This reorganization will affect first the perception of vowels and later that of consonants. If language exposure is the main determinant to perceptual reorganization, exposure to two languages must shape the phonetic repertoire of infants in a specific way. So, what happens with bilingual infants?

It is almost impossible that two languages share the very same phoneme repertoire, even for the case of similar languages. For example, English and German share a common origin and are typologically related, but they are quite different in terms of their phoneme repertoires. The same happens with French and Spanish. Furthermore, not only languages have different phonemes, but the precise acoustic realization of the same phonemes varies from language to language. Just consider how phoneme /b/ is pronounced by English and Spanish natives. Or for an even more extreme case, how phoneme /r/ is pronounced in English, French, and Italian. So, if the language of the environment shapes the way perceptual reorganization of phonemes takes place, several possibilities remain open for bilingual individuals.

As just described, we know that language differentiation occurs very early in life; in fact, it occurs before perceptual reorganization takes place. So, one possibility is that infants exposed to bilingual environments acquire two parallel phoneme systems, one for each language. Another possibility is that they melt both systems, only developing a single system where phonemes from both languages are integrated. One way of having a hint of how acquisition will eventually evolve is that of looking into adult data. One prevailing view in adult speech perception models is that bilinguals only possess one phonetic space, integrating and adapting the phonetic repertoires of both languages. However, most of these results have been obtained with successive bilinguals, that is, individuals who were only exposed to one language in the first months (or years) of their lives. The literature with simultaneous bilinguals is scarce and not all the available data fit with this notion of a single system. Finally, an additional issue is that the development of phonetic categories continues to refine well into late childhood-puberty (in particular in the production side). So, it is crucial to look into how bilingual infants and very young children establish their phonetic categories.

Very few studies have addressed the evolution of the initial perceptual capacities in the period when perceptual reorganization takes place. These studies have analyzed the evolution of vowels and consonants in Catalan–Spanish (both vowel and consonant contrasts) and French–English (a consonant contrast) bilingual infants. Let us consider each group of studies in turn.

Catalan–Spanish infants were tested in two phoneme contrasts only existing in one of the languages of exposure and not in the other. In particular, they were tested in the Catalan-specific /e-ɛ/ vowel and /s-z/ consonant contrasts. These contrasts are very difficult to be perceived by adult monolingual Spanish listeners. This is the case because Spanish only has one /e/ vowel and one /s/ consonant (in fact, these are similar situations to those that Japanese listeners face when learning the English-specific /r-l/ contrast, Japanese only has one /l/ sound). The studies of acquisition of phoneme repertoire with bilingual infants have shown a peculiar developmental pattern. Two ages were *a priori* determined to evaluate the perceptual reorganization of infants learning Catalan and Spanish. As mentioned previously, before 6 months, infants show discrimination capacities even for contrasts their parents cannot perceive. Thus, one group of participants were infants before this age (specifically, they were 4.5-month-olds). Three different linguistic backgrounds were tested: monolingual Catalan, monolingual Spanish, and Catalan–Spanish bilingual. As expected infants from all three language environments perceived the contrasts. The other age selected was beyond perceptual reorganization, for the vowel contrast it was chosen 8 months and for the consonant 12 months (perceptual reorganization takes place before for vowels than for consonants). As expected, Catalan and Spanish monolinguals behaved differently: Catalan monolinguals showed a discrimination response, while Spanish monolinguals did not. However, contrary to the hypothesis that exposure should be enough to maintain discrimination, bilinguals did not show discrimination behavior. This result was also surprising because Catalan–Spanish adult bilinguals can actually perceive and produce these contrasts. So, discrimination should be regained at some point. Another group of older bilingual infants were tested (12- and 16-month-olds for the vowel and consonant contrast, respectively), at these ages, they showed discrimination.

To what extent these results are generalizable to other phoneme contrasts and bilingual populations? The studies reviewed thus for refer to a very particular case, that is, to phoneme contrasts only existing in one of the languages and which monolingual adults would find very difficult to perceive. Other studies with infants growing up in bilingual environments have shown that this developmental pattern is widespread. In particular, the very same U-shaped pattern (discrimination, then non-discrimination, then discrimination) has been obtained with the same population and ages, but tested with a common Spanish–Catalan vowel contrast (/o-u/). However, 8-month olds have shown discrimination behavior when the vowel contrast involved acoustically distinct phonemes, in particular, the /e-u/ contrast.

Converging evidence has been gathered with French–English bilingual infants. Both French and English have the /b-p/ contrast in their phoneme repertoire. However, the specific acoustic parameters are not the same. These consonants differ in a specific acoustic parameter called the voice onset time (VOT). The important feature of French and English /b-p/ contrast is depicted in **Figure 3**(a). English–French bilinguals were tested in their ability to perceive the French and English contrast. Infants were habituated to the central exemplar [pa], and then they were tested in two test trials, a change to [ba] or a change to [p^{h}a]. Discrimination of the French boundary would be indicated by increasing looking time to [ba], whereas discrimination of the English boundary would be indicated by an increasing of looking time to [p^{h}a]. Both bilingual and monolingual young infants (aged 6–8 months) were better able to discriminate the French than the English boundary, but importantly, as expected, both groups performed similarly. Also, as expected, English monolingual infants did not show discrimination for the French contrast by 10–12 months. Again, in parallel with the Spanish–Catalan bilinguals, French–English bilinguals

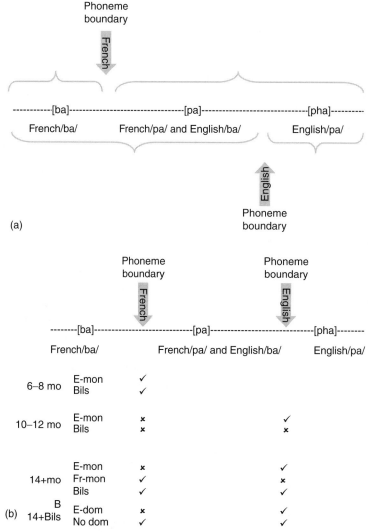

Figure 3 (a) Distribution of phoneme boundaries in the /b-p/ French and English consonant contrasts. (b) Summary of the discrimination results of /b-p/ French and /b-p/ English contrasts by monolingual and bilingual infants at different ages. From Burns TC, Werker JF, and McVie K (2003) Development of phonetic categories in infants raised in bilingual and monolingual environments. In: Beachley B, Brown A, and Conlin F (eds.) *Proceedings of the 27th Annual Boston University Conference on Language Development*, Vol. 1, pp. 173–184. Somerville, MA: Cascadilla Press.

failed to show discrimination for the French contrast at 10–12 months, when perceptual reorganization is taking place. Older bilingual infants (aged 14–17 months) regained discrimination for this contrast (**Figure 3(b)**: summary of the results of all the experiments).

Both bilingual populations were tested in totally different situations and still the results are fully consistent. What are the mechanisms underlying this peculiar developmental path for bilingual infants? The answer to this question is still under debate. However, a strong candidate is particular frequency distributions of phonemes across languages. As mentioned, Spanish has only one /E/ vowel, falling roughly in between both Catalan /e/ and /ɛ/ ones. Thus, considering that the Spanish /E/ vowel is very frequent and that Catalan /e/ and /ɛ/ are not so frequent, the frequency distribution of the three vowels in monolingual and bilingual environments would look like something similar to that depicted in **Figure 4**. The distribution of English and French consonants /d-t-tʰ/ in a bilingual environment would also look quite similar, and therefore more frequently heard, in the center (see also **Figure 4**). It has been shown that humans are very sensitive to frequency distributional cues to build up phonetic categories. It has also been shown that frequency distributions of the type that bilingual infants are exposed to for these particular sounds induce the formation of a single phonetic category. Thus, it is quite possible that particular sound distributions in bilingual environments may hamper, in some very specific cases, the creation of the appropriate phonetic categories in bilingual infants. However, this situation does not last for a long period. Both studies show that within few months, bilingual infants regain discrimination behavior. It is an open question what are the underlying mechanisms driving this change: mere frequency accumulation and computation of separate frequency statistics for each language are just two possibilities.

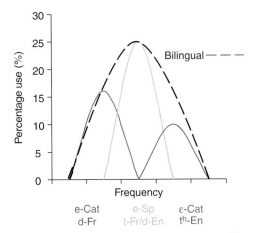

Figure 4 'Bimodal' and 'unimodal' distributions of different phoneme contrasts in Spanish–Catalan and English–French environments.

Babbling in Bilingual Infants

The studies on babbling productions in bilingual contexts are scarce. After having explored the early exposure to two languages in the early stages of the language-acquisition processes (onset of canonical babbling, vocal performance, first word production, and multiword combinations), the question whether babbling productions can offer evidence of an early differentiation of the ambient languages still remains. In monolingual infants it has been shown that babbling drifts in the direction of the speech that they hear by 10 months of age, when features of the environmental language are gradually incorporated in these early productions. Although adult listeners may not be able to identify the specific language background after hearing babbling samples from monolingual infants growing up in different linguistic contexts, the analyses of these productions have revealed differences relative to the use of the vowel space, pitch contours, and labial consonants that are characteristic of the ambient language.

By 10–14 months of age, babbling patterns are less universal and become more language-specific. The study of babbling samples from infants growing up in bilingual contexts can thus offer relevant data about early language differentiation and language dominance, two issues that were discussed above. Results from the very few studies available on these issues give preliminary support for the hypothesis that infants in bilingual contexts develop differentiated language systems during the babbling period, although this is a tentative conclusion due to the limited evidence gathered so far: a single case study from an English–Spanish infant and a group study from French–English infants. The early differentiation conclusion derives from the fact that in this single case study the infant produced a different range of sounds depending on the context and the language of his interlocutors. In contrast, the group study showed that infants babbled in a dominant language with no mixing evidence (as far as consonantal sounds are concerned), which is a more indirect evidence for differentiation. It is important to mention that the infant dominant language seems to be assessed by the acoustic saliency of the sounds under analysis instead of the proportion of exposure to each language that the infant receives. A number of variables (amount of exposure in each language, extent of infant-directed speech from the interlocutors when addressing the infant, segmental repertoires in the ambient languages, dialectal differences, etc.) must be taken into account in order to understand and clarify the results that have been obtained better.

Learning Words

Segmenting Words: Phonotactics

Studies with monolingual infants have shown that at a very early age (between 7 and 8 months), infants can segment and recognize words embedded in continuous speech. They can do it, even if a very similar stimulus is presented in the test phase (a minimal pair, that is, familiarized with 'cup' and tested with 'tup'). One particular type of knowledge that infants use is differences in the frequencies of sequences of phonemes occurring within and between words. Infants compute the transitional probabilities of segments within and across word boundaries. In the second half of the first year of life infants can use this type of information (known as phonotactics) to segment words. Because this source of information is language specific (for instance, no Spanish words can start with three consonants, while English words can), to segment the speech stream and build up appropriate lexicons properly, bilingual infants should compute two different sets of statistics, one for each language. Although there is only one study addressing specifically this issue, the results are consistent with the notion of early language dominance; that is, bilingual infants show sensitivity to the phonotactic information of their dominant language, in an equivalent way as monolingual infants of the same age.

Learning Word Forms

A major achievement in the second and third years of life is that of acquiring a sizable vocabulary. It is in this period when the 'vocabulary spurt' takes place. It has been argued that because of the relatively small vocabulary size in this age, the phonological representation of words is relatively coarse, as compared with adults' for whom fine acoustic–phonetic distinctions are represented. Nevertheless, research with monolingual infants has shown that from the very beginning infants represent words in a very detailed phonological form. For instance, they react to familiar words if slightly mispronounced. In these studies, infants are presented with two pictures of familiar objects (for instance, a dog and a car). After a short familiarization with the materials, while the images are visible, they hear a sentence either presenting a proper pronunciation (i.e., 'Where is the dog?') or a mispronunciation (i.e., 'Where is the tog?'). In these experiments, participants' eye movements are recorded. When presented with a correct pronunciation, infants look faster and longer to the right image, than when presented with the incorrect pronunciation. This difference is interpreted as an indication of infants' sensitivity of phonological lexical representations.

Research with Spanish–Catalan bilingual infants has shown that at this age they are not so sensitive to mispronunciations involving a phoneme contrast existing only in one of their languages. Bilingual infants aged 18–24 months were tested with mispronounced words made by exchanging the /e-ɛ/ vowels (as mentioned, a contrast only existing in Catalan). While infants raised in Catalan monolingual families reacted to this mispronunciation Spanish–Catalan bilinguals did not; that is, they treated the mispronunciation as correct pronunciations. This lack of reaction could be considered as an indication of less accurate lexical representations in bilinguals. However, when bilingual infants were tested with a contrast existing in both languages (/e-i/, acoustically similar to the /e-ɛ/ distinction), they reacted to the mispronunciation in the same way as monolinguals did. These results show some parallel with those previously observed with phoneme discrimination capacities. It is probable that the particular distribution of phonemes in both languages may be making some mispronunciations more salient than others.

But still, another possibility is that sound distributions are not the sole factor to explain why bilingual infants do not react to some slight mispronunciations. It could be something in the very nature of bilingual language development. Indeed, bilinguals' task is more complex than monolinguals': they must code not only information about the relationship between object/concept and form, but also they must code to which language the word belongs. Infants' attention and memory capacities are clearly limited at this early age, so the task of learning a more complex mapping between form and meaning may be putting a heavy burden on them. Under perceptually difficult situations (either because acoustic similarities, or particular phoneme distributional properties, or both), they may have their processing capacities exhausted, therefore, failing to react in the most difficult perceptual discrimination cases. This possibility is supported by studies carried out with younger infants using a word-learning task.

Although at the end of the first year of life, infants show an excellent capacity to perceive phoneme contrasts existing in their own language, they may fail to use this capacity when learning new words. In the 'switch task' infants are shown with two new objects, paired with two new words. After some trials of exposure, they are shown one object either with the correct label (nonswitch trials) or with the incorrect label (switch trials). If they can succeed in learning the new object–label pairing, infants show surprise by increasing their looking times in switch trials. It has been shown that 14-month-olds cannot learn the pairing if the two-word labels are very similar ('bih-dih'), but they succeed if the differences between both labels are perceptually salient ('nim-leef'). The problem does not lie in the infants' capacity to perceive the contrast in the similar pair at 14 months, but on the computational demands (attention and memory) of the word-learning situation. Thus, between 17 and 20 months, with better processing capacities, infants are able to learn the pairing for the similar labels in this experimental situation.

Infants raised in English–French bilingual environments have been tested with this task. If the hypothesis of a resource limitation interfering with the learning of perceptually difficult minimal pairs is correct, then, bilingual infants should show difficulties for more extended periods. The results confirmed this hypothesis. Bilinguals not only showed difficulties at 14 months, but also at 17 months. So, it seems that because of having to build two different lexicons, it is probable that bilingual infants cannot make use of all phonetic detail when learning new words. With the available data, it is impossible to decide if bilingual infants sometimes do not encode fine detail in their lexical representations or if it is access to this information that takes place later for bilingual than for monolingual infants. However, considering that a few months later bilingual infants show response patterns indicating fine phonological representation, it is unlikely that phonetic detail is not encoded in their mental lexicon.

Vocabulary Size

The fact that infants growing up in bilingual homes may store, or retrieve, word forms in a different way to their monolingual peers does not necessarily entail that their vocabulary size is different from that of a monolingual infant. However, if as mentioned, they may devote some resources to encoding to which language words belong to, it might be the case that their storage capacity is affected. As in other aspects of language development, studies about vocabulary size in infants growing up bilingual must take into consideration that although they are exposed to both languages from birth, this condition, however, is not a homogeneous one, as a consequence of differences in the proportion of exposure to each ambient language and differences in the contexts of exposure that the child may experience (differences in the distribution of languages across speakers, that is, parents/caregivers using mainly one language or speaking both languages to the child). Most of the studies have been done on populations exposed simultaneously to English and Spanish, but work with German–English and Spanish–Catalan is also available (single case studies include a wider variety of language combinations).

When vocabulary size is the measure and vocabulary in both languages is taken into account, bilingual toddlers show a total vocabulary size comparable to the same measure in monolingual children. However, in bilinguals, total vocabulary measures may differ from 'conceptual' vocabulary, when translation equivalents (words with the same meaning, usually present from the early stages of lexical development) are counted just once. This is a highly relevant issue to take into account, especially because bilingual toddlers may easily be misidentified as having smaller vocabularies than monolingual toddlers; if the tool used to measure expressive vocabulary is not well adapted to bilingual contexts a 'communicative development inventory' (CDI) should be administered for each of the ambient languages for a correct comparison with monolingual data.

Other studies have focused on the relationship between vocabulary size in each of the ambient languages and the amount of input received. Results show a positive correlation between these two factors, at least in the early stages, up to the moment when a critical mass of lexical items has been reached. It has to be mentioned, however, that beyond direct exposure provided by parents, media, and community, predominant usage of one of the languages may favor a greater than expected vocabulary growth in one of these languages (this is true for English vocabulary measures in English–Spanish homes for studies run in the US, but the situation can possibly be extrapolated to other bilingual communities in countries other than the US). Studies on expressive vocabulary development in young bilingual children should be undertaken on larger samples and on a wider variety of language backgrounds to get a more complete picture of this process.

On the receptive side, there is a single study concerned with the organization of language-relevant brain activity as a function of vocabulary size in each language. In this study, also carried out with infants being exposed to Spanish and English, electrophysiological measures (ERPs) have been measured. Infants were exposed to lists of words of both languages that the children could know or not (lists were customized for every child). The results showed that the specific brain activity pattern depended on both the number of words known for each language (separate language vocabulary size) and the total conceptual vocabulary. The results suggest that children with smaller total conceptual vocabulary (thus slower in their overall language development) are slower in the processing of lexical items of the nondominant language, but the processing of the dominant language is not affected. Although these results need to be confirmed with future studies, they are in agreement with other research (see the phonotactics section) indicating that if some delay is to be found in bilinguals' early development it is restricted to the nondominant language.

Semantics

The semantic and conceptual knowledge underlying bilingual infants' first words has not been studied extensively. Bilingual infants learn words from both of their languages early in development and it has been demonstrated that they reach language milestones such as the onset of productive language on a similar timeframe as monolinguals: They start producing single-word sentences; they then go on the production of two-word sentences and after producing multiword sentences for a while, they start using complex sentences as well.

However, comparing to monolinguals, infants acquiring two languages face another difficulty while learning words. They must solve the problem of discerning the semantic meanings and related concepts of two lexicons across their two languages. It is well known that one fundamental principle guiding monolingual children's acquisition of new words is the principle of mutual exclusivity, or the assumption that new words tend to refer to new referents or objects. Disambiguation tasks have been the most common way to study mutual exclusivity. In these studies, many objects are presented to the children, one of which does not have a known label, then a novel label is given (that might name one of the objects). The mutual exclusivity effect is evident if the child chooses the previously unlabeled object as the referent of the new word. In a study of disambiguation with 24- and 36-month-olds, bilinguals did not differ from monolinguals in their demonstration of the mutual exclusivity effect in a pointing task. In a recent study, the principle of mutual exclusivity in younger bilingual infants (English–Cantonese 18-month-olds) was examined. The results of this study indicated that both monolinguals and bilinguals have the same pattern of response in the disambiguation task, although bilinguals seemed to respond somewhat slower and less robustly. It has been argued that these results could be either due to lower exposure to and proficiency in English, or due to the dual structure of the bilingual lexicon.

Another interesting issue regards bilingual children's acquisition of translation equivalents. A translation equivalent implies to possess a word for a specific object in both languages, like ball in, for example, Spanish 'pelota' and, at the same time, for example, in English 'ball'). This question has been of interest because this would violate the principle of mutual exclusivity. The reported data have shown that bilingual children acquire many translation equivalents. In a study carried out with Spanish–English bilingual children, it was reported that infant's translation equivalents constituted around 30% of their total vocabulary. Another study of an English–French child reported 50% of translation equivalents (compared to the child's total vocabulary) at the age of 14 months, and 36% at the age of 17 months. This high rate of translation equivalents, a clear violation of mutual exclusivity, suggests that at least from this age on children seem to have two distinct lexical systems. It is possible that the ability to violate mutual exclusivity may be learned through experience of interpreting people's intentions about what words mean.

Another approach to explore conceptual knowledge focuses on the lexical-referent parings and mistakes that infants make. In a study with English–French bilingual babies it was observed that, like monolingual infants, bilingual infants rarely overextended their first words in either of their two languages. With few exceptions, a word used to indicate an object was used only to stand for that object and/or sometimes the class for related objects. It was not used to connote other associative properties of that object (actions, locations, etc.).

Taking into consideration all the infant bilingual studies we have at this point, it seems that early semantic and, thus, conceptual knowledge underlying language acquisition is equivalent in both monolingual and bilingual infants.

Morphosyntax

Research in early capacities of morphosyntactic knowledge in language production faces some specific problems in bilingual populations. Infants start producing single-word utterances, and they increase utterance length. While there is some debate about the optimal utterance length to estimate morphosyntactic knowledge in monolingual infants, this problem is even worse when bilingual infants are considered. The major problem is a consequence of differences between languages, as far as their reliance on constituent order and bound morphology. Even with closely related languages, differences arise: to say 'They did not go' (or 'They didn't go'), Spanish natives say 'no fueron' (no subject, no auxiliary), but French speakers would say 'ils ne sont pas allés' (or 'elles ne sont pas allées' if a group of women did not go; subject, two negative particles, past participle) and Catalan natives would say 'no varen anar' (no subject, past tense auxiliary). So analyzing speech productions of children who can only produce one or two words can easily lead to problems of overestimating or underestimating a child's grammar skills. To explore the morphosyntactic development we take into consideration that solid evidence refers to productions starting around 24 months or later (depending on the child abilities to produce speech).

Children who have been exposed to two languages from birth and who actually speak those languages are not different from children growing up with just one language as far as the general course of morphosyntactic development is concerned.

Bilingual children are able to produce utterances that are clearly relatable to each of their different languages from the very beginning. It is claimed that the morphosyntactic development of one language does not have any important consequence on the morphosyntactic development of the other. However, there is evidence of transfer of specific morphosyntax features from one language to the other, leaving open the possibility of interaction and cross-linguistic influence between the languages. For example, it has been reported that Australian children learning English and German simultaneously used verb–object (VO) word order much more in their German than native monolingual speakers of German (German uses both -VO and -OV word order; English uses -VO order). In another study it has been observed that language dominance could be an important factor in cross-linguistic transfer: Cantonese–English learning children were more likely to incorporate structures from their dominant into their weaker language, than vice versa.

It is important to be aware that there are few studies reporting instances of cross-linguistic transfer. They concern specific aspects of the child's developing grammars and they seem to occur only under particular conditions. Thus, isolated examples of the influence of one language on performance in the other are not sufficient to demonstrate general interdependence. It is also essential to understand properly these examples of crosslinguistic transfer. For example, although it is true that bilingual infants often produce mixed sentences (they insert words of one of the languages into sentences build with the grammar of the other language), this insertion is usually restricted to content words (most of the time nouns). This type of insertion occurs exactly in the same way when bilingual adults are trying to speak one language and they do not know (or cannot find) one word in one of the languages, but they know the word in the other. So, bilinguals (infants or adults) make use of all their resources to communicate.

Summarizing, monolingual and bilingual children acquiring the same language since birth use that language in very similar ways. They produce the same sort of utterances as similar types of errors. There is no systematic evidence of morphosyntactic influence from one language to the other in children who have been exposed to two languages since birth.

Cognitive Development

There is ample evidence indicating that children between 4 and 8 years, growing up in bilingual environments, show improved performance in executive function tasks. The usual result is that bilingual children perform in tasks of cognitive control, at the same level as their monolingual peers 1 year older. The underlying driving force of this enhanced development would be the natural training that being exposed and using two languages involves. Indeed, bilinguals need to monitor attention to two competing and active language systems continuously. In particular, when speaking, they need to select from the appropriate lexicon and grammar system the right words and syntactic structures. Research with bilingual adults has shown that they activate all their languages, even if they are in a monolingual situation; for instance, when asked to name in English the picture of a dog, an English–Spanish bilingual, not only activates the lexical entry for the English word 'dog', but also activates the corresponding Spanish word ('perro'). To be able to say 'dog' and not be confused and say 'perro', bilinguals must monitor the language production system. Different studies support the assumption that the mechanisms used by bilinguals to carry out this monitoring process are the same used in other nonverbal tasks involving executive function. The development of executive function takes place late in life. Frontal lobes, the brain substrate responsible for these functions, are the last cortical areas to mature. The impact of bilingual exposure has been studied with relatively old children (from 4 years on) but some of its effects should be noticeable with younger children. Indeed, as mentioned earlier, infants raised in bilingual environments not only are able to tell apart the two languages, but as production data show, their initial utterances indicate the ability to separate them. The extent to which bilingual exposure affects other cognitive domains very early in life is an open question that needs to be addressed.

Conclusions and Future Directions

One major problem of research with preverbal bilingual infants is that of data scarcity. Most results refer to studies carried out with Spanish–Catalan bilinguals. To what extent are these results generalizable to other language pairs?

For instance, when describing the representation of words in the lexicon, the lack of sensitivity for some phoneme contrasts was explained in terms of frequency of distribution. However, there are other factors that must be taken into consideration and deserve further research. One of them is difference between languages. For instance, Spanish and Catalan are Romance languages; thus, they share a common origin and also many words are from the same root. For instance, the Spanish and Catalan words for 'door' and 'cat' are 'puerta/porta' and 'gato/gat'. Thus, it may be the case that bilingual infants of languages sharing a common origin are used to hear different pronunciations for different objects. An important issue is that of studying infants learning typologically distant languages, so that objects are almost always labelled with very different forms. Furthermore in the study described, only cognate words of Catalan and Spanish (i.e., words with a common origin) were used. It would be interesting to test infants with noncognate words (for instance, the words 'window' and 'dog' are very different in Spanish and Catalan: 'ventana/finestra' and 'perro/gos').

However, as mentioned at the beginning of this article, taken together the results of research on very early language development of infants growing up in bilingual environments indicate that this development does not significantly differ from that of their monolingual peers: major achievements are attained at the equivalent ages. However, the mechanisms by which the two languages are acquired may not be fully equivalent to those of infants only acquiring one language. This aspect relates to studies indicating that children growing up bilingual display speedy development of cognitive control mechanisms.

See also: Habituation and Novelty; Language Acquisition Theories; Learning; Semantic Development; Speech Perception.

Suggested Readings

Bosch L and Sebastián-Gallés N (1997) Native-language recognition abilities in four-month-old infants from monolingual and bilingual environments. *Cognition* 65: 33–69.

Burns TC, Werker JF, and McVie K (2003) Development of phonetic categories in infants raised in bilingual and monolingual environments. In: Beachley B, Brown A, and Conlin F (eds.) *Proceedings of the 27th Annual Boston University Conference on Language Development*, Vol. 1, pp. 173–184. Somerville, MA: Cascadilla Press.

Cenoz J and Genesee F (2001) *Trends in Bilingual Acquisition.* Amsterdam: John Benjamins.

Genesee F, Paradis J, and Crago (eds.) (2004) *Dual Language Development and Disorders: A Handbook on Bilingualism and Second Language Learning.* Baltimore, MD: Brookes.

Kroll JF and de Groot AMB (2005) *Handbook of Bilingualism. Psycholinguistic Approaches,* (section I. Acquisition: Chapters 1 and 3, particularly). Oxford: Oxford University Press.

Birth Order

D L Paulhus, University of British Columbia, Vancouver, BC, Canada

© 2008 Elsevier Inc. All rights reserved.

Glossary

Between-family research – Involves the comparison of individuals from different families. Therefore, when birth orders are compared, the large genetic differences between families are not controlled and add much extraneous variance.

Big five personality traits – Factor analyses of comprehensive personality questionnaires typically yield five super-factors. They are named extraversion, agreeableness, conscientiousness, neuroticism, and openness to experience. This simple taxonomy of personality has proved useful in describing birth-order effects.

Birth order – The numerical sequence of a child's arrival into a family. Environmental theories focus on the functional order (actual rearing order) whereas biological theories include all births.

Intellectual achievement – This term subsumes scholastic performance (e.g., GPA, number of years of attained education) and performance on scholastic-related tests (e.g., standardized intelligence tests, SATs).

Self-fulfilling prophecy – The dynamic process whereby an expectation about birth order difference becomes a reality.

Social development – In this article, the term social development is simplified to refer to age changes in personality and political attitudes.

Teaching effect – The long-term intellectual advantage conferred by the opportunity to help one's younger siblings.

Within-family research – Within-family research involves data collected on at least one sibling as well as the target individual. In many studies, one family member reports on the whole set of siblings including himself or herself. It does not seem to matter which family member does the reporting because family members tend to corroborate each other's judgments.

Introduction

The notion that birth order has an influence on child development has undergone several cycles of popularity and disrepute. This uneven history applies to birth-order effects on social development as well as intellectual development, although the two literatures have unfolded quite independently. In this article, a brief history of this cycling of popularity in each of these literatures is provided followed by elaboration on the major theories and research.

Most discussions of the topic focus on differences between firstborn and laterborn children. This simplification results in part from a reluctance on the part of researchers to differentiate among birth orders with small frequencies. While there are sufficient numbers of first- and secondborns in most samples, the frequencies are small for thirdborns and higher. Hence all laterborns are lumped together for analysis purposes. This article will follow suit in focusing almost entirely on the firstborn vs. laterborn differences – with the exception of some notable findings regarding middle-borns and lastborns.

A Brief History

Social Development

Alfred Adler, the second born of six children, was weak, sickly, and continually tormented by his older brother.

In early childhood, Alfred envied his brother and felt that they were always in competition. But he worked hard to overcome his handicaps and became a popular member of the community. His success was such that his older brother grew to resent him.

Undoubtedly, these family dynamics played a role in Adler's seminal writings about the psychology of birth order. His ideas, published largely in the 1920s, anticipated many of the later perspectives on the subject. He suggested, for example, that firstborns are typically given more family responsibilities than laterborns and are expected to set an example. Consequently, they often become authoritarian and construe power as their natural right. This attitude can eventuate in an insecurity around the possibility of being 'de-throned' by laterborns.

Adler went further to write that achievement expectations are high for firstborns and they attempt to live up to them. Laterborns, in contrast, try to compensate for their inferiority in size and power by turning to alternative notions of achievement. For example, the laterborns might turn to more social or creative endeavors. Thus Adler's writings addressed both of the two primary domains, intellectual and personality development.

It was not until the 1960s that mainstream researchers raised the legitimacy of studying birth-order effects in personality development. Stanley Schachter, for example, conducted a series of archival and laboratory studies of birth-order differences. Other prominent psychologists (e.g., Robert Sears, Phillip Zimbardo, Edward Ziegler, and Mary Rothbart) all added to the body of research on birth order as well as its credibility. During this period, sociologists and economists also contributed both theory and data to the birth-order literature.

Although popular right up to the 1970s, the credibility of birth-order effects on personality faltered badly in 1983 with the publication of a comprehensive review by Ernst and Angst. The scope of their review was impressive: virtually every published study was included. After adding a variety of controls, including gender and family size, the authors concluded that associations between birth order and personality traits were minimal.

The reputation of birth-order effects remained in quiet disrepute until the 1996 publication of Frank Sulloway's book, *Born to Rebel*. In applying a bold new theoretical perspective, Sulloway revitalized the view that personality and social attitudes differ systematically across birth order.

Sulloway's treatment was persuasive, in part, because he offered two complementary forms of evidence. One was a catalog of captivating stories about the family life of historical figures. The second form of evidence was a meta-analysis of the large number of studies on personality and birth order. To great advantage, he organized the studies within the influential 'Big Five' or Five Factor Model of personality. That model is now generally accepted as the best organizational system (taxonomy) of personality traits.

Using that organizational system, Sulloway's meta-analysis of the apparently chaotic literature exposed a clear pattern. In particular, firstborns were more conscientious and socially conservative but less agreeable and open to experience than laterborns. These claims form the hub of debates that continue to swirl around birth-order effects on social development. Follow-up studies from other quarters have varied from highly supportive to highly critical of Sulloway's claims.

Intellectual Development

Scholarly interest in the relation between birth order and achievement can be traced to 1874 when Francis Galton published *English Men of Science: Their Nature and Nurture*. The book chronicled the lives of 180 eminent men from various scientific fields. Galton found that 48% of them were eldest sons, far higher than would be expected by chance. Anticipating later arguments, Galton provided three speculations on how the birth-order difference might come about. First was the impact of the primogeniture tradition: firstborn sons were given priority in the inheritance of family wealth. Accordingly, they would be more likely have the financial resources to continue their education. Second, firstborns were more likely to be treated as companions by parents and be assigned more mature responsibilities than their younger siblings. Galton's third speculation was that, in families with limited financial resources, firstborns received more attention and better nourishment than other siblings.

The latter two notions remain central to current debates regarding birth-order effects. Although the primogeniture tradition has waned, recent surveys by anthropologists confirm that firstborns occupy special status in every human society. Other things being equal, they are awarded more respect and given priority in legal, religious, and social matters, even when all siblings are grown to maturity.

Almost a century of sporadic studies of intellectual development yielded inconsistent associations with birth order, partly because the sample sizes were insufficient. It was not until Robert Zajonc's research in the 1960s that massive data sets were given theoretical scrutiny in major psychology journals.

Zajonc's analyses provided persuasive evidence that the intellectual achievement of firstborns tends to surpass that of other birth orders. This advantage applies across a wide range of measures including school grades, intelligence quotient (IQ) scores, and SATs. Partly due to his credibility as a hard-nosed scientist, Zajonc's theoretical and empirical analyses were taken seriously: much of his research and follow-up studies were published in medical, economics, and hard-science journals. As detailed below, his work provoked an avid interest that continues to this day.

Theories of Birth-Order Differences

As noted above, the literatures on social and intellectual development have only minimal overlap. The various theories of birth order have developed primarily in the context of one field or the other. In reviewing the five most important theories, however, this article will attempt to draw out implications for both social and intellectual development.

Confluence Model

Proposed by Zajonc, this theory explains the firstborn advantage in terms of the intellectual environment evolving within the family. With only two propositions, the theory was able to explain birth-order effects as well as intellectual deficits deriving from five other family constellation effects: family size, close child spacing, multiple births, and being lastborn or an only child.

The first proposition of the model is simply that intellectual stimulation of children has enduring benefits for their later intellectual success. Only firstborns have a period of time where they receive 100% of their parents' attention. For secondborns, the maximum quality time involves sharing the parents' attention with the firstborn. With each successive child, the available parental attention gets watered down even further. In addition, the linguistic environment becomes increasingly less mature as more children enter the family. The second proposition of the confluence model was that lastborns miss out on the intellectual stimulation involved in teaching younger siblings. We consider that second proposition in the section below on lastborns.

Zajonc's first proposition does not seem radical or especially controversial: in retrospect, it seems more like commonsense. But he spelled out the various consequences and quantified them in a simple but persusive arithmetic formula. To represent the quality of the intellectual atmosphere at any point in a child's development, one simply has to calculate the current mean mental age in the family. Integrated over the childhood years, this mean is higher for firstborns: they receive the most intellectual stimulation because they spend a larger portion of their time in a high-quality atmosphere. This stimulation stays with them in the form of superior cognitive abilities.

Intellectual deficits due to family size also follow from this watering-down mechanism. Increasing the spacing between children helps modulate this watering down effect by allowing the mental ages of the older children to increase before adding the new contributor of zero mental age. Finally, the extra deficit seen in children of multiple births follows from the extra drop in average mental age due to the addition of several zeros to the equation.

Although they are seldom spelled out, implications for social development can also be derived from the Confluence Model. Differential parental attention, even out of practical necessity, should affect the nature of the parent–child relationship across the birth order. Firstborns should be more attuned to their parents' aspirations for their children, more needy of their parents' approval, and expect to maintain the special status they enjoyed as children in future social settings. Together, these sequelae could eventuate in the different personality trait and value profiles typically found across the birth orders.

Resource Dilution Model

This theory, originally proposed by the economist Judith Blake and extended by the sociologist, Downey, goes beyond the Confluence Model to argue for a more comprehensive decrease in resources for each successive child. In particular, there is a progressive watering down of financial and educational sources such as books, travel, and tuition. Differences in such concrete parental resources across birth orders can culminate in different scores on IQ tests.

For example, parents with limited incomes may not be able to afford to send all their children to college. Any limitation in the opportunity for higher education will certainly diminish the likelihood of intellectual achievement. In combination with the decrease in parental attention, these other drawbacks handicap laterborns relative to firstborns. As noted for the Confluence Model, any special status, even if endowed arbitrarily by financial practicalities, may have implications for social development.

Writers adhering to the Resource Dilution Model seldom allude to differences in social development across the birth order. Nonetheless, it seems reasonable to speculate that the differential allotment of financial resources could influence personality. The model is consistent with a small number of studies suggesting that firstborns feel more entitled to special treatment and that laterborns experience more resentment and jealousy.

Parental Feedback Theory

This theory suggests that parents adjust their parenting style as they move from the firstborn to laterborns. This adjustment is not out of financial or attentional necessity, but out of increasing comfort and decreasing anxieties. The result is that parents are less demanding of laterborns, especially with regard to their school performance. Beyond the firstborn, parents may allocate their love and approval in a manner that is less contingent on the child's achievement.

In one of the few experimental studies examining the transmission of birth-order effects, Irma Hilton observed how mothers treated children in a laboratory setting. In the waiting-room, firstborn children were observed to remain physically closer to their mother, often holding on for security. After the children returned from a putative 'testing session', mothers were told that their child had performed extremely well or extremely poorly – based strictly on random assignment. Observation via a one-way mirror revealed that mothers of firstborns gave contingent feedback: if told their child performed well, mothers coddled and praised the child. If told their child performed poorly, mothers berated the child. Laterborns, however, received noncontingent treatment: mothers responded to the child as they had before the testing session – regardless of performance feedback.

It is easy to see how such differential treatment could set off rather different developmental trajectories for firstborns and laterborns. In firstborns, superior intellectual achievement should be accompanied by a number of personality traits: they should possess higher achievement motivation, a greater concern with approval from parents and subsequent authorities. In turn, such qualities may well diminish their popularity among peers. The need for approval from authorities should also engender more conservative political attitudes in firstborns.

Family Niche Theory

In Frank Sulloway's theory, parents play only indirect roles. Instead, birth-order effects unfold during the inevitable competition among siblings as they struggle for a family niche. Firstborns, having the first choice of niche, attempt to please their parents in traditional fashion, namely, by good performance at school and by generally responsible behavior. But, as other siblings arrive, firstborns must deal with threats to their natural priority in the sibling status hierarchy. The resulting adult character is conscientious and conservative.

Laterborns must contest the higher status of firstborns, while seeking alternative ways of distinguishing themselves in the eyes of the parents. Accordingly, they develop an adult character marked by an empathic interpersonal style, a striving for uniqueness, and political views that are both egalitarian and antiauthoritarian. In short, they are 'born to rebel'. This attempt to address birth-order differences in political orientation is unique to Family Niche Theory.

Although designed to explain birth-order differences in personality, the Family Niche Theory is not without implications for intellectual development. In fact, it makes predictions about two aspects of intellectual life – achievement and creativity. Firstborns strive to achieve via traditional academic means – conscientious striving, to be specific. This development begins with their attempt to please their parents via school success. Although traditionally distinguished as ability vs. motivation, the tight overlap between intelligence and conscientiousness has become more evident in recent work. Laterborns, in contrast, seek out creativity, even radical revolution, in their intellectual lives.

Prenatal Hypomasculinization Theory

Drawing on earlier work by Maccoby and others, Jeremy Beer and John Horn have developed a biologically based theory suggesting that the birth orders already differ at birth. The argument does not postulate an average genetic difference in the birth orders but a difference in their exposure to hormones. Previously called the 'tired mother' syndrome, the notion is that, with each succeeding male child birth, mothers expose their babies to lower levels of masculinizing hormones.

Beer and Horn derived their theory from recent findings indicating that the likelihood of male homosexuality increases with the number of older brothers. The common mechanism, they argue, is the progressive immunization of mothers to the hormones that masculinize the male fetus. Thus male children with older brothers are 'hypomasculinized' in both their sexual orientation and their personality characteristics.

According to Beer and Horn, this process eventuates in certain parallels between sex differences and birth-order effects. For example, males and firstborns should exhibit higher levels of competitive achievement whereas females and laterborns should exhibit more cooperation and flexibility. Firstborns should also be more disagreeable, and show more masculine interests. This hypothesized pattern of birth-order differences is consistent with the empirical evidence cited by Sulloway, Zajonc, and others.

To date, however, there is little direct evidence to support Beer and Horn's hypomasculinization theory. Yet the possibility that firstborns and laterborns already differ at birth is intriguing and should trigger further research on biological differences across birth orders.

Contrasting Mechanisms

Even among those writers who accept that children of different birth orders do differ in systematic ways, the disagreement over explanatory mechanisms is striking. According to the Prenatal Hypomasculinization Theory, the differences are already set at birth. For the Parental Feedback Theory, it is a change in parents' comfort level that is responsible for birth-order differences. For the Resource Dilution Theory, it is the diminishing availability of resources that aid education. For the Confluence Model, it is the devolving quantity and quality of intellectual stimulation. For the Family Niche Theory, birth-order effects are propogated by accompanying differences in age, size, knowledge, and status in the family: The oldest child will always be the oldest. Size, knowledge, and maturity differences will eventually even out but status differences can remain well into adulthood.

Of course, people spend most of their lives outside the purview of the family home and its unique interpersonal dynamics. Not surprisingly, then environmental theories typically suggest that birth-order forces on social and intellectual achievement should diminish with time. Even if accepting that the power of such differences eventually wanes, most psychologists – and lay observers, for that matter – believe that early environmental factors have a unique and enduring impact.

Modern Data: The Importance of Research Design

Each of the above theories has some intuitive appeal. But there remain serious questions about the data supporting the very existence of birth-order differences. As with many developmental debates, the key claims are not testable via laboratory-controlled experiments. Under contemporary mores, we cannot – or, rather, will not – randomly assign babies to different birth orders. Instead, social scientists can offer only correlational data and hope to clarify the developmental processes via statistical arguments.

The most persuasive birth-order studies entail a large sample of participants evaluated in an efficient experimental design that includes multiple control provisions to handle potentially contaminating variables. One critical design issue is whether the data are collected within families or between familes. Within-family studies involve a comparison of the siblings within each family. If firstborn Jason and secondborn Mark are raised entirely in the same family setting, then they are matched (in large part) on factors such as family socioeconomic status (SES), parents' child-rearing strategies, parents' personalities, family events, and many other environmental factors. Of special importance, the researcher need not be concerned with genetic differences because, on average, they do not differ among offspring of the same parents. All of these controls make for a fair comparison of Jason and Mark with respect to birth order.

In between-family studies, however, none of those controls are in place. If chosen randomly from a classroom, subject pool, street interview, or telephone survey, Jason and Mark are bound to differ on a host of environmental and genetic factors. Because those variables contribute their own (often larger) sources of variation, any birth-order differences will tend to be obscured.

Because birth-order effects are relatively small, large sample sizes are of special importance for teasing out the differences. In the case of within-family research, it is difficult to take seriously any study comprising fewer than several hundred families. For between-family studies, even larger samples are required. Because so many other factors add noise to the measurement, birth-order differences do not become apparent with fewer than 500 participants from a relatively homogeneous sample.

Debates over these methodological issues have created comparable levels of controversy in the research literatures on social and intellectual development. Yet the controversies have played out in rather different fashion in the two literatures.

Intellectual Development

In virtually every cross-sectional survey, a consistent advantage for firstborns continues to appear. Firstborns are over-represented among university students, among Nobel Prize winners, and on virtually any other concrete measure of intellectual achievement (e.g., IQ tests, SATs). Such birth-order differences, first communicated in a scientifically persuasive fashion by Zajonc and colleagues, continue to emerge in modern samples.

For the most part, however, such clearcut birth-order effects were observed in between-family (i.e., cross-sectional) data. A variety of confounds (e.g., SES, family size) make such results ambiguous. As Joseph Rodgers and others have demonstrated, when such confounds are removed, birth-order effects on measures of intellectual achivement often disappear. Unfortunately, when such important variables are statistically confounded, it is difficult to distinguish which variables are genuine effects and which variables should be controlled. By removing the effects of variables that may have similar causal mechanisms to birth-order effects, such analyses may be 'throwing out the baby with the bathwater'.

As of the writing of this article, the empirical pendulum seems to have swung back to favor the claims made by Zajonc and others. Several Norwegian researchers have recently analyzed data from virtually the entire population of their country. In 650 000 families, firstborn children showed a clear advantage in IQ, educational attainment, and later adult income.

Apart from the largest sample size, this research has the most rigorous controls, including family size and SES. The fact that education is free in Norway helps mitigate the counter-argument that family finances play a determining role. So does the finding that the birth-order effects were actually stronger for children with highly educated mothers.

Social Development

In studies of personality and social attitudes, as well, the empirical debate about birth order is characterized by inconsistency. Sulloway and others have offered large data sets to support the idea that firstborns are more conforming and conscientious whereas laterborns are more agreeable, open to experience, and politically liberal. In response, other reputable scientists have disputed the size and importance of such birth-order differences.

Again the debate may turn on the choice of within-family vs. between-family designs. In this case, however, the advocate and skeptic views are reversed. Birth-order effects are evident in within-family designs whereas minimal results emerge from between-family designs. The within-family design is typified by the method used in a 1999 article by Paulhus and colleagues. They asked a variety of large samples to report on their own families. In one study, for example, participants were asked to rate themselves and their siblings on the Big Five personality traits and on political attitudes. Results firmly supported Sulloway's predictions.

Most recently, Healey and Ellis outlined the conditions that yield the clearest birth-order effects in personality: (1) when firstborns are compared with secondborns, (2) when the age difference is 2–4 years, and (3) when children reared apart are excluded. Again, these within-family patterns confirmed predictions from Sulloway's Family Niche Theory.

With respect to between-family studies, a prototypical example is the study conducted in 1998 by Tyrone Jefferson and colleagues. Their data came from large archival samples that included both personality and birth-order data. On self-report measures, they found no significant birth-order effects on personality. On peer-ratings, the only significant finding was the usual conscientiousness advantage for firstborns. Few other studies can boast the feature of peer-raters: they provide a more objective perspective from outside of the family.

These conflicting results may have a simple resolution. Studies with weak or null birth-order effects always involve a comparison of individuals from different families. But, as noted above, families differ on a wealth of influential variables and a full range of appropriate controls is seldom available. Within-family data provide a natural control procedure for all between-family differences, including their largest contributor – genetics.

Most readers will be aware of the recent confirmation of substantial genetic effects on both intellect and personality. This consensus is helpful in understanding the conflicting conclusions drawn from within- vs. between-family studies: within-family designs remove a large component from the equation, namely, mean genetic differences between families. Accordingly, birth-order differences emerge more clearly in within-family studies.

The burgeoning behavioral genetics literature also supports birth-order claims in another way. Second to genetics, the primary source of variance is personality, values, and, even political orientation is within-family environmental variance. In other words, there are family dynamics at work making siblings more different than expected by random genetic effects. Sibling rivalry and differential parental treatment of different birth orders are likely to be part of these within-family dynamics.

Stereotype Effects

To repeat, within-family studies of personality inevitably show clear birth-order effects. Whether one asks the firstborn or laterborns, there is agreement on who is more conscientious. Moreover, this agreement seems to last a lifetime.

Yet some critics dismiss the importance of that within-family consensus, arguing instead that putative birth-order effects derive entirely from within-family stereotypes. As children grow up with siblings of different ages, real differences in size, power, maturity, and knowledge govern the intersibling dynamics. When asked later to compare their siblings, say at the age of 30 years, all family members tend to concur on the traditional family story about how the children differ. Beyond that, these critics argue, the stereotypes have no impact on people's lives.

But research from the social and developmental psychology literature indicates that self- and other-stereotypes run deeper than that. In fact, adult samples show the same pattern and size of birth-order effects as much younger samples, even when the adults have been living apart from their siblings for many years. The stability of these perceptions across the lifespan undermines the accusation that they are artifactual and makes a stereotype perspective difficult to distinguish from standard conceptions of personality.

Alternatively, is it possible that birth-order differences in that perceptions of one's siblings are a fiction inculcated by stereotypes acquired from other sources? It is hard to believe that, throughout their lives, siblings systematically ignore bona fide evidence of their brothers' and sisters' actual traits in favor of erroneous stereotypes. It seems far more reasonable to believe that such stereotypes flourish because they have (at least) a kernel of truth. Critics would have to argue further that initially false stereotypes can endure a lifetime without having any impact on personality. According to social psychological research, however, one should expect some reification due to self-fulfilling prophecies. Can the stereotypes, the self-perceptions, and the peer-perceptions all be faulty?

Critics such as Judith Rich Harris hold an intermediate position in conceding the reality of within-family personality differences, but caution that the differences remain just that – within the family. In other words, birth-order differences have no effect on life outside of the family home: only on home visits do the old familiar patterns emerge. Many readers will relate to that experience. Nonetheless, that experience may not be an insignificant portion of adulthood. Many children do go on to spend a significant amount of their adult life involved in continuing interactions with the family of origin.

Harris's notion of circumscribed personality differences is also compromised by a number of recent studies reporting on more concrete differences outside of the family. For example, firstborns show more dismissive attachment styles in later life whereas laterborns disproportionately choose occupations that involve social interaction.

To summarize, the stereotype critique is an attempt to explain away the robustness of within-family personality differences as shared fiction. Such counter-arguments must always be taken seriously, but in this writer's opinion, there is simply too much evidence for the reality of birth-order differences.

Further Complexities

Firstborns, Only-Children, and MiddleBorns

Most of this article has purposely simplified birth-order issues by limiting the discussion to a comparison of firstborn children to all laterborns. The primary reason was that, in most respects, differences among laterborns are not as apparent as is the contrast with firstborns. Yet there are a few issues where middleborns and lastborns do stand out.

The unique findings for lastborn children include both good news and bad news. As noted earlier, Zajonc found an extra decline in the intellectual achievement of lastborns – above and beyond the gradual decline due to successive birth order. A thirdborn child, for example, fares more poorly if no younger children are added to the family. This finding was confirmed in the recent large sample and tightly controlled Norwegian data (described above).

Zajonc explained this anomaly in terms of the so-called 'teaching effect'. Firstborns (and older siblings in general) often have to answer questions posed by their younger siblings and assist with their homework. At the time, the older siblings may experience these tasks as onerous. Rather than a burden, Zajonc argued, this teaching opportunity actually benefits earlier-borns, perhaps by forcing them to engage more deeply with the material they are teaching. That claim is quite consistent with the tutoring research in educational psychology, which shows that teaching benefits the teacher at least as much as it benefits the student. A lack of such opportunities can thus explain why lastborn children show an extra deficit in intellectual achievement and why only, children do not achieve as highly as other firstborns.

The good news for lastborns lies in the personal popularity that ensues from their birth order. In surveys of comparative popularity, the lastborns are voted the 'favorite child' more often than any other birth order. This popularity may well reflect an inevitable tradeoff with personal achievement. Peers prefer others who are noncompetitive and more socially oriented than achievement oriented.

These arguments can also be applied to only-children. The fact that they are also lastborns, may explain why their academic achievement does not match up to that of other firstborns; the fact that they are also firstborns may explain why they are not as popular as other laterborns.

The tradeoff between the respect accorded to firstborns and the personal popularity of lastborns often leaves the middleborns feeling left out. Studies by Canadian researchers, Salmon, Daly, and Wilson has confirmed that, in various ways, the middleborns feel less attached to the parents. For example, they are less likely than either first- or lastborns to nominate their mothers as their favorite family member.

Gender

Compared to the prominent role that gender plays in many developmental issues, it has made surprisingly little difference in birth-order studies. The intellect and personality profiles that emerge for females are comparable to those emerging for males.

Certainly, over the long history of birth-order research, a number of statistical interactions have been reported where gender was involved. When found, the results of a particular combination – say, firstborn males with secondborn females and thirdborn males – were not difficult to explain with a 'just-so story'. But the fact that such interaction effects rarely replicate suggests that the original findings were due to chance. With larger families, the number of possible combinations escalates quickly. With increasing parity in male vs. female achievement, any such interactions with birth order may eventually vanish. For these reasons and others, recent research has paid little attention to possible gender differences in birth-order effects.

A couple of recent findings constitute exceptions to this rule. An interesting finding reported by Sulloway was that secondborn boys often develop with firstborn personalities if the firstborn is a girl. Perhaps boys do not see firstborn girls as competitors and react only to their brothers. Or parents may still place more value on the firstborn male child.

The lack of difference in the size of birth-order effects has played a role in evaluating the Prenatal Hypomasculinization Theory. The credibility of that theory is weakened by the fact that its predicted larger effect size in males has not materialized in recent (tightly controlled) research.

Summary

The impact of birth order on social and intellectual development seems at once self-evident and empirically elusive. When found, the pattern is consistent: firstborns are the most intelligent, achieving, and conscientious, whereas laterborns are the most rebellious, liberal, and agreeable. In competition to explain these profiles are such diverse theories as Differentiatal Parental Feedback, Resource Dilution, Family Niche, and Prenatal Hypomasculinization.

The difficulty in confirming these birth-order differences is disconcerting. Although intially evident in most large-sample studies, the differences often disappear when key variables are controlled. The fact that significant reverse effects (e.g., firstborns less conscientious than laterborns) are rarely found, suggests that birth-order effects are at work, but that they are masked by certain research designs. Even statistical experts cannot seem to agree on how to tease apart birth-order effects from those of family size and SES.

The fact that birth-order differences are small to begin with makes them especially difficult to confirm. Indeed, all the contending theories predict small differences. In the case of IQ differences, for example, the expected firstborn vs. secondborn difference is only two IQ points. The effect sizes of birth order pale in comparison with sex differences, and most important, with temperament differences instilled by genetic and congenital factors.

As Jerome Kagan has pointed out, stereotypes about birth order are widespread and have a powerful intuitive appeal. But surely this wide appeal derives, at least in part, from some real commonality in human experience. Those of us with siblings have spent considerable time evaluating our relationships with them. The consensus within our families emerged long before we learned about birth-order stereotypes. The fact that most adults are eventually made aware of these stereotypes does not undo their validity. Even stereotypes can have a self-fulfilling effect as family members strive to live up to their expected roles.

At this point in the history of birth-order research, the informed reader must live with the fact that experts disagree and the continuing empirical debates are abstruse. Nonetheless, in this writer's opinion, the current weight of evidence favors the view that birth order does matter for both intellectual and social development.

Suggested Readings

Bjerkedal T, Kristensen P, Skjeret GA, and Brevik JI (2007) Intelligence test scores and birth order among young Norwegian men (conscripts) analyzed within and between families. *Intelligence* 35: 503–514.

Healey MD and Ellis BJ (2007) Birth order, conscientiousness, and openness to experience: Tests of the family-niche model of personality using a within-family methodology. *Human Evolution and Behavior* 28: 55–59.

Jefferson T, Herbst JH, and McCrae RR (1998) Associations between birth order and personality traits: Evidence from self-reports and observer ratings. *Journal of Research in Personality* 32: 498–509.

Paulhus DL, Trapnell PD, and Chen D (1999) Effects of birth order on achievement and personality within families. *Psychological Science* 10: 482–488.

Rodgers JL, Cleveland HH, van den Oord E, and Rowe DC (2000) Resolving the debate over birth order, family size and intelligence. *American Psychologist* 55: 599–612.

Salmon CA and Daly M (1998) The impact of sex and birth order on familial sentiment: Middleborns are different. *Evolution and Human Behavior* 19: 299–312.

Schachter S (1963) Birth order, eminence and higher education. *American Sociological Review* 28: 757–768.

Sulloway FJ (1996) *Born to Rebel: Birth Order, Family Dynamics, and Creative Lives.* New York: Pantheon.

Zajonc RB (1976) Family configuration and intelligence. *Science* 192: 227–281.

Brain Development

D Fair and B L Schlaggar, Washington University School of Medicine, St. Louis, MO, USA

© 2008 Elsevier Inc. All rights reserved.

Glossary

Afferent – A neural projection carrying ascending information from the periphery to the nervous system or providing input from one brain region to another (e.g., thalamocortical afferent).

Architectonics – The arrangement of cells (e.g., cytoarchtectonics) or other attributes such as molecular markers (e.g., chemoarchitectonic) particularly in the cerebral cortex. A feature that contributes to the characterization of a neocortical area.

Broca aphasia – A syndrome characterized by nonfluent verbal language expression coupled with the sparing of language comprehension classically, but not necessarily, due to a lesion in Broca's area within the left inferior frontal lobe.

Cortico-cortical – Neuronal projections connecting regions within the cerebral cortex.

Efferent – A neural projection carrying information away from the nervous system to the periphery or carrying the output from one brain region to another.

Epigenetic – A factor that can change the activity of genes without changing their structure. Often used to refer to a factor that interacts with genetic factors to influence phenotypic expression.

Genetic – A factor or mechanism, particularly in development, that is largely the consequence of genes.

Glia – Non-neuronal cells of the nervous system that perform a variety of functions. These cells include: astrocytes, oligodendrocytes, radial glia, Schwann cells, satellite cells, and microglia.
Perinatal – The period at or around the time of birth.
Prenatal – The period occurring prior to birth.
Retinotopic organization – A term describing the topographic representation of the retinal surface in the regions of the brain devoted to processing visual information.
Somatotopic organization – A term describing the topographic representation of the body surface in regions of the brain devoted to processing somatic motor and sensory processing.
Thalamocortical – Ascending neuronal projections from the thalamus to the neocortex. An example of an afferent projection.
Topography – Referring to the general property in the nervous system that adjacent points on a sensory surface (or within a brain area) are represented in adjacent points in brain regions to which the sensory surface (or brain area) projects.
Voxel – A three-dimensional unit of volume used in magnetic resonance imaging (MRI).
Wernicke aphasia – A syndrome characterized by fluent but nonmeaningful verbal language expression coupled with a lack of language comprehension classically, but not necessarily, due to a lesion in Wernicke's area within the posterior and superior aspect of the left temporal lobe.

Introduction

Tracing its roots back to 3000 BC, the Egyptian Edwin Smith Surgical Papyrus is the earliest written report of brain function. From this document and others, we recognize that the Egyptians deemed the heart, not the brain, as the seat of intelligence and cognition. By the fourth century BC, Hippocrates and one of his greatest enthusiasts, Galen (second century AD), ignited a sharp transition concerning the origins of thought. It became clear that the early Egyptian beliefs, although championed by greats such as Aristotle, were mistaken. At the 'heart' of thought is the brain.

Cognition is a consequence of brain function. The new acquaintance whose name you just learned, the time of your meeting tomorrow, or your spouse's birthday (presuming you have not forgotten) are all encoded in the brain. Throughout one's lifetime, this type of information/experience will continually modify brain structure.

The first two decades of life in particular represent a period of extraordinary developmental change in sensory, motor, and cognitive abilities. One of the goals of cognitive neuroscience is to link the complex behavioral milestones that occur throughout this period with the intricate changes of the neural substrate. In our view, developmental neurobiological mechanisms are complex and the linkage to the equally elaborate emergence or refinement of cognitive skills is not straightforward.

Overview

This article offers an overview on selected topics of human brain development with an emphasis on the neocortex to provide a context for relating brain development to cognitive development. The article starts with a brief description of prenatal cortical organization and characterizes the formation of the neocortex by the time of birth. This first section chronicles the genesis of neocortical layers and the initially coarse construction of neocortical areas. The second section on postnatal brain development describes lessons learned from the development of visual cortex. This section highlights the importance of both genetic and epigenetic influences on development and their relation to behavior. Also emphasized are the concepts of critical and sensitive periods which, although viewed by many in the context of behavior, are a reflection of changes in neural circuits. The third section continues with a characterization of the progressive and regressive events that manifest in the postnatal period. Such phenomena have been increasingly used in cognitive developmental models, but often metaphorically. The fourth section focuses on developmental neuroplasticity, emphasizing that neuroplasticity is mostly advantageous, sometimes undesirable, and often insufficient. The article's final section is devoted to neuroimaging. The discussion accentuates how noninvasive neuroimaging is a promising and provocative tool for the study of cognitive development, but cautions against the tendency for overinterpretation.

Prenatal Cortical Organization

Genesis of Cortical Layers

The neocortical sheet is a laminar structure consisting of six layers (**Figure 1(a)**). This laminar organization is a consistent feature across the neocortex and is relatively conserved among most mammalian species. The mature six-layer structure consists of neurons generated from precursor cells located in the ventricular proliferative zone. These neurons reach their final destination, for the most part, by traversing along radial glial guides toward the cortical surface and organize in an inside-out pattern. Neurons born early form the deepest layers of the neocortex and those born later form the most superficial layers (**Figure 1(b)**). Despite the radial migration of

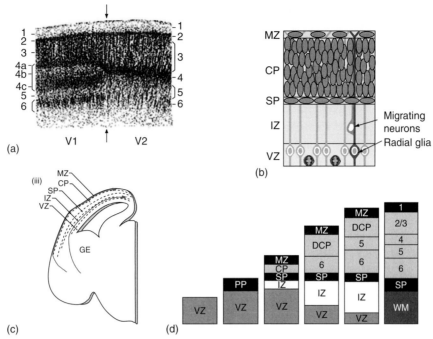

Figure 1 (a) The six layer organization of the neocortex. Provided is an image by Korbinian Brodmann of an 8-month-old human fetus. A sharp transition in the cytoarchitecture, most clearly identified in layer IV, is observed between V1 and V2 of the visual cortex. (b) The radial migration of neocortical neurons. Most neurons migrate radially along radial glial guides from the ventricular zone (VZ), through the intermediate zone (IZ), and aggregate in the cortical plate (CP). (c) The tangential migration of interneurons. Most neocortical interneurons (i.e., GABAergic interneurons) are generated in the ganglionic eminences (GE) and migrate tangentially through the IZ and marginal zone (MZ) to the neocortex. (d) Layer development in the neocortex. Neurons first generated in the VZ form the preplate (PP). The continuous migration of newborn neurons splits the preplate into the MZ, CP, and subplate (SP). In the developing cortical plate (DCP) the earliest born neurons form the deepest layers of the neocortex and those born later form the most superficial layers. (a) Adapted from Brodmann K (1909) *Vergleichende Lokalisationlehre Der Grosshirnrinde in Inren Prinzipien Dargestellt Auf Grund Des Zellenbaues*. Leipzig: J. A. Barth. (d) Adapted from O'Leary DD and Nakagawa Y (2002). Patterning centers, regulatory genes and extrinsic mechanisms controlling arealization of the neocortex. *Current Opinion in Neurobiology* 12(1): 14–25, with permission from Elsevier.

most neurons, inhibitory (γ-aminobutyric acid (GABA) ergic) interneurons, which play an important role in neuroplasticity and critical period determination (see the section titled 'The development of ocular dominance columns' later), are first born in the ventral (subcortical) portion of the proliferative zone and migrate tangentially into the developing cortex (**Figure 1(c)**).

In humans, mature layer formation begins with an initial accumulation of neurons outside the ventricular zone called the preplate (**Figure 1(d)**). By approximately 8 weeks, gestation, the continuous migration of newborn neurons splits the preplate, forming three temporary layers. These are the marginal zone, cortical plate, and subplate (going from pia to ventricle) (**Figure 1(d)**).

After subplate formation, there is a significant rise in the synaptic contacts within it. By approximately 22 weeks, gestation, the subplate is about 3–4 times thicker than the cortical plate. This growth of the subplate is accompanied by the initial (transient) projections to it from the thalamus, basal forebrain, and brainstem. As the cortical layers mature (continuing through the perinatal period), the transient synaptic contacts in the subplate are reorganized and form distinct contacts in the maturing lamina. Accompanying the loss of transient synapses is a progressive loss of subplate neurons.

The most drastic anomaly and subsequent cognitive deficits resulting from defects in neocortical neuronal migration is lissencephaly. Lissencephaly is a general term describing several disorders of migration that result in an abnormally thick, smooth, and agyric brain pattern. Affected individuals usually suffer from epilepsy and developmental delay/mental retardation.

Another anomaly, periventricular heterotopia (PH), refers to collections of neurons ectopically located (i.e., periventricularly) often under otherwise normal-appearing cortex. PH results in a less severe phenotype than lissencephaly, but is also thought to occur secondary to migration defects. Affected patients usually present with seizures in late adolescence but with normal or near-normal levels of intelligence.

Developmental dyslexia is the most common and carefully studied learning disability affecting both children and adults. Highly heritable, dyslexia is characterized by reading difficulties in individuals with otherwise normal intelligence and access to education. Recently identified dyslexia susceptibility genes appear to have roles in neuronal migration suggesting that dyslexia could, at least in part, be due to a defect in this process.

Development and Differentiation of Functional Areas

The neocortex is composed of numerous morphologically and functionally distinct areas. The developmental differentiation of neocortical areas likely corresponds to certain aspects of maturing sensory, motor, and cognitive abilities. Therefore, understanding the developmental differentiation of neocortical areas is critical to understanding cognitive development. (In functional imaging, the term 'area' has often been used interchangeably with the term 'region', such that the actual meanings have often been lost. The term 'region' is a general term that describes a circumscribed portion of cortex (or subcortex) that may consist of an area, multiple areas, or portions of an area; e.g., 'the parietal region' or 'region of interest'.)

Defining a neocortical area

The first to champion neocortical localization of functions was Emanuel Swedenborg (1688–1772). He accurately reasoned that localization was the only way to explain how higher cognitive functions were not equally affected by diverse brain injuries. Franz Joseph Gall (1758–1828), the founder of phrenology, later claimed that the brain was divided into 27 separate 'organs', each of which corresponded to specific mental faculties. Although his work on phrenology was harshly criticized and proven incorrect, Gall's insistence that the brain was divided into specific areas with distinct functions influenced other prominent figures. Paul Broca's (1824–1880) landmark case of his aphasic patient Leborgne (famously referred to as 'Tan'), as well as work by other pioneers such as Carl Wernicke (1848–1905) and Joseph Jules Dejerine (1849–1917), spawned an era of investigation that was deeply rooted in cerebral functional localization.

After over a century of work, it has become evident that ascertaining a complete collection of neocortical areas is not straightforward. Historically, the greatest difficulty in identification stemmed from a failure to establish consensus criteria for defining an area.

Current consensus is that neocortical areas can be classified based on four properties: function, architectonics, connections, and topology (FACT) (**Figure 2(a)**). Each one of these properties has its strengths and weaknesses for revealing the underlying cortical organization and none in isolation can adequately depict it. (Obtaining all of these properties in humans represents an additional level of complexity.) For instance, single-unit recording or various neuroimaging strategies might potentially identify area borders based on function. Yet,

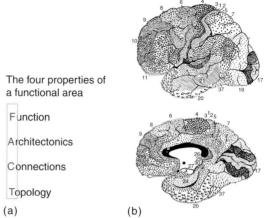

Figure 2 (a) The four properties of a functional area. The mammalian cerebral cortex neocortex is composed of several morphologically and functionally distinct areas that are defined based on these four properties. (b) Cortical areas as defined by Korbinian Brodmann with architectonics. Further analyses have shown that some of these areas are also functionally and connectionally distinct, while other areas have been further differentiated with connections, function, and topography. Although Brodmann's areas are the most recognized, there are several other renditions of cortical areas using architectonics. Adapted from Brodmann K (1909) *Vergleichende Lokalisationlehre Der Grosshirnrinde in Inren Prinzipien Dargestellt Auf Grund Des Zellenbaues.* Leipzig: J. A. Barth.

the considerable similarity in the functional properties of many brain areas makes it difficult to differentiate them based solely on their function.

The oldest and most recognized method for identifying neocortical areas is architectonics. This point is highlighted by the distinguished rendition of areas introduced by Korbinian Brodmann (**Figure 2(b)**). Brodmann's version of the parcellation of the neocortex is but one of numerous versions that emerged in the last century albeit with the greatest staying power. Although differences in cytoarchitecture have played a prominent role in area identification, architectonic transitions are neither necessary nor sufficient for marking an area boundary. Results of architectonics can be ambiguous due to limitations in staining techniques, cortical folding patterns, or from internal area heterogeneity.

Defining areas with patterned connections has also been used extensively. The deduction is that the connection boundaries of an area that receive input from another, likely define that area; however, as with architectonics, inter-area heterogeneity, as well as, individual subject connection variability, and 'noise' associated with tracer injections makes it difficult to mark area boundaries with cortical connections consistently.

Topography has also been a promising method for identifying area boundaries. Retinotopic mapping, for example, has further delineated some areas of the visual system originally defined by Brodmann with architectonics (**Figure 2(b)**). However, while somatotopic and retinotopic maps in early sensory and visual areas make topographic boundaries straightforward, topography degrades higher in the cortical hierarchy making area boundaries less discernible. As pointed out by Jonathan Horton, "What constitutes topography in regions concerned with language, motivation, or personality?"

When available, all or a combination of these sources of information that is, FACT should be used to provide a confident definition of a functional area.

Area differentiation: Protomap vs. protocortex

The extent to which genetic vs. epigenetic influences shape phenotype has been an intense discussion for over a 100 years. Throughout the 1990s, the controversy encompassed two predominant theories of neocortical area differentiation: the protomap and protocortex hypotheses. The protomap hypothesis suggested that cortical areas are prespecified and that the progenitors in the ventricular proliferative zone code area assignments as neurons are born. In contrast, the protocortex hypothesis suggested that the nascent cortical sheet is relatively homogeneous, and that neocortical areas are specified, in large part, by ascending afferent information. The controversy, now resolved (both theories are in large part correct), has led to a better understanding of how both epigenetic and genetic determinants drive the differentiation of area-specific features and areal boundaries.

Function

The specificity of areal function in the prenatal brain is not well known. This statement is not intended to suggest that neocortical areas are not functioning prior to birth. The neocortex of a fetus or premature infant is capable of receiving and responding to afferent activity. Prenatal behavior is not limited to subcortical functions. Nonetheless, using function to delineate neocortical areas in humans during the prenatal period is presently not feasible.

What can be said is that function of a particular area is malleable. In a remarkable series of experiments, Mriganka Sur and colleagues have shown that in ferrets, visual afferents can be surgically redirected to innervate presumptive auditory targets, such that they will produce physiological response to visual stimuli in auditory cortex. These rewired ferrets perceive visual cues as visual even though what is normally auditory cortex is being activated by the stimuli. These experiments and others show that, early in development, the specific function of a cortical area is malleable, can be driven by experience, and does arrive from a relatively multipotent phenotype.

Architectonics

In normal circumstances, however, by the time humans are born, an initial broad parcellation of the neocortical architecture has taken place. The primary sensory areas, including primary somatosensory, visual, and auditory cortex, can be identified by the presence of a prominent granular layer IV. In the frontal lobe, motor cortex can be differentiated by the presence of large pyramidal neurons in layer V called Betz cells and the absence of a prominent granular layer IV.

There are several lines of evidence that suggest that at least the early architectonic fingerprint is regulated by determinants inherent to the proliferative zone and independent of afferent (i.e., thalamocortical) or other epigenetic influences. However, this initial parcellation can be altered. Brad Schlaggar and Dennis O'Leary have shown that, embryonic visual cortex when transplanted to parietal somatosensory cortex in newborn rats can develop architectural and connectional features typically unique to somatosensory cortex. Other experiments have demonstrated that thalamic input can modify gene expression such that the zone of expression will eventually match that of the thalamic innervation. Although the basic phenotype of an area can occur mostly under molecular control prior to thalamic influence, the degree and range of the phenotype is affected by afferent input.

Connections

The innervation of the neocortex by thalamic afferents constitutes the first step in the creation of processing circuits. Initial area-specific, thalamocortical projections appear to be primarily controlled by guidance molecules, but activity-dependent mechanisms that refine these projections are superimposed on this process.

Early cortical projections have widespread distributions, which are refined during maturation. The restricted adult projection patterns emerge through the elimination of functionally inappropriate axons and axon branches. This process is influenced by neural activity and culminates in the characteristic patterning of callosal, intracortical, and subcortical projections.

Topography

The general topographic organization of the cortex appears to be present very early in development. Adjacent points in the thalamic nuclei project to adjacent points in the corresponding area. This arrangement exists prior to initial thalamic contacts and is likely regulated initially by guidance molecules. As with the cortical connections described above, area specific topography will continue to be tuned over age.

Postnatal Brain Development

The most notable global developmental difference between humans and other primates is the protracted period of time between birth and maturity. This prolonged developmental span is believed to allow for an extended period of juvenile learning, but is also an extension for substantial brain growth, circuit organization, and myelin formation. Very little information is available detailing these events in the human or even nonhuman primate, which makes it quite difficult to adequately relate brain development with cognitive development. Despite this caveat, the following section summarizes some basic developmental events that occur in the postnatal period in hopes of providing the framework for making this link.

Particular emphasis is placed on experience-dependent and experience-independent developmental processes. As alluded to previously, distinguishing between processes dependent on experience and those independent of experience is rather complex. The terms 'experience-dependent' and 'experience-independent' are used very loosely in the literature despite the absence of a strict dichotomy. Even within each term, further semantic partitioning is often required to clarify discussions. William Greenough has proposed that 'experience-dependent' brain changes correspond to those arising from environmental influences specific to the individual. For example, synaptic changes corresponding to the events learned in a history class would be considered 'experience-dependent'. Others have used the term 'learning' to describe such changes.

In contrast, Greenough suggests that the effect of environmental influences on brain structure common to all members of a species should be considered 'experience-expectant'. The suprachiasmatic nucleus (SCN), our internal clock, provides a helpful example of an 'experience-expectant' neural system. The SCN 'free runs' at a greater than 24 h period, such that without the sun, our sleep–wake cycle (or day) would be longer than 24 h. The SCN is, however, 'experience-expectant' in that it 'expects' the patterned light of the sun to rise and fall on a 24 h period. The SCN matches its internal cycle to the 24 h time period such that our sleep–wake cycle matches the cycles of a day. Other terms such as 'primal' or 'maturation' have been used to describe this type of change.

In the context of cognitive development, human language acquisition *per se* can be considered experience-expectant, which of the multitude of languages a child learns is experience dependent.

Of note, that the term 'experience' is not synonymous with 'activity'. Processes independent of experience can also be driven by neural activity. For instance, spontaneous waves of activity that exist in the retina prior to eye opening may influence the formation of ocular dominance columns (see section titled 'The development of ocular dominance columns' below). Thus, in the following discussions, processes related to experience and those which are strictly 'activity-dependent' are distinct.

The term molecular in the discussion below is used to signify developmental changes that occur independent of neural activity. They occur in the context of the internal environment and are independent of outside stimuli or spontaneous activity. Despite the pragmatic definition used here, it should be appreciated that molecular cues and genes can be affected by activity-driven processes. It should also be noted that drawing strict borders between these types of processes is very difficult, and as our knowledge of brain development accumulates, certain brain properties might be reassigned to different developmental categories.

Lessons from Visual Cortex

Studies of the primary visual cortex have been fundamental to understanding the mechanisms that regulate the construction of brain circuitry. The next section focuses on the development of ocular dominance columns. The formation of these circuits, guided by both a variety of molecular cues and patterns of neural activity, inform us about principal developmental concepts.

The development of ocular dominance columns

The initial description of ocular dominance columns (ODCs) and their formation was Nobel Prize winning work done by David Hubel and Torsten Wiesel in the 1960s. By using electrophysiologic recordings in the cat primary visual cortex, they were able to show that information originating from either the left or the right eye is differentially represented into columns of cortical layer IV. Since these initial accounts, ocular representation in the primary visual cortex has been one of the most thoroughly studied brain systems (**Figure 3**).

Currently, two accounts of ODC development exist. One account proposes that early developmental projections from the two eyes initially overlap in the visual cortex. During the first postnatal months, visual experience promotes a preferential stabilization of some of the cortical connections and elimination of others resulting in a segregation of layer IV projections into well-delineated columns (**Figure 3(b)**). It has now been shown that retinal inputs are not required for column formation. Activity in the form of spontaneous correlated burst of activity from the thalamus can account for their formation. This process is likely to be the result of a Hebbian-type mechanism whereby connections are strengthened by correlated activity and weakened by uncorrelated activity.

The second account suggests that 'activity-independent' mechanisms are responsible for matching appropriate targets from the lateral geniculate nucleus (LGN) to layer IV of the visual cortex. According to account, molecular cues guide axons to appropriate targets with fairly precise branching. These initial projections result in highly segregated columns with limited production of exuberant connections.

Due to evidence on both sides, it is likely that both accounts influence column formation. Molecular cues underlie the initial coarse formation while activity

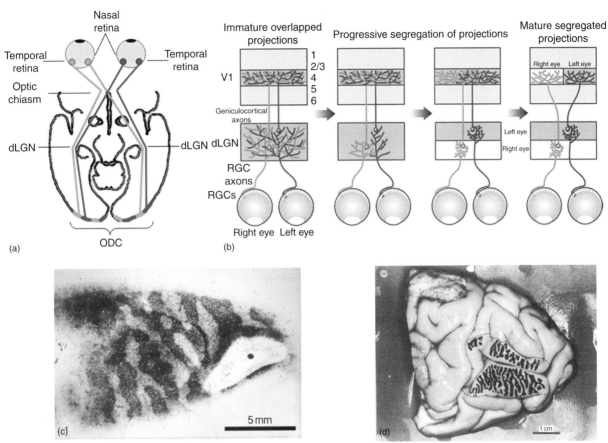

Figure 3 (a) In humans and in other mammals, retinal ganglion cells from the temporal retina of one eye and the nasal retina of the other eye encode and project the visual information from half the visual world to the same hemisphere. Ganglion cells from the temporal retina project to the ipsilateral hemisphere whereas those arising from the nasal retina cross the optic chiasm to project to the contralateral hemisphere. These projections to each hemisphere (and the lateral geniculate nucleus (LGN)) maintain their eye-specific segregation by terminating on discrete portion of the neocortex. This is the anatomical basis for ocular dominance columns (ODC). (b) There are now two primary accounts of how ODC develop. The account described, here asserts that the eye-specific patterned connections results from small-scale axon elimination. Immature exuberant projections from the two monocular inputs initially overlap in both the dorsal lateral geniculate nucleus (dLGN) and primary visual cortex (V1: layer 4c). A competitive process driven by correlated activity drives eye-specific stabilization of some of the cortical connections and elimination of others resulting in a segregation of projections in the dLGN and later layer IV projections in V1. (c) An example of ODC (identified with cytochrome oxidase) in a human section through layer 4c. (d) Projected pattern of ODC along the medial surface of the occipital lobe (outlined is the V2/V1 border). The example in (c) is located in the lower right portion of this illustration. (b) Adapted from Luo L and O'Leary DD (2005) Axon retraction and degeneration in development and disease. *Annual Review of Neuroscience* 28: 127–156 (c) Adapted from Horton JC and Hedley-Whyte ET (1984) Mapping of cytochrome oxidase patches and ocular dominance columns in human visual cortex. *Philosophical Transactions of The Royal Society of London, Series B, Biological Sciences* 304(1119): 255–272, figure 10b, with permission from The Royal Society of London.

dependent mechanisms are required to refine and maintain them. It is also likely that the relative influence of either model is species-dependent.

ODC formation has been the leading model for studying 'sensitive' and 'critical' periods. Historically these terms have been used interchangeably, while more recently, distinct definitions have emerged. A sensitive period is the time-window during which an experimental or natural manipulation of a system will strongly affect the system's development. A critical period is the point at which the effects of the manipulation are irreversible.

These concepts are often viewed from the perspective of behavior, but work in the visual system has been crucial to our understanding of these principles. Particularly relevant are experiments that elucidate the effect of monocular deprivation on ODC formation. Chronic closure of one eyelid, early in life, reveals plastic mechanisms in which the size of ODC representation corresponding to the sutured eye is significantly reduced. Conversely, the layer IV representation of the unaffected eye increases its size. In nonhuman primates, the sensitive period for this process begins at birth and slowly wanes until ∼10 weeks of age.

Interestingly, sensitive and critical periods seem to be linked to inhibitory inputs. In ferrets, the maturation of inhibitory GABA circuits lags behind excitatory circuits. The timing of this maturation correlates with the critical period. Reducing GABA function in transgenic mice can keep the critical and sensitive periods open indefinitely. Increasing GABA-mediated inhibition can prematurely shorten the span of the sensitive period.

Although often overlooked, sensitive and critical periods are a reflection of the underlying neural circuits. Demonstrating the relationship between brain anatomy and complex behavior is difficult, yet there is nevertheless a direct link between them. For example, the eyes and consequently the retina of each eye are slightly displaced such that each views the visual world from a slightly different perspective. As a result, objects represented in the retina are offset in respect to the fovea. This disparity is encoded by cells in the visual cortex and helps with our very precise ability to perceive depth, based on binocular cues. The development of stereopsis occurs after birth, during the same period as ocular dominance column formation. The rapid development of an infant's ability to perform tasks associated with binocular vision, including stereoacuity, is time locked to the end of the development of ODC, and is blocked with manipulations that prevent normal ODC formation. Thus, ODC formation is integral to the development of stereopsis.

Research on critical and sensitive periods in ODC has informed the treatment of pediatric disorders such as strabismus and congenital cataracts. Furthermore, such research has also provided perspective when considering critical and sensitive periods in relation to social, cognitive, and perceptual abilities. But caution should be taken to not overinterpret critical period data to guide specific cognitive or educational interventions without appropriate evidence to support the interventions.

Progressive and Regressive Neural Events

The development of the mammalian nervous system encompasses a wide variety of both progressive and regressive neural phenomena. The following focus is on those events most commonly referenced in cognitive neuroscience and psychology, but by no means do these represent the entire collection of progressive and regressive observations throughout maturation. We emphasize in this section that although phenomena such as myelination and synaptic pruning fit in nicely to many current theories, several questions arise regarding specifics. We recognize that cognitive neuroscientists and psychologists are motivated to integrate such phenomena into developmental models; however, the details should not be overlooked.

Broad progressive events
General growth
Humans exhibit substantial brain growth between birth and adulthood. Adult brains are approximately four times larger than infant brains. This brain growth is not linear. Maximal growth rate occurs around birth and by 6 years of age, the brain is approximately 95% of the size of the adult brain. The bulk of this early growth comes from a variety of sources including increases in synapses and dendrites (neuropil), as well as myelination. Importantly, the production of new neurons does not contribute to general brain growth (see the following).

Neurogenesis
With the exception of a few brain regions, it has become fairly well accepted that most of the neurons we are ever going to possess have migrated and are in place by the time we are born. This idea was first proposed by the founder of the neuron doctrine, Santiago Ramon y Cajal, who stated that neurogenesis is an exclusively prenatal event. While primarily true, there are three systems that continue neuron production into the postnatal period. These are the olfactory bulb, the dentate gyrus of the hippocampus, and the cerebellum.

Despite 40 years since the initial discovery of adult neurogenesis, little progress has been made as to the function in mammals. Albeit controversial, some work suggests that adult neurogenesis affects behavior. For example, in rodents exercise-induced proliferation of neurogenesis in the hippocampus can lead to increased performance in spatial learning. Conversely, pharmacologically induced decreases in neurogenesis can negatively affect behavior. Similar types of findings have been observed in the olfactory stystem.

Some insights may be gained from pathologic conditions. Brain injury can lead to abrupt modifications. General injuries such as ischemic infarction will lead to increased neurogenesis. This phenomenon can occur not only in normally neurogenic regions (i.e., hippocampus), but also at dormant proliferative sites. Sometimes these newborn neurons deviate from their normal trajectory and migrate to the injured area implicating their role in recovery.

Myelination
Although glial cells are not highly referenced in this article, their importance cannot be understated. Glia, the most abundant cells in the nervous system, account for approximately 90% of cells in the brain. Historically, their function has been limited to a structural neuronal support role. Even the name 'glia', being Greek for 'glue', downplays the importance of these cells for brain development and overall function. Among the many functions of glia (e.g., synaptic formation, radial glia guides, neurotransmitter uptake, blood–brain barrier), one of the most critical is the development of myelin sheath.

Myelination is the most commonly referenced neuroanatomical additive event that occurs postnatally. Increased myelination proceeds from sensory to motor, and last in association areas, roughly following the hierarchical organization introduced by Felleman and Van Essen in 1991. The glial cells responsible for myelination in the central nervous system (CNS) are oligodendrocytes. Like the majority of cortical neurons, oligodendrocytes arise and migrate to position prior to birth from a region in the ventral telencephalon.

White matter maturation continues at least through the second decade of life. Because of this, myelination has often been used to explain the development of several cognitive abilities. However, it is unlikely that increases in myelination can account for all of cognitive development. As Joaquin Fuster has pointed out, myelination is not a prerequisite for functional axons. Unmyelinated connections are still capable of transmitting information. Nonetheless, there remains a clear and well-established link between myelination and the functional properties of an axon. Increased efficiency of signal propagation following the addition of the myelin sheath may be important for enhancing the integration between already functioning regions.

Although oligodendrocytes migrate into their positions by the time of birth, their slow, postnatal maturation makes them particularly vulnerable to injury. Periventricular leukomalacia (PVL) is an injury of the periventricular white matter that results in cerebral palsy. It is the leading cause of brain injury in the preterm infant. The most predominant feature of PVL is the disturbance in myelination likely secondary to ischemic and inflammatory damage to immature oligodentrocytes.

With the rapid advancement of magnetic resonance imaging (MRI), particularly diffusion tensor imaging (DTI), researchers are now uncovering several other developmental disorders that may partially be secondary to abnormal white matter integrity. These disorders include schizophrenia, autism, dyslexia, and developmental stuttering.

Synaptogenesis and intracortical connections

From approximately 30 weeks, gestation, through the first 2 postnatal years, there is substantial growth in synaptic contacts throughout the cortex. The relative region-wise timing of this synaptic exuberance continues to be debated. Pasko Rakic and colleagues suggest that synaptic numbers increase uniformly throughout the cortex during this period, whereas Peter Huttenlocher and colleagues argue that synaptic numbers follow the myelination pattern described above, such that primary sensory areas increase prior to association areas. Several factors may underlie the discrepancies. Foremost are the species differences examined. Peter Huttenlocher investigated human postmortem specimens, while Pasko Rakic examined nonhuman primates. Differences in sample size and experimental techniques may also have contributed to the discrepancies.

Synapse formation is always accompanied by synaptic loss. During the period of rapid synaptogenesis, more synapses are generated than eliminated, resulting in a net gain. At the end of this period, synapse numbers plateau. The duration of this plateau is not well known in humans, but what follows (see the section titled 'Broad regressive events') is a regressive phase with a net loss of synapses that continues through adolescence. The accumulative synapse remodeling during development results in peak numbers in childhood being approximately 140–150% of those in adulthood.

By approximately 9 months of age, the development of short- and long-range (axonal) connections between brain regions is thought to be complete. In the visual system, these initial connections reflect the hierarchical organization observed in the adult brain.

Considering the various types of synapses (excitatory, inhibitory) and connections (i.e., intracortical, thalamo-cortical, cortico-cortical – including feedforward and feedback, calossal), the gross measure of synapse number *per se* may be misleading if, for example, different types of connections have differing trajectories. This issue and others will be examined further below.

The most familiar disease linked to abnormal synapse formation is fragile X syndrome. Fragile X syndrome is the most common inherited cause of mental retardation. Although there are several general developmental defects in individuals with fragile X syndrome, the abnormal morphology of dendritic spines points to a strong relationship between synapse formation and the cognitive deficits seen in those afflicted with the mutation. The partial overlap in neurobehavioral symptoms and structural abnormalities has led some to suggest a similar pathology for those affected with autism.

Broad Regressive Events
Axon retraction/synapse elimination

Several complementary techniques have revealed that the elimination of axons and synapses involves at least two different mechanisms – micro or small-scale (local retraction of axon branches) and macro or large-scale (degeneration of axons over long distances) modifications. The segregation of visual input into eye-specific patterns in the visual cortex is a classic example of a micro-change (**Figure 3(b)**). In contrast, transient inter-hemispheric connections in primary visual cortex observed during infancy are an example of a macro-change.

Dennis O'Leary and colleagues have shown in rodents that cortical layer V neurons, after early extensive interstitial branching, acquire functional appropriate connections through selective collateral elimination dictated by the cortical area in which the neuron is located (macro-change; **Figure 4**). In newborns, axons projecting from both motor and visual areas share various brainstem and spinal cord targets. Over development, neurons in motor areas eventually lose their collateral branches to visually related targets, but retain the branches to those involved in motor control. In contrast, neurons in visual areas

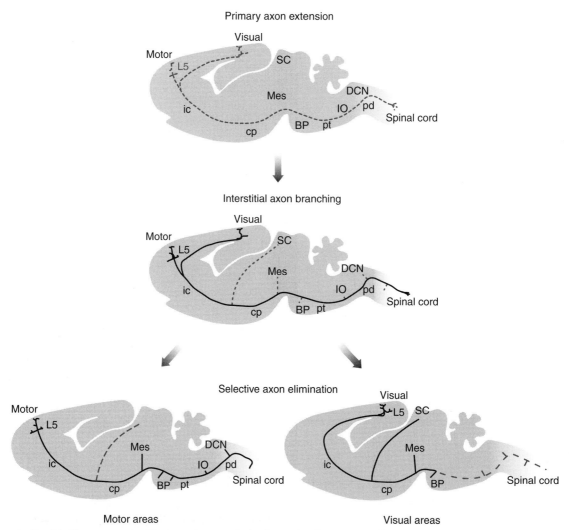

Figure 4 Provided is an example of large-scale axon elimination to develop area-specific subcortical projections of neocortical layer 5 neurons. Immature projections exhibit extensive subcortical interstitial branching, such that motor and visual neurons in newborns project to common targets in the brainstem and spinal cord. Through maturity functional appropriate connections are acquired through selective axon elimination, dictated by the cortical area in which the neuron is located. Motor area neurons eventually lose their collateral branches to visually related targets, but retain the branches to those involved in motor control. In contrast, the visual area neurons lose all collateral projections to the spinal cord and other motor-related targets and retain projections to those involved with vision. BP, basilar pons; cp, cerebral peduncle; DCN, dorsal column nuclei; ic, internal capsule; IO, inferior olive; Mes, mesencephalon; pd, pyramidal decussation; pt, pyramidal tract; SC, superior colliculus. Adapted from Luo L and O'Leary DD (2005) Axon retraction and degeneration in development and disease. *Annual Review of Neuroscience* 28: 127–156.

lose all collateral projections to the spinal cord and other targets involved in motor control, and retain projections to targets involved in vision. Interestingly, this area-specific, axon elimination and complementary maintenance is not perturbed by heterotopic transplantation of visual cortex into presumptive primary motor cortex or vice versa (**Figure 4**).

Certain aspects of this process should be considered with regard to the development of cognition. Is axon elimination uniform across all layers of the cortex? Are there different developmental trajectories for feedback and feedforward connections or inhibitory and excitatory synapses? How about for cortico-cortical, thalamo-cortical, or calossal connections? The limited amount of data available prevents a satisfactory characterization of these questions in animal models, let alone humans. However, existing evidence suggests that the developmental trajectory for both synapses and connections depends, in part, on their classification.

Some cortico-cortical connections have developmental trajectories that differ from those of the callosal and subcortical connections examined by O'Leary and colleagues. Although not a strict criterion, in the adult neocortex, feedforward projections generally arise from supragranullar layers (II, III), whereas feedback projections generally arise from the infragranullar layers (V, VI). In primates, the hierarchical nature of these projections appears to be in place early in development, but the laminar organization differs from the adult. In developing primates, a large proportion of feedback connections in early visual areas arise from the supragranular layers that are absent in the adult. Over development, a prolonged remodeling of these projections occurs. Massive pruning of early formed supragranular connections ensues with parallel production of projections from infragranular layers. In contrast, feedforward pathways appear to be largely established during early development, and rely much less on large-scale elimination of inappropriate connections.

There is also evidence suggesting that inhibitory and excitatory connections are remodeled on different timescales. Some investigators have shown a developmental lag in remodeling of inhibitory compared to excitatory connections. The remodeling of inhibitory connections becomes more focused from a more exuberant early pattern and is shaped by experience.

Cell death

Synaptic elimination and axonal retraction only partially account for the elimination of transient connections. Programmed cell death (or apoptosis) is also a prominent developmental mechanism that leads to a net loss of synapses. One example of apoptosis occurs in the developmentally transient subplate. Peak rates of apoptosis occur during the prenatal period but continue postnatally. Apoptosis is thought to be important for matching postsynaptic and presynatpic cell numbers.

Developmental Neuroplasticity

The term neuroplasticity is used in a variety of contexts but in general, refers to the brain's ability to organize itself in a novel way in response to perturbation. Perturbations can come in the form of natural experience (e.g., extended piano training), sensory loss (e.g., blindness), or intrinsic conditions (e.g., infarction).

In previous sections we briefly discussed the brain's ability to respond to significant perturbations in the developing visual cortex. The rewiring and transplantation experiments outlined above are classic examples of the brain's plastic capabilities. These types of plastic responses to extreme perturbations are available only in the earliest stages of development.

Significantly altering sensory experience can also lead to striking brain alterations, even in the adult. Michael Merzenich and colleagues showed in the adult owl monkey that correlating the inputs of two adjacent fingers by surgically connecting the skin surfaces leads to a significant change in the hand topography of the somatosensory cortex. The correlated inputs arising from the joined fingers abolished the normal discontinuities in digit representation.

Naturally occurring perturbations also provide insights into the remarkable capacity of the brain to organize itself in various ways. For instance, several groups have shown that the visual cortex of congenitally blind patients responds to tactile sensations associated with Braille reading.

Perinatal Stroke

Perinatal stroke is a particularly salient model which highlights the brain's capacity for novel organization after injury. Children with perinatal stroke are capable of acquiring relatively normal cognitive function, such as language, after experiencing a cortical insult that in adults would often lead to devastating lifetime disabilities. The fact that persistent language deficits frequently do not follow perinatal stroke even when extensive left hemisphere injury has occurred, underscores the brain's robust adaptive capabilities.

Although this developmental plasticity has long been recognized (e.g., Sigmund Freud described this clinical phenomenon in an excellent monograph written early in his career), its underlying neurobiological mechanisms are not well characterized. The most commonly referenced mechanism supporting normal language development after perinatal stroke is a functional reorganization to the contralateral hemisphere. However, other reports suggest, at times, intra-hemispheric reorganization supports the development of normal language after perinatal stroke.

A third perspective which encompasses both of these findings has recently surfaced. This model revolves around a developmental theory of typical development advanced by Mark Johnson called interactive specialization. Interactive specialization takes into account two aspects of typical development: (1) that regressive processes are not random, but selective, reduce connectivity between specific regions, span a protracted period of time, and are in large part activity-dependent, and (2) that the response properties of any given brain region are dependent on the brain's hierarchical organization. The functional specialization of regions is mediated by functional integration among feedforward, feedback, and lateral signals. There is ample anatomical support for the proposal that the brain is organized such that 'higher' cortical processes influence 'lower' cortical areas through reciprocal hierarchical networks. For example, both single-unit recordings and functional MRI (fMRI) studies have shown that attention to specific visual attributes can alter receptive fields and stimulus-driven activations. It is likely that for many regions of the brain, bottom-up, top-down, and lateral processes interact dynamically, continuously recalibrating neuronal responses to behaviorally relevant stimuli.

Johnson and colleagues suggest that these types of interactions between brain regions over development lead to the specialization of the adult brain. At birth, cortical regions and pathways are biased (due to intrinsic connectivity and architectural features) in their information processing properties, yet they are highly connected, and much less selective than in the adult (i.e., 'broadly tuned'). Johnson predicts that shortly after birth, multiple regions and pathways within the brain will be partially active during specific task conditions. But as these pathways interact and compete with each other throughout development, changes in the regional response properties will likely be observed and particular pathways will eventually dominate for specific task demands.

The interaction-driven theory of normal development described here would anticipate, as pointed out by Pamela Moses and Joan Stiles, that normal developmental mechanisms will interact with early onset pathology to yield an atypical adult functional neuroanatomy. If the balance of regional competition is altered by removal of one or more of the competing regions, as in the case of perinatal stroke, an alternate organization and developmental time course would ensue, that would largely depend on the timing, location, and the size of the stroke.

Several reports have bolstered this view. At the forefront, is work conducted by Maree Webster, Leslie Ungerleider, and Jocelyne Bachevalier. They have shown that in normally behaving adult macaques, visual recognition memory requires the interaction of inferior temporal lobe (area TE) and the medial temporal lobe (entorhinal and perirhinal areas). While inferior temporal cortex connectivity overlaps considerably between adults and infants, substantial elimination and refinement of initially widespread projections occur during development. For example, while area TE projects to the medial temporal lobe in infants and adults, an adjacent region, area TEO, projects to the medial lobe structures only in infant monkeys – suggesting elimination of transient projections. As opposed to lesions of TE in the adult animal, TE lesions in infant monkeys results in the sparing of visual recognition memory. This ability, it appears, is partially subserved by the maintenance of the normally transient TEO projections.

Adverse Effects of Neuroplasticity?

Although mostly advantageous to the developing organism, plasticity is not always beneficial and often insufficient. Residual motor function following a perinatal stroke often remains impaired into adulthood. Deficits of spatial cognition following early brain injury, albeit, more mild in children, also persist through childhood. More pronounced and multimodal deficits are associated with a diverse group of neurological disorders including fragile X syndrome. The plasticity mechanisms discussed here are not potent enough to overcome these types of perturbations.

In other conditions, extensive neuroplasticity can negatively affect function. Plasticity associated with repeated movements (such as in musicians) can lead to focal hand dystonia characterized by disabling co-contraction of agonist and antagonist muscles. The pain associated with phantom limb syndrome is also believed to be associated with cortical reorganization following amputation. It has also been suggested that in some instances altered brain activity in adults experiencing stroke can actually impair performance.

Neuroimaging Techniques for the Study of Human Development

Imaging Caveats

While most of our knowledge of postnatal human brain development comes from animal models with an extrapolation to human ontogeny, the development of noninvasive neuroimaging techniques now allows for detailed assessments of human brain maturation. MRI, in particular, has provided intriguing insights into human developmental processes both structurally and functionally.

The difficulties of relating cognition to changes in brain anatomy and physiology cannot be overstated. Although captivating, the current use of information from MRI in educational, judicial, and other social domains is often a grand misrepresentation of our current understanding of how the underlying neurobiology relates to behavior. New imaging techniques are undoubtedly valuable, but it needs to be realized that the growth of these techniques is still in the nascent stages.

One particular challenge with structural MRI involves resolution. Every MRI image is a collection of voxels (usually on the millimeter scale), any one of which consists of a mixture of neurons (axons, dendrites, cell bodies), glia (inlcluding myelin), and blood vessels. When studying gray matter development, the inability to identify all the components of a voxel makes it difficult to determine how these properties relate to maturation. For example, in some instances, increased myelination could potentially be misinterpreted as gray matter loss.

Studying the development of task induced activations with fMRI has its own conceptual and methodological concerns that require consideration. These issues include: (1) making direct statistical comparisons, (2) choosing adequate comparison tasks, (3) using a common stereotactic space, (4) assessing and accounting for performance between children and adults, and (5) using appropriate statistical measures to arrive at developmental differences and trajectories throughout development.

Irrespective of these caveats, noninvasive neuroimaging techniques performed on humans have already allowed us to explore uncharted territory in development and disease, and will continue to be a key instrument for the study of cognition.

Structural Magnetic Resonance Imaging

The current descriptions of white and gray matter development with MRI mostly agree with results from earlier histological work. The most consistent finding in white matter maturity is the linear protracted development which advances into young adulthood. In contrast, gray matter development consists of mostly nonlinear changes. Studies differ on the details, but in general, there appears to be a differential peak in gray mature volume (or density) between childhood and early adolescence that begins to decline first in sensorimotor areas and later in dorsolateral, prefrontal, parietal, and temporal regions. This general description of white and gray matter development is only a partial account of a markedly complex process.

Several research groups have successfully linked these types of structural changes over age with behavior by correlating the MRI findings with performance on specific tasks. For instance, Elizabeth Sowell and colleagues have shown that cortical thinning of the dorsal frontal and parietal lobes negatively correlates with the verbal portion of the Weschler's intelligence scale and that left hemispheric thinning negatively correlates with verbal intelligence quodient (IQ).

Functional Magnetic Resonance Imaging

fMRI allows one to display changes in task-driven activation patterns over development. It can be used in conjunction with structural MRI to study the relation of brain anatomy to brain physiology. Recent evidence suggests that the general rules of structural maturation (sensory/motor maturation followed by association areas) do not necessarily hold true for 'functional' maturation.

Association areas are not idle during specific tasks. They are actively involved in information processing despite their structural immaturity. For example, Tim Brown, Steve Petersen, and Brad Schlaggar have documented multiple developmental changes in lexical processing regions. Lower-order processing regions, particularly in the right occipital and temporal cortex, began in children as positively activated and progressed to either nonresponsive or minimally responsive in adults. Regions in the inferior frontal gyrus and fusiform gyrus, which have been historically implicated in several aspects of language processing, were equally activated in children and adults. Similar types of findings have been noted elsewhere, suggesting that many regions, despite being structurally immature, can exhibit adult-like activation patterns for specific tasks.

This observation prompts several questions. Are 'functionally' mature but anatomically immature (or regions with mature structure while functionally immature) regions exercising the same operations? How do such regions relate to behavior?

The interactive-driven view of regional specialization discussed earlier suggests that the function of any given region is mediated by the activity-dependent interactions with other regions. Perhaps then (in some cases), the role of brain regions that are functionally mature, but structurally immature (i.e., myelination, pruning, etc.), are distinct between children and adults because the regions differ in their relations to other brain regions.

Work by Donna Thal and Elizabeth Bates may address this issue. They have shown that lesions in the cerebral hemispheres in children manifest quite differently than comparable lesions in the adult brain. Thal and Bates found that the first stages of language development in children after perinatal stroke are affected by lesion location. However, the types of developmental delays are not as expected based on the typical sequela of the same focal lesions in adults. For example, early delays with word comprehension were more common with right temporal lesions, rather than left temporal (Wernicke's area) lesions as commonly observed in adult populations. Wernicke-type lesions in children resulted in expressive delays, a symptom more common in a left inferior frontal gyrus (Broca's area) lesion in adult patients.

These results suggest that the role of a given region is not necessarily matched to that of the adult. Perhaps the increased efficiency of signal propagation following the addition of the myelin sheath is important for enhancing the functional integration between regions in the cortex. This integration may result in a different network structure and hence different roles for any particular region.

Review

This article reviewed selected topics of human brain development with a focus on the neocortex. The purpose of this article was to provide a context for relating brain development to cognitive development. The prolonged developmental span in humans is important for a variety of developmental processes including brain growth, circuit organization, synaptic pruning, and myelin formation. While cognitive neuroscientists and psychologists are obliged to integrate these phenomena into developmental models and theories, there should always be an appreciation of the details. Along the same lines, the promising tools of neuroimaging have the capacity to fill many of the information gaps that currently exist in human development, but caution should be practised not to overextend interpretations.

In this article we also highlight the importance of both genetic and epigenetic phenomena in the development of neural systems. The behavioral phenomena we observe throughout development (such as critical and sensitive periods) are a reflection of changes in the underlying neural circuits. These differential aspects of brain development and the caveats that accompany them should provide a solid basis for building associations between brain and cognitive development.

Acknowledgments

The authors would like to thank our financial supporters. These include: The Washington University Chancellor's Fellowship (D.A.F.), UNCF*Merck Graduate Science Research Dissertation Fellowship (D.A.F), NIH NSADA (B.L.S.), The McDonnell Center for Higher Brain Function (B.L.S.), and The Charles A. Dana Foundation (B.L.S.).

See also: Brain Function; Cognitive Development; Critical Periods; Milestones: Cognitive.

Suggested Readings

Allendoerfer KL and Shatz CJ (1994) The sub-plate, a transient neocortical structure: Its role in the development of connections between thalamus and cortex. *Annual Review of Neuroscience* 17: 185–218.

Bates E (1999) Plasticity, localization, and language development. In: Broman SH and Fletcher JM (eds.) *The Changing Nervous System*, pp. 214–253. New York: Oxford University Press.

Belmonte MK and Bourgeron T (2006) Fragile X syndrome and autism at the intersection of genetic and neural networks. *Nature Neuroscience* 9(10): 1221–1225.

Brodmann K (1909) *Vergleichende Lokalisationlehre Der Grosshirnrinde in Inren Prinzipien Dargestellt Auf Grund Des Zellenbaues.* Leipzig: J. A. Barth.

Brown TT, Lugar HM, Coalson RS, et al. (2005) Developmental changes in human cerebral functional organization for word generation. *Cerebral Cortex* 15: 275–290.

Casey BJ, Tottenham N, Liston C, and Durston S (2005) Imaging the developing brain: What have we learned about cognitive development? *Trends in Cognitive Science* 9(3): 104–110.

De Graaf-Peters VB and Hadders-Algra M (2006) Ontogeny of the human central nervous system: What is happening when? *Early Human Development* 82(4): 257–266.

Elman JL, Bates EA, Johnson MH, et al. (1996) *Rethinking Innateness: A connectionist perspective on development.* Cambridge, MA: The MIT Press.

Fair DA, Brown TT, Petersen SE, and Schlaggar BL (2006) A comparison of anova and correlation methods for investigating cognitive development with MRI. *Developmental Neuropsychology* 30(1): 531–546.

Fair DA, Brown TT, Petersen SE, and Schlaggar BL (2006) FMRI reveals novel functional neuroanatomy in a child with perinatal stroke. *Neurology* 67: 2246–2249.

Finger S (2000) *Minds Behind the Brain.* New York: Oxford University Press.

Friston KJ and Price CJ (2001) Dynamic representations and generative models of brain function. *Brain Research Bulletin* 54(3): 275–285.

Fuster JM (2003) *Cortex and Mind: Unifying Cognition.* New York: Oxford University Press.

Gould E and Gross CG (2002) Neurogenesis in adult mammals: Some progress and problems. *Journal of Neuroscience* 22(3): 619–623.

Greenough WT, Black JE, and Wallace CS (2002) Experience and brain development. In: Johnson MH, Munakata Y, and Gilmore R (eds.) *Brain Development and Cognition: A Reader,* 2nd edn., pp. 186–216. Oxford: Blackwell.

Gross CG (2000) Neurogenesis in the adult brain: Death of a dogma. *Nature Reviews Neuroscience* 1(1): 67–73.

Guillery RW (2005) Is postnatal neocortical maturation hierarchical? *Trends in Neuroscience* 28(10): 512–517.

Hensch TK (2005) Critical period plasticity in local cortical circuits. *Nature Reviews Neuroscience* 6(11): 877–888.

Horton JC (2000) Boundary disputes. *Nature* 406(6796): 565.

Horton JC and Hedley-Whyte ET (1984) Mapping of cytochrome oxidase patches and ocular dominance columns in human visual cortex. *Philosophical Transactions of the Royal Society of London. Series B, Biological Sciences* 304(1119): 255–272.

Horton JC and Hocking DR (1997) Timing of the critical period for plasticity of ocular dominance columns in macaque striate cortex. *Journal of Neuroscience* 17(10): 3684–3709.

Inder TE and Volpe JJ (2000) Mechanisms of perinatal brain injury. *Seminars in Neonatology* 5(1): 3–16.

Innocenti GM and Price DJ (2005) Exuberance in the development of cortical networks. *Nature Reviews Neuroscience* 6(12): 955–965.

Johnson MH (2001) Functional brain development in humans. *Nature Reviews Neuroscience* 2(7): 475–483.

Johnson MH (2005) *Developmental Cognitive Neuroscience,* 2nd edn. Malden: Blackwell.

Katz LC and Crowley JC (2002) Development of cortical circuits: Lessons from ocular dominance columns. *Nature Reviews Neuroscience* 3(1): 34–42.

Katz LC and Shatz CJ (1996) Synaptic activity and the construction of cortical circuits. *Science* 274(5290): 1133–1138.

Knudsen EI (2004) Sensitive periods in the development of the brain and behavior. *Journal of Cognitive Neuroscience* 16(8): 1412–1425.

Kostovic I, Judas M, Petanjek Z, and Simic G (1995) Ontogenesis of goal-directed behavior: Anatomo-functional considerations. *International Journal of Psychophysiology* 19(2): 85–102.

Lenroot RK and Giedd JN (2006) Brain development in children and adolescents: Insights from anatomical magnetic resonance imaging. *Neuroscience and Biobehavioral Reviews* 30(6): 718–729.

Leuner B, Gould E, and Shors TJ (2006) Is there a link between adult neurogenesis and learning? *Hippocampus* 16(3): 216–224.

Levitt P (2003) Structural and functional maturation of the developing primate brain. *Journal of Pediatrics* 143(Supplement 4): S35–S45.

Lopez-Bendito G and Molnar Z (2003) Thalamocortical development: How are we going to get there? *Nature Reviews Neuroscience* 4(4): 276–289.

Luna B and Sweeney JA (2004) The emergence of collaborative brain function: MRI studies of the development of response inhibition. *Annals of the New York Academy of Sciences* 1021: 296–309.

Luo L and O'Leary DD (2005) Axon retraction and degeneration in development and disease. *Annual Review of Neuroscience* 28: 127–156.

Marin O and Rubenstein JL (2001) A long, remarkable journey: Tangential migration in the telencephalon. *Nature Reviews Neuroscience* 2(11): 780–790.

Moses P and Stiles J (2002) The lesion methodology: Contrasting views from adult and child studies. *Developmental Psychobiology* 40(3): 266–277.

Mountcastle VB (1997) The columnar organization of the neocortex. *Brain* 120(Pt 4): 701–722.

Mukherjee P and McKinstry RC (2006) Diffusion tensor imaging and tractography of human brain development. *Neuroimaging Clincs of North America* 16(1): 19–43.

O'Leary DD and Nakagawa Y (2002) Patterning centers, regulatory genes, and extrinsic mechanisms controlling arealization of the neocortex. *Current Opinion in Neurobiology* 12(1): 14–25.

O'Leary DDM, Schlaggar BL, and Tuttle R (1994) Specification of neocortical areas and thalamocortical connections. *Annual Review of Neuroscience* 17: 419–439.

Palmer ED, Brown TT, Petersen SE, and Schlaggar BL (2004) Investigation of the functional neuroanatomy of single word reading and its development. In: Sandak R, Poldrack RA, and Manis FR (eds.) *Scientific Studies of Reading: The Cognitive Neuroscience of Reading*, pp. 203–223. Mahwah, NJ: Lawrence Erlbaum.

Paus T (2005) Mapping brain maturation and cognitive development during adolescence. *Trends in Cognitive Science* 9(2): 60–68.

Price DJ, Kennedy H, Dehay C, et al. (2006) The development of cortical connections. *European Journal of Neuroscience* 23(4): 910–920.

Qi Y, Stapp D, and Qiu M (2002) Origin and molecular specification of oligodendrocytes in the telencephalon. *Trends in Neurosciences* 25(5): 223–225.

Rakic P (2002) Neurogenesis in adult primate neocortex: An evaluation of the evidence. *Nature Reviews Neuroscience* 3(1): 65–71.

Schlaggar BL, Brown TT, Lugar HM, et al. (2002) Functional neuroanatomical differences between adults and school-age children in the processing of single words. *Science* 296: 1476–1479.

Schlaggar BL and O'Leary DD (1991) Potential of visual cortex to develop an array of functional units unique to somatosensory cortex. *Science* 252(5012): 1556–1560.

Schummers J, Sharma J, and Sur M (2005) Bottom-up and top-down dynamics in visual cortex. *Progress in Brain Research* 149: 65–81.

Shaywitz SE (1998) Dyslexia. *The New England Journal of Medicine* 338(5): 307–312.

Sur M and Leamey CA (2001) Development and plasticity of cortical areas and networks. *Nature Reviews Neuroscience* 2(4): 251–262.

Sur M and Rubenstein JL (2005) Patterning and plasticity of the cerebral cortex. *Science* 310(5749): 805–810.

Toga AW, Thompson PM, and Sowell ER (2006) Mapping brain maturation. *Trends in Neurosciences* 29(3): 148–159.

VanEssen DC (1985) Functional organization of primate visual cortex. In: Peters A and Jones EG (eds.) *Cerebral Cortex*, pp. 259–329. New York: Plenum.

Webster MJ, Ungerleider LG, and Bachevalier J (1995) Development and plasticity of the neural circuitry underlying visual recognition memory. *Canadian Journal of Physiology and Pharmacology* 73(9): 1364–1371.

Brain Function

M de Haan and M Martinos, University College London Institute of Child Health, London, UK

© 2008 Elsevier Inc. All rights reserved.

Glossary

Cerebral cortex – The outer layer of the brain sometimes called the 'gray matter' in reference to its color. In humans, it plays a central role in many complex brain functions including memory, attention, perceptual awareness, 'thinking', language, and consciousness.

Developmental cognitive neuroscience – An evolving field that investigates the relations between neural and cognitive development.

Episodic memory – A type of explicit memory that refers to the memory of specific events within a spatio-temporal context.

Explicit memory – The conscious, intentional recollection of previous experiences and information.

Implicit memory – Is characterized by a lack of conscious awareness in the act of recollection. Typical instances of implicit memory include priming and procedural memory.

Long-term memory – Information that is in permanent store, but that need not be consciously accessible at all times. This includes memory for things that happened between a few hours to many years ago. Long-term memory includes memory for facts and events (explicit memory) as well as memory for skills and rules (implicit memory).

Plasticity – The adaptive capacity of the nervous system. Plasticity can occur during the normal course of learning or development, in response to brain injury or in response to alterations of sensory input.

Semantic memory – A type of explicit memory that refers to the memory for general knowledge and facts that are not tied to a specific spatial and temporal context.

Subcortex – This is the part of the brain that is underneath the cortex and that is considered older than the cortex in evolutionary terms. Its functions include basic ones such as the control of breathing and heart rate.

Working memory – A system for the temporary storage and manipulation of information. For example, working memory allows one to keep in mind a telephone number long enough to dial it once reaching the telephone.

Introduction

The human brain develops rapidly in the first years of life. At birth it is only 25% the size of an adult's brain, but by 5 years of age it is already 90% of the adult size. In parallel with this rapid brain development, dramatic changes occur in the child's ability to perceive, think about, and act in the world. However, until recently researchers studying psychological development and those studying neural development were working independently, with the former taking little notice of changes in the brain and the latter failing to consider the functional implications of such changes. Fortunately, the past decade has seen the emergence of a new field of study, called developmental cognitive neuroscience, which is devoted to studying the relationship between brain and cognitive–behavioural development. This field of study tackles complicated questions such as how the functional organization observed in the adult brain comes about, and how infants' and children's experiences influence the emergence of brain function. These questions are important to ask during early development for several reasons. First, any comprehensive model of brain or behavioral development must take both brain and behavioral factors into account, as there is little doubt that immaturity of the brain plays a major limiting factor in behavioral functioning in children or that children's interactions in the world in turn influence the brain. Second, a primary concern for those studying development is to understand how atypical development occurs and to develop intervention methods to optimize development in such cases. To accomplish this goal, it is very informative to know things such as how the brain has been injured, how this injury might influence further development of other brain regions, and the degree to which further development of this brain area is influenced by experience.

These questions are important to ask during early development for several reasons. First, any comprehensive model of brain or behavioral development must take both brain and behavioral factors into account, as there is little doubt that immaturity of the brain plays a major limiting factor in behavioral functioning in children or that children's interactions in the world in turn influence the brain. Second, a primary concern for those studying development is to understand how atypical development occurs and to develop intervention methods to optimize development in such cases. To accomplish this goal, it is very informative to know things such as how the brain has been injured, how this injury might influence further development of other brain regions, and the degree to which further development of this brain area is influenced by experience.

These lines of questioning have led to three views regarding how brain development and the emergence of behavior are interrelated. In this articles we first outline the three viewpoints of functional development: the maturation view, the interactive specialization view, and the skills learning view. Studying the different predictions of these viewpoints benefits from the use of neuroimaging tools that allow measurement of changes in brain structure during development and/or changes in the pattern of activation. Different tools are available, that differ in their strengths and weaknesses in measuring the brain and in their suitability for use with children. An overview of these different tools is provided in **Table 1**. We will describe studies using such tools to illustrate the theoretical merits and shortfalls of the three different views of functional brain development by using examples from the development of four specific functions: face processing, long-term memory, working memory, and language.

Theories of the Functional Development of the Human Brain

The adult cerebral cortex shows the characteristic of functional specialization. That is, certain areas of the cortex are particularly important for certain functions. For example, as will be described in more detail below, the fusiform face area is important for processing of faces and Broca's area is important for producing language. A key issue for those studying the functional development of the brain is to understand how this functional specialization comes about: is it present from the beginning, or does it emerge as a result of the developmental process? A related question asks, is this organization specified in the genes, or is it a consequence of input from the environment? Grappling with these questions has led researchers to identify three different processes by which cortical brain development can relate to the emergence of new functions: maturation, interactive specialization, and skill learning (see **Figure 1**). These options are not mutually exclusive, and it is possible that all these processes contribute to development. However, the three processes do make somewhat different predictions about how brain activity is expected to change when functions emerge and how the brain responds to injury and a typical experiences early on in life.

Maturation

In this view, the functional specialization observed in the adult brain is predetermined, and new functions emerge as the brain regions responsible for those functions mature (see **Figure 1(a)**). In other words, new skills come about supported by the maturation of previously immature brain areas necessary to perform these skills. Under these circumstances, we would expect to see an increase in brain activation with emergence of a skill, as a previously immature, silent brain region matures and becomes active. The maturation viewpoint predicts that damage to a brain region would result in a failure of the function it normally subserves to develop and that atypical experience would lead to a different rate of maturation of the skill in question.

Interactive Specialization

In this view, the cortex of the brain initially does not show the pattern of functional specialization observed in adults, although it may have some regional computational biases (see **Figure 1(b)**). Functional specialization comes about

Table 1 Some of the methods used in the study of brain development

Tools	Description	Suitability for infants and very young children
Electroencephalography (EEG)	EEG is the measurement of the ongoing, spontaneous electrical activity of the brain by recordings from electrodes placed on the scalp.	EEGs are frequently used in experimentation with infants and children because the process is noninvasive.
Event-related potentials (ERPs)	Similar to EEG, but records brain's electrical response to a given stimulus or action. In contrast to an EEG, ERPs are time-locked to stimulus presentation or response execution. ERPs have a good temporal resolution but more limited spatial resolution.	ERPs are frequently used in experimentation with infants and children because the process is noninvasive.
Magnetic resonance imaging (MRI)	Structural MRI is a noninvasive method for imaging the morphology of brain structures with good spatial resolution.	MRI is very sensitive to motion artifact, but structural information can be successfully obtained while infants or children are sleeping.
Functional magnetic resonance imaging (fMRI)	fMRI computes brain activity by measuring levels of blood oxygenation in the brain. This is a good tool for studying the localization of function in adults.	Since fMRI is very sensitive to motion artifact and it usually requires participants to be awake, it is typically not used with children younger than about 7 years of age. However, there have been a few studies involving younger ages.
Magnetic encephalography (MEG)	MEG is a noninvasive technique that measures the magnetic activity produced by neural electrical activity. In contrast to ERPs and EEG, MEG has good spatial resolution and, in contrast to fMRI, has a good temporal resolution.	MEG is a fairly new technique that is suitable for use with infants and children. Has been used to study sensory development in fetuses.
Near-infrared spectroscopy (NIRS)	NIRS is a form of optical imaging that computes changes in blood oxygenation and indirectly measures levels of activity in different brain regions.	It is increasingly being used with infants and young children as it is noninvasive and is not greatly affected by motion artifacts.
Positron emission tomography (PET)	PET is a nuclear medicine medical-imaging technique which produces a three-dimensional image or map of functional processes in the body.	Not suitable for use with typically developing children because a radioactive isotope needs to be injected in the subject and, therefore, the technique is invasive.

as a result of brain activity, and the function of a particular region is partly determined by its pattern of connection to other brain regions and how these regions are activated. Different cortical areas are thought to compete with one another to take on a functional role. This process of competition serves to 'sharpen' the set of functions a particular region carries out. As a result, the emergence of function is associated not just with increased activity of the particular brain region that will ultimately serve a function. Rather, it involves changes in brain activation over several regions that can include decreases in activity in regions that lose the competition and are no longer involved in that function. In the interactive specialization view there is still scope for skills to develop if the brain is damaged. This is because the initially broad functioning of the cortex would allow the possibility of flexibility in the region that would take on a particular function. That is, a new area could 'win' the competition for carrying out a particular function if the area that normally would do so was removed from the competition through injury. This would allow functional compensation, but with an atypical pattern of brain activation linked to that function as the interactive specialization view allocates an important role to experience, it predicts that atypical experience could lead to qualitative changes in the pattern of regional specialization (the brain areas that subserve a function are different from normal) rather than just quantitative changes (a simple change in the rate of development as in the maturation view).

Skill Learning

A third idea regarding functional brain development is that the acquisition of new abilities during infant and early childhood development involves similar or identical processes that occur when adults acquire new complex skills (see **Figure 1(c)**). In other words, in some circumstances it might be that humans require similar neural substrates or draw upon the same processes to acquire new functions regardless of whether they are infants or adults. This view emphasizes continuity in process across the lifespan. When adults are learning new skills, unskilled performance is often associated with activation of different brain regions than is skilled performance. If infants acquire new functions in the same way, a similar change in the areas of brain activation would be expected as new skills emerge in development. Damage to areas important for the acquisition of skills would be

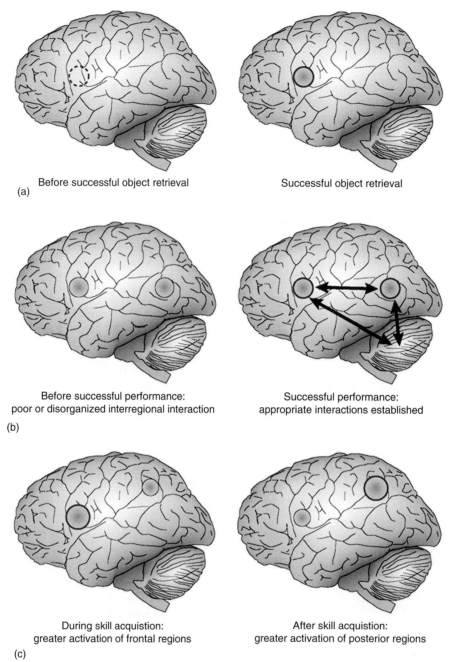

Figure 1 Theories of functional development. (a) Maturational, (b) interactive specialization, and (c) skill learning.

expected to result in widespread and long-lasting deficits in emergence of new future skills. In this view, early deprivation of normal experiences could be easily compensated in the future so long as the mechanisms of skill acquisition are still in place and could be utilized to acquire the skill in question.

A third idea regarding functional brain development is that the acquisition of new abilities during infant and early childhood development involves similar or identical processes that occur when adults acquire new complex skills (see Figure 1(c). In other words, in some circumstances it might be that humans require similar neural substrates or draw upon the same processes to acquire new functions regardless of whether they are infants or adults. This view emphasises[2] continuity in process across the life span. When adults are learning new skills, unskilled performance is often associated with activation of different brain regions than is skilled performance. If infants acquire new functions in the same way, a similar change in the areas of brain activation would be expected as new skills emerge in development. Damage to areas important for the acquisition of skills would be expected to result in widespread and long-lasting deficits in emergence of new future skills. In this view early deprivation of normal experiences could be easily compensated in the future so long as the mechanisms of skill acquisition are still in place and could be utilized to acquire the skill in question.

The three views of functional development offer different theoretical merits to the study of development. Below we illustrate these merits as well as shortcomings through examples from four specific domains of perceptual-cognitive development.

Functional Development of the Human Brain: Examples

The maturation, interactive specialization, and skill-learning views each describe how brain development relates to emergence function. Below we describe the emergence of four functions, face processing, working memory, long-term memory, and language, and evaluate how well the different view of development of brain function can account for the data in each of these domains.

Face Processing

Adults are usually quick and accurate at noticing faces and perceiving the different types of social information they display such as whether a person is familiar, how he is feeling, and where he is directing his gaze. A large body of work suggests that this expertise is supported by brain regions that are specialized for the function of processing facial information. This idea was initially put forward based on studies of patients who had lost the ability to recognize faces following brain injury. Some of these patients were severely impaired in recognizing faces, but were still able to recognize other types of objects. This was not simply because faces are more difficult to recognize than other objects, because other patients show the opposite pattern, with poor object recognition but good face recognition. This 'double dissociation' of spared-and-impaired abilities across the two groups of patients provides classic neuropsychological evidence that different brain regions are important for face and object processing. More recently, this idea has received further support from brain imaging studies of adults without brain injury. These studies have identified a region on the underside of the brain called the 'fusiform face area' because it shows greater activation for faces than for other types of objects or even other body parts. Together, the data from brain-injured patients and from brain-activation studies in intact adults are consistent with a 'content-specific' view of how the brain processes faces: certain brain areas are devoted to processing certain stimulus content, in this instance faces.

Other researchers have challenged this content-specific view, and argue that the data can better be explained in terms of a process-specific view. According to this idea, the fusiform face area is part of a brain network important for the process of acquiring expertise in perceptual discrimination, rather than a brain network specialized for processing the domain of faces. The fusiform gyrus (see **Figure 2**) just appears to be specialized for processing faces because this is the only category for which most humans acquire expertise. The content of other areas of expertise are much more variable among individuals depending on their particular lifestyles and interests. In support of this view, studies have shown that just as activation in the fusiform face area is greater for faces than objects, activation in the same area is greater when adults view objects from their individual areas of expertise than objects from other categories. For example, activation is greater for birds than cars in bird-spotting experts and for cars than birds in car experts. These types of results show that activation in the fusiform face area can be related to acquisition of perceptual expertise, although it is important to note that the fusiform face area is still more active for faces than even these expert categories.

Developmental studies of the emergence of face processing and its brain correlates can provide insight into this debate because they focus on the period when babies are first learning about faces. Those who have spent time with young infants likely know that they are very interested in faces. From just a few hours after birth, infants are generally interested in visual patterns and will shift their eye gaze and often their heads to keep a moving pattern in view. However, they do so for longer if the elements of the pattern are arranged like a face than if they are not. Within hours to days of birth, infants can also recognize the mother's face: they look longer at it than a stranger's face, even when cues from the mother's voice and smell are eliminated.

Newborns' interest in faces could be seen as evidence that the fusiform face area is functioning as a content-specific 'face' area from birth, since this interest is present

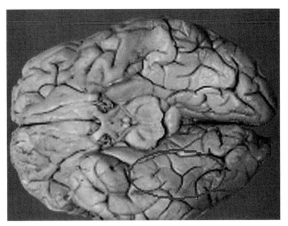

Figure 2 The fusiform gyrus in the adult brain.

from birth and before infants could have acquired expertise. This interpretation would be consistent with a maturation view: a function (orienting to faces) is possible because a brain area (fusiform gyrus) is mature. However, current theories and evidence suggest that the story may not be quite so simple. According to one influential theory put forth by John Morton and Mark Johnson, newborns' preference for orienting to faces is not mediated by the fusiform face area, but instead is supported by a subcortical system called 'Conspec'. In this view, Conspec is a reflex the newborn is born with, that works to ensure that infants frequently orient to faces in the first weeks of life. This 'face-biased' visual input then provides input to a more slowly developing cortical system, the 'Conlern', which would include the fusiform face area and other regions. Initially, Conlern functions as a general-purpose visual object-processing system, but with the help of input provided by Conspec, it begins to develop into a content-specific cortical face-processing area. In this interactive specialization explanation, the development of the cortical face-processing system can be seen in two ways: (1) the brain areas involved in face processing gradually come to respond more specifically to faces (respond more to faces and less or not at all to other stimuli), and (2) the cortical area that responds to faces becomes more focal and less widespread.

It is difficult to test the maturation vs. the interactive specialization accounts directly, because the functional magnetic resonance imaging (fMRI) techniques commonly used in adults are not well suited for studying typically developing infants (see **Table 1**). A rare exception is one study that used positron emission tomography (PET) (see **Table 1**) to examine activation of the fusiform gyrus in 2–3-month-olds, and found greater activation to faces than to pairs of lights matched in luminance to the faces. This result could be seen as consistent with the maturation viewpoint as it demonstrates that the fusiform face area is functioning by 2 months of age. However, it does not indicate whether the fusiform is specifically activated by faces (more than other objects) or more generally activated by patterned visual stimuli (compared to diodes). Studies of older children suggest that the second interpretation could be correct, because even up to 10 years of age children do not show the adult-like pattern of greater activation of the fusiform face area for faces than objects (e.g., houses).

Results from event-related potential (ERP) studies support the idea that Conlern is less 'tuned in' to faces in infants than it is in adults. These studies have focused on the development of a brain electrical response called the N170. The N170 probably reflects activation of the fusiform face area and related face-responsive brain regions. In adults, the N170 is larger and often occurs more quickly for faces than other objects. Infants as young as 3 months of age (the earliest age tested), show an N170-like response that is greater to faces than to control patterns created to have similar low-level perceptual properties but are not recognizable as a face. However, this response is not as face specific as it is in adults. For example, adults show a specific N170 response to the upright, human face, which is different even from the response to similar patterns like an upside-down face or a monkey face. Three-month-old infants do not show this specialized response, and it is not until 12 months of age that infants begin to show a more adult-like response specific to upright human faces. This pattern of findings is consistent with an interactive specialization view, where regions of cortex sharpen their functions and become more specialized with development.

Further studies suggest that the process by which infants tune in to human faces might also involve a loss of abilities. For example, in an interesting study, De Haan and colleagues found that 6-month-old infants are better than 9-month-old infants or adults at recognizing individual monkey faces. These results can be explained by the view that the development of processing faces involves a change from a more general-purpose visual-processing system to one focused on the particular cues that are especially useful for discriminating the many different faces we encounter in a lifetime. For example, a general-purpose processing system might give equal importance to eye color and the spacing between the eyes. However, eye color is likely to be of limited use for uniquely identifying many different human faces, whereas spacing between the eyes is actually a very useful cue. Thus, a specialized system would tune in to these types of useful features and tune out the less useful or unnecessary ones to establish a fast and reliable face perception system. However, this specialization might be a hindrance in some circumstances, such as recognizing monkey faces. This is because the cues that are most useful for recognizing human faces are not the same ones that are best for recognizing monkey faces. Thus, if we automatically apply our human-face-processing strategy, tuning in to cues useful for human faces and tuning out others, we will not perform very well. In this case, a general-purpose system would do better as it would process a broader range of information. Thus, 6-month-old infants are able to recognize the monkey faces because they have processed a broader range of facial features, whereas 9-month-old infants and adults apply a more specialized strategy that is less optimal. Interestingly, a follow-up study provided evidence that this shift between 6 and 9 months is dependent on experience: when 6-month-old infants were given experience in discriminating monkey faces in the form of picture books, they retained their monkey-face discrimination abilities at 9 months.

Does this evidence for the importance of experience mean that the development of face processing can be equated with the process of perceptual skill learning in adults? There remains debate on this issue. However, one line of evidence suggests that the learning that occurs in infancy may not be the same as that which occurs in adulthood. In particular, visual experience in the first months of life is critical for the normal development of face processing and, if this experience is missing, it cannot be compensated for by perceptual learning later in life. This conclusion comes from studies conducted by Rick Legrand, and Daphne Maurer and colleagues in children born with cataracts. Cataracts are a clouding of the lens that prevents patterned light from reaching the retina of the eye. These cataracts can be removed, after which the child receives contact lenses to help them see normally. Research has shown that such visual deprivation in the first months of life results in permanent deficits in perceiving certain types of facial information. This is true even though the children are tested years after their sight has been restored. These results suggest that the developing cortical face-processing system must receive visual inputs during the first months of life in order to develop normally.

Working Memory

The prefrontal cortex is a large region, covering almost one-third of the entire cortex in adults (see **Figure 3**). It is believed to be involved in high-level information processing that allows us to do things such as formulate and carry out plans and behave appropriately in response to novel or challenging situations. Neuroanatomical studies suggest that the prefrontal cortex is quite slow to mature. This is consistent with the observation that many of the skills attributed to the prefrontal cortex appear to be absent in infants and to emerge slowly in childhood and adolescence. However, an important body of research documents that the prefrontal cortex is not dormant in the first years of life but functions from at least the second half of the first year of postnatal life.

The best evidence that the prefrontal cortex functions in infancy comes from studies of spatial memory. A well-known psychologist, Jean Piaget, had documented a series of developments in spatial and object memory over the first 2 years of life. In the first 4 months of life, infants have a limited object concept, and when an object disappears from view they behave as if it no longer exists and do not search for it ('out of sight, out of mind'). From this time, babies' abilities improve, progressing from searches for partially hidden objects to full searches even when there are multiple hiding locations. In the middle of this time, at about 8–12 months, infants typically make a search error called the 'A not B' error. This can be seen in the classic search task, where there are two hiding locations. An object is first hidden in one location (A) and the infant is allowed to find it successfully. After a few successful hiding and searches at location A, the object is hidden in location B. The 'A not B' error occurs when infants continue to search in the location where they have previously successfully retrieved the object (A) rather than the location where they most recently saw it hidden (B). This occurs even though the delay between hiding and search is only a few seconds. By 12 months of age, infants' performance improves and they tend to search correctly even up to delays of 10 s. This is believed to be due to improvements in infants' abilities to guide their actions (in this case, searching) based on information that is not perceptually available but that must be held in memory (the correct location of the hidden object). Some researchers noticed the similarity between the 'A not B' task and a task of spatial memory that was known to rely on the prefrontal cortex in monkeys. Indeed, when they tested monkeys on the 'A not B' task, they found that damage to the dorsolateral region of the prefrontal cortex caused animals to make the 'A not B' error. Damage to the parietal cortex, a region involved in spatial processing, or the hippocampus, a region involved in other aspects of memory, did not affect performance on the 'A not B' task. These results support a maturational view that the improvement in human infants' performance between 8 and 12 months of age relies on development of the dorsolateral prefrontal cortex.

Further evidence in support of this view comes from brain imaging studies linking frontal activation to performance on object permanence and 'A not B' tasks. In one study, the relation between frontal brain activation as measured by near-infrared spectroscopy (NIRS; see **Table 1**) and emergence of object permanence was studied in infants longitudinally between 5 and 12 months of age. As the maturational view would predict, the researchers found that the ability to search for a hidden object was related to an increase in the NIRS measures of frontal activation. It is important to note that the researchers did not measure activity in other brain regions, so could not test the prediction of the interactive specialization view that the emergence of the skill would be accompanied by more widespread changes in brain activity. In a different line of studies, researchers used electroencephalography (EEG; see **Table 1**) and found that infants

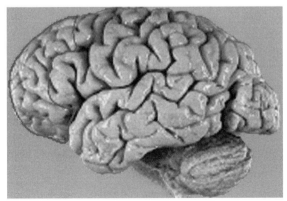

Figure 3 Lateral view of the prefrontal cortex in the adult brain.

who were successful in performing the 'A not B' task with increasingly longer delays across the second half of the first year of life showed changes in EEG over the frontal regions. In both the NIRS and the EEG studies, the links between frontal activity and object permanence or 'A not B' performance were specific. For example, there were no links between frontal activity and general playing with toys or the ability to inhibit reaching to a novel toy.

These studies using reaching tasks to investigate object permanence and A-not-B performance have suggested that these abilities emerge in the second half of the first year of life. However, studies using different methods have found evidence that these skills may be present even earlier, raising the possibility that prefrontal regions are also functioning even earlier in life. These studies use looking time, rather than reaching behavior, to assess what infants know about hidden objects. Infants are shown a display such as a ball rolling behind a box. They are then shown two outcomes when the box is lifted: either the ball appears behind the box (possible outcome) or it is gone (impossible outcome). Infants as young as 3.5 months tend to look longer at the impossible outcomes in these types of tasks. Infants' surprise when the object is missing, as shown by their longer looking, suggests that they do understand that objects continue to exist when not visible. If so, then why do infants fail search tasks at this age? One reason might be that the strength of mental representations of hidden objects is still weak at this age, and not yet sufficient to allow infants to guide their searching behavior. Another possibility is that infants do remember the hidden object, but find the performance demands of a search task (which requires the child to carry out an action e.g., lift a cover in order to obtain the goal) more difficult than a simple looking task.

Within the prefrontal cortex, there is evidence that the projections it receives involving the neurotransmitter dopamine are particularly important for cognitive function. For example, the levels of dopamine within the dorsolateral prefrontal cortex increase over the period that infant monkeys improve on cognitive tasks such as the 'A not B' and object retrieval tasks, which are known to require these regions. Evidence that the same might be true in humans comes from studies of children with the rare genetic disorder phenykeltonuria (PKU). This is a disorder which disrupts the chemical pathway for producing dopamine and so results in lowered levels of this neurotransmitter. PKU is treatable with a special diet, which is very effective in preventing the global and severe developmental delay that occurs if it is untreated. However, even with this special diet the levels of dopamine are not completely normal. The functions of the prefrontal cortex can still be affected, especially due to this region being particularly sensitive to fluctuations in dopamine levels. Thus, evidence that children with PKU show poorer performance than comparison infants would provide further evidence in support of a link between the prefrontal cortex and working memory. Studies performed by Adele Diamond have provided just such evidence: infants who followed the special diet, but who still had a moderately atypical chemical profile, performed worse on the 'A not B' task than did comparison infants or infants with PKU who had only a mildly atypical chemical profile. Do infants grow out of these problems? At older ages, the 'A not B' task is less useful because it is too easy: any differences between the PKU and comparison groups might be obscured by 'ceiling effects' where both groups do well. Instead, older children must be tested with age-appropriate tasks that still tap the key abilities to hold information in mind and resist a dominant response. With this in mind, Gerstadt and colleagues tested preschoolers on a more advanced task that is, the 'day–night' task. In this task children are required to say 'night' when presented with a picture of the sun and 'day' when presented with the picture of the moon. This requires them to keep information in mind (the rule of which word to associate with which picture) and inhibit a dominant response (to say 'day' to the sun). The results of such testing showed that the pattern of deficits observed in infants persisted at the older ages: children with PKU and moderately high phenylalanine levels showed impairments. These impairments do not reflect general developmental delay, as the same children did well on tests designed to tap the functions of the parietal cortex and the hippocampus. These findings also point to a specific impairment related to the malfunctioning of the prefrontal cortex and, thus, seem to support the maturation approach to development.

Long-Term Memory

Memory is utilized almost in every single human activity: recognizing a face, riding a bicycle, and remembering a past holiday are all typical instances of ways in which memory serves our everyday life. In the past 50 years, a lot of progress has been made in the field of memory research. For one, the importance of the medial temporal lobes (MTLs) for memory has been established. This is partly due to the description of a patient, HM, who became densely amnesic following the bilateral resection of his MTL. After his surgery, HM became unable to form new memories, yet, he was still able to learn new skills. In contrast, patients with damage to other regions of the cortex such as the basal ganglia circuit show the reverse pattern of performance, that is, they can form new memories, yet, they have difficulty in learning a new skill. These seminal findings have led researchers to advance a theoretical distinction between explicit and implicit memory.

Implicit memory refers to a set of abilities that influence overt behavior without requiring the conscious recollection of doing so (e.g., the ability to play a piano;

which a pianist seems able to just 'do', without being able to verbalize how), and explicit memory refers to the types of memories that can be brought to mind as an image or proposition without the need for perceptual support. Explicit memory includes both the memory for events known as episodic memory (e.g., remembering what color dress the piano teacher wore at the last lesson), and, the memory for facts known as semantic memory (e.g., remembering how many keys a piano has).

For some time it was thought that infants relied solely on implicit memory, with explicit memory developing only later. This was partly due to the fact that many of the tasks used to assess infant memory involve indirect measures (e.g., motor performance) similar to those often used to assess adult implicit memory, and partly due to the phenomenon of infantile amnesia, wherein most adults can recall very little from the first 3–4 years of their lives.

Explicit memory

More recently, evidence has begun to accumulate to suggest that MTL-based memory is present from very early in life. During infancy and early childhood, recognition memory has often been studied using the visual paired comparison (VPC) task. In the VPC task, subjects are familiarized with two identical items followed by the presentation of the familiar item coupled with a novel one. Attending to the novel stimulus for a longer duration is taken as a sign of recognition. Using this task, Olivier Pascalis and colleagues found that babies aged 3–4 days old can detect novel stimuli following a delay of 2 min. As children grow older they are able to withstand longer and longer delays, with babies aged 3 months old, withstanding delays of 24 h on the VPC. Performance on the VPC seems to rely on MTL regions, and more specifically, on the hippocampus (see **Figure 4**), because lesions to this structure lead to impairments in both infant monkeys and human or monkey adults. This suggests that MTL memory systems are operating, at least to some extent, early in

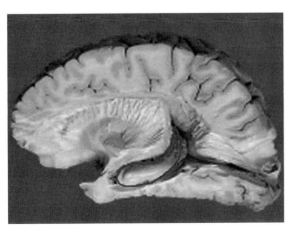

Figure 4 The hippocampal formation in the adult brain.

life. This interpretation is consistent with the maturation view: the maturity of the hippocampus allows the memory function to operate.

As infants grow, their recognition memory becomes less constrained by the perceptual similarity between the original encoding context and the testing context. In one experiment, 6-, 12-, 18-, and 24-month-olds were tested on a variation of the VPC. In this variation, objects were presented against a different background during testing from the one presented during encoding. Only the 18- and the 24-month-old babies were unaffected by this change. This increasing flexibility in being able to recognize familiar items in different contexts probably reflects the progressive development of the hippocampus since adult humans and monkeys with bilateral lesions to this structure fail this task. Specifically, success on this task may rely on the development of the dentate gyrus, that is, the major source of input from extrahippocampal regions to the hippocampus.

Another task believed to rely on the MTL is the delayed nonmatch to sample task (DNMS). In particular, lesions to the MTL lead to impairments in the DNMS task if such lesions are suffered during adulthood. In this task the subject is presented with a sample object. The subject must then remove the object to reveal a reward. Following a delay, the sample object is presented along with a novel object. Opting for the novel object is rewarded. Human infants do not succeed on this version of the task until approximately the age of 15–21 months even with brief delays of 5–10 s. This is puzzling given their early proficiency on tasks such as the VPC. Interestingly, changing the demands of the task from receiving a reward for displacing the novel object to allowing the child to play with the novel object (i.e., stimulus = reward) lowers the success threshold to the age of 6 months, with infants at this age withstanding delays of 10 min. This has led investigators to believe that, while that success on the DNMS task requires recognition, successful performance also requires additional skills such as inhibition processes and an understanding of stimulus–reward relationships. According to the maturational view, the slower development of these additional skills set the pace for developmental improvements in performance on this task.

Further evidence for the importance of the MTL in infant memory comes from studies using the deferred imitation paradigm. In the deferred imitation task, the examiner models a sequence of events for the child (e.g., placing a marble into a cup and then shaking the cup to make a rattle), and, following a delay, the child needs to reproduce this sequence of events without the benefit of prior practice. Research on the neural underpinnings of the deferred imitation task has pointed to the hippocampus as the most likely candidate. Namely, individuals who have sustained bilateral hippocampal damage during childhood or around the time of birth show impairments on this task. The same holds true for individuals that have suffered damage to the MTL during adulthood. Performance on this task shows a gradual improvement with age with dramatic improvements from the age of 6–24 months consisting of the ability to remember longer sequences and withstand longer delays. Specifically, infants at the age of 6 months show delayed memory for single actions after a 24-h delay. By the age of 9–10 months, infants begin to show memory for the sequence of actions. Moreover, by the age of 18 months infants can perform normally even when the props used in the testing phase are different from the ones used in the presentation phase. Once more this finding points to the increased flexibility of memory-retrieval processes in older infants. However, similar to the DNMS task, given the taxing nature of the deferred imitation task, it is very likely that other regions such as the prefrontal cortex contribute to the development of the requisite processes for successful performance on this task.

Further insights about the relative contributions of MTL structures to memory come from the study of children who have suffered damage to the hippocampus during infancy. These children exhibit disproportionate episodic memory deficits in the face of relatively intact semantic memory processes. One interpretation is that semantic memory processes are supported by parahippocampal regions during development and, are, thus, spared in these children. This interpretation is consistent with the maturational view, whereby perturbations in the maturation of the hippocampus disable the emergence of its corresponding function, that is, episodic memory. However, these findings may also point to the relative degrees of plasticity inherent in different memory processes. Namely, it is plausible that semantic memory is relatively spared because it is better able to reorganize in the face of injury, whereas episodic memory processes are more affected because they are less able to do so. Functional MRI studies of the pattern of activation for semantic memory would help to decide between these possibilities: the maturational view would predict a typical pattern of activation, whereas the second view would predict an atypical (reorganized) pattern.

Implicit memory

Not many studies have examined the neural correlates of implicit memory during development. One area that has received some interest is the development of conditioning. Conditioning refers to the formation of a contingency between two previously unrelated stimuli through either an association with a cue (i.e., classical conditioning) or a reward (instrumental conditioning). A common classical conditioning paradigm used both in the infancy and animal literature is the eye-blink paradigm. In this paradigm, a puff of air is blown on to the eye causing the eye to blink. This is always preceded by a tone. With time the subject responds by blinking their eye upon hearing the tone. Infants between the ages of 10 and 30 days start to show the eye-blink response. It has been shown that lesions to the cerebellum in rabbits and human adults disrupt both the acquisition and the retention of a conditioned association. Interestingly, lesions to the hippocampus do not. Seeing as the cerebellum is known to mature early in life, the reliance of classical conditioning on the cerebellum seems plausible.

Another conditioning paradigm that was originally developed by Carolyn Rovee-Collier and colleagues and has been used extensively with infants is the mobile conjugate reinforcement paradigm. In this task, a ribbon is attached to the infant's leg on one end and to a suspended mobile on the other end. In order to animate the mobile the infants need to learn to kick the relevant leg. Infants as young as 3 months old are able to learn the relationship between leg kicking and mobile movement, and, they raise their kicking rate well above baseline levels to achieve this. Infants can then be tested following a given delay to see if they have retained the learned behavior. Significant improvements in the retention of this association have been recorded across the first year of life with 12-month-old infants retaining the behavior for up to 8 weeks. However, there has been very little research on the neural bases mediating performance on this task to verify if regions such as the cerebellum are involved, or how changes in activation of this or other brain areas are related to developmental improvements in memory.

Language

Understanding the mechanisms behind language acquisition has fascinated scientists for many years. Recently, the introduction of new techniques such as neuroimaging has enabled neuroscientists to probe deeper into the mysteries of human language acquisition. Infants start babbling at around 6–8 months, move on to the one-word stage by 10–12 months, and speak in full sentences by the age of 3 years. This developmental path is followed by both deaf and hearing subjects and is irrespective of cultural background. Given our unique position in the animal kingdom regarding language and the universal nature of language acquisition among humans, one natural question that has been raised is whether humans possess innate mechanisms dedicated to language acquisition.

One way to answer this question has been to study the emergence of the hemispheric specialization for language. Research with adults has shown consistently that language processes are disproportionately subserved by the left hemisphere with lesions to this hemisphere often leading to speech apraxia or aphasia. This phenomenon has given rise to a large corpus of research in search of a reason for this hemispheric predilection. In other words, is the left hemisphere a more suitable habitat for language processes? And if so, is this tendency evident from the very beginning of language acquisition? Three lines of inquiry have been pursued to attempt to answer these questions: (1) anatomical studies, (2) functional studies, and (3) neuropsychological studies.

Whereas the left and right hemispheres might appear to be the mirror image of one another, there are some structural differences that differentiate the two. Relevant to language, the left planum temporale and the left Sylvian fissure have been found to be larger than their right counterparts. Do these structural differences reflect the impact of experience on the immature brain or do they constitute an inherent predisposition? Overall, structural studies with infants have revealed that, during prenatal development, the right hemisphere has a head start over the left, with structures such as the superior temporal gyrus appearing 1 or 2 weeks earlier on the right side. However, the planum temporale and the Sylvian fissure have been found to be larger on the left side even during prenatal life. Importantly, these areas exhibit such structural asymmetries irrespective of auditory stimulation as has been shown by studies of twins and congenitally deaf individuals. Moreover, the brains of individuals with dyslexia, a language disorder that affects reading and writing abilities, have been found to lack these asymmetries.

Are these structural asymmetries mirrored in functional asymmetries in language processing? In other words, do these structural differences contribute or lead to the left hemisphere's dominant role in language processing? Converging evidence from fMRI, ERP, and NIRS studies seem to suggest that functional asymmetries in response to language processing are evident in newborns and young infants. For example, Mehler and colleagues, used NIRS to try and detect hemispheric differences in response to normal speech, backward speech, and silence in neonates. Backward speech shares a lot of acoustic properties with normal speech making it a good baseline for the study of speech perception. Left temporal regions were found to be significantly more active in response to normal speech than to silence or backward speech; pointing to an early left hemispheric predisposition for speech perception.

In a different paradigm, 3-month-old infants were exposed to trials of four identical syllables (e.g., da), which were either followed by a fifth identical syllable (e.g., da) or a fifth deviant one (e.g., ba). ERPs, time locked to the presentation of the fifth syllable, were recorded. Recordings from a left posterior temporal site were found to be sensitive to phonetic information as evidenced by a different neural response to the presentations of the deviant and the identical syllable. Again, these findings point to the early presence of neural proclivities in speech perception.

If language processes have so consistently shown a preference for the left hemisphere, what happens to children who suffer damage to this hemisphere early on in life? It has been found that most children who suffer an early injury to their left hemisphere go on to acquire language abilities within the normal range, though, sometimes at the lower end of the spectrum. This finding is in direct contrast with the adult picture where damage to the left hemisphere often leads to aphasia. Interestingly, when direct comparisons between children with lesions on the left hemisphere and children with lesions on the right hemisphere are made, a very similar picture emerges for the two groups. A delay in language acquisition is observed in both groups relative to controls pointing to the setbacks of early injuries to overall functional development. These results support the interactive specialization theory that predicts functional compensation given an early injury. In other words, whereas some evidence does suggest that there is an early left hemispheric bias for language perception, it seems that this early bias can be overridden in the face of early injury. This conclusion is consistent with the results of PET studies of children who had neurosurgery to treat drug-resistant epilepsy. These studies suggest that, especially for language perception tasks, early left hemisphere injury is associated with enhanced activation of right-hemisphere areas. Thus, a more diffuse, widespread distribution of language networks in children compared to adults might be the explanation for children's greater recovery from left-hemisphere injury.

Summary and Conclusions

Although much of the basic architecture of the brain is laid down before birth, important aspects of neural development continue to occur after birth. The field of developmental cognitive neuroscience is aimed at understanding how these developments in the brain relate to the emergence and development of cognitive–behavioral skills. Researchers in the field have used a variety of techniques, including those described in **Table 1**, to document the changes in brain activity that occur during typical development and to understand how these processes are altered by brain injury or disease.

Investigations in the fields of face processing, working memory, long-term memory, and language have all examined how the brain areas known to mediate these skills in adults are related to advances in their development. In some cases, a maturational view, in which developments in skills are linked to the maturation of a particular brain region, appears to provide a good explanation of development. For example, there is good evidence that maturation of the dorsolateral prefrontal cortex is linked to development of spatial working memory. In other instances, the interactive specialization or skill-learning views appear to provide a better explanation. For example, development of face processing seems to involve a change from a more widespread, general-purpose visual-processing system to a more focal, face-specific one which would be consistent with both views. Additional evidence that the timing of visual experience is critical for normal development of face processing is in favor of the interactive specialization view, as the skill learning view would not expect this result. However, further studies are needed to provide a more complete account of functional brain development. For example, testing the differing hypotheses of the maturational and interactive specialization accounts requires consideration of changes in activation over the whole brain. Studies that consider activation in only limited brain regions (e.g., only dorsolateral prefrontal cortex and not other regions) might provide results consistent with the maturation view but do not truly rule out other views.

Studies of the plasticity of the brain in response to injury or alterations in sensory input illustrate that there is both remarkable flexibility as well as some constraints on functional brain development. For example, investigations of memory development following early, bilateral hippocampal injury suggest, consistent with the maturational or skill-learning views, that such early injury can result in permanent deficits. In contrast, studies of the development of speech and language following early unilateral cortical injury indicate that there is remarkable flexibility as speech and language outcomes are much better than when similar injury occurs during adulthood. These types of results are more consistent with an interactive specialization view.

The field of developmental cognitive neuroscience has clearly benefited greatly from technological advances that have allowed study of brain structure and function even in human infants. In the future, further improvements in technology and research methods will likely also prove critical, as will the integration of diverse approaches such as behavioral, neuroimaging, genetics, and pharmacology. These types of studies will provide a fuller picture of the mechanisms involved in the functional development of the human brain.

See also: Brain Development; Cognitive Neuroscience; Habituation and Novelty; Memory; Object Concept; Speech Perception.

Suggested Readings

Diamond A (1996) Evidence for the importance of dopamine for prefrontal functions early in life. *Philosophical Transactions of the Royal Society of London B. Biological Sciences* 351: 1483–1493.

Dehaene-Lambertz G, Hertz-Pannier L, and Dubois J (2006) Nature and nurture in language acquisition: Anatomical and functional brain-imaging studies in infants. *Trends in Neurosciences* 29: 367–373.

De Haan M, Mishkin M, Baldeweg T, and Vargha-Khadem F (2006) Human memory development and its dysfunction after early hippocampal injury. *Trends in Neurosciences* 29: 374–381.

Johnson MH (2001) Functional brain development in humans. *Nature Neuroscience Reviews* 2: 475–483.

Johnson MH (2004) *Developmental Cognitive Neuroscience.* Oxford: Blackwell Publishing.

Johnson MH (2005) Subcortical face processing. *Nature Neuroscience Reviews* 6: 766–774.

Nelson CA, de Haan M, and Thomas KM (2006) *Neuroscience of Cognitive Development: Experience and the Developing Brain.* Hoboken, NJ: Wiley.

Nelson CA and Luciana M (eds.) (2001) *The Handbook of Developmental Cognitive Neuroscience.* Cambridge, MA: MIT Press.

Relevant Websites

http://www.pbs.org – PBS.
http://en.wikipedia.org – Wikipedia, The Free Encyclopedia.
http://www.zerotothree.org – ZERO TO THREE.

Categorization Skills and Concepts

L M Oakes, University of California, Davis, Davis, CA, USA

© 2008 Elsevier Inc. All rights reserved.

Glossary

Categories – Collections of items that have common features; often these groups are in the world.
Categorization – Forming groups of objects that share some commonalities.
Concepts – Mental representations of groups of objects that share some set of commonalities.
Correlated attributes – The relation between multiple features that help to define some categories (e.g., birds have wings, feathers, and fly).
Dishabituation – A significant increase in looking time that infants often exhibit when shown a novel stimulus, following habituation to one or more stimuli.
Habituation – A method for assessing infants' perceptual and conceptual abilities. Habituation is a process by which infants' looking time decreases over repeated presentations with a familiar stimulus.
Multiple habituation – A method in which multiple related stimuli are presented during the habituation phase of an experiment. If infants detect the relation among those stimuli, their looking time will habituate, or decrease, over trials.
Prototype – A summary representation of a category that includes the average feature values of the encountered instances.
Representation – The mental storage of information.
Sequential-touching – A method for assessing infants' concept and categorization skills that depends on their spontaneous touching of items. When infants are presented with multiple items from two categories simultaneously, they often will touch in sequence items from one category.

Introduction

Categories and concepts are essential to understanding and organizing the rich environment around us. At every moment, we encounter new and familiar objects and people. It would be overwhelming to respond to each object, person, and event as completely new and unique. Creating a separate memory for each encounter with an item or event would result in an enormous amount of stored information, making cognitive processes cumbersome at a minimum, and quite likely some aspects of cognition would be impossible. Grouping objects into categories, therefore, helps us to more efficiently and effectively learn and remember the objects, people, and events we encounter. Moreover, understanding the referents of labels such as dog, cup, shoe, and tree requires categorizing different instances as dogs, cups, shoes, and trees, and having formed a representation that relates those instances together. Finally, inferring that a new dog will bark, that a new cup can contain liquid, that a new shoe can be put on one's foot, and that a new tree will have leaves, also depends on categorizing and forming concepts. Thus, many aspects of cognition (including memory, language, and problem solving) critically depend on concepts and categorization skills.

It should be obvious that these skills are important even in infancy. Young infants are faced with an enormous number of new objects, people, and events everyday. Making sense of this incredible amount of information is facilitated not only by remembering individual instances, but also by remembering what those instances have in common, perhaps even remembering similar items in clusters or groups. Recalling previously encountered collections of objects or general categories of actions will certainly help infants learn new words – although it is possible, and even likely, that infants learn commonalities among objects and events by hearing labels. The point is that concepts and categorization skills are an important part of cognition early in life.

Defining Categorization, Categories, and Concepts

Before discussing what we know about concepts and categorization skills in infancy, we must define our terms.

Often, the terms concepts and categories are used interchangeably, and rarely are they explicitly defined. However, understanding how infants categorize and form concepts depends on being clear about what we mean by these terms. Thus, as a first step we define these terms.

Categorization

Categorization refers to the process of forming groups of objects that share some common features. For example, dogs are all generally dog-shaped, eat dog food, wag their tails, and have puppies. Of course, this definition leaves open what a feature is – are features characteristics that you can see (such as shape, color, texture)? Can behaviors (e.g., barks, tail-wagging) and nonobvious properties (e.g., DNA) be features? The lack of a clear definition of feature contributes to a debate in the literature about whether all instances of categorization involve the same process or set of processes. For example, would we form a group of animals with the same general body and head shape in the same way as we would form a group of animals that move independently, are alive, and have similar digestive systems? Researchers have asked do we have a single process or set of processes for forming any group of items with common features, or do we have different processes or set of processes for forming groups depending on the kind of features being considered? For example, we may have one domain-general mechanism, or set of mechanisms, that allow us to detect commonalities among any kind of entities (pictures of colored shapes, speech sounds, abstract ideas) and form groups of common items. By this view, although there may be different kinds of features, the differences between those features are not important for understanding how we form categories. Alternatively, we may possess domain-specific mechanisms for dealing with different kinds of features – we use one set of mechanisms for forming groups of visually similar entities, another set for forming groups of similar speech sounds, another for forming groups of similar abstract ideas, and so on. By this view, the kind of feature being considered determines the particular categorization process invoked.

Another issue is whether categorization is itself a single process or whether categories result from several processes (such as memory, perception, and attention) working together. For example, we may possess a mental process, categorization, which is used to form groups of similar items. Like attention, perception, and memory, categorization may be a characteristic of the mind. The input to this process would be information from those other mental processes, and the output would be representations, or stored information, of a group. Alternatively, categorization itself may not be a process, but rather representations of groups of similar objects may emerge as a result of attention to, perception of, memory for, and comparison of instances. As these processes worked together, representations in memory would become linked or new representations of groups of objects would be formed. Regardless of which side one takes in such arguments, categorization refers to forming groups of objects with common features.

Categories

Categories are groups of objects that share a common feature or set of features. Usually, categories are thought to be out in the world, and often, but not always, such groups have labels (e.g., cat, flower, and car). When researchers talk about categories, it can sometimes seem like objects belong to only a single category – a particular Basset Hound, for example, is a dog. In reality, any individual item belongs to several categories – that Basset Hound is not only a dog, she is a pet, she is one of Marty's belongings, she is an animate creature, and she is a Californian. So, despite the fact that it is clear that categories are groups of similar objects, it is not always clear what real categories are (e.g., are whales only categorized with mammals, or can they also be categorized with sea creatures such as fish or sharks?).

Central to this debate is what one considers important features of categories. Features that are easily perceived – such as color and shape – are often dismissed as not important for real categories. Whales are not fish, for example, because superficial similarities in shape do not define real categories. Deep, conceptual features – such as warm-blooded and gives birth to live young – are more central. Such features often cannot be directly observed, but must be acquired through scientific methods or from an expert. For some researchers, both easily perceptible and less-obvious features are equally good types of commonalities. For others, deep, conceptual commonalities are key to true categories.

Categories are often organized hierarchically – dogs are types of animals, poodles are types of dogs. The point is that some categories encompass other categories – as you move up the hierarchy, categories become broader and more abstract (e.g., a dog and a worm are only similar in the most abstract of ways, and the features they share in common are extremely general). As you move down the hierarchy, categories become narrower and characterized by high levels of perceptual similarity (e.g., all pugs look alike, and it may be difficult to tell two pugs apart). Understanding the relation between different categories requires understanding that the same object can be categorized in many different ways. There has been significant debate in the literature about whether infants first form very general categories and only later become sensitive to narrower, exclusive categories lower in the hierarchy, or whether infants first learn the narrow, perceptually similar categories and gradually combine them to form the higher-level categories. Although there is general consensus that infants are sensitive to broad categories first, there remains significant debate about whether infants can flexibly categorize items at different hierarchical levels depending on the context.

Concept

The term concept generally refers to one's mental representations of categorical groups. Representation simply refers to how the information is stored mentally, or in the head. Not surprisingly, there is a significant debate regarding what is necessary for something to be considered a concept. Is any stored information about a collection of objects a concept? Is an infant's representation of what a group of objects looks like, without any additional information (e.g., is alive, has a brain), a concept? Or, must children store deep, nonobvious features for a representation to be considered a concept? For some researchers, concepts include both kinds of information and it is impossible to make a distinction between representations that include only perceptual information and those that include both perceptual and other kinds of information. For others, representations that include only information such as what an object looks like are not concepts, but rather are perceptual representations. For these researchers, concepts must include information about nonobvious features (e.g., can move independently, drinks), and the distinction between perceptual representations and concepts is extremely important.

There is also controversy about how to obtain evidence of concepts in infants. We can ask older children questions, probing their knowledge about categorical groups (do they know that dogs have puppies, are alive, etc.). Determining that infants have such knowledge is more difficult. Some have argued that the actions that infants perform on objects (e.g., making a dog drink from a cup) provide insight into infants' conceptual knowledge. However, even this evidence is quite controversial – how do we know that when infants make a small toy dog drink from a cup that it reflects their understanding that real, live dogs drink? This issue is yet to be resolved. Regardless of which position a researcher takes, a generally agreed upon definition of concept is that it is the mental representation of a category.

How Do We Measure Infants' Categorization, Categories, and Concepts?

How do we assess infants' concepts and categorization skills? Two methodological innovations in the late 1970s and early 1980s led to an explosion of studies examining early categorization and concepts. The following paragraphs briefly describe these methodological innovations and the procedures that emerged from them. The final two sections discuss what we have learned about infants' categorization, as well as a new framework for understanding what we have learned. The results described in these final two sections all came from the procedures described in the following paragraphs.

The Multiple Habituation Procedure

The first methodological innovation was the development of the multiple habituation procedure. In the standard habituation procedure, which has been used since the 1960s to study memory and perception, infants are shown a single stimulus on a series of trials (see **Figure 1**, top). Initially, they exhibit a high level of looking, indicating high levels of interest or processing. But as the same stimulus is shown repeatedly, looking duration decreases, indicating a waning of interest or processing. Typically, once infants' looking reaches 50% of the level that it was at the beginning, they are said to have habituated. Following this attenuation of looking, infants will show an increase in looking when a novel stimulus is shown – for example, a circle following a series of presentations with a square.

In the multiple habituation method, several different items are presented during the habituation phase (see **Figure 1**, bottom). Categorization is tested in this procedure by presenting several items from the same category – for example, several different dogs, faces, or vehicles. Researchers make inferences about how infants categorized those dogs, faces, or vehicles from how they respond to new items from the category. If infants are sensitive to the adult-defined category presented during familiarization, they should fail to dishabituate to the new items from the same category.

In 1979, Leslie B. Cohen and Mark Strauss published one of the first studies using this method to examine infants' categorization of faces. In this study 18-, 24-, and 30-week-old infants were habituated to one or more pictures of faces. Some infants received habituation trials with a single picture, some infants received habituation trials with different pictures of the same face, and some infants received habituation trials with pictures of multiple faces. Infants then were tested with a new female face. The logic was this: if infants remember the particular face(s) or picture(s) presented during the habituation phase, they should dishabituate, or increase their looking to, the new female face. But, if they have recognized the commonalities among the multiple faces or pictures seen during familiarization and the novel female face, they should fail to dishabituate (i.e., not show a significant increase in looking) to the novel female face. Only 30-week-old infants appeared to categorize the

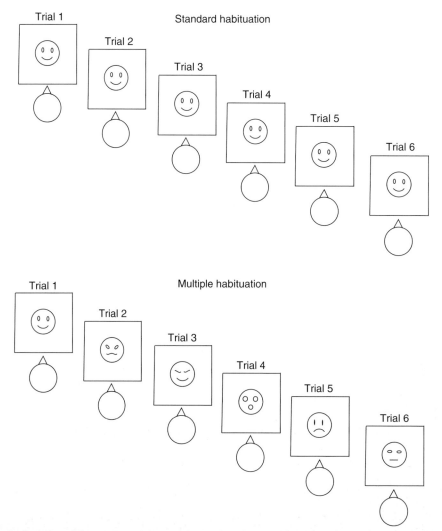

Figure 1 Schematic depiction of the sequence of events in visual habituation tasks. In the standard habituation task (top), infants are shown a single stimulus on several successive trials. In the multiple habituation task (bottom), infants are shown several different stimuli on a series of successive trials. In each version of the task, infants should look a long time on the first few trials, but their looking duration should decrease on subsequent trials as they learn about and remember the stimulus or type of stimuli.

faces. They dishabituated when familiarized with a single picture, but not when familiarized with multiple pictures of the same face or with multiple faces. The very youngest infants seemed to learn a specific picture, apparently not even categorizing different pictures of the same face as instances of a single person.

The multiple habituation procedure became the primary tool for studying infants' categorization, and many studies have shown infants respond to categories in this procedure. There are many different variations of this procedure – some researchers habituate infants as described above, others use a fixed familiarization phase; some studies present infants with pictures of objects, other present infants with real objects; in some studies items are presented one at a time and in other studies items are presented two at a time. One question that has not yet been resolved is how these methodological differences contribute to how infants categorize in these studies. Two variations of this procedure that have become widely used to study infants' categorization will be described next.

A variation: Familiarization and visual paired-comparison

Most modern studies of categorization provide infants with a relatively short familiarization period (e.g., six exposures to items from a category). Importantly, in this variation, two pictures are presented at the same time, rather than one picture as was more typical in early studies (see examples of each procedure in **Figure 2**). Thus, although infants only receive six exposures or trials, on each exposure they see two different category exemplars.

Following such familiarization, infants are then shown a pair of new stimuli, one from the nowfamiliar category and one from a different category. For example, after familiarization with horses, an infant might see a new horse paired with a dog. The logic is that if familiarization with horses causes infants to recognize, remember, or learn a narrow category that includes horses but not dogs, they will prefer the picture of the new dog to the picture of the new horse. But, if familiarization with horses causes infants to recognize, remember, or learn a broad category that includes both horses and dogs (e.g., four legged animals), then they will look equally at the new dog and the new horse. Several studies have shown that infants as young as 4 months respond to adult categories such as dog or horse when tested in the visual familiarization task.

Another variation: Object examining

Another variation that is widely used is the object examining task. The main innovation here is that rather than showing infant pictures of objects, the experimenter actually hands infants small plastic replicas of category items – for example, birds, horses, or cars (see **Figure 3**). In all other respects the task is the same as a familiarization procedure: infants are first familiarized with a series of items from within a category, and then their responding (measured as looking) to new items from the now familiar category and from a different category is assessed. The reasoning is that following familiarization with an adult-defined category such as dog, infants who are sensitive to this narrow category will be more interested in (i.e., look longer at) a novel item from a different category, such as a bird or horse, than in a novel item from the now-familiar category. Studies using this task have revealed that infants between 6 and 14 months of age are sensitive to a categorical distinction such as dog vs. horse, that perceptual similarity becomes less important in infants' attention to categories such as animal, and that infants seem to recognize global or broad categories

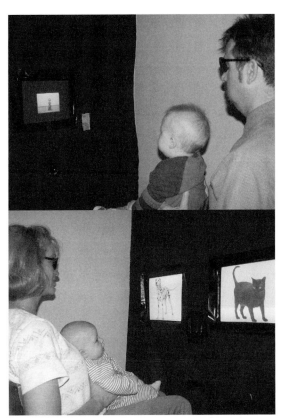

Figure 2 Examples of habituation (top) and visual familiarization (bottom) procedures used to test infants' categorization. In each procedure, infants are seated on a parent's lap, facing one or two computer monitors. The parent is provided with glasses that occlude their view of the stimuli to eliminate bias from parental response to the stimuli. An observer, seated out of sight, records infants' looking time via videorecording (in each photograph a camera is below the computer monitors) or peep holes in the display. In habituation (top) infants are presented with a single stimulus on each trial until their looking time decreases. In visual familiarization (bottom) infants are presented with two stimuli on each trial for a fixed number of trials.

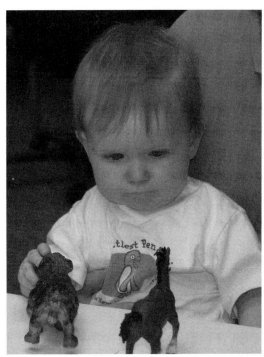

Figure 3 Example of the object-examining task. In this task, infants are presented with real, three-dimensional replicas of category items and they are allowed to play with them in any way they choose – touch, mouth, or bang them. Infants are presented with several stimuli from one category on successive trials, and then they are tested with items from the familiar category and from a novel category (as depicted here). Infants' duration of looking on each trial is recorded.

(e.g., animal, vehicle) at an earlier age than they notice exclusive or narrow categories (e.g., dog, airplane).

The Sequential-Touching Method

The second methodological innovation stemmed from studies published in the early 1980s on very young children's spatial classification or sorting. Infants and young children cannot be instructed to place similar objects into piles. Investigators observed, however, that when presented with collections that involved two groups of objects (e.g., four yellow pillboxes and four blue balls), infants in the first and second years of life engage in sequential touching of the items, or touching of several similar items in sequence. Jean Mandler adapted this task to study infants' responses to categories such as kitchen things vs. bathroom things or dogs vs. horses. In the typical version used to study categorization, infants are presented with a tray of objects from two adult-defined categories for a fixed period of time (e.g., 2 min), and their touching is observed (see **Figure 4**). If infants engage in more sequential touching of objects from one or both categories than would be expected by chance (i.e., if they selectively touch in sequence items from one category, effectively ignoring the items from the other category), then they are labeled categorizers. The proportion of children who categorize given the particular categorical contrast and/or stimulus set is used to draw conclusions about the development of categorization between 12 months and 3 years of age. Although it is difficult to uncover categorization in infants younger than 1 year with this task, a number of studies have shown that children between 12 months and 3 years of age will respond to a wide variety of categorical contrasts (e.g., animal vs. vehicle, dog vs. fish) in this task.

What Do We Know about Infants' Categorization and Concepts?

Do Infants form Categories and Concepts?

The earliest questions about infants' categorization and concept development addressed using these methods were simply do infants have concepts, or can they form categories? As described above, Cohen and Strauss's study suggested that young infants might not be able to categorize – it was not until infants were 7 months old that they responded to a category of female face – a remarkable finding given the extensive experience infants that must have had with female faces in the first 30 weeks of postnatal life.

However, subsequent studies have shown that in fact infants can and do form categories much earlier than this first study suggested. Indeed, in their original article Cohen and Strauss pointed out that infants younger than 30 weeks might be able to respond to different kinds of categories. Work in the more than 25 years since this article was published has revealed that the younger infants in this seminal study may have failed to categorize because aspects of the procedure may have made it difficult for them to detect the commonalites and differences among the items. For example, young infants may have difficulty categorizing when items are presented one at a time, as they were in this study. When items are presented in pairs, infants as young as 3–4 months can categorize male faces as different from female faces, dogs as different from cats, and triangles as different from squares. Some evidence suggests that sensitivity to these categories may emerge by 2 months, and that even newborns are sensitive to categories such as crosses vs. circles and speech sounds in some contexts.

It may be tempting to conclude that categorization is an extremely early emerging ability, and that infants form

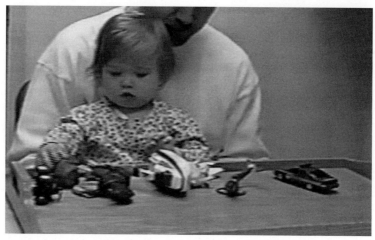

Figure 4 Example of the sequential-touching task. In this task, infants are presented with a collection of items – typically from two different categories (animals and vehicles depicted here) for a fixed period of time. Infants are allowed to manipulate and explore the objects in any way they choose. The objects they touch, and the order they touch them, are coded.

adult-like categories in the first weeks after birth. However, studies have revealed qualitative changes in infants' categorization. For example, younger infants tend to respond to broader categories than do older infants (e.g., treating dogs and horses as part of the same category, perhaps because they have four legs and tails). Different researchers have observed this pattern using different stimuli, methods, and categories. Therefore, one of the few areas of consensus in the field is that categorization in infancy develops from broad to narrow – early on, infants more easily form relatively broad categories, and later they become more sensitive to features that define narrow categories.

However, this developmental difference is not a simple broad-to-narrow developmental trajectory. For example, whether or not infants of a given age respond to a relatively broad or relatively narrow category depends on how similar the items are presented during habituation or familiarization. Infants (3–4-month-old) familiarized with a set of dogs that are very similar to one another respond to the difference between dogs and cats; infants at the same age who are familiarized with a set of dogs that are more different from one another, in contrast, respond instead to a more general category that apparently includes both dogs and cats. In addition, young infants respond to a narrow category if items are presented two at a time, side-by-side, but respond to a broader category if those same items are presented one-at-a-time. Although we do not yet know why young infants' categorization is influenced by such factors, it appears that when infants have to remember items from one trial to the next, as they do in the standard multiple habituation task, they have difficulty noticing the subtle commonalities among items that they can notice when two items are presented side-by-side.

Some problems of interpretation

So, what do we know about infants' categorization and concepts? Clearly, infants can categorize. Moreover, because in many of the studies of infants' categorization, adult-defined categories were used, these results also show us that infants are sensitive to adult-defined categories. These studies asked whether infants detect boundaries between categories important and salient for adults – dogs vs. cats, animals vs. vehicles, kitchen things vs. bathroom things. The fact that infants responded to those categories in experimental tasks provides evidence that they can be sensitive to those commonalities and differences that define such adult-defined categories. Importantly, such results do not tell us that these categories are the most salient or important from an infant's perspective – or even that the infant came to the laboratory with the knowledge of those categories. But, they do show that in particular experimental procedures with particular experimental stimuli, infants are sensitive to those categories.

Although these studies reveal infants' sensitivity to particular commonalities, it is not clear what they tell us about their 'concepts'. Recall that concepts are the mental representations infants (or adults) possess about categorical groups. Representations refer to the information stored in the head. How do we examine infants' representations? When we talk about concepts we typically are referring to enduring, long-term representations that have been built up over time. We do not usually mean a representation formed a moment ago, on the basis of limited exposure to a set of stimuli (though in theory such a representation could be a concept). One's concept of dog, for example, is based past encounters with dogs – what they look like, how they behave, and how to treat them. Habituation or familiarization procedures do not allow us to easily disentangle what infants knew before coming into the laboratory, or what categories are salient in their day-to-day lives, from what they learn over the course of the habituation period of the session. Researchers are just beginning to compare infants' responding to highly familiar stimuli (e.g., dogs for infants with dogs at home) to their responding to less familiar stimuli (e.g., dogs for infants who do not have a dog at home) to determine how learning outside the laboratory influences infants' behavior in tasks like visual familiarization. Moreover, concepts generally are thought to include more than perceptual similarities among items, and it is difficult to determine whether infants' responses in visual habituation reflect recognition of perceptual similarities vs. deeper similarities

Most researchers do assume that infants have concepts of one sort or another – although there is wide disagreement about the nature of those concepts and how to assess them. As soon as infants are old enough to act on objects, they demonstrate that they know more than just what objects look like. Infants can learn that some objects rattle when shaken, and they will attempt to shake objects that look like other rattles but not objects that do not look like those other rattles. Late in the first year, infants put toy telephones to their ears, shoes to their feet, and pretend to drink out of empty cups. These actions suggest that infants have represented more than what objects look like, and that they have concepts of those objects. Clearly, once infants are between 12 and 14 months of age and they begin to label objects, their use of labels seems to reflect concepts.

The question is whether the procedures described earlier tap such concepts? When infants are familiarized with a series of pictures of dogs and then they dishabituate to a picture of a cat, does that reflect their dog concept? When infants are given a collection of animals and vehicles and they touch the animals in succession, does this reflect an animal concept? This difficult question has been at the center of many disagreements in the study of infant categorization. There are two sources of this disagreement:

first, researchers have debated whether there are separate processes for forming concepts and perceptual categories, and second, researchers have argued whether some tasks are better able to tap concepts than others. For example, some argue that tasks in which infants touch and pick up real objects (such as small plastic replicas of objects) tap concepts better than do tasks in which infants simply look at pictures. The reasoning is that these tasks induce a kind of processing that goes beyond simply what objects look like, whereas tasks in which infants only look at pictures emphasize what objects look like. However, the same factors seem to influence infants' categorization in both types of tasks (e.g., variability among the stimulus items), casting doubt that one task is better at tapping concepts than the other.

In addition, studies using habituation of looking time have revealed more than simply infants' perceptual categories. For example, several studies have revealed a curious developmental trend that may reflect changes in infants' conceptual understanding. Specifically, younger infants actually notice more kinds of features than do older infants. This trend may reflect younger infants being open to more possibilities about how features in the world are related (e.g., the shape of a vehicle's headlights might predict whether or not the wheels go around, causal agents can have static or dynamic features), and older infants, who have learned more about the world, are constrained in the kinds of information they attend to and learn (e.g., only the appearance of the wheels predicts whether or not they go around, causal agents are more likely to be animates and thus have dynamic, moving parts). Thus, at least for some kinds of stimuli, visual habituation tasks can reveal more than infants' attention to perceptual similarities.

It is likely that this particular debate will never be fully resolved; it is extremely difficult to determine precisely what underlying representations are assessed with a particular procedure. What is clear is that although we can draw strong conclusions about infants' categorization and the categories to which they are sensitive, the conclusions we can draw about infants' concepts are more limited in large part because it is not clear how infants' behaviors in the tasks available to us reflect their underlying concepts.

What Are the Processes of Categorization in Infancy?

What we can know with confidence is something about the processes of categorization in infancy. That is, we can know not only that infants form categories, but how they form them. Understanding how infants form categories was the main focus of many early studies. Researchers examined infants' categorization of line drawings of made-up animals, schematics of faces, or geometric shapes to uncover how infants form categories. Three main characteristics of infants' categorization reveal similarities to adult categorization, suggesting continuity across development.

Summary representations

First, infants form summary representations for categories. When faced with a collection of similar items, one can either remember each individual item or form a single representation that summarizes what those items have in common. A summary representation might take one of several forms. It might include a list of features that is characteristic of all the items in a category – for example, chairs have four legs, a seat, and a back. This type of summary representation does not seem to accurately reflect how people think about categories, however. People are sensitive to the fact that categories do not have a set of necessary and sufficient features (i.e., a set of features that every member has, and that if an instance has those features it must be a member of that category), but rather category boundaries are fuzzy. For example, bean-bag chairs have none of the features in the list above and yet they are categorized with other chairs, and couches have all of those features and yet they are not categorized as chairs. It is possible, of course, that we have just not identified the right set of features, and that in fact all chairs do have some features in common that are unique to chairs.

Moreover, infants may not be aware that category boundaries are fuzzy; they may think of categories in terms of a set of necessary and sufficient features. For example, infants may have categories for objects with faces (e.g., animates), wheels (e.g., vehicles), or legs (e.g., a group that includes furniture, animals, and insects). Of course, such summary representations would cause infants to make categorization errors, at least from an adult perspective (consider the objects with legs example). An item may be miscategorized and incorrectly included in an adult-defined category if it has a highly salient feature in common with many items in that category. Indeed, in one famous example, a child used the word ball to refer to the moon and a round candle. Errors like these may indicate that the child has formed a summary representation for ball in which the feature round is necessary and sufficient. Carolyn Mervis suggested that these mistakes reflect child-basic categories – categories that are similar in some ways to adults, but that depend on slightly different features, or depend more heavily on some features, than do the categories of adults. Examples like these are not definitive, however. It is also possible that a child who calls the moon and a round candle a ball is simply noting the similarity between those different categories, or struggling to find the word in his or her limited vocabulary that comes closest to describing the object at hand. That is, errors in labeling may not reflect errors in categorization.

One summary representation that does take into account the fuzziness of category boundaries is a prototype. A prototype is the average of the category. Your prototype of a dog, for example, is not a real dog, but rather is the average of all the dogs you have seen in your life. When learning a series of animals with different length necks, therefore, the prototype formed will have the average of those neck lengths. Infants as young as 3–4 months of age have been shown to form prototypes, and by 10 months, infants clearly average features in the way just described. The formation of prototypes is a particularly important aspect of categorization. It helps to explain how items can be grouped together in a category even if they do not have all the same features, and how come some items seem to be better members of a category than others (e.g., a Labrador is a better dog than a Chihuahua). This propensity to form prototypes may be responsible for infants' preferences for attractive faces, and their ability to learn about some kinds of categories more quickly and efficiently than others.

Exemplar representation

A second finding that demonstrates that infants' categorization is like adults, is that infants not only form summary representations, but they also learn the individual exemplars. A debate in the adult literature is whether categories are represented as summary representations or as collections of instances. Theorists have pointed out that the exact same behavior is predicted if people represent individual instances or if they represent a summary representation such as a prototype. For example, a Labrador may seem like a better example of a dog either because it is closer to one's stored prototype of dogs, or because it is similar to more representations of individual dogs (e.g., German Shepherds, Golden Retrievers). Recently, however, it has become clear that adults learn the individual instances in some cases and form summary representations in others. That is, when building a representation of a new category, adults both encode individual items and they create summary representations such as prototypes of those items.

Like adults, infants also learn both individual items and form summary representations when familiarized with a series of items from within a category, depending on the particular task. When learning a collection of new female faces, for example, 3–4-month-old infants whose primary caregiver is a woman learn those individual faces; they do not learn to respond to a category of female face that is distinct from the category male face. When those same infants are familiarized with a collection of male faces, in contrast, they fail to learn the individual faces and instead respond to the category of male face as distinct from the category female face. Thus, infants can represent both the individual items and form summary representations, and which they do initially or more easily depends on factors such as the familiarity or the difficulty of the category to-be-learned.

Correlated attributes

Finally, infants' categorization is like adults in that they are sensitive to the correlations between features. For adults, categories are not defined by lists of unrelated features, but rather are defined by clusters of features (e.g., animals with feathers have wings and tend to fly). These correlated attributes are better predictors of category membership than the presence of particular features – for example, bats have wings but not feathers, and they are not birds. Thus, the presence of wings alone is not sufficient to identify an object as a bird.

Infants too are sensitive to correlated attributes. When familiarized with a completely novel category and unfamiliar items, infants in the first year of life can learn that individual features covary (e.g., that animals with long necks have wings; that purple objects squeak). By the end of the first year, infants can use those correlations to categorize objects. If, for example, they are familiarized with several long-necked animals with wings, they will recognize that a new, never before seen long-necked animals with wings is a member of the category.

Moreover, like adults, the particular correlations that infants learn are constrained by their knowledge and experience. Adults have an easier time learning correlations that make sense given their existing knowledge (e.g., a vehicle that travels in the jungle has wheels with large treads) than correlations that are arbitrary given their existing knowledge (e.g., a vehicle that travels in the jungle has numbers on the license plate). Similarly, the correlations among features that infants learn can be constrained in this way. As described earlier, infants in their second year restrict their attention to correlations that are consistent with how general principles of correlations exist in the world – for example, noticing that the appearance of wheels can predict whether or not they go round, but not that the appearance of different part can predict whether or not the wheels go round.

Summary

By focusing on the process of categorization, therefore, we have a picture of infants' categorization as similar to adults', and as a result we conclude that there is relative continuity in development. However, it is important to remember the discontinuities described earlier. Despite the fact that infants form categories in much the same way as do adults, the resulting categories they form are not identical to those of adults. Infants form broader categories, based on a larger set of correlations among features, and that include many items that have commonalities not salient to adults. The source of these discontinuities, and how to reconcile them with the clear continuity in categorization, is under debate. One possibility is that with development infants discover or become sensitive to different kinds of features. Or, what constitutes a feature might change. That is, the process itself might not develop, but the input to the process may change. Another possibility is that there is continuity in some kinds of categorization (e.g., perceptual categorization), but that other kinds of categorization (e.g., conceptual categorization) emerge later or undergo developmental change. We will gain insight into the answers to these questions by further understanding how infants form categories.

A New Framework for Categorization

A new framework of concepts and categorization is emerging, and it has the potential to change dramatically our understanding of how infants categorize, and how that categorization is related to categorization later in life. Concepts often appear to be conceived of as static representations. Researchers ask question such as: Do infants know particular categorical distinctions? Are infants' categories like those possessed by adults? When do particular concepts emerge? When examining adults' concepts, researchers have sought to identify the set of necessary and sufficient features that define those concepts, to understand how concepts are related to one another, and to examine how categories are represented.

Categories are not static, however. Rather, they are dynamic and flexibly constructed given the context and items to be categorized. Although categories may be groups of objects out in the world, how those objects can be grouped is constantly changing with the introduction of new information, salience of particular features, and encounters with new examples of existing categories. Consider, for example, an individual whose encounters with dogs included only German Shepherds, Labrador Retrievers, and Golden Retrievers. When first encountering a Chihuahua, this individual likely will not recognize it as a member of the category dog. But, as additional information is gathered (e.g., the Chihuahua is labeled dog) and subtle details are attended to (e.g., like other dogs, the Chihuahua growls and wags its tail), this individual's dog category will change to include Chihuahuas, and other similar dogs. This will change the summary representation as well as the instances stored as members of the category.

This process likely happens frequently to infants as they encounter many new objects, events, and people everyday. Consider the infant described earlier who called both the moon and the round candle a ball. If this labeling error reflects a categorization error, this child's category ball must be undergoing significant change. At the time of the labeling error, his category ball includes many round things, and does not seem to be restricted to round things that are used in games. At this point his category ball likely does not include nonspherical balls such as footballs. As this child learns about other aspects of balls – that balls are often thrown, hit, or kicked, and that balls are typically toys – his category will continue to change and his view of round objects in the world will reorganize. Indeed, this is the central idea behind the notion of child-basic categories – they are categories that map onto adult-defined categories (such as ball), but imperfectly so because the child either ignores or is unaware of some features or places too much weight on others. Such child-basic categories become adult categories as children learn more about how adults typically weight different features in making category judgments. Clearly, therefore, overdevelopmental time categories are not static. Infants do not simply learn or acquire adult-defined categories and those representations do not go unchanged over time.

Categories are dynamic on even more fine-grained timescales. Our representations for categories change - from moment-to-moment. As they learn new categories in the laboratory, adults' representations change from trial-to-trial. Similarly, infants' representations for a collection of category items change across trials. Infants who are given fewer vs. more familiarization trials with exactly the same stimulus items show evidence of having represented the items differently, suggesting that representations changed with more encounters with items. Similarly, infants' sequential-touching behavior changes over time – they shift their touching patterns from comparing individual items to examining items all from within one category, from focusing on only a single category to touching items from both categories, and from relying on one dimension (e.g., shape) to relying on a completely different dimension (e.g., material) to determine which objects to touch in sequence. Thus, regardless of the categories shown or the procedure used, infants' behavior in experiments does not reflect static, unchanging categorical representations. Not only do representations change with increased development and knowledge, but also from moment-to-moment in the context of an experimental session.

The view of categorization in infancy as a dynamic, online process has implications for how we think about infants' behavior in experimental tasks assessing categorization – particularly tasks in which infants' behavior evolves over time. When encountering a series of items in a familiarization procedure, for example, infants are actively categorizing. Infants may categorize the first stimulus in relation to their existing knowledge – though this is less likely when they encounter completely novel stimuli. If they do categorize novel stimuli, they probably begin this process once they realize that there are several different stimuli that share commonalities – perhaps as early as the first trial when presented with multiple different items at one time, and by the time they have encountered two or three different stimuli on different trials. But, this early categorization is based on encountering few stimuli. If those stimuli are extremely similar, then infants may form an overly narrow category (such as one that only includes Golden Retrievers and Labradors) that must be broadened as new items are encountered. If the first stimuli are extremely dissimilar, infants may initially form a very broad category (such as a ball category that includes any round object) that gets narrower with experience. As infants are exposed to additional items, their category changes – the new items are included in the category, and the boundaries of the category change as a consequence. This process occurs throughout the session.

This can also happen in sequential-touching tasks, in which infants freely explore collections of objects. In this case, infants likely learn new features of the objects as they explore them, and their categories change. Consider an infant faced with a collection of balls and blocks. As she first explores those objects, the differences in shape may drive her behavior. But, as she picks up and touches the objects, she may discover that some are squishy. At this point, she may form narrow categories (e.g., squishy blocks and hard blocks) or she may shift her categorization to this new dimension (e.g., squishy things and hard things, regardless of shape). The point is that even when the infant is investigating objects on her own, she can constantly discover new commonalities and revise her categorization of objects online.

Summary: The Development of Categorization

The preceding sections have detailed changes in infants' categorization behavior. We have seen continuity in how infants form categories and changes in the kinds of categories infants respond to. But what exactly is developing? Categorization itself may not develop – from shortly after birth infants show evidence of forming some categories. But, as described earlier, infants' categories do change. One possibility is that as infants' perceptual and motor abilities develop, they become able to use a wider range of features to form categories. Thus, there may not be discontinuity in the process of categorization, but rather there may be discontinuity in the input to that process. Changes in perceptual and motor abilities may also allow infants to consider more information at one time than can younger infants. That is,

quantitative changes in capacity limitations may allow the infant to consider more simultaneously information when categorizing. Indeed, there is a large literature revealing that as they develop, infants remember more information and for longer periods of time. Such changes may contribute to changes in categorization.

Not only do the categories that infants attend to change over time, but they attend to those categories in increasingly more situations with development. Infants' limited memory and other cognitive skills may make it difficult to carry out the comparisons necessary to detect commonalities and differences among items in some demanding contexts. The point is that developmental changes in categorization may in fact reflect changes in infants' other abilities.

In summary, infants' concepts and categorization skills are critically important for their developing understanding of the world. Infants can detect commonalities among items from an extremely early age. Although we do not yet know exactly why or how infants' concepts and categorization skills develop, there is a large body of evidence providing rich descriptions of those changes. This work will provide the foundation for our future understanding of the processes of categorization in infancy.

See also: Cognitive Development; Cognitive Developmental Theories; Habituation and Novelty; Language Development: Overview; Learning; Memory; Reasoning in Early Development.

Suggested Readings

Cohen LB and Strauss MS (1979) Concept acquisition in the human infant. *Child Development* 50: 419–424.

Mandler JM (2004) *The Foundations of Mind: Origins of Conceptual Thought.* New York: Oxford University Press.

Mareschal D and Quinn PC (2001) Categorization in infancy. *Trends in Cognitive Sciences* 5: 443–450.

Oakes LM and Madole KL (2003) Principles of developmental change in infants' category formation. In: Rakison DH and Oakes LM (eds.) *Early Category and Concept Development: Making Sense of the Blooming, Buzzing Confusion*, pp. 132–158. New York: Oxford University Press.

Quinn PC (2002) Beyond prototypes: Asymmetries in infant categorization and what they teach us about the mechanisms guiding early knowledge acquisition. *Advances in Child Development and Behavior* 29: 161–193.

Rakison DH (2003) Parts, motion, and the development of the animate-inanimate distinction in infancy. In: Rakison DH and Oakes LM (eds.) *Early Category and Concept Development: Making Sense of the Blooming, Buzzing Confusion*, pp. 159–192. New York: Oxford University Press.

Rakison DH and Oakes LM (eds.) *Early Category and Concept Development: Making Sense of the Blooming, Buzzing Confusion.* New York: Oxford University Press.

Reznick JS and Kagan J (1983) Category detection in infancy. In: Rovee-Collier C and Lipsitt LP (eds.) *Advances in Infancy Research*, vol. 2, pp. 78–111. Norwood, NJ: Ablex.

Cognitive Development

C D Vallotton and K W Fischer, Harvard Graduate School of Education, Cambridge, MA, USA

© 2008 Elsevier Inc. All rights reserved.

Glossary

Cardinality – In development of numeracy, the principle that the last number counted in a set represents the size of the set.
Conservation – The awareness that quantity remains the same despite change in appearance.
Décalage – Unevenness in development characterized by level of performance varying across tasks or situations.
Joint attention – The sharing of attentional focus between two people, either on one another (dyadic, e.g., mutual eye contact) or on a third entity such as an object, event, or idea (triadic, e.g., mutually looking at an object or talking about an idea).
Looking time paradigm – A methodology for studying infant cognition prior to speech by measuring differences in the time infants look at presented stimuli. Longer looking times are richly interpreted by some as indicating mental states or attitudes including 'surprise' and 'preference'.
Number line – A one-dimensional representation of numbers as sequential integers along a continuum (e.g., –3, –2, –1, 0, 1, 2, 3).
Numeracy – Contracted form of 'numerical literacy'; a proficiency with numbers and measures which requires an understanding of the number system, a set of skills for manipulating mathematical information, and ability to reason about quantitative and spatial problems.
Object permanence – A term coined by Jean Piaget to describe the knowledge that objects remain in existence even when they are perceptually obscured (e.g., knowing that a ball hidden from view by a cloth still exists under the cloth).
Ordinality – In development of numeracy, the principle that numbers follow a constant sequential order.
Perspective taking – The ability to take and coordinate different perspectives on the same thing at one time, either multiple perspectives by a single perceiver or different perspectives by multiple perceivers.
Reflex – Species-specific instinctive action elements dependent on stimulation or body position (e.g., sucking an object placed in the mouth).
Representation – Mental manipulation of concrete aspects of persons, objects, or events (e.g., "I like cookies." or "Five is bigger than two.").
Sensorimotor actions – Flexibly controlled actions and perceptions of objects, people, and events (e.g., reaching for a rattle that is seen or heard).
Skills – Organized elements of behavior – including motor actions, thinking, and feeling – that an individual can control in order to meet the demands of a given physical or social context. Skills develop in a complexity hierarchy.
Social cognition – The processing of social information, including perception, encoding, storing, retrieving, and applying social information.
Social referencing – Using another's perception of a situation in order to determine one's own response to it. In infancy, usually referencing a caregiver for information in a novel situation.
Theory of Mind (ToM) – The understanding that others have mental processes – including desires, beliefs, and perceptions – that differ from one's own.

Introduction

In this article we describe early cognitive development from the Neo-Piatetian perspective on the construction of cognitive skills. We first describe the general framework of 'skill theory' including basic tenets and useful metaphors. Then we describe cognitive development through each of three domains – including physical causality, numeracy, and social perspective taking – from infancy through approximately 5 years of age. Finally, we describe sources of variation in cognitive skills both within and across children.

The Shape of Early Cognitive Development

The current state of knowledge of early cognitive development reveals both innate knowledge in the newborn infant and consistent development through eight levels (grouped into three tiers) of cognitive skills through the first 5 years. At first, infants relate to their world by acting on it physically – reacting to stimuli and developing expectations about things and people, then acting with more and more control and forethought. In the middle of their second year, children begin to relate to the world through mental representations, holding information in mind and manipulating it, often accompanied by physical action. Though this consistent sequence of development is underpinned by spurts in brain growth, new levels do not arise simply from maturational processes, but through co-occurrence and coordination of increasingly complex skills. Despite the consistencies across children from which the knowledge of levels is derived, there is both intra- and inter-individual variation in development, showing development to be a web of interconnected skills, rather than a unidirectional ladder.

Cognitive Development as a Web

Developmental ladders and staircases

Development is often conceptualized as a ladder, a metaphor in which development moves along consistent progression toward higher stages. The metaphor of the ladder has three characteristics: (1) development follows a straight line; (2) it progresses along fixed steps in a single sequence; and (3) it is conceptualized as a forward or upward progression, without deviation to the side or movement backwards.

Developmental webs

A better metaphor than the ladder is the web of individual development, in which an individual child moves concurrently along multiple strands in different skill domains. Cognitive development encompasses many different skills developing at different rates along various trajectories toward unique developmental endpoints, and interacting and integrating with one another to produce complex behavior. The web metaphor portrays cognitive development as the complex constructive process that it is, moving along independent strands that can be linked. Indeed the web only begins to capture the complexity of development, which also involves movement up and down along strands and influences between strands. In general, (1) skills vary within a range along a strand, not just at a single level or step; (2) links between domains of development (i.e., social and cognitive development, or neurological and cognitive development) exert bidirectional influence on one another and help to explain the dynamic nature of development; and (3) development involves not only forward progression along a strand but also moving backward along a strand in order to solidify the strand or reshape earlier skills to create a new skill. This article describes several strands of cognitive development, including infants' developing understanding of physical principles, numeracy, and perspective taking. The focus on the strands for these domains grounds understanding of the developmental process, which is always based in children's specific actions in particular situations (**Figure 1**).

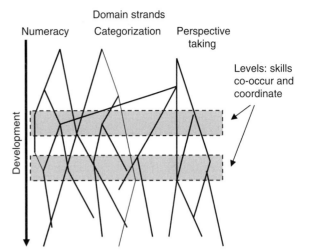

Figure 1 Developmental web showing two levels emerging in three domains. Intra-individual development of domains occurs along independent but intersecting strands, while emergence of new levels corresponds across domains. Adapted from Fischer KW and Bidell TR (1998) Dynamic development of psychological structures in action and thought. In: Damon W and Lerner RM (eds.) *Handbook of Child Psychology. Vol. 1: Theoretical Models of Human Development*, 5th edn., pp. 467–561. New York: Wiley.

The Process of Developing Cognitive Skills

Skills: The Child in Context

A skill is an ability under one's control within a specific context or task, from visually and motorically exploring a new object to maintaining multiple roles during pretend play. The concept of cognitive skill looks to performances in contexts that elicit them, rather than treating knowledge as an object that is obtained and housed in one's mind. Thus, skills are task specific, but potentially transferable to new contexts through a process of building connections. For example, a 2-year-old child may develop the skill of using a spoon to feed herself cereal from a bowl. She knows what is required in this situation, and is able to control her actions in order to do it. She may be able to transfer this skill to using a spoon to feed herself apple sauce from a bowl, but eating noodles from a bowl or eating beans with a fork are different enough that she needs to work to adapt her skill to this new situation. A skill is not a characteristic of the child herself, nor of the situation, but of the child in context – both social and physical.

Individual skills developed in later childhood and adulthood vary more in timing and sequence than those developed in early childhood (through age 5 years), where the first eight skill levels show moderate consistency within predictable age ranges. **Table 1** shows the age ranges based on research on a number of skill domains, but more research will be needed to specify the amount of variation in skill levels across children and domains.

Table 1 Levels of cognitive development in early childhood

Skill level age of emergence	Description and example of skills	Skill structure
Single reflex 3–4 weeks	Simple responses to stimuli: infant looks at object moving through visual field; grasps object placed in hand.	
Reflex mapping 7–8 weeks	Using two reflexes together in relation: infant extends arm toward object being looked at when posture allows.	
Reflex system 10–11 weeks	Coordinated system of simple responses: infant opens hand while extending arm to object being looked at when posture allows.	
System of reflex systems, which creates a single sensorimotor action 15–17 weeks	Coordination of two reflex systems: infant extends arm to and grasps object, sometimes adjusting reach as needed and relatively independent of particular postural configuration – which creates a single sensorimotor action, the flexible reach for an object.	
Sensorimotor mapping 7–8 months	Coordination of two sensorimotor actions, such as visually guided reach for an object: infant looks at an object and uses the visual information to grasp it.	
Sensorimotor system 11–13 months	Complex relations of sensorimotor action relations into a flexible system, such as visual/manual exploration: Infant uses visual information to manipulate an object and moves it to see different aspects of it. Infant also relates sound and vocalization, using single word to label object.	
System of sensorimotor systems/single representation 20–24 months	Integration of sensorimotor action systems into a concrete representation: child manipulates an object to make it carry out actions in pretend play, making a doll walk or talk, talking into a toy telephone. Child also describes attributes or actions of objects and people.	

Continued

Skill level Age of emergence	Description and example of skills	Skill structure
Representaitonal mapping 3.5–4.5 years	Coordination of two representations: child uses two objects in pretend play, relating their actions to one another, e.g., pretending that a mother doll is taking care of a child doll. Child also uses language to coordinate attributes and actions appropriate to ascribed roles, such as mother and child.	

Reference: Fischer KW and Hogan AE (1989) The big picture for infant development: Levels and variations. In Lockman J and Hazen N (eds.) *Action in Social Context: Perspectives on Early Development* pp. 275–305. New York: Plenum.

The Process of Development: Getting from One Level to Another

Convergent findings in infant research demonstrate several periods of rapid change in cognition, producing discontinuities – or shifts in level – in cognitive skills. These periods of rapid change are 2–4 months, 7–8 months, 12–13 months, 18–21 months, and 4 years. Evidence indicates that changes in growth patterns of brain activity and anatomy underpin these cognitive changes. While this association of cognition and neurology shows maturational underpinnings for shifts in skill levels, it does not alone explain development from one level to the next; available evidence does not indicate one direction of causality between cognitive skills and brain growth.

Skill levels form a hierarchy that develops in consistent sequences within domains through the process of co-occurrence and coordination. Levels are grouped into tiers, three of which fit within early childhood: the tiers of reflexes, sensorimotor actions, and representations. At each tier, children differentiate and combine the skills under their control so as to move through a series of levels that eventually create the elements of the next tier. Reflexes, which are simple elements of voluntary action by the infant that depend on inborn patterns of posture and action, differentiate and combine to produce sensorimotor actions. Sensorimotor actions, which are flexible and coordinated actions on objects, are in turn differentiated and combined to develop a third type of cognitive unit – representations. Representations are mental manipulations of concrete aspects of persons, objects, and events. This process of skill elaboration goes on through development at later years into the 20s until abstract systems are combined to create principles in adults. However, the scope of this article covers cognitive development only in early childhood – to the level of representational mappings.

Children develop more complex cognitive skills through the processes of co-occurrence and coordination. The co-occurrence of two skills, both elicited by a given task, induces the child to notice them in contrast to one another, differentiating and coordinating them by using them together in subsequent tasks. Through these processes, increasingly complex skills are built in a sequence for each domain, like cognitive building blocks. **Table 1** provides a list of the skill levels, the typical ages at which they emerge, a description and example of each level considered in this article, and a pictoral representation of the skill level to facilitate understanding of the process of building complex cognitive skills through co-occurrence and coordination of simpler skills.

Like the type of skill, developmental level is not a characteristic of the child, but of the child in context. The level of a skill, as well as its type, depends on the task itself – including the demands of the task and the child's familiarity with it. Other important sources of variation in skill level come from within the child (such as internal state) and from the supports provided to the child within the environment. Because the type and level of skill vary within their context, the structure of skill development is different from that proposed by Jean Piaget, who contended that children develop through generalized stages of skills; that is, a child at a particular stage would exhibit behaviors consistent with that stage in all tasks. Instead, children operate at different skill levels for different tasks, depending on the sources of variation described above. This is why *décalage* – a term used by Piaget to describe the variation in cognitive abilities across tasks and situations in a single child – is the rule rather than the exception in cognitive development. Even highly educated adults will use very basic, low-level skills when they encounter an unfamiliar task. Variation across children shows that the progression from one level to the next is not as simple as expectable maturation (i.e., it is not merely a result of brain development). Instead, progressing from one level to another is a result of a combination of factors, including children's maturation and their experiences performing skills.

Typical Development of Early Cognitive Skills

This section describes the typical development of early cognitive skills, from newborn through age 5 years, from the earliest levels measured through representational mappings. The focus is on the development of skills for physical causality, numeracy, and perspective taking. (To date, much less is known about the 'reflex levels' – when children are typically 4 weeks to 4 months – than the other levels. We present only what is known currently, thus descriptions of cognitive development through these levels are limited.)

Physical Causality

From basic reactions to physical objects, to intentional actions on and with objects, followed by representations of object functions and relationships to one another, young children build their knowledge of physical causality. The ability to categorize objects by their functions (or effects) contributes to children's use of objects in problem solving, as well as understanding of causality.

Newborn
Within their first few days and weeks of life, infants can demonstrate that they already know a number of things about the physical world. Newborn infants will follow a moving object with their eyes, and infants demonstrate a perception of the world as three-dimensional – for example, by showing an expectation that objects remain the same size across situations. Throughout the early months, infants' actions are seriously limited by the particular postures or positions of their body. For example, they can look at an object on the side that their head is turned, but have great difficulty following the movements of that object past the midline, where they would have to shift their body to position their head for looking at it.

Reflex levels
Single reflexes. By 3–4 weeks of age infants have a number of reflexes under their control for responding to stimuli. Some of those most widely studied are looking toward or away from an object presented in their visual field, grasping an object placed in their hand, and kicking their legs, all of which depend on their being in a specific bodily position supporting the reflex.

Reflex mappings. Beginning between 7 and 8 weeks, infants can coordinate two reflexes into a reflex mapping. For example, they can extend their arm toward an object held in their view, provided that their posture places the arm in a position to reach in that direction.

Reflex systems. Around 10–11 weeks, infants can coordinate two reflex mappings to create a reflex system. For example, they will open their hand while extending their arm toward an object held within view, so long as their body is in a position that supports this movement. Further, 3-month-old infants seem to know that they can cause events, though because their actions are primarily reactions they do not know how they carry out a means to cause the event. By tying one end of a ribbon to a mobile, and the other to an infants' foot, infants will learn that when they kick that foot, the mobile moves, and will even remember to kick that foot if shown the same mobile a week later. But if the ribbon is loose, they do not figure out how to vary their action to take account of the loose ribbon. Also, when the ribbon is removed, the infants still kick their foot, as if expecting the mobile to move. They seem to have learned 'when I act, interesting things happen'.

Sensorimotor levels
Sensorimotor actions. At 15–17 weeks, infants can combine reflex systems into single sensorimotor actions. At this point, they begin to guide and shape their reaching, extending an arm toward an object to grasp it in different positions or to adjust to it as they open their hand, and sometimes adjusting their hand if the object changes position. Through this level, children come to use a variety of different actions on objects, including systematically dropping them from wherever they sit; importantly, they do not yet look to see where objects land when dropped.

Sensorimotor mappings. At 7–8 months, infants combine sensorimotor actions into simple sensorimotor mappings. For example, an infant can now reach and grasp an object (a sensorimotor action) in order to pull it closer and look at it. Infants at this level demonstrate an ability to distinguish between objects as either animate or inanimate. By 10 months, infants show awareness of basic 'billiard ball' causality, the idea that action is caused by something. Infants who have habituated to a toy car moving after being bumped by another moving toy will look longer when the conditions of causality are not met – for example, when the car begins to move before the other toy has bumped into it to cause the movement. Infants also demonstrate expectations consistent with an understanding of forces besides personal agents, such as gravity: They will drop an object to the floor and look accurately to see where it landed (**Figure 2**).

Sensorimotor systems. Around their first birthday, 11–13 months of age, infants begin to combine sensorimotor mappings into systems of sensorimotor actions. An infant at this level can actively explore objects by moving them around to see different sides. As a result of this new coordination, infants begin to understand more about objects' relations to and effects on one another, and can use this knowledge to achieve their own goals. For example, a 12-month-old child can pull a cloth to obtain a toy that is sitting on it, and will not pull the cloth when the toy is not resting on it (indicating an understanding of the relationship of support), whereas an infant at the previous level will pull the cloth hoping to obtain the object, even if the object he wants is held above it.

> Controversy in interpretation:
> Rich vs. conservative explanations of infant behavior
>
> Rich interpretation of infants' behavior is the explanation of infant behavior in terms of adult-like mental activity. Some of the methods we describe in this article – such as habituation and looking time – lead to results which could be interpreted in either a rich or conservative way. An ongoing controversy affecting both the theory and methods in the field of cognitive development asks, is a rich interpretation of infant behavior or a conservative one more accurate and more useful for understanding the results found in studies of infant cognition?
>
> Marshall Haith put forth a heuristically challenging argument against rich interpretation, asserting that such explanations of infant behavior provoke a number of problems in the field of infant cognition. These problems include claims that very young infants have knowledge they could not yet have reasonably acquired, use of concept, minimally supported claims that certain knowledge is innate, and undermining the study of development of cognitive skills over time.
>
> On the other hand, many developmental theorists who are proponents of the 'competent infant' idea believe that conservative interpretations of infant behavior too often underestimate infants' abilities, failing to see the thoughtfulness and intentionality behind the behaviors of preverbal children.
>
> From the perspective of Skill Theory, infant behaviors such as longer looking times or preferential head-turning likely indicate the beginning building blocks of cognitive skills which will be elaborated and generalized into their adult forms later in development.

Figure 2 Controversy in interpretation: rich versus conservative explanations of infant behavior.

Infants begin to recognize rudimentary object categories based on appearances. For example, they will show surprise when a duck emerges from an occluder instead of the toy car that went behind it. Prior to this, infants rely on trajectory as the primary way to identify an object. Infants at this level will group toys by object type (e.g., plastic farm animals vs. toy cars), whereas at 9 months they show less interest in or understanding of object categories.

Representations

Single representations. Around 20–24 months, young children coordinate systems of actions to produce concrete representations. It is at this point that they begin to engage in symbolic play with objects (e.g., representing toys as having particular uses or roles), rather than functional play (simple actions on and with objects). Related to their growing understanding of causality, children's skills for manipulating objects have also become far more complex. A child will use a tool to get a toy that is out of reach, showing emerging planning and problem-solving skills.

At this level children begin to categorize objects spontaneously, carefully organizing objects by category (e.g., horses vs. pencils), stacking them or lining them up, a skill that displays their capacity to represent concrete properties of objects. Combining their skills in categorization and causality, 2-year-olds will begin to categorize things by function rather than form. Alison Gopnik and colleagues showed children a series of novel objects that looked similar to one another. Then children were shown that two of the objects shared a function. The experimenter told the children that one of the objects was a blicket, and asked which of the other objects was also a blicket. Two-year-old children chose the object that had performed the same function as the first blicket rather than one more similar in appearance.

Understanding why an object does what it does is another matter, however. Toddlers often still act as though they believe that they (or another person-agent) must act in order to make interesting events happen. When interacting with a wind-up toy, they will physically manipulate the object to perform its action rather than using the mechanism. Even when the physical demands of the task are far easier than locating and manipulating a winding mechanism, toddlers will still use more of their own force than necessary to cause an event. Besides winding up a toy unnecessarily, they will push a toy car down a ramp rather than releasing it to roll.

Representational mappings. At this level, emerging around 3.5–4.5 years of age, children begin to relate concrete representations to one another. Categorization skills are more sophisticated, and children will categorize objects by their underlying natures, and use categories to appropriately ascribe characteristics. With this more sophisticated understanding of categories, pretend play becomes much more common and complex; for example, in play children will ascribe roles to the dolls and maintain them throughout the dolls' interactions with other objects or people, using the doll as an actor or cause.

Children at this level display their knowledge of causality through their use of language, beginning to give reasonable causal explanations, as well as to make simple if–then causal predictions about simple mechanisms and interactions in the physical world, based in representations of how events occur in relation to each other. Children's explanations of the causes of events often reveal, however, the same kind of teleologic reasoning that their earlier actions displayed; young children explain events as happening 'so that' rather than 'because of'. For example, Piaget discovered that when children explain events in nature, they indicate that rain is occurring 'so that we will have water', the sun goes down at night 'so that we can sleep'. At this level, causes are still thought of as forces coming from active agents for a purpose under the agent's will, such as that the wind makes the clouds move.

Throughout early development, children's understanding of the causes that can produce effects grows from a sense of self as agent, to others as agents, and then to interactions among agents and objects. Around the age of 5 years, children understand that forces other than people cause events, but these forces are still personified. Indeed, listening to adults' explanations of events may reveal that though they may know better, they do not lose the tendency to explain events in terms of personal forces and teleological purposes.

Numeracy

Research with infants and others has revealed two number systems that people develop to mentally track numbers – an exact system used for small numbers and an approximate system used for estimating larger magnitudes. Within their first year of life, infants' abilities to differentiate varying magnitudes improve to detect smaller ratios, while the specific numbers an infant can track using the precise system increase during the course of early childhood, from just 1 and 2, to 3, then 4, then to having a sense of the number line. After children understand the number line, and sets or groups of objects represented by a single number, they begin combining components of their knowledge of number in increasingly complex ways.

Newborn

Based on habituation with looking time, infants have been shown to recognize the difference between one, two, and three objects under a variety of different testing conditions. This has been found as young as 2 and 3 days after birth. Newborn infants' attraction to visual stimuli with high contrast, and to the edges or boundaries of objects within their view, gives an indication of infants' attention to identifying singular objects, or ones. Even in their first few days, infants appear to notice the constancy (and change) of object number, though this is limited to smaller numbers.

Reflex levels

During the reflex levels, infants are learning to parse visual stimuli in appropriate places and identify objects as unitary, counting as one thing. Along with attention to high-contrast edges, infants rely on motion to determine the boundaries of an object. For most objects, what moves together stays together as one object; and infants have been shown to expect this basic principle. A lamp and coffee table both made of the same color wood may appear to be one oddly shaped object because there are no stark contrasts; however, when someone lifts the lamp from the table, anyone – including the infant – can see that they are two distinct objects. It is no surprise, then, that from birth infants will follow a moving object with their eyes. Research has also shown that infants are more sensitive to the trajectories of an object than to its surface characteristics in determining the identity of an object. An infant will show more surprise and curiosity (looking longer or looking again) toward an object emerging from an occluder when the object has changed speed or direction than when it has changed shape and color. Research with congenitally blind children and adults who have gained sight confirm the necessity of motion for identifying singular objects; a newly sighted individual tends to parse visual stimuli in inaccurate places until they see an object move.

Sensorimotor levels

Sensorimotor actions. Can infants add and subtract? At this level, studies by Karen Wynn with a series of physically impossible events show that infants as young as 4.5 months of age can add $1 + 1$. Infants saw one Mickey doll on a puppet stage, then saw the Mickey doll occluded. Next they saw a hand come from the side of the stage to place another Mickey doll behind the occluding screen; when the screen came down, they saw either one or two Mickey dolls. They had not seen the dolls together before, so that the scene of two dolls on the stage was technically novel, not seen before. However, they looked longer when there was only one Mickey on the stage, showing that they expected to see two, because one had been added to the other; they were surprised at seeing only one. The same experiment works for subtraction; when infants are presented with two Mickey dolls, and one Mickey is taken away (from behind an occluder), infants expect to see only one and show surprise when there are still two. Further, the infants showed surprise with three objects as well, leading to the conclusion that 5-month-old babies do indeed know that $1 + 1 = 2$, not 1, and not 3.

Sensorimotor mappings. Using habituation of sucking rhythm (rather than looking time), experimenters have shown that young infants' sense of numeracy extends to sounds as well, for tones and for syllables; after being habituated to words with three syllables (or to three tones), infants respond with more interest (more vigorous sucking) when they hear words with two syllables (or two tones). Testing infants' numeracy across sensory modalities, Elizabeth Spelke and colleagues used looking time to show that infants between 6 and 8 months of age prefer to look at slides of two objects while hearing two drum beats, and three objects while hearing three drum beats. It appears that infants can identify the number of sounds they hear and compare it to the number of objects they see, leading to the conclusion that infants' perception of small numbers is both general and cross-modal.

In addition to advances in the system for precise number, infants at this level are learning to discriminate smaller ratios of magnitude in both the visual and auditory modality. Using looking time as an indicator of novelty recognition, Spelke and colleagues have shown that 6-month-old infants can estimate magnitude differences of 2.0 (e.g., 8 vs. 16 objects, 5 vs. 10 objects), while 9-month-olds can detect ratios of 1.5 (e.g., 8 vs. 12 objects) as well as 2.0. Using a method in which infants' head turning toward sounds is used to indicate recognition of novelty, Spelke and colleagues have more recently shown that this same timing of magnitude recognition holds in the auditory modality as well.

The statistically sensitive infant. Another way of detecting where one thing ends and another begins is by determining the likelihood that a particular thing will follow another. In the phrase 'happy day', how does a child learn that the syllables 'hap' and 'py' are one word and 'day' another, rather than 'hap pyday'? A series of studies has shown that infants as young as 8 months old are incredibly sensitive to the statistical likelihood of word syllables being heard together, thus defining the boundaries of words within a continuous stream of sound. Other studies have shown that the same learning mechanism works with visual as well as auditory stimuli – that infants expect to see a certain sequence of pictures when they have seen the same sequence a number of times, and that they look longer when the sequence is violated.

Sensorimotor systems. Around 12 months of age, infants begin to distinguish small numbers more consistently. Conservation of number in the early months of life rarely goes beyond the number three; in only a few tasks in a few different laboratories have infants been seen to correctly conserve (or add) 4, as opposed to three, and no infants under 12 months have been observed to distinguish 4 from 5 or 6. However, getting to three is important because it shows that babies are not just distinguishing 'one' vs. 'more than one'. Around 15 months of age, after learning basic addition and subtraction of small numbers, infants combine these skills to develop a sense of basic ordinality of quantity; that is, that three is larger than two. When offered a choice, they will select the larger group of toys.

Representational levels

Single representations. At this level, young children are beginning to use verbal language more fluidly; they have a representation of the concept of more and can respond to verbal instructions to choose a line with more things in it. Piaget made the observation that for large numbers, young children will choose the longer line of objects when asked to choose which line has more. However, subsequent studies have shown that for very small numbers children around age 2 years will choose the correct line of objects (i.e., marbles) when asked which line has more, even when the one with less is made to look longer.

Representational mappings. Coordinating the concept of the ordinality of the number line with the concept that a group of objects can be represented by a single number, children between 3 and 4 years old learn the rule of cardinality; that is, for counting the objects in a set, the last number counted is the number of objects in the set. However, overgeneralization of this rule can lead to miscounting until children coordinate it with more sophisticated understandings of object identity. For example, when asked to count how many pencils are lying on the table, if one pencil is broken in two, a child of 3 or 4 will count it as two pencils, concluding that there is one more pencil in the set than there really is. Children at this level understand that you count each object in order to derive the number in the set, but have not yet coordinated what they know about object identity to take into account the unity of the broken object.

There is a spurt in the development of numeracy between ages 4 and 5 years, as many children construct the number line. That is, with the knowledge that numbers are ordinal, children at this level extend their representations of individual numbers – 1, 2, 3, and 4 – into a number line, for numbers in general to 5 and beyond.

Perspective Taking

Perspective taking is one of the foundational skills for social interaction, including the recent line of research on 'theory of mind'. Understanding of self and other is reconstructed at every level of cognitive development, and perspective taking begins at the reflex levels with actions in response to others, and in response to self. This is followed by the coordination of perceptions of and actions toward self and other at the sensorimotor levels. Then at the representational levels, children begin to coordinate increasingly complex combinations of both similarities and differences between self and other, including the very challenging matter of differences in perspectives, thoughts, and beliefs. Though Piaget described children's ability to take and coordinate multiple perspectives on a single object or concept as developing around the age of 8 or 9 years, extensive research shows how precursory skills for perspective taking develop in the first 5 years.

Newborn

From the time they are 1 h old, infants can respond to others by imitating a few simple actions they see on another's face; there is the most evidence for newborns' ability to imitate sticking out the tongue.

Reflex levels

Single reflexes. At this level, infants respond to social stimuli, such as turning toward a familiar voice or staring at a likeness of a face, so long as their bodily position supports this reflex action.

Reflex mappings. Beginning between 7 and 8 weeks of age, infants can bring together two reflexes into a coordinated reflex mapping. For example, while looking into their mother's face, they will look at her eyes in response to her voice. Infants also show some sensitivity to contingencies during interaction and begin to show upset when interactions are noncontingent, that is, when mother's responses to changes in her infant's looks and vocalizations are delayed or nonexistent.

Reflex systems. At 2–3 months of age, infants can coordinate reflex mappings into a smooth system of social responses, smiling and cooing in response to facial and vocal cues from adults, so long as their bodily position facilitates these actions. They begin to coordinate their own facial expressions, gestures, and vocal productions with those of others for a contingent turn-taking game with rhythms similar to conversation.

Sensorimotor levels

Philosophers and scientists have debated whether self-knowledge is derived from knowledge of other, or the reverse. Scientists Sandra Pipp, Kurt Fischer, and Sybillyn Jennings examined the development of knowledge of self and other in children aged from 6 months to 3 years by posing a series of sequentially ordered tasks requiring children to demonstrate knowledge of self and mother in two different domains: agency (action on self and other), and features (recognition of attributes of self and other). Their findings show that self- and other-knowledge develop concurrently, and the primacy of each depends on the particular domain (agency or feature). This is another example of intersecting strands of the developmental web.

Sensorimotor actions. At this level, infants begin to act toward others – typically caregivers – in order to elicit desired responses. They no longer merely respond, but regularly initiate interactions and manipulate others' actions. Relatedly, they begin to recognize and respond to distinct internal states in others, differentiating (as tested by looking time) facial expressions consistent with the emotions of anger, fear, and surprise in female adults. At 6 months of age, infants can interpret the goals of human actions and show surprise (longer looking time) when the human hand reaches for the 'wrong' thing (a different goal object). The effects are not seen when the task is done with a nonhuman, mechanical hand. Now that infants guide their own actions to facilitate their own rudimentary goals, they interpret others as capable of having goals or interests that likewise guide action.

Sensorimotor mappings. At this level, infants begin to coordinate a few social behaviors in order to engage, re-engage, and direct the attention of others. Around 9 months of age, infants begin to consistently engage in joint attention with another person, coordinating their actions to engage in and direct others' attention. As early as 7 months of age, infants will attempt to re-engage partners in dyadic joint attention, coordinating sensorimotor actions (such as gaze following, and some early pointing) to engage in dyadic joint attention. By the age of 10 months, infants use these behaviors consistently in social interaction, as when they engage a partner during exploration of a toy.

In the study by Pipp and colleagues, infants successfully performed agency and feature tasks directed at oneself and mother. In the agency tasks, they followed the experimenter's request to feed themselves or their mother a Cheerio. Agency toward oneself developed slightly earlier than agency toward mother. In contrast, the order was reversed for features: Infants at this level successfully identified mothers' features in the mirror, but not their own.

Identification of features in others at 10 months of age includes attribution of social qualities and rudimentary psychological attributes to individuals. In studies by Karen Wynn and colleagues, infants saw one object (a geometric shape with eyes) apparently trying to climb a hill, and another object either apparently helping or hindering the first in reaching its goal. In a subsequent scene, the climbing object moved to be near either the helper or the hinderer. Infants showed surprise (longer looking time) when the climber moved next to the hinderer rather than the helper. This surprise indicates that infants attribute some quality to the helper and hinderer, and expect a certain reaction or disposition toward these two individuals from the climber. Given the opportunity to play with one of these objects after viewing the climbing scene, infants chose the helper object rather than the hinderer.

Sensorimotor systems. Around 12 months of age, infants' social cognition becomes noticeably more complex. They begin coordinating their responses with those of others, looking to others to guide their own actions – using social referencing in ambiguous situations. There is a rapid increase in the use of pointing to direct others' attention at this level, and more consistent following of adults' pointing. Infants will also imitate adults' actions on objects, even when there is a delay between when they see the action and when they get an opportunity to imitate it. At this level infants seem to be learning that they are like others, which informs their responses to their environment. They are aligning their attitudes and actions to those of others.

In the Pipp study of self and other, infants around 12 or 13 months of age passed a simple visual recognition task by identifying in a mirror a sticker placed on theirs or their mothers' hands. On average, infants passed this visual identification task for mother at earlier ages than for self and similarly identified rouge on their mother's face in a mirror around 15 months, 3 months earlier than they identified rouge on their own face.

At 14 months of age (but not 12 months), infants coordinate more complex social information to make distinct attributions of psychological dispositions. Studies by Wynn and colleagues used an elaboration of the climber task previously described in which there were two climbers; one climber was helped and one was hindered by the same third object. Children showed the expectation that the climber who was helped would move toward the third object while the climber who was hindered would move away. That is, they did not perceive the third object as simply a helper or hinderer, but differentiated how each climber would react to it based on their experiences.

Representations

Single representations. As children move into the representational levels, they hold aspects of self and other in mind beyond their immediate experience. Around 18 months of age, children understand that other people's desires or preferences can differ from their own. Alison Gopnik and colleagues have conducted a series of experiments in which an experimenter demonstrates by facial expression and voice that she prefers broccoli to goldfish crackers, then places her hand right between the two bowls of food and asks the infant to give her more. Whereas a 14-month-old will give the experimenter more crackers (the food that the child prefers), an 18 month old will give the experimenter more broccoli. At 18 months of age children understand that the experimenter's desires are discrepant from their own. Though children as young as 18 months of age have learned that desires can differ, they do not yet understand that perspectives can differ (the apparent discrepancy here is discussed below). The inability to coordinate multiple perspectives results in humorous behavior by toddlers, such as a child covering his own eyes as he walks past his parents with a stolen cookie, believing that if he could not see them, then they could not see him.

Showing insight into others as agents with intentions, 18-month-olds will re-enact the intended, rather than observed, act of a person. Children can infer the adult's intention by watching the failed attempts, and will later do the intended action, rather than the one they saw actually done. The fact that they do not show this same intention reading when they observe a machine 'fail' at a task reveals that they are attributing internal goals and intentions to human beings.

Self and other representations show differences similar to those earlier in infancy. For the feature tasks in the Pipp study, infants recognized rouge on their own nose at around 18 months, after they had noticed it on their mother's nose, thus developing skills for other before self. For the corresponding agency tasks, infants' pretended to feed themselves and their mothers or to drink. They succeeded at this task earlier for self than for mother, thus developing skills for other before self.

Between 18 and 36 months of age, infants coordinate more and more complex representations of self and other as agent and self and other features. In the Pipp agency tasks, infants acted on another person within a prescribed interaction, interacted with another within a prescribed role, and eventually represented two distinct social roles (mother and baby) in pretend play tasks. In the features tasks, children identified increasingly abstract aspects of self and other by correctly responding to a series of questions involving self and other in spatial location ("Where is (Mommy/Child's name)?"), as actors ("Who did that?"), as owners ("Whose is that?"), in familial relationships ("Who do you belong to?"), and in gender categories ("Are you a boy/girl?"). There was a small advantage for self-knowledge in the agency tasks and for other knowledge in the features tasks. At 3 years of age, children have built complex representations of others' characteristics, including concrete visual perspectives, so that they can hide a toy so that they can see it but another person cannot.

Representational mappings. At 3 years of age, children have already built complex representations of self and other, representing basic roles and identifying features. Around 3.5–4.5 years, they begin to coordinate these representations in more and more complex ways, coming to understand many differences between self and other, as well as differences between current and past self – in visual perspectives, thoughts, and beliefs. Children use language to explicitly contrast representations. Conversations between young children and their parents recorded in the CHILDES database reveal children between 3 and 4 years of age pondering contrasts between characteristics of people such as what they like and do not like.

Between 3.5 and 4 years of age children begin to represent different, contradictory perspectives of their own and others. Extensive research on 'theory of mind' uses false-belief tasks, which require coordination of representations of beliefs and perceptions in self and other – for example, differentiating between one's own current and past beliefs, or contrasting one's current knowledge with another's ignorance of a fact or circumstance. In order to pass these tests, it is necessary to understand that people have thoughts and beliefs about things, that people can have different thoughts and beliefs from one another, that those thoughts and beliefs can change, and that those thoughts and beliefs can be wrong, as well as right.

By the age of 5 years (typically), children understand that other people have minds in a way that has much in common with adults' understanding. They know that a number of different internal states exist and have specific characteristics: thoughts, beliefs, emotions, desires, and perceptions. But they still have difficulty coordinating all of these together until later skill levels at older ages.

Variation within Children

For any given cognitive skill, the child has a developmental range of performance with a lower bound called the functional level – the child's best performance with low support – and an upper bound called the optimal level – the child's best performance with high support. The concept of developmental range is related to, but more specific than, 'Vygotsky's zone of proximal development', which includes 'scaffolding', in which a more skilled partner such as the parent actually performs part of the task jointly with the child. Developmental range encompasses what children can do on their own with and without support, or in optimal or functional (ordinary) conditions. Thus, both individual characteristics (interest, emotion) and environmental contexts shape within-individual variation in cognitive performance.

Tasks

Different tasks often produce variation in performance, even if they appear to elicit similar cognitive processes. An example of the effect of task context on children's performance in numeracy is found in studies of children's ordinality concepts. Children aged between 2 and 4 years will choose the line with more M&Ms when asked which they would rather eat, but when asked about two rows of marbles, "Which one has more?" the 3- and 4-year-olds choose the longer line with fewer marbles. When the choice in the task is based on the child's own motivation (with the M&Ms), children answer correctly, but when they must interpret the experimenter's meaning, they often answer incorrectly. More generally, different tasks elicit different performances in children, even when the tasks seem to have similar cognitive demands. Counting M&Ms is not the same as counting marbles, and counting people or buildings are different in other ways. Children perform differently in different tasks, even when adults see the tasks as equivalent.

Environmental Support

There are countless ways in which the child's environment can facilitate or hinder performance of cognitive skills. Support can take many forms, from physical support of an infant to facilitate a reach, to priming with information to facilitate success on a task. The most consistent example of varying performance in early childhood is the difference between what infants can do when they are or are not in an optimal physical position, usually supported. Eye–hand coordination illustrates this difference dramatically: A 2-month-old infant seeing an object may be able to reach out and grasp it successfully when he or she is positioned at just the right angle to both see the object and easily reach it. In other postures, however, this behavior disappears immediately; and the infant cannot perform it consistently in many different postures until several months later.

Emotions and Internal States

In order to perform at an optimal level, a child's internal state must facilitate performance. State limitations are especially severe for young infants, who must be alert but not overly aroused in order to produce organized voluntary reflex actions. Internal states continue to play a role in cognitive performance throughout life, but as children gain more self-regulatory skills, they are better able to manage internal states in order to attend to cognitive tasks.

Emotional states continue to shape performance and development even when children are alert and focused on a task. Emotions evoke particular patterns of activity and bias behavior in certain directions. In representing self and other, for example, most children from a young age naturally represent the self as good and nice, and they reserve representations of bad and mean for other people. In examining children's stories about positive and negative social interactions, Kurt Fischer, Catherine Ayoub, and their colleagues found this bias of 'me nice but you mean' in most young children. Of course, children sometimes have great fun pretending to be the bad guy as well, but in most situations children growing up in stable, supportive environments show biases toward representing self as positive.

Variation Across Children: Webs and Pathways

Given the consistent sequence and typical timing of development of early skills, what explains the variations that occur across children? Variation in development involves both the speed and timing of change and distinct pathways arising from divergent experiences, abilities, and cultures.

Timing

Children typically develop at different rates across domains, while keeping the same general order of development. They progress through the same levels of skill development, but move more quickly than their peers in some domains and less quickly in others. These variations stem from both different experiences in particular domains and diversity in ability and motivation across children. Some cognitive tests – the Bayley Mental Index, for example – test cognitive skills as if they are a singular set. In such tests, items are ordered in a single line and children are expected to pass nearly all items subsequent to their own highest item. In contrast to this, others – such as the Uzgiris-Hunt test – are composed to examine children's cognitive skills in particular domains of knowledge. In such tests, items are grouped by domain, and children may have a different score, and different ranking amongst their peers, on each scale. Either of these tests can identify differences in timing of skill development, but use of a unitary intelligence test leads to interpretation of children as generally lagging behind or speeding ahead of their peers, whereas use of a domains test leads to identification of differences across distinct contexts and tasks.

Adaptations and Perturbations

Within a traditional framework of development as a ladder going in a single direction, any variation or discrepancy is interpreted as either delay or pathology. However, within a framework viewing development as a web of interconnected skills that arise in specific contexts, variations in development are adaptive responses to differing circumstances. For example, children's representations of self and others as nice and mean in social interactions develop along distinct webs for abused children compared to nonabused and for shy compared to outgoing children.

In stories about positive and negative interactions children who have been maltreated develop along distinct but equally complex pathways: Most commonly, they build complex stories about mean interactions, and simpler, less developmentally mature stories about nice interactions. If assessments require them to focus on positive interactions, their development appears delayed or retarded, but assessments that include their natural focus on negative interactions demonstrate that they function at normal developmental levels in that domain.

Emotional differences in temperament shape children's pathways in another way: Shy (temperamentally inhibited) children show typical development of the representation of self and other as positive (nice, good), but even in pretend play, they often avoid and resist representations of negative interactions, especially when they themselves are represented negatively (as mean or bad). Uninhibited, outgoing children, in contrast, often relish pretending to be mean and thus develop richer, more complex negative representations of self and other.

Cultural Variation

People organize their mental tools and the structure of their cognition through the symbols of their cultures, as Lev Vygotsky emphasized. Cultures shape people in the developmental pathways for building the tools through participation in everyday social interactions and cultural rituals, thus producing important differences in meaning systems. In an example of cultural differences in dominant symbols, people in China and the US give different prominence and meaning to concepts and tools related to shame. Chinese culture makes shame prominent from an early age and uses it to direct behavior constructively toward prescribed cultural norms. It includes tools for coping with shame and related transgressions and teaches these tools and concepts from an early age through storytelling routines by parents and other adults. European-American culture uses shame differently, minimizing its explicit use with young children and providing few culturally supported tools for dealing with it. As a result, Chinese and European-American children differ greatly in their understanding of shame, Chinese children showing basic use of the concept by 2 years of age, whereas European-American children do not use it until around age 7 years. In China, shame is a cultural tool that shapes individual relations to social groups. In the US it is something that is unhealthy and should be avoided. People from each culture have difficulty understanding what shame means in the other.

Cultures shape important differences in many other domains as well, reflecting differential emphases in language and cultural practices. For physical properties of objects, Korean children develop an early focus on actions, while English-speaking children focus more on objects. Korean mothers use more verbs in their speech to children, talking about actions; whereas English-speaking mothers use more nouns, doing more object labeling. Korean children go on to solve certain action puzzles earlier than English-speaking children, such as obtaining an out-of-reach object using a rake-like tool. English-speaking children, in contrast, categorize objects more frequently at earlier ages than the Korean children. In general, cultures create variation in timing and developmental pathways of early skills in particular domains.

Summary

Early cognition proceeds from reflex (reaction) to intentional action and then to representation, building increasing complexity through a series of levels of development. Children build distinct, individual skills, and developmental pathways vary across domains within children, with each child forming a developmental web with many strands. At the same time cognitive skills develop in a predictable, standard hierarchical sequence in each strand, and the timing of major advances seems to correspond to spurts in brain growth. Each individual child varies her or his level of functioning dramatically as a function of support, context, and interest. Different children vary in the specific strands that they build and their connections among strands. These variations result from differences in experience – including both benign cultural experiences and extreme experiences such as abuse – as well as in interests and temperament. In developing skills and understanding, children adapt to the specific environments where they live and to their individual abilities, emotions, and other characteristics.

See also: Amnesia, Infantile; Bayley Scales of Infant Development; Categorization Skills and Concepts; Cognitive Developmental Theories; Developmental Disabilities: Cognitive; Mathematical Reasoning; Milestones: Cognitive; Object Concept; Piaget's Cognitive-Developmental Theory; Reasoning in Early Development; Theory of Mind.

Suggested Readings

Case R (1992) *The Mind's Staircase: Exploring the Causal Underpinnings of Children's Thought and Knowledge.* Hillsdale, NJ: Erlbaum.

Fischer KW, Ayoub CC, Noam GG, Singh I, Maraganore A, and Raya P (1997) Psychopathology as adaptive development along distinctive pathways. *Development and Psychopathology* 9: 749–779.

Fischer KW and Bidell TR (1998) Dynamic development of psychological structures in action and thought. In: Damon W and Lerner RM (eds.) *Handbook of Child Psychology. Vol. 1: Theoretical Models of Human Development,* 5th edn., pp. 467–561. New York: Wiley.

Fischer KW and Bidell TR (2006) Dynamic development of action, thought, and emotion. In: Damon W and Lerner RM (eds.) *Theoretical Models of Human Development. Handbook of Child Psychology,* 6th edn., vol. 1, pp. 313–399. New York: Wiley.

Fischer KW and Hogan AE (1989) The big picture for infant development: Levels and variations. In: Lockman J and Hazen N (eds.) *Action in Social Context: Perspectives on Early Development,* pp. 275–305. New York: Plenum.

Gardner H (1983) *Frames of Mind: The Theory of Multiple Intelligences.* New York: Basic Books.

Gopnik A, Meltzoff A, and Kuhn PK (1999) *The Scientist in the Crib: What Early Learning Tells Us about the Mind.* New York: William Morrow & Company.

Gruber HE and Vonèche JJ (eds.) (1977) *The Essential Piaget: An Interpretive Reference and Guide.* New York: Basic Books.

Mascolo MJ and Fischer KW (2005) The new constructivism: The dynamic development of psychological structures. In: Hopkins B, Barre RG, Michel GF, and Rochat P (eds.) *Cambridge Encyclopedia of Child Development*, pp. 49–63. Cambridge, UK: Cambridge University Press.

Stern DN (1991) *Diary of a Baby.* London: Fontana.

Vygotsky LS (1978) *Mind in Society: The Development of Higher Psychological Processes.* Cambridge, MA: Harvard University Press.

Wellman H (1992) *The Child's Theory of Mind.* Cambridge, MA: MIT Press.

Wellman H, Cross D, and Watson J (2001) Meta-analysis of theory-of-mind development: The truth about false belief. *Child Development* 72: 655–684.

Relevant Websites

http://www.gse.harvard.edu – The Dynamic Development Laboratory.
http://www.lectica.info – The Lectical Assessment System for Skill Complexity.
http://naeyc.org – National Association for the Education of Young Children.
http://www.unige.ch – The Jean Piaget Archives.
http://www.piaget.org – The Jean Piaget Society.
http://www.marxists.org – The Lev Vygotsky Archive.

Cognitive Developmental Theories

G S Halford, Griffith University, Brisbane, QLD, Australia

© 2008 Elsevier Inc. All rights reserved.

Glossary

Cognition – Includes thinking, language, learning, memory, and perception.

Epistemology – Theory of knowledge.

Natural kinds – Things that occur in nature, such as plant and animal categories. As children mature their understanding of the world and their ability to reason about it both increase to a remarkable extent. Cognitive developmental theories are designed to account for this process. There were important pioneering theories by Piaget and Vygotsky, whose ideas are still influential, but their ideas have been incorporated into a number of new theories, which we will outline.

Prototypic category – One based on the most typical example of the category (e.g., a prototype of the dog category would be the most typical dog). Prototypes are acquired automatically by exposure to examples of the category and are possibly the earliest categories to develop.

> **Transitive inference** – If there is a relation R between a and b, and between a and c, and if R is a transitive relation, then the relation R will exist between b and c (i.e., a R b and b R c implies a R c). An example would be a > b and b > c implies a > c.
> **Unary relation** – A relation with one argument. An example would be category membership – Rover is a dog, meaning that Rover is a member of the set of dogs.

Introduction

Theories of cognitive development are reviewed, beginning with pioneering theories by Piaget and Vygotsky. Neo-Piagetian theories which integrated Piagetian theory with other conceptions of cognition were developed by McLaughlin, Pascual-Leone, Case, Fischer, and Chapman. Complexity theories propose that children become capable of dealing with more complex relations as they develop. Information processing theories, neural net theories, dynamic systems theories, and theories of reasoning processes all provide models of the reasoning processes employed by children at different ages. Microgenetic analysis methods are used to study the processes of transition from one level of thinking to the next.

Piaget and Vygotsky

Some of the core ideas in Piaget's theory will be outlined first, because it is the most comprehensive and elaborate of the early theories of cognitive development.

A central idea in Piaget's theory was genetic epistemology, meaning that we can investigate how we understand the world by studying the way that understanding develops in children. An important aspect of our knowledge of the world is that objects are real and permanent, existing independently of our perception of them. How we know this has been an issue for philosophers for centuries. Piaget investigated how knowledge of object permanence develops in children by studying their reactions to vanished objects. The idea is that if an infant knows that an object still exists when it disappears from view the infant should look toward the point of disappearance, and perhaps even try to reach for the no-longer-visible object. Piaget concluded that infants had only a very rudimentary understanding of object permanence in the first few months, and that it developed over the first 2 years in a succession of substages. His conclusions have been modified by subsequent researchers, some of whom have claimed that infants' object permanence knowledge is greater than Piaget recognized. Nevertheless, the idea of investigating children's object knowledge by assessing their reactions to vanished objects persists.

Another of Piaget's key ideas was that 'logic is the mirror of thought', meaning that logic reflects properties that are inherent in thought. He tried to define the nature of thought by specifying the logico-mathematical concepts to which it was equivalent. These included notions such as function, operation, group, and lattice. However, he did not claim that human thought conformed to logic as understood by logicians, but was based on quasi-logical ideas that he termed 'psycho-logics'. Research in the latter half of the twentieth century led to reduced emphasis on logic as a basis for human reasoning. We now judge human reasoning by our ability to adapt to the environment rather than by conformity to logic. However, some of Piaget's important observations of children's reasoning remain.

Piaget carried out very extensive empirical investigations of the development of infants' and children's cognitions, and he attempted to define the way children's reasoning developed by a succession of distinct psychologics, that have come to be known as 'stages' of cognitive development. The first was the sensorimotor stage, lasting from birth to about 1.5–2 years, characterized by structured, organized activity, but not thought. During this stage actions become integrated into a self-regulating system of actions. Piaget believed that the concept of objects as real and permanent emerged as this structure was elaborated. The preoperational stage lasted from approximately 2–7 years, and during this time symbolic functions were developed, including play, drawing, imagery, and language. Thought at this stage was conceptualized in terms of what Piaget called 'function logic', the essential idea of which is representation of a link between two variables. At the concrete operational stage, lasting from 8 to about 14 years, thought was conceptualized in terms of what Piaget called 'groupings' which included a logical operation. The essential idea here is the ability to compose classes, sets, relations, or functions, into integrated systems.

Concepts such as conservation (invariance of quantity, number, weight, and volume), seriation or ordering of objects, transitive inference, classification, and spatial perspectives emerge as a result of the more elaborate thought structures that develop during this time. At the formal operational stage, beginning in adolescence, the ability to compose concrete operations into higher level structures emerges, with the result that thought has greater autonomy and flexibility.

Cognitive development depended, according to Piaget, on 'assimilation' of experience to cognitive structures with 'accommodation' of the structure to the new information. The combination of assimilation and accommodation amounts to a process of self-regulation which Piaget termed 'equilibration'. He rejected theories based on association, arguing that these were inadequate to account for cognitive development, an idea that was often thought almost heretical at the time, but would be widely accepted now. In many ways his conceptions anticipated modern conceptions of information processing and dynamic systems, to be discussed later.

A core topic in Piaget's cognitive development research was conservation, which entails recognizing that quantity remains constant when transformed without adding or removing anything. Suppose a child is shown two equal quantities of liquid in identical glasses, then one quantity is transformed by pouring it to a taller and narrower vessel. The classical Piagetian finding is that young children tend to say the quantities are now unequal because the taller and narrower vessel makes the quantity appear more. The finding that young children give nonconservation answers to these tests has been replicated many times, but there has been little consensus about the correct explanation.

Children who give nonconservation answers typically recognize that the quantity will be the same again if poured back; they also recognize that it is still the same material, that nothing has been added or subtracted and that there have been changes in two variables, that is, that the quantity increased in height but decreased in breadth. There has therefore been some mystification as to why they give nonconservation answers. Proponents of the Piagetian position held that nonconservation answers represented genuine lack of understanding of the invariance of quantity, but others have proposed that the child was misled by the transformation which made it appear that quantity or number had changed, that the child misinterpreted the words used in the test believing, for example, that 'more' referred to height of the liquid, rather than to quantity, or that there was a conflict between knowledge of conservation and appearance of the display. We will consider how some more recent theories deal with this issue later in this article.

The work of the Piagetian school has been controversial, but his empirical findings have been widely replicated. That is, children have been found to perform as Piaget reported 'on the tests he used'. For example, children undoubtedly respond as Piaget observed on the conservation tests discussed above. The major challenges to his findings have been based on different methods of assessment, the claim being that his methods underestimated the cognitive capabilities of young children. However, these claims have also been subject to controversy, and the assessments that were proposed as improvements on Piaget's techniques have not always been validated. There were also some hundreds of studies designed to train children in the concepts that they did not understand, thereby demonstrating that cognitive development could be accelerated, and depended more on experience than on development of thought structures. However, these studies did not completely eliminate limitations to what children understand at particular ages. The stage concept has also been criticized on the grounds that development is gradual and experience-based rather than sudden or 'stage-like', and the concurrence between acquisitions at the same stage has often not been as close as Piagetian theory might be taken to imply.

The work of Vygotsky was the other major influence on research into the development of thinking, and his contribution is becoming increasingly influential even today. Three of Vygotsky's most important contributions were his ideas on the relation between thought and language, his emphasis on the role of culture in the development of thinking, and the zone of proximal development. Early in the history of cognitive development research there was considerable debate as to whether thought depends on language development, or the reverse. Vygotsky proposed that thought and language have different origins both in evolution and in development. Language was initially social in character, while problem solving was initiated in motor processes. Language and thought develop independently for some time after infancy; then the young child develops egocentric speech, which is the beginning of the representational function. Finally, children develop 'inner speech' which serves the symbolic function of thought. Vygotsky emphasized the interaction between biological maturation and social experience. As the child matured, language became an increasingly important influence on the development of thought, and was the chief means by which culture was absorbed by the child.

Vygotsky proposed that the cultural input was essential to the cognitive development of the child. One of its effects is to help the child to relate concepts to larger systems, while another is to increase conscious awareness of what the child has learned. However Vygotsky emphasized that culture was not simply absorbed, but there is an interaction between spontaneous development and cultural influences, each contributing to the other. Instruction is founded on development, but instruction also influences development. This is consistent with contemporary ideas on neural plasticity, which mean that environmental factors, including experience and learning, can influence the development of the structure and function of the brain. An important consequence of this theory is Vygotsky's concept of the 'zone of proximal development', which means that new developments occur close to existing cognitive abilities. New concepts are not simply absorbed but are integrated with the mental processes of the developing child. Consequently instruction will be effective to the extent that it introduces concepts that relate to, but are just slightly more advanced than, the child's current level of understanding.

In some respects this is consistent with Piaget's notion that new knowledge is assimilated to existing structure. This is part of a larger picture in which both Piaget and Vygotsky saw cognitive development as an active organizing process that tends toward an equilibrium with its own internal processes and with the external environment. However Vygotsky differs from Piaget in placing more emphasis on cultural input, including formal instruction, in the cognitive development of the child. Piaget's work had greater early influence, but the impact of Vygotsky's work is increasing at what appears to be an accelerating rate. Both continue to have an influence on education theory.

Neo-Piagetian Theories

There were several theorists who proposed alternative explanations for Piaget's observations of children's cognitive development. G. Harry McLaughlin proposed that a child's reasoning was determined by the number of concepts that could be considered simultaneously. He proposed that the progression from infancy, to early childhood, middle childhood, and adolescence, which Piaget characterized as sensorimotor, preoperational, concrete operational, and formal operational stages, respectively, required $2^0 = 1$, $2^1 = 2$, $2^2 = 4$, and $2^3 = 8$ concepts to be considered simultaneously. This lead was taken up by a number of theorists who proposed that children's cognitive development was driven primarily by increased ability to process information. Juan Pascual-Leone proposed that cognitive development depended on increases in central-computing space, or M-space, that corresponded to the number of separate schemes that they could coordinate. The value of M was $a + 1$ at age 3 years age and increased to $a + 7$ at age 15 years. He showed empirically that older children can understand more complex concepts than younger children, where complexity is defined by the M-space required to represent the concept.

Robbie Case proposed that cognitive development depends on children learning to make better use of the available capacity. Total processing space is constant over age, but older children use their capacity more efficiently, leaving more of it available for other tasks. Short-term memory span increases with age because rehearsal becomes more efficient, using less capacity, and leaving more capacity for storage. In a number of ingenious experiments, Case and his collaborators showed that if adults' rehearsal efficiency was reduced to that of 5-year-olds' by using unfamiliar materials, their short-term memory spans for the same materials were correspondingly reduced to those of 5-year-olds'. Case also acknowledged subsequently that processing capacity increases with maturation of the nervous system, particularly the frontal lobes. Case's work remains important because it was the first to demonstrate that cognitive development depends on the efficiency with which available information processing capacity was utilized.

Later Case developed the concept of central conceptual structures, a network of semantic nodes and relations that passes through a sequence of four major neo-Piagetian stages, that Case labels sensorimotor, inter-relational, dimensional, and vectorial (or abstract dimensional). Each major stage is divided into substages known as unifocal, bifocal, elaborated coordination, and a preliminary substage that represents the transition from one major stage to another. Progression through the substages was due to working memory growth, under the influence of both maturation and experience. The transition to higher stages is achieved by coordinating two existing structures into a higher order structure. Case's theory has been applied to many domains, including science, mathematics, space, music, understanding narrative, social roles, and motor development.

Kurt Fischer's theory was based on development of cognitive skill in controlling sources of variation in a person's behavior, and was influenced by the work of Jerome Bruner as well as Piaget. There are three major stages or tiers: the sensorimotor, representational, and iconic symbolic. As with Case's theory, there is a recurring cycle of four levels within each of the major stages, and the highest level of one stage is shared with the lowest level of the next.

There is much common ground among the neo-Piagetian theories, and Michael Chapman attempted to capture this in an integrated theory. He argued that the capacity required for a given form of reasoning depends on the number variables to which values have to be assigned. The class inclusion concept has been found difficult for young children and is usually mastered in middle childhood. Suppose a child is shown some red beads (A), and some blue beads (A′), all of which are wooden (B), and there are more red than blue beads. Therefore, A and A′ are included in B (A and A′ = B), so there must be more of B than of A. However, young children have difficulty recognizing this and commonly say there are more red beads than wooden beads. Solving the problem depends on recognizing A = red beads, A′ = blue beads, and B = wooden beads. That is, it entails assigning values to three variables (A, A′, and B) that represent the classification hierarchy. Therefore, Chapman seems to have been the first to realize explicitly that the best way to analyze complexity of cognitive tasks is to determine the number of variables that have to be instantiated in parallel.

Complexity Theories

Two complexity theories have been developed. One is 'cognitive complexity and control theory', by Douglas Frye and Philip Zelazo and the other is 'relational complexity theory' by Graeme Halford, William Wilson, and Steven Phillips. Relational complexity refers to the number of entities that are related in a single cognitive representation. It corresponds to number of slots or 'arity' of relations.

A binary relation has two slots: for example, larger-than(—,—) has a slot for a larger entity and one for a smaller entity. Each slot can be filled in a variety of ways, such as larger-than(elephant, mouse), larger-than(mountain, molehill), etc. Complexity of relations can be defined by the number of slots:

- Unary relations have one slot: for example, class membership, as in 'dog' (Fido).
- Binary relations have two slots: for example, 'larger' (elephant, mouse).
- Ternary relations have three slots: for example, 'addition' (2, 3, 5).
- Quaternary relations: for example, proportion (2/3 = 6/9).

Because each slot can be filled in a variety of ways, a slot corresponds to a variable or dimension. Thus, a unary relation is a set of points on one dimension, a binary relation is a set of points in two-dimensional space, and so on. In general, an N-ary relation is a set of points in N-dimensional space.

The relational complexity metric has been applied to cognitive development, to adult cognition, to higher animals such as chimpanzees, and to industrial contexts, including air traffic control. There is a broad correspondence between levels of relational complexity and the phenomena that Piaget attributed to stages. Unary, binary, ternary, and quaternary relations correspond to preconceptual, intuitive, concrete operational, and formal operational stages, respectively. Processing capacity is an enabling factor, and concept acquisition is a function of experience, given that the relevant processing capacity is available.

The median ages at which each level of relational complexity is attained are: unary relations at 1 year, binary relations at 1.5–2 years, ternary relations at 5 years, and quaternary relations at 11 years. Concepts at a given level of complexity do not develop synchronously but are acquired by a biological growth function. Thus, ternary relations are acquired by approximately 20% of 4-year-olds, 50% of 5-year-olds, and 80% of 8–9-year-olds.

Empirical evidence suggests that a quaternary relation is the most complex that adults can process in parallel, though a minority of people can probably process quinary relations under optimal conditions. This is a 'soft' limit, meaning that increased complexity produces increased errors and decision times, rather than sudden failure. In order to handle more complex concepts, mechanisms for reducing processing loads are required. Relational complexity theory includes two such mechanisms, conceptual chunking and segmentation.

Conceptual chunking involves recoding concepts into less complex relations. However, there is a temporary loss of access to chunked relations. For example, 'speed = distance/time', is a ternary relation, but speed can be recoded into a unary relation, 'speed' (60 kmph) as when speed is indicated by the position of a pointer on a dial. However, the chunked representation does not permit us to answer questions such as "How does speed change if we cover the same distance in half the time?" To answer that we have to return to a representation of the ternary relation.

Segmentation entails breaking tasks into less complex steps, which can be processed serially. Strategies and algorithms are common ways of doing this: for example, adding one column at a time in multidigit addition.

Chunking and segmentation skills are important components of expertise. They are two of the processes that increase with age, and therefore they are important factors accounting for the way cognitive development occurs.

We will illustrate how relational complexity theory can be used to analyze class inclusion, using the example of fruit, including apples and nonapples. Fruit is assigned to the superordinate slot because it includes apples and nonapples fruit. Thus, the assignment of classes to slots in the hierarchy depends on processing the relations between the three classes, and is ternary relational.

Transitive inference is also ternary relational, according to relational complexity analyses. Consider the problem: Tom is taller than Mike, Peter is taller than Tom, who is the tallest? Process analyses have shown that the transitive inference can be made by integrating the premises into the ternary relation, Peter 'taller than' Tom 'taller than' Mike. It has been shown that integrating the premises into this ternary relation is the main information processing demand of transitive inference, and the main cause of cognitive effort, in adults and in children.

Transitivity and class inclusion are superficially different, yet they are structurally similar, and both entail ternary relations, as **Figure 1** shows. This is an example of how tasks can have equivalent relational complexity despite different domains and different test procedures. Transitivity and class inclusion were both originally Piagetian tasks, and the

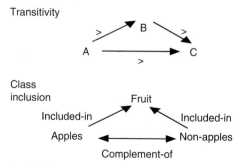

Figure 1 Similar structures in two ternary relational tasks, transitivity and class inclusion. Adapted from figure 4 in Halford GS and Andrews G (2004) The development of deductive reasoning: How important is complexity? *Thinking and Reasoning* 10: 123–145.

causes of children's failures have been controversial, but it appears that complexity is at least part of the explanation for the difficulties that young children encounter in these tasks.

Relational complexity theory proposes that understanding of conservation depends on learning relations between quantity and other dimensions like height and width. Piaget proposed that children have to recognize that when (for example) liquid is poured into a taller and narrower vessel, any increase in height is compensated by a decrease in breadth. Paradoxically however, children may recognize that width of a liquid had decreased as its height increased, yet they still fail to conserve. Relational complexity theory proposes that the reason is that compensation is a binary relation, between length and density, whereas understanding conservation requires a ternary relation between three variables, height, width, and quantity. This means conservation is a ternary relational concept, which should be attained at a median age of 5 years, like other ternary relational concepts. There is empirical evidence that supports this.

Cognitive complexity and control theory assesses complexity by the number of hierarchical levels of rule required for the task. A simple task consists of rules that link two variables, such as an antecedent and a consequent, whereas complex tasks have higher-order rules that modify the lower level rules. This adds another level to the hierarchy. The theory has been applied to the dimensional change card sort task, which has been an effective predictor of a number of important cognitive attainments in children, including theory of mind, to be considered later in this article. In a simple sorting task, cards are sorted by shape or by color, but not both. For example, a green circle might be assigned to the green category (indicated by a template comprising a green triangle) and a red triangle to the red category (indicated by a template comprising a red circle). In a complex task, sorting depends on whether the higher-order rule specifies sorting by color, as above, or by shape. If sorting is by shape, the green circle is sorted with the red circle and the red triangle is sorted with the green triangle. Children typically process a single rule by 2 years of age, a pair of rules by 3 years of age, and a pair of rules embedded under a higher order rule by 4 years of age. The transition to higher levels is achieved by reflective abstraction.

Information Processing Theory

Some theories have been based on the idea that thinking is basically a computational process that can be simulated on a computer. One example of this approach is the Q-SOAR theory of Tony Simon and David Klahr, designed to simulate children's acquisition of number conservation in a study by Rochel Gelman. Children are asked to say whether two equal rows are the same or different based on counting, then are asked to say whether they are still the same (or different) after a transformation, such as lengthening one of the rows. Inability to answer this question is represented in Q-SOAR as an impasse. The model resolves this by quantifying the sets before and after the transformation, noting that they are the same, and develops the knowledge that the transformation did not change the numerosities, and therefore is conserving.

Implicit vs. Explicit Cognition

Human reasoning, whether in children or adults, is not always conscious and intentional, but sometimes occurs at a more automatic, unconscious level. This distinction has been captured in a theory developed by Andy Clark and Annette Karmiloff-Smith. Implicit knowledge is 'knowledge in the system but not knowledge to the system'. Implicit knowledge is an effective basis for performance, but is not consciously accessible, and cannot be modified intentionally or strategically. At the next level knowledge is accessible and modifiable, but not available to consciousness and cannot be reported verbally. At the highest level, knowledge is explicit, conscious, and can be described verbally. The transition from implicit to explicit knowledge is produced by representational redescription, which means that we take our implicit knowledge and represent it verbally, in a conscious form. An example would be when we first learn a skill we can perform the relevant actions, but it is only later that we can describe what we do, and then we become capable of consciously modifying our performance.

Knowledge of Mental States

One of the most important acquisitions children make is theory of mind, or understanding of other people's mental states. One test for theory of mind is the appearance-reality task. Children are shown a cutout of a white bird, which is then covered by a blue filter, and they are asked what color the bird is really (white), and what color does it appear when viewed through the filter (blue). Children below about 4–5 years of age have difficulty recognizing that the way the bird appears is different from the way it really is, and they tend to answer that the bird is white and looks white, or that it is blue and looks blue.

Both cognitive complexity and control theory and relational complexity theory propose that inferences about other people's mental states are difficult for young children because of their complexity. Understanding the difference between the way things appear to people and the way they really are depends on understanding the relations between three variables. First there is the attribute of an object (its color in the example above). Then there is the way an object appears to people (the percept), such as whether they see it as white or blue. The relation between these two is influenced by a third variable, the viewing condition, such as whether the object is viewed directly or through a colored filter. Ability to understand how objects appear to people depends on ability to relate these three variables.

Dynamic Systems Theories

Dynamic systems theories are complex and sophisticated, but we can present the essential ideas. Technically, a dynamic system is a formal system the state of which depends on its state at a previous point in time. Dynamic systems are self-regulating, meaning that they are the result of the interaction of variables, and processes, which combine spontaneously to achieve a stable state or equilibrium. One reason why dynamic systems are important to cognitive development is that they can account for different types of cognitive growth that have been observed. That is, development is sometimes slow and steady, while at other times sudden jumps occur, resulting in new levels of functioning that appear quite different from anything that was there before. This is what led theorists like Piaget to propose that cognitive development occurs in stages, such that entirely new cognitive processes emerge when the transition is made to a new stage. Dynamic systems can show how a complex, self-regulating system can emerge from the interaction of a few variables, and offer natural interpretations of concepts such as equilibration and self-regulation which are at the core of the theories of both Piaget and Vygotsky. Links have also been made between dynamic systems models and neural net models, to be considered below.

An example of a dynamic system would be children's acquisition of the concept of conservation, considered earlier. Children of 3–4 years of age typically think that, when liquid is poured from a short and wide to a tall and narrow vessel the quantity increases, because they see the large increase in height. Understanding that the quantity remains constant typically develops spontaneously, and often appears quite suddenly, so that in a short time the child might switch from being sure that the quantity increases to being sure that it is constant. What appears to happen is that the children start to relate the three variables of height, width, and quantity, as mentioned before. That is, they realize that when you take both height and width into account, quantity remains constant, or is 'conserved'. Here the three variables are brought into a new integration, which creates a new form of stability. These variables are also related to observations that nothing was added when the liquid was poured, and that it would be same again if poured back. Quantities that formerly seemed to increase or decrease as liquids were poured from vessel to vessel are now seen as invariant over those transformations, and a lot of additional information is integrated with this conception. This development is spontaneous and is not usually taught. Indeed, attempts to teach it might be ineffective until the child is ready to make the new integration. This illustrates the self-regulating nature of cognitive development.

Microgenetic Analysis

Microgenetic methods entail detailed analysis of strategies that children use in reasoning about a concept. This enables researchers to obtain information about the processes of cognitive development, the factors that influence it, about individual differences, and how strategies for performing tasks are formed. When they reason children typically have more than one strategy available at any one time, so strategies progress in overlapping waves, and development consists of selectively strengthening some strategies. An example would be investigation of how young children learn to reach for an object using one of a number of tools supplied. The task was set up so that success depended on choosing a tool that was long enough and that had an appropriate fitting on the end. For some children modeling was used to demonstrate the appropriate action. Later a hint, suggesting the right tool to use, was provided. Children's actions progressed over the course of three problems. They began by reaching without using the tool, or by asking the parent to obtain the toy. Later they learned to use the tool. Once the children learned a tool-using strategy, it was transferred to new problems by analogical reasoning. Detailed individual differences in strategies were observed, and proficiency in the immediately preceding component of a strategy was the best predictor of progression to the succeeding component. This can be seen as illustrating dynamic development. That is, children spontaneously make the transition to a new strategy when they have mastered the previous one, consistent with Vygotsky's theory. Spontaneous switching between different strategies is also sometimes observed before the transition.

Microgenetic analysis has also been applied to conservation acquisition. Children often progressed from explanations of conservation based on one dimension (e.g., height) to explanations based on the transformation, such as pouring from one vessel to another. There are many different patterns, and the number of different explanations given was a good predictor of conservation acquisition, consistent with dynamic systems theories. It also suggests that cognitive development can progress by different pathways, but also that conflict between height and quantity might be a stimulus to conservation acquisition. Resolution of this conflict by recognizing that compensating changes in height and width are consistent with constant quantity would be a strong motivation for conservation. This would integrate the three relevant variables, as proposed earlier in this article.

Theories of Reasoning Processes

Some theories have been devoted to understanding processes that are employed in reasoning. One of the most fundamental processes in human reasoning is analogy. Indeed, natural, everyday reasoning, as distinct from reasoning by a specialist, might be considered more analogical than logical. Analogies are used in mathematics, science, art, politics, and many other areas of life. Analogy is also important in knowledge acquisition, so new concepts can often be explained by analogy with a concept that is already understood. For example, electricity might be explained by analogy with water running down pipes, so diameter of a pipe corresponds to diameter of a conductor, and so on. Concrete teaching aids, such as those used in school mathematics, are essentially analogs.

Analogy is a mapping from a base or source to a target, where both source and target are defined as sets of relations. Typically, relations are mapped but attributes are not, and the relations that are mapped are those that enter into a coherent structure. The mapping is validated by structural correspondence between relations in source and relations in target. Proportional analogies have the form A : B : : C : D (e.g., horse : foal : : cat : kitten). Horse is mapped to cat and foal to kitten. The relation, parenthood, between horse and foal corresponds to the relation between cat and kitten. Performance on these analogies depends on children having the requisite knowledge of relations. Thus young children could understand the analogy between melting chocolate and melting snowmen (i.e., solid chocolate:melted chocolate::solid snowmen:melted snowmen) because the relations between solid and melted chocolate or between solid and melted snowmen, were familiar to them. Relational complexity theory predicts that if the requisite knowledge is available, analogies based on unary relations should be possible at 1 year, those based on binary relations should be possible from 2 years, and those based on ternary relations at 3 years.

Much human reasoning has been found to be performed by mental models, in which the premises are represented by concrete analogs. We will consider conditional reasoning, using a major premise, p implies q, represented symbolically as $p \rightarrow q$. This premise would be represented initially as a mental model with this form:

$$p \quad q$$
$$\ldots$$

The first line represents a state of affairs in which p and q are both true, and there is a link between them. The dots on the next line represent implicit recognition that other possibilities exist. The representations will be 'fleshed out' to give explicit representation of other possibilities as follows (where $\neg p$ represents 'not p'):

$$p \quad q$$
$$\neg p \quad \neg q$$

Then the representation is further fleshed out as follows:

$$p \quad q$$
$$\neg p \quad \neg q$$
$$\neg p \quad q$$

This corresponds to the standard (canonical) interpretation of a conditional. The fleshing out is governed by availability of examples in memory. Consider, for example, the premise:

If X is a dog, then X has legs.
We might represent this mentally as:
Dog legs.

Now it is easy to retrieve from memory cases of nondogs that have legs (e.g., tables). Now we elaborate our mental model as follows:

Dog legs
Table legs.

Now we will not commit the fallacy of inferring that if something has legs it is a dog (known as affirmation of the consequent) because our mental model includes cases of nondogs with legs. Inference is also influenced by the complexity of the resulting representation, and children of 5–7 years of age will only be able to add one relation to the simplest model, which permits some correct inferences but also makes them susceptible to fallacies.

Theories of Infant Cognitive Development

A number of theories have been devoted to understanding the precursors of later reasoning in the cognition of infants. Image schemas in the first year of life are seen as building blocks of later reasoning. They include self-motion, animate-motion, agency, path, support, and containment. Image schemas are really implicit concepts, and they comprise linked elements, but the components of an image schema are 'fused' and are not accessible to analysis. Infants are also known to recognize cause, possibly based on some kind of innate predisposition.

Infants also have an ability to represent structure, independent of content. Seven-month-old infants who listened to 2 min segments of utterances such as 'ga ti ga', of 'li ti li' could distinguish between further utterances that that were either consistent (e.g., 'wo fe wo') or inconsistent (e.g., 'wo fe fe') with the original sequences. This was indicated because infants paid more attention to utterances with the novel structure, even though both consistent and inconsistent sentences had novel content. Thus they appeared to have represented the structure independent of content. Although this is a long way from the reasoning of adults or even older children, it is an important step toward symbolic processes.

Infant's tendency to attend to novel or surprising events has also been used to assess their quantitative knowledge. First, infants aged 6–12 months discriminate between displays with different numbers of elements, indicating that they have some conception of number. From around 5 months of age they recognize when something has been added or removed from a small set of objects. Infants also demonstrate awareness of ordinal relations such as ascending or descending sequences.

Some theories attempt to explain infant's early quantitative knowledge. The 'accumulator model' proposes that the nervous system has a pulse generator that generates activity at a constant rate, and there is a gate that opens to allow energy through to an accumulator. The gate opens for a set amount of time for each item. The total energy accumulated is an analog representation of number. For example '–' represents one, '——' represents two, and '———' represents three. According to the 'object file model' infants construct an imagistic representation of the experimental scene, creating one object-file for each object in the array. These representations of numerosity are implicit in the sense that there is no distinct symbol for the numerosity of the set and there is no counting process.

Infants can form prototypic categories. This has been demonstrated by familiarizing infants with a number of different exemplars of the same category (e.g., dogs, horses), then testing them with a novel stimulus from the same category (different dog and different horse) and a novel stimulus from a different category (a car). Children as young as 4 months of age showed a preference for the car, indicating that they had formed a category of dogs and horses.

Categories develop rapidly in early childhood and even young children can make inductive inferences about categories that go beyond observable properties. Children as young as 2–3 years of age can infer properties on the basis of category membership, even when the relevant properties are unobservable to the child. For example, if they are shown a picture of a dog and told that dog has a spleen inside, they will attribute this property to other dogs, rather than to similar animals that are not dogs.

One theorist, Susan Gelman, proposed that children's categories are based on 'essences', which are unobservable properties that cause things to be the way they are. Children's categories are based on early recognition of the causal basis of the properties of natural kinds. Another theorist, Frank Keil, showed that categories remain constant, despite changes in appearance or attempts at transformation. By about 8 years of age children recognize that an animal cannot be converted into a different species by changing their appearance or the way they behave. By contrast, children recognize that artifacts can be transformed. Thus, they appear to recognize that natural kinds have certain essential properties that are inherent in their composition, whereas artifacts can be transformed by human intervention.

Understanding the Physical World

Young children's understanding of physical phenomena is influenced by their ability to deal with complexity. If children are shown an apparatus in which a marble inserted at the top either always exits below the insertion point, or always crosses to the other side, 3-year-olds could predict on which side the marble would exit. Thus, they succeed if the exit point is always predictable by the insertion point. However if exiting below the insertion point, or crossing to the other side is indicated by whether a light was on or off, they do not succeed. Thus they succeed when the exit point was influenced by only one variable, point of insertion, but they could not take account of both side of insertion and the light signal. Four-year-olds could handle both. Thus, ability to handle the extra variable increases with age.

Children's concept of the Earth has been investigated by asking them to draw the Earth with people living on it, and to indicate the position of the sun, moon, and stars. Their conceptions reflected their attempts to reconcile what they had been taught about the Earth being a sphere with their everyday observations that it appears flat. Thus, children would draw a flattened sphere with people standing on top, or a hollow sphere with a horizontal platform inside for people to stand on, or even dual earths, one round and one flat. Their mental models showed some consistency, so if they thought that the Earth was spherical they were less likely to think it was possible to fall off the edge. To integrate everyday observation with what they are taught about the Earth being spherical children would need to know that, for example, the huge diameter of the earth makes it appear flat at any point on it surface.

The balance scale was widely used in Piagetian investigations of cognitive development. It comprises a beam balanced on a fulcrum with equally spaced pegs on each side on which weights can be placed. The beam balances when the product of weight and distance on the left equals the product of weight and distance on the right. Children's understanding of the balance scale can be defined by rules that develop progressively: with rule I children consider only weights, with rule II they also consider distance, but only if weights on the two sides are equal. With rule III they consider weight first, then distance but had difficulty if the greater weight occurred on one side and greater distance on the other. With rule IV they apply the correct principle, according to which the side with the greater product of weight and distance, goes down, but if the products on the two sides are equal the beam balances. Children progressed from rule I at 5 years of age to rule III in adolescence. Rule IV tended to be rare even in adults.

Children as young as 2–3 years have some understanding of the balance scale, and they can discriminate weights with distance constant, or distances with weight constant. These entail representing the binary relation between two weights, or two distances, according to relational complexity theory.

Neural Net Model of Balance Scale Understanding

Neural net models are designed to simulate cognitive processes by units that are connected together by variable weights. The units represent collections of neurons, and they have theoretical activation values that are intended to correspond to activations of neurons. The connection weights simulate associations between different sets of neurons. Activation is transmitted from one set of neurons to another with a strength that is determined by the weights (**Figure 2**).

Neural net models have been widely used to account for cognitive processes in children and adults and we will illustrate these developments with a model by J. McClelland of children's understanding of the balance scale, shown in **Figure 2**. There are four sets of five input units. One set, on the left side, represents number of weights, from one to five, and another set represents the number of weights on the right. The remaining sets represent number of steps from the fulcrum, on both left and right sides. There are four 'hidden' units, which are connected to the input units by connections with variable connections. Two of the hidden units compare weights and two compare distances. The hidden units are connected to the output units by another set of variable connections. Activation spreads from input to hidden units and then to output units. In **Figure 2**, the weights and distances from the fulcrum are indicated by black input units. Activations of the hidden and output units are also represented by units filled in with black. The weights are adjusted by a learning process so that the output units predict the balance state. The model's performance shows a good correspondence to the development of children's knowledge of the balance scale. Neural net models

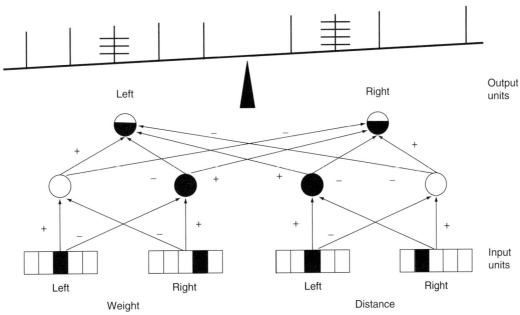

Figure 2 Neural net model of the balance scale by J. McClelland. Shading represents activation of neural units. The input units represent the weights and distances from the fulcrum and correspond to the weights and distances shown on the balance. Adapted from figure 22.1 from Halford GS (2005) Development of Thinking. In: Holyoak KJ and Morrison RG (eds.) *Cambridge Handbook of Thinking and Reasoning*, p. 533, by permission of Cambridge University Press.

are often important for the properties that emerge as they learn. In this case, training of the neural net results in the units representing larger weights, or larger distances, having greater connections to the hidden units. Thus, metrics for weight and distance emerge as a result of training, and are not predefined in the net. This is a good example of the way structure can emerge from experience with a set of phenomena.

Neuroscience Approaches

Some of the theories considered so far propose that children become able to process more complex concepts as they grow older. A probable reason for this is that the amount of information they can process at any one time increases with age. That is, their information processing capacity increases. Evidence has also been provided by Robert Kail that speed in making decisions increases with development, and this might be linked to an increase with capacity.

A theory by Quartz and Sejnowski suggests a neural basis for this capacity increase with development. They propose that, with age, increase in the number of synapses and the number of connections between neurons is responsible for this increase in capacity, and that this process is influenced by interaction with the environment. This enables more complex representations to be constructed as the child matures. It also has the important implication that brain capacity is influenced by what the child experiences during development. Spurts in brain growth, especially in the frontal regions of the brain have also been linked to transitions to higher levels of reasoning.

Summary

Cognitive developmental theories are attempts to define and explain the changes in children's concepts, their thinking and their understanding of the world, over the course of development. The pioneering theories of Piaget and Vygotsky were taken up by a number of other theorists, including the neo-Piagetian theorists, but also by others who emphasized the acquisition and organization of knowledge, and the increasing complexity of children's cognition as they developed. Some theories emphasize the nature of reasoning processes, including analogy and mental models, while others, such as dynamic systems theories and neural net models, define the processes of development. Still others, such as microgenetic analyses, are primarily concerned with ways of analyzing the development of children's cognition. Theories of the origin of cognition in infancy are also reviewed.

Although there are many theories, they tend to be complementary rather than contradictory. Cognitive development is influenced by increases in capacity to process complex information, as emphasized by neo-Piagetian theories, but acquisition and organization of knowledge are also important. Theories of reasoning processes do not contradict any of this, but relate it to what we know about how reasoning is carried out. Earlier theories, including those of Piaget and Vygotsky, have not been so much discredited as absorbed into larger bodies of knowledge. This has given us a much richer understanding of how thinking develops in children.

See also: Categorization Skills and Concepts; Cognitive Development; Humor; Milestones: Cognitive; Neonativism; Object Concept; Piaget's Cognitive-Developmental Theory; Reasoning in Early Development.

Suggested Readings

Case R and Okamoto Y (1996) The role of central conceptual structures in the development of children's thought. *Monographs of the Society for Research in Child Development* 61: v-265.

Fischer KW and Bidell TR (2006) Dynamic development of action and thought. In: Lerner RM (ed.) *Handbook of Child Psychology: Volume 1, Theoretical Models of Human Development,* 6th edn. Hoboken, NJ: Wiley.

Halford GS (2005) Development of thinking. In: Holyoak KJ and Morrison RG (eds.) *Cambridge Handbook of Thinking and Reasoning.* Cambridge: Cambridge University Press.

Halford GS and Andrews G (2004) The development of deductive reasoning: How important is complexity? *Thinking and Reasoning* 10: 123–145.

Halford GS and Andrews G (2006) Reasoning and problem solving. In: Kuhn D and Siegler R (eds.) *Handbook of Child Psychology: Volume 2, Cognitive, Language and Perceptual Development,* 6th edn. Hoboken, NJ: Wiley.

Holyoak KJ and Thagard P (1995) *Mental Leaps.* Cambridge, MA: MIT Press.

Siegler RS (2006) Microgenetic analyses of learning. In: Kuhn D and Siegler R (eds.) *Handbook of Child Psychology: Volume 2, Cognitive, Language and Perceptual Development,* 6th edn. Hoboken, NJ: Wiley.

Cognitive Neuroscience

M H Johnson, University of London, London, UK

© 2008 Elsevier Inc. All rights reserved.

Glossary

Autism or autism spectrum disorder (ASD) – A neurodevelopmental disorder that affects development and subsequent behavior including markedly abnormal social interaction, patterns of interests, and communication. Estimates of ASD within a population range from 1 in 200 to 1 in 1000.

Cerebral cortex – A brain structure, composed of neuron cell bodies, found in vertebrates. In humans it is a highly developed structure, responsible for many higher-order functions like language and information processing.

Event related potentials (ERPs) – A set of voltage changes contained within a period of electroencephalogram (EEG) that are time-locked to an event, for example, presentation of an object. This is a noninvasive technique with excellent temporal resolution.

Extinction – A milder form of spatial neglect in which stimuli in one half of the visual field are neglected only when there is a competing stimulus in the opposite field, and not when presented in isolation.

Functional magnetic resonance imaging (fMRI) – A form of neuroimaging that uses magnetic resonance to measure hemodynamic responses in relation to neural activity. This is a noninvasive technique, which allows fine spatial localization.

Near infrared spectroscopy (NIRS) – A neuroimaging technique that uses infrared resonance to measure changes in blood and tissue oxygenation in a noninvasive way, and is a relatively new form of neuroimaging. This is often used in research with infants as an alternative to magnetic resonance imaging, because it is less sensitive to movement.

Plasticity – The ability of the brain, especially in our younger ages to compensate for change. Also refers to the ability of brain regions to take on a variety of different function during early development. Plasticity decreases as brain structures become more specialized during development.

Spatial neglect – A brain-damage syndrome in which patients appear to detect visual events contralateral to their damaged hemisphere. For example, right hemisphere damage can cause a patient to fail to read the left-hand side of a book.

Synapses – Found in the nervous system, these are specialized junctions of cells that facilitate communication between cells and allow neurons to form interconnected neural circuits.

Williams syndrome – A rare genetic disorder occurring in fewer than 1 in 20 000 people. It is characterized by a distinct difference in facial features, sociable demeanor, and developmental delay in certain areas.

Introduction

Cognitive neuroscience has emerged over the past decades as one of the most significant research directions in all of neuroscience and psychology. More recently, the scientific interface between cognitive neuroscience and human development, developmental cognitive neuroscience, has become a hot topic. Part of the reason for the renewed interest in relating brain development to cognitive, social, and emotional change comes from advances in methodology that allow hypotheses to be generated and tested more readily than previously. One set of tools relates to brain imaging – the generation of 'functional' maps of brain activity based on either changes in cerebral metabolism, blood flow, or electrical activity. The three brain-imaging techniques most commonly applied to development in normal children are event-related potentials (ERPs), functional magnetic resonance imaging (fMRI), and near infrared spectroscopy (NIRS). Another methodological advance is related to the emergence of techniques for formal computational modeling of neural networks and cognitive processes. Such models allow us to begin to bridge data on developmental neuroanatomy to data on behavioral changes associated with development. A third methodological innovation is the increasing trend for studying groups of developmental disorders (such as autism and Williams syndrome) together alongside typical development. Thus, rather than each syndrome being studied in isolation, comparisons between different typical and atypical trajectories of development are helping to reveal the extent and limits on plasticity.

Brain Development

Brain development may be divided into that which occurs prior to birth (prenatal) and that which takes place after birth (postnatal). While some of the same developmental processes can be traced from pre- to postnatal life, in postnatal development there is obviously more scope for influence from the world outside the infant. A striking feature of human brain development is the comparatively long phase of postnatal development, and therefore the increased extent to which the later stages of brain development can be influenced by the environment of the child. Some degree of plasticity is retained into adulthood, but this may decline with age.

By around the time of birth the vast majority of cells are in their appropriate adult locations in the human brain, and all of the major landmarks of the brain, such as the most distinctive patterns of folding of the cerebral cortex, are in place. A number of lines of evidence indicate that substantive changes take place during postnatal development of the human brain. At the most gross level of analysis, the volume of the brain quadruples between birth and adulthood. This increase comes from a number of sources such as more extensive fiber bundles, and nerve fibers becoming covered in a fatty myelin sheath that helps conduct electrical signals (myelinization). But perhaps the most obvious manifestation of postnatal neural development as viewed through a standard microscope is the increase in size and complexity of the dendritic tree of many neurons. Less apparent through standard microscopes, but more evident with electron microscopy, is a corresponding increase in density of functional contacts between neurons, synapses.

Peter Huttenlocher and colleagues have reported a steady increase in the density of synapses in several regions of the human cerebral cortex. For example, in parts of the visual cortex, the generation of synapses (synaptogenesis) begins around the time of birth and reaches a peak around 150% of adult levels toward the end of the first year. In the frontal cortex (the anterior portion of cortex, considered by most investigators to be critical for many higher cognitive abilities), the peak of synaptic density occurs later, at around 24 months of age. Although there may be variation in the timetable, in all regions of cortex studied so far, synaptogenesis begins around the time of birth and increases to a peak level well above that observed in adults.

Somewhat surprisingly, regressive events are commonly observed during the development of nerve cells and their connections in the brain. For example, in the primary visual cortex the mean density of synapses per neuron starts to decrease at the end of the first year of life. In humans, most cortical regions and pathways appear to undergo this 'rise-and-fall' in synaptic density, with the density stabilizing to adult levels during later childhood. The postnatal rise-and-fall developmental sequence can also be seen in other measures of brain physiology and anatomy. For example, Harry Chugani and colleagues have observed an adult-like distribution of resting brain activity within and across brain regions by the end of the first year. However, the overall level of activity (as measured by glucose uptake) reaches a peak during early childhood that is much higher than that observed in adults. These rates returned to adult levels after about 9 years of age for some cortical regions. Recently, magnetic resonance imaging (MRI) has been used to study the postnatal development of brain structure. Using this method, the consensus is that brain structures have the overall appearance of those in the adult by 2 years of age, and that all the major fiber tracts can be observed by 3 years of age. Some reports suggest that after a rapid increase in gray matter up to 4 years of age, there is then a prolonged period of slight decline that extends into the adult years. Whether this decline is due to the dendritic and synaptic pruning described above remains unknown. Changes in the extent of white matter are of interest because they reflect interregional communication in the developing brain. Although increases in white matter continue through adolescence into adulthood, particularly in frontal brain regions, the most rapid changes occur during the first 2 years. For example, at around 8–12 months of age the white matter associated with the frontal, parietal, and occipital lobes becomes apparent.

Three different perspectives on human postnatal functional brain development are currently being explored. The first of these approaches, the maturational perspective, has the goal to relate the maturation of particular regions of the brain, usually regions of the cerebral cortex, to newly emerging sensory, motor, and cognitive functions. Evidence concerning the differential neuroanatomical development of cortical regions is used to determine an age when a particular region is likely to become functional. Success in a new behavioral task at this same age is then attributed to the maturation of a newly functional brain region, with maturation often assumed to be an 'all or none' phenomenon, or at least to have a sudden onset. Typically, comparisons are then made between the behavioral performance of adults with acquired lesions and behaviors during infancy. One example of this approach comes from the neurodevelopment of visual orienting and attention, where several researchers have argued that control over visually guided behavior is initially by subcortical structures, but with age and development, posterior cortical regions, and finally anterior regions, come to influence behavior.

In contrast to the maturational approach in which behavioral developments are attributed to the onset of functioning in one region or system, an alternative viewpoint assumes that postnatal functional brain development, at least within the cerebral cortex, involves a process of organizing interregional interactions: 'interactive specialization'.

Recent trends in the analysis of adult brain-imaging data have proceeded on the assumption that the response properties of a specific region may be determined by its patterns of connectivity to other regions and their current activity states. Extending this notion to development means that we should observe changes in the response properties of cortical regions during ontogeny as regions interact and compete with each other to acquire their role in new computational abilities. The onset of new behavioral competencies during infancy will be associated with changes in activity over several regions, and not just by the onset of activity in one or more additional region(s). In further contrast to the maturational approach, this view predicts that during infancy patterns of cortical activation during behavioral tasks may be more extensive than those observed in adults, and involve different patterns of activation. Within broad constraints, even apparently the same behavior in infants and adults could involve different patterns of cortical activation.

A third perspective on human postnatal functional brain development has been termed the skill-learning hypothesis. Recent neuroimaging evidence from adults has highlighted changes in the neural basis of behavior that result as a consequence of acquiring perceptual or motor expertise. One hypothesis is that the regions active in infants during the onset of new perceptual or behavioral abilities are the same as those involved in skill acquisition in adults. This hypothesis predicts that some of the changes in the neural basis of behavior during infancy will mirror those observed during more complex skill acquisition in adults.

Domains of Cognitive and Behavioral Change

Developmental cognitive neuroscience has, to date, only been applied to some aspects of perceptual and cognitive development. While several exciting new areas of development are beginning to be explored, we have selected three domains in which perhaps the most progress has been made: the developing 'social brain', speech and language acquisition, and the development of frontal cortex functions.

Developing a Social Brain

One of the major characteristics of the human brain is its social nature. As adults, we have areas of the brain specialized for processing and integrating sensory information about the appearance, behavior, and intentions of other humans. A variety of cortical areas have been implicated in the 'social brain' including the superior temporal sulcus (STS), the fusiform 'face area' (FFA), and orbitofrontal cortex. One of the major debates in cognitive neuroscience concerns the origins of the 'social brain' in humans, and theoretical arguments abound about the extent to which this is acquired through experience.

The ability to detect and recognize faces is commonly considered to be a good example of human perceptual abilities, as well as being the basis of our adaptation as social animals. There is a long history of research on the development of face recognition in young infants extending back to the studies of Robert Fantz more than 40 years ago. Over the past decade numerous papers have addressed cortical basis of face processing in adults, including identifying areas that may be specifically dedicated to this purpose. Despite these bodies of data, surprisingly little remains known about the developmental cognitive neuroscience of face processing.

Some authors have speculated that the preferential responding to faces observed in newborn infants may be largely mediated by a subcortical visuomotor pathway, whereas later developing abilities to recognize individual faces (on the basis of internal features) are mediated by the ventral stream of visual cortical processing. Much research over the past decade has focused on this 'two systems' view. With regard to a newborn's responses to faces, the majority of behavioral studies to date have found some evidence for sensitivity to face-like patterns. Although views still vary as to the specificity of this newborn bias, John Morton and the present author have speculated that the newborn bias is mediated largely by subcortical visuomotor pathways. This proposal was made for several reasons: (1) that the newborn preference declined at the same age as other newborn reflexes assumed to be under subcortical control, (2) evidence from the maturation of the visual system indicating later development of cortical visual pathways, and (3) evidence from another species (the domestic chick). Due to the continuing difficulty in successfully using functional imaging with healthy awake newborns, this hypothesis has, as yet, only been indirectly addressed. One line of indirect evidence comes from adult neuropsychological and functional imaging studies, and specifically evidence from adult patients with spatial neglect and extinction. Spatial neglect is a brain-damage syndrome in which patients do appear to detect visual events contralateral to their damaged hemisphere. For example, right hemisphere damage can cause a patient to fail to read the left-hand side of a book. Extinction is a related deficit of attention in which patients can orient to stimuli in the contralesional field, but only if they are presented in isolation and are not presented simultaneously with a stimulus in the opposite visual field. Patrick Vuilleumier and colleagues report that these patients extinguish a face much less often than other stimuli. While a variety of explanations of this phenomenon are possible, one view is that damage to cortical circuits in adults releases inhibition of a subcortical face bias. Finally, functional imaging studies in adults that include subcortical structures in their analysis, have observed activation of a range of subcortical structures in addition to the well-known areas of cortical specialization.

Turning to the neurodevelopment of face processing during infancy and childhood, it can be seen that several laboratories have examined changes in ERPs as adults view faces. In particular, interest has been focused on an ERP component termed the 'N170' (because it is a negative-going deflection that occurs after around 170 ms) that has been strongly associated with face processing in a number of studies on adults. Specifically, the amplitude and latency of this component vary according to whether or not faces are present in the visual field of the adult volunteer under study (see **Figure 1**). An important aspect of the N170 in adults is that its response is highly selective. For example, the N170 shows a different response to human upright faces than to very closely related stimuli such as inverted human faces and upright monkey faces. While the exact underlying neural generators of the N170 are currently still debated, the specificity of response of the N170 can be taken as an index of the degree of specialization of cortical processing for human upright faces. For this reason Michelle de Haan and colleagues undertook a series of studies on the development of the N170 over the first weeks and months of postnatal life.

The first issue to be addressed in these developmental ERP studies is when does the face-sensitive N170 emerge?

In a series of experiments de Haan and colleagues have identified a component in the infant ERP that has many of the properties associated with the adult N170, but that is of a slightly longer latency (240–290 ms) (see **Figure 2**). In studying the response properties of this potential at 3, 6, and 12 months of age they discovered that (1) the component is present from at least 3 months of age (although its development continues into middle childhood) and (2) the component becomes more specifically tuned to respond to human upright faces with increasing age. To expand on the second point, it was found that while 12-month-olds and adults showed different ERP responses to upright and inverted faces, 3- and 6-month-olds do not. Thus, the study of this face-sensitive ERP component is consistent with the idea of increased specialization of cortical processing with age, a result also consistent with some behavioral results (see below).

While definitive functional imaging studies on face processing in infants and young children are still awaited, evidence for increased localization of cortical processing of faces comes from a recent fMRI study of the neural basis of face processing in children compared to adults by Alessandra Passarotti, Joan Stiles, and colleagues. In this study, even when children and adults were matched for behavioral ability (in a face-matching task), children activated a larger extent of cortex around face-sensitive areas than did adults.

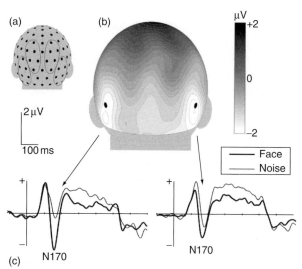

Figure 1 Scalp-recorded event-related potentials in response to faces and matched visual noise presented to adults. (a) Location on the scalp of the electrode sites selected for study (back of the head). (b) A scalp surface voltage map illustrating the distribution of voltage associated with the N170. (c) ERP waveforms from left and right posterior temporal recording sites (black spots on panel b). Note the increased amplitude of the N170 waveform to faces. Reproduced from Halit H, Csibra G, Volein A, and Johnson MH (2004) Face-sensitive cortical processing in early infancy. *Journal of child psychology and Psychiatry* 45:1228–1234, with permission from Blackwell Publishing.

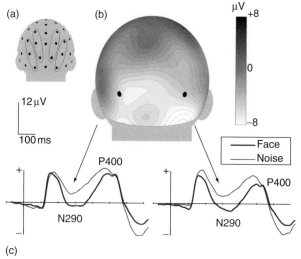

Figure 2 Scalp-recorded event-related potentials in response to faces and matched visual noise presented to 3-month-old infants. (a) Location on the scalp of the electrode sites selected for study (back of the head). (b) A scalp surface voltage map illustrating the distribution of voltage associated with the infant equivalent of the N170 (N290). (c) ERP waveforms from left and right occipital temporal recording sites (black spots on panel b). Note the increased amplitude of the N290 waveform to faces. Reproduced from Halit H, Csibra G, Volein A, and Johnson MH (2004) Face-sensitive cortical processing in early infancy. *Journal of child psychology and Psychiatry* 45:1228–1234, with permission from Blackwell Publishing.

Converging evidence about the increasing specialization of face processing during development comes from a behavioral study that set out to test the intriguing idea that, as processing 'narrows' to human faces, then infants will lose their ability to discriminate nonhuman faces. Olivier Pascalis and colleagues demonstrated that while 6-month-olds could discriminate between individual monkey faces as well as human faces, 9-month-olds and adults could only discriminate the human faces. These results are particularly compelling since they demonstrate a predicted competence in young infants that is not evident in adults.

Moving beyond the relatively simple perception of faces, a more complex attribute of the adult social brain is processing information about the eyes of other humans. There are two important aspects of processing information about the eyes. The first of these is being able to detect the direction of another's gaze in order to direct your own attention to the same object or spatial location (eye-gaze cueing). Perception of averted gaze can elicit an automatic shift of attention in the same direction in adults, allowing the establishment of 'joint attention'. Joint attention to objects is thought to be crucial for a number of aspects of cognitive and social development, including word learning. The second critical aspect of gaze perception is the detection of direct gaze, enabling mutual gaze with the viewer. Mutual gaze (eye contact) provides the main mode of establishing a communicative context between humans, and is believed to be important for normal social development. It is commonly agreed that eye-gaze perception is important for mother–infant interaction, and that it provides a vital foundation for social development.

In a series of experiments with 4-month-old infants using a simple eye-gaze cueing paradigm (in which a stimulus face looked left or right), Teresa Farroni and colleagues have established that it is only following a period of mutual gaze with an upright face that cueing effects are observed. In other words, mutual gaze with an upright face may engage mechanisms of attention such that the viewing infant is more likely to be cued by subsequent motion. In summary, the critical features for eye-gaze cueing in young infants are (1) lateral motion of elements and (2) a brief preceding period of eye contact with an upright face.

Following the surprising observation that a period of direct gaze is required before cueing can be effective in infants, the authors investigated the earliest developmental roots of eye contact detection. It is already known that human newborns have a bias to orient toward face-like stimuli (see earlier), prefer faces with eyes opened, and tend to imitate certain facial gestures. Preferential attention to faces with direct gaze would provide the most compelling evidence to date that human newborns are born prepared to detect socially relevant information. For this reason Farroni and colleagues tested healthy human newborn infants by presenting them with a pair of stimuli, one a face with eye gaze directed straight at the newborns, and the other with averted gaze. Results showed that the fixation times were significantly longer for the face with the direct gaze.

In a further experiment, converging evidence for the differential processing of direct gaze in infants was obtained by recording ERPs from the scalp as infants viewed faces. Babies, 4 months of age, were tested with the same stimuli as those used in the previous experiment with newborns, and a difference was found between the two gaze directions at the time and scalp location at the previously identified face-sensitive component of the infant ERP discussed earlier. The conclusion from these studies is that direct eye contact enhances the perceptual processing of faces in infants during the first months.

Beyond face processing and eye-gaze detection there are many more complex aspects of the social brain such as the coherent perception of human action and the appropriate attribution of intentions and goals to conspecifics. Investigating the cognitive neuroscience of these abilities in infants and children will be a challenge for the next decade.

Language Acquisition and Speech Recognition

Is language biologically special? This motivating question refers to the extent to which the human infant is predisposed to process and learn about language, and the extent to which the underlying neural circuits are 'pre-wired' to process language input. Two cognitive neuroscience approaches to this question have been taken. The first approach addresses the issue of whether there are particular parts of the cortex critical for primary language acquisition, or whether a variety of cortical areas can support this function. The second strategy has been to attempt to identify neural correlates of speech-processing abilities present from very early in life, before experience is thought to have shaped cortical specialization.

Language acquisition has become a focal point for studies designed to investigate the extent to which particular cortical areas, such as Broca's and Wernicke's areas, are 'pre-wired' to support specific functions. Two main lines of research have been pursued, with one set of studies examining the extent to which language functions can be subserved by other regions of the cortex, and another line of research concerned with whether other functions can 'occupy' regions that normally support language. The first of these approaches has been pursued through investigations of whether children suffering from perinatal lesions to the classical 'language areas' of cortex can still acquire language. The second approach has involved the testing of congenitally deaf children to see what, if any, functions are present in regions of cortex that are normally (spoken) language areas.

If particular cortical regions are uniquely pre-wired to support language, then it is reasonable to assume that damage to such regions will impair the acquisition of language regardless of when the insult occurs. This implicit hypothesis has motivated a good deal of research, the conclusions of which still remain somewhat controversial. Eric Lenneberg argued that, if localized left hemisphere damage occurred early in life, it had little effect on subsequent language acquisition. This view contrasted with the effect of similar lesions in adults or older children, and many congenital abnormalities in which language is delayed or never emerges. This view lost adherents in the 1970s, as evidence accumulated from studies of children with hemispherectomies suggesting that left hemisphere removal commonly leads to selective subtle deficits in language, especially for syntactic and phonological tasks. Similar results have also been reported for children with early focal brain injury due to strokes. These findings were compatible with studies of normal infants showing a left hemisphere bias at birth in processing speech and other complex sounds, and led some researchers to the conclusion that functional asymmetries for language in the human brain are established at birth, and cannot be reversed. This view was reinforced by a number of neuroanatomical studies that have shown differences between parts of left and right cerebral cortex in adults. For example, Norman Geschwind and Walter Levitsky reported that the left planum temporale (an area associated with language processing) was larger than the right in 65% of adult brains studied. A number of groups have looked for similar differences in infant brains as evidence for prespecified language abilities. As early as the 29th week of gestation, the left planum temporale is usually larger on the left than on the right in human infants. It is important to remember, however, that (1) this asymmetry is probably not specific to humans and (2) gyral and sucal measures only tell us about the quantity of cortical tissue within a region, and cannot therefore be used to argue for the detailed specific pre-wiring assumed by some to be necessary for language-specific processing. In addition to these reservations about the neuroanatomical evidence, many of the secondary sources that summarized the work on hemispherectomies and/or early focal injury failed to note that the deficits shown by these children are very subtle – far more subtle, in fact, than the aphasic syndrome displayed by adults with homologous forms of brain damage. Significantly, most of the children with left hemisphere injury who have been studied to date fall within the normal range, attend public schools, and certainly do better than adults with equivalent damage.

The other approach to studying the extent to which the cortical areas supporting language-related functions are prespecified is to see whether other functions can occupy such regions. This issue has been investigated in a recent fMRI study in which hearing and deaf participants were scanned while reading sentences in either English or American Sign Language (ASL). When hearing adults read English, there was robust activation within some of classical left hemisphere language areas, such as Broca's area. No such activation was observed in the right hemisphere. When deaf people viewed sentences in their native ASL they showed activation of most of the left hemisphere regions identified for the hearing participants. Because ASL is not sound-based, but does have all of the other characteristics of language including a complex grammar, these data suggest that some of the neural systems that mediate language can do so regardless of the modality and structure of the language acquired. Having said this, there were also some clear differences between the hearing and deaf activations, with the deaf group activating some similar regions in the right hemisphere. One interpretation of the right hemisphere activation is that it is evoked by the biological motion inherent in sign, but not spoken, language. A third condition addressed the issue of whether there is a sensitive period for the establishment of left hemisphere language. In this condition, deaf people read English (their second language, learned late) and did not show activation of the classical left hemisphere language regions, suggesting that, if a language is not acquired within the appropriate developmental time window, the typical pattern of adult activation does not occur.

The other general approach to investigating the extent to which language is biologically special involves attempting to identify language-relevant processes in the brains of very young infants. One example of this concerns the ability to discriminate speech-relevant sounds such as phonemes. Behavioral experiments have demonstrated that young infants show enhanced (categorical) discrimination at phonetic boundaries used in speech such as /ba/-/pa/. That is, like adults, a graded phonetic transition from /ba/ to /pa/ is perceived as a sudden categorical shift by infants. This observation was initially taken as evidence for a language-specific detection mechanism present from birth. However, over the past decade it has become clear that other species, such as chinchillas, show similar acoustical discrimination abilities, indicating that this ability may merely reflect general characteristics of the mammalian auditory processing system, and not a an initial spoken language-specific mechanism.

In a further line of behavioral experiments, Janet Werker and colleagues reported that, although young infants discriminate a wide range of phonetic contrasts including those not found in the native language (e.g., Japanese infants, but not Japanese adults, can discriminate between 'r' and 'l' sounds), this ability becomes restricted to the phonetic constructs of the native language around 12 months of age. If brain correlates of this process could be identified, it may be possible to study the mechanisms underlying this language-specific selective loss of sensitivity. Christaine Dehaene-Lambertz and colleagues presented their infants with trials in which a series of four identical syllables (the standard) was followed by fifth that was either identical or phonetically different (deviant). They recorded high-density ERPs time-locked to the onset of the syllable and observed two voltage peaks with different scalp locations. The first peak occurred around 220 ms after stimulus onset and did not habituate to repeated presentations (except after the first presentation) or dishabituate to the novel syllable. Thus, the generators of this peak, probably primary and secondary auditory areas in the temporal lobe, did not appear to be sensitive to the subtle acoustical differences that encoded phonetic information. The second peak reached its maximum around 390 ms after stimulus onset and again did not habituate to repetitions of the same syllable, except after the first presentation. However, when the deviant syllable was introduced the peak recovered to at least its original level. Thus, the neural generators of the second peak, also in the temporal lobe but in a distinct and more posterior location, are sensitive to phonetic information.

Researchers have used functional imaging methods with greater spatial resolution to investigate early correlates of speech perception. Dehaene-Lambertz and colleagues measured brain activation with fMRI in awake and sleeping healthy 3-month-olds while they listened to forwards and backwards speech in their native tongue (French). The authors assumed that forward speech would elicit stronger activation than backward speech in areas related to the segmental and suprasegmental processing of language, while both stimuli will activate mechanisms for processing fast temporal auditory transitions. Compared to silence, both forwards and backwards speech activated widespread areas of the left temporal lobe, which was greater than the equivalent activation on the right for some areas (planum temporale). These results provide converging evidence for the ERP data discussed earlier. Forwards speech activated some areas that backward speech did not, including the angular gyrus and mesial parietal lobe (precuneus) in the left hemisphere. The authors suggest that these findings demonstrate an early functional asymmetry between the two hemispheres. However, they acknowledge that their results cannot discriminate between an early bias for speech perception or a greater responsivity of the left temporal lobe, for processing auditory stimuli with rapid temporal changes.

In summary, therefore, a reasonable working hypothesis is that regions of the left temporal lobe are most suitable for supporting speech recognition. This suitability likely comes from a combination of spatial and temporal factors that may predispose this region to the processing of rapid temporal stimuli. Other regions of cortex are probably also important for the acquisition of language, and can substitute for the left temporal region if required. Language is only 'biologically special' in the broadest sense in which the human species' typical environment interacts with the architecture of cortex and its developmental dynamics to generate representations appropriate for the domain.

Frontal Cortex Development, Object Permanence, and Planning

The region of the frontal lobe anterior to the primary motor and premotor cortex, the prefrontal cortex (PFC), accounts for almost one-third of the total cortical surface in humans and is considered by most investigators to be critical for many higher cognitive abilities. In adults, types of cognitive processing that have been associated with frontal cortex concern the planning and execution of sequences of action, the maintenance of information 'online' during short temporal delays, and the ability to inhibit a set of responses that are appropriate in one context but not another. The frontal cortex shows the most prolonged period of postnatal development of any region of the human brain, with changes in synaptic density detectable even into the teenage years, and for this reason it has been the region most frequently associated with developments in cognitive abilities.

Two alternative approaches to the relation between frontal cortex structural development and advances in cognitive ability in childhood have been taken. One of these is the attempt to relate structural developments in the frontal cortex at a particular age to changes in certain cognitive abilities. A refinement of this approach is that the frontal lobes are composed of a number of regions that subserve different functions and show a different timetable of maturation. The alternative approach is based on the assumption that the frontal cortex is involved in acquisition of new skills and knowledge from very early in life, and that it may also play a key role in organizing other parts of cortex. According to this latter view, regions of frontal cortex are important in many cognitive transitions primarily because of their involvement in the acquisition of any new skill or knowledge. A corollary of this is that frontal cortex involvement in a particular task or situation may decrease with increased experience or skill in the domain. There is currently evidence consistent with both of these approaches.

One of the most comprehensive attempts to relate a cognitive change to underlying brain developments has concerned marked behavioral changes around 8–10 months of age. In particular, Adele Diamond and colleagues argued that the maturation of PFC during the last half of the human infant's first year of life accounts for a number of transitions observed in the behavior of infants in object permanence and object retrieval tasks. One of the behavioral tasks they have used to support this argument comes from Jean Piaget who observed that infants younger than 8 months often fail to retrieve accurately a hidden object after a short delay period if the object's location is changed from one where it was previously and successfully retrieved. Infants often made a particular perseverative error in which they reach out to the hiding location where the object was found on the immediately preceding trial. This characteristic pattern of error was cited as evidence for the failure to understand that objects retain their existence or permanence when moved from view. By around 9 months of age, infants begin to succeed in the task at successively longer delays of 1–5 s, although their performance remains unreliable up to about 12 months of age if the delay between hiding and retrieval is incremented as the infants age.

Diamond and colleagues tested monkeys in a modification of the above object permanence task. Consistent with the observations on human infants, infant monkeys failed to retrieve the hidden object. Further, adult monkeys with lesions to the dorsolateral region of the PFC (DLPC) were also impaired in this task. Lesions to some other parts of the brain (parietal cortex, or the hippocampal formation) did not significantly impair performance, suggesting that the DLPC plays a central role in tasks that require the maintenance of spatial or object information over temporal delays.

Further evidence linking success in the object-permanence task to frontal cortex maturation in the human infant comes from two sources. The first of these is a series of electroencephalogram (EEG) studies with normal human infants, in which increases in frontal EEG responses correlate with the ability to respond successfully over longer delays in delayed response tasks. The second source is work on cognitive deficits in children with a neurochemical deficit in the PFC resulting from phenylketonuria (PKU). Even when treated, this inborn error of metabolism can have the specific consequence of reducing the levels of a neurotransmitter, dopamine, in the DLPC. These reductions result in these infants and children being impaired on tasks thought to involve parts of the PFC such as the object-permanence and object-retrieval tasks, and being relatively normal in tasks thought to depend on other regions of cortex.

Having established a link between PFC maturation and behavioral change in a number of tasks, Diamond has speculated on the computational consequence of this aspect of postnatal brain development. Specifically, she suggested that the DLPC is critical for performance when (1) information has to be retained or related over time or space and (2) a prepotent response has to be inhibited. Only tasks that require both of these aspects of neural computation are likely to engage the DLPC. In the case of the object-permanence task, a spatial location has to be retained over time and the prepotent previously rewarded response inhibited. One experiment suggests that the PFC maturation hypothesis is not the whole story, however, and that some modification or elaboration of the original account will be required. Rick Gilmore observed that infants succeed on a task that requires temporal spatial integration over a delay at a much younger age than is indicated by the object-permanence tasks. In addition, studies by Renee Baillargeon and others entailing infants viewing 'possible' and 'impossible' events involving occluded objects have found that infants as young as 3.5 months look longer at impossible events indicating that they have an internal representation of the occluded object. In order to account for the apparent discrepancy between these results and those with the reaching measures, some have provided 'means-ends' explanations, arguing that infants are unable to coordinate the necessary sequence of motor behaviors to retrieve a hidden object. To test this hypothesis, Yuko Munakata and colleagues trained 7-month-olds to retrieve objects placed at a distance from them by means of pulling on a towel or pressing a button. Infants retrieved the objects when a transparent screen was interposed between them and the toy, but not if the screen was sufficiently opaque to make the object invisible. Since the same means-ends planning is required whether the screen is transparent or opaque, it was concluded that 'means-ends' explanations cannot account for the discrepancy between the looking and the reaching tasks. Munakata and colleagues proposed an alternative 'graded' view of the discrepancy implemented as a connectionist model.

The maturational approach to PFC development has also been extended to later childhood and adolescence. The results from a variety of behavioral tasks designed to tap into advanced PFC functions have demonstrated that adult levels of performance are not reached until adolescence or later. For example, participants from 3- to 25-years-old were tested on the CANTAB (Cambridge Neuropsychological Testing Automated Battery), a well-established and validated battery of tests previously used on adult human and animal lesion populations. This battery assesses several measures including working memory skills, self-guided visual search, and planning. Importantly for developmental studies, the battery is administered with touch-screen computer technology, and does not require any verbal or complex manual responses. Using the CANTAB, Maria Luciana and Charles Nelson found that while measures that depend on posterior brain regions (such as recognition memory) were stable by 8 years of age, measure of planning and working memory had not yet reached adult levels by age 12 years of age.

While such behavioral measures are useful as marker tasks, it is even better to use functional imaging while children perform tasks likely to engage PFC regions. This strategy has been adopted by Betty Jo Casey and colleagues who use fMRI to compare children and adults in working memory and inhibition tasks. In one experiment they used event-related fMRI while children and adults were engaged in a 'go-no-go' task. In this task, participants had to suppress their response when presented with a particular visual item within an ongoing sequence of stimulus presentations. The difficulty of the task was increased by increasing the number of 'go' items that preceded the 'no go' character. Successful response inhibition was associated with stronger activation of prefrontal regions for children than for adults.

Also, while in adults the activation of some prefrontal regions increased with increasing numbers of preceding 'go' trials (consistent with increasing need for inhibition), in children the circuit appeared to be maximally active for all trial types. Along with the poorer behavioral performance of children in this and other inhibitory tasks, these findings suggest that the functional development of some PFC regions is important for the mature ability to inhibit prepotent tendencies. The greater activation seen in children will be discussed further.

An alternative approach to understanding the role of the PFC in cognitive development has been advanced by several authors who have suggested that the region plays a critical role in the acquisition of new information and tasks. By this account PFC involvement in the object retrieval tasks is only one of many manifestations of PFC involvement in cognitive change. From this perspective, the challenge to the infant brain in, for example, learning to reach for an object, is equivalent in some respects to that of the adult brain when facing complex motor skills like learning to drive a car. A concomitant of this general view is that the cortical regions crucial for a particular task will change with the stage of acquisition. Three lines of evidence indicating the importance of PFC activation early in infancy have given further credence to this view: (1) fMRI and positron emission tomography (PET) studies, (2) psychophysiological evidence, and (3) the long-term effects of perinatal damage to PFC.

The limited number of fMRI and PET studies that have been done with infants have often surprisingly revealed functional activation in PFC, even when this would not be predicted from adult studies. For example, in an fMRI study of speech perception in 3-month-olds, Christaine Dehaene-Lambertz and colleagues observed a right dorsolateral DLPC activation that discriminated (forward) speech in awake, but not sleeping, infants. Similar activation of DLPC was found in response to faces at the same age. While this is evidence for activation of at least some of the PFC in the first few months, it remains possible that this activation is passive as it does not play any role in directing the behavior of the infant. Two other recent lines of evidence, however, suggest that this is not the case.

While developmental ERP studies have often recorded activity changes over frontal leads in infants, some recent experiments suggest that this activity has important consequences for behavioral output. These experiments involve examining patterns of activation that precede the onset of a saccade. In one example, Gergely Csibra and colleagues observed that pre-saccadic potentials that are usually recorded over more posterior scalp sites in adults, are observed in frontal channels in 6-month-old infants. Since these potentials are time-locked to the onset of an action, it is reasonable to infer that they are the consequence of computations necessary for the planning or execution of the action.

Further evidence for the developmental importance of the PFC from early infancy comes from studies of the long-term and widespread effects of perinatal damage to the PFC. In contrast to some other regions of cortex, perinatal damage to frontal cortex and PFC regions often results in both immediate- and long-term difficulties. For example, Mark Johnson and colleagues studied infants with perinatal focal lesions to parts of the cortex in a visual attention task. Damage to parietal cortical regions would be expected to produce deficits in this task in adults, but only infants with perinatal lesions to the anterior (frontal) regions of cortex were impaired suggesting that these regions were involved to a greater extent in the task in infants than in adults.

In conclusion, the prolonged anatomical development of the frontal cortex has led some to characterize the functional development of this region in terms of the differential maturation of different areas. However, increasing evidence indicates that at least parts of the PFC are functional in the first few months, and that these regions may be important for the acquisition of new skills and structuring of others parts of cortex.

Conclusions

While, even in the domains selected for review, much research remains to be done, the results that have been obtained to date suggest a simple maturational account of the development of human brain function is unlikely to accommodate the wide ranging evidence for experience-dependent effects. Similarly, while there may be some fruitful parallels to be drawn between neural changes associated with complex perceptual and motor skill acquisition in adults, and changes in brain functionality during early development, several of the primary features of early functional brain development (such as the existence of sensitive periods and initial biases) do not sit well with this approach. According to the interactive specialization view, cortical regions become specialized for particular functions partly through an activity-dependent process extending from prenatal into postnatal life.

The cerebral neocortex appears to be on a slower developmental pathway than other regions of the brain. Further, this relative delay may be exacerbated in species such as our own that have a long gestation period. Subcortical regions such as the cerebellum, hippocampus, and thalamus clearly undergo some postnatal changes, and these may be, at least partially, a response to changes in their interconnectivity with the cortex. As a whole, the human cerebral cortex has not reached adult levels of specificity at birth, but it appears that some regions of cortex may be relatively delayed compared to others. This leads us to the further question of whether all domains of cognition follow the same timetable of cortical specialization.

Some domains of cognition, such as language, appear plastic in the sense that regions of cortex are not exclusively dedicated to them from birth, but other domains, such as face processing, may have fewer options. Less extensive plasticity does not necessarily imply strict genetic determinism, however, because functions more closely tied to sensory input or motor output are likely to be more restricted to the cortical regions that have the appropriate information in their input. For example, face recognition is necessarily restricted to structures on the visual 'what' (ventral) pathway because it requires both visual analysis and encoding of particular items within a category. Language may be less constrained in the sense that it is less restricted to particular information-processing routes within the cortex. Thus, a key point about the emergence of localization of functions within the cortex is that the restrictions on localization may be more related to which cortical routes of information processing are viable for supporting the functions, rather than being due to pre-wired intrinsic circuitry within regions of cortex.

During prenatal development, spontaneous activity in sensory systems appears to play an important role in contributing to the differentiation of cortical regions. In early postnatal life infants contribute further to the specialization of their brain by preferentially orienting and attending to certain types of stimuli, such as faces. Later, social experience and interaction with caregivers may contribute further to the specialization of late developing parts of the cerebral cortex. Much of later postnatal brain development, therefore, can be viewed as an active process to which both children and their caregivers contribute. Thus, studying the postnatal emergence of cortical specialization for different cognitive functions offers the possibility of new perspectives not only on the study of perceptual and cognitive development in healthy human infants, but also for social development, education, and atypical developmental pathways. The new theoretical and methodological advances of developmental neuroscience will allow these advances.

Acknowledgments

Sections of text in this article are adapted from Johnson (2005), and the author is grateful to his various colleagues and collaborators who commented on those works for their indirect contribution to the present article. The writing of this section was primarily funded by the UK Medical Research Council (PG 9715587) and Birkbeck, University of London.

See also: Brain Development; Brain Function; Object Concept; Speech Perception.

Suggested Readings

Casey BJ and de Haan M (2002) Imaging techniques and their application in developmental science. *Developmental Science (Special Issue)* 5: 265–396.

de Haan M (2001) The neuropsychology of face processing during infancy and childhood. In: Nelson CA and Luciana M (eds.) *Handbook of Developmental Cognitive Neuroscience*, pp. 381–398. Cambridge, MA: MIT Press.

de Haan M and Johnson MH (2003) *The Cognitive Neuroscience of Development.* Hove, UK: Psychology Press.

Halit H, Csibra G, Volein A, and Johnson MH (2004) Face-sensitive cortical processing in early infancy. *Journal of Child Psychology and Psychiatry* 45:1228–1234.

Johnson MH (2005) *Developmental Cognitive Neuroscience: An Introduction,* 2nd edn. Oxford: Blackwell.

Kingsbury MA and Finlay BL (2001) The cortex in multidimensional space: Where do cortical areas come from? *Developmental Science* 4: 125–142.

Marcus GF and Fisher SE (2003) FOXP2 in focus: What can genes tell us about speech and language? *Trends in Cognitive Sciences* 7(6): 257–262.

Mareschal D, Johnson MH, Sirois S, Spratling M, Thomas M, and Westermann G (2007) *Neuroconstructivism: How the Brain Constructs Cognition.* Oxford: Open University Press.

Nelson CA (1995) The ontogeny of human memory: A cognitive neuroscience perspective. *Developmental Psychology* 31(5): 723–738.

Critical Periods

D B Bailey, RTI International, Research Triangle Park, NC, USA
J-L Gariépy, The University of North Carolina at Chapel Hill, Chapel Hill, NC, USA

© 2008 Elsevier Inc. All rights reserved.

Glossary

Canalization – Process by which the initially great range of potential narrows as a result of differentiation and the acquisition of structure and function.

Critical moment – A term usually used by cell biologists to refer to a precise moment in cell division and differentiation.

Critical period – A clearly defined period of time in the development of an organism in which an event or

experience must occur in order for to it to have its greatest impact.
Experience-dependent – Process taking place throughout life by which neural nets are formed in response to idiosyncratic stimulation to facilitate individual adaptation to new environmental challenges.
Experience-expectant – Process taking place during a critical period when neural nets are formed in the presence of stimulation that is ubiquitous in the environment and common for the species (see also 'induction').
Facilitation – The growth or consolidation of an already developed structure, function, or behavior accelerated by stimulation or experience.
Induction – A developmental event (appearance of a new structure, function, or behavior) whose occurrence during a critical period is entirely dependent upon the presence of a specific stimulation.
Maintenance – Continuous stimulation at a certain level is necessary to maintain a fully developed capacity at an optimal level of function.
Plasticity – The ability of an organism to change its phenotype in response to changes in its environment.
Sensitive period – A more loosely defined period of time in which an event or experience is more likely to have a strong effect than another time.

Introduction

A critical period generally is considered to be a point in the life of an organism in which a specific type of environmental experience is likely to exert its greatest influence. The existence and nature of critical periods has been a topic of considerable discussion among both biologists and social scientists. Research on critical periods has come primarily from the fields of embryology, neurobiology, and ethology, relying on both naturalistic and experimental studies with animals. Considerable progress has been made, but much remains to be learned both about the existence of critical periods and the basic underlying mechanisms by which they occur.

Critical periods in human development have been difficult to study scientifically, as it is virtually impossible to perform experiments on humans to prove or disprove the presence of critical periods or the effects of variations in timing of basic sensory experiences. Recently, however, researchers have used naturally occurring instances of neglect or abuse to document their effects on the developing child. As we discuss some of these cases, it will be useful to keep in mind that unlike animal studies where presumed operative factors can be brought under strict experimental control, these studies only provide correlative evidence, albeit quite compelling in some cases. In general, however, strong bases for practical application of critical periods to justify social policy initiatives (e.g., early intervention programs for infants and toddlers) or specific educational practices or experiences (e.g., early exposure to certain types of music or to a second language, based on the assumption of critical periods for musical development or second language acquisition) are still largely lacking. Typically, this debate pits the notion of a permanent deleterious effect of missed opportunities against concepts of plasticity (the possibilities for learning and brain reorganization to accommodate to new situations, even when a critical period has been passed). Despite the paucity of human research, some important conclusions can be drawn about the timing of experiences in promoting optimal infant and early childhood development.

Basic Concepts of Critical Periods

History and Terminology

In general, a critical period might best be considered a hypothetical construct to help us think about the relative power of an experience at one time vs. another. In its most classic and restrictive sense, a critical period is a point in development where a particular experience is absolutely necessary. If the experience is provided, then it allows for development to proceed normally. If the experience does not occur within the defined critical period, the organism is irrevocably damaged, or at least limited in possibilities for future growth, and it is virtually impossible to recover, even if comparable experiences are provided later. In a similar vein, exposure to environmental toxins or negative life experiences (e.g., trauma or abuse) have also been studied from a critical periods perspective. Here the question is whether the toxin or experience has an especially damaging effect during a particular age or period of development.

The concept of critical period was first articulated in the 1920s by Charles Stockard, who showed that birth defects in fish embryos, resulting from extreme temperatures or toxic chemicals, were more likely to occur or to be more serious during a period of rapid cell growth. Since the defects were less serious or in some cases did not appear if the embryos experienced toxic exposure before or after this period of rapid cell growth, he described this phenomenon as a critical moment. A decade later, Hans Spemann extended this concept to what we now refer to as stem cells. Stem cells are cells derived from embryos that are unspecialized. That is, they are not associated with a particular part of the body and therefore cannot perform any specialized functions. However, they are capable of dividing and thus replicating themselves for an extended period of time. At some point in development, likely as a result of complicated interactions among genetic, biochemical, and environmental influences, cells begin to become differentiated, a process whereby a stem cell acquires a specialized function, for example, as a heart, liver, or bone cell. Spemann used the term 'critical moment' to describe the point of differentiation. Before the critical moment, the cell has an open future, with the potential of becoming a variety of cell types. After the critical moment, the cell becomes differentiated, acquiring a specialized function. Once differentiation occurs, the cell has a constrained future, as differentiation is irreversible. In other words, once a stem cell becomes a heart or liver cell, it loses its potential for any other function.

Moving the concept of critical moments from the cellular level to the behavioral level was advanced by studies conducted by Konrad Lorenz, beginning in the 1930s. Lorenz observed that baby ducklings learned to recognize their mothers through visual and auditory exposure. Once this occurred (a process referred to as imprinting), the ducklings demonstrated that they had learned this distinction by following their mothers but not other adults. Lorenz systematically exposed ducklings to their parents, other animals, or even to humans or moving mechanical objects, varying the timing and duration of these exposures. He found that there was a very short window of time, between 9 and 18 h of age, during which imprinting was most likely to occur. Ducklings would imprint on, and subsequently follow, whatever moving object they saw during this period of time. This led to amusing situations where baby ducks were seen to prefer following humans, other animals, or even mechanical objects if they were exposed to them during what he called a critical period.

Perhaps the most well-known example of a clear critical period is the classic research conducted by David Hubel and Torsten Wiesel in the early 1970s. This research was based on the fundamental assumption that the development of the visual system depends on visual input from the environment. The discovery that normal biological development is dependent upon experience was important, but the key finding for critical periods was that the experience has to be provided during a particular time in development. Hubel and Wiesel deprived kittens of sight (by surgically closing one eye) at various periods of time during early development, systematically varying the timing and duration of visual deprivation. When the kittens were deprived of sight for 65 days, starting at 10 days of age, there was a massive reduction (from 98% to 16%) in the number of brain cells that responded to visual stimulation once the eye was opened. Essentially the kittens were blind in one eye and no amount of subsequent visual stimulation was able to allow the kittens to recover sight. But if the visual deprivation occurred before or after this period of time, the effects were less severe and, by a certain age, minimally damaging. The lack of an essential experience during a critical period of development prevented normal brain development from occurring and had a permanent damaging effect. Hubel and Wiesel preferred the term 'sensitive period' to 'critical period', however, implying a longer period of time with less well-defined boundaries.

Since these early experiments scientists have continued to look for critical periods in a number of different animals and for a range of behaviors. One example in which much research has occurred is the development of birdsong, which has been studied in a number of different species. This research shows the importance of young birds, being exposed to adult birdsong during the first year of life. Young birds who do not get this feedback produce abnormal songs as adults, even if exposed later to birdsong that is normal for their species.

Thus the history of critical periods is deeply rooted in embryology, ethology, and neurobiology, based on experimental manipulations of animals during key periods in development. A variety of terms have been used to describe the phenomenon whereby an event or stimulus has more effect at one time during development or another. Three terms have been used in the scientific and popular literature, terms that range in specificity and subsequent implications:

1. *Critical moment.* A term typically used by cell biologists to refer to a precise moment in cell division and differentiation.
2. *Critical period.* A clearly defined period of time in which an event or experience must occur in order for it to have an effect.
3. *Sensitive period.* A more loosely defined period of time in which an event or experience is more likely to have an effect than another time.

How Might Critical or Sensitive Periods Work?

If one accepts the assumption of the existence of critical or sensitive periods, the next set of questions regards their nature. What are the mechanisms by which a critical or sensitive period might operate? There has been an explosion of research in neuroscience and genetics in the past decade, and much has been learned about basic neurocognitive processes. However, we are far from a complete understanding of the mechanisms by which critical or sensitive periods operate.

While a definition of critical or sensitive periods as points in time when a specific stimulation is absolutely necessary for normal growth to occur has descriptive validity, it does not tell us why that stimulation should be necessary in the first place. In the 1983 edition of the *Handbook of Child Psychology*, Gilbert Gottlieb offered the following explanation: critical periods are points in time when novel structures are differentiating from an undifferentiated mass of cell. For that process to lead to species-specific outcomes, species-specific forms of stimulation must be encountered that are capable of bringing about the expression of the right configuration of genes in a timely manner. As Mae Won Ho and Jablonka observed, critical periods exist because natural selection does not select only for genes but genes along with a species-specific developmental context that includes endogenous and exogenous stimulus events. Accordingly, normal genetic expression depends upon the predictable and timely recurrence, generation after generation, of these stimulus events. On this view, there is as much information for development in the species-specific developmental context as there is in species-specific genes. Failure to encounter this information in a timely manner can potentially derail development from its normal course.

A compelling example is Gottlieb's own research on the origin of the capacity of the young Mallard duck to discriminate and to respond to the 'maternal assembly call' of its own species right after birth. A developmental analysis of this so-called instinct led to the discovery that depriving the developing embryo of hearing its own voice 3 days before hatching (by applying a biodegradable glue on its vocal chords) completely prevented the establishment of the postnatal capacity to selectively respond to the maternal assembly call of its own species. In order to determine which specific acoustic features of the self-produced prenatal vocalizations may have this inductive effect, Gottlieb conducted experiments by which he was able to determine that it was the rate of repetition of the prenatal vocalizations, not their pitch or absolute frequency, that had this inductive effect. More specifically, he was able to show that it was prenatal exposure to the natural variability (2–6 notes s^{-1}) around the average rate of the maternal call (4 notes s^{-1}) that was crucially important for developmental induction. Indeed, devocalized embryos exposed to an invariant embryonic call of 4 notes s^{-1} showed no postnatal preference for their species-specific maternal assembly call.

For the past few decades, explanations of critical periods have relied heavily on synaptic elimination and learning. A well-accepted theory supported by research is that during the early years of life there is a proliferation of these connections, more than is needed for successful human function. Naturally occurring events reinforce certain connections which are retained. Those not used are pruned, and new connections are less likely to develop after a certain period. If true, this theory provides a partial explanation for how a critical period might work and why it might be irreversible or at least difficult to reverse. If we start out with many connections, some of which are selectively kept as a result of experience and some eliminated, and if new connections are rarely made, then once the possibility of a connection is lost due to pruning (as is likely the case in the visual development of kittens whose eyelids were surgically closed for defined periods of time) it would be virtually impossible to regain it, unless some form of reorganization or compensation is possible.

William Greenough introduced in 1987 the concept of 'experience-expectant' processes. By this term he meant two things. First, during the period of 'brain growth spurt' that begins a few months before birth and lasts through the first 2 years of development, an overabundance of dendrites and synaptic connections are produced, 'in expectation' of the stimulation to come. Second, consistent with the concept of critical periods, for neural development to proceed normally, certain forms of stimulation must be encountered. This expected stimulation can be of a very general form, including stimulation that is often ubiquitous (e.g., patterned light) or inevitable (e.g., like exposure to gravity), but nonetheless absolutely necessary for normal development to occur. Stimulation that plays such a role is described by Gottlieb as having an inductive effect, that is, its absence always causes development to derail from its normal course. A striking example of induction is the development in the frog of neural connections between the muscles of the hind legs and the motor regions of the brain. At birth, about 200 neurons are present that 'compete' for establishing this connection. Through exercise, only one of these neurons survives in the adult animal. Depriving the young of exercise leads to a situation where many more neurons survive but none is capable of supporting the long leaps that frogs perform.

According to Gottlieb, next to induction, there are two additional roles that experience may play in development. One is that experience may have a facilitative effect. This effect is not as strong as the first because in this case normal development takes place anyway in the absence of stimulation, but its course may be accelerated when such stimulation is present. Research by Arnold Gesell illustrates this role well, showing that practice, while not necessary for the acquisition of walking, is speeded up when parents provide early and repeated opportunities for practice. The second role that experience may play is that of maintenance. Here a given function, such as vision, is fully acquired and mature in its organization but still depends upon a constant stream of stimulation to maintain its full functionality. This role is illustrated in deprivation experiments where subjects kept in the dark for extended periods report having to 'readjust' to natural light before they can see normally again. Although different in their effects, induction, facilitation, and maintenance jointly illustrate the general principle of bidirectionality between structure and function. As explained by Gottlieb, this principle implies that organs do not mature and acquire structure in a vacuum but do so guided by the exercise of their function.

The strengthening and pruning of synaptic connections can only be part of what is almost certainly a much more complicated story. First, in humans there is a relatively long period of time for synaptic development (likely continuing for at least the first 6 years of life) and synaptic pruning (likely a lifelong process). Lifespan perspectives on development show that learning occurs at all ages and thus our ability to define the onset and ending of critical periods in human development precisely is quite limited. Second, mechanisms that stimulate the onset or conclusion of a sensitive period are not well understood, and likely comprise a combination of genetic, developmental, biochemical, and environmental conditions. Third, the formation and pruning of synapses most likely occurs in the context of complicated hierarchies of neural circuits operating at different levels of complexity and integration. This is probably true even for simple behaviors, but the development of complex systems such as language or social development suggests the likelihood of multiple sensitive periods, one building on another at increasing levels of complexity and interdependence. In general, however, there is under natural conditions a 'trade-off' between the plasticity of the early stages and the eventual acquisition of functional organization. This process in which the acquisition of function entails the loss of initial plasticity has been called 'canalization' by Gottlieb.

Alternative Conceptions of Critical Periods

So far, our discussion of the concept of critical periods has been guided exclusively by a biological conception of the term. This was a good place to start because, as mentioned earlier in this article, it is in the context of developmental biological studies that this phenomenon was first observed and described. But concepts that originated in one discipline are often altered when other scientific disciplines borrow them. For a while psychologists have used this concept in ways that departed little from its original definition. But the range of phenomena of interest to them, belonging as they do to the behavioral and cognitive domains, has motivated other uses of the term, some of which are quite different from the original meaning. These alternative conceptions are seen especially in research on social development and educational psychology.

Consider, for example, the way in which the term 'critical period' was recently used by Doris Entwisle in an article where she reports on the effects of transition to formal schooling among poor African-American children. She described this event as a critical period because, for these children especially, the transition to school represents a time when factors outside the child become as important as factors inside the child. In other words, a shift is taking place during this transition in the locus of the parameters that control behavior and development. To illustrate this, Entwisle explains that African-American families often promote a conception of the self that is based on 'who you are' as opposed to 'how you perform'. By contrast, European-American families tend to create a context in which how you perform is an important factor in the acquisition of a sense of self. Thus, for European-American children, the same sense of self that promoted adjustment to the family environment now promotes integration to the school system. For African-American children, by contrast, school entry entails a discontinuity in how the self is being experienced and used to organize behavior. Here, a critical period is created by the fact that the transition to formal schooling entails a reorganization of the alignment between internal and external systems.

School entry is not necessarily a critical period for every child. The criticality of this period is not obtained by age alone or the onset of a specific maturational event, but through the fact that a particular person-situation context, often highly idiosyncratic, is being created. We illustrate this with another example from the psychology of education. Jackie Eccles showed that in the standard school system, the transition to middle school is often the beginning of a downward spiral for some adolescents that is characterized by low academic performance, low self-esteem, and school drop-out. By comparison, among the adolescents who experience the less traditional K-to-12 system, the observed proportion of these problems is much lower. She explains the difference between the two groups of students by the fact that in the first case, and to a lesser extent in the second, there is a mismatch between the needs of adolescence for belongingness, autonomy, and competence, and the large, impersonal, bureaucratic environments that inner city schools often create for their students. Another interpretation of her finding is that adolescence is a natural period of developmental vulnerability because the internal changes taking place within the individual demand a fresh alignment between biological, cognitive, behavioral, and socioecological systems. In this context, a K-to-12 system would reduce disequilibrium and personal distress by maintaining at a time of internal reorganization a familiar environment that is more likely to satisfy those basic needs of adolescence. Accordingly, how 'critical' the transition to adolescence (or to middle school) will be for each individual is not determined solely by entering adolescence *per se*, but depends upon the social circumstances in which this developmental event takes place for different individuals.

Other terms such as 'windows of opportunity' also appear in the popular literature. And the educational literature uses terms such as 'teachable moment' to refer to times when the power of a learning experience is maximized. By the time of school entry, for example, the young child is generally eager to learn what the school has to teach. For many children, the opportunity to learn the things that the adults know, like reading and counting, promises greater freedom and independence. Our best teachers know this and take full advantage of the high motivation to learn. Again, this period is not defined maturationally but rather by an event whose timing is determined by society, and subject to variation across cultures. Other researchers have recommended the term 'optimal period' to characterize a preferred time in which interventions or experiences might have the greatest impact. All of these terms share the common assumption that the timing of experience is important but that its impact may be highly variable and more or less specific in its effects. Inherent in the concepts of critical moments and critical periods are the necessary nature of the experience during precise periods of time and the irreversibility of their developmental impact. While there is nothing of absolute biological necessity about the acquisition around 6 years of age of literacy and numeracy in our American culture, failing to do so at this age has developmental consequences.

Most scientists now prefer the term 'sensitive period' over 'critical period', since precise critical periods, with the possible exception of biological maturation, are difficult to prove and may be rare. Furthermore, new revelations about the plasticity of human development and the possibilities for dramatic new treatments that could repair damage previously thought to be irreversible have forced scientists to rethink the malleability of organisms in new and important ways. Less dramatic but equally important is the fairly recent realization that the brain retains throughout life the capacity to form new connections and to reorganize itself in response to new adaptive challenges. While the evidence comes mostly from research with monkeys and rodents, there is no reason to believe that the findings cannot be generalized to our species. William Greenough also coined the term 'experience-dependent' processes. With this term he meant to highlight the fact that while there may be critical periods for the acquisition of the neural substrates that support species-specific capacities, there seems to be no time limit for the organization of neural substrates supporting individual adaptations. According to Greenough, the essential difference between the two processes is that, in the first case, dendritic proliferation is guided by genetic activity and endogenous growth factors, while in the second, dendritic proliferation is triggered by external (or self-imposed) demands for the acquisition of new capacities, new adaptations, or new skills, hence the term 'experience-dependent'. In this second case, the process by which a functional neural substrate is eventually sculpted is essentially the same: overproduction, competition, pruning, and functional validation (through exercise), of the surviving connections.

There are reasons to believe that the likelihood of finding critical periods in development diminishes as an inverse function of the degree of complexity achieved in various species through developmental differentiation. According to this principle, the more development gives rise to a hierarchy of complex systems that provide for highly sophisticated levels of behavioral control, the less likely would be the existence of tightly specified critical periods. In this regard it is informative to know that in the wake of John Bowlby's attachment theory in the early 1970s – a theory that is based largely on the ethological framework and findings obtained in avian species and apes – many suspected the existence of critical periods for attachment in human development. Lorenz, after all, had demonstrated that chicks that do not encounter a moving object within a narrow period of time shortly after birth, or became imprinted to the wrong object, suffered irreversible consequences observable well into adult life. Klaus and Kennel were among the first to take upon themselves the task of documenting the existence of such periods for attachment to the mother in our species. To do this they took advantage of situations in which mothers had been hospitalized for varying lengths of time following the birth of their babies. If a strict critical period for attachment had been operating, babies of mothers with longer stays in the hospital should have shown increasing difficulties to bond to their mother. This is not what they found. To be sure, these babies needed a longer period of habituation to their mother to warm up to her. Once this initial period passed, however, they were perfectly capable of forming an affectional bond to her. Note also that the flexibility of the attachment process in our species is further demonstrated by the capacity of the human baby to form multiple attachments.

Implications of Critical and Sensitive Periods for Early Childhood Development

What are the general implications of research on critical and sensitive periods for infant and early childhood development? Three broad conclusions are important to recognize: (1) the existence of critical periods in humans is difficult to prove scientifically; (2) without proof of critical periods, timing of experiences is still a relevant concept; and (3) emerging research on human plasticity and future treatment opportunities may provide important insights into previously held assumptions about unalterable courses of development.

Discerning Critical Periods in Humans

We can conclude with confidence that critical or sensitive periods in their original biological sense do exist, but this conclusion is largely based on research showing that animals who have been deprived of naturally occurring experiences or exposed to a toxic stimulus show varying degrees of severity and permanence of impairment depending on the timing of those experiences in development. Researchers cannot manipulate human experiences in the same way that they are able to manipulate animal experiences, and thus conclusions about critical periods in human development are more difficult to prove. It is possible, however, to approach this question by using natural occurrences of neglect, maltreatment, or exposure to noxious stimuli. In this section we examine what can be learned from studies of such occurrences. As a note of caution, let us mention at the outset that these are quasiexperimental studies, that is, the subjects in this kind of research are taken as they come, and without the possibility of controlling (as we do under laboratory conditions) for extraneous variables that may leave in place alternative explanations. To make the matter more complex, we would like, ideally, to determine whether critical periods exist not just in the formation of biological structures, but also in the developmental organization of adaptively significant behaviors, including as examples the formation of an affective bond with the caregiver, the acquisition of language, or the capacity to think abstractly. The added difficulty in these cases is that multiple neurobiological systems develop and build on each other over time to support these complex behaviors. In turn, this organization generates buffering or compensatory mechanisms not present in simpler systems or, for that matter, in species where development does not advance at that level of sophistication.

It is well known that the ingestion of lead is associated with impaired intellectual development in children. Does it matter when the exposure to lead occurs? An experiment to answer this question definitively for humans would require systematic exposure to varying amounts of lead for varying periods of time at multiple points in development. For obvious reasons, such a study would be unethical. The only way this question can be answered is by finding a large group of children who are diverse with respect to whether they were ever exposed to lead, when that exposure occurred, how much lead was ingested, and for how long. Precise estimates of all these variables are difficult to determine, since most of these data would have to be retrospective. Nonetheless, some research suggests that late in the prenatal period may be the most dangerous time for lead exposure, with effects that are more severe and more permanent than exposure at other times. Although not definitive and not a real test of a true critical period, findings such as these can help policy makers decide when and where to invest limited resources to maximize potential benefit or minimize potential harm. Of course, there is no period in development when lead exposure is good, but evidence showing that exposure during a particular window in development has much more severe or less reversible consequences than other windows would be quite useful.

Perhaps the best-known and least controversial example of a critical period in human development is the period during prenatal development when the embryo differentiates into a male if it possesses a Y chromosome or remains a female otherwise. This happens around the ninth week of gestation in our species when the Y chromosome becomes involved in the synthesis of testosterone and its release in a brain that is still undergoing differentiation and functional organization at a rapid pace. This inductive event (see Gottlieb's research mentioned earlier) is accompanied by the masculinization of the genital ridge and the brain as a whole. Not only does this transformation take place within a well-specified window of time, but the effects of testosterone release in the brain during this period are also irreversible. Once a male, always a male! We have here a very good example of a critical period at the level of biological structures, whose mechanism of action has been documented in other species, and which we know takes place via the same mechanism in our own because errors of nature have confirmed it.

Now let us consider possible critical periods at a level of organization that may be of more immediate interest to the parent, the teacher, or the psychologist. A number of recent inquiries into naturally occurring instances of early deprivation have begun to provide some answers. One of the most informative studies in this regard is the Bucharest Early Intervention Project conducted by Nathan Fox, Charles Nelson, Charles Zeanah, and Dana Johnson at the Universities of Harvard, Minnesota, and Tulane. In this project, children previously institutionalized in Romanian orphanages were placed (at 9, 18, 30, or 42 months of age) into high-quality foster care in the US and Canada and observed over a number of years for placement effects on their intellectual, social–emotional, and brain development. Compared to a noninstitutionalized group of Romanian children, those in their study were characterized by a variety of risk factors including alcohol and prenatal drug exposure, as well as abandonment, and social and material deprivation. Prior to their placement in foster care, these children were behind on virtually every measure of interest to a child developmentalist. The Bucharest Early Intervention group hypothesized that the effects of foster care placement on the various domains of developmental interest to them would fall into two broad categories. They expected developmental domains that are guided by an experience-expectant process to be quite resistant to improvements in the quality of care, while other domains, less restricted to a narrowly defined critical period, would follow an experience-dependent process and be more open to the therapeutic effects of foster care.

In general they found that the infants who were institutionalized for the shortest periods of time and who were placed early in foster care were those who showed the most rapid and complete recovery from exposure to early adverse conditions. Moreover, with the exception of physical growth, they observed improvements in virtually every developmental domain measured, including IQ, emotional expression, attention, and social development. It is perhaps through the patterns of emotional attachment these institutionalized infants displayed that the effects of early deprivation were the most striking. Zeanah and his colleagues noted among these children the prevalence of a syndrome called 'reactive attachment disorder'. This syndrome consists of two opposing but equally maladaptive responses to social contact characterized by emotional withdrawal and inhibition in the first case, and by indiscriminate, disinhibited approach of strangers in the second case. Remarkably, the research team found that over the course of 2 or 3 years of foster care placement and the experience of sensitive, child-centered interactions, these atypical behaviors were progressively replaced by more organized attachment patterns (e.g., using the caregiver as a secure base for exploration). Equally striking was the fact that the physiological measures indexing cognitive and behavioral competence (e.g., magnitude and amplitude of brain activity) also showed the same pattern of improvement over time. In every case, the effects of intervention were a joint function of the age at which placement in foster care took place and how much time had elapsed since placement. Clearly, these effects show that the cognitive, behavioral, and social–emotional domains (including their neuronal support), quite unlike basic cellular processes of differentiation, all develop following an experience-dependent process. In other words, they are not fixed by stimulation encountered within a narrow window of time. In fact, the only developmental domain that appeared so constrained by early experience in this quasiexperimental research was physical growth, a biological process more intimately tied to cell differentiation and growth.

Another domain that may be amenable to a similar type of analysis is language development – when is it important for children to hear language during the early years of life? Again, for ethical reasons it would be impossible to systematically vary the time at which a child first heard language. However, it is possible to study the rare cases of children who were deprived of language under conditions of abuse or neglect. A well-known case study is that of Genie, a child who was discovered after 13 years of being placed by her father in complete isolation in the backroom of a house where she had been strapped to a potty chair, beaten, abandoned, and prevented from any contact with other humans. By the time she was discovered, Genie could not speak, presumably because she had never been spoken to. The fact that sustained attempts to teach her language failed (she had considerable language, but could not master the most elementary rules of grammar) was taken by the linguist Eric Lennenberg as evidence that there is a critical period for the acquisition of language, somewhere between 2 and 13, he claimed, after which the biological window closes, making it impossible to acquire language later. As popular as this case has been, it remains what it is: a single case. Moreover, as pointed out by Kevin McDonald at the California State University, Genie is also an account of trauma, abuse in the extreme, and attachment failure – all factors that may, just the same, explain her failure to learn language. Under any circumstance, it would be extremely difficult to determine whether or not there is a critical period for the acquisition of language. Exposure to language in our species is virtually inevitable. Consider, for example, what a normal mother who just gave birth does when the nurse places the newborn in her arms for her to hold: she places her child in a face-to-face position and talks to her. Isolating exposure to language while keeping other factors approximately constant would be very difficult indeed.

It is also possible to study children with hearing impairments who have received a cochlear implant, an electronic device surgically implanted under the skin of individuals with congenital deafness to stimulate the auditory nerve and provide some sounds that otherwise would be impossible to detect. Studies of children who have received cochlear implants at varying ages suggest that children who receive implants before 4–6 years of age have superior speech and language development than those who receive implants after 8 years of age. These data do not provide positive proof of the existence of a critical period, but do provide useful information for clinicians and parents about the optimal timing of exposure to sound and the best time to have this surgery performed. There is, however, more than exposure to sound that is at play in the acquisition of language. The symbolic (gestural) and interpersonal aspects must also be factored in.

Time and Timing in Development

Although full proof of critical periods in humans remains difficult to obtain, timing, without a doubt, is an important consideration in infant and early childhood development. A number of researchers have pointed out that most animal research on critical periods has focused on basic sensory processes such as vision, whereas most questions of timing in human development address much more complex behaviors. These complex behaviors are likely to have less well-defined, and probably less constrained, windows of time; in fact once a window has opened for a set of skills to be learned, it is likely to remain open for a very long time. However, there is considerable evidence that although a window for learning may be open for a long time, competent development of a skill builds on earlier experiences and learning may be more difficult as one gets older.

The development of literacy is a clear example of these points. Many nonreading adults can be taught to read, and thus there is not likely to be a critical period for learning to read, at least in the classic way that developmental biologists have defined critical period. However, it is much more difficult for an adult to learn to read and the reading fluency of adult learners is likely to always be at a lower level than those who learn to read earlier. Likewise, most first graders learn to read. However, the ease of learning to read is enhanced by exposure to critical experiences during the early childhood years, such as rhyming games to build awareness of similarities and differences in sounds and early exposure to books and print materials. Thus, while the infant and preschool years may not be considered a critical period for literacy development, they pose a window of opportunity where exposure to certain types of experiences provides an important foundation that enables more complex learning to occur earlier and with greater ease.

In practice, the use of the term 'critical period' may not be accurate or useful in infant and early childhood development. And statements arguing that the first 3 years of life constitute a critical period are misleading and likely to evoke strong reactions from commentators who have a more specific definition of critical period. Nonetheless, we can convincingly argue that the first 3 years are foundational, and that appropriate experiences during this period of life make later learning easier and more efficient.

New Horizons for Human Plasticity

Some have criticized the concept of critical periods as painting an unnecessarily pessimistic view of the possibilities for change. Metaphors such as 'as the twig is bent, so shall the tree grow', suggest that certain bad experiences or the lack of key learning opportunities could permanently alter development or limit the possibilities for future growth. In reality, opportunities for learning and growth occur throughout our lives. Research on brain injury has shown how neural reorganization can occur, even in injuries sustained later in life. Neurobiological research is leading to greater understanding of learning processes, and it is possible that in the future targeted medications or gene therapy may reverse or enhance processes previously considered unalterable.

Research on stem cells could force further rethinking of the concept of critical periods, since it could lead to cell-based therapies that could repair or replace damaged tissue. For years scientists thought that only embryonic stem cells (those obtained from human embryos) had therapeutic potential because they were undifferentiated and had the potential to develop into any human tissue. Recent research suggests that adult stem cells, that previously were considered to be limited in potential therapeutic use to the tissue from which it came (e.g., bone marrow), might actually be able to lead to the creation of cells in a completely different tissue.

Three Examples of the Importance of Timing

Although critical periods may not strictly apply to early human development, timing is clearly important, and concepts such as foundational skills, windows of opportunity, and optimal times for learning are quite relevant. Three examples are presented to show the importance of timing of critical periods in early development.

Newborn Screening

Newborn screening is a public health program that rests heavily on the urgency of early treatments to prevent morbidity or mortality caused by a range of endocrine, metabolic, or genetic disorders. Newborn screening can be traced back to the 1960s when Robert Guthrie developed a screening test for phenylketonuria (PKU) using blood spots. PKU is an inborn error of metabolism in which the body is unable to process phenylalanine, a critical amino acid. If untreated, PKU results in mental retardation, small head circumference, and behavioral problems, signs of which begin to emerge by 6 months of age. However, PKU is easily treatable by a diet that dramatically lowers phenylalanine in food. To be maximally effective, the diet must be started early. Changing the diet at a later point in development does not undo the damage done if PKU is not treated early.

Today every state operates a newborn screening program for all newborns. All newborn screening is based on a fundamental assumption that early identification of children with selected conditions allows for treatments that must be provided early if they are to be effective. Interestingly, research on critical periods has not typically been used to justify newborn screening; rather the justification is generally on a condition-by-condition basis, showing the devastating consequences of the condition and the benefits of timely treatment. For example, children with galactosemia, a recessive genetic trait that emerges when two carriers have children, lack a liver enzyme required to digest galactose, most commonly found in milk products. A build-up of galactose in cells is toxic and can quickly result in liver disease, cataracts, mental retardation, or death, which can occur as early as 1–2 weeks of age. An early and immediate change in diet to a soy-based formula can prevent these consequences, although individuals with the condition must eliminate galactose and lactose from their diets throughout life. Thus timing of the identification and treatment of this condition is essential, a critical period of identification that must occur within the first few days of life. However, this is an example of a critical period in which the window for the period never closes.

Rapid changes in technology, new treatment options, and advocacy efforts have led to significant expansions in newborn screening. Technology will soon allow the possibility of identifying conditions for which there is no current treatment or for which treatment during the earliest weeks or months of life may not be critical. Debates about the desirability of expanded screening have already begun. Some have argued that no condition should be identified unless it meets a standard closely associated with critical periods, with proof that early identification and early treatment is necessary and would be less effective or even ineffective if provided later; others argue that a critical-period type standard is too restrictive, and that information about a condition has other potential benefits to families and society, even if no treatment currently exists. Important discussions are needed about the ethical, legal, and social issues that accompany rapid expansion of genetic knowledge and the benefits of newborn screening for conditions where the urgency of timing early treatments does not yet exist.

Early Education

In the 1960s, many psychologists, educators, and policy makers became concerned about the alarming rate of childhood poverty in the US and evidence showing the devastating effects of poverty on school achievement, psychosocial adjustment, and adaptation to adult life. Prominent psychologists such as Benjamin Bloom argued that since the early years were the time of greatest developmental change, this period provided the greatest opportunity for lifelong impact on development. Arguments such as these led to the establishment of Head Start (a national program of preschool education for young children living in poverty), early intervention programs (a national program of services for infants and toddlers with disabilities and their families), and a new generation of longitudinal research on the benefits of early education.

Recent follow-up studies of children participating in early intervention and preschool programs, conducted after these children had entered the early adult years, have provided strong evidence of the long-lasting benefits of early education. Children from low-income environments who participated in high-quality early intervention programs have better academic, social, and economic outcomes than children who did not participate in such programs. Data from studies such as these have provided strong support for those who advocate for initiatives such as expanding Head Start to include all eligible children, lowering the age of Head Start entry, improving quality of early childhood programs, or providing universal prekindergarten education.

But this research has not been able to answer the more fundamental question of whether the early childhood years constitute a critical period. Since some advocates have invoked the critical-periods argument in support of improving or expanding early childhood education programs, this predictably has elicited reactions from those who do not agree. Opponents argue that since no proof exists to support the general notion that the early childhood years constitute a critical period in development, increased expenditures for early childhood programs are not warranted.

This debate will never be answered conclusively. The question of whether the infant and preschool years constitute a critical period is too broad and too diffuse, and no amount of research could be done that would provide a 'gold-standard' scientific answer. But most scientists and advocates agree on two general points. First, windows for learning open at birth and remain open for a very long time, probably all of our lives. A task force on the science of early development sponsored by the National Academy of Sciences concluded:

> Early experiences clearly affect the development of the brain. Yet the recent focus on "zero to three" as a critical or particularly sensitive period is highly problematic, not because this isn't an important period for the developing brain, but simply because the disproportionate attention to the period from birth to 3 years begins too late and ends too soon.
>
> Shonkoff and Phillips (2000, p. 7)

It is difficult to argue that the early childhood years constitute a critical period, since much learning happens after this period. However, almost everyone agrees that the early childhood years are foundational. Recent publications have used the metaphor of 'brain architecture', suggesting that early childhood experiences have a uniquely powerful effect on the brain and on how brain development manifests itself in terms of later cognitive development and social processes. While claims of a critical period may be exaggerated, the early childhood period is the only time in human life that provides the foundation for all future learning.

Second, substantial data exist showing that variations in the quality of early childhood environments and experiences are associated with variations in later outcomes in school and postschool success. On the side of negative factors, clearly many children experience environmental circumstances (e.g., poverty, maternal depression, abuse or neglect, dangerous neighborhoods) that have adverse effects on academic and social development. As a result many children enter school not ready for the demands and expectations of the school environment. On the positive side, early intervention and preschool programs have been shown to improve outcomes, and high-quality programs result in better outcomes than poor-quality ones. Collectively these data show that what we do with children during the early years does make a long-term difference, irrespective of the proof of critical periods that provides sufficient evidence to support special attention to the early years.

Thus far our discussion of early education has focused on children at risk for compromised development, either as a result of poverty or as a result of a disability. A related dimension of early education has a different goal, namely the enhancement of accelerated or optimal performance by providing enriched opportunities for advanced skills early in life. For example, a number of commercial products can be purchased to help parents maximize early development through exposure to a wide range of experiences. Two questions could be asked of these products or activities: (1) do they work? and (2) must they be provided early in life to have the greatest impact? Two specific areas in which the critical-periods question has been asked are early exposure to music and early exposure to a second language. The assumption underlying both of these is that the early years constitute, if not a critical period, an important window of opportunity to maximize the likelihood of mastering a musical instrument or learning a second language.

As with all areas of human development, it is virtually impossible to answer these questions from a critical-periods perspective. Consider the case of learning a second language. Research clearly shows that early exposure to a second language can have important short-term and long-term benefits, and many of the findings are, indeed, age-related. Of course many adults would be able to learn a second language. But research clearly shows that learning a second language is more difficult for an adult than for a child, it takes longer for the adult to learn the second language, and the adult is less likely to perfect the accents and the phonetic features associated with native speakers of the second language. Thus early exposure to a second language (and probably to music or lots of other experiences) is not a necessary requirement for success, but it can make it easier to attain success or mastery. Of course, many other factors also contribute to success, among which include genetic features, motivation, enjoyment, and the context in which the experiences occur.

Critical Life Events and Teachable Moments

The notion of critical or sensitive periods is based on the fundamental assumption of a time at which an organism is particularly sensitive to environmental input. But usually this is based on a developmental or age-based perspective – the critical or sensitive period begins when the organism has reached a biological stage in development where the organism is biologically ready and environmental input is most needed, thus grounding critical periods in a maturational perspective.

An alternative view builds on notions such as critical life events or teachable moments as critical times for proper environmental input. Rather than relying on maturation reaching a certain point before input becomes important, this perspective assumes that when certain events happen, those events provide a window of opportunity for maximal environmental influence, irrespective of maturational level. The organism's maturational level might determine the nature and complexity of the environmental input likely to be most beneficial, but has relatively little bearing on the need for this input.

Some educators or psychologists refer to these times as teachable moments, a time at which the individual needs or wants to learn something or receive some type of input to help cope with a situation. Many examples of these moments are evident in the daily life of any individual. A toddler wants a toy she cannot reach or a peer has just grabbed a toy from her. A preschool child picks up a picture book and, after turning a few pages, stops and looks intently at one particular page that has piqued his interest. A preschool child just learns that her grandmother has passed away. A 5-year-old walks into a kindergarten class for his first group educational experience. A middle-school child gets stumped in the middle of a complicated experiment. A high-school student loses a friend in a tragic accident or a parent walks out of the home. An adult needs to know how to insert artwork into an electronic slide presentation.

These events vary enormously in nature and magnitude, but they share a common feature in that they all represent times during which environmental input is needed at that moment in time. Input provided before or after the event might be helpful, but the time immediately following the event is the moment in which environmental input might be most effective. When two toddlers are arguing over a toy, it provides a brief but important window of time for an adult to help model and support appropriate ways to take turns, share, and communicate. The preschool child who shows interest in a book is much more ready for appropriate and supportive adult input to build early literacy skills than one who is busy working with clay. The first day of kindergarten is a time of special vulnerability; how adults and peers interact with that child and the child's feelings of competence and belongingness on that particular day or week will have a powerful impact on feelings about school for many days to come. In all of these events, the timing of experience is likely to be a key feature in learning or adaptation.

This might be one of the most useful ways to think about critical moments – experiences that create periods of vulnerability and openness to information, feedback, or support. Hopefully research in the coming decade can be more focused on the match between the needs of the organism and the timing of environmental input.

See also: Bilingualism; Brain Development; Head Start; Language Acquisition Theories.

Suggested Readings

Bailey DB (2002) Are critical periods critical for early childhood education? The role of timing in early childhood pedagogy. *Early Childhood Research Quarterly* 17: 281–294.

Bailey DB, Bruer JT, Symons FJ, and Lichtman JW (eds.) (2001) *Critical Thinking About Critical Periods*. Baltimore: Paul H. Brookes Publishing.

Bruer JT (1999) *The Myth of the First Three Years: A New Understanding of Early Brain Development and Lifelong Learning*. New York: The Free Press.

Gottlieb G (1983) The psychobiological approach to developmental issues. In: Mussen PH (ed.) *Handbook of Child Psychology,* 4th edn. vol 2, pp. 1–26. New York: Wiley.

Greenough WT, Black JE, and Wallace CS (1987) Experience and child development. *Child Development* 58: 539–559.

Hensch TK (2004) Critical period regulation. *Annual Review of Neuroscience* 27: 549–579.

Knudsen EI (2004) Sensitive periods in the development of the brain and behavior. *Journal of Cognitive Neuroscience* 16: 1412–1425.

Knudsen EI, Heckman JJ, Cameron JL, and Shonkoff JP (2006) Economic, neurobiological, and behavioral perspectives on building America's future workforce. *Proceedings of the National Academy of Sciences USA* 103: 10155–10162.

Michel GF and Tyler AN (2005) Critical period: A history of the transition from questions of when, to what, to how. *Developmental Psychobiology* 46: 156–162.

Shonkoff JP and Phillips DA (2000) *From Neurons to Neighborhoods: The Science of Early Childhood Development*. Washington, DC: National Academy Press.

Developmental Disabilities: Cognitive

S L Pillsbury, Richmond, VA, USA
R B David, St. Mary's Hospital, Richmond, VA, USA

© 2008 Elsevier Inc. All rights reserved.

Glossary

Echolalia – The repetition of that which is said.
Etiology – The origin or cause of a medical disease or condition.
Language pragmatics – the set of rules governing the use of language in context. This includes factors such as intention; sensorimotor actions preceding, accompanying, and following the utterance; knowledge shared in the communicative dyad; and the elements in the environment surrounding the message.
Prosody – The element of language which concerns intonation, rhythm, and inflection.
Semantics – The study of meaning in language, including the relations between language, thought, and behavior.
Syntax – The way in which words are put together in a sentence to convey meaning.
Verbal auditory agnosia – The inability to understand spoken words; pure word deafness.
Verbal dyspraxia – Also referred to as childhood apraxia of speech; a nonlinguistic sensorimotor disorder of articulation characterized by the impaired capacity to program the speech musculature and the sequencing of muscle movements for the volitional production of phonemes (sounds).

Introduction

Developmental delay is the failure to achieve developmental skills at are appropriate for the age of the child. This article will concern itself with developmental disabilities in the area of higher-order cognition, as seen in preschoolers.

It is universally agreed that early recognition of developmental disability is key in optimizing functioning of the child. The age at which identification is possible varies with the nature of the developmental disability. For example, some disabilities at occur relatively infrequently, but which carry high morbidity (such as cerebral palsy, severe degrees of mental retardation, sensory impairments (blindness, deafness), lower-functioning autism spectrum disorders (ASD), and severe communication disorders), are more likely to be diagnosed in the preschool years. In contrast, disabilities at occur much more frequently but which carry lower morbidity (such as learning disabilities, mild-to-moderate mental retardation, attention deficit hyperactivity disorder (ADHD), higher-functioning ASD, Asperger's syndrome, and higher-order language disorders) often will not be diagnosed until school age. Early identification, with appropriate referrals and interventions, permits counseling for families and planning for the child's future. The child's progress is monitored over time, and interventions are modified as needed. In the very young child, there is obviously a great deal of uncertainty, both in diagnosis and prognosis. The passage of time allows greater diagnostic precision and therefore better targeted therapies.

Not all children subsequently diagnosed as having developmental disabilities will have any identifiable risk factors at birth, and many causes of developmental disability are unknown. When risk factors are present from birth or early infancy, they may be isolated or multiple, and they may interact in complex ways. Multiple risk factors can have an additive effect. However, the absence of risk factors does not guarantee typical development. Risk factors present from birth or early infancy may include:

- genetic syndromes (patterns of malformation), chromosomal abnormalities, malformations of the central nervous system (CNS);
- prematurity (although prematurity alone is a weak risk factor; its effect is probably mediated by those

complications that are seen commonly in low birth weight infants such as metabolic disturbances like hypoglycemia, severe chronic lung disease, CNS hemorrhage, sepsis, and infections of the CNS);
- conditions in pregnancy that interfere with uteroplacental circulation, oxygenation, or nutrition, which may lead to premature delivery or intrauterine growth retardation (a baby who is significantly smaller than would be predicted for his gestational age). Among these are pregnancy-induced hypertension, chronic maternal disease (such as hypertension, renal disease, and cyanotic congenital heart disease), maternal smoking, and maternal drug abuse;
- congenital infections (including cytomegalovirus, rubella, HIV, herpes, congenital syphilis, congenital toxoplasmosis);
- adverse prenatal and perinatal events such as hemorrhage from placenta previa or placental abruption, severe maternal disease (e.g., infections, seizures, trauma), anoxia (especially when the newborn is symptomatic in the immediate neonatal period with seizures, hypotonicity, and feeding problems); and
- sociocultural factors including poverty, poor access, to or underutilization of, medical care, lower maternal educational levels, physical or mental illness in the mother or other caregivers, abuse, and neglect.

Imagine the complex interplay of factors when an infant is delivered prematurely to a young, single mother who has a history of mental illness and substance abuse, and infant neorate intensive care unit (NICU) with multiple medical needs.

The pediatrician is the professional in the best position to identify the infant at increased risk for developmental disability. A careful developmental history should be obtained for milestones in the entire range of development (gross motor, fine motor, language, social, and adaptive). Parent histories may be influenced by the level of their knowledge of typical child development, and also by their readiness to acknowledge delays or atypicalities when present. The physician must, therefore, supplement the history by observation of the child's acquired skills in the office. When indicated, formal standardized screening instruments may be administered. The Denver Developmental Screening Test has been popular for many years because of its ease of administration. Another such tool, the Cognitive Adaptive Test/Clinical Linguistic and Auditory Milestone Scale (CAT/CLAMS), yields a developmental quotient (DQ) which correlates well with the 'mental development index' of the more labor-intensive Bayley Scales of Infant Development, at least in healthy children without risk factors for developmental delay. Developmental progress should be tracked over time, as the outcomes will be markedly different depending on whether the infant has suffered the consequences of a prenatal or perinatal event without ongoing insult, vs. an ongoing risk factor such as abuse or neglect, vs. a neurodegenerative disease, for example.

Earliest indicators of developmental disability may include abnormalities of tone, feeding problems, and poor response to stimuli. As the child's neurological development normally progresses from primitive reflexes and postural responses to volitional movement patterns, the persistence of primitive reflexes may be an early sign of developmental atypicality, as are asymmetries and tone abnormalities (both hypertonicity and hypotonicity). Motor delays later in the first year, such as delays in sitting and crawling, may be noted. Language and behavioral abnormalities are commonly noted in the second and third years of life. Indicators of ADHD and learning disability may be seen by the time the child is ready to enter kindergarten.

Significant progress has been made in the area of early identification and intervention for infants with developmental disabilities and those at high risk over the years since 1975, when the Education for All Handicapped Children Act (EHA) was passed. Public Law 94-142 mandated "free and appropriate education in the least restrictive environment" for children with disabilities. In 1977, this was extended to include ages 3–21 years (although coverage from ages 3 to 5 years was optional). PL 99-457 in 1986 added coverage for infants and toddlers below age 2 years with disabilities. It provided for Individual Family Service Plans (IFSPs) for the delivery of individualized services to the families of these infants and toddlers. The EHA was reauthorized in 1991; PL 101-476 gave the new title of Individuals with Disabilities Act (IDEA). Its key components were: (1) identification of children with learning-related problems; (2) evaluation of the health and developmental status of the child with special needs, determining present and future requirements for intervention, with the formulation of a plan to address each area of need with appropriate services; (3) provision of those services, both educational and related services; and (4) guaranteed due process. Under PL 101-476, it was now assured that children with disabilities and their parents were as entitled to a free and appropriate education as were those without disabilities. Children from birth to age 3 years continued to have a written plan of service known as the Individual Family Service Plan (IFSP). From age 3 to 21 years, this written plan is known as an IEP or Individual Education Plan. Autism and traumatic brain injury (TBI) were included for special education coverage by PL 101-476.

As reauthorized in 1997 in PL 105-17, so-called 'Part C' called for the provision of early intervention services for all infants and toddlers with disabilities through the creation of statewide, coordinated, multidisciplinary, interagency programs. This law did not mandate these services, but did provide partial reimbursement for their cost. Currently, all 50 states have established early intervention services for children from birth to age 3 years, addressing developmental issues in the physical, communicative, cognitive, and psychological realms, as well as self-help skills, with the goals of minimizing disability and enhancing the ability of families to meet their children's special needs. It was hoped that early intervention would also decrease the costs for special education services once they reached school age. It was left to the states to define developmental delay for the purposes of establishing eligibility for services. Services are provided both to children with demonstrated delays and to those with biological conditions that place them at high risk for delays. The states may provide services to children at risk due to environmental factors, at their discretion. At the heart of 'Part C' of PL 105-17 is its focus on family involvement and family support. Evaluation, assessment, and planning are all subject to the approval and participation of the family. Likewise, intervention services are optional. When provided, these services are rendered in the most natural setting possible, such as in the home or the day care center. Follow-up surveys of families who have been involved in early intervention services under 'Part C' have shown a generally high level of parent satisfaction with their access to services, and also their perception of optimism for the future and their own competence in caring for and advocating for their children (although less positive outcomes were seen in minorities, in families with children with complex medical needs, and in single-parent families). Another important component of PL 105-17 was the extension of coverage to include ADHD.

Any child who presents to the physician with developmental delays should receive a thorough general and neurological examination. Particular attention should be paid to growth abnormalities, congenital anomalies which may suggest a genetic syndrome or chromosomal abnormality, a congenital CNS disorder, or intrauterine infection. Abnormal skin markings may be seen in genetic disorders as well as congenital infections. Abnormalities of the eyes, heart, limbs, and abdominal organs should also be noted. As the number of physical anomalies increases, the likelihood of a genetic disorder also increases. Neurological examination should especially include measurement of head circumference, examination of the cranial nerves, and assessment of tone. Persistent primitive reflexes and any asymmetries should be noted. Testing of hearing and vision should next be undertaken, using tools that are appropriate for the age and developmental level of the child. Other tests may be obtained, as clinically indicated, and may include genetic studies, imaging of the brain using magnetic resonance imaging (MRI), electroencephalogram, and others. Specialists from pediatric neurology, cardiology, orthopedics, genetics, psychology, or psychiatry may be consulted. However, referral to the early intervention program need not be delayed pending the results of these evaluations. The early intervention interdisciplinary team includes evaluation by occupational therapists, physical therapists, speech and language pathologists, and social workers. With the establishment of the IFSP (or IEP), services may then be initiated with the cooperation of the families, with systematic monitoring of the progress of the child and his family.

Cognitive disorders in infancy and early childhood fall into three fundamental domains: disorders of communication, disorders of socialization, and visual–spatial disabilities. Within each domain, there is a continuum of severity and complexity. There is also considerable overlap among the identified domains.

Individual variations in cognitive style and temperament include activity level, rhythmicity, approach to new stimuli, adaptability, intensity, mood, perseverance, distractibility, and threshold to stimulation. Areas of concern may include withdrawal from novel stimuli, slowness to adapt, intensity of response, a predominantly negative mood, shyness, and withdrawal. While these are not considered disorders in the infant and preschool children, they may predispose the child to problems later in life.

Disorders of Communication: Developmental Language Disorders

Normal Language Development

There is a large degree of variability in the rate at which language is acquired (first words anywhere from 6 to 30 months), as well as variability in the rate of acquisition of different linguistic components, such as phonology, lexical retrieval, and syntax. For example, many normal children concentrate their early acquisition of new words to nouns, while others add verbs and adjectives at a similar pace. There is no explanation at present for these differing styles of learning, and both groups of children are normal. The wide variability in so-called normal children can make it difficult to distinguish children with developmental language disability from those normal children with an idiosyncratic initial delay who will eventually catch up. Typically, developing children have good receptive language by 2 years of age, with an expressive vocabulary of 50 words or more and some two-word phrases. A general rule of thumb suggests that, after children develop a 50-word expressive language repertoire, other individual words, as well as phrases and sentences, will generally follow quickly. Expressive language is usually well-developed by 3 years of age.

There is clear evidence that children with developmental language disorders (DLDs) are at risk for a variety of social–emotional problems in older childhood and in adult life. There are certain 'red flags' for DLDs. Children with DLDs may demonstrate early problems relative to other oral functions such as sucking, swallowing, and chewing.

Infants who fail to vocalize to social cues or to vocalize two syllables by age 8 months are suspect. Slightly older children are at risk if they acquire new words only slowly and with great difficulty, if they rely too much on contextual cues for understanding of language, if their social interactions are limited to getting their needs met, if they produce few or no creative utterances of three words or more by age 3 years, and if they show little attention and interest for language-related activities such as book reading, talking, or communicating with peers. By age 3 years, typically developing children have developed symbolic, imaginative play.

Currently available tools for assessment of early language development can result in both underdiagnosis and overdiagnosis of DLDs. As many as 40% of children identified as having DLDs in the first 2 years of life may no longer retain that diagnosis at age 3 or 4 years. Ten per cent of these children are 'normal' at school age, while others have had their diagnoses refined to mental retardation, ASD, and others. It is preferable in the very young child to overidentify DLDs, as delay in diagnosis and treatment may have long-term social, behavioral, and educational implications.

Children at Risk

Risk factors for DLDs include parental mental retardation or a family history of DLDs. Premature and small-for-gestational-age infants are also at greater risk. There is a higher concordance rate in monozygotic vs. dizygotic twins, suggesting that environmental influences alone are insufficient to explain the occurrence of DLDs. A number of gene loci have been identified, implicating 13q, 16q, and 19q as candidate genes for further study. An autosomal dominant mode of inheritance is frequently seen, but there is variability in penetrance as well as in expressivity. For the purposes of this discussion, children with significant hearing loss and those who have identifiable brain lesions have been excluded.

Subtypes of Developmental Language Disorders

DLDs are described based on the linguistic area which is most significantly disturbed.

Articulation and expressive dysfluency disorders

Phonologic (pure articulation) disorders. Most children will speak intelligibly by 2 years of age. By age 3 years, fewer than 15% of children have unintelligible speech. Minor articulation defects, such as a distortion of the "th" and "r" sounds may persist with little consequence. Phonologic awareness, however, is critically important in the acquisition of normal reading skills, and children with delayed phonologic acquisition are at greater risk for developmental reading disorders at school age.

Dysfluency (stuttering and cluttering). Some degree of dysfluency is common as language skills develop, particularly as the mean length of utterance reaches six to eight words between 3 and 4 years of age. Some children with dysfluency may be relatively fluent for days or weeks at a time, then experience a protracted interval of relative dysfluency. Both stuttering and developmental dysfluency may be influenced by factors such as the complexity of the thought to be expressed and by being rushed or when excited, happy, or angry. Between-word dysfluencies include interjecting 'um' in a sentence, repeating a phrase, or revising the sentence structure in midstream. Within-word dysfluencies include repetitions of individual sounds or syllables, prolongations of sounds, and blocks. Stuttering is a disorder in the rhythms of speech, in which an individual produces a disproportionately large frequency of within-word dysfluencies compared to normally fluent peers, particularly at grammatically important points in the sentence. It often is a genetic trait, and occurs more frequently in children with other DLDs as well as with mental retardation. It is equally common in boys and girls at its onset, but is three times more likely to persist in males. Associated behaviors such as head, torso, or limb movement, audible exhalation or inhalations immediately prior to the dysfluency, and visible muscle tension in the orofacial region are signs that the child is becoming aware that talking is difficult. In younger children, the earliest and most frequently observed associated behaviors involve the eyes (such as blinking, squeezing the eyes shut, side-to-side movements of the eyes, and consistent loss of eye contact with the listener). These behaviors are seen in stutterers and usually not in children who are simply developmentally dysfluent. Most children who begin to stutter at preschooler age will recover without specific therapy, especially those with onset prior to age 3 years, if family history is either negative or characterized by spontaneous resolution, and if there are no coexisting speech and language or learning problems. Cluttering, by contrast, is characterized by echolalia, palilalia (compulsive repetition in increasing rapidity and decreasing volume), incomplete sentences, perseveration, poor articulation, and stuttering, seen in children with fragile X syndrome.

Verbal dyspraxia. This condition, in which children are extremely dysfluent, as often been called 'dilapidated speech'. Language is produced only with great effort. Phonology is impaired, including omissions, distortions, and substitutions. Language comprehension is preserved, and intelligence is normal.

Disorders of receptive and expressive language

Each of these disorders has a receptive component. While receptive language is heavily dependent upon attentional factors, reception may be impaired independently. Reception is dependent upon spoken rate, register, and dialect. It is a mistake to assume that the child who appears to be paying attention also understands what is said to him. In an emotionally charged context, reception breaks down further.

Phonologic syntactic syndrome. This condition, which is very common, is characterized expressively by disturbances in phonology, particularly in consonant sounds and consonant clusters in all word positions. The child is extremely difficult to understand, and grammatical forms are atypical. Semantics, pragmatics, and prosody are normal. Associated neurological problems are particularly common in this DLD, as are problems with feeding (sucking, swallowing, and chewing).

Verbal auditory agnosia (VAA). Children with VAA do not understand meaningful language, despite normal hearing. VAA may be seen as a DLD, or may be acquired in association with a form of epilepsy in which the epileptogenic portion of the brain involves the receptive language areas of the temporal lobe. The prognosis for this disorder is generally poor, although better in children with the acquired variety.

Higher-order language syndromes

Lexical syntactic syndrome. This common disorder is characterized by dysfluent speech, the consequence of word-finding difficulties, and a deficiency in syntactic skills. In the absence of finding the appropriate word, the child may 'talk around' the word in what are referred to as paraphasias. Speech is intelligible because phonology is normal. The child's language production is better for repetition than for spontaneous speech. Comprehension is normal except when the child is required to process very complex utterances.

Semantic pragmatic syndrome. Children with this condition are fluent, even verbose, but their large vocabularies belie the difficulty they have with meaningful conversation and informative exchange of ideas. Their chatter and often formal style may give the impression of a high intelligence quotient (IQ). Speech in this disorder has been described as stilted, pedantic, or professorial; the speech quality may be mechanical, monotonous, or 'sing-song'. Children with this disorder are often unable to respond to 'who', 'what', 'where', 'when', or 'why' questions, but may appear to exhibit great eloquence in subject matters of their interest or fixation. Comprehension is impaired. This syndrome is often seen in high-functioning autistic children.

Outcome for Children with Developmental Language Disorders

Preschool language skills predict later reading ability. DLDs are associated with problems such as ADHD, behavioral and emotional problems, and academic underachievement. While articulation and fluency problems may be the most obvious, more subtle disorders of comprehension may be misdiagnosed as conduct disorders or oppositional-defiant disorder, owing to the emotional 'meltdowns' in the child who is chronically unable to understand the intentions and expectations of others, both peers and adults. These communication problems may persist into adulthood in more than half of these children, impairing both social interactions and career success. The effect of speech and language therapy on outcome, particularly in the more significantly affected children, is still a matter of debate. This therapy is labor intensive, and may need to continue for prolonged periods of time. Continued association with more normally conversant children in the daycare or preschool setting is helpful.

Autism Spectrum Disorders

The clinical presentation (phenotype) of autism is highly variable, as is its natural history. There are several hypotheses regarding the essential cognitive deficit in ASD. The theory of mind blindness is related to the theory of mind; it implies that individuals on the autism spectrum lack the capacity for understanding or sensing another individual's state of mind. In other children with ASDs, the ability to solve problem, to shift sets, and to plan to reach a goal are deficient. A third theory suggests that children on the autism spectrum fail to integrate information, and are deficient in Gestalt ('big picture') formulations.

ASDs are characterized by the triad of impaired socialization skills, impaired verbal and nonverbal (body language) communication skills, and restricted areas of activity and interests.

Classic autism, as originally described by Leo Kanner in 1943, is estimated to occur in approximately 1 in 1000 individuals. ASD occurs in a wide degree of severity in an estimated 1 in 150 individuals (2007). Fifty to seventy per cent of autistic individuals can be determined to have demonstrated impairments since birth (e.g., using, scoring of the infant's interpersonal interactions on home videos). There is a subtype of ASD children, 30–50%, who evidently were typically developing children until language/ autistic regression occurred at a mean age of 21 months (range 12–36 months) under the influence of unknown triggers (including potentially infectious, immunologic, or psychosocial stressors).

Etiology

There is strong evidence for a genetic (probably multigenic) basis for ASD, including a recurrence risk of 4.0–9.8% in subsequent children in a family with one autistic child. In fact, the recurrence rate would certainly be higher but for the stoppage rule, that is, parents with one severely affected child often do not have more children. Lower-functioning autistic adults commonly lack the social skills that lead to successful interpersonal relationships, decreasing their likelihood of becoming parents. Males predominate at a rate of approximately four to one. There is a high concordance rate in monozygotic twins, approximately 90%. Several candidate genes have been identified. In addition, children with certain identified genetic disorders (including fragile X syndrome, phenylketonuria, tuberous sclerosis, Angelman's syndrome, and Cornelia de Lange syndrome) may demonstrate autism symptoms.

Future genetic studies may demonstrate that, for the autism spectrum, there are indeed many specific genotypes, as opposed to a single defective gene. In addition, confusion may arise, since there are many other conditions overlap with ASDs, including obsessive–compulsive disorder, Tourette's syndrome, and ADHD. Elements of these disorders are often found within ASDs. Future research depends upon standardization of diagnostic criteria to a research level of certainty.

The recent 'epidemic' of individuals identified to be on the autism spectrum is believed by most in the scientific community as being a manifestation of increased awareness and better identification, although research is also ongoing in the areas of possible environmental triggers, especially for those children who have appeared to undergo autistic and/or language regression in the second year of life.

Diagnosis

The diagnosis of autism is based upon the presence of specific criteria. The meeting of these criteria represents an analysis of phenotype, as opposed to genotype. It is currently possible to make a reliable diagnosis of ASD at age 24–36 months in many cases, with stability of the diagnosis up to 9 years later. The DSM-IV criteria are less useful in younger toddlers, below 24 months of age, and it is not yet well understood how early symptoms map onto later symptoms. Research is ongoing to develop reliable markers as young as 6 months of age, using the lack of joint attention as the operational definition of infantile autism. (Joint attention is a platform for language development, closely linked to abstract rule-learning, which is measured by three-point gaze shifts and following the look and point gestures of others.) Children subsequently diagnosed with 'congenital' ASD typically demonstrate language delays by 14 months of age, slower than normal language development from 6 to 36 months, and decreased initiation of communication for social or instrumental purposes. Because most children who present early are identified due to delays in acquisition of language skills, the first specialist consulted is commonly the audiologist. Sixty per cent of 14-month-olds later diagnosed with ASD, and 90% of 24–36-month-olds with ASD, were seen to have stereotyped patterns and interests. In endeavoring to make the diagnosis early, the clinician is challenged to differentiate the child with early signs of autism from the range of normal variability in development.

Tools to aid in early diagnosis of autism include detailed questionnaires, specific interview techniques, and blinded reviews of home videotapes. Using such tools, it can be seen that a subset of autistic children underwent global regression prior to 24 months of age. Most studies have shown that the majority of these children with autistic regression had minor impairments prior to the onset of the regression, however. This phenomenon is well described but poorly understood. It is crucial to assess the hearing of all children with language impairment, using, when necessary, brainstem auditory evoked responses (BAERs, otherwise known as auditory evoked potentials). This will distinguish those children who are language impaired or on the autism spectrum from those who are severely hearing impaired. (Although there are children who are severely hearing impaired who also meet criteria for ASD, in general, children who are hearing impaired alone do not manifest the degree of social impairment seen in autism. However, It can be very difficult to diagnose ASD in the deaf child with significant behavior problems such as severe ADHD.) The skilled evaluation of a speech and language pathologist is also mandatory. The gamut of language disorders described earlier in this article can be seen in ASD individuals, and severely language impaired children may also present diagnostic confusion with autism, especially, again, when behavior is abnormal. Seventy to eighty-five per cent of children with ASD are mentally retarded on standard testing; this group has a generally poorer prognosis. In contrast, many other children on the autism spectrum are above average, or even superior in intellectual functioning. It should be borne in mind that measurable mental retardation does not always translate to functional retardation. Many ASD adults may take advantage of their relatively well-preserved or even enhanced abilities in the visual–spatial domain, performing such repetitive functions as data entry. Preschool children with ASD may demonstrate excellent skills in puzzle construction, for example.

Core Deficits

Social competence

Social incompetence is the hallmark of ASD. It represents a lack of intuitive social skills. Children on the autism spectrum are unable to sense the emotional state of others. The 'theory of mind' refers to the concept that autistic individuals demonstrate a lack of awareness of the internal state of others. Their play is often parallel rather than interactive, with little symbolic play. When they do engage in interactive play, they generally take a passive role. At the extremes, they may be socially unavailable, aloof, or with an intense stranger anxiety, but there are also those autistic children who are socially impaired by virtue of being 'too social', with a dramatic lack of apprehension of strangers, and a willingness to go off with anyone, even those who are totally unknown to them. Most autistic children are withdrawn and exclude themselves (and their idiosyncrasies lead their peers to exclude them as well, thus reducing their opportunities to pattern social behaviors and language on typically developing peers). Autistic individuals may exhibit difficulties with personal space, which may be represented as a reluctance to have their own individual space invaded, with no corresponding reluctance to invade the personal space of others. Lack of eye contact was thought at one time to be the hallmark of ASD, but this is not necessarily the case. Children on the autism spectrum may look at, through, or beside others. There is, for the most part, an impairment in the quantity or quality of eye engagement. Children with ASD demonstrate a lack of interest in the human face, and are more likely to concentrate on the mouth or other parts of the correspondent, rather than his eyes. (Brain imaging in adults has shown differences from normals in the cortical areas involved in the perception of facial emotion.) Sharing and turn-taking are almost always impaired. Verbal autistic children give the impression of talking 'at' others (see the discussion of language impairments in ASD, below). Socially impaired children who are also nonverbal are often hyperactive, inattentive, and aggressive. Tantruming and uncontrollable screaming – what parents often refer to as 'meltdowns' – are common, especially in the children under age 3 years. These children may be inconsolable. Sleep is often disturbed. Bowel and bladder training are difficult and often significantly delayed. Self-injurious behavior may be present, particularly in lower-functioning children. Many consider the difficulties in the domain of social cognition to be the most essential feature of ASDs.

Language impairment

Verbal and nonverbal communication deficits are an essential part of the autism triad. Language generally parallels intelligence. Echolalia, while occasionally seen as a brief developmental interlude in normal children, and infrequently seen in persistent fashion in pure DLDs, is common in children on the autism spectrum. (Echolalic speech often portends the development of more fluent speech, and therefore it is not necessarily a bad sign.) As previously stated, a thorough assessment of hearing and the evaluation of a skilled speech and language pathologist are essential. In low-functioning children, verbal auditory agnosia, phonologic-syntactic, and lexical–syntactic language disorders are seen. In higher-functioning children, pragmatic and semantic deficits are characteristic. This includes deficits in who/what/where/when/how questions and in language turn-taking. In addition, prosody is frequently impaired, such that these children speak in monotone rather than in well-modulated speech. Hyperactivity and inattention relate inversely to language competence in autistic children under the age of 3 years. It is the consensus that language competence at 5 or 6 years of age quite accurately predicts long-term prognosis, since language, as suggested earlier, determines intelligence, which then relates to functionality. Chances for a child who remains nonverbal at the age of 8 or 9 years becoming linguistically competent are very poor.

Restricted range of behaviors, interests, and activities

ASDs are characterized by behaviors that are, from the viewpoint of the observer, odd or idiosyncratic. Activities such as toe-walking, twirling, licking, flapping, rocking, opening and closing doors, and manipulating light switches are seen. Again, there is variability, and these stereotyped behaviors may appear only for a brief period of time, only to be replaced by another oddity. Motor stereotypies are repetitive actions which are complex, involuntary, and purposeless, which are carried out with predictable form, amplification and location, in the autistic individual. They usually have their onset prior to the age of 2 years. Although tics may also be seen not uncommonly in ASD individuals, these brief, uncomplicated movements usually have onset after 6 or 7 years of age. Inattention and hyperactivity may be seen in ASD, thus overlapping with ADHD. Children with ASD may have great difficulty with transitions, and may become overfocused on certain activities, especially in the visual–spatial realm, such as assembling puzzles. As mentioned earlier, preschool children with ASD behavioral idiosyncrasies serve to accentuate their social isolation.

Treatment

There have been no long-term studies comparing those individuals who received early intervention vs. those who did not. Nevertheless, it is a good presumption that early intervention can improve eventual outcomes. Of the treatment modalities currently available, those that use an operant conditioning approach appear to be the most efficacious. While all use an applied behavior analytic approach (operant conditioning), individual protocols may vary widely. There is currently no way to compare protocols.

Pharmacologic treatment is presently limited to helping with related problems (such as stimulants for hyperactivity, medications to help with sleep, anticonvulsants for coexisting seizures, etc.). Speech and language therapies and social skills training may also be of benefit.

Visual–Spatial Disabilities

Visual–spatial disabilities (VSDs) involve perceptual organization, memory, and imagery. The literature on visual–motor and spatial disabilities in young children is very limited, but impairments in this domain will significantly impact future academic success. For example, the preschooler child's ability to copy geometric shapes has predictive value for reading and math in elementary school. Motor execution is the fundamental medium for expression of function or dysfunction in the visual–spatial areas. While there are motor-free tests for perceptual dysfunction, more commonly VSDs are grouped with related disorders of motor execution as perceptual–motor disabilities, and it can be difficult to consider one without the other.

Traditional IQ tests demonstrate VSDs by the discrepancy between verbal and performance IQ. Subtests include those of design copy and memory, picture memory, and mental rotation. Other easily administered tests include requesting a child to draw or copy shapes, or to draw a human figure. There are age-related norms for both these tasks.

The etiology of visual–spatial and motor deficits in the preschooler is in the right hemisphere of the brain, as evidenced in studies comparing the copying and drawing skills and the ability to create spatial arrays of toys in children with known injury (e.g., stroke) involving the right vs. the left hemisphere.

A long-term follow-up study of premature babies demonstrated that the inability to copy a circle and a low score of sorting blocks (by shape, color, and size) at age 4 years correlated with hyperactivity and an abnormal neurological examination (so-called 'soft signs') at age 7 years. The 30% of children in the same study who showed poor execution of copying of a cross had a higher rate of diagnosis of learning disabilities and also of neurological soft signs. Poor performance on a maze task correlated with learning disabilities, ADHD, and abnormal neurological examination. Conversely, those children who demonstrated proficiency in the copying of a square at age 4 years, and who had high scores on block-sorting tasks, were actually at decreased risk for learning disabilities and hyperactivity.

Referral to occupational therapy is important for the preschooler with suspected visual–spatial and motor disability. Treatment using perceptual training programs has been reported to be helpful. Disability in this realm may seriously impair the child's perception of the world. Understanding the relationship between visual–spatial and motor disability and subsequent learning disabilities may aid in earlier recognition and special education for learning disabilities and nonverbal learning issues.

A related issue which will be discussed elsewhere in this encyclopedia merits mention here. Disorders of motor planning and execution are difficult to separate from disorders in the visual–spatial and motor realm. Disorders of motor execution can accompany paralysis, spasticity (most forms of cerebral palsy), and movement disorders, but there are also a variety of disorders of motor execution that do not result in apparent alterations in strength, tone, or posture, but rather manifest themselves by clumsiness and inadequate performance of motor acts. The true incidence of higher-order motor deficits in first graders in regular schools is estimated at somewhere between 2% and 12%. These higher-order motor abnormalities are best detected if age-appropriate sequences of individual motions are performed under an examiner's observation. These disorders of motor execution frequently occur concurrently in children diagnosed with ADHD or learning disabilities. It is a mistake, however, to consider disorders of motor execution only in the context of other conditions, because impairments in this realm are disabling in themselves.

Historically, these children often will not have met gross motor milestones such as independent walking (usually met by 10–15 months of age), climbing stairs by themselves (normally 14–24 months), riding a tricycle (2–3 years), and riding a bicycle (4–6 years). They may also have failed to meet fine motor milestones, including holding a cup (10–14 months), executing buttons and snaps (3–4.5 years), printing their own name (4.5–6 years), and tying shoe laces (4.5–6 years). On examination of gait, their walking, running, skipping, tandem gait, hopping on one foot, and climbing stairs are clearly impaired. Upper extremity functions, including finger-tapping, wrist-turning, button-pressing, finger-nose-finger, copying, drawing, and writing are also impaired. The ability to imitate nonsense gestures (dyspraxia), to pantomime to command, and to use actual objects are similarly impaired. There are age-standard normative values for performance on the Purdue Pegboard and the subtests of Kaufman that relate to hand movements and spatial memory.

In the vernacular, a clumsy child is the classic 'klutz'. The purely clumsy child exhibits slow and inaccurate fine or gross motor performance deficits. The abnormality does not pertain to impairment of strength or tone, but rather to speed and dexterity. Clumsiness is a primary cause of school failure in early grades where the demands for motor task performance are great.

Synkinesis is an involuntary movement of voluntary musculature that occurs during the course of a voluntary action. One test that can elicit this, the Fog test, requires that a child walk on the sides of his feet, either on the insides or the outsides of the sole. When the child performs this maneuver, especially when a narrow base is demanded, the arms and hands frequently enter into distorted postures. Of synkinetic movements, mirror movements are the most commonly appreciated form of synkinesis. In a finger-tapping test, mirror movements commonly occur. The demonstation of synkinetic movements can be a part of normal developmental variation, but it is abnormal in children older than 6 years. Clumsy children often exhibit synkinetic movements as well.

Dyspraxia represents a characteristic failure in a complex, voluntary act, which is more easily recognizable when the child attempts to learn more complex motor sequences. Because dyspraxia is generally not evaluated apart from clumsiness or synkinesis, it is often not described, therefore, in preschool children. The failure to appreciate the presence of dyspraxia may result in a child being regarded as lazy, oppositional, or unintelligent, and this can result in poor self-esteem, poor motivation, and poor conduct. These children may demonstrate delays in self-care skills such as dressing and grooming themselves. Their specific problems may relate to buttoning, snapping, zipping, dressing, tying shoe lace, manipulating combs, toothbrushes, and particularly scissors. They may manifest as refusing to attempt tasks such as writing and coloring, at the same time that gross motor skills may be age appropriate. Most children with dyspraxias have no identifiable brain abnormality. Dyspraxias can be elicited by asking younger children to pantomime, for instance, blowing a kiss, or waving goodbye. A child can also be asked to fold a piece of paper, fit it into an envelope, or roll up a paper to use as a pretend telescope. Practice has a significant influence in children with dyspraxia as well as in clumsy children. Unlike the clumsy child, successful performance of the task by the dyspraxic child does not improve when extra time is allotted. It is particularly important in preschoolers to note that clumsy children and children with dyspraxia are more likely to injure themselves, and parents may be wrongly accused of abuse.

Other disorders of cognitive functioning that will be seen in the older child are not well studied in preschoolers. These include deficits in memory and in executive function. Executive function refers to the ability to maintain an appropriate set of procedures for problem solving, to attain a future goal. It involves the intention to inhibit a response to defer it, to formulate a sequential, strategic plan of action, and to encode relevant material in memory for future use. Preschoolers developmentally do not demonstrate significant skills in such future-oriented behavior, but some difficulties may be noted with self-regulation, selective attention, and vigilance.

Summary

Cognitive disorders in infancy and early childhood may have long-term consequences, for learning, for social success, and for employment. Cognitive limitations and the child's frustrations related to them may lead to significant behavior problems as well. The goal of early identification and early intervention is to recognize those children at risk, as well as those children demonstrating signs of cognitive disabilities. Appropriate consultations and therapeutic regimens may then be utilized to optimize the outcomes for the child and his family. The challenge for future research is to develop the tools for practitioners to aid in early recognition. Greater precision in diagnosis will also aid in the understanding of the natural history of cognitive disabilities, and also their causes. Longitudinal studies will be helpful in comparing the outcomes of varying educational and other treatment modalities.

See also: Genetics and Inheritance; Grammar; Language Development: Overview; Milestones: Cognitive; Pragmatic Development.

Suggested Readings

Nass R and Ross G (2005) Disorders of cognitive function in the preschooler. In: David RB (ed.) *Child and Adolescent Neurology,* 2nd edn., pp. 486–510. Oxford: Blackwell.

Rapin I (ed.) (1996) *Preschool Children with Inadequate Communication: Developmental Language Disorder, Autism, Low IQ.* Cambridge: Cambridge University Press.

Tuchman R and Rapin I (eds.) (2006) *Autism: A Neurological Disorder of Early Brain Development.* Cambridge: Cambridge University Press.

Exploration and Curiosity

A Baxter, University of South Alabama, Mobile, AL, USA
H N Switzky, Northern Illinois University, DeKalb, IL, USA

© 2008 Elsevier Inc. All rights reserved.

Glossary

Competence and intrinsic motivation theories of curiosity – Theories that believe that curiosity is the result of humans' motivation to master our own environments.
Constructivist – The belief that children build their knowledge through their experiences.
Curiosity – The desire to learn or know about anything; inquisitiveness.
Drive theories of curiosity – Theories about the arousal of curiosity that propose that curiosity leads to the unpleasant sensation of arousal that is reduced by exploration.
Exploration – Relatively stereotyped perceptual-motor examination of an object, situation, or event the function of which is to acquire information.
Incongruity theories of curiosity – Theories of curiosity arousal that posit that as humans try to make sense of the world their violated expectations about the world lead to curiosity.
Play – Intrinsically motivated behaviors and behavioral sequences, accompanied by relaxation and positive affect, that are engaged in for 'their own sake'.

Introduction

Exploration and curiosity are two forces that shape the development of infants and young children. It is difficult to tease the two apart and distinguish where one ends and the other begins. There is almost a symbiotic relation between the two. For example, when infants are curious about an object, person, or event, they explore the source of the curiosity. This exploration either satisfies the curiosity or arouses more curiosity. Thus, children either decrease their exploratory behaviors or explore more, respectively. A decrease in exploratory behaviors may be accompanied by the initiation of play with the object or person. Similarly, exploration may lead to curiosity as children discover something that was previously unknown. Both curiosity and exploration stem from similar factors: uncertainty, discrepancy/incongruity, and novelty.

While both curiosity and exploration are important to child development, they have not received equal attention from researchers. Exploration has been studied more intensively than curiosity. This is probably due to the nature of the two phenomena. Exploration is readily observable but curiosity is a mental process that is inferred from affect and behavior. In fact, many studies of exploration have just assumed that children are exploring because they are curious. Researchers have investigated situations in which curiosity precedes exploration but they have ignored those in which exploration has led to the arousal of curiosity.

This article describes both of these concepts. It defines each one, charts its developmental progression in the first 3 years of life, looks at its relation to other developmental skills, and places it within the larger context of the developing infant and toddler.

Curiosity

Most theories of child development posit that curiosity plays an important role in fostering optimal development. It is a behavior believed to be present across the lifespan although the nature of its expression changes qualitatively with development. Curiosity is identified as a factor that led to human adaptation, survival, and progress throughout history. Developmentally, curiosity plays a large role in facilitating infants' and children's cognitive, social, emotional, and physical development. Developmental theories as diverse as Piaget's and Freud's viewed curiosity as a central component in development. Curiosity is the motivational component behind children's exploration. Curiosity has both positive and negative influences on people's behaviors. However, curiosity has not been well researched. This is probably due to the fact that it is mental state inferred from children's actions which makes its measurement difficult. As a result, we may not have a full understanding of the construct of curiosity.

Despite almost universal acceptance of the importance of curiosity in facilitating development, there is no consensus about what curiosity 'is'. Defining it is difficult. There is no agreement about what causes curiosity or whether it is a unitary construct or separate constructs. Some researchers view curiosity as a drive, although they disagree whether it was a primary or secondary drive. They debate whether it is internally or externally motivated. To some it is a passion for knowledge that individuals have while others believe it is a response to specific stimulus characteristics. People's 'appetite for knowledge' is thought to be curiosity.

The research on curiosity reflects the ambiguity of the concept. Multiple researchers and theorists proposed multiple multidimensional models of curiosity. Separate cognitive, physical thrill-seeking, and social thrill-seeking curiosities are posited. Some wrote about an information-seeking or cognitive or epistemic curiosity. Others described a sensory curiosity related to sensation-seeking activities. Still others thought of curiosity as a 'drive to know'. There were discussions as to whether curiosity was a state or trait variable. Research studies designed to define and understand curiosity better resulted in different conceptualizations of curiosity as well as different patterns of relations among skills related to curiosity.

Most models of curiosity view it as something (i.e., drive, emotion, cognitive state) aroused by discrepancy, uncertainty, and/or other stimulus properties leading to stimulus exploration to resolve discrepancy or uncertainty. Exploration, in turn, provides the individual with information (e.g., cognitive, perceptual, and/or sensory information) about the stimulus and additional experience with the stimulus. This either decreases the need to explore the stimulus or leads to more engagement with the stimulus. In addition, many models realize that curiosity is not aroused in all individuals by the same stimuli. Curiosity can be stimulated by objects, people, or events in the environment; whether an object, person, or event acts as a stimulus for curiosity is a function of the individual's previous experiences. Children also differ in whether they are curious about objects or people. Thus, individual differences in curiosity and its arousal are expected.

These contrasting views of curiosity are, at least partially, the result of measurement and conceptual variations among the researchers. Some studies found a great deal of overlap among the different types of curiosity they measured. Because of the methodological difficulties inherent in truly understanding what curiosity is, many researchers chose to study what causes curiosity. The major theories are reviewed below.

Theories of Curiosity

Psychologists studied the underlying causes of curiosity since its inception. Early psychologists viewed curiosity as an emotion. They believed that stimuli either elicited curiosity or fear in children. Curiosity led children to explore the environment; fear inhibited exploration. At one time curiosity was considered a basic instinct. Some theorists viewed curiosity of having a positive affective valence. They believed that the information and experiences gained through curiosity led to feelings of personal growth and competence. Other theorists differentiated curiosity into state and trait curiosity. State curiosity is situation-specific whereas trait curiosity describes individuals who generally approached most situations with curiosity. Research with adults indicated that measures of trait curiosity (e.g., descriptions of a propensity to learn new things and experience interest in many things) and state curiosity (e.g., curiosity at a specific moment in time), while positively and significantly correlated with each other, measured separate and distinct phenomena.

More recent theories viewed curiosity as derived from a drive resulting from either incongruities or a competence motivation. Thus, they viewed curiosity as a motivational construct that was central to initiating children's exploration of their worlds. They saw curiosity as an intrinsically motivated 'passion' that individuals have to acquire information. Others likened curiosity to an 'appetite' for acquiring knowledge. Data indicating that highly curious children explored environments equally in the presence or absence of their mothers but those less curious children explored more in the presence of their mothers than with an unfamiliar experimenter supported this conceptualization.

The major theories about the underlying causes of curiosity are discussed below. They differ in whether they view curiosity as arising from a drive, stimulus, or competence and intrinsic motivations.

Drive theories

Drive theorists viewed curiosity as a drive that caused arousal, which is an unpleasant state for children. As a result, children explored the object or situation leading to the arousal. The exploration led to a reduction of the arousal. Support for curiosity as a drive came from animal studies where even in the absence of physiological needs, exploratory behavior still occurred. Curiosity was motivating in and of itself and, if left unsatisfied for a period of time, the curiosity drive grew. If children had the opportunity to interact with the stimulus that aroused curiosity, the curiosity decreased with time as the drive became satisfied. This satiety was very object specific however, and not generalized as seen with other drives. Thus, curiosity about a specific stimulus can be satisfied but another item can lead to more curiosity almost instantaneously.

Among drive theories, however, there were points of disagreement. Some saw curiosity as a primary drive and others as a secondary drive (i.e., the result of a more basic drive). Some believed that curiosity arose from a lack of homeostasis within the individual. Others thought it was triggered by the stimulus.

Freud, for example, believed that curiosity was a personality characteristic. As with most of Freud's theory, the personality trait of curiosity emerged from children's sex drives. He posited that biological urges and ego mechanisms worked together to guide exploratory behaviors. Exploration was a way for children to cope with mastering the social behaviors and conflicts inherent in life. He believed that children sublimated their sex drives in one of three ways. One way was through inhibition of thought processes which was contrary to curiosity. Another was through compulsive brooding about events and objects. The final way was through the development of a type of generalized curiosity.

Perhaps the most well-known curiosity theorist was Berlyne. To him, curiosity had its basis in the stimulus and the incongruity it aroused in the individual. The stimulus' incongruity resulted from its novelty, complexity, or uncertainty. To him, curiosity had two dimensions that he labeled perceptual-knowledge curiosity and specific-diversive curiosity. Perceptual curiosity was a drive response to novel stimuli that was decreased by exploration of, and continued exposure to, the stimuli. Knowledge or epistemic curiosity reflected humans' quest for knowledge and information. Specific curiosity reflected our seeking of particular bits of information about stimuli of moderate complexity, novelty, and incongruity. Diversive curiosity was our tendency to seek out stimulation. He posited that it was related to boredom. Thus, when curiosity is strong and fear or anxiety is low, diversive exploration occurs. When curiosity is relatively weak and anxiety is high there will be stimulus avoidance. Others viewed diversive curiosity as sensation or thrill seeking not as curiosity at all.

Whether curiosity is a drive or not is unresolved; it may never be resolved. In terms of our understanding of curiosity it may not be an important issue. What is important to understanding curiosity is that it is an aversive state that arises from the environment and leads to specific responses (i.e., exploration or attaining information) to be satisfied. If it is not satisfied it will intensify. While both internal (e.g., previous experience) and external (e.g., objects, people, events) factors influence curiosity their relative impacts are not the same; the nature of the stimulus and children's previous experiences jointly determine whether curiosity is aroused.

Incongruity theories

Incongruity theorists believed that curiosity is our reaction to incongruous events or information. Piaget viewed incongruity leading to curiosity in young children. To him curiosity was the impetus for children's constructivist activities (i.e., infants' and toddlers' building their understanding of the world from their experiences with the world). To him, children were innately curious. He saw curiosity as responsible for children's striving for new information and novel forms of stimulation. He saw the importance of both 'cognitive' and 'sensory' curiosity. He believed that curiosity sprung from children's interactions with, and attempts to make sense of, the world around them. He believed that curiosity arose from environmental events that violated children's expectations of how the world worked. To Piaget curiosity resulted from the disequilibrium produced by children trying to assimilate discrepant, new information into existing cognitive structures. Piaget believed that the relation between curiosity and incongruity varied as a function of the degree of incongruity. To him, information that was not very discrepant was readily assimilated into existing knowledge structures. Information that was too discrepant was ignored. Information that was moderately discrepant led to curiosity and the accommodation of existing cognitive structures based upon the information gained after the arousal of curiosity.

Kagan, in his description of the four basic human motives, acknowledged curiosity through his 'motive to resolve uncertainty'. He expanded on traditional views of incongruity, which had focused on the violation of expectations, by including the uncertainty arising three different sources. He added the uncertainty that arises from incongruities between incompatible ideas and that arises from incompatible behavior and ideas. Finally, he added the uncertainty raised by our inability to predict the future. This broader-based view of the dimensions of uncertainty related to curiosity has given us a fuller understanding of the contexts from which curiosity evolves. While many theorists included uncertainty in their models of curiosity, Kagan pointed out that uncertainty can result from inconsistencies in ideas and behaviors as well as thinking about the future.

Competence and intrinsic motivation theories

Another cadre of theorists believed that curiosity came from our motivation to master our environment. This 'competence' or 'effectance' motivation led to curiosity. We are motivated to be in control of the world around us. Curiosity helps us figure out how things work so we can understand the world and, as a result, feel competent. For example, Gibson attributed much of infants' perceptual learning and development to exploratory and curiosity behaviors. Curiosity has been linked to the presence of uncertainty and unexpected events in infants. Studies indicated that uncertainty may be a very important setting event for curiosity. It appears to be more salient than novelty in the arousal of curiosity. Situations that do not confirm expectancies maintain curiosity as measured by infants looking toward and attending to events. This suggests that infants use curiosity to understand and feel competent in their environment.

Other theorists viewed curiosity as a mechanism that evolved to resolve conflict. They suggested that unusual events led to conflict because they did not fit children's understanding of the world. Curiosity drives children to understand the stimuli lead to knowledge and reduces the conflict. As a result, the examination of unusual events becomes an approach to future situations because the decrease in conflict reinforces the future use of that strategy. Such a use of curiosity helps infants feel competent.

Types of Curiosity

Despite these disparate views on the origins of curiosity, there is some general agreement that there are at least two types of curiosity. One is focused on the acquisition of knowledge and information and is termed 'epistemic curiosity'. The other is focused on perceptual or sensory experiences and is called 'perceptual curiosity'. Perceptual curiosity can involve physical or social sensory experiences.

Curiosity, as a psychological phenomenon, is unusual because of its highly transient nature. Once resolved, curiosity quickly disappears. Often there is disappointment when the curiosity is resolved. When activated, curiosity tends to be very intense. Individuals expend a great deal of effort toward resolving the curiosity. These factors all make studying curiosity very difficult. Researchers have struggled with their definitions of curiosity and deciding how to measure it. Debates raged about whether curiosity can be thought of as a 'state' or 'trait' variable. Is it a primary or secondary drive? Does curiosity arise from the situation, or object, or is it an internal phenomenon?

While curiosity emerges from incongruity/uncertainty, stimulus complexity, and/or novelty, the relations among these variables are complex. Data indicate that too little uncertainty, complexity, or novelty leads to boredom not curiosity. We rarely see curiosity arising during interactions with simple, familiar, and understood objects or situations.

In contrast, too much uncertainty, complexity, or novelty distresses children and results in avoidance behaviors. This can lead to fear; a protective response to encounters with dangerous objects or situations. Thus, mild-to-moderate levels of uncertainty, stimulus complexity, or novelty are associated with curiosity in young children. In such situations, children act on their curiosity to learn more about the object and the object's complexity or novelty. This helps them to understand the object and decrease their uncertainty. It is important to remember, however, that children's individual experiences influence their perceptions of the stimulus. For example, a novel stimulus may be novel to some children and not novel to others. Similarly, the objects associated with curiosity in young children do not lead to curiosity in older children or adults.

Curiosity manifests itself in many different ways. One interesting manifestation of curiosity is through impulsive behavior. When curious, individuals often immediately act to obtain the information that will dissipate the curiosity. This resulted in great discoveries and progress. However, curiosity also leads children, and adults, to act in ways that are not always in our best interests. With development we are better able to inhibit some of this impulsiveness, but some of it remains with us.

Social curiosity motivates us to interact with others. For example, the presence of a caregiver or a peer may lead to curiosity in children. Children then begin to interact with the partner which continues the social interaction and in many cases leads to the desire to engage in more such interactions in the future. In addition, the interactive partner often feels positive about the interaction because the children's curiosity has kept them involved and engaged in the interaction. Many of the social games that caregivers play with young children are based on children's social curiosity.

Developmental Progression

The nature of children's expression of curiosity changes with age and development. Young infants' curiosity is inferred through their use of prolonged visual attention to a stimulus. With age and developing perceptual and motor skills, curiosity becomes the instigator of reaching for, touching, and manipulating the object in question. With further development and the advent of speech, verbal questions about the stimulus become how curiosity is expressed. With still further development, cognitive activities become the manifestation of curiosity. Reasoning is used to fill in the missing information or resources are accessed (e.g., books, the internet) to fill in the gap. There are indications that children's curiosity increases with their mental age, such that within a group of children those with higher mental ages are also more curious.

Infants use their perceptual, physical, emotional, communication, and social skills in service of curiosity. However, there are qualitative differences in curiosity during the first 3 years of life. These differences are described below.

During the first 6 weeks of life, infants' curiosity is difficult to assess. They look around at their surroundings but little sustains their attention for too long. At about 6 weeks of age, infants' curiosity is channeled toward their own hands. They begin to show some interest in their hands and they look at them from every angle as they make new and interesting movements. Next, they begin to use their hands to engage the environment. They bat at objects, explore surfaces for different textures, and grab anything within reach. Once they have the item in hand, they will manipulate it. These manipulations are usually accompanied with intense visual inspection.

At around 6 months of age, infants have become very accomplished with using their hands to explore their environments. This puts them in contact with many new objects about which they are very curious. They are beginning to understand cause and effect relations and they curiously look for these relations during their interactions with the physical and social environments. Much of their curiosity is in response to perceptual information.

Some theorists believe that at about 8 months of age infants enter a peak period of curiosity. As they develop self-locomotion through crawling and walking, the objects that were so far away now become objects of curiosity for them. They are able to get to those objects and satisfy their curiosity about them. Objects that do not lead to curiosity in adults are fascinating to infants.

During the second year of life, infants continue to try and understand cause and effect relations. Their curiosity is shifted somewhat. They are less interested in objects *per se* but they are more curious about what objects can do. They begin to enjoy mechanical toys and they spend a great deal of time observing the consequences of different actions on objects. Their exploratory behaviors decrease and the infant becomes more interested in investigating the effects of their motor behaviors. Thus, their curiosity becomes more focused on what they can do with the stimuli rather than just what the stimuli are or look like. It is also at this time that curiosity related to discrepancies between ideas and knowledge develops. This change reflects children's changing cognitive abilities; curiosity does not only lead to exploration but to additional thoughts.

As the second year of life comes to a close and the third begins, young children shift some of their curiosity to the development of their communication and social interaction skills. Their expression of curiosity begins to rely on their verbal skills. They begin asking the name for everything and their vocabulary is growing exponentially. After their vocabulary becomes fairly well established they begin posing questions. 'What' questions are the first to appear; they relate to children's development of specific cognitive concepts. These 'what' questions are followed by 'who is what' questions and then the 'why' questions. Children who ask more questions also explore toys more than children who ask fewer questions. Again we see the link between curiosity and exploration.

As children continue to develop language, they begin to spend more time in reflection. Curiosity again changes qualitatively. It becomes more internal and exists in children's thoughts. Curiosity becomes thinking about things and then acting on them through further thought, language, or physical actions. At this time there is also an increased focus on peer relationships. Curiosity is used to try and understand others' behaviors and reactions to other children's different social behaviors. It is through these mechanisms that children begin to learn appropriate and inappropriate social behaviors.

Facilitation of the Development of Curiosity

The environments in which children are raised can either support or interfere with the development of curiosity. There have been few empirical studies of the environmental variables that influence the development of curiosity specifically; however, there are many studies investigating the facilitation of cognitive development in young children. Studies supporting a preference for novelty suggest that a caregiving and physical environment that is structured, yet varied and changeable, will support the development of curiosity and the practice of exploration skills. Too much variability however, within the environment will make it too difficult for children to understand their environments. Children's individual differences in experiences and processing capabilities are important. Too familiar an environment is as detrimental as an environment that has too much variability or too complex stimuli.

Additional research indicates that social components of the caregiving environment are also important in fostering curiosity. Although most studies in this area have been correlational and involved preschooler children and elementary-aged students, they provided evidence that social environments characterized as being positive, accepting, supportive of autonomy, and communication enhancing are associated with more curiosity in children. It also seems reasonable that a caregiving environment that fosters positive social emotional development might also support the development of curiosity. Characteristics of infants with secure attachments suggest that a caregiving environment that allows for the development of secure attachments will also lead to the development of exploration skills and a preference for novelty. A caregiving environment that is aware of and respects temperamental differences among young children should also encourage curiosity.

An environment that encourages physical development should support the development of the sensory, motor, and perceptual skills that are essential to curiosity. If infants or children have cognitive and/or physical disabilities or challenges, it is crucial that accommodations are used so that they can engage in curiosity and exploratory behaviors.

Other correlational studies reported that children who were raised in environments that encouraged autonomy had well-developed senses of curiosity. Similarly, the setting of limits encouraged curiosity, as did attending to children's excitement about new things. Directing children's attention to the sensory aspects of a new toy or situation also encouraged the development of curiosity. Finally a trusting and loving caregiver–child relationship fostered curiosity.

Relation to Other Developmental Skills

Curiosity is associated with cognitive development and intelligence. It is well established that a preference for novelty is associated with higher levels of intelligence, even in infancy. In adults, a preference for novelty is associated with creativity suggesting that there is a relation between curiosity, novelty, intelligence, and creativity.

Clearly curiosity, in its deployment in search of knowledge, influences what is learned as well as how much is learned. Curiosity provides a context for children to practice the many skills believed to be important to intellectual development. Skills such as accessing information to reduce uncertainty, detecting incongruous, complex, and novel stimuli, resolving conflicting solutions or explanations to problems, as well as hypothesis formation and testing are involved with curiosity. They are also highly valued cognitive skills. Finally, curiosity is a phenomenon that involves all developmental domains, not just cognition. Sensory skills, motor skills, communication skills, and social skills are all involved in curiosity and its expression.

Exploration

Exploration is an individuals' sensory, perceptual, and motor behaviors that are used to investigate an object, event, or person. Two different types of exploration have been described. The first is best typified by the way that young children wander around an environment, either familiar or novel, until something in the environment attracts their attention. The second type of exploration occurs when a stimulus catches children's attention, curiosity is aroused and they explore the stimulus to learn more about it. In the first example, exploration leads to curiosity and in the second curiosity leads to exploration. Psychologists have studied the first type of exploration only minimally while they have studied the second type extensively. In this article, we too will focus primarily on this second type of exploration: the exploration that results from curiosity.

Exploration is a behavior focused on the here and now. It does not have to be driven by curiosity. Children explore the objects they find readily at hand or the environment in which they find themselves. While they may use memory and schemas about previous situations, their exploration efforts are focused on where they currently are. Exploration is not a constant event, however. If children are initially very eager to explore an object their exploration of that object decreases with time, as they gather information about it. Exploratory behaviors decrease as children's familiarity with the object or event increases. Conversely, when children are hesitant to explore the object; there will be an increase in exploratory behavior across time and then a decrease as they come to 'understand' the object.

Exploration involves concentration and inspection of the object. In exploration, children use their perceptual, motor, and cognitive abilities. The purpose of exploration is to reduce uncertainty about the object, event, or person. Exploratory behaviors follow a pattern of paying attention to the object, event, or person, visual inspection of it, motor and perceptual examination, and finally physical interaction with the object or person.

The exploratory behaviors of infants and young children are well documented. Exploratory behaviors play important roles in the processes of learning about and adapting to the many environments in which children find themselves. It is through exploration that infants and young children learn about the characteristics of different objects and environments. Exploratory behaviors are related to characteristics of stimuli. Young children's exploratory behaviors result from several factors. One is an almost biological drive to explore the environment. Past experiences with objects and different environments support exploration. The state of the current environmental context drives exploration. Finally, exploration is often accompanied by neutral or mildly negative affect, suggesting that exploration is not necessarily pleasurable for the child.

Just like curiosity, exploration has been associated with stimulus incongruity/uncertainty, discrepancy, novelty, and complexity. However, exploration has different patterns of relations with these stimulus characteristics than curiosity.

Exploration is most commonly the response to moderate uncertainty. In young children the relation between stimuli uncertainty and exploration varies with the degree of uncertainty. If there is no uncertainty, children will not explore the stimulus. Too much uncertainty will lead to children inhibiting any interactions with the stimulus. A moderate degree of uncertainty, however, will lead to exploration. Thus, in reality, in uncertain situations, exploration often takes precedence over other behavioral alternatives.

There is a similar relation between discrepancy, the degree to which the stimulus is similar to known stimuli, and exploration. Stimuli that are too discrepant are not likely to lead to exploration. Stimuli that are not discrepant are more likely to encourage the activation of play or ignoring the stimulus than exploration.

The relation between novelty and exploration is different however. Research has indicated that, given the choice, infants and children prefer to explore novel toys and objects over familiar toys. Novel toys lead to higher rates of exploratory behaviors than more common toys. All novelty is not equal, however. It appears that toys with novelty along perceptual dimensions are more supportive of exploration than novelty focused on problem solving. This may be because the problem-solving toys supported more instrumental behaviors whereas the novel perceptual toys were more ambiguous and, therefore, encouraged more exploratory behaviors. No novelty induces boredom and little exploration in infants. A moderate degree of novelty seems to lead to exploration, whereas too much novelty tends to overwhelm the child and inhibit exploration, sometimes even leading to withdrawal or avoidance.

Stimulus complexity is also important to exploration. The relation between stimulus complexity and exploration is not consistent across the developmental period. Studies indicated that very young children do not explore stimuli that are too complex. For 2-year-olds, the relation between stimulus complexity and exploration is curvilinear; yet for older children it is linear. Two-year-olds explore stimuli with moderate amounts of complexity more than they do stimuli with relatively less or more complexity. Preschooler and young school-age children explore the most complex objects much more than less and moderately complex objects. Thus, with younger children the relation between stimulus complexity and exploration is the same as the relation discussed for novelty, uncertainty, and discrepancy. However, for older children more complex stimuli are associated with increased exploration and less complex stimuli with little exploration.

Modes of Exploration

Infants' and young children's exploratory behaviors are limited or facilitated by their skills in many developmental domains. In infants and toddlers, exploration often involves all of the senses. It is visual and tactile. It involves active manipulation, mouthing, and banging of stimuli, language, and thinking. We see qualitative differences in children's exploratory behaviors based upon other developmental skills.

Soon after birth, infants begin exploring their environment. Although they have a limited focal range, they will look to areas of high contrast. The caregiver's face soon becomes a favorite subject. With development, infants gain control of the movement of their eyes and learn to intentionally shift their gaze between people and objects of interest.

With further development comes visually directed grasping and reaching. This allows infants to initiate physical interactions with people and objects. Infants learn to change their grasp, to transfer objects from one hand to the other, and to put objects in their mouths to explore them more fully. Most studies of young children's exploratory behaviors have focused on their visual and manipulative behaviors. Manipulative behaviors that have been studied often include behaviors such as holding, banging, grasping, scratching, shaking, and hitting. Usually children engage in these behaviors while simultaneously looking at the object. Children learn how to vary their manipulation of objects based upon characteristics of the item. For example, children use both hands for larger objects.

Infants next learn to sit independently. This allows them to use both hands to explore and manipulate objects. This new position also allows them to visually explore more of their environment. They are now also able to manipulate objects and visually explore other parts of their environments. These changes prepare them for the next stage of exploration, being able to independently get to objects of interest.

The next development in exploration is self-locomotion. This new development allows infants to explore every nook and cranny of their environments. They can move and explore their environments at will.

As language develops, children shift from physical manipulations of objects to using questions as a way to explore their environments. As with curiosity, with age exploration is transformed into more of a cognitive activity whereby children explore more through their thoughts than through the physical manipulations of items.

Developmental Patterns

Infants' limitations in perceptual, motor, and cognitive development impact their exploratory behaviors. Initially, infants' only mode of exploring objects or environments is through their use of vision. Newborns will look around their environments and fixate on objects or people of interest. Their limited visual acuity forces them to look to objects within their focal distance or places where there is high contrast. Often, they focus on caregivers' faces. This continued visual exploration leads to the recognition of familiar caregivers and the fear of strangers that emerges in response to new interactive partners.

During the first year of life children rely on one sensory modality (e.g., vision, tactile) at a time to explore. As development proceeds they develop control over their fingers and begin to develop visually guided reaching abilities. Once infants have learned to coordinate their hand and arm movements with visual information and have prehension skills, they begin to actively manipulate objects of interest. Simply looking at the stimulus no longer meets all of their exploratory needs. This typically occurs at about 5 months of age. At this age, infants not only explore through looking at an object. Most exploratory behaviors at this age involve reaching, grasping, and mouthing of objects. Infants use both hands as they shake, hit, and finger the object. They feel it, put it in their mouths, mouth it, and gum/chew it. They also listen to it. From this point forward, most exploration involves children manipulating objects at the same time as they visually inspect them. Five-month-old infants are typically able to manipulate many objects and have a very advanced exploratory repertoire. Their sense of touch becomes well refined.

With the development of crawling, and later walking, a larger environment is opened up for infants to explore. They venture out into their environments and explore areas they could not access before. They do not need any incentives to explore because the environment itself provides a very large incentive. Both the mundane and exotic are explored. It does not matter if it is a crumb on the floor or water in the toilet; it will need to be explored thoroughly. Two- and 3-year-olds use all sensory domains to explore.

Changes in infants' cognitive development drive them toward exploring their ever-growing collection of concepts and relations in both the physical and the social realms. Exploration helps infants to 'know' their world so that novelty can be detected more easily through its contrast with the familiar. Up until about 14 months of age, infants spend a great deal of time exploring their environments. After this time however, there is a decrease in exploratory behaviors and a corresponding increase in what have been called mastery behaviors. While exploration involves examination of an object by one or several methods, mastery behaviors involve the practice of specific skills using a variety of objects. This change relates to a concomitant change in working memory that allows for the inhibition of some behaviors and facilitates goal-oriented behaviors. We see infants spend less time exploring objects but more time dropping and throwing them. They tend to practice different motor skills more and explore less. By the time that they are 2 years old they typically engage in more mastery than exploratory behaviors. The decrease in exploration also occurs because thought, rather than exploration, emerges as children's response to stimuli that are inconsistent with their knowledge base.

Developmental differences exist in infants' examining, mouthing, and banging of objects. Examining behaviors (e.g., inspection and visual attention with or without manipulation) are believed to represent an exploratory behavior. Age, related differences were found in children's latency it to examine an object. Younger infants (7-month-olds) had a longer latency to examine the object than older infants (12-month-olds) even though the two age groups did not differ in the total amount of time they spent examining the object. This difference may reflect the younger infants needing more time to process the stimulus and organize their exploratory responses. In both age groups, examination of the object preceded mouthing and banging behaviors. As exposure to the object increased, examination decreased and mouthing and banging increased. These results suggest that examination is a primary exploratory behavior and mouthing and banging are secondary exploratory behaviors. These findings suggest that the latency to examine objects and the total amount of time infants spend examining objects represent different behavioral systems. Thus, what appears to change with development is not the amount of time that infants spend exploring objects but how quickly they begin examining objects. Therefore we should evaluate several dimensions of infant exploratory behaviors because they each tell a different story about the infant's abilities.

Influences upon the Development of Exploration

There are great individual differences in young children's exploration. These differences relate to individual differences in motivation, prior experiences, and the social environments in which children develop. The motivational differences are often attributed to individual differences in curiosity which are thought to have their roots in both the genetic and environmental factors.

Studies exploring the contributions made by parents and the environment to individual differences in exploratory behaviors found interesting results. Some studies indicate that the parents of children who readily explore their environments tend to supply their children with a great deal of information about the environment. Even when separated from the parent, these children spend a relatively large amount of time exploring the environment (e.g., questioning, toy manipulation, exploring the room). When interacting with a woman experimenter, children who did not explore environments as readily were more inhibited in their exploration and questioning than when observed with their mothers. These children, however, did explore environments when guided in the exploration by an adult. Thus, children have the requisite skills for exploration; but they do not regularly use these strategies to understand their environments. Other studies of the young children of mothers with depression, indicated that they explore less than children whose mothers are not depressed. The depressed mothers' withdrawn and less-stimulating interactive styles did not encourage their children to explore. Thus, it appears that the social environment can lead to individual differences in rate of exploratory behaviors and facilitate exploration in those who do not readily explore.

Individual differences among children influence their exploration. For example, children seem to differ in terms of how much ambiguity they can tolerate. Children who cannot tolerate a great deal of ambiguity tend to explore very little. Likewise, children of mothers with depression do not explore much. Children with visual impairments and/or motor impairments explore less than children without these impairments because of the limitations that their disabilities put upon the major systems used in exploration. Finally, individual differences in experiences influence the ambiguity, uncertainty, novelty, and complexity of objects. These differences, in turn, influence whether children explore or not.

Gender differences in exploratory behaviors are documented. Infant girls explored less and remained closer to their mothers in new settings. Boys explored objects more actively than girls. Research indicated that these gender differences in exploratory behaviors linger into childhood and beyond. These gender differences have been observed in terms of children looking at objects and their manipulation of objects although the reasons for the differences are not clear. Some have suggested that they reflect differences in reactions to new or unusual objects, while others suggest that these findings might be an artifact of boys' more active mode of play.

Facilitation of the Development of Exploration

The attachment relationship between caregivers and infants is related to infants' exploratory behaviors. The different attachment classifications are based upon infants' patterns of maintaining proximity to their caregiver and exploring the environment. The phrase often heard about infants who are 'securely attached' is that they use their caregivers as a 'secure base' for exploration of the environment. This is also seen as a measure of young children's competence. A caregiver–child relationship that encourages children's exploration and object mastery also supports the development of competence. Likewise, exploratory behaviors are less common in children with ambivalent (type 'C') attachments. These children explore the environment very little. These behaviors make sense in that if parents provide information about exploration and the environment infants are likely to explore and use the parental information. If the parent does not provide such support, children may be hesitant to engage the environment because the parent does not provide them with information about safety. Type C infants have parents who typically do not provide contingent information about the environment, so they are hesitant to explore.

To encourage exploratory behaviors it is important to have environments that are appropriately stimulating to children. The environment should contain a balance of new and old activities and objects. It should allow for exploration to occur through hands-on activities. Caregiver questions will maintain exploration; asking children what an object is, and what it does. Finally, the social environment should encourage exploration rather than discouraging it by saying things such as 'Stop making a mess' or 'Do not get into things that are not yours'. In addition, children should have time to explore and be allowed to explore until their curiosity is exhausted.

Relation to Other Developmental Skills

Exploratory behaviors have been linked to the development of cognitive, communication, social, perceptual, and motor skills. It is difficult to determine if developments in exploratory behaviors lead to changes in the other domains or if changes in these domains lead to changes in exploratory behaviors. Attention is also related to children's exploratory behaviors.

Exploration and play are treated as different phenomena in the research literature. Exploration is a process of collecting sensory information to reduce uncertainty or gather information. It is accompanied by neutral or mildly negative affect. It occurs prior to, but often leads to, play. Play, defined as pleasurable activities that are engaged in for their own sake, is often described as 'children's work'. While exploration is very similar across situations, play varies from child to child, object to object, and situation to situation. Exploration and play are children's responses to different questions. Exploration is the response to the question, 'What is this stimulus and what can it do?' Play is the response to the question, 'What can I do to this stimulus?' Thus, exploration is children's responses to stimuli, while play is centered on children acting upon the object. Exploration typically precedes play in children's interactions with unfamiliar stimuli. It satisfies their curiosity and then children either ignore the stimulus or integrate it into one of their play schemas. While uncertainty is linked to exploration, play does not occur when children are uncertain or fearful. However, repeated exposure to a stimulus decreases the novelty and thus exploratory behaviors while play behaviors increase with familiarity. Play and exploration also have different affective components. Children who are playing also smile and laugh; exploration is accompanied by neutral or slightly negative affect. Play and exploration lead to the increase in independence and decrease in dependence on the caregiver that emerges in most children during development. It is in the context of exploration and play with objects, people, and situations that children come to construct meaning of the physical and social worlds around them.

Children's exploratory behaviors have always been an important component of our construct of attachment. Bowlby believed that infants would be very hesitant to explore their environments if they did not feel secure about the mother's proximity and availability. Unless the infants were sure that the parent would be there if their exploration led them to a dangerous situation, they would not explore the environment. Members of the four different attachment classifications differ in terms of their exploratory behaviors during the strange situation's three different interactional contexts: interacting with the caregiver, interacting with the stranger, and being left alone in the room. The attachment classification differences in exploration reflect temperamental and parent–child relationship differences.

The relation between novelty and exploration is an interesting one. Infants strive to explore their environments to make what seems novel, at a particular point in time, become familiar. Once familiarity has been established, children no longer use exploratory behaviors but rather interact with the toy through play. It is against this new mural of familiarity that infants again search for novelty. As a result of this never-ending process, children amass a great deal of information about their environment. This preference for novelty, which seems to drive exploration, at least in part, has been found to be positively related to the subsequent assessments of children's intelligence. Other studies have indicated that attention to novelty is related to information processing abilities throughout life.

Exploration and Curiosity

It is thought that a lack of knowledge or understanding leads to curiosity, which in turn is associated with exploration in order to acquire the missing information. Studies comparing children with individual differences in curiosity found that children who were more curious explored novel toys much more than children who were less curious. However, when more conventional preschool toys were used the children did not differ in their manipulations of the toys but the high-curiosity children played with the toys longer than the low-curiosity children did.

Interrelations of Curiosity and Exploration

Early theorists posited that curiosity and fear were common reactions to novel stimuli. The fact that novel objects elicited both curiosity and fear suggested an antagonistic relation, although both emotions were considered to be adaptive. Curiosity was thought to support one's exploration of the environment, while fear typically led to withdrawal and avoidance. Thus, relatively novel stimuli were associated with curiosity, while more unusual stimuli typically led to avoidance or withdrawal. Thus, exploration is thought to arise from curiosity and its concomitant anxiety. Exploration is one strategy children can use to decrease this anxiety.

Some researchers have taken a social learning approach to understanding the development of curiosity and exploration in young children. They suggested that parents develop curiosity in their children through modeling and reinforcement. Mothers who explored toys with their children, encouraged children's continued exploration, reinforced children's exploratory behaviors, and answered children's questions had children who asked more questions and spent more time exploring new toys. Similarly, parents who were critical of children's exploratory behaviors had children who exhibited very few exploratory behaviors. Studies comparing children relatively high and low in curiosity interacting with researchers with different interactive styles have found that regardless of the adult's interaction style highly curious children had high levels of exploratory behaviors. In addition, low-curiosity children did not explore the environment differentially when interacting with an adult who demonstrated exploration and reinforced it, an adult who was responsive but not encouraging of exploration, or an adult who was unresponsive and inattentive. Their exploratory behaviors were at low levels in all three interactive conditions.

Many quality early childhood care environments focus on the facilitation of curiosity and exploration in addition to play and creativity. These four factors, when seen in young children are thought to be evidence of participation in high-quality caregiving environments. The lack of curiosity and/or exploration in young children is often seen as evidence of psychological problems.

Parents and caregivers need to be careful about facilitating exploration and curiosity. The encouragement of these two skills in young children can be generalized in ways that may be unsafe. For example the same curiosity that leads infants to play with a new toy, can also lead children to climb up the bookcases in the living room. Thus, attention must be paid to the environment and stimulation that are available to infants and toddlers and efforts must be made to keep children safe while they are exploring based on their curiosity.

Importance to Development

Studies of the cognitive development of infants and young children point to curiosity and exploration as important to cognitive development. These effects are not limited to the infancy and early childhood years, but appear to hold for the lifespan. In addition, many of the characteristics that lead to curiosity play a role in the development of information-processing skills in human beings. Important components of curiosity: a preference for novelty, a strong desire to reduce uncertainty, and selective attention to incongruity are also important to information processing development. Curiosity and exploration also influence development in other domains as well. Children's exploration of their environments and curiosity about what they encounter foster language development. What is an object's name? What does it do? Why does it do that? Exploration and curiosity also advance social development. Children learn about how to initiate and maintain interactions with people who arouse their curiosity and who support their exploration. Social environments that do not support curiosity and exploration lead to children who do not use these skills regularly to interact with their environments. Curiosity and exploration are also linked to motor development. From children learning to control the movement of their eyes and use their binocular vision, to reaching, grasping, and manipulating objects, to self-locomotion and getting into everything, curiosity and exploration drive the refinement of children's motor skills.

See also: Attention; Cognitive Development; Habituation and Novelty; Imagination and Fantasy; Perception and Action; Play; Reasoning in Early Development; Separation and Stranger Anxiety.

Suggested Readings

Berlyne DE (1954) A theory of human curiosity. *British Journal of Psychology* 45: 180–191.

Fowler H (1965) *Curiosity and Exploratory Behavior.* New York: Macmillan.

Görlitz D and Wohlwill JF (eds.) (1987) *Curiosity, Imagination, and Play: On the Development of Spontaneous Cognitive and Motivational Processes.* Hillsdale, NJ: Erlbaum.

Henderson BB (1984) Parents and exploration: The effect of context on individual differences in exploratory behavior. *Child Development* 55: 1237–1245.

Lowenstein G (1994) The psychology of curiosity: A review and reinterpretation. *Psychological Bulletin* 116: 75–98.

Reio TG, Petrosko JM, Wiswell AK, and Thongsukmag J (2006) The measurement and conceptualization of curiosity. *Journal of Genetic Psychology* 167: 117–135.

Spielberger CD and Starr LM (1994) Curiosity and exploratory behavior. In: O'Neil HF and Drillings M (eds.) *Motivation: Theory and Research*, pp. 221–243. Hillsdale, NJ: Erlbaum.

Switzky HN, Haywood HC, and Isett R (1974) Exploration, curiosity, and play in young children: Effects of stimulus complexity. *Developmental Psychology* 10: 321–329.

Weisler A and McCall RB (1976) Exploration and play: Résumé and redirection. *American Psychologist* 31: 492–508.

Wentworth N and Witryol SL (2003) Curiosity, exploration and novelty-seeking. In: Bornstein MH, Davidson L, Keyes CLM, Moore KA, and Kristin A (eds.) *Well-being: Positive Development across the Life Course*, pp. 281–294. Mahwah, NJ: Erlbaum.

Relevant Websites

http://scholastic.com – Curiosity: The fuel of development; Encouraging new triumphs. When and how to challenge your baby to try new tasks.

http://www.naeyc.org – Early years are learning years. "I can do it myself": Encouraging independence in young children.

http://www.evenflo.com – Month 5: Exploration and Experimentation.

http://www.sesameworkshop.org – Parenting essentials for moms and dads who grew up on Sesame Street.

http://www.gfi.org – Parenting with Gary and Annie Marie: Toddlers; Toddlers and curiosity.

http://childcare.about.com – Ways to spark creativity in a child.

http://www.zerotothree.org – ZERO TO THREE.

Future Orientation

N Wentworth, Lake Forest College, Lake Forest, IL, USA

© 2008 Elsevier Inc. All rights reserved.

Glossary

Anticipatory eye movements – Eye movements that are initiated before stimulus onset and that bring the fixation point to the location of an upcoming picture.

Expectation – Hypothesized mental construct that is inferred from anticipations or faster responses during predictable sequences compared to during irregular sequences.

S1–S2 paradigm – A procedure in which paired stimuli are presented over a number of trials with a fixed interval between the first stimulus (S1) and the second (S2); used to examine physiological and behavioral anticipation.

Saccadic eye movements – Small, rapid eye movements that quickly change the point of fixation; saccadic eye movements are present at birth.

Smooth pursuit eye movements – Slow, continuous changes in eye position that occur when the observer watches a smoothly moving target; smooth pursuit eye movements appear during the first few months after birth.

Visual expectation paradigm – A procedure in which infants watch a sequence of brief pictures in alternation with blank, no-picture, intervals; the spatiotemporal structure that governs the picture sequence can be regular, and thus predictable, or irregular; used to examine anticipatory and facilitated eye movements indicative of visual expectations.

Introduction

The ability to predict what lies ahead, and adjust our behavior accordingly, is one of the defining characteristics of intelligent adaptation to a complex and dynamic environment. This article considers the emergence of this ability and its early development across several action systems including vision, visually directed reaching, posture, self-produced locomotion, and social interaction. Skills that may facilitate acquisition of future-oriented capabilities early in life are discussed as are common physiological indicators of expectation and anticipation. Progress in the developmental study of future-oriented behavior will require creative solutions to difficult methodological and conceptual challenges.

Future Orientation

We spend much of our mental lives in the future – setting goals, for example, and planning means to accomplish them, anticipating future obstacles and developing strategies to bypass them, and envisioning the scenarios we hope for as well as others we fear. The future similarly governs many of our actions – we anticipate the trajectory of a ball so that our hands can arrive in time to catch it, we stiffen postural muscles in anticipation of picking up a bag of groceries, and we articulate speech syllables differently depending on what we intend to say next. This ability to predict what lies ahead, and to adjust our behavior accordingly, distinguishes expert from novice performance and is one of the defining characteristics of intelligent adaptation to a complex and dynamic environment. But how does this capability to envision the future develop? What are the earliest forms of its expression? Which environmental or experiential factors shape its developmental course? How does the child's awareness of time emerge and differentiate into a sense of the past, present, and future?

Although the future clearly plays an important role in shaping our thoughts and actions, investigation of the early development of future-oriented processes has lagged substantially behind research on how past and present circumstances influence the behavior of infants and young children. Thus, an impressive body of literature establishes that infants, from very early in life, attend to many dimensions of the sensory information that surrounds them and that they have preferences for certain types of stimulation over others. These preferences tend to highlight certain aspects of the environment, such as edges of objects or the speech of humans, giving infants differential exposure to, and practice with, processing those attended features. An equally impressive body of literature indicates that past experience can also shape infants' preferences and activities. For example, studies have shown that newborns will modify the components of their sucking in order to hear sounds to which they were exposed when they were *in utero*. While the knowledge base concerning the influence of the future on children's behavior is much less extensive, the research that has been done suggests that infants look toward the future much earlier in life than was once thought possible, although the skills for doing so are quite limited at first and have a notably long time course.

Historical Roots

Developmental psychology's relative neglect of future-oriented processes may be traced, at least in part, to the mechanistic tradition of behaviorism. The behaviorist tradition rests on two classic discoveries. After Ivan Pavlov's discovery that salivation could be elicited by a bell simply by repeatedly pairing the bell with food, proponents of radical behaviorism attempted to explain all behavior in terms of the organism's basic biological predispositions in conjunction with the history of stimulus–response pairings to which the organism had been exposed. At about the same time as Pavlov discovered the essentials of classical conditioning, Edward Thorndike discovered the law of effect. Cats that were placed in puzzle boxes learned to escape by a process of trial and error; those responses that led to freedom were stamped in by the reinforcement of successful escape, while other responses dropped out. After Thorndike's discoveries, proponents attempted to explain all behavior in terms of the organism's reinforcement history. The discovery of the principles of classical and operant conditioning promised the early behaviorists mechanisms that might explain the emergence of intelligent behavior solely in terms of the past. Such mechanistic accounts were more parsimonious than other accounts available at the time that either invoked a nearly limitless list of instincts to explain intelligent behavior or that suffered from the logical flaw of teleology in which the cause of a behavior rests in the future and must work its way backwards in time to produce its effect. In behaviorism, in contrast, the source of explanations for the present rests in the past; the future is then free to unfold in a single linear direction that flows logically from out of the past.

It should be noted, however, that even the most ardent followers of Pavlov and Thorndike found it necessary to incorporate terms to represent the influence of the future in their behavioral equations. For example, Leonid Krushinskii, one of Pavlov's intellectual descendents, described studies of the extrapolation reflex of birds, such as pigeons, ducks, hens, crows, and rabbits. Animals were given the opportunity to eat from a moving food dish that eventually entered a tunnel. Krushinskii speculated that the animal's ability to extrapolate the movement of the food dish into the future became associated with the unconditioned response of eating in the vicinity of the dish. The capacity to make these associations explained the intelligent and future-oriented behaviors that Krushinskii observed in the animals such as running to the end of the tunnel to intercept the food that would soon emerge. Similarly, the fractional anticipatory goal response in Clark Hull's classic learning equation was Hull's clever way of bringing a representation of the goal backwards in space and time, to the start of the maze, giving the animal an incentive to run toward the goal. These examples illustrate a general tendency within the behaviorist tradition; in order to explain how animals were able to benefit from their past training, theorists had to credit their subjects with at least some capacity to look ahead into the future.

Research on Infants' and Young Children's Future-Orientation

Future-Oriented Processes in the Saccadic Eye Movement System

A number of research paradigms have yielded results that suggest that infants are capable of at least rudimentary future-oriented processing from a remarkably early age. In the 1980s, Marshall Haith and colleagues described the Visual Expectation Paradigm (VExP), a new technique for investigating young infants' visual expectations. In the VExP, infants watch a sequence in which very brief pictures alternate with blank intervals during which no picture is displayed (**Figure 1**). The pictures occur at locations according to either a random schedule, in which case successive locations are unpredictable, or according to a simple rule, such as left–right (L–R) alternation, in which case successive locations are 100% predictable. If infants detect the underlying structure that governs the predictable picture sequence, and if they use this information to form expectations about successive events, they can make anticipatory eye movements to the locations of upcoming pictures during the blank intervals before the pictures actually appear. Infants can also demonstrate expectations if they react more quickly to unanticipated pictures during predictable sequences than during irregular sequences. Thus, in this paradigm, an expectation is

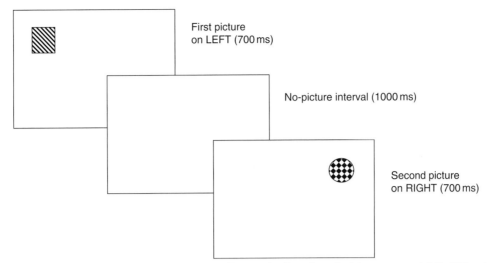

Figure 1 A schematic representation of events in the Visual Expectation Paradigm. A picture appears briefly (700 ms) on the left, followed by a blank no-picture interval (1000 ms), and then a new picture appears briefly on the right (700 ms). The sequence of 60–80 pictures is either regular (e.g., left–right alternation) or irregular. Eye movements that begin during the no-picture interval and go to the location of the upcoming picture are scored as anticipations.

seen as a mental construct whose presence is inferred on the basis of two behaviors: anticipations and facilitated reactions.

Studies using the VExP have shown that by 2 months of age, infants can rapidly form expectations about simple L–R alternation sequences and that this ability quickly expands to encompass more complicated L–L–R and L–L–L–R sequences by 3 months. In addition, a number of studies have revealed that infants use information about the spatial, temporal, and event content properties of the picture sequence to form expectations about upcoming events. For example, in 2–1 and 3–1 sequences (e.g., L–L–R and L–L–L–R, respectively) infants differentiate the spatial location at which pictures predominate by returning to it more quickly and anticipating pictures there more frequently than at the location where pictures appear less often. When the temporal duration of the interval between pictures is shortened, for example from 1 s to 700 ms, infants' anticipations happen earlier; when the interval is lengthened to 1400 ms, infants' anticipations occur later. When stable picture content appears at one location, and varying content appears at the other, infants anticipate the former more readily than the latter. Finally, by 3 months of age, infants can use a contingent relationship between location and the content of the central picture to anticipate where the upcoming peripheral picture will appear, even when the peripheral pictures do not follow a regular L–R spatial pattern.

Individual infants differ in the propensity to use spatial, temporal, and event content information to form and act upon expectations in the VExP, with the percentage of anticipations typically ranging from near zero to 30% at 3 months of age. Individual differences in the rate of anticipations appear to be fairly stable both within a single session of the VExP, with split-half correlation coefficients of approximately 0.5, and over the period of 1 week, with test–retest correlations being somewhat lower but still statistically significant. However, longitudinal analyses indicate that individual differences in anticipation rates may be somewhat less stable over longer periods, such as 1 month or more, until 6 months, when the median correlation between months averages nearly 0.70, excluding outliers. Individual differences in reaction times are similarly stable within a session, with correlations ranging from 0.45 to 0.69, and between sessions, with correlations between reaction time data collected at adjacent months typically more than 0.65, and also comparably high over periods longer than 1 month once infants reach 6 months of age. Moreover, individual differences in the VExP performance of infants at 3–4 months of age are related to other concurrent measures of cognitive processes, such as novelty preference and information processing speed; they predict later cognitive function measured at 3 years, and are correlated with parental intelligence quotient test scores.

Infants' performance in the VExP demonstrates an extraordinary ability to benefit from the regularity of the brief picture sequences. In most studies, the VExP sequence includes 60–80 picture presentations, and lasts approximately 2 min. Despite their short experience with this fairly rapid rate of information delivery, infants at 2 and 3 months quickly coordinate their eye movements with the structure of the task, anticipating some pictures and responding more rapidly than might otherwise be possible. Can infants retain information from such brief experiences and use it to anticipate more effectively at a later time? Two types of studies suggest that they can. First, infants typically perform better on their second VExP session than they do on their first, provided the two sessions occur within 1 week. Second, VExP performance in a L–R alternation sequence is generally better for infants who have seen a regular sequence on a prior occasion, even if the prior sequence followed a different regular pattern (e.g., up–down). Thus, the expectations that young infants form in the VExP appear to be retained for at least 1 week and generalize to other similar situations.

As impressive as infants' performance in the VExP is, it is vastly different from the behavior of adults in the same task who anticipate nearly every picture in a sequence of regular L–R alternation and who do so much earlier in the interpicture interval. The VExP is undoubtedly more difficult for infants than it is for adults. Infants have slower reactions, less working memory capacity, and cannot maintain a focused state of attention for nearly as long as adults can. In addition, infants may not have the same motivation to test and confirm their expectations as adults and older children do. Infants and adults no doubt bring different strategies to the task and it is possible that the infants' strategies are less task-appropriate or more difficult to inhibit. Studies have shown, for example, that, at 3 months of age, infants have a tendency to respond to picture offset in the VExP by looking further into the periphery, a tendency that must be reversed in a sequence of alternating pictures. Adults do not show this same tendency and, thus, do not have to overcome an incorrect initial response. Alternatively, infants' lower rates of anticipation may come from problems of detecting the underlying regularity in the sequence, of extrapolating from this regularity to expectations for the future, or of translating these expectations into acting before the pictures appear.

Although longitudinal analyses over the first year of life show that reaction times in the VExP speed up and become less variable, they do not show comparable changes in the rate of anticipation over the same period. If anything, the percentage of anticipation is approximately stable by 3 months, except for a decline between 9 and 12 months. What is the source of this unexpected decline in infants' tendency to anticipate? For one thing, the VExP is most likely a very different experience for a 3-month-old infant and a 12-month-old infant. Advances over the first 6 months of life in visual information processing, spatial memory, and the voluntary control of eye movements may make the VExP easier, and perhaps less captivating, for older infants. In addition, the appearance of reaching, grasping, crawling, sitting, and other developmental milestones during the first year means that many activities can compete for an older infant's attention compared to the number of tasks that can engage a 3-month-old. Thus, with a wider behavioral repertoire, and a potentially less engaging picture presentation sequence, it is possible that older infants are less motivated to anticipate upcoming pictures in the VExP compared to younger infants. Future studies will need to explore the cognitive, motivational, and behavioral factors that might limit infants' rates of anticipation at different ages in the VExP.

Future-Oriented Processes in the Smooth Pursuit Visual System

The saccadic eye movement system is functional from birth, and comes progressively under the infants' voluntary control during the first 6 months of life and beyond. The smooth pursuit system, in contrast, is not operational at birth but becomes functional some time around 2 months and improves thereafter. This onset of smooth pursuit tracking at approximately the same age as anticipatory saccades in the VExP may provide further evidence of future-oriented capabilities at this age. The reasoning is as follows. Smooth visual tracking of a steadily moving target requires extrapolation of the spatial and temporal properties of the target's trajectory. Without such extrapolation, the target will have moved out of view by the time an eye movement has occurred, forcing a saccade to regain the target. Indeed, a number of investigators have shown that prior to 2 months of age, infants typically track a smoothly moving target in this fashion, with a sequence of saccades. Beginning at around 2 months of age, however, infants' tracking becomes smoother and, when a smoothly moving object stops suddenly, infants' eyes continue to move beyond the object, for a few hundred milliseconds, along the same trajectory they were tracking, suggesting that they were using predictive tracking prior to the object's sudden stopping.

Although VExP and smooth pursuit tracking studies provide consistent evidence of future-oriented processing in the visual system by 2 months of age, there is an important methodological difference between these two types of studies; in the VExP, infants' anticipatory eye movements are generated in the absence of visual stimulation whereas in smooth tracking of a moving object, the target is always available throughout its trajectory as the infant extrapolates to upcoming locations. Can young infants track an object's motion when the object temporarily disappears? Several studies in the 1970s and 1980s tested infants' abilities to track an object that moved smoothly across regions where the movement was hidden by a screen or tunnel. Although infants as young as 5 months reportedly tracked target movement across the occluding screens in these studies, it is unclear whether these infants actually forecasted the reappearance of the target on the opposite side of the occluding screen, or merely failed to stop tracking the target when it disappeared behind the barrier.

More recent studies, using improved measurement of eye position, suggest that although young infants may not extrapolate the motion of a target across an occluder on their first experience with it, they learn to do so quite quickly, at least when the target moves in a simple linear trajectory and is invisible for a relatively brief occlusion.

By 6 months of age, infants can learn to associate specific target cues, such as shape or color, to predict the location at which a moving target will reappear from behind an occluder, even when the trajectory is a simple nonlinear one. Over the second half-year of life, infants learn to anticipate the reappearance of targets that move along yet more complicated trajectories, such as a circular path, although even at 12 months, this ability depends on target speed and the duration of the occlusion.

Future-Oriented Processes in the Visual–Manual System

For the adult, visually guided reaches are characterized by two phases: an approach phase, during which the hand is brought into the vicinity of the object; and a grasp phase, during which the fingers conform to the object's shape. The latter typically begins before the approach phase has ended. Like adults, infants as young as 5 months begin to close their hands in anticipation of contact with the target, at least on some of their reaches. This anticipatory adjustment becomes increasingly prevalent at 9 and 13 months of age, and happens progressively earlier in the approach phase. Moreover, infants preadapt their reaches and grasps in coordination with the target's direction, distance, shape, size, and orientation, with gross adjustments occurring early in development, especially when the infant's posture is stabilized, and finer adjustments appearing later, in the second half year of life.

Most remarkable, and indicative of future-oriented processing, are the findings presented by Claes von Hofsten and colleagues who report that infants from 4 to 5 months of age, at about the same age that they begin reaching for stationary objects, are able to catch objects that move in front of them in a radial path. Given the reaction time to initiate an arm movement, the inertial properties of the infant's arm, and the velocity of the object's motion, it would be impossible for infants to succeed in these catches if they aimed their reaches to the location where the target was when they launched the reach. Instead, to be successful, infants must have reached to a point ahead of the target when they initiated their reaches. This anticipatory aiming was confirmed on trials when the target motion was abruptly stopped while the reach was underway. What changed with development were the target speeds that infants could accommodate and the tendency to flexibly choose between ipsilateral and contralateral reaching strategies.

With a few notable exceptions, such as those described above, most research with infants and young children has focused on reaches for easy-to-grasp, stationary objects in an uncluttered area with the child receiving a fair amount of postural support. While it is clear from these studies that young infants use visual information to anticipate some required manual adjustments, naturalistic observations reveal many instances where infants' prehensile skills are far from smooth or effective. Consider a young child learning how to use a fork or trying to pick up a bar of soap. These tasks, and most daily activities, require the simultaneous coordination of many degrees of freedom to achieve true manual dexterity. In lifting an object, for example, adults jointly apply gripping and lifting forces whereas infants and young children apply these forces inconsistently, sometimes even applying the opposite of a needed force. How do infants and young children gain mastery over coordinating the multiple degrees of freedom required in their daily lives, and what role does predictive processing play in this development? Answers to these questions will require additional research that uses more dynamic and varied reaching tasks.

Future-Oriented Processes in the Postural and Locomotion Systems

In addition to using visual information to make anticipatory adjustments during reaching, infants also make anticipatory postural adjustments as well. In fact, some would argue that development of infants' skillful reaching must be preceded by development of postural control. Consider an infant sitting balanced on a parent's knee, receiving support only at the hips, while trying to grasp an object that is just beyond reach. Seated in this position, with limited support, the forces generated by arm and hand extensions would tend to perturb the infant's posture were they not counterbalanced by compensatory activity in the legs and trunk. Recordings of muscle activity in the trunk extensors of seated infants and the leg extensors of standing infants provide evidence of such early anticipatory postural control in infants who stabilize their posture before attempting to lean out for a reach or to pull open a drawer. Although such rudimentary anticipatory postural control has been found in infants who are just beginning to sit or stand, the timing of this control and the specificity of it improves with age and depends upon motor experience.

Anticipatory processes are also involved in the maintenance of equilibrium during self-produced locomotion. As infants learn to crawl, and then walk, they also learn to gather information through visual and haptic exploration, and they use this information to guide their movements around barriers, across gaps, down slopes, up stairs, through apertures, and across a variety of solid and deformable surfaces that support some types of locomotion better than others. For example, studies by Karen Adolph and associates show that 12-month-old infants who have just begun to walk, like younger infants who have accumulated a few weeks of crawling experience, will use the visual information of a drop-off to avoid the apparent deep side of a visual cliff. Once they have had a few weeks of walking experience, toddlers appear to recognize, in advance, the danger posed by challenges to their newly acquired walking skills, such as steep slopes or narrow bridges, and they often refuse to proceed unless there is some assistance, such as an adult's hand or a handrail. Before they continue, infants first test out the material properties of the surface they face and the type of assistance that is available.

Although infants and young children are quite skilled at picking up much of the visual and haptic information that is available to guide their movement, there are definite limits to what can be learned in advance of action. Adults have learned to interpret certain arbitrary visual stimuli, such as a mop, bucket, and caution sign, as cues to the types of surfaces that lie ahead, and they can use this information in an adaptive way. When they encounter a novel stimulus that can signal what lies ahead, adults very quickly learn to use the new cue to make anticipatory adjustments in their manner of walking, such as slowing down and taking smaller steps; as a consequence, adults are less likely to fall. Toddlers, however, require far more experience with the same novel cues before they learn to use them in an anticipatory fashion and, consequently, are much more likely to fall.

Future-Oriented Processes in Early Social Systems

The physical properties of objects, surfaces, and events provide the structure that infants can tap into to form expectations about the consequences of their own actions and to make predictions about what will happen next in the world that is beyond their control. Gravity consistently pulls objects in the same direction; one object cannot occupy a location where something else already exits; as an object approaches, its rate of expansion in our visual system indicates when it will be within reach, and so forth. Experience with repetitive sequences, as in the VExP, can provide another source of regularity that infants can use to anticipate upcoming events. It has been hypothesized that so too can the numerous repetitions of infant distress/caregiver response/infant relief cycles that occur throughout the first few months of life.

As new parents settle in to the routines of feeding, changing, burping, changing diapers, and rocking their infants, babies can begin to form expectations – both specific, as in what will happen next in the care sequence, and generalized, as in how likely is it that the social world will provide relief for the infant's distress. Perhaps these expectations explain why infants show less crying over time if parents are highly responsive to their needs in early infancy. Indeed, several studies have shown that during the first few months of life, infants will stop crying sooner when the caregiver intervenes, that infants will often stop crying even before they are picked up, and that this anticipatory quieting is specific to familiar caregiver. Of course, these results are far from definitive since it is not clear whether infants actually expect to be soothed, or whether some other explanation might account for their less persistent crying. For example, during the period from 2 to 6 months of age, infants may cry less because they develop more effective self-soothing strategies or they may stop crying when they see a familiar caregiver not because of an expectation for impending relief but because they have simply formed strong positive associations to the sight of their caregivers.

Although research has not definitively shown at what age infants begin to expect that their caregivers will be able to provide effective soothing, studies have shown that infants' early social interactions have an internal structure that can support expectation formation. For example, in early face-to-face interactions with their infants, parents often repeat sounds or gestures to which their infants have given a positive response. This combination of parental repetition of responses that are contingent on the infant's behavior is ideal for providing the basis for infants to form expectations about what their parents will do next as well as expectations about the consequences of their own behavior. Similarly, it is possible that the impressive degree of temporal coordination and turn-taking that develops between parents and infants in their early bouts of mutual gazing help infants form expectations about the general framework of social interaction; indeed, infants will protest a nonresponsive parent's face in the still-face lab procedure, an experimental paradigm in which parents adopt a neutral facial expression and stop responding contingently to the infant's behavior. Later, infants quickly learn the rules of common interactive games such as peek-a-boo and pat-a-cake and will play their role in alternation with their social partners. Thus, the daily routines that parents establish in caring for and playing with their infants and young children, and the family traditions that develop, for example, around celebrations such as birthdays and holidays, can provide the regularity that infants can use to predict what will happen next in their interactions with significant others.

Structured interviews with parents about what their infants and toddlers understand about the future suggest that parents find ample evidence in their daily interactions with their children for their infants' and toddlers' developing sense of what lies ahead. According to an interview study reported by Janette Benson and associates, parents of children from 12 to 42 months of age interpret their children's persistent attempts to accomplish a goal as evidence of a burgeoning orientation to the future. Also, parents rate their children as capable of participating in a familiar routine, and parents see this as further evidence of their young child's growing sense of the future. However, 12-, 18-, and 24-month-old children were rated as unlikely to be able to form an expectation about something unfamiliar based on being told that it will occur, while children older than 30 months were rated as showing some capacity to form expectations in this way. Parents rated other aspects of future-oriented understanding, such as wanting things done in the same order, doing things to prepare for the future, and pretending to be upset in order to get what is wanted, as increasingly characteristic of their children from 12 to 42 months of age. Parents believed that infants and young children learn about the future by being told in advance about what lies ahead. Thus, it is not surprising that parents reported talking to their children about what is going to happen in the future, even though they believed their children really did not understand what the future meant. Analyses of parents' speech to their children during brief lab tasks confirmed that parents talked about the future to their children more than they talked to them about the past, and that this tendency to talk about the future generally increased from 14 to 36 months of age. However, parents talked twice as often about the present than either the past or the future for children in this age range.

Observations of parent–child conversations and the results of the parental questionnaire studies suggest a possible sequence through which infants pass on their way toward building a firm sense of the future. At first, parents credit their infants with the capacity of extending or repeating familiar patterns and in persisting in their efforts to achieve a goal. Later, infants learn to make preparations for those familiar patterns that they can anticipate. Finally, they can use information to make vicarious expectations about upcoming events that are not simple extrapolations of a familiar pattern and they also learn to manipulate someone else's expectations.

Early Tools for Learning about the Future

Learning Temporal Patterns and Ordered Sequences

Research suggests that infants and young children possess several perceptual and cognitive resources that can be applied to the task of detecting the structure that underlies predictable future events. Young infants are remarkably attuned to variations in visual and auditory information over time. For example, newborns detect the difference between two lights that differ only in the rate at which they flash and babies have preferences for some temporal rates over others; specific preferences depend on the infant's age and current level of arousal. Spatially patterned visual stimuli, such as checkerboards or stripes, can also be discriminated based on the rate of flashing and phase reversals (i.e., black switches to white and white to black). Similarly, infants can discriminate between two auditory streams that use the same syllable (e.g., /ba/ba/ba/) but present the syllable at different rates. Differences in the global temporal patterns of visual and auditory stimuli, such as the number of cycles per second, are detected as are differences in the local temporal properties, such as rhythm, and discrepancies in the synchrony of the auditory and visual information of a multimodal event. In addition to using basic mechanisms to track the rate, duration, simultaneity, and interval between the first and second auditory or visual event, infants, at least by 4 months, also detect and remember the order of specific elements within brief repetitive sequences. By 11–12 months of age, infants can also remember and reproduce short sequences of ordered steps that produce an interesting effect. In doing so, infants show that they know what comes next, at least within the short-term timeframe of the behavioral sequence they are imitating.

Learning Contingencies in Reinforcement Paradigms

In addition to having the requisite skills to begin parsing the temporal structure of events, young infants also possess abilities that let them learn important contingencies between their behavior and reinforcing events. For example, newborns have been classically conditioned by pairing the delivery of a sucrose solution with tactile stimulation of the infant's forehead. After a number of such pairings, infants make reliably more sucking and head-orienting responses following strokes to their foreheads than infants who have not received the forehead stroke plus sucrose pairings. By 2 months of age, infants can learn to increase their spontaneous kicking when doing so activates a mobile. By 3 months of age, infants appear to generalize beyond the specific stimulus–response contingencies on which they are trained. Consider two groups of infants; one group received the same mobile on two successive days of training while the other received two different mobiles, a new one on each of the two days. On the third day, infants either received a new mobile or one they had seen before. Infants who had received the same mobile on days 1 and 2 were more likely to kick if they received that same mobile again on day 3 than if they received a new mobile. In contrast, infants who were trained on two different mobiles were more likely to kick if they received a new mobile on day 3 than if they received one of the mobiles on which they had already been trained. Thus, infants in the first group had apparently learned expectancies for the specific mobile on which they had been consistently trained whereas infants in the second group had apparently learned expectancies for mobiles to vary from one day to the next.

Learning about the Future through Conversation

Language is a third tool that infants and young children have for forming expectations about upcoming events and sharing them with others. As noted earlier, parents admit that they speak to their young children about the future before they believe their children understand what is being said. Naturalistic studies of parent–child conversations confirm that parents review the day's events with their children and preview upcoming events as well. Through participation in conversations such as these, children presumably learn skills for envisioning themselves in time and for developing a sense of the past, present, and future.

The topics of children's conversion, and their mastery of the grammatical structures for denoting the spatial and temporal locations of events, have been examined to gain insight into the child's capacity to reflect on the past and to anticipate the future. Two cautions are necessary. First, valid inferences about young children's mental processes from analysis of their speech will most likely need to come from cross-linguistic studies. This is because languages differ in the way spatial and temporal relations are coded, and some coding systems may be easier for young children to master than others. In the same vein, different ways of coding particular spatial and temporal relations may exist within a single language and these codes may differ in the demands they place on the child's cognitive processes. Consider verb tense, for example. In English, past action is generally coded by adding '-ed' to the present tense while the future is coded by inserting an auxiliary verb (e.g., 'will') before the present tense. The fact that children who are acquiring English typically master the past tense before they master the future may indicate that they understand the past before they understand the future, or, alternatively, that they merely have more trouble mastering the copula grammatical form. Second, making inferences about young children's mental processes from their speech may not accurately reflect their conceptual competence. Research indicates that language production skills typically lag behind language comprehension and this difference in developmental rate may lead to underestimating what children know when we rely on analysis of what they talk about. However, it is also possible for young children to pick up on linguistic cues as they answer researchers' questions which may lead to overestimating children's knowledge. Thus, researchers need to be especially concerned with the reliability and validity of measures of young children's language behavior.

With these caveats in mind, cross-linguistic studies suggest that young children first speak about objects and events in their immediate experience. The child's earliest future-related comments involve short-term goals or desires, for example when a child requests "more" or "again" to express continuation of a pleasant experience. Children use the present tense to refer to things they remember as well as things they intend to do. For example, a child may say "I get it!" while running to another room to retrieve a toy. Eventually, children learn to use adverbs such as "yesterday" and "tomorrow" to denote an indefinite length of time before or after the present. Later, children refer to time in the future in terms of expected events or outcomes such as "When I go to school" or "When I grow up."

By 3 years of age, children can describe what typically happens during familiar activities such as going to the zoo or attending a birthday party. Thus, when asked to describe what will happen at an upcoming birthday party, young children might answer based on recollecting the scenes that are stored in a mental birthday party script or, alternatively, by imagining themselves in a future birthday party as it unfolds. To what extent can preschool-aged children actually envision themselves in a future setting? Research by Cristina Atance and colleagues suggests that 3-year-olds can envision themselves in a familiar scene, such as in the dark or in an igloo, imagine how being in the scene might affect them physiologically, such as make them scared or cold, and anticipate the types of items that might be useful in their imagined activity, such as a flashlight or a winter coat. However, this ability to envision oneself in a different situation and reason about what that might entail is fragile with young children being particularly vulnerable to choosing items that are semantically associated with the imagined scene rather than practically related to their most likely future needs.

Physiology of Future-Oriented Processes

Researchers who have sought physiological indicators of future-oriented processes in infants and young children have most often examined changes in heart rate and the electrical potentials of the brain. Heart rate is tightly coupled to the demands for information processing in infants and adults. When a novel stimulus is introduced, a coordinated orienting response ensues that combines responses that direct the sensory receptors toward the stimulus as well as integrates changes in respiration and heart rate, thought to maximize processing of the new stimulus. This heightened attention wanes with repeated exposures of the stimulus unless the stimulus signals that something of significance is about to occur. The S1–S2 paradigm has been used extensively to study adults' physiological responses in those cases when one stimulus signals that something important is about to occur. In this paradigm, paired stimuli are presented over a number of trials, with a fixed interstimulus interval (ISI) separating the signal stimulus, S1, and the second stimulus, S2, which is usually made distinctive or imperative in some way. For example, adults may be told to count the number of S2 stimuli or to press a response button when S2 is delivered. The adult's heart rate response varies with the specific details of the S1–S2 paradigm, such as the length of the ISI, and the nature of the response required to S2, but invariably includes a phase of deceleration that reaches its lowest point just before onset of S2. This deceleration phase is thought to reflect the buildup of anticipation for S2.

Studies of heart-rate changes in neonates who were undergoing classical conditioning have produced mixed results. Some have found the anticipatory heart-rate changes seen in adults, at least in some newborns, while others have found heart-rate deceleration only during early extinction trials, when the unconditioned stimulus (i.e., S2) should have occurred but did not. Studies with older infants have produced more reliable evidence of anticipatory heart-rate decelerations, during the intervals between S1 and S2, as well as heart-rate decelerations following the omitted instances of S2 on interspersed extinction trials. The literature in this area is consistent with the hypothesis that young infants may be able to notice that a pattern has been altered before they are able to anticipate what the pattern is. Thus, retrospective pattern detection may precede prospective pattern extrapolation.

One disadvantage of using heart-rate deceleration as an index of anticipation is that the time course of the heart-rate response is somewhat sluggish. A typical ISI in S1–S2 paradigms with infants is on the order of 5–10 s; when heart-rate deceleration has been found, it typically emerges 2s or more seconds after onset of S1 and takes 6s or more seconds to reach its maximum level. It is possible that young infants might be able to anticipate events over shorter intervals before they can extrapolate over intervals as long as 5–10 s. If so, the heart-rate response may not reflect the type of anticipation that young infants can most easily generate.

Recordings of the electrical potentials of the brain have also been collected during S1–S2 studies with adults. These studies have revealed a slow brain-wave response, the contingent negative variation (CNV) that reaches its most negative point just before onset of S2. A study of electrical cortical potentials preceding stimuli in the VExP suggests that a rudimentary form of the CNV may occur in 3-month-olds during the latter part of the 1000 ms intervals between picture presentations.

Electrical potentials of the brain that precede anticipatory saccadic eye movements have also been contrasted to the potentials that precede reactive eye movements in the VExP and related paradigms. In these studies, potentials during the 500 ms preceding 3–3.5-month-old infants' anticipatory saccades were more negative over frontal areas of the brain than were the comparable brain potentials before reactive saccades. In addition, a less robust positive potential was found approximately 100 ms before the onset of anticipatory saccades in some infants. These findings suggest that the programming of saccades in anticipation of upcoming stimuli involves different brain areas than the programming of reactive saccades.

The regular alternation of pictures between the two locations of the VExP, repeated over 60–80 occurrences, gives young infants many opportunities to observe the side-to-side transitions that govern this sequence. The highly repetitive nature of this sequence means that infants can form both local expectations, such as on this trial the next picture will appear on the left, as well as global expectations, such as left pictures will always follow pictures on the right. Other studies have used a spatial cuing paradigm to examine the effects of directing an infant's attention to one location by presentation of a brief cue at that location, and then presenting a subsequent stimulus either at the precued location or at the opposite location. In this paradigm, infants may expect a stimulus to occur at the cued location, at least locally, on some trials. Cortical potentials that precede saccades to locations that have been cued have been compared to those that precede saccades to the other location in infants during the first 6 months of life. In this paradigm a robust positive cortical potential has been found in the 50 ms before the onset of saccades to the cued location, especially over the frontal areas of the brain; the amplitude of this positive potential before saccades to the cued location depends on age, with older infants more likely to show the effect. Again, these studies suggest that when attention is shifted to a peripheral location, and a target then occurs at that location, infants' programming of saccades to that location will have a different pattern of cortical activation than would occur to uncued, or unexpected, target locations.

Several studies have examined infants' cortical potentials during an oddball paradigm, a procedure in which participants watch two stimuli that appear in a semirandom sequence at a single location. One stimulus predominates, typically appearing on 80% of the picture presentations; the other stimulus, the oddball, typically appears on the remaining 20% of the presentations. In variants of this procedure, the frequent and rare pictures may occur on 80% and 10% of the trials, respectively, and a set of novel pictures may appear on the remaining trials, with a new picture chosen for each trial. Electrical potentials are typically averaged for each of the trial types from the interval just before picture onset through picture offset. In adults and children from 5 years of age through adolescence, two brain-wave responses are typically found: a positive potential with a latency of 300 ms after stimulus onset (P300) and a negative potential with a latency of 200 ms (N200). Both components typically vary as a function of the probability of the rare stimulus. The findings with infants from 2 months of age are different in form from those with children and adults. Although there are differences in the names that have been applied to the types of brain waves that have been observed in this procedure with infants, there is general agreement in finding a positive potential beginning at about 200 ms after stimulus onset, followed by a large, slow negative wave developing around 500–600 ms after stimulus onset, and a later positive slow wave peaking at approximately 1000 ms after stimulus onset. Most importantly, as with adults and children, the form of the averaged brain-wave response differs in infants for the frequent vs. rare pictures. The change in the form of the averaged brain potential is thought to reflect an expectancy that has been violated by introduction of the relatively rare picture into the sequence of repeated presentations of the frequent picture. Additional comparisons have been made of the averaged brain potentials for the frequent pictures that occur immediately before and after an oddball, respectively. Since the picture is the same in these two averages, differences in the form of the brain wave must reflect the effect of the intervening oddball stimulus.

Other Methods and Methodological Challenges

The oddball paradigm, described earlier, exemplifies a variety of techniques that have been used to gain insight into infants' and young children's expectations. These studies generally use two classes of events, rare and typical. Rare and typical events are either defined by differential familiarization during the course of the study, as in the oddball paradigm, or by the infants' experience prior to coming to the laboratory, as in the still-face procedure when the mother suddenly adopts a neutral facial expression and stops responding contingently to her infant. In either case, the experimental method involves a comparison of infants' responses following the rare event to their responses following the typical event. Presumably, when an infant gives a different response after the rare event, it indicates that a violation in the infant's expectations has occurred. In an effort to detect violations of infants' expectations, a wide variety of responses has been monitored including surprise reactions, crying or distress, suppressed motor activity, duration of looking, amplitudes and latencies of brain-wave components, heart-rate changes, and so forth. Unfortunately, these studies do not provide definitive information about infants' expectations. The rationale is as follows. It is possible that after seeing one, two, three, or more occurrences of a particular event, infants actively expect yet another repetition of this typical event to happen again and, when it does not, their expectations are violated leading to a surprise reaction. However, it is equally possible that the infant's surprise represents an after-the-fact reaction to something unusual that has just happened and it is also possible that the thing that has just happened is more difficult to process because it isn't typical. That is, it is possible that the infant was not actually expecting anything, in the sense of actively forecasting the future, at all. Thus, studies that rely on comparing infants' responses to typical and atypical events give ambiguous results: do infants' reactions reflect ad hoc responses to the rare event that just occurred, or do they reflect expectations that the typical event should have recurred but did not?

Several other research paradigms have produced results that seem relevant to questions about the early development of future-orientation. For example, studies of infants' and young children's object representation, inferential reasoning, visual and manual search strategies, and means-ends skills suggest that by 12 months, if not much sooner, infants have the knowledge sufficient to understand that solid objects will stop when they encounter a barrier, that infants can use conditional probabilities to infer causal structure, and that they can remember where to retrieve objects that have been hidden under covers in various locations. If infants do indeed possess this knowledge, it seems reasonable to expect that they could put it to use in a task that requires them to predict where a ball rolling down a slope will come to rest when it hits a solid wall that blocks its motion and, furthermore, that they should be able to use their predictions and memory to open a door at the ball's current location to retrieve the ball. However, it is not until 30 months or more that infants can perform reasonably well at this task, despite the suspicion that all of the requisite component skills are in place much earlier in development. Thus, acquisition of the knowledge or component skills needed to engage in future-oriented behavior does not necessarily imply that infants or young children will actually be able to use their skills to anticipate what is required or to act in preparation for what will occur. In contrast, infants and toddlers may be able to recognize after the fact that something odd has happened without having been able to predict what would happen in advance.

Finally, studies with adults have shown that location information may serve as an anchor for binding together the multiple properties of a single object. That is, the warmth of a campfire, its smell, the sight of the flame, and the crackle of the burning logs can all be bound together because they originate at the same location. Adults appear to use location information to help them recall object properties that were associated with that location. For example, in trying to recall a message that was once posted at a particular location, adults will look at that location, even when the message is no longer there. They look to this location, not in anticipation of seeing the message there, but as a way of retrieving the information that has been associated with the location. Studies suggest that infants may also use location information to bind together the multiple sensory inputs from multimodal events. For example, if young infants see and hear an event at a particular location, such as a talking face, when the auditory information is presented alone, infants look to the location where the face had previously appeared. But it is unclear whether infants expect to see the face at this location or, like adults, remember that the sound came from this location. Similarly, research paradigms that investigate infants' and toddlers' behavior during the interval between two events face the methodological challenge of showing that the child's behavior during the interval is truly future-oriented, predictive behavior of upcoming events rather than responses to the previous events or to an interruption in the flow of events. In the VExP paradigm described earlier, for example, infants typically made one response to picture offsets (i.e., a repetitive eye movement further into the periphery) but a different response to the upcoming picture (i.e., an eye movement in the opposite direction). Without this response difference, it would be difficult to determine when an infant was expecting upcoming pictures vs. remembering previous ones.

A Taxonomy for Classification of Future-Oriented Processes

Investigators who study learning and memory have differentiated many dimensions for thinking about past experience and for organizing the results of the numerous studies of how the past affects current behavior. There are temporal dimensions such as short-term, long-term, and the briefest of sensory registers; content dimensions such as episodic and semantic memories; and functional dimensions such as working memory or repressed memory. Similarly, investigators who study the impact of current stimuli on behavior have differentiated dimensions that are useful for classifying objects and events such as size, shape, color, number, complexity, and symmetry.

What are the relevant dimensions for thinking about future-oriented behavior? At present, no formal conceptual framework has been articulated, although a number of dimensions have been proposed (see **Table 1**). For example, one proposal has borrowed the episodic vs. semantic distinction from the study of memory and, in doing so, has speculated that infants and young children may have separate systems for thinking in general (semantic) terms about what will happen, such as Tuesday will come after Monday, and for thinking in specifically personal (episodic) terms about the future, such as "I will go to the park after lunch." Thus, according to this proposal, future-oriented thoughts can be classified on the basis of their content – events in the individual's own future vs. impersonal events in the world. Although the episodic-semantic distinction has stimulated a number of intriguing studies, it also raises some difficult questions, for example, where should we place a child's expectation that her mother will be sad when she discovers the broken vase? Do expectations about important social partners' future states belong in the personal-episodic category, the impersonal-semantic category, or somewhere in

Table 1 Selected relevant dimensions for classifying future-oriented behavior

Dimension	Range
Subjectivity	Personal (episodic) future vs. general (semantic) future
Timeframe	Milliseconds to a lifetime and beyond
Space/time dependency	Anticipation that must occur at a particular location or by a particular time vs. anticipation that does not need to be coordinated with space or time
Behavioral system	Motor, perceptual, cognitive, social
Level of abstraction	Extrapolation of a repetitive pattern, prediction from a functional relationship, creative invention of a new solution to a problem
Purpose	Fantasy/imagination, preparation, planning, problem solving
Openness to modification	Ballistic prepared response vs. ongoing modification through feedback
Degree of conscious control	Automatic or habitual vs. effortful
Complexity	Anticipating a single event vs. anticipating multiple sequential or simultaneous events

between? Thus, it is important to determine whether the episodic-semantic distinction defines a true dichotomy, a set of categories, or a self-other continuum.

As **Table 1** suggests, several additional dimensions have been proposed including the timeframe of expectations, ranging from very short intervals, measured in fractions of a second, such as those involved in making postural adjustments to accommodate intended actions, up to very long-term expectations that may extend beyond the person's own lifetime, for example in planning a legacy for one's grandchildren. In addition to unfolding according to different timescales, from milliseconds to decades, future-oriented behaviors differ in how time dependent they are. For example, in catching a falling object, certain hand and postural adjustments must happen at a particular time or in a particular sequence for the behavior to unfold smoothly whereas in other activities, such as getting ready for bed, the order and timing of events is less critical. Presumably, different timescales would place varying demands on a child's excitatory, inhibitory, coordination, and memorial resources but this remains to be established.

Future-oriented behavior occurs in different behavioral systems as well, including motor anticipation, for example, in reaching, grasping, and locomotion; perceptual and cognitive anticipation, for example, in cross-modal perceptual effects where the sight of an object can create an expectation for the object's texture, or where the context of a story primes expectations for theme-related words; or social anticipation, for example, when a child contemplates how a friend might respond to a particular birthday gift.

Future-oriented behaviors can also be differentiated by the degree of abstraction required ranging from simple extrapolation of a repetitive pattern into the future, as when we expect summer to follow spring; to prediction of a future event from knowledge of a functional relationship, as in expecting rain when dark clouds gather; to envisioning a new solution to a perplexing problem, as in creative invention.

Other dimensions include the purpose of the future-oriented behavior, for example for play or entertainment, as in daydreaming; for preparing for an expected event, as in putting things into the backpack to take to daycare; or for planning a strategy to achieve a goal, as in figuring out how to equitably divide the Halloween candy. Is the plan open to modification from feedback, as when a child shifts from an "I want" request to an "I need" request in the face of parental resistance, or must the plan be executed without modification, as when a child plans to jump across a puddle? How much conscious control is required? For example, is the child getting ready for an event that has an established routine, such as getting ready to go to preschool, or is the child anticipating a novel event, for example traveling by a new mode of transportation? Anticipated events can also vary in complexity. For example, one child may anticipate only the next event in a sequence while another anticipates the next three or four steps. Similarly, some anticipated events are fairly simple, such as the light will go on when the switch is flipped, while others are quite complex, such as the toy will light up, make noise, and begin moving when the switch is flipped.

Although the dimensions listed in **Table 1** may help us think about the development of future-oriented behavior, they do not constitute a formal, systematic conceptual framework. There are many unknowns. Is the list exhaustive? Are the dimensions relevant to all classes of anticipatory behavior? How are the dimensions related to each other? What are the assumptions underlying each dimension? How can the dimensions best be operationalized into empirical behaviors? Further research is needed to answer these questions; doing so should help us define the trajectories along which future-oriented behaviors develop.

In conclusion, the study of future-orientation in infants and young children suggests that by 2 months of age, infants can use regularity of spatial, temporal, and content information to form expectations for upcoming events and then use these expectations to adapt their eye movements to the structure of the sequence of events they are watching. This ability is followed by similar achievements in other action systems as they come under the infant's voluntary control, from smooth tracking of visual motion to eye-hand coordination, postural control and self-produced locomotion, and social communication. Infants have several capabilities that facilitate their acquisition of a future-orientation including the ability to detect the structure of temporal patterns and ordered sequences; to learn about the contingent relationships that exist between actions and consequences or between contiguous or adjacent events; and to communicate using systems of symbols. Although evidence of future-orientation appears quite early in infancy, there is a protracted period of development during which infants and children learn to coordinate progressively more degrees of freedom and to go beyond the simple extrapolation of familiar patterns.

See also: Cognitive Development; Habituation and Novelty; Imagination and Fantasy; Learning; Perception and Action.

Suggested Readings

Atance CM and Metzoff AN (2005) My future self: Young children's ability to anticipate and explain future states. *Cognitive Development* 20: 341–361.

Benson JB, Talmi A, and Haith MM (2003) The social and cultural context of the development of future orientation. In: Raeff C and Benson JB (eds.) *Social and Cognitive Development in the Context of Individual, Social and Cultural Processes*, pp. 168–190. New York: Routledge.

Haith MM, Benson JB, Roberts RJ, Jr., and Pennington BF (eds.) (1994) *The Development of Future-Oriented Processes*. Chicago: The University of Chicago Press.

Haith MM, Wentworth N, and Canfield RL (1993) The formation of expectations in early infancy. In: Rovee-Collier C and Lipsitt LP (eds.) *Advances in Infancy Research*, pp. 251–297. Norwood: Ablex.

Joh AS and Adolph KE (2006) Learning from falling. *Child Development* 77: 89–102.

Moore C and and Lemmon K (eds.) (2001) *The Self in Time: Developmental Perspectives*. Mahwah: Lawrence Erlbaum Associates Publishers.

von Hofsten C (2005) The development of prospective control in tracking a moving object. In: Riesern JJ, Lockman JJ, and Nelson CA (eds.) *Action as an Organizer of Learning and Development: Volume 33 in the Minnesota Symposia on Child Psychology*, pp. 51–89. Mahwah: Lawrence Erlbaum Associates Publishers.

Genetics and Inheritance

A Balasubramanian, J Koontz, and C A Reynolds, University of California, Riverside, Riverside, CA, USA

© 2008 Elsevier Inc. All rights reserved.

Glossary

Chromosome – A coiled double-stranded assembly of deoxyribonucleic acid (DNA) that contains multiple genes and is located in the cell nucleus.
DNA marker – A polymorphic segment of DNA that may or may not code for a protein.
Endophenotype – An intermediate trait associated with a behavior or disorder that may be more proximate to gene action.
Gene – The fundamental unit of inheritance made of DNA that governs observed physical and behavioral features. Variations in the form of a gene are called alleles.
Genotype – The combination of alleles at a particular chromosomal locus.
Heritability – The contribution of genes to individual differences in a trait; amount of trait variance accounted for in a population by genetic influences.
Phenotype – An observable trait or characteristic.
QTL (quantitative trait loci) – A gene or DNA segment that contributes to a complex phenotype.

Introduction

The nature vs. nurture debate has ended: genes and environments both influence behaviors and disorders in infancy and childhood. The hunt for specific gene candidates for behavioral traits and the environments under which gene expression may be modified is of current focus. In this article, genetic transmission, single-gene traits, complex traits, and methods to locate candidate genes such as linkage and association are outlined. Approaches that disentangle genetic and environmental influences are highlighted emphasizing the research methods and findings for a variety of psychologically relevant traits. Emerging research considering the interaction between genes and environments will clarify the complex etiologies of intellectual abilities and disabilities, temperament, and behavioral syndromes and disorders in childhood.

Genetic Transmission

Gregor Mendel (1822–1884), an Augustinian friar, discovered the fundamental element of inheritance, what we now call a 'gene', and generalizations regarding inheritance, known subsequently as the laws of segregation and independent assortment. Mendel studied multiple varieties of *Pisum sativum*, the garden pea plant, which is self-pollinating, and considered several either–or traits, including plant height (tall, short), pea shape (smooth, wrinkled), and pea color (yellow, green). From breeding experiments, Mendel determined that first-generation hybrid crosses (F1 generation) resembled only one parent. For example, the resultant offspring of a tall plant crossed with a short plant resulted in a tall plant. Indeed, tall height, smooth pea shape, and yellow pea color dominated over the recessive traits, short height, wrinkled pea shape, and green pea color, respectively. In the second generation (F2 generation), the hybrid offspring from the first generation were allowed to self-pollinate and recessive traits were again visible in 25% of the offspring; thus, the ratio of dominant traits to recessive traits exhibited was 3:1. The resulting offspring in subsequent generations (F3 and so on) led Mendel to make additional observations. The first was that plants with recessive traits only produced recessive types; for example, short pea plants crossed with short pea plants only produced short pea plants. Second among the plants exhibiting dominant traits only one-third were 'pure', that is, invariably producing plants with the dominant characteristics (tall plants only), and two-thirds were not pure types but hybrids, producing offspring which carried both dominant and recessive elements. Mendel concluded that each parent contributes equivalently to their offspring, forming pairs of inherited elements (genes) for each character. The law of segregation follows such that during the formation of germ cells or gametes (sperm and egg in humans) the pairs of genes must segregate so that at fertilization the full complement of genes are united. Mendel also studied the inheritance of combinations of traits and observed independence of inheritance, for example, tall plants produced yellow or green peas equally often as did short plants. The law of independent assortment thus states that the inheritance of a pair of genes determining one trait is independent of simultaneous inheritance of pairs of genes for other traits.

Genes

Genes control heritable physical and behavioral features in humans and other organisms. The word gene refers to both the physical and functional aspects of a segment of deoxyribonucleic acid (DNA), which contains instructions for the making of a protein. The DNA molecule is double-stranded and helical in structure with complementary strands held together by hydrogen bonds formed between base pairs, also called nucleotides: adenine (A) with thymine (T) and cytosine (C) to guanine (G). The sequence of the base pairs of a gene provides the specific instructions for the making of a protein. The sequence of DNA for a particular gene may vary resulting in differing forms of a gene, called alleles.

Genes are located on chromosomes in the nucleus of all cells. Humans possess 23 pairs of chromosomes in all cell nuclei, except germ cells in which it is necessary for procreation to contain half that number; thus, sperm and egg cells carry only 23 chromosomes. When sperm and egg unite, the fertilized egg will then contain the appropriate 46 chromosomes or 23 pairs. Chromosomes 1–22 are called autosomal chromosomes, while the 23rd pair includes the sex chromosomes, X and Y. Females have two X chromosomes while males have one X and one Y chromosome; mothers provide an X chromosome only while fathers provide an X or a Y chromosome to their resulting offspring.

Meiosis

Meiosis describes the process of cell division for reproductive cells that will result in sperm or egg cells with half the number of chromosomes. This is in contrast to the cell division that takes place in nongerm cells called mitosis, which results in daughter cells that are identical. **Figure 1** represents meiosis in females and males. Reproductive cells contain 23 pairs of chromosomes prior to meiosis, with one set maternally derived and the other set paternally derived. During the first stage of meiosis, each homologous pair of chromosomes line up (maternal chromosome 1 with paternal chromosome 1, and so on), duplicate themselves, and then between homologous chromosomes an exchange of DNA segments of equal length at the identical location occurs, called crossing-over or recombination. In the second phase of meiosis the reproductive cell divides twice more to produce four germ cells with half the complement of 23 chromosomes. In females, one reproductive cell undergoing meiosis results in one viable egg cell and three cells that are not functional, whereas in males a single reproductive cell undergoing meiosis results in four sperm cells. The resulting chromosomes in the germ cells, egg and sperm, contain DNA from maternally and paternally derived chromosomes due to crossing-over in the first phase of meiosis, ensuring added genetic variation. The segments of DNA that are exchanged during the crossing-over process is random for any meiotic division, thus it is next to impossible to recreate the exact combination of genes in germ cells produced in a single individual.

Gene Expression

As alluded to in Mendel's work, an expressed trait or phenotype is due to a combination of alleles, or forms of genes at a particular chromosomal location. If the alleles are identical in sequence, then genotype is said to be homozygous; if they differ the genotype is heterozygous. In the case of a heterozygous genotype, one set of allele instructions may dominate over the other set of instructions in expression of the protein, for example, gene expression for smooth pea coat completely dominates overexpression of wrinkled pea coat in the pea plant. A completely recessive trait, therefore, is one that is not expressed such as the wrinkled pea coat. In the case of only two possible alleles one's genotype can be homozygous dominant, heterozygous dominant, or homozygous recessive at that locus. If neither allele was dominant over the other, they would be considered to act in an additive or co-dominant manner in their contribution to the expressed phenotype. In humans, one example of complete dominance is brown vs. blue eye color. If an individual inherits the allele coding for brown eyes and the allele coding for blue eyes, brown eye color will be expressed, that is, they are heterozygous dominant. Thus, only one copy of the dominant allele is needed for the expression of brown eyes. If inheriting two blue alleles, that is, homozygous recessive, blue eye color may be expressed (assuming a homozygous recessive blue–blue genotype for the green–blue gene).

The actual mechanics of gene expression are complex and involve multiple stages. Key steps are generally described here. First, the DNA sequence is transcribed into messenger ribonucleic acid (mRNA). RNA is single stranded and has four nucleotides: A, U, C, and G. Thus,

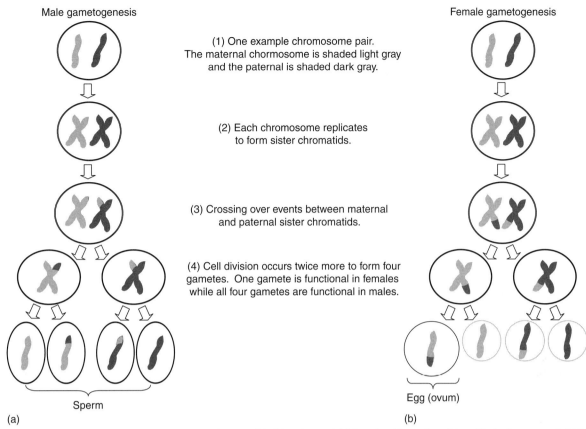

Figure 1 Meiosis. The formation of germ cells (gametes) in (a) males and (b) females. Reproduced from Hetherington *et al.* (2003) *Child Psycology*. McGraw-Hill, with permission from McGraw-Hill.

T in DNA is replaced with U in RNA. Sequences of three nucleotides are called codons and indicate amino acids, which are building blocks of proteins. For example, an mRNA sequence of CAG codes for the amino acid GLN, or glutamine. Other three-letter codons may indicate start or stop synthesizing a chain of amino acids or polypeptide chains. After DNA is transcribed into mRNA, modifications may occur including RNA splicing in which noncoding regions of the RNA, introns, are cut out and the remaining exons (protein-coding regions) are united resulting in an unbroken RNA strand. Translation of the fully mature mRNA occurs in the cytoplasm of the cell by ribosomes, the location in the cell where proteins are synthesized with instructions contained in the three-letter codons of the mature mRNA. Protein expression is influenced by multiple factors, including the physiological state of a particular cell to an individual's developmental level.

Single Gene and Chromosomal Disorders

Mendelian principles of gene transmission can be applied to parent–offspring transmission in humans, and indeed they have been invaluable to uncovering the etiology of disorders that occur as a result of rare alleles or DNA mutations. Family pedigrees are examined for systematic patterns to examine the emergence of a disorder from the maternal or paternal line.

Single-Gene Autosomal Traits

Infant and childhood disorders may be a result of rare recessive alleles for genes located on autosomal chromosomes. Phenylketonuria (PKU) is a rare genetic disorder caused by a single recessive gene on chromosome 12 that occurs in an average of 15 000 newborns per year. These newborns lack phenylalanine hydroxylase, an enzyme necessary for the metabolism of the amino acid phenylalanine. The buildup of phenylalanine can be toxic leading to brain damage and severe mental retardation. If detected at birth, the detrimental effects of PKU can be lessened with a diet lacking in phenylalanine. Following this diet from birth till early childhood can lessen the intellectual deficits.

Single-gene autosomal-dominant disorders are rarer. Autosomal dominant disorders, have less than favorable outcomes and are less likely to be passed on from one generation to another since many of the traits associated with these disorders tend to decrease an individual's likelihood of procreating. A notable exception is Huntington's disease (HD), a rare neurodegenerative disease that typically emerges in middle-to-late adulthood and is characterized by involuntary movements, changes in personality, and memory problems. The mutation for HD is located on chromosome 4: an unstable expansion of a CAG triplet repeat. The greater the number of unstable expanded triplets, the earlier this disorder is expressed. Approximately 10% of cases are diagnosed in individuals under the age of 20 years.

Sex-Linked Disorders

Some single-gene disorders are transmitted through the inheritance of the sex chromosomes, usually X-linked recessive alleles. Expression of a sex-linked disorder occurs most often in males given the greater number of genes on the X than Y chromosome; thus, only one copy of the recessive allele is necessary for expression of the disorder in males. Females are usually carriers for the disorder and can pass the recessive allele to male offspring. Males with an X-linked disorder will have normal sons, since the recessive allele on the X chromosome will only be passed to their female offspring. Fragile X syndrome is a common sex-linked disorder that is one of the leading causes of mental retardation. This disorder is characterized by cognitive deficits and mild abnormal facial traits including an elongated face with a prominent jaw, broad forehead, and large ears. Individuals may also depict behaviors characteristic of attention deficit hyperactiviy disorder (ADHD) and autism. Fragile X syndrome is caused by an expanded triplet repeat of CGG on the X chromosome. This expanded triplet repeat sequence causes the chromosome to look 'fragile', appearing as if it could physically break. This mutation interferes with transcription of a crucial RNA binding protein. The repeated sequence expands as it passes from one generation to another, increasing chances of expression in successive generations. Fragile X syndrome is more likely to be expressed in males than females. The full mutation is present in 1 in 3600–4000 male births, and in 1 in 4000–6000 female births. The disorder can be partially expressed in females in a 'mosaic' manner due to random inactivation of one of the two X chromosomes in each cell.

Chromosomal Disorders

Beyond single genes, there are chromosomal disorders that affect behavioral phenotypes. Down syndrome, also known as trisomy 21, is a rare condition in which individuals are born with an extra copy of chromosome 21 due to errors occurring during meiosis. In 2006, 1 in 733 newborns was born with Down syndrome. Down syndrome is the most common form of mental retardation; however, cognitive impairments can range dramatically but are typically moderate to mild. Physical characteristics of Down syndrome are many and include heart defects, delayed skeletal maturation, stunted height, poor muscle tone (hypotonia), and a shorter lifespan. Environmental factors may increase the likelihood of trisomy 21 nondisjunction, including older maternal age (age 35 years and older) and possibly behavioral health factors such as smoking in the case of younger mothers (age 35 years and younger).

Chromosomal aberrations are also observed for the sex chromosomes. Females with only one X chromosome have a disorder called Turner's syndrome, which occurs in 1 in 2500 females. Stunted height and underdeveloped ovaries are features. Though of average intelligence, some females with Turner's syndrome are lacking in social skills, prompting researchers to propose that sociability may be X-linked. Furthermore, parent of origin may matter; the paternal X chromosome may mediate sociability and better social interaction skills as opposed to the maternal X chromosome.

Klinfelter syndrome (KS) is a disorder resulting in males having an extra X chromosome, that is, XXY. Males with KS have an increased risk of learning disabilities, developmental delays, behavioral problems, and infertility due to the underdevelopment of the testes. One in 500 males are born with KS. When females receive an extra X chromosome, this can result in triple X or 47, XXX. Physical and behavioral features vary but may include increased height and risk of cognitive disabilities, particularly involving speech and language. One in 1000 girls is born with triple X.

Genomic Imprinting

The manifestation of particular behavioral characteristics or symptoms of disorders can be affected by which parent provided the naturally occurring allele or rare mutation, a process called genomic imprinting. Methylation, the formation of methyl groups consisting of C and G, can lead to the silencing or expression of an allele; thus, methylation can alter protein formation. Genomic imprinting may occur for spina bifida and some forms of cancers. It is also implicated in some chromosomal disorders. For example, Prader–Willi syndrome (PWS) and Angelman's syndrome are two disorders that arise from spontaneous deletions on chromosome 15; however, the expression of either disorder depends upon which parent the offspring receives the imprinted mutation from. PWS is expressed in individuals who receive the mutation from the father, while Angelman's syndrome is expressed in individuals who receive the mutation from the mother. Obesity and irrepressible appetite characterize PWS and 1 in 12 000–15 000 newborns are diagnosed with PWS. Angelman's syndrome is characterized by normal growth, but poor coordination (ataxia) and muscle tone (hypotonia), severe mental retardation, and absence of speech. One in 10 000–20 000 individuals are born with Angelman's syndrome. Factors that impact the occurrence of methylation during gamete formation are being investigated.

Locating Genes

Linkage and association analyses help geneticists hunt for genes that may be causative or associated with a disorder. Linkage analyses take advantage of violations of Mendel's law of independent assortment to find chromosomal locations where a causative gene may lie. During recombination that occurs in meiosis, segments of DNA are swapped between maternal and paternal homologous chromosomes, and indeed this process is random between meiotic events. However, the closer two genes or DNA gene markers are to one another on a chromosome the more likely they will be inherited jointly and not be split by a recombination event. Through the employment of large family pedigrees, linkage studies are used to trace the co-occurrence of particular DNA marker alleles and disorders. Ideally the DNA marker may lie in the causative gene itself or be positioned close to the causative gene. As a result of linkage studies, geneticists located the form of the gene that causes HD on chromosome 4.

While linkage studies are particularly useful in locating DNA markers, which may be near or within the potential disease-causing gene, association studies examine known genes and whether they are associated with the disease trait. The known genes may be those close to a DNA marker identified in a linkage study, or known genes that are of interest given the proteins that they code for. Polymorphisms such as single-nucleotide polymorphisms (SNPs), ideally in exons or coding regions, are identified and used in the association analyses. SNP alleles of unrelated healthy persons may be compared to a group that exhibits a disease to see if a particular allele occurs more frequently in the disease group than by chance (a case-control design). While association studies have the statistical power to detect modest effects, this approach is more likely to identify genes that do not represent true association when using unrelated cases and controls because the cases may come from different subpopulations with different gene frequencies than controls (called population stratification). However, a growing number of researchers are having more success with this technique by searching for genetic markers in family-based designs where lineage is known. For example, analyses of parents and offspring test whether offspring exhibiting a disorder may be more likely to inherit a particular allele; affected and unaffected siblings may also be used in these analyses.

Complex Traits and Disorders

Many behavioral phenotypes in infancy and childhood are complex and reflect the influence of multiple genes and environments. For example, temperament and cognitive abilities demonstrate rich variation in the population. Unlike single-gene traits, environments and genes involved in complex traits or disorders may increase (or decrease) trait values or risk of expression but may not be necessary for the emergence of the trait or disorder. The designs used to investigate the relative influence of genetic vs. environmental effects on complex behavioral traits – twin and adoption designs – take advantage of naturally occurring 'experiments' of nature or nurture. Comparing relatives who vary in genetic relatedness or who share varying degrees of their rearing environment provide a metric for calculating the relative influence of anonymous genetic and environmental factors.

Heritability. Every observed trait, or phenotype (P), is thought to result from the effects of genes (G) and the environment (E). Geneticists use certain statistical techniques to quantify genetic effects, with the heritability estimate derived from a comparison of correlations between individuals who vary in either genetic relatedness or extent to which environments are shared. Heritability is an estimate of how much trait variance is accounted for in the population by genetic factors. Thus, heritability reflects the extent to which differences in a population are due to genetic differences; estimates can vary according to population, time, and geographical contexts. Narrow-sense heritability refers to genetic variance that is explained by additive genetic effects (no dominance) and is notated as h^2_N or a^2. Broad-sense heritability refers to all sources of genetic variance including additive effects (a^2), dominance (d^2), and any other gene–gene interaction effects. Remaining differences between individuals in a population may be due to shared environmental effects (c^2) and nonshared environmental effects (e^2). In the typical behavioral genetic models estimates of heritability and environmental effects completely describe individual differences in traits; thus, when summed together they account for 100% of the trait variability.

Environmentality. Environment refers to all nongenetic factors. Shared environmental effects such as being reared in the same home, attending the same schools, and other neighborhood or regional effects make relatives more similar to one another. In contrast, the unique experiences of individuals by definition are not shared with one another and make relatives dissimilar from one another. Thus, the environmentality estimates c^2 and e^2 index the extent to which shared and nonshared environmental effects, respectively, influence individual differences in a phenotype.

Behavioral Genetic Designs and Methods

Twin designs. Geneticists have conducted twin studies since Sir Francis Galton (1822–1911), a cousin of Charles

Darwin, advocated their use in determining the influence of nature vs. nurture, though he did not distinguish between types of twins. Monozygotic (MZ) twins are commonly referred to as identical twins. They share 100% of their genes in common. This type of twinning occurs when one egg is fertilized with one sperm, and then the resulting zygote divides and separates into two genetically identical cells. MZ twinning is typically viewed as a chance event and is not believed to be heritable, though some evidence for familial effects on identical multiple births has emerged from large-scale Nordic studies. Environmental factors may include advancing maternal age.

Dizygotic (DZ) twins are commonly referred to as fraternal twins. This type of twinning occurs when two eggs are matured and released, and each egg is then fertilized by a separate sperm. These twins are expected to be no more genetically similar than typical siblings, and on average share about 50% of their segregating genes. They may be of the same or opposite sex. This type of twinning appears to be moderately heritable, with a greater maternal lineage effect noted in some studies. The chance of fraternal twins increases with maternal age.

Comparison of twin siblings may offer clues to the importance of genetic and environmental influences for behavioral phenotypes. For example, examining MZ twins who are discordant for a disease like schizophrenia, can help to explain on environmental factors that may lead to only one twin of an identical pair to have schizophrenia. Studying similarity or concordance of MZ vs. DZ twins is the most common method to estimate the extent of genetic effects. Because MZ twins share 100% of their genes in common while DZ twins share 50% of their segregating genes, MZ twins would be expected to be twice as similar than DZ when genes act in an additive fashion to influence a trait (e.g., no dominance) and shared environmental effects are not present. For example, if DZ twin similarity is greater than would be expected, that is, their correlation is greater than half the MZ correlation, then shared environmental effects are suspected to be present. If the DZ correlation is less than half the MZ correlation then dominance may be present because MZ twins are genetically identical, including any dominance effects, whereas 25% of the dominance effects are in common for DZ twins. In twins-reared-together designs, dominance and shared environmental effects cannot be estimated simultaneously thus researchers choose which to consider based on patterns of twin similarity.

Equal environments as well as random mating of parents are two key assumptions that are required to estimate heritability and environmentality estimates using twins. A third is that the twins are representative of the population. The equal-environments assumption (EEA) poses that there are no differences between MZ and DZ twins reared together in the shared environmental influences that affect their phenotypic similarity. Existing research indicates a high degree of support for the EEA for most psychological and psychiatric traits. The random-mating assumption stipulates that mates or spouses do not select one another based on (heritable) phenotypes of interest. Random mating is most certainly untrue for cognitive abilities and attitudes, with a high degree of spouse similarity present from the time of marriage. However, there is markedly little spouse similarity for most personality traits. The presence of nonrandom mating may result in inflated estimates of the shared environment if not accounted for in the statistical analyses. Infant and child twins do appear to be similar to the general population for the majority of behavioral phenotypes. It is common for twins to experience more difficult births and be physically smaller than singletons at birth. With respect to behavioral traits, twins may have greater tendency to show language delays, but approximately after 8 years of age they tend to be similar to singletons.

Adoption designs. In a typical family, parents and offspring are genetically similar and they share home, neighborhood, and regional environments. In the adopted family any similarities between the adopted offspring and the biological parent can be attributed to genetic causes, while similarities between the adoptive siblings, for example, can be thought of as due to environmental causes. Combined twin and adoption designs are even more powerful in disentangling environmental and genetic effects. Because twins are the same age, one can be sure that differences between the siblings are not due to being in different developmental periods. One variant of this design is to consider identical twins that have been reared apart, because they have identical genes but have different rearing environments. Even more powerful is to also include identical twin reared together as well as fraternal twins reared apart and together to maximize the information about heritable and rearing environmental effects.

Primary assumptions of the adoption design include no selective placement and that adoptive families do not systematically differ from the general population of families. The absence of selective placement refers to the assumption that were no selection criteria that adoptive parents match or are similar to biological parents for a particular trait or traits of interest. For traits such as physical characteristics, religious affiliation, and ethnicity there is evidence of selective placement. However, there is only nominal evidence for selective placement for behaviorally relevant traits such as education or intelligence. Where selective placement exists, statistical adjustments can be made to estimates of genetic and environmental influence, described further below. Adoptive parents are scrutinized prior to adoption to verify, for example, the absence of severe economic hardship and mental illness. To a large degree, adoptive parents represent the general population of parents; however, traits related to socioeconomic status (SES) and particularly mental health may be limited in range. A related concern is whether biological parents (and indeed the children they give up for adoption) differ from the general population. While some studies find differences in terms of levels of antisocial behavior and alcohol-use disorders, for example, differences are not routinely found across studies. The additional inclusion of intact nuclear families to adoption designs is sometimes used as a reference group given concerns regarding representativeness and when information on biological parents is limited.

Gene–Environment Relationships

Although genes and environments may be correlated or interact, these are routinely estimated as separate effects in twin and adoption designs. However, it is possible in some cases to directly test for gene–environment (GE) relationships, ideally with measured candidate genes and measured features of the environment.

GE correlation. Individuals with particular genotypes that lead to high trait values may be in environments that also facilitate high trait values whereas those with genotypes that lead to low trait values may find themselves in or chose environments that lead to low trait values. For example, parents transmit genes to their offspring and provide an environment as well. For example, parents with genes that increase sociability may provide environments with more social opportunities for their children, thus leading to higher sociability, while parents with genes leading to lower sociability may provide fewer social opportunities to their children who are less sociable, etc. This is referred to as a passive GE correlation because the parents provide both genes and environments to their children. An active GE correlation arises, for example, when a person due to their genetic propensities chooses environments that foster their capabilities or characteristics. A small but emerging research literature using longitudinal twin designs or extended family kinships of twins, for example, twins and their offspring, suggests that GE correlation may be identifiable for cognitive and antisocial traits. Though theoretically important, relatively few data are available to establish how important GE correlations may be in practice for behavioral traits.

GE interaction. Individuals with particular genotypes may be sensitive to particular environments; thus the expression of the phenotype may depend on the interplay between the particular genes and particular environments. For example, hypothetically children with allele A on gene W may be more likely to show high anxiety in novel situations but low anxiety in familiar situations than children with allele B who show equal levels of anxiety in both situations. GE interaction has been well documented in nonhuman organisms but less well established in human studies. However, with measured candidate genes or measured environmental factors, studies have begun to test this occurrence more frequently. Empirical examples of testing for GE interaction are noted below by topic.

Locating Candidate Genes for Complex Traits

For complex traits no single gene is causative but many genes may contribute in small measures. Variations of linkage and association methods may be employed to locate genes contributing to complex traits called quantitative trait loci (QTLs). As in linkage analysis for single-gene traits, in QTL linkage analysis the goal is to identify a narrow enough chromosomal region where a QTL may lie. One of the DNA markers used in the analysis may be the QTL itself or nearby it. Already known genes nearby the QTL region may be considered in subsequent association analyses that test for how much of the heritable variance may be due to the gene candidates.

Genetic and Environmental Contribution to Common Traits and Disorders

While some disorders in childhood are caused by single-gene mutations or chromosomal abnormalities, most disorders and traits are considered complex and are determined by multiple genes and environmental factors. Indeed, most behavioral traits show moderate genetic and environmental influence, though the rearing environment seems to be of small consequence in general (see **Figure 2**). The current task is to identify measurable environmental factors and locate gene candidates that are at least partly responsible for different traits and disorders. Current research on a variety of childhood traits is described in greater detail below.

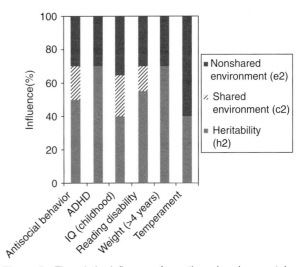

Figure 2 The relative influence of genetic and environmental factors on childhood traits. ADHD, attention deficit hyperactivity disorder; IQ, Intelligence quotient.

Cognitive ability. Twin and adoption studies have shown consistently that the heritability of general intelligence is moderate in early childhood at about 40% and continues to gain in importance through adulthood peaking at about 80% until late old-age where it drops to approximately 60%. Specific cognitive abilities, such as verbal ability, spatial ability, memory, etc., are also moderately heritable though to a somewhat lesser degree than general cognitive ability. Controversy has surrounded intelligence research for over a century because of the societal and political implications of assigning to individuals a score or set of scores to indicate their cognitive ability, that is, intelligence quotient (IQ) scores, which is predictive of school success and to a lesser degree occupational success. Embedded in this debate has been the assumption that the family environment must surely be more important than adoption or twin studies have suggested.

Studies of humans and animals have shown the importance of rearing environment in fostering or stunting intellectual growth. Some environmental aspects that cause variability in intelligence are enriched versus impoverished rearing environment (number of books and toys in the home, etc.), nutrition, quality of schools, and other life experiences. Twin and adoption studies suggest that shared or rearing environmental effects account for about 20% of individual differences in early to mid-childhood but tend to decrease to nominal levels by late adolescence. This pattern of decrease is also true for specific cognitive abilities. The decrease in shared environmental effects with age has been hypothesized to occur for a few possible reasons, including the increasing control that older children may gain over their own environment whereby they may choose particular environmental niches that suit their intellectual propensities (e.g., choosing particular classes in school, taking on hobbies, or taking part in after-school activities), an example of an active GE correlation. There is evidence for GE interaction where SES may moderate the strength of genetic influences: heritability for childhood intelligence increases as family affluence increases.

In addition to IQ tests as direct measures of ability, there is an emerging focus on possible endophenotypes. Endophenotypes for IQ would be those traits that may be closer to the neural or neuroanatomical underpinnings of ability and perhaps 'closer' to where gene action occurs. Electroencephalogram (EEG) studies have also shown heritability for multiple measures in children including coherence (a measure of interconnectivity in the brain) ranging from approximately 40% to 75% depending on location, and for alpha peak frequency (a measure of synaptic activity) at approximately 79%. Brain volume measures in adults have shown high heritability estimates (between 80% and 90%) using magnetic resonance imaging (MRI) of such structures as gray matter, white matter, cerebellar, total brain, and intracranial volume. IQ is moderately correlated with brain volume measures in adults, approximately 0.30–0.40.

Genes for intelligence are likely to be many in number and individually contributing only a small degree to individual differences. Possible QTLs for intelligence may reside in regions on chromosomes 2 and 6 that overlap with regions linked to autism, dyslexia, and reading disability. Candidate genes that code for receptors and neurotransmitters or are otherwise involved in learning and memory pathways are of particular focus in association studies. While multiple associations have been reported few have been replicated. An exception is the *CHRM2* gene that codes for cholinergic muscarinic receptor M2 and may be involved in neuronal and synaptic processes important to learning and memory.

Mental retardation. As discussed above, there are rare genetic mutations and chromosomal aberrations that can result in mental retardation such as PKU, fragile X syndrome, and Down syndrome. Multiple environmental factors may lead to severe retardation including prenatal exposure to teratogens, birth trauma, and nutritional deficiencies. On the whole, heritability of severe mental retardation is relatively low. Mild retardation, where IQs range anywhere from 50 to 75 depending on criteria used, most likely represents the continuum of intelligence found in the general population (IQ of 100 is average). Thus, it is more heritable than severe retardation at approximately 50%. The search for genes for mild retardation overlaps considerably with the search for genes for general intelligence.

Learning disabilities. Many children exhibit a learning disability that is unexplained by typical causes (e.g., head injury, mental retardation). Children who exhibit learning disorders have at minimum average intelligence and their disorder is not caused by a primary physical disability (visual, hearing, or motor), an emotional disturbance, or social or cultural conditions. Learning disorders may result in impairments in math ability (dyscalculia), writing (dysgraphia), speech (specific learning impairment or SLI), and problems with reading and comprehension (dyslexia) and affect up to 5–10% of school-aged children with boys being twice as likely to be diagnosed as girls. Genetic research has focused primarily on reading disability traits or dyslexia diagnoses. Twin studies in the UK and US suggest a moderate heritable component of 40–70% and shared environmental effects ranging from 20% to 45% across reading disability traits. Replicated linkage analyses suggest potential regions of interest on chromosomes 1, 2, 6, 15, and 18. Two gene candidates on the short arm of chromosome 6 have become of interest: the doublecortin domain containing 2 (*DCDC2*) gene and *KIAA0319*, both involved in migration of neurons in prenatal development.

Temperament. Temperament in infancy and early childhood is thought to influence the presence of behavioral tendencies and serve as a precursor to personality traits expressed later in life. The consistency of temperament in an infant or young child can best be characterized on a range of dimensions that include: activity level, attention and persistence, social skills and reactivity in social situations, and level of emotions. Temperament is theorized to be biologically driven though heritability varies across traits and studies from 20% to 60% with consistently greater similarity observed for MZ than DZ twins. Thus, genetic factors only have a moderate influence on temperament characteristics. Shared environmental factors appear unimportant to individual differences in temperament, however. Nonshared environmental factors make up the remaining variation at a minimum of 40%. Hence, not only genetics within family members but also the diversity of environmental factors across development influence temperament and eventually personality. Candidate genes of particular interest include those that are involved in the neurotransmitter systems such as dopamine, which is involved in the production of motor behaviors as well as active in a neural reward system that leads to emergence or extinction of behaviors, and serotonin, which plays a role in sleep–wake cycles, hunger, and mood amongst other domains. The dopamine D4 receptor gene (*DRD4*) has been associated with activity levels and novelty seeking, which are significant dimensions related to ADHD. Polymorphisms in the *DRD4* and serotonin transporter promoter (*5-HTTLPR*) genes have been implicated in negative emotionality and stranger anxiety/fearfulness in infants. However, these findings are preliminary and more studies must be conducted to validate the influence of these specific genes on temperament.

Autism. Autism is part of the spectrum of autistic disorders including Aspeberger's syndrome (AS) and pervasive developmental disorder – not otherwise specified (PDD-nos). Autism spectrum disorders (ASD) are discussed more fully elsewhere in this work; we only comment briefly on the emerging literature that considers autism-associated traits in population-based samples of twins. Those with ASD may exhibit varying degrees of impairments in social interactions and communication as well as demonstrate repetitive stereotyped behaviors. Twin studies have begun to consider particular symptom dimensions in the range that they occur in the general population, including social sensitivity or responsiveness, communication difficulties, and recurrent stereotyped behaviors, and suggest that these features may be strongly heritable in childhood and even adolescence, as high as 80%. Moreover, the genetic factors influencing social vs. nonsocial features may be somewhat distinct. Linkage and association analyses have yet to follow from these general population twin studies but have been proceeding in family studies with members who have autism or ASD; gene regions or candidates that have been implicated in language impairment or in neuron and synapse development have been of particular interest.

ADHD. ADHD typically emerges during the early school years, where a child exhibits an inability to pay attention for sustained periods, hyperactivity, and impulsive behavior. It affects more boys than girls, with about 5.4% of boys and 1.6% of girls having been diagnosed at some point between the ages of 5 and 17 years old. Awareness of the disorder has increased in recent years and diagnosis rates have increased as well, and it is now being recognized as persisting into adolescence and adulthood. ADHD may increase the risk of exhibiting later antisocial behavior and drug and alcohol use. It often co-occurs with learning disorders described above. Few studies have found significant shared environmental contributions, and if they do so they usually account for less than 10% of the variance. ADHD is moderately to strongly heritable with estimates ranging from 60% to 80%, if based on information garnered from parents but 10–20% lower if based on teacher reports and interviews. Some research indicates the etiological factors may be different for boys than girls; antisocial behavior is more likely to be present in boys with ADHD than girls and girls with ADHD may have more apparent intellectual deficits. Multiple-gene association studies suggest involvement of the dopamine neurotransmitter pathway, which is implicated in attention and motor activity. Gene candidates include the dopamine D4 receptor (*DRD4*), the dopamine transporter (*DAT1*), and the dopamine D5 receptor (*DRD5*) genes.

Antisocial traits. It has been divisive to consider genetic factors for antisocial behavior, by designation a social construct. However, any observed heritability may reflect underlying traits that increase risk, for example, temperament. Antisocial behaviors in childhood include rule breaking, physical aggression toward people and animals, vandalism, dishonesty, theft, and resistance toward authority. The *Diagnostic and Statistical Manual of Mental Disorders*, 4th edn. (DSM-IV) describes two disorders that represent excessive problems: conduct disorder (CD) and oppositional defiant disorder (ODD). An ODD diagnosis is a precursor to CD, with a CD diagnosis requiring the presence of more symptoms. ODD is found in about 6–11% of school-aged children while CD affects about 1–4% of children 9 years and older. More boys than girls are diagnosed with ODD and CD. The heritability of antisocial traits, including the ODD and CD disorders, is about 50% using parent-based information but may be lower if using child-based information. Shared environmental effects explain about 20% of the variation in antisocial behaviors in childhood. ODD and CD diagnoses though varying in age of emergence and severity appear to share a common genetic etiology. Similarly, antisocial traits and later criminal behavior share common genetic and environmental factors, with nonviolent criminality showing evidence of genetic influence but not violent or alcohol-involved offenses.

GE interactions may be important to antisocial behaviors and criminal offending. In adoption studies, risk of criminal behavior in adopted-away offspring is increased if the biological parents exhibited criminal behavior and further amplified if both the biological and adoptive parents displayed criminal behavior. Adoptive parents' criminal behavior did not increase the risk of criminal offending in adoptees of noncriminal biological parents. Moreover, measured environmental factors such as childhood maltreatment may transact with known genes in the emergence of antisocial traits: physical abuse in combination with the monoamine oxidase A (MAOA) allele that expresses high monoamine oxidase A may lead to a 'lower' susceptibility to exhibit antisocial behaviors compared to the MAOA allele expressing lower monoamine oxidase A. MAOA is ubiquitously involved in the degradation of the neurotransmitters dopamine, serotonin, and norepinephrine. Dopamine is implicated in antisocial behaviors as well: one of the candidate genes associated with ADHD has also been associated with antisocial traits, *DRD4*.

Childhood obesity. Childhood obesity is a growing problem in developed countries. About 15.5% of US children meet the American Obesity Association's criteria. Children are at higher risk of obesity if they have obese parents. Twin and adoptions suggest that the heritability of body weight is about 60–80% in childhood; contributions from the shared environment begin to wane after the first year of life. Thus, the primary environmental factors in childhood are attributed to unique personal environments. Environmental factors in childhood weight gain are poor diet, low activity levels, increased television watching, and other recent societal changes that promote increased sedentary behavior (e.g., video games). Aside from rare single-gene or chromosomal disorders, a search continues to find gene candidates for obesity traits and how they might interact with dietary environment factors. Gene candidates of particular interest include those associated with metabolic syndrome (e.g., *ENPP1*), insulin resistance (e.g., *CART*), and consumption behaviors, including the dopamine and serotonin pathways (e.g., dopamine D2 receptor, *DRD2*).

The Human Genome Project

In 1990, a joint collaboration between the National Institutes of Health (NIH) and the US Department of Energy (DOE) proposed the execution and completion of the Human Genome Project (HGP). A $3 billion fund was allotted and a 15-year time frame was set to complete the entire project. However, competition between the publicly funded endeavor, which ultimately included thousands of researchers in the US and six other nations, with private researchers, principally at Celera Genomics, helped to spur its essential completion 2 years earlier than expected on 14 April 2003 and resulted in a $0.3 billion savings. The aims of the HGP were to sequence the 3.1 billion nucleotide base pairs and uncover all genes located on the 24 human chromosomes, to store as well as dispense the enormous amounts of information and data generated, to produce new laboratory and computational procedures for analysis, and to evaluate moral, legal, and societal concerns that may result.

Findings from the Human Genome Project

The entire human genome was sequenced through the examination of DNA from a handful of individuals. While the public HGP collected biological samples from several male and female individuals, the sequencing efforts considered the DNA from only a few of these donors. The private Celera Genomics project used the DNA of five individuals, including both males and females of various Caucasian, African American, Hispanic, or Asian ancestries. Thus, the sequenced human genome is really a 'template' human genome since it is based upon the identification of common variations in the nucleotide base pairs in fewer than 10 individuals. It is evident that 99.9% of nucleotide base pair sequences are the same in all human beings with only 0.1% of human genome showing variation. Much of the variation is due to SNPs, which are found approximately every 100–300 base pairs. Surprisingly only 20 000–25 000 genes may be responsible for functions related to protein coding and expression; however, many of these genes appear to code for multiple rather than single proteins. Up to 97% of the human genome is thought to be replete with noncoding DNA regions including introns and intergenic regions of DNA, sometimes referred to as 'junk DNA'. However, it is becoming clearer that the label 'junk' is a misnomer. About half of the noncoding DNA consists of repetitive base pair sequences whose functions are yet unidentified, but may have been evolutionarily important at some point in time. It is also thought to include parts of older genes thought to be difficult to remove from the human genome, since they withstand removal generation after generation. Finally, regulatory DNA sequences appear to be present that affect gene transcription or expression. In addition to a smaller quantity of genes than expected, humans share close to 96% of the same genes in common with chimpanzees. The initial aims of the project have been fulfilled, leading to other issues that the researchers must answer. The goal is to understand how genes function and interact with one another.

Moral, Ethical, and Legal Implications

The impetus of the HGP on ensuing research may provide an unprecedented opportunity to screen for, and identify, a variety of inherited disorders and diseases as well as identify specific genetic mechanisms that impact complex behavioral and physical traits. More effective prevention and treatments efforts for inherited diseases may be developed in the future due to increased understanding of gene function and expression leading to efficient drug development and newer treatment options.

For instance, based on the presence and or expression of particular genes, a customized medicinal regimen could be prescribed for a patient.

Yet, moral, ethical, and legal dilemmas also stem from this advancement in the field of genetics. The implications of stem cell research and cloning have raised such concerns in recent years. Ethical quandaries could arise in the future concerning the reemergence of eugenics and the privacy/storage of genetic information. For example, should parents have the opportunity to choose what traits their unborn fetus expresses later in life – that is, eye color, height, or intellectual capacity? For example, if an unborn fetus merely presents with a genetic propensity for a particular trait, that is, expression of the trait is not certain, will parents (or society) feel compelled to intervene or abort the pregnancy because they could be born with a less than 'perfect' set of genes?

Researchers and policy makers are debating whether genetic information should be kept private or become public knowledge. If made widely available, each person's genetic information could be stored in a database and could play an ever more crucial role in the criminal justice system. DNA evidence could play a more substantive role in linking criminals with various types of crimes. In contrast, public knowledge of a person's genetic information could hamper an individual's opportunities. For instance, a person may live his life around a minor genetic flaw. Indeed, larger-scale impacts could result: persons may face discrimination as a result of minor gene defects or even on the basis of typically occurring alleles or genotypes. For example, denials of employment opportunities or insurance coverage could result from carrying specific genes – even if these 'defective' genes are never expressed. Legal safeguards regarding dissemination of genetic information and insurance coverage vary widely by country. At this point, these and other moral, ethical, and legal dilemmas are yet to be fully debated or resolved.

Conclusions and Future Directions

Most common behavioral traits and disorders in childhood show a moderate-to-strong genetic basis and small if present effect of the shared environment. This should not be construed as evidence for genetic determinism of behavior. Indeed, even single-gene traits such as PKU are amenable to environmental intervention. Importantly the field of behavioral genetics has moved from presenting estimates of the relative influence of anonymous genes and environments on behavior to incorporating measured genes and environments.

While the sequencing of the human genome has increased the pace of genetic research in behavioral domains, gaps in knowledge are considerable. For example, what functions do nontranscribed intronic and intergenic stretches of DNA serve? A multitude of hypotheses exists including that these stretches of DNA have an important influence on or regulate gene expression. A better understanding of the role(s) of so-called 'junk' DNA will lead to an improved understanding of gene function.

Increased knowledge of gene function and gene–gene interactions will illuminate biological pathways for behavioral traits. The crucial task is to uncover neural pathways and endophenotypes through which genes ply their influence and the environmental contexts under which genes are expressed. Emerging research on GE interplay suggests that both genetic susceptibility and environmental contexts are important. Genes and environmental factors are likely to be of small effect individually for most behavioral traits; thus the multifaceted pathways from small accumulating effects leading to complex behavior will long be of interest.

See also: Intellectual Disabilities; Twins.

Suggested Readings

Boomsma D, Busjahn A, and Peltonen L (2002) Classical twin studies and beyond. *Nature Review Genetics* 3: 872–882.
Bouchard TJ (2004) Genetic influence on human psychological traits. *Current Directions in Psychological Science* 13: 148–151.
Carey G (2003) *Human Genetics for the Social Sciences.* Thousand Oaks, CA: SAGE.
Gottesman II and Hanson DR (2005) Human development: Biological and genetic processes. *Annual Review of Psychology* 56: 263–286.
Hetherington et al. (2003) *Child Psycology*. McGraw-Hill.
Mendel's, Paper in English, Experiments in Plant, Hybridization (1865) by Gregor Mendel. http://www.mendelweb.org/Mendel.html.
Morgan RM (2006) *The Genetics Revolution: History, Fears, and Future of a Life-Altering Science,* 1st edn. Westport, CT: Greenwood Press.
Nervous System, How genetic disorders are inherited. http://www.mayoclinic.com/health/genetic-disorders/DS00549.
Palladino MA (2006) *Understanding the Human Genome Project. CT The Benjamin Cummings Special Topics in Biology Series,* 2nd edn. San Francisco: PB Pearson/Benjamin Cummings.
Plomin R (2003) *Behavioral Genetics in the Postgenomic Era.* Washington, DC: American Psychological Association.
Plomin R, DeFries JC, McClearn GE, and McGuffin P (2001) *Behavioral Genetics.* New York: Worth Publishers.
Posthuma D and de Geus EJC (2006) Progress in the molecular-genetic study of intelligence. *Current Directions in Psychological Science* 15: 151–155.
Rutter MJ (2006) *Genes and Behaviour: Nature–Nurture Interplay.* Oxford, UK: Blackwell Publishing.

Relevant Websites

http://genomics.energy.gov – Genome programs of the US Department of Energy Office of Science.
http://www.hdsa.org – Huntington's Disease, Society of America.
http://www.ncbi.nlm.nih.gov – National Center for Biotechnology Information; Genomic Biology, Human Genome Resources.
http://www.nichd.nih.gov – National Institute of Child Health and Human Development, Child Development and Behavior (CDB) Branch.
http://health.nih.gov – US Department of Health and Human Services, National Institutes of Health, Child Behavior Disorders.

Grammar

D Matthews, University of Manchester, Manchester, UK
M Tomasello, Max Planck Institute for Evolutionary Anthropology, Leipzig, Germany

© 2008 Elsevier Inc. All rights reserved.

Glossary

Agreement – Words are said to agree when they share a relevant feature (such as number, person, or gender). For example, with respect to the sentence 'The cats are wet' we can say that the words 'cats' and 'are' agree in number (plural as opposed to singular).

Argument – A noun phrase bearing a specific grammatical relation to a verb. For example, the arguments of the verb 'to kick' might be 'John' and 'the ball'. These arguments may be identified either in terms of grammatical relations (as a subject and direct object) or semantic roles (as agent and patient).

Auxiliary – In English, words such as 'have' in 'I have eaten', 'do' in 'They do not know' or 'can' in 'He can help'. Auxiliaries precede a main verb (such as eat, "know", or help in the above examples) and have verb like properties in that they may mark person, number, and tense. In English auxiliaries can invert with the subject of a sentence to form a question (e.g., Can he help? Do they know?).

Case – Some words are marked for case. For example, the pronoun 'I' is said to be in the nominative case and the pronoun 'me' is in the accusative case. The words refer to the same person but in different roles. Nominative case is used, for example, when the person is the agent of an action ('I am eating') whereas accusative case would be used if the person was the patient of an action ('The monster ate me'). Many languages rely heavily on case markings to express such things as who did what to whom (nominative, accusative), who received something (dative), who possesses something (genitive), where something came from (ablative), is going to (allative), or is currently located (locative), the means with which something is done (instrumental), and so on.

Construction – A grammatical construction is an abstract pattern made up of smaller linguistic units such as words and inflectional morphemes. Constructions may exist at the whole utterance level, for example, the passive construction, or they may describe fragments of utterances, for example, the noun phrase construction, or the plural construction.

Distribution – The range of environments in which a word or grammatical item may occur. For example, English nouns (e.g., dog) are often found after determiners (the dog, a dog) and before a plural suffix (dog-s).

Lexicon – The lexicon is the vocabulary of a language or a person who speaks that language.

Morphology – The form or structure of words. Words can be analyzed as being made up of one or several morphemes. For example, the word 'dogs' is made up of two morphemes: 'dog' and 's'. The sufffix -s is an inflectional morpheme, also referred to as a 'bound morpheme' because the -s cannot occur on its own but must be bound to a word.

Phrase – Sentences and clauses can be understood as being made up of phrases. For example, 'The dog quickly ate my favorite dinner' could be analyzed into three phrases: a noun phrase (the dog) a verb phrase (quickly ate) and another noun phrase (my favorite dinner). These phrases could be made up of different numbers of constituent words ('my favorite dinner', might be replaced by 'my dinner' or just 'it') but they would still play the same role in the sentence. The clustering of words into phrases that then make up sentences is sometimes referred to as the constituent structure of language.

Semantic roles: agent/patient – Also called thematic roles, these are semantic categories (e.g., agent, patient, theme, instrument, location) that describe the relationship between an argument (generally expressed as a noun phrase) and a predicate (often a verb). For example, the sentence 'John ate the apple in the park' has three thematic roles (the agent: John, the patient: the apple and the location: the park).

Semantics – The meanings of words and larger linguistic structures, such as sentences.

Syntax – The ordering of words or phrases into larger structures, particularly sentences. Syntax and morphology are often subsumed under the more general title of grammar.

Introduction

Infants begin to communicate with others about the world in the months immediately preceding their first birthdays. Typically their first means of communication is pointing and other nonlinguistic gestures. In the months immediately following their first birthdays, infants begin to learn conventional means of communication in the form of linguistic symbols. One-year-olds use linguistic symbols initially as single-unit expressions that convey what, to an adult, are complex meanings (so-called holophrases); for example, "Airplane" may mean, "There is an airplane" and "Apple!" may mean "I want an apple."

The fundamental question is how young children proceed from these single-unit holophrases to more complex forms of linguistic competence in which they comprehend and produce multiunit linguistic utterances, in other words, how they develop grammatical competence with a language. How we answer this question depends heavily on what we think grammatical competence amounts to. This is a matter of great controversy and two main theoretical views have been debated ever since the 1960s.

One view, the generative grammar view, began with the work of Noam Chomsky, who argued that the essence of human language lies in our possession of recursive procedures (abstract rules of grammar), which allow us to generate countless utterances from a finite lexicon (the store of the words we know). Many people who ascribe to the generative view argue that children must have innate knowledge of the rules of grammar since they would be impossible to learn. Indeed, Chomsky originally proposed that there must be a universal grammar that all children would have innately and that they would apply to the language they hear around them. What the universal rules of this grammar would be is currently unclear. However, it is important to bear in mind that any innate knowledge of language, if it exists at all, could only provide a starting point. There are more than 6000 different languages in the world – each with its own set of grammatical conventions – and so to acquire the specific grammatical conventions of specific languages, much will have to be learned.

Another view takes this need to learn each language's idiosyncrasies seriously and proposes that there is no innate grammar. Instead all of grammar – from the most regular of structures (e.g., 'The cat drank the milk') to the most peculiar of idioms (e.g., 'The more the merrier') – is learned. This usage-based view argues that we do not only store words (that are combined with abstract rules) but rather we store linguistic units of all sizes in memory – words and whole utterances alike. On this view, children are able to learn about grammar by forming generalizations over the examples of complex utterances that they have heard and remembered. The result is that all words, whole utterances, and generalizations are stored as symbolic associations of sound and meaning, often referred to as 'constructions'.

Taking this usage-based view, a key theoretical device we will use to trace out the development of grammar is the 'grammatical construction', which is basically a combinatorial pattern of smaller linguistic units. Constructions may be very simple, as in the English plural used to designate multiple entities of the same kind. This construction prototypically consists of a referential word (noun) plus an ending, or 'inflection', written as (-s) (e.g., boy + s > boys). But constructions may also be very complex, as in the English ditransitive construction which, prototypically, consists of a pattern of the following type: noun phrase + verb + noun phrase + noun phrase, as in "The boy gave the girl a gift," for indicating transfer of possession (see **Table 1**).

One key question for developmental psycholinguists concerns how abstractly children's early constructions are represented. The fact that children sometimes make creative errors (e.g., saying 'mouses') would seem to imply some kind of abstractness in the cognitive representation of early linguistic constructions (in this example 'any noun can combine with (-s) to form a plural'). But the question is precisely what degree of abstractness is involved and how this changes over developmental time. As documented below, grammatical development seems to be characterized by a gradual move from more concrete and local constructions/representations to more abstract and general constructions/representations during the preschool period. Again, though, this is a matter of debate and some would argue that evidence for early abstractions is a sign that children have innate principles that guide their acquisition of grammar.

Below we trace the developmental path children follow when moving from holophrases to abstract constructions. We then consider the development of some key grammatical devices, namely, word order and case marking and discuss the level of abstraction that children manifest in their comprehension and production of word order. Next, we discuss the development of inflectional morphology. We then describe a handful of the various abstract constructions children master. Finally, we return to the theoretical issues discussed in this introduction and consider some of the learning processes that are likely to underlie grammatical development.

From Holophrases to Abstract Constructions

Children produce their earliest multiword utterances to talk about many of the same things they communicated prelinguistically or with holophrases. They talk about the existence and recurrence of objects, people's action on objects, and the location or properties of objects, and people. This talk may take the form of statements (declaratives e.g., 'There's a plane!'), requests (imperatives e.g., 'Give it to me!'), questions (e.g., 'Where did it go?'), and performatives (e.g., 'Hello'). The grammatical constructions underlying these multiword utterances can come in

Table 1 Early grammatical constructions

Construction	Example/comments
Identificationals	*It's a dog.* Almost always take one of three simple forms: *It's a/the X. That's a/the. This's a/the X.*
Attributives	*There's a plane.* Often take one of two forms: *Here's a/the X. There's a/the X.*
Possessives	*(It's) X's. That's X's/my __. This is X's/your __.*
Intransitives (unergatives and unaccustaives)	*He smiled* (unergative: an actor does something) *It broke* (unaccusative: something happens to something) In the development of English unergatives such as *sleep* and *swim* predominate. The main verbs young children use in the this construction are: *go, come, stop, break, fall, open, play, jump, sit, sing, sleep, cry, swim, run, laugh, hurt,* and *see.*
Transtives	*She pushed me, I want grapes* Used early on by children to talk about both physical and psychological activities. The main verbs young children use in this construction are: *get, have, want, take, find, put, bring, drop, make, open, break, cut, do, eat, play, read, draw, ride, throw, push, help, why see, say,* and *hurt.*
Datives (ditransitives)	*John read the book for Mary* (for dative) *John read the book to Mary* (to dative) *John read Mary the book* (double object dative) Used for talking about the transfer of things between people. Some verbs are choosey about which of the dative constructions they will enter into. The main verbs young children use in these constructions are: *get, give, show, make, read, bring, buy, take, tell, find,* and *send.*
Locatives	Prepositions: *X up, X down, X in, X out, on X, off X* Verb + particle constructions: *pick X up, wipe X off,* and *get X down* Used to express spatial relationships in utterance-level constructions. Children produce two-argument locative constructions early on, for example, *Draw star on me* and *Peoples on there boat,* produced by a 20-month-old. By 3 years of age most children are able to talk about locative events with three participants, for example, *He put the pen on the desk.*
Resultatives	*He wiped the table clean* Used to indicate both an action and the result of that action. Around 2 years of age children learn various combinations of 'causing verb + resulting effect' such as *pull + up* and *eat + all gone*. Later, some children produce novel resultatives e.g. *And the monster would eat you in pieces* and *I'll capture his whole head off.*
Causatives	*He killed the deer* (lexical causative verb has causal meaning). *He made her giggle* (phrasal or periphrastic causative). Phrasal causatives supply a way of causativizing an intransitive verb that cannot be used transitively. For example, instead of saying *Don't laugh me* we can say *Don't make me laugh.* *Make* is thus the direct causation matrix verb in English, but the most frequent such verb for young English learners is *let,* as in *Let her do it.* Another common matrix verb is *help,* as in *Help her get in there.* It is unknown whether young children see any common pattern among the utterances in which these three different matrix verbs are used.
Passives	*Bill was shot by John.* *He got hurt.* Used to change the perspective from the agent of an action to the patient and what happened to it. Thus, *Bill was shot by John* takes the perspective of Bill and what happened to him, rather than focusing on John's act of shooting. English-speaking children typically do not spontaneously produce full passives until 4 or 5 years of age, although they produce truncated passives (often with *get*) and adjectival passives much earlier (e.g., *He got hurt*). Children tend to begin with stative participles (e.g., *Pumpkin stuck*), then use some participles ambiguously between stative and active readings (e.g., *Do you want yours cut?*), then finally use the active participles characteristic of the full passive (e.g., *The spinach was cooked by Mommy*). Older preschoolers occasionally create truncated passives with verbs that in adult English do not passivize, for example, *It was bandaided, He will be died and I won't have a brother anymore,* indicating some productivity with the construction.
Questions	*What did he buy?* (Object Wh question) *Who bought the house?* (Subject Wh question) *Did he buy a house?* (Yes–no question) In contrast to the above English examples, many languages form questions by using characteristic intonation (*He bought a house?*) or by the replacement of a content word with a question word (*He bought a what?*).

Continued

Table 1 Continued

Construction	Example/comments
Complex constructions	*I want to go* (infinitival complement construction)
	I think it will fall over (sentential complement construction)
	That's the doggy I bought (relative clause construction) *You do this and I'll do that* (conjoined clause construction). Complex constructions contain multiple predicates (e.g., 'want' and 'go' in the first example). Children generally start to produce complex constructions between the ages of 2 and 3 years, starting off with constructions they hear frequently and are motivated to use, such as the infinitival 'I want to X'.
Modals	*I have to go* (modal verb have used in deontic sense)
	It might be there (model verb might used in epistemic sense)
	Modality and negation are used in conjunction with argument structure constructions to talk about such things as what must, might, or should not be the case. Children are very quick to learn this using modal verbs (*can, might, could, should, must,* and so on) and negation in some form (e.g., can't) from early on to say what people have to or ought to do (deontic sense) and later in the epistemic sense.
Negation constructions	*I don't want to.*
	Negation often emerges with the ubiquitous 'no' before a statement (e.g., *No Mummy do it*) and later with sentence internal negative markers, with or without auxiliaries (e.g., *I no want that* or *I didn't caught it*).

Please note that examples are given in italics and comments in roman.

the form of word combinations, pivot schemas, item-based constructions, and abstract constructions.

Word Combinations

Beginning at around 18 months of age, many children combine two words or holophrases in situations in which they both are relevant (e.g., "all-gone apple" to announce the loss or consumption of an apple, "Daddy coffee" to describe Daddy's coffee or "Boomboom plane" to describe the noise of a plane). In these word combinations both words have roughly equivalent status. For example, a child has learned to name a ball and a table and then spies a ball on a table and says, "Ball table." Utterances of this type include both 'successive single-word utterances' (with a pause between them) and 'word combinations' or 'expressions' (under a single intonational contour). The defining feature of word combinations or expressions is that they partition the experiential scene into multiple symbolizable units – in a way that holophrases obviously (by definition) do not – and they are totally concrete in the sense that they are comprised only of concrete pieces of language, not abstract categories (e.g., noun, verb).

Pivot Schemas

Beginning at around 8 months of age, many of children's multiword productions show a more systematic pattern and the first signs of linguistic abstraction. Often there is one word or phrase that seems to structure the utterance in the sense that it determines the speech act function of the utterance as a whole (often with help from an intonational contour), with the other linguistic item(s) simply filling in variable slot(s). Thus, in many of these early utterances one event-word is used with a wide variety of object labels (e.g., "More milk," "More grapes," "More juice") or, more rarely, something like a pronoun or other general expression is the constant element (e.g., 'It's __' or 'Where's __'). Following Martin Braine, we may call these pivot schemas.

Item-Based and Abstract Constructions

Pivot schemas are a clear illustration of early linguistic abstraction and systematicity. However, although the order of slot and pivot may be fixed, this cannot be taken as a sign of a productive syntactic symbol: the order of the words is not used to mean anything. So, although young children are using their early pivot schemas to partition scenes conceptually with different words, they are not using syntactic symbols – such as word order or case marking – to indicate the different roles being played by different participants in that scene. The first signs of syntactic symbol use emerge with 'item-based constructions'. For example, if a child systematically differentiates the meaning of 'Kate pushed Jenny' from the meaning of 'Jenny pushed Kate', then we might take this as evidence of an item-based construction at least as abstract as (PUSHER pushed PUSHEE), where the order of the words is crucial to the meaning of the utterance. In this case the slot before the verb is for the pusher, whereas the one after the verb is for the pushee. Children who have grasped this function of word order can now use grammar to express 'who did what to whom'.

Using Grammar to Say Who Did What to Whom

One of the key advantages that grammatical development brings is the ability to mark agent–patient relations, the 'who did what to whom' of a sentence. Put simply, when there are several noun phrases in a sentence, agent–patient relations tell us the role each of these plays. So in the example 'Jenny pushed Kate' we need to know that role of Jenny is the pusher (or more generally, the 'agent') and Kate is the pushee (the 'patient'). The two major devices that languages use to mark agent–patient relations (also known as thematic roles) are (1) word order (as in our English example) and (2) morphological marking (e.g., case marking on nouns and agreement marking between nouns and verbs).

Word Order

In their spontaneous speech young English-speaking children use canonical word order (often referred to as SVO order – subject verb object) from very early in development. However, one key question of current theoretical debate concerns just how abstract this early knowledge of word order is. That is, do children understand the function of word order at an entirely abstract level from the outset (either in terms of marking abstract thematic roles such as agent and patient or in terms of abstract syntactic roles such as subject and object), or is this understanding first based on specific lexical items?

Several studies have revealed that children respond to word order better when the specific words used in test sentences are ones whose typical word order patterns they are already familiar with. For example, when given lots of animal toys, children barely 2 years of age respond appropriately to requests that they "Make the bunny push the horse" (reversible transitives) that depend crucially on a knowledge of canonical English word order and its function in marking agent–patient relations. However, if 2-year-olds are taught a new verb, 'dacking', to describe a novel canonical transitive action they do not perform so consistently. So, when asked to 'Make Cookie Monster dack Big Bird', 3-year-olds are consistently able to make Cookie Monster perform the dacking action on Big Bird, but many young 2-year-olds are not. This task is also made considerably harder for children if word order cues conflict with animacy cues. Thus if children are asked to 'Make the pencil kick the horse,' they are sometimes susceptible to picking up the toy horse and making it kick the pencil.

Children's production of word order also seems to be affected by the familiarity and frequency of the verb they are using. For example, in the 'weird word order' paradigm, developed by Nameera Akhtar, an adult describes a novel transitive scene by using a novel verb in an ungrammatical word order (e.g., saying "Ernie Bert dacking" to describe Ernie performing some novel action on Bert). The child is then asked to describe scenes with other characters performing this same novel action. The idea is to test whether children will adopt the adult's weird word order or prefer to use the novel verb in the canonical order of their language. Generally speaking, English-speaking 4-year-olds prefer to use canonical word order but 2-year-olds are just as likely to adopt the weird word orders as they are to switch to using a novel verb in canonical order. In contrast, with familiar verbs even 2-year-olds prefer to switch to canonical English order. Furthermore, 2-year-olds never copy a weird word order with pronouns even when novel verbs are used (i.e., they might say 'Ernie Bert dacked' but are unlikely to say 'He him dacked'). This suggests that 2-year-olds knowledge of word order may be based on words that they know well (e.g., high-frequency verbs and pronouns).

In contrast to the above findings, recent studies have suggested that even 2-year-olds show some abstract understanding of word order when undemanding comprehension tests are used. For example, when 2-year-olds are simultaneously shown two screens showing identical scenes except for their agent–patient relations (e.g., Screen 1: A dog acting on a lion; Screen 2: A lion acting on a dog) and are simply asked to 'Point to the lion weefing the dog', they point to the right scene (where the lion was the agent) at a rate above chance and do so even when novel verbs are used. Similar results have been found when children's eye movements are measured instead of their pointing gestures: the 'preferential looking' technique developed by Hirsh-Pasek and Golinkoff. In one study conducted by Cynthia Fisher and colleagues, children were shown two screens. In the first, a boy spun a girl around on a chair. In the second, a girl bent a boy over by pushing on his shoulder. After hearing test sentences like 'The girl is gorping the boy' 21-month-olds looked longer at the screen in which the girl was the agent than at the screen where the boy was acting on the girl.

When we take the results of these diverse methods together the picture that emerges is one where English-speaking children are beginning to formulate abstract knowledge of the function of word order around their second birthday. However, this early knowledge of word order starts off as weak and is open to being abandoned if other orders are modeled by an adult or if other cues, such as animacy, compete with it. At this point, then, knowledge of word order shows up in above chance performance in preferential looking tasks using highly prototypical transitives. Over the next months and years, however, it will grow in strength and abstractness and show up in tasks requiring more active behavioral decision-making and language production.

One reason it takes time for this knowledge to become robust is that understanding of word order most probably starts out as a collection of various production and comprehension heuristics, which later coalesce into a full-blown understanding, for example, of English SVO word order. When comprehending an SVO utterance a child might simply know that the first noun phrase is generally the agent, or that the noun phrase following the verb is the patient. Other heuristics for English might be based on pronouns (I-me, he-him, they-them, we-us, etc.), whose roles are not only indicated with word order but also with case marking (e.g., the agent of a transitive action is expressed with a nominative pronoun 'I/he/she', whereas the patient is expressed with an accusative 'me/him/her'). We now turn to an investigation of the development of case marking – which is much more important in some other languages than it is in English.

Case and Agreement

In many languages agent–patient relations are marked not with word order, but morphologically with case or agreement. For example, in Polish the sentence 'The giraffe is chasing the monkey' can be expressed as follows: *Żyraf-a goni małp-ę* (Giraffe + Nominative_marker chases monkey + Accurate_marker).

The ending *-a* on *zyrafa* indicates the nominative case (it marks the agent) and *-ę* on *małpę* marks the accusative case (it marks the patient). So one could just a well say *Małp-ę goni Żyraf-a* (Monkey-Acc chases Giraffe-Nom) and this would still mean 'the giraffe is chasing the monkey', since it is the case marking that does all the work in Polish not word order (although word order may be used to pragmatic effect). Case marking is used in this way in many languages ranging from slavic languages like Polish, to uralic languages like Finnish, innuit languages like Inuktitut and turkic languages like Turkish.

In the 1960s and 1970s, a number of investigators speculated that word order should be easier than case and agreement for children to learn as a syntactic device because canonical ordering is so fundamental to so many sensory-motor and cognitive activities. However, cross-linguistic research has since exploded this 'word order myth'. That is, cross-linguistic research has demonstrated that in their spontaneous speech, children learning many different languages – regardless of whether their language relies mainly on word order, case marking, or some combination of both – generally conform to adult usage and appear to mark agent–patient relations equally early and appropriately. If anything, children learning languages that mark agent–patient relations clearly and simply with morphological (case) markers, comprehend agent–patient marking earlier than children learning word order languages such as English. This is evidenced by the fact that some children learning case-marking languages over-generalize case markers in ways indicating productive control while they are still only 2 years old.

In comprehension experiments, it is clearly the case that children learning morphologically rich languages, in which word order plays only a minor role in indicating agent–patient relations, comprehend the syntactic marking of agent–patient relations as early or earlier than children learning word order languages such as English. But it should be noted that in neither comprehension nor production do we have the kind of novel word studies that could provide the most definitive evidence of children's productive knowledge of case marking. The few novel verb studies we have of case marking show a gradual developmental pattern of increasing productivity, just as with word order marking in English and similar languages.

For English, most of the discussion of case marking has centered around pronoun case errors, such as 'Me do it' and 'Him going'. About 50% of English-speaking children make such errors, most typically in the 2–4 year age range, with much variability across children. The most robust phenomenon is that children most often substitute accusative forms for nominative forms ("Me do it") but very seldom do the reverse ("Billy hit I"). This might be due to the fact that sequences like "me do it" do occur in English as fragments of well-formed sentences like "Let me do it" whereas "hit I" is a very unlikely sequence (**Table 2**).

The particular pronouns that English-speaking children over-generalize proportionally most often are the accusative forms 'me' and 'her' (and not the nominative forms 'I' and 'she'). In his work on children's errors, Matthew Rispoli has attributed this to the morphophonetic structure of the English personal pronoun paradigm: *Nominative* I/she/he/they; *Accusative* me/her/him/them; *Genitive* my/her/his/their.

It is easily seen that 'he/him/his' and 'they/them/their' each has a common phonetic core (*h-* and *th-*, respectively) whereas 'I/me/my' and 'she/her/her' do not. And indeed, the errors that are made most often are ones in which children in these latter two cases use the forms that have a common initial phoneme ('me/my' and 'her/her') to substitute for the odd-man-out ('I' and 'she'), with the 'her-for-she' error having the overall highest rate (perhaps because 'her' occurs as both the accusative and genitive form; the so-called 'double-cell' effect). The overall idea is thus that children are making retrieval errors based on both semantic and phonological factors.

Combining Word Order, Case, and Other Cues: Coalition and Competition

In all languages there are multiple potential cues indicating agent–patient relations. For example, in many languages both word order and case marking are at least potentially available, even though one of them might most typically be used for other functions (e.g., in many morphologically rich languages, word order is used primarily

Table 2 The English personal pronoun paradigm

Nominative	I	she	he	they
Accusative	me	her	him	them
Genitive	my	her	his	their

for pragmatic functions such as topicalization). In addition, in attempting to comprehend adult utterances children might also attend to information that is not directly encoded in the language; for example, they may use animacy to infer that, in an utterance containing the lexical items 'man', 'ball', and 'kick', the most likely interpretation is that the man kicked the ball, regardless of how those items are syntactically combined.

In an extensive investigation of language acquisition in a number of different languages, Dan Slobin identified some of the different comprehension strategies that children use to establish agent–patient relations, depending on the types of problems their particular language presents to them. A central discovery of this research, is that children can more easily master grammatical forms expressed in 'local cues' such as bound morphology (infections attached to words – see 'Glossary') as opposed to more distributed cues such as word order and some forms of agreement. This accounts, for example, for the fact that Turkish-speaking children master the expression of agent–patient relations at a significantly earlier age than do English-speaking children. In addition, however, it turns out that Turkish is especially 'child friendly', even among languages that rely heavily on local morphological cues. This is because Turkish nominal grammatical morphemes are:

- postposed (they come at the ends of words), syllabic, and stressed, which makes them perceptually more 'salient';
- obligatory and employ almost perfect one-to-one mapping of form to function (no fusional morphemes or homophones with several meanings), which makes them more 'predictable';
- bound to the noun, rather than freestanding, which makes them more 'local'; and
- invariably regular across different nominals and pronominals, which makes them readily 'generalizable'.

All of these factors coalesce to make Turkish agent–patient relations especially easy to learn, and their identification is a major step in discovering the basic processes of language acquisition that are employed by children in general.

A central methodological problem, however, is that in natural languages many grammatical markers occur together naturally, and so it is difficult to evaluate their contributions separately. One solution to this problem is to pit cues, like word order, case, and animacy against each other in what are called competition experiments. Elizabeth Bates, Brian MacWhinney, and collaborators conducted an extensive set of these experiments in order to establish which cues children use to comprehend agent–patient relations in a number of different languages. The basic paradigm is to ask children to pick up some toys from a table and act out utterances that indicate agent–patient relations in different ways – sometimes in semi-grammatical utterances with conflicting cues. For example, an English-speaking child might be presented with the utterance "The spoon kicked the horse." In this case, the cue of word order is put in competition with the most likely real-world scenario in which animate beings more often kick inanimate things than the reverse (the animacy cue). From an early age, young English-speaking children most often make the spoon 'kick' the horse, whereas Italian-speaking children are more likely to ignore word order and make the horse kick the spoon. This is because word order is quite variable in Italian, and so, since there is no case marking (and in this example agreement is no help because both the horse and the spoon are third-person singular), animacy is the most reliable cue available. German-speaking children gradually learn to ignore both word order and semantic plausibility (animacy) and simply look for nominative and accusative marking on 'the horse' and 'the spoon' (e.g., the spoon in nominative case is 'der Loeffle' but in accusative case it is 'den Leoffle').

Inflectional Morphology

As we have seen in the above discussion of case, many languages mark grammatical functions with inflectional morphemes (e.g., the -a and -e inflections that are added to nouns mark nominative and accusative case in Polish). In English, inflectional morphology is used to mark, for example, plurality (with the inflection (-s)) and the past tense (with the inflection (-ed)). In comparison to most of the world's languages, English is relatively impoverished when it comes to inflections. Yet the acquisition of the English plural and past tense has long been the subject of intense scrutiny and heated debate. The reason for this is that inflectional morphology had become a sort of test case for different accounts of how we learn and use linguistic generalizations in general.

The basic phenomenon under investigation is the fact that children generally start using inflectional morphology in an adult-like way. (This is presumably because they are learning each inflected word by rote.) But after a while they begin to produce the odd over-generalization, for example, saying 'mouses' and 'goed'. After a prolonged period of producing occasional over-generalizations children begin to use adult-like forms almost exclusively (although adults sometimes over-generalize, especially when under communicative pressure). This developmental trajectory of early accurate use followed by a period of errors followed by renewed accurate use is referred to as a U-shaped developmental curve. There are two main schools of explanation for this U-shape curve and for how we as adults use inflections.

Single-mechanism accounts propose that children store examples of individual inflections (e.g., dogs, cats, mice) and generalizations (e.g., noun + s marks plurality) in one and the same system. Indeed in single-mechanism connectionist models, first proposed by David Rumelhart and James McClelland, generalizations are simply the outcome of individual exemplars overlapping in representational space. Other single-mechanism accounts, such as that of Joan Bybee, propose that children learn and store enormous numbers of concrete examples and they extract two types of schema from these. Source-oriented schemas are generalizations about how an inflected form is composed of a stem and an inflection (e.g., to make a plural, take a noun stem and add -s). Such schemas explain errors of over-generalization like 'mans' and 'comed'. Product-oriented schemas are generalizations about properties of inflected forms (e.g., 'plurals tend to end with -s'). These schemas explain why children have difficulty marking the plural of nouns, like dress, that already end in -s in the singular. These difficulties lead to errors of omission, for example, saying things like 'one dress, two dress' instead of 'two dresses'.

Dual mechanism accounts of inflection, put forward by Gary Marcus, Steven Pinker, and colleagues, propose that irregularly inflected words (e.g., mice) are stored in an associative memory much like the one proposed by single mechanism theorists, whereas regularly inflected words (e.g., houses) are computed by a distinct default rule (e.g., 'add -s' for English plurals) that combines a symbol for a stem with a symbol for a suffix. While this model makes roughly similar predictions about the acquisition of morphology in English as might a schema model, it does not appear to work for languages with more complex morphology, such as Polish or Finnish, where there is not one default inflection but rather several semiregular inflections that are predictable on a phonological and/or semantic basis.

Delays in the acquisition of inflectional morphology have been taken as a key diagnostic marker of language learning difficulties, sometimes called specific language impairment (SLI). Proponents of dual mechanism models argue that this impairment reflects a specific difficulty with processing linguistic rules (as opposed to storing words). Other theorists point to four main different reasons for why inflectional morphemes might be particularly hard to acquire. First, inflectional morphemes are typically phonologically reduced, unstressed, and monosyllabic – that is, they are not very salient. Second, in some though by no means all cases, inflectional morphology carries little concrete semantic weight, for example, the English third person -s agreement marker (e.g., He runs) is in most cases almost totally semantically redundant. Third, many grammatical morphemes are pluri-functional (e.g., in English the inflection -s on a noun can mark either plurality or possession – as in 'the dog's bone'). Fourth, in some languages, the form of an inflection can change dramatically depending on which word it is combining with. For example, in Russian the form of the plural inflection depends on the gender and phonological form of the noun.

Abstract Constructions

During the preschool years, English-speaking children begin to be productive with a variety of abstract constructions. We focus here on the earliest grammatical developments at the whole utterance level, what are often called argument structure constructions. However, much development is also going on at the subsentence and suprasentence level. For example, children are learning about the major internal constituents of utterance-level constructions. Most especially, they construct nominal constructions (noun phrases) in order to make reference to things in various ways ('Bill, my father, the man who fell down') and verbal constructions (verb phrases) in order predicate for something about those things ('is nice, sleeps, hit the ball').

Table 1 presents the main grammatical constructions that have been studied with respect to the acquisition of English. Many of the constructions have equivalents in other languages, although these might not be acquired at the same rate. For example, children acquiring certain non-Indo-European languages typically produce passive sentences quite early in development. This result has been obtained for children learning Inuktitut, K'iche' Mayan, Sesotho, and Zulu. This is presumably because in these languages: (1) passives are very common in child-directed speech; and/or (2) passive utterances are actually simpler than active voice constructions (e.g., in terms of agreement).

The most abstract constructions that English-speaking children use early in development have mostly been studied from an adult perspective of grammar. As mentioned in the introduction, differing views of what adult grammar amounts to lead to differences in how people propose children develop and use grammar. For example, in some generative linguistic analyses, English questions are formed by subject-auxiliary inversion (sometimes with do-support) and Wh-movement. Put simply, this account assumes that to produce a question, the child takes a simple declarative (e.g., "John bought a house") and moves, rearranges, or inserts grammatical items to yield the question form (e.g., "Did John buy a house?" or "What did John buy?"). This account assumes that children have highly abstract representations of both declaratives and questions. However, others argue this is an unlikely explanation of early question formation for two main reasons. First, some English-speaking children use Wh-question constructions before they produce any other word combinations (i.e., before they produce the declaratives that questions are supposed to be derived from). Second, several studies of children's early questions give us no reason to suppose that these constructions are represented at a completely abstract level from the beginning. Instead most children start off with a handful of questions, at first only using 'what' and 'where', which are often pronounced as one indistinguishable wh-word (as in "Wuh dis?" for "What's this" and "Wuh dis one go" for "Where does this one go?"). Later on, questions, whether produced correctly or incorrectly, appear to be based on specific combinations of wh-words and auxiliaries.

Learning Processes

The Debate: Can Children Learn Grammar?

The question of learning processes has long divided the field of language acquisition. Those who, after Noam Chomsky, take a generativist view of language generally argue that children cannot learn language by simply creatively copying what they hear around them for two reasons. First, it is argued that children do not hear enough relevant, well-formed examples to form correct generalizations about complex structures that are heard relatively rarely (e.g., questions like 'Can the boys who can run jump?'). This is called the 'poverty of the stimulus argument'. The second argument states that, even if there were enough examples in the input of a relevant grammatical principle, there would be no way to constrain how children would generalize from the input. Children could hypothesize overly general grammars (e.g., saying 'I died him' for 'I killed him') and would have no way of knowing they were incorrect since there is very little explicit negative feedback from parents to instruct them not to do this. This is called the 'no negative evidence problem'.

If one accepts the arguments that grammar cannot be learned then the obvious solution is to propose that all children are born with substantial innate grammatical knowledge. Since any given child could end up learning one of over 6000 of the world's languages, this innate knowledge would have to apply to all languages (it would have to be a universal grammar) and children would need to adapt this universally applicable knowledge to whichever language environment they happen to be born into. This solution faces two major problems. The first concerns what a universal grammar would look like given that all the world's languages each have their own different grammatical conventions. The second concerns how children would connect any innate, language-general knowledge up to the specific language(s) they happen to be learning. There is currently no satisfactory solution to either of these problems.

On the other side of the debate, people have argued that grammar is not impossible to learn and therefore it need not be innate. Below we outline some of the mechanisms that children could use to learn about grammar. It is worth bearing in mind that, since so many grammatical conventions are specific to individual languages, it seems children would need these mechanisms no matter which theory we adopt.

Learning Mechanisms

Since language is such a complex phenomenon, it would be unsurprising if children drew on many sources of information and learning mechanisms to get going. We assume that, from very early on, children have a whole host of the prerequisites for learning grammar. These would include, on the one hand, partitioning their experience of the world into categories of entities, events, goals, etc., and, on the other, processing the speech stream into recurrent patterns to discover the phonetic regularities of the ambient language. Some of these prerequisite developments will put children in a particularly good position to learn grammar. For example, Peter Jusczyk and his colleagues have shown that infants are sensitive to prosodic information, such as the intonation contour of speech, stress patterns, pauses, and durational differences. Since these prosodic properties of speech often correlate with its grammatical organization (e.g., there are often pauses at phrase boundaries), we can assume that children are hearing language in a way that will make its structure easier to identify. Of course at some point, this understanding of language form must be linked to an understanding of its function – what we use it to talk about. We will focus here on the learning skills that are needed to bring experience of the world and experience of the speech stream together to form of a conventional spoken language with the power of expression that grammar provides.

Intention Reading and Cultural Learning

Because natural languages are conventional, the most fundamental process of language acquisition is the ability to do things the way that other people do them. This depends on a complex form of imitative learning in which children must understand other people's communicative intentions and imitatively learn how they are expressed. To understand other people's communicative intentions we basically have to know that when people are talking to us they are intending to change our thoughts or intentions (e.g., to tell us about something or get us to do something). Children's ability to read and learn the expression of communicative intentions can be seen most clearly in word learning studies in which young children have to identify the adult's intended referent in a wide variety of situations in which word and referent are not both present simultaneously.

In human linguistic communication the most fundamental unit of intentional action is the utterance as a relatively complete and coherent expression of a communicative intention, and so the most fundamental unit of language learning is stored exemplars of utterances. This is what children do in learning holophrases and other concrete and relatively fixed linguistic expressions (e.g., Thank You, Don't mention it). But as they are attempting to comprehend the communicative intention underlying an utterance, children are also attempting to comprehend the functional roles being played by its various components. This is a kind of 'blame assignment' procedure in which the attempt is to determine the functional role of a constituent in the communicative intention as a whole – what we have called segmenting communicative intentions. Identifying the functional roles of the components of utterances is only possible if the child has some (perhaps imperfect) understanding of the adult's overall communicative intention, because understanding the functional role of X means understanding how X contributes to some larger communicative structure. This is the basic process by means of which children learn the communicative functions of particular words, phrases, and other utterance constituents and, with help from pattern-finding skills, categories of these.

Schematization and Analogy

Young children hear and use – on a numbingly regular basis – the same utterances repeated over and over but with systematic variation, for example, as instantiated in item-based constructions such as 'Where's the X?, I wanna X, Let's X, Can you X?, Gimme X, I'm Xing it'. Forming schemas of this type means imitatively learning the recurrent concrete pieces of language for concrete functions, as well as forming a relatively abstract slot designating a relatively abstract function. This process is called 'schematization', and its roots may be observed in various primates who schematize everything from food processing skills to arbitrary sequences in the laboratory. In grammatical development, schematization yields what we have called item-based constructions, which can be seen as a combination of constant item(s) plus slot(s), where slots represent functional categories for the child.

Key factors that are likely to affect the formation of slots relative to constant items are 'token' and 'type frequency'. Consider the following sample of three sentences: (1) Where's the dog? (2) Where's daddy? (3) Where's your spoon?

'Token frequency' refers to the frequency with which a specific form is heard in a sample. In the above sample the token frequency of 'where's' is three and the token frequency of 'dog' is one. Token frequency should predict the selection of a constant item in a schema. This is simply because the more often a word occurs, the more easily it can be picked out as a constant. 'Type frequency' refers to the frequency with which different items of the same type (e.g., nouns referring to sought things) are heard. In the above sample the type frequency of 'sought after objects' is three. Type frequency should predict where slots are formed in relation to constant items. That is, one needs to witness a certain amount of variability before or after a constant item in order to realize that different forms can slot in around it. This variability, however, cannot be completely random. Rather the variables will all bear a common relation to the constant item (i.e., they will be of one type). Slot formation is therefore an instance of category formation.

In order to move from item-based constructions to abstract constructions, children need to form schemas that have no concrete items in common. We will refer to the learning process that achieves this as 'analogy', a form of schematization that places heavy emphasis on commonalities in relational structure. For example, despite the different number of words in the sentences (1) and (2) below, the two may be functionally aligned in that they both encode the roles of agent, action and patient. Drawing an analogy between the two would thus give an abstract transitive construction, perhaps of the form agent-causes motion-patient):

1. I kicked the ball.
2. Daddy threw it.

As is the case for schematization, the coherence of the category of variables that enters into each role (e.g., agent) is proposed to affect the ease of analogizing. This means that analogies will be formed more easily if certain items always tend to fill certain roles (e.g., if the patient role is predominantly filled by nouns denoting inanimate objects and the agent role is predominantly filled by first and second person pronouns in both constructions).

The key skill involved in analogy formation is the ability to focus on detecting similarities in relational structure. This is central to the acquisition of grammar because surface similarities between utterances often need to glossed over in order to form complex, abstract constructions. To actually use abstract constructions, though, children need to fill abstract slots with concrete words and this requires selecting words from relevant categories. For example, in the transitive construction (subject verb object) the verb slot can be filled with any word that falls into the category of transitive verbs. We now consider how children cluster words into these categories.

Constructing Lexical Categories: Functionally Based Distributional Analysis

In order to cluster words and morphemes into categories, such as 'noun', 'pronoun', 'verb', 'adjective' children must draw upon information about the word's 'distribution' and its 'function'. The term distribution simply refers to the types of neighborhood a word tends to inhabit. For example, English nouns (e.g., dog) are often found after determiners (the dog, a dog) and before a plural suffix (dog -s). So children might form rough categories by clustering together words that often share the same distribution. They could also notice functional regularities pertaining to a given class of words (e.g., that nouns tend to denote entities whereas verbs tend denote actions). However, neither distributional nor functional cues used alone would be likely to yield a very satisfactory taxonomy. Studies that have used distributional analyses to categorize English words have typically only correctly classified a certain percentage of words, mostly only nouns and verbs.

Functional analysis, on the other hand, does not explain children's early use of words such as the nonobject nouns 'breakfast' and 'night' and dual category words such as 'kiss' and 'hug', which may be used as nouns or verbs (a kiss vs. to kiss). Rather it would seem that only a combination of formal and functional cues would work and these would have to be understood in the context of each word's role in the wider communicative attempt – the whole construction or discourse turn. We refer to this combination of distributional and functional cues as 'functionally based distributional analysis', which be seen as the identification of items in a category on the grounds that they occur in the same formal contexts and perform the same communicative function within an utterance.

It is important to emphasize that this same process of functionally based distributional analysis also operates on units of language larger than words. For example, what is typically called a noun phrase may be constituted by anything from a proper name to a pronoun to a common noun with a determiner and a relative clause hanging off it. But for many syntactic purposes these may all be treated as the same kind of unit. How can this be, given their very different surface forms? The only reasonable answer is that they are treated as units of the same type because they all do the same job in utterances: they identify a referent playing some role in the scene being depicted. Indeed, given the very different form of the different nominals involved, it is difficult to even think of an alternative to this functionally based account.

Mechanisms for Constraining Generalization

As noted above, one theoretically very important question for language acquisition concerns how children restrain from adopting an overly general grammar. Children do occasionally produce sentences like 'She falled me down' or 'Don't giggle me' that are not adult-like but appear to have been formed on an analogical basis. In the two examples given the child has used an intransitive verb in the SVO transitive frame productively.

There are several mechanisms that may explain why these errors are not overly abundant and are gradually replaced with more conventional forms.

The first reason is that children appear to be very conservative learners. Naturalistic studies show that a vast proportion of children's spontaneous speech is either a direct copy or a rehash of chunks of speech they have heard addressed to them. To the extent that children repeat what adults say to them more or less verbatim, they will of course sound highly conventional in their language use.

Still, the above examples show that children do go beyond the speech they hear and combine words in a creative, sometimes unconventional, manner. Children very rarely receive direct feedback about their errors (parents do not generally say 'darling you really ought not to use intransitive verbs in the transitive construction'). However there is mounting evidence for indirect feedback. One example of this would be a recast. After hearing 'The magician disappeared the rabbit' a parent might reply by reformulating 'He made the rabbit disappear, did he?'. The pragmatic implication of such recasts is that the child's form was not conventional and the supplied alternative would be preferable.

Once children have a set of alternatives to express any given scene then they are in a far better position to recover for over-generalization errors. This is because these conventional forms will strengthen with experience and will become preferred to unlikely over-generalizations. For example, children might learn that the verb 'disappear' can appear in the periphrastic causative construction (e.g., The magician made the rabbit disappear). At the same time they will also be noticing properties of the verb 'disappear', for example, that it persistently appears in the intransitive construction ('It disappeared') but never in the transitive ('I disappeared it'). Consequently, when faced with the task of expressing that someone caused something to disappear, over-generalization to the transitive is now less likely and the new alternative form will become preferred.

The above example illustrates how over-generalization can be avoided by learning about linguistic structures in ever increasing detail and forming ever more accurate generalizations. One such late-developing generalization is the discovery of semantically governed verb classes. The idea here is that some verbs, such as those denoting a manner of motion (walk, drive, etc.), can alternate between transitive and intransitive constructions. Other verbs, such as those denoting motion in a specific direction (enter, leave, etc.) cannot take a direct object and thus only appear in the intransitive construction. Learning that the ability of a verb to alternate between constructions can be predicted from the narrow semantic class it enters into could thus also help children not to over-generalize. When this has been tested experimentally, children do not appear to use verb classes to avoid over-generalization until they are 4 years old. This would predict the U-shaped developmental curve whereby, early on, conservatism is the most likely explanation of a lack of over-generalization errors and then, as more experience with language is accrued, over-generalizations become a possibility but are gradually avoided by forming more accurate and detailed generalizations over time.

Conclusions

Above we have outlined the path that grammatical development typically takes and we have debated both the level of abstraction of children's early grammatical knowledge and the different theoretical accounts of development. To decide these debates and to be precise about how grammar actually develops, we need greater theoretical clarity and new empirical work. Those who argue grammar is not learnable must articulate what they propose children know innately and how this combines with the children's experience of particular languages in a way that yields the developments we observe. Those who argue that children could plausibly learn grammar need to test the learning mechanisms they propose in detailed studies with specific linguistic items and structures in a sufficient variety of languages.

See also: Categorization Skills and Concepts; Developmental Disabilities: Cognitive; Language Development: Overview; Language Acquisition Theories; Learning; Literacy; Pragmatic Development; Preverbal Development and Speech Perception; Semantic Development; Speech Perception; Theory of Mind.

Suggested Readings

Bates E and MacWhinney B (1989) Functionalism and the competition model. In: MacWhinney B and Bates E (eds.) *The Cross-Linguistic Study of Sentence Processing.* Cambridge: Cambridge University Press.

Bybee J (1995) Regular morphology and the lexicon. *Language and Cognitive Processes* 10: 425–455.

Clark EV (2003) *First Language Acquisition.* Cambridge: Cambridge University Press.

Hoff E (2005) *Language Development,* 3rd edn. Belmont, CA: Wadsworth/Thompson.

Marcus G, Pinker S, Ullman M, Hollander M, Rosen T, and Xu F (1992) Over-regularization in language acquisition. *Monographs of the Society for Research in Child Development* 57(4): 1–182.

O'Grady W (1997) *Syntactic Development.* Chicago, IL: The University of Chicago Press.

Pinker S (1989) *Learnability and Cognition: The Acquisition of Verb-Argument Structure.* Cambridge, MA: Harvard University Press.

Rumelhart D and McClelland J (1986) On learning the past tenses of English verbs. In: Rumelhart D, McClelland J, and Group TP (eds.) *Parallel Distributed Processing: Explorations in the Microstructure of Cognition.* Cambridge, MA: MIT Press.

Slobin DI (ed.) (1985–1992) *The Crosslinguistic Study of Language Acquisition,* vol 3. Hillsdale, NJ: Erlbaum.

Tomasello M (2003) *Constructing a Language: A Usage-Based Theory of Language Acquisition.* Cambridge, MA: Harvard University Press.

Relevant Website

http://childes.psy.cmu.edu – A database of child and caregiver speech with software tools for analysis can be found at the Child Language Data Exchange System.

Habituation and Novelty

K A Snyder and C M Torrence, University of Denver, Denver, CO, USA

© 2008 Elsevier Inc. All rights reserved.

Glossary

Declarative memory – A memory system involving structures within the medial temporal lobe (i.e., the hippocampus and adjacent entorhinal, perirhinal, and parahippocampal cortices) and midline diencephalon that is thought to support the conscious recollection of facts and events.

Dishabituation – Full or partial recovery of the orienting response that is typically observed in response to the presentation of a new or novel stimulus following habituation to a repeated stimulus.

Event-related potentials (ERPs) – Reflect the synchronous firing of neuronal populations in response to a discrete event (such as the presentation of a stimulus). They are recorded from electrodes placed on the scalp, are derived from the electroencephalogram, and provide good temporal resolution of ongoing cognitive processes.

Explicit memory – The form of memory that supports our ability to deliberately retrieve or consciously recollect, facts, events, and prior experiences.

Habituation – The decline in orienting (or responding) that is observed when a stimulus is repeated.

Implicit memory – A form of memory typically observed in terms of a facilitation or change in behavior resulting from involuntary retrieval of prior experience. Implicit memory usually occurs in the absence of conscious awareness of prior experience.

Medial temporal lobe (MTL) – The region of the brain thought to be critical for learning and memory, consisting of the hippocampus and adjacent entorhinal, perirhinal, and parahippocampal cortices.

Novelty preference – The tendency of infants to look (or orient) longer at a new or novel stimulus compared to a familiar stimulus.

Orienting reflex (OR) – The cessation and redirection of ongoing behavior that results from a sudden, unexpected, or novel event in the environment. The OR involves behavioral and physiological changes such as postural adjustments (i.e., head turning, fixating the eyes), reductions in motor activity, and autonomic responses such as vasodilation and heart rate deceleration.

Repetition suppression – The reduction in neural activity that occurs in response to a repeated stimulus. Repetition suppression occurs when the population of neurons responding to a particular stimulus decreases as the stimulus is repeated, resulting in an overall reduction of neural activity elicited by the repeated stimulus.

Introduction

Habituation and novelty paradigms have been used for more than 50 years to study perceptual and mnemonic processes in the human infant. In the first part of this article we provide a brief history and description of the different types of habituation and novelty procedures, critique the major theories and models of infant habituation and novelty preferences, and summarize major developmental trends and debates. In the second part of the article we review more recent advances in our understanding of habituation and novelty preferences using the methods of neuroscience that are now available, and provide a critical review of the debate over what kind of memory supports infant performance in these tasks.

Habituation and Novelty

Developmental psychologists have long been concerned with questions of how the mind develops. How do children acquire knowledge about the world and the ability to think, learn, remember, communicate, and feel? Research in this important domain, however, is significantly constrained by the limited behavioral repertoire of infants and young children. The typical 6-month-old, for example, can barely sit up by herself, much less understand, and follow instructions or verbally report thoughts and feelings. A significant breakthrough came when Robert Fantz in 1964 discovered that infants' looking behavior was sensitive to effects of prior experience. Specifically, Fantz discovered that infants' look less at a repeated pattern (i.e., habituation) and more at a novel pattern (i.e., the novelty preference) over time. This discovery provided researchers with an important window into early learning and memory. Methods that rely on infants' looking behavior to study cognitive development are commonly known as preferential-looking paradigms.

In the time since that seminal paper, preferential-looking methods have become ubiquitous in the field of developmental psychology and now inform most of our knowledge about cognitive development during the infancy period. A critical issue for the field of developmental psychology, however, and our understanding of infant development concerns the interpretation of infants' looking behavior. Although the empirical phenomenon itself is generally undisputed, the meaning of infants' looking behavior has always been the subject of controversy because it determines the kinds of knowledge and abilities we ascribe to young infants.

The Use of Habituation and Novelty Paradigms in the Study of Development

There are two basic types of preferential-looking procedures: the habituation–dishabituation procedure and the visual-paired comparison (VPC). These procedures both rely on the infant's inherent 'preference' for viewing novel stimuli to provide evidence for learning, memory, or discrimination. Otherwise, the procedures differ in several important respects.

The Habituation–Dishabituation Procedure

In the habituation–dishabituation procedure, a stimulus is repeated or presented for a long enough period of time until a significant decline in orienting toward the stimulus is observed. This decline in orienting is termed 'habituation'. Following habituation, the now familiar stimulus and a novel stimulus are presented one at a time, and the length of time that the infant orients toward each is recorded. If the orienting response to the novel stimulus recovers to initial levels, 'dishabituation' is said to occur.

Variants of the habituation–dishabituation procedure use different criteria to establish habituation. For example, in a 'fixed-criterion' habituation procedure, a stimulus is presented until orienting declines to a prespecified level (e.g., visual fixation declines to 3 s or less on any given trial). In a 'fixed-level' procedure, a stimulus is presented until the infant accumulates a specific amount of exposure (e.g., the infant looks at the stimulus for a total of 2 min). In the most widely used variant of the habituation procedure, habituation is 'infant-controlled': the stimulus is presented until orienting declines to some proportion of the infant's initial levels of looking (e.g., habituation is achieved when the average of the infant's last two looks is less than one-half of the average of her three longest looks). The advantage of the infant-controlled habituation procedure is that it takes into account individual differences in (1) look duration (i.e., short vs. long lookers) and (2) encoding, since one infant may require more time to encode a stimulus than another infant. This increases the likelihood that infants who reach criterion for habituation have actually encoded the stimulus, and that infants who encode the stimulus quickly do not become bored and fussy before criterion is reached.

The Visual-Paired Comparison Procedure

The VPC procedure also consists of two phases: an encoding phase and a test phase. In the encoding phase, two identical stimuli are presented side-by-side for either a fixed period of time (e.g., 30 s), or until the infant accumulates a fixed amount of looking. The length of exposure to the familiar stimulus during the encoding phase of the VPC is typically shorter than in the habituation procedure (i.e., 5–30 s vs. 1–2 min), although some researchers have used long encoding times (e.g., 1–2 min) in the VPC. Since the encoding phase of the VPC consists of relatively brief and fixed levels of accumulated looking, rather than a decline in orienting, it is typically referred to as 'familiarization' and not habituation. The test phase consists of two trials. In each trial, the familiar stimulus and a novel stimulus are presented side-by-side for a fixed period of time and the amount of time the infant looks at each is recorded. The left–right location of the novel stimulus is counterbalanced across the test trials to control for side biases in infant looking. The traditional dependent measure examined in the VPC is the 'novelty score', which is computed as the proportion of looking to the novel stimulus across both test trials combined. Greater fixation of the novel compared to the familiar stimulus (i.e., novelty preference) is inferred to reflect memory for the familiar stimulus (**Figure 1**).

Differences between Habituation–Dishabituation and Visual-Paired Comparison

The habituation–dishabituation and VPC procedures differ in several important respects. First, the amount of time

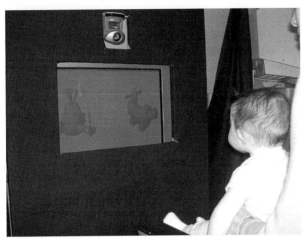

Figure 1 Six-month-old infant participating in the visual-paired comparison.

the infant views the repeated stimulus during the encoding phase is typically much longer in the habituation–dishabituation procedure than in the VPC, although some researchers have used lengthy familiarization periods in the VPC. This raises the possibility that infants may form a more robust representation of the repeated stimulus in a habituation procedure than in the VPC. Second, individual infants typically differ in the amount of time they view the familiar stimulus in a habituation procedure (due to the fact that it is infant controlled), whereas the amount of initial exposure to the familiar stimulus is controlled, and hence the same for all infants, in the VPC. Third, the familiar and novel stimuli are presented simultaneously during the test phase of the VPC procedure, whereas they are presented on different trials in the habituation–dishabituation procedure. Due to this difference in the test phases of the procedures, the VPC is considered an easier test of memory since the infant may actively compare the familiar and novel stimuli simultaneously, providing perceptual support for the comparison process. In the habituation–dishabituation procedure, however, the infant must compare each stimulus with an internal representation of the familiar stimulus, and it is a matter of debate whether the infant is actually comparing the novel stimulus with the familiar stimulus on trials in which the familiar stimulus is not present.

Thus, despite the fact that both paradigms rely on the same dependent measure (i.e., proportion of looking to a novel stimulus compared to a familiar stimulus) to provide evidence for memory, it is not clear whether the VPC and habituation–dishabituation paradigms engage the exact same cognitive processes given their procedural differences.

Limitations of Habituation–Dishabituation and Novelty Procedures

One important limitation of these procedures for the study of infant memory is that a lack of preference does not necessarily reflect forgetting since (1) null findings are inconclusive and (2) 'memory' and 'interest' are confounded in preferential-looking procedures: infants must both remember the familiar stimulus and prefer to look at the novel stimulus in order to show a novelty preference. It is possible, therefore, that null preferences might result from something other than a change in the representation of the familiar stimulus. For instance, null preferences following a delay may result from renewed interest in the familiar stimulus rather than forgetting, and age-related differences in performance may result from changes to the effect of memory on visual attention rather than memory development.

Another important limitation of these procedures is that different values of certain parameters, such as intertrial interval, may be optimal for producing habituation with infants of different ages, or encoding in the VPC under different stimulus conditions, such that spurious trends may result when using the same intertrial interval with infants of different ages, or the same familiarization periods with stimuli differing in complexity. Thus, our use of these procedures to study change across development is limited, in part, by our lack of knowledge regarding the relation between procedural parameters, stimulus conditions, and infant variables.

Major Theories of Habituation and Novelty

In general, the decrement in orienting to a repeated stimulus observed during the habituation–dishabituation and VPC procedures is considered to reflect two cognitive processes: (1) encoding (i.e., the formation of an internal representation of the repeated stimulus) and (2) a comparison of current input with an internal representation. Longer looking to a novel stimulus following habituation or familiarization is typically inferred to reflect both (1) memory for the familiar stimulus and (2) detection of the difference between the familiar and novel stimulus (i.e., discrimination). There are two major theories that attempt to explain the component processes involved in the habituation of an infant's visual attention during initial exposure and novelty preferences at test: the comparator model and optimal level theory.

The comparator model

The comparator model was proposed by E. N. Sokolov in 1963 to explain the reduction (or disappearance) of the orienting reflex (OR) with stimulus repetition or exposure. Pavlov first described the OR during his studies of classical conditioning in dogs. In what likely seemed an experimental nuisance, Pavlov noted that his subjects would fail to exhibit a conditioned response if an unexpected event occurred. Instead, the dogs would immediately orient toward and investigate this change in the environment.

The orienting response involves behavioral, physiological, and postural changes such as turning the head and fixating the eyes on the stimulus, reductions in motor activity, and autonomic responses such as vasodilation and heart rate deceleration, etc.

The concept of OR was subsequently developed by Sokolov in 1963 in his book *Perception and the Conditioned Reflex*. Sokolov viewed the OR as an adaptive response to the environment that serves to facilitate perception and learning. According to Sokolov, orienting results in the allocation of attentional resources that facilitate and promote stimulus processing by amplifying the effects of stimulation on the sense organs. When an organism orients toward a stimulus, a neuronal representation of the stimulus is constructed and stored in the cortex. Subsequent stimuli are then compared to this neuronal model. Discrepancies between existing representations and current input result in behavioral and physiological changes that amplify perception and processing of the current input. Matches, in contrast, result in behavioral and physiological changes that diminish perception and processing, and habituation of the orienting response occurs. In this way, habituation of the orienting response functions to simultaneously free the limited attentional resources of an organism from objects and events that are constant and nonthreatening in the environment, and promote the processing and evaluation of changes in the environment.

Sokolov's theory of the OR remains the most influential model of habituation today, although it has been modified and criticized over the years. For example, several researchers have argued that the stored representations to which current input is compared must not be exact copies of previously encountered stimuli, but looser representations. Otherwise, conceptual habituation or habituation to a category of stimuli (e.g., cats) could not occur. The model has also been criticized on the grounds that it does not explain certain phenomena such as why some infants never seem to habituate, or why infants continue to look at highly familiar stimuli, like a mother's face. Finally, Sokolov's assertion that the memory trace is stored in the cortex has been challenged on the grounds that lower organisms, and decorticate 'preparations' also habituate, as well as one report of habituation in an anencephalic infant.

Optimal level theory/discrepancy hypothesis

According to optimal level theories of habituation and the discrepancy hypothesis, as a stimulus loses its novelty, the infant's response should first increase and then decrease. As in the comparator model, new sensory information is compared with existing representations. In contrast to the comparator model, however, discrepancies between existing representations and new sensory information may cause the organism to either approach or withdrawal from the stimulus. Small discrepancies are thought to produce low levels of arousal, resulting in an approach response. Large discrepancies, however, are thought to produce high levels of arousal, resulting in a withdrawal response. According to optimal level theories, therefore, visual fixation is an inverted U-shaped function based on the degree of discrepancy between an existing representation and a new stimulus. In addition, optimal level theories involve an implicit motivational/interest aspect of visual attention, whereas comparator models do not.

The discrepancy hypothesis has been criticized on the grounds that the assumption that test displays can be ordered in terms of discrepancy from the infants' point of view is impossible to prove, and that evidence in support of optimal level theories is mixed. Although visual fixation to a repeated stimulus during a habituation procedure is often observed to first increase and then decrease with more exposure, many studies have shown that infants' visual fixations are an increasing function of discrepancy, rather than an inverted U-shaped function. Comparator models, however, do not readily explain the inverted U-shaped function observed in many habituation studies.

Major Developmental Trends

Although infants both habituate and show novelty preferences from birth, their performance in habituation and novelty tasks changes dramatically during the first year of life. For instance, older infants habituate more quickly than younger ones, suggesting that they encode stimuli faster. Older infants are also able to encode more complex stimuli, and discriminate smaller discrepancies between familiar and novel stimuli than younger ones. In addition, older infants appear to be able to store information in memory over longer periods of time, as evidenced by exhibiting novelty preferences over increasing delays between study and test, and form representations that are flexible across changes in the environment.

Since habituation and novelty paradigms rely on indirect measures to examine memory and discrimination, however, it is important to make a distinction between performance (i.e., whether infants' 'looking behavior' discriminates novel and familiar stimuli) and competence (i.e., whether infants' 'remember' the familiar stimulus). That is, it is possible that infants remember the familiar stimulus but fail to look longer at a novel stimulus under certain conditions. In addition, the dependent measure chosen for analysis may influence whether novelty preferences are found. In a study conducted by Adele Diamond in 1995, for example, 4-, 6-, and 9-month-old infants were habituated to three dimensional objects and then tested in the VPC. When the conventional dependent measure (i.e., novelty score) was analyzed, the infants' memory appeared to improve with age: 4-month-olds showed novelty preferences at only the shortest delay (i.e., 10 s), 6-month-olds showed novelty preferences at delays of

10 s and 1 min, and 9-month-olds showed novelty preferences at all delays tested (i.e., up to 10 min). In contrast, when the 'longest individual fixation' to each of the familiar and novel stimulus was used as the dependent measure, 4- and 6-month-olds looked longer at the novel stimulus at all delays tested. Thus, the dependent measure chosen for analysis can affect conclusions about infant memory development, especially when infant performance is considered to reflect infant competence.

In addition to age-related changes in infants' performance in habituation and novelty tasks, stimulus properties and procedural variables are also known to affect infants' performance in these tasks. For instance, stimulus complexity affects the rate at which infants habituate, as well as the size of their novelty preference at test. In general, there is an inverse relation between stimulus 'complexity' and rate of habituation: infants habituate slower to more complex stimuli. In addition, the degree of 'physical discrepancy' between the familiar stimulus and the novel stimulus (typically defined in terms of a change to one dimension, such as form, color, or orientation, of a multi-dimensional stimulus) has been found to affect the size of the novelty preference at test: the greater the 'physical discrepancy', the larger the novelty preference.

In terms of procedure variables, the amount of initial exposure to a stimulus is known to effect length of retention. For example, 6-month-old infants will exhibit retention of an abstract pattern after a 48 h delay when initial study times are long (e.g., 2 min), but will not exhibit retention after even a few seconds when initial study times are brief (e.g., 5 s). Again, however, it is important to keep in mind that failure to find a novelty preference reflects a null finding, and that it may not be appropriate to attribute this failure to forgetting.

The Role of Attention in Habituation and Novelty Detection

Habituation and novelty tasks rely heavily on the visual attention system to inform the experimenter as to the presence or absence of memory. During the first year of life, the areas of the brain that mediate attention are rapidly developing. Attention facilitates habituation and novelty detection by increasing the speed and efficiency of information processing, resulting in faster habituation and better novelty detection at test.

Attention

William James described attention as the "... taking possession by the mind in a clear and vivid form one out of what seem several simultaneous objects or trains of thought ...". Contemporary researchers, however, recognize three different types of attention: arousal, selective attention, and executive attention. Arousal is a generalized state of vigilance or alertness that serves to facilitate information processing in a wide array of brain areas and functions. Selective attention, involves the selection of specific objects or features of the environment for increased or privileged processing. Selective attention can be controlled by either voluntary/endogenous processes (i.e., voluntary attention) or reflexive/exogenous biases (i.e., reflexive attention). Selection of information rarely depends on any one factor, however, but involves a dynamic interplay between voluntary and involuntary control that involves competition between reflexive biases and the goals and intention of the individual. The final type of attention, executive attention, involves voluntary control and regulation of the allocation of attention. Advancements in our understanding of the development of the arousal system, in particular, have provided useful information for understanding infant behavior in habituation and novelty tasks.

Effects of Arousal on Habituation

The brain systems involved in arousal involve connections between the mesencephalic reticular activating system (MRAS) and widespread areas of the cortex. Sensory input can activate the MRAS via inputs to the thalamus and the mesencephalic reticular formation (MRF), which is located in the brainstem. Activation of the arousal system enhances processing in a variety of cortical areas including sensory cortices, association cortices, and the limbic system (memory and emotion), resulting in increased processing efficiency, faster reaction times, better detection, and sustained performance over longer periods of time.

The development of the arousal system and its effect on habituation and novelty detection has been studied using indirect physiological measures such as heart rate (HR) and respiratory sinus arrhythmia (RSA the cycle of breathing that occurs due to sympathetic and parasympathetic nervous system activity). This is possible because the activation of neural and endocrine systems associated with increases in arousal causes a corresponding decrease in HR and increase in RSA. For instance, the activation of certain portions of the orbitofrontal cortex has an inhibitory effect on the peripheral nervous system (PNS), slowing HR when the arousal system is engaged. In effect, increases in arousal inhibit cardiac activity as well as other peripheral physiological processes, such as body movement. As a result, attention is facilitated and performance is improved on a variety of cognitive tasks.

John Richards has proposed that the activation of the arousal system may be divided into four distinct HR-defined phases: automatic interrupt, orienting response, sustained attention, and attention termination.

Automatic interrupt is defined as the time period before the arousal system is activated. The orienting response occurs as an object in the visual field captures the infant's attention, and at the same time, HR begins to decelerate. The sustained-attention phase is characterized physiologically by maintenance of a decelerated HR and behaviorally by maintenance of fixation on the object that initially captured attention, even in the presence of distracting stimuli. It is during the sustained attention phase that stimulus information is processed. After the stimulus information is processed, the attention termination phase begins. During attention termination, attention is disengaged and HR accelerates backup to baseline levels. Most research using HR to measure arousal has focused on the orienting and sustained attention phases and their relation to performance on habituation and preference tasks.

Although the arousal system is functional from birth, it undergoes significant development during the first 2 years of life. For instance, the level of HR deceleration during the HR-defined sustained attention phase increases between 3 and 6 months, suggesting an increase in infants' ability to focus and maintain their attention. This increase in a physiological correlate of sustained attention parallels behavioral developments in habituation. For instance, 6-month-olds habituate more quickly, suggesting that they encode stimuli faster, and are able to encode more complex stimuli than 3-month-olds. Furthermore, infants who spend more time in the sustained attention stage habituate more quickly, suggesting that increased arousal is related to increased processing speed.

Effects of Arousal on Novelty Detection

If sustained attention can facilitate processing speed in habituation tasks, how does sustained attention relate to novelty detection and memory? To manipulate arousal, experimenters often expose the infant to a highly salient stimulus, such as a movie clip. Images of the to-be-remembered object are then interspersed with the presentation of the movie clip, and HR is recorded. These types of studies have found that sustained attention during presentation of the to-be-remembered object is related to greater novelty preferences at test. In fact, exposure to a stimulus for just 5 or 6 s during sustained attention results in novelty preferences at test. Furthermore, infants are more likely to show a novelty preference at test when they are 'tested' during the sustained-attention phase; if in the attention in contrast termination phase, infants tend to look equally long at the novel and familiar stimulus. Combined, the results of these studies indicate that sustained attention, or increased arousal, facilitates the infant's ability to acquire information about a stimulus, resulting in faster habituation and enhanced novelty detection at test.

What Kind of Memory Do Novelty Preferences Reflect?

In general, longer looking to a novel stimulus (i.e., the novelty preference) has been interpreted to reflect recognition of the previously seen stimulus. Although there is a general consensus that novelty preferences reflect some form of memory, there is considerable debate regarding the type of memory novelty preferences might reflect. Some researchers argue that novelty preferences reflect a form of explicit or declarative memory. Other researchers argue that novelty preferences reflect a more primitive form of memory that requires only perceptual facilitation. Given the extensive use of habituation and novelty paradigms in developmental research, understanding the type of memory that supports infants' visual preferences has important implications for our understanding of cognitive development.

Distinctions between Different Types of Memory

According to most contemporary views of memory, memory is not a monolithic function. Numerous distinctions have been made between different forms of memory or memory systems (e.g., explicit and implicit, declarative and nondeclarative, episodic and semantic, taxon and locale, fast and slow). Hypotheses about the type of memory that supports infant novelty preferences have tended to focus on two distinctions in particular: the distinction between declarative and nondeclarative memory and the distinction between explicit and implicit memory.

Declarative memory is thought to support the conscious recollection of facts and events, and to be dependent on structures within the medial temporal lobe (MTL; i.e., the hippocampus and adjacent entorhinal, perirhinal, and parahippocampal cortices) and midline diencephalon. Nondeclarative memory, in contrast, is an umbrella term that is used to refer to a collection of separate memory systems that support different abilities such as skill and habit learning, classical conditioning, priming, etc. Different forms of nondeclarative memory are thought to depend on different neural subsystems, including for example the striatum for skill and habit memory, the cerebellum for classical conditioning, and the neocortex for priming. Nondeclarative memory systems share in common the observation that memory is typically expressed through performance rather than recollection and that learning can be outside of awareness.

Although the terms 'declarative' and 'explicit' have often been used interchangeably in the memory literature, the terms 'explicit' and 'implicit' were originally proposed as labels for different 'forms' of memory (and the tests used to measure them) and not memory systems. Explicit memory refers to the ability to deliberately retrieve, or consciously recollect, facts, events, and prior experiences, and is measured by 'direct' tasks that require intentional retrieval such as recall and recognition tests. Implicit memory refers to facilitation or changes in behavior resulting from involuntary retrieval of prior experience in the absence of 'conscious awareness', and is usually measured by indirect or incidental tests such as word-stem completion and repetition priming. Researchers who make a primary distinction between explicit and implicit memory emphasize that these two different forms of memory may simply describe different retrieval circumstances (i.e., intentional vs. unintentional retrieval), and do not necessarily imply different memory 'systems' in the brain.

What Type of Memory Do Novelty Preferences Reflect?

There has been considerable disagreement regarding the type of memory reflected in an infant's preferential fixation of novelty. In an early review of the infant memory literature, Daniel Schacter and Morris Moscovitch distinguished between two broad types of memory: an 'early' form and a 'late' form of memory. The early form of memory was described as unconscious or procedural memory of the kind that is largely preserved in patients with amnesia, and was argued to be available to the infant shortly after birth. This form of memory could be inferred from facilitation in performance on tasks that did not require explicit access to prior experience, such as is typically observed in implicit memory tasks. The 'late' form of memory was described as conscious or episodic memory (i.e., explicit memory) of the type that is typically observed in recall and recognition tasks, and was argued to not be available to the infant until the latter part of the first year of life. Based on a comparison of the kinds of variables that effect infants' preferential-looking behavior and what was known about explicit and implicit memory at the time, Schacter and Moscovitch argued that the kind of memory tapped by preferential-looking tasks was mediated by the 'early' memory system.

A decade later, Richard McKee and Larry Squire tested patients who had impairments in declarative memory resulting from damage to the MTL memory system and found that these patients were impaired relative to controls in the VPC. Based on this evidence, the authors argued that novelty preferences reflect an early capacity for declarative memory that is dependent on the MTL. Similarly, Charles Nelson reviewed studies examining the performance of human adults and nonhuman primates on the VPC task following damage to the MTL, and concluded that performance on the VPC was dependent on the hippocampus. Since the hippocampus is part of the MTL system that supports explicit memory, Nelson argued that novelty preferences reflect a form of explicit memory he termed 'pre-explicit'. According to Nelson, pre-explicit memory is available to the infant during the first 6 months of life, is mediated by parts of the hippocampus that are early maturing, and supports performance on tasks involving novelty preferences over short delays. Novelty preferences over longer delays, however, were argued to reflect explicit memory and depend on later-developing areas within the hippocampus (e.g., the dentate).

The question of what kind of memory supports performance in the VPC task has important implications for our understanding of both memory development and brain development. For example, the proposal that novelty preferences reflect a form of explicit memory suggests that infants may have conscious, voluntary, or aware access to their memory from birth. In contrast, the proposal that novelty preferences reflect a form of implicit memory could be taken to imply that new learning cannot occur during the first few months of life unless a stimulus is repeated (as in a repetition-priming paradigm) or rewarded (as in a conditioning paradigm). Furthermore, since declarative and explicit memory are known to involve interactions between brain regions involved in memory storage and retrieval (e.g., the hippocampus and surrounding cortex), attention (e.g., the parietal lobe and cingulate cortex), and executive control (e.g., the prefrontal cortex) in adults, the proposal that novelty preferences reflect a form of explicit or declarative memory has implications for the development of functional interactions between these brain regions. Thus, the interpretation of infant novelty preferences raises important questions about infant learning, the development of conscious awareness, voluntary control over mental processes, and the development of functional interactions among wide-scale brain systems.

Neural Mechanisms Underlying Performance in the Visual-Paired Comparison

At the present time, the most popular view of novelty preferences is that they reflect a form of declarative or pre-explicit memory dependent on the MTL system, and the hippocampus in particular. A critical evaluation of the evidence for this view, however, and a review of the most recent evidence suggest that the MTL system is not necessary for novelty preferences. This evidence, in turn, raises the question anew of what neural systems may support novelty preferences and, critically, what 'kind' of memory novelty preferences might reflect.

Do Novelty Preferences Depend on the Hippocampus?

Encoding vs. retrieval in the Visual-Paired Comparison

Research investigating the neurobiology of novelty preferences has primarily used the VPC. It was noted earlier that the VPC consists of two phases: a familiarization phase and a test phase. During the familiarization phase, infants must transform incoming sensory information into an internal (i.e., neural) representation of the familiar stimulus. During the test phase, infants must access this representation to show differences in looking behavior to the 'familiar' and the novel stimulus (e.g., novelty preferences). Thus, successful performance in the VPC requires at least two memory processes: memory encoding, whereby sensory information is initially stored into memory, and memory retrieval, whereby previously stored information is accessed for further processing.

There are two types of scientific methods that have been used to investigate the neurobiology of novelty preferences: the lesion method and neuroimaging. In studies using the lesion method, patients with pre-existing damage to a particular part of the brain (e.g., the hippocampus), or experimental animals with induced damage to a particular brain structure, are tested in a given task. Deficits in performing the task are subsequently attributed to the damaged brain structure. Thus, for example, if patients with damage to the hippocampus perform more poorly on the VPC than adults without hippocampal damage, researchers conclude that the hippocampus plays an important role in performance on the VPC. In studies using neuroimaging neural activity in different brain structures is examined as subjects perform a task.

An important limitation of lesions studies for investigating the neurobiology of novelty preferences is that it is not possible to determine whether the lesion impairs encoding or retrieval in the VPC. Since successful encoding is a prerequisite for successful retrieval, a lesion that impairs encoding would result in performance deficits in the VPC even if retrieval is not affected. This is an important point because the measure of successful performance in the VPC, novelty preferences, is measured at test and thus reflects retrieval. Neuroimaging methods, on the other hand, are able to distinguish between neural activity related to encoding and neural activity related to retrieval in the VPC.

The neural structures that support encoding versus retrieval in the VPC have important implications for the type of memory reflected in infant novelty preferences. Importantly, involvement of the MTL system during encoding does not mean that it is also involved during retrieval. For instance, words activated during an implicit memory task (e.g., word-stem completion) may have been initially encoded via the MTL system at some earlier point in time, yet successful retrieval during the implicit task can occur in the absence of conscious awareness and does not require the MTL. This is because implicit memory involves the reactivation of previously stored representations, regardless of how the representations were initially encoded. Similarly, it is possible for the MTL system to play a role in encoding during the familiarization phase of the VPC, yet not participate in the retrieval of information that produces differences in looking behavior at test.

Evidence from lesion studies

Nonhuman primates. Evidence from lesion studies in monkeys suggests that immediate and short-term memory in the VPC depends on perirhinal cortex and visual perceptual area TE, whereas long-term memory in the VPC may depend additionally on the hippocampus. Most recently, for example, Jocelyn Bachevalier and colleagues compared the effects of selective lesions to the hippocampus, parahippocampal gyrus, and perirhinal cortex, on the performance of adult monkeys in the VPC. They reported that hippocampal lesions impaired performance at 60 s delays, parahippocampal lesions impaired performance at 30 s delays, and perirhinal lesions impaired performance at 10 s delays. In contrast, adult monkeys with lesions of visual area TE were impaired in the VPC at all delays. These data suggest that lesions to different structures within the MTL system and visual perceptual areas impair VPC performance in adult monkeys in a delay-dependent manner. Importantly, hippocampal lesions do not appear to impair VPC performance in adult monkeys unless the delay between study and test is long (i.e., >60 s).

Patients with MTL amnesia. Only two studies have examined the effects of MTL damage in humans on performance in the VPC, and the results of these studies are inconsistent. In the first study, patients with amnesia and healthy adults were tested in the VPC at delays of 0.5 s, 2 min, 1 h, and 24 h. Since amnesic patients were impaired relative to controls, the authors of this study concluded that novelty preferences reflect a form of declarative memory that is dependent on the MTL memory system. It is important to note, however, that amnesic patients were impaired relative to controls only at delays of 2 min and 1 h. Both groups showed equivalent novelty preferences at the 0.5-s delay, and neither group showed novelty preferences at the 24 h delay. Furthermore, although amnesic patients were impaired relative to controls at the 2 min delay, amnesic patients did show significant novelty preferences at this delay. Thus, patients with damage to the MTL system showed significant novelty preferences at short delays, suggesting that novelty preferences *per se* may not depend on the MTL. More recently, Olivier Pascalis and colleagues reported that a patient with selective damage to the hippocampus (i.e., patient YR) did not show novelty preferences in the VPC at delays of 5 and 10 s, and concluded that novelty preferences depend on the hippocampus.

The performance of patient YR, however, is inconsistent with findings from the patient study discussed above and from lesion studies in nonhuman primates. As reviewed earlier, selective hippocampal lesions in nonhuman primates impair VPC performance at long delays (i.e., 60 s) but not at short delays, and amnesic patients show novelty preferences at delays as long as 2 min. One possible explanation for YR's deficits in the VPC is that she also developed damage to her parietal lobe, a part of the brain that is critical for the integration of stimulus representations with eye movement plans. Thus, YR's parietal damage could have affected her looking behavior in the VPC separately from her memory for the familiar stimulus. Indeed, when asked to report which stimulus she had seen before, YR was just as accurate as adults without hippocampal damage. The weight of the evidence across patient and animal studies, therefore, suggests that damage to the hippocampus impairs VPC performance at long but not short delays.

Summary. In summary, data from patients with MTL amnesia and monkeys with MTL lesions do suggest a role for the MTL, and the hippocampus in particular, in successful performance in the VPC. These data, however, do not tell us whether the MTL and hippocampus are important for successful encoding, successful retrieval, or both. Since successful encoding is necessary for successful retrieval, and damage to the MTL is known to impair encoding, lesion data may primarily provide evidence that the MTL and the hippocampus play a role in the long-term encoding of information about the object presented during the familiarization phase of the VPC. Subjects who have not encoded the object into long-term memory would necessarily not show novelty preferences at test (a measure of retrieval), even if the hippocampus were unnecessary for successful retrieval. Neuroimaging methods can be used to examine whether the MTL and hippocampus are important for retrieval in the task.

Evidence from neuroimaging studies

John Aggleton Malcolm Brown, and colleagues have examined neural activity in rodents during a task very similar to the test phase of the VPC. Using immediate early gene (IEG) imaging techniques, neural activity in different regions of the brain can be examined by measuring the relative amounts of a protein (Fos) that is synthesized by a gene (*c-fos*) expressed when a neuron is active. Aggleton and Brown have used this technique to examine which brain areas are active when an animal distinguishes between familiar and novel objects (i.e., item memory) vs. rearrangements of familiar objects (i.e., memory for spatial relations).

Using this technique, neural activity related to item memory has been observed in occipital visual processing areas, area TE, and perirhinal cortex, but not the hippocampus. Specifically, familiar compared to novel objects elicit a decrease in neural activity in perirhinal cortex and area TE. This finding is consistent with electrophysiological evidence in both humans and monkeys that neurons in perirhinal cortex and adjacent visual association cortex (area TE) respond less to visual stimuli that were previously encountered, a phenomenon known as 'repetition suppression'. In contrast, neural activity related to memory for spatial relations has been observed in the hippocampus, but not area TE and perirhinal cortex. Combined, these findings suggest that repetition suppression in perirhinal cortex and adjacent visual association areas provides a neural basis for discriminating between new and previously encountered stimuli (i.e., novelty preferences) during the test phase of the VPC. Importantly, hippocampal neurons do not respond differentially to novel versus familiar objects, suggesting that the hippocampus may not contribute to successful retrieval in the VPC.

More recently, researchers examined whether the MTL system was necessary for successful encoding or retrieval in the VPC. In this study, researchers injected benzodiazepine, a drug that temporarily inhibits neural activity in MTL structures, into the perirhinal cortex of rodents prior to either the encoding or retrieval phase of the VPC. Injections prior to encoding abolished novelty preferences at test, whereas injections prior to retrieval but after encoding had no effect on performance. These findings suggest that perirhinal cortex, like the hippocampus, might play a role in the long-term storage of object representations during the study phase of the VPC, but may not be necessary for successful retrieval at test. Taken together, data from lesion studies and neuroimaging studies suggest that the MTL system, and the hippocampus in particular, may be necessary for encoding information into long-term memory, yet does not participate in the retrieval of information that produces differences in looking behavior at test.

Summary

In summary, the available evidence does not fully support the view that novelty preferences reflect a form of declarative or pre-explicit memory dependent on the MTL system, and the hippocampus in particular. Patients with amnesia and nonhuman primates with hippocampal damage succeed in the VPC when the delay is short. This suggests that the hippocampus is not 'necessary' for novelty preferences. In addition, adult monkeys with lesions of visual area TE, but not the hippocampus or MTL, are impaired in the VPC, suggesting that the hippocampus is also not 'sufficient' for novelty preferences. Finally, recent imaging studies in rodents indicate that the MTL system is primarily involved in long-term storage of object representations during initial encoding, but is not necessary for successful retrieval during the test phase of the VPC. Taken together, these findings indicate that the MTL, and the hippocampus in particular, may play a role in encoding information into long-term memory, yet does not participate in the retrieval of information that produces differences in looking behavior at test (i.e., novelty preferences). Instead, novelty preferences may involve reactivation of previously stored representations in the absence of conscious awareness and voluntary control, similar to implicit memory.

The Interaction between Memory and Attention in the Visual-Paired Comparison

Understanding the neural basis of habituation and novelty preferences requires that we understand how visual attention is biased toward novel stimuli. After all, memory for a previously encountered stimulus could just as well take the form of a bias in looking longer at the 'familiar' stimulus.

Robert Desimone and John Duncan have proposed a model of selective visual attention (i.e., the 'biased competition model') that can account for the bias in visual attention toward novel stimuli. The biased competition model is predicated on the assumption that the nervous system has limited processing resources, and that objects in the visual environment must compete for these resources. Attention, then, is conceptualized as "... an emergent property of many neural mechanisms working to resolve competition for visual processing and control of behavior."

In the biased competition model, competition for visual-processing resources is biased by both bottom-up and top-down neural mechanisms. 'Bottom-up' biases are defined as automatic and not necessarily related to intentions or goals. Some bottom-up biases are best described as 'stimulus-driven', such as biases toward certain colors (e.g., red), high-contrast stimuli, movement, etc. The use of the term bottom-up, however, is not intended to imply only stimulus-driven biases, but also includes biases from information stored in memory that may influence early perceptual processing via feedback mechanisms. A classic example of this type of bias is the so-called 'cocktail party' effect: the automatic orienting to the sound of one's name spoken in a noisy room even when the focus of one's behavior is elsewhere. The bias toward novelty is another example of a bias from information stored in memory.

According to Desimone and Duncan, the visual system is biased toward processing new or not recently seen objects. The neural basis of this bias is a reduction in neural activity in the visual-processing pathway with stimulus repetition, a phenomenon known as 'repetition suppression'. Repetition suppression occurs when the population of neurons responding to a particular stimulus decreases as the stimulus is repeated, resulting in an overall reduction of neural activity elicited by the repeated stimulus. This decrease in the population of neurons activated by a repeated stimulus reflects a reduction in the responses of cells that were initially activated but were not highly selective for the features of the stimulus, and is therefore thought to reflect a form of learning. In theory, the reduction in activation to a repeated stimulus would result in a smaller neural signal for familiar (i.e., repeated) compared to novel stimuli, which would in turn bias the competition for visual processing resources, and hence visual attention, toward novel stimuli. This is supported by evidence that repetition suppression is sufficient to produce orienting to a novel stimulus in monkeys. Thus, the bias in visual attention toward novel stimuli in the VPC may reflect competition for visual processing resources between the familiar and novel stimulus. Since the novel stimulus elicits a larger neural signal, visual processing resources are biased toward the novel stimulus and it has a stronger influence over behavior (i.e., eye movements and visual fixation). Thus, the biased competition model provides a mechanistic explanation for the bias toward novelty in the VPC.

This model of infant performance in the VPC suggests a plausible alternative to the hypothesis that novelty preferences depend on the hippocampus and reflect a form of explicit or declarative memory. It is consistent with the results of imaging studies in rodents indicating that repetition suppression in perirhinal cortex and adjacent visual association areas provides a neural basis for discriminating familiar and novel objects. Since repetition suppression is an intrinsic property of the visual processing pathway, and occurs independently of the hippocampus, this model also accounts for observations that patients with amnesia and nonhuman primates with lesions of the MTL succeed in the VPC when the delay between familiarization and test is short. Thus, novelty preferences may reflect the effects of repetition suppression on visual attention, independent of the hippocampus.

Electrophysiological Correlates of Infant Novelty Preferences

Understanding the neural mechanisms underlying infants' performance on preferential-looking tasks can help us to understand the type of memory that supports novelty preferences. It is very difficult to dissociate explicit and implicit memory in infants, however, since (1) measures that dissociate explicit and implicit forms of memory tend to rely disproportionately on verbal abilities not present in infants, and (2) brain imaging techniques with the requisite spatial resolution (e.g., functional magnetic resonance imaging) to assess the participation of neural structures which dissociate different forms of memory (e.g., the hippocampus vs. the striatum) are not feasible for use with infants participating in visual paradigms at this time. One brain imaging method that is appropriate for use with young infants, however, is event-related potentials (ERPs).

ERPs reflect the synchronous firing of neuronal populations in response to a discrete event (such as the presentation of a stimulus). They are recorded from electrodes placed on the scalp, are derived from the electroencephalogram, and provide excellent temporal resolution (on the order of milliseconds) of ongoing cognitive processes. There are numerous advantages to using ERPs to study cognitive development. They are noninvasive, do not require the subject to remain motionless for long periods of time, and do not require a behavioral response by the subject. Furthermore, the spatial and temporal information provided by ERPs permits the differentiation of cognitive processes that may not be directly reflected in behavior (**Figure 2**).

Two major components are typically observed in the infant ERP (see **Figure 3**): a mid-latency negative component (Nc) that peaks between 400 and 800 ms following stimulus onset and is observed over frontocentral scalp regions, and a long-latency slow-wave component (PSW) that begins around 1000 ms following stimulus onset and is maximal over temporal scalp regions. Since the Nc is thought to reflect aspects of attention and orienting, and the PSW is thought to reflect aspects of memory, ERPs are especially useful in investigating the neural basis of infants' performance on habituation and novelty tasks.

Work in our laboratory has used ERPs to investigate the neural mechanisms underlying infant habituation and novelty preferences. Our working hypothesis is that the decrease in infant attention to familiar (i.e., repeated) stimuli observed in habituation and novelty tasks reflects the effects of repetition suppression on visual attention. As a starting point, we examined the effects of stimulus repetition on infant brain activity. In one study, we recorded 6-month-old infants' brain activity while they watched alternating pictures of two different faces on a computer screen. The faces consisted of a picture of the infant's mother (i.e., a familiar face) and a picture of a female stranger (i.e., a novel face). Each face was presented for 0.5 s, and repeated between 30 and 50 times. We then compared infants' brain activity in response to the first 15 presentations of each face (Block 1) and the second 15 presentations of each face (Block 2), and found that the amplitude of the PSW decreased across blocks (see **Figures 4** and **5**) for both the familiar and the novel face. The amplitude of a component is thought to reflect the amount of neural activity elicited by a stimulus. Thus, a decrease in the amplitude of the PSW across blocks indicates that the amount of neural activity elicited by the faces decreased as the faces were repeated across trials, consistent with the hypothesis that repeated stimuli elicit smaller neural signals than novel stimuli (i.e., repetition suppression).

The results described above help to establish evidence of repetition suppression in infants. Alone, however, they do not address questions about the mechanisms underlying habituation and novelty preferences since we did not measure looking behavior. Ongoing work in our laboratory, therefore, is investigating these mechanisms by examining the relation between infant brain activity and infant looking behavior. For instance, one study examined the brain activity of infants who showed a novelty preference in the VPC. In this study, 6-month-old infants were first tested in the VPC, and then watched pictures of the familiar object from the VPC and two novel objects while their brain activity was recorded. We found that the amplitude of the PSW was greater for the two novel objects compared to the familiar object. This finding suggests that the novel objects elicited more neural activity than the familiar object, consistent with the hypothesis that decreased looking to the familiar stimulus (i.e., novelty preferences) in the VPC reflects the effects of repetition suppression on visual attention.

The major findings that have emerged from this work are that (1) stimulus repetition results in a reduction of neural activity over temporal scalp regions (i.e., the PSW) in infants and (2) infant novelty preferences are associated with a reduction of neural activity over temporal scalp regions (i.e., the PSW) for familiar compared to novel stimuli. The pattern and topography of these effects are consistent with observations of repetition suppression in visual processing areas from electrophysiological recordings in nonhuman primates, imaging studies in rodents, and neuroimaging studies of human adults. This, in turn, suggests that infant novelty preferences may be mediated by repetition suppression and could reflect a form of implicit memory. Since repetition suppression is a general phenomenon observed across many structures in the

Figure 2 Six-month-old infant wearing an electrode cap for the recording of event-related potentials.

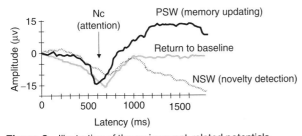

Figure 3 Illustration of the major event-related potentials (ERPs) components observed in previous ERP studies with infants. Adapted from de Haan M and Nelson CA (1997) Recognition of the mother's face by six-month-old infants: A neuro-behavioral study. *Development* 68(2): 187–210. Nc, negative component; NSW, PSW, long-latency show-wave component.

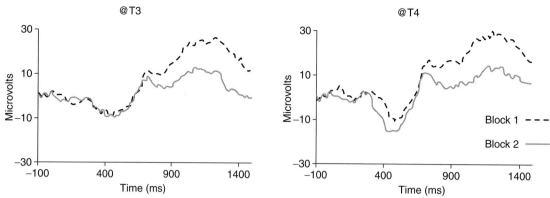

Figure 4 Grand mean event-related potential (ERP) waveforms illustrating the reduction in amplitude of the long-latency slow-wave component with stimulus repetition. Block 1 (dashed line) is the average of the first 15 presentations of the stimulus, and Block 2 (solid line) is the average of the second 15 presentations of the stimulus. ERPs are shown for representative electrodes over left (T3) and right (T4) temporal regions of the scalp. Reprinted by permission of Oxford University Press, Inc. from Snyder KA (2007) Neural mechanisms of attention and memory in preferential looking tasks. In: Oakes LM and Bauer PJ (eds.) *Short- and Long-Term Memory in Infancy and Early Childhood: Taking the First Steps Toward Remembering*, pp. 179–209. New York: Oxford University Press.

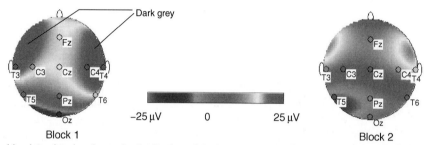

Figure 5 Topographic plots showing the scalp distribution of the long-latency slow-wave component (PSW) and changes in the amplitude of the PSW with stimulus repetition. The PSW is shown as patches of dark grey over the left and right temporal regions. Block 1 is the average of the first 15 presentations of the stimulus, and Block 2 is the average of the second 15 presentations of the stimulus. Reprinted by permission of Oxford University Press, Inc. from Snyder KA (2007) Neural mechanisms of attention and memory in preferential looking tasks. In: Oakes LM and Bauer PJ (eds.) *Short- and Long-Term Memory in Infancy and Early Childhood: Taking the First Steps Toward Remembering*, pp. 179–209. New York: Oxford University Press.

visual processing pathway, and appears to encode different kinds of information in different parts of the pathway, more information is needed concerning the specific role of repetition suppression in preferential looking and its implications for the nature of the representation reflected in infants' visual fixations.

Summary and Conclusions

An important implication of the repetition–suppression model is that longer looking to a novel stimulus may be merely a consequence of reduced neural responses to previously encoded items; it may not require explicit awareness, voluntary or deliberate control, or even a 'comparison' between new and previously encoded items. Thus, memory for a familiar stimulus may influence visual attention in a very indirect sense in that the neural activity elicited by the familiar stimulus is reduced and hence loses the competition for visual attentional resources. In this model, then, memory is an indirect, incidental influence on visual attentional preferences. Preferential looking effects may reflect attentional processes and implicit memory to a greater degree than explicit memory.

See also: Attention; Brain Development; Brain Function; Memory.

Suggested Readings

Aggleton JP and Brown M (2005) Contrasting hippocampal and perirhinal cortex function using immediate early gene imaging. *Quarterly Journal of Experimental Psychology* 58B: 218–223.

Desimone R and Duncan J (1995) Neural mechanisms of selective visual attention. *Annual Reviews in Neuroscience* 18: 193–222.

Diamond A (1995) Evidence of robust recognition memory early in life even when assessed by reaching behavior. *Journal of Experimental Child Psychology* 59: 419–456.

Fantz RL (1964) Visual experience in infants: Decreased attention to familiar patterns relative to novel ones. *Science* 146: 668–670.

McKee RD and Squire LR (1993) On the development of declarative demory. *Journal of Experimental Psychology: Learning, Memory, and Cognition* 19: 397–404.

Nelson CA (1995) The ontogeny of human memory: A cognitive neuroscience perspective. *Developmental Psychology* 31: 723–738.

Nemanic S, Alvarado MC, and Bachevalier J (2004) The hippocampal/parahippocampal regions and recognition memory: Insights from visual paired comparison versus object-delayed nonmatching in monkeys. *The Journal of Neuroscience* 24: 2013–2026.

Pascalis O, Hunkin NM, Holdstock JS, Isaac CL, and Mayes AR (2004) Visual paired comparison performance is impaired in a patient with selective hippocampal lesions and relatively intact item recognition. *Neuropsychologia* 42: 1293–1300.

Pavlov IP (1927) *Conditioned Reflexes.* New York: Oxford University Press.

Schacter DL and Moscovitch M (1984) Infants, amnesics, and dissociable memory systems. In: Moscovitch M (ed.) *Infant Memory*, pp. 173–216. New York: Plenum.

Snyder KA (2007) Neural mechanisms of attention and memory in preferential looking tasks. In: Oakes LM and Bauer PJ (eds.) *Short-and Long-Term Memory in Infancy and Early Childhood: Taking the First Steps Toward Remembering*, pp. 179–209. New York: Oxford University Press.

Sokolov EN (1963) *Perception and the Conditioned Reflex.* (S.W. Waydenfeld, trans.). New York: Macmillan (Originally published, 1958).

Head Start

J W Hagen, University of Michigan, Ann Arbor, MI, USA
F G Lamb-Parker, Columbia University, New York, NY, USA

© 2008 Elsevier Inc. All rights reserved.

Glossary

Administration for Children, Youth and Families (ACYF) – This unit replaced the office of Child Development (OCD) when the Department of Health and Human Services (DHHS) was created.

Child Development Associate Program (CDA) – A program established in 1972 to provide this educational credential to teachers and home visitors.

Family and Child Experiences Survey (FACES) – A nationally representative information system used by Head Start since 1997 to collect data on programs, classrooms, teachers, parents, and children for examining the quality and effects of Head Start.

Head Start Bureau – The administrative home of Head Start, in the Administration for Children and Families (ACF), Department of Health and Human Services (DHHS).

Head Start Program Performance Standards (HSPPS) – Comprehensive criteria establishing areas to which all Head Start Programs must conform.

National Reporting System on Child Outcomes (NRS) – Launched in 1999–2000, assesses the school readiness of 4- and 5-years olds in Head Start, producing a national outcomes report on the congressionally mandated indicators.

Office of Child Development (OCD) – This office was established by President Richard Nixon in 1969 to centralize issues concerning children and became the administrative home for Head Start.

Office of Economic Opportunity (OEO) – The federal office established under President Lyndon Johnson's administration to address directly the problems of poverty in the US.

Introduction

Project Head Start was launched by the Office of Economic Opportunity (OEO) of the US Government in the summer of 1965. A panel of experts in child development, including Edward Zigler, was recruited by OEO's Director, Sargent Shriver, to develop guidelines for Head Start. It began as an 8-week summer program for low-income preschool children to help break the cycle of poverty of their families. Julius Richmond, an MD, pediatrician, and policy maker, was its first director.

The program, now in its 42nd year, was designed to be comprehensive with components that foster cognitive, language, social, and emotional development, as well as the physical health and nutrition of children. Families were an integral part of the program, being given decision-making authority over program content and management.

Head Start is distinguished by the fact that while it is federally funded, it is locally administered by community organizations and, more recently, public school systems. Researchers and policy-based research have played major roles in Head Start, especially in its early years and then again during the past decade. There have been many program variations, such as length of providing services to children and families and age levels served. Head Start continues to be the most important, federally mandated program for young children in the US, especially those who are at risk due to family income and other environmental factors.

The Beginnings of Head Start

In the Economic Opportunity Act (EOA) of 1964, the War on Poverty was launched by the Congress of the US. The focus initially was on youth and young adults. There were provisions for several important programs, including the Job Corp, the Community Action Program (CAP), and VISTA (the domestic Peace Corps). The OEO was given the mandate to establish and flesh out programs aimed at reversing the troubling trends in domestic poverty. Head Start emerged, in part, because of the lack of promise shown by the CAP.

The director of OEO was Sargent Shriver, brother-in-law of former President John F. Kennedy, and President Lyndon B. Johnson's staff person in charge of the War on Poverty. Anticipating a surplus in the budget for OEO during this first year, he directed his staff to recommend ways to use these funds effectively. When it was made evident that almost half of the 30 million poor in the US were children, it became a mandate to found a program aimed directly at this group. The initial idea was to launch a program designed to improve the intellect and school performance of these children, so that they would have the opportunity to rise out of the grips of poverty. Shriver's wife, Eunice Kennedy Shriver, had already worked on the President's Panel on Mental Retardation and had established the Joseph P. Kennedy Jr. Foundation (named for her brother who was killed while serving in the Navy in World War II).

Sargent Shriver recalled that a Kennedy Foundation project at George Peabody College in Nashville, Tennessee (now part of Vanderbilt University) had demonstrated that the inteligence quotient (IQ) scores of black preschool children could be improved with a program designed to increase cognition as well as motivation toward school. Susan Gray, professor of psychology at Peabody, was the director of the Early Training Project in Murfreesboro, Tennessee, and her work provided the impetus for the launching of Head Start on a national scale. Professor Gray went on to be one of the leading figures not only in Head Start but in the development of the preschool education movement. Harry Levin, a professor of child development at Cornell University, also provided the US Office of Education (OE) with an endorsement of the worth of preschool programs. While Head Start has never been administratively in Education, Levin and other scholars with expertise in early child development played key roles in the initiating of and program development for Head Start.

Another relevant experience of Shriver's was his involvement with the School Board of the City of Chicago. He argued that schools, which were typically closed in the summer months, could provide the space for poor preschool children to be provided an opportunity to get a 'head start' on their education in first grade. Dr. Robert Cooke was the Shrivers' pediatrician and the science advisor to the Kennedy Foundation. He became a principal consultant with OEO to develop the model for Head Start. Since he was a pediatrician, the component of Head Start that still plays a prominent role today embracing children's health, can be attributed to Cooke. The EOA did authorize a preschool program but provided no specific direction, so Shriver and his advisors had a lot of latitude. In December, 1964, Dr. Cooke became the chair of a Head Start Planning Committee. It was a diverse group, with only two members coming from early childhood education. Edward Zigler, professor of psychology at Yale University and the first director of the Office of Child Development in Health and Human Services (HHS), became one of its members. He recalls that the committee was faced, among other things, with the dilemma of focusing on improving intelligence as a major goal of the proposed program.

Intelligence and Experience, written by a professor at the University of Illinois, James McVicker Hunt, had been published in 1961 and stirred a lot of interest but also controversy. Drawing from a wide literature, including animal research as well as human, it provided a forum for the view that proper environmental inputs could stimulate and hence improve the cognitive development of all young children. The notion of 'critical period' was also emphasized in Hunt's book, arguing that appropriate stimulation must be provided early enough if children were to benefit. The zeitgeist of the time led, in many people's view, by this pivotal book was embraced by the committee setting up the parameters for the newly launched Head Start program.

Another of the tenets of the committee was that parents should be involved in programs aimed at their children's development and well-being. Urie Bronbenbrenner, professor at Cornell University and founder of the 'ecology theory' of human development, was also appointed to the committee. According to Bronbenbrenner, "to have any lasting impact, the children's day-to-day environment – particularly their families, but also their neighborhoods and communities – must foster similar goals." His influence on the actions of the committee was apparent in the recommendations which included parents as community partners.

The notion that all children are capable of learning, given the appropriate opportunities, became a widely accepted position. The Elementary and Secondary

Education Act of 1965 included assistance of children age 5 years and older. This bill was introduced by Democrats, and the Republicans criticized it for ignoring early childhood education. It was amended to permit the inclusion of preschool programs and it passed both chambers in April 1965.

The executive branch was given flexibility in how to implement Head Start. In spite of professional advice discouraging its starting so soon, Shriver endorsed a plan to launch Head Start in the summer of 1965 as a summer only program. It was believed that a large-scale, short-term program would garner the most attention and support, especially from parents of children involved. In 1966, selected programs were offered on a full academic year basis, and by 1972, most programs were year round.

Meanwhile, Robert Cooke's Head Start planning committee issued its report, *Improving the Opportunities and Achievements of the Children of the Poor*. It strongly recommended that all programs include health, social, and educational services. Most members of the committee thought a small pilot program emphasizing quality was the way that Head Start should begin. However, the administration proceeded with its large-scale summer program, which became the nation's most ambitious attempt at staving off the problems of the youngest of the nation's poor.

The senior staff were selected by Shriver. Julius Richmond, MD, a pediatrician and dean of the Upstate Medical Center in New York, was appointed director of Head Start. Jule Sugarman was appointed as associate director, and they made a good team. Richmond started a program for disadvantaged children at Syracuse University and was committed to the value of early intervention. He insisted that meals be provided in all programs, and at least one of them was to be hot. Sugarman took leadership of day-to-day operations and brought with him considerable management experience at the federal level. He also knew how to make good use of volunteers. With this team in place, Head Start was launched as a summer program in 1965.

The launching of Head Start in the summer of 1965 had to proceed quickly, as there were only a few months to prepare. It was to be up and running in all 50 states by early summer. While many experts did not think an 8-week program would provide demonstrable effects for the children, they kept their opinions quiet. Further, the funding for individual programs was low since funds were being distributed across so many places. Many felt it was much too low. Thus, staff who were hired were mostly paraprofessional and not well trained. Later, when the program was shifted to a year-round program, the year preceding kindergarten for most children, the issue of cost per student became even more pressing.

A half million children were served by Head Start during its first summer, and the staff were sometimes parents of program participants. This had the advantage of providing employment in the local communities, but many believed it was not in the best interests of the children being served. There is little doubt that weak programs were funded during this initial phase of Head Start. It was striking, however, how quickly Head Start was hailed as being a success. In fact, its success was used to stave off the mounting criticisms of other activities of the OEO.

In the fall elections of 1966, Republican representation in Congress increased. While OEO was threatened, Head Start remained a favorite program. In fact, Republican legislators argued that it should receive more support within OEO. Shriver again fought attempts to have it moved to the Office of Education, and the educational components of Head Start were downplayed. Political battles ensued through 1968, and with the election of President Richard Nixon, Head Start was moved to the new Office of Child Development, headed by Edward Zigler, which was administratively located in Health, Education and Welfare (the predecessor of HHS). The emphasis was then placed more on demonstrating long-term effectiveness of Head Start.

The debate as to how Head Start should relate to the nation's public schools has continued through the years and will be addressed again later in this article. However, it is fair to say that since its inception, Head Start has weathered many storms, political and otherwise, and it is illuminating to try to identify the reasons for its bipartisan success and its expansions in so many ways over four decades.

The Early Years of Head Start

Intelligence and Early Intervention

Since the inception of Head Start, the debates surrounding intelligence, as measured by standard assessment instruments such as the 'IQ' or intelligence quotient tests, have flourished. Are there differences in intelligence related to characteristics of children, such as families' socioeconomic status or race or ethnicity? Can scores on tests of intelligence be raised by appropriate intervention programs? Should programs such as Head Start be evaluated on the success in improving measures of cognitive competence, which may include language, reading, mathematics, or others?

Intelligence testing has a long history in psychology and education, and the debates continue about its meaning and usefulness. Stephen J. Gould provides a fascinating account of these tests and how they have come to be used and changed over the years, and in his view, how they are misused. While originally designed to allow school systems to select children who would be candidates for special education, Alfred Binet, the inventor of the IQ test, deliberately chose a variety of diverse tasks to administer to children of different age levels. His goal was to be able to come up with a single score by combining each child's performance across tasks. In fact, Binet stated, "One might almost say, 'it matters very little what the tests are so long as they are numerous'." It did not take long for others to begin to reify the intelligence measure, and it became what many consider to be psychology's major contribution to society (whether that be a positive one or a liability).

While the tests themselves make no argument concerning from where 'intelligence' may come, it quickly became a topic of interest: is intelligence a born characteristic or is it subject to environmental inputs? Subsequent measures of intelligence include more than one score, but the debate continues whether these measures reflect actual intelligence, both now and predicting to the future for individuals. As evaluations of Head Start became formal, it was inevitable that the question of intelligence, and whether it would increase as a result of early intervention, would be addressed. Unfortunately, the early summer programs, lasting for only 6 weeks and often conducted by staff with little training in cognitive skill development or in matters of early education, became the target of mandated assessment.

A report, which came to be known as The Westinghouse Report, purported to show that the early Head Start programs did not boost intelligence for very long, and in fact reported a 'fade-out' effect. Many in the administration of Head Start, as well as scholars who were invested in the success of the program, became alarmed. Some called for earlier intervention, arguing that the summer before kindergarten was too late to provide the needed stimulation to produce longer-term effects. Issues of cultural bias and accusations of racial bias came from many quarters, and a major response has been that Head Start must be evaluated on its effectiveness in each of its areas, including health, nutrition, social development, and family factors. The importance of providing the children resources in these areas is considered later in this article.

However, those who specialized in early cognitive development argue for the importance of keeping 'intelligence' as a major area of concern in Head Start programs. Several reasons are cited that support the retention of the notion of improving intelligence in the children who participated in these programs. (1) Recent work based on highly controlled studies in the laboratory provide evidence that early experience and the rearing environment have powerful effects on both brain development and subsequent learning. (2) Studies of young humans demonstrate that specific experiences can lead to improvements in both specific skills and use of learning strategies. (3) There is increasing evidence of the range and nature of human competencies, and overall it supports the idea of early interests and skills and these lead to a wide range of abilities later in development. (4) Finally, there is now the work of the past 40 years that supports the value of early interventions, if they are high quality and appropriately educationally oriented.

Head Start began as a program to improve the chances of children succeeding in school and then later in life, and language and intellectual skills are clearly key in the pursuit of these goals.

Parent Involvement

From its inception, the belief that parents should play some sort of role in the programs comprising Head Start has been a key component. The CAP within OEO actually existed before Head Start. The concept that substantial parent involvement was necessary in Head Start was advocated strongly by Polly Greenberg, an early child educator and senior staff member of OEO in the early 1960s. Her notion was that parents were to be employees in the system and would become leaders and activists. They were skilled and committed and could make a critical difference. Greenberg left OEO just before Head Start was launched, but her legacy continued in that parents, as both employees and participants, became a mandated part of the program.

However, there was another, somewhat contradictory, view on the role of parents in Head Start, and it was implicit in the recommendations brought by many of the professionals and researchers: parents living in poverty were not necessarily good role models for their children. Thus, parents needed to be educated in the ways of parenting, often defined by the practices of the middle class. Both of these themes can be traced in the early years of Head Start, which was, after all, a program to help children and families escape the bondage of poverty.

There were advocates who felt that these two views of parents should be combined in creating the actual programs to operationalize Head Start in its first years. It is fair to say that Head Start in the early years was at best only modestly involved in community action as defined by CAP. As stated earlier, applicants for those first summer programs in 1965 included funds for paid staff, who were often paraprofessionals and sometimes parents of children in the programs as well. So parent involvement became a blend of the two 'views', that is, parents as an essential part of community involvement and parents who could benefit from involvement through training, either informal or formal.

Greenberg left Washington to launch the Child Development Group of Mississippi, which was founded by Tom Levin, MD, a psychoanalyst and social activist in New York, Art Thomas, Delta Ministry Executive Director, and Greenberg. They believed that African Americans in Mississippi needed to be incorporated into programs within their communities in order to gain political empowerment which could lead to social change. By providing parents with control in the Head Start Centers their children attended and by guaranteeing jobs for parents as well as others in the community, the stage would be set for lasting change. A core notion was that empowered parents would, in fact, serve as positive role models for their children. However, it proved to be difficult in the implementation.

By the early 1970s, research findings were interpreted to support the position that many parents in poor families lacked certain requisite skills and parenting styles to foster their children's development. Thus, training programs for parents were launched within Head Start as well as through other outlets. In a later section of this article, the descriptions of these programs and evidence concerning outcomes are discussed.

1978–89: New Issues Emerge

The first significant expansion of Head Start came with the election of Jimmy Carter in 1978 when Congress increased the budget by a third. Behind the scenes, the National Head Start Association (established in 1973) and the Children's Defense Fund had been lobbying heavily for the increase of appropriation of funds to Head Start. As a result of bipartisan support for the expansion, Head Start grew in size and scope, which continued through the presidencies of Reagan, Bush Sr., and Clinton.

One of the most significant issues that emerged after Carter's election was the proposed transfer of Head Start to the Department of Education (DOE). Renewed efforts by Republicans to move the program were revived, with the idea that after Head Start was moved to the DOE, it would then be transferred to the states. The Head Start community was shocked that the suggestion had come from a Democratic president, and mobilized a coalition of civil rights leaders, including Coretta Scott King and Jesse Jackson, to urge Carter to reject this notion. They argued that Head Start needed to be protected from take-over by segregationist/racist Southern school systems, and the rigid and bureaucratic demands of the public schools (i.e., teachers' unions, educational requirements), in general. The National Head Start Association marshaled the support of local Head Start staff and parents, along with Edward Zigler and other influential voices. Head Start was removed from the DOE bill and remained at the newly established HHS/Administration for Children, Youth, and Families (ACYF; new name for the Office of Child Development).

With Head Start's increased dollars and visibility came demands for more accountability. In 1980, at Carter's request, Edward Zigler chaired a commission to examine the state of Head Start programs and make recommendations for the program's future. The recommendations included decreasing class size, having Head Start comply with the Program Performance Standards, requiring teachers to work toward Child Development Associate (CDA) credentialing and increasing teachers' salaries.

By the time Ronald Reagan took office in 1982, inflation had affected program quality. According to Zigler, Reagan ignored the Commissions' recommendations and the situation was even more distressing: cutbacks in staff, hours, and services; increases in class size; decreases in per child expenditures; and cutbacks of more than 25% of the regional staff charged with monitoring the program.

Health

From its inception, Head Start planners viewed health as a critical component of child development. Services included physical and dental health, nutrition, and mental health. However, providing those services required agencies to partner with local community providers. By the late 1970s, local Head Starts each had a Health Services Advisory Committee (HSAC) that addressed community issues related to health. Although few comparative data were collected during that period, it was evident that the only place that low-income children were receiving health prevention services was in Head Start. Several studies that examined child health records and Head Start Program Information Report (PIR) data revealed that a much higher percentage of Head Start children had medical examinations, tuberculosis screens, and lead testing than non-Head Start children. Dental screening and examinations, and vision screenings were required by the Head Start Program Performance Standards (HSPPS). However, local programs often did not keep records, making it difficult to assess the true success of those components.

Information about mental health services was far less clear. Social and emotional development of young children was always a key component of Head Start. However, using the term 'mental health' to refer to family members was frequently viewed, by both parents and staff, as another way of categorizing people as 'crazy'. Euphemisms were used, such as 'emotional well-being', and 'emotional readiness', and problems were couched in terms, such as 'children with special needs', when actual parent workshop topics might be on substance abuse, child abuse, and developmental delays. Another issue that prevented clearer access to mental health data was that mental health coordinators (along with health and nutrition coordinators) often had multiple roles within a local agency, making documentation arbitrary and spotty. In addition, during this period, most of the mental health consultants were there to screen and assess 'identified' children. They only worked a few hours per week or even per month, and were seen as 'experts' who diagnosed and referred out to local mental health facilities. These often had long waiting lists, staff members who did not speak the language of their clients, and/or were unfamiliar with cultural mores of the local Head Start community.

Social Services

Head Start's comprehensive services model as outlined in the Head Start Program Performance Standards was designed to promote children's healthy development while making improvements in a cluster of family outcomes, including family functioning and adult growth and development. The premise underlying this approach was that there could be simultaneous support for child development and adult self-sufficiency. Changes would bolster parents' educational level, enhance career development, and reduce dependence on public assistance. Intertwined was the realization that it would be impossible to hire enough formally trained social workers to meet the needs of Head Start families. Head Start began experimenting in training paraprofessionals to deliver the services, using people from the local Head Start communities. By the late 1970s, many 'graduated' Head Start parents became Head Start staff, primarily in the areas of family support and referral.

What started as a need and an experiment soon became part of the fabric of Head Start. Staff members were usually of a similar culture to the parents, easily building rapport, and helping them through the myriad of problems endemic to poverty: housing and welfare issues, health problems, addictions, child abuse and neglect, public school liaisoning for older siblings, intergenerational family discord, etc.

As time went on, administrative staff at the local level became increasingly aware that paraprofessional staff members were not equipped to deal with the growing mental health and social services needs of families. Their own stress levels and increasing caseloads made it more and more difficult to be emotionally and professionally available to the families they served. Local social and mental health agencies also were experiencing a rise in number of people needing services, resulting in long waiting lists and increased staff frustration and turnover. Through advocacy efforts to change curricula in schools of social work, a bachelor's degree in social work became the entry level for those professionals, and was accredited by the Council of Social Work Education. This change increased the quality of social services offered to Head Start parents.

Both internal and external barriers to effective service delivery plagued Head Start during this period. Internal issues were related to record keeping, staff training and professional development, staff turnover, and hours of operation. External barriers included availability of community resources, turf conflict in partnering with community agencies, and federal and state funding issues that prevented integration of services within Head Start.

Parental Involvement

Since the EOA of 1964 mandated 'maximum feasible participation' of parents and the 1975 guidelines reaffirmed the role of parents as decision makers, parents have played a major role in the daily operations and planning for Head Start. Advocacy and decision making became a cornerstone of the program, not simply a mandated requirement. Roles included serving on management and policy committees as decision makers, volunteering, fundraising, and helping to design parenting education and self-help activities.

1989–96: A Critical Look at Head Start: Advisory Panels

During a 10-year period from 1989 to 1999, the ACYF and other professional groups assembled 'expert' panels to assess and make recommendations about future directions for Head Start. These included: *Head Start: The Nation's Pride, A Nation's Challenge* (National Head Start Association – 1989); *Head Start Research and Evaluation: A Blueprint for the Future* (ACYF – 1990); *Creating a 21st Century Head Start: Final Report of the Advisory Committee on Head Start Quality and Expansion* (Department of Health and Human Services – 1993); and *Beyond the Blueprint: Directions for Research on Head Start Families* (National Research Council (NRC)/National Academy of Sciences – 1996).

The first of these panels, conducted in 1989 by the National Head Start Association, made specific recommendations concerning future directions for improving Head Start quality, staff development and training, classroom practices and curricula, family support services and education, and federal research and evaluation efforts that encourage researchers to collaborate with community partners in early childhood and human services.

Following closely in time were the two advisory groups established by the ACYF that resulted in the *Blueprint* and *Creating a 21st Century Head Start*. The first focused on future research and evaluation and the second on quality and expansion issues. Research and evaluation recommendations included: the creation of a coordinated research strategy rather than conducting a single, large-scale study; use of diverse methodologies and multiple indicators to measure outcomes; identification of marker variables; a recognition of the importance of studying diverse children and families in diverse community settings using diverse outcome indices; the exploration of program variation in finding explanations of differential outcomes; and the enhancement of research and evaluation studies by building on existing strengths of Head Start staff and programs.

Recommendations for Head Start quality and expansion in the twenty-first century were to implement three broad principles: striving for excellence in serving children and families, expanding the number of children served and the scope of services provided that is more responsive to the needs of children and families, and forging partnerships with key community institutions and organizations in early childhood, family support education, health and mental health that are continually revitalized to fit the changing needs of families and communities, and reflect the changes in state and national social policies.

The NRC's Roundtable on Head Start research held its first meeting in November, 1994, to independently explore the parts of Head Start programming that had been understudied to that point. Subsequent meetings addressed ways of studying changes in families affected by poverty in order to help Head Start be aware of and deal with these new issues; develop innovative strategies to assess child and family outcomes; use secondary data analyses and archiving to enhance the benefits of funded research and evaluation studies; and create a forum for Head Start practitioners to discover their own research interests and needs. The resulting document, *Beyond the Blueprint*, paved the way for even more innovative ACYF research and evaluation initiatives.

1990–Present: Research/Evaluation Revived

New Funding Initiative from Administration on Children, Youth and Families /Head Start Bureau

With the appointment of Wade Horn as Commissioner of the ACYF in 1990 and the recommendations of the first advisory panels (i.e., conducted by ACYF and NHSA) came the revitalization of interest in research on Head Start. In a written communication, Horn summarized the available research on Head Start and stated that there were currently no available data on how positive Head Start effects are achieved or about how they might be enhanced or maintained over time. He felt that there was a need to address the question of "what Head Start practices work best, for whom, and under what circumstances"? He explained that this new research approach would examine how various models would impact subgroups of Head Start children, families, and communities. Since that time, a wide range of demonstration projects have been funded that included more rigorous evaluation components.

New Funding Initiative from Administration on Children, Youth and Families/Head Start Bureau

The first group of demonstration projects was formulated to address the issue of 'fade-out'. The reasoning was that there might be three causes for this purported phenomenon. One was that children needed more years of a comprehensive preschool experience. Another was that children and their families needed more intense services. The third was that the child and family services needed to be extended through second grade. To address these three potential causes, three demonstration projects were funded: the 5-year Comprehensive Child Development Program (CCDP), the Head Start Family Service Centers Project, and the Head Start Transition Demonstration Projects, respectively.

The goals of the CCDP were to provide comprehensive services to children and their families from birth to age 5 years, directly providing childcare, early education, and healthcare, and indirectly by providing parents with education, job training, and family support services. The CCDP was implemented and evaluated in 21 sites across the nation. Results of the evaluation did not show that the program did improve child development outcomes. However, limitations of the evaluation included difficulty comparing intervention and control groups since controls also had referral services and inaccurate data resulting from collection prior to full implementation by local sites.

The Head Start Family Service Centers Project was aimed at providing more intense services to families. Sixty-seven sites were selected to be representative of Head Start programs nationally for the intervention. Of that group, 26 were designated as control sites. Intervention included reducing the ratio of families to social services staff, providing staff development and training, and hiring more skilled staff. Outcomes included evaluation of family drug and alcohol use, job training and employment status, and literacy level. Results did not show significant differences between the intervention and control groups on the outcomes. The lessons learned included the difficulties in assessing social service delivery and documentation of work done with families.

The Head Start-Public School Transition Projects were designed to help children and families move from Head Start to public school kindergarten through second grade. The program included a social service component with a reduced caseload to strengthen the link between families and the school; coordinated, comprehensive health and nutrition services; and joint planning for developmental continuity of curriculum, and intensive parent involvement and education. Thirty-one local public school sites with matched control sites participated in the evaluation. Results confirmed that fade-out did not occur. Former Head Start children showed early and large gains in reading and mathematics achievement, bringing them up to the national average. What was learned were the difficulties in sustaining community-based partnerships, the variability among families living in poverty, and the challenges of conducting a randomized study where the comparison (control) schools were also engaged in transition activities, parent education and involvement, and improving their programs.

The University-Head Start Partnerships were 3-year grants to support research conducted by university faculty in partnership with their local Head Start agencies. The goal was to improve Head Start services by applying new knowledge or testing theory-driven interventions or new instruments with a variety of populations and/or in various settings. These grants were given to four to eight universities (faculty) almost every year from 1990 to 2003.

A similar 2-year grant, entitled the Head Start Research Scholars Program, was offered to graduate students who were qualified doctoral candidates or those who had completed their master's degree and were enrolled in a doctoral program.

Early Head Start (EHS) began in 1994, following the recommendations of the Secretary's Advisory Committee on Services for Families with Infants and Toddlers. ACYF designed EHS and funded the first 143 programs (not necessarily within Head Start agencies) to implement the model. At the same time, ACYF selected 17 sites (including 3001 families) from the 143 for evaluation. The evaluation used a rigorous, large-scale random assignment design that provided for both process and outcome data collection, and mirrored the program approaches and family demographics of the larger population. During that same period the Head Start Program Performance Standards were revised to include pregnant women, infants, and toddlers, who were to be served by the new initiative. The results of the evaluation are ongoing, with results of consistent patterns of statistically significant, modest improvements across a range of outcomes for 2–3-year-olds, including cognitive and language development, and social–emotional development. Additionally, EHS had significant positive effects on parenting and parent support of children's language and preliteracy development. Intervention parents made more progress toward economic self-sufficiency and mothers were less likely to have subsequent births during their first 2 years of enrollment than control group parents. The positive impact on fathers and father–child interactions was also significant, compared with controls. Families with a higher number of demographic risk factors, African American families, and families who enrolled during pregnancy made greater gains than those families in other subgroups.

Beginning in 1995, the ACYF moved to enhance Head Start program quality and outcomes through a number of strategically designed initiatives. The first of these was the Head Start Quality Research Centers Consortium, a 5-year cooperative agreement with four universities. During this period, the Consortium built partnerships between researchers and programs explored what aspects of programs contributed to positive child and family outcomes, created and refined instruments and strategies to assess classroom quality and child outcomes. Consortium members served as technical advisors to the design, development, and implementation of the Head Start Family and Child Experiences Survey (FACES).

Head Start's System of Program Performance Measures, an outcome-oriented accountability method, was initiated in 1995, on the recommendations of the 1993 Advisory Committee on Head Start Quality and Expansion, and on the mandate of the Head Start Act of 1994. The Act delineates the methods and procedures that must be used by local Head Start agencies to annually assess the quality and effectiveness of their programs. In 1996–97, a conceptual framework was developed and the measures were finalized. The 'whole child' approach to school readiness was endorsed in keeping with Goal One of the National Education Goals Panel. Defined as a complex trajectory of developmental milestones, school readiness includes physical, social, emotional, and nutritional health; language, literacy, cognitive skills, and general knowledge; and positive approaches to learning.

FACES was launched in 1997 as an integral part of the accountability process. Annually, FACES collected data on a nationally representative sample of Head Start programs, classrooms, teachers, parents, and children to study its quality and impact. The field test in 1997 collected data on 2400 children and their families on 40 Head Start programs. The sample was increased to 3200 children and families each year, in 1998 and 1999. In 2000, a new national cohort of 2800 children was selected from 43 programs. Initial results showed that Head Start classrooms have higher quality than most center-based early childhood programs; most Head Start programs have smaller class sizes and a lower child/adult ratio for 3–5-year-olds than is required by the HSPPS and the NAEYC accreditation standards; and over 79% of Head Start teachers had a CDA certificate or other early child credential. Children benefit from Head Start, showing a significant growth in vocabulary and gains in social skills and cooperative behavior. However, children with emotional and behavior problems (a relatively small number) did not change over the course of the year. Families benefit from Head Start by learning the importance of reading to their children and practicing that skill, involving their children in activities at home, participating in many areas of the program, feeling supported by Head Start in raising their children, receiving help and services for their children with disabilities, and enhancing the role of fathers in raising their children.

The Head Start Act of 1998 (PL 105–285) reauthorized Head Start funding with two new major provisions addressing staff qualifications and child performance standards, and measuring and monitoring outcomes. At least one classroom teacher had to be trained and skilled at implementing the new educational performance standards that included developing and demonstrating an appreciation of books, developing phonemic, print and numeric awareness, identifying at least 10 letters of the alphabet, recognizing a word as a unit of print, and associating sounds with written words. The ACF has given guidance on these and other legislative changes regarding the child outcomes framework, performance measures, and monitoring (i.e., self-assessment and federal on-site systems monitoring).

In 1999, following the 1998 Head Start reauthorization bill, the Department of Health and Human Services established an Advisory Committee on Head Start Research and Evaluation. The resulting document, *Evaluating Head Start: A Recommended Framework for Studying the Impact of the Head Start Program*, made several recommendations concerning future directions and requirements for Head Start research and evaluation. These included: reviewing existing and ongoing research and evaluation studies that document the impact of Head Start; exploring alternative designs and methods for studying Head Start, develop a study or series of studies of the impact of Head Start services on children and families. The resulting initiatives reflect these recommendations.

In addition to establishing the Advisory Committee, the 1998 reauthorization congressionally mandated that a national, longitudinal study be conducted on the impact of Head Start. The National Head Start Impact Study involves approximately 5000 3- and 4-year-old children whose families applied to Head Start beginning in fall 2002, across 84 representative agencies. Participating children were randomly assigned to a treatment (receiving Head Start services) or control (receiving no Head Start services) group, but the study only takes place in those communities where there are more eligible children than can be served by the Head Start program. These children will be followed through the spring of their first-grade year (2006). The primary goals of the study are to determine how Head Start affects children's school readiness as compared with the school readiness of children who have not attended Head Start.

First-year findings were reported in 2005. Highlights include the following:

Cognitive domain – small-to-moderate statistically significant positive impacts on 3- and 4 year-old children on pre-reading, pre-writing, vocabulary, and parent's reports of children's literacy skills; no significant impacts were found for oral comprehension, phonological awareness, or early mathematics skills.

Social–emotional domain – small significant impact on children entering as 3-year-olds on one of the three social–emotional constructs, problem behaviors; no significant impacts on social skills and approaches to learning, and social competencies; no significant impacts in children entering the program as 4-year-olds.

Health domain – on children entering as 3-year-olds, small-to-moderately significant impacts on access to healthcare and better health status as reported by parents; for entering 4-year-olds, moderately significant impacts on access to healthcare, but no significant impacts for health status.

Parenting practices domain – for children entering as 3-year-olds, small significant impacts in two of the three parenting constructs: higher use of educational activities and lower use of physical discipline by parents; no significant impacts for safety practices; for children entering as 4-year-olds, small significant impacts on parents' use of educational activities. No significant impacts for discipline or safety practices as compared with children who did not receive Head Start services.

Future reports will examine additional areas of potential impact and explore variations in program (i.e., classroom quality, teacher education level) and community characteristics (i.e., unemployment level, homelessness).

The ACYF/Head Start Bureau and the ACF Office of Research and Evaluation created the Head Start Quality Research Center Consortium (2001) by awarding eight universities 5-year cooperative agreements with the goal of promoting school readiness by supporting ongoing quality improvement in Head Start. Their objectives were to develop, test, refine, and disseminate interventions to enhance child outcomes; staff development, training and mentoring; and parent involvement. The Consortium used common measures in intervention/control design evaluations. Consortium findings were compiled each year into an Interim Report where they also compared their results with those of FACES. This Consortium was expanded in 2006 to include additional universities, and is ongoing.

The ACYF has been field-testing a National Reporting System on Child Outcomes (NRS) since 1999/2000. When fully implemented, it will assess the progress of approximately 500 000 4- and 5-year-olds in Head Start. It will produce a national outcomes report of children's ability and progress on the congressionally mandated indicators.

The Role of the Head Start National Research Conferences

At about the same time that the Advisory Panels were making their recommendations, Horn and one of his senior research staff members, Esther Kresh, developed their ideas for a research conference that would interest the research community. A goal was to create an avenue for attracting university researchers to conduct studies of Head Start children and families and to create evidence-based programming in Head Start. The mission of the conferences was twofold: (1) to expose practitioners to research/evaluation as the foundation for sound program development, and (2) to help researchers understand how to apply their findings to real-life situations and explain their research in terms that would be understood by Head Start practitioners and the community served by Head Start.

The eight conferences have thus far successfully addressed the goal and mission established in 1990. These conferences have become a venue for cutting-edge research in the field, as well as a forum for all of the new research/evaluation and programmatic initiatives conducted by ACYF and other related government agencies. Additionally, they have served to stimulate partnerships and collaborations among researchers and practitioners across disciplines: child development, psychology, public health, pediatrics, neuroscience, social work, and economics, to name a few. The Society for Research in Child Development (SRCD) and Columbia University Mailman School of Public Health (CUMSPH) have been responsible for developing and conducting the conferences, with the assistance of multidisciplinary program committees made up of researchers, practitioners, and policy makers who are leaders in their field, as well as the logistics partners.

An analysis of the conferences across 15 years reveals three major themes that reflect not only the state of the field of early childhood development and education, but also the transformation of Head Start research and evaluation. The three themes are: (1) cutting-edge research in child and family development, child-care, and education; (2) culturally sensitive, relevant methods and measures with sound psychometrics; and (3) partnerships among researchers, practitioners, and policy makers.

There was a clear shift in the focus of research presented at the conferences when comparing the first three (1990–96) to the later ones (1998–2006). The studies that were presented at the conferences reflected the growing sophistication of the early child development and education research communities. The later years have reflected an emphasis on context and ecology, continuities and discontinuities across child and family development, a greater emphasis on the study of outcomes, and an emphasis on positive development.

In comparing Conferences III and VII, the shift in level of comfort with sound, culturally sensitive measures and methods is apparent. In 1996, words such as 'newness', 'innovation', and 'debate' were frequently found in the titles of presentations. Random assignment to intervention and control groups and statistical methods such as hierarchical linear modeling were looked upon with caution and suspicion. In 2006, for the most part, participants voiced feelings of comfort and understanding around these issues and were interested in learning how to apply them to more complex data.

The most obvious and positive change over the course of the eight conferences has been the depth and breadth of collaboration and partnerships between researchers and practitioners. The first several conferences reflected a level of distrust and animosity between the two groups, as reflected in titles of presentations such as *Research Partnerships Action: Dynamic Struggles*. The most recent conference (VIII) had little title reference to partnerships. However, most of the presentations reflected deep and ongoing partnerships between researchers and practitioners where the presentations were a melding of discussions about process, outcomes, and lessons learned from both perspectives.

According to Aletha Huston, then president-elect of SRCD, who spoke at the 7th Conference in June 2004, "the numbers of people in attendance and the vibrancy of the [conference] program attest to the continuing impact of these conferences. The lives of children, both those in Head Start and those who profit from the gains made from the success of Head Start, are the beneficiaries."

Summary

After 42 years, Head Start remains the largest federally funded program for children in the US and is viewed as largely positive by both political parties as well as advocates for children. During Funding Year 2005, over $6.8 billion was allocated for Head Start programs in all 50 states as well as US territories. The enrollment was 906 993 children, and ranged from under 3 years (10%) to 3-year-olds (34%), 4-year-olds (52%), and 5 years or older (4%). In terms of race/ethnicity, 35% were white, 31% were black or African American, 32% were Hispanic/Latino, and 5% were American Indian/Native American. The total is more than 100% due to multiple categories for some children. There were 19 800 centers in 2005, and the average cost per child was $7287. It is noteworthy that 91% of children had health insurance, a figure attributed to the emphasis on wellness and healthcare in Head Start programs.

During the four decades of Head Start, the program has faced many obstacles, has encountered pressures from virtually all levels, including the federal government (both the administrative and congressional branches), from communities and families, from public schools, and from the academic establishment. In this article we have provided evidence for these many pressures, the changes that have occurred, the attempts to evaluate and criticize, and, perhaps most importantly, for the buoyancy and resilience of Head Start. It continues to be a program that serves almost 1 million children a year and evidence continues to accumulate that when quality is maintained the children show both short- and long-term benefits.

See also: School Readiness.

Suggested Readings

Vinovskis MA (2005) *The Birth of Head Start: Preschool Education Policies in the Kennedy and Johnson Administrations.* Chicago: University of Chicago Press.

Zigler E and Muenchow S (1992) *Head Start: The Inside Story of America's Most Successful Educational Experiment.* New York: Basic Books.

Zigler E and Styfco SJ (eds.) (2004) *The Head Start Debates.* Baltimore: Paul H. Brookes Publishing Company.

Zigler E and Valentine J (eds.) (1979) *Project Head Start: A Legacy of the War on Poverty.* New York: The Free Press.

Humor

D Bergen, Miami University, Oxford, OH, USA

© 2008 Elsevier Inc. All rights reserved.

Glossary

Humor – A quality that emphasizes a sense of the ludicrous or incongruous; something designed to be comical or amusing and to provoke laughter.

Humor development – The process of changes in humor expression and appreciation during the life span, from infancy to adulthood.

Humor frame – A setting designated as open to expressions of the ludicrous, incongruous, comical, or amusing in which actions and responses are designed to elicit laughter.

Humor-related laughter – An expression of amusement that occurs within a humor frame.

Humorous hyperbole – Extravagant exaggeration used to provoke laughter.

Incongruity humor – Action or language that is incompatible with known information, which is designed to provoke a humor response.

Joking facade – Action or language that conveys socially unacceptable meaning within a false or superficial humorous frame.

Sense of humor – The mental faculty of discovering, expressing, or appreciating the ludicrous or absurdly incongruous; a pervasive style for approaching life events.

Social laughter – Reacting to action or language intended to be humorous within a social situation without understanding the meaning of the humor.

Introduction

The term 'humor' has been used to mean many different things over the course of history, including its original Latin meaning of 'fluid' (e.g., the humors of the body such as blood and bile). Perhaps because these fluids were also associated with health and temperament, humor generally became a word associated with personality; thus, having a disposition of cheerfulness was evidence of 'good humor'. At times the term humor has also been used to define unusual types of behavior, such as those exhibited by the 'jester', the 'comic', or the 'clown'. In general, however, humor has been considered a positive comprehensive term that signals ones' well-being. In fact, humor was considered one of the 'cardinal virtues' in the nineteenth century.

The concept of humor has at times also been differentiated from other similar concepts such as wit, irony, and satire, with the differentiation being on the basis of intentionality. Humor was often seen as an unintentional dispositional characteristic, while wit, satire, and other specific humor forms were seen as intentionally generated for an audience. Today there are still multiple uses of the term humor. Sometimes it is used as an 'umbrella-term' that encompasses other terms, and at other times it is considered just one element of the comic, which also includes wit, satire, sarcasm, ridicule, irony, and many other verbal or visual actions designed to elicit laughter. In discussions of the 'sense of humor', however, the term humor is usually considered as encompassing many facets of temperament, personality, cognition, and social–emotional life, and for the purposes of this review, this encompassing definition of humor is accepted.

In regard to the humor of adults, there have been many approaches to the study of the sense of humor, including empirical investigations of temperament qualities related to humor, cross-cultural comparisons of humor-eliciting material, the relation of humor characteristics to psychological and physical health, the uses of humor as a coping mechanism, the components defining humor as a personality trait, and the characteristics of humor used by professional comedians and clowns. Humor expression in fictional literary works has also been studied extensively, as have humor-related essays incorporating specific types of humor such as sarcasm, irony, and wit. The effects of humor use on performance in teaching, business, legal, and medical fields, and in other professions have also been of research interest, as have issues of gender differences in humor and its use in promoting or countering stereotypes of women, ethnic/racial minorities, or other groups. The role of humor in adult life thus has been examined by many scholars from both theoretical and research-based perspectives, but the question of how humor develops over the course of childhood has not been a subject of as great research or theoretical interest, nor has there been much interest in studying when and whether children can be said to have a sense of humor. One reason that humor researchers may not have viewed a sense of humor as being a facet of young children's personality was probably because they were focused on the more sophisticated forms of humor that require abstract thought, which is not evident in the humor of young children. However, the types of humor that children do exhibit are not lost at later ages; adults still laugh at physical humor (e.g., pratfalls), nonsense, jests, and social games.

The study of humor as a developmental phenomenon, in which its presence and changing manifestations over the years of early and later childhood are observed, has begun to be of theoretical and research interest in more recent times. Since this interest began, there has been progress in charting the course of humor development, explaining the purpose and course of that development from various theoretical perspectives, and providing information on how to promote humor development in children. Greater attention has been given to observing and facilitating young children's cognitive, social–emotional, language, academic, and even play development, however, than to issues of humor development. This is all the more surprising because one of the first indicators of social–emotional, language, and cognitive incongruity development is the child laughter that is elicited during infant and parent peek-a-boo and other early social games. Because humor development is embedded in many other developmental achievements, attention to this domain is certainly warranted. This article discusses what is known about humor development in early childhood, theoretical perspectives on the reasons for this development, how humor development may enhance young children's overall development, and the role of adults in fostering such development.

Humor Development

Ages Infant to 3 Years

Infant laughter may be observed even in the first few months of life as a response to tickling, but those laughter responses are not considered as evidence of humor. Research indicates that these early laugh responses are probably related to emotional expression generated by the limbic system of the brain rather than to frontal lobe development. That is, they are more of an automatic response rather than a specific social response or observation of an incongruous action. Beginning at about 4–5 months, and definitely in the second half of the first year, as the frontal lobe of the infant brain begins to develop connections with the limbic system, children show the first evidences of true humor-related laughter. By 6 or 7 months, reciprocal social games such as peek-a-boo, which contain elements of behavioral expectations and routines of surprise on the part of both participants, are a primary source of humor. Observers of such interactive social games see progression from a situation in which the actions are initially controlled by the parent (parent actor/child responder) to one that is gradually taken over by the child (child actor/parent responder), with increasing expressions of child and adult laughter as the game becomes more intense and violations of expectations more elaborated by the child's actions. Humor results because the actions are 'misexpected' not 'unexpected'. The infant already knows what ordinary social interactions with the parent are like; these interactions are perceived as different because they are performed within a 'humor frame'. That is, even at this early age, young children can distinguish between 'serious' and 'humorous' behaviors in familiar adults. However, because their cognitive competence is still limited, they may have difficulty assimilating humor frame actions from unfamiliar persons and thus the incongruity behaviors of strangers may elicit fear responses rather than laughter.

There have been a number of recent studies of very young children's development of humor comprehension and expression. These studies show that infants and toddlers first use preverbal symbols, then deliberate finger and body movements, and finally symbolic play to initiate humor with parents. Toddler humor attempts include verbal humor such as mislabeling with incongruent labels, verbal puns, and nonsense word production. Two-year-old humor has been labeled 'iconoclastic' by researchers because it is often designed to gain control in social interaction situations. Toddlers self-generate much humor as well as being surprisingly sophisticated interpreters of humor events that are related to what they already know. That is, they demonstrate their increasingly sophisticated understanding of their world. Their ability to use 'practical deception' in a playful way indicates that they are beginning to have some sense that they are aware others think differently than they do. These behaviors are particularly observed in the pretend behaviors that are prominent in the second and third years of life. At this point, toddlers already seem to be aware of the 'audience' that is needed for humor to be effective. Because much toddler humor is self-generated and a response is expected from the adult, this is evidence that there is a humorous intent in the behavior.

Play and humor arise at similar times and are closely tied in infancy; however, when pretend play develops, humor begins to diverge from play to become a separate entity; that is, the 'play frame' and the 'humor frame' become differentiated. In 'serious' pretend play, the child tries to simulate the real world, using pretense to enact ordinary life events. Although often performed in the presence of others, this type of pretense can also be a solitary activity. In contrast, 'humorous' pretense requires an audience because the pretense is designed to deliberately distort reality in order to get a surprised or humorous response from other people. That is, humorous pretense is deliberately designed to get a reaction from another person and to trigger laughter. Toddlers' ability to use this type of playful deception is evidence that they are aware that the humor frame can be used to explore the ideas and expectations of other people.

In studies of parent reports of their young children's observed humor acts, a number of types of humor were described in the toddler years. Examples of toddler humor gained from parent reports include making 'funny' faces or exaggerated movements (clowning), repeating funny sounds or words (sound play), mislabeling objects or people (using incongruous language), using objects in unusual ways to elicit laughter (performing incongruous actions), provoking actions in another by calling names or grabbing possessions (teasing), and expressing joy in movement play and social games (social mastery). Another phenomenon often observed in toddlers is 'social laughter', joining into the laughter of others without understanding the meaning of the laughter. While this is not an indication of understanding humor, it is additional evidence that the child has learned the 'humor frame' and is able to interpret social occasions as either humorous or serious.

A recent study comparing the humor development of children with Down syndrome and those with autism (chronological age about 4 years but development age range of about 1–2 years) found that the children with Down syndrome who were of toddler developmental age exhibited teasing, clowning, and social laughter behaviors while the autistic children rarely did. Because autism often interferes with children's ability to interpret social interactions and connect socially with others, while Down syndrome does not interfere with children's interest in social interactions, these findings are not surprising. The children with Down syndrome were also much more likely to laugh socially without understanding the meaning of the humor event, than were the children with autism, who occasionally showed 'false' laughter when alone. Other observational studies done in early childhood programs for toddlers with special needs also have produced examples of laughter induced by social games, sound play, incongruous actions, and clowning, as well as evidence of the social laughter generated by being in a humor-related social setting. Often the teachers played a similar role to that of parents by being the initiators of these social games or other activities, but the humorous events were then continued and extended by the toddlers in the same manner that infants extend their early social games. Studies of gifted children's humor have also produced many examples of early humor development. Toddlers who are gifted often exhibit humor that is more typical of that shown in the preschool-age period. It may be that, because their knowledge base is usually more extensive, they see funniness in incongruous sounds, word use, or actions that other children do not yet notice. Often parents of gifted children indicate that one of the first reasons they suspected giftedness was because of their children's advanced appreciation and expression of humor.

Ages 4–6 Years

The age period from 4 to 6 years is a major time for humor development, and children's ability to enjoy and express humor grows exponentially. While children of this age continue to exhibit all of the forms of humor that toddlers express, they are particularly interested in incongruity humor, as their own knowledge of the world expands.

Parental reports show examples of preschool children engaging in elaborations of familiar songs and stories (making simple parodies), substituting nonsense words or using word play in elaborated sequences (usually interactively with a peer), laughing at word play with multiple meanings (having snow in the bed will make ice cold pop), describing impossible events (exaggerated tall tales), and beginning to tell pre-riddles, riddles, and simple knock–knock jokes. They also enjoy these types of humor in books and on television or DVDs, and many book authors and script writers include the types of humor young children appreciate. For example, in the book *Butter Battle* of Dr. Seuss, one child said it is funny because they fight over whether "to eat butter upside down on their bread" and "keep getting bigger and bigger things to fight with."

Pretend play continues to be a vehicle for a wide variety of expressions of humor and the presence of the social group promotes this type of humor. In one study of humor occurring in preschool settings, the greatest number of humor events were observed in pretense situations with other children. For example, one child acted as the 'baby' using an exaggerated baby style of talking and acting, and another child was the 'mother' who used unconventional objects to care for the baby (e.g., combing the baby's hair with a wood rod) and an exaggerated 'mother' voice. The entire sequence was accompanied with giggles and laughter, until the teacher told them to stop their 'silliness'. Children may use many objects in ways not intended in order to garner laughter from other children (e.g., rolling up a placemat and 'eating' it as a fruit roll, or 'kissing' a piece of paper).

A recent study found that some children were adept at using hyperbole, which requires understanding of figurative instead of literal meanings. The children made outrageously false statements about their abilities (i.e., tall tales), which then caused other children to make such claims, resulting in increasing levels of laughter. The convention of social laughter that was observed with toddlers is also evident in preschool groups, particularly in the phenomenon of 'group glee', in which some incongruous event may start a few children laughing. The laughter may then be taken up by a larger group of children until it becomes 'out of bounds'. This group glee is often a social bonding event for children, although it may be problematic for teachers.

Through these early childhood years, children gain increasing sophistication in demonstrating the more conventional types of humor, such as telling riddles and jokes. By about age 4 years, children who have older siblings or joking parents may already begin to exhibit the social convention of 'joke telling', in which they tell pre-riddles that use the form of a riddle without understanding the humorous meaning. The children know that laughter should follow the telling of a riddle or joke, but the pre-riddle has the form of the riddle without the incongruity resolution. A real riddle has conceptual incongruity or word play that makes it funny; that is, there is a misexpectation that occurs when the answer is given because the listener had one meaning of the concept or word in mind while the riddle uses an alternate but still accurate answer. The humor of a riddle such as, "Why did the girl salute the refrigerator? Because it was General Electric" is derived from the conceptual incongruity of the term 'general'. If one does not have the knowledge base to understand why a general should be saluted and that the phrase is also the name of a refrigerator maker, the riddle is not funny. After her older sister told that riddle, a preschool-age child then told this riddle: "Why did the boy salute the refrigerator? Because he was hungry." The child had the form of the riddle but was missing the conceptual incongruity dimension. Of course, the adults who heard her pre-riddle followed the social convention of laughter at the pre-riddle. This learning of the humor form of riddle and joke telling is an important stage because it then leads to the ability to tell real riddles and jokes at a later age. One way to tell whether understanding is present is to observe the humor events that do initiate young children's laughter.

By age 5 years, most children are into a riddle-telling stage from which they derive great enjoyment. The telling of true riddles is often the major humor mode of kindergarten and early elementary children. They often tell the same riddle over and over to all who will listen, and because the audience reaction is a necessary part of the humor social circle, adults usually try to express laughter at hearing the same riddle over and over as well. In studies of riddle telling, when children are asked to tell a riddle or joke, the majority of children of kindergarten or first-grade age can do so with some skill. They usually tell a riddle with lexical ambiguity (double meaning of a word) or conceptual incongruity (double meaning of a concept). They are not adept at telling narrative jokes, however. This is a skill usually reserved for children of later elementary age.

Even when children of 5 or 6 years of age can tell a credible riddle, knock–knock joke, or narrative joke, they can rarely explain why it is funny. Children's ability to explain the incongruous reasons that made their riddle or joke funny rarely occurs before second-grade level. When asked why the riddle or joke is funny they either say they do not know or they give a 'social' answer, such as 'it makes people laugh'. For words and concepts that they are very sure of, they may be able to explain the double meaning. One child told the riddle, "What is a cat's favorite color? Purr-ple" and said, "See, the cat's purr says purple." Then he added, "I made it (the riddle) up myself."

Ages 6–8 Years

By the age of 8 years, the majority of children are quite adept at telling riddles and simple jokes. They are beginning to be able to explain why they are funny, but even if they know why they are funny, when they are asked that question, it is still sometimes hard to explain. Perhaps that is because most people who tell riddles and jokes expect the listener to understand without explanation. In other words, 'getting' the joke is really a test for the listener. In fact, the child who does not get the riddle or joke is at a disadvantage, and thus social laughter (laughing even when the joke is not understood) continues to be a part of the humor dialog. Because humor development that approaches adult abilities to understand it is not accomplished until middle childhood (when abstract concepts begin to be understood), there are many occasions in which younger children will not understand more sophisticated forms of humor. The disadvantage of not understanding ones' peers' riddles and jokes can be great for children with developmental delays in cognition because they will not be 'in' on the joke. Also, a characteristic of socially isolated children is their difficulty in using humor as a way to gain acceptance by peers. In a study of gifted children, however, when the younger group (average age 8 years) and the older group (average age 11 years) were compared, most of the younger gifted children already could 'get' the joke, demonstrating advanced abilities in understanding more sophisticated forms of humor. Because humor is a great social facilitator, the inability of children with cognitive or social deficits to understand the humor of peers can be problematic for their acceptance.

Researchers have been interested in elementary age children's ability to understand incongruity in humor. When young children hear examples of humor that resolve the incongruity and examples that do not resolve it (did not really make sense), they said both were funny, while older children thought the one with incongruity resolution was funniest. Other studies of this issue have found mixed results and it is likely that the knowledge base of the particular children would make a difference in what humor they find funniest. Studies of spontaneous humor in school, on playgrounds, and in other nonhome settings have found that boys usually express more humor. Teachers usually rate the sense of humor of boys and girls similarly in early childhood grades but rate boys as having a greater sense of humor at later ages, although there is no difference between boys' and girls' ratings of their own sense of humor. Parents also rate their children's humor similarly regardless of gender, and parents of young children often report earlier humor expression in daughters, perhaps due to the earlier language development of many girls. The reason that 'public' expression of humor is more noticeable in boys may be due to the social expectations children learn as they get older. At later ages, girls often serve as the audience while boys are allowed more humor expression, but this appears to be a result of social convention rather than humor understanding.

Theoretical Explanations of Humor Development

Children's ability to express and comprehend humor has been considered a meaningful indicator of their development by theorists from a number of different perspectives, including anthropological/sociological, psychodynamic, and constructivist ones.

Anthropological/Sociological/Communication Theory

The anthropological/sociological theoretical perspective on humor has also been supported by communication theorists. In this view, the very early adult–child interactions, such as the peek-a-boo example given earlier, are vehicles for communicating shared cultural understandings and frames for appropriate behaviors. When adults interact with infants in a playful way, they give signals such as smiles, open mouths, exaggerated language, and expressive body movements that help children understand that these interactions are playful, not serious interactions. Thus, infants and toddlers learn early what behaviors can be exhibited in the 'not serious' (i.e., humorous or playful) interactive frame, which helps children differentiate the boundaries between these types of social interactions. The interactions also contain the metacommunication that within this humorous frame, the role one takes differs from the role taken in nonhumorous situations. According to these theorists, even at this very young age, children are learning to differentiate humorous and serious communication interaction signals. That is, they learn the cues for 'this is humor'. Such cues as exaggerated facial expressions, high-pitched and emphasized voice quality, intense play gazes, and smiles and laughter that are exhibited in social games such as peek-a-boo enable infants of 4 or 5 months of age to distinguish playful from serous modes. They show their understanding by their smiles, laughter, excitement, and other positive affect. An interesting test of this theoretical view can be observed if an unfamiliar adult attempts to play peek-a-boo with an infant or if a familiar adult increases the arousal level too quickly or intensely. Either of these actions may result in a fearful rather than a humorous response from the infant because the infant is less able to read the cues for humor in those situations. Thus, the early humor context must be both safe and playful. From this theoretical perspective, children's ability to develop a good sense of humor is based on these early adult–child social play experiences, which transmit to the child the metacommunication knowledge of humor as an appropriate communication frame. One implication of this perspective is that the human capacity for humor develops best if these types of social interactions begin in the first year of life. An interesting research question is whether high levels of adults' social skill in expressing and comprehending humor could be traced to their earliest humor-related social interaction experiences. It is the case that some children are less able to interpret communication interactions appropriately and distinguish when a humor frame is being used in a communication event. This also happens when an adult is in a new cultural environment (either a different country, family constellation, or professional group) because the signals for the humor frame may be unfamiliar. From this theoretical perspective, humor can be used to bond a social group and also to limit membership in the group by having humor communications that only those 'in the know' can understand.

Psychodynamic Theory

Another theoretical perspective on humor comes from psychodynamic theory, which began with Sigmund Freud's interest in the meaning of adult joking behavior. Freud was particularly interested in the joking behavior of adults because he thought that jokes revealed much about adults' unconscious emotions and motives by allowing them to express otherwise prohibited ideas (e.g., hostile and sexual) in a socially acceptable manner (it's only a joke!). He reserved the word 'humor' for its use as a method of coping with difficult situations in which fear, sadness, or anger might be the likely emotions generated. For example, people living in oppressive regimes often use humor to help them cope, as do those with severe illnesses or others in dire life circumstances. Although Freud's major focus was on adult joking, as part of his discussion of this topic he described three stages of joking development, beginning in early childhood. He called the first 'play' (ages 2–3 years), which involves repeating sounds or practicing unusual actions with objects to 'rediscovering the familiar'. This stage has little cognitive purpose but it does indicate how children of toddler age juxtapose objects or actions in incongruous ways and find that funny because they know their actions with the objects are not correct. According to Freud, this stage is followed by a 'jesting' stage (ages 4–6 years), which Freud saw as the originating point for 'nonsense' humor. It is the first stage that requires an audience, but the child does not expect the adult to get particular meaning from the jest. By this age children know most adults expect reasonable behavior so jesting is an attempt to get their reaction to absurd behavior. Finally, true 'joking' behavior begins about age 6 or 7 years, and this mode gradually becomes more refined and extends through adulthood, resulting in expert use of the 'joke façade', which allows expression of tendacious feelings (i.e., hostility, sexual thought) to be expressed in public. An example of a child's humor play in the first stage is the 2-year-old who first pushes his toy car along the floor but then begins having it do 'tricks' such as flipping over, going in circles, or driving up the wall, all of which behaviors are accompanied by laughter.

At the jesting stage, adults may enter in and allow themselves to be 'fooled' by the child's jest. For example, a child might call all the adults in the family 'mommy' and they might go along with the jest by responding as a mother would respond rather than telling the child he or she has made a mistake. Even at this early age, jesting may help children cope with anxieties about their abilities, especially in situations where they have just mastered some concept or experience but are still anxious about their knowledge or skill. For example, they may find it very funny to give their wrong name or say the wrong name of animals even though they know the correct names. The joking facade learned in the later age period starts out very crudely, perhaps with jokes about body functions, but as children grow older they become adept at using this form in various ways. For example, 'insult' jokes are very popular by middle childhood. This perspective on humor is useful in explaining how it can provide a vehicle for many types of emotional expression. Although not all adult humor has a hostile or sexual overtone, much of the humor used by professional comedians, in literature and other media, and in everyday social interactions, does have such connotations. The ability to laugh at such humor does not just depend on whether one understands the joke but on whether the meaning is derogatory of the group to which one belongs. Some interesting analyses of differences in humor understanding between males and females have been reported in a number of studies. These studies usually reported that men had a greater sense of humor (i.e., found cartoons funnier); however, the researchers often used humor-eliciting cartoons that were derogatory toward women. It is not surprising that the researchers reported women found the cartoons less funny than did men. Thus, the ability to understand the joke is not the only factor in humor appreciation; the nature of its message is also a factor.

Constructivist Theory

The constructivist theoretical perspective, described by Piaget, has also affected understanding of humor development. Much humor is derived from the recognition of cognitive incongruity, and is thus evidence of knowledge construction. Even for young children, humor has an incongruity recognition element that requires knowledge of what is correct or expected in actions, language, concepts, or meanings. When incongruous or unexpected (i.e., surprise) events occur, there is a humor response. Often humor is triggered by the realization that there is an incongruous visual, verbal, or conceptual event. Such an event may be spontaneous, such as a verbal mistake, or it may be planned, such as a riddle with word play. Incongruity-based humor is also the vehicle for many advanced types of humor, such as wit and hyperbole. In order for incongruity to be considered humorous, however, the individual must have knowledge of what would be the 'reasonable' or expected assumption. Then, if there is a juxtaposition of two unrelated ideas, a substitution of one idea for another, or a misexpected consequence that occurs, the event is seen as humorous.

From the Piagetian constructivist perspective, children's stages of humor development parallel their cognitive development, and thus at an early age they only perceive incongruous actions as funny. For example, an infant or toddler may laugh at seeing a picture of a dog wearing a hat, or at being swung up and down by a parent. The actions of the peek-a-boo game and of the car doing tricks on the wall are other examples in which there is an incongruous element that triggers laughter. By about age 2 years, when children begin to have a command of language, they will also begin to find humor in incongruous language and sound play. Language becomes a major means of expressing humor in rhymes with funny sounds, repetition of noises, and calling people or animals by the wrong name. These are funny because the child now knows what 'should' be said and is deliberately creating an incongruous element. The child of about age 4 years has a rather sophisticated knowledge regarding the basic concepts of the world and so conceptual incongruity, in which ordinary conceptual elements are put together in incongruous ways become funny to the child.

Television cartoons in which the characters do things that are conceptually incongruous are common elicitors of conceptual incongruity humor beginning about age 4 or 5 years. For example, trees that dance or flowers that talk may elicit laughter because the children know that trees and flowers do not act in those ways. They also delight in 'mistakes' made by people who do not know as much as they know. Depending on the child's facility with language, word play with multiple meanings becomes a major vehicle for humor by age 5–7. Children of these ages love to tell riddles with word play elements; that is, where a word has a double meaning and is used in the riddle. The riddle 'Why are Saturday and Sunday the strongest days?' with the answer being 'Because the rest of the days are week (weak) days' is an example of word play with multiple meanings. For young children, this humor has an incongruity recognition element that requires knowledge of what is correct or expected in actions, language, concepts, or meanings. When incongruous or unexpected (i.e., surprise) events occur, there is a humor response. In the early childhood years (kindergarten through third grade) riddles and 'knock–knock' jokes are prime examples of the use of these incongruity elements in humor. Humor gradually changes from being a product of concrete thinking to more abstract levels, paralleling cognitive development. As children begin to laugh at sophisticated humor in cartoons, books, or other media, they demonstrate their increasing knowledge base and ability to understand more subtle conceptual incongruity and linguistic multiple meanings. Thus, in the constructivist view, humor is both a vehicle for demonstrating cognitive development and a means for extending such development. The essential knowledge base for finding humor funny expands at later ages; however, it is still the case that if the realm of knowledge is not familiar (e.g., physics, geography, politics, music), adults will not find the humor attempts funny.

Other Theoretical Explanations

There have been other theoretical versions of explanations for the functions of humor, but these have not typically been related to children's humor development. However, in regard to adult and adolescent humor, one perspective suggests that the desire to show 'superiority' is a motive for much humor, and this explains a type of humor often called 'disparagement' humor. This type of humor is directed at some 'out' group in order to make the 'in' group laugh. Many comedians use a version of this, which is 'self-disparagement' in order to make the audience feel superior to them. Another perspective stresses the 'relief' function that humor can give to emotional or social stresses, and this view is closely tied to psychodynamic and to communication theory, because it suggests that the use of humor in stressful social situations opens lines of communication, relieves tension, and allows the group to bond. This then enables greater productivity to occur because underlying emotional and social strains may be dissipated. The incongruity perspective, which forms the basis of constructivist explanations of humor development, has also been discussed by others. For example, Immanuel Kant saw humor as a form of cognitive incongruity, because it transforms existing expectations by juxtaposing ideas and circumstances in a surprising or unexpected way. The ability of humor to change ones' train of thought may also lead to creative and unconventional ways of problem solving. That is, humor may 'shake up' thought and make it more productive. Although laughter often accompanies humor, laughter may also occur in nonhumorous situations. For example, laughter may signify pride, uncomfortableness in unfamiliar situations, or embarrassment.

Humor Development in Relation to Other Developmental Domains

Interest in children's humor has also been promoted by evidence that humor development appears to be related to other developmental domains.

Cognitive Development

Because there is a body of evidence that shows how children's understanding of humorous incongruity is closely tied to the sequence of cognitive development outlined by Piaget and other constructivist theorists, the tie between humor and cognition seems to be evident. Early indications of humorous responses to incongruous actions, language, or concepts seem to parallel young children's thinking because when young children recognize incongruous actions and language and respond with laughter, they are demonstrating what they already know about their world. Their engagement in the humor frame appears to include some sense of a separate self-identity, and when they later begin to initiate incongruous acts and utterances in order to get responses, they show that they have in mind some expectations of how others will react, which is related to 'theory of mind' development. Theory of mind is defined as the ability to understand that other people have minds that may be thinking different thoughts than oneself. When children try to 'fool' other persons through the children's actions or language, it seems that they must have some idea that the other persons will have different thoughts. That is, they must predict the 'difference in mind' of the other persons because that is what will allow them to be fooled (misexpectations). At later ages, when they laugh at increasingly sophisticated humor in cartoons, books, or other media, and when they begin to tell pre-riddles, riddles, and jokes, they are demonstrating their increasing knowledge of conceptual incongruity and linguistic multiple meanings. By observing what children think is funny at each age, one can chart quite easily how their knowledge is being constructed. When children can tell true riddles and simple jokes and can explain the conceptual incongruity or multiple meanings that make the riddles and jokes funny, they are clearly demonstrating their knowledge. They also gain sophistication in understanding some specific types of humor. For example, children's comprehension of irony begins about age 5 or 6 years but is not fully developed until about age 10 years. In studies of the humor of children age 11–12 years, researchers have found that they have reached the stage of beginning to understand abstract concepts and to 'play' with these concepts in their humor. Of course more sophisticated cognition continues to show development in adolescent and adult humor expression, but the basic cognitive stage progress is evident in the jokes of middle childhood. Children reveal the knowledge they have gained and their understandings of the world, and thus, what they think is funny changes with their cognitive growth. One study found, for example, that when children had just mastered the concept of conservation, they found humor that needed that understanding most funny. Cognitive appraisal techniques also enable them to use humor as a coping mechanism. While 'nonsense' humor continues to be appreciated even into adulthood, adult humor is highly cognitive, requiring recognition of subtle incongruities in concepts and language, and a great deal of factual knowledge from many knowledge systems.

Language Development

Play with language almost always leads to laughter and many of children's earliest attempts at humor involve language or nonsense sound play. Infants gain pleasure from manipulating the sounds of language, and toddlers and preschoolers enjoy engaging in language chants and playful rhythmic exchanges with peers and siblings. Although these humor-related activities with language may seem to be nonserious, through their elaboration and repetition, children are also practicing the phonological, syntactic, semantic, and pragmatic aspects of language. Young children's sound and word play in chanting or rhyming is usually accompanied by increasing bouts of laughter, but it also serves as a way to practice the syntactic forms of language. They also play with the meanings of language and make up words to express their ideas, as well as using language as an accompaniment to their play. In pretend play, they narrate their actions, negotiate with peers, and to try out the language of various roles (e.g., using a 'Teacher' voice.) Their riddles and knock–knock jokes are often funny because of language misexpectations. They develop parodies of familiar songs such as substituting 'I hate you' for 'I love you' in the Barney theme song, and they adore books that have multiple meanings in the words (a favorite is 'Amelia Bedelia'). They enjoy 'Mad-Libs' which substitute similar syntactic but dissimilar meaning forms of language into stories. They tell 'tall' tales and sing favorite playground rhymes. Indeed, much of the language culture of early childhood is deliberately designed to cause laughter.

Social–Emotional Development

Humor, from infancy on, develops best within social interaction settings. Even toddler humor attempts require an 'audience' and humor often serves as a get-acquainted strategy, a bonding mechanism, and a reliever of social tension. Expression of humor requires an ability to interpret social cues (serious or humorous occasion), and a 'safe' environment in which children can take the risk of humor expression. Depending on their socialization in early childhood, as well as their own personalities (e.g., outgoing or shy), children show a wide range of social uses and extensiveness of humor expression. The humor exhibited in the social interactions of preschoolers at play, the kindergarten or first-grade child's riddle telling, and the 'jokes' that are told by 8-year-olds all require social skill. Recent studies of bullying in schools have differentiated behaviors that may elicit or escalate bullying. Although not true of such behaviors in general, at least a portion of the teasing behaviors that may escalate to bullying can be dealt with by humorous responses. Children can make use of humor an effective social strategy in dealing with at least some forms of such teasing by learning to interpret various forms of humor and responding appropriately to the ambiguous messages often conveyed in teasing behavior. When elementary-age children rated the responses to teasing interactions in videotape examples, the children judged hostile and ignoring responses as less effective than humorous responses. Most children learn to distinguish humor-related teasing from hostile teasing; however, teachers may not be aware of many types of the teasing behaviors present in school settings. Given that teasing and other humor-related behaviors, such as clowning, are often a social problem in schools and that certain groups of children are more likely to be teased, to clown, or to use humor in hurtful ways, and given that many variations of humor, including teasing, are pervasive in human society, it is important to help children learn how to interpret and use humor in ways that facilitate their social competence rather than in ways that harm others or make them open to being victims of bullying. In reports of older children who have performed antisocial actions in school, there is often information about their social isolation; it is at least possible that their ability to use humor as a way to bond with the social group was not well developed. Knowing when to interpret an action or a verbal comment as 'this is humor' is an important social skill. Most older children and adolescents will rate a peer who has a 'sense of humor' very positively; thus, a sense of humor fosters social acceptance and friendship.

Physical and Motor Development

One of the major ways humor is initially expressed is in social games that have physical elements. Although physical play, especially when it leads to exuberant laughter, is often frowned upon in school, is also an important vehicle for humor in early childhood. Toddler humor most often has a physical and motor element, and even in preschool, the types of humor that involve physical activity and motor skill are prominent. Laughter almost invariably accompanies interactive physical play; thus such play enhances not only physical development but also humor development. The 'rough-and-tumble' play of childhood can be distinguished from fighting behavior by the humor-related signals (reciprocity, open facial signals, laughter). Recent research showing that frontal lobe development may be enhanced by physical activity has not yet shown linkages to humor. However, because the limbic systems' involvement in emotional expression and the fact that laughter is a strong accompaniment to incongruous actions suggests that research on physical and motor development should also record the accompanying humor elicited by physical and motor actions in young children.

Individual Differences in Humor Expression

Having a 'sense of humor' may be affected by genetic and experiential differences. For example, children vary on the temperament dimension of 'playfulness', which includes ability to show manifest joy and appreciate humor. Also, adults have temperamental differences in the amount of optimism/pessimism or sadness/bad mood they self-report. Experiences related to humor expression in families may also affect children differentially. For example, some families encourage joking and teasing, while others do not. Safety factors in an environment are also relevant for humor expression; with more humor usually being expressed in settings where individuals feel comfortable. Humor may also be initiated as an attention-getting device for a certain group of individuals, as the 'class clown' demonstrates. Finally, people of groups that have been stereotyped by humor are not as likely to enjoy humor that reflects those stereotypes.

Methods for Fostering Humor Development

It is evident from both research and general observation that adults play a major role in encouraging children's humor development. By appreciating children's humor attempts, initiating humor that children can understand, and exposing children to many humor examples, adults can foster this development. However, there is wide individual variation in how much parents and teachers encourage humor development. Humor is often seen as a peripheral skill rather than an essential one. Part of the answer to the puzzle of why some children are adept at using humor and some are not may lie in the social interactions of parents and children in the children's earliest years. Similarly, the emotional tone of educational environments, which may encourage or discourage humor, may contribute to children's development of varied humor strategies. One study using teachers' self-report of their encouragement of humor in the classroom showed that elementary teachers were even less likely to encourage humor than were middle school teachers. Many parents and educators are unaware of the research on humor development and do not realize that humor is one of the many domains of development that progresses from infancy to late elementary years. Thus, they may not be cognizant of ways that they can help young children learn how to use humor as a facilitator of social competence. This discussion suggests ways that the use of humor can be a positive feature of home and educational environments.

The Role of Parents and Other Caregivers

Since the earliest development of humor occurs in the first year of life, the role of parents and other caregivers is very important in helping infants understand the difference between humorous and serious social interactions. Of course, the ability to discover the humor frame in many other social settings develops over many years, but its first manifestation is an important building block for later humor development. Caregiver physical and social play, using the signals of exaggerated voice and facial expression will enable infants to begin their understanding of humor. Other important adult humor facilitation techniques in the toddler years are sharing in children's laughter at incongruous actions and language, acting as the audience when toddlers make humor attempts, being a model of playfulness and humor, and continuing to respond when the humor act is repeated over and over.

When children begin jesting (i.e., teasing) behaviors, adults can be 'fooled' again and again and can give exaggerated humorous responses. They can also 'tease back' in kind ways so that children learn to note the ambiguity of the teasing act and interpret it correctly. Adults can also provide opportunities for peer humor interactions and allow the long sound, word, and action nonsense interactions among peers to escalate without cutting them off too soon. They can provide material and activities that encourage humor appreciation, such as CDs with silly songs and books with funny stories or pictures, and they can provide other media experiences for children that are appropriate for their humor development level. They can participate with their children in these activities and talk about the incongruity elements that occur that make them funny.

When children begin pre-riddle telling, adults can respond to the form of the riddle with laughter, and they can tell riddles that have simple meanings to enable their children to get the understanding of the conceptual and word play aspects of riddles. They can read riddle books to their children to enable them to have a source for riddle telling. They can ask about the reasons why a riddle or joke is funny so that their children can begin to articulate that understanding, and give their own explanations so that children's understanding will grow. They can be tolerant of socially inappropriate and crude joking attempts, knowing that these are just practice for the refinement of the joking facade. When true joke telling begins, adults need to have patience because the telling of the joke may take a while. It is often hard to get the narrative of a joke correctly told on the first try. Because the use of humor as a coping strategy is important to learn, adults can also model this skill by being lighthearted and creative in dealing with problems that occur. For example, an exaggerated, joking response to a child's minor complaint can help the child gain perspective. Most importantly, they can create a climate in the home that signals humor is welcome. If children learn about humor at home, they will be able to carry that knowledge to other settings and interpret humor attempts in those settings appropriately.

The Role of Teachers and Other Adults

All of the techniques discussed for home use can also be used in the school, playground, or other environments. However, in addition, there are some ways that humor development can be enhanced in educational settings, and these techniques may result in greater learning and motivation to learn. Obviously, the educator should never model humor that ridicules, insults, or demeans any groups in stereotypic ways. (Although children find teacher 'self'-disparagement humor funny.) Classroom humor can be very useful in developing social bonds with children in the class and stimulating positive rapport among teacher and students.

In relation to specific techniques for facilitating learning through humor, one way that humor can be used in learning environments is as an attention-getting strategy. If children are to learn particular concepts, they must be attending to the information. A humorous story or joke about a topic can often increase children's initial attention to the topic and attention can be maintained better if some incongruous changes or positive emotional events are built into the activity. Of course, the humor has to be appropriate to the age level of the children. Humor can also increase children's motivation for learning so having some projects that involve learning 'funny' facts or requiring incongruous actions or language can also be helpful. When tension inducing situations are present, for example, at standardized testing times, having some humor-related activities to provide relief from tension can be very useful. Within the curriculum objectives, humor can sometimes be used to teach the concepts. For example, phonological knowledge can be learned as well by having children make up nonsense words that rhyme as by having them use a list of real words, and investigating cartoons that comment on a historical event can provide additional information on the social effects of that event.

While all of these ideas can lead to planning for humor in the classroom, educators also can promote humor development just by conveying an openness and acceptance of children's humor expression within the educational setting. Humor is sometimes used 'iconoclastically' to deride the values and conventions of an educational setting, as the 'class clown' knows, and of course, it can be used deliberately to hurt other students through teasing or bullying. These less desired forms of humor can be controlled best if all of the students in the class are socially skilled in humor expression and understanding, and comfortable within the 'humor frame'.

Summary

Humor is a term with many meanings, many uses, and many variations. While it has long been recognized as a feature of adult life, it is also a pervasive part of young children's lives, because it is a basic human quality. Much in now known about the course of young children's humor development, and there are some useful theoretical explanations for its development and purposes. There is also evidence that a sense of humor is highly related to children's competencies in cognitive, language, social–emotional, and physical-motor realms. The development of humor can be facilitated by the adults in children's lives, if they understand how humor develops, and know how to provide both home and educational environments that help young children to become skilled humor users.

See also: Cognitive Development; Cognitive Developmental Theories; Language Development: Overview; Play.

Suggested Readings

Bergen D (2000) *Enjoying Humor with Your Child (ACEI Speaks Series).* Olney, MD: Association for Childhood Education International.

Bergen D (2006) Play as a context for humor development. In: Fromberg DP and Bergen D (eds.) *Play from Birth to Twelve : Contexts, Perspectives, and Meanings*, pp. 141–155. New York: Routledge.

Loomans D and Kolberg K (1993) *The Laughing Classroom: Everyone's Guide to Teaching with Humor and Play.* Tiburon, CA: H. J. Kramer.

McGhee P (2002) *Understanding and Promoting the Development of Children's Humor.* Dubuque, IA: Kendall-Hunt.

Ruch W (ed.) (1998) *The Sense of Humor: Explorations of a Personality Characteristic*, pp. 329–358. Berlin: Mouton deGruyter.

Sinclair A (1996) Young children's practical deceptions and their understanding of false belief. *New Ideas in Psychology* 14(2): 152–173.

Sobstad F (1990) *Preschool Children and Humor.* Trondheim: Skriftserie fra Pedagogisk institutt, Univeritetet i Trondheim. Rapport nr. 1.

Imagination and Fantasy

J D Woolley and A Tullos, The University of Texas, Austin, TX, USA

© 2008 Elsevier Inc. All rights reserved.

Glossary

Fantasy – A subset of imagination in which the imagined entity, object, or scenario is more extravagant or less constrained by reality.

Imagination – The formation of mental imagines of entities or events that are not present to the senses.

Individual differences – Characteristics of children's biological, social, environmental, or genetic makeup that make them different from other children the same age. Without individual differences, all children of the same age would develop similarly.

Object substitution – Involves using one object to stand for another. For example, children might pretend that a cardboard box is a castle.

Pretend play – An activity in which children's behavior involves some form of nonreality. It often involves some or all of the following six behaviors: (1) self-pretense, (2) object substitution, (3) animation of objects, (4) pretending about imaginary objects, (5) pretending to be another person or entity, and (6) pretending to have imaginary companions.

Pretense – Involves mental, verbal, or physical engagement in nonreality.

Role play – Involves imagining and acting out the role of another person or creature. It can involve acting like another person, behaving toward a toy as if it is really what it represents, or interacting with a pretend being, such as an imaginary companion.

Introduction

Walk into any preschool classroom, and evidence of young children's imagination abounds. In one corner of the room you might observe children playing dress-up, in another the products of a finger-painting project, and in another a child building a castle out of colorful blocks. Many consider the preschool years to represent the peak of imaginative and fantastical thinking. In this article we explore the origins and development of imagination and fantasy from its earliest observable manifestations in older infants and toddlers through its peak in the later preschool years.

We must begin by considering what we mean by imagination and fantasy. The word 'imagination' is certainly used in a multitude of ways to mean many things: "use your imagination," "she or he's got a good imagination," "I can't imagine what it would be like," are some common examples. In its most basic sense, imagination is the formation of a mental image of something that is not present to the senses; it is the act of conceiving of an alternative to reality. Imagination is the ability to think of things as otherwise than we see them or as different from how they exist in the world. Imagination can include thinking about the immediate future (e.g., imagining how good a cookie would taste) and the distant future (e.g., imagining being a grown-up), as well as the more prototypical uses found in the quotes above. Fantasy is most often taken to be a subset of imagination, or imagination that is somehow farther removed or less restricted by reality. For example, a fantasy may involve slaying dragons or time travel, things that are impossible, but would not include improbable imaginations like winning the lottery or traveling to the moon.

The ability to engage in imagination and fantasy underlies many activities in which adults engage, including art, music, fiction, appreciation of movies and plays, and other more mundane activities as well, such as planning one's future. Imagination allows one to experience different realities without actually living them. Teenagers, for example, can imagine what it would be like to be a doctor or an architect, what it would be like to have children or to live in another country. The capacity to imagine provides an alternative universe to envision different futures. Thus, imagination is believed to be critical for children to grow into their future selves. In the next section, two important questions will be addressed: (1) What are the origins of imagination and fantasy? (2) When do children come to share this important ability with adults?

One problem that is faced in seeking answers to these questions is that external manifestations are required to discern the presence of imagination. That is, without some kind of behavior, it is difficult to know when someone is imagining, especially in infants. The traditional developmental perspective is that infants do not imagine or participate in fantasy, and that this ability develops with age. This perspective is not based on evidence that infants do not imagine; rather, it is based primarily on a lack of evidence that they do. Psychologists have not yet developed a method to assess the presence of imagination in infants. Part of the reluctance to attribute imaginal abilities to infants stems from Piaget's proposal that mental representation is not possible until toddlerhood. However, given that recent research in cognitive development is uncovering earlier evidence of object permanence, imitation, and other representational abilities previously thought to be absent in infancy, it seems reasonable to consider that imagination may be present earlier too. We can consider this possibility from a theoretical perspective, but from an empirical perspective researchers are still limited to external signs of imagination, most notably, pretense. Thus we begin with this question: When do children begin to pretend?

Imagining, Pretending, and Fantasizing: The Developmental Course

Imagination and Pretending

As with imagination and fantasy, we must first consider what we mean by pretending or pretense. Pretending or pretense are mental activities involving imagination, in which alternative identities are projected onto reality. Pretend play is the behavioral manifestation of pretense. While pretense can be a solely mental activity (such as daydreaming), pretend play involves physical activity and thus can be observed and documented. A wide range of behaviors can be classified as pretend play. **Table 1** shows five criteria that have been proposed for symbolic or pretend play. These include: (1) familiar activities may be performed in the absence of necessary material or a social context (e.g., pretending to stir soup in an empty pot), (2) activities may not be carried out to their logical outcome (e.g., when pretending to go out to dinner, children do not actually leave the house and drive to a restaurant), (3) a child may treat an inanimate object as animate (e.g., offer food to a teddy bear), (4) one object or gesture may be substituted for another (e.g., a block becomes a pot), and (5) a child may carry out an activity usually performed by someone else (e.g., pretending to be a doctor).

As shown in **Table 2**, children engage in the following six forms of pretense: (1) self-pretense (e.g., a child pretends to be asleep), (2) object substitution (e.g., a child uses a stick as a spoon), (3) animation of objects (e.g., a child feeds a stuffed bear), (4) pretending about imaginary objects (e.g., pretending to drive an invisible car), (5) pretending to be (or act) like someone else, and (6) pretending to have imaginary companions. Many of these forms of pretense are readily observable in any preschool classroom across the US. However, pretend play is clearly not limited to classrooms.

Researchers have observed pretend play in a wide range of cultures; thus, it is believed to be universal in its occurrence. Not only does pretend play seem to be prevalent across cultures, there are also certain specific aspects of pretend play that appear to be universal. One of these is children's use of objects in their pretend play. Most of children's pretend play occurs in relation to toy objects such as blocks and baby dolls. When toys are not readily available, children often use objects from nature. A second universal characteristic of pretend play is its interactive context. Although solo pretend play does occur, caregivers, siblings, and peers are most often an

Table 1 Five criteria for pretend play

Criterion	Example
1. Familiar activities performed in the absence of necessary material	Pretend to stir soup in an empty pot
2. Activities not carried out to logical outcome	Children pretending to go out to dinner do not actually drive to or from the restaurant
3. Treat inanimate object as animate	Offer food to a teddy bear
4. Object or gesture substituted for another	A block is used as a pot
5. Child may carry out activity usually performed by someone else	Pretend to be a doctor

Table 2 Six forms of pretense

Pretense form	Example
1. Self-pretense	Pretending to be asleep
2. Object substitution	Using a stick as a spoon
3. Animation of objects	Feeding a stuffed bear
4. Pretending about imaginary objects	Pretending to drive an invisible car
5. Pretending to be someone else	Impersonating Spiderman
6. Pretending about imaginary other	Having an imaginary friend

essential component of children's pretend play. Since cross-culturally children engage in pretend play, the question often arises as to how this ability develops.

Symbolic pretense was proposed by Piaget to derive initially from imitation of oneself, which extends to others as children get older. The primary trajectory is from solitary play toward play with others, or sociodramatic play. The earliest observed indications of pretending are at around 12–13 months, and children's pretending abilities develop significantly between the ages of 15 and 24 months. In addition, the incidence of pretend play increases significantly between the ages of 1 and 4 years. Based on Piaget's work, children are believed to progress through three basic levels in this pathway. Children first reproduce regular actions. Here, the child's own body can be a prop (e.g., pretend sleeping). Next they show similar actions but with one part missing (e.g., cup with no liquid), and begin to incorporate objects as props into their play. For example, if they are pretending to scramble an egg, they may use a stick to represent the whisk and their cupped hand to represent the bowl. With age, the ability to pretend with substitute objects continues to improve, and children also become more able to imagine scenarios in a purely cognitive realm without the aid of objects or body parts. For example, a child may be able to pretend to make scrambled eggs without using any props. Finally, children start performing pretend actions on others, acting out others' actions, and coordinating joint pretense. This is the developmental trajectory of pretend play in general. In addition, there are subsets of pretend play that also provide a glimpse of how pretense develops.

Role play is a type of pretend play that involves children's ability to imagine and act out the role of a person or creature. There are three different ways children can participate in role play: (1) by acting like another person (e.g., pretending to be a mother), (2) by treating a toy as if it is what it represents (e.g., by acting as if a baby doll is sleeping), and (3) by structuring interactions around a pretend being (e.g., having a conversation with an imaginary companion). Role play is quite common in typically developing humans but limited in nonhumans (although there is some evidence in great apes and bottlenose dolphins). The most frequent context for role play is with other children, most often siblings or peers. This type of pretend play, in which children enact roles with one another, is often referred to as sociodramatic play. Factors that influence this sort of play include the age of the partner, the child's relationship to the partner, and the child's culture.

The social relationship between mother and child facilitates the development of children's pretense. The mother's participation in play increases the duration, complexity, and diversity of children's pretend play. Mothers often begin introducing pretense to their 12-month-olds through nonliteral comments such as "I bet your doll is really hungry – she hasn't eaten since breakfast." By 18 months, mothers begin to add requests to their nonliteral comments. For example, mothers of younger children might scaffold the pretend play by making a request such as "Why don't you scramble an egg for your doll?" At this age, children will often go along with their mother's request and engage in the pretense, but they are less likely to initiate the pretense or create the plot on their own. There is considerable development between the ages of 1 and 3 years in the extent to which young children initiate play themes. Younger than 2 years, mothers initiate most play; they suggest ideas, and pull children from solo to joint play. After age 2 years, children become increasingly more likely to initiate themes of pretend play on their own. Even so, mothers continue to play an important role in maintaining and enhancing children's initiatives. While research is just beginning to investigate the role of fathers in caretaking, studies have shown that fathers scaffold their toddlers' pretend play similarly to mothers. However, there are sex differences in the play themes that fathers initiate with their children. Fathers tend to use explicit guidance in initiating traditional, male play themes with their sons, such as playing with cars or tools. In contrast, with their daughters, fathers are more implicit in their guidance and suggest domestic themes, such as cooking. This research demonstrates the utility of the parental role in initiating pretend play, providing more support for the suggestion that parents use pretend play as a vehicle for teaching social/gender roles, and in general for preparing the toddler to socialize with family and peers.

Sibling relationships also play a unique role in children's pretending. Children's ability to engage in joint pretend play can be enhanced by their participation in a warm and affectionate sibling relationship. Younger children's pretend play can be scaffolded by the involvement of an older sibling. The sibling most often sets up and directs the pretense, with the younger sibling occasionally making unique contributions. Siblings give each other more control and input into the pretend play situation than do mothers, and also require a higher level of cooperation from each other. Thus, siblings and parents appear to play unique but complimentary roles in the development of joint pretend play.

Cultural differences in beliefs about the value of pretend play can affect the frequency of others' involvement in children's pretend play and the orientation of the play. Some research has shown that mothers from different cultures have different goals about the role of pretend play, and that these goals influence the themes they initiate with their children. For example, Chinese caregivers have been shown to use play to teach morals and social routines, whereas Irish-American parents often use play to involve children in fantasy. These goals are often reflected in the children's play themes. For example, in a study comparing children from these cultures, the Irish-American children's play centered around themes such as superheroes, and Chinese children's play more often focused on social behaviors, such as cooking dinner. Most of these sorts of play scenarios involve role play with peers or family members, which is often considered the most sophisticated form of pretense. We will now turn our attention to a less common and more highly debated form of role play in which children interact with imagined others.

Imaginary Companions

The creation of imaginary companions is arguably one of the most imaginative types of pretend activity in which children engage. The incidence of imaginary companions in preschool children ranges from 13% to 75%, depending on the definition used by the researcher and the method of study. Whereas some researchers only include children with invisible companions, others include children who animate their stuffed animals. Some researchers require parental validation of children's reported imaginary companions whereas others do not. According to Marjorie Taylor, who has studied children with imaginary companions extensively, imaginary companions represent a high level of pretend play not found in any other species besides humans. Unlike everyday pretend play, the creation of an imaginary companion represents a pretense activity that is often sustained for a long period of time; a child may have the same imaginary companion for weeks or even months. Although earlier research had indicated that imaginary companions rarely last beyond the preschool years, recent research reveals that having an imaginary companion is as common in the early elementary years as it is in the preschool years. However, there is not much stability in this type of role play; often a child's imaginary companion in preschool will not be the same one that the child has in the early elementary years. In identifying children with imaginary companions, researchers consider three types of activity: (1) creating an invisible companion, (2) impersonating a known character, like a superhero, and (3) endowing a stuffed animal with animate characteristics and/or personality.

The clinical portrait of children who create imaginary companions has been somewhat negative, suggesting that these children are lonely, shy, or friendless. However, Taylor's extensive research indicates that children who create imaginary companions differ very little from other children in most respects. They do seem to display advantages in areas such as sociability, creativity, and positive affect in play with other children (we discuss these patterns more fully in the section on individual differences). Children create imaginary companions for a variety of reasons; their companions provide them with fun and companionship, a vehicle for dealing with anger or fear, and help in coping with problems. In most cases, children begin to create imaginary companions during the preschool years and eventually give them up for a variety of reasons, including lack of interest, creation of a new imaginary companion, and parental intervention through engagement in more social activities.

Parents often wonder whether it is normal or acceptable for their children to have imaginary companions. Should a parent intervene and stop a child from talking to an imaginary companion? As previously mentioned, people have historically wondered if children with imaginary companions were mentally ill. However, recently parents in Western culture have come to accept that pretend play is a valuable component of children's development and that having imaginary companions can be an important part of that development. Whereas not all parents are aware of their children's foray into the world of imagination, a majority of parents are knowledgeable and respectful of their child's interest in imagination. Some parents even facilitate their child's relationship with the imaginary companion; in one reported case, parents set an extra place at the dinner table each night. However, in some religious groups, such as the Mennonites, imaginative play and imaginary companions are discouraged by adults. Researchers have found that this discouragement does not successfully squelch the child's engagement in pretense. Rather, the intervention often forces the children to be more secretive in their pretend play and creation of imaginary companions. Thus, research has found that children with imaginary companions are engaging in a fairly common and potentially beneficial form of play that in many cases seems to be an integral part of their development.

Fantastical Beings

Children in many cultures exhibit strong beliefs in fantastical beings. As we have discussed, family or peers initially supply the themes for very young children's pretense, but later in the preschool years, children begin to initiate and create the play themes on their own. Individual children and adults are similarly involved in the creation of imaginary beings. When children create the fantastical beings themselves we call them imaginary companions, but cultures also create fantastical beings and introduce them to children. In Western culture, these culturally supported fantastical beings include specific event-related beings such as Santa Claus and the Tooth Fairy and also generic beings such as fairies and monsters. What is the developmental course of children's participation in fantasy worlds around these beings?

Children in Western culture participate in numerous rituals around culturally supported fantastical beings. These rituals include leaving cookies for Santa Claus on Christmas Eve, hunting for Easter eggs, and checking for monsters under the bed. Participating in rituals involving fantastical beings serves important roles for both parents and children. The Tooth Fairy ritual, for example, provides a vehicle for parents to maintain what many perceive as the innocence and magic of childhood. This ritual can also aid children in a period of loss, and provide them with empowerment in the form of money, a symbolic form of adult society. Santa Claus inspires more complex rituals, and arguably also serves as a vehicle for parents to prolong in their children what they see as a period of innocence and magic. Santa Claus rituals can also provide a means of behavioral control for parents (e.g., parents' threat of Santa putting coal in the Christmas stocking rather than toys). Some have proposed that children's experiences with these fantastical beings play an important role in the development of faith and spirituality. Specifically, children learn to believe in something that they cannot see or experience directly, and this ability is thought to facilitate later belief in God and other religious entities.

What Do Children Understand about Imagination and Fantasy?

The first part of this article has focused on what children do – when and how they start imagining and pretending, and when they tend to have imaginary companions and engage in rituals around them and other fantasy figures. The remainder of the article will be devoted to addressing what children understand about imagination and fantasy. At the heart of this issue is children's understanding of the distinction between reality and nonreality. In other words, do children realize that when they are pretending to eat a cookie, that they are not really eating a cookie; do they perceive a difference in the reality status of Santa Claus and that of their parents?

When do children differentiate the real from the unreal? It is difficult to assess the presence of this distinction in infants. It has been shown that by 9 months of age, infants behave differently toward objects and photographs of those objects, reaching more often for the objects themselves when the two are presented simultaneously. Thus, infants do distinguish between real objects and physical representations of those objects. Although it is clear that these young infants treat objects and pictures differently, it is unlikely that a concept of reality or nonreality underlies this behavior. However, by 19 months of age, children do appear to have a concept of a picture as something that is not real. Children's understanding of the properties of real objects vs. the properties of not-real objects continues to develop through the preschool years.

The most convincing evidence that children make this distinction comes from observations of their early language. Thus, we again focus our attention on toddlers and preschool-age children. Recording of children's conversations shows that, by 2.5 years of age, children use the words 'real' and 'really' to make a number of contrasts between the real world and various alternatives. Children use the word 'real' to contrast reality with a wide range of alternatives, the most common being toys, pictures, and pretense. For example, a child might point to a stuffed animal and say: "That's not a real dog; it's just pretend." Thus at a fairly young age children are beginning to carve the world into things that are real and things that are not real.

Understanding of Pretending and Imagination

When do children begin to understand that pretense, in particular, is distinct from real life? For a child to be truly pretending he or she must understand that what he or she is doing is different from reality. If a child who appears to be pretending to play with a toy cookie begins to take a (real) bite of the cookie, then it is more appropriate to say that this child thought he or she had a real cookie rather than that he or she was pretending. Research shows that, by 3 years of age, children are able to identify both a real object (e.g., a block) and the pretend identity someone has assigned to it (e.g., an airplane). One way to test children's understanding that pretend objects and actions are distinct from real ones is to interfere with children's pretending and observe their reactions. Interference may involve another person entering the room or one of the play participants leaving, or it may be subtler, such as one participant changing the plot of the pretence (e.g., "Now let's pretend this table is a cave instead of a tower"). Young elementary-age children can handle an interruption to their pretend play quite well and can incorporate the source of the interruption into their pretense. Preschool-age children do not handle interruptions well and often will terminate the pretense game if interrupted. These findings suggest that older children have a better grasp on the boundary between fantasy and reality than do younger children. However, more extreme violations of the pretend-real boundary seem to bother both younger and older children. For example, in one study, a researcher actually bit into a pretend cookie. If children confused the pretend cookie with a real one, this sort of action should not have bothered them. However, it did. Even preschoolers were clearly shocked by this action, indicating that they were able to maintain the pretend-real boundary while playing.

To engage in pretend play with others, children must also learn to tell when other people are pretending and to interpret their actions accordingly. Imagine a child who has not shown any evidence of pretending, and then imagine what that child thinks when her mother pretends to pour tea into an empty cup and hands it to her. Research shows that, when pretending with their children, mothers act differently than when they are really performing an action. For example, they look at their child longer when pretending than when they really perform the same action in real life, they smile more when pretending, and they make more exaggerated movements. By the age of 2 years, children are able to pick up on these cues and to become engaged appropriately in pretense. Children of this age also learn to understand that an object has taken on a pretend identity. Between the age of 2 and 3 years, children develop the ability to identify the pretend outcome of another's action. For example, if a child sees someone pretend to give a doll a bath, he or she will appropriately pretend to dry the doll off. The ability to imagine a pretense scenario and actively engage another person to join in the pretense develops around this same age.

Children of 3–5 years of age also understand that objects of imagination differ from real physical objects in important ways. In one study, children were told stories about characters who were thinking of something (e.g., thinking about a cookie), characters who were 'pretending' something (e.g., pretending to have a cookie), and characters who really were in possession of an object (e.g., had a cookie). Then children were asked to make judgments concerning three criteria – behavioral-sensory properties, publicness, and consistency. For example, children were asked, for each character, whether he could see and touch the cookie (behavioral-sensory evidence), whether someone else could do these things (publicness), and whether he could eat the cookie at some point in the future (consistency). Children claimed that, unlike real physical objects, imagined objects could not be seen, touched, or acted upon by themselves or others. Children as young as 3 years are also able to comment on and manipulate their mental images. For example, children claim that, just by thinking about it, they can make an imagined balloon stretch or imaginary scissors cut.

Children's explanations of their responses to these sorts of questions reflect their rich knowledge of imagination. For example, when asked to explain why a child could not eat a cookie that she was just thinking about, 3-year-olds offered explanations like "Pretend ones aren't real ones," and "he or she wants to eat it and he or she can because it's not imaginary." Other children replied, "Cause it's invisible; cause you just imagine it" (4-year-old), and "Because if you're blind or not you can still see things in your imagination" (5-year-old). The frequency with which children spontaneously used the word 'imagination' in these studies, along with the richness of their comments, strongly suggests that preschool-age children know quite a lot about the mental nature of imagination, and about the not-real status of imagined entities.

Other research shows that in addition to understanding these important properties of imagination, children also understand how imagination is different from other mental states. For example, by the age of 3 years, children understand that knowledge reflects reality more than does imagination. That is, if one person claims to know something about the world, and another states that he or she is just imagining, children will expect the world to reflect the contents of the former person's mind.

In addition, children understand that if a person thinks that something is the case, he or she will be more likely to act upon that mental state than if he or she is only imagining a particular outcome. For example, if a child thinks that a box really contains a toy, he or she will be more likely to eagerly rip the box open than if he or she is just fancifully imagining that the box contains a toy.

The research we have discussed shows that children understand some basic differences between imagination and reality. In addition to understanding these differences, it is important that children also understand the causal relations between imagination and reality. Most adults in Western culture believe that one cannot cause physical events with one's imagination. Research with children shows that, by the age of 3 years, children understand that objects of their imaginations do not come to life. This is especially clear with respect to everyday objects – children know that even though they imagine a pencil in an empty box, the box will remain empty. However, emotion can sometimes disrupt this understanding, or at least its expression. That is, even though a child knows that monsters are not real, the thought of a monster under a bed might be enough to make a child refuse to go into his room at night. Indeed, research shows that children have a more difficult time displaying their understanding of the causal relations between imagination and reality when they are asked to pretend or imagine scary things, like monsters. In one study, preschool children were shown an empty box and were asked to imagine a monster inside. All children agreed that the box was empty. However, when they were left alone with the box, they exhibited fear and avoidance of it. Although this behavior might suggest that children confuse fantasy and reality, one must consider that adults may engage in similar behaviors. For example, an adult might cover his or her eyes when watching a scary movie, or might cry while reading the tragic conclusion to a love story. These sorts of reactions suggest separate emotional and cognitive systems, and have led researchers to propose that emotional reactions to imaginary objects may develop independently of a child's understanding of the reality status of the entity.

Imaginary companions are a classic area in which children have been thought to be confused about the nature of imagination. Children often exhibit complex behavioral routines around their imaginary companions (e.g., insisting that a place be set for them at the dinner table). Because of this, children are traditionally thought to believe that their imaginary companions are real. However, children with imaginary companions are, for the most part, quite clear about the fantasy status of their imaginary companions. They understand that they are not real, and often, if engaged in a discussion about their imaginary companion with a researcher, feel compelled to clarify to the researcher that, "She's just pretend, you know."

One interesting question is whether children with imaginary companions differ from children without imaginary companions in their general understanding of the mental nature of imagination. As mentioned earlier, historically children with imaginary companions were thought to be exhibiting early signs of mental illness and therefore to have difficulty understanding that imagination is a mental activity different from reality. However, research has shown that, when given standard tasks to assess their understanding of imagination, children with imaginary companions do not perform differently from children without imaginary companions. However, children with imaginary companions do show a higher level of engagement in fantasy play than children without imaginary companions. Thus, although children with imaginary companions may be more highly disposed to engage in fantasy than children without imaginary companions, their understanding of the mental nature of imagination is comparable to their peers.

What Do Children Understand about Fantastical Beings and Events?

The traditional view of young children is that they are credulous, forming firm beliefs in everything their parents tell them about the world. Some have even proposed that such credulity is an adaptive mechanism in childhood, helping children to stay safe in a dangerous world. Others have argued that, because of the way beliefs are formed, young children lack the cognitive resources necessary to doubt claims they hear others make about fantastical sorts of entities and events. These general arguments suggest that children would indiscriminately hold strong beliefs in fantastical beings and events.

Fantastical events. Do children understand that certain kinds of events are not possible in the real world? By the age of 4 years, children are quite good at differentiating events that are possible in reality from those that are impossible. For example, children understand that events like turning applesauce into apples or walking through a wall are impossible. Older preschool-age children can even make this distinction when they see pictures of fantastical events. In one study, researchers showed 3–5-year-old children a set of pictures taken from children's storybooks, some realistic (e.g., a mother bird feeding its young), and some fantastical (e.g., a rabbit sweeping the floor while another rabbit bakes a cake). Children were asked to indicate whether the depicted events could really happen. Results indicated that 3-year-olds had considerable difficulty with the task, but by the age of 5 years children were able to identify the pictures correctly. As with causal relations between imagination and reality, emotional content appears to affect such differentiation. When depicted real situations invoke fear, children are more likely to incorrectly claim that they are not real, even when they are able to successfully differentiate real from pretend nonemotional scenarios.

Young children seem to differ from adults regarding their beliefs about the reality of magic. In one study, 4–6-year-old children were told a story about a box that supposedly transformed pictures into the real objects they represented. Almost all children understood that this sort of box could not exist in reality. However, later on, the researchers presented a box to the children and suggested that it was the same sort of box as in the story. When left alone with the box, the majority of the children tried in some way to use the box to create real objects. When it did not work, they expressed disappointment. Thus, even though they seemed to understand that this sort of box was not possible, they still tried to work magic on it. This research shows that, although children seem to have some skepticism about magic, they are not entirely sure that it does not exist in the real world.

When children do not understand how an unusual event might have happened, they tend to attribute it to magic. However, there are age differences in what children mean when they attribute an event to magic. Younger (preschool-age) children seem to believe that magic is a real force in the world, one that can make seemingly impossible events possible. Older children are more likely to conceive of the event as a trick, or as someone's attempt to deceive them. However, even though younger children are more likely to believe in certain magical events, they are able to tell the difference between a magical and an ordinary event. For example, preschool-age children know that putting a marble in a box with one's hand is an ordinary event, whereas moving a marble with one's mind is magical.

Fantastical beings. Fantastical beings often generate extreme emotions in children, ranging from acute terror over the monster under the bed to gleeful adoration of Santa Claus. The extreme behavioral reactions of children to fantastical beings contribute to the common belief that children are confused about fantasy and reality. Researchers have assessed children's understanding of the reality status of a variety of fantastical entities. In one study, children were presented with pictures of generic supernatural creatures like witches and dragons, specific fantasy figures from popular culture such as Big Bird and Smoky the Bear, and real entities like birds and frogs. Children received both free sorting tasks, in which they were asked which pictures went together, and a task in which they were asked to categorize each item as being 'real' or 'pretend'. On the categorization tasks, even kindergartners were able to properly place these entities into pile of 'real' and 'pretend', with this ability continuing to develop through the grade-school years. However, until grade 6, children rarely spontaneously used fantasy status as a dimension with which to categorize entities. Thus, it appears that, in young children, the fantasy–reality distinction is in place, but the ability and motivation to use it in the same way that adults do continues to develop throughout childhood.

It is important to distinguish between two types of fantastical beings: generic beings, such as monsters, and specific event-related beings, such as Santa Claus. With regard to generic fantastical beings, recent studies show that, with a few exceptions, preschool-age children understand that they are not real. Young children can put pictures of monsters, ghosts, and witches into a 'make believe' box and pictures of everyday entities like dogs into a 'real' box. In contrast, many young children in Western culture appear to hold strong beliefs in specific event-related fantasy figures, most notably, Santa Claus, the Easter Bunny, and the Tooth Fairy. Results of research investigating these beliefs confirm that the majority of preschool-age children raised in families that celebrate Christmas believe that Santa Claus is real. Age is a significant determinant of the degree of children's beliefs in these figures. By the age of 8 years, belief in Santa Claus has declined significantly, with less than 25% of 8-year-olds still believing. Parents also report that their young children believe that event-related figures such as the Tooth Fairy and the Easter Bunny are real (e.g., exist in the real world), but report a lesser degree of belief in nonevent-related figures such as dragons, witches, ghosts, monsters, and fairies.

Event-related fantasy figures are often strongly tied to religious beliefs, and as such, it is possible that non-Christian children lack many of the associated experiences. In a sample of American Jewish children aged 3–10 years, level of belief in Santa Claus was found to be significantly lower than belief levels in Christian children. However, surprisingly, belief in the Tooth Fairy was significantly lower as well. One possible explanation is that a child's first experience with fantasy figures may color attitudes toward subsequent ones. Children typically learn about Santa Claus first, and to Jewish children he is presented as unreal. When they later hear about the Tooth Fairy, they may also assume that she is unreal.

Researchers have attempted to address what sorts of factors influence initial acceptance of the existence of fantastical beings. In one study, researchers introduced preschool- and elementary school-age children to a novel fantastical being, the Candy Witch. The Candy Witch was presented as a nice witch who visits children on Halloween, and trades a new toy for unwanted candy. They found that among older preschoolers, children who participated in the Candy Witch ritual in their home exhibited stronger beliefs in the Candy Witch than did those who did not. Among children who participated in the ritual, older children had stronger beliefs than did younger children. Belief in the Candy Witch remained high 1 year later. Children who believed in more fantastical beings when they were introduced to the Candy Witch also had stronger beliefs than children who believed in fewer fantastical beings. Thus, parental support, age, and the number of fantastical beings in which a child already believes, all influence the extent to which a child will form a belief in a fantastical being. Overall, despite having a clear understanding of certain important aspects of the fantasy–reality distinction, beliefs in the real existence of certain culturally supported fantastical beings persist into the early elementary-school years.

Fantasy in the media. Storybooks and television often transport children to imaginary worlds and introduce them to fantastical beings and processes. Thus, an important question concerns children's understanding of the reality status of the material they encounter in interactions with these media. Do children believe that Big Bird is real? What about all the people and creatures they encounter for the first time in books?

Young children do exhibit some confusion about the reality status of objects, people, and events on television. One might expect that children mistakenly believe that everything they see on television is either inside the television or is really happening somewhere else. However, by the age of 4 years, and possibly somewhat earlier, children understand that the things that they see on television are not real, physical objects; they understand that they are pictures. With regard to televised events, rather than being credulous and believing that events on television are real, 5-year-old children have a bias to claim that all events on television are fictional. By age 7 years children learn to recognize cues indicating that certain television shows or events are real, whereas others are not. Specifically, children learn to distinguish between realistic shows such as the news and documentaries and fictional shows like sitcoms.

Most early research on storybooks showed that young children's interpretations of stories are that they are events that happened in the past – they are historical rather than fictional. From this research it was concluded that children begin to doubt the reality of stories at around age 5 or 6 years of age, and that not until age 7 years did they let go of literal beliefs in fiction. More recent research indicates that reality/fantasy differentiation regarding storybook events develops toward the end of the preschool years. By age 4 years, children know what sorts of events are possible in fairy tales versus in reality. For example, when questioned about the possibility of a child passing through a wall, 4–6-year-old children understand that this sort of event cannot happen in the real world but could happen in fairy tales.

Research involving reading children entire storybooks (vs. presenting them with isolated events) reveals even earlier understanding. This research shows that, by the age of 3 years, children begin to differentiate realistic, fantastical, and religious stories in terms of the reality status of the characters and events. Three-year-olds are more likely to judge story characters as real than are 4- and 5-year-olds, but most preschool children judge storybook characters as not real with all story types. This is important, as it indicates that young children may, in fact, be skeptical about storybook content, rather than credulous, as many have believed. Children of all ages understand that events in realistic stories can happen in real life more so than events in fantastical stories. Interestingly, 5-year-olds are more likely than younger children to claim that events in religious stories can happen in real life. Religious background plays a role in these judgments, with children from more highly religious backgrounds being more likely to claim that religious events really happened. Now that we have reviewed when children understand the difference between reality and nonreality, we can address what factors might make some children develop this distinction earlier than others, or might simply make some children think differently about it.

Individual Differences in Imagination, Pretense, and Fantasy

Most of the research discussed in this article has addressed age norms in the development of imagination and fantasy. However, as many have observed, some children simply seem more attracted to or more engaged in imagination and fantasy than others. Some researchers have proposed that this reflects a general personality disposition, which has been referred to as fantasy proneness or fantasy predisposition. Those with a greater fantasy predisposition are thought to be better able to create alternative environments of the sort employed in pretend play. Others have suggested that children who pretend more are those that are more socially skilled. Others have suggested that creativity is an important factor. Although it is not certain what is at the root of these differences, they have been observed at many levels.

Researchers have uncovered individual differences even in those aspects of pretense that seem simplest and most basic. For example, regarding object pretense, children of the same age vary in their willingness to use imaginary objects – some children need objects to represent pretend identities whereas others can more easily conjure an imagined representation. There also appears to be significant variation in role play pretense, both in terms of factors that are considered to contribute to individual differences and factors believed to be a result of these differences (in most cases it is impossible to infer the direction of causation). One increasingly common finding is that children who engage in more role play are more socially skilled than other children. They have a better understanding that different people may have different ideas, different desires, and different emotions, and tailor their interactions with people accordingly.

Familial factors also appear to affect role play. Having an older sibling is associated with more role play, perhaps because siblings provide increased opportunities for role play. Some studies have shown that living in poverty can affect fantasy play. These studies show that, although children living in poverty are capable of engaging in high-quality fantasy play, they engage in it less often than do other children, and they show less diversity in the themes of their pretend play. However this may be due more to motivational factors than to cognitive or social limitations, as the simple presence of fantasy-promoting toys can increase the frequency of high-level play in these children. The fact that there are no social class differences in the onset of pretend play or in its development during the first year or so supports this interpretation.

There are sex differences in the types of role play in which children participate. With regard to the objects used in their pretend play, patterns follow traditional gender stereotypes. For example, girls often involve dolls in their pretense and boys often involve trucks. Girls and boys also differ in the themes that are the focus of their pretend play. Boys most often play adventures, fantasy characters, superheroes, and television-related roles, whereas girls most often pretend-play family roles, house, and dress-up. The characters that children pretend to be also differ by sex, with boys' impersonated characters more likely to be fictional and girls' more likely to be real.

As in role play, there are sex differences regarding imaginary companions. Girls are often reported as being more likely to have imaginary companions than are boys. However, some studies report no gender differences in the frequency of imaginary companions. Boys and girls differ more obviously in the kinds of companions they create. Girls are more likely to create true imaginary companions who serve as playmates. Boys, however, more often impersonate superheroes and other characters. Although this is different from actually having a companion, the level and type of imagination involved is quite similar. Paralleling this, girls' imaginary companions are more often invisible beings, whereas boys' are more often based on toys. Some research also shows that boys may begin to create imaginary companions later in their development than girls.

There are also other individual differences with regard to the creation of imaginary companions. First-born and only-children are somewhat more likely to have imaginary companions. This may be partially due to a need for companionship. However, as mentioned previously, children who create imaginary companions differ very little from other children in most respects. With regard to personality, there are very few significant differences between children with and without imaginary companions in the incidence of behavior problems. Children with imaginary companions do show some slight behavioral advantages over those without, in areas such as cooperation and aggression. Although the common stereotype of these children suggests that they are more shy and withdrawn than children without imaginary companions, research does not confirm this difference. Research comparing children with and without imaginary companions also reveals no differences in intelligence between the two groups, and very slight differences in creativity, favoring children with imaginary companions. Children with imaginary companions also appear to be better able to take another person's perspective, that is, to understand that someone else may have different thoughts, beliefs, or desires. This is thought to be a critical component of social interaction.

With regard to belief in fantastical beings, one might expect that children who pretend more often or who have imaginary companions would be more likely to believe in Santa Claus and other fantasy figures. However, there does not appear to be a relation between these factors; children who are highly involved in fantasy in their daily lives are not more likely to believe in fantastical beings. As discussed earlier, children who already believe in multiple fantastical beings are more likely to believe in a new fantasy figure. It is not clear whether this reflects a personality factor, a cognitive facilitation, or some aspect of those children's culture. Parental promotion of belief, however, does distinguish children who believe strongly in fantastical beings from those who do not. Children whose parents encourage belief through participation in activities centered on particular fantastical beings are more likely to believe in fantastical beings than are children whose parents do not promote these activities. Thus, parental encouragement can create individual differences in children's beliefs in fantastical beings.

Summary and Conclusion

The first section of this article presented a developmental portrait of children's imagination and fantasy. While little is known about the possibility of infant imagination, by the first birthday, parents begin to engage their children in pretense through statements about nonreality. Later, parents scaffold children's pretense by initiating themes during pretend play. By 2–3 years of age, children frequently engage in pretend play on their own and with peers, and begin to offer their own comments about reality and nonreality. Parents encourage pretend play for socialization purposes and to develop children's ability to form mental representations. By preschool age, children begin to engage in role play, they develop beliefs in fantastical beings such as Santa Claus, and they may invent their own imaginary companions. Between the ages of 3 and 5 years, children hone their skills in distinguishing reality from nonreality, but their practiced differentiation can be thwarted when the topic is highly emotional.

The second section of the article reviewed children's understanding of imagination and fantasy. When children pretend or imagine, do they understand that the contents of their thoughts are not real? Again, it is difficult to know if preverbal infants understand this distinction. However, around the age of 2.5 years, children begin to differentiate reality from nonreality in their everyday language, making comments such as "Bo-Bo is not really a bear." Preschool children demonstrate their understanding between mental verbs such as 'thinking' and 'pretending' and physical verbs such as 'holding'. For example, preschoolers understand that a child who is thinking about a cookie or pretending to have a cookie cannot really eat the cookie, unlike a child who is holding the cookie. By the early elementary school years, children are adept at separating the physical world from the mental world, and are able to switch between the two easily. For example, when mothers interrupt children's pretend play, children are able to disengage from the pretense, interact with their mothers, and then return to the pretend play scenario where they left off. Thus, children demonstrate a keen understanding of the difference between their mental and physical worlds. While this ability is useful for compartmentalizing play themes in childhood, adults also use it when they mentally rehearse scenarios before actively engaging in real life situations. In the late preschool and early elementary school years, children also demonstrate an understanding that imaginary companions, fantastical beings, and events exist primarily in their minds and in storybooks and are not real.

The third section explained how individual differences play a role in children's development and participation in imagination and fantasy. Children who are more interested in fantasy participate more in pretend play, which has been shown to be related to the development of social skills. Children who engage more in pretend play demonstrate better socialization with family, peers, and others. Familial encouragement has shown to be important in the development of pretense and fantasy. Parents and older siblings can encourage pretend play by providing themes for the play. Children whose families and culture encourage belief in fantastical beings show a higher level of belief than children who receive little encouragement. Lastly, birth order and gender have been shown to affect the creation of imaginary companions. Children who are firstborns or only children are more likely to invent imaginary companions than are children with older siblings. With regard to sex differences, boys tend to conjure superheroes for imaginary companions, whereas girls are more likely to fabricate completely invisible, imaginary companions.

In conclusion, imagination and fantasy are an integral part of children's social and cognitive development. Pretense emerges early in development and appears to be present in all cultures. From a cognitive perspective, the ability to differentiate reality from a variety of alternatives – imagination, fantasy, books, and television – is critical to children's ability to learn about the world. From a social perspective, pretending and imagining can help children overcome emotional difficulties and can facilitate social interactions. More research is needed to understand the origins and early development of imagination and fantasy, as well as the various factors that affect children's ability to make the fantasy-reality distinction throughout the preschool and early elementary years.

See also: Birth Order; Cognitive Development; Exploration and Curiosity; Future Orientation; Humor; Play.

Suggested Readings

Clark CD (1995) *Flights of Fancy, Leaps of Faith: Children's Myths in Contemporary America.* Chicago, IL: University of Chicago Press.
Harris PL (2000) *The Work of the Imagination.* Malden, MA: Blackwell Publishers Inc.
Mitchell RW (ed.) (2002) *Pretending in Animals and Children.* Cambridge, UK: Cambridge University Press.
Taylor M (1999) *Imaginary Companions and the Children Who Create Them.* New York, NY: Oxford University Press.

Imitation and Modeling

A N Meltzoff and R A Williamson, University of Washington, Seattle, WA, USA

© 2008 Elsevier Inc. All rights reserved.

Glossary

Binding problem – Binding refers to the mechanism by which a particular motor response is 'glued to' perceptual input – usually a visual or auditory stimulus.
Intermodal – A connection that spans across perceptual modalities, for example, touch to vision or audition to vision. Watching someone else speak provides intermodal input because they are seen as well as heard.
Invisible or opaque imitation – A term used to refer to a particular kind of imitation in which the behavior of the model and imitative response cannot be perceived within the same modality. Facial imitation qualifies: Although the actor can see the model's face, she cannot see her own face. It remains invisible.
Proprioception – The perceptual process by which we monitor our own body position in space and the relation between our moving body parts. If you close your eyes and move your fingers, hands, or feet you can 'sense' the form your body takes through proprioception. You monitor your own facial expressions through proprioception.
Social cognition – Perception and cognition about other people (as opposed to space, objects, numbers). Social cognition typically involves processing other people's internal states including their wants, thoughts, and emotions; but more elementary levels may involve processing how other people act and other basic social information.

Introduction

Human infants are avid learners, and as Aristotle noted, young humans excel in learning by watching and imitating. Imitative learning is a means by which human infants profit from information that has been learned by previous generations. It provides a mechanism for the transmission of acquired characteristics from one generation to the next. Imitation is faster than independent discovery (the type of learning emphasized by Piaget) and safer than trial-and-error learning (the type of learning emphasized by Skinner).

The imitative skills of human infants go hand in hand with the motivation of adults to teach their young. Adult pedagogy, in the form of purposely showing a child what to do, is so common that it is often taken for granted. Adult modeling and infant imitation are important pillars of human culture and early apprenticeship learning.

Humans as the Imitative Animal

Imitation provides an efficient channel through which the young incorporate behaviors, skills, customs, and traditions. Bona fide instances of imitative learning in animals are rare enough to be noteworthy. Animal behavior texts devote discussion to the unusual case of a troop of Japanese macaques that began washing their sweet potatoes in the sea after watching a few juveniles who invented this technique. In contrast, even casual observation of human behavior reveals myriad instances of imitation in young children – the imitation of parental postures, facial expressions, and tool use. It is commonly observed that a little girl will reach into her mother's purse to pull out the treasured lipstick and apply it to her lips or studiously poke at the keys of the parental computer. Parents often discourage the particular behaviors, but they persist in part because children see these actions everyday and copy them.

In the 1930s, Margaret Mead highlighted the role of childhood imitative learning in non-Western societies. She published photographs from her research of the Balinese people in Indonesia. Mead's plates provide snapshots of behavior that would be unusual in Western infants and may be partly attributable to imitation of experts in that culture. One photo shows an infant just under 1 year of age who is wielding a machete-like knife. Another shows an older infant playing a 'tjoengklink', a bamboo musical instrument, using the distinctive manual techniques employed by adult experts.

A bold experiment in comparative psychology from the 1930s also underscores the special imitative prowess of *Homo sapiens*. Ironically, the goal of this study was to downplay the genetic bases of differences between humans and apes. The authors sought to attribute behavioral differences to differential rearing conditions. The Kelloggs raised an infant chimpanzee alongside their infant son, providing them with environments as identical as possible. Both were diapered, talked to while playing on the Kelloggs' laps, hugged, and so on. Much to the researchers' disappointment, the infant chimpanzee never grew to be very human-like. But the report reveals that the human infant may well have learned from watching the chimpanzee. The boy was reported to scrape paint off walls with his teeth, to engage in certain mauling play tactics, and most dramatically, to imitate the food barks and grunts of the chimp when he saw the chimp's favorite food. It seems likely that these behaviors were performed by the human child in imitation of the ape – a direction of transmission that had not been anticipated by the Kelloggs.

Distinguishing Imitation from Other Forms of Social Learning

So far the concept of imitation has been used in a commonsense way to mean that the observer duplicates the act that the model performs. Researchers have sought an operational definition of imitation that can be used in designing experiments on infants and nonhuman primates. Imitation seems to require that three conditions are met: (1) the perception of an act causes the observer's response; (2) the observer produces behavior similar to that of the model; and (3) the equivalence between the acts of self and other plays a role in generating the response. In imitating, the goal of the observer is to match the target behavior. Equivalence need not be registered at a conscious level, but if it is not used at any level in the system (neurally, cognitively, computationally), then lower-order nonimitative processes may be more parsimonious.

Several decades of careful analysis and experiments have taught us that it is useful to distinguish imitation from other closely related behaviors. These fine-grained distinctions are useful because (1) the underlying mechanisms may be different and (2) research has shown that true imitation is more prominent in humans than in other species. There is wide consensus that distinctions need to be drawn among imitation, social facilitation, contagion, and stimulus enhancement.

Social facilitation is an increase in the production of a target behavior due to the mere presence of a conspecific. Suppose an adult waves bye-bye to a young baby. In response the baby may flap her arms, duplicating the motor pattern that was demonstrated. This could be an imitative response, but if the arm flapping is due to the child being excited at seeing an adult, it would be more sensibly classified as social facilitation.

Contagion is a term that emerges from the animal literature. It covers an increase in an instinctual behavior pattern upon observing a similar pattern by a conspecific. For example, some animals increase their eating behavior upon seeing their conspecifics eat. In this case the observer is neither learning a new behavior nor sculpting a behavior in its repertoire to match what it sees. Seeing another animal eat triggers feeding behavior in the observer and the shared biology assures that the stimulus and response take the same form.

Stimulus enhancement and local enhancement refer to the fact that the model draws the observer's attention to a stimulus object or location in performing a target act. Jane Goodall noted that the juvenile chimpanzees in the Gombe Stream Reserve were often attracted to the place where the adults fished for termites and played with the same sticks the adults used. If the young chimps later use the sticks to obtain termites, this could be because they discovered the use of the stick through their increased chance manipulations rather than through a strict duplication of the adult's actions.

In addition to these classical distinctions, comparative researchers such as Michael Tomasello and Andrew Whiten have attempted to differentiate imitation from what they call emulation. In both there is an attempt to match. In the former it is the bodily act that is copied; in the latter it is the end-state or outcome. For example, if the adult puts one block on top of another with a flourish, the child might copy: (1) the distinctive motor pattern used by the model, which is imitation or (2) the end result of one block on top of the other using any means available (called emulation). A current debate is whether these should be considered different processes or whether they are two exemplars of the more general category of imitation, one oriented toward the bodily act and the other toward the end-state.

Origins of Imitation in Humans

The Binding Problem

There is no question that children are avid imitators, but there is debate about when imitation begins. Questions about development and mechanism are intertwined. At issue is how infants come to 'glue' together an observed stimulus with a matching response of their own. What links the observed behaviors of others to one's own body parts and movements, underwriting the imitative response? We will call this the binding problem. Others have referred to this conundrum as the mechanism question or the correspondence problem. The use of the term 'binding' has an advantage of remaining neutral with respect to the psychological processes and neural underpinnings involved. Whatever one's theory of imitation, the stimulus and response are linked, bound, or connected in some way.

There are three classical theories of how infants first come to match the acts of others and solve the binding problem: operant conditioning, associative learning, and Piagetian theory.

Learning to Imitate by Operant Conditioning

In the 1950s, Skinner developed the idea that imitation is simply a special case of operant conditioning where the stimulus and response happen to match. He noted that pigeons can be conditioned to peck a key when they see other pigeons peck. If a pigeon (P-1) pecks at a key and an observer pigeon (P-2) is reinforced with food for pecking upon seeing this event, P-2 will eventually be shaped to peck when seeing P-1 pecking. Note that P-2 did not produce this act because it was motivated to match the other animal's behavior. All that has happened is that the behavior of P-1 became a discriminative cue for eliciting a conditioned response in P-2. The observer pigeon could be conditioned to perform a nonimitative act just as easily. The similarity of the stimulus and response plays no role.

Strong operant conditioning theorists hold that there can be no infant imitation without a prior period of shaping which binds the discriminative cue to the response. For example, when a young infant sees a mother perform a simple act such as shaking a rattle, the infant at first does not know what movements to recruit to copy this act. Rather, the parent needs to shape the child's response through operant conditioning. Mom shakes the rattle, and the infant responds with random motor acts. Mom selectively reinforces those acts that are similar to her own shaking movements. Over time, the mother's motions come to serve as a discriminative cue (a light would do as well) that elicits the reinforced act (the baby's rattle shaking).

Infants and young children may learn certain acts in the ways described, but there are two drawbacks to this theory as a complete account of imitation. First, it cannot easily account for the imitation of novel acts – acts that the caretakers have not explicitly shaped up. Second, most ethnographic reports of parent–child interaction do not report the type of extensive shaping procedures needed to account for the range of acts infants and young children can imitate.

Learning to Imitate by Associative Learning

A second theory of the origins of imitation, and a possible solution to the binding problem, is based on associative learning. In this view, the infant's act and the adult's act are bound together by temporal contiguity. The prototypical learning case arises because parents tend to imitate their children. When the baby waves her hand, the parent enthusiastically waves back; when baby bangs an object, the parent bangs one in order to play a reciprocal game. According to the theory, infants come to associate their own acts with the similar ones of the parents. Thus, when they see the parent's act in the future, they produce the matching act that has been associated with it through regular temporal contiguity. In a sense, infants come to imitate adults to the extent that the adults have previously imitated their infants.

There have been many reports of parents enthusiastically copying their infants. These exchanges are so well timed that social theorists in the 1980s, such as Berry Brazelton and Hanus Papousek, described them as a gestural dance. There is ample opportunity for infants to bind together the acts of self and other in these reciprocal imitation games. However, the associative learning view would have a difficult time explaining the imitation of novel acts that have not served as familiar games in the past. Moreover, many observers of parent–child interaction remark that parents embellish and vary their infant's behavior, rather than simply mirroring it. This would predict associations between nonidentical behaviors and consequently imitative errors of a type that have rarely been observed. (A variant of this view holds that infants learn to imitate others through associating an action such as shaking a rattle with the outcome; and then when the adult later produces the outcome the infant generates the associated motor actions. Again the challenge is provided by the imitation of novel acts that are not familiar games for the infant.)

Piaget's Theory of Imitative Development

It is clear that human beings, at some age at least, are capable of spontaneously imitating novel adult displays for which there is no previous training history, no physical molding of the body, and no coaxing in any way other than the brief presentation of the model. Jean Piaget devoted his book *Play, Dreams and Imitation in Childhood* to the ontogenesis of this capacity. He was not concerned with specially trained matching responses (or pseudoimitation as Piaget calls it). In his view imitation is intertwined with cognitive development and unfolds in a series of invariantly ordered stages.

Piaget postulated six stages in infants' imitation, and for ease of summary they will be collapsed into three major levels. In level-1 (0–8 months of age; sensorimotor stage 1–3) infants are restricted to the imitation of simple hand movements and vocalizations. For example, the Piagetian 6-month-old would be expected to imitate a simple hand-opening gesture or an /a/-vocalization even if the infant had never been specifically trained to do so. Piaget's notion is that both of these types of imitation are similar in that they can be accomplished on the basis of an intramodal matching process. In principle, the infant could directly compare the adult's hand movements with those of his own visible hand, and thereby use vision as a guide in the matching process. Similarly, the infant could use audition to monitor both his own and the model's vocalizations and to guide his own vocalizations until they sounded like the model's. From Piaget's cognitive-developmental perspective, visually guided manual imitations are analogous to auditorially-guided vocal imitations.

In level-2 (8–18 months of age; sensorimotor stages 4–5) infants first become capable of imitating facial behaviors and novel acts. The fundamental claim made by Piaget is that the difficulties involved in manual and vocal imitation pale in comparison to those involved in facial imitation. Because infants cannot see their own faces, they cannot directly compare their own acts with the ones they see. According to Piaget, facial imitation (or invisible imitation as it is sometimes called) is a landmark cognitive achievement that is first passed during stage 4 of the sensory-motor period.

Finally, level-3 (18–24 months; sensorimotor stage 6) is characterized by the emergence of deferred imitation – the ability to perceive a behavior at one point in time and then, without having responded in the presence of the demonstration, to delay the duplication for a significant period. Deferred imitation directly implicates mnemonic and representational capacities, and Piaget predicted that it emerged synchronously with other complex cognitive abilities such as high-level object permanence (the search for invisibly displaced objects), symbolic play, and insightful problem-solving prior to action. All these synchronous developments constituted what Piaget termed stage 6, the last purely sensory–motor stage of infancy before the emergence of language.

In summary, Piaget's cognitive-developmental hypothesis is that infants gradually become able to imitate events that are farther and farther removed from the immediate sensory field. First they imitate those involving intramodal comparisons (manual and vocal acts), next those involving cross-modal comparisons (facial acts), and finally those implicating a stored representation of the modeled act (deferred imitation). Piagetian theory makes at least three strong predictions that have sparked considerable empirical work in over the past 30 years: (1) facial imitation is impossible before about 8 months of age (stage 4), (2) deferred imitation is impossible until about 18 months of age (stage 6), and (3) infants will progress through the stages in an invariant order, it being impossible to reach higher stages without having achieved the milestones of the preceding stage. As we will see below, these predictions have not received support in empirical tests, which has in turn generated new theorizing about the roots and development of imitation.

Imitation of Facial Acts

In many circumstances it is difficult to determine whether the stimulus-response matching is rooted in operant conditioning, associative learning, Piagetian development, or another process altogether. The problem, in most cases, is that one does not have full knowledge of the child's (or animal's) reinforcement and learning history.

Using a novel act as the target is one way to address this issue. A different approach is to test infants before they have had a chance to learn to link the stimulus and response through conditioning or association. Such demonstrations of imitation prior to the required learning would weigh against the operant conditioning and associative learning views. The Piagetian account can explain early manual and vocal imitation, because infants can compare their own acts with the ones they see. Infants cannot, however, see their own faces. If they are young enough they will never have seen their own faces in a mirror. Piaget predicts that facial imitation is beyond the cognitive abilities of the infant younger than about 8–12 months of age. Because it provides such a powerful test of extant theories of imitation, developmental psychologists have actively investigated the first appearance of facial imitation in human infants.

In 1977, Meltzoff and Moore reported the surprising results that 12- to 21-day-olds imitated four different gestures, including facial and manual movements. The infants confused neither actions nor body parts. They responded differentially to tongue protrusion with tongue protrusion and not lip protrusion, suggesting that they can identify the specific body part. They also responded differentially to lip protrusion versus lip opening, showing that different action patterns can be imitated with the same body part. This was later confirmed and extended by research showing that infants differentially imitate two different kinds of movements with the tongue. Published studies document a range of acts that can be imitated, including mouth opening, lip protrusion, tongue protrusion, selected emotional expressions, head movements, and simple hand and finger movements. In all, there are more than 30 published studies of early imitation from more than 13 independent laboratories. Attention has shifted beyond tests of the raw existence of early behavioral matching to investigations of the basis and functional significance of this behavior.

These findings argue against the classical solutions to the binding problem. Current approaches to this question investigate both the neural and psychological processes used for linking the observation and execution of isomorophic acts. Two discoveries are key. First, early imitation is not restricted to immediate duplication. In one facial imitation experiment, the infants had a pacifier in their mouths so that they couldn't imitate during the demonstration. The pacifier was then withdrawn, and the results showed that the infants initiated their imitation in the subsequent 2.5 min response period while looking at a passive face. Second, infants correct their imitative response. They converge on the match without feedback from the experimenter. An infant's first response to seeing a facial gesture is the activation of the corresponding body part with a gradual homing in on the action demonstrated.

The Active Intermodal Mapping Hypothesis

Meltzoff and Moore proposed that facial imitation is based on active intermodal mapping (the Active Intermodal mapping (AIM) hypothesis). The key claim is that early imitation is a matching-to-target process. The active nature of the matching process is captured by a proprioceptive feedback loop. The loop allows infants' motor performance to be evaluated against the seen target and serves as a basis for correction. AIM proposes that such comparison is possible because the observation and execution of human acts are coded within a shared framework. It is termed a supramodal act space because it is not restricted to modality-specific information (visual, tactile, motor, etc.). In this view, although infants cannot see their own facial expressions, they still have perceptual access to their facial movements through proprioception. AIM does not rule out the existence of certain basic acts that can be imitated on first try without the need for feedback, but it allows proprioceptive monitoring and the correction of responses for novel acts.

This hypothesis of a supramodal framework that emerged from developmental science fits well with proposals from cognitive science about action coding (the common coding thesis of Wolfgang Prinz) and discoveries in human social neuroscience using functional magnetic resonance imaging by Jean Decety, Marco Iacobani, and others concerning shared neural circuits for the perception and production of action. Nonetheless, newborn humans are different from monkeys, who are in turn different from human adults. More analytic work is needed to determine whether the current convergences are merely surface similarities or more substantive (see the section on mirror neurons). Moreover, young infants do not imitate the full range of gestures copied by adults; thus, mechanisms of developmental change will need to be articulated.

Using Imitation to Learn about Objects

Imitation of Novel Acts from Memory

Moving beyond the binding problem and granting children the ability to copy the behaviors of others, another important question to consider is how children make use of this ability. For imitation to serve as a powerful learning mechanism in infancy and early childhood, infants will need to imitate not only facial gestures and other simple body acts, but also tool-use and other object-related behaviors. Moreover, they will need to imitate novel acts after significant memory delays. Human parents engage in purposeful pedagogy, often demonstrating a new skill at a time and place far removed from when the infant has an opportunity to imitate. If the human young could not imitate after a lengthy memory delay, this would necessarily constrain theories about the role of imitation in the transmission of culture. Thus if we want to draw inferences about cultural transmission, we need to know about imitative generalization across time and space.

In the 1980s, Meltzoff conducted a series of relevant studies. One study with 14-month-olds had three features: (1) imitation was tested after a 1 week delay, (2) infants were required to remember not just one demonstration but to keep in mind multiple different demonstrations, (3) novel acts were used. One of the acts was to bend forward from the waist and touch a panel with one's forehead which made it illuminate. This unusual act was not observed in more than 100 infants in free play, and certainly qualified as a novel display (baseline measures were also taken in the experiment).

Infants in the imitation group were shown six different acts on different objects on the first day of testing. They were not allowed to touch or handle the objects. They were confined purely to watching the displays. Infants were then sent home for the 1 week delay. Upon returning to the laboratory, the infants in the imitation group were presented with the objects. In a baseline control group, the adult meets the infants in session 1, but he did not manipulate the test objects; he simply talked pleasantly to the mother and child. The second session assessed the spontaneous likelihood of the infants producing the target acts in the presence of the adult, and this controlled for social facilitation. Contagion and stimulus and local enhancement were ruled out through a third group called the adult-manipulation control. For this group, the adult played with the same objects during session 1; but he did so using different

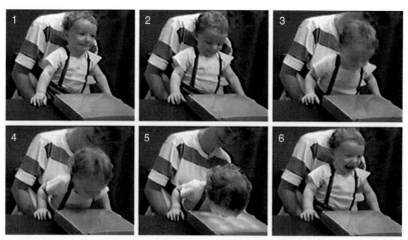

Figure 1 Fourteen-month-old infants can imitate novel acts such as touching their head to a panel. After successful imitation, infants often smile at the adult as shown in plate #6. This article was published in *Journal of Communication Disorders*, Vol. 32, Meltzoff, AN, *Origins of theory of mind, cognition, and communication* 251–269, Copyright Elsevier 1999.

movement patterns. For many stimuli, such as the head-touch gesture, even emulation was ruled out, because in the adult-manipulation control group the end-state (the panel light turning on) occurred but was activated through a different means than the novel head-touch act. The results showed significantly more target acts in the experimental group than in each of the controls, providing clear evidence for deferred imitation from memory after the delay (**Figure 1**).

Rachel Barr, Harlene Hayne, and colleagues have reported that infants as young as 6 months old can perform deferred imitation, which is especially significant given Piaget's prediction that deferred imitation first emerged at about 18 months. Patricia Bauer and Leslie Carver have shown that infants imitate novel sequences of behaviors from memory. Taken as a whole the studies on deferred imitation of object-related acts all suggest that infants imitate multiple targets, including novel ones, after lengthy delays, which suggests that imitation is capable of playing a significant role in human development prior to linguistic instruction.

Imitation of Peers Outside the Dyad

The ecology of child rearing is changing in the US. With the increase of women in the work force, infants are spending increasingly more time with peers in daycare settings. In most of the previous experiments adults were used as models. However, other children can also be important sources of information for how things work and the appropriate ways to act in different social situations. Do infants take advantage of this source by learning from and imitating their peers in daycare centers and other sites?

In one study, by Elizabeth Hanna, 14-month-old naïve infants observed tutor infants. These tutors had been previously trained to play with the toys in novel ways. After observing the peer play with five objects, the naïve infants left the test room. When they later returned and were presented with the test objects in the absence of the peer, they imitated. Further research extended to a daycare setting in which the demonstration was not one-to-one. Instead the tutor infant played with objects as a large group of naïve infants in a daycare center simply observed. The naïve infants were not allowed to approach or touch the toys. After a 2 day delay, a new experimenter (not the one who had accompanied the tutor) brought a bag of objects to the infants' homes and laid them out on a convenient table or floor. Neither the parent nor this new experimenter had been present in the day-care center 2 days earlier. The results showed significant imitation, providing evidence for deferred imitation across a change in context (a shift from daycare to home site). The fact that infants can transfer their imitative learning to a different environment from the one in which they observed the model, can do so after a long delay, and will imitate peers as well as adults, again supports the idea that imitation may play a role beyond the laboratory.

Using Imitation to Learn about People

Imitation and Social Communication

Children use imitation to learn about the physical world, to learn causally efficacious ways of manipulating objects and tools. However, typical children also use imitation for social purposes, such as communicating, sharing, and affiliating with others. What should be imitated to engage another person socially differs in a number of interesting respects from what should be imitated in an instrumental task such as using a tool. Behaviors used in the context of solving physical causality problem involve causally relevant manipulations of the inanimate world. Those used for social purposes can be more arbitrary and unconventional as long as there is a shared history. The imitation of unusual social acts is often incorporated into identification routines (a private 'handshake' or cultural practice) and used in communication to establish and maintain common ground. Important cultural conventions often revolve around arbitrary acts; the in-group knows the routine, which fosters group membership and cohesion. Thus, the criteria used for choosing what to imitate may be very different for achieving physically causal ends versus social-communicative goals.

Moreover the motivation to be like the social other is an important component of human imitation. The research suggests that infants and young children actively strive to match the form of their acts to those they see. Human infants do not need to be motivated by food in order to imitate; imitation is its own reward, a goal in itself. The motivation to 'be like' the other may be less compelling to nonhuman primates and children with autism (see section titled 'Autism'). It suggests a drive for social connection and communication in typically developing children.

Roots of Social Cognition

Scholars concerned with social understanding have often commented on the wide gulf between knowing the self and the other – dubbed the 'problem of other minds'. We experience our own thoughts and feelings but do not see ourselves from the outside as others see us. We perceive visual and auditory signals emanating from others but do not directly experience their mental states. There is a gulf that divides us. Analogously and for similar reasons, developmental scientists are struck by the binding problem in behavioral imitation. Infants experience their own bodies and movements from the inside, but watch the movements of others from a completely different point of view. There seems to be a gap between the behaviors they see and their own behaviors. The solution to this binding problem is the Holy Grail of imitation research. There are preliminary attempts to explain how infants bridge this gap, ranging from mirror neurons to the AIM hypothesis, but more work is needed to provide detailed models at both the psychological and neuroscience levels.

The fact that typical children have the capacity for behavioral imitation provides them an important foothold in social development. Human parents often engage in reciprocal imitation games. The same neurocognitive machinery that enables infants to imitate may make them sensitive to being imitated by others. In this case infants would be recognizing a match between themselves and others instead of producing one. In 2007, Meltzoff articulated a model of early social cognition called the 'Like-Me Framework' which proposed that parental imitation of children's behavior holds special significance not only because of the temporal contingencies involved, but because infants can recognize the structural congruence between the adult's acts and their own. The detection that something out there in the world is 'like me' and can do what I do could have cascading developmental effects. Children may use analogical reasoning to make crucial inference – entities who externally act like me may also share my internal emotions, intentions, and desires. According to this view, imitation is not only an aspect of early social cognition but an engine in its development.

The Regulation of Imitation

Adults are not blind imitators. They choose when, what, and whom to imitate. Developmentalists are beginning to investigate the regulation of imitation by children. The results are intriguing because they show that children do not automatically imitate what they are shown. Instead, there is a high degree of flexibility in childhood imitation.

Regulation of Imitation by Goals and Intentions

Children do not always imitate what you do, but often what you mean to do. If an adult makes a mistake or is unsuccessful in his attempt to complete a task, children will copy the intended goal instead of the outcome they observed. For example, Malinda Carpenter and Michael Tomasello showed 14–18-month-olds two actions that produced an interesting effect on an object. One of these acts was done in an accidental way and verbally marked by saying, "Woops!" The other act was done cleanly and the adult looked satisfied saying, "There!" The children skipped over the accidental acts and imitated those that appeared purposeful.

Actions do not have to be linguistically marked for children to understand the goal of the adult's act. Children will also use patterns of behaviors to infer the model's goal, even if he does not successfully achieve it. For example, Meltzoff showed 18-month-olds an adult who repeatedly pulled at the ends of a barbell-shaped object, as if striving to pull it apart. When given a chance to manipulate the object, the children firmly wrapped their hands around the ends and yanked the object apart. Even though they had never seen the completed act, the children inferred the goal of the act from his try-and-try again behavior. The children did not slavishly imitate the unsuccessful motion by letting their fingers slip from the object, but instead completed the intended goal. This and other related work strongly suggests that infants can interpret what the adult is trying to do and re-enact the goal of the act, not what was literally done.

Regulation of Imitation by Emotions

A recent study by Betty Repacholi investigated whether 18-month-old infants will regulate their imitation based on another person's emotional reaction to the target act. For example, a model performed a series of novel acts on objects and a bystander either became angry (indicating these were forbidden acts) or remained pleasantly interested in what the model was doing. After this emotional reaction, the bystander adopted a neutral face. The toddler watched this interaction between the two adults, and the question was whether they regulated their subsequent imitation based on the bystander's reaction to the model's action. A second factor that was manipulated was whether the bystander was looking at the toddler when she was given a chance to imitate. The experimental conditions included: (1) the bystander left the room, (2) the bystander was present but had her back turned, and (3) the bystander was looking at the toddler. Each of these three conditions was crossed with whether the bystander had exhibited anger or interest in the action when it was shown.

The results showed that if the adult had not exhibited anger at the action, the toddlers imitated at high levels regardless of whether or not the adult could see them. But if the adult had exhibited anger at the action, then the toddlers were significantly less likely to imitate the acts only when the adult was monitoring their behavior. If the previously angry adult left the room or had her back turned, the toddlers' imitation was not reduced.

It was not just the fact that the bystander expressed anger that accounted for the results. These effects cannot be explained by emotional contagion, because the infant had the chance to 'catch' the adult's emotion equally well in all groups. Instead the toddlers' were regulating their imitation based on the conjunction of two factors: (1) whether the bystander had a negative reaction to the act and (2) whether the bystander was watching what the toddler did. Evidently, toddlers regulate their imitative response based on the emotional reactions that others have to the target act and whether the emoter can monitor their imitative reactions or not. Toddlers seem to realize that they can be a target of other people's perception and will not imitate an action when the emoter is watching them produce those actions. Imitation is thus not automatic and inflexible, at least by 18 months of age. Instead, toddlers choose when to imitate.

Regulation of Imitation by Prior Experience and Success of the Model

Rebecca Williamson and colleagues further investigated whether children are blind imitators or if they flexibly employ imitation depending on the circumstances. In one series of studies 3-year-old children were tested to see if they were more open to imitating another person's technique if the child had a prior experience of difficulty with a task. Children were randomly assigned to two independent groups. One group had an easy experience and the other a difficult experience in achieving an outcome, such as opening a drawer to retrieve an object. For the difficult group the drawer was surreptitiously held shut by a resistance device. Then the model demonstrated a distinctive technique for opening the drawer. The same distinctive technique was demonstrated to both the easy and difficult groups. The results showed that children were significantly more likely to imitate after a prior difficult experience with the task. These results fit together well with work in school-age education emphasizing the value of hands-on prior experience in structuring a student's understanding. The gist of the educational research is that some prior experience confronting difficulties with a problem can help the student be more ready to learn from an expert, as was also shown here.

In a related study, children watched a model who demonstrated a particular technique, but for half the children the technique led to success and for the rest it led to the model's failure. The results showed that children took the model's efficacy into account and preferentially imitated the actions when they led to success. Moreover, studies by Stephen Want and Paul Harris show that preschool children learn from seeing not only a successful model, but the learning steps that led up to that performance. Children who saw the model make mistakes and correct the behavior were more likely to imitate the successful act than those who did not see the errors. Mark Nielsen adapted this procedure for 12-month-olds. If the infants first saw an adult try but fail to open a box with his hand, they were more likely to imitate his subsequent demonstration of how to use a certain tool to succeed. Taken together, this research suggests that infants and young children are not blind imitators, their imitative responses are altered depending on a larger envelope of the model's behavior.

Infant Imitation as an Emerging Interdisciplinary Field

Mirror Neurons

There has been an explosion of interest in imitation in the neuroscience community. This owes to the fact that in the late 1990s Giacomo Rizzolatti, Vittorio Gallese, and a team of other neuroscientists in Parma, Italy discovered neurons in the premotor cortex of the monkey's brain (area F5) with peculiar properties. These were dubbed mirror neurons because they fire both when the monkey performs certain goal-directed acts, such as grasping food, and also when they observe another perform the same act. These neurons code the act regardless of whether it is performed by the self or the other. Mirror neurons bring together the observation and execution of motor acts.

Following the initial discovery of mirror neurons in monkeys, Marco Iacobani, Jean Decety, and others reported that there are neural circuits in adult humans that have similar mirror properties. These shared circuits become activated whether the adult performs a certain act, for example, raising and lowering his index finger, or merely observes another person doing so.

Some have theorized that mirror neurons provide the neural substrate for imitation – that they solve the binding problem. However, the existence of mirror neurons may not solve the psychological puzzle involved in imitation. First, even though their brains house mirror neurons, monkeys are notoriously poor at imitating (once stimulus enhancement and contagion are controlled). This shows that imitation requires more than this neural tissue. Second, neuroscientists have yet to map the ontogenesis of mirror neurons. Adult monkeys have repeatedly watched themselves grasp objects. Mirror neurons could code visuomotor associations forged from such learning experiences. Such gradual learning, if it occurs, would suggest that mirror neurons are the product of observation–execution associative pairings and may not underlie them in the first instance. Mirror neurons may develop.

There are two ways of testing whether mirror neurons develop through experience. One is to test newborn monkeys who have not had a chance to watch themselves reach. A second approach is selective rearing in which the experimenter arranges a situation that prevents monkeys from visually monitoring their own grasps, for example, by wearing a collar that blocks the view of their hands. The critical question is whether mirror neurons can be found in the brains of such animals. If they have functioning mirror neurons, it would suggest that mirror neurons do not emerge from learned associations of repeatedly seeing oneself grasp an object. This experiment has yet to be done.

Moreover, canonical mirror neurons cannot be the whole story of human imitation. Mirror neurons are best suited to explaining immediate resonance phenomena. John Braugh and colleagues have reported motor resonances in adults, such as when a therapist and patient unconsciously adopt the same posture (he calls these chameleon effects). But such immediate motor resonances, while they exist in adults and children, do not exhaust the imitative capacities of adults or even of infants and young children. They do not easily explain the following empirical demonstrations: (1) imitation of novel acts, (2) the correction of the imitative act so that it more closely resembles the target, (3) deferred imitation 1 week or several months after the stimulus has been withdrawn, and (4) the regulation of imitation – infants and toddlers do not imitate under certain circumstances and there is flexibility in their choosing what and whom to imitate. Current research is dedicated to investigating the nature, scope, and limits of the mirror neuron system in monkeys and adults in order to discover what additional factors are needed to generate and control imitation.

Autism

Children with autism have a core deficit in the ability to communicate with others and in understanding others' thoughts, feelings, and actions. It has long been known that children with autism have deficits in a cluster of skills such as language, symbolic play, and social reciprocity. More recently, there has been great excitement surrounding the empirical studies establishing that children with autism also show atypical performance on a variety of imitation tasks. This has been demonstrated in both high- and low-functioning children with autism, even after careful matching against mental-age controls.

In 2001, Justin Williams and colleagues suggested that children with autism might have a mirror neuron deficit. Regardless of the debate surrounding this claim, research by Peter Hobson and colleagues reveals that children with autism have more difficulties with certain aspects of imitation than with others, and this will need to be taken into account. Hobson presented tasks in which children were shown how to perform a novel act using a certain style or manner of doing so. His results showed that the children with autism often achieve the same outcome as the adult; however, they do not use the same style. Using the terms introduced earlier, the children could emulate the adult and recreate (aspects of) the end-state; but they did not imitate the distinctive way the adult moved. Further research is needed to characterize the precise nature of the imitative deficit in children with autism, and to distinguish when different aspects of behavior (means, ends, goals, intentions) are imitated. It is also possible that children with autism lack the fundamental motivation to imitate social others, to 'be like' their social partners.

Robotics

In computer science, researchers are becoming increasingly interested in robotic imitation. One motivation is that roboticists want to build robots that interact more naturally with humans. They have noted that imitative responses are part and parcel of natural social exchanges and may help make robots more user-friendly. Another motivation is that it is burdensome or impossible to write code that anticipates all of the complex, novel acts that a user may want the robot to perform. An imitative robot would allow you to teach it to act in much the same way you teach a pre-verbal child – by showing them what to do. If you want your robot to pour a cup of tea, demonstrate how to pour your particular tea pot in front of the robot's sensors and a processor would translate the observed actions into commands to the robot's effectors.

It has quickly become apparent that solving the binding problem is not an easy task – in this case the issue is how to connect an observed action performed by a human to the corresponding action performed by the robotic device. In 2007, Chrystopher Nehaniv and Kertin Dautenhahn published a collection of the recent advances in robotic imitation in one volume that also includes work from developmental and evolutionary psychology. The hope is that biological models of imitation can be used in the design of robots that can learn by imitation; and conversely that work in robotics will help sharpen developmentalists' ideas about underlying mechanism.

Summary and Future Directions

Imitation provides a mechanism, prior to language, through which the human young learn by watching others. Researchers have adopted a definition of imitation that distinguishes imitation from other related concepts (e.g., social facilitation, contagion, and stimulus enhancement). This has allowed them to address three crucial issues: existence, mechanism, and function of imitation. At the psychological level, the AIM mechanism holds that the perception and production of human acts are mediated by a common code, a 'supramodal' framework. Neuroscientists debate whether mirror neurons underlie infant imitation, or whether additional neural machinery is needed to explain the full range of imitative phenomena evident in human children. Regardless of this debate, the capacity for flexible deferred imitation of peers and adults suggests that imitation is a powerful learning mechanism and plays a role in the transmission of human culture.

Future work on imitation will rely on techniques in developmental cognitive neuroscience to more fully explicate the mechanisms binding together perception and production. Other future work will focus on robotics. Computer scientists seek to design robots that can learn by observing and imitating others; and they are increasingly turning to developmental science for a 'biologically plausible' model of imitative learning. Finally, the bridge to autism is promising, because children with autism have core deficits in social understanding, including dysfunctions in imitation. Cutting-edge interventions aimed at promoting imitation skills in young children with autism may have more general effects of improving their understanding of people.

Acknowledgments

Support was provided by grants from the National Institute of Child Health and Human Development (HD-22514), the National Science Foundation (SBE-0354453), and the Tamaki Foundation.

See also: Cognitive Developmental Theories; Learning; Piaget's Cognitive-Developmental Theory; Symbolic Thought.

Suggested Readings

Heyes CM and Galef BG, Jr (1996) *Social Learning in Animals: The Roots of Culture.* San Diego: Academic Press.
Hurley S and Chater N (eds.) (2005) *Perspectives on Imitation: From Neuroscience to Social Science,* vols. 1 and 2. Cambridge, MA: MIT Press.
Meltzoff AN (1999) Origins of theory of mind, cognition, and communication. *Journal of Communication Disorders* 32: 251–269.
Meltzoff AN (2007) 'Like me': A foundation for social cognition. *Developmental Science* 10: 126–134.
Meltzoff AN (2007) The 'Like Me' framework for recognizing and becoming an intentional agent. *Acta Psychologica* 124: 26–43.
Meltzoff AN and Prinz W (eds.) (2002) *The Imitative Mind: Development, Evolution and Brain Bases.* Cambridge: Cambridge University Press.
Nadel J and Butterworth G (eds.) (1999) *Imitation in Infancy.* Cambridge: Cambridge University Press.
Nehaniv CL and Dautenhahn K (eds.) (2007) *Imitation and Social Learning in Robots, Humans, and Animals: Behavioural, Social and Communicative Dimensions.* Cambridge: Cambridge University Press.
Piaget J (1962) *Play, Dreams and Imitation in Childhood.* (Attengno C and Hodgson FM (Trans.)) New York: Norton.
Rogers SJ and Williams JHG (2006) *Imitation and the Social Mind: Autism and Typical Development.* New York: Guilford.

Intellectual Disabilities

D J Fidler and J S Jameson, Colorado State University, Fort Collins, CO, USA

© 2008 Elsevier Inc. All rights reserved.

Glossary

Adaptive behavior – The ability of an individual to perform behaviors that evidence age-appropriate and culturally appropriate levels of personal independence and social responsibility.

Behavioral phenotype – The observable expression of behavioral traits; in this case a profile of behaviors associated with a specific genetic disorder.

Diagnostic overshadowing – The tendency of a clinician to attribute co-morbid psychiatric symptoms to the presence of mental retardation/intellectual disability or a syndrome associated with mental retardation/intellectual disability.

Dual diagnosis – The diagnosis of comorbid psychiatric disorders in addition to intellectual disability.

Early intervention – A comprehensive set of services that are provided to children from birth to age three and their families to enhance a child's developmental potential.

Familial mental retardation – According to Zigler, mental retardation that results from the interaction between inherited and environmental factors, leading to a designation.

Indirect effects – The impact that behavioral characteristics associated with specific genetic disorders impact family members, educators, and other members of the community.

Individualized education plan – A plan that describes the educational program that has been designed to meet the unique needs of a child receiving US special education services (ages 3–18 years); it outlines the needs, goals, strategies, and methods of assessment that will guide instruction and intervention strategies.

Individualized family service plan – In the US, contains information about the services necessary to facilitate a child's development (ages 0–3 years) and enhance the family's capacity to facilitate the child's development; family members and service providers work as a team to plan, implement, and evaluate services tailored to the family's unique concerns, priorities, and resources.

Mental retardation/intellectual disability – According to the 2002 definition from the American Association of Mental Retardation, "a disability characterized by significant limitations both in intellectual functioning and in adaptive behavior as expressed in conceptual, social, and practical adaptive skills" that originates before the age of 18 years.

Organic mental retardation – According to Zigler, mental retardation that results from a biological insult on the genetic, neurodevelopmental, or pre/perinatal level.

Special education – Specially designed educational instruction, including supplementary aids and related services that allow a child with a disability to benefit meaningfully from his or her educational program.

Undifferentiated mental retardation – According to Zigler, mental retardation that cannot be reliably attributed to either organic or familial causes.

Introduction

According to the most current definition put forth in 2002 by the American Association on Mental Retardation (AAMR), the term mental retardation refers to "a disability characterized by significant limitations both in intellectual functioning and in adaptive behavior as expressed in conceptual, social, and practical adaptive skills." To highlight the developmental nature of mental retardation, this definition specified that cognitive limitations and adaptive behavior deficits must originate before the age of 18 years. The AAMR also stipulated that there are additional assumptions that should be made when applying the current definition of intellectual disability/mental retardation. First, functioning difficulties must be understood within the context of the community and environments that are appropriate for an individual's chronological age and cultural background. Second, appropriate assessment techniques that lead to a diagnosis of mental retardation must take both cultural/linguistic background and issues related to motor, sensory, and communicative functioning into account. The third assumption relates to the recognition that challenges in functioning often occur simultaneously with areas of strength in functioning. Fourth, one of the main purposes of identifying an individual's challenges relates to developing a profile of supports to address the individual's needs. And the final assumption of the AAMR definition relates to the idea that well-planned support systems implemented over time should lead to improvement in the functioning of the individual with intellectual disability/mental retardation.

While this definition of the construct 'mental retardation' is widely used in clinical and educational settings, it is the product of many decades of change. The most recent changes relate to the use of the term 'mental retardation' itself, which has increasingly fallen out of favor in both the advocacy and practice communities. In 2006, the majority of members of the AAMR voted to change the name of their organization to the American Association on Intellectual and Developmental Disabilities. This is the culmination of a larger movement worldwide to discontinue the use of the term mental retardation, in favor of terms such as intellectual disability, cognitive disabilities, and the more global term developmental disabilities. Thus, while the term mental retardation is still currently used in clinical and some educational settings, the term is becoming increasingly obsolete as organizations formally adopt other, more socially acceptable, terms. For the purposes of this article, the term mental retardation will be used to discuss any historic issues involving the definition of the phenomenon, but the term intellectual disability will be used for all current issues and topics. In addition, to illustrate the complex nature of this construct, in the following sections we will focus on the history of mental retardation/intellectual disability in the US, though additional cross-national information will be included in the discussion of service delivery.

Definition and Categorization

Definition History

In addition to changes in terminology, throughout much of the twentieth century, the behavioral sciences have struggled to operationalize a definition of mental retardation that defines accurately and humanely the specific characteristics that are common among individuals in this category. The many changes in terminology and the definition of mental retardation/intellectual disability reflect a century-long history of challenge regarding the science and study of individuals with impaired or delayed cognitive development. These struggles have led to many definitions, technical terms, and clinical criteria that often changed in accordance with broader political and societal movements. Regardless of the variations, the definition of mental retardation has had importance beyond the scientific community as throughout much of its recent history, the definition has had a direct impact on eligibility for services from government agencies.

The earliest definitions of mental retardation focused mainly on intellectual functioning exclusively, with the use of IQ tests serving as the main diagnostic criterion. In the 1920s, the AAMR introduced a classification scheme that categorized individuals according to the severity of their impairments, dividing the IQ ranges by 25 point ranges, with the cut-off IQ score for mental retardation designated at 75. With the introduction of the first edition of the Diagnostic and Statistical Manual in the 1950s, the term mental deficiency was introduced by the American Psychiatric Association (APA), with severity of impairment denoted by the terms mild deficiency (IQ range 70–85), moderate deficiency (IQ range 50–69), and severe deficiency (IQ of 49 and below). In one of the many controversial turns in the definition's history, this competing definition put forth by the APA designated the cut-off for mental deficiency at 10 IQ points higher than the earlier AAMR definition. This is the first of several differences between the APA and AAMR definitions to come in the latter part of the twentieth century. While these early definitions focused exclusively on intellectual functioning and IQ scores, during the first half of the twentieth century various opinions were expressed that IQ-only definitions were insufficient to characterize the true nature of mental retardation. By the 1930s and 1940s, the discussion of the definition of mental retardation widened to include competence in one's own environment. This led to an updated AAMR definition in the 1960s, that included impairments in a construct titled 'adaptive behavior', in addition to subaverage intellectual functioning that originates in the developmental period. This 1960s definition also raised the IQ score cut-off to 85, in line with the APA definition at the time, and established five categories of severity of impairment: borderline, mild, moderate, severe, and profound mental retardation.

Those who have analyzed the history of the definition of mental retardation often note that this change mirrored the 1960s movement to be more inclusive in providing services to individuals in need. However, it is also noted that changes in the IQ cut-off raised the number of individuals who met at least the borderline definition of mental retardation to 16% of the general population, with concerns raised that there was an over-representation of minorities included in this range.

In addition, the introduction of the adaptive-behavior aspect of the definition proved controversial, with difficulties relating to reliability of assessments of this dimension, and the practicality of its use in actual diagnostic situations. The 1970s definition of mental retardation put forth by the AAMR made some minor changes in wording, specifying that subaverage general intellectual functioning must be 'significant', and that it must 'exist concurrently' with adaptive-behavior deficits. But one change had a strong impact, as the IQ cut-off was lowered to 70, lowering the percentage of individuals meeting the criteria to roughly 2% of the general population. Minor wording changes were also made to the AAMR definition in the 1980s, with specifications that the onset of mental retardation should occur before the age of 18, rather than the more general wording regarding manifestation during the developmental period as mentioned earlier. Perhaps the most controversial changes to the AAMR definition of mental retardation were introduced in the 1990s. Substantial changes were made to the AAMR definition of mental retardation, with specification that an individual must show impairment in two of 10 specific adaptive behavior skill areas. In addition, another major change related to the categorization scheme, that shifted from an IQ-based 'severity of impairment' approach to categorization of 'intensities of needed supports' (intermittent, limited, extensive, and pervasive), though the use of this system was challenged by the lack of readily available instruments for measuring these levels of need. Finally, this definition imprecisely identified the IQ cut-off as '70 to 75 or below', leaving the range of individuals meeting the criteria ranging from 2% to 5% of the general population. These changes proved to be so controversial that many organizations and agencies rejected the categorization scheme, and some voiced the need to develop their own definition for mental retardation. Others, like the APA, opted to adopt the new categorization scheme, but maintained clarity regarding an IQ cut-off with their prior designation of 70 (rather than 70–75). The 2002 definition of mental retardation, however, has reverted back to a severity of impairment categorization scheme and more general notions of adaptive behavior.

Adaptive Behavior

The term adaptive behavior refers to the ability of an individual to perform behaviors that evidence age-appropriate and culturally appropriate levels of personal independence and social responsibility. The inclusion of the adaptive behavior construct in the formal definition of mental retardation in the latter half of the twentieth century reflected awareness that intellectual functioning was not the sole predictor of one's ability to function in society. In addition, the inclusion of this construct was meant to encourage clinicians and educators to focus on remediation of disabilities, rather than simply categorizing children according to specific groups.

Adaptive behavior assessment became an important means of identifying behaviors that facilitated deinstitutionalization in the 1960s and brought about an increased awareness of the need for rehabilitation for individuals with disabilities in their communities. With the shift in focus from treatment and service delivery in the 1960s to normalization and legal rights in the 1970s, legislation was passed in some states that designated adaptive behavior assessment as a crucial measure of functioning. This reflected a concern that without adaptive behavior assessment and consideration of performance outside of academic contexts, there would be an over-representation of minorities in special education settings. By the 1980s, adaptive behavior assessment was seen as foundational for developing instructional approaches that would prepare individuals for living in their communities. The 1980s also brought about increased research attention into the construct of adaptive behavior in individuals with intellectual disability, leading to some specific criticism of the construct from researchers' perspectives. Some researchers argued that problematic aspects of the adaptive behavior construct – including lack of cohesive factor structure, lack of consensus regarding the best method for assessment, differing opinions regarding the relationship between intelligence and adaptive functioning – limited its utility.

Over the last few decades, the notion of adaptive behavior shifted from a broad concept to a more specific delineation of competence in specific areas. In the 1992 definition of mental retardation, adaptive behavior was redefined as adaptive skills comprising the following areas: communication, self-care, home living, social skills, community use, self-direction, health and safety, functional academics, leisure, and work. While these skill areas were thought to be related to the need for supports, and thus improved the characterization of individuals with mental retardation, these changes did not silence the debate regarding the utility of the adaptive behavior construct. Among the main criticisms of the construct was the argument that, practically speaking, most clinicians did not use the construct when making a diagnosis. The 2002 definition of mental retardation has reverted back to the term adaptive behavior (instead delineating adaptive skill areas), with a renewed focus on adaptation in conceptual, social, and practical areas; however, the debate over the use of the construct in clinical and educational settings continues.

Two-Group Approach

Amidst these definitional issues, an additional view for categorizing individuals with mental retardation became prominent in the latter half of the twentieth century. This new categorization approach arose when researchers began to note that there are more cases of children with IQ scores lower than 50 than would be expected, based on a normal statistical distribution. Various theorists began to speculate that there were various pathways leading to mental retardation, culminating in Edward Zigler's argument that there are two distinct groups of individuals with mental retardation. The first pathway is through the interaction between inherited and environmental factors, leading to a designation of familial or cultural mental retardation. The second pathway is through a biological insult that could happen on the genetic, neurodevelopmental, or pre/perinatal level, leading to a designation of organic mental retardation. Zigler argued that the distinction between familial and organic mental retardation is so important that it should be included alongside intellectual functioning for the classification of individuals with mental retardation. Included in this scheme was also a group of individuals with 'undifferentiated' mental retardation, for whom a reliable assignment to a group was not possible. This undifferentiated group has historically received very little research attention, and thus, Zigler's approach has been called the 'two-group' approach for its primary distinction between mental retardation due to organic versus nonorganic causes.

Within this two-group approach to categorization, additional designations were made by Zigler and his colleagues. Within the familial group, they included children who had at least one parent with mental retardation; isolated cases of children who had parents of normal intelligence and from appropriate home environment, but inherited low intelligence; and children who experienced sociocultural deprivation. Within the organic group, Zigler included children with chromosomal disorders, metabolic disorders, neurological impairments, congenital birth defects, and perinatal complications. He theorized that children in the familial mental retardation group would show 'similar sequences' of development, and thus would pass through the stages of typical development in the same sequence as typically developing children, albeit at a slower pace. He also argued that children in the familial mental retardation group would show 'similar structures' of development, thus showing the same organization of developmental constructs as typically developing children. It is important to note that Zigler did not argue that the similar sequence and similar structure hypotheses would apply to children in the organic mental retardation group. Subsequent researchers argued for a more 'liberal' application of Zigler's developmental theories, suggesting that children with organic etiologies of mental retardation, such as Down syndrome, may conform to the similar sequence and similar structure hypotheses as well.

Etiology-Specific Approach

As an extension of Zigler's two-group approach to classifying individuals with mental retardation, Robert Hodapp, Jake Burack, and other researchers in the developmental approach argued that greater differentiation was needed within the organic mental retardation group. Specifically, they argued that it would advance both science and practice in mental retardation to distinguish among children with different organic syndromes, particularly among children with different genetic disorders. There are currently over 1000 known genetic disorders associated with intellectual disability that have been identified to date. Research on a small subset of these disorders suggests that there are identifiable patterns of outcome associated with these disorders, which may inform both the basic science of gene–brain–behavior pathways, as well as the delivery of educational and intervention services for individuals with intellectual disability.

In the past few decades, many research endeavors have been aimed at characterizing behavioral phenotypes, or the various patterns of behavioral outcomes associated with specific genetic disorders. Though there have been debates over what constitutes a behavioral phenotype, especially with respect to the issues of specificity and pervasiveness of specific symptoms, there is some emerging consensus regarding a middle ground. Elisabeth Dykens' definition of a behavioral phenotype includes the probabilistic notion that children with a given genetic disorder may have a heightened probability of showing a specific outcome or set of outcomes relative to children without the syndrome. Implicit in her definition is the notion that not every child with a specific genetic disorder will show the phenotypic outcomes associated with the disorder, and that an outcome need not be totally unique to a specific group.

In further discussion on the uniqueness of the effects of genetic disorders, Robert Hodapp has noted that some outcomes are partially specific, or shared characteristics among a handful of disorders, and some characteristics are totally specific, or unique to a specific syndrome. Amidst these debates, research on behavioral phenotypes has become increasingly advanced in recent years, involving the use of more sophisticated developmental protocols, brain-imaging techniques, and genetic sequencing. These studies have made it possible to characterize the impact of genetic disorders such as Down syndrome, fragile X syndrome, Williams syndrome, Prader–Willi syndrome, Smith–Magenis syndrome, and 5p-syndrome on development in the areas of cognition, language, social and emotional functioning, motoric functioning, and outcomes related to psychopathology.

Dual Diagnosis

While the term 'intellectual disability' has referred to individuals with cognitive impairments and difficulties with day-to-day adaptation, individuals with intellectual disability are often at risk for showing other behavior problems beyond those captured in this definition. As a result, many individuals have been dually diagnosed with both intellectual disability and other co-morbid conditions, such as psychiatric disorders. The reported prevalence of individuals with dual diagnoses varies from study to study, with some reports as high as 40–50% of children with intellectual disability in middle childhood showing some degree of psychiatric symptomatology.

In addition, children with specific causes of their intellectual disabilities may be vulnerable to some psychiatric conditions, but not others. For example, individuals with Prader–Willi syndrome show increased rates of obsessive-compulsive behavior, including hoarding behavior, as well as well-documented obsessive food ideation symptoms. Children with Williams syndrome are at increased risk of showing difficulties in the area of anxiety and heightened fear responses. While children with Down syndrome tend to show lower levels of psychopathology than other children with intellectual disability, there is evidence to suggest that these individuals are at increased risk for autism and autism spectrum disorders, relative to the prevalence rates observed in the typically developing population.

Diagnosis of a comorbid psychiatric condition along with intellectual disability may pose many challenges to clinicians and therapists. Researchers in this area have noted that many clinicians are prone to attribute the behavior problems associated with psychiatric conditions to the diagnosis that a child already has, leading to the phenomenon called diagnostic overshadowing. In other words, the diagnosis that a child already has – for example, Down syndrome – becomes the explanation for poor communication and impairments in social interaction, rather than exploring the alternative possibility that the child might meet criteria for autism as well. This is notable in that impairments in social interaction are unusual in most children with Down syndrome, who tend to show competence in achieving early intersubjective milestones in infancy and toddlerhood. Thus, understanding the relative contributions of the intellectual disability and a possible comorbid disorder may make it possible to improve the precision with which decisions are made regarding appropriate services and intervention strategies.

Yet, making dual diagnoses of this nature can be challenging for a number of reasons. First, the manifestation of a psychiatric disorder may be modified in an individual with intellectual disability. For example, an anxiety disorder may manifest itself differently in a child who has pronounced expressive language delays versus a child who has an age-appropriate ability to express his/herself. In addition, when a child has pronounced intellectual disability that are in the severe or profound IQ score range, additional difficulties present themselves with regard to accurate dual diagnosis. If a low-functioning child with Down syndrome shows many of the behavioral hallmarks of autism, including poor joint attentions skills, poor initiation, language delays, or a lack of pretend play, it is possible that the child simply has not yet reached an overall developmental level wherein a clinician would expect to observe those behaviors. As a result, an autism diagnosis may not be appropriate in this situation, especially if these deficits are observed in the context of some other, more basic behaviors that evidence impairment in social interaction (e.g., sharing enjoyment or interest).

Identification, Intervention, and Education

Identifying Young Children with Intellectual Disability

Evaluation of young children during the first 2 years of life involves identifying children who already show pronounced developmental delays, as well as identifying children who are at high risk of showing later developmental delays. Newborn assessment begins in the earliest moments of life with Apgar scoring. Lower Apgar scores indicate an increased risk of neurological impairment, and newborns with low scores generally require close observation during the first weeks of life. Additional screening during the first few months of life includes assessment of reflexes and screening for genetic abnormalities via blood testing, if needed.

The pathways into the referral process vary internationally. For example, in Spain and many other countries, children are monitored by pediatricians or pediatric nurses, who use protocols that detect warning signs for developmental delays during regular visits. The Israeli early intervention system stresses both the importance of parent-initiated referrals, as well as referrals through the public well-baby care centers that are found throughout the country. In addition, infants determined to be at greater risk because of low birth weight or other factors, are referred to a child development center for closer monitoring. In Sweden, referrals can come from parents or Child Health Services, but often children who do not have established disabilities are referred by preschool professionals because of the general system of preschool services provided to all children in that country.

Though systems for identifying children with or at risk for intellectual disability vary greatly internationally, there are some features that are commonly found. In general, the first line in detecting developmental delays involves those professionals who have the greatest interaction with infants, including pediatricians and other healthcare workers. If delays are suspected, additional professionals are recruited into the clinical team, including developmental specialists, social workers, and other interventionists. Subsequent to the newborn-screening process, additional evaluation of development can take place throughout infancy, with measures such as the Bayley Scales of Infant Development and the Mullen Scales of Early Learning.

Specific assessment of the development of areas such as language, social–emotional functioning, and adaptive behavior can also be conducted with standardized measures that have become the norm for typically developing infants and other infants with delays. Because of their psychometric properties, in the US, commonly used measures in infancy include the Preschool Language Scales IV, the Reynell Developmental Language Scales, the Battelle Developmental Inventory, the Brazelton's Neonatal Behavioral Assessment Scale, and the MacArthur Communication Development Inventories (Infant and Toddler form). For preschool-aged children, assessment of various aspects of development continues. To assess cognitive development, commonly used measures include the Wechsler Preschool and Primary Scale of Intelligence – Revised and the Stanford Binet. Language assessment is often assessed using the *Peabody Picture Vocabulary Test* (3rd edn.) and the *Preschool Language Scales* (4th edn.). Social and adaptive behavior development is often measured using the Vineland Adaptive Behavior Scales and the AAMR Adaptive Behavior Scales.

In general, children with lower IQ scores tend to be identified earlier in development than children with more mild impairments. Thus, the prevalence of children with IQ scores below 50 or so remains somewhat steady throughout development. In contrast, children with milder intellectual disability tend to be identified later in development, often upon beginning formal schooling. As a result, the prevalence of children with mental retardation tends to increase for children once they reach school years.

Early Intervention

Beyond identification of intellectual disability in young children, a primary goal of early assessment is to enable children with identified intellectual disability to receive appropriate early intervention services. Early intervention is a comprehensive set of services that are provided to children from birth through the early childhood years (generally lasting through to ages 3–6 years, depending on the country) and their families to enhance a child's developmental potential. The family-focused approach to early intervention is found in many different countries, including the US, Austria, Canada, the UK, Israel, Spain, and Sweden, among others. The structure and implementation of early intervention services internationally varies greatly. In this section, we explore the model implemented in the US, though references for additional information are given ahead about early intervention in other countries.

In the US, federal law Individuals with Disabilities Education Act (IDEA), with the 1997 Amendment (Public Law 105–17), specifies that children under the age of three years are eligible for early-intervention services should they show delays in one or more areas of development or if they have a diagnosis of a condition that is generally associated with developmental delays. Named 'Part C', early-intervention services include a few over-riding principles: families are at the center of the early-intervention process; and services should be provided to young children within natural contexts (typically the child's home). A service coordinator is assigned to each child to act as the family's main point of contact for the provision of these services. In many cases, early intervention involves a teacher (or an early-intervention specialist), various therapists, the family, and the child, working together to minimize the effects of the child's disability on his or her development. Specialists in the area of family training, counseling, respite care, home visits, physical therapy, occupational therapy, speech-language therapy, audiological services, and many other areas may be included in this team according to each individual child's and family's needs.

In the US early intervention involves the development of an individual family service plan (IFSP), which is created by a team in order to identify both short- and long-term goals and strategies for early intervention. The IFSP contains information about the services necessary to facilitate a child's development and enhance the family's capacity to facilitate the child's development. Through the IFSP process, family members and service providers work as a team to plan, implement, and evaluate services tailored to the family's unique concerns, priorities, and resources. According to IDEA, included in the IFSP are the following elements: (1) Current level of functioning – this section includes a detailed description of the child's present levels of development in all areas (cognitive, communication, social or emotional, and adaptive development). (2) Resources – this area outlines the family's resources and concerns relating to enhancing the development of their child. (3) Desired goals and outcomes – this section lists the major outcomes to be achieved for the child and the family. It includes the criteria, procedures, and timelines used to determine progress; and whether modifications or revisions of the outcomes or services are necessary. (4) Access to early intervention services – specific early-intervention services are identified that are necessary to meet the unique needs of the child and the family. This section also indicates the frequency, intensity, and the method of delivery for recommended services. (5) Integration into environments with typically developing peers – this section describes the natural environments in which services will be provided, including reasoning as to the extent, if any, to which the services will not be provided in a natural environment. (6) Timeline – the timeline documents the projected starting and ending dates for delivery of services. (7) Identification of service provider – this section, unique to the IFSP, identifies the specific service provider who will be responsible for implementing the plan and coordinating with other agencies and persons. (8) Plans for transition into the formal educational environment – this final section identifies the steps to support the child's transition to preschool or other appropriate services upon reaching the age of three.

Special Education

Special education services refer to specially designed educational instruction, including supplementary aids and related services, that allow a child with a disability to benefit meaningfully from his or her educational program. These strategies include both instructional accommodations and developmentally designed learning environments inside the classroom and outside intervention programs with specialists. The changes in attitudes toward educating children with intellectual disability are reflected in the twentieth century history of disability law in the US. Prior to the passage of IDEA, in the US, the standards for educating children with disabilities varied tremendously among states. When it was first enacted in 1975, IDEA introduced the notion of guaranteed 'free, appropriate public education' to children with disabilities and mandated that, to the 'maximum extent appropriate', they be educated with their non-disabled peers in the 'least restrictive environment'. In addition to creating standards for the education of children with intellectual disability and other conditions, IDEA brought into the public schools slightly more than 1 million children with disabilities who had previously received only limited educational services.

Beyond guaranteeing children an education that was free and appropriate, an important shift in education for children with intellectual disability in the US came in the stipulation that children should be educated in the 'least restrictive environment'. Prior to this landmark legislation, children with disabilities who were permitted into public schooling environments were often assigned to self-contained classrooms. The implementation of IDEA in educational settings was not without controversy. Teachers and administrators cited issues related to a lack of preparation and training to accommodate the needs of children with developmental delays, and parents of typically developing children expressed concerns over the issues of equity and access to quality. In particular, some parents were concerned that the quality of the education that their child would receive might be in some way compromised by the presence of a child with intellectual disability in the classroom.

The concept of full inclusion calls for teaching students with disabilities in regular classrooms, rather than in special classes or pull-out sessions, and is now adopted in many countries, including the UK and Australia. In the US, federal special education law states that, to the 'maximum extent appropriate', children with disabilities should be educated with nondisabled peers in the 'least restrictive environment possible'. While inclusion has grown more common, most severely disabled students are still typically included in regular education classes for only a few subjects a day, such as art or physical education. The inclusion of children with disabilities in the general education classroom and access to a developmentally appropriate curriculum has improved in recent years with increased training for teachers in all classrooms and a better understanding of intervention strategies and assessments.

Individualized Education Plan

Education planning for older children with intellectual disability

From age 3 to 21 years, children with intellectual disability in the US may qualify for special education services through the public educational system. Criteria state that the child must have a disability that interferes with their ability to benefit from a regular educational program. Within an educational environment, specialists, educators, and parents work together to identify common goals and strategies to assist the child with developmental disabilities in achieving critical developmental milestones. Once a child reaches the age of 3, they no longer receive an IFSP through Part C services. Rather, children over the age of three are given an individualized education plan (IEP) to guide their development and learning both in and out of the classroom. Each child's IEP describes, among other things, the educational program that has been designed to meet that child's unique needs. It is created in collaboration and reviewed at least once per year, possibly more often, if requested by a parent or teacher.

The IEP includes pertinent information outlining the needs, goals, strategies, and methods of assessment that will guide instruction and intervention strategies. Included in the IEP are the following elements: (1) Current performance – the IEP must describe the child's current performance (known as present levels of educational performance). The statement about current performance includes how the child's disability affects his or her involvement and progress in the general curriculum. (2) Annual goals – these are goals that the child can reasonably accomplish in 1 year. Goals are broken down into short-term objectives or benchmarks. Goals may be academic, address social or behavioral needs, relate to physical needs, or address other educational needs. The goals must be measurable; it must be possible to quantify whether or not the student has achieved the goals. (3) Special education and related services – this section outlines the particular intervention strategies and how they will be implemented during the child's time at school. (4) Participation with nondisabled children – addresses the amount of time spent in a classroom with typically developing peers and the amount of time in pull-out intervention programs. (5) Dates and places – the IEP must state when services will begin, how often they will be provided, where they will be provided, and how long they will last. (6) Measuring progress – the IEP must state how the child's progress will be measured and how parents will be informed of that progress.

The IEP differs from the IFSP in several ways. First, the IFSP revolves around the family, as opposed to the educational environment where older children spend the majority of their day. The IFSP includes outcomes targeted for the family, while the IEP focuses primarily on the eligible child. The IFSP includes the notion of natural environments that encompass home or community settings such as parks, childcare, and gym classes. This community-oriented focus allows for learning interventions in everyday routines and activities, rather than limiting the implementation to formal educational settings. Finally, it names a service coordinator who will assist the family during the development, implementation, and evaluation of the plan.

Etiology and Education Planning

With a new wealth of knowledge regarding the impact of specific genetic syndromes on behavioral outcomes, there is a growing awareness that this information might be used to inform intervention and educational planning for children with intellectual disability. Given that children with different genetic disorders can be predisposed to very different profiles of strength and weakness in areas such as cognition, language, social–emotional functioning, and other important areas of development, it may be possible to incorporate these profiles into the educational planning process for children with different disorders. This approach can be incorporated into educational programming for children in primary and elementary education settings, as well as early intervention programs for infants, toddlers, and preschool-aged children.

In terms of instruction in educational settings, it has been recommended that aspects of a child's syndrome-specific predispositions be used to modify the presentation of materials and to inform the selection of instructional techniques. For example, children with Williams syndrome are predisposed to deficits in various aspects of visuospatial processing, but they show relative strengths in the area of verbal processing. Children with Down syndrome show the opposite profile, evidencing pronounced deficits in verbal processing and strengths in visual processing. Thus, in coordinating instructional techniques for a child with Down syndrome and a child with Williams syndrome – even if they show similar overall severity of impairment – it would be advantageous to take into account these diverging profiles with subtle modifications. A simple example might be to support verbal instruction with visual scaffolds for a child with Down syndrome, and to support visually based instruction with verbal scaffolds for a child with Williams syndrome. A teacher who is informed regarding these information-processing profiles might make such decisions seamlessly, without needing to disrupt his/her instruction in a larger class setting, with great impact. Other etiology-linked aspects of learning may be taken into account in this type of instructional modification, including executive function, simultaneous/sequential processing, and motivation.

In terms of early-intervention planning, it may be possible to use information regarding etiology-specific predispositions to identify potential areas of vulnerability during the earliest stages of development. Interventionists may take into account, for example, that the majority of middle childhood-aged children with Down syndrome show strengths in receptive language and pronounced delays in expressive language. When treating a toddler with Down syndrome, rather than waiting for a distinct split between receptive and expressive language to emerge in order to begin to address the issue with intervention, an interventionist could use knowledge about this predisposition to target a potential split from very early stages of development. They may choose to monitor early precursors of expressive language to identify an evidence of a disrupted pathway, and make effective intervention-planning decisions from the beginning. Thus, using an etiology-specific approach it may be possible to monitor areas of later strength and weakness from the earliest stages of development in order to detect and target subtle manifestations of a later, more pronounced, profile.

Critics argue that such an approach might not be cost-effective in that not all children with a given syndrome show a given outcome. In addition, there are concerns regarding defining groups too narrowly in the educational system such that it becomes both costly and cumbersome to address the needs of each identified group. These issues will doubtlessly be explored in debates regarding special education policy in upcoming years. Yet, as scientific research in the area of behavioral phenotypes continues to become more sophisticated, it may be inevitable that families and educators work together to connect phenotypic learning profiles in various syndromes with educational pedagogy.

Families of Children with Intellectual Disability

Though a great deal of attention was placed on the definition of mental retardation during the first half of the twentieth century, little attention was placed on families of individuals with mental retardation. In the 1960s, however, families became a focus of research attention as a greater emphasis was placed on improving child outcomes. It was theorized that families can have a direct influence on a child's achievement and their adaptation to their environment, and targeting home environments might be an important way to improve outcomes for children with mental retardation.

The main focus of initial research on families of children with mental retardation was on negative outcomes in the family, with an emphasis on issues such as social isolation, divorce, sibling identity, and parental depression. Case reports focused largely on parental experiences of mourning and the responses of parents to the loss of the 'ideal' typically developing child they had expected. More current research continues to focus on negative outcomes to some degree, though the focus of such work has been updated to include issues such as work–family balance and quality of the spousal relationship. In addition, more recent work has focused on the notion of stress in families of children with intellectual disability, where such a child is viewed as one stressor in the larger family environment. The notion of stress in this line of research refers to a perceived disparity between the situational demands and one's ability to respond to them. Thus, in families of children with intellectual disability, stress may result from a mismatch between the demands of caring for a child with cognitive impairments and the resources available to the family to address those needs.

Recent research on outcomes in families of children with intellectual disability has also begun to focus on positive aspects of the parenting experience, such as feelings of satisfaction and enjoyment. Parents in these studies have reported feelings of reward in watching their child make small achievements, enjoying the various aspects of everyday life, enjoying when demands were decreased, or the child's prognosis was good. Other positive outcomes in research on families of children with intellectual disability are parents reporting that their child with intellectual disability may provide challenges but also makes them feel needed, and even provides a sense of purpose in life. Research on families of children with intellectual disability has also focused on coping style and family supports. Factors impacting parental coping involve demographic factors such as Socioeconomic status, and also cognitive factors such as being problem-focused versus emotion-focused. Social support networks can influence outcomes like maternal stress and family adjustment, though some characteristics of support networks, such as increased density (many members of the support network are known to one another), may be less helpful than others.

Specific child characteristics may also have an impact on family outcomes as well. Some studies show that the child's age is positively correlated with family stress. These findings may support a 'wear-and-tear hypothesis', where the stress associated with parenting a child with a disability builds up over time. Other studies do not show this positive association between child age and stress, and some suggest that there is a lack of linearity in the relationship between the two. A nonlinear model of stress in families of children with intellectual disability suggests that specific periods in the child's development may increase a family's vulnerability to stress, while other periods of time may place families at lower risk for stress. For example, certain age milestones throughout development may lead parents to make normative comparisons to typically developing children, leading to 'wistful' thoughts about what their child may have been experiencing if they did not have intellectual disability.

Another child characteristic that has been shown to impact family outcomes is maladaptive behavior. Problem-behavior, associated with outcomes such as parental depression, pessimism, time demands, dependency and management, lifespan care, and maladaptive behavior, is a stronger predictor of parenting stress than some other possible factors, such as severity of cognitive impairment. Family outcomes may also be influenced by the specific etiology of the child's intellectual disability. It has been hypothesized that genetic disorders predispose children to specific outcomes, and that these outcomes may indirectly affect family stress, coping, and other outcomes. Robert Hodapp termed this phenomenon the indirect effects of genetic syndromes associated with intellectual disability, and has shown that different genetic disorders indirectly affect families in various ways. For example, families of children with Down syndrome report lower levels of overall family stress than families of children with other genetic disorders, such as Williams syndrome, and Smith–Magenis syndrome. These findings have been replicated in several studies, and possible reasons for the disparity may be related to child-personality characteristics, lower levels of maladaptive behavior, perceived immaturity, and parent-demographic characteristics.

Summary

In the past century, important advances have been made in both science and practice in intellectual disability. The needs of children with intellectual disability and their families have moved to the center of education service delivery in many countries, and early-intervention practices have become standard in many countries for children who are at risk or identified as having intellectual and developmental disabilities. However, the historical struggle to define and treat intellectual disability in the most humane and appropriate ways will likely continue into the next century. As attitudes continue to shift, it is likely that the political, economic, and social environments will continue to intersect and influence the ways in which children with intellectual disability are identified and educated.

See also: Bayley Scales of Infant Development; Genetics and Inheritance.

Suggested Readings

Borthwick-Duffy SA, Palmer DS, and Lane KL (1996) One size doesn't fit all: Full inclusion and individual differences. *Journal of Behavioral Education* 6: 311–329.

Dykens EM (1995) Measuring behavioral phenotypes: Provocations from the 'new genetics'. *American Journal on Mental Retardation* 99(5): 522–532.

Guralnick MJ (1997) Second-generation research in the field of early intervention. In: Guralnick MJ (ed.) *The Effectiveness of Early Intervention*, pp. 3–20. Baltimore, MD: Paul H. Brookes Publishing.

Guralnick MJ (2005) *The Developmental Systems Approach to Early Intervention*. Baltimore, MD: Paul H. Brookes Publishing.

Hodapp RM (1997) Direct and indirect behavioral effects of different genetic disorders of mental retardation. *American Journal on Mental Retardation* 102: 67–79.

Hodapp RM (2004) Behavioral phenotypes: Beyond the two group approach. *International Review of Research in Mental Retardation and Developmental Disabilities* 29: 1–30.

Hodapp RM and Fidler DJ (1999) Special education and genetics: Connections for the 21st century. *Journal of Special Education* 33: 130–137.

Lipsky DK and Gartner A (1998) Factors for successful inclusion: Learning from the past, looking toward the future. In: Vitello SJ and Mithaug DE (eds.) *Inclusive Schooling: National and International Perspectives*, pp. 98–112. Mahurah, NJ: Lawrence Erlbaum Associates.

MacMillan DL and Reschly DJ (1997) Issues of definition and classification. In: MacLean WE, Jr. (ed.) *Ellis' Handbook of Mental Deficiency, Psychological Theory and Research*, 3rd edn., pp. 47–74. Mahwah, NJ: Lawrence Erlbaum Associates.

Relevant Websites

http://www.aamr.org – AAIDD, The American Association on Intellectual and Developmental Disabilities.

http://www.assid.org.au – Australasian Society for the Study of Intellectual Disability.

http://www.dh.gov.uk – British Department of Health, Providing Health and Social Care Policy, Guidance and Publications.

http://www.iassid.org – International Association for the Scientific Study of Intellectual Disabilities.
http://www.mencap.org.uk – MENCAP, Understanding Learning Disability.
http://www.psych.org – The American Psychiatric Association.
http://www.thearc.org – The Arc.
http://www.cec.sped.org – The Council for Exceptional Children, The Voice and Vision of Special Education.
http://idea.ed.gov – U.S. Department of Education, Promoting Educational Excellence for all Americans.

Language Acquisition Theories

S Goldin-Meadow, University of Chicago, Chicago, IL, USA

© 2008 Elsevier Inc. All rights reserved.

Glossary

Canalization – Canalization in genetics is a measure of the ability of a genotype to produce the same phenotype regardless of variability in the environment. More broadly, canalization refers to the developmental path of least resistance, the path typically followed by a species.

Corpus – A large collection of spontaneously produced utterances.

Ergative languages – An ergative language is one in which the subject of an intransitive verb (e.g., 'Elmo' in "Elmo runs home") is treated in grammatical terms (word order, morphological marking) similarly to the patient of a transitive verb (e.g., 'Bert' in 'Elmo hits Bert') and differently from the agent of a transitive verb (e.g., 'Elmo' in 'Elmo hits Bert'). Ergative languages contrast with nominative languages such as English; in English, both the subject of the intransitive verb ('*Elmo* runs home') and the agent of a transitive verb ('*Elmo* hits Bert') are placed before the verb, whereas the patient of a transitive verb is placed after the verb ('Elmo hits *Bert*').

Morpheme – A meaning-bearing linguistic form that cannot be divided into smaller meaning-bearing forms, for example, 'unbearable' is composed of three morphemes, *un*, *bear*, and *able*.

Morphology – The study of how morphemes are combined into stems and words.

Motherese/parentese – The kind of speech that mothers (and others) produce when talking to infants and young children. It is characterized by higher pitches, a wider range of pitches, longer pauses, and shorter phrases than speech addressed to adults (also referred to as child-directed speech or infant-directed speech).

Null-subject languages – Some languages allow pronouns to be omitted from a sentence when the referents of those pronouns can be inferred from context (e.g., Japanese); other languages do not allow pronouns to be dropped (e.g., English). Languages that only allow omission of the subject pronoun are called 'null-subject languages' (e.g., Spanish, Italian).

Predicate – The portion of a clause that expresses something about the subject.

Segmentation – The breaking down of a unit into smaller parts; for example, the word 'dislike' can be broken down into two smaller parts (in this case, morphemes), 'dis' and 'like'.

Specific language impairment – A delay in language development in the absence of any clear sensory or cognitive disorder (as labeled in the *Diagnostic and Statistical Manual of Mental Disorders*, 4th edn.).

Subject – The element in a clause that refers to the most prominent participant in the action of the verb; often (but not always) this participant is the one that does or initiates the action named by the verb.

Syntax – The study of how words combine to form phrases, clauses, and sentences.

Transitional probabilities – A conditionalized statistic which tracks the consistency with which elements occur together and in a particular order, baselined against individual element frequency; for example, if B follows A every time A occurs, the transitional probability for this A–B grouping is 1.00.

Introduction

The simplest technique to study the process of language learning is to do nothing more than watch and listen as children talk. In the earliest studies, researcher parents made diaries of their own child's utterances (e.g., Stern and Stern in the 1900s, and Leopold in the 1940s). The diarist's goal was to write down all of the new utterances that the child produced. Diary studies were later replaced by audio and video samples of talk from a number of children, usually over a period of years. The most famous of these modern studies is Roger Brown's longitudinal recordings of Adam, Eve, and Sarah.

Because transcribing and analyzing child talk is so labor intensive, each individual language acquisition study typically focuses on a small number of children, often interacting with their primary caregiver at home. However, advances in computer technology have made it possible for researchers to share their transcripts of child talk via the computerized Child Language Data Exchange System (CHILDES). A single researcher can now call upon data collected from spontaneous interactions in naturally occurring situations across a wide range of languages, and thus test the robustness of descriptions based on a small sample. In addition, naturalistic observations of children's talk can always be, and often are, supplemented with experimental probes that are used with larger number of subjects.

Thus, it is possible, although time-consuming, to describe what children do when they acquire language. The harder task is to figure out how they do it.

Many theories have been offered to explain how children go about the process of language learning. This article begins by reviewing the major accounts. We will find that, although there is disagreement among the theories in the details, all modern-day accounts accept the fact that children come to the language-learning situation prepared to learn. The disagreement lies in what each theory takes the child to be prepared with: A general outline of what language is? A set of processes that will lead to the acquisition of language (and language alone)? A set of processes that will lead to the acquisition of any skill, including language? The article then goes on to describe theoretical and experimental approaches that have been applied to the problem of determining the constraints that children bring to language learning. We end with an analysis of what it might mean to say that language is innate.

Theoretical Accounts of Language Learning

Behaviorist Accounts

Consistent with the psychological theories of that era, prior to the late 1950s language was considered just another behavior, one that can be acquired by the general laws of behavior. Take, for example, associative learning, a general learning process in which a new response becomes associated with a particular stimulus. Association seems like a natural way to explain how children learn the words of their language, but it is not so simple. Quine's famous theoretical puzzle highlights the problem: Imagine that you are a stranger in a foreign country with no knowledge of the local language. A native says 'gavagai' while pointing at a rabbit running in the distance. You try to associate the new response 'gavagai' with a particular stimulus, but which stimulus should you choose? The entire rabbit? Its tail? Its ears? The running event? The possibilities are limitless and associative learning solves only a small piece of the problem.

In addition to association, imitation, and reinforcement were also proposed as mechanisms by which children could learn the grammatical 'habits' that comprise language. However, even the most cursory look at how children learn language reveals that neither of these mechanisms is sufficient to bring about language learning.

Children learn the language to which they are exposed and, in this broad sense, learn language by imitation. But do children model the sentences they produce after the sentences they hear? Some do, but many children are not imitators. Moreover, the children who are imitators do not learn language any more quickly than the nonimitators. Even the children who routinely imitate do not copy everything they hear – they are selective, imitating only the parts of the sentences that they are able to process at that moment. Thus, imitation is guided as much by the child as by the sentences the child hears.

What about the responses of others to children's sentences? Parents might positively reinforce sentences their children produce that are grammatically correct and negatively reinforce sentences that are grammatically incorrect. In this way, the child might be encouraged to produce correct sentences and discouraged from producing incorrect ones. There are two problems with this account. The first is that parents do not typically respond to their children's sentences as a function of the grammatical correctness of those sentences. Parents tend to respond to the content rather than the form of their children's sentences. Second, even if children's grammatically correct sentences were treated differently from their grammatically incorrect sentences, it is still up to the child to determine what makes the correct sentences correct. For example, if the child says the grammatically correct sentence, "I colored the wall blue," and mother responds with positive reinforcement (thus ignoring the sentence's troubling content and focusing on its form), the child still has to figure out how to generalize from the sentence; she needs to understand the patterns that generate the sentence in order to recognize that one analogous sentence (e.g., "I saw the wall blue") is not grammatically correct while another (e.g., "I pounded the clay flat") is. In other words, there would still be a great deal of inductive work to be done even if children were provided with a set of correct sentences from which to generalize.

The behaviorist account of language was dealt a devastating blow with the publication in 1959 of Noam

Chomsky's review of BF Skinner's *Verbal Behavior*. Chomsky argued that adult language use cannot be adequately described in terms of sequences of behaviors or responses. A system of abstract rules underlies each individual's knowledge and use of language, and it is these rules that children acquire when they learn language. When viewed in this way, the language acquisition problem requires an entirely different sort of solution.

Nativist Accounts

The premise of the Chomskian perspective is that children are learning a linguistic system governed by subtle and abstract principles without explicit instruction and, indeed, without enough information from the input to support induction of these particular principles (as opposed to other principles) – Plato's problem or the poverty of the stimulus argument. Chomsky went on to claim that if there is not enough information in the input to explain how children learn language, the process must be supported by innate syntactic knowledge and language-specific learning procedures. The theory of Universal Grammar (UG) formulates this *a priori* knowledge in terms of principles and parameters that determine the set of possible human languages. UG is assumed to be part of the innately endowed knowledge of humans. The principles of UG provide a framework for properties of language, often leaving several (constrained) options open to be decided by the data the child comes in contact with. For example, word order freedom is a parameter of variation. Some languages (English) mandate strict word orders; others (Russian, Japanese) list a small set of admissible orders; still others (Warlpiri, an Australian aboriginal language) allow almost total scrambling of word order within a clause. Input from a given language is needed for learners to set the parameters of that language.

One important aspect of this theory is that setting a single parameter can cause a cluster of superficially unrelated grammatical properties to appear in the language. For example, the null-subject parameter involves a number of properties: whether overt subjects are required in all declarative sentences (yes in English, no in Italian), whether expletive elements such as 'it' in 'it seems' or 'there' in 'there is' are exhibited (yes in English, no in Italian), whether free inversion of subjects is allowed in simple sentences (no in English, yes in Italian), etc. The prediction is that the input necessary to set the null-subject parameter results in the simultaneous alignment of all of these aspects within a child's grammar. There is, at present, controversy over whether predictions of this sort are supported by the child language data.

Innate knowledge of the principles underlying language is, however, not sufficient to account for how children acquire language. How are children to know what a noun or a subject is in the specific language they are learning? Children obviously need to identify subjects and verbs in their language before they can determine whether the two are strictly ordered in that language, and before they can engage whatever innate knowledge they might have about how language is structured. Thus, in addition to innate syntactic knowledge, children also need learning procedures, which may themselves be language-specific.

One example is a set of rules linking semantic and syntactic categories. Under this hypothesis, children are assumed to know innately that agents are likely to be subjects, objects affected by action are likely to be direct objects, etc. All they need do is identify (using context) the agent in a scene; the linking rules allow them to infer that the term used to refer to that agent is the subject of the sentence. Their innate knowledge about how these elements are allowed to be structured can then take over. Again, controversies exist over whether child language data support these assumptions (e.g., ergative languages do not straightforwardly link agents with subjects and yet are easily acquired by young children).

Social/Cognitive Accounts

The nativist position entails essentially two claims: (1) at least some of the principles of organization underlying language are language specific and not shared with other cognitive systems, and (2) the procedures that guide the implementation of these principles are themselves innate, that is, centered in the child and not the child's environment. Note that, while these two claims often go hand-in-hand, they need not. One can imagine that the principles underlying linguistic knowledge might be specific to language and, at the same time, implemented through general, all-purpose learning mechanisms (although such mechanisms must be more complex than the mechanisms behaviorist accounts have offered). This position has come to be known as a social or cognitive account of language learning.

For example, by observing others' actions – where they look, how they stand, how they move their hands and faces – we can often guess their intentions. Young children could use this information to help them narrow down their hypotheses about what a word means. In fact, if a speaker looks at an object while uttering a novel word, a child will assume that the speaker's word refers to that object, even if the child herself is not looking at the object. In other words, children can use general cues to speaker intent to guide their guesses about language.

Children do not sound like adults when they begin to speak – clearly, there is developmental work that needs to be done. The question is what type of work is required? One possibility, favored by some nativists, is that children have in place all of the grammatical categories and syntactic principles they need; they just lack the operating systems that will allow those principles to run. The developmental work to be done does not, under this view, involve a changing grammatical system.

Another view suggests that the child's language changes dramatically during development, transforming from a system based on semantic categories to one based on syntactic categories. This transformation could be determined maturationally or guided by innate linking rules. However, the transformation could also result from an inductive leap children make on the basis of the linguistic data available to them, in conjunction with the cognitive and/or social skills they bring to the task – this inductive leap is at the heart of all social or cognitive accounts of language acquisition.

Cognitive underpinnings are obviously necessary but they may not be sufficient for the onset of linguistic skills. For example, the onset of gesture plus speech combinations that convey two elements of a proposition ('open' plus point at box) precedes the onset of two-word combinations ('open box') by several months, suggesting that the cognitive ability to express two semantic elements is not the final stumbling block to two-word combinations. More than likely, it is the inability to extract linguistic patterns from the input that presents the largest problem.

Social and cognitive accounts claim that there is, in the end, enough information in the linguistic input children hear, particularly in the context of the supportive social environments in which they live, to induce a grammatical system. Ample research indicates that adults alter the speech they direct to their children. Speech to children (often called 'motherese') is slower, shorter, higher-pitched, more exaggerated in intonation, more grammatically well-formed, and more directed in content to the present situation than speech addressed to adults. And children pay particular attention to this fine-tuned input, interpreting it in terms of their own biases or operating principles (e.g., paying attention to the ends of words).

However, one problem that arises with postulating motherese as an engine of child language learning is that child-directed speech may not be universal. In many cultures, children participate in communicative interactions as overhearers (rather than as addressees) and the speech they hear is not likely to be simplified in the same ways. Nevertheless, children in these cultures become competent users of their grammatical systems in roughly comparable timeframes. These observations suggest that there may be many developmental routes to the same end – a reasonable conjecture given the robustness of language.

One very interesting possibility that skirts the problem that children do not universally receive simplified input is that the children may do the simplifying themselves. For example, young children's memory limitations may make them less able to recall entire strings of words or morphemes. They would, as a result, be doing the analytic work required to abstract linguistic regularities on a smaller, filtered database (the 'less is more' hypothesis). This filtering may be just what children require to arrive at their linguistic systems. Moreover, it is a general process that children around the globe presumably bring, in equal measure, to the language-learning situation.

Connectionist Accounts

Connectionism is a movement in cognitive science whose goal is to explain human intellectual abilities using artificial neural networks (also known as neural nets). Neural networks are simplified models of the brain composed of large numbers of units (the analogs of neurons) and weights that measure the strength of the connections between those units. In a connectionist account, behavior is shaped by selective reinforcement of the network of interconnected units. Under this view, language development is a process of continuously adjusting the relative strengths of the connections in the network until linguistic output resembles linguistic input.

In a sense, connectionism is more of a technique for exploring language learning than an explanatory account. But connectionism does come with some theoretical baggage. For example, most connectionist models are based on the assumption that language (like all other cognitive skills) can be explained without recourse to rules.

Connectionism offers a tool for examining the tradeoff between the three components central to all theories of language learning – environment (input to the system), structures the child brings to the learning situation (architectures of the artificial system), and learning mechanisms (learning algorithms). For example, a great deal of linguistic structure is assumed to be innate on the nativist account. Connectionism can provide a way to explore how much structure needs to be built in to achieve learning, given a particular set of inputs to the system and a particular set of learning mechanisms. As another example, networks have been shown to arrive at appropriate generalizations from strings of sentences only if the memory span of the network for previously processed words begins small and gradually increases (reminiscent of the 'less is more' hypothesis described earlier). In principle, connectionism is agnostic on the question of whether the architecture of the system (the child) or the input to the system (the environment) determines the relative strengths of each connection. However, in practice, most connectionists emphasize the importance of input. And, of course, the unanswered question is what determines the units that are to be connected in the first place.

Constrained Learning

All theoretical accounts agree that human children are prepared to learn language. But what are they prepared with? Do children come to the learning situation with specific hypotheses about how language ought to be structured? Or do they come with general biases to process information in a particular way? This second view suggests that the strong inclination that children have to structure communication in language-like patterns falls out of their general processing biases coming into contact with natural language input.

The language that children learn must, at some level, be inferable from the data that are out there. After all, if linguists manage to use language data to figure out the grammar of a language, why can't children? But linguists can be selective in ways that children are not able to be. Linguists do not have to weigh all pieces of data equally, they can ask informants what an utterance means and whether it is said correctly, and they have at their disposal a great deal of data at one time. The question is – what kinds of learning mechanisms can we realistically impute to children that will allow them to make sense of the data they receive as input?

One learning mechanism that has been proposed is known as statistical learning. The assumption underlying this mechanism is that children are sensitive to the patterns in their input, and can perform rapid and complex computations of the co-occurrences among neighboring elements in that input. By performing statistical computations over a corpus, children can pick out the recurring patterns in the data and thus are less likely to be misled by individual counter-examples.

However, children must also face the problem that a corpus can be analyzed in many different ways. How do they know which computations to perform on a given corpus? Perhaps children are only able to perform a limited set of computations. If so, this limitation would effectively narrow down the range of possible patterns that could be extracted from a database. Thus, one way that children may be prepared to learn language is that they come to language learning ready to perform certain types of computations and not others.

To discover which computations young language learning children are able to perform, we can provide them with a corpus of data constructed to exhibit a pattern that can be discovered using a particular computation. If the children then extract the pattern from the data, we know that they are able to perform this type of computation on a corpus. As an example, 8-month-old infants were exposed to a corpus of nonsense words playing continuously on an audiotape for 2 min. The corpus was arranged so that the transitional probabilities between sounds were 1.0 inside words, but 0.33 across words. The only way the infant could figure out what the words in the corpus were was to (1) pay attention to these transitional probabilities and (2) assume that sequences with high probabilities are likely to be inside words and that sequences with low probabilities are likely to be the accidental juxtapositions of sounds at word boundaries. The infants not only listened differentially to words vs. nonwords, but they were able to discriminate between words and part-words (part-words contained the final syllable of one word and the first two syllables of another word; they were thus part of the corpus the infants heard but had different transitional probabilities from the words). The 8-month-olds were not merely noting whether a syllable sequence occurred – they were inducing a pattern from the sounds they had heard, and using a mechanism that calculates statistical frequencies from input to do so.

Infants are thus sensitive to the transitional probabilities between sounds and can use them to segment speech into word-like units. Can this simple mechanism be used as an entry point into higher levels of linguistic structure? If, for example, children can use transitional probabilities between words (or word classes) to segment sentences into phrases, they could then use this phrasal information as a wedge into the syntax of their language. In other words, children may be able to go a long way toward inducing the structure of the language they are learning by applying a simple procedure (tabulating statistical frequencies) to the data that they receive. A related domain-general approach that has been taken to the problem is the Bayesian inference framework, a tool for combining prior knowledge (probabilistic versions of constraints) and observational data (statistical information in the input) in a rational inference process. The theoretical assumption underlying all of these approaches is that children come to language learning equipped with processing strategies that allow them to induce patterns from the data to which they are exposed.

The open question at the moment is – how sophisticated do the data-processing strategies have to be in order for children to induce the patterns of their language from the input that they actually receive? Can children get by with the ability to calculate transitional probabilities, building up larger and larger units over developmental time? Or are there units over which children are more, or less, likely to calculate transitional probabilities? For example, children may (or may not) be able to calculate statistical probabilities over units that are not immediately adjacent (i.e., dependencies between units that are at a distance from one another, for instance, in the sentence, 'the cats on the couch are beautiful,' the verb 'are' is plural because it depends on 'cats', the subject of the sentence, which occurs several words earlier). Some of the constraints that children exhibit during language learning may come from the processing mechanisms they bring to the situation.

Two questions are frequently asked about language processing mechanisms. (1) The task-specificity question – are the mechanisms that children apply to language learning unique to language, or are they used in other domains as well? (2) The species-specificity question – are the mechanisms children apply to language learning unique to humans, or are they used by other species as well?

The task-specificity question can be addressed with respect to statistical learning by providing children with nonlanguage input that is patterned (e.g., musical patterns, visual patterns) and observing whether young infants can discover those patterns. They do, suggesting that calculating transitional probabilities is a general purpose data-processing mechanism that children apply to their worlds. The species-specificity question can be addressed with respect to statistical learning by exposing nonhumans to the same type of language input that the human infants heard, and observing whether they can discover the patterns. It turns out that cotton-top tamarin monkeys can extract word-like units from a stream of speech sounds just as human infants do. But, of course, tamarin monkeys do not acquire human language. The interesting question, then, is where do the monkeys fall off? What types of computations are impossible for them to perform? This theoretically motivated paradigm thus allows us to determine how the mechanisms children bring to language constrain what they learn, and whether those constraints are specific to language and specific to humans.

Constrained Invention

When children apply their data-processing mechanisms to linguistic input, the product of their learning is language. But what if a child was not exposed to linguistic input? Would such a child be able to invent a communication system and, if so, would that communication system resemble language? If children are able to invent a communication system that is structured in language-like ways, we must then ask whether the constraints that guide language learning are the same as the constraints that guide language invention.

Language was clearly invented at some point in the past and was then transmitted from generation to generation. Was it a one-time invention, requiring just the right assembly of factors, or is language so central to being human that it can be invented anew by each generation? This is a question that seems impossible to answer – today's children do not typically have the opportunity to invent a language, as they are all exposed from birth (and perhaps even before birth since babies can perceive some sounds *in utero*) to the language of their community. The only way to address the question is to find children who have not been exposed to a human language.

In fact, there are children who are unable to take advantage of the language to which they are exposed. These children are congenitally deaf with hearing losses so severe that they cannot acquire the spoken language that surrounds them, even with intensive instruction. Moreover, they are born to hearing parents who do not know a sign language and have not placed their children in a situation where they would be exposed to one. These children lack an accessible model for human language. Do they invent one?

The short answer is yes. The children are able to communicate with the hearing individuals in their worlds, and use gesture to do so. This is hardly surprising since all hearing speakers gesture when they talk. The surprising result is that the deaf children's gestures do not look like the gestures that their hearing parents produce. The children's gestures have language-like structure; the parents' gestures do not.

The children combine gestures, which are themselves composed of parts (akin to morphemes in conventional sign languages), into sentence-like strings that are structured with grammatical rules for deletion and order. For example, to ask an adult to share a snack, one child pointed at the snack, gestured eat (a quick jab of an O-shaped hand at his mouth), and then pointed at the adult. He typically placed gestures for the object of an action before gestures for the action, and gestures for the agent of an action after. Importantly, the children's gesture systems are generative – the children concatenate gestures conveying several propositions within the bounds of a single-gesture sentence. For example, one child produced several propositions about snow shovels within a single sentence: that they are used to dig, that they are used when boots are worn, that they are used outside, and kept downstairs. The gesture systems have parts of speech (nouns, verbs, adjectives), are used to make generic statements (as in the snow shovel example), and are used to tell stories about the past, present, future, and the hypothetical. The children even use their gestures to talk to themselves and to talk about their own gestures.

In contrast, the children's hearing parents use their gestures as all speakers do. Their sloppily formed gestures are synchronized with speech and are rarely combined with one another. The gestures speakers produce are meaningful, but they convey their meanings holistically, with no componential parts and no hierarchical structure.

The theoretically interesting finding is not that the deaf children communicate with their gestures, but that their gestures are structured in language-like ways. Indeed, the children's gestures are sufficiently language-like that they have been called home signs. It is important to note that the deaf children could have used mime to communicate – for example, miming eating a snack to invite the adult to join the activity. But they do not. Instead, they produce discrete, well-formed gestures that look more like beads on a string than a continuous unsegmentable movement.

Segmentation and combination are at the heart of human language, and they form the foundation of the deaf children's gesture systems. But segmentation and combination are not found in the gestural input children receive from their hearing parents. Thus, the deaf children could not easily have taken data-processing strategies of the sort that have been hypothesized and applied them to the gestural input they receive in order to arrive at their home-sign systems. Although it is clear that children must be applying data-processing strategies to the particular language they hear in order to acquire that language, it is equally clear that children can arrive at a language-like system through other routes. A communication system structured in language-like ways seems to be overdetermined in humans.

The deaf children invented the rudiments of language without a model to guide them. But they did not invent a full-blown linguistic system – perhaps for good reason. Their parents wanted them to learn to talk and thus did not share the children's gesture systems with them. As a result, the children's systems were one-sided; they produced language-like gestures to their parents, but received nonlinguistic co-speech gestures in return.

What would happen if such a deaf child were given a partner with whom to develop language? Just such a situation arose in the 1980s in Nicaragua when deaf children were brought together in a group for the very first time. The deaf children had been born to hearing parents and, like the deaf children described above, presumably had invented gesture systems in their individual homes. When they were brought together, they needed to develop a common sign language, which has come to be called Nicaraguan Sign Language (NSL). The distance between the home signs invented by individual children without a partner and the sign system created by this first cohort of NSL can tell us which linguistic properties require a shared community in order to be introduced into human language.

But NSL has not stopped growing. Every year, new deaf children enter the group and learn to sign among their peers. This second cohort of signers has as its input the sign system developed by the first cohort. Interestingly, second-cohort signers continue to adapt the system so that the product becomes even more language-like. The properties of language that crop up in this second and subsequent cohorts are properties that depend on passing the system through fresh minds – linguistic properties that must be transmitted from one generation to the next in order to be introduced into human language.

NSL is not unique among sign languages; it is likely that all sign languages came about through a similar process. As another recent example, a community was founded 200 years ago by the Al-Sayyid Bedouins. Two of the founders' five sons were deaf and, within the last three generations, 150 deaf individuals have been born into the community. Al-Sayyid Bedouin Sign Language (ABSL) was thus born. ABSL differs from NSL in that it is developing in a socially stable community with children learning the system from their parents. Because ABSL is changing over time, the signers from each of the three generations are likely to differ, and to differ systematically, in the system of signs they use. By observing signers from each generation, we can therefore make good guesses as to when a particular linguistic property first entered the language. Moreover, because the individual families in the community are tightly knit, with strong bonds within families but not across them, we can chart changes in the language in relation to the social network of the community. We can determine when properties remained within a single family and when they did not, and thus follow the trajectory that particular linguistic properties took as they spread (or failed to spread) throughout the community. This small and self-contained community consequently offers a unique perspective on some classic questions in historical linguistics.

Because sign languages are processed by eye and hand rather than ear and mouth, we might have expected them to be structured differently from spoken languages. But they are not. Sign languages all over the world are characterized by the same hierarchy of linguistic structures (syntax, morphology, phonology) and thus draw on the same human abilities as spoken languages. Moreover, children exposed to sign language from birth acquire that language as naturally as hearing children acquire the spoken language to which they are exposed, achieving major milestones at approximately the same ages.

However, the manual modality makes sign languages unique in at least one respect. It is easy to use the manual modality to invent representational forms that can be immediately understood by naive observers (e.g., indexical pointing gestures, iconic gestures). Thus, sign languages can be created anew by individuals and groups, and are particularly useful in allowing us to determine whether language-creation is constrained in the same ways that language learning is.

Computational and robotic experiments offer another approach to the problem of language invention. These studies explore whether communication systems with properties akin to those found in natural human language can emerge in populations of initially language-less agents. There are two traditions in this work. The first functional approach assumes that linguistic structure arises as a solution to the problem of communication, for example, as a way of limiting search through possible interpretations. The second structural approach does not rely on communication pressure to motivate change but rather examines the emergence of structure as the system is passed from one user (or one generation of users) to the next. Studies in this second tradition have found that a compositional system with recursion, grammatical categories, and word order inevitably results from passing an initially unstructured communication system through generations of learners. These are just the properties found in the deaf children's home-sign gesture systems, but the home-sign systems are not passed through a series of learners and are instead invented by individual children who are the sole users of their systems. Once again, we find that there is more than one way to arrive at language-like structure. In general, modeling studies, combined with observations of actual cases of language learning and language invention, can help us appreciate the range of circumstances under which language-like structure can arise and the mechanisms responsible for that structure.

Is Language Innate?

Children are likely to come to language learning constrained to process the language data they receive in certain ways and not in others. The constraints could be specifically linguistic, but they need not be. Constraints are assumed to be internal to the child at the moment when a particular skill is acquired. But are they innate?

Innateness Defined as Genetic Encoding

The problem of innateness has been addressed repeatedly and elegantly in other disciplines, especially ethology, and many definitions of innateness have been proposed. One of the most common, albeit not the earliest, definitions of an innate behavior is that it have a genetic base. Some have claimed evidence for grammar genes – not for a single gene responsible for all the circuitry underlying grammar but for a set of genes whose effects are relevant to the development of the circuits underlying parts of grammar. The dispute is whether the genes are specific to the grammatical aspects of language.

What might it mean to claim that language has a genetic base? At one level, the claim is obviously true – equipped with the human genetic potential, humans develop language. But what does this claim buy us if our interest is in understanding how children learn language? We could study twins, both fraternal and identical, to explore the phenomenon of language learning. However, in this regard, it is important to note that, in twin studies conducted to explore the genetic basis of intelligence (i.e., IQ), the focus is on differences among individuals relative to a normative scale. In contrast, claims about the innateness of language are claims about the commonalities among people, not the genetic differences between people. In arguing that language is genetically based, there is no obvious claim that two individuals who are genetically related have linguistic systems that are more alike than two individuals who are not genetically related. All humans who are genetically intact have, at base, comparable linguistic systems – comparable in the same way that all human bodies have two arms and two legs. The details of the arms of any two unrelated individuals (their length, width, definition, etc.) are likely to differ (and those differences may or may not be grounded at the genetic level) but the basic twoness and structure of the arm is constant across all genetically intact humans – so too for language.

So why then (assuming we are not geneticists) should we care about the genetic base of language learning? Perhaps we should not. Of all of the very large number of definitions and criteria that have, over the years and over the disciplines, been applied to the term innate, one could argue that the definition that is least central to the notion's core is having a genetic base. A useful definition of innate need not be anchored in genetic mechanisms.

Innateness Defined as Developmental Resilience

An alternative definition of an innate behavior is that it is developmentally resilient. A behavior is developmentally resilient if its development, if not inevitable, is overdetermined in the species; that is, it is a behavior likely to be developed by each member of the species even under widely varying circumstances. The way we traditionally explore the boundaries for the development of a behavior is to manipulate the conditions under which that behavior is typically developed, extending the range until the behavior no longer appears. For obvious ethical reasons, we cannot tamper with the circumstances under which children learn language. But we can take advantage of variations in language-learning conditions that occur naturally, and thus explore the boundary conditions under which language development is possible.

Resilience in the face of external variation

Language learning is not infinitely resilient. When human children are raised by animals, they do not develop language. And when children are raised by inhumane parents who mistreat them physically and emotionally, including depriving them of a model for language, they do not develop language. But given a reasonable social world, children seem to be able to develop language under a wide range of circumstances.

Consider first the effects of variability in the way adults speak to children within a culture. Adults in each culture tend to use a distinct register of speech with their children. There is, however, variability across adults in how much they talk to their children and in the frequency with which certain constructions are used. Variability in the amount of talk a child hears has been shown to affect that child's rate of vocabulary growth, and variability in how often a particular construction is used in speech to a child has been shown to affect how quickly the child develops that construction. However, despite the effects of input on the pacing of language learning, there is no evidence that the particular way in which an adult speaks to a child affects whether or not language is ultimately learned by that child.

Indeed, the amount of input a child receives can be quite minimal and still the child will learn language. For example, hearing children born to deaf parents often get very minimal exposure to speech. But it turns out that they do not need much; 5–10 h a week of exposure to hearing speakers is typically sufficient to allow language learning to proceed normally. As another example, twins share their language-learning situation with one another, making the typical adult-twin situation triadic rather than dyadic. Nonetheless, language learning proceeds along a normal trajectory, although often with mild delays. A child may develop language more or less quickly, but almost all intact children in almost all linguistic environments eventually develop language.

The resilience of language learning in the face of across-culture variability is even more impressive. Cultures hold different beliefs about the role that parents need to play to ensure the child's acquisition of language. Not surprisingly, then, children around the globe differ in how much, when, and what types of language they receive – not to mention the fact that, in each culture, the child is exposed to a model of a different language. Indeed, many children are exposed to input from two different languages and must learn both at the same time. Despite the broad range of inputs, children in all corners of the earth learn language and at approximately the same pace.

Resilience in the face of internal variation

Language learning is also resilient in the face of many organic variations from the norm, variations that alter the way children process whatever input they receive. For example, intermittent conductive hearing losses from repeated middle ear infections can cause a child's intake of linguistic input to vary over time in amount and pattern. Despite this variability, spoken language development for the most part proceeds normally in children with this type of hearing loss. As a second example, blind children live in a nonvisual world that is obviously different from the sighted child's world, and that offers a different spectrum of contextual cues to meaning. However, this difference has little impact on language learning in the blind child.

Organic variation can be much more severe and still result in relatively intact language learning. For example, grammar learning in the earliest stages can proceed in a relatively normal manner and at a normal rate even in the face of unilateral ischemic brain injury. As a second example, children with Down syndrome have numerous intrinsic deficiencies that complicate the process of language acquisition. Nevertheless, most Down syndrome children acquire some basic language reflecting the fundamental grammatical organization of the language they are exposed to (the amount of language that is acquired is in general proportion to their cognitive capabilities). Finally, and strikingly, given the social impairments that are at the core of the syndrome, autistic children who are able to learn language are not impaired in their grammatical development, either in syntax or in morphology, although they do often have deficits in the communicative, pragmatic, and functional aspects of their language.

Interestingly, even when children do have trouble learning language, some properties of language (the resilient ones) are spared. For example, a basic understanding of the organization that underlies predicates appears to be intact in children with specific language impairment (children who have neither hearing impairment, cognitive deficit, nor neurological damage yet fail to develop language normally). However, these children have difficulty with morphological constructions. As another example, children who are not exposed to a usable language until adolescence have no trouble mastering word order when learning language late in life, but do have difficulty with morphology. Some properties of language appear to be robust, and some fragile, across a variety of circumstances and internal states.

There may be no greater testament to the resilience of language than the fact that children can invent language in the absence of a model for language. A combination of internal factors (the fact that the children are profoundly deaf and cannot acquire a spoken language) and external factors (the fact that the children have not been exposed to a conventional sign language) together create the unusual language-learning circumstances in which the deaf children described earlier find themselves. Despite their lack of a model for language, these children still communicate in language-like ways.

In sum, language development can proceed in humans over a wide range of environments and a wide range of organic states, suggesting that the process of language development may be buffered against a large number of both environmental and organic variations. No one factor seems to be ultimately responsible for the course and outcome of language development in humans, a not-so-surprising result given the complexity and importance of human language.

Mechanisms that Could Lead to Resilience

Another way of describing the language-learning process is that the range of possible outcomes in the process is narrowed. This narrowing or canalization is often attributed to genetic causes. However, canalization can also be caused by the environment. Consider an example from another species. Exposing a bird to a particular stimulus at one point early in its development can narrow the bird's learning later on; the bird becomes particularly susceptible to responding to that stimulus, and buffered against responding to other stimuli. Note that, in order for acquisition to be universal when the environment is playing a canalizing role, the relevant aspect of the environment must be reliably present in the world of each member of the species. In a sense, the environment must be considered as much a part of the species as its genes.

For language, it looks as though there is a basic, resilient form that human communication naturally gravitates toward, and a variety of developmental paths that can be taken to arrive at that form. In this sense, language development in humans can be said to be characterized by equifinality, an embryological term coined to describe a process by which a system reaches the same outcome despite widely differing input conditions. No matter where you start, all roads lead to Rome.

Are there any implications for the mechanisms of development that we can draw once having identified language as a trait characterized by equifinality? Two types of systems seem possible:

1. A system characterized by equifinality can rely on a single developmental mechanism that not only can make effective use of a wide range of inputs (both external and internal) but will not veer off track in response to that variability, that is, a mechanism that is not sensitive to large differences in input. The gross image that comes to mind here is a sausage machine that takes inputs of all sorts and, regardless of the type and quality of that input, creates the same product.

2. A system characterized by equifinality can rely on multiple developmental mechanisms, each activated by different conditions but constrained in some way to lead to the same end product. The analogy here is to several distinct machines, each one designed to operate only when activated by a particular type of input (e.g., a chicken, pig, cow, or turkey). Despite the different processes that characterize the dismembering operations of each machine, the machines result in the same sausage product. At first glance, it may seem improbable that a variety of developmental mechanisms would be constrained to arrive at precisely the same outcome. However, it is relatively easy to imagine that the function served by the mechanisms – a function that all of the developmental trajectories would share – might have been sufficient to, over time, constrain each of the mechanisms to produce the same product. Communicating via symbols with other humans might be a sufficiently constraining function to result in several mechanisms, each producing language-like structure.

Which of these scenarios characterizes what actually happens when children learn language is an open question. But what is clear is that language-like structure is overdetermined in human children. Many paths lead to the same outcome, and whatever developmental mechanism we propose to explain language learning (or language invention) is going to have to be able to account for this equifinality.

Language is Not a Unitary Phenomenon

Until now we have been discussing language as though it were a unitary phenomenon, as though it were obvious what the appropriate unit of analysis for language is. However, it is clear that language is not a unitary whole, particularly when it comes to issues of resilience and innateness.

Children who are not exposed to a conventional language model create communication systems that contain some, but not all, of the properties found in natural human languages. Thus, the absence of a conventional language model appears to affect some properties of language more than others. Even when linguistic input is present, it is more likely to affect rate of acquisition for certain properties of language than for others. Further, when language is acquired off-time (i.e., in late childhood or adolescence) certain properties of language are likely to be acquired and others are not. Thus, some properties of language are relatively resilient, while others are relatively fragile. Moreover, there is some evidence that the same properties of language (e.g., using the order of words to convey who does what to whom) are resilient across many different circumstances of acquisition – acquisition without a conventional language model, with varying input from a language model, and late in development after puberty. Thus, language as a whole need not be said to be innate.

The definition of innate that best fits the language-learning data is developmental resilience. This notion operationalizes innateness by specifying the range of organisms and environments in which language learning can take place. There clearly are limits on the process of language development; children raised without human interaction do not develop language. But the process of language development can proceed in children with a range of limitations and in children raised in environments that vary radically from the typical. What we see in exploring this resilience is that certain aspects of language are central to humans – so central that their development is virtually guaranteed, not necessarily by a particular gene but by a variety of combinations of genetic and environmental factors. In this sense, language is innate.

See also: Bilingualism; Grammar; Imitation and Modeling; Language Development: Overview; Learning; Literacy; Pragmatic Development; Preverbal Development and Speech Perception; Semantic Development; Speech Perception.

Suggested Readings

Bishop D and and Mogford K (eds.) (1988) *Language Development in Exceptional Circumstances.* New York: Churchill Livingtone.
Bloom P (ed.) (1993) *Language Acquisition: Core Readings.* New York: Harvester Wheatsheaf.
Brown R (1973) *A First Language.* Cambridge, MA: Harvard University Press.
Fletcher P and and Mac Whinney B (eds.) (1995) *The Handbook of Child Language.* Oxford: Blackwell Publishers.

Gleitman LR and Newport EL (1995) The invention of language by children: Environmental and biological influences on the acquisition of language. In: Gleitman LR and Liberman M (eds.) *Language Vol. 1, Invitation to Cognitive Science Series*, pp. 1–24. Cambridge, MA: MIT Press.

Goldin-Meadow S (2003) *The Resilience of Language: What Gesture Creation in Deaf Children Can Tell Us About How All Children Learn Language.* New York: Psychology Press.

Lust BC and and Foley C (eds.) (2004) *First Language Acquisition: The Essential Readings.* Oxford: Blackwell.

Mac Whinney B (ed.) (1987) *Mechanisms of Language Acquisition.* Hillsdale, NJ: Erlbaum.

Pinker S (1994) *The Language Instinct: How the Mind Creates Language.* New York: Morrow.

Slobin DI (ed.) (1985–1997) *A Cross-Linguistic Study of Language Acquisition,* vols 1–5. Hillsdale, NJ: Erlbaum Associates.

Tager-Flusberg H (ed.) (1994) *Constraints on Language Acquisition: Studies of Atypical Children.* Hillsdale, NJ: Erlbaum Associates.

Wanner E and and Gleitman LR (eds.) (1982) *Language Acquisition: The State of the Art.* New York: Cambridge University Press.

Language Development: Overview

E Lieven, Max Planck Institute for Evolutionary Anthropology, Leipzig, Germany

This article is reproduced from the *Encyclopedia of Language and Linguistics,* 2nd edition, volume 6, pp. 376–391, © 2006; Elsevier Ltd.

Glossary

Grammar – The study of classes of words, their inflections, and their functions and relations in a sentence.
Morphology – The system of word-forming elements and processes in a language.
Phonology – The study of speech sounds.
Semartics – The study of the meaning of words.
Syntax – The way in which words are put together to form phrases, clauses, or sentences.

Introduction

All over the world, children learn to talk on a roughly equivalent timetable. They do so by learning the language or languages of their environment. There is considerable debate over what cognitive, social, or specifically linguistic, innate capacities they bring to language leaning. This article begins with a brief timetable of development and then focuses in turn on the major aspects of language learning in terms of infancy, learning words, learning morphology, early grammar, later grammar, and the learning of pragmatic and metalinguistic skills. It concludes with some brief reflections on atypical development. The relevant theoretical issues are covered as they arise in each section and are considered again in the last section on learnability and constituency.

During infancy, children develop a wide range of cognitive and social skills together with a developing ability to segment the speechstream into meaningful units. They usually produce their first recognizable words somewhere between 10–18 months of age and their first multiword utterances between 14–24 months. By age 3 years, children are often able to produce quite long utterances and are beginning to be able to combine more than one clause into coordinate and subordinate constructions (e.g., relative clauses, cleft sentences). Between the ages of 4 to 7 years, there are major advances in children's ability to take the perspective of the listener into account and to produce coherent discourse and narrative sequences. These abilities, as well as the ability to reflect on language as an object of knowledge, develop throughout the school years and are much influenced by the extent of literacy or other complex language (for instance, ritual language) to which children are exposed.

Throughout this developmental timetable, there are major individual differences in the ages at which children reach these points and, in addition, in the balance of skills that a particular child may manifest at a particular point in time. There are also individual differences in how children tackle any of these tasks. This is an important point to remember when considering theories that rely for their confirmation on a particular order of development or on a particular relationship among different skills. It is also important to remember that many children (perhaps most) grow up hearing and, to some extent at least, learning more than one language. The evidence to date is that doing so does not have a significant impact on the developmental timetable for language learning in the early years.

Overview of Development

Infancy

Children are born with the ability to discriminate their mother's voice from that of other women and to discriminate speech from nonspeech, presumably because of their experience in the uterus. In the earliest months of life, they seem able to discriminate sounds produced in the languages of the world, but this ability diminishes until, by 8 to 10 months, their ability to discriminate between sounds is confined to the sounds of their native language(s).

Experiments with children between 6 to 10 months of age indicate a developing sensitivity to the prosodic indicators of major phrasal units in the speechstream. Thus, 9-month-old infants prefer to listen to speech that is segmented using pauses at major clause boundaries, rather than within clauses, whereas there is no difference in listening preferences for 6-month-olds. Around 7.5 months infants also become able to identify words in the speechstream. Experiments with English-, Japanese-, and French-learning children have shown that children can discriminate words that they have heard before from those that they have not, even when the words were embedded in speech. They can also discriminate highly frequent words in their language from low-frequency words, and words that are typically learned early by children from words that are not typically learned early.

Experiments with children about 10 months of age have indicated that they are sensitive to the ordering of words in their language, thus being able to discriminate normal English sentences from ones in which determiners and nouns were reversed (e.g., *kitten the*) or ones in which some grammatical morphemes were replaced by nonsense syllables. Older children (at 18 months but not at 15 months) can discriminate sentences in which the combination of auxiliary and verb was correct (*is running*) from those in which it was not (*can running*). Finally, using simple artificial languages, it has been claimed that infants between 7.5 to 17 months are able to recognize strings with the same ordering rules, but with different 'vocabulary' after a short exposure. However, it seems that this discrimination is possible only when there are patterns of repetition in the 'vocabulary items'.

These experiments show a clear path of development during the first 12 to 18 months of life. As children's experience with language develops, so do their segmentation, word recognition, and pattern recognition skills. These skills are obviously central to the child's ability to parse the input and to start to connect it to meaning. It is important to note that all these experiments depend on the infant's ability to discriminate one stimulus from another. They do not have to understand or use the stimuli in communication nor connect them to any meaning in the environment.

However, infants do make huge developmental strides in their cognitive and social development during the first 12 months of life. Cognitively, infants (probably from birth) have clear expectations about the ways in which objects will behave, and these expectations develop in sophistication over the first year of life. Before their first birthday, they are able to form categories of objects based both on form and, to some extent, on function.

During the first 6–8 months of life, children develop the ability to interact with others, to make demands, and to resist them. At around 8 to 9 months, there is a major 'step change' as the infant starts to understand that others have intentions that may be different from their own and to incorporate this understanding of other minds into their behavior; for instance, imitating the perceived intentions of others and showing objects that they know their interactant has not seen. Infants aged 12–18 months are clearly starting to associate attention sharing, demanding, and assisting others with specific gestures that they use and, also perhaps, with systematic vocalizations. This development is highly correlated with word learning, as it seems to be the beginning of the attempt to match form to meaning.

Thus, by about age 10–12 months, infants are ready to put the patterns that they have extracted together with their communicative and meaning-inference skills. It is this combination that is the true start of human language learning.

How many of these developing abilities are unique to humans, and how many are shared with the other great apes or primates? This is obviously a contentious issue, and researchers of different theoretical persuasions have made very different claims. Much more research remains to be done to tease apart the exact nature of the skills and their precise developmental sequence. However, a number of experiments have indicated that many of the pattern recognition skills shown by human infants may be shared by other primates. In contrast, the intention-reading and communicative skills shown by infants in the last trimester of their first year do seem uniquely human, though nonhuman primates show some precursors of these abilities, especially those few who have been reared in a 'human' environment.

Early Comprehension and Production

The time when children first start to show signs of comprehension and to start producing words varies. However, because much depends on how comprehension and production are defined, it is difficult to give an exact range of variation. Comprehension of individual words such as *No* starts very early, and children can use contextual cues to interpret the utterances of those around them without parsing much of what they hear. Although most well-controlled studies of early word learning have found that comprehension is achieved in advance of production and starts early, production is more variable, with some children producing their first words (as reported by parents) at around 10 months, whereas others might not produce more than a few recognizable words before 16 to 18 months. For most children, progress in comprehension and in production is highly correlated, but there are reports of some children whose comprehension outstrips their production by much more than the normal extent.

Studies have shown that, even when infants know a word, it will take 15-month-olds much longer to process it and to look to a matching picture than it will older infants. Thus, 15-month-olds need to hear the whole word before looking to the matching picture, whereas 18- and 24-month-olds process it 150 and 300 ms faster, respectively. These two older groups shift their gaze before the word has ended, using the ongoing phonological information to discriminate the matching picture from a distractor. This development of automatization is clearly one of the major processes taking place between the earliest word-meaning mappings and the point where vocabulary learning develops rapidly.

The production of utterances also goes through a long process of automatization and refinement. Initially, infants' utterances can match the adult form quite closely. However, they go through a subsequent stage in which each child produces a wider range of words, most of which are reduced to a phonological 'template.' The nature of this template varies from child to child, though it always bears a phonological and segmental relationship to the particular language being learned. Children vary greatly in how accurately they can produce the phonology of their language and in how long it takes for this accuracy to develop. They may also differ early on in the extent to which they pick up on the major tunes of the language, as some children tend to produce shorter and more well-articulated utterances.

Some early words are highly context dependent – for example, Piaget's classic example of his daughter, Jacqueline who used *voua-ou* (wow-wow) to refer to everything that could be seen from the balcony – but it seems to be the case that children also produce relatively context-independent words from early on (e.g., *more* to request a number of items, not just food). Context dependence is similar to 'underextension' in which the child uses the word to refer to a limited set of referents. This contrasts with overextension where the word is used to refer to a wider group of referents than in the adult language (an example is the use of *Daddy* to refer to all men whom the child encounters). Much early word comprehension and production shows both characteristics and initially is not stable.

One of the most striking aspects of very early speech is its phonological inaccuracy. Analysis makes it clear that the phonological errors that children produce are systematic. Individual children drop syllables or substitute a particular sound of their own for sounds in their language (for instance, *Puggle* for *Puddle*) while still being able to hear the difference between their own production repeated to them and the 'real' word. Children will not, in fact, accept a repetition of their version of a word as being the 'real' word. This phenomenon raises interesting issues for the relationship between comprehension and production. There is major theoretical debate, however, concerning how it should be analyzed. The debate is between a 'templatic approach,' which characterizes the process as the child assimilating words to a production template or an optimality theoretical approach that sees the child as seeking to resolve a set of constraints on production, such as 'faithfulness' (i.e., getting as close to the model as possible) and 'markedness'.

A second issue is the extent to which children's communicative behavior in these early stages is already 'linguistic' in the sense of being conventionalized, context free, and combinatorial. Thus, researchers have suggested that children's early communicative acts (e.g., showing as a precursor of declaratives and demanding as a precursor of imperatives) develop into 'protolinguistic' symbols; that is, each child uses a specific set of sounds and gestures to convey different meanings.

Learning a Vocabulary and Developing Meaning

After an often slow start, children's vocabulary grows exponentially, with new words being added at a rate of 9 to 10 words per day between the ages of 2 and 6 years. In industrialized and urbanized societies, children add about 3000 words per year for each year in school. Vocabulary size is related closely to the amount of Child-Directed Speech (CDS) in the early years and to various measures of family talk and schooling in the later years.

For children learning many languages, including English, nouns form the largest single category of words, but children also learn a wide range of words from other categories (e.g., *want*, *me*, *no*, *what*). The extent to which nouns predominate early on varies among children learning the same language and among children learning different languages. Young children, under certain pragmatic conditions, require only a minimal number of exposures to a novel noun and its referent to learn its meaning.

One issue concerns when children form categories of the words that they are learning. The answer to this depends, in part, on how a category is defined, but evidence suggests that a category of nouns develops relatively early in many languages; that English-speaking children can substitute the determiner *a* for *the* early (while taking many years to learn the full range of determiners and their scope); and that fully fledged categories of verb and adjective take more time to develop.

When children learn a new word, what meaning do they give it? It could be the meaning the word has in the language that they are learning or a meaning based on their cognitive categorizations of the world. For instance, children the world over might already have developed nonverbal categories of 'in-ness' and 'on-ness' during infancy, and when they learn words that express the relation between objects, they might initially match these words to these pre-existent categories. There has been considerable research on this issue, and it seems that this is not what happens. Instead, children seem to learn the word and its referent together. Thus, English-learning children use the prepositions *in* to refer to one object contained within another and *on* to refer to one object supported by another, irrespective of how tight the fit is between the objects. However, Korean-learning children use the verb *kkita* to refer to one object inside another only if the fit is tight (e.g., a cassette in a box) and for other tight fit relations between objects (e.g., one object stuck to another with Velcro). The verb *nehta* is used to refer to a loose fit, regardless of whether one object is inside another or on top of it. Children do under- and over-generalize, but they seem to do so along the lines of categorization indicated by their language.

How does a child know what someone is referring to when that person uses a word? In principle, the speaker could be referring to any part of the scene. This problem of reference was elucidated most clearly by the philosopher, Quine. The general answer is to suggest that children come to word learning with some already pre-given interpretative skills. One group of researchers has suggested that these skills are in the nature of innate constraints; for instance, the child initially assumes that a word applies to the whole object and that a novel word will not apply to an object for which the child already has a word. Another group suggests that these skills derive from the pragmatics of the situation that the child already knows about. A series of experiments indicating that children pre-verbally know what is relevant to a situation and to the perspective of another and that, simply through using context, they can find the referent for a word they have never previously seen paired with the referent, suggest that the latter explanation is more likely to be correct.

Another major debate in the literature is over the status of nouns as the first category to be learned. In 1982, D. Gentner claimed that nouns are universally easier to learn and that they initiate the process of category learning. She argued that this occurs not only because the use of nouns tends to be very frequent in CDS but also because their reference is more transparent – to concrete, imageable objects – and children already have developed a considerable knowledge of objects and their behavior pre-verbally. In opposition to this theory, researchers have argued that children learn a range of words, not just nouns, from the beginning and that there are languages, such as Korean, in which the proportion of nouns in the lexicon does not exceed the proportion of verbs (more or less broadly defined). This issue has not been resolved: on the one hand, it *is* easier in many languages to learn many object words; on the other hand, children are also building up other categories of their language from the beginning. Developing categories helps the child segment the other words they hear, and the relative growth of these categories depends on the characteristics of the language being learned and the way it is used in CDS.

Learning Grammar

Learning Morphology

Inflections change the grammatical meaning of words. Languages differ greatly in the amount and kind of inflectional morphology that they show. English has very little inflectional morphology (plural – *s* and past tense –*ed* are two examples). Free morphemes also mark grammatical meanings in languages. For instance, in English, *he* indicates the nominative masculine pronoun (subject argument), whereas *him* marks the accusative masculine pronoun (direct or indirect object argument). The English pronoun system shows irregularity: each pronoun in the English paradigm changes somewhat differently between nominative, accusative, and genitive (e.g., *he, him, his, we, us, our*). In addition, multiple meanings are encoded in one morpheme: number, case, and gender. Other languages encode meaning much more extensively and systematically with both inflectional and free morphemes. Inflections can mark either a local meaning (e.g., plural on a noun in English) or a relational meaning (e.g., plural on a verb to agree with the subject or object; a case marker on a noun as a function of its syntactic role). In either case, productive inflectional marking involves constituency: the ability to understand how plurality is marked on the whole noun phrase within the language being learned and how the noun phrase is coordinated with marking on the verb phrase. Thus, in some languages, determiners, adjectives, and nouns are all marked for plurality and/or case and/or gender, in others not; in some languages there is both subject and object marking on the verb and/or its auxiliaries and in others not.

Children may start by rote learning some frequent words together with their inflections while omitting non-salient inflections (omission errors). Later, children may over-generalize and use incorrect forms (errors of commission). For instance, in English, children leave out tense markers (*It go there* for *It goes there*), over-regularize past tense marking (*goed* for *went*), and use incorrect forms (*I think her was crying for me*). In languages in which all words in a class carry an inflection, the child may initially use only one inflection and over-generalize it to all members of that class.

A central question is when children become productive with morphology. Researchers from different theoretical persuasions tend to interpret the data in predictably different ways. Those arguing for early, abstract knowledge point to the fact that children learning highly inflected languages produce words with inflectional marking from the beginning, usually accurately. Those who emphasize that the abstract representations underlying inflectional morphology are learned point to the potentially rote-learned nature of early inflectional marking and the limited range of items with which particular inflections are used.

There have been many different ways of defining productivity in naturalistic corpora: for instance, percentage provision in obligatory contexts, use of the same inflection on a number of members of the class, or use of different inflections on the same word. Inevitably, these measures yield different results, depending on how stringent the criteria are and how good the sampling is. Methods are being developed that control for the range of forms in the child's lexicon and then compare the degree of productivity between the child's system at different developmental points and between the child's system and the adult's. For two children learning Spanish, a language with rich inflectional morphology on verbs, this method has shown that productivity develops even after the child can provide all the forms and that the children's range of inflectional provision on the same verbs as their parents, even when the range of inflections is controlled for, is still significantly different at age 2.6 years.

How quickly children learn the morphology of their language seems to depend on the following factors and the interaction among them: type frequency (how many different lexemes are inflected in the same way) and token frequency (the relative frequency of different surface forms) in the input; salience (can they be heard?); transparency of meaning (is the semantics accessible?); formal complexity (is one meaning or more encoded?); and the regularity and distributional consistency of the inflectional paradigm. In such languages as Turkish, in which suffixes are added in a consistent order and with consistent form to indicate local meaning (e.g., plural, location, possessive), children seem to be at least partially productive relatively early. Other languages present more difficulty – those in which the morphemes are: (1) portmanteau (more than one meaning is combined in one form; e.g., the nominative for 'water' in Russian is *vodá*; the dative plural form is *vodám*); (2) distributed (e.g., marked with a free form and an inflection, Serbo-Croatian locative markers); and/or (3) in complex and partial paradigms (e.g., Polish case endings).

One sure way to know that children have a productive system is to test for their ability to mark words that they have never heard before ('nonce' words). Otherwise, one can never know whether each word and its accompanying inflection have been learned from the input on a one-by-one basis. In Berko's classic 'wug test,' children are first introduced to a novel creature called *a wug*, and then another of these creatures is produced. The child is then asked, *Now we have two – ?* We know that children have productive plural morphology if they answer *wugs*.

This method can be extended to other word classes. For instance, experiments with novel verbs in English suggest that productive past tense morphology for verbs develops somewhat later than does plural morphology for nouns. Note that this is also a way of determining what type of category is represented in the child's system and its level of abstraction (for instance, action verbs only or all verbs or concrete nouns only or all nouns). Nonce experiments have not been conducted in many languages other than English, but their wider use would certainly help clarify some very complex issues in the learning of inflectional morphology. However, they are not easy to conduct with children younger than age 2, and children learning some languages may be partially productive before this age.

Because inflectional morphology can be extremely complex and children seem to demonstrate early sensitivity and productivity, it is often used as a testing ground for debates about whether children have very early abstract linguistic representations. An example is the extensive debate on past tense marking in English. Children start by producing a small number of forms (many of them irregular) and subsequently start to over-generalize the regular *–ed* marker to irregular verbs (e.g., '*runned*' rather than '*ran*'). Children concurrently use the correct form and may continue to over-regularize some forms for many years. Proponents of early abstract representations argue that, once children have learned the past tense rule, they seek to apply it to all new forms that they learn and stop doing so only when they learn the new irregular form that 'blocks' the application of the rule. This model is called the 'dual route model': one route for regulars and one for irregulars. The claim is that this learning occurs even in languages, unlike English, for which the rule is not the most frequent form (i.e., is a 'minority default' rule). Challenges to this position come from 'single-route models' that claim: (1) the developmental pattern of marking can be closely modeled in connectionist networks that have only one (not two) mechanisms; (2) these networks can also model the development of marking in languages in which the 'default' marking is not the most frequent; (3) detailed studies of children's marking in languages either with a 'default' or with no default show a long process of development during which children over-generalize a variety of markers, depending on such factors as frequency and phonological similarity, before arriving at the adult system; and (4) the fact that over-generalizations continue for a long time after the child has learned the correct form does not suggest that there are two entirely separate processes involved.

As well as being a potential window on the nature of children's underlying syntactic abstractions, inflectional morphology can also provide a window on the development of children's underlying semantic representations. An example of this is the 'aspect before tense' debate. Here, the issue is whether children are initially sensitive only to the aspectual features of situations and their marking on verbs (e.g., punctual or durative events: *hit* vs. *singing*) or also to the temporal features (past vs. present events: *sit* vs. *sat*). Because languages differ greatly in how these features are coded on verbs, crosslinguistic comparison of children's development has been essential in this debate. Methodological problems and the complexity and inter-relatedness of the tense and aspect systems in different languages mean that we do not yet have a final answer to this issue.

Early Syntactic Development

Children's first utterances containing more than one word appear between 18 to 24 months of age. Almost all researchers agree that, in the early stages, some utterances are rote learned as a whole (e.g., *what's that?*), and others may be slot-and-frame patterns (e.g., *where's X gone?* or *more X*, where X denotes a range of referents). However, there is disagreement as to the extent of these low-scope patterns: what part they play, if any, in children's developing linguistic representations; and how utterances that are considered not to derive from them should be represented. For instance, when it is suggested that the child is using rules for the combination of underlying categories, the hypothesized categories can be very varied. One suggestion would be semantic categories; for instance 'agent' and 'action verb' to generate an utterance like *Lion swim*. However, a different researcher might analyze the same utterance in terms of syntactic relations, such as 'subject' and 'intransitive verb.' In the case of any particular utterance, these alternatives cannot be distinguished: A corpus of utterances (the larger, the more reliable) must be analyzed together with clear definitions of productivity before it is possible to suggest whether the utterance is likely to have been generated productively and on the basis of what linguistic representations. As noted for morphology, naturalistic data never allow one to be completely certain that an utterance is productive.

Many of children's early utterances are missing features that are provided in adult speech: subjects are frequently omitted, as are function words (e.g., auxiliaries, complementizers, prepositions). Utterances often lack finiteness marking (e.g., no third person –s on main verbs in English; nonfinite for finite verbs in Dutch and German).

Children's utterances also reflect features of the input very closely. Thus, English-speaking children's early verbs are those that occur most frequently in the input, children mark verbs in accordance with the most frequent marking on those same verbs in the input, and they use verbs in the argument structures that their mothers use most frequently. In fact, whatever system one looks at, there are strong correlations with frequency in the input. This is not, however, the only factor affecting the child's use: as with phonology and semantics, complexity and salience also play a role, together with, most importantly, what the child wants to talk about.

None of these facts are in serious dispute in the literature; however, their interpretation certainly is. The major divide is between those who interpret them as indicating that the child has early abstract and, specifically, linguistic knowledge (for some researchers, innate) and those who argue that abstraction develops throughout the process of learning language. Clearly, even though children's utterances show a great deal of lexical specificity and partial marking, they could still reflect underlying abstract linguistic knowledge, limited by these four factors:

1. lexical learning of the forms of the language
2. learning the syntactic features particular to the language
3. processing constraints on production (e.g., a limit on the length of what the child can produce)
4. late biological maturation of some part of the system that underlies the abstraction.

Each of these factors is briefly considered below.

In addition, all theories need to account for the patterns of errors that children show. Those maintaining the existence of innate linguistic knowledge must answer this question: If children have innate grammar, why do they make errors that seem to reflect the lack of knowledge of fundamental linguistic systems, such as tense, agreement, and the provision of arguments? Those maintaining that abstractions are constructed must determine how the interaction between the child's current system and the input explains the pattern of errors.

In the case of (1) above, it is obvious that, whatever the underlying system, children have to learn the specific forms of their native language. The clear implication is that claims to underlying structure or the lack of it should not be made until it is established that the child is able to fully comprehend or produce the forms reflecting the hypothesized abstraction.

Within nativist linguistic approaches, one solution to the issue of how children use the hypothesized Universal Grammar (UG) to work out the syntactic particularities of their input language (point 2 above) is to suggest that they have to set a range of parameters as the result of hearing (a small number of) utterances. Within this literature, there are major debates on the number of parameters, whether or not they are initially set, and how many settings there can be (one, two, or more). An example is to hypothesize a 'head direction parameter' that determines how children identify the input language as being 'left' or 'right branching.' In principle, children then know how to order words across a range of phrasal structures (e.g., noun phrases, prepositional phrases, and verb phrases). Alternative constructivist accounts would suggest that children do this on the basis of the particular strings that they learn from the input, from which word-order patterns are subsequently abstracted in conjunction with the learning of word classes. This hypothesis would make it easier to account for the many instances of inconsistency of head direction in languages. The success of the Principles and Parameters approach in its own terms depends on the number of parameters being relatively small and on agreement among researchers as to how the specified settings can account for the range of relevant phenomena in language development. At the present time, it is not clear that either of these conditions can be met.

In the case of processing constraints (3 above), there clearly are length constraints on what the child produces. Probably, the single most obvious aspect to the lay observer of children's developing language is that children's utterances get longer as they grow older. However, is this an output limitation imposed on a much fuller underlying abstract representation, or does it reflect what the child has actually learned up to this point? For instance, if children are processing the input by using already identified strings as the basis for building new strings, doing so would also yield increasingly long utterances over time. In addition, the way in which patterns were added would mean that the distribution of marking would also change over time. Research incorporating this type of learning mechanism has been successful at modeling children's patterns of finiteness marking not only in English but also in Dutch and Spanish.

An alternative linguistic nativist approach is to hypothesize that, although UG is innate, some parts of the system are on a later maturational timetable, which can account for some of the early error patterns shown by children (point 4 above). Two well-known accounts that use this approach are Borer and Wexler's attempt to explain the late use of full eventive passives by English-speaking children and Wexler's Agreement-Tense Omission Model (ATOM). In the first, the authors suggest that children are late with eventive passives because 'argument-linking chains' are a late biological maturation. This theory cannot account for the fact that full passives emerge early in some languages.

The ATOM model (of which the Optional Infinitive hypothesis for typically developing children and the Extended Optional Infinitive hypothesis for children with SLI are earlier versions) predicts that, because prematuration children are subject to 'the unique checking constraint,' they will only be able to check either for tense or for agreement. This constraint is intended to account for patterns of incorrect finiteness marking found in young children's speech across a range of languages. One aspect of this model concerns agreement marking. Because, in the model, children can only check for either tense or agreement, a pattern of errors is predicted that, in English, sometimes results in non-nominative pronouns appearing in subject position (e.g., *me* for *I* errors or *her* for *she* errors). The only error predicted *not* to occur at levels greater than noise is the use of a non-nominative pronoun (e.g., *me, him, her, them*) with a finite verb that agrees with the subject (e.g., *Me am going, Her wants that*), because this would result from both tense and agreement having been checked. However, researchers have shown that if agreement rates are broken down by the specific pronoun, errors with *her* in subject position and an agreeing verb occur too often to be disregarded as noise. One implication of this analysis is that it is important to analyze errors in terms of the particular form, rather than to sum across a category defined by the adult system, because the child's system may not be operating at this level of abstraction.

The other main theoretical approach to children's syntactic development argues that grammatical abstraction emerges from interaction between the input and innate learning mechanisms and that these are *not* restricted to the domain of syntax. Constructivist approaches maintain that children start by learning low-scope constructions based around specific words or morphemes. These constructions become more complex, and abstractions (for instance, of tense, agreement, subject, and transitive) build up. Initially, a child may have no understanding of the internal structure of a construction (e.g., *what's that?*), but uses it as a whole with a specific meaning. As development proceeds, functional distributional analysis based on the relation between a form and (child-identified) functions leads to representations of constructions developing internal structure. Patterns of relationships build up between constructions and their parts, in a process of increasing complexity and schematization (**Table 1**).

One critical aspect of this theory is that, once a slot develops in a construction, it will be paired with a meaning: thus, a 'noun phrase' slot always denotes a referent. In time, the child will learn to refer in increasingly complex ways; for instance, in English with a range of determiners and adjectives. Constituency thus develops hand in hand with the function of the constituent in the construction and becomes increasingly schematic.

M. Tomasello (2003) provided the most comprehensive statement of this position to date. He suggested that, rather than having to postulate innate syntactic categories or linking rules, it is possible to account for the development of abstract categories and constructions on the basis of general communicative and cognitive processes, such as intention reading, analogy making, and distributional

Table 1 Examples of different types of constructions and their meanings

Form	Meaning	Level of abstraction
What's that?	Requesting a name	Rote-learned
It's a <Noun>[1]	Naming <referent>	Slot-and-frame
Double object construction: <Noun> <Verb> <Noun> <Noun> Mary gave John the ball	Agent-Verb of transfer-Recipient-Transferred Object	Schematic

[1] < > denotes an open slot.

analysis. The critical aspect of this approach is that utterances have meanings as a whole and that, for children to be able to work out what role a word or inflection is playing in an utterance, they have to know, first, what the whole utterance means and then, in a process that Tomasello calls 'blame assignment,' identify the part of the meaning for which the particular form is responsible. In this approach, abstract constructions develop through analogies based on semantic similarity between the meanings of different item-based constructions; for instance, *A hits B*, *X loves Y*, *C pushes D* may give rise to the transitive construction and its syntactic roles.

Tomasello's 'verb island hypothesis' was an early example of such an approach. He claimed that children initially build up constructions around individual verbs, rather than having more general and abstract categories, such as subject, direct object, and transitive verb, from the beginning. Thus, a child who knows the verb *hit* may have a slot before the verb for the 'hitter' and one after for the 'hittee' without having the abstract representation of a transitive construction. A wide range of production experiments that test English-speaking children's ability to use novel verbs in transitive constructions supports this claim. Although most children aged just over 2 years old are already using verbs they know in some two-argument constructions, the ability to demonstrate this knowledge with a verb they have never heard before develops between the ages of 2 and 3 years and can be affected strongly by the experimental method employed.

The verb island hypothesis has been challenged by studies using the preferential looking paradigm. They suggest that children can discriminate between a transitive utterance that matches a scene they are looking at and one in which the argument roles are reversed at younger ages than those shown for success in production experiments. Some researchers have suggested that this indicates that children are innately equipped either with a notion of subject or with rules that link the notion of agent to subject. However, it seems difficult to argue for an innate notion of subject, because subject is not a universally identical category across languages.

Other researchers, less contentiously, suggest that children are already sensitive to the number of arguments in an utterance and their relationship to a causative scene with two actors and that this allows them to make the preferential-looking discrimination. Because children are sensitive pre-verbally to causation and many already know how to name people and objects by the time they take part in preferential-looking studies, this finding seems plausible – particularly because there seems to be a correlation between the child's vocabulary level and success in these tasks.

Children's avoidance of using ungrammatical transitives and intransitives in production experiments also suggests earlier sensitivity to some aspects of verb argument structure. In addition, experiments show that English-speaking children manage to use the transitive construction with a novel verb somewhat earlier when case-marked pronouns, rather than nouns, are used as arguments. It may be that languages, such as German, with relatively clear case-marking of argument roles, also assist children in schematizing these roles somewhat earlier. Pine *et al.* have argued for patterns building up not only around verbs but also around other high-frequency markers, such as *I + Verb* or *Verb + it*. Thus, the child, as well as building up a 'transitive verb' category, would, at the same time, be learning that *I* and other frequent referents in first position can be in a range of semantic roles in relation to the verb. Childers and Tomasello found supporting evidence for this suggestion. Thus, more recent constructivist accounts suggest that the abstract transitive construction builds up from a number of different sources: pre-verbal knowledge of causality, the ability to match arguments in an utterance to referents in the environment, the development of other lexically specific constructions around pronouns, and high-frequency items. The combination of these factors may result in the child being able to perform correctly in some tasks using less fully specified representations than would be required for others (e.g., using a novel verb that has never been heard before in a transitive construction).

From a constructivist perspective, there is initially no necessary relation in the child's system between one construction and another; for instance, between a declarative and a *wh*-question that would be related in the adult system as would be maintained in any analysis based on one or other generativist theory of island constraints (e.g., movement, gaps or checking). However, such relationships do develop. This can be seen from children's increasing conversational flexibility as they question previously mentioned constituents, manipulate topic and focus, and, in English, expand contracted auxiliaries, insert DO-support when rephrasing a previous utterance, and so on. Many experimental studies also show that children become increasingly able to hear a nonce form in one construction (for instance, an active) and to transform it into another (a passive). For linguistic nativists, this should be a relatively automatic outcome of children's abstract linguistic representations.

However, within constructivist approaches, these relations are seen as being learned. This learning occurs in part through the identification of the same meaning-based categories in different constructions and in part through relating the overall meanings of constructions to each other. For instance, the simple active statement, *I want a banana*, communicates something different from the cleft: *It's a banana I want*. Children's over-generalizations of constructions are explained relatively easily within this framework: For instance, when a child says *Don't giggle me* (meaning *Don't make me giggle*), she has analogized *giggle* as having causative meaning and therefore placed it into a causative transitive construction. There are, however, considerable problems both for linguistic nativists and construction-based accounts in explaining how children cut back from such over-generalizations.

Later Syntactic Development

As children's language develops, major changes occur at both clausal and sentential levels. Noun phrases and verb phrases increase in complexity: for instance, although English-speaking children use *a* and *the* early on, it may take many years before they can operate with more complex determiners and their scope (*some, every,* and *each*). Likewise, children may be able to use some auxiliaries (e.g., *I'm X-ing, Can I Y?*) and verb complement structures (e.g., *I want to play out*) from early on, but the full development of complex verb phrases takes considerable time. At the sentential level, although English-speaking children produce many questions between the ages of 2 and 3 years, initially most of these are with contracted copulas (*What's that?, Where's X?*) or contracted auxiliaries (*What's Mummy X-ing?, Where's Y gone?*). Some questions with subject-auxiliary inversion (*Can I X?, Are you Y-ing?*) also start appearing during this period, but it is not until approaching age 3 and older that children start to show considerable flexibility in the range of subjects, auxiliaries, and *wh*-words that they can use in inverted *yes/no*- and *wh*-questions. Clause coordination and subordination (e.g., complement structures, causatives, relative clauses) also develop over a considerable time period – both when these structures start to appear and when they increase in internal complexity.

In principle, it is rather difficult for linguistic nativist theories to explain this slow and somewhat patchy development of complex syntax and the accompanying errors that children make. Once the lexical forms are learned, why should children make uninversion errors (*Where she is going?*) or find some embedded relatives easier than others? Linguistic nativist explanations of children's later syntactic development all start from the claim that children could not learn the abstract basis of these constructions because the constituents involved could not be abstracted from a surface analysis of the input. Errors are accounted for in two ways: (1) they arise from the particularities of the language being learned and not from the absence of the abstract representations of Universal Grammar; or (2) children have full competence and errors arise from faulty methodologies. In constructivist accounts, complex constructions, such as *wh*-questions or relative clauses, begin as item-based or with simpler structures that then build toward greater complexity and schematicity.

Uninversion errors in English-speaking children's *wh*-questions have given rise to several different linguistic nativist accounts. For example, it has been proposed that questioning arguments is easier than questioning adjuncts.

An alternative account, related to the particularities of English, suggested that the errors in children's inversion are explained by the fact that only main verb BE can invert (unlike in German where all main verbs can invert in questions) and DO-support is also unique. Recent constructivist accounts have explained inversion errors in terms of the relative frequency of *wh* + auxiliary combinations in the input. Thus, it has been suggested that children are learning correct inversion from high-frequency combinations of a *wh*-word plus a specific form of the auxiliary and that uninversion errors occur when they have not yet learned the correct combination and produce a 'groping pattern' by putting together a known *wh*-word and a known declarative.

However, the overriding argument, from the linguistic nativist position, against the possibility of learning syntax is that children can deal with complex constructions that could not have been learned from the input. An example is extraction from embedded clauses in *wh*-questions: *Who do you think John likes?* In UG accounts, children operate with abstract formalisms that relate the object of the embedded clause first to the object of *you think* and from there to the position at the front of the sentence. These formalisms could not, it is argued, be learned from the sequential probabilities of strings on the surface of the input; in addition, the structures are rare to nonexistent in the input and therefore could not be learned as a whole. Whether this latter point is the case awaits much denser sampling of the input, but it should be noted that this type of extraction is not possible in German and that a much wider range of extraction occurs in Italian. This considerable cross-linguistic variation therefore requires, in UG terms, a complex parametric account and, from the point of view of the language learner, close attention to the particularities of the language.

From a constructivist point of view, children solve these tasks by building up their knowledge of constituency and using already established form-meaning mappings to identify potential constituents in novel constructions. Thus, although children may not have had previous experience with the type of sentence noted above, they will already know constructions that identify the matrix *wh*-clause as a constituent asking for an act of reference, thus allowing them to attempt to identify the referent of the embedded relative. For instance, English-speaking children's early relative clauses tend not to be restricted (i.e., adding more information about a referent: *The cow that the dog bit ran away*), but presentational (i.e., introducing a topic: *That's the cow that goes there*). Presentational relatives do not involve embedding one clause within another; the main clause is usually a copula (one of the earliest constructions that English-speaking children learn), and the relative clause is not presupposed information but contains the new information to be conveyed. It has been suggested that all these factors make these constructions easier to produce and also make them the basis for the development of more complex relative clause structures. The idea that already existing constituents can be used to work out the meaning of a novel construction is supported by a modeling study in which a connectionist network was shown to generalize correctly to previously unlearned constructions on the basis of having learned a variety of simpler constructions.

Developing Pragmatic and Metalinguistic Skills

Children are immersed in communicative interaction with others from infancy, but there are many aspects that take years to develop. Coordinating reference across speaker and listener roles involves manipulating and understanding given and new information, deictic and anaphoric pronouns, temporal information, and so on. In most of the cultures studied, these skills develop initially in conversations with others, and children's attempts to narrate sequences of events start to develop slightly later. Both conversation and narrative require the ability to ground utterances and to refer to referents in ways that require complex cognitive, communicative, and linguistic skills. Children also have to learn to adjust their speech to the genre of the task (conversation, personal narrative, reporting, arguing) and to fit the social context in which they are communicating (for instance, levels of politeness and formality.

Conversation

Early conversations with young children typically show a great deal of scaffolding. Thus, background and setting and the identification of referents are provided by the child's interlocutor. Around the age of 2 years, children are more fluent participants when the conversation is highly 'scripted' around routine activities and when they can join in a multiparty conversation at moments that they choose. Between the ages of 2.6 to 3.0 years, the first, more subtle, discourse particles start to be used (for instance, in English, *now* and *just*), but their range and presence continue developing up to and beyond the school years. Topic continuity in terms of responding to questions and maintaining the topic over a number of turns also improves radically between the ages of 2 and 4 years. Clarification requests by children and children's responses to them show clear development as well: Children respond to clarification requests with more nuanced answers as they get older, and they also make more of them, though even at the age of 7 years, children in a referential communication task do not make clarification requests either as much or in as focused a way as is required by the task. Children's rhetorical skills develop throughout the school years, with the ability to bring arguments to bear, to return to a conversational topic, and to introduce new topics in an appropriate way, all taking many years to perfect.

Narrative

Children's early narratives tend to be a set of short utterances with no attempt at cohesion among them. For a child to be able to narrate an event to another who was not present requires taking into account the hearer's lack of knowledge of the timing of the event, its sequence, and the participants. This is a complex task in itself, and children also have to learn to coordinate sequences of utterances to keep track of referents and events such that, for instance, already referred-to participants are referred to in one way, and novel ones in another.

Once children start being able to produce some coordination between utterances in a narrative, they often use very repetitive devices: for instance, maintaining reference to the same referent as thematic subject throughout the story (e.g., using *He* at the beginning of every utterance) or using *and then* at the beginning of every utterance to coordinate the action. Clearly, the development of narrative abilities is based on the development of a range of skills: Children must be able to take into account the perspective of the listener in terms of what the listener does and does not know. They must also know the linguistic devices of the language that coordinate clauses within utterances (e.g., temporal sequencing, subordination) and across utterances (e.g., the use of pronouns for anaphoric reference), and they must know how their language encodes perspectives; for instance, in English, manner of motion tends to be encoded in the verb, whereas in Spanish it tends to be encoded in adverbials.

Metalinguistic Skills

Children gradually become able to consciously reflect on language, to correct their own and others' utterances, and to notice features of language at all levels: Rhyming relationships, the explanation of metaphors and idioms, and grammaticality judgments. A. Karmiloff-Smith has incorporated language development and metalinguistic awareness into her general theory of the development of cognitive skills. In this approach, the early period of language learning is concerned with skill automatization: children have to learn the forms of the language and to use them relatively effortlessly. Once language becomes relatively fluent and automatic, it can become an object of reflection.

Karmiloff-Smith also discussed children's increasing awareness of the plurifunctionality of forms. She sees metacognition as going through several stages in which initially awareness is implicit and only later, as a result of 'representational redescription,' does it become available to conscious reflection.

For many children, the process of moving to conscious awareness of the forms of language and how they fit together is almost certainly aided by learning to read and write. It has been argued that many of the structures that linguists are concerned with can only be found in written texts and thus that children only learn them during the school years. Competence is, therefore, still developing, rather than being either innate or language development being 'all over by 3.0.' How rapidly these skills develop and how far children get with them is related to the complexity of the language that they hear at home and at school and to levels of literacy.

Clearly, literacy cannot be the only way in which speakers become aware of language as an object of reflection. Preliterate children already show some metacognitive awareness of aspects of language as indicated by Karmiloff-Smith; for instance, they can sometimes correct ungrammatical utterances in naturalistic and experimental situations. There must be many aspects of oral interactions that also afford this ability; for instance, argumentation, speech making, traditions of oral narrative, and the learning of complex ritual language are all likely to be media through which speakers and listeners come to be able to reflect on linguistic structure and its meaning. The important point is that these genres may contain much more complex language than children are likely to learn early on. Thus, language competence, often in the structures in which linguists are most interested, continues to develop over many years.

Atypical Development

Some children grow up in situations that are radically different from those in which typically developing children learn an oral language. The study of these children's atypical development often throws light on the processes involved in language learning and their inter-relationships, though caution should be exercised because one has to see the child and his or her situation as a whole. It is therefore impossible to treat these cases as controlled experiments in which only one variable is changed.

First, from the study of children who grow up from birth in a home where the language used is one of the sign languages of the world, it is clear that these children go through the normal stages of language development on the same timetable as children learning oral languages. Sign languages differ from oral languages not only in the obvious dimension of the medium but also, as a result, in the degree of simultaneity of signs and in the ways in which the face and hands are used grammatically and suprasegmentally. Thus, comparisons between the ways in which children learn the morphology, syntax, and pragmatics of oral and sign language can be extremely illuminating.

There are two groups of children whose nontypical development has been of particular interest to the study of language development: children whose language seems relatively poor by comparison with their nonverbal cognitive levels (children with SLI) and children with Williams's syndrome, whose language seems relatively advanced compared to their very low level of nonverbal cognitive development. Researchers coming from a more linguistic nativist background have claimed that these two syndromes are evidence for an innate basis to grammatical development (compromised in SLI, preserved in Williams's syndrome) that is separate from more general cognitive development. In the case of SLI, the issue is the nature of the biological compromise. Most children with SLI have a range of problems with language, some of which may be more typical earlier and some later. Articulatory and phonological problems, together with delayed inflectional marking, are typical early problems that often resolve, leaving apparent grammar-only problems later on. There is certainly no agreement in the field that the pattern of impairment in SLI children indicates the presence of an innate module for syntax, though some have made claims to this effect.

In the case of Williams's syndrome, it is clear that these children also suffer from a wide range of problems with language and that none of them ever reach the language levels of age-matched, typically developing controls. Karmiloff-Smith *et al.* emphasized a developmental model for these children that suggests that, although language development is atypical from the outset, the problems that children demonstrate change with development and depend on the strategies for producing language that they have developed at earlier stages in the absence of the processes available to typically developing children. Here, too, then, there seems no clear evidence for a specific innate module for syntax.

Learnability and Constituency

The field of language acquisition has been dominated until recently by the so-called learnability issue; namely, that children cannot learn correct syntax from only positive evidence (the so-called poverty of the stimulus argument). Chomsky's various versions of a postulated innate Universal Grammar were attempts to provide these constraints, and the various nativist proposals outlined above aimed to show how these constraints explain different aspects of language development.

Several solutions have been proposed, all of which involve changing the premises of the learnability problem in one way or the other, usually to make the generation of sentences in the language probabilistic, rather than all or nothing. Although the leap from the higher reaches of statistical theory to the details of children's language development is rather large, this solution actually accords quite well both with constructivist approaches to language learning that emphasize the larning of the distributional probabilities in the input and to various attempts to model computationally how distributional probabilities might lead to phrasal learning. Despite not incorporating any model of semantics, these attempts have been quite successful at detecting distributional regularities in the target language that could form one basis for the establishment of categories and of syntagmatic learning.

However, language learning must go beyond the mere learning of immediately sequential probabilities between words. Simply calculating the transitional probability between one word and the next will ignore constituency and produce ungrammatical sentences. This was the basis for Chomsky's 1957 attack on the behaviorist theory of language development. Sentences involve constituents; the subject noun phrase, however long it is, agrees with the main verb, regardless of how many subordinate clauses occur in between; the relationship between an inverted question and its declarative version involves the relationship between the *wh*-word and the whole questioned constituent, independent of the length of the constituent or what occurs between it and the main verb. Thus in *The boy wearing a green hat who I saw yesterday in the park is very nice*, the subject NP (*The boy*) must agree with the main verb (*is*). The relationship between *Is the boy who is wearing a green hat nice?* and *The boy who is wearing a green hat is nice* is that the first *Is* in the question parallels the second *is* in the declarative; otherwise, we would have *Is the boy who wearing a green hat is nice?*

From a constructivist point of view, the crucial extra ingredient is that children are intention readers and meaning makers and that they learn about constituency by building up increasingly complex paradigmatic slots that connect form to meaning. Thus, a child who has heard and used literally hundreds of thousands of copula sentences of the form – *The boy's nice*; *The bus is red*; *They're the ones I want*; *They are really really good*; *The ones over there are the ones I want*; *The boy wearing a green hat is nice* – will know that *the boy wearing a green hat* refers to a particular object or person. This learned structural knowledge of constituency is then used to parse and produce the more complex embedded structures.

Conclusion

Humans have developed language and it has a biological basis. Yet, precisely what this basis is (or, more likely, bases are) still needs a great deal of precise specification. For instance, localization of language in the brains of adults is much more determined than it is in children: Children who have early damage to the areas of the brain that subsume language in adults can learn language to normal levels and will have language represented in other parts of the brain as adults. Thus, it seems that language modularity, and the relative independence of syntax and semantics that characterizes the results of some experiments with adults, may be an outcome of development, rather than being pre-given. Chomsky's insistence on a separation between syntax and meaning, as well as the claim that syntax is essentially unlearnable and therefore that there must be an innate module for grammar, has ultimately had a negative impact on the scientific study of how children learn to talk. However, many of the issues raised by researchers working within this tradition, especially with regard to the development of more complex syntax, present challenges that have not yet been met fully by those who suggest that, whatever else is innate, syntax is learned through the application of general cognitive skills to the communicative tasks set for children by those around them.

Both positions face a number of challenges. In both, there is a need for greater specification of the processes involved so that proposals can be tested empirically. The challenge to linguistic nativists is to specify in advance the postulated performance limitations and late maturing processes precisely enough so that, rather than invoking them on an *ad hoc* basis to deal with counter-evidence, they can be used to make falsifiable predictions. In addition, these accounts often lack any notion of development: how does what a child is doing at one stage affect what happens next? Finally, because there are input effects at all levels of language acquisition, such theories tend to under-theorize the role of the input, not just in the quantity required by the child but also in the ways in which its precise characteristics are reflected in the child's system and how this interacts with any hypothesized innate knowledge.

The challenge to constructivists is to specify more precisely the ways in which the cognitive and communicative development of the child and the distributional information in the input interact to generate the patterns of learning and of errors and to test this with a wider range of languages and a wider range of input densities and conditions. There is a long way to go, even in the study of English language learning, to say nothing of other languages, in specifying the precise ways in which children expand their inventory of constructions and how they become increasingly schematic.

Children are creative communicators from the start. The question is the basis of this creativity, its scope, and how it develops.

See also: Bilingualism; Grammar; Imitation and Modeling; Language Acquisition Theories; Literacy; Pragmatic Development; Preverbal Development and Speech Perception; Semantic Development; Speech Perception.

Suggested Readings

Aguado-Orea J (2004) *The acquisition of morpho-syntax in Spanish: implications for current theories of development.* Ph.D diss., University of Nottingham.

Bates E (1976) *Language and context: the acquisition of pragmatics.* New York: Academic Press.

Bates E, Bretherton I, and Snyder L (1988) *From first words to grammar: individual differences and dissociable mechanisms.* Cambridge: Cambridge University Press.

Berman R and Slobin D (1994) *Relating events in narrative: a crosslinguistic developmental study.* Hillsdale, NJ: Erlbaum.

Bernhardt B and Stemberger JS (1998) *Handbook of phonological development.* San Diego: Academic Press.

Bowerman M (1988) 'The "no negative evidence" problem: how do children avoid constructing an over-general grammar?' In: Hawkins JA (ed.) *Explaining language universals.* Oxford: Blackwell.

Bowerman M and Choi S (2001) 'Shaping meanings for language: universal and language-specific in the acquisition of spatial semantic categories' In: Bowerman M and Levinson S (eds.) *Language acquisition and conceptual development*, pp. 475–511. New York: Cambridge University Press.

Carey S and Bartlett E (1978) 'Acquiring a single new word' *Paper and Reports on Child Language Development* 15: 17–29.

Carpenter M, Nagell K, and Tomasello M (1998) 'Social cognition, joint attention and communicative competence from 9–15 months of age' *Monographs of the Society for Research in Child Development* 255.

Chang F (2002) 'Symbolically speaking: a connectionist model of sentence production' *Cognitive Science* 26(5): 609–651.

Clark E (2003) *First language acquisition.* Cambridge: Cambridge University Press.

Crain S and Thornton R (1998) *Investigations in Universal Grammar: a guide to experiments on the acquisition of syntax.* Cambridge, MA: MIT Press.

Croft W (2001) *Radical construction grammar: syntactic theory in typological perspective.* Oxford: Oxford University Press.

Dąbrowska E (2004) *Language, mind and brain.* Washington, DC: Georgetown University Press.

Demuth K (1992) 'The acquisition of Sesotho' In: Slobin DI (ed.) *The crosslinguistic study of language acquisition,* vol. 3, pp. 557–638. Hillsdale, NJ: Lawrence Erlbaum.

Diessel H (2003) *The acquisition of complex sentences in English.* Cambridge: Cambridge University Press.

Drozd K (2004) 'Learnability and linguistic performance (plus commentaries)' *Journal of Child Language* 31: 431–457.

Elman J, Bates E, Johnson M, Karmiloff-Smith A, Parisi D, and Plunkett K (1997) *Rethinking innateness: a connectionist perspective on development.* Cambridge, MA: MIT Press.

Fenson L, Dale P, Reznick JS, Bates E, Thal D, and Pethick S (1994) 'Variability in early communicative development' *Monographs of the Society for Research in Child Development* 242(59): 5.

Fernald A, Pinto J, Swingley D, Weinberg A, and McRoberts G (1998) 'Rapid gains in speed of verbal processing by infants in the second year' *Psychological Science* 9: 28–31.

Fodor J (2001) 'Setting syntactic parameters' In: Baltin M and Collins C (eds.) *The handbook of contemporary syntactic theory*, pp. 730–767. Oxford: Blackwell.

Gentner D (1982) 'Why nouns are learned before verbs: Linguistic relativity versus natural partitioning' In: Kuczaj S (ed.) *Language Development,* vol. 2, pp. 301–333. Hillsdale, NJ: Erlbaum.

Gobet F, Freudenthal D, and Pine JM (2004) 'Modelling syntactic development in a cross-linguistic context' In: Sakas WG (ed.) *Proceedings of the First COLING Workshop on Psycho-computational Models of Human Language Acquisition*, pp. 53–60.

Gomez RL, Gerken L, and Schvaneveldt RW (2000) 'The basis of transfer in artificial grammar learning' *Memory & Cognition* 28(2): 253–263.

Hart B and Risley T (1995) *Meaningful differences in the everyday experience of young American children.* Baltimore, MD: H. Paul Brookes.

Hickmann M (2003) *Children's discourse: person, space and time across languages.* Cambridge: Cambridge University Press.

Huttenlocher J, Vasilyeva M, Cymerman E, and Levine S (2002) 'Language input and child syntax' *Cognitive Psychology* 45(3): 337–374.

Jusczyk P (1997) *The discovery of spoken language.* Cambridge, MA: MIT Press.

Karmiloff-Smith A (1994) 'Precis of beyond modularity: a developmental perspective on cognitive science (with peer commentary)' *Behavioral and Brain Sciences* 17(4): 693–706.

Karmiloff-Smith A, Brown JH, Grice S, and Paterson S (2003) 'Dethroning the myth: cognitive dissociations and innate modularity in Williams's syndrome'. *Developmental Neuropsychology* 23(1&2): 229–244.

Köpcke K (1998) 'The acquisition of plural marking in English and German revisited: schemata versus rules' *Journal of Child Language* 25: 293–319.

Leonard L (1998) *Children with specific language impairment.* Cambridge, MA: MIT Press.

Lewis JD and Elman J (2001) 'A connectionist investigation of linguistic arguments from poverty of the stimulus: learning the unlearnable' In: Moore JD and Stenning K (eds.) *Proceedings of the Twenty-Third Annual Conference of the Cognitive Science Society.* Mahwah, NJ: Erlbaum.

Lieven E (1997) 'Variation in a crosslinguistic context' In: Slobin DI (ed.) *The crosslinguistic study of language acquisition,* vol. 5, pp. 199–263. Hillsdale, NJ: Lawrence Erlbaum.

Lieven E, Behrens H, Speares J, and Tomasello M (2003) 'Early syntactic creativity: a usage-based approach' *Journal of Child Language* 30: 333–370.

MacWhinney B (2004) 'A multiple process solution to the logical problem of language acquisition (plus commentaries)' *Journal of Child Language* 31: 883–914.

Mandler J (2000) 'Perceptual and conceptual processes in infancy' *Journal of Cognition and Development* 1: 3–36.

Maratsos M (2000) 'More overgeneralisations after all' *Journal of Child Language* 28: 35–54.

Markman E, Wasow J, and Hansen M (2003) 'Use of the mutual exclusivity assumption by young word learners' *Cognitive Psychology* 47(2): 241–275.

Miller J and Weinert R (1998) *Spontaneous spoken language: syntax and discourse.* Oxford: Clarendon.

Morris W, Cottrell G, and Elman J (2000) 'A connectionist simulation of the empirical acquisition of grammatical relations' In: Wermter S and Sun R (eds.) *Hybrid neural symbolic integration.* Berlin: Springer Verlag.

O'Grady W (1997) *Syntactic development.* Chicago: University of Chicago Press.

Peters A (1997) 'Language typology, prosody and the acquisition of grammatical morphemes' In: Slobin DI (ed.) *The crosslinguistic study of language acquisition,* vol. 5, pp. 135–197. Hillsdale, NJ: Lawrence Erlbaum.

Pine J, Lieven E, and Rowland C (1998) 'Comparing different models of the development of the verb category' *Linguistics* 36: 4–40.

Pine J, Rowland C, Lieven E, and Theakston A (2005) 'Testing the Agreement/Tense Omission Model: why the data on children's use of non-nominative 3psg subjects count against the ATOM'. *Journal of Child Language* 32: 2.

Plunkett K and Juola P (1999) 'A connectionist model of English past tense and plural morphology' *Cognitive Science* 23(4): 463–490.

Ravid D and Tolchinsky L (2002) 'Developing linguistic literacy: a comprehensive model (plus commentaries)' *Journal of Child Language* 29: 417–447.

Rice M and Wexler K (1996) 'Towards tense as a clinical marker of specific language impairment in English-speaking children' *Journal of Speech and Hearing Research* 41: 1412–1431.

Rowland C and Pine J (2000) 'Subject-auxiliary inversion errors and wh-question acquisition' *Journal of Child Language* 27(1): 157–181.

Santelmann L, Berk S, Austin J, Somashekar S, and Lust B (2002) 'Continuity and development in the acquisition of yes/no question: dissociating movement and inflection' *Journal of Child Language* 29: 813–842.

Slobin DI (1985) 'Crosslinguistic evidence for the language-making capacity' In: Slobin DI (ed.) *The cross-linguistic study of language acquisition,* vol. 2, pp. 1157–1256. Hillsdale, NJ: Lawrence Erlbaum.

Slobin DI, Gerhardt J, Kyratztis A, and Guo J (1996) *Social interaction, social context and language: essays in honor of Susan Ervin-Tripp.* Mahwah, NJ: LEA.

Tomasello M (1992) *First verbs: a case study of early grammatical development.* New York: Cambridge University Press.

Tomasello M (2000) 'Do young children have adult syntactic competence?' *Cognition* 74: 209–253.

Tomasello M (2003) *Constructing a language.* Cambridge, MA: Harvard University Press.

Tomasello M and Stahl D (2004) 'Sampling children's spontaneous speech: How much is enough?'. *Journal of Child Language* 31: 101–121.
Valian V (1991) 'Syntactic subjects in the early speech of American and Italian children' *Cognition* 40: 21–81.
Vihman M (1996) *Phonological development.* Oxford: Blackwell.
Weist R, Pawlak A, and Carapella J (2004) 'Syntactic-semantic interface in the acquisition of verb morphology' *Journal of Child Language* 31(1): 31–60.
Wexler K (1998) 'Very early parameter setting and the unique checking constraint: a new explanation of the optional infinitive stage' *Lingua* 106: 23–79.
Wexler K (2002) 'Lenneberg's dream: learning, normal language development and specific language impairment'. In: Schaffer J and Levy Y (eds.) *Language competence across populations: towards a definition of specific language impairment.* Mahwah, NJ: Lawrence Erlbaum.

Learning

R L Gómez, The University of Arizona, Tucson, AZ, USA

2008 Elsevier Inc. All rights reserved.

Glossary

Classical conditioning – A process of behavior modification by which a learner comes to respond to a previously neutral stimulus. When the neutral stimulus is repeatedly paired with an unconditioned stimulus, it begins to elicit the desired response even in the absence of the unconditioned stimulus.

Discrimination – After familiarization with novel information, infants are tested for learning in terms of their ability to differentiate a stimulus consistent with their learning experience versus a stimulus that is not consistent, measured in terms of the time they orient to the two stimulus types. Discrimination, and hence learning, is said to occur if attention to the two stimulus types differs across a group of infants.

Frequency – The number of times a unit occurs.

Generalization – A process involving abstraction away from specific stimulus materials that leads to perception of higher-order regularities or rules. Generalization enables learners to recognize new examples that are similar, but not identical, to previously encountered examples.

High-amplitude operant sucking procedure – Infants in this procedure are tested in a reclining seat, facing forward toward a colorful display. The infant sucks on a blind nipple (one without a hole) connected by a rubber hose to a pressure transducer that produces a signal on a polygraph machine. High-amplitude sucks (the top 33% of responses) are reinforced to a particular stimulus. After time, the infant's sucks will diminish as the infant becomes familiar with the stimulus. At that point a new stimulus is introduced. An increase in the quantity of high-amplitude sucks is interpreted as the infant having noticed a difference in the old and new stimulus.

Joint probability – The probability of two units occurring together.

Observational learning – A process by which learners acquire behaviors by observing others then imitating what they have observed.

Operant conditioning – A process of behavior modification in which the probability of a specific behavior is increased by applying positive reinforcement after the occurrence of the behavior. The occurrence of a behavior can be decreased through negative reinforcement.

Statistical learning – The discovery of structure in perceptual information in terms of the statistical properties of perceptual units. In language the perceptual units can be phonetic segments, syllables, or words. Taking English as an example, certain phonetic segments (e.g., the -ng sound in any word ending in '-ing') are statistically probable at the ends of words, but are nonexistent at the beginnings of words, whereas this segment can occur with high statistical probability at the beginnings of words in some languages.

Transitional probability – The probability of the occurrence of one unit given another (the probability of event B given event A is the joint probability of event A and event B divided by the probability of event A).

Introduction

Learning is a relatively stable change in behavior that results from exposure to a novel stimulus. Developmentalists have long been interested in learning because of its potentially important role in cognitive development. Learning is a fundamental process that operates in concert with other perceptual and cognitive processes, but the extent of its contribution to early cognition (in contrast to the contribution of biological constraints) is largely unknown. One goal of current research is to identify core infant learning mechanisms in an effort to better characterize the infant's initial state. Before detailing the research to date, the author briefly reviews the history of learning as it has pertained to issues in child development.

The impetus behind human development, whether caused by nature or nurture, has been debated for centuries. John Locke (1632–1704) espoused the view that children were born with a *tabula rasa* (blank slate) and must therefore acquire all knowledge through experience. In contrast, Jean-Jacques Rousseau (1712–78) emphasized the role of innate knowledge in development. An emphasis on learning re-emerged in the last century with Pavlov (1849–1936) who showed with classical conditioning that an unconditioned response (a reflex such as salivation) could be trained to respond to a conditioned stimulus (CS; the sound of a bell) if the CS was paired with an unconditioned stimulus (US) such as food. Eventually, the food could be taken away to show that the CS was sufficient for producing the response. Based on these principles, John B. Watson (1878–1958) advocated a psychology of learning called behaviorism. This movement dominated theories of human development in the early half of the twentieth century. In particular, B. F. Skinner (1904–90) developed a theory of learning based on principles of operant conditioning, emphasizing the role of reinforcement and punishment in shaping specific behaviors. His work culminated in the book *Verbal Behavior*, which attempted to explain how a complex skill (such as language) could be acquired by principles of operant learning, where learners receive reinforcement for particular linguistic behaviors. However, in 1957, Noam Chomsky argued that Skinners' theory was inadequate for explaining the complex rules that underlie human language, rules that enable children to understand sentences they have never heard and generate novel sentences. Chomsky also rejected the notion that the processes advocated by Skinner could explain how human children can acquire language so rapidly. Chomsky rejected the simple processes proposed by Skinner in favor of the notion that children are biologically prepared to acquire language such that fundamental principles of language are hard-wired into the circuitry of the brain.

Although Chomsky's arguments were directly relevant to language acquisition, they reflected a paradigm shift spreading across the field of psychology at that time. The notion that human behavior could be explained in terms of associative learning principles was widely abandoned in favor of theories emphasizing underlying cognitive processes. Other scientists also argued that simple associative learning principles were inadequate for explaining human behavior. For instance, Lashley (1890–1958) pointed out that many human endeavors, such as language, involve hierarchically organized behaviors as opposed to chains of stimulus response associations. Additionally, in 1961, Albert Bandura showed that children could learn through vicarious observation (observational learning) without need for direct reinforcement. In the area of language acquisition, learning theories were replaced by theories emphasizing inborn principles and parameters (where principles are rules common to all languages and parameters are rules capturing the possible differences between languages).

In recent years the tide has turned back toward an emphasis on learning. This has been driven by the success of computer models demonstrating that simple associative systems can accomplish fairly complex learning, as well as broad acceptance of the fact that the perceptual input to learners is rich in statistical information. Finally, experimental work with infants has led to exciting discoveries regarding early learning abilities suggesting that human learning is more powerful than originally conceived in behaviorist theory. This experimental work, and precursors to it, is the focus of this article.

The remaining sections summarize some of the early work on learning before detailing recent experimental work on infants' ability to detect statistical structure. The article ends by posing open questions and challenges for learning research.

Early Work on Learning

Much of the earliest research on infant learning was methodological in nature. Driving questions were whether human infants were even capable of learning and if so, what types of learning they would exhibit. Researchers were also interested in determining when learning might begin to take place in development. Before these questions could be answered, fundamental methodological details had to be worked out. For instance, it was important to rule out the possibility that a change in behavior reflected acclimatization to a stimulus or a response to a particularly appealing reward, behaviors that mimic but do not reflect learning. Additionally, a number of early studies failed because researchers did not know how much or how little exposure to a stimulus would promote learning or which types of rewards were needed.

The earliest studies investigated whether infants could be classically conditioned to associate a conditioned stimulus with an unconditioned response by pairing a CS with an UCS. In 1920, John B Watson and Rosalie Raynor exposed an 11-month-old child named Albert to an UCS (a loud sound) each time he touched a CS (a white rat). The loud sound caused Albert to cry and withdraw his hand, so that subsequently, merely seeing the rat led to the same behavior, demonstrating memory of a learned stimulus–response pairing.

Infants just a few hours old can be classically conditioned also. In 1984, E M Blass and colleagues followed a stroke on the forehead (the CS) by immediate oral delivery of sucrose to infants through a glass pipette (the UCS). A control group was exposed to the same number of CS–UCS pairings, but the time interval between the pairings varied across trials. Another control group received only the UCS in order to rule out the possibility that repeated deliveries of sucrose itself would result in a change in behavior. During an extinction phase where infants received the CS but not the sucrose delivery, the experimental group cried when the sucrose was not delivered whereas infants in the two control groups did not. All three groups experienced withdrawal of sucrose, so this in itself could not explain the experimental group's behavior. Their behavior could only be explained in terms of their having learned the predictive CS–UCS relationship. This study, and others in this general vein, established that infants could be classically conditioned from birth.

Researchers were also interested in determining whether infants were capable of learning using operant principles. Operant conditioning involves reinforcing a naturally occurring response to increase or decrease the rate of that response. For instance, positively reinforcing a response leads to an increased rate of that behavior. This is in contrast to classical conditioning, which involves a learned association between a CS and UCS. The first study to obtain evidence for operant conditioning in newborns was conducted in 1966 by Siqueland and Lipsett. They paired differential auditory stimuli with an unconditioned tactile stimulus (stroking the infant's cheek). The stroking produces an unconditioned rooting reflex to that side and by necessity a head turn. In their study, when the pairing of the positive auditory stimulus (a buzzer) and the tactile stimulus produced a head turn, this was always followed by a positive reinforcer (administration of sugar water). However, a head-turn in response to the pairing of the tactile stimulus and the negative auditory stimulus (a tone) was never reinforced. Responding to the presence of the positive auditory stimulus increased over time whereas responding to the negative auditory stimulus decreased suggesting that infants were discriminating between the two types of auditory stimuli based on operant conditioning.

An operant paradigm that has been used extensively to study learning and memory in infants since then, is the mobile conjugate reinforcement procedure developed by Carolyn Rovee-Collier in 1969. In this procedure, an infant is placed on his back in a crib beneath a mobile. A ribbon runs from a suspension hook on the mobile to the infant's ankle (in the reinforcing condition) or from a hook that will not move the mobile (the nonreinforcing condition). First, a measure of baseline kicking is obtained by observing the number of kicks in the nonreinforcing condition (a pretest). After obtaining a baseline measure, the ribbon is tied to the suspension hook so that when the infant kicks he moves the mobile, resulting in a high rate of kicking and attention to the mobile. Memory of the learned experience can then be assessed after various delays by positioning the infant beneath the mobile, attaching his ankle to the nonreinforcing hook (to prevent additional learning), and measuring the number of kicks he produces. Learning is evidenced by a greater rate of kicking relative to baseline when infants are tested with the same mobile as compared to a different one. This procedure was used to show that 2-month-old infants could remember a learning experience occurring 24 h earlier.

Infants and young children do not necessarily need reinforcement to learn. In a seminal study of observational learning reported in 1961, Bandura showed that 4-year-olds who simply observed an adult beating up a Bobo doll were more likely to direct similar behaviors toward the doll in subsequent play than were children in a control condition who did not see an adult exhibiting such behavior. This type of learning is referred to as observational because learners imitate an observed behavior with no stimulus–response pairing or any kind of reinforcement. Observational learning does not appear to have a lower age limit. In deferred imitation, another type of observational learning, an experimenter models a sequence of actions and the infant is later tested on the ability to reproduce the behavior. In 1992, Patricia Bauer and Jean Mandler showed that infants as young as 11.5 months of age can learn and later imitate novel actions in an event sequence like making a rattle. Events were simple, consisting of two or three actions, but infants readily reproduced the actions in their correct order. Interestingly, the type of sequence matters, such that arbitrary sequences involving a series of events that are not causally related (like banging, turning, and stacking a ring on a dowel) are much more difficult to learn than causally related actions that require actions to be performed in a certain order (such as making a rattle by putting a ball in a paper cup, joining the mouth of the cup with the mouth of another paper cup, and shaking). In a different experimental paradigm demonstrating observational learning, Rachel Barr and colleagues in 1996 showed that infants as young as 6 months of age can remember and imitate portions of a sequence they have observed being modeled. The sequence, consisting of removing a mitten from a puppet's hand, shaking the mitten (causing a bell inside the mitten to sound), and placing the mitten back on the puppet, was imitated by the infants after a 24 h delay. In most cases, exposure was very brief. The event sequences were modeled just twice with 11.5-month-olds and six times with the 6-month-olds. Additionally, infants as young as 2 months of age can engage in learning without feedback as shown by Naomi Wentworth and Marshall Haith in a study reported in 1992. Infants were exposed to an alternating left–right pattern of visually presented pictures.

On one side (left or right) the picture was always the same and on the other side the picture varied. Infants showed learning of the visual content of the picture as evidenced by their tendency to anticipate the location of the stable picture and to respond to it more quickly as compared to the location of the unstable picture.

Given these findings it becomes important to ask just how early learning occurs in human development. Given the results detailed above, it is reasonable to think that learning may occur as soon as infants are able to process sensory information, indeed that they might even begin learning *in utero*.

One of the earliest indications of fetal learning was the finding that newborns prefer their mother's voice to that of another female speaker. They also prefer sentences from their native language to sentences from another language. Passages read in French produced higher sucking rates in French newborns than passages read in Russian. Other studies have shown that these preferences are not specific to French. Therefore such preferences must be shaped by prenatal experience with maternal speech. What might infants be learning? We know from intrauterine recordings that low-frequency components of maternal speech, including its rhythmic qualities are audible *in utero* and infants born prematurely at 24 weeks are able to react to sounds, raising the possibility that learning may begin this early.

In 1986, Anthony DeCasper and Melanie Spence showed that newborns, whose mothers read a passage aloud each day during the last 6 weeks of pregnancy, were able to discriminate the passage from an unfamiliar one at birth. Two-day-olds were tested, using a high-amplitude operant sucking procedure, to see whether the familiar passage would be more reinforcing than an unfamiliar one, even when read in another woman's voice. It was, suggesting that infants had learned features from their training passage involving its prosodic (or rhythmic) qualities over and above features specific to their mother's voice. The passages were not read aloud before the newborns were tested, and thus learning must have occurred *in utero*. A later study, by DeCasper and colleagues, used heart rate as a dependent measure to test learning in 37-week-old fetuses. Mothers recited one of two rhymes out loud, once a day, over 4 weeks. At 37 weeks' gestational age the fetuses were stimulated with recordings of the familiar and unfamiliar rhymes. The familiar rhyme elicited a decrease in fetal heart rate, whereas the unfamiliar one did not, suggesting discrimination of the two passages, and hence learning.

Statistical Learning

Despite the success of these early studies, learning was not studied in its own right for many years. In the past 10 years, however, researchers have begun to document learning of statistical regularities in perceptual input. Statistical learning, the ability to track probabilistic patterns, is an important mechanism because probabilistic structure abounds in the information available to our senses.

Statistical structure can take many forms including the frequency of individual units, joint probability, or the transitional probability of one unit given another. Joint probability is defined as the probability of two units occurring together. Transitional probability is the probability of the occurrence of one unit given another (the probability of event B given event A is the joint probability of event A and event B divided by the probability of event A). There are other forms of statistical structure but common to all forms is the requirement that units occur with some regularity that lends itself to mathematical description (and presumably also to computation).

As an example of statistical learning, a problem infants must solve in speech perception is identifying words in running speech. This is a daunting task because words are rarely demarcated by pauses. One popular proposal is that infants might learn a few words spoken in isolation and use the boundaries of these known words to discover the boundaries of words that co-occur. However, useful information is conveyed in the higher transitional probabilities occurring between syllables in words as compared to the lower probabilities of syllables spanning words. In a landmark study reported in 1996, Jenny Saffran, Richard Aslin, and Elissa Newport showed that very young infants are able to capitalize on this kind of information. For instance, in the phrase 'pretty baby', the syllables 'ba' and 'by' occur within a word, whereas 'ty' and 'ba' span words. As such 'by' is more highly predicted by 'ba' than 'ba' is by 'ty'. Saffran and colleagues implemented this idea experimentally by exposing 8-month-old infants to continuously running syllables such as tupirotiladogolabudabikutupirodabikugolabu.... where tupiro, dabiku, tilado, and golabu were words that were presented in random order. For instance, in the first four syllables in this particular example 'tu pi' and 'pi ro' are syllables within words, whereas 'ro' and 'ti' are syllables spanning words.

Although statistical learning occurs in multiple modalities, much of the research has been conducted in the context of language acquisition. In these studies infants are exposed to artificial language materials they have never heard before. In natural language cues are correlated making it difficult to pinpoint the locus of learning, but artificial languages are devised with particular learning cues in mind, enabling more precise control over the input to learners. Artificial languages also control for prior exposure and therefore provide insights into learning capabilities at a given point in time instead of tapping a developing sensitivity midstream.

A typical study involves a familiarization phase followed by a test. Length of familiarization in infant studies varies from 2 to 3 min. Most studies counterbalance stimulus materials so that half of the infants are exposed to one version of the language and half to another version. At test, infants are exposed to strings from both versions so that what is grammatical for one group is ungrammatical for the other (e.g., version A strings violate the constraints of version B and vice versa). This ensures that the structure of the language, instead of something idiosyncratic about the sound tokens, is responsible for learning. Infants are tested using procedures for recording the amount of time they attend to different stimulus types. If learning has occurred, a group of infants should listen differentially to strings conforming to their training language versus strings that do not conform.

Statistical learning appears to play a role in the formation of speech categories, in the identification of word-like units in running speech, in the ability to track adjacent and nonadjacent word dependencies, and in generalizations involving the acquisition of categories and their relationships in speech. Learning research has also investigated whether infants can learn in the presence of noisy input and whether they can use prior experience to bootstrap learning of more difficult patterns from simpler ones. That research, as well as research conducted in the visual modality, will be summarized with the goal of describing a range of statistical learning studies including research conducted in the author's laboratory.

The Role of Frequency in the Formation of Speech Categories

Infants are sensitive to a wide range of speech contrasts very early in development. An example is the contrast between the consonants /b/ and /p/. Very young infants even discriminate contrasts that do not occur in their native language but by 8–10 months of age, discrimination only occurs for those contrasts in their native language. This finding is widely recognized as experience dependent, but until recently we did not have a very good candidate for the process underlying this change. One possibility, found in the literature on statistical learning, is that infants use statistical information to home in on phoneme categories. Although phonemes may vary acoustically along a dimension, such variation is not random. It patterns bi-modally such that the most frequent tokens of one category occur at one end of a dimension and tokens from another category occur at the other end. This is in contrast to a unimodal distribution in which the most frequent tokens occur between two ends of a continuum. Will distributions with these different characteristics influence infants' ability to distinguish speech contrasts such that exposure to bi-modal distributions results in discrimination of a speech contrast, whereas exposure to a unimodal distribution prevents discrimination?

In the earliest infant experiment exploring this hypothesis in 2002, Jessica Maye, Janet Werker, and LouAnn Gerken familiarized 6- and 8-month-olds with one of two distributions of eight speech sounds on a /da/–/ta/ continuum (the voiced unaspirated /d/ in day and the voiceless unaspirated /t/ in stay) (**Figure 1**). Infants this age can make this discrimination, but if perception of speech sounds is malleable then exposure to a unimodal distribution should interfere with discrimination whereas exposure to a bi-modal distribution should preserve it. This pattern of findings would support the proposal that sensitivity to the frequency distributions of speech sounds is instrumental in learning. Infants in both unimodal and bi-modal conditions heard the same eight speech sounds along the continuum, but those in the bi-modal distribution condition heard speech sounds near the end (2 and 7) most frequently whereas infants in the unimodal distribution condition heard the middle speech sounds (4 and 5) most often. After familiarization, infants were tested on their ability to discriminate alternating speech sounds (the endpoints 1 and 8) from nonalternating ones (repeats of speech sounds 3 or 6). Only infants in the bi-modal condition discriminated alternating from nonalternating speech sounds, supporting the idea that exposure to the bimodal distribution led to preservation of two categories of speech sounds whereas exposure to the unimodal distribution resulted in the formation of one. In subsequent studies Jessica Maye and colleagues have shown that exposure to a bi-modal frequency distribution can also enable detection of an initially undetectable speech sound contrast. Thus, the ability to learn the frequency characteristics of speech sounds can blur distinctions between previously known categories or they can enable the formation of new ones.

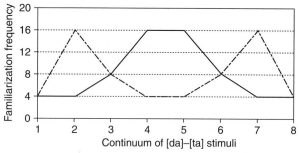

Figure 1 Bimodal versus unimodal distributions of [da]–[ta] stimuli during familiarization in a study of speech-category formation. The continuum of speech sounds is shown on the abscissa with Token 1 corresponding to [da] and Token 8 corresponding to [ta]. The ordinate axis plots the number of times each stimulus occurred during the familiarization phase. The presentation frequency for infants exposed to a bimodal presentation is depicted by the dotted line, and for the unimodal presentation by the solid line. Reproduced from Maye J, Werker J, and Gerken LA (2002) Infant sensitivity to distributional information can affect phonetic discrimination. *Cognition* 82: B101–B111, with permission from Elsevier.

The Role of Joint Probability and Transitional Probabilities in Visual Statistical Learning

Infants are also able to keep track of joint probabilities in learning the most frequent associations between objects in visual sequences. Natasha Kirkham, Jonathan Slemmer, and Scott Johnson in a study reported in 2002 familiarized infants, ages 2, 5, and 8 months, to a continuous series of objects, presented one at a time in sequence. The stimuli were six shapes (e.g., turquoise square, blue cross, yellow circle, pink diamond, green triangle, red octagon, where the square was always followed by the cross, the circle by the diamond, and so on). The infants were then tested to see if they would discriminate legal pairs of objects from illegal ones (e.g., turquoise square followed by the pink diamond) by manifesting longer looking times to the illegal combinations. All three age groups showed discrimination, demonstrating early sensitivity to joint probability in visually presented stimuli (**Figure 2**).

In a study reported the same year, Josef Fiser and Richard Aslin showed that infants can track transitional probabilities in objects co-occurring in visual scenes by 9 months of age, but because these studies have not yet been conducted with younger infants it is not known whether there is a lower limit on the ability to track transtitional probabilities.

The Role of Transitional Probabilities in Segmenting Words in Continuous Speech

As described briefly earlier, infants can also keep track of more complex statistics, such as transitional probabilities in sequences of syllables, and they can use this information to discover word boundaries. Such learning has been tested in 7- and 8-month-olds by exposing them to continuous streams of four randomly ordered three-syllable words (e.g., tupiro, dabiku, tilado, golabu in a string such as tupirotiladogolabudabikutupirodabikugolabu....). Although syllable pairs within words occurred with identical joint frequency to those occurring between words, higher transitional probabilities for syllables within words versus those spanning words, can provide cues to word boundaries. Take a phrase like 'naughty puppy'. The syllable transition in 'naugh-ty' has a higher transitional probability than the transition 'ty-pu' because 'naugh' in the word 'naughty', is more likely to predict 'ty' than 'ty' is to predict 'pu'. Jenny Saffran has shown in a series of studies that infants are able to use the differences in transitional probabilities within-words versus between-words to identify word boundaries in running speech such that they show longer listening times to part-words (words that span word boundaries, e.g., bikuti) than to words (e.g., tupiro). This pattern of listening makes sense if we assume that once infants have learned the words, they will find them less interesting, and hence will listen to them for a shorter time than they will listen to novel part-words. Infants can also track transitional probabilities in tone sequences, showing that such learning is not confined to linguistic stimuli.

Even though such learning is not specific to a particular context if it is relevant for language, one might predict that when infants segment syllable sequences (as opposed to tone sequences) they should treat these as candidates for words. This would be evidenced by a greater likelihood of discriminating words and part-words in the context of English sentence frames. If the segmented syllable strings have a word-like status, then we might expect infants to listen longer when words (as opposed to part-words) are embedded in English frames ("I like my tupiro" vs. "I like my bikuti"). This is because if syllable strings are 'candidate words' they should sound more natural in the context of familiar natural language frames than part-words, and infants should listen longer. However, it could be that infants are doing nothing more then discriminating legal from illegal patterns of syllables (tupiro vs. bikuti). Thus, an important control is one where the words and part-words are embedded in nonsense frames (such as "Zy fike ny tupiro"). If infants are treating words and part-words alike, then performance should be the same in English and nonsense frame types: as in English frames they should listen longer to nonsense strings with embedded 'words' as compared to part-words. Jenny Saffran found that 8-month-olds only discriminated words and part-words in English sentence frames suggesting that they treat the words they segment as more language-like than the part-words. Another clue that infants treat segmented nonsense words as candidates for

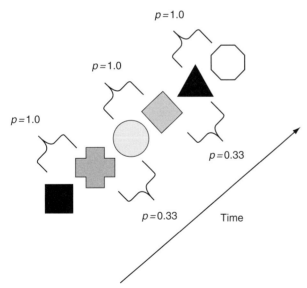

Figure 2 A depiction of stimuli used in a visual learning study to assess learning of joint probability. Reproduced from Kirkham NZ, Slemmer JA, and Johnson SP (2002) Visual statistical learning in infancy: Evidence for a domain general learning mechanism. *Cognition* 83: B35–B42, with permission from Elsevier.

real words is the fact that older 17-month-olds more readily map newly segmented words onto word meanings than part-words onto word meanings. Katharine Graf Estes, Julia Evan, Martha Alibali, and Jenny Saffran first exposed infants to a continuous stream of nonsense words, with transitional probabilities as the only cue to word boundaries. For half of the infants, two of the nonsense words were paired with visually presented objects. For the remaining infants the word forms used to label the objects were part-words. If the segmented units are treated as candidates for real words, infants should be more likely to map the word labels to objects than the part-word labels, and they were.

How Infants Might Tune in to Long Distance Dependencies

The research summarized early on shows that infants are adept at tracking sequential dependencies between adjacent elements. Indeed, this tendency occurs across species (for human, nonhuman primates, and rats), across development (in infants and adults), and even under incidental learning conditions, suggesting that it may be a default. However, many dependencies occur across longer distances, especially in language. Some examples are dependencies between auxiliaries and inflectional morphemes (e.g., *is* quickly runn*ing*), and between nouns and verbs in number and tense agreement (The boy*s* in the tree *are* laughing). If the tendency to track adjacent structure is pervasive, how might learners begin to track more remote dependencies in sequential structure?

Rebecca Gómez investigated this question in 2002 by familiarizing infants with one of two artificial languages. Language 1 sentences followed the patterns aXb or cXd (e.g., pel-wadim-jic, vot-kicey-rud). In Language 2 the relationship between the first and third elements was reversed to aXd or cXb such that pel sentences ended with rud, and vot sentences ended with jic (pel-wadim-rud, vot-kicey-jic). The a, b, c, d, and X elements were restricted to the same positions in the two languages and adjacent dependencies were identical (aX occurred in both languages as did Xd) so that strings could only be distinguished by learning the relationships between the nonadjacent first and third words. The size of the pool from which the middle element was drawn was also manipulated (set-size = 3, 12, or 24) while holding frequency of exposure to particular nonadjacent dependencies constant (see **Figure 3**). The purpose of this manipulation was to determine whether high variability in the middle element would lead to better perception of nonadjacent dependencies even though these were equally frequent in all three set-size conditions. The motivation for the variability manipulation was the observation that long-distance dependencies in natural language between frequently occurring words such as 'is' and '-ing' occur with a large number of verbs as opposed to a small number (e.g., 'is running', 'is playing', 'is sleeping'). Perhaps the variability of verbs contributes to detection of the long-distance dependencies. Infants as young as 15 months of age acquired the nonadjacent dependency when the intervening element came from a set of 24 possible words, but not when intervening set size was smaller (3 or 12). One might have expected the added noise to impede learning; however, high variability appeared to increase the perceptual salience of the nonadjacent words compared to the middle word, resulting in learning.

Generalization in Learning

Rebecca Gómez and LouAnn Gerken in a study published in 1999 familiarized 12-month-olds with strings from an artificial grammar in one vocabulary and tested them on strings in entirely new vocabulary (e.g., infants heard FIM-SOG-FIM-FIM-TUP and were tested on VOT-PEL-PEL-JIC). Although the constraints on word-ordering remained the same between training and test, vocabulary did not.

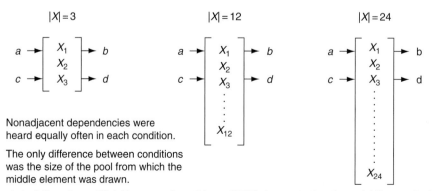

Figure 3 An abstract depiction of an artificial language from Gómez (2002) demonstrating the variability manipulation that showed that adjacent dependencies that are sufficiently low, as they are in the set-size 24 condition, will result in nonadjacent dependency learning.

Infants could not distinguish the two grammars based on transitional probabilities between remembered word pairs because of the change in vocabulary. The infants made the discrimination suggesting that they had abstracted something about grammatical structure above and beyond pairs of specific words. In the same year Gary Marcus and his colleagues reported similar findings for younger 7-month-olds. Infants in their studies were familiarized with ABA versus ABB (wi-di-wi vs. wi-di-di) patterns. Infants discriminated strings with the training pattern from those with a different pattern despite a change in vocabulary (e.g., ba-po-ba vs. ba-po-po).

These are important findings but it is crucial to ask to what degree such learning extends to real-world problems such as those faced by children learning language? The infant abstraction abilities documented in these studies are dependent on learning patterns of repeating and alternating elements (e.g., ABB, ABA, ABBC), a form of generalization that is fairly limited in language. Whereas recognizing ba-po-ba and ko-ga-ko as instances of the pattern ABA entails noting that the first and last syllables in sequence are physically identical, most linguistic generalizations involve operations over variables that are not perceptually bound. If we compare the pattern-based representation ABA to the category-based representation Noun Verb Noun, abstracting ABA from ba-po-ba involves noting that the first and third elements in a sequence are physically identical, and thus recognition is perceptually bound. In contrast, the Noun Verb Noun relation holds over abstract categories that do not rely on perceptual identity. "Muffy drinks milk" and "John loves books" share the same category-based Noun Verb Noun structure, despite the obvious physical dissimilarities between category members such as milk and books. Given this observation, researchers have begun to examine learning involving abstract variables.

The ability to perceive category relationships among words in strings is essential to linguistic productivity.

For instance, an English speaker must be able to generalize from a novel string like "The pleg mooped" to "Is the pleg mooping?" Generalization is extremely powerful – once a novel word is categorized children can automatically apply all of the syntactic constraints associated with other words in its category. How do children achieve such generalization? Although semantic information most certainly factors into such learning, infants must parse syntactic categories in the speech they hear in order to link them with semantic referents. This involves learning phonological regularities within words of a category (e.g., noun or verb), and co-occurrence relations between categories (e.g., determiner and noun). An infant who is able to parse the relevant categories in speech has a leg up on the ultimate task of mapping meaning to syntactic phrases.

One way to investigate this kind of learning with artificial languages is to give categories arbitrary labels such as a, X, b, and Y. Words from these categories are then combined to form legal phrases. For instance, aX and bY might be legal in a language whereas aY and bX are not. To give an example, imagine that a-elements correspond to 'a' and 'the' and b-elements to 'will' and 'can' (see Table 1). Infants will only be successful at discriminating a new legal phrase (e.g., 'a cat') from an illegal one ('a eat') if they have learned that a-elements go with nouns (the Xs), but not with verbs (the Ys). As in natural language, where the set of determiners has very few members and the set of nouns is large, a- and b-categories have fewer members than Xs and Ys. Also, in natural language nouns and verbs tend to have distinguishing phonological features. For instance, in English nouns tend to have more syllables than verbs. Therefore, it is important to incorporate such phonological features into the aX bY language.

Rebecca Gómez and Laura Lakusta in 2004 reported research asking whether 12-month-olds could learn the relationship between specific a- and b-words and features defining X- and Y-categories. During training infants heard one of two training languages. One language

Table 1 A paradigm for investigating category abstraction

Natural language example	X_1	X_2	X_3	X_4	X_5	X_6
a_1 = the	boy	girl	ball	dog	cat	car
a_2 = a	boy	girl	ball	dog	cat	car
	Y_1	Y_2	Y_3	Y_4	Y_5	Y_6
b_1 = will	jump	run	play	sleep	eat	wait
b_2 = can	jump	run	play	sleep	eat	wait
Artificial language example	X_1	X_2	X_3	X_4	X_5	X_6
a_1 = alt	coomo	fengle	kicey	loga	paylig	wazil
a_2 = ush	coomo	fengle	kicey	loga	paylig	wazil
	Y_1	Y_2	Y_3	Y_4	Y_5	Y_6
a_1 = ong	deech	ghope	jic	skige	vabe	tam
a_2 = erd	deech	ghope	jic	skige	vabe	tam

The top half of the table demonstrates the paradigm with natural stimuli with phrases like 'the boy' and 'will jump'. The bottom half of the table demonstrates the paradigm with artificial language stimuli. Infants are familiarized with phrases like 'alt fengle' and 'erd ghope' then are tested to see if they will generalize correctly to strings with new X and Y words (an example of a new aX string is 'alt roosa' and a new bY string is 'erd pel').

consisted of *aX* and *bY* pairings, the other of *aY* and *bX* pairs. *X*s were two-syllable words and *Y*s were one syllable so that infants could use syllable number as a feature for distinguishing *X*- and *Y*-categories. At test, for example, infants trained on *aX* and *bY* pairings had to discriminate these from *aY* and *bX* pairs. However, in order to assess generalization, all *X*- and *Y*-words were novel. The infants successfully discriminated the legal from illegal pairs, suggesting that they had learned the relationships between the *a*- and *b*-elements and the abstract feature characterizing *X*- and *Y*-words (syllable number). Similar learning may occur in natural language, where children exposed to English may pick up on distributional regularities distinguishing nouns and verbs and link these to specific function words.

Although this study was important for determining whether 12-month-olds could learn to associate *a*- and *b*-words with different category features, the next step is to determine whether infants can form categories of *a*- and *b*-words by themselves. This is an important ability in natural language. For instance, once children form the category of determiner, if they hear a novel word predicted by 'the' they will know to use 'a' with that word also. At a more general level, this kind of learning feeds into the ability to use the occurrence of words of one category to label the syntactic category of a following word (e.g., using the presence of a determiner in the phrase 'a dax' to label the novel word 'dax' as a member of the noun category).

How might this kind of learning be realized in our artificial language paradigm? After learners have associated *a*- and *b*-words with *X*/*Y*-cues, they might then go on to categorize individual *a*- or *b*-elements based on their joint association with particular *X*- and *Y*-cues (for instance, in natural language, children would form a category containing 'a' and 'the' based on features that tend to occur with nouns and not verbs; see **Table 2**). Once function-word categories are formed, children can rely on memory for a phrase they have heard (e.g., 'the dax') and the fact that 'the' and 'a' are in the same category to make an inference about a phrase they have not heard (e.g., 'a dax'), regardless of whether the novel word has a defining feature.

LouAnn Gerken and colleagues in 2005 investigated such learning with 17-month-old American infants by exposing them to Russian words in which feminine word stems appeared with the case endings –oj and –u and masculine word stems appeared with the case endings -ya and –em. Case endings in these experiments were equivalent to *a*- and *b*-elements. Additionally, cues distinguishing *X*s and *Y*s (feminine and masculine words) were present for a subset of the items. For instance, three of six of the feminine *X*-words contained the derivational suffix -k (e.g., *pol<u>k</u>oj*, *pol<u>k</u>u*) whereas three of the masculine *Y*-words contained the suffix -tel (e.g., *zhitelya*, *zhitelyem*). Infants were familiarized with a subset of stimuli and were tested to see if they would attend differentially to novel *aX* and *bY* stimuli versus ungrammatical *aY* and *bX* ones even when the distinguishing suffix was absent (e.g., generalizing to *vannoj* and *pisarem* after hearing *vannu* and *pisarya*). The infants were able to do this, showing that they had categorized *a*- and *b*-words (using the feminine and masculine case endings). Having heard *vannu* (for which the distinguishing suffix was absent) they were able to treat *vannoj* equivalently. This finding is important for showing that by 17 months of age, infants can form categories and dependencies between them from distributional cues in speech.

Current Issues

The results of the studies in the growing literature on infant statistical learning reveal precocious learning abilities in young infants. The findings are intriguing and raise more general questions. For instance, can infants learn any kind of predictable structure or are there limits on their ability to detect statistical structure? Are the changes lasting or are we only measuring short-term discrimination? If learners are changed by their experiences, do prior learning experiences shape subsequent ones? And finally, does statistical learning observed in the lab have any connection to learning in the real world?

The first question has to do with the robustness of infant learning, especially when the information in perceptual input is noisy. In language all children are exposed to inconsistencies of one type or another during acquisition, in adults' informal speech, in children's own ungrammatical utterances, and in the ungrammatical utterances of other learners (such as playmates and siblings). Inconsistencies also occur naturally in language, for instance, in English the degree to which verbs take the regular -ed ending for the past tense, or in Spanish the extent to which feminine nouns end in -a. Other instances of

Table 2 Steps in syntactic category-based abstraction

1. Learners associate *a*-words with *X*-features and *b*-words with *Y*-features.
2. They can then form a functor-like word category of '*a*-elements' based on the joint association of individual *a*-words with particular *X*-features. For instance, in English 'the' and 'a' belong to the category of determiners.
3. Once function-word categories are formed, children can rely on memory for a phrase they have heard (e.g., 'the dax') and the fact that 'a' is in the same category as 'the' to make an inference about a phrase they have not heard (e.g., 'a dax'), regardless of whether the novel word has a defining feature.

noise in linguistic input are less widespread, such as when children are exposed to nonnative language input (a deaf child who is exposed to American Sign Language through a hearing parent who has not achieved proficiency in this language). In all of these instances, children must distinguish grammatical from ungrammatical instances, and they must generalize beyond the data to which they are exposed, making it important to ask how well infants learn on exposure to probabilistic structure.

Rebecca Gómez and Laura Lakusta investigated this question by familiarizing 12-month-olds with artificial languages with three levels of probabilistic structure. In the 100/0-condition all of the training strings were from the infants' 'predominant' training language. In the 83/17-condition, approximately 83% of the training strings were from the predominant language (the remaining 17% of the strings were from the other language and thus constituted noise). In the 67/33-condition, the split between the predominant and nonpredominant training languages was 67% and 33%. Infants in the 100/0 and 83/17 conditions learned equally well, whereas learning was diminished in the 67/33-condition. The findings suggested that infants are able to track regularities in probabilistic input even when the regularities do not occur with perfect probability (as was the case with the 83/17 ratio) and so infant-learning is robust to some noise. However, learning does need to be based on some minimum degree of regularity, as demonstrated by the fact that infants in the 67/33-condition failed to learn.

Another question has to do with determining whether the learning observed reflects a permanent change. Otherwise, statistical learning studies may simply be registering acclimation to a particular stimulus. Familiarization in statistical learning studies is typically brief (3 min or less) and testing is immediate. Given that very young infants show forgetting of short-term memory after a 15 s delay it is important to determine whether discrimination extends past this window. Very little work has explored long-term memory of a brief learning experience, but recent studies by Rebecca Gómez, Richard Bootzin, Almut Hupbach, and Lynn Nadel show retention of an artificial language after delays of 4 and 24 h. These findings are important for ruling out the possibility that statistical learning studies only measure short-term effects; however, more information is needed regarding how memories for statistical patterns persist and how they affect later learning experiences over the long term. Should parents worry that exposing their children to artificial languages might affect their natural language learning? They should not. Exposure in the lab is brief in comparison to the overwhelming experience children have with their natural language, and although infants may remember their learning experiences, their learning of natural language will take precedence over information they have acquired in the laboratory.

A third question has to do with whether and how learning at one point in time impacts learning at another point. Jill Lany and Rebecca Gómez recently investigated this question in the context of learning of categories in sequential structure. They familiarized 12-month-olds with aX and bY strings where X- and Y-elements were distinguished by different morphological endings (e.g., -ee or -oo). Infants had to learn that a-elements went with Xs and not Ys (and vice versa for b-elements). After familiarization with the aX/bY structure the infants were able to detect the a-X and b-Y relationships in a more complex language involving long-distance dependencies (e.g., in acX and bcY sentences). This language was particularly challenging because the intervening c-element required the infants to track nonadjacent dependencies between a- and X- and b- and Y-elements. Infants with prior experience with consistent aX and bY pairings were able to generalize to the nonadjacent acX/bcY structure over infants in a control group. This finding is important for showing how infants might scaffold learning of complex structure from learning of more simple forms and is particularly significant because of previous work showing that infants this age are unable to track nonadjacent dependencies.

A fourth question has to do with whether the learning observed in the laboratory scales up to real-life learning. One way to determine this is to ask whether the output of learning can be used as input to real-life learning processes. As discussed previously, Jenny Saffran and her colleagues have addressed this issue in the context of language acquisition in several studies by showing that infants prefer to listen to newly segmented artificial words in the context of natural language sentences frames (as opposed to nonsense frames), and also more readily learn a mapping between these newly segmented words and novel objects (as opposed to a mapping of a nonword and an object). Another approach is to determine whether statistical learning and real-life learning show similar developmental trajectories. Although learning occurring in the real world is far more complex than that observed in the lab, similar developmental trajectories would be partial support for a shared process. Initial evidence for this comes from work by Rebecca Gómez and Jessica Maye showing that the ability to detect long-distance dependencies in an artificial language comes online at 15–18 months, roughly the same time infants begin to detect long-distance dependencies in natural language.

Finally, certain kinds of statistical learning (frequency, joint probability, and transitional probability learning) occur across a broad range of organisms and across different modalities. This suggests that statistical learning may be a very general process and raises questions about how it interacts with other processes and mechanisms known to be involved in memory change. One such mechanism is sleep. New studies with adults show that sleep is instrumental in memory consolidation such that it enhances memory, improves generalization, and also leads to qualitative change. A recent study reported by Rebecca Gómez, Richard Bootzin, and Lynn Nadel tested the effects of sleep on infant learning. Infants who napped in a 4-h interval between familiarization and test were able to generalize a rule in an artificial language. In contrast, infants who did not nap had excellent memory for the strings of the artificial language but they did not generalize. Generalization is a critical form learning that results in greater flexibility. Such learning plays an essential role in cognitive development by sustaining sensitivity to previously encountered information, while enabling learners to generalize to novel cases.

Another important mechanism involved in memory change is memory reconsolidation. According to the literature on this phenomenon, memory is much more dynamic than previously thought. Previous research suggested that memories become crystallized as the result of a consolidation process, varying only in their access. But recent evidence shows that consolidated memories are open to change because when they are accessed, they go into a labile state. Once in this state, memories can be enhanced, altered, or overridden depending on new information encountered. Studies with rats and humans have found that a consolidated memory can be overwritten by new information when exposure to it follows memory reactivation. When the memory is not reactivated, exposure to the new information has no effect. Such a process has important implications for understanding how children recover from erroneous generalizations (if children's memories can be overwritten by new learning after reactivation of erroneous information) and could also explain how new learning becomes integrated with existing knowledge if it can be shown that new information is merged with old information as part of the reconsolidation process. Almut Hupbach, Rebecca Gómez, Oliver Hardt, and Lynn Nadel have recently shown that such merging does indeed happen, suggesting that reconsolidation can be a constructive process in learning.

Summary

In sum, infants show remarkable learning abilities ranging from the ability to detect statistical patterns of varying complexity to the ability to generalize from these patterns. Learning is rapid, and appears to occur early in development. Infants show learning for a range of different types of statistical structure including frequency, joint probability, and transitional probability. These particular forms of statistical learning occur across species, across development, and with no explicit intent to learn suggesting that they may be fundamental in learning. Infants also show learning over different types of units including phonetic segments, syllables, words, and visual objects, and they learn at different levels, for instance, at the level of specific syllables or words or at the level of generalization. Although many questions remain with respect to bridging statistical learning and learning in the world in terms of (1) understanding how learning in the lab scales up to real-life learning, and (2) delimiting the robustness of learning in terms of infants' ability to find signal in noise, their ability to retain their learning experiences, and their ability to build on what they have learned, such learning is sure to play a central role in development.

To go full circle in terms of the history of learning, it is important to note that while the field of learning in the 1960s and 1970s focused primarily on reinforcement issues and paradigms, it has since moved to a greater appreciation of how much infants seem to learn from simple observation of regularities in their environment, both in the language and in other domains. Even so, there are still critics of learning points of view. One classic argument against learning is that simple learning mechanisms are not sufficiently powerful to explain learning of complex information found in the world (such as in language). However, in contrast to the simple learning mechanisms documented by the behaviorists, statistical learning appears to be quite powerful, with mechanisms capable of tracking vast amounts of information as well as engaging in generalization. Such sophistication raises the possibility that infant-learning may contribute substantially to the acquisition of complex skill. Yet, no matter how powerful infant-learning turns out to be, it must certainly be constrained by the biological dispositions learners bring into the world. Just how much is contributed independently by learning, how much by the child's biological preparedness, and how much arises in the interaction of the two, has yet to be determined. Ongoing and future studies will be important for specifying the kinds of learning mechanisms children are born with and how they develop.

See also: Categorization Skills and Concepts; Cognitive Development; Imitation and Modeling; Language Acquisition Theories; Memory; Preverbal Development and Speech Perception; Semantic Development; Speech Perception.

Suggested Readings

Aslin R, Saffran J, and Newport E (1998) Computation of conditional probability statistics by 8-month-old infants. *Psychological Science* 9: 321–324.

Gerken LA, Wilson R, and Lewis W (2005) 17-month-olds can use distributional cues to form syntactic categories. *Journal of Child Language* 32: 249–268.

Gómez RL (2002) Variability and detection of invariant structure. *Psychological Science* 13: 431–436.

Gómez R and Gerken LA (2000) Infant artificial language learning and language acquisition. *Trends in Cognitive Sciences* 4: 178–186.

Gómez RL and Lakusta L (2004) A first step in form-based category abstraction by 12-month-old infants. *Developmental Science* 7: 567–580.

Gómez RL, Bootzin R, and Nadel L (2006) Naps promote abstraction in language learning infants. *Psychological Science* 17: 670–674.

Kirkham NZ, Slemmer JA, and Johnson SP (2002) Visual statistical learning in infancy: Evidence for a domain general learning mechanism. *Cognition* 83: B3–B42.

Maye J, Werker J, and Gerken LA (2002) Infant sensitivity to distributional information can affect phonetic discrimination. *Cognition* 82: B101–B111.

Saffran J (2003) Statistical language learning: Mechanisms and constraints. *Current Directions in Psychological Science* 12: 110–114.

Saffran J, Aslin R, and Newport E (1996) Statistical learning by eight-month-old infants. *Science* 274: 1926–1928.

Literacy

C M Connor and S Al'Otaiba, Florida State University, Tallahassee, FL, USA

2008 Elsevier Inc. All rights reserved.

Glossary

Alphabetic principle – The concept that letters and letter combinations represent individual sounds, or phonemes, in written words.

Comprehension – Understanding the meaning of what one is reading, the ultimate goal of all reading activity.

Decoding – The ability to determine the pronunciation of a word employing knowledge of sound symbol correspondences; the act of deciphering a new word by sounding it out.

Emergent literacy – An early stage of early reading development that occurs prior to formal schooling and includes skills, knowledge, and attitudes that are developmental precursors to conventional forms of reading and writing.

Expressive language – Language that is spoken.

Fluency – Ability to read text quickly, accurately, and with proper expression, that allows the reader to focus on meaning.

Lexical access – The process of mapping a printed word onto a specific meaning in the reader's memory.

Lexical semantics – The study of meanings of words and their relationships.

Lexicon – The mental dictionary or body of word knowledge that includes memory of the meanings and pronunciations of words; also referred to as vocabulary.

Literacy – Broadly, the skills involving processing written language including listening, speaking, reading, and writing.

Metalinguistic – An awareness of language structure and function that allows one to reflect on consciously manipulating the language; for example, understanding that the sounds in 'dog' are /d/ /o/ /g/ and not 'bow-wow', or the sound a dog makes.

Morpheme – The smallest meaningful unit of language. For example, 'preview' has two morphemes: 'pre-' and 'view'.

Morphemic or structural analysis – An analysis of words formed by adding prefixes, suffixes, or other units of meaning to a base or root word.

Morphology – The study of word structure including inflection, derivation, and the formation of compounds; refers to how words are formed and relate to each other.

Morphosyntactic awareness – An awareness of the connection between grammar and word forms.

Onset – Most syllables contain an onset, or an initial consonant or consonant cluster before the vowel; (e.g., in the word 'lap', the onset is 'l'. In the word 'star', the onset is 'st').

Phonemic awareness – The ability to notice, think about, or manipulate the individual phonemes (sounds) in words and to understand that sounds in spoken language work together to make words; the highest level of phonological awareness (awareness of individual phonemes in words).

Phonics – The relationship between letters and the sounds they represent – also, reading instruction that teaches the correspondence between sounds and symbols.

Phonogram – A series of letters that represents the same phonological unit in different words, such as 'igh' in 'light', 'sight', and 'sigh'.

Phonological awareness – A sensitivity to, or explicit awareness of, the sound structure of words in a language, including awareness of phonemes

in individual words, sentences, syllables, and onset-rime segments.
Receptive language – Language that is heard.
Rime – The part of a syllable following the initial consonant or consonant cluster that includes the vowel and any letters that follow it; different from rhyming. (For example in the word 'lap', the rime is 'ap'. In the word 'star', the rime is 'ar')
Semantics – The study of the meanings of words and phrases; the ways in which language conveys meaning.
Vocabulary – All of the storage of information about word meanings and pronunciations necessary for communication. Readers need to know many word meanings to comprehend text.

Introduction

In the enactment of the No Child Left Behind Act our society has recognized literacy as a right and not a privilege. Yet teaching all children how to read and write proficiently has proved to be difficult. Indeed, the most recent results of the National Assessment of Educational Progress (NAEP), which has been called the nation's report card, reveals that we fail to teach more than one-third of our students to read proficiently by fourth grade. Yet at the same time, our understanding about how children learn to read and become literate members of society has increased greatly since the mid-1980s. In this article, we focus on what we have learned about how children learn to read and the essential skills that comprise proficient reading. We will start with a brief history of literacy instruction and will then discuss the salient but complex links between children's oral language skills and their literacy abilities, the emerging insights offered by neurological research, and how links between language and literacy have important implications for designing effective instruction from preschool through third grade. As we will show, unlike talking, reading and writing must be taught and so we will discuss literacy development in the context of instruction – in both home and school environments. Moreover, accumulating research reveals that the impact of any particular instructional strategy depends on the language and literacy skills children bring to the learning environment. Additionally, we will discuss reading disabilities in the context of 'response-to-instruction', and how definitions of reading disabilities are changing.

We use the terms 'literacy' and 'reading' throughout this article. Generally, when we refer to reading, we mean a specific set of skills. However, our use of the term literacy carries broader implications and includes the knowledge and skills that facilitate learning. The hallmarks of proficient literacy are the ability to comprehend, or understand what is read, to learn from what is read, and to express ideas in written form. We will also briefly touch on emergent literacy in the context of children's developing skills.

The History of Literacy Instruction

The history of literacy instruction has been characterized by contention and division and reflects a debate in the field of education that finds its early roots in romanticism and the traditional versus progressive movements. Fruits of this debate can be traced across the content areas, such as math and science, but have been most public in the recent Reading Wars, which, as we will discuss, pitted whole-language against code-based instruction.

Until the early 1800s, *Webster Spellers*, introduced in 1782, provided the most popular method of reading instruction in the US. The *McGuffey Readers*, which slowly replaced the *Webster Spellers*, incorporated both alphabetic and phonics methods while promoting the virtues of honesty, thrift, and kindness. Then, in 1832, stating that learning should not be 'tiresome drudgery' (as exemplified by the McGuffey reader), John Miller Keagy introduced the whole-word method. Proponents of the method, also advocates of romanticism, stated that learning to read should be 'as natural as learning to talk', predating the claims of contemporary whole-language approaches. In the 1930s through the 1950s, the Dick and Jane series, using the whole-word method, gained widespread popularity. In 1955, Flesch wrote *Why Johnny Can't Read*. This book reached the national bestseller list and further charged the bitter debate about phonics versus whole-word. Coupled with rising criticism of public education, the general press proposed phonics as the solution to reading problems, while this stance was rejected by educators and educational researchers as opinion rather than science.

In 1967, Chall's *Learning to Read: The Great Debate*, which had been commissioned by the Carnegie Corporation of New York, was supposed to settle the debate. However, as Chall soon discovered, comparing reading methods' efficacy was complex. Moreover, no one method of instruction fully insured reading success for all children. Teachers frequently used a combination of old and new methods. For example, Chall observed that phonics instruction survived in the 1930s because some teachers "got out their old phonics charts, *closed the doors*, and hoped the supervisor or principal would not enter unannounced" (p. 7). One clear message from the research was that an early emphasis on decoding and phonics (i.e., code-focused) instruction appeared to be critical for children's reading success.

Throughout the 1970s, the notion that learning to read was like learning to talk or that it was a 'psycholinguistic guessing game' was emerging. These ideas formed the foundation of the 'whole-language' approach. Its proponents suggested that learning to read was a natural process (in line with romanticists' principles and social constructivism); children needed only to be exposed to 'authentic' text and coached by their teacher to enable them to succeed and to construct their own knowledge. While highly similar in many ways to the largely discredited whole-word look-say approach, educators were enthusiastic. The response to whole language was, in part, a reaction to the overemphasis on script, drill, and workbooks that was typical of the 1970s and early 1980s. Whole-language approaches de-emphasized explicit and systematic teaching of phonics, tended to empower teachers, and promoted using interesting books and instilling a joy for reading over a focus on basic skills and phonics. Nevertheless, researchers in the 1990s rediscovered what Chall had found in the 1960s – many children required systematic and explicit instruction in phonics, phonological awareness, and fluency (i.e., code-focused instruction) and explicit instruction in comprehension strategies if they were to become successful readers. Although the debate continues, the most current research has shown that elements of both whole-language and code-focused instruction are important for developing readers.

Learning to Read versus Learning to Talk

Speaking a language is a common human characteristic found within every human society – and reading is not. Although linguists may get contentious on the topic, there are no public debates regarding how to teach children how to talk. Yet schools' failures make headlines and every year the National Assessment of Educational Progress (NAEP) shows that one-third of children are not reading proficiently whereas we assume that virtually all the children are talking proficiently. Indeed, when provided even a marginally acceptable linguistic environment, adequate hearing, and cognitive wherewithal, epidemiological studies show that approximately 93% of children learn to talk without any specific instruction or intervention. There appears to be a 'language instinct'. That is not to say that the child's home and learning environments do not matter. If they did not, all of us would speak the same language and all children would have very similar language abilities. Children do show widely different language abilities within a normal range and a large part of this variability can be traced to the home linguistic environment. Nevertheless, following highly predictable timetables, babies babble, toddlers talk, and 3-year-olds carry on conversations.

The same highly predictable and resilient development is not evident for literacy. Although some children learn to read almost regardless of instruction, and many children who receive good instruction overcome initial difficulties and successfully learn to read, too many children (by some estimates 30–60%) fail to reach functional levels of literacy. Some of these children who struggle with learning to read have learning disabilities; fewer have specific language impairments or other communication challenges, such as deafness. However, the reason that most of these children fail to learn how to read and write proficiently is because they do not receive the amount, intensity, and types of instruction that they need.

Accumulating evidence reveals that the effect of any particular type of instructional strategy depends on students' reading and language skills. Connor and Morrison recently showed that what is effective for a student who reads competently, may not be effective for a student still struggling with basic decoding skills. These child-by-instruction interactions have been found across school communities, across the country, and across grades from preschool through third grade. Moreover, the results of their recent random field trial reveal that, at least in first grade, these child-by-instruction interactions are causally implicated in students' letter-word reading and reading comprehension skill growth.

As we will discuss in more detail, this emerging theory of literacy teaching and learning relies on conceptualizing literacy as a phenomenon or construct composed of multiple dimensions that cross the boundaries between oral and written language, that affect each other reciprocally, and that are greatly influenced by the learning opportunities provided. Increasingly, researchers are showing that proficient literacy requires children to have a strong foundation in oral language – including lexical and semantic knowledge (e.g., vocabulary), metalinguistic awareness including phonological awareness, and strong overall receptive and expressive language skills coupled with explicit and systematic instruction in decoding, comprehending, and writing text. Any part of the system that breaks down (e.g., phonological awareness) impacts the entire system.

Brain imaging techniques, known as hemodynamic studies (e.g., functional magnetic resonance imaging (or fMRI), evoked-response potential (or ERP), and neuromagnetic (or MEG) are improving, which allow researchers to examine the brain activity of children and adults while they complete tasks like reading words. A number of interrelated neural systems are activated during reading. However, there is now an accumulation of evidence that brains of individuals with reading disabilities show different, and less-efficient patterns of processing (including under- and overactivation of specific neural circuits or differences in onset latencies within certain regions). These most-researched areas include the temporo-occipital region, the temporoparietal region, and the left inferior frontal regions, which are related to phonetic decoding. Recent work has also focused on networks within the posterior temporal and temporo-occipital cortex that appear to support sight word reading. For example, good readers employ their left temporo-parietal region to process letter–sound correspondences. A less-effective pattern (including underactivation of the posterior temporal and temporoparietal cortices and overactivation in the inferior frontal and right posterior temporal cortices) is found when imaging brains of individuals with reading disabilities.

Interestingly, researchers have also begun to use imaging before and after intensive explicit decoding and other code-focused interventions and have demonstrated changes in brain activation in individuals with reading disabilities. Pre- to postintervention changes in brain activity indicate a more normalized pattern within the specific brain areas that, research has shown, support word-reading accuracy. Moreover, these changes also account for significant variance in pre- to post-treatment growth in children's oral-reading accuracy scores. Such research is important because it confirms that the brain is malleable and fluidly organized. Although early intervention to prevent reading difficulties appears easier than remediation later in life, even adult brains respond to training and become more efficient at reading. Furthermore, it appears this positive reorganization endures.

For these reasons, any successful conceptualization of literacy development will integrate characteristics of both students and instruction into the model. Nevertheless, understanding the components that comprise proficient literacy skills is critical. Thus, we will first discuss the language skills that appear to contribute directly to proficient literacy as well as skills that are specific to the skill of reading, keeping in mind that they are all part of a complex system that supports literacy.

Language

Our ability to use language to communicate feelings, ideas, emotions, and plans is a unique human ability that affects every aspect of our lives. It is the medium by which we learn and teach. By 3 years of age, most children are using language for relatively sophisticated purposes, as any parent knows. Toddlers negotiate nap time, they express joy, anger, and frustration, they even begin to deceive and manipulate. By 4.5 years, children are masters at communicating, ready to maneuver through the complexities of home, community, and school interactions. When children learn to talk, they increasingly become part of their family and social community. Moreover, children develop proficient language skills unless they encounter neurological, physical, or environmental barriers, and even then they may learn to compensate.

Generally, linguists describe language as comprised of various components although these are only theoretically discrete, and interact and support one another. These include the individual sounds of language (phonemes), vocabulary, semantics (the meaning of what is said), morphemes (the smallest units of language that carry meaning, like '-ed', which marks past tense, or '-s', which marks plurals), syntax (the ways in which we order words, use pronouns and verbs, and structure sentences), and pragmatics (the ways in which we use language, such as how we take turns talking, decide who gets to talk, and use language that is appropriate for the setting). In contrast to these linguistic skills, which are largely unconscious, metalinguistic awareness is the conscious use and manipulation of language (e.g., an appreciation of nursery rhymes, the deft skill of punsters, the ability to say 'ink' when asked to say 'link' without the /l/); it is integral to the process of learning to read and provides an important link between language and reading. Moreover, as the medium of teaching and learning, oral language is the essential foundation of literacy instruction.

There are also important social and pragmatic aspects to language that have implications for children's learning. For example, children who do not learn the rules about how to talk in the classroom (e.g., tell stories with a beginning, middle, and end or to answer questions in order to show what they have learned) may encounter difficulty within the school environment both on the playground and in the classroom. Due to problems interacting with peers and teachers, these students may be at a disadvantage during class discussions and during peer-learning opportunities.

Links between Language and Literacy

In general, children who achieve at the highest academic levels use oral language with flexibility, fluency, and skill. Children who start kindergarten with stronger oral language skills become the most proficient readers and writers by high school. At the same time, children with specific language impairments are much more likely to experience reading disabilities than are their peers with typical language skills. Accumulating research reveals three language skills most frequently identified as components of reading – vocabulary, metalinguistic awareness (including phonological awareness), and listening comprehension (i.e., receptive oral language skills).

Children's vocabulary is highly predictive of their literacy. Moreover, there is accumulating evidence that vocabulary influences the types of instruction that will be more effective for particular children. The National Reading Panel identified it as one of the key component skills of reading. Children with stronger vocabulary skills are, on average, better readers and better able to take advantage of a wider range of literacy instruction activities. While there is some evidence that it is very difficult to change the rate of vocabulary development, other evidence indicates that explicit vocabulary instruction can improve students' reading skills.

Phonological awareness, a type of metalinguistic awareness, is the ability to consciously manipulate the individual sounds (i.e., phonemes) within words and, as we will discuss below, is considered a critical skill for proficient reading. Children who could, for example, respond 'horse' when asked what word is left in 'racehorse' without 'race' or who could blend onsets (first sound 't') and rimes (the rest of the word 'oy'; answer 'toy') were consistently better readers than were children who could not do these tasks. However, there is also evidence that learning to read contributes to phonological awareness. Identified by the National Reading Panel as a key skill of proficient readings, we will discuss phonological awareness, in the context of instruction, more fully later in this article.

Emerging research indicates that other aspects of metalinguistic awareness are also intricately linked with children's developing literacy. Children's morphosyntactic awareness, which is the ability to manipulate the grammar and structure of language (e.g., that 'public' and 'publicity' share the same root and that adding – er to the end of 'farm' changes the meaning of the word to the person who farms, the 'farmer') is related to reading comprehension.

Listening comprehension or receptive oral language is a key part of the Simple View of Reading, one of the most consistently supported theories of reading. Originally proposed by Hoover, Gough, and colleagues, the Simple View of Reading states that proficient reading is the product of decoding and listening comprehension. Because proficiency is the product and not the sum, a breakdown in either component leads to less proficiency. For example, children with specific language impairments are much more likely to have reading difficulties than are children with similar cognitive abilities but who do not have language impairments.

The links between language and literacy are proving to be more intricate than the simple relation between letters and sounds and the Simple View of Reading suggest, however. This is largely because language develops. For example, Scarborough reported that the strongest predictors of whether children might develop reading disabilities were how accurately they pronounced words and the complexity of their sentences when they were 20 months of age. However, by the time they were 42 months, vocabulary predicted more strongly than did pronunciation. By 5 years of age, only phonological awareness differentiated between children with reading difficulties and those without.

Literacy Skills

Development of Literacy Skills and Phases of Learning

While it is increasingly apparent that, for many children, proficient literacy will not develop in the absence of explicit instruction, there are phases that most children who receive appropriate instruction will experience as they follow the path toward proficient literacy. Ehri describes these phases as: 'pre-reading', 'learning to read', and 'reading to learn', which, not surprisingly, overlap and support one another.

Pre-reading phase

During the pre-reading phase, very young children begin to develop the fundamental language skills that are necessary for learning to read and, as they hear books being read to them, they learn the foundation of code-focused skills: print awareness and phonological awareness. Their growing receptive language skills enhance their understanding of what they hear, build their vocabulary and listening comprehension skills, and enable verbal thinking skills that are essential for reading comprehension. As their expressive language develops, they learn to communicate their thoughts. The onset of the code-focused aspect of this phase depends on exposure to print, that is when they hear books being read, and it extends through preschool and kindergarten. During this period, young children can learn that print represents spoken words, and they may be interested in letters and reciting or singing the alphabet song.

Parents and educators capitalize on young children's budding interest by providing learning opportunities so children may also begin to acquire some initial awareness of the phonological structure of words (i.e., that words can be divided into parts (or phonemes) or that they can have the same beginning or ending sounds). With support, children may also start to recognize some very familiar words by sight including their own names, names of playmates, family members, and favorite characters. Further, children in this pre-reading phase begin to use visual memorization and context cues to recognize familiar signs and words such as '7-Up', 'milk', or 'Cheerios'. Although they may at times correctly identify the first letter in a word like 'milk', children are not yet able to independently use the correspondence between letters and sounds to read. Children frequently engage in pretend reading and, with guidance, begin to develop basic concepts about print (holding the book upright, pointing to words as they tell the story, left to right orientation).

The learning-to-read phase

While students continue to develop the language, listening, and critical thinking skills, they began to acquire during the pre-reading phase, a sign that students are entering the learning-to-read phase is that they shift from using distinctive visual features to recognize words (i.e., the M in the McDonalds arches), to using the relations between letters and sounds in words (i.e., grapheme phoneme correspondence) as their main clue to a word's identity. Thus, during this stage, effective instruction supports students' mastery of the alphabetic principle so that they can reliably use the correspondences between letters and sounds in words to identify words they have never seen before in print.

For most students, this stage begins in kindergarten when they begin to 'sound out' at least a few letters in a word. At the very beginning, because they are still trying to guess the word, they are not very accurate. But throughout kindergarten and into first grade, if students are explicitly taught how to use letter–sound correspondences to phonetically decode new words, they can reliably sound out more of the phonemes in words (particularly the vowels), and they become more accurate readers. The accuracy of their reading is also enhanced when they realize that another important clue to the identity (and mistaken identity) of new words comes from the meaning of what they are reading. So, as students master this learning-to-read phase, they learn to integrate information about letter–sound relations with their background knowledge and their sense of the meaning of the passage, to find a word that matches the sounds they have decoded and that also 'makes sense'. In addition, with enough practice, they begin to accurately identify more words by sight and they build more reliable representations for words in their memory. When students have been taught to map the sounds in words to spellings, these representations may be created quickly and efficiently. However, students who do not yet understand these letter–sound mappings will have more difficulty learning to recognize words at a single glance and will have more difficulty entering the next phase of reading, 'reading to learn'.

The reading-to-learn phase

In this phase, students continue to develop and integrate language, listening, and critical thinking skills as they start to gain new information from a broader array of reading materials and genres. Additionally, students will encounter increasingly more unique words and multisyllabic words. Thus, learning explicit strategies to decode complex words and implicit strategies to integrate new vocabulary with what they already know will support their improving skills. Guided practice to use both types of strategies as students analyze text and read critically and to generalize these strategies to different text structures and genres also supports developing literacy. In essence, the reading-to-learn stage never ends because the students' vocabulary and other language skills, background knowledge, and strategies become increasingly sophisticated.

Components of Reading and Effective Instructional Practices

The report of the National Reading Panel, published in 2000, emphasized five key components of reading. These components are phonological awareness (as discussed, one of the most salient links between language and literacy skills), phonics (knowing the rules that relate letters and clusters of letters to sounds and morphemes), fluency (the ability to read facilely with appropriate intonation and prosody), vocabulary (as discussed previously, includes both size of lexicon and semantic flexibility), and comprehension (including foundational language and specific text-related strategies). We discussed phonological awareness briefly and vocabulary more extensively in the previous section on language. In this section, we focus further on phonological awareness, phonics, fluency and reading comprehension while keeping in mind that each dimension is highly related to the others and together – along with other skills – comprise a system of proficient literacy.

Phonological awareness

Phonological awareness, a metalinguistic skill, is among the most important links between children's oral language and literacy skills. Instruction in phonological awareness trains children to recognize and manipulate individual sounds, or phonemes, as well as clusters of phonemes (e.g., rimes) in spoken words. It is this ability that allows students to map or link the sounds in words with the letters that represent these sounds in written words. Converging research has shown that students who do not develop this ability at the discrete level of the individual phoneme (phonemic awareness), struggle with learning to read and spell, and are at risk for reading disabilities. Fortunately there is a robust research base demonstrating that students can be taught to develop their phonemic awareness skills through systematic, explicit instruction. Additionally, combining phonological awareness instruction in the presence of text and linking this instruction to letter–sound instruction appears to be more effective and to contribute to stronger reading skill development for students.

Ideally, most children receive such instruction and develop phonological awareness during the 'pre-reading' phase. Initially, they are taught and thus learn to identify words that rhyme or words that start with the same sound, then they can blend and segment short words at the onset and rime level (e.g., /c/ /at/ is 'cat'). Eventually, with instruction, they are able to blend and segment at the level of the individual sound (i.e., the sounds in 'man' are /m/ /a/ /n/), to count the sounds in words, and to manipulate and delete sounds (e.g., say 'mat', then say it again without the 'm'). However, many children, particularly those at risk for reading difficulties, continue to struggle with these later, more difficult phonological awareness skills well into the learning-to-read phase.

Phonics

Phonics instruction teaches children about the regular relations between spoken sounds and letters in words and morphemes (the smallest unit of meaning in language). It is important that they learn about the alphabetic system so they can use phonics to decode and to write new words. After reviewing recent research on reading from a number of disciplinary perspectives, Raynor and colleagues concluded that 'mastering the alphabetic principle' was essential to becoming a good reader. Students who do not master phonics during the learning-to-read phase will lack efficient strategies to sound out words they have not seen before. Thus, phonics instruction, just like phonological awareness instruction, should be systematic and explicit. Many individuals who have reading difficulties are not able to use phonics knowledge when they encounter novel words, particularly multisyllabic words, and continue to need explicit instruction well into the learning-to-read phase.

Fluency

Fluency instruction and practice helps students develop skills to read text accurately, quickly, and with appropriate intonation and prosody. Research indicates that fluent readers not only recognize individual words quickly and automatically, but they are able to simultaneously comprehend the meaning of what they are reading. Not surprisingly, fluency and reading comprehension operate to support each other in a reciprocal fashion, especially for young readers. To begin to develop readers' fluency, it is helpful to provide a fluent adult model of reading, or to allow children to practice through partner reading. Then, once students have acquired the skills to read accurately, fluency develops most directly through extended reading practice. Fluency development is a goal of the instruction during the learning-to-read phase. Thus, the real key to helping students move beyond the learning-to-read phase is for teachers to systematically teach phonological decoding skills while at the same time building a large vocabulary of words that children can recognize by sight and for which they can develop mental representations. In fact, it is the latter accomplishment that appears to be a prerequisite for fluent reading. As students learn to recognize more words at a single glance, they become more fluent readers, which, in turn, supports their ability to self-monitor and self-correct when a word does not make sense. However, if students are not taught to read accurately and fluently above a second grade developmental level, they will make too many mistakes. In turn, they will not be able to build the phonological representations for words in their memory, which is the foundation for getting information and building new vocabulary from what is read.

However, fluency with increasingly difficult or unfamiliar material continues to develop long after entering the reading-to-learn phase and is a life-long challenge for most individuals with reading difficulties. Improving students' reading fluency may compensate for weaker vocabulary skills. For example, first graders with lower vocabulary but higher oral reading fluency scores achieved reading comprehension scores, on average, that were highly similar to their peers with stronger vocabulary scores.

Reading comprehension

Reading comprehension requires the reader's active extraction and construction of meaning from text. Many factors can influence the reader's comprehension of text, including the other components of proficient reading and the instruction they receive. Children's spoken language skills provide a foundation for proficient reading comprehension but, in the absence of effective instruction, are not sufficient for developing proficient literacy. Vocabulary, for example, is one of the stronger predictors of reading comprehension. Children may have the decoding skills required to read an unfamiliar word, but if the word is not part of their lexicon, they may not be able to attach meaning to the decoded text. On the other hand, if they cannot decode the word to begin with, their vocabulary skills will not help them understand what they are reading.

As the RAND report reveals, there is compelling evidence that 'accurate and fluent (automatic) word recognition is a prerequisite for adequate reading comprehension'. Children's background knowledge and exposure to the world around them may affect how well they understand what they read, as may children's home literacy environment. Children enter the process of understanding what they read with very different skills and backgrounds, which appears to influence the types of home and classroom reading experiences that will most effectively support their learning of comprehension of text.

Explicit instruction contributes significantly to children's reading comprehension growth, especially in the early grades. For example, explicitly teaching children comprehension strategies leads to stronger reading comprehension specifically, and reading proficiency generally. The National Reading Panel meta-analysis identified a number of different strategies that, when taught, positively affected children's reading comprehension skills and, in some cases, generalized to improved overall reading proficiency. The most effective instruction included multiple combinations of strategies (e.g., reciprocal teaching). A list and descriptions of comprehension strategies are provided in **Table 1**.

Literacy Learning Environments

For many children, the process of becoming fully literate begins at home and in preschool. However, traditionally, the teaching of reading and writing begins when children start formal schooling in kindergarten. First grade is most clearly identified as the time during which children are expected to master the basics of reading. However, children begin school with highly notable individual differences in both their language and emergent literacy skills. These individual differences appear to be the result of home, parenting, preschool, and social/cultural

Table 1 Description of comprehension strategies

Comprehension instruction is intended to increase students' comprehension of written or oral text. This includes instruction and practice in using comprehension strategies and demonstration of comprehension abilities. Comprehension activities generally follow or are incorporated into reading or listening of connected text (e.g., silent sustained reading followed by a comprehension worksheet, comprehension strategy instruction using a particular example of connected text, an interactive teacher read aloud during which the teacher models various comprehension strategies). Research suggests that using strategies in combination is generally more effective that focusing solely on one strategy.

Strategy	Description
Previewing	Previewing includes activities that involve thinking about what might occur in a story based on the illustrations (including taking a 'picture walk' through a book), cover, title, etc. Previewing activities always precede reading and involve predictions about the general content of a text, which helps to distinguish it from Comprehension>Predicting. Previewing often leads into activating prior knowledge related to the story.
Schema building	Schema building includes activities that involve clarifying a concept and building background knowledge. For example, the teacher tells the students about the middle ages while reading a fairy tale.
Question response and generation	Questioning includes activities that involve generating or answering questions regarding factual or contextual knowledge from the text (e.g., What did Ira miss when he went to the sleepover? What was the name of _____?). Other comprehension activities incorporate questioning including 'activating prior knowledge' (e.g., when the teacher uses a question to scaffold children in activating personal knowledge related to the text: "When you go to an amusement park, what do you expect to see?"), comprehension monitoring (e.g., when the teacher uses a question aimed at stimulating students' metacognitive assessment of whether they comprehended the text: "Did I understand what happened there?"), or 'predicting' (e.g., when the teacher asks students to predict what will happen next: "What do you think the lost boy will do now?").
Activating prior knowledge	Activating prior knowledge includes activities that involve activating students' personal knowledge as it relates to the content of text in order to facilitate comprehension. An example would be asking "Have you ever slept over a friend's house?" when reading Ira sleeps over. This relates to the student's personal knowledge.
Comprehension monitoring	Comprehension monitoring includes activities that involve stimulating students' metacognitive awareness regarding their comprehension of text or sharing strategies to provoke students to think about whether they are fully understanding. Generally, these activities involve thinking about one's own understanding of a particular text and whether the text is making sense (e.g., the teacher pauses and says "Did that make sense to you? If not, how can we fix it?" or "Wait, did I understand that?" or "That didn't make sense to me. Let's go back and reread"). These may include identifying areas of difficulty while reading, using think-aloud procedures to pinpoint difficulties, looking back in the text, restating or rephrasing text, or looking forward to solve a problem.
Predicting and inferencing	Predicting and inferencing include activities that involve predicting future events or information not yet presented based on information already conveyed by the text (e.g., making predictions from foreshadowing). Predicting occurs while reading a story and involves specific details or events.
Highlighting/identifying	Highlighting/identifying includes activities that involve picking out the important details conveyed through a text. Examples include verbally listing, underlining, highlighting, or otherwise noting major points. Highlighting differs from 'summarizing' because it explicitly involves identifying the important details within text.
Summarizing	Summarizing includes activities that involve generating an overall statement or identifying the main ideas of the content of the text. This activity condenses the text to the main points. This might include generating a sentence that tells the story or drawing a picture in response to the text just read.
Retelling	In retelling activities, students are asked to retell a story using their own words. This differs from summarizing because a retell ideally mimics the text structure and includes as many details of a text as possible.
Context cues	Context cues include activities in which students are using pictures, the title, or previous parts of the text to understand a new event or new information presented in the text. For example, a teacher might advise a child to look at picture to identify the setting of a story. It should be noted that this strategy is generally considered a weak substitute for fluent phonological decoding.
Graphic/semantic organizers	Graphic/semantic organizers include activities in which students are using graphic or semantic organizers (e.g., Venn diagrams, story webs) in order to aid their comprehension. Graphic/semantic organizers are frequently used to help students organize their writing efforts.
Comparing/contrasting	Comparing/contrasting includes activities that involve making comparisons across or within texts. For example, asking "how are lions and tigers the same and how are they different?"

influences children experience, as well as children's cognitive abilities, social skills, and temperament. Moreover, the impact of this instruction depends, in large part, on the language and literacy skills children bring to the classroom. In this article we focus on two important learning environments, the home and the classroom, fully recognizing that preschool, community, and other important learning environments exist.

Home

Learning to read is a long-term process that begins with emergent literacy, the period of time between birth and when children begin to read and write conventionally. The interplay between language and literacy is highlighted in the practice of parents (and teachers) and children reading together. Shared book reading is one of the most successful methods that parents and teachers can employ to enhance children's language and emergent reading skills. Over 30 years of converging research findings support the importance of reading aloud to children to develop vocabulary, improve reasoning skills, introduce story grammar, and build knowledge about the alphabetic principle. A particular focus of this work has been to contrast the frequency of book reading in middle- versus low-socioeconomic status (SES) homes. The gap in book reading experiences is startling. At the start of school, Adams estimated that children from low-SES families have experienced only 25 h of book reading, whereas children from middle-SES families have experienced between 1000 and 1700 h.

Moreover, there is a well-documented predictive relation between the frequency of early parent–child book reading and later reading skills. Bus and colleagues conducted a meta-analysis of 33 studies, which demonstrated that the frequency of children's preschool reading experiences accounted for at least 8% of the unique variance in children's reading scores in elementary school. Furthermore, findings from longitudinal studies have shown that the frequency of children's preschool reading experiences predicted their reading, spelling, and intelligence quotient (IQ) scores into seventh grade. Children's development of early reading habits is associated with their later familiarity with popular books and stronger comprehension skills in high school. The more book titles elementary school children recognize (an indicator of their 'print exposure'), the greater their growth in vocabulary, spelling, and reading comprehension skills. These findings appear to support what Stanovich termed 'the Matthew effect' in which most children who experience rich early literacy experiences grow to be good readers and it is difficult for children with impoverished early literacy experiences to ever catch up.

Classroom Instruction

So far, we have focused on the components of language and literacy that comprise proficient reading skills and noted that, in the absence of effective instruction, children may not learn how to read. The classroom learning environment is highly complex and relies on both the teacher and the students as they interact around literacy learning and incorporates both the content of the instruction (phonics, comprehension, etc.), how this instruction is implemented, and the knowledge and skills both the students and the teacher bring to the learning environment. Starting with teacher characteristics that, research shows, do and do not contribute to student learning, we will then present multiple dimensions of instruction and, finally will discuss how the impact of this instruction appears to depend on the language and literacy skills children bring to the classroom (i.e., child-by-instruction interactions). Of note, as we discuss effective instruction, we are defining it as the combination of practices, methods, and strategies that lead to stronger student literacy outcomes.

Characteristics of effective teachers

Surprisingly, teachers' years of education, holding a credential, and their years of experience do not consistently predict student outcomes, especially early literacy outcomes. While we would expect that more experienced teachers and those with masters or other advanced degrees and credentials would be more effective teaching children how to read, accumulating research shows that the link is weak and indirect. Other sources of influence, such as the characteristics of children in the classroom, are much better predictors of students' outcomes. More direct assessments of teachers' knowledge about language and literacy have been shown to predict students' reading outcomes more directly. The implementation of research-based (also called evidence-based) instructional practice supported by rigorous teacher knowledge in the area of language, literacy, and teaching is associated with stronger student outcomes. Teachers who know more about the components of language and literacy and how to implement instruction effectively (e.g., use assessment results to determine learning goals for individual students) and who actually enact this knowledge and skill in the classroom tend to be more effective than teachers who know less about language and literacy instruction.

Accumulating research clearly documents that teachers' greater warmth and responsiveness to their students (in contrast to detachment) during teacher–student interactions is associated with stronger student outcomes. There is also evidence that teachers who coach their students and are more interactive are more effective than are teachers who tell their students information and offer fewer opportunities for teacher–student interactions. Also well supported by research is that teachers who can clearly impart classroom rules and routines, organize and manage their classrooms well, plan ahead, explain instructional concepts and how to do the activities supporting these concepts clearly are more effective than are unorganized teachers who do not plan or who are unclear in their instruction.

Multiple dimensions of instruction

One reason the reading wars raged is because, traditionally, classroom instruction has been viewed as one-dimensional – whole-language or phonics – or as too complex to reduce to simple pieces (e.g., social constructivism or critical theory). Certainly, teaching and learning are highly complex processes and attempts to measure them necessarily fail to capture some of their complexity. Fruitful emerging conceptualizations present teaching and learning as multidimensional with the model becoming more complex as additional dimensions are considered. As we have discussed, literacy itself is multidimensional so using a parallel argument, if literacy has multiple dimensions, then examining sources of classroom influence on literacy multidimensionally will be more informative than examining their impact globally at the curriculum level. As research on classroom instruction continues, more dimensions will be identified. Here we present four of the more salient dimensions, teacher- versus child-managed, code-versus meaning-focused, student- versus classroom-level, and change over time. These dimensions operate simultaneously and may be conceptualized as two tables with teacher- versus child-managed as columns and code- versus meaning-focused as rows with a table for classroom and another table for student-level instruction.

The dimension teacher- versus child-managed instruction is a continuum that ranges from the teacher lecturing while students listen (teacher-managed) to more interactive teaching (teacher/child-managed) to peer interactions (peer-managed) to children working independently. Overall, this dimension captures who is focusing the child's attention on the learning task. For example, the teacher discussing a book with the students would be teacher/child-managed. Students working independently on seat work would be child-managed. Students working in groups or buddy reading would be peer-managed (a type of child-managed instruction). There is evidence that all three (teacher/child, child, and peer) contribute to student learning although children who struggle with reading generally require more time with the teacher (i.e., teacher/child-managed instruction).

The dimension code- versus meaning-focused instruction has been well established throughout the extant literature and finds its roots in the Simple View of Reading (proficient reading is the product of decoding and comprehension) and the Reading Wars (phonics vs. whole language). Code-focused instruction is designed to help children grasp the alphabetic principle, to gain phonological awareness, to blend and segment words, to learn spelling and phonics, and to read words fluently. Meaning-focused instruction is designed to support students' efforts to understand what they read and includes vocabulary, reading aloud, reading independently, writing, grammar, and comprehension strategies.

If we consider two dimensions – teacher-versus child-managed and code versus meaning-focused – these dimensions together form a grid upon which any literacy activity can be placed (**Table 2**). So, for example, children reading together in the library corner would be considered peer-managed meaning-focused instruction. The teacher explaining to children how word families work (b-at, c-at, h-at) would be an example of teacher/child-managed code-focused, and children doing phonics worksheets at their desks would be an example of child-managed code-focused instruction.

The classroom- versus student-level dimension considers the extent to which instruction is the same or different for each child in the classroom. When the teacher is reading aloud or conducting a phonics lesson to the entire classroom, this would be classroom level. All of the children are being provided essentially the same information. Even if children are working in small groups or individually (e.g., seat work), if they are all doing substantially the same thing (e.g., reading the same book), then that is classroom-level instruction. In contrast, when children are engaged in substantially different activities at the same time, this is considered student-level instruction. A key characteristic is that student-level instruction is individualized and may be provided in small groups or when children work individually (e.g., centers with different activities, tutoring one child while the rest do other activities). Specific types of activities, for example, book

Table 2 Examining two dimensions of instruction simultaneously

	Teacher-managed	Child-managed	Peer-managed
Code-focused	• Alphabet instruction • Letter–sound correspondence • Phonological awareness • Phonics • Word fluency	• Alphabet worksheets • Letter–sound correspondence activities • Phonological awareness activities • Phonics • Word fluency	• Alphabet practice • Letter–sound correspondence activities • Phonological awareness • Phonics • Word fluency
Meaning-focused	• Vocabulary instruction • Comprehension strategies • Connected text fluency • Read aloud • Discussion • Model writing	• Vocabulary practice • Comprehension strategies • Independent fluency practice • Sustained independent silent reading • Independent writing	• Vocabulary activities • Comprehension strategies • Connected text fluency buddy reading • Read aloud pairs • Discussion • Buddy writing or writer's workshop

reading, can occur on both the classroom and student levels. For example, in one classroom, a teacher might read aloud to the entire class (teacher/child-managed, meaning-focused, classroom-level), while in another, a teacher might read aloud to a small group of children (teacher/child-managed, meaning-focused, child-level) while the rest of the children engage in substantially different activities such as writing in their journals (child-managed, meaning-focused, child-level).

The dimension change over time addresses the amount of time spent on specific instructional activities from grade to grade, as well as during the school year. Literacy instruction in second grade differs substantially from instruction in first or third grade. At the same time, many teachers change their instructional emphasis over the course of a single school year. For example, a teacher might begin the year with a strong focus on explicit, teacher-managed decoding instruction that decreases by winter and spring as children master basic skills. Researchers have also found that for first graders with weaker vocabulary scores, small amounts of child-managed, meaning-focused (e.g., independent reading and writing) activities at the beginning of the school year that decreased over the first grade year was associated with stronger decoding skill growth. The opposite pattern held for children with strong vocabulary skills, for whom consistently high amounts of child-managed meaning-focused instruction related to stronger decoding skills.

Using these dimensions provides a better representation of the complexity of teaching and learning (although not fully) because, as research shows, even in whole-language classrooms, some time is spent in code-focused activities and any code-focused core curriculum includes opportunities for children to read connected text (a meaning-focused activity). Effective teachers individualize instruction (i.e., provide student-level instruction), balancing the amounts and types of reading instruction, across multiple dimensions, based on children's assessed learning needs. Viewing reading instruction multidimensionally rather than as 'whole-language' or 'skill-based' has been instrumental in revealing that the impact of any given instructional strategy depends on the vocabulary and reading skills students bring to the classroom (i.e., child-by-instruction interactions).

These child-by-instruction interactions reinforce the reciprocal nature of teaching and learning. This means that there is not one 'best way' to teach reading. Although, as we have discussed, children must master the alphabet principle on their path to proficient reading, providing intensive instruction in the alphabetic principle to students who can already read *Charlotte's Web* will probably not advance their reading skills. In the same way, providing sustained opportunities to read *Charlotte's Web* independently for a child who has not mastered fluent phonological decoding will most likely lead to frustration and less learning. As discussed, research shows that instruction that takes into account the unique constellation of skills children bring to the classroom is more effective than the traditional 'one size fits all' and 'every child on the same page' approaches. Moreover, as research continues, we are becoming more sophisticated in developing ways to predict and recommend optimal patterns of instruction for children based on their language and literacy skills.

Individualizing student instruction and new definitions of reading disabilities

The need for strengthening early reading instruction is underscored when we consider that the incidence of students identified as having a learning disability, which includes children with dyslexia (i.e., specific reading disability), during elementary school has grown exponentially (by over 200%) since the establishment of the learning disabilities (LD) category in 1977. Moreover, most LD students are identified because they are experiencing difficulty learning to read.

The modal age at which children qualify for services as LD is 11 years old, by which time reading difficulties become increasingly difficult to remediate. There is a critical need for more effective early reading interventions especially considering that, as we discussed, current data indicate that 36% of students in the US cannot meet basic standards of reading competence by the end of fourth grade. The NAEP data indicates that the situation is even more critical for poor and minority students because 56% of low-SES, 61% of African American, and 57% of Hispanic students (noting that many African American and Hispanic students are also low-SES and that these percentages overlap) were not able meet the fourth grade basic reading standards.

There is a vital need for effective early identification and interventions for students who struggle to read, keeping in mind that past and current research clearly demonstrates that remediating reading difficulties is more difficult after students have struggled in learning to read for several years. Torgesen reports that once students fall behind in reading fluency, even the most powerful remedial interventions are not able to help most of them to catch up. Other negative consequences of early reading difficulties include weak vocabulary growth, less motivation to read, and fewer opportunities to develop or practice reading comprehension strategies. Moreover, several longitudinal studies have shown that reading trajectories are distressingly stable: children who are poor readers at the end of first grade almost never acquire average level reading skills by the end of elementary school.

Response to intervention (RTI) has largely been conceptualized as a general education initiative to reduce the incidence of students identified as having LD with a focus on prevention, by providing students, who fail to progress in learning to read, with evidence-based instructional services immediately, rather than waiting for children to fall far enough behind to qualify to receive special education services. RTI stems from widespread concern about the number of children not reading at grade level, which has led researchers and practitioners to question the validity of using the traditional IQ–achievement discrepancy to identify students with LD. Proponents of RTI have criticized this discrepancy approach, which requires students to demonstrate up to two standard deviations of difference between their IQ and their reading achievement, for several reasons: (1) the large increase in the numbers of students with reading disabilities and variability in state-to-state prevalence figures, (2) the disproportionate representation of diverse students among those labeled with LD, (3) instructional needs of students labeled with LD are not reliably different from poor readers without the label (i.e., LD is essentially the low tail on a bell-shaped curve), and finally (4) that without the label, many children who need early literacy intervention, especially children from high poverty backgrounds, do not receive it.

Although there is no single RTI model, broadly speaking, all RTI models include a multilayer process that often involves extensive school reform. Teachers receive professional development that precedes or coincides with implementation of RTI that aims to support implementation fidelity and instructional effectiveness. There are some differences in how response to intervention has been conceptualized and operationalized. At one end of the continuum of current RTI models, students with similar reading deficits are given evidence-based interventions that have been shown to 'work' for other students with the same deficits. Teachers or interventionists are then expected to follow a standardized treatment protocol and implement the intervention with fidelity. At the opposite end of the continuum are models that address these deficits by individualizing instruction based on a problem-solving model. Between the two ends of the continuum are models that provide a combination of standardized and individualized intervention – often beginning with what works and increasingly tailoring instruction based on progress monitoring. A useful conceptualization presents RTI instruction in three tiers.

RTI begins with effective Tier 1 classroom intervention, which presupposes that this instruction will result in almost all children becoming literate. However, as we discussed, the research suggests that the effect of instruction depends on the language and literacy skills children bring to the learning opportunity. Thus, what is effective for a student with strong language and reading skills may be ineffective for the student with weaker language and literacy skills. For Tier 1 instruction to be effective, the strategies used should be tailored to each student's strengths and weaknesses. One encouraging development is the 'Individualizing Student Instruction Project'. This study by Connor and colleagues uses a web-based software program called Assessment-to-Instruction or A2i, to help teachers provide effective individualized instruction to all the children in their classroom. The software uses algorithms to recommend specific amounts and types of instruction for each child in the classroom using each student's assessed vocabulary and reading skills. In a random field trial, after 4 months, children demonstrated significantly stronger growth in letter-word skills when their teacher individualized instruction (i.e., used small groups with appropriate learning goals and planned instruction using A2i) compared to a control group and to children whose teachers had access to the software but did not use it consistently. By the end of the school year, children in the treatment group achieved stronger reading comprehension skill growth, overall, than did children in the control classrooms.

Next, students not making adequate progress receive Tier 2 – more intensive (3–5 days per week for 15–30 min) supplemental small group intervention delivered by classroom teachers, reading specialists, or other interventionists (i.e., research staff); student progress is monitored more frequently. One example of a successful Tier 2 intervention that may be delivered by well-trained paraprofessionals or community mentors is Tutor-Assisted Intensive Learning Strategies, or TAILS developed by Al Otaiba. TAILS was field tested in a randomized field trial involving 12 kindergarten classrooms in four high-poverty elementary schools. Al Otaiba and colleagues found that children who participated in TAILS 4 days per week achieved significantly stronger letter-word, phonological awareness, and passage comprehension growth compared to children in the control classrooms. Moreover, the effect sizes were large.

Lastly, students still not making adequate progress receive Tier 3 interventions, provided in even smaller groups (one to three children) by a skilled intervention specialist, such as a special education teacher, speech-language pathologist, or reading specialist. Tier 3 sessions may be conceptualized as a mix of general and special education that is more responsive to individual children's needs and might include up to 1 hour of extra instruction per day.

Conclusion

In this article, we have conceptualized literacy as a construct comprised of multiple dimensions, which cross the boundaries between oral and written language, that affect each other reciprocally, and that are greatly influenced by the learning opportunities provided to children as they develop into proficient readers. Accumulating and compelling evidence reveals that proficient literacy requires children to have a strong foundation in oral language including lexical and semantic knowledge, metalinguistic awareness including phonological awareness, and strong overall language skills, coupled with explicit and systematic instruction in decoding, comprehension, and writing. Time to practice these skills using engaging text also contributes to proficient reading. Any part of the system that breaks down undermines this complex and dynamic system and children fail to become proficient readers. Moreover, children themselves are active agents in this system. The language, literacy, temperament, self-regulation, motivation, and other characteristics children bring to literacy learning contribute significantly to their success or failure in learning to read by influencing how they respond to learning opportunities and by shaping how parents and teachers may respond to them.

Rigorous educational research establishes the causal impact of various literacy interventions on children's learning and incorporates randomized studies. Underlying most recent efforts is the notion that we will never find a silver bullet – the perfect curriculum or the high-quality program that will meet the needs of all children. Emerging evidence that child-by-instruction interactions are causal in nature, means that school- and classroom-based programs that are high quality for one child (i.e., positive outcomes) may be poor quality for another (negative outcomes) with a different set of skills and attributes. Systematic application of research that takes into account the links between language and literacy, the strengths and weaknesses children bring to classroom, individualizing instruction and monitoring children's response to this instruction, will help us better understand the complex and dynamic construct of literacy and support all children as they become literate members of our society.

See also: Grammar; Language Acquisition Theories; Preverbal Development and Speech Perception; School Readiness; Semantic Development; Speech Perception.

Suggested Readings

Adams MJ (1990) *Beginning to Read: Thinking and Learning about Print.* Cambridge, MA: The MIT Press.
Al Otaiba S, Schatschneider C, and Silverman E (2005) Tutor assisted intensive learning strategies in kindergarten: How much is enough? *Exceptionality* 13: 195–208.
Chall JS (1967) *Learning to Read: The Great Debate.* New York: McGraw-Hill Book.
Connor CM, Morrison FJ, and Katch EL (2004) Beyond the reading wars: The effect of classroom instruction by child interactions on early reading. *Scientific Studies of Reading* 8(4): 305–336.
Connor CM, Morrison FJ, Fishman BJ, Schatschneider C, and Underwood P (2007) The early years: Algorithm-guided individualized reading instruction. *Science* 315(5811): 464–465.
Ehri LC (2002) Phases of acquisition in learning to read words and implications for teaching. In: Stainthorp R and Tomlinson P (eds.) *Learning and Teaching Reading*, pp. 7–28. London: British Journal of Educational Psychology Monograph Series II.
Morrison FJ, Bachman HJ, and Connor CM (2005) *Improving Literacy in America: Guidelines from Research.* New Haven, CT: Yale University Press.
Neuman SB and Dickinson DK (2001) Handbook of early literacy research. In: Dickinson DK and Neuman SB (eds.) (2006) *Handbook of Early Literacy Research,* Vol. 2. New York: Guilford Press.
NRP (2000) *National Reading Panel report: Teaching children to read: An evidence-based assessment of the scientific research literature on reading and its implications for reading instruction* (No. NIH Pub. No. 00-4769). Washington DC: U.S. Department of Health and Human Services, Public Health Service, National Institutes of Health, National Institute of Child Health and Human Development.
Snow CE (2001) *Reading for Understanding.* Santa Monica, CA: RAND Education and the Science and Technology Policy Institute.
Snow CE, Burns MS, and Griffin P (eds.) (1998) *Preventing Reading Difficulties in Young Children.* Washington, DC: National Academy Press.

Relevant Websites

http://isi.fcrr.org – Individualizing Student Instruction.
http://www.nrp.org – Making Minneopolls Neighborhoods Better Places to Live, Work, Learn and Play.
http://www.fcrr.org – The Florida Center for Reading Research.
http://www.ed.gov – US Department of Education, Promoting educational excellence for all Americans.

Mathematical Reasoning

K McCrink and K Wynn, Yale University, New Haven, CT, USA

© 2008 Elsevier Inc. All rights reserved.

Glossary

Accumulator model – A proposed system which underlies an organism's ability to represent approximate magnitudes.

Core systems – A suite of conceptual systems which are responsible for specific evolutionarily advantageous cognitive tasks.

Dyscalculia – A selective impairment in number processing. Can be either acquired (through strokes or lesions in the brain) or are developmental (present from birth).

Evolutionary continuity – The idea that traits and capacities found in common ancestors will likely be found in all subsequent evolutionary branches.

Habituation – The technique of repeatedly presenting a certain stimulus until the observer has thoroughly processed the item of interest.

Intermodal – Going from one sense, or modality, to the other.

Object file – A mental 'tag' placed on a visually presented object, which helps track the object in case of occlusion or disappearance.

Weak-Whorfian view of number – The learning of number words, and the particular native language, influences the already developing exact number calculations in children.

Weber fraction limit – The ability to discriminate two stimuli is dependent not on the absolute difference between the two values, but rather their proportionate difference. The amounts 20 and 10 are the same 'mental distance' away as 2000 and 1000, because these pairs share a Weber fraction of 2.0.

Introduction

Number and the Core Systems View

Numerical comprehension is thought by many psychologists to be part of a suite of domains that comprise our 'core systems'. These conceptual systems, originally proposed by Elizabeth Spelke, correspond roughly to the major academic subjects (such as physics, geography, math, and psychology) and, at least in the evolutionary environment, provided a platform for relatively inexperienced organisms to quickly grasp critical aspects of incoming information. These systems predate our current evolved state, are by and large shared with our common mammalian ancestors, and are present during infancy. They are automatically engaged, largely impervious to explicit second-guessing, and specific to the domain and task of interest; they represent only a circumscribed set of entities (such as magnitudes or faces) and use these representations to address a certain set of tasks (such as enumeration, deciding whom to approach, etc.).

The benefit of having a sensitivity to number and an ability to compute over numerical values is apparent when one examines the literature on animal cognition. Although many of the current methods and models take place in an artificial learning environment, some of the most striking evidence for the ecological utility of a number system comes from studies that capitalize on natural surroundings. American coots who are able to count the number of eggs in their nest can avoid devoting resources to extraneous eggs deposited by local parasitic birds. The foraging literature on species as varied as ducks and rats illustrates a number- and time-based ability to maximize the yield of depleting food sources. These findings highlight the significant survival advantage that would be conferred to individuals who happened to possess these numerical abilities.

A General Model of Numerical Processing

There has been overwhelming evidence for two main distinct systems that support numerical cognition, each of which has its own neural circuitry. The first component is the ability to represent and operate over approximate numerical magnitudes. This ability to represent inexact magnitudes is found not only in adult humans, but also in infants and animals. Although there are several models one could posit to account for magnitude approximation, a prevalent model with empirical support is the 'accumulator model' proposed by Warren Meck and Russell Church. This model, originally developed to account for perceptual and numerical competencies in rats, postulates a mechanism composed of a sensory source for a stream of impulses, a pulse former that gates this stream of impulses to an accumulator for a fixed duration (around 200 ms) whenever an object or event is counted, an accumulator that sums the impulses gated to it, and a mechanism that moves the magnitude from the accumulator to memory when the last object has been counted. The output of the accumulator can be either magnitude-based ('roughly 10') or time-based ('roughly 10 s'). (Because this article focuses on number alone, we will for the purposes of brevity set aside the dual nature of this mechanism. It is, however, a vital aspect of the full model and there are major similarities between counting and timing processes). This mechanism is subject to psychophysical laws, namely Weber's fraction limit, which states that the variability of perception of magnitude increases with the amount to be represented (i.e., representation becomes more approximate and discrimination between quantities less exact as the magnitude in the accumulator increases). The accumulator can enumerate both large and small amounts across several different modalities, during both sequential and simultaneous presentations. In adult humans, the intraparietal sulcus is thought to house the mechanism for approximating magnitudes; it is active when quickly estimating a large number of visually presented objects, and also when approximating the result of an addition problem (but not when calculating the exact solution). Much of the research on infant number is assumed (either explicitly or implicitly) to be tapping into this evolutionarily ancient magnitude system. Critically, this mechanism is thought to give rise to a sense of magnitude that is conceptual and ultimately independent from the sensory modality in which it was perceived. A scene of 10 objects will activate the same circuitry that represents 10 incoming tones, yielding an identical 'number sense' across the two modalities.

The second component of a mature numerical system is, in actuality, not inherently arithmetical at all but rather language-based. Located in the left angular gyrus, its main role is to serve as a retrieval system for facts that are stored in verbal memory, such as automated small number addition facts or the multiplication table. In tandem with the approximate magnitude system, it aids the exact, uniquely human calculations of complex math problems such as counting to precisely 10, discriminating 100 from 101, determining derivatives, and solving for 'x'. As children's linguistic skills develop, so does their ability to comprehend and keep track of precise amounts and verbally manipulate these magnitudes.

There is some evidence that, in addition to these two central components, a third non-numerical mechanism contributes to mature number processing. This system is found in the posterior superior parietal lobule, is responsible for orienting attention, and was originally thought to be mainly active during visuo-spatial tasks. This has led to speculation that the numerical estimation system is somehow spatially oriented, perhaps corresponding to a mental 'number line'. Recent adult work on operating over approximated numbers and numerical judgments by hemispheric-neglect patients has provided evidence that there is indeed a link between space and number, mediated by attentional processes. However, there is to date very little work in the developmental literature on this third system. Consequently, in this article we will focus on the developmental origins of the two primary components of number comprehension: the approximate magnitude system and exact verbal numerical representations.

Developmental Origins of Number Processing

The Approximate Number System in Infancy and Early Childhood

Research on approximate magnitude representations in infancy is a relatively new topic. Classic psychophysical work looking at numerical representation in animals has been present for over 50 years in the animal literature. With the popularization of the concept of 'evolutionary continuity', infant researchers began in earnest to study number across multiple populations and age groups. Beginning in the early 1980s, experimental evidence that preverbal infants also possess an inherent capacity to represent and manipulate numerical magnitudes began to emerge. Infants are able to discriminate between two numbers of items (such as 8 and 16) if the values are sufficiently disparate. These numerical representations are independent from perceptual variables (such as area or contour length), are highly salient to infants, and are represented in an abstract and sensory-independent fashion.

In one of the first studies on approximate magnitude representation in infancy, Fei Xu and Elizabeth Spelke habituated 6-month-old infants to displays containing either 8 dots or 16 dots. At test, the infants were given alternating trials of 8 dots and 16 dots. The infants dishabituated to the novel number, showing successful discrimination of these larger values. In a second experiment using an identical design, infants failed to discriminate 8 from 12. Subsequent research illustrates that infants this same age also succeed at discriminating 16 from 32, but fail to discriminate 16 from 24. These results indicate that young infants' representations are highly imprecise. Interestingly, the discrimination function obtained in these studies displays the Weber fraction signature of scalar variance, in that the ratio of the two values rather than their absolute difference determines their discriminability. This scalar variability, or 'noisy' representation, is a hallmark of the accumulator model outlined above, suggesting that both infants and animals use a similar mechanism for approximating magnitudes.

The ability to discriminate between two represented amounts is not restricted to the visual domain. Jennifer Lipton and Elizabeth Spelke studied 6- and 9-month-old infants in a tone discrimination task. After habituation to a set number of sounds, both groups of infants were able to discriminate a test item consisting of a novel number of sounds. However, as with previous studies, this ability to represent sounds was inexact, and it also sharpens with age; younger infants could only tell apart items that differed by a factor of 2 (such as 16 and 8), while older infants were able to discriminate items both at a factor of 2 (16 and 8) and a more difficult discrimination ratio of 1.5 (12 and 8). Infants also have been shown to represent other units besides visual objects and sounds. After being habituated to a set number of puppet jumps, 6-month-old infants will look longer to a moving puppet when it is jumped a novel number of times, as compared to a number that was previously shown to the infant. The children are able to make this discrimination on the number of jumps alone, since extraneous perceptual variables such as duration and tempo of the sequence were controlled. Further, these infants are able to tabulate these distinct countable units despite the presence of continuous extra motion, such as head waggling, that the puppets were performing. Infants are also able to discriminate between distinct numbers of moving objects and collections of objects.

Some of the most compelling evidence for an abstract number sense is work that addresses the intermodal nature of these representations. In an early study, Prentice Starkey, Elizabeth Spelke, and Rochel Gelman presented 6–8-month-old infants with visual displays of either 2 or 3 objects while 2 or 3 drumbeats played in the background. The infants looked preferentially to the visual displays that matched the auditory input. Although the replicability of this study has been controversial, several recent studies, using somewhat different methods, have clearly shown a similar capacity to detect magnitudes that are identical across the senses. For example, 5-month-olds who are given 2 or 3 objects to handle (while a sheet prevented them from viewing the objects) exhibit a preference for displays that contain a novel number of objects relative to the previous tactile phase. To summarize, the number mechanism that infants possess can be used to: (1) tabulate many types of countable units, (2) produce representations that can be matched across sensory modalities, and (3) yield an inexact representation of magnitude which gets sharper throughout the first year of life, such that discriminability of the two values rests on the proportionate difference between them.

The Special Case of Small Numbers of Objects: Object Tracking and the Object–File System

The research program on infants' numerical capacities has not always revealed a clear-cut competence with respect to discriminating two magnitudes. Indeed, there are experiments that show a lack of numerical understanding in a domain that would be, intuitively, the easiest – small sets of objects. This has led some researchers to suspect that infants' numerical competence is a result not of a numerical representation system, but rather of an automatic and precise system for tracking and reasoning about individual objects in the world, via 'object files' or other object tracking mechanisms. According to the strong version of this account, each individual object in an array is mentally tagged as an open 'file', and any numerical differences between two sets are detected by a one-to-one correspondence function. Thus, when faced with two sets that mismatch, the infants look longer not because of a difference in magnitude, but because there is an open (and now missing) object file. These object files are used to establish location and track individuals as they move about the world. Critically, just as the accumulator mechanism has a distinct failure point (the Weber fraction limit), so too does the object-tracking mechanism. It shows a set-size limit of roughly 3 to 4 objects, and is disengaged when dealing with a large number of objects.

There are several pieces of evidence that support the presence of this system. Lisa Feigenson, Susan Carey, and Marc Hauser presented 10- and 12-month-old infants with two amounts of graham crackers, placed one at a time in separate containers, and tested which container the children crawled to. The infants were able to choose the container that had more when the number of crackers was less than four, easily telling apart 1 from 2, and 2 from 3. When one container held four or more crackers, the infants chose randomly (even failing to discriminate 1 cracker from 4). Furthermore, the infants did not attend to number when the overall amount of cracker 'stuff' was controlled for, and crawled evenly to both buckets, showing a lack of sensitivity to number. The authors took this finding as support for a numerical system that was not really numerical at all, but rather based on tracking and discriminating individuals in a display. Fei Xu found that when continuous extent variables in a display were controlled for, 6-month-old infants were able to discriminate 4 objects from 8, but not 2 from 4. This failure is also found with respect to discriminating action units. Infants (6-month-olds) can discriminate 4 from 8, but not 2 from 4, puppet jumps when all available perceptual variables are controlled for (such as sequence duration, jump duration, jump rate, and extent of jumping motion). Some research has even found that infants habituated to a small number of objects (either two or three squares) look longer to test displays that exhibit a new amount of contour length relative to that previously seen, and fail to look longer to a new number of objects when contour length was controlled. When infants are habituated to a set of either 1, 2, or 3 items whose sizes vary systematically, longer looking is only exhibited to the test displays that contain a new amount of surface area, and looking continues to decline at test when an array containing a new number of objects is shown.

So how can one reconcile the massive literature on successful number discrimination, the majority of which is well controlled, with this new evidence of failure? One hypothesis is that this special case of tracking small numbers of objects engages a system in addition to the magnitude approximation mechanism that is constantly churning in the background. This tracking system does its job in a very accurate and task-specialized fashion. It knows where objects should be and can predict where they are going, keeps tabs on continuous extent variables such as summed area and contour length, and uses this information to guide the infants' behavior. In a hierarchy of systems that interpret incoming information, the object-tracking system was built for a specific situation and takes precedence when a certain condition, like the presentation of a small number of objects, is met.

Evidence for the approximate magnitude estimation system still abounds. The proposed object tracking mechanism cannot be the entire story of infants' enumeration capacities, as one sees arithmetic prowess in areas not covered by this mechanism. For example, the set-size limit of object tracking means that any well-controlled study that goes beyond these limits of 3–4 objects is tapping into an inherently numerical system. There is also evidence for discrimination of small numbers of entities that are not visual, such as tones. Seven-month-old infants are able to distinguish between two sets of tones, even when these tones are in the small number range (such as 2 tones vs. 4), and this discrimination function is nearly identical to the Weber fraction limit found in work on large number discrimination.

This controversy has two main consequences: it highlights one of the main challenges to studying number in infancy, and it leads to a fuller understanding of how exactly our numerical processing works. These studies show us that, in addition to the broader methodological issues one deals with when studying a nonverbal population, the variable of interest, numerosity, is naturally confounded with purely perceptual variables. These continuous extent variables, such as area and contour length, are an additional cue to perceived number. If participants in these tasks behave differently to a test item, it may be because of a change in these linearly related dimensions, such as a new amount of brightness, or a differing amount of area than previously shown. When experimenters took care to control for these perceptual dimensions, they uncovered the possible presence of an alternative system (the object-tracking mechanism) which is so attuned to the qualities of the individuals that it trumps the processing of numerical information. This 'two-systems view' (recently outlined by Lisa Feigensen and colleagues) is still in the early stages of being developed, but is promising as a key to reconciliation of the curious pattern of successes and failures in the developmental literature.

Going Beyond Discrimination: Using the Approximate Number System in Arithmetic Operations

Although discriminating two numerical sets is undoubtedly a critical ability, many of the advantages of numerical capacity identified by researchers (e.g., foraging calculations) rest on the ability not only to represent numerical values, but to compute over them. We can now examine the child's ability to go beyond simple discrimination and use these represented magnitudes as parts of an arithmetic computation. Here too the developmental origins are located in early infancy, indicating an unlearned basis that serves as the foundation of our arithmetical capacity. For example, 11-month-old infants are able to order numerosities in either a descending or ascending manner. Infants habituated to a sequentially presented set of carefully controlled arrays of objects (4, 8, and 16 objects for the ascending group, or 16, 8, and 4 for the descending group), then tested with a new sequence of arrays in either a novel ascension (3, then 6, then 12), or a novel descension (12, then 6, then 3), look significantly longer when the type of ordering at test is a mismatch for what they had been habituated to. They are able to extract from the habituation scenario a concept of 'small → big' or a concept of 'big → small' and generalize on the basis of that criteria. This ability, like the majority of findings outlined here, is not unique to humans. In an earlier study, rhesus monkeys had been trained to respond in an ascending ordinal fashion to 1, 2, 3, and 4 objects (1 → 4), while varying perceptual factors such as size, shape, and color. These monkeys were given displays during a testing phase that showed novel large numbers (5, 6, 7, 8, and 9), and they responded by ordering these new magnitudes in an ascending fashion (5 → 9).

Karen Wynn tested 5-month-olds' simple addition and subtraction capacities by using a small set of objects to act out a computation (such as 1+1 or 2−1). The infants in the addition condition saw a single Mickey mouse doll hop onto the stage, and a rotating screen rose to occlude it. A hand from the side of the stage came out and moved a second doll to join the first behind the screen, then exited the stage as an empty hand. A second group of infants saw a complementary action played out, where instead of addition the operation was subtraction. Two dolls were placed on the stage, and covered. A hand came and took away one of the dolls, leaving the stage with one doll. The screen then came down to show either a correct outcome, or an incorrect outcome produced by manipulating a trap door behind the screen. Infants who witnessed the addition event were more likely to look longer to the outcome of 1 doll over 2 dolls, while infants who saw subtraction looked longer to 2 dolls than to a single doll. This 'flip' in looking time preference was driven by the preceding operation; each group of infants looked longer to the wrong outcome, despite this outcome being different across groups. This experiment has recently been replicated and extended using an intermodal addition paradigm. First, infants are familiarized to a display of a doll hitting the bottom of the stage and producing a tone. They are then shown several arithmetic events involving the addition of tones and objects (such as 1 object + 1 tone = 2 or 3 objects), and are able to detect the incorrect outcomes of these problems. Infants appear to compute the basic arithmetic operation of addition across sensory modalities.

There were several criticisms to the Wynn study, and to some extent all studies that use a similar paradigm and number of objects. In the case of the original study, the amount of continuous extent (area of the dolls) was confounded with the total number. Melissa Clearfield and Kelly Mix performed several follow-up studies which hypothesized that this confound was responsible for infants' performance, and that if these variable were manipulated there would be no significant effect of number. They habituated infants to two or three squares of the same size, and then showed the infants test displays which had either a novel number of objects, or a novel total area. The authors found that infants looked longer to the test displays that showed a novel surface area compared to those displays that showed a novel number of objects. This experiment has been replicated to show that this pattern of preference for novel continuous extent variable also holds when the child is tested with a novel contour length as well. These results, while interesting, are limited in interpretation due to the fact that the variables at test are not merely controlled for, but rather 'pitted against' each other. This research raises the invaluable point that babies are indeed very sensitive to continuous extent variables, and perhaps may even give higher priority to detecting them than to detecting numerical violations. The research as to whether this is truly the case is still ongoing, with researchers such as Elizabeth Brannon finding that, in fact, infants in her studies have a bias toward numerical discrimination over area and contour length discrimination.

The sheer fact that small numbers of visual objects were being manipulated in Karen Wynn's original addition and subtraction study makes it difficult to disentangle claims about represented magnitudes from hypothesized object-tracking systems. Even in the case of intermodal addition and subtraction, the possibility remains that the familiarized pairing of objects and tones resulted in the engagement of the object-tracking system. One simple way to get around the possible engagement of this alternate system is to take the identical paradigm and methodology of Wynn, but move them out of the domain of small number. One has reason above and beyond the small-number work on addition and subtraction to believe that infants would be able to perform operations over large nonverbally represented magnitudes, as animals as varied as monkeys and pigeons have shown this ability in numerous studies. Rhesus macaques are able to spontaneously compute the outcome of both small- and large-number addition problems (such as $2+2$, or $4+4$) and the limit on this ability is set by the Weber fraction of the possible outcomes. Pigeons are able to compare a constant number of flashes with the number remaining after a numerical subtraction of two comparison magnitudes of flashes.

To look at infants' ability to perform these large-number operations, we presented 9-month-old infants with a computerized display of addition or subtraction events. Half the infants saw displays in which 5 objects dropped down from above, constantly changing shape and gradually moving to the right side to become occluded. Five more objects dropped down and went behind the occluder. The other half of the infants saw the complementary subtraction movies in which 10 objects fell down, an occluder rose, and 5 objects moved off screen. All infants then saw two alternating test displays of either 5 objects or 10 objects. These test displays had the same amount of summed area and overall contour length, leaving only number as the difference between the two sets. The addition group looked longer when presented with test displays of 5 objects, the incorrect outcome of $5+5$. The subtraction group showed the opposite pattern, and looked longer at the test displays of 10 objects (the incorrect answer to $10-5$). This study establishes that performing computations such as addition and subtraction do not only occur in the non-numerical context of object-tracking; rather, the systems that provide an approximate sense of magnitude are able to provide representations for use in arithmetic operations. Follow-up studies have confirmed that the representations used in these computations are inexact. While the infants were generally quite good at determining incorrect vs. correct outcomes (even succeeding at $4+5=6$ or 9, and $10-4=6$ or 9), their performance suffered when trying to discriminate two outcomes that were very close together. When presented with difficult problems such as $7+5=12$ or 9, or $14-5=9$ or 12, the infants looked similarly to each outcome irrespective of whether it was correct or incorrect.

Hilary Barth and colleagues have conducted several studies on young children using a similar computerized addition and subtraction paradigm. In one such study, 5-year-old children were shown arrays of large numbers of objects and given the two tasks of comparison and addition. In the comparison task, a group of blue dots comes from offscreen and becomes occluded. A group of red dots then comes down from offscreen and the children are asked whether there are more blue dots, or red dots. In the addition task, a group of blue dots goes behind an occluder, and a second group of blue dots moves to join the first set. A group of red dots comes from off screen, and the child is again asked if there are more blue dots or red dots. In both these tasks, the children were able to correctly answer, above chance performance, which array was larger. Five-year-olds have also been found to correctly compare and add two sets of items across different sensory modalities. Barth also found that children could perform both the comparison and addition tasks when given a combination of objects and tones, and that their performance was just as accurate when dealing with multiple modalities than their performance in a single-modality version of the tasks. Thus it appears that this magnitude information was put into an abstract numerical code, distinct from the sensory code through which it was initially perceived.

But what of more complicated operations, assumed to come online later in life via schooling and experience? These computations, such as multiplication, division, and statistics have only recently been indirectly tested in young infants. For over 50 years animal theorists have noticed that animal foraging behavior appears to rely on computational processes that use time, amount, and discrete number as relevant variables in operations that are analogous to division and multiplication. For example, in a case alluded to earlier, many animals will 'rate match' when foraging. Mallard ducks will distribute themselves to two experimenters at opposite ends of a pond in a proportion that is equivalent to the relationship between the size, number, and rate of tossed bread morsels. Although it is of course impossible to perform these sorts of experiments with infants, it is a reasonable hypothesis that such an evolutionarily critical computation will be present from early on in our development, and can potentially manifest itself in other ways through careful testing.

To examine this hypothesis, we presented 6-month-old infants with a test of proportional understanding, by habituating them to a series of slides displaying a constant ratio of object type A (pellets) to object type B (pacmen). At test, the infants were shown either an entirely new ratio of pellets to pacmen, or a new example of the old ratio. If infants dishabituate to the never-seen ratio, but not the new example of the old ratio, this would be evidence for an ability to extract a common proportion and generalize on the basis of this relationship. Several manipulations were performed within this basic design, and examined whether infants can detect a change in proportion of perceptual variables (such as area), conceptual variables (such as number), the difference between ratios that are quite disparate (such as 4:1 vs. 2:1), and the difference between ratios that are closer together (such as 3:1 vs. 2:1). Incredibly, these young infants readily distinguish between scenes that contain a different numerical proportion of object A to object B. They can also tell the difference between scenes that contain a different proportion of pellet area and pacmen area. This ability to equate proportions disappeared when we decreased the disparity between the two ratios; the infants looked similarly to test outcomes of 2:1 and 3:1 irrespective of what they were previously habituated to.

This ability to comprehend ratios has also been found in early childhood. Children with the age of 4 and 5 years tested with a variety of stimuli (such as animals with varying degrees of head-to-tail ratio, or two line segments that exhibited a particular length ratio) are able to reliably determine which test stimulus exhibits the same proportion as the standard when they have the comparison readily available. This research, as well as the infant research outlined above, is in stark contrast to earlier work by classic developmental scientists such as Piaget on ratios and proportions which does not find competence when testing schoolchildren. In fact, many schoolteachers and students say that understanding of fractions and proportions is one of the hardest basic math lessons to learn. Although there is very little research that directly tests hypotheses that could reconcile these two findings, one idea is that the use of implicit measures such as looking time (in the case of the babies) or direct comparison of perceptual ratio (in the case of the competent schoolchildren) taps into a slightly different, less-conscious system than those commonly used when testing or teaching ratios. When one learns about ratios in school, it is in a very concrete, exact way that does not necessarily recruit the same representations that are being used in the experiments on estimated ratios.

This ability to understand proportion is, to our knowledge, one of the most computationally complex operations shown in infants to date. It is also a finding that confirms that attention to ecological validity (here, in the evolutionary sense of the term) is a critical component to establishing and elucidating the suite of possible processes that infants possess. Using the wealth of animal literature will be critical to pinpointing those abilities that are most likely to be found as part of our underlying cognitive architecture.

The Role of Language in Numerical Development

Learning to Count

With the immense competence shown by preverbal infants, one would have very little reason to think that a mature numerical understanding would be an arduous process. This is, however, exactly the case. As with many of the core knowledge systems, the aspects of the world that are salient to nonverbal organisms do not necessarily manifest themselves in the explicit day-to-day behaviors children perform as they develop. One of the very first steps in transitioning from a nonverbal representation of quantity to a mature verbal system is learning to count. Rochel Gelman and Randy Gallistel outlined three basic principles that must hold in order to successfully count a set. The child must understand that as an ordered list of words is applied to the items, each linguistic tag applies only to a specific item in the set (the one-to-one correspondence principle). The stable-order principle states that the count list must be applied the same way across different counting situations. The cardinal principle states that the final word used when counting the set represents the total number of items (the cardinal value). In order to successfully count, children must map the number of the set represented by their magnitude system to these ordinal, symbolic terms used by the linguistic system.

Rochel Gelman performed a classic series of 'magic' studies with young children. In these experiments, children were presented with two plates, each of which had a differing number of toys. Half the number of children were trained that the plate containing a greater number of toys was the 'winner', and the plate with the smaller quantity the 'loser'. The other half were trained on the reverse labels, with small-quantity plates being 'winners' and large-quantity plates 'losers'. After training the children to distinguish winners from losers, the experimenter covered the plates and surreptitiously transformed the plates. These transformations were either numerical in nature (such as changing 2 objects to 3), spatial (rearranging where each object was on the plate), or identity-based (changing the type of object on the plate.) When the plates were uncovered, the experimenter asked them to distinguish anew the winner and loser plate, and justify their decision. Children as young as 2.5 years of age appealed to concepts of numerosity and were not 'fooled' by other numerically extraneous transformations. Gelman concludes that children, even if they are counting poorly, understand that this counting process gives a representation of number that lends itself to arithmetic reasoning, and are able to apply these counting principles from a very early age.

Other researchers believe that, although young children are giving the appearance of competence, they are actually performing the task without true comprehension of what it means to count. Karen Wynn tested children ranging from 2.5 to 4 years of age and asked them to give a certain number of toys from a pile (the give-a-number task). They were also given a counting task, and were asked to count sets ranging from two to six items and then report how many there were to the experimenter (the how-many task). Although some children were able to count to correctly perform the give-a-number task (the

Counters, whose average age was 3.5 years), the younger children (the Grabbers) failed to count in order to solve the task, instead grabbing several dolls to hand to the experimenter. This failure is more striking when one considers that these children had in place a very solid counting routine, and could count the six items in the pile with no problem. The Grabbers failed to understand that the count list they happily produce is what determines the specific number of a collection of items. Counters and Grabbers also exhibited different behavior in the how-many task. Children who counted in the give-a-number task were able to distinguish between their own correct and incorrect counts, and were three times as likely to reply with the last number word they produced after a correct count than they were when their initial count was incorrect. The Grabbers were equally happy to give whatever number word they had stopped at as their answer to the experimenter, irrespective of whether this count was correct or not. Through this study, and other studies that examine the protracted development of counting, Wynn posits that a true conceptual understanding of the count list, and the principles that guide counting, is only available to children come early childhood (roughly 3–4 years of age.)

There is evidence to suggest that it is the particular linguistic context of differing types of number words that scaffold the child into a mature understanding of number. Children are able to determine that a particular word picks out a specific quantity of items (and therefore, it is a number word) if that word occurs in certain syntactic frames and not others. For example, in a database that examines naturalistic speech to young children, adults speaking to 1- and 2-year-olds used number words to apply over individuals, when denoting discrete unchangeable values, and when describing the quality of a set of objects. These syntactic frames correspond to the level of knowledge described by the Grabbers in the give-a-number task above. Thus, it follows that how these number words are presented in the syntax of the child's language will interact with pre-existing numerical systems to guide children toward a greater understanding of arithmetic principles.

Linguistic Effects on Number Comprehension and Encoding

The impact of language on arithmetic development is more striking when one examines cross-cultural studies that map the linguistic idiosyncrasies of a language to altered patterns of numerical development. A well-established example in the developmental literature is that of the Chinese language. The construction of the first ten counting words is completely arbitrary (yi, er, san is equivalent to one, two, three), as in English and most other languages. The numbers that follow ten, however, are perfectly regular and embody the structure of the base-10 system. For example, 35 is expressed as Three-Ten-Five, or $3 \times 10 + 5$. This intuitive system, markedly different from the relatively opaque English counting system, is thought to contribute to the superior performance of Chinese-speaking pupils over English-speaking pupils. Children (4-, 5-, and 6-year-old) who speak Chinese are able to count higher and more competently than an age-matched group of US children. First-graders in San Francisco who know the Chinese counting system are more likely to represent numbers in base-10 form (by segregating a collection of 35 objects into groups of 10, 10, 10, and 5 for the experimenter) than English-system first-graders, who simply present 35 objects. The idea of place value, a concept that many American children struggle with in school when learning precise computations, is inherent to the way Chinese number words are expressed.

In addition to symbolic number words, the Chinese language is more transparent with respect to mathematics terms used for complicated domains such as algebra and trigonometry. For example, the literal translation for the symbol of 'mode' from Chinese to English is 'frequent number'. In an ingenious study on the conceptual differences between Chinese and English numerical systems, and how this may prompt differential learning, Yi Han and Herbert Ginsburg created a set of 'Chinglish' words by literally translating Chinese symbols into the English words for those symbols. These Chinglish terms were rated to be more conceptually clear, as the inherent compound structure is well-suited to portray complicated mathematical ideas. The authors then examined three groups of junior-high-school students, all of whom were ethnically considered Chinese: monolingual English speakers, bilingual English/Chinese speakers, and monolingual Chinese speakers. The students who could speak Chinese performed better on a test of mathematical concepts, and level of Chinese reading ability correlated positively with performance level during the test. This was not merely a situation in which underlying cognitive factors drive success in both math and language, as the level of English-speaking ability was not correlated with performance on the math test in the bilingual and English-speaking groups.

Olivier Houde and colleagues have studied the relative influence of several languages on early arithmetic development. In one study, they found that the dual use of the word 'un' in the French language as both an indefinite article ('an') and a number word ('one') led to a phase of development in which qualitative differences in arithmetic performance could be observed between French-speaking children and English-speaking children. Using a task that mimicked Karen Wynn's violation-of-expectation experiment with young infants, the experimenters performed a puppet show of the arithmetic problems $1 + 2 = 2$, 3, or 4, and $2 + 1 = 2$, 3, or 4. The children were then asked if each outcome was 'okay' or 'not okay'. English-speaking, but not French speaking, 2-year-olds were able to correctly determine the outcome of all the addition problems. The French 2-year-olds were selectively impaired on those problems that start off with 'un' object on the stage. By 3 years of age, both groups of children were able to do both types of problems. The authors argue that this shows an effect of language on the child's conceptualization of the situation at a fundamental, arithmetic level. The child could not compute the answer to the problem, because the mental application of the tag 'un' put the child in a situation that was syntactic, and not numeric. Follow-up studies by the same group have found an identical pattern of results with Spanish and Finnish children. Spanish-speaking children, whose word for 'an' overlaps with their word for 'one' (*uno/una*), showed a performance deficit relative to Finnish-speaking children (whose language does not conflate the article with the number word) when given addition problems that start off with a single object on stage. These findings support a weak-Whorfian view that some aspects of language influence the pattern of conceptual development in the numerical domain.

Evidence for this weak-Whorfian view also comes from the literature on how adults behave when placed into a new learning situation. Bilingual students who were taught a set of new numerical operations, new exact equations, and novel numerical or non-numerical geography and history facts show a lag when tested for exact calculation problems ('$86 + 26 = 112$ or 102'?) or numerically based facts ("After which election did the King execute several governors?") outside of the language in which they had encoded them. However, this discrepancy is not present when the students retrieve information on approximate numbers (such as determining the approximate logarithm or cube-root of a value) or recall non-numerical facts ("Where did the band of farmers meet?") that they had learned in the other language. Thus, language appears to play a critical role in the encoding and storage of particular types of numerical information but not others, and this role corresponds nicely with the proposed number systems of approximate magnitude representation and exact verbal calculation.

Abnormal Numerical Development

In the condition of developmental dyscalculia (DD), a child with otherwise normal mental abilities shows a deficit in mathematical abilities. Brian Butterworth, via the 'defective number module hypothesis', posits that this deficit arises from a genetic defect in the specialized numerical systems common to all humans. Evidence for a genetic component of DD comes from studies with twins. While the baseline rate of the disorder is somewhere around 6% of the general population, dizygotic twins (who share half of genetic material) have a 39% concordance rate and monozygotic twins (whose genetic material is identical) have a remarkably high 58% concordance rate. DD is frequently comorbid with other learning disabilities, such as dyslexia and attention deficit hyperactivity disorder (ADHD). Although this is suggestive of an across-the-board deficit in processing information, there is evidence that cases of pure dyscalculia exist. One investigation into 8- and 9-year-old children with dyscalculia, dyslexia, or no learning disability found that children with dyscalculia had deficits specific to math that extended qualitatively and quantitatively beyond those shown in the other two groups. These cases provide us with the opportunity to examine what exactly it means to represent and manipulate number, and the limits of the supplementary systems used in arithmetic tasks.

There are many different types of DD, with widespread deficits seen in some patients, and other patients who suffer only from specific deficits. These specific deficits tend to roughly correspond with the circuits outlined above, namely the approximation system and the rote verbal calculation system. In several case studies on 'acquired dyscalculia' (a deficit that came about as a result of injury to the developed brain), Stanislas Dehaene and colleagues have found a dissociation between magnitude approximation and exact calculation. One patient, N.A.U., was able to determine whether a simple approximated arithmetic calculation was incorrect (such as $2 + 2 = 9$), but was unable to say if exact, small-number calculations were correct or incorrect, judging such rote, precise, arithmetic problems as $2 + 2 = 3$ to be correct. Two other dyscalculiac patients who exhibited a double dissociation between the systems of approximation and exact calculation have been studied. A patient with a lesion of the inferior parietal lobe was impaired in tasks that tested the manipulation of approximate quantity, but was able to perform rote, exact tasks such as the multiplication problems one finds on a grade-school multiplication table. Another patient, who had a lesion of the left subcortical region, was impaired on operations that involved rote, verbal calculations and unimpaired on tasks that involved the manipulation of magnitudes.

These studies, while generally supportive of the outlined component model of number processing, are not able to address questions of numerical development *per se*, as they study adult humans who had many years of schooling and experience before impairment. It is entirely possible that outside cultural norms regarding how to classify number concepts had come to shape the organization of numerical knowledge. In order to examine the way in which our minds are initially organized, the population of children with dyscalculia is of interest. These children have been impaired from birth (assuming the defective number module hypothesis is correct), with official diagnoses generally given as they started schooling and failed to progress normally. And they too, show deficits that are specific to the proposed number components. Children with DD exhibit immature strategies for dealing with basic arithmetic, such as counting on their fingers instead of retrieving rote facts. These children do not exhibit difficulties on just the verbal tasks of recall, however. Butterworth also discovered a reverse distance effect in children who had severe DD. Normally, it is much easier to determine that magnitudes that lie far apart on the number line (such as 4 and 12) are different, and this task gets more difficult when deciding if magnitudes that are on roughly the same area of the number line (such as 10 and 12) are different. Children with severe DD sometimes exhibit the opposite pattern; they are better able to determine the difference between numbers that are similar (15 and 14) than numbers that are disparate (15 and 10), presumably because they are using a non-magnitude-based counting process. Although there are only a handful of neuroimaging studies done with DD patients, they are suggestive of brain abnormalities analogous to that found in adult patients with acquired dyscalculia. If one examined two groups of adolescents, one of which was unimpaired and the other which exhibited specific deficits on numerical operations, the impaired adolescents would have overall significantly less gray matter in the left intraparietal sulcus, an area that is found to be selectively active during magnitude approximation and calculation tasks in adults.

On the strongest possible account of the defective number module hypothesis, children who are impaired have been impaired since birth. An intriguing way to test this hypothesis would be to use the early tests of mathematical understanding outlined previously to pinpoint which children may have problems in the future. One can do this in an 'educated-guess' manner by studying the relatives (siblings or children) of those who have already been diagnosed with dyscalculia. If scientists are able to correlate later numerical competence based on their performance as infants, this would be extremely important at both the theoretical and applied level. First, it would suggest that the abilities we see in infants are indeed related to our adult arithmetic abilities and are recruited later on in development. Second, it would confirm the idea of a genetic basis for developmental dyscalculia. Third, it would allow psychologists to pinpoint those children who would benefit the most from an intervention to improve their arithmetic skills.

Sex Differences in Arithmetic Development

The idea that males are superior to females on arithmetic tasks has been omnipresent for quite a long time, both scientifically and anecdotally. There are many different types of claims about sex differences and mathematics. Some people believe that there are intrinsic differences from birth with respect to male and female competence. Others believe the differences are indeed present, but have come about as a function of socialization or only happen as hormone levels fluctuate. The developmental literature on mathematical ability is therefore extremely relevant to this debate, as it has the ability to pinpoint if and when differing capabilities arise.

First and foremost, there is no compelling evidence from the developmental literature on number systems in infancy that the genders innately differ on any of the tasks relevant to this debate. Although some work has shown a tendency for male infants to focus more on objects (thus, presumably, leading to a more mechanical and mathematic way of thinking) and female infants to focus more on faces (suggesting a predisposition for socializing), the specific experiment of interest has not been replicated and, in fact, goes against several other well-replicated studies that show equal levels of interest to both objects and faces by female and male infants. There is a tendency, by around adolescence, for boys to outperform girls on such standardized tests as the math portion of the SATs. This difference grows larger as one moves up the age range. David Geary and colleagues posit that the main factor mediating this difference between genders is not mathematical reasoning ability *per se*, but rather a sex-based difference on how each sex chooses strategies-when faced with different tasks. Females are more likely to solve complicated problems by using verbal calculations, whereas males resort to a strategy of spatial imagery. It is true that spatial imagery is, on average, stronger in men than women, but only as hormonal levels fluctuate in the female body. Non-ovulating females show similar performance to an average male. This unreliability is, perhaps, a reason for females to adopt a non-spatial strategy as a first pass at arithmetic problem solving. Because the SAT-M is composed of questions that are more easily solved by using spatial imagery, a difference in overall mathematics scores emerges.

The psychological processes of socializing girls and boys with respect to math achievement reveals a lopsided picture of parental influence on arithmetic development. Parental justifications of their childrens' success in mathematics courses have been examined by researchers in several cultures (such as America, Finland, and Israel). These experiments have found that parents of boys are more likely to attribute success to inherent, natural ability, while parents of girls believe their child's success is due to effort. People tend to associate effort with diligence and, unflatteringly, conformity. Thus, a boy who does well in math is considered to possess a very highly valued trait (natural ability), while a girl who performs similarly is seen as having the less-admirable trait of a good work ethic. (Ironically, the parents of the boys are doing their children no favor, as attributions of natural ability in the classroom yield a less motivated student than attributions of effort.) To summarize, it appears that eventual sex differences in mathematical ability are due to many factors, including socialization, test construction, and deployment of differing problem-solving strategies in a mathematical context.

Conclusion

The above review of the current and classic literature on numerical understanding shows a deep continuity between nonhuman animals, infants, and adults. By informing our infancy research with established phenomena in the animal literature, we are closer to discovering the 'fundamentals' of our nature. The capacity to represent amounts, and to productively use these representations, indicates an important and rich network of systems that have evolved to support a core capacity of arithmetic understanding. This line of research starts to address the broader issue of how humans process and organize information from our environment, and how this activity changes across development.

Although the mechanisms outlined above are undoubtedly critical to a mature number system, they are only a small step toward the entire package of complicated mathematical discovery. There are some concepts that do not lend themselves to being represented as a magnitude, an object, or even a word. Concepts such as infinity, zero, derivatives, and *pi* are unique to the world of theoretical math. The systems outlined above must be built upon and improved throughout development, and meshed with other core capacities such as physics, mechanics, biology, and linguistics. It is through this combination of domains that we are able to use our mind to its fullest extent.

See also: Habituation and Novelty; Neonativism.

Suggested Readings

Barth H, La Mont K, Lipton J, and Spelke ES (2005) Abstract number and arithmetic in preschool children. *Proceedings of the National Academy of Sciences USA* 102(39): 14116–14121.

Butterworth B (1999) *The Mathematical Brain.* London: Macmillan.

Dehaene S (1997) *The Number Sense: How the Mind Creates Mathematics.* Oxford: Oxford University Press.

Dehaene S, Piazza M, Pinel P, and Cohen L (2003) Three parietal circuits for number processing. *Cognitive Neuropsychology* 20(3–6): 487–506.

Feienson L, Carey S, and Hauser M (2002) The representations underlying infants' choice of more: Object files versus analog magnitudes. *Psychological Science* 13: 150–156.

Feigenson L, Dehaene S, and Spelke E (2004) Core systems of number. *Trends in Cognitive Science* 8(7): 307–314.

Gallistel CR (1990) *The Organization of Learning.* Cambridge, MA: MIT Press.

Geary DC (1996) Sexual selection and sex differences in mathematical abilities. *Behavioral and Brain Sciences* 19: 229.

Gelman R and Gallistel CR (1978) *The Child's Understanding of Number.* Cambridge, MA: Harvard University Press.

Han Y and Ginsburg H (2001) Chinese and English mathematics language: The relation between linguistic clarity and mathematics performance. *Mathematical Thinking and Learning* 3: 201–220.
Hubbard E, Piazza M, Pinel P, and Dehaene S (2005) Interactions between number and space in parietal cortex. *Nature Reviews Neuroscience* 6(6): 435–448.
Kimura D (1999) *Sex and Cognition.* Cambridge, MA: MIT Press.
Lipton J and Spelke E (2003) Origins of number sense: Large-number discrimination in human infants. *Psychological Science* 14(5): 396–401.
McCrink K and Wynn K (2004) Large-number addition and subtraction by 9-month-old infants. *Psychological Science* 15: 776–781.
Meck W and Church R (1983) A mode control model of counting and timing processes. *Journal of Experimental Psychology: Animal Behavior Processes* 9(3): 320–334.
Spelke ES (2000) Core knowledge. *American Psychologist* 55: 1233–1243.
Wynn K (1990) Children's understanding of counting. *Cognition* 36: 155–193.
Wynn K (1992) Addition and subtraction by 5-month-old human infants. *Nature* 348: 749–750.
Xu F (2003) Numerosity discrimination in infants: Evidence for two systems of representations. *Cognition* 89(1): B15–B25.
Xu F and Spelke E (2000) Large number discrimination in 6-month-old infants. *Cognition* 74(1): B1–B11.

Memory

H Hayne, University of Otago, Dunedin, New Zealand
J Richmond, Harvard University, Boston, MA, USA

© 2008 Elsevier Inc. All rights reserved.

Glossary

Classical conditioning – A form of learning in which a previously neutral stimulus (conditioned stimulus or CS) is presented in conjunction with another stimulus (unconditioned stimulus or US) that elicits a particular response (unconditioned response or UR). Over successive pairings of the CS and US, the CS begins to elicit the same response (conditioned response or CR).
Encoding – The process by which information is stored in memory.
Habituation – A decline in responding to the repeated presentation of the same stimulus.
Memory retrieval – The process by which information that is stored in memory is accessed.
Reminder treatment – The presentation of a stimulus prior to the retention test; presentation of this stimulus facilitates memory retrieval and improves retention.
Retention – A term that is analogous to memory or remembering; retention interval refers to the delay between the end of the learning session and the outset of the test session.

Introduction

Relative to other primates, human infants enter the world in a relatively altricial, or immature, state. Although most of their senses are well developed at birth (e.g., hearing, taste, touch, and smell), their visual acuity is initially very limited. The newborns' motor skills are also very immature and it will take years before they attain the motor milestones that their other primate cousins attain at or around the time of birth. If we look at the nature of the human brain, we can begin to understand the source of the human newborn's immaturity. Unlike other primates whose brain growth peaks during mid-gestation, human brain growth peaks at about the time of birth; thus, at the time they are born, human infants are more neurologically immature than other primates. After birth, the human brain continues to mature for at least another 20 years (and perhaps even longer), but changes in the brain occur very rapidly during infancy and early childhood. What are the consequences of this brain growth on infants' cognitive skills, particularly on their memory? How does the infant's memory skill change as he or she matures? Begins to crawl? Acquires language? These are some of the questions that we will try to answer here.

The task of measuring memory in human infants is one that is fraught with difficulty. Unlike human adults, preverbal infants cannot draw on language to express their memory for a past event. As a result, researchers must rely on infants' overt nonverbal behavior as an index of their memory. In other words, researchers must find ways for infants to 'show' us rather than 'tell' us what they remember. In addition, infants are often unpredictable research participants; their attention span is typically short and their emotional state can change very rapidly. For these reasons, tasks that are designed to assess memory during infancy must be brief; when the experimental session is long, attrition rates are often very high. Studying age-related changes in memory across the infancy period is also particularly challenging because the changes that occur in language, motor skill, and attention that take place over the first 2 years of life make it difficult to design a single task that can be used with infants of different ages. Despite these challenges, researchers have developed a number of experimental techniques that have allowed us to study memory development over the first 2 years of life.

Newborns

At the time of birth, the average human newborn weighs approximately 3400 g or 7.5 lbs. Despite excellent auditory, olfactory, and taste capability, newborn infants' visual acuity is extremely limited. Based on three different assessment methods, newborn visual acuity is estimated to be about 20/640. In terms of gross motor skill, human newborns cannot sit, crawl, or roll over and they do not have the fine motor control required to reach for or grasp objects. In fact, most newborns cannot support the weight of their own head for more than a few seconds.

Historically, many researchers believed that because of their physical immaturity, infants were unable to learn or remember during the first few months of life. Initial research on learning and memory in newborns confirmed this belief. When newborns were tested using habituation or classical conditioning procedures that were originally developed to study nonverbal memory in human adults or other animals, researchers consistently found that newborns were incapable of retaining information for more than a few seconds at best.

Gradually, however, researchers began to take a different approach to studying the memory ability of newborns. Rather than focusing on the newborns' inability to learn and remember arbitrary relations between novel stimuli and their consequences, researchers began to examine what newborns might learn and remember about meaningful stimuli in their environment. This shift in focus has challenged the claim that newborns lack memory skill. In fact, the results of these experiments have uncovered some remarkable memory abilities in human newborns.

The first step in studying memory in newborns is to find a way for infants to demonstrate that they remember. In order to do this, researchers must harness a behavior that newborns can master. Although the range of behaviors that they exhibit is somewhat limited, researchers have been able to capitalize on newborns' ability to suck, look, turn their head, and stick out their tongue.

High-Amplitude Sucking

The high-amplitude sucking task capitalizes on a behavior that newborns do exceptionally well – sucking. In this task, infants learn to suck on a non-nutritive nipple; by changing the pattern of their sucking, infants can produce changes in the environment. In a landmark study, DeCasper and Fifer used the high-amplitude sucking procedure to study newborns' memory for their own mother's voice. In that study, a standard baby bottle nipple was placed in the infant's mouth. One end of a piece of flexible tubing was connected to the nipple and the other end was connected to a recording device. This arrangement allowed the researchers to measure and record the pattern of the infant's sucking bursts. In addition to sucking on the nipple, the infant was also fitted with a set of headphones that allowed the experimenters to present the infant's mother's voice or the voice of another, unfamiliar woman.

For each infant, baseline suck rate was established during a 5-min period in which no voices were presented. Following this baseline period, some infants were required to increase the duration of the pause between successive sucking bursts and some infants were required to decrease the pause between successive sucking bursts. When infants met their target criterion (i.e., increased or decreased pause length), their mother's voice was played through the headphones. When they did not meet their target criterion, another woman's voice was played through the headphones. DeCasper and Fifer found that although the infants were less than 3 days old at the time of the test, they altered their suck rate to maintain contact with their mother's voice. The results of this study showed that these newborns had already learned something about the characteristics of their mother's voice and that they would alter their own behavior to maintain contact with it.

These data raise another interesting possibility. On the basis of their findings it is tempting to conclude that the infants' preference for their mothers' voice was based, at least in part, on their experience with her voice prior to birth. We know that infants can hear *in utero* and that the volume of their mother's voice is sufficient to reach their ears, but is there any evidence that they learned the characteristics of her voice during the prenatal period? Because all of the infants in the DeCasper and Fifer study had at least some postnatal contact with their mothers, it was impossible to rule out the role of postnatal learning in their findings. In an attempt to study what infants might remember about a 'prenatal' auditory stimulus, DeCasper and colleagues conducted another study in which he asked pregnant women to read one of three prose passages out loud to their fetus, twice a day during the last 6 weeks of their pregnancy. Two to three days after these infants were born, they were given the opportunity to alter their suck rate to produce the passage that their mother had read during her pregnancy or to produce another passage. DeCasper found that infants altered their suck rate to maintain contact with the familiar story irrespective of who read it during the test (i.e., their mother or another unfamiliar woman). Taken together, studies conducted by DeCasper and colleagues clearly show that the ability to remember emerges at the time of birth, if not earlier!

Visual Preference

Despite their limited visual acuity, research has shown that newborn infants do learn and remember the basic characteristics of their mother's face within the first few days after birth. In the visual preference task, for example, infants are given the opportunity to look at their mother or at an unfamiliar woman when both women are presented simultaneously. Both women are silent during the task so that infants cannot use their mother's voice as a cue. Under these conditions, newborns spend more than twice as much time looking at their mother relative to the other, unfamiliar woman. Furthermore, when the women change their right/left position during the test, infants track their mother's position and continue to look longer at her face. Additional research has shown that newborns' recognition of their mother's face depends, at least in part, on her hair line. When the women's hair is covered by a towel, for example, newborns show no visual preference for their mother over another unfamiliar woman during the test.

Head Turning

Although most human newborns cannot support the weight of their own head for long periods of time, if the weight of their head is supported by a hand or a pillow, they can (and do) turn their head from side-to-side. A number of researchers have capitalized on this behavior to study newborns' memory for both olfactory and auditory stimuli. For example, newborn infants will turn their head in the direction of odor cues from their mother's body or breast milk when they are pitted against similar cues from another infant's mother.

Presumably, infants learn and remember the characteristics of their mother's smells on the basis of their prolonged daily contact with her. What about other stimuli that are encountered less often? Can infants learn the characteristics of these stimuli as well? To answer these questions, some researchers have used head turning procedures to study newborns' memory for stimuli encountered for the first time during the experimental session. In one experiment, for example, researchers examined habituation of head turning in 1–2-day-old newborns. During the habituation phase of the experiment, the experimenter, supporting the infant's head, positioned the infant midway between two speakers. One of two words (beagle or tinder) was played from the speakers, one at a time. On the initial trials, infants turned their head toward the speaker from which the word was played. Over trials, however, the infants presumably became bored with the word and they started to turn away from the speaker. The next day, when infants were tested again, those infants who were tested with the original word were less likely to turn toward the speaker than infants who were tested with a new word or than infants who had never heard the original word before. In short, these newborns exhibited some memory for their brief experience with the word the day before.

Imitation

Imitation is a monkey-see, monkey-do activity in which a child copies a behavior that he or she has seen performed by someone else. Imitation is an important way by which children acquire a wide range of new behaviors during the course of their daily lives and researchers have capitalized on this opportunity to develop more standardized procedures that can be used to study imitation in the laboratory. In these experiments, an infant watches as an adult performs an action or series of actions, and the infant's ability to reproduce that action or actions is assessed immediately or following a delay.

Research conducted using imitation procedures has shown that even newborns readily learn by watching and repeating the actions of others. In one study with 6-week-old infants that was conducted by Meltzoff and Moore, an adult demonstrated a particular facial gesture (e.g., sticking out his tongue) and the infants' ability to imitate this gesture was assessed both immediately and after a 24 h delay. They found that these very young infants not only imitated the model's action at the time of the original demonstration, but they also repeated the action when they encountered the model again the following day.

Summary

In contrast to the view that newborns have little or no memory ability, a large body of research has now shown that newborns learn and remember a great deal about biologically relevant stimuli that are associated with their survival – they learn the basic characteristics of their mother's voice, face, and smell and they remember this information when they are tested after a delay. Furthermore, newborns also exhibit some, albeit limited, ability to learn and remember information about new stimuli and new actions that are not intimately tied to survival. Over the next several months, however, the ability to accomplish these memory tasks improves dramatically.

3–6-Month-Olds

Human infants undergo some remarkable changes between 3 and 6 months of age. Their visual ability increases dramatically, and by the age of 6 months, their average visual acuity is roughly equivalent to that of adults (e.g., 20/40). In terms of gross motor skill, most infants begin to roll over sometime between 2 and 4 months of age, and they begin to sit unsupported by approximately 5 months. Infants begin to engage in visually guided reaching by about 4 months of age and they rapidly get better and better at holding and manipulating objects. Consistent with these changes in perception and motor skill, infants also make great strides in their ability to learn and remember about the world around them.

Visual Recognition Memory Paradigm

The visual recognition memory (VRM) paradigm that researchers now use to study infant memory evolved from experimental procedures that were originally designed to study visual perception in human infants and nonhuman primates. In this task, the infant is typically seated on the mother's lap facing a pair of computer screens or video monitors (see **Figure 1(a)**). The VRM procedure typically involves two phases; a familiarization phase and a test phase. During the familiarization phase, infants are presented with a visual stimulus, either for a fixed period of time, or until a fixed amount of looking time is accumulated. Following a delay, infants are presented with a pair of stimuli, one that is the same as the familiarization stimulus and one that is new (see **Figure 1(b)**).

Infants' visual behavior is recorded during the test phase of the VRM procedure and it is analyzed to determine the amount of time that they spend looking at the novel stimulus and the familiar stimulus. Memory is inferred if infants exhibit a novelty preference, spending a greater proportion of time fixating the novel stimulus than the familiar stimulus. Forgetting is inferred when infants exhibit a null preference, fixating the novel and familiar stimuli equally during the test.

Novelty preferences in VRM performance have been reported in infants from birth; however, the amount of familiarization time that is required for infants to exhibit novelty preferences changes with age. Susan Rose and colleagues have shown that with limited familiarization time, infants will initially exhibit a preference for the familiar stimulus. This preference shifts toward novelty with longer familiarization times. For example, Rose reported that while both 3- and 6-month-olds exhibited familiarity preferences when they were allowed only 5 or 10 s familiarization, 6-month-olds required only 15 s of familiarization to exhibit a novelty preference, while 3-month-olds required 30 s of familiarization. These results illustrate significant age-related changes in the speed of encoding across this age range.

The maximum retention interval after which infants will exhibit a novelty preference in the VRM procedure also changes with age. Although young infants typically exhibit retention on the VRM task after delays ranging from minutes to days, by 6 months of age, infants may exhibit novelty preferences after delays as long as 2 weeks. Although testing is most commonly discontinued after the retention interval at which infants exhibit a null preference (i.e., forgetting), some researchers have tested infants on the VRM task after delays ranging from 1 min to 3 months. Lorraine Bahrick and colleagues have shown that 3-month-olds may exhibit novelty preferences when tested after short delays, null preferences when tested after intermediate delays, and familiarity preferences, which can also be interpreted as evidence of retention, when tested after long delays. Bahrick argues that performance on the VRM task may be best characterized along a continuum from novelty preference to familiarity preference.

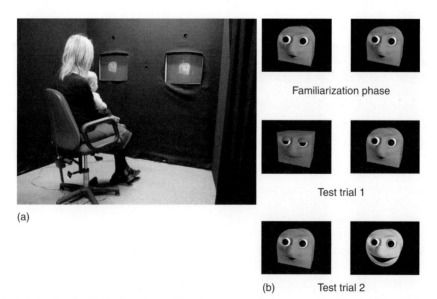

Figure 1 (a) An infant during the familiarization phase of the visual recognition memory (VRM) paradigm. (b) Sample stimulus presentation schedule during the familiarization and test phases of the VRM paradigm.

There is now considerable evidence that the VRM task may measure a fundamental component of cognitive ability that is continuous across development. Individual differences in the magnitude of infants' novelty preference have been shown to predict childhood intelligence quotient (IQ) at age 11 years. In addition, VRM performance is sensitive to a number of risk factors for developmental delay, including prematurity, prenatal drug exposure, and Down syndrome.

Operant Conditioning Procedures

The mobile conjugate reinforcement procedure is an operant conditioning task that was originally developed by Carolyn Rovee-Collier. In this task, infants learn to kick their foot to produce movement in an overhanging mobile, which is attached to their foot by a ribbon. The term 'conjugate reinforcement' refers to the fact that the rate and vigor of reinforcement (i.e., movement in the mobile) is directly proportional to the rate and vigor of the infant's responding (i.e., kicking). In other words, the more or harder the infant kicks, the more the mobile moves.

Infants are typically trained in the mobile procedure in two 15 min sessions that take place on consecutive days. During each session, infants are placed on their back in their crib and a mobile is suspended from a flexible mobile stand. Each training session begins with a period of nonreinforcement (see **Figure 2(a)**). During this period, a ribbon is tied around the infant's ankle, but rather than being attached to the active mobile stand, it is attached to an empty mobile stand. In this way, the mobile is visible to the infant, but kicks do not produce movement in the mobile. The purpose of this nonreinforcement phase is to measure the infant's baseline kick rate, before the contingency between foot kicks and mobile movement is introduced. Following this baseline phase, there is a period of reinforcement. During this phase, the ribbon is attached to the stand containing the mobile, and the infants' kicks produce movement in the mobile (see **Figure 2(b)**). Each training session ends with another brief period of nonreinforcement. During this period, the ribbon is again attached to the empty mobile stand, and infants do not receive reinforcement for foot kicks. The period of nonreinforcement at the end of each session provides a measure of immediate retention. Learning in the mobile conjugate reinforcement paradigm is operationally defined as a kick rate that exceeds the baseline kick rate by a factor of 1.5 during 2 out of any 3 consecutive minutes of reinforcement. A number of studies have shown that infants as young as 3 months meet or exceed this kick rate within the first session of training (see **Figure 2(c)**).

The mobile conjugate reinforcement paradigm can be used to study memory simply by inserting a delay between the end of the final training session and the beginning of the test that is scheduled days or weeks later. Memory in the mobile conjugate reinforcement task is assessed during another period of nonreinforcement at the outset of the test session. Retention is inferred on the basis of two relative response measures. First, the baseline ratio expresses the degree to which the infant's kick rate during the test exceeds his or her kick rate prior to learning. Memory is typically inferred if the baseline ratio is significantly greater than 1.0. Second, the retention ratio expresses the degree to which the infant's kick rate during the test matches his or her kick rate at the end of

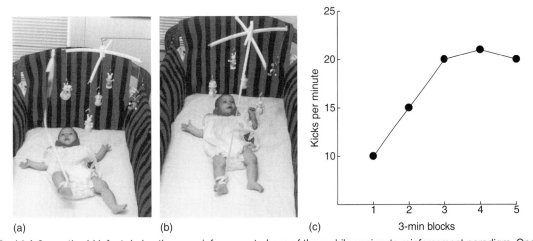

Figure 2 (a) A 3-month-old infant during the nonreinforcement phase of the mobile conjugate reinforcement paradigm. One end of the ribbon is tied to the infant's ankle and the other end is secured to an empty mobile stand. In this arrangement, the infant can see the mobile and feel the tug of the ribbon when she kicks, but her kicks are ineffective in producing mobile movement. (b) A 3-month-old infant during the reinforcement phase of the mobile conjugate reinforcement paradigm. During this phase, the ankle ribbon is attached to the stand supporting the mobile. In this arrangement, kicks of the infant's foot produce corresponding movement in the mobile. (c) The mean number of kicks per min by a group of 3-month-old infants trained in the mobile conjugate reinforcement paradigm.

training, prior to the retention interval. Retention ratios that approach 1.00 indicate that little or no forgetting has occurred over the delay.

Although the mobile conjugate reinforcement task is suitable for use with infants from 2 to 6 months of age, it is necessary to adjust the task to account for age-related changes in motor skill and speed of learning. Because they are more likely to roll over during the training and test sessions, 6-month-old infants are placed in an infant seat during each session. Furthermore, the duration of the training sessions varies slightly as a function of age. For example, while 3-month-old infants are typically trained in two sessions that are 15 min in duration, 6-month-old infants only require 6-min training sessions to learn the same task, so their training sessions are typically abbreviated.

Research conducted using the mobile conjugate reinforcement paradigm has clearly documented that the duration of infant memory increases linearly as a function of age. For example, 2-month-olds exhibit memory for 1 day, 3-month-olds exhibit memory for 8 days, and 6-month-olds exhibit memory for 14 days (see **Figure 3**, open circles). The duration of retention in an analogous task, the train task, continues to improve over the next 12 months.

Although infants eventually forget in the mobile conjugate reinforcement paradigm, Rovee-Collier and colleagues have shown that the memory may still be retrieved and expressed if infants are exposed to a brief reminder treatment prior to the test. In the initial demonstration of this phenomenon, Rovee-Collier found that when 3-month-old infants were briefly exposed to the moving mobile 24 h prior to the test, forgetting was alleviated after a 2–4-week delay. During the reminder treatment, infants were placed in an infant seat to restrict movement of their legs. During the test, however, infants were again placed supine in the crib. In the absence of a reminder treatment, infants did not kick during the test; when infants were given a reminder, their kick rate during the test was virtually identical to their kick rate at the end of the final training session 2–4-weeks earlier. Furthermore, infants continued to exhibit memory in the task for several days after the reminder treatment.

Subsequent research has shown that if 6-month-old infants are given a 2-min exposure to the moving mobile 20 days after the conclusion of training, they also exhibit retention when tested 24 h later, and will continue to remember for 14 days, the same length of time that 6-month-olds typically remember the task in the first place. Taken together, these studies show that although forgetting occurs very rapidly at 3–6 months of age, the memory is not always permanently lost and, given the appropriate conditions, the memory can be restored, allowing infants to profit from their prior experiences over very long delays.

Research using the mobile conjugate reinforcement paradigm has also shown that young infants form remarkably detailed memories of the mobile that is present during training as well as detailed memories of the context in which training occurs. Studies in which researchers have manipulated aspects of the mobile or the testing environment have shown that relatively small changes in the cues that are available at retrieval will disrupt infants' memory for the mobile task. For example, 3–6-month-old infants will not exhibit retention if they are trained with one mobile and tested with a different mobile. In fact, at 2 and 3 months of age, memory for the mobile is so specific that infants do not exhibit retention during the test if more than one out of the five objects that make up the mobile is changed during the test.

Memory performance by 3–6-month-olds is also highly context-specific; memory retrieval is impaired if aspects of the incidental learning environment are changed between training and the test. Rovee-Collier has shown that infants do not exhibit retention if they are trained in one room of their house but are tested in another, or if they are trained in the presence of one distinctively colored crib bumper but are tested with a different crib bumper. These results suggest that young infants encode a considerable amount of detail about the mobile and the testing environment; however, the specificity of the memory representation prevents infants from generalizing their memories if aspects of the cue or context are manipulated. In the end, the highly specific nature of infants' memories may actually work against them because, in the real world, cues and contexts rarely occur the exact same way twice. As we

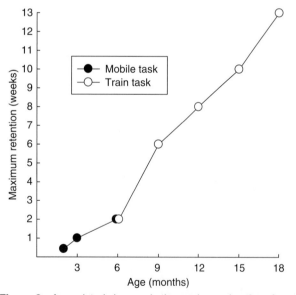

Figure 3 Age-related changes in the maximum duration of long-term retention by 2–18-month-old infants who were tested in either the mobile conjugate reinforcement paradigm (open circles) or in the train paradigm (closed circles). As shown here, 6-month-olds perform equivalently on both tasks. This figure was redrawn from Hartshorn *et al.* (1998) and has been reprinted with permission from John Wiley & Sons, Inc.

will see below, a major hallmark of memory development during the second year of life is an increase in the flexibility of memory retrieval.

Electrophysiology

Event-related potentials (ERPs) represent transient changes in the brain's electrical activity that occur in response to the presentation of a stimulus. Electrophysiological measures of memory are particularly useful in studies with infants because ERPs can be measured from the scalp (see **Figure 4**). Furthermore, although ERPs may be correlated with behavior, they do not require an overt motor or linguistic response. As such, ERPs may be recorded from infants of different ages using the same paradigm, or may be recorded from the same infant tested on an ERP paradigm at a number of different ages. Although ERP techniques have poor spatial resolution (it is difficult to localize where the electrical activity recorded at the scalp is generated in the brain), the temporal resolution is very high. This feature allows researchers to precisely assess the timing of the neural events that underlie the memory processes in the brain.

There are a number of characteristic components of the infant ERP waveform that have proven to be of interest in the study of memory development. The Nc (negative central) is a mid-latency negative component that is evident in electrodes that are positioned over the central front of the scalp. This feature of the infant ERP waveform is thought to reflect obligatory attention. Although it is not considered a direct index of memory, the Nc is often modulated by stimulus novelty. In contrast, late slow wave activity is thought to index memory processing more directly. Following the Nc, the infant ERP response may take one of three forms: a positive slow wave (PSW), negative slow wave (NSW), or return to baseline (see **Figure 5**). The PSW is thought to index memory updating of a partially encoded or forgotten stimulus. The NSW is often seen in response to a novel stimulus that is presented in the context of familiar stimuli and is thought to reflect novelty detection. A return to baseline is interpreted as evidence of a fully encoded stimulus that does not require additional processing.

ERPs are used to study infant memory using one of two different paradigms. Researchers sometimes record ERPs in response to stimuli with which the infant is presumably very familiar, and compare the ERP waveform to that elicited by stimuli that the infant has not yet experienced. For example, in some studies, researchers record ERPs in response to pictures of the infant's mother's face relative to the face of an unfamiliar woman. These studies have shown that in 6-month-old infants, the amplitude of Nc component is larger in magnitude in response to the mother's face relative to the stranger's face. Following the Nc, the ERP in response to the mother's face returns to baseline, indicating complete encoding. The response to a stranger's face, however, takes the form of a PSW, indicating that the infant may be encoding new details of the stranger's face during the course of the testing session. Similar studies using auditory paradigms with younger infants have shown that the Nc and slow wave components also differentiate between mother's voice and that of a stranger. In 6-month-old infants, these components also differ when infants are presented with pictures of their favorite toy and a novel toy. Collectively, these results have led researchers to suggest that the brain systems that are necessary for infants to form representations of people and objects in their environment and to discriminate novel and familiar stimuli are functionally mature during the first months of life.

Given the extensive experience that infants have with their mother's face (or even their favorite toy), ERPs recorded in response to such stimuli can only tell us so much about the neural correlates of infant learning and memory. For these reasons, the majority of infant ERP studies have used a modified oddball paradigm in which

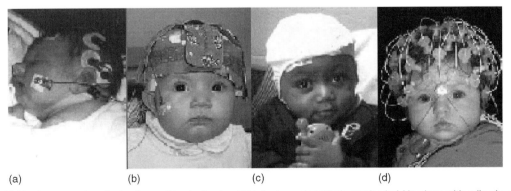

Figure 4 (a) Newborn wearing single disposable electrodes; (b) infant wearing 16 electrodes held in place with adhesive foam pads and Velcro headbands; (c) infant wearing a 32-channel electro-cap; and (d) infant wearing a 64-channel electrogeodesic sensor net. From C. A. Nelson.

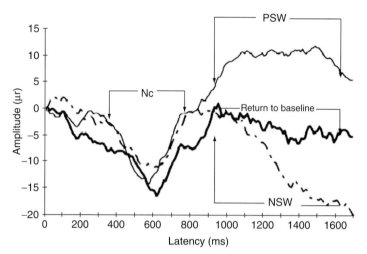

- Nc (negative component)
  - middle latency response occurring 400–800 ms after stimulus onset attentional response
- PSW (positive slow wave)
  - later latency response occuring 800–1700 ms after stimulus onset memory updating
- NSW (negative slow wave)
  - later latency response occuring 800–1700 ms after stimulus onset detection of novelty
- Return to baseline
  - later latency response occuring 800–1700 ms after stimulus onset
  - present for stimuli not requiring memory updating and not detected as novel

Figure 5 Example of the components observed in the infant event-related potential during a visual recognition memory task. From de Haan M and Nelson CA (1997) Recognition of the mother's face by six-month-old infants: A neurobehavioral study. *Child Development* 68: 187–210.

infants are familiarized with new stimuli at the outset of the session and they are tested for recognition of these newly familiar stimuli relative to a novel stimulus. In the oddball paradigm, infants are familiarized with two stimuli. Following familiarization, one of these stimuli is presented on 60% of the test trials (frequent familiar) and the other is presented on 20% of the test trials (infrequent familiar). A novel stimulus is presented on the remaining 20% of trials.

Studies using the oddball paradigm have shown that while the Nc is evident in the ERP waveform of infants across a wide range of ages, there is considerable change in the pattern of slow wave activity in response to novel and familiar stimuli across the first year of life. For example, in 4-month-old infants, slow wave activity does not differentiate between frequent familiar, infrequent familiar, or novel stimuli; in 6-month-old infants, frequent familiar stimuli elicit a return to baseline, indicating complete encoding, while infrequent familiar stimuli elicit a PSW, indicating some kind of updating. In 8-month-old infants, familiar stimuli, whether presented frequently or infrequently, elicit a return to baseline. This pattern of results indicates a gradual improvement in memory capabilities between 4 and 8 months of age. While 4-month-olds are unable to distinguish between any of the stimulus categories, 6-month-olds maintain a representation of a familiar stimulus provided that the stimulus is presented relatively frequently. If the familiar stimulus is presented infrequently, the representation is forgotten rapidly, and requires additional updating. Eight-month-old infants, however, are able to maintain a representation of the familiar stimulus even when it is presented infrequently, as evidenced by a return to baseline for both the frequent familiar and infrequent familiar stimulus presentations.

Electrophysiological measures of infant memory are often more sensitive than behavioral measures. Several studies have now shown that the Nc and slow wave components differentiate between novel and familiar stimuli under conditions in which infant's looking behavior on tasks such as the VRM paradigm does not. In addition, ERP studies of infants at risk for neurodevelopmental delay (i.e., pre-term infants, infants of diabetic mothers, infants who have suffered hypoxic injury) have yielded memory deficits in the absence of detectable differences in standardized measures of cognitive development.

Summary

Infant memory between 3 and 6 months of age is typically measured by assessing changes in infants' behavior (i.e., looking, kicking) or brain response (i.e., event-related potential) as a function of their prior experience. Infants of this age are able to demonstrate memory; however, there are age-related changes in the speed with which infants learn and the delay after which they will exhibit retention. In addition, infant memory during this period is characterized by extreme specificity; small changes in the stimuli or learning environment disrupt memory retrieval.

6–12-Month-Olds

Developmental changes in motor abilities continue during the second half of the first year of life, expanding the range of behaviors that can be used to index infant memory. Between 6 and 12 months of age, infants are increasingly able to grab and manipulate objects using their hands. Researchers have capitalized on this ability in the design of operant conditioning and deferred imitation tasks that are typically used to measure memory during this period.

Operant Conditioning – Train Task

Although the mobile conjugate reinforcement paradigm is ideally suited for infants up to 6 months of age, changes in motor capabilities, interests, and motivation render the task less interesting for older infants. To continue the study of memory development in infancy, Carolyn Rovee-Collier designed an equivalent task that can be used with 6–18-month-olds. In the train task, infants learn how to press a lever to produce movement in a toy train (see **Figure 6**). Like the mobile task, training begins with a brief period of nonreinforcement before the contingency between lever presses and train movement is introduced. Each training session also ends with a period of nonreinforcement. Retention is typically tested after a delay and memory is inferred from infants' response rate during the nonreinforced test period, relative to response rates during baseline (baseline ratio) and following training (retention ratio).

Although reinforcement in the train task is not 'conjugate' like it is in the mobile task, in every other sense the two tasks are equivalent. Six-month-old infants learn the train task at the same rate and remember it for the same length of time that 6-month-olds remember the mobile task. At this age, memories for the train task are similarly disrupted by a change in train set (i.e., cue) or testing room (i.e., context). Forgotten memories for the train task may be also reinstated by administering a brief reminder treatment.

Infants' ability to exhibit long-term retention continues to improve gradually between 6 and 12 months of age. For example, while 6-month-olds will remember the train task for 2 weeks, 9-month-olds will remember the task for a maximum of 6 weeks, and 12-month-olds will remember the task for 8 weeks (see **Figure 3**, closed circles). Similarly, the rate at which infants learn about the contingency between their behavior (i.e., lever presses) and its consequences (i.e., train movement) continues to improve during this period, requiring researchers to adapt the learning phase of the task to suit the age of the infant; for 6-month-olds, the training involves 6-min periods of reinforcement, however, 9- and 12-month-olds will learn the task with only 4-min periods of reinforcement.

Infants' memory for the train task becomes less susceptible to changes in cue and changes in context as infants approach 1 year of age. Six-month-olds will not exhibit retention if the train set (i.e., cue) or testing room (i.e., context) is changed between the learning and test phases. Older infants, however, will generalize responding to a new train set or a new context provided that they are tested after a short delay. At the extreme end of the forgetting function however, infants' memories continue to be disrupted by changes in the retrieval cues at the time of the test well into the second year of life.

Deferred Imitation

Although neonates will exhibit imitation for facial gestures, it is not until the second half of the first year of life that infants' motor skills are sufficiently developed to allow them to imitate actions that can be performed with objects. In the deferred imitation task, the experimenter demonstrates a sequence of actions using novel objects. During this demonstration phase, the experimenter does not label the objects or describe the actions verbally; infants are allowed to watch but are not allowed to touch the objects or practice the actions. Following a delay, infants are given the opportunity to reproduce the actions that the experimenter performed earlier. Memory is inferred if infants in the demonstration group produce the target actions at a higher rate than do infants in a control group who had the same amount of experience with the objects, but did not see the actions demonstrated.

When defined in this way, infants as young as 6 months of age will exhibit deferred imitation after a 24-h delay; however, younger infants require more encoding time than older infants to exhibit the same level of performance after a delay. Using a deferred imitation task in which a set of novel actions are demonstrated with a hand-held puppet, Hayne and colleagues have shown that following a 30 s demonstration period, both 6- and 12-month-old infants will imitate the actions immediately, however, only

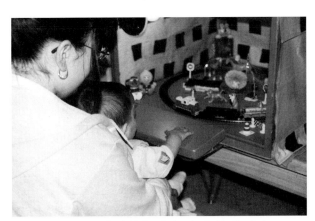

Figure 6 A 6-month-old infant being tested in the train paradigm.

12-month-olds will do so after a 24-h delay. If 6-month-olds are shown the actions for a 60 s demonstration period, however, they too are able to demonstrate retention when tested after a delay. These results point to age-related changes in both the speed of encoding and the duration of retention across this period.

Like performance on the train task, deferred imitation between 6 and 12 months of age is characterized by extreme specificity (see **Figure 7**). During this period, small changes in the objects (i.e., cue) or learning environment (i.e., context) can disrupt infants' retrieval of imitation events. For example, 6-month-olds fail to exhibit retention when the demonstration occurs in their home but the test occurs in the laboratory (or vice versa). This retrieval failure occurs irrespective of the cue present at the time of the test (see **Figure 7**, context change). In contrast, 12-month-old infants exhibit the same level of retention irrespective of whether they are tested in the same or a different context. At both 6 and 12 months of age, changes in the cue (i.e., puppet) disrupt memory retrieval and impair performance (see **Figure 7**, cue change). Both 6- and 12-month-old infants do not exhibit retention after a 24-h delay if they are shown the target actions with one puppet (i.e., a pink rabbit) but are tested using a different one (i.e., a gray mouse). In fact, 12-month-old infants do not exhibit retention if the test puppet differs from the demonstration puppet in color only (i.e., a pink mouse to a gray mouse) or in form only (i.e., a pink mouse to a pink rabbit). It is not until well into the second year of life that infants begin to use their memories in a flexible manner to perform a deferred imitation task across changes in cue (see **Figure 7**, 18-month-olds).

Infants' experiences influence their emerging ability to use their memory flexibly. With the onset of independent locomotion, infants begin to learn that objects work in a similar way even when they are moved to a new environment. Research has shown that 9-month-old infants who are crawling and 12-month-old infants who are walking are more likely to exhibit generalization across changes in cues and contexts than are their noncrawling and nonwalking counterparts. Although it is tempting to argue that individual differences in motor skill simply reflect individual differences in maturational status, the relation between motor development and cognitive development is quite specific. For example, infants with higher levels of motor skill perform equivalently to infants with lower levels of motor skill on standard tests of deferred imitation; the difference between the two groups only emerges when infants are asked to solve problems that involve changes in cues and contexts (i.e., that require representational flexibility).

Even stronger evidence that the relation between motor skill and cognitive development reflects maturation alone, is derived from studies of the relation between motor ability and language skill. For example, infants with higher levels of motor skill perform equivalently to infants with lower levels of motor skills on global tests of language, but they outperform infants with lower levels of motor skill when it comes to the comprehension and production of prohibitive language in particular. We know that as infants begin to crawl, parents begin to use more prohibitive language (e.g., "Stop." "Don't touch."); apparently this experience facilitates language learning in this specific domain. Although it is not possible to rule out maturation entirely, the highly specific nature of the differences in representational flexibility and language skill has lead many researchers to argue that the ability to crawl or walk provides new experiences and poses new challenges.

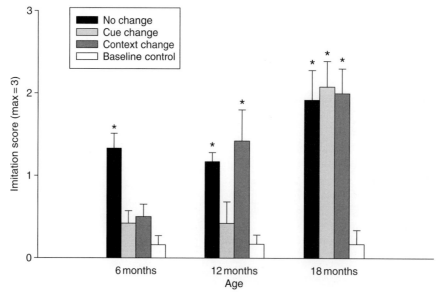

Figure 7 Age-related changes in generalization across cues and contexts by 6-, 12-, and 18-month-old infants who were tested in the deferred imitation paradigm. Asterisks indicate scores significantly greater than baseline.

It is these experiences and challenges that ultimately drive changes in both representational flexibility and language skill during the infancy period.

Summary

There continues to be a gradual improvement in infants' encoding and retention during the second half of the first year of life. Although memory during this period continues to be highly specific to the conditions that were present at encoding, coincident with the onset of independent locomotion, there are some improvements in infants' ability to use their memory flexibly. Independent of the task that is used to measure memory, 12-month-old infants are able to exhibit retention even when aspects of the learning context have been changed. The ability to generalize memory across changes in cue continues to develop into the second year of life.

12–24-Month-Olds

The second year of life is characterized by two major changes in infant development. First, most infants take their first tentative steps sometime around their first birthday. Second, infants' ability to both comprehend and produce language increases dramatically between their first and second birthdays. How do these changes in motor development and language acquisition influence memory ability? As described above, the onset of upright locomotion, like the onset of crawling, influences the flexibility of memory retrieval. When chronological age is held constant, for example, infants who can walk show more flexible memory retrieval than do infants who cannot yet walk.

Second, language acquisition also plays a major role in memory development during the second year of life. Most of the research on the relation between language development and memory development has relied on the deferred imitation paradigm described above. Even before they can produce many words themselves, infants can use an adults' language to facilitate their memory performance in the deferred imitation task. For example, when the demonstration and the test sessions are narrated by an adult who labels the objects and describes the actions and the outcome of the event, 18-month-olds infants exhibit superior memory performance than they do when the demonstration and the test session do not include these linguistic cues (see **Figure 8(a)**).

By 24 months of age, infants can use an adult's language to facilitate generalization to novel test cues. For example, when tested with more complex stimuli and target actions, memory retrieval by 24-month-olds is impaired by changes to the stimuli at the time of the test (see **Figure 8(b)**). If the experimenter provides a unique verbal label for the stimuli during the demonstration and uses the same label to refer to the new stimuli at the time of the test, then infants exhibit the same level of memory performance irrespective of whether the test stimuli are the same as or different from the stimuli present at the time of the demonstration (see **Figure 8(b)**).

Summary

Although the speed of encoding and the duration of long-term retention continue to increase between 12 and 24 months of age, the most important change in memory development during this period is an age-related change in the flexibility of memory retrieval. Between

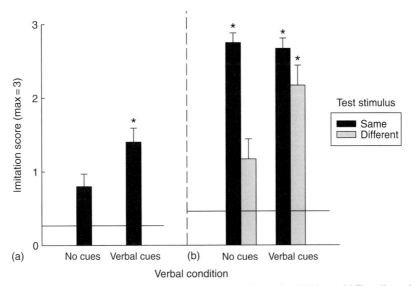

Figure 8 (a) The effect of adults' language cues on long-term retention by 18-month-old infants. (b) The effect of adults' language cues on generalization by 24-month-old infants. In both parts, the imitation score of the baseline control group is indicated by the solid line.

12 and 24 months, infants begin to retrieve and use their memories in a wider range of circumstances. They also begin to exploit new retrieval cues, including words provided by an adult.

Conclusions

Taken together, the research outlined here supports three general principles of infant memory development. First, the speed of original encoding increases as a function of age. Data collected using the VRM paradigm, the mobile conjugate reinforcement paradigm, the train paradigm, and the deferred imitation paradigm have all confirmed that older infants learn faster than younger infants. Put another way, if encoding time is held constant in any of these procedures, older infants learn more during a given episode than younger infants.

The second general principle of memory development is that the duration of long-term retention increases as a function of age. Even when the level of original encoding is held constant by increasing exposure time to the stimulus or by extending the duration of the training session, older infants remember longer than younger infants. This age-related increase in retention allows older infants to profit from their prior experience over longer periods of time. Greater retention also allows older infants more opportunity to accumulate information over successive learning episodes, particularly if those episodes are separated in time.

Third, the flexibility of memory retrieval increases as a function of age. During early infancy, infants can retrieve and use their memories if and only if they re-encounter the original cue in the original learning context. If either the cue or the context is different, then retrieval suffers. As a function of both age and experience, however, infants gradually begin to exploit cues that are different from those encountered during original learning. Clearly, both language acquisition and motor development play an important role in this process. Age-related changes in the flexibility of memory retrieval allows older infants to use their memories in a wider range of circumstances and it may also allow them to learn from a wider range of sources including picture books, television, and photographs.

Age-related changes in encoding, retention, and retrieval that take place during the infancy period continue to take place throughout early childhood. By the end of the infancy period, children begin to acquire their native language and as they do, they also begin to express the contents of their memories linguistically. It is important to note, however, that children's ability to use language in the service of memory pales by comparison to their nonverbal memory skill or to their ability to use language in the here-and-now.

Furthermore, children do not readily map their emerging language skill onto their nonverbal representations which means that most of the memories that we form during the infancy period do not survive the transition to language. It has been argued, for example, that the failure to translate our early, pre-verbal memories into language may be one source of childhood amnesia – the universal inability of adults to recall events that took place during their infancy and early childhood.

For decades, many researchers expressed a relatively dim view of mnemonic capacity during the infancy period. Based on a substantial body of research, we now know that infants can and do exhibit sophisticated memory skills beginning at birth. The next new challenge for research on infant memory development will be to establish the critical link between age-related changes in memory performance and maturation of the human central nervous system. Thirty years ago, this goal was little more than a pipe dream, but as our ability to study the human brain in action becomes increasingly more sophisticated using electrophysiological and imaging techniques, we are slowly moving closer to making this dream a reality.

Acknowledgments

Preparation of this article was supported by a Marsden Grant from the Royal Society of New Zealand to Harlene Hayne.

See also: Amnesia, Infantile; Attention; Brain Development; Habituation and Novelty; Language Acquisition Theories; Language Development: Overview; Milestones: Cognitive.

Suggested Readings

Bahrick L and Pickens J (1995) Infant memory for object motion across a period of three months: Implications for a four-phase attention function. *Journal of Experimental Child Psychology* 59: 343–371.

de Haan M and Nelson CA (1997) Recognition of the mother's face by six-month-old infants: A neurobehavioral study. *Child Development* 68: 187–210.

DeCasper AJ and Fifer WP (1980) Of human bonding: Newborns prefer their mothers' voices. *Science* 208: 1174–1176.

Hayne H (2004) Infant memory development: Implications for childhood amnesia. *Developmental Review* 24: 33–73.

Meltzoff AN and Moore MK (1994) Imitation, memory, and the representation of persons. *Infant Behavior and Development* 17: 83–99.

Rose SA and Feldman JF (1997) Memory and speed: Their role in the relation of infant information processing to later IQ. *Child Development* 68: 630–641.

Rovee-Collier C (1997) Dissociations in infant memory: Rethinking the development of implicit and explicit memory. *Psychological Review* 104: 467–498.

Milestones: Cognitive

M W Daehler, University of Massachusetts, Amherst, MA, USA

© 2008 Elsevier Inc. All rights reserved.

Glossary

Analogical problem solving – Transfer of a solution principle applicable for solving one problem to another problem that can be solved using the same solution principle.
Explicit memory – Recall of information that had been acquired at a specific time and place.
Habituation – Gradual decline in intensity, frequency, or duration of a response over repeated or lengthy occurrences of the same stimulus.
Implicit memory – Recognition or recall of information not available to conscious reflection or awareness of its having been acquired at a specific time or place.
Means-ends behavior – Deliberate actions that must be performed prior to achieving a goal.
Norms – Measures of average values and their variations for the onset or display of some aspect of development.
Object identity – Ability to anticipate an object's reappearance after a brief interval of time.
Object permanence – Realization that objects continue to exist and can be retrieved even when not in view.
Psychological causality – Recognition that the actions of humans or other agents are influenced by intentions or other mental, emotional, or motivational factors.
Scripts – Organized memories for commonly experienced events.

Introduction

The major milestones or markers indicating various cognitive achievements in infants and young children during specific developmental ages (0–1 month, 1–6 months, 6–12 months, 12–18 months, 18–24 months, and 24–36 months of age) are identified and described. These milestones provide useful practical information about important intellectual changes and challenge researchers and theorists to explain the mechanisms underlying how cognitive structures and processes are acquired and develop.

Virtually everyone who studies children and their development would agree that there are momentous changes in attention and memory, planning, problem solving, language, reasoning, and a host of other intellectual domains over the first 3 years of life. Developmental psychologists have long been enamored with describing these changes. Even the efforts of some of the earliest observers, those who maintained a diary of their own children's developmental progress, typically focused on documenting when their children accomplished some task or demonstrated some level of competence. For example, Charles Darwin reported that his 5-month-old son already seemed to be making connections among events in his world; at that age he would become upset if not taken outdoors soon after being dressed in a hat and cloak. At 7 months of age this same child looked around to find his nurse upon hearing her name, and Darwin noted that one of his children readily imitated a variety of actions at 11½ months of age. Furthermore, at a little over 3 years of age one of Darwin's children recognized a picture of his grandfather and remembered a series of events that had taken place upon visiting him 6 months earlier. If psychologists are to understand the processes and mechanisms responsible for development in any domain, it is imperative that an accurate assessment of the child's progress in achieving various cognitive skills be obtained.

Milestones most frequently have been linked to the first appearances of various motor behaviors, for example, the ability to roll over from back to stomach, to sit upright without support, to crawl on all fours, or to walk without assistance. In a similar vein, the onset of various language skills such as babbling, first words, and the appearance of two-word utterances have been viewed as milestones. The idea of milestones applied to the emergence of cognitive skills has been less frequently voiced by developmental researchers, perhaps because behaviors that unambiguously signal a new-found cognitive skill often must be inferred from performance on tasks designed to measure such an accomplishment rather than being directly observed as they are exhibited in the child's day-to-day behaviors. As a consequence, the ingenuity and creativity of the researcher in devising procedures that assess a particular cognitive ability is often a major factor in determining when infants or very young children have reached a specific level of accomplishment.

Norms, measures of average times and their variability among children for achieving some aspect of development, are exceedingly useful for a number of reasons. Norms often serve a practical function. Knowing that an infant or young child is demonstrating satisfactory progress in a domain that typically undergoes change can signal whether biological or experiential factors are hindering, or perhaps promoting, some cognitive capacity. For example, several reflexes routinely displayed by the 1 month old are no longer exhibited by the healthy 6 month old. These changes are generally accounted for in terms of the maturation of various regions of the cortex; failures in this normal progression may be an indicator of brain damage. From a similar perspective, precocious intellectual advances may signal the benefits of certain kinds of experience for development.

Documenting the emergence of new cognitive abilities may also serve a theoretical function. A child who demonstrates the capacity to use symbols or representational insight, for example, awareness that a word, a picture, a map, or a model can stand for or serve in the place of a real object or event, reveals a new level of conceptual understanding that needs to be considered within any explanation of cognition and its development. For Piaget, the transition from being able to act upon objects and events in the world to using symbolic representations in place of those objects and events served as the key cognitive advance to distinguish two stages of intellectual competence differentiating the child older than 18–24 months of age from the infant or younger child. If researchers are to recognize theoretically important changes and fully understand the processes underlying some developmental capacity, they must begin by documenting when that capacity has emerged.

Keep in mind, however, that variability is an essential aspect of measuring the onset of intellectual markers in development. Although an age may be identified when children, on average, are capable of some ability, this average is based on information obtained from many different children. Any single child may be several weeks or months younger or older than another child before exhibiting some cognitive ability, yet fall well within the range of acceptable deviation from the so-called 'typical' child. Thus although we can describe milestones or, perhaps more appropriately, markers for intellectual development, when they are exhibited is probably better considered within a broader conceptualization regarding age than at time X or time Y.

Variability in displaying some capacity may even be found when observing the same infant. For example, variability can occur if a procedure is modified, that is, the task or situation used to assess some level of competence is changed. Thus in one context the infant may be said to have some cognitive skill but if evaluated with a different procedure, for example, when the processing load becomes too great, he or she may not appear to have the skill or to even have lost it. Nevertheless, this variability can be the impetus for further efforts to understand what processes and mechanisms are central to the emergence of cognitive markers.

Table 1 summarizes, within relatively broad age ranges, some of the major cognitive achievements demonstrated by infants and very young children who are described in additional detail here. Developmental researchers, however, are not always in agreement concerning the time these various capacities emerge. Nevertheless, these disagreements can have positive consequences in that they provide additional challenges for investigating and understanding the basic processes and structures that comprise cognition and its development in humans.

0–1 Month of Age

Before developmental psychologists began to study carefully their behaviors and had established procedures for asking questions that would shed light on their capacities, the general view was that infants were quite limited in terms of their cognitive skills. Research carried out, particularly beginning in the 1960s and continuing at a rapid pace yet today, has refuted this historical assumption and has revealed surprising competencies at far younger ages than ever anticipated. For example, even the newborn shows evidence of some cognitive skills.

Recognition Memory

Newborns have basic recognition memory capacities. When shown the same object over and over again, they will look at it for less and less time. They are displaying habituation, that is, a decline in intensity, frequency, or duration of a behavior. This decline is not due to fatigue or some other processing limitation since infants often display recovery of attention when a new stimulus is presented. Instead, newborns must be recognizing (remembering) that the repeatedly presented object is the same and that a new one is different. Recognition memory is even possible for events to which the infant was exposed prenatally. Newborns and very young babies respond differently to music that they have repeatedly heard while in the uterus compared to music that they have not heard before. In addition, they discriminate and prefer their mothers' voices over the voices of strangers. For example, a neonate is more likely to engage in sucking at a particular rate that results in the opportunity to hear the voice of his or her mother reading than sucking at another rate that has the consequence of hearing a stranger reading that same passage. Recognition memory for simple visual objects, their size, shape, and color, begins to be evident typically within the first month after birth.

Basic Learning Processes

Infants also show the capacity to learn shortly after birth. Within a matter of hours or days after delivery, newborns can modulate their rate or manner of sucking to more successfully ingest milk or to obtain some other reinforcer

Table 1 Summary of major markers in cognitive development from birth to 3 years of age

Age[a]	Cognitive capacity
0–1 Month	Demonstrates recognition memory for simple visual arrays for short durations
	Capable of being operantly conditioned using behavioral systems such as sucking and head turning
	Responsive to classical conditioning
1–6 Months	Able to recognize events experienced days and weeks earlier
	Possesses object identity, memory for the location and movement of a briefly occluded stimulus
	Displays some core physical knowledge of objects (e.g., solidity; need for support)
	Makes inferences about the continuity of an object when portions are occluded (object unity)
	Aware of numerosity (1–4 objects)
	Exhibits perceptual categorization (based on perceptual attributes)
6–12 Months	Shows consistent increases in the durability of short-term memory
	Demonstrates explicit recall memory for a sequence of actions over several weeks
	Searches for a hidden object (object permanence)
	Infers causality between physical objects (mechanical causality)
	Begins to understand goal-directed and intentional actions
	Shows planning and means–ends problem solving
	Operates with an egocentric frame of reference in terms of spatial tasks
	Comprehends the meaning of a few common words
	Demonstrates conceptual categorization (based on role, function, or meaning)
12–18 Months	Shows long-term recall involving a series of action over several months' duration
	Exhibits an awareness of intentionality and psychological causality
	Produces single word utterances that reflect overextensions, underextensions, or overlap with typical concepts
	Initiates pretense activity initially involving self, then includes another person or toy
	Differentiates pictures from objects
	Succeeds in solving simple analogical problems
18–24 Months	Provides first indications of strategic behavior to assist memory
	Acquires a concept of self
	Understands that the desires of others may differ from one's own
	Reaches goals through the appropriate selection of and use of tools
	Uses interesting objects (e.g., models) as representations for other objects
24–36 Months	Recalls conventional scripts for routinely experienced events
	Reorients pictures as well as objects to be upright
	Begins to use maps and models as symbols
	Able to employ arbitrary substitute objects in play and demonstrates simple kinds of sociodramatic play

[a]Infants and very young children often show individual differences in the ages at which they display the various developmental achievements summarized in this table.

such as visual or auditory stimulation. For example, as already indicated, they will quickly learn to suck at a faster or slower rate depending on whether it results in hearing the mother's voice rather than a stranger's voice. Very young infants also display the capacity to be classically conditioned. For example, they learn to turn their head toward the sound of a tone that has repeatedly signaled the availability of milk. Not surprisingly, 1- and 3-month-olds are likely to display such learning more consistently and in fewer numbers of conditioning trials than the newborn whose central nervous system is less fully mature.

1–6 Months of Age

Recognition Memory

Recognition memory for visual events experienced days and weeks earlier becomes evident beginning around 2–3 months of age. For example, if 3-month-olds are given the opportunity to make brightly colored elements of a mobile move and produce sound by kicking a leg to which a ribbon from the mobile has been attached, they learn to do so in a matter of minutes. When shown the mobile again 2–8 days later, but with the ribbon no longer attached to their leg, they display more active kicking than when the mobile is not present; they appear to remember that the kicking would make the mobile move. If presented the opportunity to learn the contingency between the mobile and their kicking on more than one day, retention of the relation is extended several more days. Perhaps not surprising is that memory for the specific elements of the mobile such as the particular shapes and colors of the items in it, tends to be lost fairly quickly over that time; any similar mobile, even with somewhat different elements, is sufficient to increase kicking rate. More surprising, however, is that surrounding aspects of the setting in which the learning has taken place such as the colors and patterning of the crib bumper are important cues to remembering; memory is less likely over short periods of time when these contextual features change. Even more remarkable is that a reminder of the mobile, such as showing infants its movement independent of their kicking activity many days after memory for the array has apparently been lost, encourages some infants as young as 2 months of age, and most infants at 3 months of age, to remember the kicking activity for nearly 1 month. Thus infants at a very early age display competence in performing behavioral responses that have had consequences on their environment over surprisingly long durations of time. Moreover, by 5 months of age, even after only briefly seeing a visual array, infants will recognize it as long as 2 weeks later.

Knowledge of Objects and Events

Infants around 3–4 months of age also begin to display knowledge of core principles of some of the physical characteristics of objects. One core principle is object identity. Object identity refers to the ability to remember and to anticipate an object's reappearance after being hidden for a brief period of time. Thus, a representation of at least some of its properties such as its location and direction of movement has been formed. As one illustration of this capacity, if shown an object passing behind an opaque barrier, babies attend to it more, as if surprised, if it reappears at some position other than the edge of the barrier where expected to re-emerge than if it reappears at the edge where it should re-emerge. As another illustration, an opaque barrier whose forward edge rotates upward in front of an object so as to hide it from view, but then continues to rotate as if the object is no longer behind the barrier to stop its continued motion, draws more attention from 4-month-olds than when the barrier stops its motion about the point where the hidden object normally would prevent its continued movement.

Infants this young may have some awareness of other properties of objects. For example, they attend longer, again as if somewhat surprised, when a solid object appears to pass through another solid object than when it does not. Moreover, they seem to understand that an object will fall if it is pushed past the edge of a supporting surface. Yet at 3 months of age, they accept any contact with the surface as sufficient to uphold the object; it is not typically until about 7 months of age that they seem to appreciate that a substantial proportion of the object needs to be supported by a surface to prevent it from falling. In addition, at about 2–3 months of age, infants infer that a rod whose two ends can be seen protruding from behind a barrier comprises a unified object, that is, a continuous rod rather than two separate segments. This knowledge of object unity becomes evident when the two visible ends show various kinds of coordinated movement; newborns do not make this inference and seem to interpret the end segments as two separate, unconnected objects even though there are coordinated movements between the visible ends.

Even 1-month-olds may have some capacity for representing numerosity. When repeatedly shown the same number of items in different arrays, say two, they show increased attention if three items are shown. However, the evidence infants process numerosity for between one and three items is especially compelling beginning around 5 months of age. At about this same time, infants may also have some basic understanding of addition and subtraction, again among small numbers of items. For example, if infants are shown one object before it is covered by a screen, then watch as a second is placed behind the screen, they respond differently when the screen is removed if they see only one object than if they see the expected two objects. Similarly, if they see two objects before they are covered by the screen and observe one being removed from behind that barrier, they look longer, when the screen is removed, if two objects come into view rather than only one perhaps an indication of being somewhat surprised by two still being there. This finding, however, has been difficult to replicate consistently; explanations for these behaviors based on perceptual processes rather than a conceptual understanding of arithmetic may provide an alternative, more parsimonious explanation for some of these results.

Perceptual Categorization

A major question that has prompted considerable research throughout infancy is how soon after birth babies conceptualize different objects as members of the same category. Considerable evidence supports the conclusion that infants by around 3 months of age recognize different exemplars of cats or dogs or horses as belonging together and some findings show that they process exemplars of broader classes such as mammals or birds or furniture as belonging together. But substantial disagreements continue over whether this recognition is driven by an understanding of conceptual representations or is better considered in terms of the similar perceptual attributes that category members may share such as specific features, that is, color, shape, movement, and so on. Infants as young as 3 months are able to notice the correlation among simple features of stimuli such as color and shape; thus perhaps from repeated experience with exemplars belonging to a category, infants this young are beginning to abstract commonalities or prototypic components that serve to promote a conceptual representation for that category. Not surprisingly, however, at this age these representations are likely to be implicit and developed without any conscious awareness on the part of infants.

6–12 Months of Age

Short-Term Memory

Short-term memory in infants after about 6 months of age is often assessed by a measure of its durability, that is, the length of delay the infant can withstand in order to successfully find a hidden object from among one of several different locations. Research generally reveals that infants of about 7 months of age can remember where an object was hidden for only a couple of seconds but that their short-term memory increases on the order of about 2 s per month over the next several months; thus by about 12 months of age they can tolerate delays of about 12 s. This ability may, of course, be affected by any number of methodological factors and the above estimates should be considered conservative since some studies report somewhat greater durability of memory in infants of this age.

Recall and Long-Term Explicit Memory

Some evidence exists that an implicit memory for a particular event experienced around 6 months of age may still be retained up to about 2 years later. But explicit memory, the conscious recall of information linked to the specific occurrence of an event, now becomes evident during the second 6 months of life. Explicit memories are typically measured by verbal recall in older children. However, infants under 18–24 months of age do not have the verbal abilities needed to report explicit memories. Thus imitation of actions performed on objects provides some of the best evidence for explicit memory in infants. For example, a sequence of three or four actions with a toy may be modeled for the child. If the infant imitates those actions in the same order as they were modeled, he or she is displaying a kind of recall very similar to that of an older child who remembers a short series of words verbally. In comparison to 6-month-olds who show little evidence of recall of such a sequence of actions, a substantial proportion of 9-month-olds reproduce the multistep actions with the toy even when tested up to 1 month later.

Object Permanence

Knowledge about the properties of objects shows further advances in children 6–12 months of age. Infants begin to display object permanence, or the realization that objects continue to exist and can be retrieved even when out of sight. For example, at about 8 months of age, infants actively implement searching for an attractive object that they have just been shown but which has then been hidden behind a cloth. For many developmental psychologists, this search behavior is theorized to signal the onset of a more sophisticated level of representation or a more active type of memory than that associated with object identity for which 3-month-olds demonstrate competence.

Object permanence undergoes a protracted developmental progression. Eight-month-olds may search for a toy that has been hidden under a single cloth. However, if they retrieve it from that location several times and it is then hidden under a second cloth, they are not likely to initiate a correct search for it, returning instead to the original location in which they had repeatedly found it during their previous efforts to retrieve the toy. This incorrect search, described as the 'A-not-B' error, usually is no longer made by infants as they approach 1 year of age and may be due to an increasing ability to inhibit an inappropriate response or the development of greater memory strength for the more recent event relative to repeated earlier events.

Causality

Philosophers have long speculated about when children begin to understand causality. An appreciation of physical causality or awareness that one object can influence another may occur as early as 6 months of age at least when simple launching events are observed. For example, infants may be repeatedly shown a moving object that makes contact with a second object which, in turn, moves as if in response to its contact with the first object. At some point the causal sequence is reversed; the second object moves to make contact with the first which then moves. Infants shown this display demonstrate a substantially greater increase in attention when this sequence is reversed compared to a reversal of a sequence where the first object is shown stopping short of making contact with the second before the second appears to move on its own. Infants appear to have recognized something unique about the relationship between the two objects in the first context, that is, when they make contact with each other, but not in the second where the movement takes place independent of direct contact. This understanding of causality, however, is quite fragile at 6 months of age. For example, when the objects are simple such as balls that strike one another the effect is found around 6–7 months of age, but behaviors suggesting an understanding of causality involving more complex, toy-like objects are not evident in infants until they are several months older. This delay presumably stems from the greater amount of information involved in processing the more complex stimuli which leaves fewer cognitive resources for imputing a causal relationship between them. By the end of the first year infants seem to understand additional aspects of causality, for example, a larger object striking a smaller one will normally have a greater impact than a smaller object striking a larger one.

Goal-Directed and Intentional Action

In addition to an early understanding of causality, infants around 6 months of age begin to infer that some actions, especially those associated with humans, are directed toward a goal. The basic procedure involves infants observing a person repeatedly reaching for and grasping one of two different objects. Each object appears in its same location on each trial so that the person is always reaching in the same direction. Once the attention of the infants to this repeated action declines to a predetermined level, a change is introduced. The location of the two objects is reversed and the person then either reaches to grasp the same object (now in a different location so that the path of reaching has changed) or reaches in the same direction as on preceding trials to grasp the object that had not been acted on before. Infants from 6 to 12 months of age show far greater recovery of attention when the direction of reach stays the same and a different object is grasped than when the direction of reach changes in order to grasp the same object. The novelty of reaching for and grasping a different goal object appears to attract far more attention than the perceptual change introduced by changing the direction of reaching. Moreover, this difference is more typically found when the actions are initiated by a human; infants are less likely to display the same kind of response when an inanimate claw or ambiguous agent is used in the sequence of events.

Evidence that infants at about 9 months of age have a somewhat more sophisticated understanding of goal-directed behavior comes from research in which a person attempts to hand small toys to the child. In some cases the initiator accidentally drops a toy before the baby can take it, but in other cases, he or she pulls the toy back out of reach as if belatedly deciding not to give it to the infant. Nine-month-olds seem more frustrated by the latter condition than the former, whereas 6-month-olds do not respond differently to these two events. These findings suggest that underlying the child's conceptualization of goal-directed behavior may be some early appreciation of intentionality in human agents. Other research provides further support for this view. For example, 12-month-olds who watch a sequence in which a larger ball rolls toward a barrier and then appears to 'jump' over the barrier to make contact with a second, smaller ball respond in a manner suggesting that the first ball's actions are intentional. Adults watching this scenario often describe it in terms of a 'mother' (the larger ball) intending to get to its 'baby' on the other side of the barrier. Infants seem surprised when the barrier is no longer present but the larger ball continues to jump gratuitously, that is, no longer has to perform this action as part of its 'intention' to reach the small ball.

Planning and Means–Ends Problem Solving

A major achievement associated with problem solving is the ability to plan for and initiate the sequence of steps that may be necessary to reach a goal. This capacity, often termed means–ends behavior, is first clearly displayed by infants between 8 and 12 months of age. Prior to this time infants who are shown an attractive toy placed out of reach, but on a cloth that is within reach, will typically initiate a 'direct action attack' toward the object, completely disregarding the possibility that the cloth could serve as a tool for obtaining the toy. These actions may include extending their reach and leaning as far forward toward the object as possible, perhaps even attempting to crawl on the table or hard surface supporting the cloth and the toy if that is an option. Should these behaviors fail to achieve the goal, infants may be left with one final recourse, entreating their caregivers to serve as instruments for obtaining their goal. However, around 8 months of age babies are far more likely to reach for and grab the edge of the cloth on which the toy has been placed and pull it (and the toy) toward themselves. By 12 months of age they can combine several means–ends steps that may be necessary to reach the goal. For example, if shown a toy on a cloth to which a string is attached, but the string cannot be reached because of a barrier, babies will first knock over the barrier, reach for the string, and use it to pull the cloth supporting the toy in order to retrieve it.

Egocentric Spatial Framework

The 6- to 12-month-old's understanding of space is often described as egocentric, that is, heavily weighted toward the use of their own body for determining the location of an object. For example, 9-month-olds will have little difficulty repeatedly finding an object hidden in a well located on either the left or right side of their body. But if the baby is then moved to the opposite side of the room, he or she will typically choose the well on the same side of the body, that is, the incorrect location, instead of updating spatial information based on his or her having been repositioned. Frame of reference for infants this age is heavily governed by the body.

Nevertheless, this limitation is not absolute; for example, if distinctive landmarks or features differentiate the two locations such as the color of the wells, infants this age may be able to override their egocentric orientation and correctly locate an object after being repositioned.

Meanings of Words

Word production typically will not begin until about the end of the first year. Nevertheless, understanding the meaning of commonly spoken words that the infant hears is probably well underway by this time. For example, by about 6 months of age infants will look in the direction of their mother or father when they hear 'mommy' or 'daddy', respectively, but not to an unfamiliar woman or man. Similar responses to objects for which infants have repeatedly heard the name before become evident by about 9 months of age and they are able to respond to simple requests spoken by another person. Thus word comprehension is possible well before word production.

Conceptual Categorization

Whereas debate continues with respect to whether children younger than 6 months of age have concepts or are able to classify different members of a category together on the basis of more than their perceptual similarity, there is consensus that categorization clearly has become meaning-based or conceptual by 12 months of age. Infants now apply actions that they have seen someone perform on one member of a category, such as pretending to feed a toy dog, to other toy animals but not to vehicles or exemplars of other categories. Since infants may not yet be producing verbal utterances by this time, these early concepts are likely image-based. Nevertheless, even though the members of different categories may share considerable overlap in their perceptual features, the behavior of infants of this age provides considerable ammunition for concluding that inferences are being made on the basis of the similarity in role or function of objects identified as belonging together. These early concepts may also be relatively global, for example, at the superordinate level such as mammals, vehicles, furniture, and food or even at higher levels such as animate objects and artifacts as well as at more basic levels such as dogs, cats, chairs, and tables.

12–18 Months of Age

Advances in Long-Term Recall

Noteworthy during the first half of the second year of life is the increase in recall memory over longer and longer periods of time. For example, at 16 months of age, most infants are not only capable of reproducing an ordered sequence of three or four actions on objects when shown the objects 1 month later, but even when tested 3 and 6 months later. If the sequence is seen at 20 months of age, infants recall them as much as 12 months later.

Intentionality (Human Agency)

Although infants very likely begin to understand some aspects of goal-directed behavior and intentionality in others before they reach a year of age, this knowledge shows further development during the first half of their second year. Before 1 year of age infants will often use another person's gaze to redirect their own looking. However, now they begin to appreciate that looking at an object has a goal-directed quality on the part of that other person. Using procedures similar to those designed to explore their understanding of goal-directed reaching at 6–12 months of age, 1-year-olds respond more when another person looks at a different object located in the same place as the object at which he or she had been gazing than when the individual redirects his or her attention to the original object now repositioned in a different location. The same can be said for pointing which may be understood as an intentional behavior even before 1 year of age. Moreover, the emergence of and understanding of the message being communicated by pointing is correlated with the child's initiating his or her own pointing to direct the attention of another.

These findings do not necessarily mean that children this age have a complete understanding of intentions in others, for example, that some mental state is motivating the other person's behavior. However, these and other accomplishments do suggest that among the toolbox of cognitive resources becoming available at this time is an appreciation of psychological causality. For example, in one study 14-month-olds observed adults performing a simple activity. However, the demonstrations were accompanied either by a verbal comment that suggested that the activity was completed as intended ('There!') or that the outcome was accidental ('Whoops!'). The children were more likely to imitate the activity when the adult's comment suggested it was intentional. Moreover, 18-month-olds are as likely to complete a simple activity that they see an adult complete successfully as one that they see the adult attempting to complete, but not being successful at; they seem to have recognized the intention of the adult even though they did not observe the goal being achieved since, if just given the materials on their own, infants this age generally did not produce these activities. Nor are they as likely to imitate these activities when mechanical devices are shown performing them. Inferring the intentions, goals, and plans of a human agent seems essential to infants imitating these activities and this understanding may provide an important stepping stone for the very young child in eventually learning to regulate their social interactions based on the mental states of others.

Word Production

Few milestones in development are met more enthusiastically by parents than the production of their children's first words. Such utterances typically emerge toward the end of the first year of development and generally increase to about 50 different words by about 18 months of age. Although the production of words is an interesting behavioral milestone in itself, realizing that an arbitrary symbol such as a word can represent an object or event reflects a major advance in cognitive development. The beginnings of comprehension of the meanings of some words very likely came about sometime between 6 and 12 months of age; now that understanding extends to infants' production of their own words.

Not surprisingly, the meanings for early words may not quite match up with typical adult meanings for those words. Children at this age and for several more years may overextend the meaning of their initial words, that is, apply them to far more referents than normally acceptable. For example, the word 'ball' may initially be used to label an orange, the moon, or any other round object. They may also underextend their meaning, that is, provide the label to far fewer referents than normally considered appropriate by adults standards. For example, they may apply the word 'dog' to only those that walk through their yard and not to those seen riding in a car. Perhaps even more frequently, they may both overextend a word to some inappropriate referents yet at the same time underextend them by failing to include some typical referents of the concept. One culprit underlying these kinds of errors may be an overemphasis on the similarity in perceptual features of categorically different referents (when overextension occurs) or insufficient similarity in perceptual features (in the case of underextension). Errors based on similarity (or lack of similarity) of functional characteristics may occur as well. Finally, most of the earliest words that are acquired refer to things (i.e., are nouns) rather than actions (i.e., verbs) or other parts of speech.

Pretense

In addition to the use of words to represent some object, other clear signs that children are beginning to understand that one thing can represent another is evident in the onset of pretend behavior. The earliest appearance of this activity varies widely from one child to another, but many children display simple forms of pretending soon after 1 year of age, for example, simulating drinking from an empty toy cup. At this age, children are unlikely to have any appreciation that pretense involves a mental activity; moreover, the pretense behavior often appears as an extension of well-learned sensorimotor behaviors applied to similar, thus not completely arbitrary objects. As they near 18 months of age, toddler's make-believe activity often begins to include a cohort, another person or toy such as a favored doll, who becomes the recipient of feeding or combing or comforting activities that children, at a younger age, only might have applied to themselves.

Pictorial Competence

Infants less than 1 year of age attempt to treat pictures of objects somewhat the same way as the objects themselves. They may rub the picture and make finger and hand motions as if attempting to grasp the depicted object and as if confused about the differences between the physical properties of two-dimensional and three-dimensional stimuli. These responses diminish with development so that by 18 months, infants are displaying them very infrequently. In response to pictures, infants are now much more likely to apply labels or verbal expressions. In addition, a label learned for a pictured object can be readily generalized to its three-dimensional referent. Two-dimensional sequences of actions such as those presented via television are imitated and remembered just as when real people serve as models indicating that information can be gained from two-dimensional stimuli as well as three-dimensional stimuli.

Analogical Problem Solving

Analogical problem solving refers to the ability to extend some principle for solving a problem to another problem which, at least in terms of its specific features, seems very different. For the most part, even adults are not always very good at analogical problem solving, but the beginnings of this ability can be observed during the first half of the second year. As already indicated, infants around 12 months of age will knock over a barrier to reach a string attached to a cloth on which an attractive toy has been placed, pulling the string and attached cloth toward themselves to reach the toy. But even those who do not spontaneously demonstrate this problem-solving skill will often perform it if it is modeled for them by a parent. Moreover, once they have demonstrated competence on one task of this type, they are able to transfer it to others that require the same solution even though barrier, string, cloth, and desired goal are quite different from the one on which they first learned this solution principle; they seem to understand that the problems are analogous to one another. However, children under 1 year of age are less successful in demonstrating transfer and only do so if there are substantial perceptual similarities among the elements of the various problems.

18–24 Months of Age

Strategic Memory

The development of various strategies for assisting memory accounts for much of the improvement in recall throughout later childhood; nevertheless, the earliest implementation of one rudimentary strategy can be seen beginning around 18 months of age. At this time, if shown an object hidden at a particular spatial location but not allowed to search for it immediately, toddlers begin to point to or look toward that location on occasion as if to reconfirm that the object is still there even though they are engaged in other activities during the delay. In contrast, if the object is clearly visible during the delay, they initiate such actions far less frequently. Although children this age are unlikely to be consciously aware of its benefits to memory, such behavior is a primitive manifestation of far more sophisticated mnemonic strategies children acquire as they become older.

Self-Recognition

Evidence from several different types of observations converge in suggesting that by 18 months of age toddlers form a concept of themselves as individuals different from other individuals. The household mirror has become a valuable tool for demonstrating the earliest evidence of this accomplishment. For example, if a spot of rouge is surreptitiously placed on the nose or forehead of children, toddlers between 15 and 18 months of age are much more likely to touch or rub the spot on their own body whereas younger infants touch or rub the spot on the image they see in the mirror. Even children who have no experience with mirrors typically display such self-recognition activity before they reach 24 months of age. In addition, by 2 years of age, children respond differently, smiling and verbalizing about themselves, when they see their own photograph as opposed to the photograph depicting another child of a similar age. Common, too, at this time, is the onset of personal pronouns such as 'I' or 'me' when talking about themselves.

Desire in Others

As already indicated, infants recognize some aspects of intentionality in the behavior of others well before 18 months of age. However, toward the end of their second year, they start to display a greater appreciation for psychological factors that underlie the actions and goals initiating behaviors. By the age of 2 years, toddlers realize that they themselves have desires or emotional states and that the desires or emotional states of others may not match their own. If given a choice between a preferred or a nonpreferred food, children are highly likely to choose the preferred. However, if informed by the facial or verbal expressions of another person that this individual would rather have the nonpreferred food, children will offer that alternative to him or her. Although at this age toddlers are unlikely to understand that others have mental representations of desires, the realization that the actions of others are governed by motivations that do not always correspond to their own serves as an important step to acquiring a fuller understanding of the psychological states of others.

Tool Use

Children's tool use becomes far more sophisticated at this time. For example, if shown how a tool such as a rake can be used or alternatively, if given a hint to use it to retrieve a toy that is too far away to reach, toddlers now readily generalize such information to other problems by choosing a tool that is rigid, long enough, and contains a feature permitting the toy to be pulled toward themselves from among the various alternatives.

24–36 Months of Age

Scripts as Organizational Underpinnings for Autobiographical Memory

Beginning around 30 months of age; undoubtedly facilitated by their burgeoning verbal abilities, children begin to recount events that have been commonly experienced such as eating out at a restaurant or getting ready for bed. These scripts, or organized descriptions for commonly experienced events, usually lack specific details but highlight the key, routine components often involved in recurring activities and appear to serve as the basis for much of autobiographical memory. Children this young do not normally recall specific events that have occurred to them, that is, they still show infantile amnesia or the inability to remember the details of any particular experiences, but they nevertheless have clearly begun to organize their retention of general information around sequential, context-specific routines.

Advances in Pictorial Competence

Although children recognize that pictures of objects are different from the three-dimensional objects they represent, they continue to have limited appreciation of the spatial orientation governing how to view pictures. If shown a picture book, it typically matters little to them if a parent is holding the book upside down nor do they show preferences for pictures of objects that are upright vs. upside-down; in contrast, clear preferences for uprightness are displayed for real objects. However, by 30 months of age, even pictures are perceived as having an appropriate orientation.

Models as Symbols

Although infants, perhaps even before the end of their first year, seem to understand symbols, for example, that a word can be used to represent some external referent, the range of symbols that can serve this representational capacity expands between 24 and 36 months of age. Objects that are meaningful and interesting in themselves now can serve as representations. Consider pieces of furniture in a room in a dollhouse. For young children these items are usually items interesting in and of themselves, for example, things to play with. However, the furniture and room can also serve as a representation of a normal, life-size room. Thus, if told that a toy is located behind a piece of furniture in the dollhouse, and that a similar toy is located behind the equivalent piece of furniture in the regular room, we would have little difficulty finding it in the regular room. However, it is not until children are typically nearly 36 months of age, that they are successful on such a task. They appear to lack the capacity to form two different representations for the dollhouse, one as an interesting array in and of itself and one as a symbol for the regular room. Not surprisingly, when using photographs depicting the dollhouse furniture to indicate the location of the toy, children at 30 months of age are already successful presumably because the primary function of pictures is to serve as a representation of something else.

Pretense and Sociodramatic Play

Pretend activities now become substantially more complex. For example, beginning around 2 years of age arbitrary objects (e.g., a block or a stick) can be incorporated into make-believe play; toddlers are not limited to using somewhat realistic representations of objects as part of their play adventures. In addition, an agent such as a doll may become actively engaged in participating in a pretend routine; it takes on a separate role in the play activity, for example, it is used to feed itself or another doll. Finally, by about 30 months of age, these advances contribute to the onset of modest forms of sociodramatic play where the child begins to coordinate roles among themselves and others (parents, siblings, dolls) in their imaginary world, a skill that becomes far more sophisticated and frequently displayed as children move into the preschool years.

Challenges and Opportunities

As these examples illustrate, memory, understanding of the physical and social world, conceptual development, representational abilities, and planning and problem solving undergo tremendous changes in infants and young children during their first 3 years. Identifying and determining when these new cognitive accomplishments first emerge has been one outcome of the enormous efforts of many developmental researchers engaged in ingenious and creative approaches enticing infants and very young children to provide answers about what they know and understand. The description of these milestones and indicators of early cognitive development remains incomplete. In the years to come newly discovered methods for gaining insights into the major achievements occurring in infancy and early childhood will undoubtedly provide a more accurate, more complete, and more informative picture of when and under what circumstances various markers of intellectual development are exhibited. These advances are likely to provide further distinctions and refinements to complete the many gaps that remain unfilled concerning this topic.

In contrast to other areas such as physical and language development where milestones in development are often of interest, the research on cognition has provided little information concerning the range and variation among children with respect to when various intellectual accomplishments are achieved. Developmental psychologists have, for the most part, carried out their research on samples of European or American children growing up in middle- or higher-income families. Within these populations, little attention has been given to what proportion of children display various cognitive abilities weeks, or even months, earlier or later than the 'average' child. In other words, we know little about how much variability exists from one child to another in displaying various cognitive accomplishments. This information is important since it can inform us about whether caregiving practices or factors associated with cultural, socioeconomic, or other family variables have an influence on the development of these capacities.

In closing this discussion of milestones pertaining to cognitive development one further idea needs to be emphasized. Such descriptions should not be the endpoint but rather the beginning of our explorations into cognitive development. Describing when infants and young children accomplish various cognitive skills tells us very little about how these structures and processes came about or the practical implications and theoretical importance of their acquisition. In fact, many other articles included in other sections of this encyclopedia address these kinds of issues and should be considered an important additional step to understanding the remarkable changes in cognition that take place during infancy and early childhood.

See also: Bayley Scales of Infant Development; Brain Development; Categorization Skills and Concepts; Cognitive Development; Cognitive Developmental Theories; Developmental Disabilities: Cognitive; Mathematical Reasoning; Memory; Object Concept; Piaget's Cognitive-Developmental Theory; Reasoning in Early Development; Self Knowledge; Theory of Mind.

Suggested Readings

Bauer PJ, Burch MM, and Kleinknecht EE (2002) Developments in early recall memory: Normative trends and individual differences. *Advances in Child Development and Behavior* 30: 103–152.

Cohen LB and Cashon CH (2006) Infant Cognition. In: Damon W, Lerner RM, Kuhn D, and Siegler R (eds.) *Handbook of Child Psychology: Vol. II. Cognition, Perception and Language,* 6th edn., pp. 214–251. Hoboken, NJ: Wiley.

Flavell JH, Miller PH, and Miller SA (2002) *Cognitive Development,* 4th edn. Upper Saddle River, NJ: Prentice-Hall.

Pelphry KA and Reznick JS (2003) Working memory in infancy. *Advances in Child Development and Behavior* 31: 173–227.

Siegler RS and Alibali MW (2005) *Children's Thinking,* 4th edn. Upper Saddle River, NJ: Prentice-Hall.

Troseth GL, Pierroutsakos SL, and DeLoache JS (2004) From the innocent to the intelligent eye: The early development of pictorial competence. *Advances in Child Development and Behavior* 32: 1–35.

Woodward AL (2005) The infant origins of intentional understanding. *Advances in Child Development and Behavior* 33: 229–262.

Neonativism

A Needham and K Libertus, Duke University, Durham, NC, USA

© 2008 Elsevier Inc. All rights reserved.

Glossary

Canalization – Extent to which the development of a process is constrained by environmental factors. Highly canalized processes do not have a wide range of phenotypes available to them, whereas less highly canalized processes do.

Contrastive evidence – A type of evidence that comes from observing the outcomes of events in which a physical principle is in operation and when it is not (e.g., when an object receives adequate support it remains stable in space and when it receives inadequate support it falls down). Comparison of these two events within a physical principle may be essential for coming to understand the physical principle.

Core knowledge – Knowledge that is fundamental to reasoning about objects, events, and people. Many theorists consider this knowledge to be innate.

Experience-dependent – Term to describe a process that may or may not develop (or may develop in very different ways), depending upon the environmental input.

Experience-expectant – Term to describe a process that depends upon a certain kind of environmental input at a certain time in development in order for it to develop appropriately.

Interactionism – A range of approaches to explaining origins that all involve some amount of influence of factors intrinsic to a process and those extrinsic to it.

Introduction

Adult humans have remarkably complex cognitive skills. We can write novels in which we create whole worlds quite different from our own; we do the science to build rockets that take people into space, and have made discoveries that help us cure diseases that used to kill people. In recent years, we have also started to understand the basis of our cognitive skills, our brain, in more detail. For example, we have discovered areas in the brain that are specialized for particular functions. We believe there is a language area (or areas – one for production and another for comprehension); we believe there is a face area; we believe there is an area that processes biological motion. Furthermore, we can also predict about where each of these areas is likely to be in any individual. Our brain may be one of the most complex structures on our planet and we are just beginning to understand how it is organized and how it functions. Indeed, it is still far from clear whether the organization of our brain that research has uncovered was destined to be this way because of factors that were established millions of years ago or whether it reflects the product of an active process that is shaped by the consistency in the environment in which it develops.

These and related questions are discussed within the context of the nature/nurture 'debate', which has probably garnered more attention and anger than any other question in developmental and cognitive science. Because of the unique opportunity to produce evidence that directly addresses the importance of nature and nurture, research on infants has provided a high-profile battleground for addressing these influences on knowledge. However, this opportunity comes with some challenges. Research with infants is notoriously difficult, as there are relatively few responses they can give. Typically, indirect measures are taken and interpretation is required to make conclusions of theoretical interest. Further, negative findings could always be interpreted in light of competence/performance differences – perhaps a suitably sensitive measure has not yet been found to tap into this underlying competence.

Some investigators remain enmeshed in the nature–nurture arguments while others have rejected these traditional views and have put forth the strong claim that this dichotomy is false because there is no way to separate these factors, even conceptually, and therefore no way to somehow estimate the effects of one in the absence of the other. An illustration of this view comes from Susan Oyama, who argues, "Since the genome represents only a part of the entire developmental ensemble, it cannot by itself contain or cause the form that results. But then, neither can its surroundings.". It is striking that, after so many years of study there remains such a multiplicity of views on this topic. It is a testament to the strength of the metaphors contained in the nature–nurture tug-of-war that so little agreement has been achieved and it shows the continued need for precise and clear definitions of what is meant by terms like innateness, nativism, and environment. As Oyama's quote demonstrates, many philosophers and researchers find that any conceptualization that partitions the developing system along the lines of internal/external, biological/environmental is inherently flawed, because the components of the developing organism have a recursive quality in which characteristics of the organism (typically thought of as nature) serve as environmental influences for subsequent developmental change. At different scales or levels of analysis, environment can be conceptualized very differently, and it is always possible to continue asking how earlier and earlier forms of the ability or organism came into being and whether that process could have been influenced by factors extrinsic to that particular developmental change. In sum, it is impossible to overestimate the complexity of development.

Explaining the Origins of Behavior and Knowledge

How can we think of these different influences on the body, on behavior, and on cognition? Specifically, when we think of the origins of our many skills, what kinds of explanations do we give and what kind of explanations are we willing to accept? In this essay, we first consider the historical foundations of nativism and then move on to the current issues influencing researchers' thinking about these basic notions.

A History of the Notion of Nativism

Where does our knowledge come from and how are we able to learn so many complex skills throughout our lifetime? The questions about the origins of knowledge and human behavior are maybe as old as the human species itself and whole branches of science and philosophy are still investigating this issue. Especially in philosophy, the epistemological question about where knowledge comes from and how it is acquired has a long-standing tradition. Two basic forms of knowledge can be distinguished: *a priori*, knowledge that is independent of experience, and *a posteriori*, knowledge that is derived from experience (empirical knowledge). Early philosophers used these terms to distinguish between knowledge that is acquired through experience and knowledge that is derived from basic principles that were assumed to be predefined (axioms).

Ancient times

The notion of *a priori* knowledge can be traced back to Socrates in Plato's dialog Meno (380 BC). In the course of this dialog Socrates proposes that it is not necessary for us to acquire new knowledge, instead we already have all knowledge and just need a reminder. To support this claim, Socrates demonstrates how a boy can produce a geometrical theorem even though this boy has never been taught geometry before. According to this line of reasoning, all knowledge is *a priori*. Along the same lines, the philosophical notion of rationalism argues that all knowledge can be, in principle, derived from some basic principles and deduction alone. Assuming that these basic principles are in place (are axioms in the system) then no experience is required to obtain new conclusions. Similarly, the question about the origins of human behavior can be seen from this perspective. Are our behaviors and traits predetermined *a priori* or are they acquired *a posteriori*? Or in more modern terms: is our behavior defined by aspects of our biology (nature) or does our environment (nurture) define how we will behave?

An early account of the influence of nature on human behavior can be found from Hippocrates and thinkers of his time (around 400 BC). They suggested that four fluids (humors) can be found within the body and that the mixture of these fluids determines the personality of a person – essentially arguing that behavior is driven by intrinsic factors or nature. The two classic notions about knowledge (Socrates) and behavior (Hippocrates) described above can be subsumed under the heading of nativism. Both accounts share one important aspect: something is considered to be given, something in our body – nowadays preferably in the brain – is innately predisposed for a certain task.

Influences of early modern philosophers

These ancient versions of the nativist idea often referred to a divine source of the innate knowledge or behavior. This notion remained popular in the seventeenth century. The famous philosopher Rene Descartes (1596–1650) assumed the existence of a benevolent god that has created our bodies in a way that allows us to extract truthful information from our surroundings. Moreover, Descartes made a strong distinction between our mind and our body (Cartesian Dualism) that holds that our mind is different from our physical body. For Descartes our mind was nonphysical substance and its main function is thought (res cognitans). With respect to the mind, Descartes also expressed a strong nativist argument in that he claimed that some of the most basic truths (truths of reason) are innate, that there is a basis of innate knowledge in the human mind upon which all further knowledge can build. This idea stands in strong opposition to notions from empiricists.

Most famously, the British empiricist John Locke (1632–1704) described the human mind as a 'tabula rasa', a blank slate, at the onset and all knowledge is build onto this void. One of the ancient forefathers of this position is Aristotle who first introduced the empiricist principle that all knowledge about the real world is based on experience through the senses. Following Aristotle, the Stoics (around 300 BC) were the first to formulate the idea of the human mind as a clean slate but at the same time also maintained the notion that some universals are innately present in the mind of all humans. Later, Jean-Jacues Rousseau (1712–78) formulated a similar notion when he proposed that humans have an innate tendency to be good but that external experiences influenced this innate tendency and could eventually override it. These early accounts of a combination of empiricist and nativist ideas expressa general dissatisfaction with the idea of an *a priori* foundation of the human mind that derives from an unknown (probably divine) source but at the same time acknowledges the need to assume a foundation for our mind to grow on (even if our mind is a blank slate, there is still the slate that is innate).

Innate modules

In the early nineteenth century Franz Josef Gall (1758–1828) presented a new idea concerning the organization of the mind. His theory became known as 'phrenology' and is concerned with the localization of mental functions in the brain. Gall believed that the shape of the skull, the bumps on our head, reflects how pronounced certain character traits of cognitive abilities are in an individual. The theory of phrenology stated that the brain is the seat of our mind and that its size and shape directly reflects individuals' traits and personalities. More important, different cognitive functions or traits were believed to be localized in particular areas of the brain. Thus, the mind was seen as a modular system with specialized areas that subserve a specific trait. This idea provides arguments for a nativist position in that it suggests that the global organization of the mind into functional compartments is predefined by nature.

The idea of modules continues into the twenty-first century, as researchers have identified, in a surprisingly close parallel to Gall's general idea, specific areas of the brain (of course not apparent on the skull!) that are responsible for conducting different cognitive functions. For example, Jerry Fodor, in his well-known nativist treatise *Modularity of Mind*, proposes that functions like language and perception are accomplished via specialized processes or modules in the brain. These modules have specific characteristics, including that they conduct their computations very quickly and their processes are informationally encapsulated – in other words, we are not aware of the processes by which we perceive various components of the visual world, and these processes are typically not influenced by other knowledge we may have about the stimuli. Although it is of course possible that these areas of the brain are trained up through development to provide this automatic and quick processing, Fodor and others who share his perspective believe that these modules do not need training of any sort. Rather, these functional modules are in place prior to any relevant experience.

Advances in science eventually lead to the discovery of the genome and its role in heritability. Gregor Mendel (1822–84) first proposed the existence of genes and studied their role in inheriting traits from parents to offspring. The existence and idea of genes provided a new basis for nativist arguments by filling in the place that had been occupied by divine intervention before. Basic innate notions and predispositions of the mind could now be explained in terms of the 'blueprint' found in the genome. One of the first scientists to explore the role of genes with respect to human behavior was Sir Francis Galton (1822–1911). One of the goals of Galton's research was to identify the influences of environmental factors and hereditary factors on human development and to what extent one could act on the other. Galton was also the first to use the terms nature and nurture to distinguish between the genetic endowment and our experiences. However, Galton did not provide an answer to the question of whether nature or nurture defines human behavior. However, his research and his techniques foreshadowed future research that has been essential in the nature–nurture debate. In particular, Galton was one of the first scientists to methodically study twins in order to estimate the different contributions of shared genes or a shared environment. In his view, the evidence favored the influence of nature, the hereditary factors.

Behaviorism and nativism

Following the dawn of the twentieth century the psychologist John B. Watson (1878–1958) started the psychological movement of behaviorism. This train of thought would become most dominant in American psychology for the first half of the twentieth century. Most behaviorists favored the nurture side in the debate about nature and nurture. For example, Watson himself made a strong claim about the influence the environment can have on an organism:

> Give me a dozen healthy infants, well-formed, and my own specified world to bring them up in and I'll guarantee to take any one at random and train him to become any

type of specialist I might select – doctor, lawyer, artist, merchant-chief and, yes, even beggar-man and thief, regardless of his talents, penchants, tendencies, abilities, vocations, and race of his ancestors. I am going beyond my facts and I admit it, but so have the advocates of the contrary and they have been doing it for many thousands of years.
John B. Watson (1924, p. 82)

The learning mechanisms uncovered by behaviorism like classical or operant conditioning seemed to provide enough basis for nurture to fundamentally influence the behavior of an animal. However, another psychological movement around the same time, psychodynamics, provided a more balanced view where nature and nurture influenced each other. Carl Jung (1875–1961), for example, introduced the notion of innate archetypes that influence the personality of a person. In contrast, to uncover the reasons for a certain behavior, behaviorists claimed that an analysis of the current environment and the history of the environment and the animals' behavior are sufficient. According this view there was no or only little need for innate capabilities. However, exactly this point led to a now famous discussion about the mechanisms of language acquisition in Noam Chomsky's response to the book *Verbal Behavior* by Burrhus F. Skinner (1904–90). Chomsky challenged the behaviorist view and instead, with respect to language acquisition in particular, proposed the existence of linguistic universals that all languages have in common and therefore seem to be part of a universal grammar. Chomsky argued that a small set of rules is built into the human brain and that these rules help us to acquire a language – even in the presence of impoverished or incorrect models from which we learn. This form of nativism, for the first time, is highly specific about what is innate and why this innate knowledge is crucial for normal development and stands in contrast to classical nativism. This view suggests that children are biologically prepared for a certain task – like language acquisition – by their genes or the structure of their mind.

Constructivism

A different approach that provided the theoretical grounding for the systematic study of cognitive development was put forward by Jean Piaget (1896–1980). According to his theory, children construct their own cognitive structures over protracted periods of time interacting with objects (his theory is referred to as a constructivist theory). Piaget believed that a steady state or equilibrium of cognitive activity was present early in life and maintained throughout development via the processes of assimilation and accommodation. What the child experiences is compared with the existing knowledge structures, and is either consistent or inconsistent with these structures. If too much inconsistent evidence is collected, a disequilibrium results and the cognitive structures are reorganized through a process of accommodation. These processes of assimilation and accommodation lead to a progression to each successive developmental stage.

One critical component of Piaget's theory is that representational abilities were relatively late to develop. Indeed, he believed that infants must first construct the world of real, three-dimensional objects (through their actions upon these objects) and only then could begin the process of re-creating these objects in representational form in the mind. From this perspective, it was not until approximately 2 years of age that children could form 'true' representations of objects. Thus, infants lived in a very different world from adults – a world in which objects (and presumably people) were totally unpredictable. These strong claims, apparently supported by his observations, at first did not encourage researchers to study the abilities of infants. However, over the years researchers have developed new and more sensitive methods to study infants and made some critical discoveries that provided new arguments for a new nativist position.

A new form of nativism

Gaining arguments from novel and carefully designed studies, a new form of nativism emerged. For this new form of nativism, the study of child development is of critical importance. Piaget was the first to create a comprehensive theory of cognitive development on the basis of his rich and detailed set of observations about children's abilities and behaviors at several ages. His theory included several different stages of development that were defined by the abilities of the child. In addition to being valuable for these reasons, Piaget's theory served as a framework against which new ideas were proposed. One way to test Piaget's theory is by asking if it is possible to see evidence for the presence of an ability earlier then predicted by Piaget. For example, a theoretical perspective called the competent infant or rational infant approach grew up in strong opposition to Piaget's theory. According to this approach, infants were substantially more sophisticated than Piaget gave them credit for. Presumably, if sensitive enough tests were devised, one could discover newborn competences abounding in every cognitive domain, making development a bit of a pointless process to study. However, the data that are now available from studies of early infant abilities are not consistent with this perspective. There are many changes that happen with development, and one might argue that it is these changes that are important to characterize and understand. The competent infant movement did have a lasting impact on the field, though, in the form of questioning some of the basic tenets of Piaget's theory that applied to infants' cognitive development.

Arguing with more subtlety and precision, researchers such as Renée Baillargeon and Elizabeth Spelke argued that success in Piaget's tasks required more than just conceptual competence – motoric competence and planning were also required. To be judged as having a representation of the existence of a hidden object, infants had to reach for and uncover a hidden object. This requires considerable skill in planning, problem solving, and motor control. Even though infants' goal is likely to play with the toy, they cannot fulfill that goal directly, they must first grasp the toy's cover and remove it. So, clearly infants could have the competence – a representation of that hidden toy – without being able to reveal this in their performance.

Piaget's high threshold for granting children cognitive skills coupled with a new interest in the subcomponents of the skills required to succeed in his tasks led researchers to investigate these subcomponents. Visual measures were used that did not require infants to plan an overt 'this is my answer' solution to the tasks. These visual tasks were hypothesized to be less demanding of infants' cognitive resources than Piaget's manual tasks were. These new tasks were built upon basic patterns of infant looking behavior, such as that they tend to look longer at novel or unexpected events than at familiar or expected ones. Thus, two events could be created that were superficially very similar but that differed in a component critical for the principle being tested.

For instance, two events could proceed in a nearly identical fashion, but one would contain a violation of object permanence and the other one would not. This procedure was used in one study where infants were shown a car that rolled down a ramp, traveled behind a screen and across the apparatus floor. Prior to seeing this event, infants had been shown what was behind the screen. All infants saw a toy behind the screen but for half of the infants the toy was positioned on top of the ramp, while for the other half it was placed behind or in front of the ramp. The rationale of the researchers was that if infants represented the existence of the toy on the track, they should look reliably longer when the toy was blocking the tracks and the car seems to pass through the space occupied by the toy, emerging unscathed from the far end of the screen. The results supported this conclusion with infants as young as 4.5-month-old of age.

These results and many others like them called into question Piaget's explanation of cognitive development in at least two ways. First, the timetable Piaget sketched out for the ages at which different cognitive structures develop was inconsistent with these new findings. Infants showed more and earlier understanding about the physical world than Piaget's theory predicted. Perhaps more importantly, the mechanism by which Piaget thought infants acquired these knowledge structures – self-produced actions on objects – was not fully functional at the point in development that these competences were discovered. Both of these factors, especially the second one, were problems for Piaget's theory and called for new theories and explanations.

These new approaches that attempted to more accurately understand infant behavior and development, often in contrast to Piaget's perspective, are referred to as neonativism. However, instead of postulating completely preformed innate abilities, here the focus is often on constraints on learning. These constraints are not learned themselves. Thus, there is a nativist component to these approaches, but in most cases, the emphasis is on how learning takes place and how abilities change over development. This could be at least in part because we do not yet have a good way to characterize or talk about unlearned components of behavior or skill.

The early abilities revealed by these measures that do not require overt behavior on the part of infants are sometimes referred to as core knowledge and are thought to provide the basis for future learning. According to many core knowledge theorists, these core knowledge systems are thought to have developed through the evolution of our species and to be independent of input from the environment. Research with young infants has shown that infants have a concept of object permanence and a rudimentary understanding of number and numerical transformations. These findings and the interpretations offered for them have stirred a heated debate about infants' early cognitive abilities and the origins of these abilities. Specifically, there are some researchers who consider it likely that learning mechanisms that support rapid learning on the basis of relatively few observations are not learned but that content about objects, people, or language is learned. However, more extreme nativist perspectives hold that actual cognitive content is part of the innate endowment, built into the organism through evolution. This debate on the origins of cognitive skills continues to be one of the most discussed topics in developmental psychology.

What is Nativism?

Nativism assumes that some abilities or skills are 'innate'. Therefore, the first and most important point we need to consider when discussing nativism is the precise definition of 'innateness'. What do we mean when we use the word 'innate'? Researchers typically mean that a given structure, behavior, or ability cannot be learned or does not need to be learned and is not dependent upon exposure to environmental stimuli. On the one hand, that a behavior or ability is innate can be seen as a specific expectation already present in the animal's mind the first time he or she encounters a situation in the world. In such a case, the knowledge of the animal was truly independent of prior experience. On the other hand, it can also mean that a specialized learning mechanism or constraint is innate to the cognitive structure of the animal. In this case, experience is necessary for the ability to be learned or expressed but at the same time an innate mechanism is necessary to derive this ability from the experience. The former view represents a strong form of nativism that claims that actual substantive knowledge is innate. The latter represents an interactionist perspective that acknowledges the need for experience with the environment but at the same time assumes the existence of innate mechanisms that constrain learning from the environment.

As our discussion of the history of nativism has shown, the function and quality of innate abilities has become more and more concrete in the last century. Especially, research with infants has developed finer measures enabling us to study infants' expectations and beliefs as well as their brain function. In the following we consider some concrete instances from the developmental psychological literature. One recent example concerns the existence of a Spelke object early in infancy, named for Elizabeth Spelke who has conducted much of this pioneering research. Evidence from Spelke's lab as well as from other labs studying early physical knowledge indicates that very early in life, infants have a tendency to assume that the world is populated with three-dimensional (3D) objects that are bounded, have substance, are lasting in time and space, and move in predictable ways. Spelke has argued that this knowledge is part of our genetic endowment. We do not need to learn about these properties of the physical world because we already have them built into our system to prepare us for the world we live in. It should be noted that these expectations are very basic, not complex or elaborate, and are probably required in order to learn anything about physics (because physics is in its essence about how objects move relative to each other).

Evidence for this claim comes from a variety of studies with infants. At the core of this research and similar research using habituation or violation of expectation paradigms is the finding that infants show a strong novelty preference. For example, when exposed to a series of photographs from one category (e.g., dogs) infants will show an increase in looking duration if a new category (e.g., cats) is shown after repeated exposure to the first category. Similarly, if infants have an already formed expectation about how the world works and functions (e.g., that objects fall without support) then they should be surprised and look longer if researchers present them with an event that violates this expectation (e.g., a floating box) as compared to an expected event (e.g., a box being supported by a hand). This basic finding about infants' novelty preference has been used repeatedly in infant research to study infants' understanding of the world. For example, several studies from Spelke's own lab investigate as directly as possible the ways in which infants expect objects to behave. In one of these studies, infants were shown events in which an object moves along a straight path from left to right or from right to left. Between the infant and this path of motion were two narrow screens. Infants were shown test events in which the object disappeared as it moved behind each screen. The difference between the two test events was in whether the object was visible between the two screens: in the possible event the object was visible between the two screens, whereas the object disappeared between the two screens in the impossible event. Thus, Spelke and colleagues asked whether infants expect objects to move along spatiotemporally continuous paths – do they expect that to get from point A to point B, objects must travel through every point between A and B? Alternately, infants could expect that objects can disappear at location A and reappear at location B, as has been initially suggested by Jean Piaget. Spelke's results, significantly longer looking at the impossible than at the possible event, supported the former of these two possibilities: infants do expect objects to travel along spatiotemporally continuous paths.

These and other results have led some researchers to speculate that object persistence (part and parcel of the Spelke object), the notion that objects are bounded, have substance, are lasting in time and space, and move in predictable ways, is innate.

Of course, showing that this is the case is quite difficult, especially given the concerns raised about the meaning of innateness discussed earlier. Ideally, one would want to show that the ability could not possibly have been learned. Two factors constrain if an ability can be learned, first its overall difficulty and second the time that is available to learn the ability. As we will see below, we must even consider the possibility that learning takes place prior to birth. While still in the uterus, the fetus has access to a surprisingly large amount of information (not necessarily visual, but certainly tactile and auditory) about the physical world. Thus, it is possible that an ability that is present at birth is not innate but learned by the fetus in the uterus. Therefore, it is important for a nativist argument to show that an ability is not learnable given the time and exposure to situations that would allow an infant to learn the ability.

The concept of learnability comes from formal learning theory and is a mathematical and computational framework. One domain where this framework has been used is language acquisition. The key issue of learning a first language is the question how it is possible for a child to extract the grammatical rules and structure of a language given the limited and often ill-formed language examples they are exposed to? One answer to this question is to assume that infants are prepared to learn languages that follow the general structure found in all human languages. Thus, infants are able to pay attention to the important properties of language that are needed for successful learning. Such learning could be based on the statistical properties of natural languages but it could also be aided by innate structures such as a universal grammar.

Baillargeon and colleagues have also addressed this issue of learnability. In their work on learning about the physical world in infants, Baillargeon and colleagues have shown that 'contrastive evidence' is an important source of information for infants to learn the critical components of any physical principle. Contrastive evidence refers to observing the outcome of an event when a physical principle is maintained and what happens when it is not maintained. For instance, when learning about support relations between objects, contrastive evidence is obtained when infants see the consequences when an object is adequately supported by another (i.e., it remains stable on top of that object) and they also see the consequences when an object is inadequately supported by another (i.e., it falls to the ground). Results from a variety of studies indicate that infants learn about the principles of support and other physical principles such as occlusion and containment when they have access to contrastive evidence. However, Baillargeon points out that infants cannot observe contrastive evidence for object continuity as they watch parents interact with objects or as they do so themselves, because such evidence does not exist in our physical reality. There is never a clear-cut set of events in which objects are continuous in one case and not in another – this is essentially object implosion or disintegration, which are not physically possible and therefore not observable. Baillargeon's extensive body of research led her to conclude that this contrastive evidence, available for all other physical principles she has investigated and critical for learning, is not available for object persistence. Despite this, infants show evidence of expecting objects to be lasting in time and space in most every visually based paradigm used to test it. Taken together, these pieces of evidence lead to the logical conclusion that the persistence of objects need not be learned.

One possibility we will consider in more detail later is how learning in the prenatal environment could have an influence on postnatal ability. Here it seems as though the observations necessary for learning about the persistence of objects is not available in the visual environment postnatally, but perhaps the first learning done about objects actually occurs prenatally, in the dark fluid environment of the uterus. It is difficult to know what kind of relevant experiences fetuses might have in the uterus, because as far as we know, fetal learning about objects has not been studied at all. Until this has been studied, the cautious approach would be to not make assumptions about the origins of these abilities.

Perhaps this analysis has made clear how difficult it is to find unequivocal evidence for innateness in humans. Below we will consider other reasons why the use of the term innate is often at odds with producing findings, interpretations, and theoretical claims that are clear.

Struggling with Definitions

It turns out that exactly how to define 'innate' is nontrivial. Patrick Bateson has explained his concerns that there are different possible meanings for the word 'innate'. He puts forth six possible meanings: (1) present at birth; (2) a behavioral difference caused by a genetic difference; (3) adapted over the course of evolution; (4) unchanging throughout development; (5) shared by all members of a species; and (6) not learned. These different meanings or connotations are present throughout the literatures in different subfields of psychology, ethology, and biology, raising at least two major questions regarding meaning. First, if evidence for one of these conclusions is demonstrated, can another (or all six) be inferred? Certainly not. But this is a common logical error in the literature. Further, an author might use the term in one limited way, but readers may infer a different or broader use of the term. As a solution to this problem, Bateson implores scientists to "Say what you mean (even if it uses a bit more space) rather than unintentionally confuse your reader by employing a word such as innate that carries so many different connotations." Thus, if a scientist has evidence that a given ability is present at birth, Bateson asks that he or she simply states that fact and not be tempted to make inferences beyond that actual finding. Employing this simple measure would reduce confusion about what precisely is meant by the claim that something is innate. Researchers must be aware that our findings have implications for other researchers from related or even unrelated disciplines. Furthermore, caution with this matter is warranted because an ability that is present at birth could have been learned in the uterus and therefore does not automatically support a nativist argument.

Why These Differences in Meaning Are Important

It may seem that some of Bateson's six meanings are just synonyms for each other. For example, isn't 'present at birth' the same as 'not learned'? One example will show how they can be quite different. Studies with humans and animals have shown that the sensory and cognitive systems of the fetus allow for learning to take place prior to birth. For example, a series of studies with human infants conducted by Anthony DeCasper and colleagues showed that newborn infants prefer listening to their mothers' voices to other female voices. Some researchers might have been tempted to make the conclusion that this ability is innate, after all 'present at birth' is one of the meanings ascribed to innate. Then, we would be tempted to make additional conclusions, such as this ability is not learned, that it is caused by a genetic difference, etc.

However, it turns out that this was just part of the story. The full story was that newborn infants did not just prefer their mothers' voices. They also preferred listening to a story their mother had read aloud everyday during her last 6 weeks of pregnancy (they showed this preference even when their mother was not reading either story). Thus, it was not just that the newborns preferred their mother's voice, they preferred things that she said! Now we can see more clearly that the preference newborns show for their mother's voice is very likely due to the experience they have with her voice while still in the uterus.

So, perhaps fetal learning is something special about early human cognition, but other animals would not show evidence of it. After all, we know that animals display species-specific action patterns that are sometimes quite elaborate, and perhaps these are truly not learned or influenced by experience. However, the research of Gilbert Gottlieb has shown that fetal experience influences ducklings' perceptual judgments, proximity-seeking behavior, and vocal behavior.

Fetal ducklings that do not hear themselves or their siblings vocalize prior to or immediately posthatching are different from ducklings with typical auditory experience in many ways. The ducklings that did not receive auditory input prior to hatching did not discriminate between their own species' maternal call and those of other similar species as well as ducklings who did hear these early calls. Although the ducklings with typical auditory experience only seek proximity to an audio speaker emitting their own species' maternal call, those without auditory experience with their species' maternal call seek proximity to the speaker when it emits many different calls. Thus, newly hatched ducklings without typical auditory experience fail to discriminate between their own species' call and other similar calls. They also failed to produce these calls as well as ducklings with typical auditory experience. These findings show that abilities that had typically been thought of as innate (identifying and producing their species' maternal call) are actually dependent upon certain experiences. Further, we see that it is not always straightforward to determine which prenatal experiences support which postnatal abilities.

Thus, early preferences and behaviors (and, presumably, cognitive skills) can be set up and traced back directly to experiences that were received prior to birth. However, these paths of influence are not always what we might expect them to be. At this point we do not yet know enough about the prenatal environment or about how human fetal experiences can set up particular expectations, thoughts, or behaviors in the newborn. Therefore, we cannot make claims about which of these skills are certainly not influenced by various experiences they have prior to birth.

Various Forms of Interactioninsm

Another account of the role of experience in development has been put forth by William Greenough and colleagues. According to this approach, there are some events that are so prevalent in the environment of the developing organism that the system develops in such a way that these events are 'expected' by the organism. Thus, the mammalian visual system is only partially developed at birth and requires a steady diet of patterned visual stimulation for normal development to continue. Once the organism leaves the uterus, patterned visual stimulation is available essentially whenever the eyes are open, as long as the infant is in a typical environment of any kind. These kinds of processes are called experience-expectant and will not develop into their typical form if certain experiences are not available at certain times. In addition, he proposes that other processes are experience-dependent – not so constrained by time and by appropriate input and likely resulting in more variability across individuals.

Another way researchers describe how much the environment contributes to the development of a trait or ability is by using the concept of 'canalization'. This term comes from Waddington's classic metaphor of trait development involving a ball rolling through a landscape that allows for more or less lateral movement from environmental influences or winds that might blow the ball to another portion of the landscape and a different instantiation of the trait. If the ball began in a deep canal or was highly canalized, presumably hurricane-force winds would be necessary to push it off track. A process is highly canalized if it is not very vulnerable to the influences of the environment. Less canalization means that more variability is expected from environmental influence. The appeal of this metaphor lies in its capturing the dynamics of the whole organism–environment system rather than trying to separate these two in ways that are untenable. Thus, this metaphor replaces the dichotomy of nature and nurture with a continuous scale of environmental and biological influences on development. Another strength of this view is that it makes no claims about the starting point or ending point of a developmental process. This avoids unnecessary confusion about origins and puts the emphasis on process.

Such accounts of development have been called interactionist approaches since the influences and interplay of both biology and environment are considered. However, even in this very general sketch of an interactionist approach different camps of researchers prefer to focus on different aspects of development. While researchers generally agree that some learning mechanisms are available relatively early in life to support further development, one can choose to focus either on understanding the learning mechanism itself or to focus on understanding what is learned. Even if researchers seem to agree on how the developing system works in general and which processes are necessary for development, they could still disagree on which process or learning mechanisms are employed first, are most important, are dependent on each other or just plainly most interesting. Thus, while a less rigid form of nativism that assumes only a limited number of core processes to be innate may be indistinguishable from a similar form of empiricism, the theoretical positions underlying these views can differ greatly on where they place their emphasis. Thus, among researchers there is also a graded continuum of views and perspectives on nativism and empiricism. Differences between two views are often quantitative rather then qualitative. New and highly sensitive methods in the cognitive neurosciences will allow researchers to identify more core processes in development. However, if these new findings are interpreted as evidence for nativism or for empiricism will remain a matter of the theoretical position of the researcher.

Conclusions

Nativism is an approach to understanding human cognition that has a long and rich history within philosophy and even today is considered by many to be an important component of how we explain human nature. Although nativist explanations have stirred many heated debates, we suggest that the utility of this term has to do with the level of analysis at which the argument is targeted. For more philosophical approaches to psychology and human nature, the concept of innateness may well be useful and appropriate. However, for more biologically oriented approaches that are in the realm of neuroscience, the concept of innateness is nearly impossible to define and impossible to use with precision. How to resolve this conflict in boundary areas that span these levels of analysis is a challenging question for the future of our disciplines. Often it is nearly impossible to make this distinction and in 1967 William Kessen pointed out that "... the division of he world of infant studies into naturist and nurturist is at best misleading ..." We agree and suggest that, for now, abandoning the use of the word 'innate' unless further clarification is also offered may be the most useful way to go forward.

See also: Cognitive Development; Cognitive Developmental Theories; Habituation and Novelty; Learning; Mathematical Reasoning; Object Concept; Piaget's Cognitive-Developmental Theory.

Suggested Readings

Baillargeon R (1999) Young infants' expectations about hidden objects: A reply to three challenges. *Developmental Science* 2: 115–163.
Bateson P (1991) Are there principles of behavioural develoment? In: Bateson P (ed.) *The Development and Integration of Behaviour: Essays in Honour of Robert Hinde*, pp. 19–39. Cambridge: Cambridge University Press.
Fodor JA (1983) *The Modularity of Mind.* Cambridge: MIT Press.
Gottlieb G (1971) *Development of Species Identification in Birds: An Inquiry into the Prenatal Determinants of Perception.* Chicago: University of Chicago Press.
Oyama S (2000) *The Ontogeny of Information: Developmental Systems and Evolution.* Durham, NC: Duke University Press.
Spelke ES (1990) Principles of object perception. *Cognitive Science* 14: 29–56.
Spelke ES (1998) Nativism, empiricism, and the origins of knowledge. *Infant Behavior and Development* 21: 181–200.
Spelke ES (2000) Core knowledge. *American Psychologist* 55: 1233–1243.

Object Concept

S P Johnson and K C Soska, New York University, New York, NY, USA

© 2008 Elsevier Inc. All rights reserved.

Glossary

A-not-B error – In simple hiding games, infants will sometimes search at a location where they had previously found an object (the 'A' location), even after watching it hidden someplace else (the 'B' location).
Action systems – Locomotor, manual, and oculomotor (eye movement) behaviors that may play a central role in developing object concepts.
Allocentric reasoning – Coding of spatial location in terms of landmarks in the environment (compare egocentric reasoning).
Ecological approach to perception – A theoretical view suggesting that the way to understand human cognition is to study the moving, acting human as he or she exists (and evolved) in real-world contexts.
Egocentric reasoning – Coding of spatial location in terms of the observer's own viewpoint (compare allocentric reasoning).
Electroencephalography (EEG) – Recording of differences in small electrical currents produced by the brain and measured at the scalp; they reflect the brain's response to a specific visual or auditory stimulus.
Neural synchrony – A common firing mechanism among circuits of neurons in the brain that work together to code an event.
Object concept – The ability to represent objects in the absence of direct perceptual support, including some (internal) cortical activity that registers the presence of a hidden object or hidden object part beyond what is available via sensory input, as well as some (external) behavioral manifestation of the representation.
Objectification – Knowledge of the self and external objects as distinct entities, spatially segregated, persisting across time and space, and obeying certain commonsense causal constraints.
Prefrontal dorsolateral cortex – A part of the brain that is thought to be important in short-term memory and inhibition of habitual behaviors.
Visual preference paradigms – Methods used to probe learning, memory, representation, and discrimination in preverbal infants, based on the tendency of infants to look longer at visual stimuli that are novel, interesting, or otherwise discriminable.

Introduction

Adults experience a world composed of objects at various distances. We perceive these objects as continuous and enduring even when they are out of view, part of a mature system of object concepts. We consider theories of how object concepts develop in infancy, focusing on the seminal views of Jean Piaget, and more recent alternatives based on innate concepts. We then present evidence from a variety of paradigms designed to elucidate the precise mechanisms of object concept development. This evidence points to emerging action systems and neural development as providing crucial support for object concept development.

Object Concept

We live in an environment filled with countless objects, each of which occupies a unique spatial location. Objects in the world tend to be predictable; for example, we know that inanimate objects do not move in the absence of some outside force, objects cannot be in two places at once (nor two objects in the same place), and objects do not vanish out of existence and then reappear. But the visual environment that is seen 'directly' (i.e., the light that is reflected to the eye from visible surfaces in the environment) changes with every head and eye movement, and objects themselves may move out of sight and subsequently return to view. Nevertheless, our experience is not a world of transitory, intangible, disembodied shapes, but rather one of substance, volume, and depth.

Do infants also experience a world of solid objects? Or might they instead perceive only what is directly visible, failing to infer the permanence of objects without, say, extensive experience, a certain level of brain maturation, or both? Note the similarity of these questions to the classic 'nature–nurture' issue, the subject of long and fierce debates. The origins of object perception have interested philosophers for centuries, and discussions have often centered on the extent to which knowledge of objects is gained from visual, manual, or some other active experience, or is the product of innate (unlearned) cognitive skills. Systematic empirical approaches to these vital questions were unavailable until the early twentieth century with the publication of a succession of books by Jean Piaget. He introduced a series of tasks posed to his own young children in an attempt to chart the development of object representations – amongst other cognitive skills – across infancy. Some of these tasks are described subsequently. Also described are alternative theoretical views, followed by discussions of studies that examine carefully how object concepts might develop across the first several months after birth. These studies, by and large, are consistent with Piaget's theory, although the scope of the theory, in hindsight, appears to have been limited.

Piaget's Theory

Piaget presented a theory of object concepts that comprised development of knowledge of objects in tandem with their spatial relations, because one cannot perceive or act on objects accurately without awareness of their positions in space relative to other objects. The foremost explanandum of Piagetian theory was objectification, the knowledge of the self and external objects as distinct entities, spatially segregated, persisting across time and space, and obeying certain commonsense causal constraints. Piaget suggested that objectification is rooted in the child's recognition of her own body as an independent object and her own movements as movements of objects through space, akin to movements of other objects she sees. This constitutes a transition from egocentric to allocentric reasoning. Over time, thinking and reasoning about objects become detached from actions, and actions are placed on the ongoing, observed series of surrounding events in the construction of the reality of time and space. That is, it no longer becomes necessary for the infant to act upon on object for her to gain an understanding of its properties. The progression from egocentric to allocentric spatial reasoning and to a mature object concept was revealed to Piaget and other developmental psychologists by changes in infants' behavior in the normal, day-to-day flow of activities, and when confronted with a series of tasks that Piaget devised.

Objectification was thought to be an outcome of coordination of actions. Initially, behaviors are simply repeated, one at a time and then become organized into more complex strings of action sequences. At the same time, infants begin to explore novelty, as when trying new behaviors, or using familiar actions with no clear prediction of outcome. These behaviors are evident in everyday play activities, as when Piaget observed his daughter repeatedly hide and reveal a toy under a blanket. Piaget proposed that these simple games led the child to establish spatial relations among objects, such as above, below, and behind, largely by manual experience. For example, infants who are learning to reach (at 4–6 months) soon discover which objects are within reach and those that are not – a kind of depth perception. Therefore, both direct experience (to learn when search is successful or not) and deduction (reasoning from general principles to specific instances) contribute to the developmental process.

Development of action systems, spatial concepts, and object concepts was organized into six stages. Initially (during stages 1 and 2), infants exhibited a kind of recognition memory, for example, seeking the mother's breast after losing contact shortly after birth, and within several months, continuing to look in the direction of a person's exit from the room. These behaviors were not systematic, however, and Piaget considered them more passive than active. For Piaget, active search, initiated by the child, was a critical feature of mature object concepts.

More active search behavior emerged after 4 months, and marked the beginnings of true objectification during stage 3. Piaget outlined five examples, in roughly chronological order. The first of these was visual accommodation to rapid movements, when an infant would respond to a dropped object by looking down toward the floor, behavior that became more systematic when the infant himself dropped it. A second behavior, interrupted prehension, refers to the infant's attempts to re-acquire an object that was dropped or taken from her hand if it is out of sight momentarily and within easy reach. (The infant will not search yet, however, if the object is fully occluded.) Deferred circular reactions describes the infant's repetitive gestures when interrupted during some object-oriented play activity, resuming the game after some delay (necessitating memory of the object, the actions, and their context). Reconstruction of an invisible whole from a visible fraction was evinced, for example, by retrieval of an object from a cover when only a part of the object was visible. Finally, the infant became capable of removal of obstacles preventing perception, as when he pulls away a cover from his face during peekaboo, or withdraws a fully hidden toy from beneath a blanket. This behavior marked the transition to stage 4.

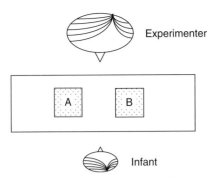

Figure 1 Schematic overhead view of an infant and experimenter participating in a hidden object search task designed to elicit the A-not-B error.

During stage 4, beginning at about 8 months, the infant will search actively for a hidden object under a variety of circumstances. Searches may be erroneous, however, when the object is hidden first at a single location followed by (successful) search, and then hidden in another location as the infant watches (see **Figure 1**). Here, the infant may remove the obstacle at the first location the object was hidden, even though she saw it hidden subsequently somewhere else. This response has come to be known as the A-not-B error. Piaget also described an intriguing incident when one of his daughters, aged 15 months, saw her father in the garden. When asked, "Where is papa?" she pointed to the window of his office in the home, as if there were two papas: "papa at his window" and "papa in the garden." These behaviors mark awareness of and search for a vanished object, but their erroneous nature, according to Piaget, indicated a fundamental limitation of the emerging object concept: There is not yet true objectification. During stage 4, the object is considered an extension of the infant's own behavior, and identity of objects is not preserved across perceptual contacts. That is, if an object appears at a particular place as a function of a child's activity, there is no concept yet of continuity across time and space.

Objectification is completed across the next two stages as the infant first solves the problem of multiple visible displacements, searching at the last location visited by the object (stage 5), and then multiple invisible displacements (stage 6). Finally, the infant searches systematically at all potential hiding locations visited by the object. For Piaget, mature search revealed detachment of the object from the action, and knowledge of the infant's body itself as one object among many, brought into an allocentric system of organized objects and events.

Evaluating Piaget's Theory

Piagetian theory has received a great deal of interest, in particular the A-not-B error, but a number of researchers have explored earlier developmental patterns as well. The theory enjoys strong support for many of the details of behavior that Piaget described, but many researchers have questioned the reasoning behind the developmental changes in these behaviors.

Consider first the A-not-B error. There have been hundreds of successful replications of the effect in 8–12-month-old infants. Nevertheless, the basis for the error, and what it reveals about object concept development, remain a matter of relentless dispute. Three examples of research paradigms that have examined Piagetian claims help to illustrate this controversy. Adele Diamond has used the A-not-B error as an index of brain development, specifically an area known as 'prefrontal dorsolateral cortex', which is thought to be important in short-term memory and inhibition of habitual behaviors (so-called 'inhibitory control'). According to Diamond, the A-not-B error occurs in infants because there is a difficulty in maintaining a short-term representation of the object and its location, plus a difficulty in inhibiting a tendency to reach at a 'primed' location. Renee Baillargeon has suggested that the A-not-B error is a poor index of infants' object concepts, because of a general lack of coordinated manual search behavior in infants who are still learning to reach appropriately. Finally, Linda Smith and Esther Thelen have claimed that the A-not-B error tells us nothing at all about object representations or concepts, because the error arises from specific task demands, reaching history, and the experimental context. Infants even produce the error in the absence of any hidden toy!

Turning next to other evidence of early object concepts, numerous experiments have revealed that by 2–4 months of age, infants appear to maintain representations of partly and fully hidden objects across short delays. These experiments rely on 'visual preference' paradigms, using techniques developed in the 1960s and 1970s by Tom Bower and further refined by Elizabeth Spelke and others. These paradigms built on methods pioneered by Robert Fantz, who discovered that infants tend to lose interest in repetitive visual stimuli, and recover interest to novel stimuli. Some researchers, in addition, have devised a variant of the novelty-preference paradigm known as the violation-of-expectation method, which relies on the assumption that infants will look preferentially in general at odd or unusual events. A well-known example was described by Renee Baillargeon and colleagues, who showed 5-month-old infants a stimulus consisting of a rotating screen that appeared to move through the space occupied by a previously seen object. They reported that infants looked longer at the event in which the screen 'passed through' the object relative to the event in which the screen stopped at the object's location (see **Figure 2**). The first event, therefore, was claimed to violate the previously seen object's solidity, but the second event was consistent with an expectation of solidity.

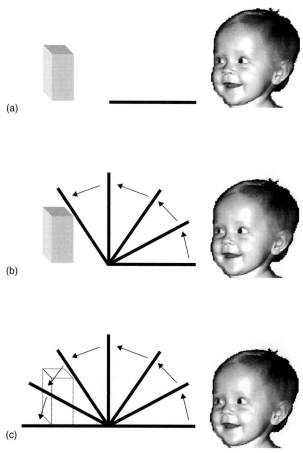

Figure 2 Schematic depiction of the events used to probe young infants' object representations across short intervals of occlusion. (a) The infant sees a box and a screen that is flat on the table. (b) The screen rotates up to the box and stops, a so-called possible event. (c) The screen appears to rotate through the space seen to have been occupied by the box, an impossible event. Reproduced with permission from the parent.

The outcomes of these experiments are by and large consistent with Piaget's claims: evidence for the rudiments of object concepts, in place early in infancy, which are elaborated with learning and experience. Reaching errors in the context of multiple hiding locations have been observed in many experiments but remain a source of controversy, and it is unclear what such behavior reveals. Also in question is a central tenet of Piaget's theory of object concept development: the idea that early object concepts are egocentric, not allocentric. Few active theoreticians would likely agree with this notion, and the evidence that Piaget offered in support of this proposal seems weak relative to other aspects of the theory. On the other hand, two ideas originating in Piaget's theory have been supported by more recent research: first, the possibility that newborn infants do not perceive occlusion (and therefore no functional object concept), and second, the importance of the infant's own behavior in constructing object representations. These ideas are discussed in subsequent sections of this article.

In summary, Piaget inspired decades of fruitful research that have documented clearly the development of object concepts within several months after birth. These concepts guide detection of anomalous visual stimuli (such as impossible events), guide reaching toward previously seen objects, and are manifest in recordings of cortical activity as infants view occlusion stimuli. Despite this progress, fundamental questions remain in the extent to which object representations develop with experience, learning, and general maturation. These questions are considered in subsequent sections of the article.

Nativist Theory

Central to nativist theory are the tandem possibilities that some kinds of knowledge form a central core upon which more diverse, mature cognitive capacities are built, and that some kinds of knowledge are unlearned. Philosophical discussions of innateness are ancient; historically, these discussions have centered around the extent to which human knowledge must necessarily be rooted in, or is independent of, postnatal experience. Plato and Descartes, for example, proposed that some ideas were universal and available innately because they were elicited in the absence of any direct tutoring or instruction, or were unobservable in the world, and thus unlearnable (e.g., concepts of geometry or God). With the advent of rigorous testing methods in the last century, the debate began to shift from the role of innate concepts to the role of innate process in shaping knowledge acquisition. Donald Hebb, for example, noted the 'intrinsic organization' that characterized the neonate's electroencephalogram, which he postulated as a contributing mechanism of subsequent perceptual development,

Violation-of-expectation methods, too, are controversial, because we can never be sure why infants look longer at violations – it has been suggested, for example, that the violation in this example is interesting because there is more motion in the event. Nevertheless, there are dozens of corroborative and related findings that young infants perceive objects as persistent and whole across short intervals of time and space. Simple reaching measures, for example, are consistent with this interpretation: young infants have been found to reach in the dark toward an object in a previously visible location. In addition, recordings of brain activity in infants, in particular electroencephalography (EEG) (differences in small electrical currents at the scalp over the brain), have revealed object representations that are maintained under occlusion. This evidence comes from coordinated bursts of neural activity that may reflect short-term memory for objects that were recently hidden.

based primarily on associative learning. Innate process was an important facet of Gestalt perceptual theory as well: dynamic forces of electrical activity in the brain were thought to guide general perceptual organization, alongside experience with specific object kinds. For researchers advocating an innate process, the innateness is not any knowledge per se, but the ability for the child's developing brain to quickly and easily pick up many types of information.

More recently, theories of innate concepts have again become more common: concepts of objects as obeying certain real-world, physical constraints, such as persistence and identity across occlusion, and solidity. Three arguments have been offered for such hypothesized innate object concepts. First, veridical object knowledge can be elicited in very young infants under some circumstances, suggesting that early concepts emerge too quickly to have been derived from postnatal learning. Second, infants' detection of apparent violations of simple physical events has been proposed to reflect weighing 'contrastive' evidence. To nativists, though, young infants would not have had sufficient opportunities to observe conditions under which an object behaves in a manner consistent or inconsistent with a particular concept. If this is a principal mechanism of development of object concepts, it follows that a concept of persistence across occlusion must be innate, because it cannot have been acquired from observing contrastive evidence in the real world. Third, there is evidence that nonhuman animals' mechanisms for tracking objects across occlusion may operate in similar ways to those of humans, suggesting that object concepts were programmed via evolutionary pressure.

The majority of evidence for early object concepts comes from experiments in which looking times are recorded relative either to a familiarization stimulus (i.e., a novelty preference) or to some aspect of object knowledge that the infant is purported to bring to the task (i.e., a violation of expectation). As noted previously, there is evidence from a variety of laboratories and experimental settings for short-term representations of objects under occlusion that are functional by 2–4 months after birth. Nevertheless, the question of developmental origins cannot be addressed merely by noting competence at a young age. Evidence for innate object concepts would come from, for example, functionality at birth, emergence in the absence of experience, or stability across development, and at present no such evidence exists. Moreover, experiments on infants' perception of partly occluded objects, reviewed next, cast doubt on the viability of nativist theory to explain early object concepts.

In the 1960s, Tom Bower devised a clever task to examine infants' discrimination of the perceptual equivalence of two visual stimuli. The stimuli were identical, except one was partially occluded (see **Figure 3**). An operant conditioning procedure was employed with 1-month-old infants, with sucking rate as the operant response (the infant was required to suck on a pacifier for the visual display to appear). The infants were first exposed to a partly occluded triangle, and reduced sucking rates were interpreted as evidence of perceptual discrimination. The infants maintained sucking rates in response to a complete (unoccluded) triangle, taken as evidence for phenomenal identity, and perception of the partly occluded triangle (the training stimulus) as having a definite form behind the occluder. Presentation of triangle parts (separated by a gap) resulted in decreased response, taken as evidence that these incomplete forms were perceived as different than the partly occluded triangle – in other words, the infants perceived the partly occluded triangle as complete. In experiments with 4-month-olds, Philip Kellman and Elizabeth Spelke were unable to replicate the finding of perceptual completion on the basis of static information; they reported that only motion was effective in specifying unity. After habituation to a partly occluded rod, the infants looked longer at two rod parts than at a complete object, but only when the rod parts moved relative to the occluder (see **Figure 4**). These experiments challenge the notion that young infants perceive object completion on the basis of Gestalt perceptual information such as good continuation, but leave open the question of development of perceptual completion in infancy.

This question was addressed by Alan Slater and colleagues, who replicated the methods of Kellman and Spelke with newborns, tested less than 3 days after birth. In contrast to 4-month-olds, newborns responded to a partly occluded object display solely on the basis of its visible parts, failing to perceive completion behind the occluder. Scott Johnson has found that under some conditions, 2-month-olds perceive object unity, as when the occluder is made narrow and the distance of perceptual interpolation is reduced, relative to a display in which

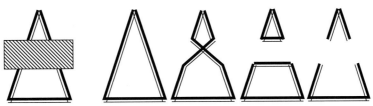

Figure 3 Training (left) and four test stimuli used in the Bower experiment on 1-month-olds' perception of a partly occluded wire triangle.

older infants are able to achieve perceptual completion. Johnson and colleagues reported similar patterns of evidence in experiments examining perception of continuity of object trajectories (see **Figure 5**). Four-month-olds perceived continuity only when the object was out of sight for a very brief period of time; when out of sight for a more extended duration, the infants appeared to perceive only the visible segments of the object trajectory,

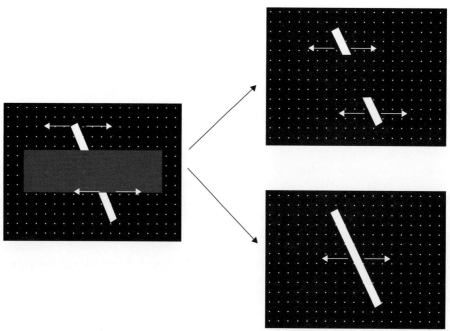

Figure 4 Events presented to young infants in investigations of perception of partial occlusion. After habituation to the partly occluded rod at left, infants view displays depicting either the rod segments that were formerly visible (top), or a complete version of the rod (bottom).

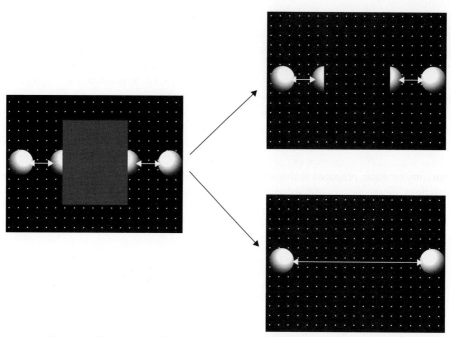

Figure 5 Events presented to young infants in investigations of perception of object trajectories under occlusion. After habituation to the partly occluded object trajectory at left, infants view displays depicting either the trajectory segments that were formerly visible, without the occluder present (top), or a continuous version of the trajectory, again with no occluder (bottom).

failing to perceive persistence. In other words, they behaved in like manner to the newborns in the experiments described previously, responding only to what is directly visible. Six-month-olds seemed to perceive continuity even under the longer occlusion duration.

Consider these results in the light of nativist theory. All evidence to date indicates that perception of occlusion is not available to newborn infants; instead, developments in perceptual completion occur across the first several months after birth. Without perception of occlusion, of course, a functional object concept is impossible, and therefore we conclude that there is no innate object concept as such. Nevertheless, some potential mechanisms of development are consistent with, and indeed rely on, innate structure and process. These are presented in subsequent sections of the article.

Evaluating Nativist Theory

As noted previously, there is evidence from a variety of laboratories and experimental settings for representations of objects as solid bodies that are spatiotemporally coherent and persistent; these representations appear to be functional by 2–4 months after birth. Obtaining such evidence for competence in these tasks at a young age is an important step in determining how object concepts develop, but the arguments discussed previously do little to shed light on this important issue. Nativist theory draws praise, however, for the cultivation of exciting, alternative perspectives on questions of cognitive development and for serving as the inspiration for the generation of an abundance of data. Development is always a matter of building new structure upon the old, whether the structures under consideration are concrete, such as arrangements of neural connections, or more abstract, such as object concepts. The ultimate value of nativist theory, instead, may be the attention it calls to the potential role of more general developmental processes that may operate outside experience, even while lacking specific proposals for how this might occur in the case of object knowledge. The infant is delivered to the world outside the uterus an active perceiver, endowed with the readiness and ability to acquire information, prepared to discover the patterns and regularities in the events she views in the surrounding environment. An understanding of the state of neonates' perceptual systems may be a more well defined question under the purview of nativism than is development of object concepts.

In summary, nativist theory has provided provocative claims for innate concepts, yet provides little insight into developmental mechanisms. One problem with nativist theory is a failure to consider evidence from experiments that investigate object perception in newborns and very young infants. In the next section, we consider alternatives that may hold more explanatory power.

Developmental Mechanisms of Object Concepts: Action Systems

In the previous sections of the article we presented and critiqued two theories, each of which captures a part of the larger picture of object concept development. From Piagetian theory comes the notion that object concepts likely take many months to mature, from an initial response to missing (occluded) object parts to the ability to solve complex hiding tasks. In addition, the possibility that the infant's own behaviors have a direct role in concept development is appealing, and Piaget described evidence from hiding tasks to support this idea. Nativist theory stresses the importance of development that occurs outside experience. This viewpoint is correct for some perceptual skills: newborn infants distinguish between separate regions of visual space that constitute visible surface fragments, they retain information for short intervals, and there are distinct visual preferences at birth (e.g., edges are preferred over homogeneous regions). Nevertheless, there is strong evidence that infants are not born with object representations or concepts. In the remainder of the article, we will address the question of how perceptual completion might develop in infancy. We will return to the issue, initially suggested by Piaget, of action systems in developing object concepts: locomotor, manual, and oculomotor (eye movement) behaviors that appear to provide a crucial supportive – or perhaps causal – role in early object perception.

The possibility that action and motor development can promote the understanding of object properties has a long history within developmental psychology research. As noted previously, Piaget placed the actions of infants at the forefront of his theories of perceptual development. On Piaget's theory, the sensorimotor period is characterized by increasingly coordinated actions that permit infants to learn about objects in the world, and motor skills were thought to be the primary means by which object knowledge was constructed into a representational system. Piaget popularized the idea that the active child could – through exploration of objects – obtain information relevant for future understanding of several properties, including object permanence and perceptual completion.

Building upon the idea that the actions of the developing child could promote learning about the visual world, Eleanor Gibson posited several areas in which exploratory skills facilitate object knowledge. Newborns use visual scanning to obtain information about important events in the world. Over the next few months, infants become increasingly skilled at coordinating eye movements with head movements. For Gibson's approach to object perception, this nascent exploratory system allows infants to learn about the events of the visual world. Manual exploratory systems grow increasingly skilled around 4 months, giving infants even more opportunities to learn about the distinctive features of objects. As self-locomotion begins around 8 months, infants use their own actions to situate objects within the three-dimensional (3D) world and discover the layout of an environment on their own. In Gibson's 'ecological' approach to perception, infants' object knowledge is grounded within action as the two form a mutual, self-reinforcing loop. The interplay of perception and action in the infant's object concept reflects the realm in which object knowledge takes place in the mind of ecological developmentalists. The real world is where actions take place, where cognition is used, and where the infant learns and grows. Action is constant and inherently meaningful for the developing infant.

The theoretical link of perception and action within development takes on a more unidirectional role for other researchers. For instance, Joseph Campos, Bennett Bertenthal and colleagues have proposed that developments in independent locomotion likewise can ignite a host of new skills. The authors have been major proponents of the organizational nature of self-locomotion for many domains including social, spatial, and object perception, and emotional development. On their perspective, there is a hierarchal and nested relation among motor development and cognitive and perceptual skill acquisition. The onset of locomotion provides various experiences and processes that in turn stimulate a range of psychological reorganizations. For example, locomotion involves a continual updating of one's position in space, and this in turn may lead to improvements in spatial reasoning: learning to keep track of specific target locations, encoding spatial relations among targets, using landmarks for spatial coding, and so forth, leading then to more effective search strategies. Emily Bushnell and Jean-Paul Boudreau proposed that motor development may necessarily lead perceptual development within several domains. Depth perception and knowledge of 3D object structure, for example, were hypothesized to be deeply rooted in action development. On their view, coupled visual–manual exploration affords infants the most direct, well-controlled, and veridical perception of 3D forms, and kinetic cues to form can be revealed through infants' exploration. These two proposals are examined in more detail in the following sections.

Object Concepts and Search Behavior

Self-locomotion may help the infant understand spatial transformation of layouts because he or she is actively in control of the visible changes to the world. When infants are moved passively through the world, they may encode spatial relations egocentrically, in Piagetian terms, but overcome this as active locomotion changes the way the infant experiences the world. Additionally, when under active control, there are many redundancies to the information about the objects in the environment and their displacements as the infant moves, including motor commands, vestibular changes (balance and sensing body movements), and visual signals.

Karen Horobin and Linda Acredolo were the first to provide conclusive evidence that locomotor development was linked to performance on traditional Piagetian hidden object tasks. Across several different versions of an A-not-B task, infants aged 8.5–10 months who had more independent locomotor experience were consistently more successful at locating the hidden object. The authors observed that infants who had more independent locomotion experience displayed more attentiveness visually to the hiding of the objects to be searched for. Thus, simple attention to the task relevant information seems to improve with self-locomotion, in addition to search behavior. Follow-up studies by other researchers found that it was not simply hands-and-knees crawling that provided benefits to object search, but experience with independent locomotion through the use of a walker was also able to facilitate improved action-object knowledge. Additionally, unlike previous work, all of the infants in the sample were of the same age – the simplest way to control for age (or more likely maturation *per se*) as the factor at work in the progression of object search. Results like these indicate that locomotor experience, and not the age of the child alone, account for the success on object search tasks.

Martha Ann Bell and Nathan Fox continued this line of inquiry, recording electroencephalogram (EEG) and examining locomotor skills in the same infants. Frontal EEG signals have been linked to success on object permanence tasks with a delay period inserted. At the onset of crawling experience in infancy, there is also increased coherence of EEG activity over frontal cortex, which may be related to increasing organization of neural networks within the frontal lobe. The frontal lobe, as discussed previously, is of importance for inhibition and short-term memory. In these experiments, infants at 8 months with any amount of locomotor experience or a high amplitude frontal EEG signal were found to be highly successful on the search tasks. Interestingly, there was no interaction between measures of brain maturation and self-locomotion as predictors of success on the search tasks. The authors concluded that there may be multiple pathways to the same result, and that success on object permanence tasks may be driven by different means for different children – locomotor skills for some and cortical maturation for others.

A problem for those proposing that the onset of self-locomotion is crucial for object concepts are results, some of which were described earlier, that infants as young as 4 months of age seem aware of the existence of hidden objects, when tested in purely visual assessments. Bennett Bertenthal attempted to reconcile these apparently conflicting findings by appealing to a potential dissociation between registering and interpreting object events and acting upon objects. Visual processing in the cortex follows two distinct pathways, one for recognition and one for action. Bertenthal proposed that the ventral, recognition pathway may be precocious and drive looking behavior. The dorsal, action stream, on the other hand, may develop later; spurred by locomotor experience, this pathway achieves competency later. Self-locomotion clearly plays a role in aiding infants' searches for hidden objects, yet does not appear to influence looking behaviors in a violation of expectation paradigm.

Manual Learning and Experience

Amy Needham has demonstrated that manual experience with objects can aid infants in understanding their physical boundaries. In her early work, Needham showed that infants at 4.5 months of age were found to 'expect' two objects with distinct shapes, sizes, and colors to be physically separate, even if the objects were immediately adjacent (i.e., in direct contact). This finding was made by observations of infants' looking times as they watched two distinct looking objects either move together or move apart as a hand pulled on them. Infants were predicted to look longer and be more interested in the event that violated their expectation of the objects' physical properties (the violation-of-expectation paradigm discussed earlier). That is, if they assumed the two objects were physically joined, then pulling on one should move both objects together, whereas if they were disjoined, pulling on one should only move the one object.

Needham then examined how manual object exploration might be involved in the development of boundary perception. She reported that infants in a particular age group who were the most active explorers were those who consistently responded with longer looking toward the event display in which the two objects moved together. Infants of all exploratory skill levels have shown evidence of being able to assign object boundaries based on spatial information alone (an ability that may be related to perceptual completion, according to Needham). Yet, only when infants become truly proficient manual explorers do they utilize the featural information of objects to segregate them. The more active manual explorers examined (visually) the objects in a separate object exploration task for at least two-thirds of the time they spent holding it. Compared to the less active explorers, the active explorers may have had more general experience learning about objects and thus segregated the two new objects shown to them in the looking time part of the experiment while the less active explorers did not Object exploration thus appears to be linked to the ability to segregate and assess the boundaries of objects in infancy.

In experiments designed to examine the facilitation of these skills in younger infants, Needham gave 3-month-olds 2 weeks of experience using sticky mittens, small gloves covered in Velcro that stuck to small objects, also covered in Velcro. These tools allowed the infants a chance to view their own actions and the effects they had on objects at an age when their fine motor skills (notably fingering and bimanual grasping) were compromised compared to older infants. Infants given mitten experience were significantly more likely to switch between visual and oral exploration of objects without mittens compared to same-aged controls. The intervention appeared to boost attentiveness toward the visual properties of the objects and spurred infants' engagement with novel objects. There were no reported improvements in fine (motor skills, however). It seems that learning about the contingencies of actions on the physical world spawned new interest in objects and may have driven sensitivities to relevant and novel aspects of objects, learned primarily through action-based learning.

Integrating Information Over Time and Space: The Role of Eye Movements

Object manipulation is surely a vital part of the acquisition of object knowledge, but it cannot contribute in any meaningful way to the developmental origins of perceptual filling-in, because these origins appear earlier in development than does skilled manual exploration. The oculomotor system, in contrast, is largely functional at birth and matures rapidly, and even neonates scan the environment actively. There are important developments at around 2–3 months, however, in scanning 'efficiency'; young infants sometimes tend to fixate specific parts of a visual display rather than all the visible surfaces. Recent studies have found that overcoming this tendency – that is, engaging in more broad-based scanning – is associated with perceptual completion in 3-month-old infants. Infants who exhibited less efficient scan patterns, measured with an independent target search task, tended to perceive a partial occlusion display in terms of its constituent parts only (not as a whole). Infants who exhibited more efficient scan patterns provided evidence of unity perception. This implies that one way in which infants come to perceive partly occluded surfaces as coherent objects occurs via an active process of comparing the visible parts and integrating them into a whole.

Oculomotor Learning and Experience

Learning about occlusion and perceptual filling-in might be a deductive process: repeated exposure to many instances of objects becoming occluded and re-emerging, and subsequent identification of partly occluded objects as continuous, via an associative process. Occlusion and disocclusion are common occurrences in the real world: infants are exposed to multiple instances of such events routinely in the normal visual environment, and young infants are adept at rapid associative learning. Recent evidence from an anticipatory eye movement paradigm showed that when 4-month-old infants viewed a repetitive trajectory, they tended not to look ahead to where the ball was about to emerge from behind the occluder, in contrast to 6-month-olds, who showed a higher proportion of anticipations. But when 4-month-olds were first presented with a few trials with an unoccluded trajectory, followed by the occlusion stimulus, their rates of anticipation were roughly equivalent to those of the older infants. In other words, given experience, the 4-month-olds' performance was boosted to the level of the older infants. This effect fades after a short delay (30 min), however, suggesting that repeated exposures to multiple instances of hiding and revealing events, across weeks or months of developmental time, are necessary to ensure robust learning about these kinds of trajectory. Nevertheless, this research provides evidence that oculomotor development coupled with everyday visual experience may be an important mechanism behind the development of some kinds of object concept.

Developmental Mechanisms of Object Concepts: Neural Systems

For the sake of the present discussion of developmental origins of object concepts, it is worth highlighting some of what is known about cortical mechanisms of perceptual filling-in, and how such mechanisms might develop in infancy. Perception of connectedness across a spatial gap may be accomplished with relatively low- and mid-level mechanisms (i.e., cortical areas V1 through inferotemporal cortex), and development consists of at least two kinds of neural maturation. First, long-range cell-to-cell interactions in early visual areas connecting neural circuits coding for common edge orientations may reach sufficient maturity within several months after birth to support unity perception under some circumstances. Second, there are improvements in firing patterns of cell assemblies across the brain by reduction of neural 'noise'.

Perception of object persistence under occlusion may be accomplished by somewhat higher-level mechanisms (i.e., centered in inferotemporal and perirhinal cortex) that support neural activity coding for objects that have become occluded, and that guide overt behavioral responses. These behaviors include anticipatory eye movements in young infants, and reaching behaviors in older infants. This progression toward appropriate search in the context of complex hiding tasks is consistent with a view positing age-related strengthening of neural representations, such that with development, stronger representations support success at enacting appropriate behaviors across a wide range of situations involving occlusion. One candidate mechanism, mentioned previously, may promote development of many kinds of organized cortical activity: 'neural synchrony'. Processes such as binding of object features and location or coordination of object representations and object-oriented action have been hypothesized to be linked to neural synchrony. Neural circuits that participate in a common goal engage in synchronized activity, firing in brief bursts in the 40 Hz range. Evidence has emerged that there are changes in synchronized activity in infants that accompany perceptual changes, when perception of object occlusion is compared to perception of nonocclusion events.

A final piece of evidence highlighting the importance of neural developments to theories of object concepts comes from a recent experiment in which infant rhesus monkeys were tested in an object trajectory experiment similar to one described previously, with human infants. Eye movements were recorded as the monkeys viewed a target object move back and forth behind an occluder; patterns of oculomotor anticipations provided an index of object concepts. The youngest monkeys tested (5 weeks old) showed similar rates of anticipation to 4-month-old humans, and the proportions of anticipation improved with age. The rate of improvement, however, was dramatically faster in monkeys relative to humans. Other visual functions, as well, mature far more rapidly in monkeys. If simple visual experience were the sole mechanism, we would not find this great a difference in developmental timeliness between humans and monkeys. These results suggest that cortical maturation may support object concept development, rather than a specific period of experience viewing objects in the environment.

Conclusions

We discussed claims and evidence from two theories of object concept development: Piagetian theory and nativist theory, and we presented evidence from a wide range of experimental paradigms that that no single account can embrace the multitude of cortical and behavioral changes that underlie the emergence of object concepts in infancy. Significant progress, nevertheless, has been realized. We now know where to look for answers: the rudiments of veridical object concepts are evident in the first 6 months after birth. We know also the kinds of tools to use: assessments of eye movements, for example, and cortical development (e.g., recording EEGs) have revealed important hints to behavioral and physiological changes that accompany development of object concepts in young infants. The multipronged approach advocated in this article rejects polemic debates between the roles of nature or nurture, debates which, when it comes down to the details of developmental process, are ultimately meaningless. There is no pure case of development caused in the absence of either intrinsic or external influences. The question is what mechanisms are responsible for perceptual and cognitive development. There are many mechanisms, and, therefore, no one correct approach to the question of development of the object concept.

See also: Cognitive Development; Cognitive Developmental Theories; Habituation and Novelty; Neonativism; Piaget's Cognitive-Developmental Theory; Symbolic Thought.

Suggested Readings

Atkinson J (2000) *The Developing Visual Brain.* New York: Oxford University Press.

Cohen LB (1998) An information-processing approach to infant perception and cognition. In: Simion F and Butterworth G (eds.) *The Development of Sensory, Motor, and Cognitive Capacities in Early Infancy: From Perception to Cognition*, pp. 277–300. Hove, East Sussex, UK: Psychology Press.

Diamond A (1990) The development and neural basis of memory functions as indexed by the AB and delayed response tasks in human infants and adult monkeys. *Annals of the New York Academy of Sciences* 608: 267–317.

Elman JL, Bates EA, Johnson MH, Karmiloff-Smith A, Parisi D, and Plunkett K (1996) *Rethinking Innateness: A Connectionist Perspective on Development.* Cambridge, MA: MIT Press.

Gibson EJ (1988) Exploratory behavior in the development of perceiving, acting, and the acquiring of knowledge. *Annual Review of Psychology* 39: 1–41.

Johnson SP (2003) The nature of cognitive development. *Trends in Cognitive Sciences* 7: 102–104.

Piaget J (1954) *The Construction of Reality in the Child* (M. Cook, Trans.). New York: Basic Books (Original work published 1937).

Spelke ES and Newport E (1998) Nativism, empiricism, and the development of knowledge. In: Damon W and Lerner RM (eds.) *Handbook of Child Psychology, Vol. 1: Theoretical Models of Human Development*, pp. 275–340. New York: Wiley.

Perception and Action

B I Bertenthal, Indiana University, Bloomington, IN, USA

© 2008 Elsevier Inc. All rights reserved.

Glossary

Action system – Functionally organized action requiring continuous and dynamic perceptual modulation of the many factors (i.e., inertia of limbs, posture, direction, and distance of target) necessary for executing a response.

Affordance – Perceptual information about an object or surface specifying a possibility for action. This information is only perceived if the action is within the motor repertoire of the actor.

Coordination and control – Coordination involves organizing the multiple parts of a goal-directed action into proper relation with one another. For humans, coordination is a formidable task that involves almost 800 muscles that act to generate and dissipate energy at approximately 100 joints. Control involves tuning the specific parameters of a movement (e.g., displacement, amplitude, and speed of limb movements) to the local conditions in order to optimize coordination.

Embodied knowledge – Pragmatic or sensory–motor knowledge about the physical or social world that enables a spatially coordinated action even when the goal is not conscious or continuously visible. This knowledge can be contrasted with symbolic knowledge that involves a representation of the world that can be mentally transformed and linguistically coded.

Haptic perception – An active tactile process (pertaining to touch) that involves both sensory and motor systems to identify an object. In the human hand, tactile information is provided by the receptors in the skin, the muscles, and the joints. For example, if we hold a cube, we perceive it through the skin of our fingers and the position of our fingers.

Mirror neurons – These neurons are located in the ventral premotor cortex of the monkey's brain and discharge when the monkey performs a goal-directed action, as well as when the monkey observes a conspecific or human experimenter perform the same action.

Perceptuomotor scaling – The timing and force of motor responses are modulated by the relevant perceptual information. Each response is different (e.g., crawling vs. walking) and necessitates a different scaling between the perceptual information and the response synergies (i.e., interactions between the components of the response, such as muscles, limbs, joints, etc.).

Predictive tracking and reaching – Pursuing a moving target that disappears behind another object or surface and anticipating its reappearance based on the spatiotemporal information specifying the movement of the target prior to its disappearance.

Proprioception – The sense of position and movement of the limbs that is derived from sensory receptors in the joints, tendons, and muscles. This information is used to specify the orientation of the body in space and the direction, extent, and rate of movement of the limbs.

Simulation – Representing an observed action performed by someone else by covertly activating the same action in one's motor system.

Introduction

Traditional research on motor development focused primarily on how movements were generated by 'motor programs' in the central nervous system. The Russian physiologist, Nikolai Aleksandroich Bernstein (1896–1966) was one of the first to recognize that spatially coordinated behaviors involved more than simply programming muscular responses, because other factors such as inertia of the limbs, reactive forces from the support surface, and initial postural conditions always combine with active muscle forces in producing complex chains of multisegment movements. All of these factors, or degrees of freedom, necessitate that active muscle forces are modulated by a combination of different sources of perceptual information specifying the self and the environment to ensure a functionally organized and goal-directed response.

As actions continue to change over time so will the modulation of the perceptual information. In essence, perception and action form a continuous loop in which, according to James Gibson (1904–79), "we must perceive in order to move, but we must also move in order to perceive." All spatially and temporally coordinated behaviors require the coupling of perception and action. For example, reaching for an object is guided by perceptual information specifying the relation between the self and the environment which changes as the reach progresses. These perceptual changes produce adjustments to hand and arm movements to insure that a reach is successful, which, in turn, modify the perceived relation between the reach and the target. Similarly, perceptual information is necessary to maintain a balanced posture during the reach, but again the perceptual information changes as the posture is adjusted to that information.

This cycle of perceptual changes and motor responses is dynamic and continuous. Neither perception nor action alone is sufficient to simultaneously maintain postural stability and perform goal-directed actions. Moreover, each time the same action is performed (e.g., reaching for a glass), the initial conditions between the actor and the goal (e.g., distance and size of the glass, posture, inertia of the limbs) will differ requiring variations in the movements and the response.

In view of these many factors that must simultaneously contribute to the execution of a goal-directed action, it would be misleading to conceptualize perception and action as independent processes. Instead, it is much more parsimonious to view these processes as opposite poles of a functional unit or action system. The earliest developing action systems will be those related to supporting biologically adaptive functions, such as orientation, exploration, locomotion, manipulation, and communication.

Origins of Perception–Action Coupling

When are perception and action first coupled? Until recently, the answer to this question was dominated by Jean Piaget's (1896–1980) view of sensorimotor development. He proposed that perceptions and actions are initially independent but become gradually coordinated with experience. The implication is that the behavior of the neonate is essentially reactive and not sensitive to contextual information. More recent findings from studying infants reveal a very different picture of the early behavioral organization of the young infant.

Perceptuomotor Behavior of Neonates

Newborn infants are capable of performing a number of actions that are regulated by perceptual information. For example, they turn their eyes in the direction of a sound, visually scan differently in the light and the dark and concentrate their fixations near high contrast edges, visually track moving targets, increase the frequency of hand-to-mouth contact following oral delivery of a sucrose solution, and show hand extensions toward a visible target. Until the availability of more sensitive instruments for measuring neonatal responses, these behaviors were often overlooked because they are quite fragile and inconsistent. For example, one reason that neonates show difficulty in tracking moving targets is that their heads are not yet independent of their trunks which are quite unstable and subject to intermittent movements.

It thus appears that newborns enter the world prepared to perceptually control some actions, especially those that are essential to their survival and adaptation. This preparation is a function of both the intrinsic organization of the brain, as well as behaviors that are practiced in the uterus. For example, the proprioceptive guidance of the hand to the mouth is established in utero by the beginning of the second trimester of pregnancy, and is readily observed in neonates. Furthermore, the mouth is more likely to remain open during arm movements when the hand goes directly to the mouth than when it first touches other portions of the face. The opportunity to practice this behavior in the uterus no doubt contributes to the degree of specificity that is present in its control at birth.

Some behaviors may not be practiced *in utero*, but nevertheless show a rudimentary perceptuomotor coupling from birth that is necessary for their functioning. Indeed, newborns are intrinsically biased to move their arms in such a way that their hands remain in the field of view. While lying supine with arms pulled down by small weights, newborns will resist this force on the side of the body to which their head is turned (see **Figure 1**). Interestingly, the resulting posture is consistent with a neonatal reflex, known as the tonic neck reflex, and is similar to the posture assumed by a person fencing. This behavior is not, however, simply a function of a reflex, because infants viewing a video monitor localized on one side but displaying the opposite hand, resist the weight with the hand opposite to the direction in which they are looking. Moreover, newborns viewing their hand in a dark room

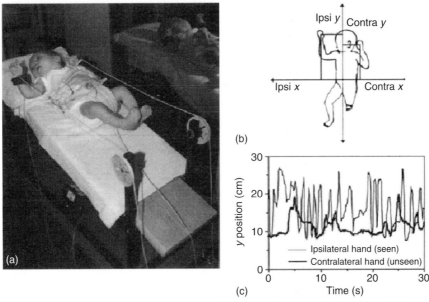

Figure 1 (a) An 18-day-old baby participating in the experiment. (b) Schematic representation of how the hands were measured in terms of *x* and *y* coordinates. (c) A typical time series showing the changing *y*-axis location of both arms waving without weights attached. Reprinted with permission from van der Meer ALH, van der Weel FR, and Lee DN (1995) The functional significance of arm movements in neonates. *Science* 267: 693–695. Copyright (1995) AAAS.

keep it positioned within a narrow beam of light and move their hand when the beam moves. This behavior is extremely adaptive because it biases infants to visually explore information that can be gathered by one of the principal information acquisition devices available from birth – the hands. In sum, infants are born prepared to coordinate their movements with perceptual information, especially when the coupling will benefit their acquisition of new information about themselves and their environment.

Even though some actions are spatially coordinated from birth, this coordinative pattern represents only a skeletal structure that will continue to develop for a long time to come. The development of perception–action systems involves a confluence of factors that include neural and biomechanical changes, as well as task and environmental factors. As infants continue to practice performing these actions, they will develop improved coordination and control. In the case of sucking, these changes take place very quickly. Within a few days after birth, the sucking system functions with considerable precision to optimize the intake of nutrients. Neonates learn very quickly to adjust the change in sucking pressure to the flow of milk that changes from suck to suck. They can also learn to modify their sucking in an experimental situation that provides them with access to their mother's voice. By 5 weeks of age, infants can use sucking as a means to bring a picture into focus. These latter two examples show that even early action systems are not limited to specific biological functions and that they can be used as a means to an arbitrary goal, such as listening to the mother's voice, as well as serving to fulfill an intrinsic goal, such as gaining nutrients.

Adaptation to Changes in Brain and Body

Although practice and experience are certainly necessary for the development of these action systems, they are not sufficient because the developing infant is also changing in body size and strength and the brain is developing as well. For example, the optical components of the eye are still growing at birth, the photoreceptors will continue to mature and migrate toward the center of the retina (i.e., fovea) during the first few months, and the synaptic connections between neurons of the central visual pathways in the brain will continue to develop for some time. These changes will improve the resolution of the visual image, which will contribute to improvements in the accommodation and convergence of the eye, as well as greater acuity for perceiving visual patterns. Likewise, the perception of relative depths and distances in the spatial layout will become more precise with the neural development of the visual system.

A more specific example of how the incompletely developed visual system constrains the functioning of an action system involves the saccadic localization of visual targets. When young infants detect a visual target flashing or moving in the peripheral portion of their visual field, they will move their eyes to center their gaze on the target. This movement involves a direct mapping between the retinal location of the target and the neuromuscular stimulation of the appropriate eye muscles, which changes as a function of the distance of the eyes from the visual stimulation. This mapping is present from birth, yet the localization process is imprecise and involves multiple saccades (rapid eye movements that jump from one location to another) before the target is foveated. It is not until 4 months of age that localization is accomplished with a single saccade. One factor contributing to this development is learning the precise relation between the neural pulse duration innervating eye muscles and the saccade magnitude necessary for rotating the eye to the correct position. Nevertheless, it is surprising that the calibration process takes over 4 months to complete, especially since it is estimated that infants make between 3 and 6 million eye movements by 3.5 months of age. It has been hypothesized that the reason for this lengthy process is that the mapping of retinal locus onto an oculomotor command is constrained by the changing distribution of photoreceptors on the retina. This situation makes it necessary for the infant to adapt continually to this changing sensorimotor relation during early development.

Although some action systems are present at birth, it is clear that many others will develop in the months and years to come, and all of them will become better tuned and coordinated as a function of both neural development and experience. In the remainder of this article, we will discuss some of the organizing principles by which this development occurs with illustrative examples from the different action systems that play a pivotal role in early development.

Principles of Perception and Action

Reciprocity between Perception and Action

Sensitivity to surfaces and objects

Perceptual control of behavior depends on the detection of the relevant perceptual information, as well as the coordination of responses necessary for the action system. As simple actions, such as pursuit tracking of moving targets, saccadic localization, or hand–mouth coordination are practiced and repeated, they become better controlled and coordinated, which demands that the necessary perceptual information is detected with increasing specificity. An excellent example of this mutual reciprocity between perception and action is revealed by research on the minimum audible angle necessary for detection of a change in sound-source location. In this task infants are expected to turn their heads to the right or left of midline if they are capable of localizing the sound. The minimum detectable difference decreases rapidly between 8 and 24 weeks of age and then continues to decrease more gradually through 80 weeks of age. It is noteworthy that the most rapid improvement occurs during and just following the time that infants are developing independent control of their heads and torso. Until they develop enough control to stabilize their heads, it is not possible for them to localize a sound source with sufficient resolution to differentiate sounds that are close together.

Another compelling example of the reciprocity between perception and the improved coordination of actions involves haptic perception. Adults detect many different properties of objects, such as size, texture, weight, hardness, and temperature, from haptic explorations. In the case of a blind individual, touch would serve as the principal means for learning about the material properties of objects. Some of these properties, such as size and temperature, demand minimal control of the hand and fingers, whereas other properties, such as weight and shape, require much greater control. Intriguingly, the ages at which infants first discriminate different object properties correspond to the developmental changes in the control of the hand and fingers. For example, infants discriminate size within the first few months, but texture, temperature, and hardness which involve tactile exploration are not detected until around 6 months of age, and weight and shape which involve grasping and lifting are not detected until even later.

In the preceding two examples, motor development facilitated the perceptual sensitivity of infants to the properties of surfaces and objects over time. There are two other sources of perceptual information that are involved in the development of actions. One source is proprioceptive and it involves the positions, orientations, and movements of body segments relative to each other. The final source is the perceived relation between self and environment and it involves the position, orientation, and movement of the whole or a part of the body relative to the environment. Let's consider how motor experience contributes to these two latter sources of perceptual information.

Sensitivity to movements of the body

The development of self-produced locomotion on hands-and-knees involves a rather protracted period of development. Most infants begin to crawl with their abdomens on the ground by around 7 months of age. During this initial period of crawling, infants show considerable variability in their locomotor strategies and explore many different patterns of interlimb coordination, including pulling themselves with only their hands, or lurching forward by pushing up with their legs, or moving one limb at a time, or even moving all four limbs at the same time. The support of their abdomens on the ground enables infants to engage in any interlimb pattern of movement without risk of losing balance or falling. During this period of development, they are able to explore a wide variety of different interlimb patterns for locomoting.

Once infants develop sufficient strength to support themselves on hands-and-knees, they quickly converge on an interlimb pattern of moving diagonally opposite limbs (e.g., left arm and right leg) simultaneously and 180° out of phase with the other pair of limbs. The selection of this specific pattern is a function of perceiving the optimal coordinative structure to ensure balance while minimizing the expenditure of energy. These are intrinsic goals that drive the infant to select the optimal locomotor gait pattern from among the many variations that were previously explored. This process by which behaviors go through a period of considerable variation before a stable new organization develops is repeated often in development, and is especially common in the development of motor skills, such as stepping, sitting, and standing.

Sensitivity to the relation between self and environment

The last source of perceptual information is concerned with the relation between the body and the environment. Does the development of self-produced locomotion contribute to infants' sensitivity to this source of information? This question has been addressed by investigating whether prelocomotor and locomotor infants are differentially sensitive to whether a surface is traversable. Although some surfaces are more easily traversed than others, for example, a roadway vs. a narrow footpath along a mountainside, most afford some form of locomotion. One dramatic exception is a surface that ends abruptly at a precipice or cliff.

This type of surface has been simulated in the lab with a 'visual cliff', which consists of a large sheet of plexiglass suspended 4 ft above the floor (see **Figure 2**). A narrow board is placed across the middle, dividing the plexiglass into two sides. On one side (referred to as the shallow side), a textured checkerboard pattern is placed directly under the glass, so that it appears as a rigid and supportable surface. On the other side (referred to as the deep side), the checkerboard pattern is placed 4 ft below the glass, so that this side simulates an apparent drop-off. In most studies, infants are placed on the centerboard and encouraged to cross to the mother who alternates standing across from the deep and shallow sides of the cliff. The question of interest is whether infants will be less likely to crawl across the deep side than the shallow side of this apparatus.

The visual cliff was designed originally to test depth perception, but more recent research suggests that infants are sensitive to depth information prior to the age when they begin crawling. If avoidance of the deep side of the cliff was specifically a function of depth perception, then all infants should avoid the deep side from the earliest age at which they could be tested. This is not what is observed, however. Infants' avoidance of the deep side is related to their crawling experience – infants who have been crawling for 6 weeks are much more likely to avoid the deep side of the visual cliff than infants who have been crawling

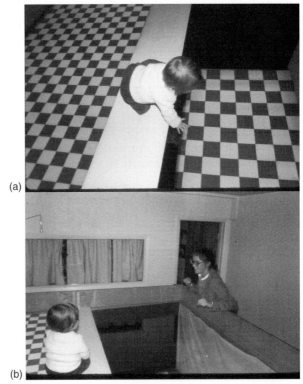

Figure 2 A photograph of the visual cliff with the baby sitting on the centerboard. (a) Baby is looking down at the edge of the apparent drop off; (b) baby is looking across the deep side of the cliff at the mother.

for only 2 weeks. Converging evidence come from studies measuring infants' heart rate as they are lowered toward the deep or shallow sides of the visual cliff. Prelocomotor infants show heart rate deceleration (indexing interest and attention) to the depth information as they are lowered onto the deep side of the cliff. By contrast, locomotor infants with a few weeks of crawling experience show heart rate acceleration (indexing wariness or fear).

Why is perceptual information about the traversibility of surfaces interpreted differently by locomotor and prelocomotor infants? The answer is that the information specifying the apparent drop-off is only perceived as something to avoid when it is relevant to controlling the action of locomotion. If infants are not yet able to locomote, then this perceptual information can still be perceived, but it will not be perceived as a danger because this appraisal is specifically related to locomoting beyond the apparent drop-off. In essence, the visual cliff surface represents an 'affordance', or a possibility for action. This affordance is only perceived if the action is available to the infant. Thus, the perception of affordances and the motor status of the infant are intimately related.

Infants learn to perceive affordances for locomotion from their everyday crawling and walking experience. As infants acquire more experience with crawling, they become more accurate in perceiving whether or not these surfaces afford traversability. For example, infants become more accurate with experience in choosing which sloping surfaces can or cannot be descended. Moreover, their perception of the traversability of surfaces changes when the possibility for locomotion is manipulated by loading them with weights or extending their leg length with platform shoes. Similarly, varying the slant, friction, or rigidity of the support surface, etc., also alters the perceived possibilities for locomotion.

The preceding perceptual judgments are all scaled to the motor capabilities of infants. This is an important point to emphasize because it implies that the learning of specific perceptuomotor skills cannot be generalized. The perceptual learning that accrues during the period of crawling is not transferred to upright locomotion. At the onset of walking, infants who avoid steep slopes when crawling show no hesitation in attempting to walk down these same slopes. Perceptual learning of affordances is highly specific and the mapping between vision and posture that emerges with the development of crawling will require a new mapping with the development of walking. This lack of transfer is not surprising given that each new form of locomotion involves a different set of response synergies that need to be coordinated and controlled by the perceptual information.

In sum, the development of perception and action is reciprocal. Improvements in the tuning of perceptual sensitivities enable finer control of motor responses. Likewise, changes in body size and shape, strength, postural control, and coordination of multiple body parts enable perceptual experiences that were heretofore unnecessary or unavailable. These changes in perception and action are cyclic and repetitive, and enable infants to continually improve their fit between their own action capabilities and the perception of their bodies and the affordances in the environment.

Planning and Prospective Control

Significance of future-directed information
Our actions, like those of all animals, must be coordinated with the physical and social environment, and this coordination demands perceptual guidance and control. In walking along an unpaved, narrow path, for example, we select which surfaces to contact and which to avoid. Likewise, when reaching for a fork, we guide our hand to select this utensil and simultaneously avoid or inhibit our hand from reaching for the spoon or knife. These actions are accomplished in real time and their control requires more than feedback following their execution. It is only possible to modify a movement that has not yet been executed, which is why it is necessary to predict what will happen next and prospectively control the action. Information needed for the specification of upcoming events is available from the spatial and temporal changes in the optic and acoustic arrays. As adults, we readily appreciate the spatial and temporal components in the control of actions. For example, we know that it is necessary to be in the right place at the right time to catch a ball, meet a person, or give a lecture. Likewise, infants show considerable sensitivity to the spatiotemporal coordination necessary for the control of actions.

Unlike neonatal reflexes that are automatically triggered by specific stimuli (e.g., Moro reflex – extensions of arms and legs with loss of support), actions are goal directed and they often involve multiple body parts that are hierarchically organized into a single system. For example, the eyes, head, and trunk must be coordinated when tracking a moving target that continues beyond the immediate field of view. Thus, actions must be scaled to the spatial and temporal changes in our body, as well as in the external world. Even a simple reach for an object requires the ability to predict what will happen next to the moving limb, as well as to the object that is to be grasped. Prospective control involves implicit knowledge of the body schema, as well as knowledge of the spatiotemporal regularities that govern physical and social events in the external world.

Smooth visual pursuit tracking
What sorts of prospective information are available to infants and how is this information used for controlling their behavior? One of the earliest examples of prospective behavior involves the smooth visual pursuit of moving targets. In order to track an object smoothly it is necessary to anticipate its future position from its past history of movement, because the motor commands for moving the eyes in response to the movements of the target are not instantaneous but delayed by the inertia of the eye, as well as the rate of neural transmission. Smooth pursuit is present from birth, but it is intermittent and limited to large targets. As the eyes begin to trail the target, infants' eye movements become jerky because they are forced to execute corrective saccades (rapid eye movements from one fixation to the next). Beginning around 6 weeks of age, smooth pursuit improves rapidly and attains adult levels by 14 weeks of age for targets that move smoothly and gradually slow down before reversing directions. By 20 weeks of age, infants successfully track targets that cycle back and forth and abruptly change direction.

This evidence for early pursuit tracking is even more remarkable when one considers that it often requires the coordination between head movements and eye movements. Some head movements are unrelated to fixation, and both visual and vestibular mechanisms are involved in compensating for these movements to some extent from birth. Between 3 and 5 months of age, head movements increase in response to a moving target, but for quite some time lag behind the target because of the greater inertia associated with the head. In order to stabilize gaze on the target, the eyes must lead the target to counteract the delayed head tracking. Thus, smooth pursuit involves the coordination of eye tracking and head tracking which continues to improve as infants develop better control of their heads and greater sensitivity to target velocity.

Reaching for stationary and moving objects

A similar pattern of jerky and inconsistent movements accompanies the initial development of reaching which begins sometime between 12 and 18 weeks of age. When adults reach for a stationary object, they execute a single movement unit characterized by the arm initially speeding up and then slowing down as it approaches the target. The trajectory of the arm movement is smooth and precise requiring only a slight adjustment at the end to grasp the object. By contrast, infants initially execute multiple movement units as their reaching arm gradually approaches the object; each movement unit brings the hand closer to the object, but the reach takes longer and is more circuitous. Over the next few months, the reach becomes better scaled to the distance and location of the object reflecting the development of an ensemble of factors including neuromuscular mechanisms, the control of posture, improved distance perception, and a more precise mapping between perceptual information and the motor responses necessary for executing the reach.

At approximately the same age that infants begin reaching for stationary objects, they begin catching objects attached to a moving rod. By 4.5 months of age, infants can catch an object moving at $30\,\mathrm{cm\,s}^{-1}$, and by 8 months infants can catch objects moving at $125\,\mathrm{cm\,s}^{-1}$. Successful catching requires that the infant predict the future location of a moving object and program arm and hand movements to arrive at that location just prior to the arrival by the object. Infants typically reach for a stationary object with their ipsilateral hand (corresponding to the same side of the body midline as the object), but they will often switch to their contralateral hand when catching an object oscillating back and forth in front of them. The choice of the contralateral hand insures more time to execute the arm and hand movement before the arrival of the object, and thus represents additional evidence of prospective control by infants.

Predictive tracking of briefly occluded moving objects

One of the critical skills necessary for predictive tracking and reaching is the prediction of the future location of a moving target. If a moving target is briefly occluded, it is necessary for the observer to represent the object's trajectory in order for the eyes to anticipate where the target will reappear. Tracking is predictive if, after following a moving target before occlusion, infants shift their gaze to the far side of the occluding surface before it reappears. This visuomotor behavior begins to emerge between 3 and 5 months of age depending on the width of the occluder, the duration of occlusion, and the velocity of the target.

Jean Piaget suggested that predictive tracking is an epiphenomenon of motor persistence – the prediction of the reappearance of the target is a function of failing to stop tracking when the target disappears rather than a function of representing the continuity of the target's trajectory. Recent evidence reveals, however, that motor persistence cannot account for such predictive tracking, as infants rarely track smoothly and continuously once the target disappears. Instead, they tend to stop and fixate on the occluding edge for a brief period of time, and then make one or two saccades to the other side of the occluder. In addition, infants predictively track along circular trajectories by 6 months of age, but this is also inconsistent with a motor persistence explanation which suggests that tracking should follow only a straight line trajectory.

Another possibility is that prediction develops from some form of contingency learning. Infants as young as 2–3 months of age learn to predict sequential alternations of targets appearing in two locations. This same type of learning is probably not sufficient, however, for explaining infants' predictive tracking of a moving target, because the likelihood of this response increases following 2 min of visual experience with an unoccluded object. During this familiarization period, the moving object is always visible so there is no opportunity for learning the contingency that a target disappearing in one location would reappear some time later in another location. Instead, it appears that infants extrapolate from the preceding spatiotemporal information to predict the reappearance of the target. In other words, infants represent the trajectory of the moving target to predict its future location.

One of the most important spatiotemporal properties of objects concerns the way they appear and disappear behind nearer objects. Consider, for example, a typical street scene where pedestrians and vehicles are continuously appearing and disappearing from view as they move, or you, the observer, moves. Adults interpret moving objects that disappear gradually behind an occluding surface as continuing to follow the same trajectory; moving objects that disappear abruptly or implode (shrink rapidly in size) are interpreted as following a discontinuous path. In a recent experiment, 5–9-month-old infants were observed tracking these different events (see **Figure 3**). The results revealed that they were more likely to predictively track a moving object that disappeared naturally (via occlusion) than unnaturally (via abrupt disappearance or implosion) (see **Figure 4**). These results are significant because they show that infants predict the reappearance of objects based not only on their trajectories and the location of the occluding surfaces, but also based on the spatiotemporal changes associated with their disappearance.

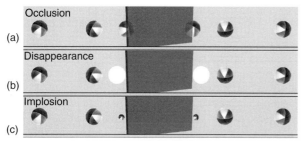

Figure 3 The three horizontal panels depict the location and appearance of the rolling ball at different times during the stimulus event. (a) Occlusion. The ball gradually disappears behind the right side of the occluding surface (located in the center of the display), and then after 2 s reappears from behind the left side of the occluding surface. Note that the shaded portion of the ball is meant to depict its nonvisible portion behind the occluding surface. (b) Instantaneous disappearance. The ball abruptly disappears when it reaches the location of the white circle and abruptly reappears 2 s later at the location of the second white circle on the other side of the occluding surface. (c) Implosion. The rolling ball rapidly decreases in size as it approaches the occluding surface and rapidly increases in size as it reappears 2 s later on the other side of the occluding surface. Note that the ball completes disappearing or begins reappearing at the same exact time that the ball abruptly disappears or reappears in the instantaneous disappearance event. Reproduced from Bertenthal BI, Longo MR, and Kenny S (2007) Phenomenal permanence and the development of predictive tracking. *Child Development* 78: 350–363, with permission from Blackwell Publishing.

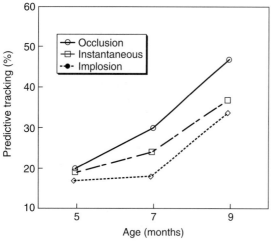

Figure 4 Mean percent tracking as a function of age and stimulus condition (occlusion, instantaneous disappearance, implosion). Reproduced from Bertenthal BI, Longo MR, and Kenny S (2007) Phenomenal permanence and the development of predictive tracking. *Child Development* 78: 350–363, with permission from Blackwell Publishing.

Embodied knowledge

Infants do not necessarily represent the identities and spatial locations of moving objects at the same age they represent the trajectories. Even 9-month-old infants sometimes fail to notice a change in the identity (e.g., shape, color) of a moving object following a brief occlusion. (Interestingly, this finding is as true for adults as it is for infants because the same spatiotemporal information specifying the continuity of an object can sometimes obscure a change in its featural identity – a phenomenon known as change blindness.) Likewise, infants around the same age sometimes fail to represent the spatial location of a moving object during a brief occlusion. For example, 9-month-old infants can predictively reach for a briefly occluded moving object. If, however, the object does not reappear, infants search in a variety of locations but do not search behind the occluding screen, suggesting that they do not represent the spatial location of the hidden object at the same time that they represent its trajectory. In sum, infants developing representations of objects emerge piecemeal rather than all at once.

In this section, we have emphasized prospective control of smooth pursuit and visually directed reaching, but there are many other examples of prospective control that develop within the first year. For example, infants learn to posturally compensate for a loss of balance, lean toward objects that are out of reach, anticipate the size, shape, and orientation of objects that they are attempting to grasp, and guide their locomotion around obstacles. It is often suggested that infants become successful across all these tasks as they develop the capacity to represent future events. This interpretation is partially correct, but it is not the whole story.

Knowledge of the future is embodied in the specific actions performed by infants. Prospective control depends upon the developing coordination and control of multiple body parts that are continuing to change in size, shape, flexibility, and strength in conjunction with the perceptual and cognitive information necessary to forecast future events and plan adaptive actions. Thus, future-oriented behaviors emerge piecemeal from specific experiences that infants encounter through their actions. It is the dynamic interplay between actions and goals in specific contexts and tasks that fosters the development of prospective control.

Perception and Action are Context Specific

As previously discussed, actions are a product of a multiplicity of factors including physical, physiological, and energetic components. Different tasks and contexts make different demands on these components, and thus the same action will not necessarily be observed in different contexts. For example, some neurologists report that pre-reaching movements by neonates are much better coordinated when the head is stabilized than when it is unsupported. This finding is especially important because it illustrates how passive support from the environment can interact with the active control and coordination of body movements.

Coordination of leg movements

One of the best examples of context specificity in the control and coordination of actions involves the alternating step-like movements of neonates when held upright with the balls of their feet touching a flat surface. Within a few months, these movements disappear when infants are held upright, but not when infants are lying on their backs or stomachs. These differences can be explained by a simple biomechanical calculation showing that more energy is needed to lift a leg to full flexion while upright than while supine. Although gravity is a constant force in the environment, it only becomes a constraint after the newborn period when infants begin experiencing rapid weight gains that decrease the ratio of muscle to subcutaneous fat in the legs. Experimental manipulations that change the weight of the legs or the resistance of the leg to flexion (e.g., submerging infants in torso-deep water) show that the presence or absence of stepping is systematically related to the interaction between physical strength and leg resistance. These experimental manipulations highlight the importance of context in determining whether or not a specific action will be observed at a particular age.

The development of reaching in different postures is another example of the context specificity of motor control. Coordinated reaching is only possible in the context of a stable body posture that also enables stabilizing the visual target. When infants incapable of sitting without support (22–26 weeks of age) are placed in a fully supported posture (e.g., supine or reclined), they tend to reach for objects with both hands. By contrast, infants capable of sitting without support (28–38 weeks of age) reach with one hand, regardless of body posture. The younger infants reach with only one hand when placed in an unsupported seated position, because they must compensate for a loss of balance by recruiting the other hand to help stabilize their body in this position. In this context, infants shift to a different response because the demands on balance are different, not because they have undergone a change in neural or muscular control.

Scaling perceptual information to motor responses

Another reason for the importance of context specificity is that successful performance requires scaling the changing perceptual information to a specific motor response. The scaling learned in one context does not automatically generalize to new motor responses in the same or different contexts. This lack of generalizability explains why crawling infants who have learned whether or not it is safe to traverse surfaces that are sloped at different angles are unable to transfer this learning a few months later to walking down these same surfaces. As a consequence, infants must relearn whether or not it is safe to traverse these surfaces when walking as opposed to crawling.

This same lack of generalizability is observed with regard to using visual information to control posture. In adults, posture is specified by proprioceptive, vestibular, and visual flow information. It is a goal-directed behavior, even though it is typically not consciously controlled. The goal is to maintain a stable body posture relative to some frame of reference usually specified by gravity and the surface of support. When a perturbation of this position is sensed, a postural compensation is initiated. This perturbation can be specified by one or more sensory inputs, such as visual motion, which is sufficient to induce a postural compensation. When an observer sways forward, visual information radially expands in the optic array, and this expansion typically leads to an automatic postural compensation in the opposite direction. Likewise, swaying backward results in visual information radially contracting and inducing a compensation in the opposite direction.

Some postural compensations are even elicited by neonates. When reclined newborn infants are stimulated by radially expanding patterns of visual information observed on video monitors, they show sensitivity to this information by pushing back with their heads. These compensations are detected by a pressure transducer and are scaled to the speed and direction of the visual motion. In other words, infants apply more backward force to their heads as the visual motion information is perceived as moving faster. Although this finding suggests that infants are already sensitive to optical flow information for controlling posture at birth, it is still necessary for them to learn how to compensate to visual motion information for controlling other postures, such as sitting and standing.

A good deal of the research on the development of postural control has involved a 'moving room' (see **Figure 5**). In this paradigm, the infant sits or stands on a stationary floor while the walls and ceiling move forward and backward. This movement produces visual flow information congruent with the head and body moving in the opposite direction, and induces a compensation of the infant's posture. Sitting infants begin to show compensations at 7–9 months of age, a period that straddles the development of this posture. During this period infants show improvements in the speed and consistency of these compensations suggesting that some period of time is necessary to learn to regulate the amount of force necessary to compensate for the perceived displacement. Similarly, infants begin to show compensations while standing between 12 and 15 months of age, but these compensations are not present immediately with the development of independent stance. Some period of learning to scale the new response synergies to the optical flow information is required before infants show the ability to maintain their balance when perturbed by the moving room. In sum, infants must learn to modulate or control each new motor response *de novo*, even if the perceptual information

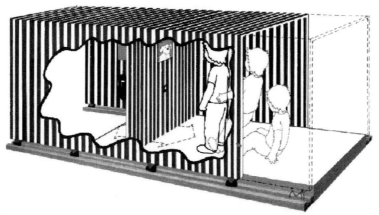

Figure 5 Schematic drawing of the moving room apparatus. As the walls move toward the infant, self-motion in the opposite direction is perceived inducing a postural compensation in the same direction as the walls are moving. As the walls move away from the infant, the opposite response is induced. Reproduced from Bertenthal BI, Rose JL, and Bai DL (1997) Perception-action coupling in the development of visual control of posture. *Journal of Experimental Psychology: Human Perception and Performance* 23(6): 1631–1643.

(e.g., optical flow for specifying postural sway) is readily detected and processed.

Development of reaching in the light and dark

Before concluding this section, there is one important caveat that should be discussed. Context specificity is important only if the changes contribute to the assembly of the action. At face value, this point is obvious, but there are many nonobvious examples in development. Consider, for example, young infants reaching for objects in the light or the dark. Historically, the prevailing view has been that reaching is initially visually guided, but more recent studies show that infants reach as accurately in the dark for sounding or glowing objects as they reach in the light for the same objects.

In one longitudinal study testing infants between 6 and 25 weeks of age, infants first contacted the object in both conditions at comparable ages (light – 12.3 weeks; dark – 11.9 weeks), and they first grasped the object in the light at 16.0 weeks and in the dark at 14.7 weeks. Infants could not see their hands or arms in the dark suggesting that proprioceptive information was sufficient to guide reaching. Additional studies reveal that there are no differences in the reaching of young infants even when more precise kinematic measures (speed, number of movement units, straightness, etc.) are used.

By contrast, adults and even 15-month-old infants show significant differences when reaching in the light and dark. These differences are most likely attributable to the specificity of the reaches. Whereas adults and 15-month-old infants scale their reaching and grasping to the size and shape of the object, infants, just beginning to reach, apply the same undifferentiated response to all objects. Thus, contextual differences relating to the ability to see the arm and hand do not affect the reaching behavior of young infants because scaling the reach and grasp to match the size and orientation of the object is not yet integrated into the organization of this behavior.

Action Understanding

Common coding of the observation and execution of actions

Recent neurophysiological, neuroimaging, and behavioral evidence suggest that perception and action share a common representation or code for the observation and execution of actions. This common code implies that visual percepts of observed actions are mapped directly onto our motor representation of the same action. As a consequence, an action is understood when its observation leads to simulation (i.e., representing the responses of others by covertly generating similar responses in oneself) by the motor system. Thus, when we observe a hand grasping a glass, the same neural circuit that plans or executes this goal-directed action becomes active in the observer's motor areas. It is the motor knowledge by the observer that is used to understand the observed goal-directed action via covert imitation.

Although this theory for explaining how we understand actions dates back to the 1890s and the ideomotor theory of William James (1842–1910), direct evidence supporting this view emerged only recently with the discovery of mirror neurons in the ventral premotor cortex of the monkey's brain. These neurons discharge when the monkey performs a goal-directed action, as well as when the monkey observes a human or conspecific perform the same or a similar action. Thus, these neurons provide a common internal representation for executing and observing goal-directed action. Human neuroimaging and transcranial magnetic stimulation studies have shown activation of a homologous frontoparietal circuit during both the observation, as well as the imitation of actions.

This neurological evidence is complemented by recent behavioral evidence showing that the observation of actions facilitates or primes responding to similar actions. For example, people automatically and unconsciously mimic each others' gestures when they are casually talking to each other. Also, people tend to respond more quickly to a stimulus when the response involves imitation as opposed to some arbitrary action. The availability of specialized processes in the brain for mapping perceived actions onto the motor system suggests that infants should be intrinsically prepared for directly matching the observation and execution of actions.

Simulation and understanding of actions

Some of the best evidence for this matching system in infants comes from observing their perseverative search errors. In the classic, Piagetian A-not-B error, 8–12-month-old infants first search correctly for an object they see hidden in one location on one or more trials, but then continue to search at that same location after seeing the object hidden in a new location. Recent accounts of this error emphasize the role of repeated reaching to the initial location. If an observation–execution matching system is functional in young infants, then simply observing someone else reach repeatedly to the same location should be sufficient for eliciting this error. This prediction was confirmed when 9-month-old infants observed a human agent hiding and finding the object, but not when they observed two mechanical claws performing the same actions. It thus appears that this matching system is limited to actions performed by human agents. Moreover, this error was restricted to observing the experimenter hiding and finding the toy with her ipsilateral hand. At this age, infants are biased to use their ipsilateral hand when reaching for objects, and thus their motor experience with their contralateral hand is less developed. A consistent finding with adults is that covert simulation of observed actions is limited to those actions that are within the motor repertoire of the observer, and the same qualification appears to apply to infants as well.

Direct matching between the observation and execution of actions enables not only covert simulation but prediction of the outcome or effects of the action. When adults perform a goal-directed action their eyes precede their hands in moving toward the goal. Likewise, when observing someone else perform a goal-directed action, the eyes move to the goal before the agent completes the action. Twelve-month-old infants show similar anticipatory eye movements when observing goal-directed actions (i.e., placing objects in a container) performed by a human agent, but not when observing a 'mechanical motion' event in which the objects move without the intervention of a human agent. These differences between the observation of human actions and mechanical events suggest that the observation–execution matching system is specific to the perception of human actions.

An important principle of the direct matching theory is that actions are understood in terms of their goals and not their movements. For example, human infants understand that the goal structure of an action is based primarily on the object toward which it is directed. By contrast, the way in which the action is accomplished is less important. For example, infants differentiate between a human agent reaching and grasping for two different objects, but do not differentiate between reaching and grasping for the same object even when it involves a new path or a new location. Six-month-old infants are sensitive to this difference, but 3-month-old infants are not. If, however, the younger infants are given a few minutes experience reaching with 'sticky mittens' (allowing them to artificially grasp small objects), then they, too, discriminate between a change in the goal of the action and a change in the movement of the action. It thus appears that even minimal experience with a goal-directed action is sufficient for infants to map their observation of the action onto some preliminary motor representation of the action. Currently, it is unclear whether this preliminary motor representation is transient or persists for some extended period of time and could be reinstated with additional motor experiences.

Developmental origins of common coding

It is very likely that some version of the direct matching system is functional from birth. Newborn infants imitate oro-facial gestures (mouth opening and tongue protrusion), even though they've never seen their own face. The origins and developmental trajectory of this behavior are consistent with an observation–execution matching system.

It is well established that fetuses perform mouth opening and closing and tongue protrusion while *in utero*. Thus, these gestures are already part of the neonate's behavioral repertoire at birth. The evidence also suggests that neonates are more likely to match the modeled gesture after it has been presented for some period of time (~40 s), rather than immediately. This finding is consistent with a motor simulation explanation in which activation would be expected to build up gradually as the gesture is observed, as opposed to an explanation predicting an immediate response because of the availability of higher-level processes from birth. Finally, the empirical evidence suggests that the likelihood of automatic imitation increases until around 2 months of age, and then declines and virtually disappears by 5 months of age. It is during this same window of time that neonatal reflexes are gradually inhibited, suggesting that similar cortical inhibitory processes may serve to suppress neonatal imitation.

As the spontaneous elicitation of these overt facial gestures becomes gradually inhibited with age, they do not disappear entirely. Instead they become subject to volitional control such that the infant determines when and how they are elicited – imitation is no longer automatic, and the observation of a facial gesture will not necessarily lead to its execution by the infant. Thus, rather than reflecting a precocial social ability of the infant as suggested by some theorists, neonatal imitation may reflect a striking inability of the infant to inhibit activation of the motor system by direct matching mechanisms. Similar compulsive imitation is observed in adults after lesions of areas of the frontal lobe involved in inhibitory control, and even in healthy adults when attention is diverted.

Although overt imitation of facial gestures ceases with the development of inhibition, covert imitation continues and provides specific knowledge about these gestures when observed in others. Very recent evidence suggests that this same developmental process is played out at different ages for many other important behaviors (e.g., gaze direction, visually directed reaching and grasping, vocalizations of sounds). As these behaviors are practiced, the infant develops greater control of their execution, as well as knowledge of their effects or outcomes. The development of these motor schemas enables infants to covertly simulate and predict the effects of similar actions performed by others. This reliance on the developing control of self-produced actions explains why action understanding continues to develop with motor experience.

Change Mechanisms

Recent research on the development of perception and action offers new insights into how behavior changes with age and experience. In contrast to conventional views of behavioral development which emphasize stable patterns of performance that are interrupted by temporary and abrupt changes, new findings emphasize that variability is often present in the performance of infants and contributes to both further development and greater flexibility in different situations. Although we typically associate variability with the outcome of an action (e.g., location of a thrown dart relative to the bull's eye), it is also related to the execution of an action (e.g., relative coordination of eye, hand, and feet in throwing the dart). Both sources of variability are relevant to the development and improvement of new behaviors.

Variation and Selection

Variability in behavior is always present, but its function changes with age and experience. Consider, for example, visual control of posture while sitting in a moving room. When 5-month-old infants are tested they show large and random amplitudes of postural sway, but this variability declines significantly by 7 months of age. Surprisingly, this variability increases again at 9 months of age. The reason for this flip-flop is that 5-month-old infants cannot control their balance while sitting, whereas most 7-month-olds are learning to sit without support. During the learning of a new skill, infants, as well as adults reduce degrees of freedom by stiffening some joints to minimize unsafe and poorly controlled limb movements. By 9 months of age, infants are more secure with their new sitting posture and they reduce muscle stiffness, which results in greater amplitudes of postural sway. In this example, the variability in maintaining a balanced posture is first attributable to poor control of the necessary response synergies, but later variability is attributable to the need for greater flexibility to compensate for postural perturbations. Additional examples of increased variability in movement patterns accompanying the development of new levels of behavioral organization include toddlers learning to descend slopes and infants stepping on motorized treadmills.

One question unanswered by the above examples is how infants learn new perception–action couplings. The traditional view is that infants are prescribed by some genetic plan or abstract cognitive structures to follow a fixed and sequential progression of stages in the development of new behaviors. A radically different proposal is that learning follows a stochastic process (i.e., probabilistic as opposed to deterministic outcome) in which a multiplicity of developmental factors (e.g., neurological, physical, cognitive, social) induce new forms of behavior. As infants explore new behaviors that emerge with organismic (e.g., increases in muscle strength or improvements in distance perception) or environmental changes (e.g., maintaining balance against gravity in more challenging postures or responding to new task demands by parents), a distribution of implicit (e.g., minimization of energy) and explicit (e.g., intentions) goals motivate the infant to store and repeat those actions that are optimally successful.

An excellent illustration of this process is observed in infants' learning to reach. Initially, reaching for an object involves a number of discrete movement units that decrease over time. Infants initially show considerable variability in the direction and amplitude of each movement unit, but this variability decreases as they learn to select those movement units that optimize performance. It thus appears that the development of smoother and more accurate reaching is consistent with a self-organizing system in which specific visuomotor mappings are selected from a much larger distribution in order to optimize the goal of contacting the object.

Summary

Infants engage in goal-directed and exploratory behaviors from birth, and their actions become better coordinated as the perceptual information becomes more differentiated and mapped to more specific response synergies. In turn, the development of new and more complex responses requires greater perceptual specificity and greater prospective control. This mutuality and reciprocity between perception and action demands that the development of new behaviors is dynamic and multidetermined. In contrast to earlier views of behavioral development reflecting patterns of stability interrupted briefly by transitions to new behaviors, the development of perception and action show significant periods of variability in real and developmental time. This variability introduces new movement patterns or actions for achieving specific goals and also offers greater flexibility in adapting actions to task demands.

See also: Brain Development; Cognitive Developmental Theories; Future Orientation; Imitation and Modeling.

Suggested Readings

Adolph KE and Berger SE (2006) Motor development. In: Kuhn D and Siegler RS (eds.) *Handbook of Child Psychology, Vol. 2: Cognition, Perception, and Language*, 6th edn., pp. 161–213. New York: Wiley.

Bertenthal BI and Longo MR (2008) Motor knowledge and action understanding: A developmental perspective. In Klatzky R, Mac-Whinney B, and Behrman M (eds.) *The Carnegie Symposium on Cognition, Vol. 34. Embodiment, Ego Space, and Action*, pp. 319–364. Mahwah, NJ: Erlbaum.

Bertenthal BI, Longo MR, and Kenny S (2007) Phenomenal permanence and the development of predictive tracking. *Child Development* 78: 350–363.

Bertenthal BI, Rose JL, and Bai DL (1997) Perception-action coupling in the development of visual control of posture. *Journal of Experimental Psychology: Human Perception and Performance* 23 (6): 1631–1643.

Clifton RK, Rochat P, Robin DJ, and Berthier NE (1994) Multimodal perception in human infants. *Journal of Experimental Psychology: Human Perception and Performance* 20: 876–886.

Thelen E (1995) Motor development: A new synthesis. *American Psychologist* 50: 79–95.

van der Meer ALH, van der Weel FR, and Lee DN (1995) The functional significance of arm movements in neonates. *Science* 267: 693–695.

von Hofsten C (2003) On the development of perception and action. In: Valsiner J and Connolly KJ (eds.) *Handbook of Developmental Psychology*, pp. 114–171. London: Sage Publications.

Relevant Website

http://www.sidgrid.ci.uchicago.edu – Social Informatics Data Grid.

Piaget's Cognitive-Developmental Theory

J P Byrnes, Temple University, Philadelphia, PA, USA

© 2008 Elsevier Inc. All rights reserved.

Glossary

Accommodation – Changing a mental structure in order to assimilate a new idea.

Assimilation – The mind's ability to incorporate an experience or new information into an existing mental structure.

Concrete operational thought – A representational form of thought characterized by reversibility, the ability to consider two dimensions, hierarchical categorization, and seriation; focused on concrete reality rather than hypothetical possibilities.

Conservation – A belief that the amount of something stays the same despite superficial transformations in the appearance of an object or array of objects.

Constructivism – The belief that concepts are neither inborn nor immediately learned through exposure to the world; rather, knowledge is build up, step by step.

Empiricism – The belief that knowledge can be acquired through the senses.

Equilibration – Restoring the balance between assimilation and accommodation.

Formal operational thought – A representational, reversible, multidimensional, and abstract form of thought; focused on both concrete reality and hypothetical possibilities.

Functionalism – A belief in the goal-directed and adaptive nature of thought.

Nativism – The belief that concepts are inborn.

Object permanence – Understanding that an object continues to exist even when it is out of view.

Preoperational thought – A nonreversible form of representational thought that is unidimensional and grounded in perceptual similarity.

Reflective abstraction – Contrasts with simple abstraction in which the properties of objects (e.g., its redness) are merely 'read off' the objects. As children coordinate actions to achieve certain ends, the mind discovers commonalities across these coordinations, reorganizes and reconstructs them, and projects this construction onto a higher plane of thought.

> **Reversibility** – A quality of thinking in which an observed transformation can be mentally 'undone'.
> **Schemes** – Goal-directed behaviors that are repeatedly utilized in situations to discover the properties of objects.
> **Sensorimotor thinking** – Objects are understood with respect to what actions can be performed on them; limited to the here and now.
> **Structuralism** – A belief in the importance of discovering the inherent organization and the form and content of thought.

Introduction

It is sometimes said that one of the hallmarks of genius is the ability to recognize the deep significance of seemingly ordinary phenomena that are 'right under everyone's noses'. Many of the phenomena that Jean Piaget examined have been well known to parents and early childhood educators for hundreds of years. For example, most parents have probably hidden a toy under a pillow to see if their toddlers will search for it, or heard their child say "I think the moon is following us" as they travel at night in a car or train. Piaget's unusual insight was these phenomena were manifestations of characteristic kinds of thinking in children; in other words, children's behaviors had a lot to say about the kinds of knowledge structures that they held in their minds. In addition, however, Piaget moved well beyond these naturally occurring behaviors by probing children's minds using a variety of novel experimental tasks. His explanations of children's spontaneous and elicited behaviors resonated with some scholars, but evoked strong criticism from many others. Regardless of whether scholars were trying to support or disconfirm his account, Piaget's work influenced several generations of researchers by identifying the kinds of competencies that should be investigated at specific ages. For example, few developmental psychologists examined phenomena such as object permanence or conservation of mass before Piaget brought these competences to the attention of developmental psychologists. Moreover, criticism of his methodologies likewise prompted many to devise extremely clever procedures to reveal competences at ages earlier than he found. Piaget's theory was particularly revolutionary to scholars of the infancy period in that it was one of the first to provide a detailed account of infant cognition and tried to show the continuities between infant and later cognition. Even 26 years after his death, Piaget's works are still cited over 2000 times per year.

Although it is not feasible to provide a comprehensive summary of Piaget's work in a brief encyclopedia entry, it is possible to present some of the main themes of his work and the controversies that these themes evoked.

Major Themes

The following four themes capture the essence of Piaget's perspective. (1) Of the three possible epistemological stances regarding the origin of knowledge (i.e., nativism, empiricism, and constructivism), constructivism is the most viable and compelling alternative. (2) The development of children's thinking can be described as a progression through four levels or stages of thought. (3) Of the various epistemological stances regarding the nature of knowledge (e.g., structuralism, functionalism, behaviorism, and connectionism), structuralism and functionalism are the most viable and compelling alternatives. (4) Of the four factors that explain the changes in thought that occur over time (i.e., biological maturation, physical experience, social exchange, and equilibration), equilibration is the most significant. In what follows, these themes are discussed in turn.

Constructivism. When Piaget first began his career in the 1920s, he had recently finished his graduate studies in the area of philosophy. His interest in philosophy affected all aspects of his subsequent empirical work in the area of cognitive development in the sense that he collected data to largely show that the two primary philosophical perspectives on the origins of knowledge, that is, empiricism and nativism, were incorrect. Empiricists such as philosopher John Locke and psychologist Edward Thorndike believed that people's minds are 'blank slates' when they are born, though the mind has an inherent ability to form associations between events that co-occur in the environment and can be perceived through their senses. For example, if a father nearly always wears his favorite hat when he goes out, the sight of his hat hanging on a hook may cause his children or spouse to think of him. Empiricists believe that events in the world have a natural regularity to them that is registered in the mind (e.g., the cycle of day followed by night). Thus, empiricists would argue that people could develop a concept of time by merely observing the cycles of days, months, seasons, and so forth.

Nativism is the polar opposite of empiricism. Nativists such as the philosopher Immanuel Kant and linguist Noam Chomsky believe that the world is neither regular nor organized. In addition, they argue that conceptual relations (e.g., causality and time) could not be sensed in the same way that colors or temperature could be sensed. Together, these two beliefs imply that concepts could not be acquired through simple exposure to the world. If the latter proposition is true, then it follows that the vast majority of important concepts must be inborn. As such, these concepts should be evident in a newborn or emerge in an all-or-none fashion at a particular point in time as a child's brain matures. Nativists suggest that people are born with concepts of causality, time, space, and so on in order to make sense of stimulation that makes no inherent sense.

After much reflection and experience testing children, Piaget found problems with both empiricism and nativism. As a result, he created a third alternative: constructivism. He agreed with the nativist view that people have concepts that they impose on the world to make sense of it but disagreed with the claim that these ideas were inborn. He agreed with the empiricist view that the world has a certain regularity and structure to it that children come to know through experience but disagreed with the idea that concepts are learned immediately through exposure to the world. His middle-ground stance was that exposure to the world and children's activities cause them to create mental precursors to more fully developed ideas. He felt that children's minds take these precursor components and continually build more sophisticated ideas out of them.

For example, when children are born, they lack voluntary control over their arm and hand movements. Everything is reflexive. Soon, however, they gain some voluntary control and begin creating 'grasping' and 'pushing' schemes out of reflexes (hence, reflexes serve as precursors to the schemes). Schemes are goal-directed behaviors that are repeatedly utilized in situations to discover the properties of objects. Early on, the grasping and pushing schemes are not interconnected. By around 8–12 months, however, a child who wants an attractive toy hidden behind a barrier can combine the grasping and pushing scheme together in order to retrieve the toy. Children are not born with this knowledge of how to put the two schemes together, nor can they be taught this earlier in the first year even though they have the two schemes. Children themselves think of putting the two schemes together to attain a goal (i.e., get the toy). Later on, the act of counting objects will serve as a precursor to the mathematical idea of sets, and grouping actions will serve as a precursor to mental addition and subtraction. Still later, children will combine addition and subtraction together with the insight that subtraction is the opposite of addition. In effect, actions have a certain logical structure to them that serve as a template for conceptual relations.

As a second example, consider Piaget's meticulous characterization of the slow, progressive acquisition of the concept of object permanence in infants. Infants who understand object permanence recognize that an object continues to exist even when it is out of view. Object permanence is not something that could be sensed, so it poses immediate problems for empiricists. However, if it could be shown that infants are not born with this idea either, or that it does not emerge in an all-or-none manner, such findings would be a serious blow to Kant's nativism as well. Kant used the example of the concept of space as a prototype for the claim that people are born with mental structures that help them organize their sensory experiences. One cannot have a concept of space unless one has a concept of objects and the space between these objects. If Piaget could show that children are not born with a concept of permanent objects, he would show that Kant was wrong about children being born with a concept of space.

Piaget documented six substages in the acquisition of object permanence that occur between the ages of birth and approximately 18 months. Each successive substage represented a small but significant advance on earlier understandings. These findings suggest that (1) object permanence is not present from the start (as nativists would predict), (2) it does not appear to be learned immediately (as empiricists would predict), and (3) it does not emerge in an all-or-none fashion at one point in time (as maturational empiricists would predict). Instead it truly develops, in Piaget's view.

In the first two substages, the infants confronted with hidden objects either seem oblivious to their disappearance or simply continue to stare at the location where an object was last seen before it disappeared. In the third substage, the infant may now look for an object that has, for example, fallen off her highchair instead of merely staring at the location where it fell off. However, the child may give up if the object is not immediately found and will not attempt to retrieve a desired object that is placed under a blanket in full view. In the fourth stage, the child will finally search for the hidden object placed under a blanket but makes an interesting error when the object is placed successively under two blankets in turn: instead of looking under the second of the two blankets, the child looks under the first (the so-called A-not-B error). In the fifth substage, the child no longer makes the A not-B error, but will not engage in search behaviors when the movement of the object to specific locations is not observed. For example, imagine a setup in which a child watches as an adult places a small desired toy inside a cup. The adult next moves the cup behind a small screen and surreptitiously dumps the toy out of the cup behind the screen. When the adult's hand re-emerges at the other side of the screen and the child looks inside the now empty cup, she does not immediately look behind the screen. By the sixth substage, however, infants finally do engage in search behaviors even when invisible displacements are used (as in the cup example).

In Piaget's view, all of the major concepts that he investigated are built up or constructed in this step-by-step manner. Eventually, children acquire the kinds of conceptualizations that are evident in adults. He documented the various substages in all of his books on the development of specific concepts. Note that Piaget did not deny the existence of inborn capacities (e.g., he recognizes that reflexes are inborn) or the capacity of the mind to acquire rote associations (as he pointed out in his book on memory). His point was that the full-blown, adult versions of concepts such as object permanence, causality, class inclusion, conservation, number, space, and time were neither inborn nor learned through associative mechanisms involving the senses.

Four levels of thought. Having identified the small steps that occur in the development of major concepts between birth and adulthood, Piaget then grouped chronologically arranged sets of these achievements into four levels of thought: sensorimotor, preoperational, concrete operational, and formal operational. For some concepts, for example, the first six substages that emerge between birth and 18 months might be called sensorimotor thinking, the next six that emerge between 18 months and 5 years of age might be called preoperational thinking, and so on. Each level is characterized by how children view the world.

When the world is viewed from the standpoint of sensorimotor thinking (birth to about 18 months of age), objects are understood with respect to what actions can be performed on them. For example, a bottle, a toy, and a finger are all the same because they are 'suckables'. In addition, sensorimotor thinking is limited to the here-and-now. Children who can only reason at the sensorimotor level (e.g., infants or severely retarded older students) cannot think about the past or things that might happen in the future, according to Piaget. They simply perceive objects in current view and try to use a motoric scheme to interact with these objects.

After motoric schemes have been repeated many times to attain goals, children's minds form abstract, mental versions of these schemes. As a result, children can imagine themselves doing something before they do it. Once children can think in this representational way, they have moved into the preoperations level (begins around 18–24 months of age). In addition to being able to imagine future events, children can also think about things that happened to them in the past. Thus, preoperational children are freed from the here-and-now. Piaget called this kind of thought representational in the sense that children can re-present absent objects to their consciousness for consideration. Children who look for the hidden toy in the cup example described earlier do so because they imagined the dumping action of the adult. Thus, the sixth substage for object permanence is actually preoperational thought. Although preoperational thinking is more advanced and more adaptive than sensorimotor thought, it is limited in four ways. First, it has overly strong ties to perception, perceptual similarity, and spatial relations. For example, some 3-year-olds believe that a family exists only when the family members hug. When they are spatially separated, the family no longer exists. Similarly, many preschoolers think that an arrangement of five pennies spread out in a row contains more pennies than a pile of five pennies.

When preschoolers mentally group things, they rely heavily on perceptual similarity. For example, they think that 'dogs' and 'horses' are both 'doggies' and that 'goldfish' and 'whales' are both 'fishies'. Grouping things by perceptual similarity, of course, is not a good idea because few categories are defined this way. For example, categories such as 'doctor', 'country', 'dictator', 'polynomial', and 'acid' are not defined by the visual appearance of members of these categories. Most categories in fields such as science, mathematics, and social studies are defined in a nonperceptual, abstract way. As a result, a Piagetian perspective predicts that the real definitions of these categories would be difficult for preschoolers to grasp.

The second limitation of preoperational thinking, according to Piaget, is that it is unidimensional; that is, children can think about only one aspect of something at a time. For example, when they are asked to sort objects into categories, they use just one dimension (e.g., size) rather than multiple dimensions (e.g., size and color). In addition to studies of categorization, Piaget revealed unidimensionality in his many studies of conservation. Conservation is the belief that the amount of something stays the same despite superficial changes in appearance. In his classic 'beaker' task, for example, children are shown two short, wide glasses that have the same amount of juice. When the juice of one is poured into a taller thinner glass, the level of the juice is higher than in the remaining short glass. Preschoolers only attend to the height of the glasses and not the width in judging which of two glasses has more juice in it. After pouring, they think the tall glass has more juice even though they just said the two short glasses had the same amount. Beyond these conservation examples, it is easy to show how many concepts that are presented in school are multidimensional (e.g., the definition of a 'square' or a 'republic'), so this second limitation would cause problems for students if it persisted after preschool. The tendency to focus on just one dimension or view things only from one's own perspective has been called centration.

The third limitation of preoperational thought, according to Piaget, is that it is irreversible; that is, preschoolers often cannot mentally imagine something that has just be done (e.g., a ball of clay being rolled into a sausage) being 'undone' (e.g., the sausage being rolled back into a ball). Piaget likened this limitation to a movie projector that cannot play movies in reverse. Again, most subjects in school contain ideas that involve reversibility. In math, for example, addition is the opposite of subtraction and '-5' is the opposite of '5'. In history classes, it is common to speculate whether some trend could ever be reversed (e.g., Russian citizens going back to repressive communism after tasting freedom and capitalism). Hence, preoperational children tend to think of things in terms of their static configuration instead of thinking of them in terms of a dynamic, reversible transformation.

The fourth limitation of preoperational thinking, according to some early works of Piaget, is that children have difficulty distinguishing between reality and fantasy.

For example, they sometimes have difficulty telling the difference between real people and television characters, and also are bothered by nightmares that seem awfully real.

For Piaget, these four limitations of preoperational thinking are overcome when children develop the concrete operational mode of thought around age 5 or 6. In particular, concrete operational children are no longer limited to using perceptual similarity when they group things. However, although children can understand somewhat more abstract properties, these properties still must be something one can point to or concretely describe (e.g., 'warm-blooded' for 'mammals'). In addition to going beyond mere perceptual similarity, concrete operational children also do not confuse spatial arrangements with actual quantities. For example, they know that rolling a round clay ball into a sausage shape has no effect on the amount of clay present. In addition, children can think about two dimensions at once and can also mentally 'undo' a real event that has happened. Hence, concrete operational thought is marked by its reversibility. Finally, concrete operational children do not confuse reality with fantasy and are more concerned with playing games by the rules than with assimilating the world to their own fanciful desires. In fact, they seem to be overly concerned with 'the way things are'.

In some cultures, thinking that is (1) freed from perceptual relations, (2) reversible, (3) two dimensional and (4) realistic would be sufficient for full adaptation to that culture. In most industrialized cultures, however, people apparently need more than that if Piaget is correct in his assertion that minds adapt to the demands placed on them. For example, many things in school require comprehension of more than two dimensions and the ability to go beyond reality to think about hypothetical possibilities (e.g., give a reasoned answer to questions such as, would the Vietnam war have ended earlier if President Kennedy had not been assassinated?). Moreover, some ideas cannot be defined by pointing to something or using concrete descriptions (e.g., the fourth dimension; conservatism; the 'limit' of a function). Students who can think about multiple dimensions, hypothetical possibilities, and abstract properties are capable of the formal operations level of thinking (begins usually around age 10 or 11 years).

One further way to characterize the differences in thinking that occur with age is to consider two overarching assumptions of Piaget's theory: (1) thinking becomes increasingly abstract with development and (2) thinking becomes increasingly logical with development. By abstract, Piaget meant, removed from immediate perception and action. Thinking that is closely tied to perception or action is lower-order thinking (e.g., sensorimotor or preoperational thought). Thinking that is less tied to perception and action is higher-order thinking (e.g., concrete and formal operational thought). Moreover, as a child moves between one level of thought and the next, his or her thinking becomes more abstract because each stage transition produces thinking that is one step further removed from immediate perception and action. Thus, preoperational thought is more abstract than sensorimotor thought because the former is one step removed from immediate perception. Similarly, concrete operational thinking is more abstract than preoperational thinking because it is two steps removed from immediate perception, and formal operational thought is more abstract than concrete operational thought because it is three steps removed.

When children reach the concrete operations level for some content area, they are capable of reasoning with symbols that do not resemble their real-world referents. For example, the symbol '3' does not resemble a collection of three objects and the word 'animal' does not look like any particular animal (unlike mental images that may actually resemble their referents). In freeing the mind from particular concrete referents, children can think about the symbols themselves. Thus, although the symbol '3' can refer to a set of three apples or three trucks, one can ignore which objects it refers to in, say, judging that when one takes away one object from any set of three objects, one is always left with two objects (no matter what those objects are). Then, when children reach the formal operations level, symbols can stand for sets of symbols. For example, 'X' can stand for '3', '4', or any other number.

In order to be ultimately capable of abstract reasoning, Piaget argued that children need to interact with objects or actual content. For example, preoperational children need to count actual sets of objects and form many sets of three things in order for their mind to create structures that help them comprehend symbols such as '3'. In particular, through the process of reflective abstraction (see glossary for definition), children's minds abstract across sets of object-oriented actions to form schematic representations of set size. Similarly, they need to work on many sets of arithmetic problems (e.g., $3 + 4 = 7$) before their mind will abstract a schema that would promote an understanding of algebraic formulas (e.g., $x + y = z$). In essence, experiences with objects, arithmetic sentences, and so forth are the 'grist' for the schema-abstraction 'mill'. Thus, Piaget would argue against the idea that nothing should be done to promote abstract thinking until children reach a certain age. Rather, he would argue that children should be given experiences that help them construct precursory ideas to later ideas. Abstract thinking will not emerge on its own without ample experiences.

As for the second assumption that thinking becomes more logical with age, Piaget meant that thinking literally conforms to the canons of logic. Long before Piaget did his experiments, philosophers devised laws and theorems that were argued to be universal truths. One such theorem was the assertion that 'If $A > B$ and $B > C$, then $A > C$.' Piaget was well versed in logic and was quite surprised to see that 7-year-olds could make such transitive inferences long before students are exposed to the idea of transitivity in logic or math courses. In a typical task, a child might be shown an array of three sticks that increase in size. The apparatus is such that the relative sizes of sticks can only be seen two at a time. First, stick A and stick B are uncovered to reveal that stick A is larger than stick B; Then, stick A is covered again while stick B and stick C are now exposed, revealing that stick B is larger than stick C. Whereas a preoperational child would have to examine each item mentioned in a transitive statement in order to reach the correct conclusion (e.g., look at all three sticks simultaneously to know that the first stick is larger than the third), concrete operational children would know the answer without actually comparing the first and third item (e.g., the first and third stick).

In addition to transitive inferences, concrete operational thought conforms to logical analyses in two other ways. First, philosophers have claimed that logical thinking requires that things be classified in such a way that valid inductive and deductive inferences can be drawn. To insure the validity of categorical inferences, it is important to have correct definitions of categories such as 'squares' or 'mammals'. The definition of 'squares' is correct if it properly includes all of the things that are squares and properly excludes all of the things that are not squares. According to a classical perspective in philosophy, the best way to create correct definitions is to use lists of necessary and sufficient attributes. For squares, for example, the necessary and sufficient attributes are that the object has to have (1) four sides, (2) equal sides, and (3) 90° angles. Anything that has all three attributes is a square and anything that lacks one or more of these attributes is not a square. Piaget argued that whereas preoperational children categorize things together if they merely look similar (e.g., a trout and a whale are both fish), concrete operational children categorize things using necessary and sufficient criteria. Thus, once again concrete operational thought is more logical than preoperational thought.

The third way that concrete operational thought is more logical pertains to the notions of negation and reversibility. Concrete operational children connect categories and operations to their opposites. For example, all of the things that are 'dogs' are grouped together with all other animals that are not dogs through the superordinate category of 'animals'. This hierarchical grouping allows a child to fully comprehend class-inclusion relations (e.g., that dogs and cats are both animals). In addition, each mental operation is linked to an opposite operation that 'undoes' the former. For example, addition is linked to its opposite, subtraction. By linking things to their opposites, children gain a sense of logical necessity. That is, they feel that their deductions must be true. Thus, when asked, "If all of the dogs in the world were to die, would there be any animals left?", concrete operational children would say, "Of course! Dogs are not the only kind of animals!"

Formal operational thinking extends the logical aspects of concrete operational thinking in new ways. In the first place, inductive, deductive, and transitive inferences can now be applied to both real things and hypothetical ideas. In addition, children become capable of performing valid experiments because formal operational students examine combinations of variables and use the isolation of variables (IOV) technique to test their hypotheses. The IOV technique involves varying only one factor while holding all other constant. Moreover, the abstract quality of formal operational thought helps children to step back from a chain of inferences and judge the validity of these inferences, regardless of the content. For example, consider the syllogism, 'All frogs are mammals. Mammals are warm-blooded. Therefore, frogs are warm-blooded.' Even though the content of this syllogism is factually incorrect (frogs are not mammals), formal operational thought helps an adolescent or adult ignore this fact and recognize that the conclusion follows if we temporarily assume the truth of the prior premises.

Structuralism and functionalism. Historical analyses of Piaget's 60-year career suggest that there were periods of time in which he alternated between his structuralist and functionalist tendencies. Whereas nativism, constructivism, and empiricism have to do with the origin of knowledge, structuralism, and functionalism have more to do with the nature of knowledge. For Piaget, a structuralist is someone who examines multiple instances of some phenomenon, identifies the inherent organization of parts within this phenomenon, and uses formalisms to describe this organization. For example, linguist Noam Chomsky examined large numbers of declarative sentences (e.g., 'Bill eats red apples' and 'The burly man hit the small dog') and noted that they all had the same basic structure: a sentence (S) can be decomposed into a noun phrase (NP) and a verb phrase (VP). In formulaic terms, this abstraction could be written as S $\rightarrow$ NP + VP. The formula represents the form of the structure and the specific words (e.g., 'Bill') represent the content that fills in the placeholders or variables in the formula (e.g., NP). Piaget argued that all mental structures have both form and content. The form stays the same but the content varies.

For his part, Piaget identified the form and content of mental structures at each level of thought. For example, the form of sensorimotor structures is the scheme and the content is the objects that are acted upon by the scheme. At the preoperations level, Piaget proposed the existence of 'one way mappings' or representations that link beginning states to end states of some event in a unidirectional way. Later writings suggested that these mappings were not unlike mathematical functions such as $y = f(x)$. If an initial state of some apparatus were to be substituted for the 'y', an outcome state 'x' is the output of the function. Relying on such structures, children can be quite skilled at predicting outcomes after observing events for some time. However, these mental functions lack the ability to reverse (e.g., given the output, what was the input?). At the concrete operations level, Piaget emphasized form and content related to hierarchical categories and ordered series. For example, many categories can be expressed in the formalism, $A + A' = B$, in which A stands for a category (e.g., dogs), A' stands for its complement class (e.g., nondogs) and B stands for the superordinate category (e.g., mammals). In the case of ordered series, various objects can be arranged in terms of increasing magnitudes based on specific characteristics (e.g., height, weight, color, and loudness). These series can be represented using formalisms such as $A > B > C$, etc. At the formal operations level, Piaget emphasized logical relationships such as implication. Propositions such as 'If today is Tuesday, I have math class' and 'If an animal barks, it is a dog' can be represented using formalisms such as $P \rightarrow Q$ (i.e., P implies Q).

During his structuralist period, Piaget endeavored to characterize the mental structures of children and his books are full of formalisms to represent these structures. His major foray into functionalism came about shortly after his children were born and he searched the scholarly literature for plausible accounts of infant development. He discovered the work of American scholar James Mark Baldwin who was a key figure in the functionalist school of thought during the late 1800s and early 1900s. Piaget incorporated many of Baldwin's insights and constructs into his own theory (e.g., Baldwin coined the terms primary, secondary, and tertiary circular reactions). Functionalists differ from structuralists in their emphasis on the goal-directed and adaptive nature of thought. The functionalist perspective emerged on the heels of Darwinian theory in the late 1800s that emphasized the idea of adaptation to the environment. It also was created as a counterpoint to the structuralist perspective of the mid-1800s that seemed to ignore the usefulness of knowledge for solving real problems. Piaget's functionalist tendencies were evident in his books on infancy in two ways. First, he argued that intelligence is first manifested in development when infants combine schemes together to achieve goals at around 8–12 months of age. Second, he claimed that intelligence consists in transforming or adapting mental structures to make them more in line with reality.

What was unique about Piaget's perspective was that he attempted to integrate the structuralist and functionalist perspectives into a single account. That is, he tried to show that when certain structures emerge in development, children use these structures to attain goals and solve problems. Moreover, when children attempt to apply structures to a particular problem and discover the inadequacy of their solutions and ideas, this experience helps promote changes in these structures. In the next section, the latter notion is developed more fully.

Four factors of development. Developmental psychologists make a distinction between developmental states and developmental mechanisms. Developmental states are like snapshots that describe the current complement of skills possessed by an individual at a particular point in time. In Piaget's theory, the four levels of thought described above are examples of successive developmental states that children pass through. In addition to describing the succession of states, however, theories also posit developmental mechanisms that explain why it is that children progress from one state to the next (e.g., why children move from the sensory-motor level of thought to the preoperations level). Piaget's developmental mechanisms included four factors: biological maturation, physical experience, social exchange, and equilibration.

With respect to biological maturation, it is important to avoid common misconceptions about Piaget's stance toward this factor. The fact that children in developed countries demonstrate the four levels of thought at similar ages has led some to conclude that Piaget was a maturational nativist. In reality, Piaget did acknowledge the similarity of age changes as possibility having a maturational component but he also expected that all children would go through his four stages at roughly the same ages mainly because he assumed that the physical structure of the world was pretty much the same for all children. Hence, children's mental structures would tend to run up against the same reality regardless of whether they lived in Switzerland, the US, or Africa. As he argued in his 1983 chapter in the *Handbook of Child Psychology*,

> It is clear that maturation must have a part in the development of intelligence, although we know very little about the relations between the intellectual operations and the brain. In particular, the sequential character of the stages is an important clue to their partly biological nature and thus argues in favor of the constant role of the genotype and epigenesis. But this does not mean that we can assume there exists a hereditary program underlying human intelligence: there are not 'innate ideas' (in spite of what Lorenz maintained about the a priori nature of human thought). Even logic is not innate and only gives rise to progressive epigenetic construction. Thus, the effects of maturation consist essentially of opening new possibilities for development; that is, giving access to structures that could not be evolved before these possibilities were offered. But between possibility and actualization, there must intervene a set of other factors such as exercise, experience, and social interaction.

Thus, if children do not interact with the physical and social world, they will not develop the structures associated with Piaget's four stages by the time they reach physical maturity in adolescence. Thus, brain maturation is a necessary but not sufficient condition for the development of knowledge. However, as the preceding quote illustrates, experience interacting with objects is not sufficient either. He acknowledged that social exchanges between children and their parents, teachers, and peers often precipitated intellectual advances through the medium of language, but also pointed out that such exchanges could not account for the progressive changes that occur during the sensorimotor period or the shift between sensorimotor and preoperational thinking. In both cases, children are preverbal and unlikely to understand what other social agents are saying. It is for this reason and the insufficiency of the other three factors that he appealed to one further factor: the construct of equilibration.

'Equilibration' pertains to restoring the balance between two competing tendencies in the mind: assimilation and accommodation. Piaget used the notion of 'assimilation' to describe the process of incorporating experiences and information into existing knowledge structures in the mind. Metaphorically, children find a 'home' for this information in their existing knowledge structures. To say that a child has assimilated an idea or experience is to say that he or she understood the idea or experience. Piaget thought that mental assimilation was analogous to the biological assimilation that takes place when the human body extracts what it needs from food and incorporates the extracted nutrients into existing organs and tissues.

Sometimes an idea is so discrepant from what a child believes or knows that it cannot be assimilated. Piaget used the notion of 'accommodation' to describe the process of changing the existing configuration of knowledge in the mind in order that the troublesome idea can be assimilated. In most cases, assimilation is always partial in the sense that children only assimilate that portion of an experience that is consistent with their current understanding. Unless an experience or idea is identical to previous ones, every act of assimilation usually precipitates accommodation of knowledge as well. For example, when a child encounters a new species of dog for the first time and is told that it is a dog, this information finds a home in the existing network of ideas (i.e., it is assimilated), but the network is also changed as the child's mind creates a new representation corresponding to the new subtype of dog (i.e., there is accommodation).

In his book, *Play, Dreams, and Imitation*, Piaget argued that "...imitation is a continuation of accommodation, play is a continuation of assimilation, and intelligence is a harmonious combination of the two." This quote suggests that when one assimilates, one inserts one's own ideas into reality; when one accommodates, one's schemes and ideas come into closer conformity with reality and tend to be fairly direct copies of it. Play and fantasy, moreover, are examples of overassimilation (i.e., putting too much of one's ideas into reality). In contrast, children engage in overaccommodation when they try to directly copy the actions of someone (without putting their own 'spin' on the actions).

To illustrate assimilation and accommodation further, consider the following example. Young preschoolers who are passengers in their parents' cars often think that the moon is following them when they drive at night. The physics of the explanation of what is actually happening is too abstract for young children to comprehend, so they could not assimilate even this explanation if it were provided. Ultimately, however, their knowledge of the physical world will change enough that they may eventually understand the explanation as young adults.

Piaget argued that confronting discrepant ideas is absolutely essential for knowledge growth. If children never had experiences or heard information that contradicted the erroneous ideas that they construct by themselves, they would never develop the correct conceptions. Thus, the 'readiness' idea of waiting until a child's mind matures enough to teach a topic to them is actually an implication of nativism, not Piaget's constructivism. Piaget did not believe that ideas were inborn as nativists do; rather, he believed that children build up their ideas step by step.

Moreover, Piaget argued that assimilation and accommodation work in opposition to each other. The central tendency for assimilation is to keep the existing knowledge structure the same and find a place for new information in this structure. The central tendency for accommodation, in contrast, is to change the existing knowledge structure. It is not possible to keep things the same and change them at the same time. Thus, only one of assimilation or accommodation 'wins out' in a given situation. This 'battle' between these processes means that change in children's misconceptions can be frustratingly slow for teachers. That is, even when a misconception is repeatedly pointed out and explained to children, they may cling to the erroneous idea for some time. Perhaps this implies that assimilation normally takes precedence over accommodation. When the battle is resolved over some idea and a balance is restored between assimilation and accommodation (i.e., equilibration has occurred), children's understanding usually moves to a higher plane and often becomes more abstract as well. For example, in order for a child to come to understand that dogs and people are both animals, they have to change their concept of 'animal' in such a way that it is more abstract (e.g., 'a living thing that can move itself' from 'furry four-legged things').

Piaget argued that equilibration was particularly adaptive because the changes that are incorporated into mental structures are such that the mental system of ideas becomes capable of anticipating future problems that might arise. That is, the change not only allows a child to assimilate a particular idea that once was difficult to grasp, it also helps the child grasp related ideas that he or she has not yet encountered. In this way, equilibration works in a manner analogous to how the immune system creates structures (i.e., antibodies) that can deal with problems that arise in the future (i.e., re-occurrence of a virus that was encountered before).

Criticisms of the Theory

Although Piaget's account has enjoyed a certain degree of acceptance in fields such as developmental psychology and education (especially the latter), many psychologists began to challenge his claims and findings soon after his account was first introduced to American audiences in the early 1960s. At a general level, the majority of critics felt that the tasks used by Piaget to reveal various levels of competence were too difficult and underestimated what children knew. For example, some argued that infants who did not search under blankets in object permanent tasks might still understand that objects exist when not in view. Searching was an undue, extra burden on young infants, they argued. To reveal object permanence in nonsearching infants, critics created several clever apparatuses. In one, 3–5-month-old infants watched as a solid screen repeatedly rotated up and away from them through a 180° arc, in the manner of a drawbridge. The screen appeared to start by laying flat on a table with one side down. It rose up and completed its arc by resting again on the table with the opposite side now facing up (in the manner of a card being turned over in solitaire). After observing the screen make a complete arc a certain number of times, test trials began. Here, a box was placed in a position behind the screen that would normally interfere with the screen's movement such that it would rest and stop on the box, rather than complete its arc and rest on the table. Half of the trials were 'possible' events in which the screen did stop and rest on the box. The other half, however, were impossible trials that used a rigged box that could collapse into a flat surface. Here, the screen completed its 180° arc and rested on the table. To an observer, the box seemed to vanish. Infants were attributed an understanding of object permanence if they showed surprise expressions and looked longer at the impossible trials than the possible trials.

In studies of older children, some critics argued that Piaget's various conservation tasks were very misleading and tricked young children through perceptual illusions. They argued that tasks should be modified to be less misleading. For example, instead of showing children the level of liquid rising in a tall, thin beaker as the liquid is poured from a short, wide beaker, the tall beaker should be hidden from view as the liquid was poured. Other critics felt that Piaget used too strict of a criterion in many of his tasks by not only requiring a right answer, but also requiring appropriate explanations and the ability to resist being persuaded by arguments to the contrary.

Thus, they often created nonverbal versions of his tasks in which children could merely point to the correct answer.

A third way to counteract Piaget's suggestion that a child of a certain age could not understand a particular concept was to conduct training studies in which correct answers and verbal feedback were provided on repeated trials. For example, a child who initially failed to realize that the amount of clay in a clay ball is not increased when it is rolled into a sausage shape, might be asked to repeatedly weight the clay before and after the transformation, or be given a verbal rule of some sort (e.g., 'Even though it looks like it has more, it really doesn't').

In the 1960s, 1970s, and 1980s, training studies and studies using modified Piagetian tasks routinely revealed apparent competences in age groups younger than Piaget found. For example, whereas Piaget suggested that object permanence did not typically emerge until around 8 to 12 months of age, researchers using modified versions of object permanence tasks (e.g., the screen task described above) revealed an apparent understanding in 5- and 6-month-olds. Similarly, whereas Piaget revealed concrete operational skills in 5- to 8-year-olds using his original tasks, researchers using training tasks and modified versions of Piaget's tasks (e.g., nonverbal tasks) revealed apparent competence in 4- to 7-year-olds. As more and more of such findings emerged in the literature, the standing of Piaget's theory in the field of psychology began to diminish.

Other problems for the theory grew out of findings that suggested that:

1. Children who succeed on one measure of concrete (or formal) operations do not always succeed on other measures of concrete (or formal) operations; if competence is task-specific rather than domain-general, the notion of children being in a 'stage' of thought loses its credibility and meaning.
2. Only about 40% of adolescents and adults pass Piaget's original formal operations tasks; if passage through the four stages is a universal consequence of interacting with the physical and social world, all adolescents and adults should attain the level of formal thought.
3. Children and adults do not seem to base their mental categories on necessary and sufficient criteria; rather, categorization is based on the formation of prototypes for each category (e.g., robin in the case of bird) and the presence of characteristic features that most but not all members of the category have.
4. Young preschool children have less trouble differentiating fantasy and reality than Piaget suggested.

To all of the aforementioned empirical problems for the theory, influential philosophers and linguists have also argued against the theory on logical grounds. In most cases, these critics have had strong nativistic orientations that led them to take issue with Piaget's constructivism.

For example, philosopher Jerry Fodor argued that constructivism is logically impossible. His thesis centered on Piaget's suggestion that children eventually acquire mental systems that have a logico-mathematical character to them. Fodor made the interesting observation that Piaget seemed to be saying that children acquire increasingly powerful mental 'logics' in which each successive logic was able to account for more truths about reality. But just as Gödel's famous mathematical proof showed that it is impossible to derive a more powerful logical system out of a less powerful logical system (e.g., model logic out of truth functional logic), it is impossible to derive formal operations out of concrete operations. Anything that is new about formal operations could not be present in concrete operations. If anything new does emerge, then, it must have been 'known' all along. Hence, Fodor argued that the only viable way to explain the emergence of formal operational thought is some form of maturational nativism.

Collectively, the empirical and philosophical problems identified by critics of the theory led to its ultimate demise in the field of psychology. As noted earlier, though, this does not mean that the theory no longer has influence. On the contrary, many scholars still look to the theory as a starting point for their own investigations to familiarize themselves with the various phenomena that Piaget examined. Few doubt the reality of the phenomena that Piaget observed; controversies arose over Piaget's explanation of these phenomena. In addition, many contemporary scholars appear to be amenable to the idea of constructivism and seem to prefer it to more extreme forms of nativism.

Relatedly, many of the newer theoretical proposals that have been advanced in recent years have a constructivist flavor to them, but tend to emphasize domain-specific competencies (e.g., within-topic qualitative changes in insight) rather than domain-general competencies and stages. Finally, of all the cognitive-developmental theories that have been proposed to date, Piaget's theory is one of the few that is capable of predicting slow, conservative changes in conceptualizations and young children's difficulty in understanding abstract ideas.

See also: Cognitive Development; Cognitive Developmental Theories; Milestones: Cognitive; Neonativism; Object Concept; Reasoning in Early Development.

Suggested Readings

Bereiter C (1985) Toward a solution of the learning paradox. *Review of Educational Research* 55: 201–226.
Brainerd CJ (1978) The stage question in cognitive-developmental theory. *Behavioral and Brain Sciences* 1: 173–213.
Chapman M (1988) *Constructive Evolution. Origins and Development of Piaget's Thought.* Cambridge: Cambridge University Press.
Gruber HE and Vonèche J (1995) *The Essential Piaget.* Northvale, NJ: Aronson.
Piaget J (1952) *The Origins of Intelligence in Children.* New York: International Universities Press.
Piaget J (1983) Piaget's theory. In: Mussen P and Lerner R (eds.) *Handbook of Child Psychology,* 4th edn., vol. 1, p. 117. New York: Wiley.
Piaget J and Inhelder B (1969) *The Psychology of the Child.* New York: Basic Books.

Play

M Sumaroka and M H Bornstein, National Institutes of Health, Bethesda, MD, USA

© Published by Elsevier Inc.

Glossary

Exploratory play – Play that is directed toward the tangible properties and functions of objects.
Imaginary companion – Invisible vividly imagined characters that children play and talk with, while recognizing their unreality.
Individual differences – Variability in development and behavior as the result of different biological, cognitive, social, and environmental factors.
Interpersonal play – Direct, interactive social involvement with other participants in play with the purpose of entertainment.
Object play – Play that focuses on objects and events.
Primary circular reactions – Activities repeated for their own sake.
Security of attachment – A relationship between caregiver and child characterized by mutual trust.
Symbolic (pretend) play – Make-believe activities, in which children create symbolic uses of objects, pretend roles, and scenes.

Introduction

Play is important to children's lives and stimulates their development in many ways.

There are two main categories of play: interpersonal and object play. Interpersonal play implies participation in social interactions, such as face-to-face routines, social games, and physical play. Object play involves exploration and concentration on a toy, its functions and properties. Each kind of play contributes to psychological growth (e.g., children learn to control and express emotions); cognitive maturation (e.g., they develop creative abilities); mastery (e.g., they learn to concentrate and elongate attention span); social (e.g., they understand behaviors and feelings of others), communicative (e.g., they acquire social skills), and cultural (e.g., they rehearse traditional roles and behaviors) development. Particular types of play depend on many factors, among which are developmental capabilities of the child, play partners, and context.

Children's abilities change through the course of development, allowing parents to initiate more complex games. For example, 2–3-month-old infants are mostly entertained by repeating simple body activities, such as repeatedly kicking their legs. By 4 months of age, infants are capable of manipulating and exploring objects. When infants reach 1 year, they become interested in physical characteristics of objects (e.g., color, texture, and shape). In the second year of life, children develop symbolism and pretense in play. They start to substitute objects for one another and imitate actions and situations, at first centering pretense on themselves and, later, involving others and objects. Children's evolving sophistication of play reflects their progression in cognitive functions, such as representation, perception, language, and attention.

Many psychologists and philosophers have studied play and its influence on the development of children. Among the main theories of play are: surplus energy theory, relaxation and recreation theory, practice theory, and recapitulation theory. Psychologist have also suggested that play helps children to rehearse certain survival skills, has anxiety-relieving qualities, and fosters psychosexual development. Researchers have related play to social, cognitive, therapeutic, and emotional functions in the child.

Development of play is often stimulated by parents and other partners who initiate and participate in child play. Play partners differ in many aspects. For example, mothers usually focus on object play, developing children's visual, language, and representational abilities, whereas fathers are prone to initiate physical play, stimulating motor and communication skills; peers and siblings tend to involve children in pretend play and stimulate social competence.

Along with play partners, children's gender also influences their types and kinds of play. From birth, children are traditionally offered different toys, infants' rooms are often decorated in 'gender appropriate' colors, and parents are more permissive during play with boys and more directive in playing with girls. Around 4–5 years of age children start to choose certain gender-segregated types of play and toys and prefer playmates of their own gender, which can be explained by biological, cognitive, and social-learning theories.

Societies around the world have different understandings of the role of play and play partners. Many cultures regard play as an exclusively children's activity and parents do not participate in play. In other cultures parents may by the first and main play partners for their infants and, usually, initiate play and direct it as participants. Through play, cultures rehearse social role behaviors, introducing expected duties and responsibilities.

Types and Functions of Play

Play is practically synonymous with childhood. Play seems to be children's primary and most enjoyable activity, and it is a prevalent form of children's interactions with parents, siblings, and peers. It is usually associated with joyful and fun pastimes for children of all ages, yet play is also a very important force in child development, because it incorporates cognitive, social, emotional, and motivational skills. Therefore, play is a broadly beneficial activity that transcends simple enjoyment. There are no specific activities ascribed to play because it can take numerous forms, and any activity might be identified as 'play' when it meets the criteria of certain types and functions. Play is acknowledged to be complex and resists definition by any single characteristic or set of actions.

Types of Play

There are two main types of play that are evident from infancy: interpersonal (dyadic) forms of play and object-focused (extradyadic) engagements. These types of play are distinguished according to identifiable characteristics. Each type of play demonstrates patterned developmental change, serves unique functions, and is meaningful in child development. Throughout development, many changes occur in types of play as well as in their frequency of occurrence.

Interpersonal play

Interpersonal play is a social activity that appears to be prevalent during the first few years of life and has the goal of having fun. It requires direct interaction of the participants and is normally characterized by high degrees of pleasure derived by both parties. Interpersonal play involves various dyadic exchanges, such as face-to-face interactions, social games or routines, and physical play.

Face-to-face interactions balance repetitive bouts and creative variations of shared affect; they are framed as playful through specific vocalizations or gestures within the stream of ongoing parent–child communication. This type of play has mainly affective characteristics, and parents seem to engage in it with the goal of teaching infants to enjoy interpersonal interactions. Imitation is a typical component of face-to-face play interactions. Face-to-face play often occurs at home during other task-oriented activities (e.g., mothers engage into face-to-face interactions while feeding or changing the baby). Face-to-face play is typical of early infancy and decreases in frequency and duration as infants reach their first birthday.

Although face-to-face play is common in early infancy, interpersonal play is not confined to this period. When face-to face interactions decrease in occurrence, parents and children begin to get involved in social games and routines, such as peek-a-boo and pat-a-cake. The unstated goal of these social routines is to teach the child set formats of social exchange and their variations, as well as to try on different roles and take progressively greater responsibility. The role of parents is usually to facilitate the game, and the child's role often involves motor behaviors that are meaningful within the context of a particular game.

Physical play is another prevalent form of interpersonal play which occurs most frequently between 1 and 4 years of age. Research distinguishes among three types of physical play: rhythmic stereotypies, exercise, and rough-and-tumble play. Rhythmic stereotypies are usually a solitary form of play that emerges during the first year of life and includes gross motor movements. Onset of exercise play starts at the end of the first year and includes motor behaviors in the context of play. Exercise play can be solitary or interpersonal. Rough-and-tumble play peaks in the preschool years. It includes kicking, wrestling, and pushing in the friendly context of play. Rough-and-tumble play can escalate in levels of aggression; thus, parents must teach children the acceptable limits of rough-and-tumble physical play and explain how to maintain friendly interactions to control their behaviors.

Object play

At the age when children begin to notice objects, mothers adjust their playful interactions from interpersonal to extradyadic, focusing attention outwards from the dyad toward objects in the environment. Thus, strictly interpersonal interactions moderate in complexity to match newly developing skills in the child.

Parental direct involvement in child object play is usually less active, and characterized by less mutual engagement than interpersonal play, because the child is often preoccupied with toys. At the time children begin to focus on objects, parents actively promote and encourage such attention by showing new objects and demonstrating the functions and properties of objects, thus encouraging children to explore and learn about their surroundings.

Functions of Play

Play serves various adaptive functions. It also contributes to several different developmental areas: psychological, cognitive, mastery, social, communication, and cultural.

Through the psychological functions of play, children learn to control their state of arousal, develop self-regulation capacities, resolve conflicts, and address traumas.

Appropriate stimulation also helps children to develop self-regulation capacities. Play enables children to experience a broad range of feelings and emotions, from fun and enjoyment to anger and sadness. Parents are the best play partners for children in terms of intensifying and prolonging their pleasure in the first few months of life. From the beginning of life, parents support babies' experience of joy by playing with facial expressions, vocalizations, and touch, and evoking gaze, smiles, and laughter from their infants. During the course of typical face-to-face interaction games, mothers build and repeat predictable sequences of actions and vary them based on their infant's response. The infant's growing awareness of contingency in these interactions adds to feelings of mastery, in addition to enabling greater tolerance for higher arousal states. Parental selective imitation of infant behavior also enables infants to mark important acts as meaningful, thereby reinforcing certain behaviors to and facilitating mutual understanding.

Object play gives parents and children an opportunity to share their joys and frustrations while exploring objects, and struggling to accomplish goal-directed activities. During object play, parents devote much more time to talking about children's inner states and emotional expressions. These activities later help children verbally label their emotions as well as correctly link their inner states to emotional expressions.

Children experience and express a wide range of emotions such as joy and sadness, fear and excitement, or pleasure and anger. Play can be a unique platform for experiencing certain emotions, for example, aggression and anger that are caused by behaviors that might not be safe or appropriate to display otherwise. During interpersonal play, children also have an opportunity to 'practice' particular life events in a playful nonthreatening manner. A well-known example is the peek-a-boo game that gives the infant a chance to experience and control emotions related to separation and reunion. By representing traumas and conflicts symbolically through play, children can release forbidden impulses and also test alternative outcomes and solutions in conflict resolution.

The cognitive functions of play are to receive and exchange information, develop skills and representational abilities, and engage in creative and divergent thinking. In infancy, caregivers use play to foster speech-like sounds and babbling, thus stimulating child language development. Joint play advances communication between child and caregiver, and parent–child object play adds opportunities for children to expand their lexicon, learning new names for objects, their qualities, and effects they can produce.

Language use in child–parent play depends on the toys presented and settings of play, however; parents' speech toward children varies if they are playing with dolls, vehicles, or shape-sorters. When playing with dolls, parents tend to talk more and use a greater variety of words, ask questions, and name and label objects and contexts. By contrast, when play involves shape-sorters, parents tend to give directions and use attention-stimulating techniques. Play with vehicles produces the least amount of parent–child communication; parental vocalizations involve mostly pretend noises and imaginative sounds. Different play contexts also provide children with different opportunities for language acquisition. Caregivers direct children's attention to objects in the environment, encouraging them to explore, and later practice new skills. Both exploratory and pretend types of play promote flexibility, creativity, and divergent thinking in children.

New behaviors and skills help children to combine actions and objects in novel ways, promoting mental flexibility. For example, imaginary play is linked to creative performance and problem solving. It stimulates the development of representational thinking by allowing children to reflect on the past and anticipate the future using language and gestures. Joint play with caregivers brings the quality of children's play to a new level. During play with a caregiver, children are expected to (and often do) exhibit higher levels of play (more sophisticated pretense and symbolism) than when playing alone. Empirical evidence shows that children's play with parents is more sophisticated, complex, diverse, frequent, and sustained than is their solitary play. Higher complexity of parent–child play is believed to advance children's abilities.

The functions of play that enhance mastery cultivate a sense of self-efficacy, motivation, and persistence toward goal achievement. Over the course of the first 2 years of life, children practice new skills and engage in multipart tasks in playing with objects. During this time parents offer essential support – first, by focusing children's attention; next, by sustaining children's attention; and finally, by fostering mastery motivation on structured tasks. Mothers who encourage their 2-month-olds to orient and explore objects in the environment have infants who explore objects more at 5 months. Additionally, parents' stimulation and responsiveness to infants at 6 months is associated with infant persistence on problem-solving tasks at 13 months.

Parents' achievements in supporting persistence and efficacy in children's goal-directed behaviors are attributable to their responsiveness to children's initiatives, accuracy in assessing children's need for help, and effectiveness in assistance. Mothers who encourage and physically aid or coach their 18-month-olds when playing, have children who persist on structured tasks.

Through joint play, parents can help children find different, innovative uses of objects thus helping children to think 'outside the box' and develop their imagination. For example, while engaged in symbolic play, parents often make objects and toys perform different roles, shifting among different imagined or real scenarios and situations. When parents give children opportunities to play freely with materials, they enhance innovative uses of objects, flexible approaches to problem-solving tasks, and more divergent thinking on tasks. Development of attachment between children and parents also affects children's mastery capacities. Research links security of attachment to exploration. Security allows children to explore more, while in turn, exploration promotes competence. Play sophistication is associated with a longer attention span and greater persistence in problem-solving. Curiosity motivates children to explore the world, and pretend play enables them to master novel and complex environments in small scale.

The social functions of play create a base for future successful interactions and relationships by fostering children's understanding of others' feelings, intentions, and perspectives. During play, children practice reciprocal patterns of communication. Positive emotional exchanges in game rituals with parents, and later, with siblings and peers, allow children to achieve greater levels of joy than they might on their own. Role-playing, in particular, is associated with the ability to accept multiple points of view. Shifting between pretense and reality enhances children's ability to compare and contrast various perspectives, which is positively associated with social competence. In the social domain, play supports the development of mutual accordance and adjustment, or attunement, and it provides a foundation for more advanced forms of social understanding. Parent–child object play has been linked to the later quality of childrens' relationships with peers. For example, mothers' involvement in symbolic play with children between 2 and 4 years predicts their peer competence at 5 years. Children's play with their parents serves as a foundation for enhanced competence with peers, once peer interactions become prevalent in children's lives. Some forms of interpersonal play serve as a medium through which children learn norms, rules, and limits that are acceptable in society. Through games and rituals, children learn the limitations and boundaries of their behavior, first, within the family and, later, with peers. Games like peek-a-boo and pat-a-cake translate culturally appropriate elements of social interaction and set the stage for learning rule-bound conventional behaviors.

Play helps children to develop their communication skills. Through playful interactions, children learn key elements of social exchange, such as engaging a partner's attention, turn-taking, terminating social encounters, and role-reciprocity. Through face-to-face play, children learn to frame certain social exchanges as playful as well as to discern meaningful acts, and read certain expectations within a particular social interaction. Sometimes face-to-face interactions do not go smoothly; sometimes a mother may vary her vocalizations or movements too quickly and thus lose the child's attention. It is important that both partners remain attuned to each other. Through mutual involvement, face-to-face play allows parents and children to establish, maintain, and construct their relationship on the basis of common expectations, and vocalizations in play allow creative variation in interpersonal exchanges.

Play serves a variety of cultural functions, by embodying accepted social roles and values. Through culture-appropriate play, children learn local norms of behavior and are exposed to cultural traditions. Expectations about the roles of different individuals within a society start with the notion of who is an appropriate play partner. In some cultures, it is considered inappropriate for parents to play with children. Thus, Mexican, Guatemalan, and Indonesian parents typically avoid participating in play with their children. In other cultures, such as Turkish and American, parents think of themselves as good play partners for their children. The cultural functions of play begin early in life. For example, when playing with their infants, Japanese mothers more often direct attention to themselves, whereas American mothers encourage attention to objects in the environment. When the child gets older, Japanese mothers more often involve their toddlers in 'other-directed' interpersonal pretense play, whereas American mothers more often encourage their toddlers to engage in independent object play. In this way, Japanese mothers foster generally allocentric collectivist values in play which are typical of their culture, whereas American mothers foster generally idiocentric individualist values which are typical of theirs.

Toys are cultural objects that children learn to play with in particular and culturally appropriate ways. Through participating in complex play, caregivers demonstrate traditional ways of object use. For example, when a mother models a telephone conversation during pretend play, she first dials the number, waits for a response, and only then begins to talk. If, while imitating the telephone conversation, the child forgets to dial the number, or mistakes the order of action, the mother may adjust child's actions, thus teaching the correct way of play. Parent–child object play is also a medium through which children practice real-life scenarios (e.g., doctor–patient, mother–baby). Children's knowledge of cultural activities also contributes to the structure of parent–child play. When children play with familiar toys, they are more likely to facilitate pretend play, while parents serve as an audience. In contrast, when novel toys are used in the course of parent–child play, parents are more likely to start and organize the pretense.

The Developmental Progression of Play

Play develops with the child. It begins as inspection and manipulation and moves gradually to symbolism and pretense.

For the first 2–3 months of the child's life, objects in the environment are not very important for play purposes. According to Jean Piaget, during this time infants engage in 'primary circular reactions' – activities repeated for their own sake. For example, infants may coo repeatedly or open and close their fingers repetitively, suck their thumbs, or blow bubbles; while lying awake, they may arch their backs and drop their bodies onto the mattress over and over again.

Around 4 months of age, infants develop skills to manipulate objects, but even then, they are more interested in the actions they can perform than in any object characteristics. Thus, babies may look at a toy in their field of vision, but when holding an object in their hands they bring it to their mouth rather than visually study it. Even when two objects appear related to one another – a cup and a spoon, for instance – the infant often still focuses on actions, banging the spoon in the cup rather than on the objects. Remove the spoon, and the infant is likely to continue the action.

A major change in complexity and quality of play occurs when infants approach the end of the first year. At about this time, infants engage in three different types of exploratory play: functional, relational, and functional–relational. When infants are involved in functional play, they play with toys in the way the toys were designed to be played with, like rolling a car on its wheels. In the course of relational play, infants bring together two unrelated toys (e.g., a car and a cup) with no signs of pretense. In functional–relational play, children bring two objects together and use them in the meaningful way (e.g., load a container with blocks).

Thus, first-year play is predominantly characterized by sensorimotor manipulation. In their play infants explore the environment around them, deriving information about objects: their properties, physical characteristics, functions, and effects. Because children's activities are tied to the physical properties of objects, rather than being representational, this type of play is called exploratory or nonsymbolic. In the course of development of exploratory play, infants first direct their actions and attention toward a single object and later incorporate several objects in their play. Initially these objects may be treated inappropriately with respect to function, and only later children learn to treat them appropriately. For example, during the first months children may mouth a cup, but when they get a little older they may bang a spoon and a cup. Only later with age does the child use a cup and spoon appropriately, by stirring the spoon inside the cup.

Until the second year of life there are few signs of pretense or symbolism in children's play. Pretense requires representational skills. Because representational skills only slowly emerge, pretend play does likewise. Additionally, object substitution emerges as a clear indicator of more advanced symbolic play. When the young child builds a tower out of blocks, the tower now means more to the child than the characteristics of the blocks themselves. This suggests that there are two distinct kinds of representations reflected in object substitutions: primary representations and metarepresentations. Primary representations reflect tangible properties of objects (their shape, color, substance). Thus, objects can be used for different purposes. Younger children tend to restrict object substitutions according to perceptual features, such as shape and color. The child can talk on the toy telephone, utilize a cloth as a toy blanket, or pretend a red ball is an apple. Older children are able to use metarepresentations – representations of objects in unusual ways, independent of their physical characteristics. Thus a banana can be a telephone, and blocks can be served as pastries.

When pretend play first emerges, children tend to engage into self-directed pretense, centering pretense on their own bodies and actions. Children may pretend to be asleep, to eat from toy tableware, to read a book, or to talk on a toy telephone. Older children 'decenter' pretense by involving not only themselves but surrounding objects in pretend actions. They can make a doll read a book or make a set of buttons to go for a walk as if they were people. Even after the advent of decentration, play becomes more elaborate, when children combine sequences of pretend actions into a coherent scenario and make pretend plans for the future, such as hosting tea parties, cooking dinners, taking dolls to school, and going to work.

Thus, in the second year, children's play actions take on more of a nonliteral quality. The goal of play now appears to be symbolic or representational. Play becomes increasingly generative, as children enact activities performed by self, others, and objects in simple pretense scenarios, pretending to drive toy cars, eat from empty plates, or talk on toy telephones. Symbolic or pretend play also follows a sequence in development. At first symbolic play is self-directed, later it begins to include pretense schemes that apply to others. In the same way, single-scheme pretense appears before multischeme pretense. Finally, pretense with substitution objects develops.

This developmental progression of play is a generalized version of the sequential changes in representation that take place in early childhood. The majority of children follow this developmental pattern, although there are also wide individual differences in the rates of children achieving each level of development and in the quality of each level of achievement.

Play and Other Related Functions

Engaging in play requires the activation of different cognitive factors such as attention focus and mental representation. Thus, play, especially solitary play with objects, often serves as a mirror of cognition. Infants' perceptual exploration of objects facilitates the development of representation. While playing with an object, rotating, banging, mouthing, or squeezing it, a child receives different perceptual experiences that relate to the same object. As the central nervous system develops, cognitive processing grows, and children are exposed to novel situations that allow them to experience the presence and absence of objects. Children express their interest in the temporary absence and presence of objects or others by engaging in peek-a-boo games or intentionally dropping objects. These experiences extend perceptions in the developing child gradually promoting the distinction between perceptual experiences that rely on focal sensorimotor attention and representational experiences that transcend the here and now. Children's representational play is a platform for this distinction.

In parallel with their growing play sophistication, infants exhibit tremendous development in related areas of cognition. Thus, the growth of language and engaging in pretend-play scenarios during the second year of life, both reflect the development and increasing sophistication of children's representational capacities. In the domain of language, for example, children begin to understand and produce sound sequences that function as true naming as they shift away from the context – 'restricted' use of words and phrases to more 'flexible' uses across contexts. At the same time, their attention span becomes longer and more controlled. Children can coordinate and focus their attention, disregarding extraneous distractions.

Pretense play appears to have least two independent components – play that is associated with language as well as play that is associated with attention. The two reflect different underlying mental capacities. Advances in play and language go together. Children who perform well in one domain of development usually do well in the other. Apparently, language and pretense play share a representational nature. In language, as in pretend play, objects, people, and actions are represented symbolically. In contrast to this association between language and play, children's play competence is separately associated with their attention span. The mastery motivation side of play provides an explanation of the association between play and attention. Motivation to master the environment often results in sustained periods of object exploration, or attention focus, and thereby increased competence. Some theories suggest that ability to stay on task is necessary to bring play to higher levels of sophistication. Over the first 2 years, children regulate their visual attention and gradually move from nonsymbolic to symbolic play.

A Short History of Research on Play

Play is a part of the child's daily life in every society. Many philosophers and psychologists have been interested in child play, tried to define it, explain the reasons that motivate children to engage in play, and discuss the benefits and outcomes of play for children.

Early theories of play tended to divide into four groupings based on function:

1. *Surplus energy theory.* Charles D. Spencer argued that there is a universal need for people to engage in mental and physical activities. Because young children do not have responsibilities, they expend their surplus energy through play.
2. *Relaxation and recreation theory.* Moritz Lazarus suggested that work exhausts people mentally and physically, and sleep and rest are insufficient to recover. To achieve full recreation ('re-creation'), people need to engage in actions unrelated to real life and released from the constraints of work.
3. *Practice theory.* Karl Groos opined that a period of immaturity is specifically designed for complex organisms to practice skills that are necessary for survival during adulthood.
4. *Recapitulation theory.* Luther Gulick and Granville Stanley Hall considered play to be a cathartic factor in child development. Play constitutes an outlet for certain instincts and, by weakening them, enables children to acquire more complex behaviors of adults in society.

Many theorists have addressed other specific aspects of the development of play. For example, William Stern suggested that gender-specific games, such as girls playing with dolls and boys play-fighting, foster maternal instincts in women and aggressive instincts in men, respectively. Lili Peller linked the evolution of child play to progression in psychosexual development. Sigmund Freud suggested that the purpose of play is wish-fulfillment released from the constraints of reality. Karl A. Menninger emphasized the anxiety-reducing benefits of play.

Among the most influential child psychologists of play are Erik Erikson, Lev Vygotsky, and Jean Piaget. Erikson thought of play as a way children work through tensions; he advanced the use of play for therapeutic purposes. Piaget viewed play as a tool for cognitive assimilation. Vygotsky argued that caregivers serve as important play partners who help to shape child play in its social context.

Contemporary theorists consider play to have more than instinctual and psychoanalytic functions, but also include normative emotional, cognitive, communicative, social, and cultural functions.

Play in Relation to Play Partners, Gender, and Culture

Children's growth and development are shaped by various biological, cognitive, and social factors. Play, among other developmental processes, is strongly influenced by these aspects. It varies across families, genders, and cultures. To understand child play, it is often crucial to determine the child's playmates, the gender of the child, and where the play occurs.

Play and Play Partners

Early theorists tended to focus on children's solitary play. Vygotsky changed the way the child's playmates were viewed, by introducing the notion that child play is shaped by the context of social interactions. Although play emerges from the child, adults provide the play environment and objects used in play, inducing and stimulating play. Children often initiate pretend play, but they also complete play scenarios begun by others as well as imitate the play they see. Collaborative play interactions are believed to advance play sophistication in children, bringing the child to higher levels of development.

Various play partners stimulate the development of play, and they do so in different ways. It is difficult to underestimate parental contributions to children's cognitive development through play.

At all ages, mothers are more effective than other play partners in controlling and regulating emotional arousal in play and by providing appropriate stimulation. Mothers who are more knowledgeable about play are likely to prompt their children to play at more sophisticated levels than mothers who are less knowledgeable. Generally, mothers are more likely to initiate symbolic play than nonsymbolic play with their toddlers and remain involved until the pretend scenario is completed. Depending on their children's capabilities and age, mothers take different roles in pretend scenes, sometimes facilitating the game and sometimes participating as audience. Children actively seek maternal involvement in pretend play, thus indicating their understanding of symbolic play as a joint activity. In addition, maternal initiation of symbolic play predicts the quantity of children's engagement in symbolic play and maternal responsiveness to child play predicts the quality of later child play. Child's gender influences the style of maternal play. Thus, mothers of girls tend to direct their daughters' behavior during the course of play, more than do mothers of boys, who direct them less and let them explore more. As play partners, mothers and children seem to adjust to one another, each bringing the play level of one close to the play level of the other.

Multiple studies have shown the importance of father's involvement as a playmate in infancy and childhood. While in general, fathers participate in caregiving less than mothers do, fathers tend to spend more of 'together time' playing with their infant. The ways in which fathers play with their children during the course of development differ consistently from the ways that mothers do. Different styles of play encourage development of various skills and abilities in infants and children. For example, fathers usually engage in physical games, such as lifting and bouncing, while mothers prefer educational, visual games, most of the time involving toys. During object play, mothers follow infants' gaze, notice changes of attention from one object to another, and let infants explore and choose objects of interest; fathers, in contrast, change infants' attention by initiating physical play.

Fathers' engagement in physical play is most frequent in toddlerhood and gradually declines after that. Even with the decreased engagement in physical play, father's participation is significantly higher than mother's participation in physical games. Through late childhood fathers remain frequent partners in outdoor activities, trips, and the like.

Both mothers and fathers respond appropriately to the changes in their children's abilities, by switching to more complex play patterns. Parental knowledge about play development is an important factor in fostering interactions with children.

Aside from parents, siblings and peers are also effective play partners for children and impact social and gender-typed roles of the society by engaging in culturally appropriate, and eschewing inappropriate, play behaviors. After the first year, play interactions with siblings and peers increase in prevalence and may be more intense than those with parents. Parents and siblings stimulate cognitive skills differently through play, often with different outcomes. Parents use play as a tool for learning and communicating knowledge about the real world, whereas siblings and peers often 'play for play's sake'. Like adults, older siblings have more competence and are capable of bringing child play to more sophisticated levels. Peers share similar developmental achievements; therefore, they relate to each other more as equals, without necessarily creating an intellectual hierarchy.

Aside from peers and siblings, older children often have imaginary companions – invisible individuals that are invented and vividly imagined. Even though children pretend to talk or play with imaginary companions, they usually acknowledge that imaginary companions are not real. More girls than boys are known to have experiences with imaginary companions. In the beginning of the last century, these experiences were thought to indicate mental and developmental deviations and were strongly discouraged. In the middle and at the end of the last century, scientists assumed that children with experiences of imaginary companions grow to be more creative than children without such experiences. Recent findings disprove that notion, suggesting that there is no difference in creativity in children who have an imaginary companion compared to those who do not have such experiences.

Gender Segregation of Play

Around their fourth or fifth birthday, children's play becomes remarkably gender-segregated in terms of preferred toys, playmates, and play styles. Girls prefer to play with girls; they are less interested in rough, outdoor play, but are more interested in playing with dolls. Boys play with other boys, prefer cars and constructors, and enjoy rough, outdoor games. If one looks at toys that boys and girls choose and ask to buy, children tend to ask for more gender-stereotyped toys than their parents tend to choose. While they both may request clothing, sports equipment, and educational toys, boys usually desire action figures and toy vehicles, and girls ask for dolls and toy household items.

Biological, cognitive, and social-learning theories have been marshaled to explain this phenomenon. The biological perspective includes hormonal theories. It holds that sex-typed behaviors develop due to the influence of hormones (especially androgens), during critical stages of development. Because of hormonal changes in the brain, sex-typed behaviors are altered. Differences in levels of prenatal androgens contribute to observed sex-typed behaviors such as toy choices. For example, androgenized girls (girls exposed to high prenatal levels of male hormones) prefer typical boys' toys over girls' toys.

The cognitive perspective invokes gender constancy and the gender schema concept to explain gender-specific play. Gender constancy refers to children's understanding of belonging to a certain gender identity group and this identity does not change with time, social settings, or appearance. When children achieve gender constancy, they develop skills to categorize behaviors in terms of being male or female (gender schema). These schemas influence subsequent sex-typed behaviors. For example, when a girl categorizes cooking as an example of female behavior, she will more likely play with kitchen-sets than with a tool kit.

According to the social-learning perspective, children's gender play behaviors develop as a result of social–environmental influences. Traditional views on childrearing cause different treatment of children based on their gender, thus different sex-typed behaviors are reinforced. Adults fill infants' cribs with toys that are considered to be gender-appropriate to the child. Older children imitate sex-typed behaviors of caregivers and other adults; appropriate sex-type behaviors are later encouraged by parents and peers through positive and negative responses. Same-sex play is supported by peers who see it as appropriate, while crossgender play does not usually elicit positive responses. Observational learning contributes the development of gender-segregated play as well. While playing 'house', for example, girls pretend to do dishes imitating mothers, and boys emulate fathers by pretending to fix appliances.

When they play with different toys, children acquire different play experiences and thereby develop different skills and abilities. Traditional boys' toys, such as constructors and action figures, stimulate sustained attention, creative thinking, and fantasy play that is centered on constructiveness, social pretense, and competitiveness. Because many of boys' toys, such as electric trains and radio-controlled cars, can move on their own, they may stimulate visual tracking and spatial skills. Girls' toys, such as dolls, dolls' accessory packs, and tea sets, stimulate nurturance and fantasy play that centers on domestic life. Girls' toys are usually more colorful and appealing than boys' toys, but often are less mobile. In general, instructions and accessories for dolls point to what can be done to the doll (e.g., groom it, put on make-up, dress up), whereas directions and accessories for action figures advise what can be done with the toy (e.g., fight with weapon).

Certain categories of toys are played with equally by both boys and girls. Gender-neutral toys, such as play-doh, slinkies, and doctor kits, promote artistic and creative abilities. Gender-neutral toys change across time and culture. Contemporary girls play with sports equipment as much as boys do, but several decades ago most sports toys were considered to be boy toys only. In the countries of the former USSR, most physicians were women; thus, doctor kits were considered a strongly feminine toy, whereas in the US they are seen as masculine or gender-neutral.

When toys are rated from strongly gender-stereotyped to gender-neutral, violence emerges as a feature associated with masculine toys (e.g., weapons, toy soldiers, and certain video games); use of such toys is also associated with aggressiveness in pretense play. Toys and accessories, such as perfumes and make-up, are believed to focus girls on the value of physical attractiveness.

Moderately gender-stereotyped and gender-neutral toys (e.g., books, puzzles) tend to have higher educational value and to stimulate development of cognitive skills.

Play and Culture

The vast majority of research on developmental milestones, individual variation, and parent–child interactions in play has been conducted by Western researchers among families in the West. This monocultural tradition imposes limitations on the findings and extant theories of play. Characteristics of growth and development that appear universal can turn out to be culturally specific and vice versa.

Even though virtually all children around the world may engage in prevalent types of play, parental involvement in play differs across cultures. In some cultures, especially in hunting-and-gathering and agricultural village ones, play is regarded as mainly an amusing child activity. Children tend to find play partners among their peers rather than among adult caregivers (e.g., Mayan and the native peoples of the Americas). Parents do not practice direct teaching through play, rather they assist and direct children in group play with their siblings or peers. In contrast, other cultures view parental participation in play as an important developmental activity. In these cultures (e.g., North America), parents are the first and main play partners of children during the first years of life. This is often due to the widespread belief that children learn through play, and that play helps to develop cognitive, social, motor, and affective skills.

Parents in different countries hold different attitudes toward stimulating children's play. European and North American cultures traditionally encourage independence and autonomy, whereas Asian, South American, and African societies tend to emphasize interdependence and obedience to elders. For example, during mother–child pretend object play, US American children engage in more complex play, when mothers encourage their children's independent activity and praise them. By contrast, Japanese children respond with more complex pretend play when their mothers lead and direct joint activities.

In many cultures, interpersonal play is viewed as an activity through which parents and children strengthen their attachment and learn to exchange emotions in shared experiences. In these cultures, interpersonal play is a usual daily interaction. Interpersonal play can be also affected by child-care arrangements and everyday cultural practices. For example, in many traditional cultures, mothers use devices such as slings to carry infants and free their hands for work; this practice eventuates in less opportunity for face-to-face interpersonal play. Rather than engaging in face-to-face play interactions, these mothers structure interpersonal games that involve a third person; their own role is to direct the infant's gaze toward others.

These examples show that even though interpersonal games between parents and children are rare in some cultures, infants still engage in games with partners other than parents. Those interactions enable children to master modes of communication appropriate to their culture.

For example, the Gusii of southwestern Kenya avoid eye-to-eye contact during social interactions. This behavior derives from cultural superstitions about the possible dangers of visual contact. Even though mothers provide children with sufficient physical contact, they tend to restrain playful interactions and avoid eye-to-eye gaze. Gusii infants are viewed as incapable of interpersonal interactions; although mothers respond to infants' needs and demands, they do not engage them in play nor do they facilitate interactions. However, when specifically asked to perform face-to-face interactions, Gusii mothers and infants resemble Western dyads in many ways. Nonetheless, the dynamics of their interactions differ. Their duration of playful interchanges is shorter, and their interactions do not revolve around peaks of stimulation and affect arousal. This dynamic might be the result of different cultural beliefs.

Gusii parents might view their role as protecting the child from overexcitement and distress rather than as being a source or partner of playful stimulation.

In play, cultural settings cannot be underestimated: they constitute means of play forms and organize children's experiences, provide rules and information to construct knowledge about the society, and teach appropriate roles and behaviors.

Summary

Play is a complex activity that is described best according to its types and functions. Different types of play, such as interpersonal play and object play, contribute to psychological, cognitive, and mastery in addition to social, communication, and cultural development. Types of play develop gradually with the growth of child. The infant first engages in exploratory play and progresses to symbolic play. This progression serves as an indicator of cognitive development of the child: advances in play are correlated with progress in mental representations, attention, and language acquisition. Play develops in the context of gender and culture. Toy preferences of boys and girls differ due to biological, cognitive, and social factors; play partners vary by culture due to different cultural attitudes toward play and appropriate play partners.

Acknowledgment

Preparation of this article was supported by the Intramural Research Program of the NIH, NICHD.

See also: Cognitive Development; Cognitive Developmental Theories; Exploration and Curiosity; Imagination and Fantasy; Imitation and Modeling; Language Development: Overview; Piaget's Cognitive-Developmental Theory; Symbolic Thought.

Suggested Readings

Blakemore Owen JE and Centers RE (2005) Characteristics of boys' and girls' toys. *Sex Roles* 53: 619–633.

Bornstein MH (2007) On the significance of social relationships in the development of children's earliest symbolic play: An ecological perspective. In: Göncü A and Gaskins S (eds.) *Play and Development: Evolutionary, Sociocultural, and Functional Perspectives*, pp. 101–129. Mahwah, NJ: Lawrence Erlbaum Associates.

Bornstein MH and O'Reilly AW (eds.) (1993) *The Role of Play in the Development of Thought*. San Francisco: Jossey-Bass.

Pasterski VL, Geffner ME, Brain C, Hindmarsh P, Brook C, and Hines M (2005) Prenatal hormones and postnatal socialization by parents as determinants of male-typical toy play in girls with congenital adrenal hyperplasia. *Child Development* 76: 265–278.

Pellegrini AD and Smith PK (1998) Physical activity play: The nature and function of a neglected aspect of playing. *Child Development* 69: 577–598.

Piaget J (1983) Piaget's Theory. In: Kessen W and Mussen PH (eds.) *Handbook of Child Psychology: Vol. 1. History, Theory, and Methods,* 4th edn., vol. 1, pp. 103–128. New York: Wiley.

Rubin KH, Fein GG, and Vandenberg B (1983) Play. In: Mussen PH and Hetherington EM (eds.) *Handbook of Child Psychology: Vol. 1. Socialization, Personality, and Social Development,* 4th edn., vol. 1, pp. 752–833. New York: Wiley.

Tamis-LeMonda CS, Užgiris IČ, and Bornstein MH (2002) Play in parent–child interactions. In: Bornstein MH (ed.) *Handbook of Parenting,* 2nd edn., vol. 5, pp. 221–241. Mahwah, NJ: Lawrence Erlbaum Associates.

Pragmatic Development

N Akhtar and K Herold, University of California, Santa Cruz, Santa Cruz, CA, USA

© 2008 Elsevier Inc. All rights reserved.

Glossary

Communication – The exchange of ideas and/or feelings, often via speech, but also via gestures, eye contact, etc.

Comprehension – Understanding of words, gestures, etc.

Conventional symbols – Usually words, but also sometimes arbitrary gestures, that are understood by the community to have a particular meaning.

Deictic gestures – Gestures such as pointing that refer to something in the nonlinguistic context.

Ellipsis – The omission of certain words or phrases from a sentence, especially when that information can be retrieved from the preceding linguistic context.

Joint attention – A state achieved when two (or more) individuals attend to the same thing at the same time and are mutually aware of the other's focus of attention.

Morphology – The branch of linguistics concerned with word structure.
Narratives – Telling of a sequence of events in a particular order.
Pragmatic bootstrapping – Using one's understanding of communicative intentions to learn language.
Pragmatics – The branch of linguistics concerned with the uses of language for the purpose of communication.
Production – Expression or use of words, gestures, etc.
Proto-words – Phonetic forms used by very young children with a consistent meaning, but that are not considered conventional words in the adult language.
Scaffolding – The graduated assistance provided by adults to infants and young children to aid them in their cognitive or linguistic development.
Social referencing – Checking in (usually via gaze) with a social partner to judge his/her reaction to something.
Still-face paradigm – A method used in infant social development research whereby a parent interacting with his/her infant is asked to stop interacting verbally and to provide no facial expressions.
Symbolic gestures – Gestures (e.g., a thumbs-up) that stand for or represent something else.
Syntax – The branch of linguistics concerned with sentence structure.

Introduction

Pragmatics is the branch of linguistics concerned with the use of language for the purpose of communication; it is concerned with the use of language in context. Pragmatic approaches to language acquisition focus on the fact that children's primary motivation in acquiring language is to communicate with others, and they learn language in the context of conversational interactions (i.e., in communicative contexts). Since the emphasis is on communication, pragmatic development begins in the prelinguistic period, as infants begin to communicate before they start using any linguistic forms.

Babies can be said to communicate from birth in that their reflexive cries tell their caregivers that they need food or comfort. Researchers make an important distinction, however, between unintended acts that communicate information (e.g., shivering communicates that an individual is probably feeling cold) and acts that are intended to communicate. In a classic paper published in 1975, Elizabeth Bates and her colleagues distinguished between the perlocutionary (pre-intentional) stage in which babies behave in ways that have communicative effects and may be interpreted by adults as communicative (e.g., crying, smiling, vocalizing) and the illocutionary (intentional) stage in which infants demonstrate increasing control over their (nonverbal) communicative behaviors, and can establish and maintain attention on a shared 'topic'.

Most researchers agree that intentional communication begins in earnest around 9–10 months. This is widely recognized as the period in which both the ability to produce intentionally communicative acts and the ability to comprehend the communicative intentions of others really takes off. In this article, we provide a description of the most notable developments in infants' and children's communicative abilities, beginning with a brief description of some of the pre-intentional behaviors in early infancy that are interpreted as communicative by infants' caregivers. We then describe some of the intentionally communicative acts of late infancy, focusing on gestures. Finally, we examine toddlers' learning and use of conventional symbols (words), their subsequent production of phrases and sentences, and the development of the ability to engage in extended discourse in the preschool years. In each section, we describe the major communicative milestones of the period and discuss the abilities that are hypothesized to underlie attainment of these milestones.

In particular, it is infants' ability to read the intentions of others that is considered to play a very important role in their communicative development. Quite contrary to the Piagetian view of the egocentric child, the emphasis now is on infants' and toddlers' skills of perspective-taking. With new methods of assessing infants' comprehension, huge strides have been made recently in establishing that infants are sensitive to the goal-directedness (intentionality) of others' behavior from a relatively early age. Indeed, it is around the same age (9–10 months) as they themselves begin to engage in intentional behavior that they also show evidence of understanding the intentions of others. Initially, however, babies do not communicate intentionally. Their behavior communicates information to their caregivers, but they lack the motor, cognitive, and social skills necessary to engage in intentional acts of communication.

Early to Mid-Infancy

Newborns cannot behave intentionally, but they are born with certain visual and auditory preferences that enable them to enter into social interactions. For example, they prefer human voices to other types of sounds, and will sometimes even stop crying in order to attend to someone talking softly to them. On the basis of prenatal auditory experience, they also prefer to listen to their own mother's voice rather than another woman's voice. These preferences for speech ensure that babies will get plenty of exposure to the language they are going to be learning. In terms of visual preferences, newborns like to explore complex stimuli – stimuli with lots of contrast and contours; in particular, they like to look at human faces. A preference for faces means babies will spend a great deal of time looking at the faces of their caregivers, and often caregivers will interpret the resulting eye contact as an intention to interact. Among adults, mutual gaze generally signals an intention to communicate. Even if a baby doesn't have this intention when it gazes at its caregiver's face, the caregiver (at least in Western middle-class cultures) will tend to interpret the baby's behavior as intentionally communicative. Caregivers sometimes interpret clearly noncommunicative sounds (like burps) as communicative signals by acknowledging them and responding to them in some way. This contingent responsiveness of caregivers may play an important role in showing infants that their behaviors have a predictable impact on people. Then, eventually, when they are cognitively mature enough, infants will start to intentionally act to get reactions from their caregivers.

Early on, however, it is the caregiver who takes most of the responsibility for social interactions. In some sense, caregivers create the illusion of a communicative interaction with a newborn. In early infancy, babies are not themselves very good at turn-taking. What looks like turn-taking behavior seems more a function of what the caregiver is doing than what the infant might be doing. For example, during nursing, infants produce sucking bursts and they pause in between them. Often the mother will do or say something during these pauses. Initially newborn babies do not really initiate or maintain turn-taking interactions but their pauses give mothers the opportunity to turn feeding sessions into social interactions. The same is probably true of what are known as 'proto-conversations'. In these face-to-face interactions the caregiver and infant seem to be engaging in a conversation in that the caregiver says or does something, the infant appears to respond by smiling or vocalizing, and they go back and forth in this manner. It may be that early on what looks like turn-taking is actually the caregiver skillfully inserting behaviors into pauses in the baby's ongoing behavior. Gradually, however, as infants get older and enter the mid-infancy period, they start to take a more active role in these kinds of interactions.

In the mid-infancy period, infants start to show more awareness of social interactions. The evidence for increased awareness comes from studies of infants' participation in routine games and from what is known as the 'still-face procedure'. Games such as peek-a-boo have a predictable sequence and over time infants develop an anticipation of 'what happens next' (also known as script knowledge or event knowledge). Thus, when parents or researchers interrupt the regular sequence by not doing what they normally do, the infants respond by trying to get the adult to continue, sometimes even taking the adult's turn in the game themselves. Similarly, in the still-face paradigm, researchers ask parents to engage their infant in a face-to-face interaction and then at a signal from the experimenter, they are asked to adopt a still face and stop interacting with their infant. What usually happens is that the infant will first attempt to re-engage the parent and when those attempts fail, become distressed. Both sets of results are interpreted as the baby being sensitive to the normal structure of a social interaction. It is interesting that allowing the parent to continue to touch the baby during the still-face can attenuate the effect, indicating that a sense we often neglect in the realm of communication – touch – also serves to communicate to young infants.

Around 4–6 months there is a noticeable change in social interactions as infants start to become more interested in objects out in the environment. Their interactions with their caregivers start to be centered on objects and they don't spend as much time in face-to-face interactions. Adults tend to follow the infant's interests and talk about what the infant is looking at or playing with, leading to episodes of what is known as joint attention. These episodes – when adult and infant are focused on same thing – set the stage for more complex social and linguistic achievements, but at this early stage they are achieved mainly through the adult's efforts to follow what the infant seems to be interested in.

Over this period of time, babies also gain control over their muscles and therefore develop control over a wider range of behaviors – including communicative behaviors such as smiling, gazing, and vocalizing. Developing motor skills thus plays a role in how well and quickly infants can respond to their social partner's communicative behaviors, and probably also in the next big step in the infant's communicative repertoire: the production of gestures. Gestures play a very important role in early communication and they provide one way of assessing whether a given child is on track in terms of early language development. One of the difficulties in assessing language delays or problems in young children is that there is such a wide range of what is normal in terms of when a child utters their first word, so it is difficult to know whether a given child is simply a late bloomer or truly delayed. Researchers have found that these two groups of children can be differentiated by their comprehension of words and their use of gestures; those with poor comprehension of words and low use of gestures are the ones who continue to show signs of delay 1 year later. The infants with high comprehension of words and use of gestures tend to catch up to their age level 1 year later. Early use of gestures is therefore an important predictor of subsequent language development.

Summary

In early infancy babies engage in several social behaviors that enable them to interact with others and have communicative effects. Adults are primarily responsible for initiating and maintaining these early interactions. In mid-infancy, infants' interests shift to objects; caregivers tend to follow their infants' interests and initiate and maintain episodes of joint attention with them. It is not until the last part of the first year that infants begin to clearly initiate episodes of joint attention themselves by, as we discuss in the next section, pointing to something and then checking to see if the caregiver has followed the point.

Late Infancy

Around 9–12 months, infants begin to take a more active role in establishing periods of joint attention. For example, they will follow an adult's gaze to determine what the adult is looking at, and they start using points to actively manipulate their caregiver's focus of attention. It seems that at this age they are starting to understand that another's focus of attention can be different from their own, and that one needs to ensure that one's social partner is focused on the same thing to communicate about that thing. This is also the age at which social referencing first appears. Social referencing involves infants checking their caregiver's expression when they're in an uncertain situation – essentially trying to get information from their caregiver about a new situation or object. So, it is around the end of the first year, when babies start to use communicative gestures, that there is strong evidence for truly intentional communication.

Initially, infants primarily use deictic gestures (sometimes accompanied by vocalizations) such as pointing, showing, and giving. A variety of behaviors have been used to establish the intentional nature of infants' early gestures. First, babies tend to use them only or primarily when they have an attentive audience. Second, they tend to alternate gaze between their addressee and the event or object of interest, suggesting they are checking to see if their message has been received. And third, they make attempts to repair failed messages by repeating and/or elaborating the message when there are signs that their social partner has not attended to the message or has misunderstood it.

Repairing failed messages is a particularly good indication that preverbal infants can communicate intentionally as it shows that babies recognize when their communicative goals have not been achieved, and they are able to (and motivated to) adjust their behavior to achieve their goals. For example, when parents misunderstand or ignore their 1-year-old infant's communicative signals, the infant is likely to repeat the original signal, to augment it in some way (with additional vocal emphasis or the addition of a gesture, for example), or to substitute another signal for the original one. Infants will produce repairs of failed messages when they have failed to achieve some desired object (e.g., a special toy), but will also do so when their goal is simply to share their interest in something. Some experimental studies show that somewhat older toddlers will repair failed messages even when they have achieved their instrumental goal, suggesting even more strongly that the ultimate goal is to communicate, not just to get what they want. This and other findings like it have been used to argue that, in addition to using language as an instrument to get things done, infants and toddlers are also motivated from very early on to acquire language to express themselves and share their interests.

Pointing

Language is used, by children and adults, for both instrumental and sharing functions, and so are early gestures. Perhaps the most studied deictic gesture is the point – the extension of the index finger to an object or event. Early studies described two distinct functions of 1-year-old infants' points: imperative (instrumental pointing to request the object pointed at) and declarative (pointing to share interest in the object or event pointed to). Subsequent studies have confirmed this distinction that imperative points involve using a person as means to obtain an object (the goal), whereas declarative points involve using an object as a means to obtain adult attention. Declarative pointing is therefore seen as involving a deeper understanding of others as having attentional states that can be manipulated. Indeed, the claim is that the use of declarative pointing implies an attribution of an internal psychological state (as opposed to mere agency) to the addressee. While some studies have shown a nearly simultaneous emergence of the two types of points, others suggest that declarative points may develop a few months later than imperative points. Later emergence of the declarative point and the fact that use of it (and not of the imperative point) correlates with an independent measure of intention understanding, supports the view that declarative points rely on a more complex social–cognitive understanding.

Michael Tomasello has argued quite strongly that the infant's use of declarative points means that she has in some sense an understanding of others as intentional agents with mental states such as attention. The claim is that when babies use imperative points they may simply be using their social partner as a tool; that is, imperative points may rely on understanding of adults as causal agents but not necessarily as mental agents. Declarative points, on the other hand, are not used to obtain material goals, but simply to direct attention and to share an experience; thus, they appear to be more purely communicative, as they do not involve any instrumental goals.

While some researchers argue for attributing less sophistication to 1-year-old infants, and intentional understanding certainly develops in complexity over the first few years of life, there is considerable evidence to support the view that intentional understanding is present in nascent form at the end of the first year. In this regard, it is interesting that autistic children show a dissociation between the two types of points – they have difficulty with declarative pointing (both comprehension and production) but not with imperative pointing. The same dissociation is seen in human-reared apes. This dissociation provides additional support for the conclusion that declarative points may index a deeper understanding of others' minds than imperative points. While this is one possible interpretation, it is also possible that the dissociation is due to motivational differences rather than an inability to detect others' mental states; that is, not using declarative points may be related to less interest in sharing sights and sounds with others. We know of no studies that have attempted to tease apart the motivational versus sociocognitive explanations, but recent studies may lead in that direction.

These studies describe a third function of prelinguistic pointing: to provide information. In these studies, 12- and 18-month-olds spontaneously pointed to an object they inferred the experimenter needed to complete a task. This type of point is particularly interesting because it appears to involve both the cognitive ability to understand the experimenter's need for information and the motivation to cooperate with and help the experimenter. It would be interesting to conduct a similar study with autistic children to see if they are motivated to engage in this type of pointing. Finding that these children do not point to inform would not be very instructive on its own. However, if they, for example, looked to the object the experimenter needed but did not point to it, that might provide evidence that they possess the sociocognitive capacity to determine what the experimenter needs, but lack the motivation to provide that information. For present purposes, however, it is sufficient to note that all three types of pointing that toddlers engage in – imperative, declarative, and informative– are examples of intentional communication that involve directing the attention and/or behavior of others.

It is widely agreed that 1-year-old infants use intentional vocalizations and gestures to communicate, but there is less consensus on the number and variety of specific meanings or communicative intentions their vocalizations and gestures express. As discussed previously, pointing is used for imperative (instrumental) as well as declarative (sharing, commenting) and informative purposes, but prelinguistic infants also make use of varied intonation patterns to produce requests for actions, to greet their social partners, to protest or reject the actions of others, and so on. Eventually they begin to use words for these and other communicative functions.

Symbolic Gestures

Before they start using words, however, many infants and toddlers produce symbolic gestures in interactions with their caregivers; for example, sniffing to label a flower. These gestures appear to be used for the same communicative functions as early words; that is, to request, comment on, and label objects, and to describe children's experiences. Some of these gestures are learned within interactive routines, but some seem to be spontaneously generated by children themselves. Regardless of how they originate, these gestures seem to be generalized and used in a contextually flexible way (i.e., in different contexts for different communicative functions), much as early words are, and so their acquisition probably relies on the same social and cognitive skills that word learning does (see the next section). The production of symbolic gestures emerges earlier than word production probably because infants and toddlers have better control over the large muscles used in forming a gesture than they do over the many tiny muscles used to articulate words. One interesting finding is that children who are trained to use multiple symbolic gestures may have an advantage (compared to children with no training) in subsequent verbal comprehension and production. With or without training, it is possible that children's early use of symbolic gestures can facilitate or bootstrap their subsequent communicative development in several ways.

One possibility is that once babies start producing some symbolic gestures, adults around them start to treat them differently – they may talk to them more because there is more to communicate about. So, infants who produce more symbolic gestures may receive more verbal input overall than, for example, a baby who only points. A related possibility is that once babies start producing gestures, it is easier to read their minds and figure out what they are focused on – so that makes it easier to establish joint attention with them and determine their specific communicative intentions. If the baby makes the sign for 'Hungry', for example, the parent might respond with "Oh, you're hungry," thereby providing a verbal label for what the child is feeling at the time. In this way the children might receive more relevant verbal input. Finally, another possibility is that by using symbolic gestures and being understood children might become even more motivated to talk and be even better understood. These are all hypotheses at this point and remain to be tested systematically.

It is important to note that almost all of the developments in preverbal intentional communication we have described have also been demonstrated by captive apes: for example, pointing, gaze following, gaze alternation, and even communicative repairs. There are a few important differences, however. One is that the apes tend to use their communicative gestures for imperative purposes only. Second, to our knowledge, they do not invent novel symbolic gestures as young human infants do. Finally, the apes in these studies do not appear to use their human-like communicative behaviors in communication with conspecifics, suggesting that these are behaviors that they learn only through training and that the learning does not transfer to their interactions with one another. These differences between apes and children suggest that apes' understanding of communicative signals may be qualitatively different from the understanding of human toddlers; that is, the apes may only appreciate the impact of their gestures on the overt behaviors of the humans who interact with them, and not any impact on their mental states. An alternative hypothesis is that human-reared apes may have the same cognitive level of understanding of internal states as young children but they may, in sharp contrast to human infants, lack the motivation to share these states with others.

Summary

Near the end of the first year of life, a variety of preverbal behaviors (gaze following, gaze alternation, communicative repairs, pointing, vocalizations, and symbolic gestures) demonstrate not only that infants have the ability to communicate intentionally, but also that they have come to understand others as intentional beings like them. Although nonhuman primates in captivity also engage in some of these behaviors, they seem to do so in qualitatively different ways from human infants, for example, using pointing only for instrumental purposes, and not using it to communicate with other apes.

Early Word Learning and Use

Before beginning to use conventional symbols (words), some children produce transitional communicative forms known as phonetically consistent forms or proto-words. These forms function as words in that they are used intentionally for consistent communicative functions but are unlike words in that they are not fully conventional symbols in the adult linguistic system, for example, saying "baba" to request one's bottle. Use of proto-words is a significant development because it indicates very clearly that toddlers understand that specific sound patterns can be used for specific communicative intentions, a necessary precursor for word-learning.

On average, infants demonstrate the first signs of word comprehension at approximately 9 months of age, but don't start to spontaneously produce words until around 12 months. While there are huge individual differences in the age of onset of word comprehension and production, the lag between comprehension and production is a very robust finding. This lag is probably due, in large part, to the difficulties associated with coordinating the many nerves and muscles involved in speech production. Indeed, early difficulties with articulation may also explain why toddlers' first words tend to include the same phonemes they used most frequently in earlier babbling. Toddlers' earliest words also tend to be used for similar communicative intentions as their preverbal gestures, but as children acquire more words, they learn to use those words in new ways; that is, the variety of communicative intents expressed increases, as does the intelligibility of children's productions. Children also gradually develop the capacity to take into account multiple aspects of the interaction context in producing different speech acts. Finally, as in the prelinguistic stage, they continue to negotiate communicative breakdowns with their caregivers but they are more adept at tailoring the reformulations of their initial utterances to the type of feedback provided by their social partner. For example, they respond differently to specific versus general queries of their utterances ("What does he need?" vs. "What?") and they are able to monitor their own speech for errors and respond appropriately when queried.

Many researchers now view children's ability to discern others' communicative intentions as playing a critical role in early word-learning. In brief, the view is that words are used primarily to direct the attentional states of addressees, and that children match the sound patterns they hear to their interpretations of what the speaker is trying to get them to attend to. If words are used by speakers to direct the attentional states of their listeners, then the child listener's goal in communicative contexts is to try to understand what a speaker is directing their attention to with a given word. Indeed, Bruner has argued that an act of reference is actually an intention to invite the listener to engage in joint attention.

Many experimental studies have shown that 18- and 24-month-old toddlers can use a variety of pragmatic cues to establish joint focus with their interlocutors, and thereby determine their communicative intentions. These include gaze direction, facial expressions, event or script knowledge as well as sensitivity to the prior discourse topic. Children's use of these cues enables them to attend to the appropriate referents and learn the words their caregivers use, but it also indexes a motivation to establish joint attention with others. In all of these studies, the onus is on the child participant to establish joint attention with the adult in order to learn the word the adult used. Clearly, young children are very motivated to do so.

It is also important to note, however, that in all of these studies the children were engaged in a dyadic interaction with the experimenter. One interesting question is whether toddlers are also able to determine the communicative intentions of a person who is not interacting with them. This is an important question because anthropologists suggest that in many communities, young children do not experience as many one-on-one interactions with adults as the children we typically study, yet they do not appear to be greatly delayed in language-learning. Children growing up in these contexts seem to be quite good at monitoring others' interactions, which leads to the hypothesis that they may learn a great deal of language by listening in on the conversations of others. Indeed, children in all cultural contexts probably learn a great deal of language in this way. For this reason, researchers have begun to examine young children's ability to learn new words through overhearing – that is, through monitoring third-party interactions.

The main findings so far are that 2-year-old children are equally good at learning a new object label through overhearing as when they are directly addressed. Older 2-year-olds are able to learn a verb through overhearing as well. Eighteen-month-old infants are also able to learn a new object label through overhearing but it is not as easy for them as it is for 2-year-olds. Another recent study has shown that 18-month-old children can monitor and comprehend communicative gestures that are not directed to them.

These are interesting findings, but it is not clear to what extent the experimental contexts used in these studies are similar to the everyday contexts in which children overhear new words. In these studies, the children in the overhearing condition were seated as onlookers to the adults' interaction but there was nothing to really distract them from that interaction. There was nothing else that was particularly interesting going on; certainly, the most interesting thing in the room was the interaction between the two adults who were playing with fun toys. But in real life, children don't just sit down and pay attention to others' conversations. There are generally other things going on that compete for their attention. If children are truly motivated to attend to others' communicative intentions, they should do so even when they are engaged in an interesting activity themselves. More recent studies have shown that 2-year-olds can also learn new words through overhearing when they are engaged in another distracting activity. These experimental studies of word-learning through overhearing along with naturalistic observations of children's attention to third-party conversations demonstrate that toddlers are motivated to monitor the communicative intentions of people who are not even interacting with them, giving them multiple sources from whom to learn words.

It is probably true that many (if not most) children spend a significant amount of time in multispeaker environments in which they are not always directly addressed; therefore, overhearing contexts may represent a vital part of young children's early language learning experiences. The vast majority of studies of early language learning focus on dyadic contexts; only a few relatively recent studies have systematically examined children's word-learning through overhearing. Future studies will need to explore the cognitive skills that underlie children's ability to learn through overhearing, and whether children who grow up in societies where they are expected to learn through observation are actually better at learning through overhearing than children growing up in communities that emphasize direct teaching.

Summary

Children first use nonconventional forms (proto-words) to communicate, and at around 12 months begin producing more traditional words, with varying success. While their intent is quite often to highlight their own wants and needs, they also use words to communicate their perspectives in attempts to share those perspectives with others. They repair misunderstood utterances, and use words to direct the attention of the person they are communicating with. Young children are quite skilled at learning new words, even when those words are not being directed to them. These findings indicate that children can monitor others' interactions, and can learn words from overheard conversations as well as from conversations in which they are directly involved.

Multiword Speech

Before toddlers begin to combine words, they first combine gestures with words, for example, pointing to a book and saying "mommy" to indicate something like "That book belongs to my mom". These gesture-plus-word combinations are said to 'pave the way' for two-word combinations as children who are first to produce gesture-plus-word combinations are also first to produce word–word combinations. One way in which gesture–word combinations may facilitate the production of word–word combinations is that they may lead parents to 'translate' the communicative intents children express with gesture–word combinations into word–word combinations, providing an appropriate models for children on how to verbally express their communicative intents.

Early word combinations allow the child to begin to rely somewhat less on the nonlinguistic context to get their communicative intentions across. In the one-word stage, their holophrastic (one-word) utterances can only be interpreted with heavy reliance on context and even then the child's intent may be ambiguous. Although two-word utterances can also be ambiguous, they provide a bit more information about what the child has in mind. Across the languages that have been studied in detail, children's early word combinations tend to be used for a similar range of communicative functions. For instance, toddlers make requests, reject and negate others' assertions, describe and comment on actions and locations, talk about possessions, etc. They also ask questions, often yes/no questions that are marked with rising intonation, but 'where' questions are also frequent. In their two-word utterances. toddlers tend to mark new information with stress, suggesting that they take the context (and perhaps the listener's perspective) into account when formulating their early multiword utterances.

There is not as much known about the communicative intentions of children in the later stages of linguistic development when they start producing full-length sentences. This is likely because the emphasis (of most researchers) appears to shift to matters of form (morphology and syntax) rather than function (pragmatics) when children start speaking in longer sentences. Formalists define language as a system of abstract rules for combining various parts of speech, independent of the contexts of use of those rules. Functionalists, on the other hand, define language as the use of symbols and rules for combining those symbols for the purpose of communication. While the differences between formal and functional approaches to language may appear to be merely differences in emphasis – after all, both form (structural rules) and function (communication) are crucial aspects of human language – because of their focus on communication, functionalist approaches tend to be more developmentally friendly. However, most of the research on children's developing syntactic abilities is not framed in terms of communicative intentions because grammar has been considered by many theorists and researchers to be a completely autonomous linguistic module. More recent functional approaches to grammatical development are promising, but it remains true that most of the research on the early development of syntax and morphology does not explicitly examine the communicative functions of the various constructions children are learning to comprehend and produce.

It is noteworthy, however, that some longitudinal studies have found positive correlations between measures of pragmatic development and grammatical development, and some researchers believe that joint attention may play an important role in grammatical development. This is consonant with Tomasello's view that "learning words and learning grammatical constructions are both part of the same overall process," the process being reading the communicative intentions of the people speaking those words and constructions. The process is slightly different in the case of grammatical constructions because the child has to pay attention to (and abstract) a pattern of symbols and link that pattern to the speaker's communicative intent. In this view, sentence-level constructions are, like words, essentially pairings of form and function (communicative intent). It is certainly the case that different syntactic constructions can provide different perspectives on the same scene or event (e.g., the passive vs. active transitive construction in English), and children and adults do use different syntactic constructions to convey different communicative intentions. We know of no empirical research, however, that has directly addressed the question of whether children learn syntactic constructions in the same way as they learn words; that is, through "pragmatic bootstrapping" or attention to speakers' intentions. The fact that autistic children sometimes show a dissociation between pragmatic and syntactic abilities – producing grammatically correct utterances that are often pragmatically odd – suggests that pragmatic development alone cannot account for the development of syntax.

Ochs and Schieffelin's description of the language socialization of Kaluli children, however, provides illustrations of the role of pragmatics in some aspects of grammatical development. They found that there are several grammatical forms that are frequent in input to Kaluli children but the children themselves do not use them because it is not culturally appropriate for them to do so, for example, command forms of a verb that the society's rules dictate can only be used by adults to children and not vice versa. The children show comprehension of these verb forms at a young age (by 19 months) but they do not use them themselves. Similarly, there are grammatical forms that are relatively infrequent in the input that the children do pick up and use. The main point is that children do not just learn the words and constructions that they hear frequently – they are paying attention to the pragmatic contexts in which those words and constructions are used, and they use the ones that best fit their communicative goals within the constraints of the cultural context. Indeed, Ochs and Schieffelin conclude that "children's use of particular grammatical forms at particular moments of their language development is profoundly linked to social and cultural norms, expectations, and preferences which may not be explicit and are not easily counted or detected."

Summary

Children's early ability to combine gestures with words facilitates their ability to combine words with each other. As children move from two-word combinations to multiword utterances, they rely somewhat less on the extralinguistic context and more on linguistic means for expressing their communicative intentions, although context remains vital to communication throughout development. The new linguistic skills that allow children to produce complex constructions also allow young toddlers to engage in extended discourse, the topic of our final section.

Extended Discourse

In the preschool years, children begin to engage in extended discourse on various topics; that is, they become better conversationalists and tell better stories. To do these things effectively, they need to adapt to their audience and use linguistic devices such as ellipsis pronouns, and various causal connectives to maintain coherence and cohesion across utterances. They have to monitor their listener's comprehension and, in general, they need to use social perspective-taking and their developing linguistic skills to ensure this comprehension. In addition, children learn to use mental state terms such as 'think', 'want', and 'believe' to convey their own feelings and perspectives as well as those of story protagonists. Although conversations often contain narrative sequences, we discuss these two types of extended discourse – conversational development and narrative development – separately.

Conversational Development

Becoming a skilled conversationalist is important because it plays a role in peer relationships; children who are good at conversation are more effective at interacting with their peers and better liked by them. But becoming an effective conversationalist is a difficult task because it involves coordinating many different skills, both linguistic and nonlinguistic. For example, one has to plan what one is going to say, monitor and comprehend one's partner's responses, time one's turns appropriately, maintain relevance to the topic at hand, maintain an appropriate distance, use eye contact appropriately, and so on. There are also a number of conversational rules (some of which vary by culture and subculture) that children must learn, including of course the famous Gricean maxims of Quantity (say enough, not too much or too little), Quality (be sincere or truthful), Relation (be relevant), and Manner (be clear).

As young preschoolers are generally more egocentric than older children their contributions to conversations are not always relevant, and may not provide enough information in a clear manner to their conversational partners. Young children sometimes appear to assume that their listeners have access to the same information as they do. Motivation seems to play an important role in conversational competence, however; when engaged in referential communication tasks in a laboratory, preschoolers appear less competent than when engaged in more meaningful situations in which they are highly motivated to get their message across. In real-life situations, children will try various ways of repairing or reformulating their initial utterance when it is clear that their partner has misunderstood them. Some studies have shown that children will adjust the type of repair they use in different communicative situations. For example, toddlers are more likely to simply repeat their initial utterance (or say it louder) when queried by their mother and more likely to reformulate it when queried by an adult stranger, suggesting that they may be sensitive to the fact that strangers are less likely to understand them whereas their mother may not have heard what they said. Similarly, toddlers also respond differently to different types of requests for clarification. They tend to repeat all of what they had said when asked "What?" but they give only the requested information when asked a more specific question ("You want what?"). In general, these studies of communicative breakdowns show that even young children have some rudimentary knowledge of appropriate conversational behavior: they recognize when communication fails and have a variety of means for repairing breakdowns. They are also clearly motivated to achieve communicative success, as they engage in repairs even when they get what they want but their conversational partner has indicated a misunderstanding verbally.

There are individual differences in how successful young children are at turn-taking; some do not wait for their partner to stop speaking (although it must be noted that in some communities, this type of overlapping speech is the norm), while others wait too long before taking their turn. In general though, young children appear to be relatively good at conversational turn-taking. Other aspects of conversational exchange, however, seem to undergo more protracted development. These include the abilities to smoothly initiate, maintain, and end conversations. Young children are generally not very skilled at initiating conversations, but they are more likely to do so with family members than strangers. When interacting with peers, young children are less likely to maintain a topic over several conversational turns than they are when interacting with adults. This is most likely due to the responsive scaffolding of the adults children typically interact with.

Through their interactions with parents, siblings, peers, and teachers, children learn that they should speak differently (use different speech registers) in different social settings. For example, in school they typically speak differently to teachers than to their peers, and are more likely to use politeness markers such as 'please' and 'thank you' with adults than with other children. Language socialization studies have shown that in many cultures parents actively teach children when to say what; however, politeness consists of far more than simply knowing when to use the appropriate words. It also involves understanding various social roles and how they relate to the use of different linguistic forms. In some communities, children are required to use different lexical and grammatical forms with different individuals. Children in these communities attend to how males and females speak differently, and to the various relationships among individuals, and who speaks how to whom, in order to learn with whom to use different grammatical forms. They are generally not directly instructed in these understandings but come to them through keen observation of others' interactions. As with all pragmatic developments, the development of politeness relies heavily on children's social understanding.

Narrative Development

Narratives are similar to conversations in that both involve perspective-taking and a certain degree of linguistic skill. In both it is important to provide relevant information in a clear and unambiguous way. But conversations and narratives differ in one significant way. Whereas conversations are dialogues between two or more participants who essentially build on and provide a context for each other's contributions, narratives involve, for the most part, decontextualized monologues. There is in some sense necessarily less scaffolding because a narrative usually involves a longer stretch of speaking, and children therefore have to rely more on their linguistic skills in getting the message across. This may explain why narrative skill has been linked to literacy development. Children who are good at producing coherent narratives appear to have an advantage in learning to read, perhaps because experience with decontextualized language plays an important role in literacy.

Children's earliest narratives occur in the context of conversations so they have lots of responsive support initially, but as they get older they depend less on adults' scaffolding, and their contributions become longer, more coherent, and more complex. They often begin by recounting stories with adult encouragement, and typically construct their stories in response to prompts or other adult scaffolding behaviors. Very young children also learn to tell stories by narrating ongoing events. This is especially prevalent in pretend play, when children will often narrate their constructed imaginary situations to one another. By 4–5 years of age, children have typically learned a 'story grammar', or a set of rules that provide the structure for a good story. These rules vary by culture, and children tend to adopt the storytelling structures of their parents, and others in their community.

A 'good' narrative often has a specific organizational pattern. The speaker presents an explicit topic, and discusses it in a way that clearly states the relations among a sequence of events. For many narratives the grammar consists of an introduction that orients the listener followed by an organized sequence of events that leads to some type of conclusion. The setting or introduction includes the place and the characters involved. This is generally followed by a sequence of events or episodes and then some kind of ending or resolution. Older children's narratives are more sophisticated in several ways – they include mention of the characters' motivations and internal states, they describe multiple events and, in general, there are more explicit connections made between the events so that the story actually 'flows'. Good narratives make use of various linguistic devices to achieve coherence and cohesion. These include conjunctions (and, but, or), causal connectives (because, so), temporal connectives (then), the appropriate use of pronouns, definite and indefinite articles, etc. These devices bridge different parts of the narrative in appropriate ways and, in some cases, are essential to maintain coherence of the narrative as a whole.

Summary

In early childhood, children begin to engage in extended discourse. They learn culturally specific rules of conversation and politeness, and become sensitive to the need to use different speech registers in different settings. Their emerging linguistic skills as well as their increasing ability to take others' perspectives enable them to produce more coherent and cohesive narratives. Early interactions within the family set the stage for these developments and while some parents actively socialize these skills, children also learn a great deal through observation of 'how things are done' in their communities.

Concluding Remarks

Intentional communication begins with infants' use of gestures to request and comment on objects and events. Toddlers progress to using words for these and other communicative functions, then combine gestures with words, and then combine words with words. There appears to be some continuity between these stages of communicative development in that infants' use of symbolic gestures predicts their use of words and their use of gesture–word combinations predicts their use of word–word combinations. The ability to produce effective narrative sequences is positively correlated with subsequent literacy skills, but there is little evidence on the relations between earlier communicative developments and the ability to engage in extended discourse.

We have noted throughout our review that social–cognitive abilities (e.g., understanding of others as intentional/mental agents, perspective-taking) provide the foundation for pragmatic development. Pragmatic development is also inextricably linked to children's motivation – evident at a very early age – to communicate with others and to interpret others' communicative intentions. While intention-reading skills have been demonstrated in some nonhuman primates, the motivation to connect with others and share experiences is postulated to be unique to humans. It is perhaps this distinctive combination of social–cognitive skills and motivation to communicate that sets human children apart and enables them to progress as rapidly as they do through the various stages of pragmatic development.

See also: Grammar; Literacy; Preverbal Development and Speech Perception; Semantic Development; Theory of Mind.

Suggested Readings

Adamson LB (1996) *Communication Development During Infancy.* Boulder, CO: Westview Press.

Akhtar N and Tomasello M (2000) The social nature of words and word learning. In: Golinkoff RM and Hirsh-Pasek K (eds.) *Becoming a Word Learner: A Debate on Lexical Acquisition*, pp. 114–135. Oxford: Oxford University Press.

Baldwin DA (2000) Interpersonal understanding fuels knowledge acquisition. *Current Directions in Psychological Science* 9: 40–45.

Bloom L (1998) Language acquisition in its developmental context. In: Kuhn D and Siegler RS (eds.) *Handbook of Child Psychology, Volume 2: Cognition, Perception, and Language*, pp. 309–370. New York: Wiley.

Bruner JS (1983) *Child's Talk: Learning to use Language.* New York: Norton.

Ninio A and Snow CE (1996) *Pragmatic Development.* Boulder, CO: Westview Press.

Tomasello M (2003) *Constructing a Language: A Usage-Based Theory of Language Acquisition.* Cambridge, MA: Harvard University Press.

Preverbal Development and Speech Perception

R Panneton, Virginia Tech, Blacksburg, VA, USA
M McIlreavy, University of Georgia, Athens, GA, USA
N Bhullar, Widener University, Chester, PA, USA

© 2008 Elsevier Inc. All rights reserved.

Glossary

Bootstrapping – The ability of infants and children to use their conceptual knowledge in one domain (e.g., syntax) to create new understanding in a second domain (e.g., word meaning).

Categorical perception – The ability to detect a change in a given speech sound along a continuum; not gradual changes but in instances of discrete categories.

Iambic pattern – A weak–strong pattern for multisyllabic words in which primary linguistic stress does not occur on the first syllable (e.g., in English, sa-lute).

Perceptual attunement – The process by which infants initially show broader, less-constrained acuity in discriminating between various elements, but with more experience, maintain discrimination of some contrasts but not others.

Phoneme – A basic sound unit of a spoken language. Each unit consists of a distinctive sound that comprises a given language.

Phonology – The branch of linguistics that focuses on the sound systems of different languages.

Prosody – The intonation, rhythm, and stress in speech. Also known as suprasegmental because these features are not limited to single sounds but extend over syllables, words, or phrases.

Statistical learning – An approach to understanding language in terms of identifying speech sounds that have high probabilities of occurring together.

Stress timed language – A language class in which there are stressed syllables appearing at a roughly constant rate and where nonstressed syllables are shortened.

Trochaic pattern – A strong-weak pattern for multisyllabic words in which primary linguistic stress occurs on the first syllable (e.g., in English, sís-ter).

Voice-onset-time (VOT) – Refers to the length of time that passes between the beginning of vibrations of the vocal cord and the release of a consonant.

Introduction

During the first year after birth, most humans are continuously embedded in a social milieu within which they acquire information about people and objects, emotions and expectations, causes and consequences. Along with growing social awareness and knowledge, infants begin to understand and produce gestures in their native language system (vocal and manual) that convey their perceptions, feelings, and intentions, as well as those of their social partners. Often, when we think about language acquisition, we focus primarily on word learning. For hearing infants, it involves much more than this, including the perception and production of individual sounds, combinations of sounds, intonations, stress patterns, orderings of units (words, phrases, sentences), and accents. Language also involves movement in the face (e.g., lips and mouths), body posture, and interpersonal routines.

As complicated as this may seem, most toddlers are making requests, naming objects, identifying people, and beckoning attention by the age of 18 months. Without a doubt, infants listen to and learn from the communication that is directed to them. According to an influential model by developmentalist Anne Fernald, vocal communication between caregivers and infants serves development in the preverbal period in three ways: (1) speech captures and maintains infants' attention to others; (2) speech conveys emotion to the infant, not only about the speaker's feelings, but also about the speaker's interpretations of the infant's feelings, helping to regulate emotional experiences; and (3) speech provides lexical/linguistic information necessary for native language learning. Importantly, all of these functions continuously influence infants and children, although certain milestones within each function may be age-related (e.g., infants may be more sensitive to some aspects of vocal emotion during early as opposed to later infancy).

The aim of this article is to characterize the functions listed above via the existing literature on language-related accomplishments that take place for many infants in their first postnatal year, with an eye on the processes that nurture and shape language development. To do so, we will first briefly consider how developmental psychologists are able to ascertain infants' understanding of language when they are not yet producing it, and when infants appear to be sensitive to language-relevant information. Next, we will discuss language learning during infancy from two perspectives: from a social/emotional view that describes the richness of the interactive framework within which almost all early language learning takes place; from a perceptual/biological view that describes the various components of language which infants can and do perceive in the course of learning how to communicate, and how the biology of infants is becoming organized and specialized in ways that promote language processing. Both of these perspectives have generated a considerable amount of research, and contribute in important ways to the ultimate organization and structure of children's emerging communicative competencies. We will also consider aspects of preverbal development that highlight the importance of ecology in considering just how infants learn language in their everyday environments (outside of ideal laboratory settings) but are not yet well understood, and in need of future research attention.

How Do We Study Language Perception in a Nonverbal Infant?

It is easy to understand why the topic of language learning in infants has garnered so much attention and inquiry

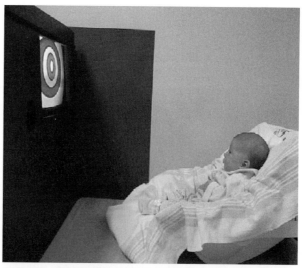

Figure 1 Photograph of a 1-month-old infant in a speech preference procedure. Whenever the infant looks at the target, a speech sample begins to play, for the duration of the look that initiated that particular trial. From the Infant Perception Laboratory, Department of Psychology, Virginia Tech.

from developmentalists. Almost all infants learn language and are trying to actively communicate with others by the end of the first postnatal year (**Figure 1**).

But ironically, it is difficult to go about studying language learning when our primary subjects do not yet use it! Developmental researchers have dealt with this by devising interesting techniques that capitalize on several aspects of infants' rapidly improving perceptuomotor skills. For example, as infants get older (usually by 4 months of age), they become proficient at controlling their own head movement, and can independently (**Figure 2**) turn to the left and to the right. One popular task used in language perception research takes advantage of this skill by allowing infants to hear certain words when they turn to their right (e.g., native language words) compared to other kinds of words on their left (e.g., foreign language words). In this particular task, we would conclude that infants recognize and prefer their native language if they turned their heads more often to the right (we would also test more infants with these words on their left to make sure there was no turning bias). There are quite a few different kinds of behavioral techniques that are used to ask questions about infant language processing, and capitalize on (**Figure 3**) different behavioral competencies. However, a full presentation of these methods is beyond the scope of this article. Thus, we summarize the most commonly used behavioral tasks for studying language perception during infancy in **Table 1**.

In addition to the clever behavioral methods that researchers have developed for the purpose of understanding preverbal development, this field of study has also greatly benefited from advances in a variety of psychophysiological techniques. Efforts to adapt brain-relevant development. A sample of such neuropsychological methods are summarized in **Table 2**, and we will integrate findings from this literature with those from behavioral studies as we present some of the major findings from research on preverbal development. In doing so, it is important to acknowledge that the infant brain is not simply a smaller version of that found in the adult. Studies on the organization of adults' nervous systems clearly show that certain areas of the brain tend to be specialized for language (e.g., left temporal cortex), and that when such areas are compromised through disease or injury, language impairments are highly likely. Infants' brains are quite different in both structure and function, and we should exercise appropriate caution in drawing parallels between findings with infants and adults. In spite of this caveat, it is important to explore evidence for similar and different neurological/neurophysiological mechanisms that appear to be related to various aspects of early language learning, for our understanding of both typical as well as atypical infant development.

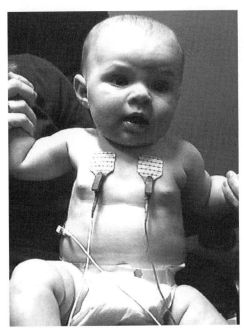

Figure 2 Photograph of an infant in a speech preference study who has been readied for the recording of heart rate (HR) activity. Two pediatric electrodes are attached to the infant's chest (above the breast bone) and a third is attached to the infant's lower right side (this electrode acts as a reference). The infant's HR activity is then recorded online during the procedure, and is event-marked so that it is possible to examine changes in HR activity during each experimental trial. From the Infant Perception Laboratory, Department of Psychology, Virginia Tech.

The Beginnings of Human Speech Perception

Late in prenatal development (at the start of the third trimester), human fetuses can hear (i.e., detect and/or react to sound). Fetuses are exposed to a variety of acoustic information, much of which consists of maternal speech sounds. Prenatally occurring maternal speech can be considered vibroacoustic because it resonates through the mothers' skeleton; maternal speech also occurs in a higher frequency band than most other *in utero* sounds, and it is louder at the fetal ear than typical airborne voices as it gets amplified by the bone structure of the female body. Prenatal work has shown that fetuses respond to their mothers' voices with greater heart rate changes (more heart rate decelerations, indicative of increased attention). After birth, newborns prefer their mothers' voice compared to an unknown female's voice, perhaps due to their exposure to the maternal voice *in utero*. Interestingly, newborns do not prefer the voices of their fathers, suggesting that male voices are not as readily available for fetal perception.

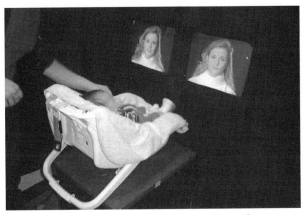

Figure 3 Picture of an infant in the two-choice preference procedure. When the infant looks at the monitor on the right, one speech stream will play. When the infant looks to the left, a different speech stream will play. Preferences can be discerned by calculating the magnitude of looking in each direction. Reprinted with permission from Dr. Janet Werker's website: http://infantstudies.psych.ubc.ca/meth_two.html.

recording procedures for use with infants and young children, such as scalp electroencephalography (EEG), magnetic resonance imaging (MRI), and optical topography (OT), have led to a greater understanding of neural structure and function (**Figure 4**) underlying language

A more direct demonstration of fetal learning comes from a study with pregnant women in Paris, who read a nursery rhyme aloud three times a day for 4 weeks toward the end of their pregnancies. Prior to delivery, two nursery rhymes were presented via loudspeakers to the fetuses; the one the mothers had been reciting and a novel rhyme. The fetuses showed significant changes in heart rate to the familiar rhyme but no change in heart rate to the unfamiliar rhyme. Other evidence of prenatal language learning has shown that when pregnant women recite a passage regularly, 2–3-day-old newborns modify their sucking patterns in ways that allow them to hear the

Table 1 Current behavioral methodologies for studying infants' language perception

Testing method	Examples of primary tasks	Dependent measure
Habituation	Infant is presented with a sound (e.g., the phoneme /ba/) repeatedly and then is tested with the familiar sound and a novel sound (e.g., /pa/)	If infant attends more to novel than to familiar sound.
Preference	Infant is presented with a visual display accompanied by one sound (e.g., native language) then by the same display accompanied by a second sound (e.g., foreign language); sounds stay on as long as infant looks at the display	If infant looks longer at the visual display when one of the two sounds is available.
Conditioned head turn	Infant is presented with a continuously repeating background sound (/ba/) which occasionally switches to a novel sound (/pa/); when infant looks in the direction of the sound that changes, reinforcement is delivered	If infant turns head to the side whenever sound changes compared to when there is no change.
Recognition/ matching	Infant is presented with two side x side visual displays of a speaking head and hears a centrally located sound-track that corresponds to one of the displays	If infant looks longer to the side that corresponds to the sound-track.
Segmentation	Infant is presented with a stream of acoustic input (e.g., phonemes, words, sentences) and then tested in a head-turn task with two different sound types (familiar on one side; novel on the other).	If the infants looks more the side that produces the familiar (or sometimes novel) stream of sounds.
Word/object pairing	Infant is repeatedly shown object A paired with word A, and a object B paired with word B. During test the infants sees+hears object A + word A, but also sees+hears a recombination (object A + word B).	If the infant attends longer on the 'switch' trial (object A + word B) than on the familiar trial.

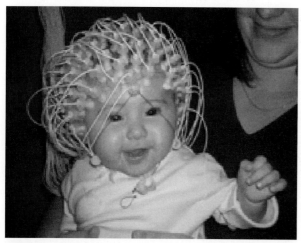

Figure 4 Picture of an infant wearing a high-density EEG cap for scalp recordings of brain activation patterns. Reprinted with permission from Dr. Laurel Trainor's website: http://www.psychology.mcmaster.ca/ljt/.

familiar passage. Newborns prefer recordings of their mothers' voices filtered in ways that mimic how such voices sound *in utero* over unfiltered versions that newborns experience after birth. Also, newborns prefer recordings of their native language (even when spoken by unfamiliar females).

Although it is unclear which aspects of maternal language are perceived prenatally, it appears that some information specific to the mother (her vocal signature) and her native tongue (language rhythm) are evident in the prenatal environment, and that this experience biases the newborn toward certain language sounds after birth. In contrast, one recent study with newborns suggests that not all early biasing comes from prenatal experience with mothers' voices. In this study, newborns showed a preference (**Figure 5**) for nonsense words (e.g., 'neem') over nonspeech sounds that shared every acoustic dimension with the nonsense words, except the spectral properties that allowed the words to sound 'speech-like'. Similar findings have come from our laboratory with 1-month-olds in which they showed a preference for normal speech over speech that was filtered to preserve its pitch patterning, but obscured the words (this is in contrast to the study mentioned above in which newborns preferred to hear a filtered version of their mother). From these results, it appears that infants are more likely to pay attention to speech sounds than nonspeech sounds (when the voice is someone other than their own mother), even from the earliest days after birth, and may reflect a strong perceptual bias toward language.

Such behavioral findings are supported by recent neurophysiological studies on whether there is an early developmental sensitivity to language-specific information in newborns. For example, using both OT and functional MRI (fMRI), researchers have found greater activation (e.g., increased blood flow) in language-specific brain regions in both Italian and French newborns to forward speech, compared to the same speech played backwards or to silence. Interestingly, other studies have found that newborns are more responsive to displays of the human face than to

Table 2 Current psychophysiological methodologies for studying infants' language perception

OT (optical topography)	The recording of changes in vascular blood flow from the scalp by measuring the absorption of infrared light in the brain (2–3 cm from the surface); cerebral blood flow increases in areas that are more active depending on the task. Optical fibers are placed on the scalp to both emit and detect changes in blood flow. Can be administered during sleep.
EEG (electroencephalogram)	The recording of electrical activity from the scalp, which reflects patterns of cortical activation/deactivation caused by synchronous firing of neuron assemblies. Although the temporal resolution of EEG activity is poor, it is a useful measure of the relationship between patterns of brain activity in relation to perceptual/cognitive function. Must be administered while awake.
ERP (event-related potential)	The recording of electrical activity from the scalp, similar to EEG except that the change in cortical activation/deactivation is time-locked to the onset of a discrete event. Of primary interest is the latency to significant changes in the amplitude of activation patterns (i.e., waveforms) that reflect brain activity during event processing. Can be administered during sleep.
MMN (mismatch negativity)	An ERP waveform component that is generated by an unexpected change in some repetitive string of events (e.g., a sudden change in the pitch of successive tones). MMN is evoked in response to changes in the physical features of a sound stimulus such as frequency, location, intensity and duration and also changes in patterns of sound. Can be administered during sleep.
fMRI (functional MRI)	The recording of changes in cerebral metabolic activity (blood volume shifts and blood oxygenation) in specific areas of cortex as a function of task parameters. The spatial resolution of fMRI (localization of cortical sources) is superior to EEG, but temporal resolution is similar to ERP. Can be administered during sleep.
Heart rate change	The recording of average length of interbeat intervals (heart period) during event processing. Increases in heart period reflect heart rate deceleration (associated with attention) whereas decreases in heart period reflect heart rate acceleration (associated with alerting or attention termination). Administered while awake.

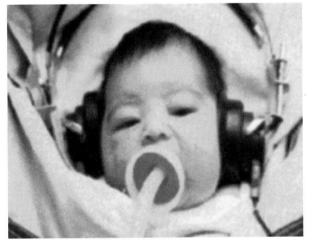

Figure 5 Picture of a 2-day-old newborn wearing headphones and sucking on a non-nutritive nipple that allows her to hear certain speech recordings, depending on when and how she sucks. Reprinted from Dr. Willam Fifer.

almost any other visual scene, suggesting that from birth, the human infant is highly attuned to visual and auditory concomitants of language. This face + voice sensitivity may be advantageous for infants' perceptual, emotional, and cognitive development during the numerous interpersonal interactions they are about to experience.

The Social and Emotional Ecology of Infant Language Learning

Language learning after birth takes place in a rich, interactive context in which caregivers, siblings, and others communicate with infants in order to regulate their attention, modulate their emotions and arousal levels, and teach them about themselves and the world around them. Moreover, infants are also surrounded by ongoing communication events between other partners and have numerous opportunities to observe dynamic properties of these exchanges. Thus, the consideration of early language learning is best served by a full description of this social milieu, especially with regard to the emergent communication patterns between infants and others.

Across many of the worlds' cultures, adults interact vocally with infants via speech and song. Infant-directed speech (IDS) often sounds considerably different from the speech that adults use when interacting with other adults, that is, adult-directed speech (ADS). When comparing the two, IDS is characterized by higher pitch, greater pitch variability, fewer words per utterance, longer pauses between utterances, slower rate, more repetition, and greater hyperarticulation (speech that is clearly enunciated). Generally, these are referred to as 'prosodic modifications' in that they primarily influence the way that speech 'sounds' to the listener. Adults often modify speech prosody to convey emotion, increase emphasis, and highlight intention, particularly in their speech to infants and children. When addressing infants, such modifications occur in the speech of mothers, fathers, other adults, and even children, and occur within a wide variety of language cultures (French, Italian, German, Japanese, Mandarin, Spanish, Australian, British English, American English, Japanese Sign Language, American Sign Language).

Several studies have shown that infants (especially when young) prefer IDS over ADS, although this depends on certain aspects of the testing context. For example, 1-month-olds show no preference for IDS over ADS when both are spoken by their own mother. However, they do prefer IDS when both are spoken by an unknown female. This further suggests the potency of the maternal voice for infant attention, possibly due to prenatal experience with the mother's voice, as young infants' preference for the maternal voice can override their preference for IDS. In contrast, 4-month-olds prefer IDS over ADS even when both are spoken by their mothers, showing their emerging interest in this enhanced speaking style and perhaps the diminished potency of the maternal voice as infants age. When paired with a smiling female face, female IDS effectively increases infants' attention, but female ADS does not. As infants get older, IDS has been found to increase attention, aid in emotion regulation, highlight linguistic information, and enable infants to better discriminate speaker gender, speech content, and temporal synchrony of facial information (coordination of lips, voice, and face movements).

Recently, it has been argued that infants' attention to IDS is primarily due to their perception of its emotional valence, especially for positive vocal emotion or 'happy talk'. Typically, IDS is emotionally rich, which may help to highlight the communicative intent (**Figure 6**) of the speaker. In fact, adults more accurately classify speaker intent when listening to IDS compared to ADS utterances. Interestingly, when IDS and ADS are equated for emotion valence (both speech types are rated by adults as 'happy'), infants show no preference for IDS over ADS. Likewise, when pitch characteristics are held constant, but one group of IDS utterances are judged as 'happy' and another judged as 'sad', infants prefer the happy speech. Therefore, it may be more accurate to say that infants are particularly drawn to speech that conveys a high degree of positive emotion, and that IDS is more likely to do so (at least in some cultures) than ADS. This being said, it is not the case that happy speech is the only speech to which infants respond, as IDS is often employed and effective when calming distressed infants or prohibiting activity in older infants. The vocal components of soothing and prohibitive speech are not the same as those in happy speech, yet infants readily respond to both.

The manner in which adults convey their emotions in speech to infants changes developmentally across the first postnatal year. It has been found that mother's adapt their patterns of interaction (including their voices but also facial and body gestures) according to the age of their infants. More specifically, mothers modify their voices primarily to calm and soothe a newborn and gently introduce them into social interactions. There is also an important social dynamic that is evident in these early communicative patterns not only for the infant but for adults as well. Studies that have compared caregivers' speaking and singing styles both in the presence and absence of their infants have found that mothers exaggerate their prosody more when interacting with their infants. That is, they sing and speak in a higher pitched voice, with a slower tempo, place more pauses between phrases, and have a more loving tone but only when their infant is actually present. Comparatively, the extent of these prosodic modulations declines when mothers sing as if their infant was present.

Although infants and caregivers contribute uniquely to the social situation, most often the caregiver is the more responsible agent for the coordination of the social interaction. Over time, these interactions lay the foundation for infants' understanding of their own emotions as well as the emotional messages being expressed to them. From 3 to 9 months, mothers typically alter their different intonation patterns that help optimize interactions (elicit attention and encourage participation), particularly as this is a time in which infants are able to initiate and contribute as an active partner in the social interchange. Infants appear to differentiate these interactive patterns, even by their vocal characteristics alone. When familiarized with different female voices, all conveying the same intention (e.g., eliciting activity), infants do not increase their attention to a new voice with the same intention, but do increase their attention to a new voice from a different intention category (e.g., calming). Additionally, 5-month-olds have shown differences in facial affect when presented

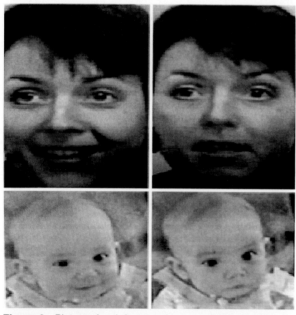

Figure 6 Picture of an infant watching two videos of a female speaker. On the left, she is presenting IDS, and on the right she is presenting ADS. Note the differences in emotional expression on the infant's face to these two interactive styles. Reprinted from Werker JF and McLeod PJ (1989) Infant preference for both male and female infant-directed talk: A developmental study of attentional and affective responsiveness. *Canadian Journal of Psychology* 43: 230–246.

with approval and prohibitive IDS (more smiling to approvals, more negative emotion to prohibitives). Interestingly, infants did not show any affective differences in response to approval and prohibitive ADS. These results suggest that infants can discriminate affective vocal expressions occurring in IDS and that it is more effective than ADS in eliciting infant emotion.

By 9 months, mothers actually attenuate some of the vocal exaggerations associated with positive emotion, replacing them with an increase in their use of directive utterances ("Don't put that in your mouth, sweetie."). As we will see in the next section, it is during this time that infants are becoming more aware of and tuned into the linguistic structure of their language, and thus may not rely as much on exaggerated vocal emotion to maintain their attention to speech. In fact, recent evidence from our laboratory suggests that the preference for IDS over ADS seen in younger infants is somewhat weaker in 8-month-olds. One interesting question that arises from studies investigating infants' speech preferences is whether the vocal emotion in IDS differentially affects infant learning at various ages. In her recent dissertation project, N. Bhullar found that 11–13-month-old infants discriminated a change in a target word carried in a set of IDS sentences (that remained constant) when they were presented by a dynamic female speaker who was portraying a happy expression. In contrast, another group of same-aged infants did not discriminate the word change under similar conditions except that the female speaker was portraying a sad expression.

In one of the few psychophysiological studies to focus on the perception of emotional prosody in speech, 7-month-old infants' event-related potentials (ERPs) were compared to happy, neutral, and angry speech. The amplitude of the first negative ERP wave was greatest for angry speech over frontal areas of the infants' brains (indicating more emotional attention to this event) and the amplitude of the first slow, positive ERP was greatest for happy and angry speech over temporal areas, but not so for neutral speech. This ERP pattern suggests enhanced sensory processing of emotionally loaded linguistic events (happy and angry speech). These psychophysiological data support the hypothesis that infants are primarily responsive to the emotional valence of speech, but they do not address the issue of whether infants prefer one emotional valence to another (e.g., happy over angry speech).

To this point, it is clear that the language ecology of the infant is replete with speech that appears tailored to their interests and needs, even if the primary motivation of adults who talk to infants is to convey their feelings of warmth and nurturance. From this input, infants construct their initial understanding of their native language, so we now turn to those processes that allow infants to decipher the information they will need to become competent communicators with those around them.

Infants' Perception of the Speech Stream

As is clear from the section above, the input to the infant is a critical aspect of language development. Given the complexities of language, however, it is not immediately obvious how any given language learner, but especially an infant, manages to listen to, comprehend, and then produce meaningful speech. As it turns out, infants can (and do) attend to many different aspects of language, and this perceptual multiplicity is highly adaptive because perception at one level almost always informs the perceiver about language at other levels (in the developmental literature, this is called 'bootstrapping').

By way of illustrating this point, we will discuss infants' perception of prosody (the intonation and rhythm patterns of language) and phonology (the individual speech sounds of language) as each pertains to the acquisition of language-relevant information. Although prosody and phonology continuously interact in natural speech (see **Figure 7**), it has been fruitful to consider them as separate sources of information for infants' language learning. Recall that prosody can reside above the level of individual speech sounds (e.g., the emotional tone of utterances), but it can also be linguistically relevant. Prosodic features provide important cues for phrase, clause, and word segmentation, and contribute to languages' stereotypical sounds.

Phonology often refers to individual speech sounds, such as consonants, vowels, clicks, and tone changes (e.g., in Thai) that are linguistically significant. The world's languages vary greatly in phonotactic structure, with some languages allowing certain combinations of speech sounds while excluding others (e.g., th- but not dp- at the start of an English word). Phonology also involves the combinations of phonemes into higher-order elements that are lexically meaningful (morphemes, syllables, words). Clearly, infants learning a language must perceive and produce its phonotactic elements, so a considerable amount of research has concentrated on this developmental process.

Perception of Prosody

Because the prosody of IDS is highly exaggerated and infants' attend more to IDS than to other speaking styles, IDS is likely to be advantageous for its language-promoting properties. One such prosodic source is linguistic rhythm, which varies across the world's languages. Some languages are stress-timed (their rhythm is determined by differential vocal emphasis on certain syllables) whereas others are syllable-timed (their rhythm is fairly constant because all syllables receive similar emphasis, but some syllables may receive stress primarily through consonant/vowel lengthening) or mora-timed (their rhythm is influenced more by voicing durations, in that some syllables contain vowels that are longer than others). Within stress-timed languages (such as English

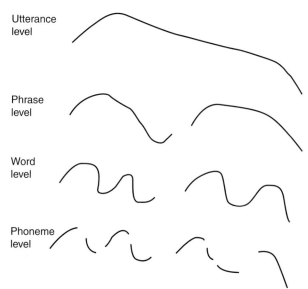

Figure 7 Hierarchical levels of pitch contours in human speech, starting with phonemes (lower portion) and ending with utterance level intonation contours (upper portion). Reprinted from Sagisaga Y (1990) Speech synthesis from text. *IEEE Communications Magazine* 28: 35–41.

and Dutch), some are dominated by a strong–weak trochaic pattern (as in English words such as '*fé*line' and '*per*son') compared to a weak–strong iambic pattern (such as the English words 'sus*tain*' and 'de*cide*'). Other kinds of prosodic features include intonation contours as they relate to communicative intent (e.g., rising pitch movement toward the end of a sentence to convey a question), lengthening of vowels in final syllables to indicate that a sentence is coming to an end, and periods of silence that indicate separation between successive utterances/words.

As early as 4 days old, newborns discriminate their native from a non-native language, even if the speech is acoustically filtered but leaving the prosodic contours intact. However, no discrimination is seen if newborns hear these filtered contours played in reverse, suggesting that the dynamics of forward pitch movement in speech is one early source of familiarity for infants. Newborns can distinguish between two languages with different stress/rhythm patterns (e.g., Dutch and Japanese) but have considerable difficulty discriminating two languages within the same stress category (e.g., Dutch and English). With more experience and better perceptual skills, 4-month-olds (and older infants) begin to show discrimination between languages within the same rhythm class, such as Spanish and Catalan, and even between two accented versions of the same language (American English and British English). In general, it appears that language stress or rhythm is one of the first ways in which infants begin to categorize languages, with broad rhythmic classes acting as perceptual 'anchors' from which they refine their perception of differences across and within their own and other languages.

Several neuropsychological studies have found support for infants' perception of linguistic prosody, one of the major cues for speech segmentation (e.g., stress patterns, phrases, clauses, words). Five-month-old, but not 4-month-old, German infants showed significant mismatched-negativity (MMN) effects in brain activity while hearing strings of bisyllabic words with their native stress pattern (e.g., trochaic) punctuated by an occasional word with a different stress pattern (e.g., iambic). Although these results show infants' attunement to the prevalent stress pattern in their native language, the results are slightly different from those found with behavioral studies. As mentioned above, infants show preferences for their native stress patterns in individual words at around 7 months of age, but not earlier. Thus, the discrepancy is in the finding that 5-month-olds discriminated a change in syllable-level stress whereas no preference for dominant native stress pattern has been seen until about 7.5 months of age. This most likely reflects younger infants' sensitivities to cues that do differentiate words before they are able to perceive that one such pattern predominates in their own native system. This is similar to the finding that younger infants discriminate both native and non-native phoneme contrasts, before they become attuned to those that are present in their own language. However, it would be interesting to couple the use of ERP and behavioral protocols in the same sample of infants to verify that discrimination using one technique does not necessarily predict discrimination in the other, contingent on infant age.

With age and experience, infants' perception of prosodic stress/rhythm continues to improve, helping infants with a particularly difficult task: segmenting ongoing speech into syllables and words, particularly in the second half of the first postnatal year. Studies have shown that by 6 months, American infants prefer native over non-native words (e.g., English vs. Norwegian), and by 9 months, infants prefer bisyllabic words with the predominate stress patterns of their native language (e.g., trochaic or iambic), even if the words are filtered to reduce phonetic information. Within this same age range, infants are also able to use stress patterns to isolate words from sentences, but more so if the words reflect their language's dominant stress pattern. For example, American 7-month-olds recognize words like *doc*tor and *can*dle (trochaic) after hearing these in sentences, but they do not recognize words like gui*tar* (iambic), suggesting that infants use the strong syllable (the one with the primary stress) as the start of a word. Of course, as infants get older, they become more adept at extracting words from sentences with any given stress pattern, including weak syllables, but this is a harder perceptual feat and no doubt requires more language experience.

There is evidence that 2–3-day-old infants can use prosodic cues to help mark the onset of phrase and clause boundaries in continuous speech. These cues are helpful to newborns because they highlight certain units of language and allow for further processing (they can focus on phrase-level vs. sentence-level strings). Likewise, 6-month-olds listen longer to IDS sentences in which natural clauses are bounded by short pauses compared to sentences in which pauses have been artificially inserted, suggesting that even silence can act as a perceptual cue to phonological boundaries. Interestingly, this same pattern is seen in older infants with words in that they prefer pauses between words rather than within them, but only when the words are not filtered. This is important because the finding that this preference does not emerge when the word-level information is not available demonstrates that as infants grow older and gain more experience with language, they progressively integrate both prosodic (e.g., pauses) and phonological (e.g., specific consonants and vowels) cues for speech segmentation.

Infants may also integrate across prosodic and phonological levels in their speech preferences given the results of several recent experiments in our laboratory. We have found that American 6-month-olds prefer Australian female IDS over American female IDS (even when the same sentences are being spoken), but not if the speech is low-pass filtered (the words are no longer available). In other experiments, we also found that 10-month-olds preferred native utterances (i.e., American) over non-native utterances (e.g., Mandarin), but only within IDS; when using ADS, no preferences were found. It is possible that when listening to ADS, infants did not attend as much to the phonological information in order to recognize utterances as native speech. In sum, the prosodic aspects of language are readily perceived by infants during the entire first postnatal year, and appear to provide important cues to native language structure and to breaking into the speech stream in order to learn about its lexical elements. Next we consider infants' perception at this more elemental level.

Perception of Phonology

Phonemes are the basic sound units in any given language that have become incorporated into formal language systems. For many of the worlds' languages, phonemes consist of various combinations of consonants (C) and vowels (V). For other languages, a phoneme can also be defined as a CV+tone combination. For example, in Thai, ma(rising pitch) is a different phoneme from ma (falling pitch). Phonemes can be differentiated at many levels, such as: (1) their place and/or manner of articulation (e.g., whether the lips are closed or open during production), (2) their voicing properties (e.g., whether activity in the larynx begins prior to full production), and (3) degree of aspiration (or airflow) during production.

From the newborn period onward, infants from all language cultures appear capable of discriminating phonemes (notice a change from one to another), with two features of early phoneme perception being especially noteworthy. First, infants (like adults) perceive phonemes categorically. That is, they discriminate the phonemes /ba/ and /pa/, because they come from two distinct categories (according to an acoustic feature called voice onset time). However, they do not discriminate two versions of 'pa' [pa_1 vs. pa_2] or two versions of ba [ba_1 vs. ba_2] even though acoustically these pairs are just as distinct as the ba/pa contrast, yet they do not cross category boundaries.

The second interesting aspect of phoneme perception is that younger infants respond categorically to speech contrasts that are present in their native language, and also to those that are not present in their native language (i.e., non-native phonemes they have not previously heard). This is true for both consonants and vowels, suggesting that early phonetic perception derives from more general auditory competencies. However, with age and experience, infants continue to discriminate native phonemes, but have more difficulty discriminating non-native speech sounds. This has generally been referred to as perceptual attunement, resulting from infants' increasing attention to and encoding of native language information.

Interestingly, this pattern of initial perceptual openness followed by progressive narrowing across infancy is seen in other domains. For example, younger infants discriminate between pairs of human faces as well as primate faces, but older infants only maintain discrimination of human faces, even if the primate faces are accompanied by distinct vocalizations. Most recently, infants have even shown discrimination of video presentations of both native and non-native phonemes (with no sound track) at younger ages, but not at older ages. In the older group, only discrimination of native visual phonemes was evident.

Neurophysiological studies support these general behavioral patterns (categorical perception and perceptual attunement). Newborns and slightly older infants show distinct ERPs to categorical changes in consonants, especially those involving voice-onset-time differences. Such category-specific ERPs have been observed over several cortical areas, some involving the right or left hemisphere, and some involving both. Interestingly, distinct ERPs occur in infants when listening to phonemes with place-of-articulation differences but these effects are observed primarily over the left temporal areas (a more adult-like pattern). Discrimination of changes in phoneme categories (both consonants and vowels) has also been observed using MMN measures. For example, newborns show a distinct MMN pattern when presented with two Finnish vowels. MMN has also been observed in English 8-month-olds to the CV pairs /da/ and /ta/. In a similar study, MMN was recorded from Finnish infants at 6 and 12 months of age in a longitudinal design, and from Estonian 12-month-old infants. Both groups of infants were tested for their discrimination of changes in Finnish and in Estonian vowels. The results showed a significant MMN response in the 6-month-olds to both native (Finnish) and non-native (Estonian) vowels, and also in the 12-month-old Estonian infants to their native vowels. However, all infants at 12 months showed diminished MMN to non-native vowels.

Likewise, in a longitudinal ERP study, American infants at 7 and 11 months of age were presented with native and non-native speech contrasts. The results showed no difference in ERP latency or magnitude in speech-related components to either native or non-native contrasts at 7 months of age, but only the native contrasts elicited these same ERP patterns at 11 months of age. This is consistent with the behavioral data reported with non-native speech discrimination. We might expect, then, that the underlying biological substrates that subserve language processing are the same across infants and adults. Infants between 13- and 17-months of age also show larger amplitude ERP responses to known than to unknown words, with this difference evident in both hemispheres in the frontal, parietal and temporal lobes. By 20 months of age, however, this ERP enhancement is restricted to the left hemisphere over the temporal and parietal lobes only, indicating a gradual specialization of the neural systems for processing words (and much more akin to the pattern seen in adults). These results were further corroborated in a study with 14- and 20-month-olds in which they heard known words, unknown words that were phonetically similar to the known words, and unknown words that were phonetically dissimilar from the known words. Both age groups showed higher amplitude ERP responses to known than to unknown words. However, the 14-month-olds' ERP responses were similar in amplitude for known words and phonetically similar unknown words which imply that these words were confusing. In contrast, ERP responses in the 20-month-olds to the phonetically similar unknown words were the same as those to the unknown words. These findings show that the older infants improved processing of phonetic detail with experience compared to the younger infants.

Thus, young infants show consistent brain-related responses to different speech sounds (supporting the behavioral evidence) but their brain-localization patterns in response to different phonemes appears to depend (at least to some extent) on the nature of the information in the speech sounds that make them distinct. Vocal-timing differences appear to be represented more diffusely in the infant brain whereas place/manner of articulation takes on a more adult-like representation (left-temporal localization). This could be due to less cortical specificity for timing in general (because timing is a process involved in many domains of perceptual functioning) and/or because there are multiple pathways available for speech processing in the developing nervous system, given that the infant is less experienced with speech in general. This latter possibility may help to explain one study which examined infants' processing of their native language compared to a non-native language and to backwards speech. The results showed that areas of cortex in infants' brains that are activated by the native language are not completely confined to the primary auditory areas but include those similar to adults in their localization (temporal region) and lateralization (left hemisphere). This early lack of specificity has also been found using ERP methods with 6-month-olds, in which same-component ERPs to words are equally large over temporal and occipital (typically referred to as visual cortex) brain regions. Interestingly, between 6 and 36 months of age, there is a gradual decrease in the ERP amplitude to vocal words (i.e., decreased processing) over occipital areas but the amplitude remains unchanged over temporal areas.

Such findings point to a common process of perceptual attunement to culturally relevant information throughout the first postnatal year. In terms of language development, infants begin building linguistic representations of phonemes so that their subsequent perception is guided by the fit between an incoming speech sound and these phonemic representations. We have also seen that prosodic information appears to assist infants in this focusing on important elements of speech (prosody bootstraps the discovery of phonemic detail). But what happens if the speech stream that infants' hear is prosodically attenuated, as is more likely the case when the caregiver seeks to soothe and calm a distressed infant. Such soothing speech is more likely to be lower in pitch, pitch variance, amplitude, and slow. Therefore, are infants not as perceptually attuned to language in these instances? Would infants not learn language if only an ADS style of speaking was available to them?

Perception of Conditional Probability

These questions can be addressed by studies examining another process that appears to facilitate infants' segmentation of words, called statistical learning. Statistical learning occurs when perceivers are sensitive to the conditional probabilities of the occurrence of adjacent events, over time. When applied to speech, statistical learning refers to the conditional probability that one phoneme will follow another. For example, if the probability of 'mas' being followed by 'cot' is high (let's say close to 90%), then a listener might anticipate the sequence 'mascot'. Such sensitivity to conditional probabilities leads to the perceptual grouping of high probability strings (or phoneme clusters), allowing listeners to parse units (e.g., words) from the speech stream relatively rapidly and efficiently. Recently, 8-month-old infants were played continuous strings of speech sounds with no prosodic cues present (e.g., pagotiku...pagotikitula) in which the conditional probabilities of some phonemes (pagoti) were higher than others. In a subsequent test, infants showed different amounts of attention to 'words' such as 'pagoti' compared to nonwords such as 'dotapa' (the conditional probability of this string was very low). So even in the absence of prosodic cues, infants can use other information to help find words in speech. Nonetheless, other recent studies have found that when infants have a choice between prosodic and conditional probability cues for segmentation, they tend to rely on prosody first.

In sum, the speech that is characteristically available during interactions between adults and infants appears to be organized in a way that facilitates language processing. In fact, even adults who are learning words from a non-native language benefit from this same kind of speaking style. These benefits derive from the structure of the input itself, especially that the prosodic and phonotactic characteristics are exaggerated in ways that make speech information more perceptually available. Overall, the evidence from neurophysiological studies supports those using only behavioral measures of infants' speech processing abilities (e.g., phoneme discrimination; discrimination of linguistic stress). However, the correspondence between adults and infants regarding cortical patterns of localization for speech is less clear. Some level of cortical organization for speech is apparent, but the precise patterning of area-specific increases in activation is dependent on method and/or speech information. Clearly, this is an area of concern for future infant speech research, and will no doubt benefit from continued improvements in technologies as well as infant-specific cortical models.

Relating Research from the Laboratory to Infants' Language-Learning Ecology

To this point, we have considered the nature of speech to infants and how it appears to be ideally suited to maximize attention and highlight information that needs to be culled from the speech stream in order to learn language. We have also seen that to some extent, early language perception is subserved by patterns of cortical organization that promote language processing (e.g., specialization of the left hemisphere for speech). In this last section, we turn to a slightly different issue in considering the context in which language learning takes place, and whether the current literature on infants' perception of speech can address issues of ecological validity. Ideally, language learning takes place in a quiet environment, one in which the speech signal can easily be attended to and identified, processed and stored for later use. In contrast, most infants face more challenging learning situations in their daily lives. Infants acquire language in homes filled with sources of multisensory information (sounds, sights, smells, textures), that can include multiple caregiver and siblings, and an endless list of potential distractors and competitors for attention. In the laboratory, most of this complexity is substantially reduced to make the perceptual task more accessible to the infant, and to increase the likelihood that learning will occur, but this is done at the risk of potentially misrepresenting the natural context for language learning, and so may reduce external validity. We will review the results of studies that have brought some of this natural complexity into the laboratory in interesting ways, and then we will also make suggestions for how future studies can be designed to more accurately model the language learning ecology during infancy.

Given that most natural language learning situations contain more than one sound source at any point in time, infants must be able to separate speech from background distraction, a process known as streaming. Compared to adults, infants appear to be at a disadvantage for streaming because they have: (1) higher auditory detection thresholds (sounds, including speech, need to be louder before they can be detected), (2) higher auditory discrimination thresholds (sounds, including speech, in both quiet and noise, need to be more discrepant before a change from one to another can be detected), and (3) more difficulty localizing sound in space. Also, unlike adults, infants do not listen more selectively to the frequency band within which most speech sounds occur, which means they are attending to other areas of auditory space that are not necessary for perceiving language.

Nonetheless, infants do perceive speech and learn much about their native language in spite of noisy environments and limitations in their perceptual skills. Once again, it may be IDS that helps to facilitate speech perception under demanding conditions. A series of experiments have found that infants can successfully match a voice track with its complementary video of a female speaker when a distracting male voice has been superimposed on her speech, if she is using IDS; if she is using ADS, no such matching occurs. Similarly, infants are able to learn words being repeated by a female IDS speaker even when a male distractor voice is superimposed on hers. However, they do not learn words if these voices are reversed (i.e., the words are delivered by a male ADS speaker with a female IDS distractor voice superimposed on his). Infants show this same kind of enhanced attention when the speaker's voice is someone they know (e.g., their own mother) compared to an unknown female. Thus, the combination of IDS and familiarity appears to help infants focus on both speakers and what is being said.

The ability of familiarity to aid infants' speech perception was shown in a similar study in which infants listened longer to a female speaker when she uttered the infant's own name compared to when she uttered the names of other infants, even when several background female voices were superimposed on the target voice. Importantly, infants' recognition of familiar words in the speech stream (e.g., their own names) also seems to increase the saliency of adjacent words, allowing infants to better process them. It is thought that frequency of sound patterns that are heard repetitively early in the first year are the first steps in building a lexicon. Around 6 months of age, infants respond more to utterances that contain their names than to those containing other infants' names (matched for syllable structure). Capitalizing on this finding, researchers familiarized 6-month-olds with utterances containing the infants own names or others' names, along with target words directly before and after the embedded name. They found that the infants were more likely to recognize isolated target words in a subsequent test when they had occurred adjacent to the infant's own name.

There are many cognitive processes associated with an infant's ability to comprehend speech in noise that are relevant to language learning. Speech stream segregation involves infant discrimination of speech from other sources of information (particularly other acoustics), perceptual identification of speech and cues occurring from a specific speaker, and selective attention to that speaker. If there is a deficiency in any of these cognitive processes, an infant's ability to hear speech in noise will be impaired. Further, it has been suggested that if an infant does have difficulty discriminating speech in a noisy environment it may have underpinnings for later language development, as poorer ability to segregate streams of speech could potentially lead to slower language acquisition. This variability in infant performance has yet to be fully explored.

Finally, most existing studies on infants' language learning have employed methods that rely primarily on the presentation of language (whether phonemes, words, or utterances) either in the absence of a face and/or in the presence of an arbitrary visual event (e.g., a checkerboard). However, language learning often takes place in face-to-face interactions between infants and caregivers, and there is often concurrent information about how the sound looks as it is articulated, the timing of the sound with its visual movement in the face, whether or not it is exaggerated in its production (both vocally and facially), and the ways in which speech is complemented by gestures. An important demonstration of the power of face+voice information on infants' perception of consonants is provided by studies involving the McGurk Effect. For example, 4.5-month-old infants were familiarized with a female speaker who was mouthing the phoneme /ga/ but the video was accompanied by her voice saying /ba/. When adults view this video, they perceive a blended phoneme of either /da/ or /tha/. When the infants were tested after familiarization, they only paid attention to the phoneme /ba/, suggesting that they perceived this phoneme as novel even though it is actually the one they heard during familiarization. So, the infants most likely perceived the blended phoneme, like adults, rather than the actual phoneme. This demonstrates the power of the face to influence infants' perception of speech, but this aspect of language learning has largely been ignored in previous research.

Taken together, it is clear that the field of infant speech perception has made great strides toward our understanding of one of the most interesting and important feats in development. With our focus on new and exciting questions, coupled with our continued creativity in designing laboratory tasks that capture the essence of the natural context in which language is learned, this field of research will continue to contribute to our ability to fully characterize language acquisition, and all of its inherent complexities.

See also: Bilingualism; Grammar; Habituation and Novelty; Language Acquisition Theories; Language Development: Overview; Learning; Literacy; Pragmatic Development; Semantic Development; Speech Perception.

Suggested Readings

Aslin RN, Jusczyk PW, and Pisoni DB (1998) Speech and auditory processing during infancy. In: Kuhn D and Siegler RS (eds.) *Handbook of Child Psychology: Vol. 2. Cognition, Perception, and Language*, pp. 199–254. New York: Wiley.

Jusczyk PW (1997) *The Discovery of Spoken Language.* Cambridge, MA: MIT Press.

Kitamura C and Burnham DK (2003) Pitch and communicative intent in mother's speech: Adjustments for age and sex in the first year. *Infancy* 4: 85–110.

Lavelli M and Fogel A (2005) Developmental changes in the relationship between the infant's attention and emotion during early face-to-face communication: the 2-month transition. *Developmental Psychology* 41: 265–280.

Mehler J (1995) Maturation and learning of language in the first year of life. In: Gazzaniga MS (ed.) *The Cognitive Neurosciences*, pp. 943–954. 943–954. Cambridge, MA: MIT Press.

Sagisaga Y (1990) Speech synthesis from text. *IEEE Communications Magazine* 28: 35–41.

Werker JF and Curtin S (2005) PRIMIR: A developmental framework of infant speech processing. *Language Learning and Development* 1: 197–234.

Werker JF and Desjardins RN (1995) Listening to speech in the first year of life: Experiential influences on phoneme perception. *Current Directions in Psychological Sciences* 4: 76–81.

Werker JF and McLeod PJ (1989) Infant preference for both male and female infant-directed talk: A developmental study of attentional and affective responsiveness. *Canadian Journal of Psychology* 43: 230–246.

Werker JF and Vouloumanos A (2001) Speech and language processing in infancy: A neurocognitive approach. In: Nelson CA and Luciana M (eds.) *Handbook of Developmental Cognitive Neuroscience*, pp. 269–280. Cambridge, MA: MIT Press.

Reasoning in Early Development

E K Scholnick, University of Maryland, College Park, MD, USA

© 2008 Elsevier Inc. All rights reserved.

Glossary

Analogical reasoning – Based on the discovery that two systems have some similar internal relations, inferences are made that there additional ways the systems correspond to one another.

Basic level – The most accessible level of categorization in a hierarchy because the instances in the class are fairly similar but also are fairly distinct from members of other categories. In the hierarchy of poodles, dogs, and canines, 'dogs' is the basic category.

Deduction – Drawing the implications of a sentence according to a set of laws.

Essentialism – The belief that for each category of things found in nature, whether they are animals, vegetables, or minerals, there is an underlying invisible essence that causes things to be the way they are.

Induction – Reasoning from knowledge of one particular to another particular or from a particular fact to a general law.

Modus ponens – A form of conditional reasoning which permits a deduction from an if-statement 'If p, then q'. When p is true, then q must also be true.

Modus tollens – A form of conditional reasoning which permits a deduction from an if-statement 'If p, then q'. If q is false, then p must be false, too.

Natural kinds – Classes of entities occurring in nature such as animals, plants, and minerals. Instances of a class seem to share a common essence (see essentialism).

Pragmatic schema – A set of rules for social interactions, such as permissions and obligations.

Introduction

Why does the topic of reasoning belong in a volume devoted to infants and preschoolers? Should we expect toddlers to exercise the rules of thought that enable the derivation of new information from earlier material? Suppose the child is promised, "If it is sunny, we will go to the zoo tomorrow." When the child wakes up the next day and learns the zoo trip is canceled, can we expect her to rush to the window to see the rain? If the toddler is told that he needs exercise to make him strong, will he infer that his dog does, too? Clearly having strong reasoning skills would be advantageous to young children in their quest to grasp the intricate patterns that shape our universe and our daily lives. The child would not have to repeat the same lesson every time a new event or object appeared. The early emergence of reasoning would explain how easily children learn to name objects, embark upon a vocabulary spurt, figure out how to combine words, and construct a grammar. But the realm of deduction has been the exclusive purview of philosophers and geometers, and induction and analogy are the tools of scientists and inventors. Are there really practicing Aristotles in the nursery? If so, what enables them to do it? Maybe they are simply practicing 'toy' versions of reasoning with miniature tools that will grow in size, power, and complexity just as their body grows throughout childhood.

The study of early reasoning is fascinating because it tracks the origins of processes that uniquely characterize our species. These origins have been controversial because the cognitive revolution in psychology was accompanied by a second revolution in developmental psychology which eradicated the barriers between mature and infant thought. Additionally computational models have redefined the nature of the processes by which inductions, deductions, and analogies are accomplished and the methods by which they are studied. The debates about whether, when, and how youngsters reason are intimately linked to the process of taking reasoning from the nursery into the laboratory and using laboratory data to model thought.

A Framework for Understanding Issues in the Development of Reasoning

The deduction about the zoo trip was triggered by a sentence with a subordinate if-clause followed by a main clause, or in formal logic, an initial premise with antecedent (if p) and consequent (then q) clauses. A second premise provided new information that denied the consequent (not q, no trip). Conditional logic dictates the conclusion about the status of the antecedent precondition (not p, no sun). 'If' often signals that the original premise is hypothetical. Who knows tomorrow's weather? The sentence describes a familiar event. The toddler has visited the zoo under diverse weather conditions and knows that thunderstorms ruin excursions. Pragmatically, the parent has promised an excursion under certain preconditions. In daily life, interpretations of conditional premises draw upon knowledge of logic, syntax, social interactions, and events, and the child who is developing competence in reasoning is simultaneously gaining social and linguistic competencies which may support reasoning. There are multiple redundant cues and multiple redundant processes by which the information can be extended. But the scientific study of psychological processes is analytic and focuses on single processes at their simplest level. This reductionist approach presents barriers to the study of children's reasoning. Each facet of reasoning, its syntax, semantics, pragmatics, and logical form, facilitates reasoning. As each is removed, reasoning becomes harder and more inaccurate and young children seem less competent. Moreover, our models of reasoning and its origins become impoverished because they do not encompass the multiple inroads available to children depending on the circumstances and skills of the child.

The definition of reasoning is also elusive. Four new pieces of information could follow the premise, "If it is sunny, we will go to the zoo." Two focus on the antecedent if-clause and either affirm the precondition of a sunny day (modus ponens) or deny it, citing rain, and then leave the reasoner to decide whether there will be a zoo trip. Two others focus on the consequent, either affirming that the zoo trip occurred, or as in the modus tollens example that canceled the trip, denying the consequent clause, leaving the reasoner to infer the weather conditions. Modus ponens reasoning is accessible to toddlers but college sophomores studying logic err in the inferences they draw from affirming the consequent or denying the antecedent because the inference is indeterminate. The if-premise states what happens when its precondition is satisfied, but says nothing about what happens when it is not satisfied. The abysmal performance of adults on problems with indeterminate answers led to claims that some or all of conditional logic falls outside the province of mature reasoners, much less children. The more encompassing the definition of reason, the more likely complex processing will be required to exhibit the skill, and competence will appear late in development.

There are also levels of understanding of reasoning, and where the bar is set may determine the age of emergence and the level of competence attributed to the reasoner. Children may know the agenda for a zoo trip on a sunny day. Do children also know that canceling the excursion on a sunny day would make their mother a liar? Forms of inference and their ramifications, like falsification strategies, may not emerge simultaneously. Just as President Clinton once tried to evade his questioners by noting that it depends on what the meaning of 'is' is, analyses of reasoning depend on what the meaning of reasoning is.

Debates about the emergence of reasoning fall into three camps. The first camp inspired the question, "What's the topic of reasoning doing in this volume?" Reasoning is a higher order skill best studied with abstract materials, and embedded in two interlocking systems, of mutually entailing rules and conscious awareness of their conditions of operation. The rules are idealizations that most individuals rarely attain. Only logicians and scientists reason with any facility. The rules exemplify what children can aspire to master. The study of logic in childhood is either an oxymoron or a search for the roots. The second, opposing view posits scientists in the crib, born with either powerful reasoning devices that undergird learning or powerful belief systems about domains like biology or social behavior that support reasoning. The early emergence of reasoning demonstrates the power of our evolutionary endowment to prepare children to adapt to the world. The third view is developmental. There are pronounced changes in children's reasoning skills. This perspective encompasses lively debates about starting points, developmental mechanisms, benchmarks of change, and final destinations. Some researchers ground early reasoning in dumb mechanisms like attention, perception, and association that become smarter and more abstract. Alternatively the initial theory of the world that undergirds reasoning may undergo radical changes. The choice of theory and its characterization of young children reflect prior choices of the definition of reasoning and the contexts in which it is studied. This article provides a survey of 2–5-year-old's inductive, analogical, and deductive inference performance that bears on these debates.

Induction

Induction extends information known about one particular to another or from a particular to the general. Scientists use induction when they take a pattern in a sample of data as the basis for a general law. It is also a tool for everyday learning. My collie Spot likes to chew on bones. Other collies like Rover should like to chew on bones, too. There is no certainty that Rover likes to chew on bones, but knowledge of dogs might enable toddlers to guess what might please a new dog. The inference is based on the assumption that the unfamiliar target instance (Rover) is like the familiar Spot in some respect. Therefore, Rover might resemble Spot in other ways. Debates about induction revolve around three issues: (1) the meaning of 'like', the original linkage that supports induction; (2) the properties of the familiar or source stimulus, Spot, that children are willing to project onto inductive targets like Rover; and (3) the mechanisms enabling linkage of the base and target and projection of properties.

If Spot and Rover were identical twins, the task of inferring similar food preferences would be simple. Animals that look alike in one way might be alike in others. Perceptual similarity enables the inference. But if Rover is a poodle, a wolf, or a tiger, would the child assume these animals share Spot's food preferences? They would have to search for the category to which both the dog and the target animal belong. Children would then need to draw upon their knowledge of dogs, canines, or animals as the basis for induction. The base and target are both dogs, canines, or animals so they must have similar body structures. Because the child might not recognize that dogs and tigers are both animals, they might not recognize they share some common properties. Thus induction might depend on knowledge of categories. The likelihood of inferences also depends on properties. If the property projected is visible like diet, validating an inference is easy. But if the property is invisible, like having an omentum, then ordinary observation cannot validate inductions. The child must have a theory or causal narrative that explains why all dogs or all canines or animals probably have an omentum. Because induction tasks can differ in the relations between the base and target entities and the properties that are projected, there are different stories of the origin and course of induction in early childhood.

Every theory acknowledges that even infants recognize common categories such as females and males and can make simple inductions from one member of a narrow category to another. Twelve- to 14-month-olds who learn that a novel object is squeezable will attempt to squeeze highly similar objects. They will even make inductions about objects that are not close replicas if the objects share the same name. Word learning indicates inductive capacities, too. When my son began to label dogs 'woof-woof', he called every dog by that name as well as neighborhood cats.

Susan Gelman claims that this early appearing inductive capacity is deployed to make inferences about members of certain kinds of categories. The infant starts with a cognitive bias to carve the world into pieces, each associated with a story justifying the way the world is sliced. Those stories enable the child to make inductions among events, entities, and phenomena in each realm because they obey the same laws or they have the same infrastructure. A key line of demarcation is between natural entities, such as animals and minerals, and artifacts like automobiles and buildings. Susan Gelman's research on induction focuses primarily on living creatures and a naive biological theory, essentialism, that explains their appearances and behaviors. Upon hearing that one creature is called a 'bird' and another, a 'bat', the child has an all-purpose theory to explain why different creatures receive different names. All creatures within each named category have a common invisible essence that accounts for why they are the way they are and do what they do. We often hear people say things like "Boys will be boys." This belief bias is a placeholder for later, more scientific explanations invoking genetic causation for traits, behavior, and appearances.

The structure of categories provides a tool for testing theory-based induction as opposed to perceptually based induction. Although members of a category usually resemble each other, not all members of a category look alike. Angelfish do not resemble sharks but both are fish because their internal anatomy supports the capacity to live under water and they have similar reproductive systems. Appearances can also be deceiving. Dolphins look like sharks but they breathe air and bear live young. If children made inductions simply on the basis of perceptual appearances they would infer that a novel property of sharks also characterizes dolphins. But if they had a theory of fish 'essences' they would instead assume that sharks and angelfish share the same properties. Susan Gelman demonstrated that young children's inductions were governed by an essentialist theory. She showed children two line drawings, for example, an angelfish and a dolphin. Each animal was named and children were told a property. "This fish stays underwater to breathe. This dolphin pops above water to breathe." They then saw a picture of a shark, and were asked whether it breathes like the fish (angelfish) or the dolphin. Four-year-olds' choices were based primarily on category membership. The same pattern of induction is shown by 32-month-olds. For example, when they saw a picture of a bluebird which they were told lives in a nest, they acknowledged that other bluebirds lived in a nest and so do dodos who do not look much like bluebirds. They did not think that pterodactyls, the flying winged dinosaurs, lived in nests. The children usually made the correct inference that birds and dinosaurs have different living places. For young children the trigger for an essentialist induction is naming. If they heard the name of the creature or knew its name, they decided that the weird dodo bird lived in a nest while the pterodactyl, despite its bird like appearance, lived elsewhere. Without those labels most answers were based on appearances.

Young children do not make inductions indiscriminately. When categories are labeled by proper nouns like 'Tabby' which denote individuals, they do not make category-based inferences. Adjectives won't suffice either, perhaps because they do not tap into the categories that index causal essences. If the property is transient or accidental, such as 'fell on the floor this morning' inductions are less because it is also unlikely to play a causal role in defining identity. Category labels appear to play an important role in triggering children's inductions, and Susan Gelman theorizes that they may help children construct essentialist categories. When she observed parents reading picture books to young children, she found that they used generic common nouns like 'dolphin' more frequently to describe animals, which are the subject of essentialist theories, than artifacts. Their children show the same labeling bias, using generics especially for animate terms. These labels also draw attention to the stability and coherence of categories and thus indirectly support the child's inferences. Thus growth in inferential skill in the biological domain might reflect changes in the understanding of categories or revisions in the theory of natural kinds.

The mechanism for inference is referral of the base instance, for example, angelfish, to a higher order category, fish, and projection of essential properties of one fish to other category members. But angelfish are fish, vertebrates, and animals, too. Given a familiar animal with a novel property like having an omentum, how far up the category hierarchy do children go in making inductions? Research on the scope of induction in young children echoes research on categorization. The toddler's categories are very broad, animate or inanimate, plant or animal, but they quickly form categories at the basic level where there are sufficient commonalities among category members to form a coherent set, and also enough distinctiveness to easily differentiate one category from another. Sharks are finned, scaly, and gilled, but dogs are not. But it is difficult to discriminate nurse sharks from tiger sharks. Basic level categories are also usually assigned a single noun name, for example, shark rather than tiger shark. Induction follows the same route. With age, the scope of induction narrows. Two-year-old wills will generalize a property like "needing biotin to live" from animals to plants. But 3–4-year-olds prefer to make property inductions within basic categories like fish or birds. Experts in fields narrow their inferences further because they know that species of fish and birds may behave very differently. For example, penguins do not fly. The privileged level for experts' reasoning is very narrow because their category hierarchy includes more differentiated subspecies. When preschoolers in families who lived in rural areas or who worked in biological fields were tested, they, too, were more discerning in their inductions. They would project what they knew about one subspecies to another but not to broader categories. Category-based induction may reflect changes in children's theories of categories in different domains.

Although preschoolers make categorical inductions, unlike adults, they do not fully understand what constitutes good evidence for inductions. Some inductions are more convincing than others. For adults, inductive inferences are stronger if they are based on a great variety of examples. This is termed categorical coverage. You are told both cats and buffalos have cervicas inside them. Additionally cows and buffalos have ulnaries inside them. Based on this information what do you think kangaroos have inside them, cervicas or ulnaries? Because cats and buffalos are two very different species, cervicas may be a very general property of animals and could apply to kangaroos, which also fit under the animal umbrella. But buffalos and cows are both hoofed mammals, and a kangaroo is a marsupial. So it would be safer to claim the kangaroo has cervicas than ulnaries. Adults also believe that the more similar the source and target animals, the stronger the inference. If both a zebra and a horse possess ulnaries, it is safer to conclude a donkey possesses ulnaries than a kangaroo does. Kindergartners acknowledge that information about animals similar to the target of the inference provides a more reliable base for induction than information about source items dissimilar to the target. But they do not believe that the strength of an inference is related to the span of category coverage. Seven-year-olds recognize that categorical coverage matters, too, but only if they are reminded they are making inferences to all the animals.

Why should children do so well on making inferences but not on judging the strength of the evidence? Why should they be more sensitive to similarity evidence than category coverage? These judgment tasks present more information to process. Each argument set includes several instances. The overburdened 5-year-old may reduce the information by choosing a single similar animal in the base set to compare with the target. Additionally, children had to take the extra step of generating the relationship between the target and the inclusive class, animal, which forms the basis for inference. When the target of inference was labeled an animal, it made the task easier for 7-year-olds. The rules are also subtle. Diversity and similarity are opposite sides of the coin, yet both strengthen arguments. Success on these tasks requires metacognitive understanding of the rules of inference and their domain of application. Although kindergartners can easily make simple inferences, they may be stymied when the tasks require conscious awareness of the ground rules for induction.

There is another possibility. Even kindergartners know arguments are stronger if the base and target animals are similar but they do not appreciate the role of category coverage. Vladimir Sloutsky has claimed that early inductive inference is mediated by similarity and shifts toward categorization later. Sloutsky refined Gelman's research in two important ways. He obtained information about children's judgments of similarity and then he assessed children's performance on category, similarity, and naming tasks to tease apart their relative contributions to induction. Susan Gelman usually asked children to choose between a source of inference that looked like the target or that belonged to the same category as the target. But the mere appearance and categorical matches varied in their resemblance to the target items. Since some categorical inductions were harder than others, perhaps similarity accounted for these variations. So Sloutsky asked 4- and 5-year-olds to judge whether the mere appearance or the shared category picture was more like the target and also elicited inductions. He found that children were more likely to make essentialist categorical inductions if the category match closely resembled the target item and the mere appearance match was not very similar to the target. In short similarity supported the categorical induction. Conversely if the mere appearance match was indeed rated as very similar and the category match was dissimilar, the child was more likely to make inductions based on appearance. Therefore, Sloutsky asserted that categorical induction is not a higher order reasoning skill but is governed by simpler perceptual and attentional mechanisms that are the foundation for later developing categorical knowledge.

Susan Gelman argued that labels influence essentialist inductions by enabling children to detect essentialist categories and apply essentialist knowledge. Vladimir Sloutsky provided evidence that 4-year-olds use names for another purpose, enhancing the similarity between category members. He created a set of imaginary animals and then asked children to make similarity judgments. For example, there were two animals, equally similar to the target animal. When the animals were unnamed, the children chose at random. If the target and one animal were both called 'lolos' but the other animal was a 'tipi', the child chose the animal with the same name as the target as more similar to the target. Maybe labels influence induction in the same way, by enhancing the resemblance between the source and target of induction. He then demonstrated that when children were presented with tasks requiring similarity judgments, categorization, naming, and induction, their performance was highly correlated. In Sloutsky's view, initially, induction, naming, and categorization are based on similarity, which is grounded in deployment of simple attentional and perceptual mechanisms. Naming enhances the similarity between instances, and similarity-based category structure supports induction. Early induction is a bottom-up process, not a theory-driven one. During the elementary school years, induction becomes more knowledge-driven as a result of exposure to schooling. His view falls within a rich tradition describing a developmental shift from similarity to knowledge-based approaches.

The debate between Susan Gelman and Vladimir Sloutsky returns us to the issues raised in the introduction. The basis for induction may depend on the pull of the task. When the stimuli are line drawings that are lean on perceptual detail and that depict familiar natural kinds, these inputs tap a rich linguistic and conceptual knowledge base that primes theory-based induction. Increase the stimulus detail and decrease stimulus familiarity by using artificial creatures and the child relies more heavily on similarity. When the child is ignorant of the category, similarity may be the default strategy.

Attempts to partial out similarity from categorical understanding reflect the attempt to isolate single mechanisms even though the components of induction are intertwined. The search for a single mechanism leads to varying just one aspect of induction or finding cases at the edge where the several sources of input may conflict. Category members usually resemble one another and resemblance is the basis for initial category formation. However, there is also considerable variation among members in a category and some instances overlap with other categories. The categorizer and inductive reasoner always indulge in a guessing game about whether a feature possessed by one member applies to another and where the category boundaries end. Essentialism helps the reasoner to make inductions in the boundary cases where similarity is insufficient or misleading. These are the cases Gelman probes, and these are also the challenges reasoners are more likely to encounter as they gain deeper acquaintance with categories. Essentialist theory enables children to sharpen the categorical divide by creating a mythical entity shared by all the diverse members that accounts for their membership in the category. Essentialist theory also helps the child decide which properties are good candidates for defining class membership and making property projections.

Analogical Reasoning

At first blush, the process by which the knowledge of elephant anatomy is extended to rhinos seems dissimilar to the process by which one infers that dark is to light as night is to day. Because the Miller analogy test, which contains these 'proportional' analogies in the form, $A:B::C:D$, is often required for entrance to graduate school, analogical reasoning seems to be another skill that prompted the query, "Why do discussions of higher order reasoning appear in an encyclopedia on early childhood?" However, the processes and origins of induction and analogical reasoning have much in common. Like inductions, analogies extend current knowledge to new instances. In induction, the reasoner encounters a new instance, relates it to an old one, and projects the properties of the familiar instance onto the new instance, based on the guess that the two instances are the same in some way. Analogies involve the same processes on a broader scale. Again, there is a familiar base or source and an unfamiliar target the individual wishes to understand. Reasoners use their representations of the relational structure of the well-known source to find correspondences in the unfamiliar target on the assumption that target and source work the same way. For example, preschoolers often use humans as an analogical base to make inferences about animals, rather than an abstract essentialist theory. They assume that the anatomical functions of humans are also possessed by creatures resembling them.

Like the study of categorical induction, descriptions of the timetable of emergence for analogical reasoning reflect assumptions about the nature and origin of the reasoning process and the choice of tasks. Some theories postulate a single analogical skill. Usha Goswami assumes there is an inbuilt powerful capacity ready to go in infancy providing the baby has sufficient experience to extract the likenesses on which analogies build. The engine is ready to go, but the child needs knowledge to fuel it. Growth of analogical reasoning reflects gains in knowledge. Three-year-olds can solve pictorial analogies depicting familiar causal relations, such as bread:sliced bread::lemon:?. They do not complete the analogy by choosing the same object, a lemon, with the wrong causal transformation, or the wrong object with the right transformation, or an object resembling a lemon. Instead they choose a lemon slice. Both adults and preschoolers are competent reasoners but adults, who are more knowledgeable about causal and categorical relations, can construct more analogies.

Graeme Halford counters that the engine needs to increase its horsepower and a maturational timetable governs the expansion of engine power. Performance depends on the number of variables that need to be related in a representation of a problem regardless of problem content. Lemon: sliced lemon is a binary relation linking two terms and the analogy between slicing bread and slicing lemons is another binary relation. Halford claims that 2-year-olds can process these binary relations, but three-term relations, such as the transitive inference, a>b, b>c, and therefore a>c, cannot be solved until 5 years of age. However, Trabasso has provided evidence that with appropriate training, 3-year-olds can solve transitive inference problems.

These views, which posit a generic prowess, are problematical because analogical reasoning performance varies. Two-year-olds, given the appropriate linguistic and perceptual prompts, can grasp analogies, so more than processing capacity is at issue. Accounts based on knowledge fail to explain why adults often fail to apply what they know to structure a new domain. Dedre Gentner's theory of analogical development addresses these issues and also provides a framework for resolving controversies on induction and deductive reasoning. She exemplifies the approach that introduced this article. Her theory is as follows. Because our environment contains multiple overlapping sets of cues, it provides multiple bases for detecting correspondences and drawing analogies. Often appearances and relational structure are correlated and these correlations provide support for analogies. In animals, appearance, anatomy, and function are often related. The growth of analogical skill reflects changes in the child's representation of the diverse facets of source and target phenomena with a shift from solely representing perceptual similarities to greater emphasis on structural relations. Early global similarity detection becomes more analytic. This lays the groundwork for detection of isolated superficial relations that gradually become deeper and more integrated.

Babies form analogies. Neonates imitate an adult sticking out her tongue at them by forming an analogy between the adult's behavior and their own. Upon witnessing an adult using a rake to reel in a desirable toy, in the absence of a rake, toddlers select a similar tool to attain the same end. But their ability to form analogies and apply the right means-end behavior is fragile and context-dependent. Babies can match objects that are very similar if not identical. Slightly change the object or its setting and the perceived correspondence between objects vanishes. Early mapping is global and context dependent.

However, with increasing familiarity with objects, children start to differentiate each object's properties and to form categories of similar but not identical objects. The advent of the ability to name objects both capitalizes on this ability and strengthens it. Upon hearing a new name, for example, 'dog' the child applies it to poodles and dachshunds and the acquisition of nominal terms prompts the child to look for other instances belonging to the same categories. Knowledge becomes more abstract, analytic, and portable. In addition to perceptual features, members of categories share functional and causal resemblances, too. Dogs communicate, breathe, grow, and reproduce in the same way. Increased familiarity with objects in a category exposes the child to relations among properties of objects and these relations become accessible for use in analogical reasoning. At this point children can detect relational analogies like dog:puppy::horse:foal. Understanding of these relations will, in turn, become more abstract and the concept of birth will be applied to planets, not just the origin of babies.

These changes are influenced by linguistic experience and the opportunities to make comparisons between objects. Languages employ a set of relational terms, such as 'middle', prepositions, such as 'on', and inflections, such as '-er', to draw attention to dimensions and their interrelations. Different grammars vary in the extent to which they require encoding various relations and the ease of encoding. Homes also differ in the extent to which they prompt children to make the perceptual comparisons that underlie extraction of dimensions of similarity and to coordinate dimensional information into deep, coherent networks.

Dedre Gentner's research on the origins of analogy focuses most intensively on preschoolers although she has also tested the role of similarity and relational components of analogy in college students and through computer modeling. In her research children are asked to find correspondences between two series of objects, such as two sets of objects arranged in descending size order. In one experiment, 3- and 4-year-olds were shown a sticker on the bottom of an object in one set and asked to locate the corresponding sticker in the other set (by going to the same location). In the baseline conditions, the items in the series differed only in size, three clay pots arranged in descending order from large (pot 3) to medium sized (pot 2) to small (pot l). When the experimenter showed a sticker under the middle pot in one series, the child had to pick the middle pot in the other series. Size and position jointly determine the correspondence. In a contrasting condition, the objects differed in identity as well as size and position. Each series contained a plant, a dollhouse, and a coffee mug. Three-year-olds performed poorly on the sparsely detailed stimulus set, but were usually correct when the object's size, identity, and position jointly contributed to correspondence. The 4-year-olds produced few errors with either stimulus set. The younger child needed more cues to map ordinal relations.

In order to ascertain the comparative strength of perceptual vs. relational similarity in determining correspondences, the two sources of similarity were placed in opposition. As before, both the child and adult had a series of three objects differing in size (see **Table 1**). The adult revealed a sticker that was pasted on the object that was the middle size in her series. The child was to infer that the middle object in the child's series would have a sticker, too. The child's choice was to be guided by relational size information. However, the child's series presented a conflict because the child could instead use other absolute perceptual cues. In the 'sparse' condition, there was only one perceptual conflict, absolute size. The stimuli in both the child's and adult's set were pots. But the sizes of pots differed. Let us designate the relative sizes as 1 through 4. The adult's pots were arranged in descending size order 3, 2, 1 with the sticker under pot 2. The child's pots remained arranged in descending size order, but the sizes in the second series were 4, 3, and 2. Pot 2 was the middle pot in one series but the smallest in the other. To find the corresponding pot, the child must ignore the absolute size of each middle pot to focus on its relational position. In the rich detail condition, a second source of perceptual conflict was added, the identity of the objects. Thus in the adult series, there was a big house, smaller cup, and an even smaller car. The sticker was under the cup which occupied the middle position in size and location. The contrasting series contained a very large vase, followed by the large house and the smaller cup. Now the large house was in the middle position. To find the sticker, the child must ignore the identity and absolute size of each middle object to focus on its middle relational position. When object identity was not a competing cue, the performance of 5-year-olds in the task was superlative. They ignored absolute size to focus on ordinal position. But when the stimuli differed in identity, 5-year-olds' performance deteriorated although it was still above chance. Four-year-olds could not handle either task.

In order to understand the contributors to age changes, Dedre Gentner and colleagues tried to bolster 3-year-olds' attention to ordinal relations. The child was taught to apply names for a familiar series, 'Daddy, Mommy,

Table 1 Where is the child's sticker?

Series	Biggest	Middle	Smallest
Sparse			
Adult's	Large pot(3)	Medium pot(2) with sticker	Small pot(1)
Child's	Very large pot(4)	Large pot(3)	Medium pot(2)
Relation of child's sticker to adult's pot with sticker			
Size	Wrong	Wrong	Same
Relative position	Wrong	Same	Wrong
Rich			
Adult's	Large house(3)	Medium cup(2) with sticker	Small car(1)
Child's	Very large vase(4)	Large house(3)	Medium cup(2)
Relation to child's sticker to adult's toy with sticker			
Size	Wrong	Wrong	Same
Relative position	Wrong	Same	Wrong
Identity	Wrong	Wrong	Same

Baby', to families of stuffed bears and stuffed penguins and to select the animals in both series that played the same familial role. Armed with this knowledge, they were able to solve even the difficult task of detecting relational correspondences with competing cues (cross-mapping) with rich stimuli because relational language made position in an ordinal series more salient than object similarity. The family series helped the child attend to the relational structure of the analogy.

Finding corresponding ordinal positions in two size series is a comparatively simple task. Dedre Gentner has also assessed analogical performance on higher-order relational reasoning and the contribution of language and perceptual comparison to its development. In these tasks the child saw one series and must find a series that matches it. One series consisted of three circles increasing in size and the child had to choose between two triads of squares, which were either arranged in ascending size order or in random order. Higher-order relations were introduced in two ways. One involved a cross-dimensional match. The standard showed circles increasing in size but the correct match depicted squares increasing in brightness from black to white. The match is based on representing both the source and choice stimuli as increases. Alternatively, the circles differed in direction. Instead of increasing in size, the squares decreased in size. Both stimuli incorporated linear size changes. The most challenging task changed both direction and dimension. The series of circles increasing in size was to be mapped to three squares decreasing in brightness. The basis for matching is very abstract, linear change. Performance should increase in difficulty as the number of differences between the source and target increased. The same direction-same dimension match ought to be easier than either the same direction-opposite dimension or the opposite direction-same dimension matches and these in turn should be easier than the opposite direction-opposite dimension match. Four-year-olds performed above chance only in the same direction-same dimension condition which requires minimal relational abstraction. Six-year-olds performed above chance in all four conditions but were hampered somewhat by changes in either dimensionality or direction. Eight-year-olds had difficulty only when both aspects of the match were changed. These older children seemed to be shifting toward a higher-level relational analysis.

Again Dedre Gentner used training to diagnose determinants of the shift in reasoning. Even analogical reasoning in same dimension, cross-dimensional matches seemed beyond 4-year-olds' reach. When they learned relational terms, such as 'more and more' their analogical reasoning improved. Perceptual training also boosted performance. When 4-year-olds were given practice on the same direction-same dimension tasks, one dimension at a time, they were then able to find correspondences across dimensions. Gentner attributed the change to more abstract encoding. After repeated experience with size series the child begins to code them economically and abstractly as 'increases' and repeated exposure to brightness series produces the same economical code. Once the two series are both represented abstractly as increases, the child is prepared to do cross-mapping.

Rather than treating analogy as a readymade tool for the infant, Gentner asserts that analogies exist at different levels of abstraction from object correspondence to higher order relational correspondence. The more the task relies on global similarities, the easier the process and the earlier its emergence. Everyone finds analogies based on perceptual similarities easier than analogies requiring cross-relational or higher-order relational mapping. With age access to more conceptual analogies increases. Expertise brings with it the detection of a network of dimensional relations that becomes deeper and more coherent and more accessible for use as a source of analogies. That expertise is fostered by verbal interchanges and perceptual comparisons. The initial steps in analogical reasoning belong in a article like this, but the ability to draw analogies continues to change across the lifespan as the individual learns to abstract the deep causal structure of knowledge. These developmental shifts in analogical reasoning are similar to the course of deductive reasoning.

Deduction

There is agreement that induction appears very early despite debates on the mechanisms enabling its emergence and use. There is less agreement about the emergence of deduction, due to Jean Piaget's claims that logical competence emerges in adolescence and subsequent research demonstrating that even adult logic is flawed. These data appear to support the belief that discussion of logical reasoning does not belong in volumes devoted to infants and preschoolers.

The problems college students encounter can be illustrated with a selection task devised by Peter Wason. Imagine a pack of cards with letters on one face and numbers on the other. A rule explains the design of the cards. "If a card has a vowel on one face, the other side has an even number." You view the faces of four cards, showing A or B or 4 or 7. What cards must be turned over in order to verify the rule (if A is on one face, then 4 is on the back)? The problem can be solved by applying a truth table for conditional logic, such as **Table 2**. In conditional statements, the occurrence of the event in the antecedent if-clause necessitates the co-occurrence of the event in the consequent, main clause. If the antecedent is false, predictions of the consequent are unwarranted. Two cases falsify the rule, a vowel card but the wrong digit, an odd number, on the back, or conversely, an

Table 2 A conditional truth-table for "If it has a vowel, it has an even number"

Card content	Vowel	Consonant
Even number	True	True
Odd number	False	True

odd number with a vowel on the back. College students usually do not choose the converse case. The task requires grasping the pattern within the entire truth table, generating a strategy to falsify the pattern, and applying the strategy to abstract and arbitrary content. Why would anyone expect preschoolers to succeed on this task? Can they succeed when the material is meaningful and the task is simplified?

The selection task entails verifying two types of inferences. Modus ponens calls for the joint presence of the antecedent(p) and consequent(q). "If there is a vowel, there is an even number." Modus tollens is the contrapositive, the denial of the consequent implies denial of the antecedent (not p, not q). Odd number cards do not have vowels. By their third birthday, children make these inferences during conversations.

Mark (44 months): If you want no raisins in it, then you call it bran. (p.q).
And I want no raisins in it. (p).
So I call it bran (q) (Modus ponens).
Father: If you don't eat food, you're going to die. (p.q).
Ross (49 months): If he wants to be alive (not q).
He 'll have to eat his food (not-q) (Modus tollens).
Father: If you're not hungry (and eat the rest of your dinner), then you can't eat cracker jacks. (p.q).
Abe (43 months): If I'm not hungry, I can... I'll just sneak in the car and get some. (p not q). (Refutation):

These interchanges, drawn from the CHILDES database, differ from the Wason task in crucial respects. The children make deductions when they wish, not on demand, as in the laboratory. In the Wason task, the reasoner must simultaneously make modus ponens and modus tollens inferences and realize what would falsify each. Conversational inferences rarely combine all three elements of the Wason task. Additionally, children's inferences are often joint. The parent produces the initial if-premise and the child supplies the second premise and deduction. Consequently, even before producing 'if', 2-year-olds refute and make inferences from their conversational partner's premises. Adults scaffold and prompt deductions. Adult use of if-statements and particularly, "What if?" questions is correlated with the frequency of children's inferences. Older children are more likely to produce inferences from their own initial premises.

Unlike the Wason task, conversation is meaningful. Two of the examples reflect a popular conversational topic, social control. Rule statements produce resistance (refutations) or concessions (modus ponens). Note that two of the examples also refer to the child. Children are more likely to make inferences when the premise mentions them than when it does not. When the content is meaningful, children's inferences are often quite sophisticated. In the following example from the CHILDES database of conversations, Mark makes an essentialist deduction by using predicate logic to apply information about a general class to a specific instance.

Father: If you have blood you'll die.
Mark (51 months): Do dinosaurs have blood?
Father: Some blood.
Mark: Some blood, then they'll die.

Children also exploit the hypothetical nature of if-sentences to refute parental premises. Abe's father states, "If you're ice, you better get outside (in the cold) or you'll melt." Abe's refusal is justified by explaining that warmth melts ice, but Abe is not ice, only as cold as ice.

When investigators have simplified the traditional laboratory tasks of deduction, they also have unearthed early conditional inferences. Martin Braine's theory of mental logic posits that deduction evolved along with language to handle the comprehension of discourse and to integrate diverse pieces of data. Even before children speak, they grasp contingent, causal, and probabilistic information and they represent these relations in a format that provides a template for comprehending 'if'. Once children have mapped the template onto 'if', they automatically make the inferences. Upon hearing the precondition expressed in an if-clause, even young children expect the main clause to predict the consequences of satisfying that precondition (if it snows, schools will close), and a subsequent discussion of the status of the precondition (it is snowing). They then automatically use modus ponens logic to infer a school holiday. Braine's research focuses on testing the deductions which should appear when young children begin to comprehend and produce the connectives, 'if', 'and', and 'or' and negation ('not').

Braine claims these deductions are produced by a packet of reasoning schemes. Each form of premise cues a simple reasoning program that functions like a computer routine that takes in premises and spits out inferences. The routines are universally available, and can be applied almost effortlessly and flawlessly, even by young children. Many of these schemes are definitional, determined by the meaning of the conjunction. When I say, "I have a cat. I have a dog," it is true that I have both a cat 'and' a dog, and it would be contradictory to deny that I have a cat. Reasoning with 'and' is based on making lists including every item. Understanding of 'or' is derived from experiences selecting some items for the list. Modus ponens reasoning with 'if' reflects understanding the meaning of contingencies. However, some logical routines, like modus tollens, require more steps than others and are generated from combinations of other routines. These produce slower and more inaccurate inferences because they make more demands on memory. Unlike the universal schemas which constitute a natural logic, the latter routines are acquired through education in analytic thinking. This is the same kind of thinking that allows people to reason from counterfactual content.

Although Martin Braine acknowledges that reasoners can use various resources, including their pragmatic knowledge of threats and promises, to bolster employment of reasoning schemes, his research eliminates the influence of these cues by using arbitrary content, such as, "If there is a fox in the box, there is an apple. There is a fox. Is there an apple?" Second graders handle modus ponens problems easily.

Preschoolers can make modus ponens deductions on laboratory tasks with meaningful content and even solve problems akin to the Wason task. They have little difficulty with evaluating the implications of permission rules and detecting violations. A permission rule requires some precondition to be satisfied before an action is taken. If children want to go outside (action), they must don their coat (precondition). Four-year-olds know the kind of naughty behavior that would violate the rule, a little girl outdoors but coatless, an action taken without satisfying its precondition, and they can justify why she is naughty. Sally needs her coat! Three-year-olds know what violates the rule but cannot explain why. It might be argued that the children were simply remembering what happened to them when they tried to go out without a coat but the children do as well with arbitrary, unfamiliar permission rules.

Children's understanding of the logic of permission rules is not surprising. In daily life protective authority figures impose limits on child behavior, and children push these limits. Children know what happens when they violate the permission rules. They also understand obligations, such as "If I give you candy, you must share it with your brother." When they encounter problems that fit these familiar pragmatic schemes, they easily make deductions. There is debate about whether these schemas are inherent or derived from experience. Perhaps children are born with the ability to comprehend the social contracts that make it possible to live harmoniously in a group. Alternatively children may slowly accumulate different social scripts for permissions, promises, and obligations.

There is evidence that children understand the logic of other kinds of rules. Four-year-olds know when a stated contingency is false. Suppose your nephew states, "If I play soccer, I always wear red sneakers." You know that seeing your nephew on the soccer field shod in blue sneakers would prove him a liar. Four-year-olds would agree. However 4-year-olds knowledge is very specific. When it is a permission rule, they can tell who disobeys it but they cannot tell what evidence would falsify the rule. When the statement describes a descriptive sequence like the soccer playing example, they know what evidence falsifies it, but they cannot describe when someone violates the rule. It appears as if they possess certain very specific reasoning scripts enabling them to detect when meaningful pragmatic rules are followed and violated and other scripts detailing meaningful sequential rules and the conditions for their falsification. They possess pieces of deductive competence but not an abstract, coherent set of rules.

Although children's early deductions seem to be content-specific, sometimes young children seem to be able to set aside their own belief system to make deductions. For Jean Piaget, the hallmark of formal reasoning is the ability to represent any conditional problem as an instantiation of an abstract formula. Under some circumstances 4-year-olds who hear a patently false sentence like "All snow is black" followed by the query, "Tom sees some snow. Is it black?" can use modus ponens logic to answer in the affirmative. They disregard their own knowledge if the counterfactual nature of the situation is made salient by explaining that Tom lives in an alternative universe, or by requesting the child to construct an imaginary picture of the dark precipitation. These instructions alert the child that the sentence is to be taken at its face value for the moment so that the child no longer is as concerned with ascertaining whether the sentence is true but ascertaining what conclusion can be drawn if the speaker believes it to be true. Similar instructions enable 4-year-olds to make modus ponens inferences from the abstract proposition, "All mib is black."

Early representations have been described as knowledge in pieces. Two-year-olds know when rules are broken and lies are told. Three- and 4-year-olds dispute and draw conclusions from their conversational partners' if-statements. In laboratory tasks, 4-year-olds show fragments of deductive competence with if-statements stating contingencies and pragmatic rules. The more information available for use, the more expert the child appears. It is difficult to ascertain which piece is privileged, because each piece, syntactic, semantic, or pragmatic can trigger a procedure for generating a new deduction or a reminder of a past deduction. Deduction, like induction and analogy, is the product of multiple abilities and is achieved by multiple routes. Whether anyone but logicians or computer programmers ever operates on a purely abstract basis is debatable. Nature is not abstract. Natural logic may not be either.

Four-year-olds' mastery of logic is incomplete. Modus tollens reasoning often eludes them. Like many adults, they do not appear to operate with a complete logical truth table that includes indeterminate problems. Unless the conditional rule expresses a familiar pragmatic scheme, preschoolers, like adults, are challenged by the Wason selection task which requires integration of the complete truth table Although 4- and 5-year-olds can determine whether a rule statement is empirically correct, they are not particularly sensitive to logically incompatible arguments and logical necessity. Supposing that seeing is believing, 4-year-olds may not recognize that deductions are a source of a reliable belief. However, the presence of older siblings, who are undoubtedly eager to point out the child's flaws in reasoning, prompts growing sensitivity to self-contradictions. Exposure to schooling and tasks like reading that require inferences to integrate information reinforces the realization that deductions may provide a valid source of knowledge. During the school years, children add metalogic to their own logic.

As in the realm of analogies, the basis for deduction shifts. Initial concrete and experientially based deductions give rise to inferences based on specific abstract schemas such as permission. Eventually children may generate deductions derived from deep relations among schemes and general logical rules. This passage through the levels may be very experience- and task-dependent, but it begins in early childhood, making reasoning an appropriate topic for a article like this.

See also: Categorization Skills and Concepts; Cognitive Development; Cognitive Developmental Theories; Piaget's Cognitive-Developmental Theory.

Suggested Readings

Braine MDS (1990) The 'natural logic' approach to reasoning. In: Overton WF (ed.) *Reasoning, Necessity and Logic: Developmental Perspectives*, pp. 133–157. Hillsdale, NJ: Erlbaum.

Gelman SA (2003) *The Essential Child: Origins of Essentialism in Everyday Thought.* New York: Oxford University Press.

Gentner D (2003) Why we're so smart. In: Gentner D and Goldin-Meadow S (eds.) *Language in Mind: Advances in the Study of Language and Thought*, pp. 195–235. Cambridge, MA: MIT Press.

Goswami U (2001) Analogical reasoning in children. In: Gentner D, Holyoak KJ, and Kokinov BN (eds.) *The Analogical Mind: Perspectives from Cognitive Science*, pp. 437–469. Cambridge, MA: MIT Press.

Moshman D (2004) From inference to reasoning: The construction of rationality. *Thinking and Reasoning* 10: 221–239.

Scholnick EK (1990) The three faces of if. In: Overton WF (ed.) *Reasoning, Necessity and Logic: Developmental Perspectives*, pp. 159–182. Hillsdale, NJ: Erlbaum.

Sloutsky VM and Fisher AV (2004) Induction and categorization in young children: A similarity-based model. *Journal of Experimental Psychology: General* 133: 166–188.

School Readiness

F J Morrison and A H Hindman, University of Michigan, Ann Arbor, MI, USA

© 2008 Elsevier Inc. All rights reserved.

Glossary

Child-by-instruction interactions – Not all literacy instruction yields the same gains for all children. Rather, children's learning from instruction depends in part on the skills and levels of understanding that they bring to the learning situation. These child-by-instruction interactions have been found in preschool through third grade. This principle yields two important implications related to the multidimensional nature of school readiness. First, even children who are 'ready' will not have identical skills and interests; in other words, there are multiple patterns and degrees of readiness. Second, upon school entry, the amount and type of instruction that will optimize children's learning is very likely to vary across children.

Dimensions of instruction – Recent research points to four salient dimensions of instruction. These include the (1) explicit focus of instruction (explicit vs. implicit), (2) manager of the students' attention (teacher-vs. child-managed), (3) content of the instruction (code-based or word-level vs. meaning-based or higher order), and (4) change in amount of instruction over the school year. As instruction is multidimensional, it is important to consider how each of these aspects of a child's classroom environment supports or even hinders readiness.

Dimensions of parenting – While sometimes considered as a multidimensional construct, data suggest that three proximal dimensions of parenting most directly contribute to children's literacy skills. These are (1) the family learning environment, (2) parental warmth/responsivity, and (3) parental control/discipline. A separate distal dimension has been posited, parental knowledge and beliefs, which operates primarily through the other three proximal sources. These dimensions exert independent influences on different aspects of a child's behavior and can be either independent of or correlated with one another.

Ecological perspective – Set forth by Uri Bronfenbrenner, the ecological perspective on child development suggests that children grow and learn in the midst of a complex system of forces. Some forces are very proximal, or close, such as parents and teachers. Others are more distal, or distant, such as employment trends. These proximal and distal forces shape the ways in which children develop; for example, a child learns the language that his or her family speaks at home. These forces can also shape one another; parents and teachers might share information and learn from one another, changing the ways that they interact with children to better support their learning. Finally, children shape these forces. For example, a child who is very talkative and asks many questions will likely demand more verbal interaction from their parents and/or teachers than would a child who rarely initiates conversation, which might well affect the number of words the child learns. This perspective, then, posits that development is a complex process influenced by many interacting forces in a child's environment, including the child him- or herself.

School readiness – School readiness includes both cognitive and social–emotional skills. Many assessments of school readiness measure general cognitive skills, including language and problem solving, as well as concrete academic concepts such as identifying letters, numbers, colors, and parts of the body. Social–emotional skills necessary for participation in a classroom community include self-regulation of one's own attention, behavior, and emotion; as well as knowledge of interpersonal relations, including cooperation and conflict resolution.

Introduction

The effort to understand and improve children's literacy skills and school achievement in America has begun to focus increasingly on their readiness for school, for a number of reasons. First, it is becoming evident that meaningful individual differences in important language, cognitive, literacy, and social skills emerge before children begin formal schooling in kindergarten or first grade. Second, this early variability is influenced by a number of factors in the child, family, preschool, and larger sociocultural context. Third, these contributing influences do not operate in isolation, but interact with each other in complex ways to shape children's variable trajectories. Finally, the early schooling experiences of American children are highly variable, in some cases exacerbating the degree of difference found among children prior to school entry. Children who enter the primary grades without core competencies in early language, literacy, self-regulation, and interpersonal relations are at far greater risk than their more knowledgeable peers of encountering difficulty in reading and in academics more generally. Cumulatively, these trends have sharpened scientific and societal focus on the process of school transition as a unique and important milestone in the academic development of children and as a foundational experience for early school success. In this context, understanding the nature and sources of variability in children's school readiness has received heightened attention.

In this article, a working conceptualization (or model) of the nature and sources of children's literacy development across the school transition period, from roughly 3 years of age to third grade will be presented. The empirical literature on the major factors contributing to school readiness and early literacy skill growth will then be reviewed. Finally, the implications for research and for improving literacy in the US will be considered.

Conceptualizing School Readiness and Transition

Working from the ecological perspective first asserted by Uri Bronfenbrenner, scientists have attempted to develop a coherent conceptualization of the process of school transition. **Figure 1** depicts a working model of the major factors shaping children's literacy development and their independent and combined influences over the school transition period. Four features should be noted. First, the model includes and distinguishes those processes that occur prior to school entry from those operative once school begins. At the same time, the model

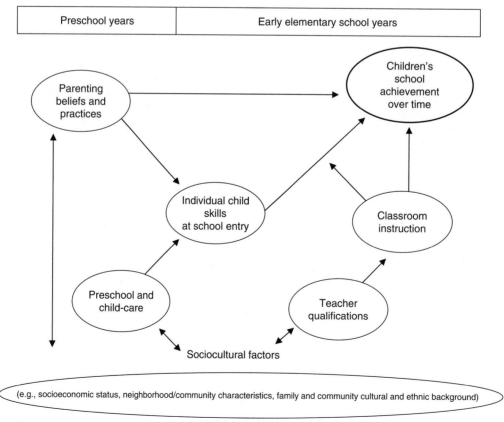

Figure 1 Model of the sources of influence on literacy development.

depicts the continuity of influences (e.g., from parenting) across the two periods.

Second, the model attempts to capture the interplay of distal and proximal factors in shaping children's literacy trajectories. In particular, the mediational role of proximal factors linking distal factors to literacy outcomes is depicted. Hence, in the preschool period, the contribution of sociocultural factors, like parental education or income, is shown as operating through their effect on more proximal parenting or preschool influences. Likewise, during early schooling the impact of teacher education or experience is seen in the model as manifesting itself primarily through the ongoing instructional activities of the teacher in the classroom.

Third, the model includes some of the important components within each of the larger factors. For parenting, research has highlighted the unique influence of the learning environment, parental warmth/responsivity, and control/discipline. Finally, the model depicts some of the important interactions among these factors, recognizing the emerging consensus that these factors do not operate in isolation. For example, while the home learning environment contributes directly to children's literacy growth and self-regulation skills, parental control/discipline contributes to literacy growth primarily through its impact on self-regulation. On a broader plane, accumulating evidence increasingly highlights the need to capture the complex interplay of forces shaping children's literacy trajectories across the school transition period. For these reasons, understanding children's school readiness must necessarily include consideration of the environmental context of early development as well as the role of early formal instruction in enhancing or impeding children's early skill growth.

Before Children Get to School

Child Factors

Whether through inherited genetic or acquired differences, child characteristics by themselves and in interaction with environmental factors shape the course of children's early development. In reality, these child qualities are what we mean when we typically refer to 'school readiness'. While most scientists now view readiness as a two-way street (with schools needing to be ready to deal with children's individual differences), there is still intense interest in factors within the child that are most crucial for school readiness and successful school transition.

One of the most important policy goals to emerge in the last decade is that all children will arrive at school 'ready to learn'. But what exactly does 'ready to learn' mean? What knowledge and skills are important prerequisites for children's success in school, how many children are not 'ready to learn', and what are the consequences?

As researchers investigate the construct of school readiness, they include both cognitive and social–emotional skills. For example, standardized assessments of school readiness usually assess general social interaction, cognitive skills, and concrete academic concepts such as identifying letters, numbers, colors, and parts of the body. Social–emotional skills necessary for participation in a classroom community include self-regulation of one's own attention, behavior, and emotion, all of which aid children in learning from instruction, following directions, and persisting through challenges. Further, the focus on large- and small-group activities and play in many early classrooms requires that children build knowledge of interpersonal relations, including cooperation and conflict resolution.

Unfortunately, too many of children in the US are not ready for the transition into a formal schooling environment, either socially or academically. Among a national sample of almost 3600 teachers studied by Sara Rimm-Kauffman, Robert Pianta, and colleagues, over one-third maintained that about half of their class or more began kindergarten socially and emotionally unprepared for the demands of the classroom. Considering that these teachers managed classrooms with an average of 22 students, this estimate translates into a staggering number of children. Teachers reported that at least half or more of the students in their class had difficulty following directions (46%), difficulty working independently (34%), and difficulty working as part of a group (30%) when they began school. Other pressing problems included students' lack of academic skills (36%), disorganized home environment (35%), or lack of any formal preschool experience (31%). Note that these teachers identified as many social–emotional skills as they did academic and cognitive skills.

These skills matter a great deal. Accumulating research reveals that a child's profile of literacy and social competence in early elementary school is highly predictive of academic achievement in junior high and high school, as well as whether students will drop out of high school. Consequently, children's ease with the transition to school and their cognitive and social/behavioral skills at kindergarten entry have meaningful implications for their later educational and vocational success.

The bulk of our discussion of readiness will focus on the role of oral language, literacy, and self-regulation skills. Nevertheless, there are a number of issues of particular concern to parents and teachers that are important to consider initially.

Entrance Age

A child's age at kindergarten entry is often a source of concern for parents and teachers. Older kindergartners have experienced almost 1 year more of language and literacy exposure than their younger classmates, and may be more socially mature. National surveys indicate that 9% or 10% of parents delay their child's entrance to kindergarten, especially if they are among the youngest in their classroom (i.e., their birthday falls close to the school cutoff date). Earlier research may have unduly influenced parents' fears by suggesting that younger children were at greater risk for poor academic performance, grade retention, and special education referrals.

More recent investigations have utilized a variety of methods to evaluate how young children perform in school compared to their older peers. Researchers have compared: (1) children who entered school when eligible with children who delayed entrance for 1 year; (2) the oldest and youngest children in the same grade; and (3) same age children in different grades. This last technique has provided the most rigorous strategy for distinguishing effects of experiencing a year of schooling from maturational (age) effects. However, across all of these methods, any early discrepancies that favored older children in kindergarten significantly diminished by second or third grade. Overall, younger children benefit from formal instruction as much as do their older peers and are able to match the performance of older classmates within a relatively short amount of time.

While these studies persuasively demonstrate that entrance age, in and of itself, is not a useful predictor of early academic achievement, two issues remain unresolved. First, although the early effects of entrance age appeared short-lived, the long-term effects have not been adequately examined. It is possible that despite substantial reductions in entrance age gaps during early elementary school, the influence of age on cognitive and social domains may reemerge as schooling requirements become more complex and student-managed. A recent analysis of approximately 14 000 children from the National Education Longitudinal Study (NELS) offered encouraging evidence that the early narrowing of the entrance age gap is maintained throughout formal schooling. For example, no significant differences emerged between younger and older kindergartners across a range of long-term educational and social outcomes, such as high-school dropout, college attendance, behavior problems, and arrests. Second, it is also still not clear whether entrance age is an independent risk factor, or whether the risk is produced when being young at school entry is combined with other child factors, such as weaker cognitive skills or social immaturity. For example, the largest discrepancies in school success are between older and younger students who were in the lowest 25th percentile of cognitive ability. Nevertheless, while some questions remain to be addressed, chronological age at school entry does not appear to be an important source of school readiness.

Gender

Gender differences in verbal and mathematics abilities have been tracked for decades. Early reviews in the 1970s indicated that discrepancies detected at young ages were generally small, whereas consistently significant sex differences that favored boys in verbal, mathematics, and spatial abilities did not often emerge until 10 or 11 years of age. In contrast, later evidence revealed girls' advanced verbal abilities and comparable mathematics and memory performance to boys'. By the end of the 1980s, the size of the gender differences in math and verbal skills had substantially declined. The gender gaps in academic achievement not only narrowed, but disparities in math performance actually began to favor females.

So, now that the women who entered the workforce and pursued professional degrees in the 1970s and 1980s are sending their own sons and daughters to school, what has happened to the gender gap? According to 2003 NAEP data, female students in fourth and eighth grade outscored male students in reading by an average of 7–11 points. In contrast, the mathematics gap is much smaller, with boys scoring higher than girls by only 2 or 3 points. Furthermore, the magnitude of these gender gaps has remained fairly consistent since the early 1990s.

It is important to keep in mind that these national data reflect academic achievement, but not necessarily school performance. Girls' achievement, especially in math and science, was once a major educational concern, but researchers and educators are now arguing that a 'new gender gap' has emerged in American schools: as recently noted in the *New York Times* "Every time I turn around, if something good is happening, there's a female in charge,' says Terrill O. Stammler, principal of Rising Sun High School in Rising Sun, Md. "Boys are missing from nearly every leadership position, academic honors slot, and student-activity post at the school. Even Rising Sun's girls' sports teams do better than the boys'." On a larger scale, data suggest that, by high school, girls now show higher grades and higher scores on achievement tests. This new achievement disparity continues after high school as well. For more than 10 years, women have surpassed men in earning postsecondary degrees (e.g., bachelors or masters degrees), and current projections anticipate a widening of the gap in men's and women's educational attainment over the next decade.

So how early do these gender differences appear? Female toddlers exhibit greater rates of vocabulary production and language complexity, expression, and comprehension. However, these differences are usually small in size and diminish by 20–24 months of age. In preschool measures of emergent literacy, significant gender discrepancies are generally not found or weakly favor girls.

Some researchers are currently arguing that, rather than gender *per se*, disparities in social maturity or the socialization practices that girls and boys experience may also place girls at an advantage both in the classroom and the workplace. James Garbarino, professor and author of *Lost Boys: Why Our Sons Turn Violent and How We Can Save Them*, contends that "Girls are better able to deliver in terms of what modern society requires of people – paying attention, abiding by rules, being verbally competent, and dealing with interpersonal relationships in offices." Along these lines, higher levels of self-discipline, or self-regulation, may undergird girls' greater achievement. It is important to recognize that, in and of itself, focusing on gender may not be terribly illuminating in helping us understand the growing divergence among boys and girls in school success. In a sense, gender, like socioeconomic status (SES), is a distal factor that operates through more proximal sources of influence/characteristics, like parenting, social maturity, or self-regulation.

Cognitive Skills and IQ

Another commonly recognized characteristic of children that greatly contributes to literacy acquisition is their intelligence. Although this attribute goes by many names (e.g., IQ or cognitive competence), in a classroom, it is readily evident that some children are able to learn and apply new information with greater ease and accuracy than their peers. Efforts to somehow measure or quantify these abilities are generally constrained by children's language development. In other words, if we want to examine the influence of children's intelligence on the variability in children's literacy skills at kindergarten entry, the earliest we could administer a standardized IQ test would be around age 2 years, when children are better able to produce answers to questions. In response, psychologists have also utilized more global mental and psychomotor scales, such as the Bayley Scales of Infant Development (BSID), to assess major areas of infants' and toddlers' cognitive development, such as sensation, perception, memory, and language. Scores on the BSID at 2 years of age have been useful for detecting language delays and are strongly associated with later academic and language skills during the preschool and elementary school years. In recent decades, cognitive researchers have devised several techniques to obtain indicators of infants' cognitive development at very young ages, presumably when performance would better represent biological traits rather than environmental experiences. For example, infants' abilities to distinguish new from familiar sounds or pictures during the first year of life predict cognitive scores 2–8 years later.

Not only are there age issues to consider when assessing children's intelligence, but researchers continue to disagree about the aspects of intelligence to include in standardized tests. Most IQ tests contain verbal (e.g., vocabulary, comprehension, general information) and quantitative (e.g., arithmetic, problem-solving, spatial reasoning) components that can be aggregated to form a global score. However, Howard Gardner has argued that each individual possesses multiple intelligences that include naturalist, musical, bodily-kinesthetic, interpersonal, and intrapersonal domains, in addition to the more traditional intelligence domains of linguistic, logical–mathematical, and spatial skills. Despite the controversy surrounding the content of IQ tests, children's verbal and quantitative abilities in preschool and early elementary school do predict a variety of later academic outcomes, such as grades and standardized test scores of reading and mathematics, and even high school dropout. Further, IQ scores are often among the most predictive of factors for academic competence, over and above measures of SES, parenting practices, and children's social and behavioral skills.

Nevertheless, it is important to reiterate that while western culture reifies intelligence as a heritable trait, IQ scores are not good indicators of genetic characteristics. For instance, since verbal ability assessments are related to children's language comprehension skills, environmental effects on children's vocabulary development cannot be underappreciated. Adopted children's IQ scores increased substantially more if they were adopted into families of higher SES than of lower SES households. More specific still, IQ scores of preschool children in high-poverty communities showed significant growth after exposure to high-quality curriculum in school for just 1 year, and even greater gains with continued enrollment in the program. Therefore, these indicators or proxies of cognitive competence that researchers rely upon are clearly responsive to environmental enrichment.

Language/literacy skills

One of the most important discoveries of the past two decades has been the critical role that language plays in early literacy development. Several language skills independently contribute to reading acquisition, and there may be interactions among these components over the course of learning to read. Of particular focus has been the role of phonological skills (particularly phonemic awareness) in learning to read. Increasing competence at consciously manipulating the component sounds in the speech stream facilitates the child's task of 'cracking the code', that is, learning the symbol-sound correspondence rules and utilizing them in ever more sophisticated ways to derive accurate word pronunciations. Locating the smallest units, phonemes, within a word seems to be the most critical level of segmentation for early word decoding. Children who have difficulty at this level, for whatever reason, experience significant problems progressing in word decoding. Vocabulary, both receptive and expressive, has also been shown to predict early reading skill. The number of different words a child understands, as well as the number s/he speaks, helps word decoding efforts and may facilitate growth of phonological awareness. Finally, children's knowledge of the alphabet when they enter kindergarten is one of the best predictors of learning to read. Letter knowledge predicts more advanced phonological awareness and better word decoding skills throughout elementary school.

There is some uncertainty at present about how and when each of these component skills exerts its influence. Some studies have demonstrated that vocabulary uniquely predicts early reading skills only through kindergarten, after which it contributes indirectly via its association with phonological processes, which continue to predict reading well into early elementary school. Other recent studies appear to find an independent contribution for vocabulary and other oral language skills through third grade. There is agreement, though, that development of early oral language facility, including vocabulary, is essential to later comprehension skills.

Self-regulation

As noted above, increasing attention in recent years has been paid to a class of skills that has been variously called executive functioning, learning-related social skills, social competence, and self-regulation. They refer to the co-ordination of processes involved in response inhibition, sustaining attention over time, and planning and organization in working memory. They contribute, among other things, to a child's ability to work independently, control impulses, and complete tasks on time. There is a growing sense that difficulties with self-regulation among American children are contributing in major ways to the literacy problems in the nation.

Children with poor learning-related social skills at the beginning of kindergarten have been shown to perform more poorly academically at school entry and at the end of second grade. Likewise, a child's skill at sustaining attention and restraining restlessness predicts academic functioning in first grade. The close connection between social and academic skills persists throughout school. Adolescents rated more highly by teachers and peers on complying with rules and expectations outperformed their lower scoring peers on measures of academic achievement. Clearly, development of self-regulation is an important task for preschool children over the school transition period and one that has sustained influence throughout a child's life.

Motivation

Motivational skills refer to students' values and beliefs when approaching school tasks, including their engagement with the material, interest in the topic, beliefs about self-efficacy as well as their attributions of success or failure and their goal orientations. The study of motivational processes in education has a long history, yet surprisingly little research has been conducted on young children. This is unfortunate since, in practically every other area of academic functioning, it has become clear that the seeds of later success are sown during the preschool years. Hence laying a foundation of academic engagement, coupled with a strong sense of mastery and self-efficacy prior to school entry, could be expected to reap long-term benefits throughout a child's academic career. Clearly, more systematic empirical inquiry is needed on the early roots of motivational processes in children and their influence on academic functioning.

As with language and literacy skills, it is clear that multiple sources of influence, including parenting and schooling, shape growth of social and motivational processes, though research is just beginning to delve into the nature and impact of these relations.

In summary, research since the mid 1980s has clearly revealed that a number of potent forces, independently and in combination, shape the literacy development of preschool children. Factors in the child, family, preschool, and broader sociocultural context all contribute to create the significant variability American children present when they walk in the school door.

Sociocultural Factors

Several decades of research have documented strong connections between SES and academic achievement. Likewise, accumulating evidence has established links between race/ethnicity and school success, particularly the persistently poorer performance of African-American students compared to their European-American peers. These factors are obviously linked, since the poverty rate among black families in the US continues to be higher than it is for White families. Recently, scientists have attempted to disentangle the independent and combined influences of social, economic and racial/ethnic influences on academic development.

Socioeconomic disadvantage and academic achievement

Whether measured by income, education, or occupational status, socioeconomic factors are substantially linked to a child's school success. The National Assessment of Educational Progress reports that 9-, 13-, and 17-year-old students from families with less than high school education scored lower on tests of reading, math and science than did children whose parents completed some education after high school. More significant for our discussion is the recent realization that children from low-SES families start school behind their more affluent peers and progress more slowly through the early years of elementary school. More recent work has unearthed that children from lower-SES families demonstrate delays in language and emergent literacy skills. In a pioneering study, Betty Hart and Todd Risley found that preschool children from welfare families had smaller vocabularies compared to children from working-class and professional families as early as 3 years of age. Moreover, their rates of vocabulary acquisition were much slower.

How does SES affect academic achievement? Despite the strong association between socioeconomic disadvantage and poor school performance, it is not obvious how SES factors operate to shape children's academic trajectories, especially in the preschool years. In their efforts to probe more deeply into the mechanisms underlying the SES–performance connection, scientists have distinguished between direct and mediated pathways of influence.

Direct pathways reflect influences that operate directly on the child to affect academic performance. For example, poor children are more likely to have experienced negative perinatal events, like prematurity or low birth weight, in addition to poorer nutrition and healthcare in early childhood, all of which can directly limit a child's cognitive growth and potential. Yet, increasingly, scientists are describing the impact of SES as operating through more immediate influences in the child's environment. For instance, mothers living in poverty are less likely to receive adequate prenatal care, which could contribute, in part, to the connection between SES and prematurity. Researchers describe these as mediated pathways, where SES is viewed as a distal variable that exerts its influence through a more immediate or proximal variable. The wholeprocess is described as a mediated relation. Scientists are increasingly seeing the effects of SES as mediated through more proximal factors, one of which is parenting. Parents living in poverty are less likely to talk to their preschool children; they communicate with a more limited vocabulary, offer fewer questions or descriptive statements to them, and are more repetitive. In general, parents with fewer economic and/or educational resources are less likely to provide the stimulating home environments children seem to require if they are to be maximally ready for school. The important insight gained from seeing SES in this mediated fashion is that improving a family's economic circumstances alone may not translate into improved parenting, the more immediate causal agent shaping the child's development.

Race, ethnicity, and academic achievement

Similar issues have surfaced in trying to explain the disparities across racial and ethnic groups in academic attainment. Clearly, race and ethnicity, in and of themselves, are distal variables that won't directly affect academic performance. Their influence must be mediated by more proximal sources. Since most progress in understanding these complex relations comes from the study of differences between African-American and European-American students, we will focus on this issue here.

Of particular import is the Black–White test score gap. In general, African-American children do not perform as well academically as their European-American counterparts on the NAEP. While some variation has been noted over the last three decades, sizable differences have persisted throughout the period in which scientists have been tracking children's performance.

The most common explanations for 'the gap' have leaned on socioeconomic and sociocultural factors. In particular, the higher rate of poverty among African-American families has been offered as an obvious cause for poorer performance in black children. Likewise, the legacy of racial discrimination, which limits opportunities for Black children, has been put forth as a contributor to lower academic attainment.

While these factors are reasonable and, no doubt, play some role in the gap, two recent findings have caused scientists to reassess the nature and sources of the black–white discrepancies. First, it has become clear that the test-score gap is not limited to lower-SES groups. Black middle-SES children are performing more poorly than their white peers. Second, the gap in academic performance emerges before children begin school. These two findings have caused researchers to look more deeply into the proximal environments of black families for a more comprehensive understanding of the roots of academic problems. For example, studies from the Center for Disease Control and Prevention have found that infant mortality rates are higher in black families, and more significantly, this difference occurs independently of SES.

Perhaps the most salient and controversial proximal factor implicated in the Black–White test score gap is parenting. Mounting evidence has pointed to differences across racial groups in the types of learning experiences provided to children and other aspects of the literacy environment. These differences also seem to extend to middle-class parenting practices. While the reasons for these differences in parenting are not clearly understood, and many distal factors are implicated, the focus on parenting and related proximal causes is yielding a clearer, more comprehensive picture of the complex forces contributing to the continued underperformance of black children.

Early Childcare and Preschool

Over 60% of the almost 20 million preschoolers in this country will spend some amount of time in alternate care. Hence, researchers have become increasingly interested in the psychological consequences of childcare for children under 5 years of age as well as its impact on school transition and later school functioning. In addition, for children most at risk for school failure, intensive interventions during the preschool years have attempted to help children at risk for academic failure (e.g., children living in poverty) catch up to their peers and be equally ready for school. In this section we will first review the evidence on the impact of childcare on children's cognitive and social development. Next we will summarize the evidence on the outcome of early interventions for children at-risk of academic underachievement.

Is day care good or bad for children?
While stated rather simplistically, the above question accurately captures the essence of the debate on the impact of early childcare for preschool children. The importance of this question can be appreciated by realizing that the Federal government undertook to fund a major national study of the nature and consequences of early childcare in the late 1980s. That study, the National Institute of Child Health and Human Development (NICHD) Study of Early Childcare, as well as others, have yielded valuable insights on the role of childcare experiences in children's development and school performance.

As we stated above, the question of whether childcare is good or bad oversimplifies the issue. Closer examination reveals that two variables – quality and quantity of care – are crucial to understanding the role of childcare in children's lives. In broad terms, higher-quality childcare produces positive effects on children's cognitive, language, and literacy skills, while high quantities of care (defined as more that 30 h per week) have been associated with poorer social outcomes. Even these conclusions do not capture the complexity of the role of childcare. Parents are active agents in choosing alternate care for their child, and more educated mothers have been shown to be more sensitive and responsive to their children than mothers with less education. The more educated and responsive mothers likely chose higher-quality childcare, monitored it more closely, and could afford to pay for it. In fact, when direct comparisons have been made between parenting and childcare environments, the impact of the quality of parenting was 3–4 times greater than that of childcare on children's language and social skills. Nevertheless there is early evidence that, independent of quality, children who spend more than 30 h per week in center-based care may be less socially competent and somewhat more disruptive to other children and teachers.

Thus, in answer to our original question, research over the last two decades permits us to conclude that, in and of itself, daycare is neither good nor bad for preschool children. High-quality childcare enhances children's cognitive growth, while high amounts of childcare per week may put children at risk for slightly poorer social outcomes.

Are early intervention programs for at-risk students effective?
Here, too, the question of program quality is central to answering this question. High-quality interventions can significantly enhance development. But poor-quality programs can impede children's progress. High-quality preschool interventions have been shown to significantly improve children's prospects for academic success, to promote stronger language and literacy development, and to demonstrate significant return on investment over children's lifetimes.

A number of interventions have been implemented for at-risk children. The most visible (and controversial) is Head Start, the mixed outcomes of which illustrate the crucial importance of ensuring high-quality programs for producing consistently positive effects. Some of the more prominent and successful model programs include the Perry Preschool Project, the Abecedarian Project, the School Development Program, and the Chicago Title 1 Child–Parent Centers. In virtually every instance, children receiving these interventions showed significantly stronger academic and social skill development compared to equally at-risk children not enrolled in such programs.

On balance then, the mounting weight of evidence demonstrates that high-quality childcare and interventions for at-risk children can and do improve the psychological well-being of preschool children, enhance their school readiness, and improve their chances for successful school transition.

But what defines high-quality care? Examining the characteristics of programs that work, like those listed above and others, there are at least five crucial elements of high-quality early care programs:

1. Strong support for parents. Successful programs coupled intensive intervention with home visits, parent education, and parent involvement.
2. Intensity. Programs that were more available to children all day, 5 days a week, such as the Abecedarian project, tended to produce stronger, more durable outcomes for children.
3. Starting earlier. Programs that yielded greater cost-benefit ratios (e.g., Abecedarian and Chicago Title 1) began their interventions when participants were infants.
4. Well-qualified teachers. Programs with more teachers who were certified produced more consistently positive effects than those with fewer certified teachers.
5. Rich linguistic and literacy environment. Perhaps most fundamental to success was an explicit focus on improving the language and literacy skills needed for early school success. Included were emphases on vocabulary, syntax, world knowledge, phonology, alphabet knowledge, and elementary word decoding.

In summary, the nature of a child's experience in alternate forms of care outside the home can have a measurable effect on subsequent psychological development and preparation for school. While perhaps not as crucial as parenting (to which we will turn next), high-quality experiences in a childcare environment can improve cognitive functioning in children at risk. Alternatively, for some children, more than 30 h per week in childcare, particularly prior to 1 year of age, may pose some short-term risks for their social behavior. On this latter point, it would, therefore, seem prudent to examine current parental leave policies to see if giving parents more leave time with young infants might reduce the number of hours infants spend in childcare and forestall some of the problems that may arise.

Parenting

Throughout the previous sections we have referred to parenting as a critical mediator of the effects of SES, as well as being inextricably linked to the influences of childcare. While it would seem obvious that parenting is an important, and perhaps the most important, factor shaping a child's development, again, the picture is not so simple. Recent work on the genetic bases of development has challenged the once-dominant position of parental socialization as the primary instrument through which human nature is molded. Further, efforts to improve parenting in at-risk families have proved to be surprisingly unsuccessful. In this section we will review these issues and, while we will conclude that parenting is a critical source of children's development, we will need to broaden our conceptualization of parenting in order to appreciate its full sweep and power.

Does parenting matter?

Until the mid-1980s, parenting was tacitly assumed to be the preeminent force shaping children's development. Most developmental theories accorded parents primacy over genetics, peers, and other contextual influences. Nevertheless, in the past two decades, behavior-geneticists and others have challenged this simple view. Utilizing twin and related research methods designed to separate genetic from environmental influences, researchers have found that: (1) children's development can withstand substantial variability in parenting practices and emerge intact; and (2) other socializing forces, particularly peers, can exert long-term influence on selected personality traits.

This work has had the salutary effect of yielding a more balanced view of the complex forces shaping human development. More recent work has attempted to gauge the intricate interplay of parenting and genetic and other factors and its effects on child development. As an example, in a French study of late-adopted children (3–5 years old) with below-average IQs, those children who were adopted into higher SES families exhibited substantially greater IQ gains (19 points) by 11–18 years of age than did children adopted into lower SES households (8 points). This finding neatly demonstrates that children with similar genetic characteristics make differential progress depending on the SES of the family in which they are reared; this difference is, presumably, mediated in part by differing parenting practices.

Can parenting be modified?

One way to examine the power of parenting is to conduct intervention studies to examine whether programs actually improve parenting skills and, subsequently, whether there are corresponding increases in children's literacy skills. Two strategies have been adopted: (1) family-focused early childhood education (ECE) coupled with home-based services; and (2) exclusively parent-focused home visiting programs. Recent reviews have concluded that home-based interventions alone, without a center-based child-intervention component were surprisingly ineffective in improving children's cognitive skills. Many of these adult-based efforts did not substantially increase parental outcomes (e.g., educational attainment), which, in part, may explain why their children's cognitive performance did not improve.

If parenting is so important to a child's development, then why haven't the interventions been more powerful? Actually, there are several reasons these efforts may have fallen short. First, as the authors themselves noted, case managers in these studies quickly found that they needed to deal with a number of family crises and chronic adversities, like inadequate housing, lack of food and heat and legal problems, and that it was difficult to move beyond crisis intervention to work on parenting-for-literacy. In addition, there were sizable differences across families in the uptake of services or the 'dosage' effect. Specifically, since participation in these interventions was, ultimately, voluntary, parental participation varied widely, with about half the scheduled visits actually taking place. Significantly, when eligible families were split by their participation level, children in families with greater involvement made greater gains than did their peers whose families participated less. Finally, it should be noted that smaller, more focused interventions (e.g., around book reading) have yielded measurable gains in children's oral language skills.

What is parenting anyway?

Most of the intervention efforts to improve parenting have been relatively limited in time and scope. For example, in the Comprehensive Child Development Program, parents received training from a home visitor for a maximum of 13 h (30 min, biweekly), which may be insufficient to promote and maintain lasting change over time in parental habits. Further, interventions that focus primarily on one aspect of parenting may necessarily be limiting their impact. Research over the past 20 years has clearly demonstrated that parenting for literacy involves more than reading to children and even more than providing a rich literacy environment.

It has become useful to think of parenting not as a single construct, but as varying along a number of dimensions, with three proximal dimensions being most salient for shaping literacy skills. These are: (1) the family learning environment, (2) parental warmth/responsivity, and (3) parental control/discipline. A separate distal dimension has been posited, parental knowledge and beliefs, which operates primarily through the other three proximal sources. These dimensions are conceived to exert independent influences on different aspects of a child's behavior and to be potentially independent of one another (although correlated in most instances). For example, parents who provide a rich learning environment for their child might not necessarily also give the child the high degree of emotional warmth needed for emotional security nor the rules, standards and limits needed to develop cognitive or moral self-regulation.

Family learning environment

In large national datasets, measures of 'cognitive stimulation' or 'home learning' have predicted preschoolers' IQ and receptive vocabulary, as well as reading, math and vocabulary skills in elementary school. Analyses with a sample of preschool children and their families recently revealed that the home learning environment positively predicts code- and meaning-related skills, as well as self-regulation skills. Recent efforts have focused on identifying more precisely the connections between specific parental behaviors and child outcomes. This work has revealed a high degree of specificity in the impact of the learning environment; namely, parental behaviors such as book reading, promote language development but do little for specific literacy skills like letter knowledge and word decoding. In contrast, deliberate efforts by parents to teach these emergent literacy skills to their children help to promote their alphabet and word decoding skills but do little to enrich vocabulary.

Language-promoting behaviors include frequent labeling and describing of objects in the environment. The overall amount and complexity of parental speech to children predicts their vocabulary and complex grammar acquisition. Beyond size and content, the manner of speaking and interacting with children contributes to oral language growth. Children with relatively limited vocabularies in the Betty Hart and Todd Risley study received a greater proportion of commands and prohibitions from their parents. In other work, parents who maintained longer periods of joint attention on an object had children with larger vocabularies.

Shared book-reading has generally been demonstrated to be a powerful tool, for some children, to enhance vocabulary development. In randomized experiments, book reading styles that involve actively labeling and describing illustrations or encouraging and assisting children's storytelling significantly enhance vocabulary development.

In general, literacy-promoting activities by parents may require more explicit instruction than do those that nurture oral language growth. When parents explicitly teach their children how to name and print letters and words, children's print knowledge improves as does later word decoding and comprehension skills in school.

In summary, parents' efforts to promote language and literacy in their children can substantially improve their development and school readiness. An important insight has been gained in recognizing the high degree of specificity in what parents do and what children learn.

Parental warmth/responsivity

The degree to which parents display open affection to their children, offer physical or verbal reinforcement and show sensitivity to their feelings and wishes is predictive of preschoolers' literacy and language skills as well as their later school achievement. Mothers' sensitivity to children's developmental progress during the first 2 years of life has been shown to predict cognitive and language skills later in preschool, kindergarten and first grade. More responsive mothers are more likely to reduce the length of their utterances to their infants so that children can better comprehend them. Other research has shown that at-risk groups of children can make substantial progress when mothers interact with them in a highly responsive manner. A classic situation combining elements of the learning environment along with warmth/responsivity is shared book-reading, especially during bed-time. In addition to the benefits to cognitive and language skills, shared book reading promotes emotional closeness, affection, and provides the child with the undivided attention of a loving parent. Such interchanges may nurture self-regulation and emotional well-being.

However, recent work on parenting of preschoolers in one middle-class sample revealed that parents rated their warmth/sensitivity, as gauged by 13 items on a questionnaire, as very high (on average, 4 out of a scale from 1 to 5, with no respondent reporting a 1 or 2). Analyses relating this factor, along with the two other dimensions of parenting, to children's code, meaning, and self-regulation outcomes suggested that high levels of warmth were negatively associated with children's code-focused learning, but not linked to any other outcomes. One interpretation of these findings is that parents with very high levels of warmth might engage in permissive behaviors that actually impede children's learning of the challenging but constrained skills related to decoding words. This raises questions for future study regarding the distinction between responsiveness and permissiveness, both as grounded in research and in the minds of parents, as well as optimal levels of these parenting practices for children's early learning.

Parental control/discipline

Though less well researched, the degree to which parents establish rules, standards and limits for a child's behavior creates a structured and supportive context for literacy development. Book reading, for example, affords parents the opportunity to resist children's fidgeting and squirming, and to sustain their attention until the story is finished. In one study, parents' use of disciplinary practices did not directly predict literacy outcomes, but did reliably predict self-regulation measures (e.g., cooperation, independence and responsibility), which in turn contributed positively to literacy skill levels at kindergarten entry; similar results have been found among preschool children and families.

In summary, the weight of evidence at this point supports a strong role for parenting in shaping children's literacy development, albeit in complex ways. Future research will evaluate whether and to what extent more intensive and comprehensive interventions (encompassing more dimensions of parenting) will yield measurable improvements in the literacy attainment of at-risk children.

Once Children Begin School

Stability of Language and Literacy Skills

Children who begin school with strong language skills tend to be more successful academically throughout their school career than are those with weaker language skills. Students who start first grade knowing the letters of the alphabet and with a firm grasp of other emergent literacy skills achieve stronger reading skills by the end of first grade than do students with weaker skills. Indeed, some have proposed a critical period for reading development encompassing the first three elementary school grades. Research reveals that students who fail to reach grade expectations by third grade are unlikely to experience success in school later on. The stability of students' language and literacy development may be one reason that the achievement gap between children from low-SES and high-SES families is both pervasive and persistent. As we discussed in the beginning of this article, children from low-SES families begin school with language and early reading skills that fall well behind those of their more affluent peers, with multiple sources of influence on this development – home, parenting, preschool, and child characteristics.

The Effect of Schooling and the Specificity of Learning

In the face of this stability, some have questioned whether schooling has any appreciable direct effect on children's cognitive development. However, there are studies that demonstrate causal effects of schooling on children's literacy skill growth. Some of these studies utilize a natural experiment employing the rather arbitrary birth date that school districts mandate for school entry. Children who just make or just miss this cut-off birth date are essentially the same age chronologically, but those whose birthdays fall before the cutoff date start first grade while those whose birthdays fall just before go to kindergarten. In this way, the schooling and maturational effects on children's development can be examined separately. If both groups demonstrate similar rates of growth in a particular skill, then that skill is most likely a product of maturation – there is not a 'schooling effect'. On the other hand, if children who are the same age but a grade ahead demonstrate rates of skill growth that are greater than their age-peers who are a grade behind them, then there is a 'schooling effect'.

First-grade schooling effects are evident for alphabet recognition, word decoding, phonemic (individual sounds within words) awareness, general knowledge, addition, short-term memory, sentence memory, and visuo-spatial memory. Yet there are no schooling effects for receptive vocabulary, rhyming, conservation of number and quantity, addition strategies, and narrative coherence. Children demonstrate similar rates of growth in these skills regardless of whether they are in kindergarten or first grade. For example, for 89 children who attended the same school district, and taking into account cognitive abilities and parents' education, there were kindergarten but not first-grade effects for letter naming. There were kindergarten and first-grade effects for basic reading skills, including word decoding. There were only first-grade effects for general information, mathematics, and phonemic segmentation (identifying the individual sounds in words).

These results are particularly revealing if we consider the three phonological awareness tasks. These tasks differed only in the level of segmentation the child was asked to complete – syllabic, subsyllabic, and phonemic. For the syllabic segmentation task, children were asked to identify the number of syllables in a word. For example, 'cucumber' has three syllables, 'cu-cum-ber'. In the sub-syllabic task, children were asked to say the first sound in each word. For example, /t/ is the first sound in the word 'toy'. For the phonemic task, children were asked to count the number of sounds in a word. For example, rest has four sounds, /r-e-s-t/. The study revealed that there were schooling effects but only for specific skills. For syllabic segmentation, neither first grade nor kindergarten had an effect on growth in these skills. For sub-syllabic segmentation, both first grade and kindergarten affected growth. In contrast, first grade but not kindergarten had an effect on phonemic segmentation. Additionally, emerging research reveals that once the amount and type of instruction students receive is taken into account, the schooling effect disappears. Thus, the schooling effect is most likely the result of instructional differences in kindergarten and first grade. In other words, learning is highly specific and related to the explicit focus of the instruction students receive. In first grade, children are provided with more time in activities that support their decoding skill growth, which results in first graders' stronger decoding skills when compared to their same-age peers who are in kindergarten.

Parents' and Teachers' Beliefs about Readiness

Apart from the research presented above, evidence indicates that parents and teachers have their own perceptions and beliefs about what skills comprise readiness, and these views in many ways outline the arena in which the translation of research into practice must occur. Recent research has illuminated several fundamental trends in parent and teacher attitudes and beliefs about readiness. First, evidence indicates that, overall, both parents and teachers are aware that children must be 'ready' for school and feel pressure to achieve this readiness, reporting a sense that demands for early learning are high. At the same time, many express a lack of clarity concerning what skills are needed or how they can be nurtured and assessed.

Second, despite possible confusion, parents and teachers do report conceptualizations of what readiness entails, and they share many of the same perceptions. For example, both parents and teachers of preschoolers were more likely to identify a child as ready to move from preschool to kindergarten if the child was well within the chronological age window for attendance, appeared to be adaptable (e.g., did not have outbursts and could manage in different social environments), demonstrated interpersonal skills, and displayed task persistence. These results are consistent with prior work indicating that both parents and teachers perceive social skills, particularly those related to self-control and interpersonal cooperation and compliance, as important for readiness.

Yet some evidence of fairly systematic differences between parents' and teachers' beliefs about readiness is apparent. Several studies suggest that parents more frequently assert academic components to readiness, including competence in English and in basic concepts. In contrast, teachers differed from parents in that their ideas about readiness also included gender, indicating that girls tended to be more ready than boys, and inhibited behavior, suggesting that children with more independent, outgoing behaviors were more ready than those who were shy. Across kindergarten teachers involved in the Early Childhood Longitudinal Study – Kindergarten Cohort, some disparities were apparent along sociodemographic background variables; female teachers were more likely to emphasize social development, while younger teachers were more likely to emphasize academics.

The findings above indicate not only that parents' and teachers' views of readiness are not identical, but that, on average, neither the average parent nor the average teacher conceptualizes readiness in the complexity set forth by prior research. Thus the final trend we will discuss, related to the relative malleability of parents' and teachers' views on readiness, is of particular import. A primary influence on teachers' beliefs about readiness are their administrators and colleagues, and emerging data suggest that parents glean much of their information from booklets and other materials provided by the school, which are often few in number. One future task, then, will likely involve disseminating information in ways that can be easily understood and applied to foster early learning.

Conclusions

As the foregoing discussion illustrates, the conceptualization of school readiness has undergone significant revision in the last two decades, from a simple child-centered notion to a deeper appreciation of the broad range of influences shaping a child's trajectory across the crucial school transition process. We have learned a great deal about how parents, preschools, early elementary schools and the larger sociocultural milieu contribute independently and interact to influence a child's growth. Fuller understanding of the complex pathways children follow will ultimately pave the way for successful efforts to ensure that all children are maximally ready to benefit from their early schooling experiences.

See also: Bayley Scales of Infant Development; Cognitive Development; Head Start; Language Development: Overview; Literacy.

Suggested Readings

Bornstein MH (2002) *Handbook of Parenting*, 2nd edn. Mahwah, NJ: Lawrence Erlbaum Associates.

Bowman BT, Donovan S, and Burns MS (2000) *Eager to Learn: Educating Our Preschoolers*. Washington, DC: National Academy Press.

Chall J (1967) *Learning to Read: The Great Debate* New York: McGraw-Hill Book Co.

Dickinson DK and Newman SB (2006) *Handbook of Early Literacy Research*, vol. 2. New York: Guilford Press.

Dickinson DK and Tabors PO (2001) *Beginning Literacy with Language*. Baltimore: Paul H. Brookes Publishing.

Morrison FJ, Bachman HJ, and Connor CM (2005) *Improving Literacy in America: Guidelines from Research*. New Haven: Yale University Press.

National Reading Panel (2000) *Teaching Children to Read: An Evidence-Based Assessment of the Scientific Literature on Reading and Its Implications for Reading Instruction* (Summary). Washington, DC: National Reading Panel.

Neuman SB and Dickinson DK (2006) *Handbook of Early Literacy Research*, vol. 1. New York: Guilford Press.

Relevant Websites

http://www.childtrends.org – Children's home and school experiences in the United States, as well as their health and well-being.

http://nces.ed.gov – Children's home lives, their preschool and early elementary educations.

http://www.ed.gov – Major recent research findings pertaining to reading and education more generally, as well as descriptions of initiatives to help children learn to read.

http://nces.ed.gov – Students' performance reports, including on measures of reading skills, over the last decade, as well as break-downs of achievement by race, gender, and socioeconomic status.

Self Knowledge

A E Bigelow, St. Francis Xavier University, Antigonish, NS, Canada

© 2008 Elsevier Inc. All rights reserved.

Glossary

Ecological self-knowledge – Perceptually based knowledge of self within the local physical environment, for example, awareness of one's spatial relation to objects in the environment.

Episodic memory – Memory of a specific event that occurred at a particular time and place.

Generic event memory – Memory of a script for a routine event, that is, memory of the general sequence of what happens in the event.

Intermodal perception – The ability to integrate perceptions from different modalities, such that perceptions of an object from one modality allow recognition of the object in another modality.

Interpersonal self-knowledge – Perceptually based knowledge of self in interaction with others, for example, awareness that one's actions affect others' behavioral responses.

Joint attention – Child's ability to attend to an object or event and a social partner at the same time, knowing that the partner is also attending to the child and the same object or event.

Means-end understanding – The ability to combine actions, originally learned separately, to achieve new goals.

Secondary emotions – Emotions requiring the ability to sense how self-actions might be perceived by others, for example, embarrassment or pride.

Social contingency – Social responses to selected behaviors of a partner that immediately follow the behavior and match it in intensity, affect, and tempo.

Social referencing – Checking the emotional or behavioral cues of others to determine self-action in an uncertain situation.

Introduction

The development of self-knowledge is one of the oldest and most fundamental concerns in psychology. At the end of the nineteenth century, William James distinguished between the 'Me' and the 'I'. The 'Me' corresponds to the self-reflective sense of self that is identified and recalled. Traditionally within psychology, it is this sense of self that was the focus of study. During the second year of life, infants begin verbally to refer to themselves and they communicate their desires and feelings through language. At approximately the same time, they show recognition of themselves in mirrors. Such behaviors indicate children have begun to have a reflective concept of themselves.

During the past few decades, infancy research has had a resurgence of interest in the development of self-knowledge and has focused more closely on what is meant by the 'I'. The 'I' is the sense of self as a differentiated entity distinct from other objects and persons, yet capable of operating upon them. For example, in reaching for objects, infants express a sense of self as capable of acquiring objects that are perceived as graspable within a reachable distance. Such a sense of self does not require representational thought, conscious identification, or recognition, and as such it is present in preverbal infants long before children have a conceptual sense of themselves.

Humans share many aspects of the 'I' with other animals. Yet the 'Me', with its reliance on language or other representational systems and indications of visual self-recognition, may be uniquely human or shared only with few evolutionarily advanced species.

Although the development of the 'I' and the 'Me' may be independent, much of recent research on self-knowledge supports the notion that conceptual self-knowledge is rooted in earlier developing preconceptual knowledge of self. Infants' ability to sense themselves as objects of reflection and recognition does not develop suddenly in the second year, but rather emerges from earlier forms of self-understanding. By the second year, infants' sense of self has already evolved from simpler beginnings and self-knowledge continues to develop through early childhood and beyond. There is not one form of self-knowledge, or even two as James proposed, but many that build upon each other in complex ways.

What factors affect developments in early self-knowledge? Changes in the brain provide the foundation for these developments. Brain changes are rapid during infancy and early childhood and underlie cognitive developments important to self-knowledge, such as in visual processing, language development, and memory retention. There is debate about whether these brain changes are due to maturational factors, as traditionally thought, or are activity-dependent, that is, are based on the actions and perceptions of infancy that are universally experienced because of the similarity in human infants' environments. Whether critical brain changes are dependent on experience or not, experience plays a primary role in the development of self-knowledge. Theorists differ on the relative importance of experience in the physical vs. social environments for developments in self-knowledge. For early forms of preconceptual self-knowledge, some theorists propose that infants' engagement in the social and physical world have equal importance, but others support the dominance of infants' interactions with others because people tend to be particularly responsive and engaging with infants, allowing them more readily to notice the effect of their actions. For children with the ability to reflect upon themselves, self-knowledge is especially influenced by how others respond to them and help shape their emerging sense of who they are. Young children's experience in the world, perhaps particularly with others, is fundamental to their developing understanding of self.

Perceptually Based Self-Knowledge

Newborns spend much of their time caught up in physical states of sleep, drowsiness, fussiness, or crying that inhibit their focus on the external environment. The one exception is the quiet alert state, where infants are fully awake without excess distracting limb activity. In this state they can take in the surroundings visually, as well as through their auditory, tactile, taste, and olfactory senses. This perceptual information is the basis for infants' early self-knowledge. Essential to this self-knowledge is infants' ability to notice the relation between their own actions and perceived changes.

Ulric Neisser proposed that infants have access to two forms of perceptually based self-knowledge very early in life, probably from birth: the ecological self, which is self in relation to the physical environment, and the interpersonal self, which is self in relation to other people. These early perceptually based forms of self-knowledge do not disappear when other forms of self-knowledge are added; rather they remain reality-based sources of information about self in the physical and social world.

The ecological self is the sense of self within the local physical environment. Knowledge of the layout of the environment seen from the perspective of the self and knowledge of how that relationship changes with movement through space positions the ecological self in the environment. Young infants show evidence of the ecological self quite early. They react to looming objects by pulling back or moving away, which is not a simple reflex. When the object is a looming aperture, such as a framed window, infants as young as 3 months do not move away but rather lean forward to see what the window may reveal. When put in specially designed rooms that have walls that move, creating optic flow much like we see from windows of moving cars, infants make posture adjustments as if to maintain their position in the perceived moving environment. Such posture adjustments are clearly evident in crawling and walking infants, and also in the head adjustments of infants as young as 2 months. As infants' physical capabilities and knowledge of the world grow, infants' sense of their ecological self expands as well. For example, as infants develop locomotor abilities and increased strength, more objects are perceived as potentially attainable. Aspects of ecological self-awareness are shared with other species. Many animals with developed visual systems respond as young children do to the physical environment and to perceptual events in it, such as looming objects and optic flow.

The interpersonal self is the sense of self within the social environment and is manifested in actions such as mutual gaze and reciprocal responding. Such activities are clearly perceivable and no inferences to internal states being communicated are required. The interpersonal self is not necessarily embedded in a sense of relationship; rather it is based specifically on perceptual information. Like ecological self-knowledge, infants show evidence of interpersonal self-knowledge very early. When engaged in face-to-face interaction with a social partner who suddenly becomes still faced, that is, silent and unmoving, infants as young as 2 months, and possibly younger, react to the still face with less attention and decreased positive affect. When the partner reengages, the infants become happier and attentive again, indicating that they were reacting to the disruption in the social interaction rather than to boredom with a prolonged visual display. The replay effect is even stronger evidence for infants' interpersonal self-knowledge. To demonstrate this effect, infants engage in face-to-face interaction with a social partner over live video. Both the infant and the partner see and hear the other in real time over closed circuit television. The videotape of the social partner is then played back to the infant. In the playback, the infant-directed facial expressions and vocalizations of the partner are present as they were moments before except that the partner is no longer responding to what the infant is currently doing. Infants at 4 months, and in some studies at 2 months, show disinterest and less positive affect to the replay, similar to their reaction to the still face. When live video interaction with the partner is resumed, infants become engaged again, indicating that they are aware of when others' behaviors are responsive to their own.

Perceptions relevant to ecological and interpersonal self-knowledge can coexist in the same event, yet they are distinct. The two forms of self-knowledge are based on different information and can be salient on different occasions. Despite their early development, the coordination of ecological and interpersonal self-knowledge is thought to occur toward the end of the first year with the emergence of joint attention. In joint attention, infants are capable of attending to a person and an object at the same time, thus understanding that the object of their own focus is attended to by another person who simultaneously is also attending to them.

Evidence of the separate development of ecological and interpersonal self-knowledge comes from studies of children who have impairments or difficulties with acquiring one of these senses of self but not the other. Children with autism typically have difficulty with interpersonal self-knowledge but not with ecological self-knowledge. They have difficulty acquiring information from the behavior of others and understanding how others' behavior is affected by their own. Yet they have little trouble relating to the physical environment and objects in it. Children with autism also have problems engaging in joint attention, which in part may be due to the discrepancies between their development of interpersonal and ecological self-knowledge.

Children born totally blind show a pattern of disturbance in early self-knowledge that is the reverse of children with autism. To be sure, blind children's knowledge of their interpersonal selves is hindered. Many important avenues to the formation of interpersonal self-knowledge, such as mutual gaze, are absent in blind children. They have difficulty perceiving what others are attending to and, therefore, understanding the emotional reactions of others. Others also have difficulty knowing where blind children's attention is focused because there is neither visual orienting nor pointing, and their facial expressions are more neutral. Nevertheless, blind children's knowledge of their interpersonal selves can flourish if they perceive others' actions as contingent on their own behavior, a perception that is difficult but not impossible without vision. Tactile and vocal responses to the children's actions allow the children to sense the effect of their behavior on others. Interpersonal self-knowledge is attained as the children become aware that they can influence the actions of others in predictable ways.

Blind children's ecological self-knowledge is more fundamentally challenged. They cannot readily perceive the physical layout of their environment, the objects in the environment, the spatial relations among the objects, or the spatial relation of self to the objects and the physical space. Sound cues do not initially convey to blind infants an object's location or sustained existence. Their difficulty understanding their position within the physical environment and to objects in it delays reaching and locomotion, which further impedes the infants' interaction with and exploration of the environment. Blind infants' ecological self-knowledge is initially thought to be indicated by their reaching for objects on external sound cues. By their reaches, they convey their awareness of themselves as positioned within the physical world with objects to which they can gain access through their own actions. It is not surprising that blind infants' demonstration of joint attention, through acknowledgement that both they and another are sharing in the same event or object, occurs after their ability to search for objects on sound cues. Yet knowing where one is in physical space, where objects are in relation to each other and to self, and how these relations change with self-movement are lifelong challenges for blind children.

Bodily Awareness

Although very young infants can perceive the social and physical world around them, they are particularly interested in watching and discovering their own bodies. A distinguishing feature concerning perceptions of their own bodies vs. external objects, both animate and inanimate, is the perfect contingency between self-actions and perceived changes. With the exception of watching one's mirror reflection or live video image, perfect contingency is present only in self-actions on the self, such as sucking on one's own fingers or watching one's hand move; the perceptual feedback is consistent and simultaneous with self-action. From the beginning, infants show behaviors suggestive of an ability to differentiate self-actions from others' actions. Newborns show differential responding to their own hand spontaneously touching their cheek, generating double touch in that the hand feels the cheek and simultaneously the cheek feels the hand, and having another person's hand touch their cheek; they show rooting behavior to the latter but rarely to the former. They also show expectation of results of their actions on their own bodies. In moving their hands to their mouths, newborns open their mouths in anticipation of the hand entering. Young infants' familiarity with self-actions on the self may originate in prenatal experience. The fetus in the latter months of pregnancy has tactile contact with its own body and babies are often born with marks on their hands and arms from prenatal sucking. Newborns' differential responses to self vs. external actions may be attributed to reflex reactions built into the nervous system or to reinforced stimulus-response associations. But by 2 months of age, infants show active exploration of the effects of their own actions. For example, when given pacifiers which when sucked above a baseline pressure either produced sounds with pitch variations that were analogs to the pressure variations applied by the sucking or pitch variations that varied randomly, 2-month-old infants modulated their sucking to the pacifiers differently. Although sound from both pacifiers was produced by the infants' sucking, infants more actively explored the effects of their sucking in the analog condition.

Infants' capacities for intermodal perception facilitate their ability to distinguish self from other people and objects. Piaget thought that young infants experienced their perceptions from different modalities as unrelated and only gradually came to the awareness that perceptions from separate modalities can specify the same object, for example, mother's voice and her visual image originate from the same person. Research on infant development from the past several decades shows such thinking to be incorrect. From birth infants have the ability to integrate their perceptions from different modalities, such that they are able to perceive objects in one modality and recognize them in another. For example, 1-month-old infants who have sucked on, but not seen, a tactually distinctive pacifier visually discriminate that pacifier from a novel one when given a choice of looking at two different distinctively shaped pacifiers. Intermodal perception facilitates infants' understanding and organization of the external world, but also greatly aids in their awareness of their own bodies.

In the first few months of life, infants spend extended periods of time in self-exploration, for example, kicking, vocalizing, touching their bodies, watching their limbs move. These experiences are absorbing and do not include other people or objects. Such activities provide numerous opportunities for infants to experience intermodal perception of their own bodies and to notice the perfect match between their actions and perceived changes. When watching their hand move, infants see the movement as they proprioceptively feel the movement; when vocalizing, they hear sound as they feel air passing through their throat and mouth. Such actions help infants form their body schema; what belongs to their own body and what are its limits.

By 2–3 months of age, infants become more interested in the relation between self-action and external responses in the environment, both social and nonsocial, than in self-actions on the self, perhaps because effects of the latter have become familiar. External responses to infants' actions show high but imperfect contingency rather than perfect contingency. Imperfectly contingent responses occur immediately after self-action rather than simultaneously with self-action and do not occur in response to every self-action. Studies in which infants are given a choice of watching actions that are perfectly matched with their own bodies' movement, for example, live video displays of their legs kicking, vs. actions that are similar but not perfectly matched with their bodily movement, for example, video displays of another infant's legs kicking, indicate that infants over 3 months of age prefer to watch the displays that are not perfectly matched to self-actions, but younger infants do not. The shift to focusing attention on imperfect contingencies present in the environment or in others' social behavior rather than on intrinsic sensations is adaptive. Infants' ability to detect differences between perfect and imperfect contingencies is acquired early and may be one of the first ways they distinguish self from other.

Self-Efficacy

By noticing the relation between their own actions and resultant external changes, infants develop self-efficacy, a sense that they are agents of the perceived changes. Although infants can notice the effect of their behavior on the physical environment, it is in early social interactions that infants most readily perceive the consequence of their actions. People have perceptual characteristics that virtually assure that infants will orient toward them. They have visually contrasting and moving faces. They produce sound, provide touch, and have interesting smells. In addition, people engage with infants by exaggerating their facial expressions and inflecting their voices in ways that infants find fascinating. But most importantly, these antics are responsive to infants' vocalizations, facial expressions, and gestures; people vary the pace and level of their behavior in response to infant actions. Consequentially, early social interactions provide a context in which infants can easily notice the effect of their behavior.

Parents are generally infants' most frequent and consistent social partners and as such their behaviors are those that most profoundly affect infants' emerging sense of self-efficacy. The responses that are most effective in facilitating infants' early self-knowledge are socially contingent and reflect the infants' own behavior. In naturally occurring interactions with young infants, parental responses are primarily imitations of infants' actions. These imitations are not exact but rather match the infants' actions in intensity, affect, and tempo. Infants' early perceptual capacities allow them to recognize these imitative behaviors as mirroring their own. From the beginning of life, infants are aware of the matching quality of their behavior and that of others. Infants may more easily recognize the external effect of their behavior when the actions of others mirror the behavior the infants produce. Some theorists propose that in mirroring infant behavior, which exposes infants to external perceptual manifestations of what they are internally experiencing, parents facilitate infants' early understanding of their own experience.

Parents are selective in responding to infant behaviors. The infant actions that parents respond to tend to be those in which the parents perceive emotion that they, either with or without awareness, wish to reinforce, modify, or share with the infants. These emotions vary among parents because of the parents' own emotional histories and expectations regarding infants. Consequently there are individual differences in the range of parental social responsiveness. What is important for infants' sense of self-efficacy is that the presence of contingent responsiveness to them be such that the infants notice the effect of their actions on their parents' behavior. Thus, individual differences in parents' contingent responsiveness to infants' actions can affect infants' development of their self-efficacy.

The contingent responsiveness present in early parent–infant interactions has been shown to influence infants' subsequent sensitivity to various contingency patterns in others' behavior. Infants become accustomed to particular levels of contingency that they experience in their family interactions, creating optimal contingency levels through familiarization that are reflected in infants' responsiveness to new people. Maternal contingencies to infant behavior are relatively stable within mother–infant pairs but vary across the population. This stability within dyads and variability in the population is present in infants' first year, possibly by the time infants are 3 months old. Infants' detection of and preference for imperfect contingency at this age undoubtedly helps them orient toward people, but because people are imperfectly contingent to different degrees, infants are particularly oriented toward people whose levels of contingency are similar to the levels with which they have become familiar.

This principle goes against the intuitive expectation that infants should be increasingly responsive to increased social contingency because in such conditions the association between self-action and external consequences would be more evident, thereby facilitating infants' self-efficacy. Indeed, research does indicate that the more responsive parents are to infants, the more infants are able to rely on their own self-efficacy. For example, infants whose cries are readily responded to in early infancy cry less in later infancy. This contradicts learning theory, which would predict that responding to crying would reinforce the behavior and thus increase it. But infants' learning processes are complex. By having their cries responded to, infants learn that their own actions are effective in getting their needs met, increasing their sense of self-efficacy. Then at later ages when they run into difficulties, they are more likely to trust their ability to deal with the problems, often succeeding, and therefore needing to cry less. Infants whose parents are less responsive to their cries maintain higher levels of crying throughout infancy. Intermittent reinforcement has been proposed as an explanation, yet all infants experience some intermittent responsiveness from their parents, making this explanation inadequate. Parental responsiveness facilitates infants' understanding that they are effective agents in the world, which in turn influences infants' readiness to seek the effects of their self-actions. Yet infants develop sensitivities to particular levels of perceived social contingency based on past experience and, as a consequence, they are most responsive to other external stimulation that has similar levels of contingency.

Evidence for this principle comes from studies in which infants participated in face-to-face interaction with mothers and strangers. When infants interacted with strangers whose responsiveness to them was similar to that of their mothers, infants' responsiveness to the strangers was much like their responsiveness to their mothers. However, when strangers' responsiveness to the infants was dissimilar to that of the mothers, either by being more contingent or less contingent than the mothers, the infants were less responsive to the strangers relative to their mothers. Such evidence is depicted as a U-shaped curve when infants' responsiveness to mothers (Im) minus infants' responsiveness to strangers (Is) is plotted against mothers' responsiveness to infants (Mi) minus strangers' responsiveness to infants (Si). The significant quadratic trends shown for vocal contingency in **Figure 1** and for smiling contingency in **Figure 2** are from adult–infant interactions involving 4- to 5-month-old infants. Similar significant quadratic trends have been found for adult–infant interactions involving 2-month-olds, indicating that infants show a preference for familiar contingency levels from

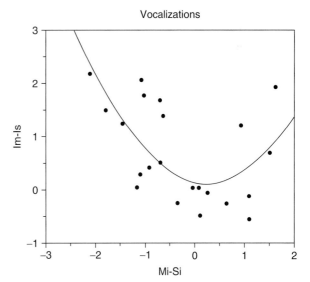

Figure 1 The relational plot of the differences between the infants' contingent vocal responsiveness to mothers and strangers (Im-Is) and the difference between mothers' and strangers' contingent vocal responsiveness to the infants (Mi-Si). Reprinted from Bigelow AE, Infants' sensitivity to familiar imperfect contingencies in social interactions. *Infant Behaviour and Development* 21: 149–162, Copyright 1998, with permission from Elsevier.

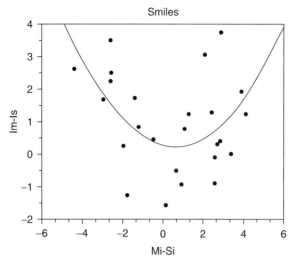

Figure 2 The relational plot of the differences between the infants' contingent smiling responsiveness to mothers and strangers (Im-Is) and the difference between mothers' and strangers' contingent smiling responsiveness to the infants (Mi-Si). Reprinted from Bigelow AE, Infants' sensitivity to familiar imperfect contingencies in social interactions. *Infant Behaviour and Development* 21: 149–162, Copyright 1998, with permission from Elsevier.

the time they first show an interest in imperfect or social contingency.

Individual differences in parental contingency levels also may influence infants' ability to regulate their levels of stimulation. Initially parents do much of the work in maintaining and regulating infants' emotional engagement in interactions. But infants can influence the level of engagement by averting their gaze when stimulation becomes too high and by reengaging with attention and positive affect when seeking more stimulation. Sensitive parents adjust their interactive behavior to the infants' current level of excitement, while also frequently arousing them to high but manageable levels of stimulation where the potential for learning is at its peak. Infants' experience with parents as regulators of interactions influences infants' ability to accommodate to wider ranges of stimulation and to self-regulate their own levels of engagement in the absence of the parents. In novel situations, the most arousing and interesting levels of contingency are those that are familiar. Infants with parents who respond to them at low levels of contingency may be most engaged in social situations in which low levels of responsiveness are present, and thus, they may have difficulty detecting the impact of their actions. Infants with highly contingent parents may be more sensitive to and interested in people who are highly responsive to them. In so doing they may learn more readily about their own effectiveness.

The sensitivity infants show to the social contingency levels in their parental interactions raises concerns for infants who are exposed to persistent low levels of parental responsiveness. It is not uncommon for periods of low parental contingent responsiveness to occur as a result of parental illness, grief, or other emotionally distracting circumstances. But such periods tend to be temporary; infants are compelling forces for reinstating parental attention. Yet for some infants, low levels of contingency persist in their most intimate interactions. Children of depressed mothers are such a population. Infants of depressed mothers are exposed to minimal contingent responsiveness and reduced synchronous behavior in their maternal interactions. Initially the infants attempt to engage their relatively unresponsive mothers, but by approximately 3 months of age, they tend to mirror their mothers' depressed activity and affect. When with nondepressed social partners, these infants continue to be relatively unresponsive, and interestingly, seem to elicit depressive behavior from these partners. Either with or without awareness, the nondepressed partners adopt lower levels of social contingency, perhaps because it is at these levels that the infants can be most engaged. The infants' familiarity with low levels of contingency within their maternal interactions generalizes to their interactions with others regardless of the contingency patterns provided. Thus the infants' experience with minimal contingent responsiveness in their social interactions may be easily perpetuated. Extended experience with low levels of social contingency may impair infants' ability to sense their self-efficacy, adding to the difficulties in cognitive, social, and emotional developments for which children of depressed parents are at risk.

Self-Reflective Awareness

Self-reflective awareness requires the child to take an outside perspective of self. Children's ability to take the role or perspective of another has a developmental trajectory that extends beyond infancy and early childhood, yet it is in this time period that the ability emerges. In the latter part of the first year, infants are no longer just engaged with the social and physical world through perception alone; that is, their sense of themselves is not limited to the immediacy of direct action and perception. Although younger infants can relate their actions to similar past experiences and, therefore, have expectations of the outcomes of their actions, infants at the end of the first year begin to act more intentionally with goals in mind. They start to use symbols to convey those goals to others and use tools as aids in acquiring those goals.

Infants achieve what Piaget called means-end understanding. They are able to differentiate goals from the means that bring them about and can choose among alternative means to achieve their goals. For example, infants may have an action pattern for reaching to retrieve objects and an action pattern for batting or striking objects to push them away. When faced with a desired toy that is partially blocked by another object, like a pillow, they can use the striking action, which was not associated with retrieving objects, as a means to remove the pillow in order to get the toy. Or if a desired toy is placed on a table out of reach but on a cloth that the infant can grasp, infants at the end of the first year will pull the cloth to get the toy, whereas younger infants tend simply to reach for the toy with growing frustration. Infants become able to combine actions with intention to achieve specific goals.

Infants also show intentional behaviors in their interactions with others and begin to treat others as beings with intentions that can be different than their own. Prior to the use of language, infants can use gestures to solicit help in obtaining desired objects. They point or reach for an object while glancing back and forth between the object and an adult. In so doing, infants not only are indicating their desire for the object but also are attempting to engage the adult's help; they are attempting to affect the adult's intention with their own.

In addition, infants can direct others' attention with the goal of sharing their interest in an object or event. Infants' gestures of pointing, showing objects, gazing, and accompanying affective expressions are used as directives for adult participation in object play. The goal is purely social and indicates infants' awareness that others' attentional focus can be different than their own but can be changed to match their own focus.

Although infants can use adults as social tools by following others' gazes to find interesting objects from about 6 months of age, beginning around 9 months of age, they engage in joint attention. They can actively coordinate their attention to both an object and a partner, knowing that the partner is attending to them and to the same object that they are. The prototype joint attention episode involves an infant and an adult playing with a toy and the infant looks from the toy to the adult's face and back to the toy. Initially infants are simply checking to see if the partner is attending to the object they are manipulating. Later in coordinated joint attention, they can show or give the object to the partner as a means of more actively participating in triadic interactions with adults and objects.

Infants' use of symbols increases during their second year. Knowledge that others' attention and intention can be different than their own facilitates infants' acquisition of language. They understand that novel labels used by adults generally refer to objects adults are focused on, which can be different from the objects on which the infants are focused. They also can reformulate their own communication when adults appear to have misunderstood them. Eventually, the use of symbolic gestures and language allows infants to move from a focus on the here and now to interactions that include multilayered temporal and spatial events.

In the second year, infants also can make inferences about others' intentions in their actions. For example, after watching an adult perform two actions in sequence, one of which is perceived to be intentional and the other as accidental, infants readily imitate the perceived intended action and tend to ignore the perceived accidental action regardless of which action came first. Perhaps even more impressive, infants who watch an adult perform a failed action on an object, for example, miss a bucket when attempting to drop a toy into it or unsuccessfully attempt to pull two objects apart, will complete the action for the adult. That is, infants read intention into the adult's action and can imitate the intended, but unwitnessed, action.

Around the same time, infants begin to use others to acquire emotional information through social referencing. When encountering a novel and uncertain situation, such as meeting a dog, a remote controlled toy, or a stranger, the infant will look to a trusted person, usually the parent, to see how that person has assessed the situation. Is the parent pleased, indicating encouragement for the infant to approach the new object, or is the parent wary, indicating retreat? In social referencing, infants show awareness that others have access to information that they themselves do not. Social referencing also indicates infants' knowledge of others' perceptual experience as different from their own. In order to ascertain whether the parent's emotional cues are related to the object of concern, the infant typically must turn away from the object to look at the parent and then must determine whether the parent is focused on the object in question. This involves a sophisticated knowledge of space and an awareness of where another's line of vision would intersect with their own if they themselves were looking at the object.

Thus, infants show intentional actions in their social encounters as well as in their encounters with the physical environment. They use adults' actions to change their own behavior and attempt to change adults' behavior with their own actions. Inherent in infants' use of communicative gestures, acts of joint attention, language use, imitation of intended goals, and social referencing is their awareness of intentionality in others' behavior. Whether infants' understanding of themselves as intentional comes before their understanding of others as intentional is debated. But it is likely that intention in self-actions comes first. Infants' experience of intentionality in self behavior, through formulating goals independent of actions and then pursuing them, prepares infants to understand others as intentional agents, whose attention to objects and events may be shared, followed, or directed. Integral to this understanding is infants' knowledge of themselves to be like others yet distinct from them.

During their second year, infants not only are objects of thought to themselves, but they also begin to realize they can be objects of thought to others. One way this is manifested is in the emergence of secondary emotions. Primary emotions involve a direct response to an event;

knowledge of, or concern for, others' reactions is not necessary. Primary emotions include emotions such as joy, anger, and surprise. These emotions can be witnessed in infants during the first half year of life. Secondary emotions, sometimes called self-conscious emotions, involve a sense of seeing self from the outside, sensing how self-actions might be perceived by others. The emotions of embarrassment, shame, and pride involve a projected sense of self to another's perspective. In their second year, infants can show a marked sense of embarrassment, typically manifested when doing a task or a performance that can be evaluated by others, and sometimes in the context of protracted attention by others.

Incidents of secondary emotions increase in early childhood. Between 2 and 3 years of age, children begin to evaluate their actions against social expectations by holding in mind the standards of others and their own behavior at the same time. Significant others play a major role in the development of secondary emotions. How others respond to young children's actions influences how children evaluate their own behavior. Such self-evaluations are beginning points of self-esteem and can either enhance or injure children's growing sense of self-competence.

Visual Self-Recognition

How infants learn to recognize their own image as themselves is still an open question. Watching one's mirror reflection is a unique experience in many ways. The perceptual information pertinent to self-recognition is distinct from one's own body yet generated by it. Self is perceived from the perspective of an outside observer. Most theorists agree that visual self-recognition does not emerge suddenly but rather develops gradually, building on earlier aspects of self-knowledge.

Criteria for self-recognition vary among studies. Typically, baseline measures are taken of the infant's self-directed behaviors in front of a mirror or live video and then surreptitiously a mark is made on the infant's face or head, and subsequent self-directed behaviors to the marked area in front of the mirror or live video are noted. Significant increases in touching the marked area of the face or head indicate the infant knows the reflected image is of self. Such measures originated from studies showing self-recognition in chimpanzees. Alternative criteria for self-recognition include infants' self-labels of their reflected images, their coy or embarrassed behaviors in front of a mirror, and their turning to find interesting objects that appear behind them in the mirror. Although justifications, as well as criticisms, can be made for each of these criteria, the timing of self-recognition is quite similar by each of the measures, lending credence to them all. Self-recognition occurs for most infants near the end of their second year.

Although self-recognition occurs rather late in infancy, infants have an early interest in mirrors and other reflective surfaces. Initially, infants are more attentive to the reflected images of objects or other people rather than to their self-images, probably because they readily see that two identically looking objects or people seem to be present and this attracts their interest. Then, beginning around 3–4 months of age, infants' attention is directed toward the self-image. Smiles, vocalizations, touching the image, and even attempts to look behind the mirror become prevalent. Infants appear to treat the image in a social manner as if there were an interesting baby behind the glass, although studies of infants' responses at this age to their reflected image and to a socially responding partner show infants to be more responsive to the social partner.

Toward the end of the first year, infants' behavior toward their mirror image takes on a new dimension. Infants begin to test the correspondence between the action of the image and their own behavior. They study the movements of their reflections while systematically varying these movements. Most characteristic is repeated limb activity while observing the limb in the mirror image or a repeated bobbing, bowing, or bouncing while attending to the image, at times turning away and then quickly back to the image as if to try to catch it off guard. Movement testing behavior indicates that infants are exploring the uniqueness of their reflected self-image and its perfect match to their behavior. Movement testing behavior accelerates around the time of self-recognition. The realization that the movement of the self-image is perfectly matched to the infant's movement may be an initial cue to self-recognition. That is, the first recognition of the visual self-image may be the recognition of self-movement.

Figure 3 shows infants' movement testing behavior to different video conditions in a longitudinal study of the development of self-recognition beginning when infants were 18 months of age. On each monthly session, infants were shown a playback of a video of themselves taken at the beginning of the session (discordant condition), a live video of themselves (simultaneous condition), and a video of a similarly aged infant in the same setting (other child condition). The mean age of self-recognition in the simultaneous condition in this study was 22 months. Movement testing to this condition was clearly higher than in the other conditions and showed an increase prior to self-recognition.

Infants' interest in the movements of their mirror image may be due to advances in their imitative abilities and awareness. Around the time infants show an interest in movement testing with their reflected images, they show development in their ability to imitate novel behaviors not in their repertoire of actions and in their deliberate attempts to adjust their behavior to more accurately

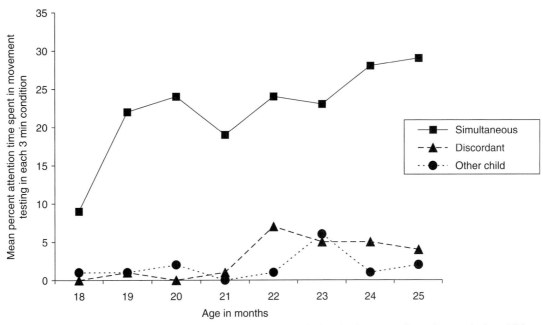

Figure 3 Mean percentage of attention time spent in movement testing in the simultaneous, discordant, and other child conditions from ages 18 to 25 months. Adapted from Bigelow AE (1981) The correspondence between self and image movement as a cue to self-recognition in young children. *Journal of Genetic Psychology* 139: 11–36, Copyright (1981), with permission from Heldref Publications.

match that of a model. As infants' imitative ability becomes more precise, they may notice that the actions of their reflected images are unique. The images consistently, simultaneously, and perfectly match their own movements, unlike that of a social partner.

Within a few weeks to a few months after infants can recognize themselves in mirrors or live video, they can recognize themselves in still images, such as picking out pictures of themselves from a series of photographs of babies, and on videotape that is not concurrent with their present movement. In the study depicted in **Figure 3**, self-recognition in the discordant condition occurred at a mean age of 24 months. Between self-recognition in the simultaneous and discordant conditions, movement testing increased in the discordant and other child conditions, although movement testing was virtually nonexistent prior to this time as can be seen in **Figure 3**. The infants may have been trying to identify the images in these conditions by means of the same process that facilitated recognition in the simultaneous condition, that is, by attempting to test for a correspondence between self and image movement. In these conditions, however, there was no visual feedback of a correspondence so the attempts were short-lived.

Infants eventually become aware that their reflected self-image has unique visual characteristics, that is, it is always the same-looking child who moves exactly like self. Once they understand that particular image to be of self, they can match that image to other self-images that do not have exact correspondence to their current movement.

Thus, the process of self-recognition may begin with infants' interest in the correspondence between self and image movement, which leads to the realization that the image that shows such correspondence with self-movement is a self-image, and be followed by the children's development of mental representations of what they look like to which they can match the images they see.

Interestingly, studies of 2- and 3-year-old children's reactions to their delayed video images indicate that, although the children can recognize their delayed video images as self-images, they have difficulty recognizing the images as of themselves in the present unless the delay is less than 2–3 s. Young children's recognition of self-images in the present is dependent upon their ability to detect the temporal matching of their current action and the action of the self-image.

The temporal limits of recognition of self-images in the present correspond to the timing necessary for infants to detect socially contingent responses to self-action. The responses of others are perceived to be socially contingent only if the responses occur less than 2–3 s after the infants' own behavior. Adults show similar temporal limits to the perception of social contingency.

Experience with social interaction may be important for self-recognition. Such speculation is supported by findings that show chimpanzees raised in isolation, unlike those raised with other chimpanzees, do not perform self-directed behavior when watching their mirror reflection. Perhaps it is necessary to experience the contingency between self-actions and those of a socially responding partner before it is possible to become aware that the unique simultaneous matching between self and image action is an indication that the image seen is a self-image.

Early Autobiographical Self-Knowledge

Our autobiographical self-knowledge consists of our memories of important events in our lives that help define who we are to ourselves and others. There are large individual differences in the age of first memories, as well as the number of memories reported from early childhood. Rarely do people report memories from before 2 years of age. Most people have some sporadic memories from the years 2–4, with more accessible memories from middle childhood.

Freud labeled this phenomenon of little or no memory of early life infantile amnesia. He proposed the cause to be repression of memories that were too arousing for the ego, such as the child's early sexual desires. It is unlikely that Freud's explanation is the reason for the absence of self-memories from early childhood; all memories of very early childhood tend to be absent, not just those that are emotionally arousing or might be associated with the young child's sensual pleasures.

Piaget proposed a cognitive explanation. He thought that memories from early life are stored differently than memories from later childhood and adulthood, and therefore, the retrieval systems to those memories are not accessible or, at best, indirect. From a Piagetian perspective, thought in infancy is a product of the babies' ongoing perceptions and motor actions. Babies think about what they currently perceive and what they are doing. In later infancy, these sensorimotor processes connect to previous learning in new ways, as in means-end understanding. Yet infants still do not have representational thought. From the end of infancy at about 2 years of age through the preschool period, young children's thought is representational but is not yet logically organized, making access to memories fragmented. Thus, events that occurred in infancy and early childhood are not stored in ways that are easily retrievable by older children and adults.

More recently, cognitive theorists have proposed that until children have a concept of self as an individual with unique characteristics, as evidenced specifically by mirror self-recognition, there is no framework around which to organize their personal memories and formulate their autobiographical past. Thus, autobiographical memory depends on developments in specific self-constructs.

Developments in children's memory storage and retrieval systems and constructs of the self are important to children's ability to remember their own lives, but such developments may not fully account for the emergence of autobiographical memory. These theoretical positions cannot readily explain the large variation in age and number of early memories. Children across cultures develop neural cognitive structures relating to storage and retrieval of memories at approximately the same age, and visual self-recognition is acquired within a narrow age range even in cultures with little or no experience with reflective surfaces.

Social cultural theorists propose that autobiographical memory emerges gradually and is influenced by multiple factors that interact in a dynamic fashion. Important to autobiographical memory are advances in neural cognitive structures in the brain that facilitate encoding, consolidation, storage, and retrieval of memories; conceptual developments of the self that include a subjective view of how events make one feel and think, which has its basis in infants' understanding of intentionality in self and others; language development, especially in narrative skills; developments in temporal concepts, particularly of self in time; and conversations with others about events the children have experienced. The importance of conversations with others is particularly intriguing and may help explain variations in age and number of early memories.

There are individual differences in the ways parents and others discuss children's life experiences with them. Some parents are more elaborate than other parents in their discussions with children about events in their lives, both at the time of the events and in reminiscing about them. In trying to help children remember, elaborative parents provide verbal props, expand on whatever fragments the child contributes, and are detailed in their descriptions. Less elaborative parents tend to repeat their questions rather than become more expansive in their detail and are more pragmatic in their questioning about the past, for example, where did you put your sweater. The differences among parents' conversations with children about events in the children's lives are most evident when talking with 2- and 3-year-olds because children at this age tend to contribute little original information to conversations about past events, resulting in the discussion being carried primarily by the parents' comments. Although parents tend to become more elaborate as children grow older and acquire more narrative skills and parents tend to emphasize different topics with sons than with daughters, individual differences in how elaborative parents are in their conversations with children are robust. Parents' reminiscing styles correlate over time and show similar patterns with multiple children in the family. One of the reasons there are such large individual differences in age and number of early autobiographical memories may be due to individual differences in how parents discuss events in young children's lives with them.

How do conversations with children about events in their lives affect autobiographical memories? Autobiographical memories are episodic memories, which are memories of specific events that happened at specific times and places. Children as young as 2.5 years report episodic memories, but whether they have autobiographical memories is questionable. Not all episodic memories become autobiographical memories. For instance, yesterday's lunch may be remembered today, but unless the lunch was extraordinary for some reason, it is unlikely that it will become part of one's autobiographical self knowledge. In talking with children about events in their past, children are helped to reflect on the events, which may facilitate the consolidation of specific episodic memories into autobiographical memories.

To children of 2 and 3 years of age, routine events, rather than one time events, are particularly important. Young children are trying to figure out the world and themselves in it. Their particular interest is in how things are done and what to expect next. The scenarios of routine events are scripts or generic event memories, for example, bedtime scripts may involve taking a bath, getting into pajamas, getting a story read to you, having a glass of water, getting a goodnight kiss, hugging your teddy bear. When a novel event occurs, young children can hold it in their memories for a period of time. If a similar event occurs within that period, the event is remembered longer. Two-year-olds have been shown to remember an event for 3 months if it reoccurred within 2 weeks of the original occurrence. After an event occurs several times, it tends to become a generic event. For example, going to the zoo may be a memorable episodic event for a 2.5-year-old, but after several trips to the zoo, the child forms a script for zoo trips but does not remember what specific animals were seen on which trips. The underlying principle is that events must reoccur for young children to have sustained memories of the event, but those memories tend to get transformed into generic event memories.

But when parents, siblings, and others talk to the child about experiences the child has had, the experiences are reinstated; the child revisits the event in conversation with the other person. Unlike generic or script memories, the revisits are not similar actual events, but rather involve mentally reinstating the specific episodic event. All autobiographical memories may be products of mentally reinstating specific episodic events. The difference between the establishment of autobiographical memories in early childhood and in later childhood and adulthood may be that, for young children, the mental reinstating of episodic events is facilitated by others.

The influence of children's conversations with parents and others on children's memory implies that autobiographical memory is subject to social construction. What is salient to the parent from a particular event in the child's life may not be what was salient to the child at the time, yet the parent's version is what is discussed, especially in early childhood when information contributed by the child is minimal. Children's reports of private memories that do not involve discussions with others tend to become more prevalent in the late preschool years. Although this may be because of increases in children's narrative skills, it is also when children become more facile in using their thought processes to reminisce and reflect upon happenings for themselves, essentially reinstating the event in their minds without help from others. Yet social cultural theorists do not propose that conversations with others cause children's memories. Although children with parents who are elaborate in their discussions of past events report longer and more detailed descriptions of their past experiences, children with less elaborative parents do not necessarily have fewer memories.

From the perspective of social cultural theory, the frequency and manner of parents' reminiscing with children about events in the children's lives affect the development of several skills important to autobiographical memory. Parental conversation styles that are elaborate, both when events occur and when reminiscing about them, may help children organize their memories, which makes them more accessible. Parent–child conversations about the child's past may facilitate the child's understanding of self in time through focusing on the child's experience in temporally specified events. Potentially, such conversations also may allow more opportunity for the parent and child to disagree on the facts (e.g., whether talking to Santa was scary or not) and thus facilitate children's understanding of memories as representational and that self and others can have different perspectives of the past, allowing for the creation of a truly personal past. Children's discussions with others about their experiences help them distinguish specific episodic events as significant from other events in their lives and to integrate such memories into their life story. Parent–child conversations about the past influence the way children think about their lives, the sense they make of their experiences, and how they share their experiences with others.

Conclusion

Early forms of self-knowledge prepare the way for later more complex forms of self-knowledge to develop. Through experience with their own actions and perceptions, infants distinguish self-action from the actions of others or events in the physical world. They become aware of their own bodies and the effects their actions have on the physical and social environment. These effects become predictable and anticipated. Infants become intentional in their actions and begin to read intention in the actions of others. They become self-reflective, learn to recognize their own images, and begin to form their life narrative. In the first few years of life, self-knowledge progresses from simple beginnings to sophisticated forms of self-understanding that continue to develop throughout life.

Experience is crucial to early developments in self-knowledge. The child's experience when alone and when engaged with the physical environment provide the child with important information relevant to the self, but much of the experience most salient to self-knowledge occurs within social contexts. In early infancy, responding others facilitate infants' ability to distinguish self from other and to learn that they are effective in producing external changes. In later infancy, self-recognition may depend on children's awareness of the difference between the movements of their reflections and those of a socially responding other. The development of intentionality is enhanced through engagement with others by facilitating infants' understanding that their intentions and those of others are distinct yet can be changed through their own behavior. Others' communications with children influence how children begin to value their abilities and remember their own lives. Social encounters provide the fertile ground for young children to acquire self-knowledge. In early life, as well as throughout life, knowledge of self is embedded in interactions with others.

See also: Amnesia, Infantile; Milestones: Cognitive.

Suggested Readings

Bauer PJ (2007) *Remembering the Times of Our Lives: Memory in Infancy and Beyond.* Mahwah, NJ: Erlbaum.

Bigelow AE (1981) The correspondence between self and image movement as a cue to self recognition in young children. *Journal of Genetic Psychology* 139: 11–36.

Bigelow AE (1998) Infants' sensitivity to familiar imperfect contingencies in social interaction. *Infant Behavior and Development* 21: 149–162.

Carpenter M, Nagell K, and Tomasello M (1998) Social cognition, joint attention, and communicative competence from 9 to 15 months of age. *Monographs of the Society for Research in Child Development* 63. (4, Serial No. 255).

Lewis M and Haviland-Jones JM (eds.) (2000) *Handbook of Emotions,* 2nd edn. New York: The Guilford Press.

Neisser U (ed.) (1993) *The Perceived Self: Ecological and Interpersonal Sources of Self Knowledge.* New York: Cambridge University Press.

Nelson K (1993) The psychological and social origins of autobiographical memory. *Psychological Science* 4: 7–14.

Nelson K and Fivush R (2004) The emergence of autobiographical memory: A social cultural developmental theory. *Psychological Review* 111: 486–511.

Rochat P (ed.) (1995) *The Self in Infancy: Theory and Research.* Amsterdam: North-Holland/Elsevier.

Rochat P (ed.) (1999) *Early Social Cognition: Understanding Others in the First Months of Life.* Mahwah, NJ: Erlbaum.

Stern DN (2000) *The Interpersonal World of the Infant: A View from Psychoanalysis and Developmental Psychology.* New York: Basic Books.

Semantic Development

J Bhagwat and M Casasola, Cornell University, Ithaca, NY, USA

© 2008 Elsevier Inc. All rights reserved.

Glossary

Agent – In linguistics, a grammatical agent is the recipient of an action that is carried out.

Bootstrapping – The idea that knowledge about one aspect of language (e.g. syntax) can help children learn about another aspect (e.g., semantics).

Count noun – A noun which can be used with a numeral (e.g. one ball, two dogs) and can occur in both singular and plural form, as well as with adjectives of quantity such as every, each, several, most, etc. (e.g. every ball, several dogs, most apples).

Intermodal preferential looking paradigm – (IPLP) In the standard IPLP, the infant is seated on a parent's lap in front of two laterally spaced video monitors. A concealed centrally placed audio speaker plays a linguistic stimulus that matches only one of the displays shown on the screens. The variable of interest is the total amount of time that the infant spends watching the matching vs. nonmatching screen.

Joint attention – Characteristic of certain interactions between child and adult wherein the child follows the focus of the adult's attention to a third entity or event in the environment. It may include the child's attempts to redirect the adult's attention to the entity of the child's interest. Joint attention is often achieved via eye-gaze, pointing, and verbal signals.

Mass noun – A mass noun cannot occur in singular/plural. This type of noun cannot be used with a number unless a unit of measurement is specified (e.g., two piles of sand, three bottles of water).

Mean length of utterance (MLU) – A measure of linguistic productivity in children. It is traditionally calculated by collecting 100 utterances spoken by a child and dividing the number of morphemes (a morpheme is the smallest linguistic unit that has

meaning) by the number of utterances. A higher MLU is taken to indicate a higher level of language proficiency.
Patient – In linguistics, a grammatical patient is the participant of a situation upon whom an action is carried out.
Pragmatics (pragmatic) – The study of language as it is used in a social context. Pragmatics is concerned with how language meaning and language use are dependent on the speaker, the addressee, and other features of the context of utterance.
Referent – Any entity (including objects and events) that can be named or labeled. (Naming and labeling are used interchangeably throughout this article. The terms entity and referent have also been used interchangeably.)
Syntax (syntactic) – The study of the rules that govern how words combine to form phrases, and how phrases combine to form sentences.

Introduction

Broadly defined, semantic development describes how children learn the meanings of words. The term comes from the branch of linguistics called semantics: the study of the meaning system of language. Thus, semantic development could be defined as the acquisition of words and their meanings. To know the meaning of a word is to possess a certain mental representation or concept that is associated with a certain linguistic form.

However this process of mapping word to meaning is no easy task. Many of us have had the experience of being surrounded by a roomful of people speaking an unfamiliar tongue. Often, all one can perceive is a string of speech with few cues that tell us where a particular word begins and where it ends. Even after one has identified a word, there is the problem of determining the object or event to which the word refers. An often-cited example that beautifully illustrates the nature of this problem was first outlined by the linguist Willard V. O. Quine in 1960. Quine posited an imaginary linguist visiting a culture whose language bears no resemblance to the linguist's language. A rabbit wanders by and the native exclaims, "Gavagai!" The term gavagai could refer to any number of logically possible referents, including the rabbit, the name of that specific rabbit, all mammals, all animals or even all objects. It could mean white and furry, refer to one particular part of the rabbit's body, or alternatively refer to the act of running. Given that there many possible referents for a single word, how does a child solve this problem?

Word learning can be viewed in terms of steps that the child undergoes in arriving at the meaning of the word. The child must (1) identify the relevant entity from the ongoing stream of activity in the world, (2) parse or segment the relevant piece of sound from the ongoing stream of continuous speech, and (3) establish a mapping between the entity and that sound. Some researchers would add a fourth step: the child must develop an understanding that a word stands not only for the specific entity that it names, but also that it applies to other members of that category. For instance, knowing that the word 'dog' refers to a particular kind of domestic animal would imply knowing that the word 'dog' refers to all dogs and not simply an individual dog. The process or ability by which the name for an entity can be extended to other members that belong to that entity's category is known as generalization.

Others have broken down these steps further, particularly in terms of language comprehension. There is substantial evidence that children comprehend (i.e., understand) language earlier than they can produce it. Researchers have discriminated between different types of comprehension, such as recognitory comprehension, and symbolic comprehension. In recognitory comprehension, children form an association between a referent and a label. This type of comprehension is an early type of comprehension and is often considered a precursor to learning the meanings of words. Once children break away from this simple association between word and referent and begin to understand that a word does not merely co-occur with a referent but that the word stands for it or refers to it, they have acquired symbolic comprehension, a more advanced type of comprehension. Symbolic comprehension of the word 'dog' implies that the child understands that 'dog' does not merely refer to a particular dog but refers to the whole category of dogs. Thus, this definition of symbolic comprehension includes the aspect of generalization, described above. Some of the studies that will be discussed in this article examine recognitory comprehension, whereas others examine symbolic comprehension. Both are equally important in the broader study of semantic development.

First Words

Comprehension

Although infants in their first year produce few words, they nonetheless possess a sizeable receptive (i.e., comprehension) vocabulary. Numerous studies have shown that infants comprehend language earlier than they can actually produce it. Maternal reports document that word learning, both productive and receptive, begins at about 9–12 months. Similarly, naturalistic studies have shown that infants in this age range respond appropriately to verbal commands. However, the earliest traces of comprehension may begin as early as 4.5 months. Jusczyk and colleagues found that 4.5-month-olds listened significantly longer to repetitions of their own names than other names, and by about 6 months of age, they were able to recognize their own names in fluent speech. Six-month-old infants also demonstrate comprehension of the labels 'mommy' and 'daddy'. When shown side-by-side videos of their own parents, infants looked longer at the video of the named parent than the unnamed one (i.e., when hearing 'mommy' or 'daddy'). Thus, infants' comprehension of their own names and their caregivers' names is evident by 6 months. Comprehension of other labels has been shown to emerge by about 8 months.

In the infants' second year, comprehension continues to outpace production. Although 14-month-old infants, on average, produce only about 10 words in total, children of this age are reported by their parents to understand roughly 50 words. Moreover, by about 13–14 months of age, infants can learn to link words to objects under experimental conditions that provide only limited exposure to the novel labels and their referents. When the experimental condition involves an actual experimenter providing a label, this ability is evident by 13 months of age. For example, in one study by Amanda Woodward and colleagues, 13-month-old infants were shown two novel objects. One object was labeled nine times as 'dax'. The other object was not labeled, but the researcher drew equal attention to this nonlabeled object by using general linguistic phrases such as, "Ooh, look at that". When asked to find the 'dax' and put the 'dax' down a toy chute, infants chose the labeled objected more often than expected by chance. In contrast, when asked to simply 'pick one' to put down the chute, infants displayed no preference for the labeled object. These results provided some of the first evidence that infants can learn a new label after only nine exposures. Similarly, when the labels and objects are presented via video (without a live experimenter), infants of 14 months can form links between the labels and the objects. Infants of 12 months, however, have difficulty with this task, suggesting that infants develop the ability to quickly form associations between novel words and objects between 12 and 13 months of age. More recently, however, infants as young as 9 months of age have shown that they can quickly map a label onto an object, but only if the object is perceptually salient (i.e. interesting and attractive to the infants). Just as infants in their first year improve in their ability to quickly link words to objects, they also begin to learn that words hold a special status relative to other sounds. Whereas infants of 13 months are willing to accept a range of sounds, from words to whistles, as labels for objects, infants of 18 months accept only words as labels.

Production

At about 12 months of age, infants start producing their first words. These first words are usually single words, produced in isolation, giving this phase of language development its name: the 'one-word stage'. By the time they are 18 months, most English-learning toddlers have a productive vocabulary of about 50 words. During their second year, many children undergo a vocabulary spurt or naming explosion – a marked increase in the rate at which new words are added to their vocabulary. Even those children who do not show evidence of a marked increase in rate, still greatly increase the total size of their productive vocabularies during this time. By 24 months of age, children comprehend and produce hundreds of words and also start to combine them systematically to form phrases.

The very first words, at least for English-learning children, often include sound effects, such as moo and meow; words for routines such as peek-a boo, bath, bye, all gone; and names for people such as mommy and daddy. There is substantial evidence for significant individual differences between children in the single-word stage. Some children adopt what is known as a referential style. They begin by learning single words including a large percentage of common nouns or object labels in their first 50–100 words, and then begin combining them into phrases and sentences. Other children have more heterogeneous vocabularies including a number of rote-learned and unanalyzed multiword phrases, including strings of words for social and instrumental purposes such as 'thank you', 'go away', 'I want it', 'don't do it', and 'no'. This style has been called the expressive style. Similarly, there are certain patterns of word use that often are observed in the early productions of children. For example, children learning their first words often use a single word for several different referents, an example of overgeneralization. Thus, a child may initially use the term 'kitty' to refer to all animals or the term 'ball' to refer to all round objects, such as oranges, door knobs, or even the moon. The reverse phenomenon is undergeneralization wherein a child is conservative in his/her first uses of a word. For instance, the child may use car to refer to only the family car without generalizing it to other cars. Similarly, a specific word may be used only in a particular context, as in a child who only uses 'car' when watching cars move below the living room window.

Reasons for such generalization patterns remain unclear. It has been suggested that children may overgeneralize or undergeneralize even though they perceive differences in these referents. It is possible that their limited vocabulary compels them to use a single word for different referents. Alternatively, it is also possible their understanding of the world itself is limited. Whatever the reasons, all children eventually abandon these over- and undergeneralizations.

Learning Words: Theories and Mechanisms

Before launching into a discussion on the specific mechanisms and processes of word learning, it is worth noting that traditionally, most word learning theories have focused on how children learn the meanings of nouns. Although the reasons for this bias have also been hotly debated, some possible reasons might be that for children learning English, nouns tend to be more predominant in children's early vocabularies than other types of words (such as verbs), and nouns appear to be learned more quickly and easily than these other word types. At the same time, there have always been a few researchers, such as Lois Bloom and colleagues, who drew the attention of the field to the presence of other types of words in children's early vocabularies. Bloom's work set the stage for studies on how children learn verbs and other action words (see work by Michael Tomasello, Jane Childers, Diane Poulin-Dubois, and colleagues), adjectives (Sandra Waxman and colleagues), as well as cross-linguistic studies on how specific properties of a language can influence the way children learn that language (Melissa Bowerman, Soonja Choi, Twila Tardif, and colleagues). In the light of new findings, researchers such as Roberta Golinkoff, Kathy Hirsh-Pasek, and others have proposed more comprehensive and integrative theories of word learning, outlining not only how children learn to map words onto objects (as was the focus in many theories of early word learning) but also, actions.

In recent times, there is increasing consensus that children use multiple resources in order to hone in on the meanings of words. This complex network of resources comprises the child's own preferences (i.e., biases); the child's developing conceptual knowledge; social cues that are offered by communicative partners; as well as linguistic and grammatical cues that can be gleaned from the actual language that the child is learning. The theories that are discussed in the followings sections focus on one or more of these resources in order to explain early word learning by children.

Constraints Theories

Constraints theories, initially proposed by Ellen Markman and colleagues, offer a solution to the Quinean conundrum by proposing that children approach the word learning task biased to make certain assumptions about word meanings. These biases are also referred to as constraints, predispositions, expectations, or assumptions. Recall that the Quinean example suggests that children must venture different guesses in determining the referent of a new word. According to the constraints theories, rather than generating countless hypotheses about the possible meaning of a particular word, children are naturally predisposed to attend to certain aspects of the word learning situation. Traditionally, constraints have been viewed as specific expectations that children have about word meanings. Thus, these expectations are assumed to be specific to the domain of language learning. However, there is increasing evidence that suggests that constraints may be better viewed as default assumptions that the child relies on, in the absence of other social and linguistic cues, rather than viewing these expectations as absolute linguistic constraints. In the sections that follow, we discuss some of the different kinds of constraints that have been proposed to explain word learning.

The whole-object constraint

The whole-object bias, first proposed by Ellen Markman, predicts that children assume that new words refer to objects rather than their parts or properties. For instance, when provided with a novel object and a novel word, children often assume that the word refers to the whole object rather than parts of the object, or a property of the object (e.g., its color), or the substance that its made of. For instance, 2-year-olds were shown a novel object and were told that it was 'a zom'. They were then shown other novel objects, some of which matched the original object in form (i.e., they were identical in shape, size, texture and material, but not color), and others which matched the original only in color. Subsequently, when the children were asked to find 'another zom', they almost always chose the form match rather than a color match. However, when simply asked to 'find another one', children often chose the color match over the form match. The results suggest that a label plays a role in drawing attention to the whole object rather than a property of the object.

Taxonomic constraint

A second constraint, also initially proposed by Ellen Markman, is the noun-category bias that predicts that hearing a novel label actually leads children to form a category of objects. The taxonomic assumption predicts that children correctly extend object labels to members of a class (category) and not to thematically related objects. When presented with a novel label for dog, preschool-age children extend the label to other kinds of dogs and are thus more likely to put two toy dogs together in such tasks. In contrast, without a label, children are more likely to choose a thematically related object, such as placing a dog with a bone or a rabbit with a carrot. Even infants of 12 months seem to understand that count nouns refer to categories of objects. Indeed, infants of this age can use a novel noun to aid them in grouping objects into categories. In one study, infants were introduced to toys from two different categories (e.g., vehicles vs. animals). During a familiarization phase, infants were presented with toys from within a category (e.g., four different cars, belonging to the vehicle category) and the experimenter labeled each toy with the same novel label (e.g., 'avi'). Next, in the test phase, infants were presented with another toy from the same category (e.g., another car) and a toy from a different category (e.g., a plane or an animal). A control group of infants experienced the same procedure but no label was used to name the toys. Only the infants who heard the novel label during the familiarization phase discriminated between the categories of animals vs. vehicles, as measured by the time they spent attending to a toy from the familiar category as compared to a toy from another category. Thus, hearing the novel label drew infants' attention to certain commonalities between objects, leading them to form a category. This pattern was not evident when the infants were presented with the same toys without hearing a novel label, suggesting that infants of 12 months are developing an understanding that a count noun will refer to categories of objects.

Mutual exclusivity constraint

Another extensively studied constraint bias is the principle of mutual exclusivity. This bias predicts that children prefer a single label for an object or object category because children assume that a novel word will not label an already-named object, but instead, will label an unfamiliar object. In support of this view, several studies conducted by Markman and colleagues have demonstrated that when presented with a familiar object with a known label and a novel object, children tend to map a novel label onto the novel object rather than onto the familiar object. This effect has been demonstrated in infants as young as 15 months.

Sociopragmatic Theories and Cues to Word Learning

The sociopragmatic theories of word learning view the child as embedded in social networks and social contexts. These theories propose that children depend on communicative interactions with other people (usually adults) to provide cues about the possible meanings of words. Specifically, the child's earliest words depend on his/her ability to perceive and understand the actions of other persons as intentional. For instance, if an adult calls out the child's name and points to a referent in their common environment, the child understands that such pointing is purposeful and intentional – the act of pointing is an indication of the adult's intention to draw the child's attention toward that referent. This social understanding develops through the child's communicative interactions with others. Furthermore, such communicative interactions have been found to play a crucial role in the child's overall cognitive development and are not restricted to language learning. Thus, the sociopragmatists argue that word learning recruits general cognitive processes as opposed to cognitive processes that are specialized for language learning.

How does children's understanding of others' intentions aid them in word learning? Studies by Dare Baldwin and colleagues demonstrate that when learning new words, infants rely on a wide variety of social cues, such as direction of the speaker's eye gaze, head direction, body posture, pointing, source of the sound (whether the label is coming from a visible human source or coming from an disembodied voice with an unknown source), gestures, and facial expression. Some of these cues facilitate the creation of joint attention between the adult and the child, and provide information about the intentions of the speaker. Joint attention has been shown to facilitate word learning in several experimental and naturalistic studies.

Evidence from experimental studies

A series of experiments by Michael Tomasello, Nameera Akhtar and their colleagues have demonstrated that children use their understanding of others' intentions to learn new words. For instance, 2-year-olds and even 18-month-olds were able to use intentions and emotional cues to correctly infer the meaning of new words. Children observed as an experimenter expressed the intention to find an object, used a novel label for this desired object, and subsequently searched for the object. For some children, the experimenter did find the objects, whereas for other children, the experimenter failed to find the object. However, in both situations, children understood that an adult's intention to find an object and subsequent excitement at finding the object (or subsequent disappointment at not finding the object) suggested that the novel label referred to this specific object and not other objects that were also present and with which the adult also played.

As children become older, their understanding of the intentions and knowledge and beliefs of others becomes more sophisticated and they continue to recruit this expanding social understanding to learn the meanings of new words. For instance, 3–4-year-olds resist learning new words if the speaker displays signs of ignorance about the new words, but they readily learn the word when the speaker seems knowledgeable. Similarly, preschoolers prefer learning labels from an adult who has previously labeled an object correctly as compared to an adult who has been shown to label objects incorrectly in the past. In fact, although preschoolers usually assume that adults are better sources of information than their peers, children of this age sometimes consider another child as a more reliable source of information than an adult, if the child previously has proved to be reliable and the adult unreliable.

Parental input: Individual, socioeconomic and cultural factors

Both quality and quantity of maternal language input have been shown to play critical roles in children's early semantic development. Important studies by Michael Tomasello, Nameera Akhtar and their colleagues have found that some mothers engage more often in joint attention, by following their child's attentional focus rather than attempting to redirect the child's attention. Children of these mothers show more rapid vocabulary development and larger vocabularies than children whose mothers often attempt to redirect their attention. In fact, maternal following of the child's attention when the child was about 13 months old accounted for 60% of the variance in children's vocabulary at 22 months of age.

Those mothers who provide more language input overall also use a richer vocabulary, repeat the same words more times, and use longer utterances. Children of such mothers are found to have larger vocabularies than those whose mothers provide less input overall. For verb learning particularly, using several different sentence frames for each verb provides clues to the meaning of the verb and can thus aid verb learning. In fact, such mothers also tend to respond frequently and contingently to their children's vocalizations and these children often start talking sooner and reach the 50-word milestone at a younger age than children of less responsive mothers.

Furthermore, certain conversational settings such as book reading and meal times have been found to incorporate most of the above mentioned characteristics. In fact, time spent by children in book reading with an adult is found to predict vocabulary development. Children in families where mealtimes are used as opportunities for conversation, including extended narratives of family members recounting their days, have been found to show advantages in vocabulary development. Thus, the positive relation between verbal responsiveness and child language milestones could be an effect of engagement (i.e., responsiveness) as well as an effect of the amount and nature of the input.

Socioeconomic status has also been found to affect children's opportunities for communicative interactions and the availability of language input. An influential study by Betty Hart and Todd Risley in the mid-1990s found that socioeconomic status (SES) related differences in vocabulary-size in children were noticeable from the beginning of speech and they increased with development. Studies show that higher-SES mothers are much more likely to demonstrate all the input characteristics that have been related with advanced vocabularies in children, as compared to lower-SES mothers. When SES, input to children, and children's language development are all measured, it becomes clear that differences in input across SES account for the differences in children's language outcomes. Thus, differences of SES in children's vocabulary development reflect differences in experience and not ability.

Certain cultures do not consider infants as appropriate conversational partners and children are usually not addressed directly. Nonetheless, in these cultures, joint attention is often achieved by mother and child focusing on a common topic. In some cases, infants are held in such a way that they can see adults talking and see what adults are talking about. In such situations where children rely predominantly on overheard speech and thus do not get language that is segmented for their benefit, children begin talking by producing large memorized chunks of language, which they only later analyze into component words. Such patterns have been found among the Walpiri people of Australia, the Mayans in Mexico and the Inuit. In fact, this pattern of language acquisition is also found to be characteristic of children who find themselves suddenly immersed in a foreign language (such as children whose families move to a new country) and must rapidly learn this language without explicit instruction.

Similarly, Italian and Argentinean children are found to produce significantly more words for people (e.g., aunt, grandmother, cousin) than their US counterparts. These differences are thought to reflect differences in the amount of contact children have with extended family members. Nevertheless, it is important to note that these differences have been found in vocabulary composition and not vocabulary size.

Attentional Mechanisms

Recently, Linda Smith, Larissa Samuelson, and colleagues have offered a third perspective on the word learning problem. Similar to the sociopragmatic view, this perspective on word learning also argues for cognitive processes that are more general in nature, rather than specific to language. In this view of word learning, the earliest word learning can be best accounted for through attentional mechanisms. Children notice objects, events, and actions that are most perceptually salient in their environment. They associate the most frequently used label with the most salient candidate. Thus, a general cognitive mechanism such as attention is sufficient to account for how young children first map words onto referents. Furthermore, such an account also explains how different general mechanisms could combine in ways that would lead to more sophisticated word learning.

How exactly does an attentional mechanism account for word learning? Just as children tend to associate labels with whole objects, there is evidence suggesting that children attend to shape while learning new words (also known as the shape-bias). It is important to note that the shape-bias operates under the caveat of experience, so that children start attending to shape only after they have had sufficient experience with language. Whereas the very first words may be learned through a simple trial-and-error process, once the child has accumulated a vocabulary of about 50 words, the child has learned that names are usually associated with shape, that is, objects with very similar shapes usually have the same name. Thus, every time a novel word is heard, attention is drawn to the shape of the referent object. This association is the engine that propels word learning forward, leading to more and more complex associations between words and real-world referents.

To illustrate using a specific example, by about 2 years of age, English-learning children have been shown to extend novel labels on the basis of shape for objects with a rigid shape. Researchers introduced 2-year-olds to a novel object made of a distinctive substance (e.g., a circular piece of wood), while saying, "This is my blicket." This neutral sentence frame suggests that 'blicket' could refer to the whole object, or to the substance (e.g., wood). In the test phase, children were shown an object of the same shape but different material (e.g., a circular piece of clay) as well an object of the same material in a different shape (e.g., pieces of wood) and asked to 'find the blicket'. Despite the neutral sentence frame in the initial phase, children chose the object similar in shape (e.g., the circular piece of clay), rather than pieces of the original material (e.g., wood). However when the named entity was a nonsolid substance (e.g., sand), children of the same age were more likely to extend the name to other referents that were similar to the original in its material and color. Other studies have shown that when the named entity has properties that are typical of animate things – eyes, feet, limbs – slightly older children (2.5- to 3-year-olds) generalize the name to objects that match the named example in both shape and texture, presumably because they associate animate objects as having certain commonalities in texture, such as furry, scaly and so on. These findings demonstrate how increasing attention to a progression of commonalities across objects leads to the association of labels with these commonalities resulting in word learning. These findings highlight how a general cognitive mechanism such as attention can be shown to aid word learning.

Since the shape-bias is believed to be contingent upon sufficient experience with language, it is possible that specific properties of the language will influence the emergence of this bias. For instance, English makes a grammatical distinction between count and mass nouns (i.e., objects and substances). Specifically, English marks nouns as count nouns (e.g., a ball) or mass nouns (e.g., some water, bottle of water). Importantly, in English, entities having distinctive shapes are usually encoded as count nouns (e.g., balls, dogs, and most object labels) whereas entities that do not have distinctive shape are usually encoded as mass nouns (e.g., water, sand and most substance labels). This particular feature of English is thought to account for the shape-bias that is displayed by English-learning infants. English-learning children must learn that when a count noun is used (with count-noun syntax, such as 'this is a ball'), it is most likely to refer to an object, which has a distinctive shape. On the other hand, when a mass noun is used (with mass noun syntax, such as, 'this is some sand'), the label most likely refers to substances (e.g., water, sand). Thus, because English language syntax makes a distinction between count and mass nouns, English-learning children are more likely to attend to whether or not a novel object has a distinctive shape. However, they may be more likely to attend to substance, and ignore shape cues when mass-noun syntax is used.

By this reasoning, children who are learning a language that does not make a grammatical distinction between count and mass nouns (such as Japanese), should not show a preference to attend to either shape or substance. In a study with Japanese and American 2-year-olds, Mutsumi Imai and Dedre Gentner found that American 2-year-olds tended to extend novel labels for simple objects (e.g., a circular piece of clay) on the basis of shape. Specifically, when told that a circular piece of clay was 'my blicket' and asked to 'find the blicket' from a circular piece of wood and some differently shaped pieces of clay, American 2-year-olds were more likely to choose the circular piece of wood. In contrast, Japanese 2-year-olds did not show a preference to extend the name for a simple object on the basis of shape; instead, they were equally likely to choose other differently shaped pieces of clay and a circular piece of wood when asked to 'find the blicket' in Japanese. These findings suggest that specific characteristics of the English and Japanese language play a role in children's tendency to extend (generalize) novel names.

Combining Syntactic and Pragmatic Cues

Recall that in all the studies examining children's ability to learn novel labels for a referent, the novel labels were presented in a neutral sentence frame (e.g., "This is my blicket") so that children could not use syntactic cues in inferring the meaning of these labels. However, there is increasing evidence that by about 2 years of age, children are sensitive to syntactic or grammatical cues, and are even able to combine syntactic and pragmatic cues when deciding on the referents of novel labels.

For instance, D. Geoffrey Hall and colleagues found that when 2-year-olds were presented with a novel word in a syntactic frame that suggested that it was a proper noun (e.g., "This is Zav") in the presence of a familiar toy animal (such as a cat or a teddy bear), the toddlers assumed that 'zav' was a name for the animal. They were unwilling to extend this name to other similar toy animals, and preferred to restrict it to a particular individual. In contrast, when presented with a novel label in a syntactic frame that suggested that the label was a count noun (e.g., "This is a zav"), toddlers extended this label to other toy animals that belonged to the same category as the original animal, indicating that they interpreted the noun as a name for a category of animals such as all cats, rather than the name for a particular individual animal.

However, this understanding was evident only for categories with which children were already familiar. If, instead of a toy cat, a novel animal such as a llama was labeled using proper noun-syntax (e.g., "This is Zav"), 2-year-olds assumed that the name labeled the entire category of llamas, and not just that particular llama.

Similarly, 2-year-olds have different expectations about the labeling norms for animate and inanimate objects. When an inanimate object was labeled using either a count noun- or proper noun-syntax, 2-year-olds did not show a systematic preference in the way they extended either label (i.e., 'Zav' or 'a zav'). Thus, children are able to use syntactic information (the sentence frames) as well pragmatic information (the fact that only animate entities typically have names and that each entity typically has just one name) in order to learn new words.

Hybrid Models of Word – Learning

In recent years, there is increasing consensus that children recruit a wide variety of cues and exploit multiple sources of information in order to learn their first words. The emergentist-coalition model of word learning, proposed by Roberta Golinkoff, Kathy Hirsh-Pasek, and George Hollich, is a hybrid model that outlines the diverse cues in the real world that children recruit in word learning. They argue that children use a combination of cues, such as attentional, social, cognitive, and linguistic to learn new words. Despite their availability, not all cues are equally utilized in word learning. Younger children may rely on only a subset of the available cues. For instance, although 12-month-olds are sensitive to speaker's eye-gaze, they do not appear to use this cue to aid them in word learning until they are about 18 months old. Rather, younger infants rely on perceptual salience of the object in order to decide on the referent of a new label. Older, more experienced learners rely on a wider set of cues and on some cues more heavily than others. Given these developmental changes, the emergentist model suggests that the word learning constraints may be better viewed as the products and not the root causes of semantic development. That is, word learning constraints may be expectations that emerge in the child with increasing experience with the world and the language that surrounds them.

Nouns vs. Verbs: Is there a Noun Bias?

A comparison of the findings on children's verb vs. noun learning has led many to note that many children, especially those learning English, seem to learn nouns (usually object labels) earlier and more easily than verbs. In one of the very few studies that directly compared the learning of novel nouns and novel verbs, Jane Childers and Michael Tomasello found that under a variety of conditions (where frequency of exposure was varied), 2-year-olds showed a more robust ability to learn nouns as compared to verbs. In fact, 2-year-olds in this study were able to remember and understand an action in a nonverbal task but still had trouble learning a name for it (i.e., a verb). What could be the reasons for these differences?

In two highly influential papers, Dedre Gentner and colleagues proposed that the answer may lie in the concepts to which these words usually refer. Nouns usually label concrete entities, whereas verbs and prepositions usually label events such as actions, motions, and spatial locations. These events tend to comprise components such as manner (the way in which something moves), instrument (the means by which it moves), path (the direction in which it moves), and result (the outcome of the movement). When a child sees a boy kicking a ball and hears, "Look, the boy's kicking the ball," the child must learn which component of the kicking action the adult refers to when saying 'kicking'. The question arises of whether the word 'kick' refers to the contact action, the trajectory, or the landing action.

Verbs are inherently relational. They often imply the presence of an actor to carry out that action and often have referents that exist only briefly. Nouns refer to an entity that is usually perceptually concrete and apparent as a whole unit, has distinct boundaries, is unchanging, and persists over time. These differences may explain why children seem to attach labels to objects more easily than actions. In fact, researchers have cited these differences to explain the whole-object bias. A novel label may heighten attention to a novel object over a novel action because objects are more perceptually apparent as distinct, whole units in comparison to an action, such as 'kicking' which may be observable for a brief time. It is important to note, however, that actions or relational concepts are not harder to understand *per se*. Evidence from experimental studies demonstrates that infants as young as 9 months are able to form categories of motion but are not able to map a verb onto these categories until much later.

An added difficulty with verbs, prepositions and other relational terms is that they often are encoded differently across languages (unlike most object labels). For instance, in English, meanings of motion verbs are usually centered around the manner of motion, with the path of motion encoded as a separate element (e.g., fly away, tiptoe across). In contrast, in romance languages such as Spanish and French, motion verbs often encode the path of motion with manner added as an optional separate element (e.g., *partir en volant* (to leave flying); *traverser sur la pointe des pieds* (to cross on tip-toes)). Consequently, a child who is faced with the task of mapping a label onto a verb must not only isolate the word, but must also learn the specific encoding patterns of his/her language.

In the light of these cross-linguistic differences, some researchers have proposed that the so-called noun bias may not be as universal as previously thought. Studies examining vocabulary development in children learning some languages other than English suggest that linguistic and cultural factors play a role in explaining the patterns of semantic development that are observed in children. The input to English-learning infants is characterized by frequent and salient object labels. Western mothers often focus on concrete objects and provide a higher proportion of nouns in their speech to their infants. During this early stage, mothers also tend to use grammatically simpler and shorter sentences in their speech. This kind of input is found to correlate with early vocabularies that start with single words, with a high proportion of object labels and nouns, and later start comprising novel combinations of those words. Some languages such as Korean and Mandarin are more verb-friendly (i.e., verbs are more salient and more frequent in the input). Korean and Mandarin mothers are less object oriented; their speech contains proportionately more verbs and fewer nouns, and the vocabularies of the children learning these languages are less dominated by nouns than their English-learning counterparts.

Verb Learning

Although much of the research has focused on children's learning of labels for objects, children's earliest vocabularies do contain words that refer to actions (verbs such as 'cry', 'kiss', 'bite', 'eat') and events, such as 'bye-bye' and 'all-gone'. Experimental studies have shown that at about 16 months, infants demonstrate comprehension of verbs such as 'wave', 'eat', 'bounce' and 'roll'. Observational and experimental studies have noted that children's early verbs are usually context-bound and that these verbs have restricted meanings as compared to adult uses of these verbs. Janellen Huttenlocher and colleagues, for example, noticed that many of children's first verb meanings referred specifically to self-involved actions and did not include actions produced by others. Similarly, Michael Tomasello and colleagues found that the youngest word-learners start out by learning verbs one at a time. Furthermore, each verb is initially associated with only certain sentence frames. For instance, 25-month-olds were taught a series of novel verbs, each of which was introduced in a limited set of sentence frames. Thus, one verb might be introduced in a frame with an agent but no patient (e.g., 'Ernie's gaffing'), another might be introduced with a patient but no agent (e.g., 'blicking Ernie') and another might be introduced with both (e.g., 'Ernie's ziking Cookie Monster'). When children's spontaneous productions of these novel verbs were recorded and analyzed, it was found that children of this age rarely used a verb in a sentence frame that they had not heard previously. These results, as well as findings from a diary study of a child's early verb acquisition, led these researchers to conclude that children are initially conservative in their use of verbs, restricting a given verb to a narrow range of sentence structures and usages.

In other studies, Diane Poulin-Dubois, James Forbes, and colleagues found that 18–20-month-olds generalized a familiar verb (e.g., 'kick') when the actor was different but not when the manner or outcome was different. For instance, infants perceived a video of a woman kicking three balls across the floor and into a box as being different from a woman who turned around and kicked the balls with her heels (a different manner). The first action also was perceived as different from an action wherein the woman kicked the balls and the balls bounced off an obstacle placed behind the box and rolled back in the direction of the woman (a different outcome). In contrast, older children of 26 months extended a familiar verb such as kicking to new actors and new manners. Nonetheless, neither age group extended these verbs when the outcome changed. Such findings and others suggest that young children's representations of familiar action verbs change from 20 to 26 months.

Sources of Information about Verb Meaning

As we have seen in the preceding sections, young children can recruit a wide variety of cues to learn new words, particularly object labels and other nouns. Not surprisingly, children similarly rely on several sources of information when learning the meanings of verbs. The following studies provide examples of some of the cues that children recruit in order to learn the meanings of novel verbs.

Sociopragmatic Cues

Children draw on their understanding of speakers' intentions in order to interpret new words (such as verbs) for actions. For instance, children use pragmatic cues to decide whether a new word is the label for an action or an object. When the action, as opposed to the object, was the new element in the communicative context, or when the experimenter made obvious preparations related to the novel action prior to introducing the new word, children interpreted the word as a label for the new action rather than an object label. Similarly, when shown video events of people performing certain actions, 2-year-olds are sensitive to the intention (via eye-gaze) of the actor in the event and can use this information to determine whether the novel label refers to the object or the action in the event.

Two-year-old children also understand that speakers usually label only intentional actions and not accidental ones. Similarly, children of this age understand that if the speaker uses a label while expressing an intention to perform an action, and then is not able to successfully perform that action, the label still refers to that unaccomplished action, presumably because the speaker expressed the intention to perform it.

Syntactic Bootstrapping

Researchers such as Lila Gleitman, Barbara Landau, and others have proposed that children use information from sentence frames as clues to verb meanings. The proposal that sensitivity to sentence structure guides the acquisition of verb meaning is known as syntactic bootstrapping. Thus, an understanding about the components of a sentence such as the agent and patient of the verb may help children in determining the meaning of the verb.

Findings from studies using the intermodal preferential looking paradigm (IPLP) have been used as evidence to support the argument for syntactic bootstrapping. For instance, Letitia Naigles presented 2-year-old children with a single videotaped event, involving a duck and a bunny. Each actor was performing two actions simultaneously. One action was causal (the duck pushed down on the bunny's head, causing the bunny to squat) and the other action was noncausal (both the duck and the bunny waved their arms in large circles). As children watched these events, they heard a novel verb. For some children, the verb was embedded in a transitive sentence ("The duck is gorping the bunny"), and for others the verb was embedded in an intransitive sentence ("The duck and the bunny are gorping").

After the introduction of the new verb, children were shown two video scenes simultaneously, each of which contained only one of the actions seen in the first video. Thus, one screen showed one character pushing the other into a squat. The other screen showed both characters moving their arms around in large circles. As these two events were presented, children were asked "Where's gorping?" and the amount of time they looked at each screen was recorded. Children who had heard the verb in the transitive frame looked longer at the causal action (pushing down) and the children who had heard the verb in the intransitive frame looked longer at the noncausal action (arm circling). Thus, the children inferred that a transitive sentence frame (e.g., "the duck is gorping the bunny") suggested a causal action and the intransitive frame (e.g., "the duck and the bunny are gorping") suggested the noncausal action.

A more recent study suggests that even 21-month-olds can use the word order of a sentence to interpret the meanings of novel verbs. Children watched two videos side-by-side. One of these videos depicted one cartoon character (e.g., a duck) performing an action on another cartoon character (e.g., a bunny). The other video depicted the reverse: the bunny performing an action on the duck. Half of the children saw these two videos and heard a sentence such as, "The duck is gorping the bunny", while the other half saw the same two videos and heard a sentence such as, "The bunny is gorping the duck". Those children who heard the former sentence (i.e., "the duck is gorping the bunny") looked longer at the video where the duck was performing an action on the bunny. The opposite was found for the children who heard the latter sentence (i.e., "the bunny is gorping the duck"). Further, when the same two videos were shown with sentences such as, "He is gorping the bunny" or "He is gorping the duck", children looked longer at the appropriate video. These results suggest that, even before the age of 2 years, children expect the subject of the sentence to refer to the agent of an action and they expect the object of the sentence to refer to the patient of the action. These results suggest that young children can use the sentence frame to inform them about the meaning of the verb.

Conclusion

Numerous experimental studies on children's semantic development have provided insights into the processes by which children learn how to map words onto real world referents. These processes include not only the sociopragmatic, linguistic, and contextual cues that children recruit but also the assumptions children make about the meanings of new words. Taken together, the evidence suggests that early word learning is a complex interplay of children's cognitive abilities, their emerging conceptual understanding of the world around them and their experience with their specific native language or languages. In any one situation, children are able to use multiple sources of information simultaneously in order to hone in on the meaning of a word.

Furthermore, early semantic development is also highly influenced by the child's environment. Factors as diverse as structural characteristics of the language, cultural influences, maternal sensitivity, and responsivity to children's needs and abilities, and socioeconomic status of the family are found to have powerful impacts on children's semantic development. In addition, these factors too combine and complement each other to predict language outcomes in children.

See also: Attention; Bilingualism; Birth Order; Categorization Skills and Concepts; Grammar; Language Acquisition Theories; Language Development: Overview; Pragmatic Development; Preverbal Development and Speech Perception; Speech Perception.

Suggested Readings

Bloom P (2000) *How Children Learn the Meanings of Words.* Cambridge, MA: MIT Press.
Bowerman M and Levinson S (eds.) (2001) *Language Acquisition and Conceptual Development.* Cambridge, UK: Cambridge University Press.
Hall DG and Waxman SR (eds.) (2004) *Weaving a Lexicon.* Cambridge, MA: MIT Press.
Hirsh-Pasek K and Golinkoff RM (eds.) (2006) *Action Meets Word: How Children Learn Verbs.* Oxford: Oxford University Press.
Hoff E (2006) How social contexts support and shape language development. *Developmental Review* 26: 55–88.
Woodward AL and Markman EM (1998) Early word learning. In: Damon W, Kuhn D, and Siegler RS (eds.) *Handbook of Child Psychology: Vol. 2. Cognition, Perception and Language,* 5th edn., pp. 371–420. New York: Wiley.

Separation and Stranger Anxiety

A Scher and J Harel, University of Haifa, Haifa, Israel

© 2008 Elsevier Inc. All rights reserved.

Glossary

Anxiety – The psychological and physiological reaction to an anticipated danger, real or imagined.
Distress – An intense negative reaction to adverse events. The reaction may be emotional and/or physical.
Person and object permanence – The understanding that people and objects continue to exist when they are not directly observed.
Separation anxiety – A distress reaction in response to separation from the primary caregiver.
Separation anxiety disorder (SAD) – Developmentally inappropriate and excessive anxiety concerning actual or anticipated separation from the caregiver, most often the parents.
Stranger anxiety – The fearful, distressed response that infants exhibit when approached by an unfamiliar person, in the second half of the first year.

Introduction

In the second half of the first year, infants show signs of distress when approached by an unfamiliar person and when their primary caregiver leaves. The study of these phenomena underscores the link between advances in the child's ability to mentally represent people and events, along with changes in the emotional tie to the caregiver. Separation anxiety is an important psychological construct within a number of emotional development theories. While the reaction is normative, some children develop a separation anxiety disorder.

Reactions to the Approach and Disappearance of People

The second half of the first year of life is a time of major cognitive and emotional discoveries and challenges. In this period, infants not only explore and manipulate the environment more actively, but they also start expressing clear social preferences and apprehensions. While infants happily exchange smiles with strangers during the first months of their life, in the second half of the first year they begin to exhibit a clear preference for specific social partners, typically their parents. Moreover, at this stage when parents leave the room, even for a short time, babies often become distressed and start crying. Another trigger for distress during this period is the approach of an unfamiliar person. Upon encountering strangers, infants of this age observe the unfamiliar face intently, turn their heads away, and sometimes cry. In the developmental literature, the emergence of these distress responses – to separation and to strangers – is considered a major developmental milestone. When describing the reaction to the approach of an unfamiliar person, researchers use the terms wariness, apprehension, distress, fear, and anxiety depending, partially, on the theoretical perspective they are using to explain the response. In psychoanalytic theory, the reactions to the disappearance of the familiar caregiver and to the approach of an unfamiliar person are conceptualized as anxiety: separation anxiety and stranger anxiety.

Stranger Anxiety

Around 6–8 months, when infants are approached by an unfamiliar person, a new response appears: the expression of wariness and distress. At this stage, infants react to encounters with unfamiliar people who try to engage them in ways they are not used to, including becoming sober and quiet, staring and frowning, lowering the gaze or turning the head away, getting a frightened expression, or even starting to cry or scream. These responses are particularly striking when they show up with family acquaintances or relatives who were greeted with smiles a month or so earlier. While there is variation in the form, intensity, and duration of the response, infants across diverse cultures show some degree of wariness toward strangers which tends to peak toward the end of the first year of life and generally decreases thereafter.

The contextual variables that affect the intensity of the stranger anxiety response include proximity and accessibility to the mother. More distress is shown when the mother is not present in the room; when the mother is holding the infant, the reaction is least intense. A sudden and abrupt approach of the stranger, as opposed to a slow warm-up period, also intensifies the distress reaction. Research on stranger characteristics is mixed, suggesting that infants react more favorably to child than adult strangers (presumably because children are perceived as more like themselves), while findings regarding stranger gender are inconclusive.

The emergence of the anxious response to strangers, which is widely acknowledged in child development textbooks and often discussed in the popular parenting media, was a topic of focused research during the 1960s and 1970s, but has received less attention in recent years. A review of the empirical studies reveals discrepancies and disagreement as to the prevalence of the behavior, the age at which it is first observed, and how it fades across time. In a number of reports, the reaction to strangers is described as emerging between 6 and 8 months or even earlier, while others conclude that the phenomenon is first evident only toward the end of the first year. There is also considerable discrepancy concerning the specific ages in which the response peaks (9–10 months according to some reports, 12–15 months according to others) and diminishes (toward the end of the first year vs. during the course of the second year). The different timetables described in these studies partially reflect differences in methodology. Still, a fairly consistent finding is that sometime in the second part of the first year infants display a noticeable new response to unfamiliar people – showing signs of distress when approached by strangers. What makes this response particularly interesting is that it underscores the important links between emotion and cognition.

Cognitive Advances Underlying the Response to Strangers

Object permanence

In the latter part of the first year infants are capable of evaluating situations and responding to them in a more complex way. Advances in sensory–motor capacities allow more regulated attention to relevant components of novel situations and more awareness of violated expectations. The examination of these evolving capacities is the hallmark of Jean Piaget's theory of cognitive development. Piaget was interested in how infants develop an understanding that objects are independent of themselves, occupy physical space, and continue to exist even when they do not see them. Piaget used the term object permanence to describe this capacity and suggested that the concept of people as permanent develops before the understanding of the permanence of objects. This is important for conceptualizing the infant's developing discrimination of the mother from the other. However, the prediction that the anxious reaction to strangers would occur only after the achievement of object permanence (typically around 12 months of age) is not supported, given that this phenomenon may appear as early as 6 months.

Research on the maturation of distance vision has indicated that it is not until 6 months of age that infants reach adult-like discrimination, allowing them to identify familiar faces from different angles and distances, and across a wide variety of situations. Nonetheless, we know that infants learn to recognize and differentiate between their parents and other people at a much earlier age; for example, it has been shown that newborns are able to identify the face, voice, and smell of their mothers already in the first weeks of life. Extensive research over the past few decades suggests that infants learn to recognize the invariant features of people and objects, as well as the concepts of appearing and disappearing and occupying different locations, earlier than Piaget claimed. Using internalized schemes and representations to bring past experience to bear on the present, young infants engage in detecting regularities and discrepancies in stimuli, and form expectations about events. Through repeated exposures during the early months, infants come to distinguish between the familiar and the unfamiliar. But why do they start expressing apprehension, avoidance, and distress when encountered by a less familiar or a strange person?

Incongruity between the familiar and the unfamiliar face

A number of investigators have argued that the reaction to unfamiliar people results from an incongruity between the stranger and the internalized schema of the familiar caregiver. Donald Hebb's cognitive theory, which links perception and behavior to the neuronal network, offers insight into infants' fearful response to strangers. Hebb argued that perceptual experiences establish memory traces in the form of neural circuits, and that these are activated when a new perceptual experience is sufficiently similar to a previous one. But when the new stimulus is not similar enough to maintain continued smooth transmission in the neural circuit, the ensuing disruption produces a distress reaction. According to this explanation, an approaching adult could seem somewhat familiar to an infant at first, but then turn out to be different from the well-established mental representation of the familiar caregiver, and this disruption stirs up emotional distress. The intensity of the reaction to novel experiences depends on the extent to which the child has developed an internal representation of the stimuli and the degree of discrepancy between the new situation and the internalized schema. According to the incongruity principle, it is the discrepancy between the novel face and the internalized standard (e.g., the caregiver) that is responsible for the distress reaction, not social interaction with the stranger *per se*. However, as noted earlier, infants can discriminate between their mothers and strangers already in the first weeks of life, but they do not show fear of strangers until 6 or 8 months of age.

Jerome Kagan, who has been studying the links between children's cognitive capacities and emotional reactivity for over 30 years, maintains that perceptual experiences and memory traces yield interest rather than fear in infants younger than 6 months; in older infants, who are better able to generate explanations about new and unexpected events, a discrepant event that they cannot explain generates emotional distress. This developmental account adds to the incongruity model in that it links the newly acquired capacity to explain the discrepancy between the familiar and the strange to distress when the explanation fails. Although this concept is plausible, it is difficult to test.

Brain maturation

During the latter part of the first year, the ability to retrieve knowledge from memory and use this information for performing tasks improves dramatically. Adele Diamond, who studied the development of memory functions and their neural basis, provided evidence that links the improvement in infants' search for hidden objects to the maturation of the prefrontal cortex, including the growing differentiation of gamma-aminobutyric acid (GABA), an inhibitory neurotransmitter known to play an important role in the regulation of anxiety and behavioral reactivity. Another critical development during this period is the integration of the limbic and endocrine systems into the memory networks. The capsula interna, which links the cerebal cortex with the amygdala, develops mature myelin around 10 months of age, allowing increased connectivity and efficient integration between the two systems. As the amygdala is also linked to the hypothalamic–pituitary–adrenal (HPA), or the stress axis, the improved connectivity between stimulation, interpretation, and emotional processing also increases the involvement of the stress axis in the processing of experiences.

Fear and Anxiety as Indicators of Emotional Advances in the First Year

The 8-month anxiety

Although distress reactions to strangers were described by the pioneers of infant observation at the turn of the nineteenth century, the first systematic study of the phenomenon was conducted by Rene Spitz. As a psychoanalyst working with infants in group care, he methodically observed and recorded behavioral patterns that marked the changing relations between infants and the social environment. The observations were documented in a film entitled *Anxiety: Its Phenomenology in the First Year of Life*, and discussed in a 1950 paper on the manifestation of anxiety in the first year. The naturalistic observations showed that between 6 and 8 months, infants no longer responded with smiles when unfamiliar visitors approached them, and instead showed apprehension and distress. While the specific behaviors of different children varied (e.g., turning the head away, covering the face, or screaming), the common denominator was an avoidant response, refusal to contact, and distress. Spitz called this pattern the 8-month anxiety and considered it the earliest manifestation of psychological anxiety.

According to Spitz, the 8-month anxiety is unique and differs from earlier expressions of fear, for instance, a fearful reaction to repeated inoculation. In reacting to a stranger, the infant is responding to a person with whom no previous unpleasurable encounters have been experienced. So why manifest wariness and anxiety? Using psychoanalytic reasoning, Spitz argued that the response to approaching strangers is triggered by the realization that, since the unfamiliar person is not the mother, mother has left. The anxiety results from an inference process involving the comparison of the stranger to an internal representation of the mother, and the fear of losing her. In attributing the 8-month anxiety to the infant's wish for the mother and the disappointment that the approaching person is not her, Spitz underscored the role of the infant's affective communication in the caregiving process, and attributed to the 8-month anxiety a major organizing role in the evolving psychological self.

Fearfulness as a marker of a new level of emotional organization

Inspired by Spitz's work, Robert Emde and colleagues conducted a longitudinal investigation of emotional development in the mid-1970s. Following a sample of 14 infants throughout their first year, at home and in the laboratory, the researchers collected an elaborate database that included naturalistic behavioral observations, interviews with mothers, structured tests, as well as EEG recordings. Emde, like Spitz, identified two organizing principles of emotional development that emerge in the course of the first year: the social smile and stranger distress.

Around 2 months of age, infants typically show the milestone of social smile, which is a marker for inquisitive, active engagement with their surroundings. At this age, infants' curiosity is on the rise as they develop and master new ways to maintain and increase interesting stimulation (e.g., shaking a rattle). Whereas Piaget viewed sensory–motor schemas of exploring and understanding the world (e.g., hand–eye coordination, mouthing) as the major organizers of experiences in the first year, Emde and colleagues emphasized the role of emotionality as a key organizer. The appearance of the social smile marks a new way of interacting with the world. Whereas crying, the key organizer in the first weeks of life, conveys an urgent need for change and a plea for alleviating discomfort, smiling signals positive engagement, an invitation for the continuation of a pleasurable exchange. Emde observed that by 2.5 months, infants smiled regularly in response to the faces of their parents, as well as the faces of unfamiliar individuals. By 4 months, the infants in the study showed more smiling and motor responsiveness in the presence of their mothers than with other people. At around 5 months, some infants curiously studied and compared their mother's face with that of strangers, and between 5 and 7 months, they stared soberly at strangers faces.

Around 8 months, the infants in Emde's study manifested a distress reaction to unfamiliar people which, according to his model, marks the second shift in emotional expression. While the average age was 8 months, considerable variation among the infants was observed; as to the duration of the response, 11 of the 14 infants manifested distress for 2 consecutive months and eight continued to show stranger distress into the third month. In their attempt to explain the roots of the fearful response to strangers, Emde and colleagues acknowledged the importance of the infant's changing relationship to the mother and the cognitive advances of the second part of the first year, but also suggested a new focus: the emergence of the capacity for fearfulness.

Evidence from numerous studies shows that around 7–9-month infants not only show distress to strangers and unfamiliar surroundings, but also start to manifest wariness of heights, mechanical toys, masks, etc. Before this age, distress was nonspecific, mostly a reaction to physical discomfort, whereas the new distress responses are linked to specific stimuli in the environment, as evidenced by the fact that infants look and evaluate before displaying distress. Cardiac measurements support the idea of a developmental shift in the capacity for fear. At 5 months of age, the approach of an unfamiliar person led to heart-rate deceleration in the infant, accompanied with a facial expression of delighted curiosity, but at 9 months, the stranger's approach was associated with cardiac acceleration, frowning, gaze aversion, and crying. Emde argues that from a social communication perspective, the fearful reaction to the approach of a stranger conveys a clear message to the mother: a preference for her company and a plea not to be left alone with unfamiliar people. This new message to the primary caregiver is linked to another major emotional milestone of infancy: separation anxiety.

Separation Anxiety

Sometime in the middle of the first year, when infants understand that people exist even when they are out of sight (person permanence), they react to the everyday recurring disappearances of their parents by attempting to maintain proximity through the behaviors available to them, including crying, cooing, and crawling. In manifesting these responses, infants not only indicate their desire to stay in proximity with the caregiver but also the development of ways to control distance and separation. During this stage, infants increasingly initiate interaction with their parents and actively protest when their primary caregiver departs, even for a moment. By the first birthday, behaviors that indicate separation distress are even more clearly detected, with infants tending to become agitated and upset upon separation.

The Normative Course of Separation Anxiety

Separation distress, signaled by crying in response to parental separation, may be observed as early as 4 or 5 months of age, but most accounts identify 8 months as the age when separation anxiety emerges. Distress from brief separations continues to characterize toddlers' behavior well into the second year of life; the normative response typically peaks around 12–18 months and then fades after 2 years of age. In diverse cultural contexts, such as the Kalahari Bushmen, the Israeli Kibbutz and Guatemala, infants display distress in response to separation from their mothers; this is considered a normative part of development and its emergence is viewed as a major milestone in the formation of the emotional tie between the child and primary caregiver. The reaction to separation from the mother appears to be a universal phenomenon; however, specific parenting practices and cultural experiences may impact the timing and the intensity of the response. For example, in cultural settings where infants experience constant physical contact with their mothers distress to separation was observed earlier than 8 months; Japanese, as compared to Western toddlers were found to express more intense reactions to separation from their mothers. The use of an inanimate companion such as a blanket or doll (also known as a transitional object) is one of the ways toddlers attempt to alleviate separation distress. While separation anxiety gradually fades for the majority of children after the second birthday, some children will continue to express extreme distress in the face of parental separation. In many cases, these children will be subsequently diagnosed as suffering from separation anxiety disorder (SAD), a psychological disorder briefly discussed in the final section of this article.

The role of cognitive and social factors

The emergence and decline of separation distress has been linked to the cognitive advances of the first and second year. As with stranger anxiety, object permanence has been suggested as one of the determinants of the response to the disappearance of the familiar caregiver. In a series of experiments on infants' early representational capacities, Chris Moore and colleagues demonstrated that while infants younger than 6 months are able to detect violation of identity of objects (characteristics of the objects), they only appear to understand the concept of permanency of objects at 9 months. However, Piaget suggested that understanding person permanence comes earlier, and Mary Ainsworth's observation of infants and mothers in Uganda revealed that around 4–6 months, when mothers left the infants and went out of sight, some of the infants appeared distressed and cried. Silvia Bell, who compared object vs. person permanency, confirmed that indeed the concept of persons as permanent objects appears before infants understand the permanency of inanimate objects.

The understanding that the parent continues to exist when out of sight, together with advances in motor control, are believed to shape the process of active searching for the caregiver (e.g., crawling). In the same vein, advances in cause–effect reasoning shape infants' responses; they begin to grasp that calling or crying increases the likelihood of the parent's reappearance. The establishment of an integrated and enduring representation of the caregiver plays a critical role in the formation of the emotional tie between the child and parent, but it is less clear why infants at this stage show distress when separated from their primary caregivers.

Drawing on the concept of discrepant event, discussed earlier with respect to stranger anxiety, Kagan maintained that the infant is likely to display separation anxiety when the sight of the mother leaving is a discrepant event which the child is unable to prevent and/or integrate with previous experiences. It was found that infants showed less distress in a home setting when the mother departed through a door she used frequently, compared to when she exited through a door she rarely used. The decline of separation distress in the latter part of the second year is believed to be associated with the toddler's increased cognitive capacity to understand the circumstances of the separation and maintain the expectation that the parent will return. For example, when the mother left the room through a door rarely used, it was found that some of the toddlers approached the door and engaged, on and off, in play with toys, but did not cry.

In the second half of the first year, as infants gain better control of posture and movement and become more active explorers of their environment, they appear to pay extra attention to the location of other people, both caregivers and strangers. Infants at this stage frequently monitor their relative proximity to the caregiver; while venturing away from their mothers, they tend to frequently look toward their mother's face. Social referencing, an active search for others' emotional expression as a source of information to help clarify uncertain events, begins around 8–9 months. At this age, infants can understand that facial expressions have emotional meanings and they make use of others' emotional expressions to guide their own behavior with reference to specific situations and events. By monitoring their parents' facial expression, infants obtain information as to the danger or safety of their planned actions. When infants encounter a potentially dangerous setting, such as a visual cliff (a glass-covered table with an illusionary deep drop), they make use of parents' facial information to regulate their actions; when mothers smile, infants typically cross the deep part whereas when mothers show fear, infants avoid crossing.

The Developmental Significance of Separation

In psychoanalytic theorizing, separation anxiety in infancy is viewed as a consequence of, on the one hand, the capacity to mentally represent the mother, and on the other hand, the interpretation of her absence as 'losing' her. In other words, the cognitive ability to keep the mother in mind even in her absence not only triggers feelings of longing, but also stirs up the distress of separation. To understand the anxiety produced by separation, it is essential to conceptualize the significance of the absence and its implications from the perspective of the infant. When separated from the primary caregiver, infants lose a significant regulator of their needs, not only physical but, just as crucially, emotional.

Consequences of Separation in Animals

Significant insights into the formation of the emotional bond between infant and mother, and the detrimental consequences of maternal separation, come from studies of animal behavior, specifically the work of Harry Harlow and Stephen Suomi with monkeys, and Myron Hofer's studies with rats. For example, rat pups emit initial separation calls and their heart rate falls significantly after separation, regardless of supplemental heat. By studying a number of systems, such as those controlling sleep and arousal, activity level, and sucking, Hofer and colleagues identified changes in the activation of these systems that resulted from maternal separation and concluded that through ongoing interactions, mothers regulate their offspring, and that the loss of the maternal regulators has serious consequences, including a decrease in growth hormone secretion. In demonstrating the regulatory function of mother–infant proximity, animal models have significantly advanced our understanding of the neurobiological nature of separation distress, and provided important clues as to how proximity-maintenance shapes the well-being of mammals, including humans.

Physiological and Behavioral Correlates of Emotional Distress

Studying emotional distress among infants and young children presents many challenges of measurement and interpretation. Since fear and distress involve complex neural interactions and coordinated activities of psychobehavioral, physiological, and hormonal systems, measurement can take place at different levels. Facial expressions provide one avenue. Charles Darwin underscored the innateness, universality, and survival value of children's fear and distress responses when he documented, in a series of photographs, facial expressions displayed by different youngsters in circumstances of pain, hunger, and discomfort. Since then, a number of researchers have devised detailed measurement systems for coding facial expressions that index specific emotions (e.g., Izard's MAX coding system and Baby FACS, which is based on Ekman's Facial Action Coding System). In the MAX, for example, criteria of distress/pain expression include closed eyes and a squared and angular mouth, whereas in the fear expression, eyelids are lifted and the mouth corners are retracted straight back. Vocal response is another way to study the expression of distress, but there is still a debate whether infants cry distinctively when they are physically as opposed to emotionally distressed.

Measuring cortisol, a blood-borne hormone that increases under stress, has significantly advanced our understanding of children's responses to daily normative challenges, as well as the long-term effects of poorly regulated stress levels. For more than two decades, Megan Gunnar has been studying children's stress by measuring cortisol; she showed that the quality of the mother–child tie regulates levels of cortisol secretion. Children who experience secure relationships with their mothers show stable cortisol levels even when emotionally upset, whereas in insecure mother–child relationships, even minor challenges raise cortisol levels.

The way different children react to stress-producing stimuli has been studied within the conceptual framework of temperament. Kagan, who longitudinally studied children with different reactivity levels to unfamiliar stimuli, found that inhibited infants were more fearful as toddlers and were more likely to manifest symptoms of anxiety at school-age compared to uninhibited infants. Together with other studies, these findings point to a relative stability across time in children's reactivity. Temperamental disposition is one source of individual variability in the ways children cope with fearful events. Mothers' behavior is another determinant. For example, recent findings from Nathan Fox's laboratory show that infants who received insensitive caregiving display higher levels of right frontal electroencephalogram (EEG) asymmetry and fearfulness to unfamiliar stimuli compared to infants whose mothers were more responsive and sensitive in their daily caregiving behavior. The ways in which temperament, social learning, and caregiving variables jointly modulate stranger and separation anxiety during infancy have yet to be comprehensively investigated. The focus of the subsequent section is separation anxiety from the standpoint of the psychoanalytic and the attachment perspectives.

The Mother–Child Dyad and Separation Anxiety

Freud's description of his nephew playing with a reel of string is the first account in psychological literature describing a toddler coping with separation and anxiety. The child, in his crib, was throwing the reel and pulling it back again. Freud maintained that for the playing child, the reel represented his mother, who had to leave him several times. The play sequence helped the child gain control over his mother's disappearance and return, which in real life was an experience he endured passively, anxiously, and as beyond his control. Since then, many theoreticians have tried to describe children's reactions to separation and differentiate between the normative and disturbed variations.

The concept of separation is central to two influential theories of emotional development: John Bowlby's Attachment theory, and Margaret Mahler's Separation–Individuation theory. Both of these theories had a major impact on the way we understand separation reactions and separation anxiety today. Both these theories emphasize the relationship between the child and the parent (especially the mother) as the regulating factor of separation reactions, both normative and pathological.

Attachment as a window on separation anxiety

John Bowlby, the founder of attachment theory, was among the first to emphasize the human infant's biological disposition to participate in relationships, and proposed that the formation of the mother–child tie is controlled by mechanisms that evolved as a result of evolutionary adaptedness. This tie – the attachment relationship – is shaped through interactions in which proximity to the caregiver plays a significant role. In his book, *Separation: Anxiety and Anger*, Bowlby discusses the situations that trigger fear in children and lists four main categories: noise, strange people/objects/places, animals, and darkness. He also notes that being alone significantly increases the likelihood that fear will be aroused by these stimuli. In studies of infants' fear of strangers, the presence of the mother served as a moderator of the intensity of the distress: in the absence of the caregiver, infants were more fearful. It was found that the proximity to the mother was particularly significant around 12 months of age; Bowlby explains that as their emotional tie to mother becomes better consolidated, their knowledge of objects and situations becomes more sophisticated, and their ability to move in space becomes more skillful, infants are better able to coordinate moving away from a fearful situation toward the comforting proximity of the attachment figure, usually mother.

From an evolutionary perspective, proximity to the parent allows protection and thus provides a survival advantage; a predisposition to seek the protection of caregiver is particularly advantageous in times of danger and distress. According to Bowlby, attachment behavior – responses that aim to keep the caregiver in proximity to the baby – evoke caregiving behavior that promotes infants' sense of security. Attachment is a primary survival system, akin to other instinctual systems like feeding and sexual behavior, and is irreducible to other drives. Infants are born with the motivation and capacity to form emotional ties with their caregivers, and to use them as a source of comfort in times of danger and stress. During the first 6 months of life, the infant learns to prefer the primary caregiver as a source of comfort and security, thus creating an attachment bond. The attachment system is activated by external danger conditions (for instance, darkness, loud noise, sudden movements) and by internal conditions (such as illness, fatigue, pain). When the system is activated, the child seeks proximity to the caregiver to attain a sense of security. The caregiver can alleviate the child's distress by different means, depending on various factors including the child's age and the level of anxiety aroused. With young children, physical contact is the most effective response; with older children, more distal means like talking are also effective. When the danger is serious, even older children (and adults) may need physical contact to relieve the distress and anxiety.

Attachment theory explains why situations of separation or threats of separation arouse anxiety in people of all ages, but since children are more dependent on the protection provided by the caregiver, they suffer more intense separation anxiety. Bowlby and his coworkers described the sequence of typical reactions when young children are separated from parents. Children first protest, then show despair, and if the caregiver does not return, they subsequently show detachment. When the child perceives a threat of separation, she/he protests by crying, clinging, expressing anger, and looking for the parent; the protest is often expressed around sleep, at bedtime, and in the course of the night. When in despair, babies looks sad, move slowly and sometimes cry persistently, withdraw, and even act hostile. In the detachment phase, the child seems to return to normal behavior and is willing to accept comfort from unfamiliar adults. The problematic behavior shows up upon the parent's return: the child ignores the parent, or avoids and walks away. These behaviors might alternate with crying and extreme clinging, showing the child's suffering and anxiety regarding a possible future separation from the parent.

A key principle in attachment theory is the interrelation between the attachment, fear, and exploration systems. For example, the activation of the fear system generally heightens the activation of the attachment system and deactivates the exploration system. Bowlby maintained that the biological function of the fear system, like the attachment system, is protection. Because the two systems are inter-related, frightened infants increase their attachment behavior and seek protection; the fear not only triggers a desire to escape from the frightening stimulus but also a search for the anticipated security provided by the attachment figure. Separation anxiety occurs when attachment behavior is activated by the absence of the attachment figure, but cannot be terminated because the caregiver is not available to provide security. With the cognitive advances of the latter part of the first year, infants become capable of expectant anxiety in situations that seem likely to be threatening or in which the attachment figure is likely to become unavailable. As discussed, the presence or absence of the mother was found to attenuate or enhance the fear of strangers – in attachment terms, the proximity and trust in the availability of the attachment figure makes the infant less fearful. As the attachment and exploratory systems are linked, a child who is anxious about separation or does not have a secure relationship with the caregiver is expected to be inhibited in exploration and learning.

Separation anxiety in secure and insecure children

Attachment research identified different patterns of relationships between the infant and the attachment figure. Empirical studies, particularly those that use Ainsworth's Strange Situation procedure, differentiated between secure and insecurely attached infants. Secure children represent their relationship with mother as providing a sense of security, while insecure children encounter difficulties in attaining a sense of security, developing unique strategies to counteract this. Avoidant children tend to minimize their signals of needing mother, while anxious ambivalent children tend to exaggerate them; they have learned which strategies are most effective in eliciting caregiving from their mothers. The different attachment patterns are schematically represented in the child's mind as internal working models, guiding the child's behavior in relationships and specifically in stressful and emotionally charged situations. For secure children, the represented relationship with the attachment figure potentially provides security and alleviates anxiety, even in the absence of mother. Children with secure attachments are better equipped to cope with situations evoking negative emotions, including separation anxiety, than children with insecure attachments. For example, in Bell's study of person and object permanence, it was found that infants with secure attachment more actively searched for their mothers.

The separation–individuation process

Margaret Mahler was the first psychoanalyst to observe nonpatient mothers and infants as a source of information about emotional development, making her an innovator at a time when the accepted investigation method in psychoanalysis was the reconstruction of infancy from adult patients' narratives. In Mahler's opinion, the human infant's physical birth does not coincide with his or her psychological birth. The psychological birth involves a separation–individuation process, which is based upon the child's maturation and dependent not only on the child, but on the mother and eventually the father too. The process has two components which usually develop at the same pace: separation, the attainment of an experience of separateness from mother as opposed to nondifferentiation from mother (a different body), and individuation, the attainment of a sense of having specific, individual characteristics (being somebody).

Mahler describes several stages in the infant's journey from a state of nondifferentiation between infant and mother to a state of differentiated representations of self and mother, as well as in the attainment of differentiation between inner and outer worlds. Grasping these differentiations is an important step in the child's ability to function independently from mother without experiencing too much separation anxiety. The child who successfully goes through the separation–individuation process is one who can separate from the actual mother since he/she has an internally represented mother who is available to comfort the child when distressed, frustrated, and anxious.

The first two stages, labeled by Mahler as the 'normal autistic' and the 'symbiotic', span the first half-year of life. The infant's emergence from what Mahler referred to as 'symbiosis' marks the beginning of the separation–individuation process proper; the infant is 'hatching' from the mother–infant unit and turning his or her attention toward the world out there. In the differentiation phase, the infant, still in his mother's arms, starts exploring mother, pushing his body away from her and looking at her from a distance, pulling her hair, and fingering her face. The infant is comparing the mother who is known to the unfamiliar elements in the environment. The peek-a-boo game, much enjoyed at this age, is an exercise in separation, a way of facing this basic fear in a controlled, pleasurable atmosphere.

When the child is able to move away from mother (e.g., by crawling), the 'practicing' phase begins, peaking with the attainment of walking. With the achievement of this milestone, children are able to move further away from mother, and new cognitive abilities enable them to further explore the world outside them and enjoy new experiences. The child is at the height of feelings of omnipotence, in love with the world and with his or her own skills. Still, periodically the child will return to mother for emotional support when he momentarily becomes aware of being alone and anxious.

During the second half of the second year the toddler enters the phase of 'rapprochement' (approaching again) which lasts to about 2 years of age, considered one of the most sensitive, difficult periods of the separation–individuation process. During this phase, the toddler experiences the need to explore and function without mother, but at the same time, the need for mother is rediscovered because the growing awareness of separateness is anxiety-arousing. Reapproaching the mother is, on the one hand, a source of comfort to the infant, but it also triggers fear of regressing to earlier states of less differentiation and loss of independence and identity. Mothers find it difficult to adjust their behavior to the changing moods of the child who is clinging one moment and pushing her away the next. Mahler contends that both mother and toddler experience the loss of earlier ways of being with each other during this phase. The toddler experiences anger and sadness, and expresses these feelings by separation protest and temper tantrums. As the child explores separation from the mother, the father becomes a valuable alternative, a less conflicted caregiver figure for the child.

One of the main achievements of the rapprochement phase is the mastery of separation anxiety. Toddlers who have successfully resolved the conflicts of rapprochement enter the next phase, beginning around the third year of life: consolidation of identity and the beginnings of integrated self and other representations. The integration of the maternal representation, including positive and negative aspects of mother, establishes in the child's mind an 'internal mother' who is always with him/her and available to comfort the child when separated from his or her parents, or feeling anxious or distressed.

Although Mahler's theory, and mainly her first two subphases came under severe criticism, it is a rich source of insights and understanding of normative separation anxiety, as well as the more pathological separation reactions. Toddlers at risk for developing problems, including different degrees and forms of intense separation anxiety, are those with developmental limitations (e.g., regulatory disorders), those whose mothers have failed to respond sensitively to the child's needs during the separation–individuation process, and those experiencing an inordinate number of separations.

Separation anxiety as a marker of emotional development

Both Bowlby and Mahler underscored separation-related experiences and theorized about their developmental significance. Bowlby focused more on the observable aspects of the behavior, whereas Mahler emphasized the implicit, subjective experiences of the child. Both theories provide a detailed description of the child's development from a state of needing the actual, physical presence of the parent and experiencing distress and anxiety when separated from the parent, to a stage when the parent and the relationship with the parent are represented in the child's mind, consequently lessening the need for the parent's actual presence. In both theories, the representation of the caregiver takes the role of the comforting parent when anxiety is aroused. The qualities of the representation, and thus its effectiveness in reducing anxiety, are dependent on the child's experiences with the parent. Children who have had more positive experiences, whose parents are more attuned to their needs, are expected to form more positive representations of themselves, their caregivers, and their relationship. Whereas Bowlby gives more room to the real, objective aspects of the relationship, and assumes a closer correspondence between the real relationship and the child's representation of it, Mahler adds the child's subjective experience of the relationship, and the child's own drives and fantasies, as an additional formative factor of the representation. In both theories, the separation and reunion of the child and the caregiver, as well as the anxiety induced by the separation and its regulation, serve as key theoretical constructs for explaining child development in general, and emotional development in particular.

Maternal separation anxiety

The way in which mother and child negotiate separations has been a topic of continued developmental research. While separation anxiety has been typically addressed from the perspective of the child, mothers also experience distress when separation occurs. Bowlby postulated that caregiving is governed by a behavioral system which is reciprocal to attachment and is biologically predisposed to protect the child. The system is activated by the child's distress, for example, when separated from the parent, or by the caregiver's perception of danger to the child (e.g., at night); when the caregiving system is strongly activated, the parent seeks proximity to the child in order to insure protection. In situations of danger, real or imagined, when separated from the child, and the provision of care and safety cannot be maintained mothers experience anxiety.

Maternal separation anxiety has been studied by Ellen Hock, who defined it as an unpleasant emotional state that reflects concern and apprehension about leaving the infant. Maternal separation anxiety involves feelings of guilt, worry, and sadness that accompany short-term separation from the child. As mothers' separation concerns are likely to shape their tolerance of staying apart and their behavior upon return, it has implications for child behavior and development. For example, it has been found that high levels of maternal separation anxiety was linked to infants' sleep difficulties as well as to SAD in older children.

Separation Anxiety Disorder in Young Children

While SAD occurs most frequently after age 5 years (and is thus outside the age group addressed in this article), it is nevertheless important to include a brief description of the characteristics and correlates of the disorder as in some cases children as young as 2 years old are diagnosed. SAD is one of the most common disorders in childhood; prevalence estimates for SAD in community samples range from 3% to 13%. Though it is common and causes much distress to child and family, in most cases it is not severe and does not predict future emotional disorders. The clinical presentation of SAD includes a variety of signs of anxiety; it is not easy to differentiate between severe normal separation anxiety and the pathological variety, or among the different types of anxiety disorders (panic disorder and general anxiety disorder).

Differentiating Separation Anxiety Disorder from Normal Separation Reactions

SAD is suspected when the child expresses excessive anxiety upon actual or anticipated separation from the caregivers, most often the parents. Age is one criterion in diagnosing pathological separation anxiety. Although children older than 3 years are not supposed to show separation anxiety under regular circumstances, when ill, fatigued, or in a strange environment, they might exhibit signs of anxiety even at later ages. In diagnosing SAD, clinicians need to observe whether the child regresses to behaviors that were present at earlier ages; for example, children who stopped wetting the bed might begin bedwetting again as part of a SAD. An additional criterion in diagnosing SAD is the severity of the anxiety reaction. Children often cling, protest, and cry when separated from their parents and/or appear sad and distressed when their caregiver is away. However, children who throw up, cry for hours, and cannot be soothed, exhibit severe nightwaking and bedtime settling problems, and/or suffer from persistent depressive mood might be suffering from SAD. Another criterion often used in diagnosis is the pervasiveness of the reaction. Children who react anxiously or show physical distress in every situation unless they are in close proximity to their parents could be suffering from SAD. Some children express fears that something terrible might happen to them or to their parents, are afraid of being alone, refuse to go to sleep, or express a fear of monsters. Others complain of more diffuse feelings that are disturbing them and have difficulty describing why they are troubled. Children suffering from SAD try to coerce their parents not to separate and may react to separations with anger and aggression. Since some young children suffering from SAD are unable to verbalize their feelings and distress, it is important to look out for physical and somatic symptoms that may be signs of emotional distress. To assess separation anxiety in infants and very young children, the DC: 0–3R (Diagnostic Classification of Mental Health and Developmental Disorders of Infancy and Early Childhood) may be used. Although the DC: 0–3R is intended to diagnose children in the first 3 years of life, it is maintained that SAD is difficult to diagnose at this early age (for reasons we have delineated before).

Clinical and Etiological Consideration

While there is some evidence that secure attachment serves as a protective factor against psychopathology, the link between insecure attachment and anxiety disorders proved difficult to establish. Nevertheless, in the clinical literature on SAD, the child's and parent's failure to develop a secure realtionship is considered a key factor. It is assumed that this failure might arise for different reasons, including the child's temperament or parental mental problems that lead to compromised parent–child relationship. Normal anxiety reactions might become chronic or exaggerated by specific life events or circumstances. Children experiencing prolonged separations, death of a parent, traumatic events like war, as well as children living with anxious, overprotective, or neglectful parents are more vulnerable to SAD. In young children, even experiences such as vacations or illness might cause difficulties with separation. Bowlby stressed that separation anxiety might be heightened in children who are chronically exposed to actual separations or threats of separation, making them more vulnerable to normally occurring separation events. Clearly, not all children experiencing the above conditions and circumstances develop SAD. So far, risk factors rather than causes of the disorder have been identified. Although the causes of SAD are still unknown, parents who consult with professionals are often told that their own anxiety about separation negatively influences the child's ability to cope with separation. Informed by both the psychoanalytic and the developmental approach, many clinicians view sensitive parental responsiveness to the child's needs and attachment security as protective factors against SAD.

Finally, with respect to intervention and prognosis, clinicians maintain that children who are effectively and timely treated for SAD develop into mentally healthy individuals. When untreated, children with SAD may be at risk for depression and other anxiety disorders. In young children, sleeping and eating problems can be related to SAD; if not treated properly, more complicated problems in these areas might develop. Given the multiple contributing factors, difficulty in diagnosis, and different intervention approaches, there is a need for more research in the field, including longitudinal investigations of the antecedents and consequences of SAD, as well as intervention studies.

Suggested Readings

Cassidy J (1999) The nature of the child's ties. In: Cassidy J and Shever PR (eds.) *Handbook of Attachment: Theory, Research and Clinical Applications.* New York: Guilford Press.

Eisen AR and Schaefer CE (2005) *Separation Anxiety in Children and Adolescents: An Individualized Approach to Assessment and Treatment.* New York: Guilford Press.

Emde RN, Gaensbauer TJ, and Harmon RJ (1976) *Emotional Expression in Infancy: A Biobehavioral Study.* New York: International University Press.

Fonagy P and Target M (2003) *Psychoanalytic Theories: Perspectives from Developmental Psychopathology.* London and Philadelphia: Whurr Publishers.

Spitz RA (1965) *The First Year of Life: A Psychoanalytic Study of Normal and Deviant Development of Object Relations.* New York: International Universities Press.

Witherington DC, Campos JJ, and Hertenstein MJ (2001) Principles of emotion and its development. In: Bremner G and Fogel A (eds.) *Blackwell Handbook of Infant Development*, pp. 427–464. Oxford: Blackwell.

Speech Perception

G W McRoberts, Haskins Laboratories, New Haven, CT, USA

© 2008 Elsevier Inc. All rights reserved.

Glossary

Acoustic invariance – A single, unique acoustic form for a category of speech sounds; phonemes in speech generally lack acoustic invariance across speakers, or within speakers across phonetic context or rates of speech.

Acoustic resonance – Physical properties of closed chambers or cavities, which strengthen the intensity of some frequencies of sound, while dampening other frequencies.

Coarticulation – Simultaneous or overlapping movement of articulators during speech production.

Contingency – The dependency of one event on another; in infant perceptual testing, a temporal contingency is established between sound presentation and a behavior under the infant's control; for example, sound may be presented only when an infant fixates a visual target, and fixation must be maintained for continued sound presentation.

Discriminate – The ability to distinguish or notice the difference between two speech sounds.

Fundamental frequency or F0 – The base frequency of a voice, determined by the rate of opening and closing of the vocal folds; it is the physical correlate of the perceptual quality of pitch.

Habituation – A reduction in behavioral response to a repeated stimulus.

Infant-directed speech – A register or style of speech used when adults speak to infants (infant-directed speech, or IDS) or young children (child-directed speech, or CDS); differs from speech directed to other adults (adult-directed speech, or ADS) prosodically, linguistically, and in discourse features.

Morpheme – Minimal distinctive unit of grammar, of which there are two types: free morphemes can occur as separate words, and bound morphemes cannot occur separately, but must occur as affixes to words.

Phoneme – The smallest unit in the sound system of a language.

Pressure transducer – A device that converts variations in pressure into a voltage that can be measured; attached to a nipple, it allows the strength and frequency of infant sucking to be recorded and used to control sound presentation in a discrimination test.

Prosody – Variations in pitch, loudness, rhythm, and rate of speech.

Introduction

Speech perception refers to the ability to perceive linguistic structure in the acoustic speech signal. During the course of acquiring a native language infants must discover several levels of language structure in the speech signal, including phonemes (speech sounds) which are the smallest units of speech. Although phonemes have no meaning in themselves, they are the building blocks of higher-level, meaningful linguistic units or structures, including morphemes, words, phrases, and sentences. Each of the higher-level units are composed of units at the next lower level using rules that are specific to each language (i.e., morphology, grammar, or syntax). Thus, sentences are made up of phrases, phrases are composed of words, and words are made up of morphemes. Each of the meaningful units are composed of one or more phonemes. In a very real sense, the ability to perceive differences between and categorize phonemes provides the underlying capacity for the discovery of the higher levels of language structure in the speech signal. In this way, infants' speech perception abilities play a fundamental role in language acquisition. Although infant speech perception has traditionally focused on discrimination and categorization at the phoneme level, research over the past two decades has shown that infants are also beginning to become sensitive to a variety of higher-level linguistic structures in speech. This article outlines the current state of knowledge about how infants begin to perceive linguistic structure in speech during the first year of life, and the methods used to study infant speech perception.

Why Speech Perception Is Difficult

Infants' discovery of language structure in speech is not a trivial task because phonemes lack acoustic invariance. That is, the acoustic properties of specific phonemes in fluent speech can vary dramatically based on several factors. The acoustic characteristics of speech sounds that listeners use in perception directly reflect the acoustic resonance properties of the vocal tract, which in turn are determined by moment to moment changes in the shape of the vocal tract during speech production. In addition, because the size and shape of speakers' vocal tracts vary, so do the specific acoustic properties of any particular phoneme. The rate at which speech is produced also introduces variations in the characteristics of speech sounds. In particular, as the rate of speech increases, speakers' articulatory gestures (the movement patterns of articulators, such as the tongue tip) fail to reach the positions attained with slower rates of speech. This means that the vocal tract shape associated with a speech sound varies as a function of speech rate. Finally, although speech unfolds over time, speech sounds are not produced in a strictly serial manner. Rather, the production of speech sounds overlaps in time due to a phenomenon referred to as coarticulation. One example of coarticulation can be seen when the word 'two' is spoken. The vocal tract movements for the vowel /u/ in 'two' includes a lip movement called rounding. However, it is common to see this lip movement occur throughout the word. Lip movement occurs during the /t/ even though it is not a normal part of the production of that phoneme, nor is it necessary, since the word 'two' can be produced without lip rounding during the /t/. One result of this coarticulation is that the sound of the /t/ is different when the lips are rounded compared to when they are not. In general, because coarticulation is common in fluent speech production, the acoustic information that specifies any particular speech sound is highly context dependent. That is, the acoustic properties of speech sounds can depend significantly on the preceding and following speech sounds. These, and other, sources of variation in the speech signal mean that there is no absolute acoustic signature (acoustic invariance) for any speech sound. In language acquisition, this lack of invariance in the acoustic specification of speech sounds is a complicating factor in speech perception. Additionally, it must also complicate the development of speech production, because infants' and young children's vocal tracts cannot physically produce many of the specific acoustic patterns they hear in adult speech.

Methodologies for Studying Infant Speech Perception

The limited behavioral repertoire of infants kept their ability to perceive speech unstudied until appropriate methods were developed beginning in the late 1970s. Unlike the case of vision, where observable behaviors, such as direction of eye gaze, are reliable indicators of perception, there is no overt behavior that indicates listening. Researchers interested in infants' auditory and speech perception capabilities had to develop methods that used behaviors infants had under their control as indirect measures of perception. For example, by coupling the presentation of speech (or other sounds) to behaviors that infants can control, such as fixating a visual target or sucking at a certain rate or pressure, these behaviors can be used as indices of infants' interest in the sounds. When infants look at a visual target more to make one sound play longer than another, it is inferred that the greater looking is related to more interest in the sound. Thus, the duration of looking (or the amount of sucking) is used as an index of infant listening or attention to the sounds. Procedures that use contingencies between infant behavior and sound presentation are sometimes referred to as 'infant-controlled' procedures because the infant controls the duration of sound presentation on each trial. There are other procedures used to study infants' speech perception that do not use contingencies, and thus are not infant controlled. However, these procedures still require infants to produce an observable behavior, such as turning their head in a particular direction to either choose between two sounds, or to indicate they heard a change in the sound that was playing.

The focus of this article is on two aspects of infant speech perception: (1) infants' ability to discriminate between different speech sounds or categories of speech sounds; (2) infants' preference to listen to some forms of speech or speech with specific types of structure over others. Both sucking and gaze patterns have been used as behavioral indices in each of these approaches to infant speech perception. The next section describes several approaches to infant speech sound discrimination. A later section describes infant speech preference procedures and their uses in studying the development of speech perception.

Infant Speech Discrimination Procedures

Infants' ability to discriminate or categorize speech sounds has often been studied using procedures that involve habituation. These procedures are typically divided into two phases, habituation and test. Early studies of infant speech perception exploited infants' sucking reflex as a response measure in the high-amplitude sucking (HAS) procedure. In this procedure, infants suck on a non-nutritive nipple attached to a pressure transducer, which measured the amplitude of the sucking. Spontaneous sucking levels without sound presentation are measured during an initial period to establish each infants' baseline sucking amplitude. After the baseline is established, the habituation stimulus is presented contingent on the infants maintaining a sucking amplitude greater than the mean of the baseline period. More recent studies have tended to use infants' gaze as a response measure. In this case, infants are presented with a simple image, such as a checkerboard, as a visual target. When the infant fixates the target, the habituation stimulus is presented contingent on the infant maintaining fixation. When the infant breaks fixation for a period greater than 1 or 2 s, stimulus presentation stops and the trial ends.

For both sucking and gaze measures, a criterion is used to determine when infants have habituated. When the behavioral response is sucking, the criterion is typically a decline in the sucking rate by 20% for two consecutive minutes. When gaze is the behavioral response, the habituation criterion is usually set at 50% of average looking on the first two trials, or the two longest trials. Habituation occurs when the behavioral response is below the criterion (e.g., 50% of the average of the first two trials) on two consecutive trials. Once the behavioral response indicates habituation, the habituation stimulus is changed to the test stimulus on the subsequent trial.

Consider an example in which a researcher wishes to test infants' ability to discriminate between two syllables differing in their initial consonant, such as [ba] and [pa], using the visual habituation procedure. During the habituation phase, infants would be presented with either a single token or multiple tokens of the habituation stimulus (e.g., [ba]) repeated at a short interval (e.g., 500 ms). When the infant fixates the visual target, the habituation stimulus is presented. Typically, a trial continues until the infant stops the target behavior for a specified duration (e.g., looks away for longer than 1 s) or the trial reaches a maximum time (e.g., 20 s). Because stimulus presentation is contingent on the infant maintaining fixation, the duration of the trial is taken as an index of interest in the stimulus being presented. Over several trials the infant becomes more familiar with the stimulus and habituation occurs, resulting in less looking at the visual target. The looking time on each trial is compared to the predetermined habituation criterion. When the criterion is reached on consecutive trials, the test phase begins and the test stimulus (e.g., [pa]) is presented on the next trial. The number of trials in the test phase varies. Often only two or three trials are presented, but testing can also continue until the infant is habituated to criterion on the test stimulus.

Usually 18–24 infants are tested per age group in discrimination experiments. Mean looking times for the last two habituation trials and the test trials are calculated for each group of infants. If infants notice the difference between the habituation stimulus and the test stimulus, the expectation is that they will look (or suck) more to hear the novel (unhabituated) stimulus. An increase in looking during the test phase relative to the end of the habituation phase indicates response recovery or dishabituation. To establish that discrimination did or did not occur, a comparison is made between the last two trials from the habituation phase and the first two trials from the test phase. If looking during the test phase is statistically greater than during the last trials of the habituation phase, discrimination is inferred. If the difference is not statistically different, failure to discriminate is inferred. Because infants can exhibit some degree of spontaneous recovery after several short stimulus presentations, such as the final trials of the habituation phase, a no-change control group is often employed. Infants in the control group continue to hear the same stimulus after reaching habituation criterion. Thus a second important comparison is between the test trials of infants in the test and control groups. To rule out the possibility that infants in the test group exhibited spontaneous recovery, their looking times in the test phase must be statistically greater than the no-change control group, as well as their own final habituation trials.

The visually reinforced head turn (VRHT) procedure differs from the HAS and infant gaze procedures in that it does not involve habituation and is not infant controlled. Rather, it requires infants to notice a sound change in a continuous stream of recurring syllables and look toward a visual reinforcer within a brief time window after the sound change. This procedure typically involves two sessions. In the first session, infants are trained on the procedure, and in a second session they are tested on the stimulus for comparison of interest. During the training phase, a visual reinforcer, usually an animated toy in a smoked plexiglass box, is used to train infants to produce a head turn when a change occurs in a repeated background sound (e.g., from a high tone to a low tone). During training, the visual reinforcer is activated just prior to a sound change. Over the course of training, the interval between the sound change and activation of the reinforcer is reduced and finally reversed, so that activation occurs after the sound change. When the infant reliably anticipates activation of the reinforcer by turning toward the reinforcer after a sound change, but before the reinforcer is activated, the testing phase can begin with the stimuli of interest. During a second session, usually on a separate day, a procedure refresher may occur prior to testing to establish that the infant still looks to the reinforcer within a brief time window after the sound change. Testing then occurs on the stimulus comparison of interest. During testing, the infant is distracted from the visual reinforcer by a research assistant displaying an interesting object. This reduces false positive responses, in which the infant looks to the reinforcer when no sound change has occurred.

Each of these procedures has both advantages and disadvantages. The habituation approach works well from the neonatal period into the second year of life. However, the sucking measure works best with infants up to 4-months of age, after which infants are prone to rejecting the nipple. The visual fixation method works well across a wide range of infant ages and is now the generally accepted method of choice. The VRHT procedure requires adequate head, neck, and postural control from the infant, and therefore does not work well with infants younger than about 4 months. In addition, some subjects are usually lost because they do not reach criterion during the training phase. However, this procedure has the advantage of providing reliable data for individual infants, while the habituation procedures can only be used for group comparisons. Although it may be possible to modify habituation procedures to provide individual data, attempts to do so have not proved successful at this time.

Infants' Phonetic Discrimination

In order to understand important issues involved in the study of infant speech perception, it is helpful to have a bit of background on how speech sounds are made and classified. Speech sounds are produced by complex coordinated interactions among the components of the vocal tract. During speech production, air from the lungs induces the vocal folds to vibrate, producing a buzz-like sound source that is filtered by passing through several cavities in the vocal tract, including the pharyngeal, oral, and nasal cavities. Speech production involves movement of the vocal tract articulators, including the tongue, velum, and lips, which change the sizes and shapes of the cavities, altering their resonance properties. It is the resonance properties of these cavities that filter the sound source and account for most of the differences in the sounds used in speech.

Phonetics, the study of how speech is produced and perceived, generally distinguishes between two classes of phonemes, consonants and vowels. One basis for this distinction is related to differences in how these sounds are produced. Vowels are produced with a relatively open and unobstructed vocal tract, which allows air and sound to move freely through the vocal tract. Changes in the height and front–back position of the tongue, along with rounding or spreading of the lips, produce most of the differences in vowels in English. Other languages also distinguish vowels based on whether air flows only through the oral cavity, or through the nasal cavity, which results in a nasalized sound.

In contrast to vowels, consonants are produced by introducing a constriction of the airflow. Consonants can be classified by the type and location of the vocal tract constriction used in their production. Many types of constrictions, or manners of articulation, are used in languages around the world. The most common types involve a complete closure or one of several kinds of partial closure. Stop consonants (e.g., /p/ or /d/), are produced with a full closure of the vocal tract that results in a complete stoppage of air flow, whereas fricatives (e.g., /s/) involve a less-than-complete degree of constriction that results in a turbulent air flow. There are several other manners of articulation, some of which are not used in English. Two manners of articulation not used in English are click and ejective. Clicks are used in Zulu and some related languages in Southern Africa. Production of clicks involves a suction type closure and release. Another common manner of articulation is called ejective. Ejectives are produced using a closure of the vocal tract in the mouth and also squeezing the vocal folds together. Air that is trapped between the vocal tract closure and vocal folds is compressed by moving the larynx upward. When the closure in the oral cavity is released, the built-up air pressure is released with a distinctive sound.

Each manner of articulation can be produced at various places within the vocal tract and can involve the tongue, lips, teeth, hard and soft palate, as well as other parts of the vocal tract. One common constriction location involves a closure at the lips, and is referred to as bilabial. Examples of other common closures involve the tongue and any of several locations along the roof of the mouth, including the teeth (interdental), the ridge behind the teeth (alveolar), the hard palate (palatal), or the soft palate (velar).

Consonants are also classified as being either voiced or voiceless. Voiced means vocal fold vibration occurs during the constriction or constriction release. This contrasts with voiceless (or unvoiced) consonants, where vocal fold vibration begins some time after the constriction is released. The difference in when the vocal folds begin to vibrate is referred to as voice onset time (VOT), or the time from when the constriction is released until the vocal folds begin to vibrate. In English, voiced consonants have a VOT from about 0 to 40 ms, meaning the onset of vocal fold vibration can be simultaneous with, or up to 40 ms after, release of the closure or constriction (e.g., /b/ or /z/). In unvoiced consonants, vocal fold vibration begins from about 60 to 100 ms after the constriction is released (e.g., /p/ or /s/). Thus, the consonant inventory of a language is dependent on which combinations of articulatory features, including voicing, manner of articulation, and places of articulation, are used. The phoneme inventory of languages differ substantially in the number of vowels and consonants that are used. Anyone acquiring a language must be able to distinguish among the phonemes, as well as produce them.

Infants' Discrimination of Phonemes

Early research on infant speech perception focused mainly on the ability of young (e.g., 1–6 month old), English-learning infants to categorize and discriminate between pairs of speech sounds from the phonetic inventory of English. These early studies established that young infants are very good at discriminating a wide variety of speech sounds. Later research investigated how infants perceive speech sounds that do not occur in their native language, the discrimination of longer segments of speech, and the role of visual information in infants' speech perception.

In 1971, Peter Eimas and colleagues reported the first study of infant speech perception. This study used the HAS method described previously to show that infants between 1 and 4 months of age were able to discriminate between two stop consonants that differed in VOT ([ba-pa]). Additional studies by Eimas and others investigated infants' discrimination of sounds differing in place of articulation. These studies showed infants discriminated [ba]-[ga], [bae]-[dae], [fa]-[øa], [va]-[øa], and [ma]-[na]. Infants were also shown to discriminate between sounds that differ in the manner of articulation, including [ra]-[la], [ba]-[wa], and [ba]-[ma].

After several early studies demonstrated that infants could discriminate various consonant contrasts, other researchers investigated infants' perception of vowels. These studies showed that 1–4-month-old infants also discriminate among a variety of vowels, including [a]-[i] (e.g., hod vs. hid), [i]-[I] (e.g., hid vs. heed), [a]-[aw] (e.g., hod vs. hawed). Thus young infants also appear to be very good at discriminating among vowels. As noted earlier, the lack of acoustic invariance in speech sounds is a potential problem in discrimination, since the same sound produced by different talkers will have different acoustic characteristics. Several experiments by Patricia Kuhl and colleagues have shown that infants are able to categorize and discriminate among vowels, even when they are spoken by different speakers (e.g., males and females), or have irrelevant acoustic variation (e.g., pitch contour).

Overall, these early studies established that young infants up to about 6 months of age are able to perceive the differences between consonants that differed along articulatory dimensions including VOT, place of articulation, and manner of articulation, as well as discriminate between many vowels. Initially, infants' discrimination of consonants was tested with syllables that differed in their initial consonants (e.g., [ba]-[pa]). Other studies showed that infants could also perceive differences between syllables that differed in their final consonants, or when consonants were between two vowels, and in multisyllable contexts. For example, young infants were shown to discriminate consonants in syllable-final position (e.g., pat vs. pad), between two vowels (e.g., [aba] vs. [apa]), and in two-syllable sequences (daba vs. daga). In order to more closely approximate natural speech, discrimination of consonants embedded in longer stretches of speech was also investigated. In these studies, 1–4-month-old infants were shown to discriminate between sequences of three syllables when only a single consonant differed (e.g., [marana] vs. [malana]).

Categorical Perception

As noted earlier, the acoustic properties of the same speech sound can vary significantly when produced by different speakers, or by the same speaker in different phonetic contexts. Faced with this variation, human perceivers 'categorize' speech sounds. That is, they are able to ignore irrelevant acoustic variation and focus on the properties that identify a phoneme as a member of a specific speech sound category. Because attention is focused on similarities among items of the same category, discrimination of different tokens or versions of a speech sound that are within a single category is usually difficult compared to speech sounds that are from different phonetic categories. That is, two spoken versions of [ba] sound more alike and are thus more difficult to discriminate than a [ba] and a [pa].

The sounds [ba] and [pa] in English differ in many ways, but one of most prominent differences is VOT. When producing [ba], the vocal folds begin to vibrate almost simultaneously with the opening of the lips, whereas with [pa] there is a noticeable lag in the onset of vocal fold vibration. It is possible to produce a VOT continuum of equal steps (e.g., 10 ms) from 0 (i.e., vocal fold vibration simultaneous with lip opening) to 80 ms (i.e., vocal fold vibration starts 80 ms after lip opening). On such a continuum, the endpoints (i.e., 0 and 80 ms) are heard clearly as [ba] and [pa], respectively. When native English-speaking adults are asked to label each token from the continuum, they typically show a rather abrupt shift from one category to another rather than a gradual change. That is, they may label items up to 40 ms as [ba], and items over 60 ms as [pa], while items at 50 ms might be labeled as [ba] half the time and [pa] half the time. Thus, a category boundary appears to exist between 40 and 60 ms. If asked to discriminate between pairs of sounds at 20 ms intervals along the continuum, it will be difficult to distinguish between two tokens on the same side of the category boundary, such as +10 and +30 ms, but easy to discriminate tokens that are from different sides of the boundary, such as +40 and +60. In other words, discrimination is poor within categories (e.g., two [pa]'s or two [ba]'s), but good when the pairs cross a category boundary (i.e., one [ba] and one [pa]), even when the physical difference between the items in the two pairs is equal. The degree to which native-language phonemes are perceived categorically varies. For example, stop consonants are usually perceived very categorically, while vowels are perceived less categorically.

Early studies showing young infants' ability to discriminate among various speech sounds were often followed by studies of categorical perception of the same sounds. These studies suggest that young infants, like adults, have categorical perception of consonants that differ in VOT, place of articulation, and manner of articulation. However, it should be noted that the procedures for establishing categorical perception are necessarily somewhat different for adults and infants, because infants are unable to directly identify speech sounds. Thus, the conclusion that infants perceive speech categorically relies on results showing that infants have more difficulty discriminating items that are within the adult categories than items that fall across category boundaries.

Audio-Visual Speech Perception

Speech is usually considered to be an acoustic event, and speech perception is typically seen as perceiving the acoustic structure of speech. However, there is strong evidence that under some circumstances visual information from the face of a speaker can influence the perception of speech. Two kinds of influences of visual speech information have been studied in infants. In some studies infants have been shown to look longer at a video of a speaking face that matches a speech sound than at a face that is mismatched. For example, 6-month-old infants have been shown to look longer at a matching face for some consonant–vowel syllables. Four-month-old infants have been shown to look more to a face that matches some vowels from the native language, and perhaps non-native vowels. Some studies suggest the ability to match visual and acoustic speech information may be present at birth or very early in the postnatal period.

Another way visual information can influence speech perception is to alter how speech sounds are perceived. When a video of a speaker's face saying [ba] is combined with audio [ga], many (though not all) adults and children perceive [da] or [tha]. Thus, the auditory and visual information have been integrated to form a novel percept. Other combinations are also possible. This phenomenon was first demonstrated by Harry McGurk and John MacDonald in 1976, and is referred to as the McGurk Effect.

A fascinating study by Larry Rosenblum and colleagues demonstrated that 5-month-old infants also appear to show the McGurk Effect. Rosenblum and colleagues habituated infants with video clips that contained a matched face (visual) and voice (auditory) saying [va], and then tested them on three kinds of trials that paired different auditory information with the original visual [va]: (1) the original auditory [va]; (2) auditory [ba]; and (3) auditory [da]. Infants differed in the rate at which they habituated to the three test stimuli. They were slower to habituate to audio [da] paired with visual [va] (perceived as [da] by adults) than when either auditory [va] or [ba] was paired with the visual [va] (both perceived as [va] by adults). These results suggest that the infants perceived the auditory [da] with visual [va] as different from either of the other two. That is, it appears the infants heard the visual [va] and auditory [da] as something other than [va], just as adults do, though it is unclear from these results that they heard the same [da] that adults hear. Other studies have confirmed these results in showing that infants appear to be susceptible to the McGurk Effect. Thus, this form of auditory–visual speech perception appears to emerge early in infancy. However, recent studies suggest that there may be large individual differences in infants' integration of auditory and visual information for speech, just as there are for adults.

Infants' Perception of Non-Native Speech Sounds

The early studies of infant speech perception clearly demonstrated that infants are quite adept at discriminating and categorizing a wide range of speech sounds. As a wider range of phoneme contrasts, language environments, and ages of infants were studied, it became clear that infants did not always discriminate all speech contrasts. For example, several studies suggest that infants have difficulty distinguishing between some fricative sounds, and even some vowel contrasts that are present in their native language. Other studies show that some speech contrasts were discriminated by infants from one language environment but not another. Still other studies clearly show that infants can discriminate between some speech sounds not present in their ambient language environment which adult speakers of their native language could not discriminate. Thus, the accumulating evidence suggested that the speech perception abilities of young infants must eventually become attuned to their native language. Beginning in the 1980s, the issue of how infant speech perception develops from a language-general ability that prepares infants to acquire any language to a language-specific ability became a central theme of research.

In a seminal series of experiments, Janet Werker and colleagues showed that infants' attunement to their ambient language environment begins by the end of the first year of life. Werker and colleagues tested English-learning infants between 6 and 12 months of age on a native-language phonetic contrasts ([ba] vs. [da]), as well as two non-native phonetic contrasts that adult and child native-English speakers could not discriminate. One of the non-native contrasts included two stop-consonants from Hindi. The phonemes were [ta], with a dental place of articulation (similar to English [ta]), and [ta] which has a more posterior place of articulation referred to as retroflex. Also included was a velar-uvular ejective contrast, [k'ae] vs. [q'ae], from the Native American language Nthlakapmx (also referred to as Puget Salish). The 6–8-month-old English-learning infants discriminated all three contrasts. However, the 8–10-month-olds discriminated the non-native sounds less well than the younger infants, and the 10–12-month-olds were generally unable to distinguish the non-native sounds. Both groups of older infants retained the ability to discriminate the native-language [ba]-[da] contrast. This showed that infants' sensitivity to at least some non-native speech contrasts declines significantly by 10–12 months.

These findings initially seemed to suggest that the decline in discriminability was due to a lack of experience with the speech sounds. That is, while young infants could discriminate speech sounds that did not occur in their native language, exposure or experience with the speech sounds seemed to be necessary to maintain that ability. However, research by Catherine Best and colleagues showed that the decline in perceptual sensitivity at 10–12 months only occurred for some non-native speech sounds. In one study, English-learning infants from 6 to 14 months of age, and English-speaking adults were tested on their ability to discriminate click contrasts from the Zulu language. The Zulu click sounds are very different from anything in the inventory of English speech sounds, and thus represent an example of speech sounds that English-learning infants and English-speaking adults would never experience in a speech context. The results of this study showed that native English-speaking adults were able to discriminate among several click consonant contrasts. Both older and younger infants were tested on a subset of the clicks the adults discriminated and were also able to discriminate the clicks. Thus, while it seems clear that exposure to language influences the development of speech perception, the results with the Zulu clicks demonstrated convincingly that it is not necessary to have experience with specific speech sounds in order to be able to continue discriminating them. The results of this study reframed the issue of the development of speech perception to why discrimination of some non-native speech sounds declines, while others continue to be well discriminated.

Best and colleagues have investigated this question in a series of studies, in which the discrimination abilities of younger and older infants were compared to that of adults on a variety of non-native speech contrasts. In these studies, the discrimination pattern for adults is usually established first, followed by infant tests. To establish the pattern of discrimination ability, each infant is usually tested three times, using two non-native phonetic contrasts, and a native-language contrast. Across several studies, English-learning infants and English-speaking adults have been tested on a wide variety of non-native sounds, including several additional Zulu contrasts (lateral voiced-voiceless fricatives [ɮa]-[ɬa]; voiceless aspirated velar stop-ejective [kʼa]-[kʼa]; plosive-implosive bilabial stop [b]-[ɓ]), a bilabial-alveolar ejective distinction from Tigrinya (Ethiopian) ([pʼa]-[tʼa]), the Nthlakapmx velar-uvular ejective contrast [kʼae] versus [qʼae] from Werker's earlier study, as well as English bilabial-alveolar stop consonants [ba]-[da] and English alveolar voiced-voiceless fricatives [sa]-[za]. Younger infants discriminated all of the non-native contrasts. Older infants discriminated the clicks and fricatives from Zulu, the Tigrinya ejectives, and the stop-consonants and fricatives from English. They failed to discriminate the Nthlakapmx velar-uvular ejective contrast, confirming Werker's earlier results. However, even among the contrasts that were discriminated at both ages, the younger infants performed better than older infants on all tests except the Tigrinya [pʼa]-[tʼa] and the English [ba]-[da], which were discriminated equally well at both ages.

Infants' perception of non-native vowels has been studied less than non-native consonants. However, the studies that have been done suggest the development of vowel perception proceeds differently from the pattern seen for consonants. One difference is that the influence of the native-language environment on vowel perception may occur as early as 6 months of age, whereas similar effects for consonants do not emerge until 10–12 months.

In addition, there appear to be directional asymmetries in vowel discrimination that are not commonly reported with consonants (but may nonetheless exist). These asymmetries reflect the fact that infants discriminate better when they are habituated to one vowel (e.g., vowel A) and tested on a second vowel (e.g., vowel B), than when habituated to vowel B and tested on vowel A. As described earlier, different English vowels are produced by changing the height and front–back position of the tongue, as well as rounding, protruding, or spreading the lips. A vowel space can be defined based on the extremes of tongue and lip positions. For example, for /i/ (as in 'heed') the tongue is high and to the front of the oral cavity, and the lips are spread. The vowel /u/ (as in 'who'd') is produced with the tongue high and to the back of the oral cavity, with the lips rounded and protruded. The vowels /ae/ (as in 'had') and /a/(as in 'hod') are produced with the tongue low (on the floor of the oral cavity), and more to the front and back of the oral cavity, respectively. Other vowels are produced with less extreme positions. The vowels /i/, /u/, /ae/, and /a/ define the limits of the English vowel space, and are thus considered most peripheral (i.e., nearest the periphery) in the space. There is some evidence that the asymmetries in vowel discrimination are related to the degree of peripherality within this vowel space. Vowels that are more peripheral in the space appear to act as reference points, so that discrimination is easier when infants are habituated to vowels that are less peripheral in the space and then tested on more peripheral vowels.

Several theoretical models have been proposed to account for the results of infant non-native speech perception studies. The model that most adequately accounts for the results, especially with non-native consonants, is Catherine Best's perceptual assimilation model (PAM). This model assumes listeners hear non-native speech sounds in terms of their native-language phonetic categories whenever possible. This is called perceptual assimilation. Within PAM, listeners can assimilate non-native phoneme contrasts into their native categories in several ways. Two contrasting non-native speech sounds can: (1) be assimilated into a single native-language category (single category, or SC assimilation); (2) be assimilated into two different native-language phonetic categories (two category, or TC assimilation); (3) be assimilated into two native-language categories, but with different degrees of goodness (category goodness, or CG assimilation); and (4) fail to be assimilated into any native-language category (nonassimilable, or NA). Based on the earlier discussion of categorical perception, it should be clear that discrimination for SC assimilation will be very difficult (at or near chance levels) under most circumstances, but discrimination will be quite easy (near ceiling levels) in TC assimilation. In the case of CG assimilation, discrimination is intermediate between SC and TC. Finally, when non-native speech sounds are so different from any native-language phoneme that assimilation does not occur (NA), discrimination will be very good because the sounds will be perceived as nonlinguistic, allowing perceivers to compare them on acoustic dimensions that would be irrelevant or unavailable in phonetic perception. Predictions from PAM about the degree of discriminability of non-native sounds (especially consonants) have been tested extensively with English-speaking adults, who have also provided descriptions of their assimilations of non-native phonemes into native-language categories. In general, the predictions have been upheld. Although older infants often show the same pattern of discrimination as adults, Best and colleagues believe that infants' speech sound categories are not fully developed by the end of the first year. Rather, they suggest that infants' perception of speech sounds becomes increasingly sensitive to information about how the sounds are produced (i.e., phonetic or articulatory information). Thus, near the end of the first year of life, infants are beginning to perceive many, but not all, of the details that specify how native-language speech sounds are produced. Therefore, their pattern of discrimination (assimilation) of non-native speech sounds becomes increasingly adult like, but further development occurs as access to more fine-grained detail is achieved through infancy and into early childhood.

In conjunction with earlier studies, research on the perception of non-native phonemes shows that infants enter the world as 'language-general' speech perceivers, able to discriminate among most of the speech sounds of the world's languages, and over the first year or so of life, become attuned to many of the specifics of their language environment to become 'language-specific' speech perceivers.

Speech Preferences in Infancy

The research on phonetic discrimination abilities provides clear evidence of infants' underlying speech perception capabilities, as well as the timeline of some of the developmental processes involved in acquiring a native-language phonology. The development of infants' speech perception from language general to language specific over the course of the first year focuses attention on the early influence of the ambient language environment on language development. One question of interest is whether infants attend preferentially to some aspects of the language environment over others. The auditory preference procedure has been used to address this question. Whereas discrimination procedures assess infants' ability to detect differences between smaller units of speech, such as phonemes or syllables, preference procedures allow researchers to study how infants respond to longer samples of speech that more realistically approximate what they normally hear. As a result, studies of infant speech preferences have taken a significant role in research on the development of speech perception and language development. Early studies of speech preferences focused on infants' preference to listen to speech over nonspeech sounds, and infant-directed speech (IDS), or child-directed speech (CDS) over adult-directed speech (ADS). More recent studies have used speech preferences to investigate the development of sensitivity to various aspects of native-language structure in speech.

Auditory and Speech Preference Procedures

Auditory preferences in infants were first demonstrated in 1968 by Bernard Freidlander. The procedure involved an apparatus with two large knobs, a speaker, and an activity recorder. By manipulating the knobs, infants could activate one of two recorded audio samples. The activity recorder collected the amount of time each sample was played. Infants aged 11–15 months showed a preference by listening more to some sounds, such as their mothers' voice, more than other sounds, such as simple musical passages. Friedlander's apparatus was later modified for use with younger, less mobile infants. A related procedure was developed for use with young infants by Anne Fernald. Fernald's procedure required only a head-turn response to activate sounds that played from speakers located to the infant's right or left. No contingency was required to continue sound presentation. Eventually, infant-controlled variants were developed using both gaze and sucking.

Two versions of the auditory preference procedure are in common use today. Both are infant-controlled procedures that use gaze as the behavioral measure. In one variant, a single visual target is located directly in front of the infant (central fixation preference). The other approach is a direct descendent of Fernald's procedure, and requires a head turn to one of two visual targets located on the infant's right or left (head-turn preference). In the central fixation procedure, infants fixate a centrally presented visual target, such as a checkerboard. Stimulus sounds are played through a speaker located directly below the visual target. Sound presentation on each trial is contingent on the infant maintaining fixation of the target. When fixation is broken for more than 1 or 2 s, the sound ends, the visual target is removed, and the trial ends. After a brief delay, the visual target returns, signaling the availability of the next trial.

The head-turn procedure is somewhat more complicated than the central fixation procedure. It uses two speakers, each 90° to the infants' right and left. Small red lights are usually placed near the speakers, and directly in front of the infant. A test typically begins with several presentations of stimuli from each speaker to familiarize infants with the procedure and train them to turn toward the lateralized lights and speakers in order to initiate a trial. Trials begin with the central red light flashing. When the infant orients to the flashing light, it is extinguished and one of the lateral lights blinks to indicate a stimulus is available. Stimulus types can be associated with a specific side, or can be randomized to either side. Infants are required to make a criterial head turn (e.g., at least 45°) to initiate a trial, and they must maintain the head turn to continue sound presentation on each trial.

Both procedures are infant controlled, and typically use 12 trials, evenly divided between two types of speech presented on alternate or randomized trials. As in the discrimination procedures discussed previously, fixation time on each trial is used as an index of interest or listening. Fixation times are averaged across trials of each stimulus type, resulting in a mean for each stimulus type.

While both procedures are in current use, the central fixation procedure seems to have several advantages over the head-turn procedure: (1) it eliminates the effects of lateral biases evident in some infants; (2) it does not require training or familiarizing infants with head turning to initiate trials; and (3) observers are not required to judge whether infants maintain a sufficient degree of head turn to continue a trial.

Infants' Speech Preferences

The first study to address young infants' speech preferences was performed by Anne Fernald, who investigated 4-month-old infants' listening preference for IDS by female speakers compared to speech by the same speakers to another adult, or ADS. Fernald used the noncontingent head-turn procedure described earlier. Her results showed that infants turned to the side that activated the IDS speech samples more often than the ADS speech samples. In other studies infants have showed more positive affect when listening to IDS than ADS.

Other studies have explored a variety of aspects of infants' preference for IDS over ADS. For example, it appears that infants' preference for IDS is present from very early in the postnatal period. And while some studies suggested that the preference for IDS might decline or disappear in older infants, more recent studies show that infants as old as 16 months of age continue to show a preference for IDS over ADS. Still other studies have demonstrated that infants will attend to IDS in an unfamiliar language over ADS from the same language, and also prefer male speakers' IDS over the same speakers' ADS.

The acoustic basis for infants' preference for IDS over ADS has been somewhat in dispute. One early study showed that 4-month-old infants listened more to sine-wave analogs of the F0 contours of IDS than ADS, but not to sine-wave analogs of the amplitude envelope or temporal structure of IDS. Thus it appeared that the higher F0, wider F0 range, and expanded intonation contours typical of IDS were the acoustic basis of infants' preference. Several recent studies have noted that early studies of IDS preference often confounded the prosody of IDS with affect, because IDS typically contains expressions of positive emotion. These studies have shown that IDS prosody by itself, in the absence of expressions of positive affect, is not sufficient to result in a preference by infants at 6 months of age. In addition, when prosodic factors such as F0 range are controlled, infants prefer to listen to ADS containing positive affect over IDS that does not contain positive affect. Thus, it appears that by 6 months of age, infants may be attending more to the positive affective expressiveness of IDS, even if other prosodic characteristics of IDS are absent. Nonetheless, in spontaneous interactions with infants, the typical prosodic characteristics of IDS, including higher F0 and wider F0 range, will normally be highly correlated with positive affect.

Beyond establishing infants' preference to listen to IDS over ADS, auditory preference procedures have been used to study infants' detection of a wide variety of linguistic structures in speech, such as patterns of lexical stress (e.g., pres'-ent vs. pres-ent'), locating words in sentences, native-language phonotactics (the legal sound patterns that can make words in a language), and repeated utterances. These studies have provided important insights into how infants become attuned to the properties of their native language. One example is infants' ability to perceive differences between languages based on prosodic patterns. Several studies have shown that very young infants will listen longer to speech from languages that have rhythmic patterns that are similar to their ambient language (e.g., French) over languages with different prosodic patterns (e.g., Russian). However, not until 6 months do they show a preference for their own language over other languages with similar prosodic structure (e.g., English vs. Dutch).

Another use of the preference procedure is to pair it with familiarization to stimuli for which infants initially have no preference. Peter Jusczyk and Richard Aslin used this procedure in a landmark study showing that by 7.5 months of age, infants begin to segment words from fluent speech. In their initial study, infants were familiarized with a repeated list of single words spoken in isolation (either cup or bike). The infants were then tested for a listening preference with sentences containing the familiarized word and similar sentences containing the unfamiliar word. Although 6-month-old infants showed no preference, 7.5-month-old infants had a preference for the sentences containing the familiarized word. Follow-up studies reversed the procedure, familiarizing the infants with the sentences that contained the word, and then testing on the familiarized word repeated in isolation vs. the unfamiliar word. The outcome confirmed the initial results, showing that infants listened longer to the familiarized words. Additional studies showed that infants failed to prefer words that differed from the familiarized target by one phoneme, such as 'gike' instead of 'bike'. Taken together, these results provide evidence that infants are able to remember phonetic strings that occur in running speech soon after the middle of their first year of life.

See also: Grammar; Language Development: Overview; Preverbal Development and Speech Perception; Semantic Development.

Suggested Readings

Best CT (1995) A direct realist perspective on cross-language speech perception. In: Strange W and Jenkins JJ (eds.) *Cross-Language Speech Perception*, pp. 171–204. Timonium, MD: York Press.

Best CT and McRoberts GW (2003) Infant perception of non-native consonant contrasts that adults assimilate in different ways. *Language and Speech* 46: 183–216.

Eimas PD, Jusczyk P, and Vigorito J (1971) Speech perception in infants. *Science* 171: 303–306.

Fernald A (1992) Maternal vocalizations to infants as biologically relevant signals: An evolutionary perspective. In: Barkow JH, Cosmides L, and Tooby J (eds.) *The Adapted Mind: Evolutionary Psychology and the Generation of Culture*, pp. 391–428. Oxford: Oxford University Press.

Jusczyk P (1997) *The Discovery of Spoken Language.* Cambridge, MA: MIT Press.

Jusczyk P and Aslin RN (1995) Infants' detection of sound patterns of words in fluent speech. *Cognitive Psychology* 29: 1–23.

Kuhl PK and Melzoff AN (1984) The intermodal representation of speech in infants. *Infant Behavior and Development* 7: 361–381.

Polka L and Bohn O (2003) Asymmetries in vowel perception. *Speech Communication* 41: 221–231.

Rosenblum LD, Schmuckler MA, and Johnson JA (1997) The McGurk effect in infants. *Perception and Psychophysics* 59: 347–357.

Werker J and Tees RC (1984) Cross-language speech perception: Evidence for perceptual reorganization during the first year. *Infant Behavior and Development* 7: 49–63.

Symbolic Thought

S M Carlson and P D Zelazo, Institute of Child Development, Minneapolis, MN, USA

© 2008 Elsevier Inc. All rights reserved.

Glossary

Cognitive flexibility – The capacity to consider and selectively attend to more than one aspect of a situation or problem.

Executive function – Conscious control over thought and action, including resistance to interference, set-shifting, and withholding a dominant response; reflection on the self is implicated, as are processes of working memory and inhibitory control.

Inner speech – Silent self-directed talk, preceded developmentally by private speech in which children talk aloud to themselves; utilized to facilitate problem solving.

Intentionality – The property of 'aboutness' or directedness that can be said to characterize the relation between a symbol and its referent (i.e., the stimulus represented by the symbol), as well as between conscious thoughts and their content.

Mediation (symbolic) – The knowing substitution of a symbol for a direct experience of a stimulus, which allows behavior to be controlled in light of the symbol rather than the stimulus itself.

Psychological distancing – Cognitive separation from the immediate perceptual/behavioral environment through the use of representation and reflection.

Reflection (self) – Awareness and conscious consideration of one's own sensations, perceptions, thoughts, and behavioral tendencies.

Zone of proximal development – Transitional period in cognitive development in which the child is close to achieving explicit understanding of a concept or success on a problem, but cannot do so without guidance or scaffolding from more knowledgeable others.

Introduction

Symbols are ubiquitous in children's lives. They include paintings on the wall, pictures and written words in books, traffic signs, numbers, scale models, maps, toy replicas, and communication signals in gesture and speech. How children come to understand and use symbols is a key question because symbolization allows children to engage in a wide variety of sophisticated intellectual activities (e.g., language, mathematics, art) that are unique to our species. Research suggests that the development of symbolic thought follows a gradual course that is closely tied to the development of self-reflection and that depends importantly on cultural practices and social interaction.

Definition and Overview

Symbolic thought is thought that involves symbols, or things that represent (or stand for) something else. To play their constitutive role in symbolic thought, however, symbols must be intended to be representational by the person using them. By definition, then, symbolic thought requires some degree of self-reflective understanding of the relation between the symbol (e.g., a drawing of a dog) and the referent (e.g., the dog drawn). A drawing may represent a dog, but only if someone understands it as such.

Discussions of symbolization and symbolic thought often make reference to two key (and related) constructs: mediation and intentionality. First, like all thought, symbolic thought mediates between stimuli and responses. In symbolic thought, however, a symbol (e.g., a word, picture, number, visual image, or even an idea) is knowingly substituted for a direct experience of a stimulus, which allows behavior to be controlled in light of the symbol rather than the stimulus itself. This type of mediation may be referred to as symbolic mediation.

Second, the term intentionality – in the philosophical sense – refers to the property of aboutness or directedness that can be said to characterize the relation between a symbol and its referent (i.e., the stimulus represented by the symbol): the symbol is about, or in some sense directed at, the referent. Again, this is a property of all conscious thought; symbolic thought is simply a special case. In the case of symbolic thought, however, an agent is aware of the intentional relation between the symbol and the referent: he or she knows that the symbol represents the referent. Many of the cognitive and behavioral consequences of symbolic thought may derive from this feature of reflection on the intentional relation and the concomitant psychological distancing from stimuli (i.e., from reality) that takes place.

Symbolic thought develops gradually during infancy and early childhood. We suggest that it progresses through a series of levels corresponding to increasing degrees of reflection on the nature of the symbol-referent relation. These levels, which correspond to the age-related increases in reflection identified in Philip David Zelazo's Levels of Consciousness model, may be summarized briefly (see **Figure 1**).

1. At the first level, spanning from birth to approximately seven months of age, there is no evidence of symbolic thought. Conscious thinking is representational (i.e., it is intentional) and it mediates between stimuli and responses, so there is a sense in which it is symbolic, but in the absence of reflection on one's representations, behavior is tied directly to stimuli (i.e., behavior is 'stimulus bound').

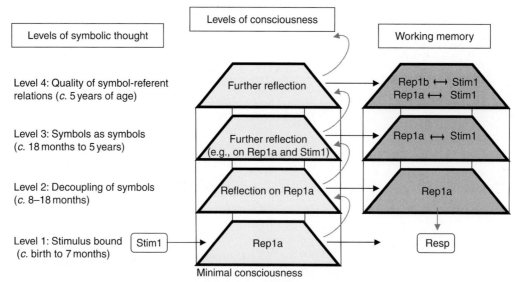

Figure 1 Consequences of reflection for symbolic thought. Development of the capacity to reflect on the contents of one's own consciousness, resulting in higher, more reflective levels of consciousness, allows for more aspects of symbols and symbol-referent relations to be considered and maintained in working memory. Reflection is interposed between perception of a stimulus (Stim1) and responding (Resp). The contents of minimal consciousness at one moment, together with new information about a stimulus, are fed back into minimal consciousness. Figure illustrates the different contents of working memory made possible by different degrees of reflection. Rep1a and Rep1b are alternate symbolic representations of the stimulus.

2. During the latter half of the first year, infants acquire the ability to keep representations of stimuli (i.e., symbols) in mind even in the absence of the stimuli themselves (e.g., as when objects are hidden and infants search for them). At this point in development, however, infants still do not reflect on the relation between the symbol and the referent – instead they merely substitute the symbol for reality – so their thought is not properly called symbolic according to the definition provided earlier. Nonetheless, there is a decoupling of symbols from referents, and this is an important step in the development of symbolic thought.
3. During the second year of life, children begin to treat symbols 'as' symbols, as when they engage in pretend play. This developmental advance marks the beginning of genuine symbolic thought insofar as there is, for the first time, reflection on the fact that there is a relation between symbol and referent. Children's symbolic thought is still limited, however, and they generally fail to consider the nature or quality of the symbol-referent relation.
4. Finally, further increases in children's reflection during the preschool years allow children to consider the quality of the symbol-referent relation (e.g., detecting ambiguity in which referent is being symbolized), and eventually to consider multiple symbol-referent relations in contradistinction (e.g., allowing them to appreciate irony).

Development of Symbolic Thought

Thinking about symbolic thought in this way allows us to trace its development from simple consciousness (referred to as minimal consciousness) through the conspicuously self-reflective instances seen in some forms of art. The foundations of symbolization are inherent in infant perception. According to Jean Piaget, infants and toddlers interact with the world in terms of sensorimotor schemes and schemata. A scheme is a behavioral category, and a schema is an abstract representation of the distinctive characteristics of an event – it is a category in terms of which stimuli are interpreted. A father's finger, for example, might be experienced by a young infant as a suckable thing, and this description might trigger the stereotypical motor scheme of sucking. Sensorimotor schemata are modified through practice and accommodation (i.e., learning can occur), and they can be coordinated into higher order units. In contemporary parlance, schemata would be referred to as representations.

Level 1: Intentionality and Mediation Without Reflection

Several decades' worth of research on infant visual perception, attention, categorization, and memory indicates clearly that human infants process stimuli in terms of representations, and that these representations may be modified by experience. Rather than responding directly to stimuli, infants (and indeed, fetuses during the third trimester) seem to respond on the basis of representations, or interpretations, of these stimuli. The behavioral consequences of this representational mediation include habituation, pattern completion, and expectation, among many other phenomena. In all cases, infants go beyond the information that is given in any particular presentation of a stimulus.

Infants' perception of color serves as a good example. Despite continuous variation in the wavelength of light, infants reliably categorize this continuous spectrum in the same way as human adults. For example, they may show greater attentiveness when a shade of red changes to yellow than when a lighter shade of red merely replaces a darker shade of red, despite the fact that both differences correspond to comparable differences in the relevant dimension of the physical stimulus (i.e., in the wavelength of reflected light). Different instances of red are assimilated to a single category of color; they are represented as red.

Interestingly, infants' categories may be quite abstract, as demonstrated by research on cross-modal perception. For example, if infants suck on a nubby pacifier without being able to see it and then are shown that pacifier alongside a smooth one, they will usually look longer at the nubby pacifier. They will also look longer at other stimuli that share the feature of having a discontinuous surface, like the nubby pacifier, as opposed to a continuous surface, like the smooth pacifier. For example, they will look longer at an incomplete circle. One interpretation of this finding is that infants may categorize stimuli without regard to sensory modality and interpret the sucked-upon pacifier as a discontinuous thing. When shown another example of discontinuity, they may recognize this characteristic and be more or less interested in it depending on the results of their initial processing of discontinuity.

The representations underlying infant categorical behavior are symbolic insofar as they function in ways that allow them to stand for classes of stimuli, and these representations are likely to provide a foundation for subsequent developments in symbolic thought. However, these representations are probably not symbols that can be used in the absence of current stimulation. Young infants obviously display evidence of memory and learning, but this evidence seems to be tied to ongoing perceptual processing. For example, young infants show recognition memory, responding differentially to a familiar vs. a novel stimulus, but there is no clear evidence of recall memory in the absence of the remembered stimulus. In short, young infants might be said to be stimulus bound.

Level 2: Thinking about Representations in the Absence of Stimuli

In contrast, toward the end of the first year of life, most infants begin to exhibit behaviors suggesting that they are responding not to current stimulation but to information maintained in working memory or recalled from past experience. This advance becomes apparent when an infant watches an adult hide an object under a cloth and must wait a short period of time before being allowed to reach for it. Six-month-olds will not reach under the cloth for the hidden object, presumably because they forget that the object was placed there ('out of sight, out of mind') – although some understanding of the object's continued existence may be demonstrated using more sensitive (albeit more ambiguous) measures such as looking times. Twelve-month-olds, however, will reach for the object even after a 30-s delay period, presumably because they are able to maintain a representation of the hidden object and respond in light of this representation rather than in light of the current stimulation (i.e., no visible object). The representation of the object – a symbol that stands for the object – can now be decoupled from the object itself and considered in the absence of the object. These improvements enable infants to relate an event in their environment to similar events in the past. As a result, they begin to anticipate their mother's positive reactions when the two are in close face-to-face interaction, and they may behave as if inviting her to respond. Infants may also develop new fears, such as those of objects, people, or situations with which they are unfamiliar – that is, which they cannot relate to past experiences using recall memory.

Infants make robust advances in recognition memory during their first year, but it is not until the end of the first year that there is convincing evidence for recall memory. As noted, recall memory involves remembering an event or object that is not currently present – retrieving a representation of it. One way to demonstrate recall memory is via delayed imitation. Imitation may be defined as behavior that duplicates that of another person. One-year-olds become capable of imitating an act some time after they have actually observed it; for example, they may imitate a novel action they witnessed 1 day – or even 2 weeks – earlier, especially if placed in the same physical setting. These findings suggest that infants are able to hold in mind schematic representations – particularly of the actions of caregivers – for increasingly longer periods of time, and these representations stimulate re-enactment through imitation, even when the evocative stimulus is not present.

Level 3: Treating Symbols as Symbols

Keeping a symbolic representation in mind, however, is not the same as treating it as a symbol. Jean Piaget argued that deliberate symbolization typically emerges during the second half of the second year of life, and contemporary analyses are generally consistent with this account. Many authors agree that there are changes during the second year in children's reflective awareness, and these changes should allow them to consider the relation between a symbol and a referent. Pretend play is a good example. In the earliest forms of pretense, one treats something (a pretense object) as something else (a real object), such as treating a bowl as a hat. Not only is there a decoupling of a representation from what is represented, as in level 2 of symbolic thought, but there is also some degree of reflection on the relation between the symbol and the referent: the child knows he or she is treating the bowl as a hat.

Over the course of the second year, children become more likely to perform pretend actions (e.g., talking on the telephone) with pretense objects (e.g., a spoon) that bear little physical resemblance to the real objects. They also are increasingly less likely when pretending (or symbolizing, more generally) to respond on the basis of the actions suggested by the real objects. Thus, in this context, one sees increasing independence from the literal context, and an increasing reliance on imagination. Piaget observed his daughter Jacqueline at 15 months place her head on a pillow and close her eyes, thus simulating the gestures of sleep using the real props associated with sleeping. Only later in development did she substitute a symbol for the pillow – resting her head on her bear and a plush dog. As Lev Vygotsky put it: "It is remarkable that the child starts with an imaginary situation that initially is so very close to the real one. A reproduction of the real situation takes place." Eventually, however, children become capable of creating symbolic representations on the basis of more subtle suggestions, and we might say that their representations are less dependent on external context and more internally determined.

These developments continue into the third year, and may be seen in domains other than pretend play. By 3 years, for example, children are capable of simple metaphor (e.g., playing with two wooden balls of different size as if they symbolized a parent and child). At this age, children also become more likely to perform pretend actions without objects altogether (such as pretending to drink from an imaginary cup), and they may begin to create imaginary companions with detailed biographies. Children's drawings also become symbolic during the second and third years and begin to contain forms that look like (or at least are intended to represent) animals, people, and various objects. These developments all appear to be refinements of a basic ability to treat a symbol as a symbol, and to transcend the limitations of reality via imagination.

An important developmental milestone occurring in the third year is the growing realization that an object can be understood both as a thing itself and as a symbol for something else – that is, dual representation. For instance, a mature understanding of pictures requires the reconciliation of two fundamental requirements: identifying the representation with its referent, while, at the same time, recognizing the distinction between referent and representation. Evidence suggests that children's conceptual understanding of pictures (e.g., photographs and drawings) develops gradually. Even infants can recognize objects in pictures and discriminate depicted objects from actual objects, although they sometimes try to manipulate a picture as if it were the object itself, such as 'grasping' a pictured bottle. By 20 months of age, this confusion about pictures typically is overcome. At age 2 years, however, children still have difficulty using photographs or live video to guide their search for a hidden toy in a simple object-retrieval task (e.g., a photo of a toy hidden behind a sofa). In contrast, 2.5-year-olds readily use pictures for this purpose.

Two-year-old children's use of pictures to guide search for hidden objects may indicate some understanding of representational specificity – that the picture is not merely a picture of a toy behind a sofa, but rather is a picture of the particular toy hidden behind the sofa in the laboratory room. This understanding may emerge relatively early for photographs and video in part because these media are familiar and in part because they function primarily as symbols – children are rarely encouraged to consider pictures as objects in themselves (e.g., with particular formal properties such as size and texture). Rather, children habitually 'look through' pictures to what the pictures represent.

Two-year-olds' use of photographs and video to guide search is in contrast to their difficulty using three-dimensional (3D) scale models. In one experimental paradigm introduced by Judy DeLoache, children's understanding of the symbolic relation between a scale model and the larger space it represents is assessed using a procedure in which children are first familiarized with a life-size room and a miniaturized scale model of that room. Then the child watches as an attractive toy (e.g., a tiny Snoopy dog) is hidden within the scale model (e.g., behind the miniature sofa). Next, the child is invited to find an analogous toy that has been concealed in the corresponding place in the room itself (e.g., a large Snoopy dog hidden behind the full-sized sofa). Lastly, the child is returned to the model and asked to retrieve the miniature toy, as a check on children's memory for the hiding location. The results were dramatic. Across numerous studies and manipulations of the procedure, 2.5-year-olds failed to search correctly for the object in the analogous location (less than 20% did so), despite accurately remembering the original hiding event. By contrast, most 3-year-olds had no difficulty retrieving the object in either location (about 80% did so). One interpretation of these results is that the 3D model is a salient object (like a dollhouse), and this interferes with their appreciation of it as a symbol.

As a result, they have difficulty looking through it to what it represents, and instead treat the model only as an object in itself.

This representational insight has also been investigated with respect to children's understanding of toys as symbols. In one set of studies by Michael Tomasello and colleagues, young children were asked to select objects that had been previously represented by either a gesture or a symbol. For example, when the target object was a hammer, the experimenter used her fist to make a hammering motion in the gesture condition, and showed children a miniature hammer from a dollhouse in the symbol condition. Children of 18 months correctly selected the real hammer on test trials only in the gesture condition, whereas 26-month-olds performed well in both conditions. The younger children apparently failed to see the toy replica as a symbol for the larger object, in addition to seeing it as a toy. Understanding pretense gestures might come earlier than understanding toys because, like photographs, gestures do not generally demand dual representation; as with words, the primary function of gestures is symbolic – to represent something else. Again, however, it should be noted that using measures of preferential looking, other researchers have shown that recognition of the relation between iconic toy symbols and their real-world referents begins to emerge earlier, around 14 months of age.

Limitations on children's developing understanding of symbol-referent relations can be seen not only in their failures to use symbols to make inferences about reality, but also in their confusion about the relevance of stimulus properties and symbol properties. For example, toddlers continue to make 'scale errors' with iconic symbols. That is, they sometimes treat a miniature or gigantic replica as if it had the functional properties of the thing it represents (e.g., trying to climb into the driver's seat of a doll-sized car). Even older children continue to struggle with non-iconic symbols. They appear to operate on the assumption that perceptual similarity of the symbol and referent matters. In reading, writing, and understanding maps, preschool children are more likely to select an item that looks like the referent than one that does not, such as a word written in red ink to stand for 'tomato'. They also reject symbols based on a lack of perceptual similarity, such as claiming that a red line on a map cannot represent a road because roads are not red.

The increasing capacity for reflection on symbols as symbols during the early preschool years allows for much more control of symbolic thought. As we have described, this is apparent in terms of both transferring information from external symbols to their real-world analogs, as well as overcoming errors of misappropriation of certain perceptually salient symbols to real-world functions. Nonetheless, difficulties in attending selectively and flexibly to different aspects of the symbol-referent relation persist at this level of symbolic thought. For example, research has explored 3- to 5-year-old children's ability to respond to pictures on the basis of their formal properties (i.e., the way in which something is represented) as well as on the basis of their content using a match-to-sample task in which children were shown a sample picture (e.g., a blurry bird) and test pictures that matched the sample according to content (e.g., a nonblurry bird), form (e.g., blurry gloves), or neither (e.g., a nonblurry violin). Whereas most 5-year-olds were successful at matching pictures according to both content and form, 3-year-olds often failed to match according to form. These findings provide support for the notion that younger children still 'see through' pictures, experiencing particular difficulty with the dual requirement of representing pictures with respect to both their semantic and formal properties. That is, 3-year-olds seem particularly captured by content, and have difficulty attending to form in the presence of conflicting content information.

Another study found that preschoolers are indeed capable of responding to formal features of pictures – in particular, to the artistic style of paintings. In this study, preschoolers (3–5 years of age) were presented with slides of paintings in which artistic style (i.e., artist) and subject matter were varied independently. Children of all ages were capable of making both style and subject matter matches. When shown abstract paintings, for example, children were able say that two paintings by the same artist were more similar than two paintings by different artists. However, children exhibited a strong reliance on subject matter over style when these cues conflicted (e.g., when asked whether a still life by Seraut was more similar to a portrait by Seraut or a still life by Brueghel, they selected the two still lifes).

Related phenomena have been observed in even older children. Six-year-olds have difficulty evaluating paralinguistic cues (i.e., how a speaker's voice sounds) in the presence of conflicting propositional content (i.e., what is said). For example, children erroneously reported that a speaker was happy when she uttered a positive proposition in a sad voice (e.g., "My mommy gave me a treat" in a sad voice). Subsequent experiments demonstrated that 6-year-olds could respond on the basis of paralinguistic information when it was not in conflict with propositional content. For example, they could judge whether a speaker was happy or sad when she spoke a foreign language. Moreover, when children heard conflicting sentences and were first told to judge on the basis of content, and then told to switch and judge on the basis of prosody, children who noticed the conflict and described it when asked, tended to switch successfully. This finding reveals the important link between the complexity of children's representation of the problem, made possible by increases in reflection on multiple aspects of the communicative symbols, and their ability to resist interference from a salient aspect of the problem.

More generally, these findings situate the development of conceptual understanding of representations in the context of general changes in cognitive development, including the well-established changes in executive function that occur from 3 to 6 years of age. Executive function refers to conscious self-control of thought, action, and emotion, including resistance to interference, set-shifting, and withholding a dominant response; reflection on the self is implicated, as are processes of working memory and inhibitory control. It is closely associated with the development of prefrontal cortex. The limitations seen in children's symbolic thought at level 3 may be in part attributable to a tendency in early childhood to focus attention on highly salient but misleading or interfering aspects of stimuli. With increasing reflective capacity and control, children are able to inhibit a dominant way of construing things (e.g., seeing only the subject matter in pictures) and entertain more abstract and flexible representations (e.g., appreciating stylistic similarities and differences).

Level 4: Reflection on the Quality of the Symbol-Referent Relation

The epitome of symbolic thought is language, which uses words or symbols to transcend concrete reality and allows intangibles to be manipulated (as in mathematical symbols). Although infants begin to link words with their referents in speech beginning around 12 months, research on children's understanding of language has revealed changes during the preschool period in children's evaluation of the quality of the symbol-referent relation. For example, even 5-year-olds tend to confuse what is meant with what is said when they hear ambiguous verbal messages. In one study, an experimenter and a child sat on opposite sides of an opaque screen, and each had his or her own set of cards, which varied along two dimensions (e.g., large/small and red/blue flowers). They then played a game in which they took turns choosing a card from their set and describing it in a way that allowed the other participant to choose the identical card from his or her set. On some turns, when the experimenter acted as the speaker, the utterances were intentionally ambiguous. For example, the child might be told: "Pick up the red flower," an expression that described both the big red flower and the small red flower. Subsequently, the child was asked to make a judgment about what was said. Children heard one of three types of utterance: a disambiguated version of the original utterance (e.g., "Did I say 'the big red flower'?"), a verbatim repetition of the original utterance (e.g., "Did I say 'the red flower'?"), or an incorrect version of the original utterance (e.g., "Did I say 'the blue flower'?"). Five-year-olds were quite good at rejecting the incorrect version (81% of the time) and at accepting the verbatim repetition (76% of the time). However, they incorrectly accepted the disambiguated version 60% of the time. Thus, children behaved as if the two utterances were indiscriminable, suggesting they did not recognize the referential ambiguity. Indeed, similar to younger children's understanding of visual representations, children appear to 'see through' linguistic expressions to the intended referent, failing to 'see' expressions in and of themselves.

Related phenomena in later childhood include the development of understanding of irony and sarcasm, as well as the nuances of artistic representation and aspects of scientific reasoning (e.g., relations between theory and data). These developments may also be made possible by age- and experience-related increases in children's reflection on their symbolic representations. Reflection allows children to consider complex sets of relations among symbols and various symbol-referent relations (e.g., ideal vs. actual models of reality), setting the stage for still more abstract and imaginative relations in adolescence.

Facilitation of Symbolic Thought

Now that we have described the developmental progression of symbolic thought in terms of increases in reflection, we next turn to the question of how it might be fostered by experience and enculturation. First, by using representations, one comes to understand more aspects of the representing relation. Lev Vygotsky viewed this as an instance of a more general developmental law: ". . . [C]onsciousness and control appear only at a late stage in the development of a function, after it has been used and practiced unconsciously and spontaneously." Recent work has also emphasized the transformative effect of using representations. For example, there appears to be a correlation between when children start using pictures to guide search for a hidden object and when they start producing pictures. Drawing may provide insight into the artist's intention to represent a particular referent – it may provide a first-person appreciation of this intention.

At the very least, using symbols provides an opportunity for the discovery of certain of their properties – including properties of symbols in general and the special properties of the particular types of symbols used. For example, training in the use of maps diminishes children's tendency to be overly literal in their interpretation of them (e.g., thinking that 'north' is always straight ahead). This work suggests that children can overcome symbol-referent errors with increasing experience. Similarly, research has shown that early pretense with parents and siblings jumpstarts children's own progression through the stages of pretending, perhaps because it provides both modeling and practice, and alerts children to the possibilities inherent in pretend play.

Second, as Lev Vygotsky emphasized, a key influence on the development of symbolic thought is the appropriation and internalization of the 'tools' of a particular culture. These tools are cultural practices, such as the use of speech, writing, numbers, and music. Vygotsky described a process whereby the formal structure inherent in these cultural practices is first acquired in overt behavior and then reflected in one's private thinking through a gradual process of interiorization. An essential piece of the reflection process we have described is the notion that symbolism is recursive: symbols feed and fuel symbolic thought, with the outcome being increasingly higher levels of conscious reflection on external and, eventually, internal symbols. But the foundation of this process is basic symbolization. Hence the symbols or 'tools' that a culture, school, or home provide for children will determine, in part, the kinds of reflective symbolic thought in which children engage – for example, symbolic thought involving numerals, words, and even whole mythologies. Cultural differences also will determine which symbol systems are most valued and imparted to children earlier in development. For example, Chinese children's rapid learning of counting in comparison with North American children might be mediated by both a difference in the structure of the numbering system (a base-10 system) and a high cultural value placed upon mathematical skills.

It is important to note, however, that the influence of practice and the provision of cultural tools on the development of symbolic thought will be constrained by age-related, domain-general limitations on the complexity of the conceptual relations children can formulate – and ultimately on the degree of self reflection in which they can engage. For example, no amount of training or practice appears to help 2-years-olds appreciate the relevance of the 3D scale model to the location of the large toy in Judy DeLoache's search task. This finding is consistent with Lev Vygotsky's zone of proximal development principle; children are most receptive to intervention at certain points in development that are under biological as well as contextual control.

The Role of Symbolic Thought in Problem Solving

We have discussed some of the possibilities for how symbolic thought is derived and fostered in development. Next we consider where it leads children; in other words, what does symbolic thought 'buy' them? In addition to providing the raw materials for the imaginative enjoyment of objects and simulation of real-world events in pretend play, symbolic thought plays an essential role in children's increasingly sophisticated problem solving ability.

Although symbolic thought figures prominently in play, it may also be initiated by recognition of a discrepancy or a problem to be solved; it may be elicited by a sense of novelty, surprise, complexity, incongruity, or ambiguity. Once initiated, however, how might symbolic thought contribute to success in problem solving? One possibility is emphasized by the psychological distancing hypothesis of Heinz Werner and Bernard Kaplan, and more recently developed by Irving Sigel. By way of the substitution of symbols for stimuli themselves, one's attention is moved away from the concrete and motivating (e.g., appetitive) properties of the stimuli and toward a more abstract characterization. The dimension in which this movement is hypothesized to occur is referred to as psychological distance.

Psychological distancing may facilitate problem solving in several ways. First, simply by decreasing the salience of certain aspects of a stimulus or problem, psychological distancing may help children to resist a temptation to respond impulsively – to select prepotent but inappropriate responses. Second, symbols may permit one to notice alternative aspects or implications of a problem that were not initially obvious. This, in turn, may allow a wider range of possible responses to be entertained and executed.

Research has indeed shown that symbols can provide degrees of distance from reality, which then might make it possible to reflect on the self and govern one's responses more effectively. For example, in Walter Mischel's delay of gratification task, children need to wait alone in the presence of food rewards if they want to receive the larger reward; otherwise, if they do not wait until the experimenter returns, they can take only the smaller reward. A symbolic strategy that was highly effective in extending preschoolers' delay times involved a cognitive transformation in which children were asked to pretend that the marshmallows in the experiment were 'white fluffy clouds'. Presumably this symbolic ideation decreased the salience of the food reward, thus enabling children to delay gratification.

A more direct demonstration of the role of symbols in psychological distancing comes from the Less is More task, developed by Stephanie Carlson. In the Less is More task, children are presented with two piles of candy, one large and one small, and must point to the small pile in order to obtain the large pile. Three-year-olds, compared to 4-year-olds, have difficulty inhibiting their tendency to point to the preferred, larger reward. In one study, 3-year-olds were trained on symbolic representations for the quantities of treats, in increasing degree of separation from reality, before being given the task (e.g., one-to-one correspondence with rocks vs. a mouse and elephant to stand for small and large amounts, respectively). Children in the symbol conditions performed better than children presented with real treats, and improved as a function of the degree of symbolic distancing from the real rewards.

Like symbol substitution, verbal labeling also seems to promote psychological distancing, and the facilitative effects of labeling have been examined on several tests of executive function in children. Alexander Luria assessed the effects of labeling on a Go-Nogo task. When 3-year-olds were asked to accompany their manual responses (i.e., pressing on Go trials) with self-directed commands such as 'Press', they were better able to regulate their responses. By contrast, when 3-year-olds were asked to accompany their nonresponses (i.e., withholding responding on Nogo trials) with self-directed commands such as 'Don't press', their performance deteriorated. Older children's performance improved when they labeled both Go and Nogo trials. One possibility is that younger children can regulate their behavior using the concrete, physical, expressive aspect of labels, but they have difficulty using the more abstract, semantic aspects when these aspects conflict with the expressive aspects or with children's prepotent tendencies. This pattern is similar to the examples described earlier (e.g., children's difficulty using the semantic meaning of a 3D scale model). Preschool children seem to have difficulty reflecting on and using multiple aspects of a symbol, and instead they rely only on the most salient aspects.

The fact that labels may help children to reflect on their symbolic representations was shown by Sophie Jacques and colleagues in work using the Flexible Item Selection Task. On each trial of the task, children are shown sets of three items designed so one pair matches on one dimension, and a different pair matches on a different dimension (e.g., a small yellow teapot, a large yellow teapot, and a large yellow shoe). Children are first asked to select one pair (i.e., selection 1), and then asked to select a different pair (i.e., selection 2). To respond correctly, children must represent the pivot item (i.e., the large yellow teapot) according to both dimensions. Four-year-olds generally perform well on selection 1 but poorly on selection 2, indicating inflexibility. However, asking 4-year-olds to label their basis for selection 1 (e.g., "Why do those two pictures go together?") improved their performance on selection 2. This was true whether children provided the label themselves or whether the experimenter generated it for them. These results suggest that labeling does not simply change the relative salience of stimuli and re-direct children's attention to the postswitch dimension, but instead may facilitate reflection on their initial construal of the stimuli, allowing them to recognize that, for example, they initially represented the large teapot as a teapot but now may represent it as a large thing.

Mature symbolic thought is marked by fluency, originality, and flexibility of one's approach to problems, in other words, thinking 'outside the box'. As these examples suggest, symbolic thought appears to assist problem solving at least in part by improving cognitive flexibility. Being able to consider more than one alternative to a situation is fostered by representing and reflecting upon the situation from more than one angle. Dual representation – thinking about a representation in two different ways at the same time – is a crucial requirement not only for understanding the semantic meaning of representations but also for problem solving more generally. Examples include appreciating that a single reality can be understood in different – sometimes conflicting – ways, as in the appearance-reality distinction, and by different people, as in the false belief task. Similarly, social role-play, common by age 4 or 5 years, fosters thinking about other points of view. When pretending to be someone else, children are simulating the other's beliefs, desires, and emotional responses to situations. Perhaps not surprisingly then, some researchers have reported that training children to pretend to be another person improves their ability to take that person's perspective.

This last observation highlights an important pathway in the development of cognitive flexibility. As with pretend play, the development of perspective taking is characterized by a decreasing reliance on external support and an increasing reliance on imagination. Consistent with a long tradition of work on social mediation and dialogic thinking, symbolization facilitates the imaginative appreciation of other people's perspectives, and then, with practice, the ability to adopt alternative perspectives becomes internalized – engaged in symbolically – resulting in cognitive flexibility.

Clearly, then, symbols not only play an instrumental role in the development of cognitive flexibility, but they also provide the medium in which much flexible cognition occurs. In particular, a great deal of conscious, directed thinking appears to occur in terms of potentially silent, self-directed speech – or symbolic rules. By formulating and using rules, children essentially talk their way through challenging problems. This notion is consistent with the Vygotskian view that 'private speech' has an adaptive function in the self-regulation of behavior. Private speech is overt speech that is not addressed to a listener, when one essentially is talking to oneself. According to Lev Vygotsky, it is a stage that serves to move children from social speech and overtly verbal thought toward the gradual internalization of dialogic interpersonal language (e.g., between the child and caregiver), leading ultimately to 'inner speech' (i.e., verbal thought that takes place with no outward signs). The central premise for a link between private speech and self-regulation is that 'talking through' the features of a problem enables children to 'think through' the problem more effectively, by regulating their representations, response selections, and monitoring of outcomes. Indeed, as we have described, several studies have demonstrated empirically that private speech during problem solving is positively related to task performance. By reflecting on the rules that they represent, children are able to embed these rules under higher order rules that control their application. For example, in the Less is More task described earlier, children are able to say to themselves, "Yes I want the larger pile of candy, but in this game, if want the larger pile, then I have to point to the smaller pile." The use of higher order rules allows children to respond flexibly across a wider range of situations (i.e., including counterintuitive situations like the one in the Less is More task).

Summary

The ability to create, utilize, and think with and through symbols is a remarkable ontogenetic achievement. We have defined symbolic thought as thought that knowingly involves symbols, or things that represent (or stand for) something else. Two key features of symbolic thought are symbolic mediation (the symbol is understood to be a buffer between direct experience of a stimulus and action upon the stimulus) and intentionality (the symbolizer is aware of the intentional relation between the symbol and what it stands for).

We proposed that the development of symbolic thought proceeds gradually through a series of hierarchical levels. The levels are characterized in terms of the degree of reflection on the symbol-referent relation and are hypothesized to correspond to concomitant increases in self-reflection that are manifested in children's executive control over thought and action more generally. First, infants exhibit mediated thought in various ways but there is no reflection on the symbol-referent relation. Second, toward the end of the first year, infants can substitute a representation for reality (such as holding in mind an absent stimulus) but there is still no clear reflection on the relation. Third, beginning in the second year, there are major and dramatic advances in children's ability to treat symbols as symbols, that is, to reflect on the duality of symbols as being both objective and representational. Examples included children's understanding of pictures, toy replicas, scale models, and maps. However, we pointed out several limitations in children's symbolic thought and confusions that are only gradually overcome at this level. Finally, in the later preschool and early elementary school years, increases in self-reflection enable children to reflect further on the nature of symbol-referent relations, to disambiguate them, and to consider multiple such relations from a higher order perspective, including the understanding of irony.

We next considered ways in which symbolic thought is facilitated. In accord with Lev Vygotsky's sociocultural view, we asserted that using symbols and, relatedly, having certain symbolic 'tools' available in a given culture, will direct the development of symbolic thought in a recursive fashion. Lastly, we provided examples of the ways in which symbolic thought aids children's problem solving ability by way of psychological distancing (e.g., noniconic images, verbal labeling), consideration of multiple alternative perspectives or solutions, and inner speech or rule use. In this way, the development of symbolic thought corresponds to well-established increases in executive function that occur in infancy and early childhood. Age-related increases in both symbolic thought and executive function are made possible by increases in self-reflection, but symbolic thought, executive function, and self-reflection also interact to influence performance in a wide range of situations.

There are several up-and-coming research directions on symbolic thought in early childhood. One is identifying the neural underpinnings of self-reflection in order to move descriptions of this process – evident in children's behavior – to another level of analysis, a level that might help to explain deficits in symbolic thought in certain populations of children (e.g., children with autism). Another new direction is to examine more closely how it is that 'experts' (parents, teachers, older siblings) transmit information about symbols and promote their use (thus influencing the development of symbolic thought both directly and indirectly), and how these practices vary within and across cultures. Finally, there are advances to be made in our understanding of the role of symbolic thought in problem solving, particularly with respect to the conditions in which symbols provide specific or generalized effects (e.g., positive transfer from symbolic to real contexts), and the mechanisms by which these effects occur (such as distancing and inner speech). Addressing these important questions about symbolic thought will contribute to our own reflections on what is perhaps the fundamental developmental achievement of human cognition.

See also: Artistic Development; Cognitive Development; Cognitive Developmental Theories; Imagination and Fantasy; Object Concept; Piaget's Cognitive-Developmental Theory; Play.

Suggested Readings

Baldwin JM (1897) *Social and Ethical Interpretations in Mental Development: A Study in Social Psychology.* New York: Macmillan.

Bruner JS (1983) *In Search of Mind: Essays in Autobiography.* New York: Harper & Row.

Carlson SM, Davis A, and Leach JG (2005) Less is more: Executive function and symbolic representation in preschool children. *Psychological Science* 16: 609–616.

DeLoache JS (1995) Early understanding and use of symbols: The model model. *Current Directions in Psychological Science* 4: 109–113.

Lee K and Karmiloff-Smith A (1996) The development of external symbol systems: The child as a notator. In: Gelman R and Au T (eds.) *Perceptual and Cognitive Development: Handbook of Perception and Cognition,* 2nd edn. 185–211. San Diego, CA: Academic Press.

Luria AR (1961) *The Role of Speech in the Regulation of Normal and Abnormal Behavior.* In: Tizard J (ed.). New York: Liveright Publishing Corporation.

Mischel W, Shoda Y, and Rodriguez ML (1989) Delay of gratification in children. *Science* 244: 933–938.

Piaget J (1947/1966) *Psychology of Intelligence.* New Jersey: Littlefield, Adams, and Company.

Sigel I (1993) The centrality of a distancing model for the development of representational competence. In: Cocking RR and Renninger KA (eds.) *The Development and Meaning of Psychological Distance,* pp. 91–107. Hillsdale, NJ: Erlbaum.

Vygotsky LS (1962) *Thought and Language.* In: Hanfmann E and Vakar G (trans.). Cambridge, MA: MIT Press (original work published 1934).

Werner H and Kaplan B (1963) *Symbol Formation: An Organismic Developmental Approach to Language and the Expression of Thought.* New York: John Wiley.

Zelazo PD (2004) The development of conscious control in childhood. *Trends in Cognitive Sciences* 8: 12–17.

Theory of Mind

J W Astington and L A Dack, University of Toronto, Toronto, ON, Canada

© 2008 Elsevier Inc. All rights reserved.

Glossary

False-belief task – An experimental task that assesses young children's ability to attribute beliefs to others. Children are given different information about a situation – for example, an object is moved from one place to another, witnessed by child but not other, or a familiar container has some unexpected content seen by child but not other. Children are asked what the other will do, or think, or say. About 4 years of age they respond correctly by attributing to the other a belief that is different from their own, and false from their point of view.

Intentional causation – The idea that intentions are fulfilled only if a person's intention causes the action that brings about the outcome, despite the fact that one's desires may be fulfilled, however, the outcome is achieved.

Interpretive diversity – The understanding that two people may make different interpretations of the same external stimulus and that both interpretations may be legitimate.

Metarepresentational understanding – The ability to represent one's own and another person's different relationships to the same situation. Children who pass false-belief tasks demonstrate such metarepresentation, as they understand that another person will act on the basis of his or her mental representation, even when this is a misrepresentation of the actual situation in the world as represented by the child.

Modularity theory – The theoretical explanation of theory-of-mind development that proposes that theory of mind depends on maturation of a particular brain structure – an innate cognitive theory-of-mind module. While experience might be required as a trigger, the module will not be modified in differential ways by different experiences.

Simulation theory – The theoretical explanation of theory-of-mind development that proposes that mental-state concepts are derived from children's own direct experience of such states. The theory says that children can understand other people's behavior through a process like pretence. They can imagine having the beliefs and desires that the other person has, and imagine what they themselves would do if they possessed those imagined beliefs and desires.

Theory of mind – People's understanding of themselves and others as psychological beings, whose beliefs, desires, intentions, and emotions differ. Theory of mind underlies the ability to understand human behavior, as people explain their own actions, as well as attempt to interpret and predict other people's actions, by considering mental states.

Theory–theory – The theoretical explanation of theory-of-mind development that proposes that children's theory of mind develops via a process of theory construction and change, analogous to construction and change in scientific theorizing. With this view, children construct a theory about the mind, whereby their concepts of mental states are abstract and unobservable theoretical postulates used to explain and predict observable human behavior.

Introduction

Theory-of-mind research investigates children's understanding of people as mental beings, who have beliefs, desires, emotions, and intentions, and whose actions and interactions can be interpreted and explained by taking account of these mental states. Children's understanding of mental life was first investigated by Jean Piaget early in the last century and it has been of interest to psychologists ever since, for example, in studies of perspective taking and metacognition. However, recent years have seen an explosion of research in the area and given it a new name: theory of mind.

What is a Theory of Mind?

Developmental psychologists often refer to children's theories of different domains – for example, physics or biology – by which they mean that children have an integrated set of concepts underlying their understanding of how things work in a particular domain. The characteristics of theories in general and theory of mind in particular are shown in **Table 1**.

Theory of Mind

Children's theory of mind underlies their ability to understand human behavior. It is called a theory of mind rather than a theory of behavior because much of people's behavior depends on what goes on in their minds. We explain our own actions by referring to our beliefs, desires, and other mental states, and we attempt to interpret and predict other people's actions by considering their mental states. Such mentalistic explanations, interpretations, and predictions of human behavior are fundamental to social interaction. Theory of mind is therefore an important part of social understanding or social cognition.

The term theory of mind might seem to portray children as little psychologists or philosophers but this is not what is intended – children do not hold the theory explicitly as a psychologist or philosopher would. They cannot articulate their theory of mind, but rather we have to infer it from what they say and do in naturalistic and experimental situations. Both are required because the natural setting shows the child's abilities as an interacting participant within the social world, whereas the experimental setting allows for more control, in order to reveal the precise level of the child's own understanding.

However, the fact that theory of mind is inferred from behavior leads to the vexing question of whether the child 'has' a theory of mind in a first-person sense or whether it is merely a third-person ascription. That is, is theory of mind a psychologically real structure underlying the child's behavior or is it merely a way of describing the child's behavior – as if it were guided by a theory of mind? It may be that only verbal self-ascription can provide unequivocal evidence for theory of mind in a first-person sense but this is not possible for preverbal children or nonhuman primates.

It is worth noting that the term first entered the developmental literature after it had been applied to nonhuman primates in a landmark article by David Premack and Guy Woodruff entitled, 'Does the chimpanzee have a theory of mind?' These researchers reported that they had shown a chimpanzee videotapes, in which a man was faced with a problem (e.g., trying to get bananas that were hung out of his reach) and the animal then had to choose between two photographs, one of which depicted the solution to the problem (e.g., the man standing on a box). The animal chose the correct photograph significantly more often than the other one. The researchers claimed that this demonstrated that chimpanzees have a theory of mind, which they defined as a system of inferences about mental states that can be used to make predictions about behavior (e.g., the man 'wants' bananas and so he will stand on a box to get them).

The focus of Premack and Woodruff's study was on the animal's recognition of the man's desire or intention. However, other researchers' commentaries on the article made it clear that the critical inference revealing theory of mind is the attribution of belief – in particular, in a case where observer and observed have different beliefs about a situation. Only in this case can one be certain that the observer is actually attributing a mental state to the observed and not merely responding as he himself (or she herself) would do in the same situation.

Understanding False Belief

The commentaries on Premack and Woodruff's article led two Austrian psychologists, Heinz Wimmer and Josef Perner, to develop the 'false-belief task', which assesses whether children have a theory of mind in the Premack and Woodruff sense. That is, it shows whether a child can make inferences about mental states, in order to predict behavior. In the task, children are told a story that the experimenter acts out with toy figures and props. A character in the story has a false belief about a situation and the child has to predict what that character will do (see **Table 2**).

At the end of the story children are asked a question about the character's subsequent action, which in this example is: 'Where will Maxi look for the chocolate?' They are also asked where he put it and where it is now. Numerous studies have shown that children of about

Table 1 Characteristics of theories and theory of mind

Theories	Theory of mind
Make ontological distinctions and define a domain	Distinguishes between mental and real and defines mental world
Coherent set of inter-related concepts	Concepts of mental states: belief, desire, intention, emotion, etc.
Underlie explanations and predictions within the domain	Explains, predicts, and interprets human behavior
Change in light of counter-evidence to predictions	Changes and develops throughout childhood, especially early childhood

4 years of age and older say that Maxi will look where he put it, in the cupboard. However, younger children say that he will look in the drawer where the chocolate now is, even though they remember where he put it at the beginning of the story.

The catch is that children have to recognize that the story character's belief about the location of the chocolate is different from their own. That is to say, this is one of those cases where the observer (the child) and the observed (Maxi, the boy in the story) have different beliefs about a situation. Children can respond correctly only by attributing to the boy a belief that is different from their own, and false from their point of view. They further have to recognize that the boy's belief is what guides his actions, even though it is false.

This simple demonstration reveals a most important aspect of theory of mind. Children who can correctly predict that the boy would look for the chocolate in the cupboard understand that people act not on the basis of the way things actually are in the world but on the basis of the way they 'think' that they are. That is, successful performance on the false-belief task demonstrates an understanding of the idea that people's relationship to the world is mediated by their mental representation of it. Children who pass the false-belief task understand that the world is represented in mind and that people act on the basis of their mental representation even when this is a misrepresentation of the actual situation in the world. To be precise, they are capable of 'metarepresentation' – that is, they not only represent a situation but they can also represent their own and another person's different relationships to this situation. Expressing it this way draws on a philosophical work on the representational theory of mental states, which has informed research on children's theory of mind and which is briefly described in the following section.

Mental Representation

Mental states such as beliefs and desires are representations that mediate our activity in the world. They are also referred to as 'intentional' states, not with the everyday meaning of 'deliberate' or 'on purpose' but with a technical meaning from the philosophical literature: 'aboutness'.

Intentional states are always 'about' something. One does not just have a belief, for example, but rather one has a belief about something – this is the content, or propositional content, of the intentional state. Such states are often described as attitudes to propositions. That is, a person has a certain attitude toward the propositional content – such as holding it to be true or wanting it to happen – and this attitude denotes what type of mental state it is, as shown in **Table 3**.

A person can hold different attitudes to the same propositional content, resulting in different mental states. For example, the boy can 'believe' the chocolate is in the cupboard, 'hope' the chocolate is in the cupboard, 'want' the chocolate to be in the cupboard, and so on.

Beliefs and Desires: Truth and Fulfillment

There is obviously a difference between believing something to be true and wanting something to be the case, even when the propositional content of the belief and the desire are the same. This difference is due to a difference in the nature of the representational relation. There are two basic types of relation, characterized by truth/falsity or by fulfillment/unfulfillment, as shown in **Table 4**.

Belief-type states are true or false, whereas desire-type states are fulfilled or unfulfilled. If the propositional content of a belief corresponds to the way things actually are in the world, then the belief is true. If it does not correspond, then it is false. If it is false, it can be made true by changing the belief – by making the mind fit the world. This is described as a mind-to-world 'direction of fit'.

Desires (and also intentions) are different from beliefs because they are neither true nor false. They are fulfilled or unfulfilled. If the propositional content of a desire does not correspond to the way things actually are in the world,

Table 2 Example of a 'false-belief' story

Mother returns from a shopping trip with some chocolate. Her little boy, Maxi, puts the chocolate away in the cupboard. Then he goes outside to play. Mother takes the chocolate from the cupboard and uses some to make a cake. Then she puts the remaining chocolate away in a drawer, not in the cupboard, and goes upstairs. Maxi then comes back inside, hungry and wanting some chocolate.

Table 3 Examples of intentional states

Attitude (type of mental state)	Propositional content (what it is about)
Believe	Chocolate is in cupboard
Want	Eat some chocolate
Intend	Open the cupboard

Table 4 Two basic types of intentional state

Beliefs	Desires and intentions
True or false	Fulfilled or unfulfilled
Caused by events in the world	Bring about changes in the world
Changed to fit the world: 'mind-to-world' direction of fit	World has to change to fit them: 'world-to-mind' direction of fit

then the desire is unfulfilled. However, it cannot be fulfilled by changing the desire. In order to fulfill the desire, things in the world have to change to fit the representation that is held in mind. That is, desires and intentions have a world-to-mind direction of fit.

Predicting and Explaining Behavior

As mentioned, theory of mind is used to explain and predict human behavior. The basic premise is that actions are produced by desire and belief in combination (**Figure 1**).

That is, people act to fulfill their desires in light of their beliefs. This is why false beliefs lead to misguided actions. If a person's belief and desire are known, one can predict how the person will act (as in the false-belief task). Alternatively, if the desire is known, a misguided action can be explained by attributing a false belief to the person.

In fact, intentions are mediators between desires and actions. If someone desires something they may form an intention to obtain it, which causes them to act in a way that will lead to fulfillment of the desire (**Figure 2**).

That is, a desired outcome can be achieved through the action of a person whose intention causes the action. Actually, desires may be fulfilled however the outcome is achieved (the dotted line in **Figure 2**) but, importantly, intentions are fulfilled only if the person's intention causes the action that brings about the outcome. This is known as intentional causation.

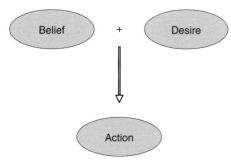

Figure 1 The basic premise of theory of mind.

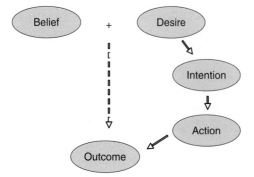

Figure 2 Intended actions are means to desired outcomes.

Development of Theory of Mind

The ability to explain and predict human behavior using concepts of false belief and intentional causation typically develops toward the end of the preschool years. However, children's first awareness of mental life begins much earlier. There is, indeed, no single moment when children acquire a theory of mind. On the contrary, their understanding changes and develops from infancy on into the school years, so that perhaps it would be better to refer to children's theories (rather than theory) of mind. **Table 5** highlights the major development occurring at each of the stages which are described in the following sections.

Social Perception in Infancy

When Premack and Woodruff asked, "Does the chimpanzee have a theory of mind?" they took it for granted that human beings do. Their definition of theory of mind – a system of inferences about mental states that can be used to make predictions about behavior – was taken up by developmental psychologists and the question became: "When does the child acquire a theory of mind?" Inge Bretherton and colleagues gave one of the first answers, arguing that infants' ability to engage in intentional communication implies that they have a theory of mind, at least an implicit and rudimentary one. However, most theory-of-mind research during the 1980s focused on preschool children's success on the false-belief task as providing evidence for theory of mind. It is only more recently that there has been much investigation of developments during the infancy period that may underlie theory of mind. This is now a burgeoning area of research.

It is obvious that even young infants 'have' beliefs, desires, and intentions (e.g., they become upset when their desires are frustrated or show surprise when their expectations are unrealized) but this is different from having 'awareness' of belief, desire, and intention, and attributing such states to others. It is the latter that is theory of mind, and it is debatable whether theory of mind in this sense is developed during infancy. However, infants do have some important precursors to theory of mind.

Table 5 Development of theory of mind

Period	Age range	Major development
Infancy	Birth–18 months	Social perception
Toddler and early preschool	18-month-olds to 3-year-olds	Mental-state awareness
Preschool	4- and 5-year-olds	Metarepresentation
School age	6 years onwards	Recursion and Interpretation

From birth, infants are interested in other people and prefer social over nonsocial stimuli. They attend to human faces and voices more than to nonhuman sights and sounds and they can soon discriminate the mother's face and voice from those of others. Infants can also imitate human facial movements from very early in life. Even newborns can imitate – for example, by protruding their tongue in response to an adult's tongue protrusion. Infants only see the other's face and only feel their own response yet, in some way, they can connect the visible bodily actions of the other with their own internal state, thus demonstrating that they can match their own actions to those of another individual. This ability – referred to as 'cross-modal matching' – shows that infants can make a connection between self and other, at least at some primitive level, which is important because the similarity between self and other is at the heart of theory of mind.

Infants soon begin to participate in social interactions with those around them. Around 2 months of age they start to interact by smiling and vocalizing (e.g., cooing and, later, babbling). At first these interactions are dyadic, in that only two participants – infant and adult – are involved. However, around 9 months of age triadic interactions appear, in which both participants are focused on the same object. For example, the infant and adult may engage in turn-taking with a toy, continuously switching their focus between each other and the toy. Such 'joint attention', which is the ability to coordinate attention with others by following gaze or pointing gestures, is a major feature of infant social behavior. It is more than just looking at the same thing but involves mutual awareness (at some level) that both are engaged with the same object. Between 9 and 12 months of age, infants develop the ability to follow an adult's eye gaze or an adult's point even to objects not in their line of sight. Also, if the adult points or gazes and there is no evident object of attention, the infant will look to the adult, as if checking back. Likewise, when infants point, they will look toward the adult as well as toward the object to monitor the other's attention.

At this stage infants also begin to engage in social referencing, in which they look to an adult (often their mother) when they are unsure how to react in an ambiguous situation and then respond in accord with her positive or negative emotional expression. Social referencing is triadic, in that infants are able to respond to their mother's reaction to an object.

Dishabituation experiments, in which infants look longer at a novel stimulus than one seen earlier, are used to demonstrate their sensitivity to mental states. Findings show that infants can distinguish between agents (that have goals) and inanimate objects (that do not). They are more sensitive to the goals of an action than to the physical movements involved. They understand actions as goal-directed and linked to perceptions/emotions. They are also more sensitive to interruptions in action that occur before a goal is achieved than to interruptions occurring as the goal is achieved. They also respond differentially based on knowledge states of the agent.

In sum, infants have many abilities relevant to social understanding (see **Table 6**).

These early developing behaviors may be referred to as social perception, social intuition, person perception, intersubjectivity, or even 'early' or 'implicit' theory of mind – but, the latter is controversial. Although there is general agreement on the behavioral findings, there is much disagreement over their interpretation. The debate centers on whether the appropriate level of analysis is behavioral or mental. That is, some researchers maintain that infants are merely able to detect statistical regularities in behavior, whereas others claim that infants understand the subjective nature of psychological experience – that is, they are aware of other people as intentional agents, whose behavior is governed by goals and perceptions. Yet other researchers argue that this is a false dichotomy and that interpersonal perception only later splits into separable bodily and mental aspects. Although this debate is not yet resolved, it is clear that infants display behaviors that are relevant to theory of mind. Certainly, social perception is not supplanted by later-developing aspects of theory of mind but rather it continues to exist and underpins the complexities of social understanding right on into adulthood.

Mental-State Awareness in Toddlers and Young Preschoolers

Important changes come at about 18 months of age, when children clearly begin to show awareness of the subjective nature of psychological experience. This depends on their ability to think about more than what is directly perceived. Although infants think about things in the world, they do not think of alternative possible worlds. Around the middle of the second year, children can think and talk about absent and hypothetical situations. This is seen in Piagetian sensorimotor stage 6 behaviors, such as, finding invisibly displaced objects, and solving problems by

Table 6 Theory of mind in infancy

Social perception in infancy, from birth to 8 months of age

Characteristic behaviors and abilities
- Imitation
- Dyadic smiling and vocalizing
- Joint attention:
  Follow other's pointing and gaze
  Direct other's attention with point and gaze
  Social referencing
- Discriminate animates from inanimates
- Discriminate goals from movements
- Sensitive to agents knowledge state

insight. It is also revealed as language develops – toddlers can talk about past and future events and things out of sight or only imagined. For example, a child building a tower out of blocks may say 'uh-oh' as the tower collapses. This use of 'uh-oh' indicates the discrepancy between what the child imagined would happen and what actually happened. What is important is that the child is able to think of the hypothetical and compare it with the reality.

The ability to imagine a possible alternative reality is also seen – perhaps best seen – in young children's pretend play, which begins to develop at about 18 months of age. Through pretend play (e.g., pretending that a banana is a telephone), toddlers show that they can distinguish between the object – the banana – and thoughts about the object – the banana as a telephone.

The ability to distinguish between objects and thoughts about them can also be demonstrated in experimental tasks. For example, 3-year-olds can tell the difference between a boy who is thinking about a cookie, and a boy who has got a cookie. That is, they know which boy can see, touch, share, or eat the cookie. They know that people's thoughts are private, they cannot be seen or touched, and sometimes, as mental images, for example, they can be made to come and go at will.

Toddlers' awareness of the subjective nature of psychological experience is also seen in their recognition of people's intentions and desires. For example, 18-month-olds can use the direction of a speaker's gaze to infer the referent of a novel word. When adults are labeling objects, they understand that the word the adult is using refers to the object the adult is currently looking at, not the one they themselves happen to be looking at. That is, children of this age clearly attribute communicative intentions to the other person. They can also recognize intention in an adult's behavior. For example, if 18-month-old infants watch an individual attempt to perform a task but fail (e.g., attempt to push a button with a stick, but miss the button) and are then given the opportunity to handle the objects themselves, they will demonstrate the intended task, rather than imitate the way in which the other person failed (i.e., the infant will push the button with the stick). That is, they are aware of what someone wants to achieve.

Also at this age, children can recognize that there may be a difference between what they want and what another person wants. For example, if an experimenter shows pleasure toward one food and disgust toward the other, 18-month-old infants understand that they should give her the one toward which she showed pleasure, even if they themselves prefer the other food. Three-year-olds are able to reason more explicitly about desires and emotions. For example, if they are told what a story character wants, they are able to predict what the character will do to fulfill this desire. Further, they can predict the character's emotion based on whether or not the desire is fulfilled. That is, they understand that people will feel happy when they get what they want and will feel sad when they do not.

During this period children also begin to show some understanding of how people get to know things. For example, 2-year-olds know that in showing something, they have to orient it toward the person. Two-year-olds also take account of people's knowledge states when asking others for assistance, in that they will give more information to someone who is ignorant about the situation. Three-year-olds understand that if an object is hidden inside a box, only those who have looked inside the box will know what is inside.

A developing awareness of mental states is seen in children's language too. Around 2 years of age, children start to talk about what people 'want' and 'like' and 'feel'. They produce explicit contrasts – distinguishing between what they want and what another person wants, or between what they wanted and what they got or what happened. Toddlers also talk about emotions, using terms like 'happy, sad, mad', and so on. When they are 3 years of age they also talk about what people 'think' and 'know'.

In sum, it is clear that 3-year-olds are aware of the subjective nature of psychological experience (see **Table 7**). They know that there is a difference between thoughts in the mind and things in the world; they are aware of people's wants, feelings, perceptions, and knowledge; and they use mental-state terms in their talk.

There is more to theory of mind, however, than being aware of mental states and reasoning about action based on desire. As mentioned earlier, mental states are representations that mediate our activity in the world. The two basic types of mental state – desires and beliefs – differ in the nature of the representational relation. Desire-type states are characterized by fulfillment/unfulfillment, whereas belief-type states are characterized by truth/falsity. Three-year-olds understand that people act to fulfill their desires and they are able to use information about a person's desire to explain or predict actions or emotions. However, 3-year-olds do not understand truth and falsity; therefore, they cannot take into account that people act to fulfill their desires in light of their beliefs even when they are mistaken (recall 3-year-olds' failure on the false-belief task described in an earlier section).

Table 7 Theory of mind in toddler and early preschool period

Mental-state awareness, 18-month-olds to 3-year-olds

Characteristic behaviors and abilities
- Distinguish between mental and real
- Pretend play
- Aware of intentions, desires, and emotions
- Desire-based reasoning
- Aware of perception and knowledge acquisition
- Use mental-state terms

Metarepresentational Ability in Older Preschoolers

Understanding truth and falsity and taking false beliefs into account in predicting action depend on the development of metarepresentational understanding. This is the understanding that people's beliefs, desires, and intentions are mental representations that mediate their actions in the world and their interactions with others in the world. Children with this understanding think of beliefs, desires, and intentions as representations that are produced by the mind as a result of certain experiences and that effect actions in the world in certain specific ways. They have the ability to represent their own and another person's different relationships to the same situation – as clearly demonstrated in successful performance on the false-belief task.

Children's understanding of false belief is undoubtedly the most striking and most studied aspect of their theory of mind. As described earlier, this research began in the early 1980s with the task devised by Heinz Wimmer and Josef Perner, in which a story is acted out for children. A character in the story is off the scene when an object that he has left in one location is moved to a different place. The character therefore has a false belief about the object's location. When he returns to the scene, children are asked where he will look for the object or where he thinks it is. By 4 or 5 years of age, children recognize that the character's representation of the situation is different from their own and they can predict the character's action based on his false belief.

One criticism of this 'change-of-location' false-belief task is that children have to follow a complicated story narrative and have to attribute beliefs to dolls. Researchers attempted to make false belief easier for 3-year-olds, by letting children actually experience a false belief themselves, and then asking them about another person's belief in the same situation. For example, they showed children a familiar candy box, all closed up, and then let them find out that it contained pencils, not candy. Then they put the pencils back and asked what another person, who had not seen inside the box, would think was inside it. Most 3-year-olds claimed that the other person would think there were pencils in the box but by 4 or 5 years of age children realized that the other person would think as they themselves had done, that it had candy inside. That is, they could represent and distinguish between their own and another's different relationships to the same situation.

The traditional Piagetian explanation of 3-year-olds' failure on this 'unexpected-contents' false-belief task is that such young children are egocentric and thus cannot understand that other people may have beliefs different from their own. However, 3-year-olds' lack of understanding is more profound. In this experiment, children were also asked what they themselves had thought was in the box before it was opened. Three-year-olds found it as difficult to remember their own previous false belief as to predict the other person's false belief. They could not metarepresent, that is, they could not represent themselves as representing both the past and the present situations and see that what was true for them in the past was false for them in the present.

Children's performance on these types of false-belief task is an extremely robust, much-replicated finding. In fact, a recent meta-analysis determined that there were no age differences in children's ability to attribute false beliefs to others or to themselves in the past. In addition, children's success did not differ based on the experimental procedures used, for example, the change-in-location-story task or the unexpected-contents-box task. These meta-analytic findings support the argument that there is a genuine conceptual change – that is, the development of metarepresentational understanding – underlying performance on different types of false-belief task.

The development of metarepresentational understanding is associated with the development of a number of other behaviors and abilities. False-belief task performance correlates with children's recognition of the relative certainty implied by use of the term 'know' over 'think' or 'guess'. In addition, since deception is the intentional creation of false beliefs, once children understand false belief, they are able to understand deception and to act deceptively or to tell lies. Some researchers claim that there is evidence for deception and lying earlier, before children understand false belief, but this is controversial. It may be that younger children act intentionally in ways that affect others' beliefs even though that may not be their motive in so acting – rather, they may just want to affect what the other person will do.

Metarepresentational ability also underlies children's understanding of the distinction between appearance and reality. For example, children are shown a piece of painted sponge that looks just like a rock, and then they squeeze it and discover that it is really a sponge. Once they know it is a sponge, 3-year-olds say that it looks like a sponge, but by 4 or 5 years of age children understand that its appearance is misleading – it looks like a rock but it is really a sponge.

At this age children also come to understand aspects of knowledge acquisition. They realize that information comes from different sources, that is, beliefs are derived from perception (e.g., feeling or seeing) or from communication (e.g., being told). They can remember the source of their own information and they remember, if they have just learned something new, that they did not know it previously. By 4 or 5 years of age, children also understand that different sensory modalities yield different kinds of information, for example, seeing gives information about color, whereas touching gives information about texture.

The development of metarepresentational ability also allows for a new understanding of desire and intention. Recall that intentions are mediators between desires and actions – although a desire may be fulfilled however the outcome is achieved, intentions are fulfilled only if the person's intention causes the action that brings about the outcome (intentional causation). As discussed earlier, toddlers have some understanding of desire and intention but they may think of both as mental states that motivate actions and outcomes, without distinguishing between the two types of state. Metarepresentational ability allows them to differentiate between desire and intention and to recognize cases of fortuitous success – in which the desire is satisfied even though the intention is unfulfilled. This ability also allows children to understand cases where two people's desires are in conflict, that is, situations where the satisfaction of one person's desire necessarily means that the other person's desire is not satisfied.

Emotional understanding continues to develop in 4- and 5-year-olds. In particular, toward the end of this period, children can make belief-based emotion attributions, for which they have to assess whether characters believe their desires will be fulfilled, not simply whether the desires will be fulfilled. Children also come to understand the distinction between appearance and reality in the emotional realm. For instance, they recognize that people might feign happiness even when they are sad, for example, because their desires are unfulfilled.

In sum, the development of metarepresentational ability in the later preschool period underlies a range of new behaviors and abilities that become apparent during this period (see **Table 8**).

Once metarepresentation is clearly established, children reach a new level of understanding of social interactions – including surprises, secrets, tricks, and lies. Of course, there are further developments in social cognition after the preschool years, which can be construed as further development in theory of mind, although research on social cognition during the school-age years has been less specifically focused on theory of mind.

Table 8 Theory of mind in older preschool period

Metarepresentational ability, 4- and 5-year-olds

Characteristic behaviors and abilities
- Understand false belief in self and others
- Understand deception
- Distinguish appearance and reality
- Understand aspects of knowledge acquisition
- Distinguish between desire and intention
- Understand intentional causation
- Understand belief-based emotions

Recursive and Interpretive Abilities in School-age Children

One of the main developments in theory of mind at the beginning of the school years is an understanding of mental-state recursion, that is, the embedding of one mental state in another (e.g., 'Mother thinks that Maxi thinks that the chocolate is in the cupboard'). Children become aware that people have beliefs, not just about the world, but about the content of others' minds (e.g., about others' beliefs) and, like people's beliefs about the world, these too may be different or wrong. Such beliefs about beliefs are referred to as second-order beliefs. Tasks designed to assess children's second-order false-belief understanding show that it develops by about 7 years of age. Somewhat earlier, children acquire the ability to understand second-order representations involving desires and intentions, such as understanding that someone wants to make another person believe something. Somewhat later, children acquire the ability to deal with third-order representations involving beliefs, desires, intentions, and emotions (e.g., 'Mother wants Maxi to think that she intended to hide the chocolate' or 'Mother thinks that Maxi wants her to know that he could not find the chocolate').

Such recursive ability underlies the more mature understanding and use of complex language, particularly indirect speech acts, such as irony and metaphor, that develop during the school-age years. In indirect speech there is a distinction between what a person means and what their words appear to mean; that is, what is actually said is not really what is meant. In verbal irony, for example, someone says something that is false but does not intend the listener to believe it to be true, but rather to recognize the falsity and interpret the statement as funny or sarcastic. Likewise, metaphors are not intended as statements to be literally interpreted but are used to create poetic images. Children's understanding of irony and metaphor begins to develop during the early school years, although it takes some years to reach maturity.

The ability to comprehend recursive mental states also underlies an increasing sensitivity to the interpersonal dynamics of social situations. For example, during the early school years children come to understand 'white lies' where something untrue is said to protect a person's feelings. They also recognize when someone has produced a 'faux pas' and unintentionally revealed secret information or created hurt feelings. As well, they can invent or select persuasive strategies, which require the manipulation of a person's mental states in order to get them to believe or do something. Children's use of language during the school-age years also reflects their more sophisticated understanding of the mind, as children begin to comprehend and produce more complex mental-state terms, such as 'interpret', 'infer', 'doubt', and many more.

Other developments in the early school years involve increasing understanding of knowledge acquisition and of the mind as an active interpreter of information. For example, around 7 years of age children recognize interpretive diversity, that is, they understand that even given the same external stimulus, two people may make legitimate but different interpretations of it, which requires more than understanding the possibility of true vs. false beliefs. Also by age 7 years, children come to understand the role of inference in knowledge acquisition and to recognize ambiguity and referential opacity. Children of this age also have a simple understanding of evidence for belief and can distinguish between the cause of a phenomenon and a person's reason for believing it. This allows them to engage in scientific reasoning by evaluating evidence.

Understanding the mind as an interpreter of information is related to understanding the dynamic nature of mental activity. Until the early school years, children are unaware of the stream of consciousness that fills the waking mind and they are not able to introspect about their own thinking. Preschool children can report the content of their mental states – but without recognizing that it is produced by the mind's activity. Participation in formal school activities may facilitate children's introspective abilities. Indeed, the investigation of a number of metacognitive abilities that are demonstrated in school tasks, such as metamemory and comprehension monitoring, began during the 1970s, before the explosion of research into children's theory of mind. Undeniably, although such metacognitive abilities, as well as the social cognitive abilities described earlier in this section, can be interpreted in the framework of children's theory of mind, it is fair to say that much of the research predates the theory-of-mind field and even now is conducted somewhat independently of it (**Table 9**).

Differences in Development

The preceding section provides an overview of typical development of theory of mind from infancy through the early school years. Although approximate age norms are given, there are marked individual differences in typical development. In addition, there are variations in development in atypical populations. Furthermore, the overview is derived from research conducted primarily with samples of middle-class, Western children – however, theory-of-mind development may not be universally the same across cultures. Therefore we need to consider individual differences in typical development, diverse atypical developments, and cultural differences in theory of mind.

Individual Differences

The main focus of research so far has been on examining factors, both within the child and in the child's environment, that are associated with the development of false-belief understanding, which some children achieve soon after they are 3 years of age and others not until age 5 years. A number of factors, such as executive functioning, language ability, and social competence, are correlated with the understanding of false belief – both contemporaneously and across time in longitudinal studies. The causal or consequential nature of such earlier or later correlates is a matter of some debate, requiring careful consideration.

Executive functioning. Executive functions are self-regulatory cognitive processes, such as inhibition, planning, resistance to interference, and control of attention and motor responses. During the years from 3 to 5, children's performance on executive function tasks is correlated with their performance on false-belief tasks. This may be because executive function tasks require suppression of a habitual response in favor of a new response and, likewise, in standard false-belief tasks children must resist making the more salient (incorrect) response. This suggests that there are executive functioning demands embedded within false-belief tasks. However, most researchers believe that the relation between theory of mind and executive function extends beyond the fact that false-belief tasks require inhibition. Some argue that executive functioning is actually required for children to develop a theory of mind, in that children must be able to control their own representations of the world before understanding others' representations. Others argue that the relation is in the opposite direction, in that children must understand mental states before they are able to control their own actions. Yet a third group propose that the relation between theory of mind and executive function is due to the acquisition of the general ability to reason about complex problems relating to selective attention. In turn, this ability improves performance on both false-belief and executive function tasks.

Fantasy and pretense. Pretend play is a context in which children can simulate feelings and desires they do not currently hold and imagine states of the world that do not currently exist. Researchers argue that pretend play

Table 9 Theory of mind in school-age children

Recursive and interpretive abilities, 6 years and older

Characteristic behaviors and abilities
- Understand second- and higher-order mental states
- Recognize interpretive diversity
- Understand indirect speech, for example, irony and metaphor
- Aware of white lies, faux pas, and persuasion
- Use and comprehend complex mental-state terms
- Understand inference, ambiguity, referential opacity
- Aware of stream of consciousness, introspect

encourages theory-of-mind development and this is supported by data showing that preschoolers who score higher on theory-of-mind tasks engage in more fantasy and pretense. There is also evidence that acting out roles in pretend play precedes and supports false-belief understanding, whereas explicit assignment of roles and plans for joint action in pretend play follow and result from false-belief understanding.

Language ability. It is well established that there is a strong relation between language ability and theory-of-mind development that is independent of age. In 9- to 15-month olds, joint attention behaviors are correlated with language production and comprehension and may be instrumental in language development at this stage. Subsequently, many studies have shown relations between false-belief understanding and various language skills, including general language, receptive vocabulary, semantics, and syntax. Moreover, it is likely that there is a causal relation involved such that children's linguistic development supports their theory-of-mind development at this later stage. Longitudinal studies show that changes in children's false-belief understanding are predicted by their language competence but the reciprocal relation (i.e., prediction of language development by false-belief test scores) is much weaker. It is not likely that the verbal requirements of false-belief tasks can alone explain these findings since the correlations are found for a wide range of theory-of-mind measures, some less verbal than others.

The role of language in the development of theory of mind is complex, reflecting the multifaceted nature of language, which includes pragmatics, semantics, and syntax. Pragmatic ability allows children to participate in communicative exchanges, where they hear mental terms used in complex syntactic structures. From this experience they acquire awareness of different points of view, concepts of mental states, and mastery of the syntax for representing false beliefs. Both the social environment that provides this input and the child's own cognitive resources that make use of it are needed for the child's theory of mind to develop.

Family environment. A number of studies show that the kind of conversational experiences that children have is related to theory-of-mind development. In particular, children whose mothers use more mental terms in their conversations acquire false-belief understanding at an earlier age than children whose mothers use fewer such terms, even when the children's own language ability is taken into account. However, it is certainly possible that it is not the use of mental-state terms in particular that is important for children's understanding of the mind, but rather, that use of mental-state terms is an easily countable measure that is likely to be found in mothers who also tend to introduce varying points of view into conversations with their children. In addition, both parenting style and disciplinary strategy are associated with children's false-belief understanding. As might be expected, children whose parents explain and discuss, rather than only punish unacceptable behavior, score more highly on false-belief tasks.

Children from larger families develop false-belief understanding sooner. Perhaps this is because they have more experience of tricks, jokes, and teasing among their siblings, or perhaps because they are more exposed to talk about thoughts and wants as parents try to settle disputes among the children. Other studies have shown a similar effect for children who interact with more adults and who interact with older children including both siblings and peers. The relation between family size and performance on theory-of-mind tasks is stronger in the case of children with poorer language skills. This means that children with poor linguistic competence can acquire an understanding of false belief through social interaction with siblings in their home.

Evidence from the attachment literature also demonstrates the importance of the family environment and parenting style to theory-of-mind development. Children who are classified as having secure maternal attachments in infancy develop false-belief understanding at an earlier age than children with less secure attachments. Some researchers argue that mothers' 'mind-mindedness', that is, their propensity to treat their infants as individuals with minds, is an important factor in determining attachment security, as well as underlying their children's developing awareness of other minds.

Social competence. One might expect that children's developing theory of mind would be related to their social competence – that is, children's awareness of others' mental states should have consequences for their relationships with others and for their social behavior in general. And indeed, research shows that individual differences in false-belief understanding are associated with actual differences in behavior in the social world. These behaviors are: communication abilities, as seen in more connected and more informative conversation; imaginative abilities, as seen in more frequent and more sophisticated pretend play; ability to resolve conflicts and to maintain harmony and intimacy in friendships; teacher ratings of global social competence; happiness in school; and peer-rated empathy and popularity. Importantly, in most if not all cases, the relations with false-belief understanding are independent of age and language ability. Conversely, preschoolers who are rejected by their peers and who do not have stable friendships tend to perform more poorly on theory-of-mind tasks. However, the directionality of this finding is not known. It is possible that these children's low scores on theory-of-mind tasks are due to their limited opportunities to engage in pretend play and the use of shared mental states with other children. On the other hand, it is possible that these children's lack of social understanding weakens their ability to develop friendships and gain acceptance from peers. Either way, children with a better understanding of false belief tend to be more successful in their social relationships.

However, theory-of-mind understanding is also related to children's antisocial behavior. For example, children who are bullies have sophisticated theory-of-mind abilities and the skill of manipulating other people's beliefs. As well, children who show a highly developed understanding of mental states tend to be better at lying. These paradoxical findings of the effects of theory of mind on social behavior have led some researchers to suggest that the concept of theory of mind be separated into 'nice theory of mind' (prosocial behavior requiring theory of mind) and 'nasty theory of mind' (antisocial behavior requiring theory of mind). In fact, research has suggested that these truly are distinct cognitive abilities. Yet the consequences of theory-of-mind development are perhaps most striking in their absence, suggested by studies of atypically developing populations.

Atypical Development

Autism. Children with autism show impairments in communication and social interaction. Because of these deficits, there has been intensive investigation of theory-of-mind development in autism. Although autism is not usually diagnosed until after 2 years of age, children at risk for autism do not show the typical joint attention behaviors of late infancy and do not engage in pretend play. Later in the preschool years, they do show some understanding of others' desires, although their ability lags behind that of typically developing children. Most striking, though, is their difficulty in understanding other people's beliefs, as shown in their performance on the false-belief task. Only about 20% of children with autism succeed on standard false-belief tasks. This finding has been replicated numerous times in many different studies. Children with autism also tend to fail theory-of-mind tasks that require deception and have difficulty understanding belief-based emotions.

As in typical development, autistic children's false-belief understanding is predicted by their language ability, perhaps to an even greater degree than for typically developing children. Notably, children with autism require far higher verbal mental age to pass false-belief tasks than typically developing children do. Some researchers suggest that high levels of language ability allow these children to pass false-belief tasks by working around their lack of intuitive social understanding. However, even with high levels of language ability, few individuals with autism develop the ability to understand second-order false beliefs and they have particular difficulty with nonliteral language use, such as sarcasm, irony, white lies, and metaphor.

One thing that is clear is that the difficulty that children with autism have in passing theory-of-mind tasks is not due to a lack of intelligence. Evidence for this comes from the fact that children with Down syndrome tend to be successful on false-belief tasks, despite the fact that their intelligence scores are, on average, significantly lower than those of individuals with autism.

Sensory impairments. Theory-of-mind development in children who are deaf differs depending on their family environment. Deaf children with hearing parents are delayed in their false-belief understanding, whereas deaf children with deaf parents are not. This is because, even though both groups of children engage in social interaction, the children with hearing parents are delayed in their acquisition of sign language, which again shows the important role of language in theory-of-mind development. Deaf children whose language development is delayed fail false-belief tasks even though the tasks are adapted to their mode of communication and they completely understand the basic story facts in the task. Furthermore, they find nonverbal theory-of-mind tasks just as difficult and their performance on such tasks is predicted by their level of language development.

Children who are blind cannot see facial expressions and gestures and tend to have delayed language development. These children too show delays in theory-of-mind development, particularly in understanding false belief. There are also studies indicating deviations from typical theory-of-mind development in children with cerebral palsy, Williams syndrome, and fragile X syndrome.

Behavior problems. A few studies have examined theory-of-mind development in children with behavior problems but the findings are somewhat inconsistent, with some studies suggesting a mix of enhanced and impaired performance on theory-of-mind tasks in 'hard to manage' preschoolers and others describing no deficit in theory-of-mind competence in school-age children with attention deficit hyperactivity disorder (ADHD).

Cultural Differences

Theory-of-mind development has been investigated primarily in middle-class children in North America, Europe, and Australasia. Most researchers assume that it is a universal development, or at least that there is a universal core to theory of mind that is acquired in the early years. In support of this idea, research shows that Chinese and Japanese children's theory-of-mind development is quite similar to that of Western children, with slight variations in timing and perhaps more emphasis on social roles in the explanation of behavior. However, these children are also generally from middle-class, literate cultures. There are a few studies of children in unschooled, nonliterate populations, such as Baka and Mofu of Cameroon, Tolai and Tainae of New Guinea, Quechua of Peru, and Mopan Maya children in Central America. The findings from these studies are somewhat contradictory – some indicating development comparable to that in Western children, and others indicating delays or differences in development.

However, cross-cultural research, in which tasks like false-belief tasks are adapted for local use, may not be the best way to investigate cultural diversity in theory of mind. Western theory of mind, which explains and predicts behavior by imputing mental states to self and others, underlies the design of such tasks. Yet other cultures may have quite different conceptions of mind, or the concept of mind may not exist in every culture. That is to say, there could be ways of interpreting social behavior that do not necessarily rely on theory of mind. It is possible that theory of mind is not universal and not all cultures explain and predict behavior as people do in Western society. This issue could be effectively addressed by collaborations among developmental psychologists and anthropologists.

Furthermore, evidence provided by ethologists and comparative psychologists is also relevant here. If nonhuman primates were shown to possess theory of mind, then it would be more likely that theory of mind is universal in the human species – at least its basic core, even if there is cultural diversity in its further development. As mentioned, research on children's theory of mind was initiated by reports of theory of mind in the chimpanzee. In more recent years, however, the issue has been highly controversial. Although most researchers agree that chimpanzees do not understand false belief, there is disagreement over whether they do understand simpler psychological processes, such as seeing, or whether they are simply able to detect statistical regularities in behavior without any awareness of mental states or ability to reason about mental states.

Importantly, these debates – concerning the universality of theory of mind in humans, and whether theory of mind is a unique cognitive specialization in humans – inform ongoing debate on how to explain theory-of-mind development.

Explanations of Theory-of-Mind Development

Theory of mind is defined as an integrated set of mental-state concepts underlying the interpretation of human social activity that develops gradually from infancy onwards. Various competing theories have been put forward to explain how this development comes about. The characteristics of theory of mind described in the first section of this article are associated with one particular explanation, one that gives a literal interpretation to the term 'theory of mind'. The proposal is that children's theory of mind develops via a process of theory construction and change, analogous to construction and change in scientific theorizing. That is, the theory says that children construct a theory about the mind, which has led to this view being referred to as the 'theory–theory' (see **Table 10**). On this view, children's concepts of mental states are abstract and unobservable theoretical postulates used to explain and predict observable human behavior. The concepts are coherent and interdependent, and the theory can interpret a wide range of evidence using a few concepts and laws. The theory is not static but is reorganized over time when faced with counter-evidence to its predictions.

A somewhat similar explanation is provided by 'simulation theory' (see **Table 10**). However, on this view, mental-state concepts are derived from children's own direct experience of such states and are not postulated in some process of abstract theorizing. The theory says that children are intuitively aware of their own mental states and can understand other people's behavior by a process of simulation, using their abilities for pretence that develop early in the preschool years. Children can imagine having the beliefs and desires that the other person has, and imagine what they themselves would do if they possessed those imagined beliefs and desires.

Another explanation is provided by 'modularity theory'. On this view, theory-of-mind development depends on maturation of a particular brain structure – an innate cognitive theory-of-mind module. Like theory–theory, modularity theory regards children's concepts of mental states as abstract theoretical entities, organized into causal laws that can be used to interpret a wide range of evidence. However, the theory is not acquired

Table 10 Theoretical explanations of theory-of-mind development

Theories	Characteristics
Theory–theory	Children construct theory of mind through a process of theorizing
Simulation theory	Children simulate others' experience based on their own
Modularity (nativist) theory	Theory of mind depends on maturation of an innate cognitive theory-of-mind module
Social-constructivist theories	Theory of mind is collaboratively constructed in linguistically mediated social interaction
Domain-general theories	Theory-of-mind development depends on domain-general developments, for example, in executive functions

through any process of 'theorizing', but rather the theory-of-mind module is innate and matures. The module constrains development in a precise way – the theory is not subject to revision based on experience. Although experience might be required as a trigger, the module will not be modified in differential ways by different experiences, which predicts that the acquisition of a theory of mind will be a universal human achievement.

These three views – that posit theory construction, simulation, or an innate module – all focus on theory of mind as an individual cognitive achievement in which children construct or employ a conceptual structure – the theory of mind. An alternative view gives social factors a much greater role in theory-of-mind development. 'Social constructivist theories' assert that theory of mind is embodied in the folk ways and speech practices of a culture and theory of mind develops as children participate in interaction and dialogue with more knowledgeable members of the culture. Importantly, social constructivist views are not passive enculturation explanations that allow the child no active role. Rather they recognize the contribution both of the child and of the social environment, arguing that children's understanding of mind is collaboratively constructed in linguistically mediated social interaction.

Against the aforementioned four views, other researchers argue that children do not develop a domain-specific theory about the mind. Rather, theory-of-mind development is a reflection of domain-general changes in cognitive processes, such as executive function, working memory, or reasoning abilities (**Table 10**).

Evidence for and against each of the proposed theories is hotly debated and there is no overall consensus clearly supporting one theory over all the others. The same empirical evidence is used to support different theories and, furthermore, evidence that some researchers use to refute a particular theory is dismissed by others as not relevant. Indeed, some researchers maintain that the differences between some of the theories (e.g., theory-theory and simulation theory) are philosophical differences that cannot be refuted by empirical evidence.

Many researchers argue that the striking absence of theory-of-mind abilities in children with autism occurs because of impairment in the theory-of-mind module, which is taken as evidence in support of modularity theory. However, cultural variation in theory of mind speaks against modularity theory and in favor of social constructivist theories. Researchers generally agree that domain-general resources are needed for successful performance on theory-of-mind tasks but the origin of domain-specific mental-state concepts still requires explanation.

In recent years, substantial attention has been paid to the role that the brain plays in theory-of-mind reasoning, with an attempt to isolate brain regions that are specific to this ability. However, most of this research has focused on adult participants, making it difficult to draw conclusions about how theory of mind develops. The limited research conducted with young children has attempted to examine the relationship between functional brain development and theory-of-mind development. Findings suggest that the neural systems associated with children's ability to reason about mental states (i.e., theory-of-mind reasoning) are independent of those associated with other kinds of reasoning (e.g., reasoning about reality). There is also evidence to suggest that it is the frontal lobes in particular that are required for theory-of-mind reasoning, and that this may be lateralized to the left hemisphere of the brain. Given the recent rise in interest in cognitive neuroscience research, significant future work in this area is to be expected and this may inform the debate over theoretical explanations of theory-of-mind development.

See also: Attention; Cognitive Development; Cognitive Developmental Theories; Grammar; Imitation and Modeling; Milestones: Cognitive; Pragmatic Development; Symbolic Thought.

Suggested Readings

Astington JW (1993) *The Child's Discovery of the Mind.* Cambridge, MA: Harvard University Press.
Astington JW and Baird JA (eds.) (2005) *Why Language Matters for Theory of Mind.* New York: Oxford University Press.
Baron-Cohen S (1995) *Mindblindness: An Essay on Autism and Theory of Mind.* Cambridge, MA: Bradford Books/MIT Press.
Carpendale J and Lewis C (2006) *How Children Develop Social Understanding.* Oxford: Blackwell.
Carruthers P and Smith PK (eds.) (1996) *Theories of Theories of Mind.* Cambridge, UK: Cambridge University Press.
Malle BF and Hodges SD (eds.) (2005) *Other Minds: How Humans Bridge the Divide between Self and Others.* New York: Guilford Press.
Moore C (2006) *The Development of Commonsense Psychology.* Mahwah, NJ: Erlbaum.
Perner J (1991) *Understanding the Representational Mind.* Cambridge, MA: Bradford/MIT Press.
Tomasello M (1999) *The Cultural Origins of Human Cognition.* Cambridge, MA: Harvard University Press.
Wellman HM (1990) *The Child's Theory of Mind.* Cambridge, MA: Bradford/MIT Press.

Twins

L F DiLalla, P Y Mullineaux, and K K Elam, Southern Illinois University School of Medicine, Carbondale, IL, USA

© 2008 Elsevier Inc. All rights reserved.

Glossary

Conjoined twins – When an egg divides, leading to monozygotic twinning, but the division occurs late in development and therefore is incomplete, the two resulting embryos may not completely separate, leading to partial fusion, or conjoined twins. Twins may be joined physically at different places and to different extents, and we are not certain what causes this.

Gene–environment (GE) correlation – Genes and environment can be correlated three different ways. Passive GE correlation happens when both genes and environment come from the parents and thus are correlated. Reactive GE correlation happens when people in the environment react to something genetically influenced in the child, making the child's genes and subsequent environment correlated. Active GE correlation occurs when a child chooses an environment partly because of his or her genetic make-up.

Heritability – The extent to which genetic make-up influences behavior is called heritability. Genetic influences on behavior are indirect via proteins that are coded for by genes and that have effects on the brain. Heritability is a statistic that is specific to the population for which it is calculated. The comparison between monozygotic (MZ) and dizygotic (DZ) twins can be used to calculate the heritability of a particular behavior.

Twin research – Twins are a wonderful natural experiment because MZ and DZ twins can be compared to provide information about the extent to which genes influence behavior. MZ twins share 100% of their genes, whereas DZ twins share approximately 50% of their genes. Therefore, if MZ twins are more similar to each other on a particular behavior than DZ twins are to each other, then genetic influences can be assumed to be important for influencing that behavior.

Twins – Twins are children who are conceived at the same time from the same mother. There are two types of twins: MZ, when one egg is fertilized by one sperm and then the zygote splits in two, forming two genetic copies, and DZ, when two separate eggs are fertilized by two separate sperm, resulting in two siblings who share approximately 50% of their genetic material.

Introduction

Twins occur when two fetuses share the same uterus during a pregnancy. Overall, twins occur in approximately 1 in 32 births in the US. When this happens, resources must be shared during development in the uterus. This causes most twins to be born prematurely and with a lower birth weight than normal infants. Single births have a gestation period of approximately 40 weeks, whereas twin births normally range from 34 to 36 weeks. Twins are usually born in quick succession and are often kept for observation due to low birth weight and increased possibility of complications found in multiple births.

Two basic types of twinning can occur (monozygotic (MZ) and dizygotic (DZ)) depending on the number of eggs (zygotes) that are fertilized during pregnancy. MZ twins, sometimes known as identical twins, are the result of a single egg that is fertilized during conception that then splits into separate embryos. MZ twins, therefore, are 100% genetically the same because they result from a single fertilized egg. This causes them to look very similar and to be the same sex. (There are rare exceptions to this, however, as noted below.) After they split, these separate embryos develop into two fetuses that share the uterus during pregnancy. MZ twins may share the same amnion (the inner fetal membrane that contains the amniotic fluid) and placenta (the organ joining the mother and fetus that allows transfer of oxygen and nutrients to the fetus and waste from the fetus), or just share the same placenta. MZ twins occur in about 1 in 250 of all births.

Dizygotic twins, sometimes called fraternal twins, develop when two eggs are released at about the same time and both become fertilized. These eggs then develop into two separate fetuses. Because DZ twins are a result of two different eggs, they are as genetically similar as siblings and they share on average 50% of their genes. Opposite sex twins can occur in fraternal pairs because different sperm fertilize the two eggs, and sex is determined by whether the sperm carries an X or a Y chromosome. Thus, DZ twins do not necessarily look alike and may have differing features as well as similar ones. Dizygotic twins occur in about 1 in 36 of all births.

Since the 1990s, multiple births, especially dizygotic, have become more common as a result of infertility treatments, although multiple births may also occur naturally. In addition, certain maternal factors such as higher maternal age and race may contribute to multiple births.

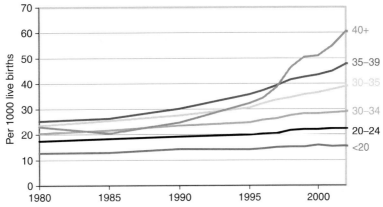
Figure 1 Twin birth rates by age of mother: US, 1980–2002. Source: National Vital Statistics System, NCHS, CDC.

The risk of having multiples doubles in women over the age of 35, partly because these women are more likely to use fertility drugs to conceive (see **Figure 1**). Also, women who are African American have a greater likelihood of having multiples.

Multiple births of three or more children can be comprised of any combination of MZ and DZ pairs. For instance, a single fertilized egg can split (resulting in twins), and then one of those can split again (resulting in genetically identical triplets). Similarly, three different eggs can be released simultaneously and can be fertilized by three different sperm, resulting in dizygotic triplets. Combinations of each of these can also occur, resulting in a combination of MZ and DZ multiples. DZ multiples are more common and often result from infertility treatments, such as implanting multiple eggs in the uterus or giving a woman fertility drugs that increase the likelihood of her releasing multiple eggs simultaneously. The overall rate for triplets is 1 in 535 of all births, and the frequency for having more than three children at once is even smaller at approximately 1 in 8700 of all births.

More unusual types of twinning can occur as well. Conjoined twins are the result of a fertilized zygote that fails to split completely. This causes the bodies of the twins to be fused together during development in the uterus. Conjoined twinning occurs on an average of 1 in 50 000 births, with only about 1 in 200 000 live births. Conjoined twins have a low survival rate, between 5% and 25%. Conjoined twins are most often males prenatally, but more females survive to birth, with the most common type of conjoining occurring at the front chest wall.

Other unusual outcomes of twinning can result in twins of opposite races or identical twins of opposite sex. Twins of opposite races occur only in DZ twins but can happen in two different ways. Two eggs can be released during ovulation and can be fertilized by two different fathers. Also, in an extremely rare situation, if both parents are of mixed race and if two eggs are released and fertilized by the same father, it is possible that the mother's and father's genes will contribute in such a way that one twin inherits only one skin color while the other twin inherits the other. Identical twins of opposite sex are also very rare and result from chromosomal birth defects that determine sex.

Other rare kinds of twinning are vanishing twins, thought to occur when multiple eggs are fertilized but one dies *in utero* and is reabsorbed by the mother. This usually occurs very early in pregnancy. Another case can occur when one twin fails to develop in the uterus, which can be detrimental to the other developing fetus. This is known as a parasitic twin and is similar to a conjoined twin. When this happens, the undeveloped twin is absorbed into the body of the developing fetus. The remains of this twin may appear as remnants such as teeth or bones in the healthy body of the surviving twin.

Twin Behaviors

Although there have been few systematic studies of twins as a special population, we do have some information about typical twin development and behavior. Twins are born into a unique and special situation by virtue of having a same-age sibling right from the early prenatal period. This can lead to both positive and negative consequences. For one thing, twins immediately have a same-age peer throughout development, and this typically yields a very close friend who is always there in their own home. However, twins must also share resources, beginning in the uterus and extending throughout childhood because they share parental attention and both emotional and financial resources of their parents. These consequences of being a twin can lead to behavioral outcomes that may be different from those for singleton, nontwin children. Some of the areas in which this has been examined include prosocial behaviors, psychological closeness, shyness, school behaviors, and language development.

Prosocial Behaviors

There do not appear to be differences in early social behaviors in same-sex vs. opposite-sex DZ twins during the preschool years. This is somewhat surprising if we assume that twins who have a co-twin who is more different from them (opposite-sex twin pairs) would have more experience with differences in playmates and therefore would be more socially prepared to interact well with other children. However, thus far it appears to be the case that DZ twins do not differ in their social competence based on whether they have a same-sex or an opposite-sex co-twin. They do appear to show poorer social competence than singletons, though. In general, preschool twins show less social independence and fewer friendships with other children than do singletons.

As twins get older, this trend begins to shift. At age 5 years, there is no difference between MZ and DZ twins in terms of their prosocial behaviors with nonfamiliar, same-age peers, but both types of twins show fewer prosocial behaviors than do singletons. However, in adolescence this difference in prosocial behaviors seems to disappear, although twins in this older age group begin to show more aggressive behaviors than do singletons.

Studies of the prosocial behaviors of twins are in the early stages, but they point to a possible risk for twins to exhibit less prosocial behavior than singletons. Twins at ages 3–5 years have been shown to have fewer friends and to exhibit fewer prosocial behaviors when they interact with other children. It has been hypothesized by researchers such as Nancy Segal that these behaviors may result from twins becoming used to playing with a same-age sibling who shares both genes and environment with them, and therefore they are less interested in playing with other children or are less able to communicate well with them on a social level. This behavior may put twins at risk for later social interaction difficulty, and therefore research on the causes of this lack of prosocial behavior must continue.

Psychological Closeness

MZ twins appear to share a special bond that sets them apart from other types of relationships. This does not appear to be a result of parental training, because even twins whose parents try to treat them differently are likely to behave similarly and to develop this bond. This bond can be so strong that it persists even when something happens to set the twins apart, including such severe events as partial paralysis or even death. MZ twins typically define their co-twin as their 'best friend'. This does not mean that these twins never fight. In fact, they frequently do, and they are as likely as DZ twins to describe their rate of fighting as 'sometimes' on a scale from never to sometimes to always. The important point is that these fights do not detract from their love for each other or from their feelings of closeness. It is not unusual for MZ twins to bicker constantly but then to stand up for each other if anyone else should try to harm either one of them.

Dizygotic twins also share a special bond, but it does not seem to be of the same quality as the bond that MZ twins share. DZ twins tend to be less close to each other than are MZ twins. They probably are more comparable to nontwin siblings in terms of psychological closeness. Nonetheless, many do have special bonds with their co-twins. There has not been a reported difference in closeness between same-sex and opposite-sex twins, but this may be because it has not been explored in research. DZ twins appear to share the same sort of feelings toward each other as other nontwin siblings share, although their feelings of closeness may be slightly increased simply by virtue of their growing up at the same time together in the same family environment.

Differences in cooperative behavior have been demonstrated by Nancy Segal and colleagues for school-age twins, with MZ twins being more cooperative with each other than were DZ twins. However, this difference did not extend to their cooperation with other children. This suggests that the bond they feel with each other is special and is not simply training for how to behave in general with other children. MZ twins may be more cooperative because they are so much more similar to each other and therefore it is easier for them to work together toward a common goal. They understand each other's styles and they conceptualize the work in more similar ways than do DZ twins.

Comparable studies of twin closeness have not been conducted with infants or preschoolers. It would be very interesting to know at what age twins begin to sense this special bond and to become aware of the presence of another person who is so similar to them and who shares the environment with them. Infants begin to show social referencing and separation anxiety toward the end of their first year of life, demonstrating an awareness of the differences in the people around them. It is likely that it is about the same time that twins, especially MZ twins, might begin to form the special bond between them that becomes the basis for their closeness as they grow.

Although few investigations of twin closeness during infancy have been conducted, twin attachment behavior (a close emotional bond between the twins) has been examined. In 1994, Nathan Gottfried and colleagues demonstrated that the presence of the co-twin served as a source of security during the absence of the mother which is a highly stressful event for this age group (18–34 months). Even though the twins exhibited lower levels of distress when their co-twin was present during the mother's absence, the twins did not actively soothe or comfort each other. This suggests that early co-twin attachment provides some degree of comfort and acts as a buffer in stressful situations experienced during infancy.

Shyness

It is possible that MZ twins are shyer than either DZ twins or nontwins because they are used to interacting with another child, their co-twin, who is genetically the same as them and therefore is probably physically and behaviorally like them. Because they spend so much time with these genetically identical co-twins, they may not learn how to interact with other, different children as well. Therefore, they may feel more uncomfortable with others and show shy behaviors. If this is true, then it also would be expected that DZ twins would be less shy than MZ twins, but they might be shyer than nontwins because they are used to interacting with another child (their co-twin) who is quite similar to them, often more so than other children. However, it is also possible that twins may be less shy than nontwins for the opposite reason. They are used to interacting with another child their same age, and therefore they may feel more comfortable interacting with other children.

Research exploring these two possibilities has been sparse. However, some researchers have studied shyness in twins in order to better understand genetic influences on this behavior (see the section on 'Internalizing behavior') rather than to compare twins to nontwins. One study by Lisabeth DiLalla and colleagues in 1994 noted that 2-year-old MZ twins appear to score higher on measures of shyness than do DZ twins. Another study by Lisabeth DiLalla and Rebecca Caraway in 2004 on 5-year-old children has demonstrated that both MZ and DZ twins behave more shyly than do nontwins when they interact with unfamiliar peers. Thus, twins appear to be shyer than nontwins, perhaps because they are so used to playing with a genetically similar playmate (their co-twin) and therefore are shyer about playing with someone they do not know as well. However, parent ratings actually have shown exactly the opposite trend, with twins being rated as less shy than nontwins. This might be a result of parents seeing their two twins playing together so frequently that when they rate the twins, they imagine them as being fairly outgoing. If this is the reason for the different results, then parent rating biases are playing an important role and it is necessary to consider this carefully whenever parent ratings are utilized. Parent ratings are frequently used when infants and young children are studied, so it is important to be careful about the results that are obtained.

Although there is little scientific evidence concerning how shy twins are, they do appear to be more inhibited when they are interacting with unknown children their same age. This is not consistent with parent reports, but it is enough to suggest that this might be an area that requires further exploration. In addition, parents of twins often are concerned when one twin appears to be much shyer than the other twin. This is an area that has not been addressed in twin research and it also bears further examination.

School Behaviors

One issue that twins but not singleton children experience is whether to place the twins in the same or in different classrooms during the school years. In general, this decision is made by the specific school system that the twins attend and often this decision is made without consulting the opinion of the twins' parents. Legislation has been proposed by a few states such as Minnesota that would require twins to be kept in the same classroom at the parents' request. There are two competing reasons why twins should be kept together or separated in the classroom. Proponents of placing twins in separate classrooms claim that the close social relationship of twins may impede their development by not allowing the growth of their individuality and independence. Conversely, proponents of keeping twins in the same classroom claim that separating twins may be more stressful and lead to distress and emotional difficulties for these twins because it is the first time the twins may have spent a significant amount of time apart. Although educators, the school systems, and parents may have differing opinions about whether or not it is best to separate twins at school, there has been little research conducted to address this debate.

Researchers have focused primarily on the impact of class separation on internalizing behaviors (fear, shyness, withdrawal, depression), externalizing behaviors (aggression, disruptiveness, impulsivity), and academic achievement. Lucy Tully and colleagues examined the impact of placing twins in separate classrooms and found that twins who were placed in different classrooms when they began school exhibited more internalizing problems than those twins who were placed in the same classroom for the first year of school. These internalizing problems persisted over time for MZ twins. This indicates that placing twins in separate classrooms may be more distressing for MZ twins than for DZ twins.

The impact of class separation on externalizing behaviors differs from that of internalizing problem behaviors. There is evidence that twins who are separated do not exhibit more externalizing problems than those twins who were not separated. In 2007, Lisabeth DiLalla and Paula Mullineaux investigated the impact of separating twins on problem behaviors reported by multiple informants. For MZ twins identified with conduct problems (behaviors characterized as noncompliant, aggressive, and rule-breaking) before beginning school, separating these twins actually increases the incidence of conduct and peer problems as rated by teachers and parents. This indicates, at least for conduct and peer problems, that MZ twins may have fewer behavioral problems when placed in the same classroom.

With regard to academic achievement, there appear to be benefits for keeping MZ twins in the same classroom but there are some advantages to separating DZ twins after the first year of school. In 2003, Lacy Tully and colleagues found that MZ and DZ twins who are placed in separate classrooms are likely to have poorer reading abilities than twins who are placed in the same classroom. Later separation in school may be beneficial for DZ twins. When DZ twins are separated after the first year of school, they tend to be rated by teachers as working harder than DZ twins who are placed in the same classroom. Later separation in school may be beneficial for DZ twins. When DZ twins are separated after the first year of school, they tend to be rated by teachers as working harder than DZ twins who are placed in the same classroom. The long-term affects of early separation on academic achievement was examined in 2005 by van Leeuwen and colleagues. No significant differences in academic performance on mathematic and language exams were observed between the groups of twins who always had been separated in school and those twins who had never been separated in school. Interestingly, those twins who had experienced both separation and nonseparation performed the best on the mathematic and language exams.

Overall, research has indicated that separating twins in school may not be beneficial for twins with regard to problem behaviors and academic achievement. In addition, there is some indication that the impact of school separation may differ for MZ and DZ twins. Currently, the research that has been conducted on the effects of classroom separation has focused on the early school years. It is possible that keeping twins in the same classrooms is only beneficial during the early schooling experience. Additional research on the impact of separation during later elementary school and beyond must be conducted to determine if the advantages of keeping twins in the same classrooms persist.

Twin Language

Twins experience a unique childhood because they coexist with a companion (their co-twin) with whom they learn and grow. The twins are at a similar developmental level by virtue of being the same age. The language development of twins is often not the same as singleton children but may lag behind by about 3 months. This has been attributed in part to low birth weight, which is common among twins. Another possible explanation is that twin children have co-twins who are so developmentally and socially intimate that a separate form of communication may arise, possibly interfering with normal language development. This unique form of communication has been termed twin language, criptophasia, autonomous language, and secret language. In the past, the lack of a concrete definition of twin language has made identifying nontraditional language development in twins difficult. 'Private language' and 'shared understanding' are two well-defined terms used in twin language studies. Private language is defined as comprehensible communication solely used between twins. This type of communication has often been called secret language as it is not used to communicate with others. Shared understanding is verbal communication not comprehensible to persons outside the twin pair but comprised of language not used exclusively within the twin pair. Around 40% of twins develop some personal way of communicating with each other. This occurs most frequently with identical twins, which may reflect a closer social relationship between those twins. While the most obvious cases of twin language are verbal adaptations of normal language, many twins also develop nonverbal methods of communicating as well.

The verbal communication that takes place between twins is most often an adaptation of language learned from parents and others in the twins' lives. This type of speech is not a new language altogether as speech often adheres to the sentence structure and grammar of 'normal' language. Twin language has been proposed as a form of immature speech during the process of normal language development. These examples of twin language are seen to emerge during periods when normal language development would take place, around 2 years of age and older. Twins usually grow out of using unique speech. Often, placement of twins in different classrooms or introducing playmates who are capable of normal language enhances normal development. These steps foster language development as twins' lack of interaction with others is thought to increase the likelihood of using twin language.

Social factors have been linked to the development of twin languages. The lack of outside interaction has been shown to contribute to using twin language. Twins who participate in nonverbal play, do not attend preschool, and do not have any older siblings appear to be most likely to use a unique twin language. Nonverbal play is thought to decrease the need for verbalization. Attending preschool and being in the presence of older siblings may act to introduce social forces that require a twin to participate in ordinary language exchanges, thus fostering normal development. A risk factor that may contribute to special twin language development is that twins receive less verbal communication and more nonverbal communication from their mothers than do singletons. Mothers of twins have also been shown to exhibit less affection and more controlling behaviors than do mothers of singletons. This may be a product of a more stressful environment from raising two same-aged children compared to one child. The combination of social isolation and less parental communication may result in the development of a special twin language.

Twin language is a remarkable phenomenon. The fact that a variation of normal language develops between children who are so young, and that it is often incomprehensible to those outside of the twin pair, contributes to the fascinating nature of twin language. Even though this language is often foreign, even to parents of the twins, the language component of this communication indicates a step toward normal language development. The often isolated nature of the social world of twins contributes to the intimate communication that may form between twins. This interesting step in the development of language reflects the unique social and developmental world that twins experience.

Why and How We Use Twins to Study Behavior

Unlike behavioral studies conducted with other species, studies of human behavior are limited to naturally occurring genetic and environmental variation. Fortunately, nature has provided a naturally occurring experimental situation through twinning that can be used to identify the impact of genes and environment on human behavior.

Comparing MZ and DZ Twins

By comparing MZ and DZ twins, we are able to test the relative influence of genes and the environment on human behavior. It is this comparison between MZ and DZ twins that allows us to begin to disentangle the impact of genetic and environmental influences on human behavior. This can be done because MZ twins share 100% of their genes and DZ twins share, on average, 50% of their genes. If genetic influences are important for a particular behavior, then MZ twins will be more similar to each other than are DZ twins for that behavior. If environmental influences are important, then MZ and DZ twins will be fairly similar for that behavior. This is because shared environmental influences impact MZ and DZ twins equally.

There are two basic types of twin studies: twins reared together and twins reared apart. Twins reared together are twins who are not separated and who are raised in the same home. Sometimes twins are separated at birth or shortly thereafter and are adopted into different families and raised in different environments. Twins reared apart still share the same percentage of genes (100% for MZ twins and on average 50% for DZ twins) as twins reared together, but MZ and DZ twins share none of their environment when they are raised apart. Thus, any similarities between twins reared apart would be due to genetic influences, whereas similarities between twins reared together may be due to genes or environmental factors and can only be determined by comparing the two twin types.

Heritability

Heritability (h^2) refers to the amount of phenotypic variation among individuals that is due to genetic influences. This statistic can be roughly estimated by subtracting the DZ twin correlation for a trait from the MZ twin correlation for that trait and doubling the difference. Thus, we can determine whether genes are impacting a behavior and how much they impact that behavior. For example, if the MZ correlation for intelligence quotient (IQ) is 0.86 and the DZ correlation for IQ is 0.60, then roughly 52% (twice the difference between 0.86 and 0.60) of the difference observed among individuals for IQ is attributed to genetic influences. This also tells us that the other ~50% of the differences in IQ scores are due to environmental influences.

Environment

There are two types of environmental influences: shared environment (c^2) and nonshared environment (e^2). Shared environment, also called common environment, includes the aspects of the environment that are shared among twins. By definition, both MZ twins and DZ twins share 100% of their shared environment. This includes environments such as their home environments, neighborhood environments, and school environments. Shared environmental factors are those factors shared by individuals that make them more similar. Conversely, nonshared environment, also called unique environment, refers to aspects of the environment that only one member of the MZ or DZ twin pair experiences and makes the twins less similar to each other. Examples of nonshared environment include one twin experiencing an illness that the other twin does not, having different teachers at school, participating in different activities, and socializing with different friends. Just as with heritability, we can estimate how much impact shared environment (c^2) and nonshared environment (e^2) have on behavior. Shared environmental influences are estimated by subtracting h^2 from the MZ twin correlation. Nonshared environment is estimated by subtracting the MZ twin correlation from 1.0. Any error variance is represented in the nonshared environment estimate. Using the MZ and DZ twins from the above example, where the MZ correlation was 0.86 and the DZ correlation was 0.60, shared environment would explain 34% of the variance in IQ scores and nonshared environment (and any error) would explain 14% of the variance in IQ scores. Heritability (h^2), shared environment (c^2), and nonshared environment (e^2) always equal 1.0, which represents 100% of the genetic and environmental influences impacting a behavior.

Genetic Influences on Environmental Influences

Certain measures traditionally have been believed to represent children's environments (e.g., how often mothers name objects when interacting with infants). However, we now know that there are genetic influences on these measures of the environment. This suggests that parents are responding to differences in children's genetically influenced characteristics and therefore are creating differences in the child's environment that are related to the child's genetic propensities. These are called gene–environment correlations.

The Equal Environments Assumption

One of the most important criticisms of the twin method is that MZ twins may experience a more similar environment than DZ twins. Critics suggest that MZ twins may be treated more similarly because of being labeled as MZ twins and because it is easier to identify MZ twins based on physical appearance than DZ twins. This may cause people to create a more similar environment for them because of the label or their similar appearance. This criticism challenges the 'equal environments assumption' (EEA), which is based on the belief that the environment that MZ twins experience is not significantly more similar than the environment that DZ twins experience. If this assumption is violated because MZ twins experience a more similar environment than that of DZ twins, then the estimate of genetic influence would be overestimated. Several studies have specifically investigated the EEA, and in general the assumption appears to be supported for most behaviors. Likewise, the effects of mislabeling twin pairs (e.g, labeling MZ twins as DZ twins) have shown that zygosity (MZ or DZ) is a better predictor of how similar twin behavior is than parents' perceptions of zygosity.

Gene–Environment Correlation and Interaction

Twin research allows us to consider the extent to which environment and genes affect behaviors. This method was essential for advancing our understanding of behavior, from the belief during most of the twentieth century that all behavior can be attributable to environmental influences to our more recent understanding that our genetic make-up also plays an important part in influencing our behaviors.

However, the picture is much more complicated than we originally thought. The interplay between genotype and environment is difficult to disentangle conceptually and even more difficult to measure. For instance, infants who live in chaotic homes often are more temperamentally difficult. We must ask 'why' these infants are this way. It is possible that their environment is so noisy and unstructured that they respond by behaving in a difficult manner (they may cry more, they may be hard to soothe). However, it is also possible that difficult infants make their parents so tired and anxious that the home environment provided by the parents becomes more chaotic. Finally, it is possible that these infants and their parents share genes that make them difficult in infancy and more chaotic and unstructured in adulthood.

At the basis of this question is the issue of genotype–environment (GE) correlation. These correlations probably occur with most of the behaviors that we study, but they are extremely difficult to measure. There are three types of GE correlations (see **Table 1**). The first is 'passive' GE correlation. This occurs when a child gets both genes and environment from the parent. Infants of course inherit their genotype from their parents, and also they are raised in the home environment that is shaped by their parents. Thus, their genes and their environment are correlated with each other. The second type of GE correlation is called 'reactive' or 'evocative'. This occurs when children behave a certain way that is partly genetically influenced, and then this behavior evokes certain responses from the people around them, thus influencing their environment. Again, in this case the genes and the environment are now correlated with each other. The third type of GE correlation, which does not occur until children are older, is called 'active'. With this, children (or adults) choose a particular environment based in part on personal attributes that are genetically influenced. Once again, genes and environment are correlated with each other when this happens.

One other way in which genes and environment work together is through gene–environment interaction. This happens when people with certain genotypes respond differently to a specific environment than do people with other genotypes. For example, an infant who is temperamentally reactive (partly as a result of genetic

Table 1 Three types of gene–environment correlation

Type of correlation	Definition	Typical ages	Example
Passive	Genes and environment come from the same source (the biological parent)	Birth through adolescence, but most important early in life	Child inherits athletic ability from parent, and parent constantly plays ball with child (thus, genes and environment are correlated)
Active or evocative	Child evokes certain environments from others based in part on his or her genetic make-up	Throughout life	Child is genetically athletically inclined, therefore parents and coaches encourage athletic activities for the child
Active	Child actively seeks environments that match with his or her genetically influenced preferences	Childhood and throughout adulthood	Child is genetically athletically inclined, therefore he or she chooses to attend a college with a strong athletic department

make-up) may be overwhelmed by a chaotic home environment and may cry and fuss quite a lot, whereas an infant who is temperamentally easy may find this same environment to be stimulating or at least may not be bothered by it. Thus, it is not only genes or only environment that cause certain behaviors, but it is also the complex way in which these two influences work together that lead to certain behavioral outcomes.

It is critical to understand genetic effects because if we ignore them then we incorrectly interpret findings of environmental effects as either stronger or weaker than they really are. This has important implications for policies and intervention programs. If we assume that the environment is responsible for making children either aggressive or smart or sociable, but in fact their genetic make-up is also important for these behaviors, then the intervention programs that are designed will be inadequate. Thus, a greater understanding of the ways in which genes and environment work together to lead to behavioral outcomes in children will add important information that we can use when designing programs to help children maximize their potential in all areas.

Twin Study Results on Normal Development

The study of twins allows us to learn more about genetic and environmental influences on various behaviors, including temperament, cognition, and social behaviors. This section details information we have learned about these behaviors in general from studying twins and reviews evidence from twin studies about genetic effects that we believe are generalizable to all children.

Temperament

Experiments with twins have yielded valuable information useful for understanding aspects of personality and development in nontwins as well. One of these areas is temperament, which is a stable, early developing tendency to experience and express emotion in a particular way. For example, children may be perceived as fussy, easygoing, or shy depending on how they respond to everyday situations in life. Temperament is attributed to both biological and environmental factors. Individual biological differences in emotional expression have been based on reactivity and self-regulation. Self-regulation is the active control of emotional expression. Examination of self-regulation measures such as attention, approach, avoidance, and behavioral inhibition (inhibition to new stimuli, or extreme shyness) have indicated that biological influences on temperament are dependent on the child's level of maturation. Physiological measures such as heart rate, cortisol levels, and brain activity have been used to study how reactive children are to new stimuli. In periods of competition, decreased positive emotional expressions are seen in conjunction with increased cortisol levels and increased heart rate. Inhibition in children has also been related to an increase in heart rate during novel situations, suggesting a physiological bias for behavioral inhibition.

Genetic effects on temperament have been studied extensively from infancy to adulthood using twins. Recent research on infants and toddlers has found that many temperamental traits are moderately influenced by genes. In general, negatively valenced traits such as aggression have shown evidence of being largely genetically influenced. Positively valenced traits such as happiness show moderate genetic influence with more environmental effects. Inhibition has shown moderate genetic influence and small effects of the environment, although extreme inhibition has shown very strong genetic effects.

Environmental factors that children experience have also been shown to affect the development of temperament. The main sources of environmental influence on temperament appear to be parent–child relationships. One important aspect of the mother–child relationship is synchrony, which is a state of shared focus, with communal exchanges between interacting partners. Synchronous mother–child pairs rated high on positive emotion and engagement yielded children who were rated as more socially competent. Mother–child pairs rated high on negative emotion and low engagement predicted children who were more aggressive and less socially competent. Mother–child synchrony is beneficial for the child by providing the child a guide for later patterns of social and emotional response. More recently, the emotional impact of such parental relationships has been researched. One twin study found that fearful and pleasurable aspects of temperament in 3–12-month-old children were associated with low or high amounts of parental sensitivity, respectively, as seen in parent–child interactions.

Twins have been invaluable in the study of temperament. They have helped researchers explore the biological, genetic, and environmental effects on temperament. It is through the use of twins that we are able to uncover how these processes unfold in normal human development.

Cognition

Twins also have been instrumental in elucidating the impact of genetic and environmental influences on cognitive ability across the lifespan. By comparing MZ and DZ twins' similarities on measures of cognitive ability over the course of development, we are able to determine whether the impacts of genetic and environmental factors are stable from one age to the next. Genetic influences have been indicated for measures of general cognitive ability with genetic and environmental influences each accounting for, on average, 50% of the observed variance for measures of cognitive ability. Although both genetic and environmental influences impact cognitive ability, the balance between genetic and environmental influences changes over the lifespan. Heritability estimates of cognitive ability appear to increase with age, from less than 20% in infancy, to 40% in early childhood, to 50–60% in early adulthood, and finally increasing to 80% in late adulthood. This indicates that genetic factors become increasingly important for cognitive ability and the impact of environmental influences decreases over the lifespan.

Cognitive ability is considered to be fairly stable over the lifespan. This does not mean that cognitive ability does not change over the course of development or that the cognitive ability of a 6-month-old is the same as that of a 6-year-old. What stability in cognitive ability reflects is the relative constancy of individual differences or the extent that children's rank order in comparison to peers is constant. In general, infants' performance on cognitive measures of novelty preference, memory, and learning spatiotemporal rules is related to their performance on cognitive measures during childhood, although infant measures of sensory and motor skills which reference the infant's developmental level are not highly related to their later performance on cognitive measures during childhood.

Twin studies have also been utilized when examining cognitive growth over time and the changing impact of genetic and environmental influences. Infants' scores on standard measures of cognitive ability are comparable for MZ and DZ twins from 3 to 12 months, which does not suggest genetic influences on these behaviors at these ages. This is also true of some measures of specific cognitive abilities in infants, such as visual anticipation of patterns. However, some other measures of specific cognitive abilities, such as recognition of novel faces, appear to show slightly greater genetic influences. During early childhood, MZ twins begin to perform significantly more similarly than DZ twins on measures of cognitive ability, suggesting new genetic influences. Additionally, Ronald Wilson in 1983 found evidence indicating that the pattern of change in cognitive abilities over time is more similar for MZ twins than for DZ twins, indicating that the spurts and lags experienced during early cognitive growth are being influenced by genes.

The use of twins in studying the development of cognition has led to a better understanding of the impact of genetic and environmental influences on cognitive development.

Externalizing Behaviors

Externalizing behaviors refer to acting out behaviors, such as being aggressive or engaging in delinquent activities (including things such as stealing or vandalizing). Children who engage in these behaviors typically may have more difficulty making friends or fitting in well with society. Children who engage in many of these behaviors often drop out of school or are neglected or rejected by their peers. By understanding the development of problem behaviors, perhaps we can help these children have better and more productive lives in society. Twin research has been valuable in shedding light on some of the causes of externalizing behaviors in children.

Although most research on the genetic effects on externalizing behaviors in children has been conducted on school-aged twins, there is some recent work examining the heritability of externalizing problems in preschoolers and some work specifically on 2- and 3-year-olds. Research on older children, aged 5 and up, mostly suggests that there is a heritable effect on externalizing behaviors, meaning that part of the reason why children either do or do not exhibit externalizing behaviors has to do with their genetic make-up. However, genes only account for about half of the influence on these behaviors. The rest seems to be a result of nonshared environmental influences which are influences that make children less similar to each other. This is counter-intuitive because many have believed that the ways in which parents raise and discipline their children are responsible for behaviors such as aggression. However, the research based on twins does not support this, or, if discipline is an important influence, the twin research suggests that it must vary across children within the same family.

One possible problem with much of the early research on twins and externalizing was that most researchers relied on parent ratings of children's behaviors. It is possible that parent ratings are biased and that parents may rate MZ twins more similarly because they look more alike. Therefore, it is also important to have other types of ratings on children before we can state confidently that externalizing behaviors are genetically influenced. Fortunately, a few recent studies on 5-year-old twins using teacher reports and observational ratings from testers have been conducted. The results of these studies support the earlier work based on parent report, that aggressive behaviors in 5-year-olds do have genetic influence.

The question still remains whether these behaviors are genetically influenced even earlier, especially during the first few years of life. Very few twin studies have examined infants' externalizing behaviors, but these appear to support a genetic influence on these behaviors even at such young ages. One study examining parental ratings of aggression during the second half of the first year of life showed a strong influence of genetic factors on externalizing behaviors. In addition, at ages 2 and 3 years there also appears to be a large influence of genotype on aggressive and acting-out behaviors. Studies from Canada and Denmark have shown this, suggesting that these results are not specific to certain cultures. However, these findings rely on parent ratings. In the future, it will be important to show the same effects using other, unbiased methods of rating children's aggression as well.

Empathy and Prosocial Behaviors

Prosocial behaviors, which include helping, sharing, and caring for others, have been studied much less than problem behaviors, and therefore we know less about them in terms of what causes them. Initial twin studies examing prosocial behaviors indicate a slightly different pattern from externalizing or acting-out behaviors. Although there appear to be genetic influences on prosocial behaviors, there are also notable environmental effects. Because these behaviors are so important for humans, it makes sense that they should be taught and reinforced in the family environment. There is some evidence that the shared family environment is indeed an important influence on prosocial behaviors in young children, which supports this view.

Prosocial behaviors and empathy are difficult to measure in infancy and parent reports are often used. Parent reports are based on behaviors such as showing concern when another is hurt and offering to help another person. However, as with externalizing problems, parent reports may be subject to rater bias, with parents rating MZ twins more similarly than DZ twins. Thus, it is always important to utilize other sources, such as behavioral ratings of twins by trained coders.

In the MacArthur Longitudinal Twin Study, researchers Carolyn Zahn-Waxler, Joann Robinson, and colleagues have attempted to examine empathy in infants from 1 to 3 years of age by observing infant twins' responses to their mothers' demonstrations of pain, such as pretending to hurt her foot. They also observed twins' responses to hearing another child cry. Whether or not these behaviors are equivalent to more mature versions of empathy is uncertain. However, the researchers did find that MZ twins responded more similarly to each other than did DZ twins, suggesting a genetic influence on these behaviors. These results were not corroborated by parent reports of empathetic behaviors of the infants, which failed to show evidence of genetic influence on empathy.

Thus, there is still much to learn about the causes of empathy and prosocial behaviors using twins. There is evidence that genotype has an impact on these behaviors. However, until further research is conducted, using multiple methods of assessment, we cannot be certain about these findings. As with externalizing problem behaviors, it is most likely that the reason that genotype is a significant influence on prosocial behaviors is via the link with temperament. It is probable that genotype influences temperament, which in turn manifests a direct influence on both problem and prosocial behaviors in children.

Internalizing Behavior

From birth, infants interact differently with the world around them. Some infants respond and interact with others freely. Other infants will warm up to others only after a period of time. There are also those infants who never warm up to others and are withdrawn and timid in social situations. Shyness and inhibition are precursors of a child's developing personality during childhood.

Being shy or inhibited can last into the early childhood years. A general trend has been found for children to become less inhibited as they age, displaying better inhibitory control. Studies on twins have shown that behavioral inhibition can be attributed to both genetic and environmental factors. The genetic component of inhibition and shyness also contributes to its stability over time. In twin studies, behavioral measures of shyness for children have shown a moderate correlation with later inhibition in different situations. Also, inhibited behavior between MZ twins has been observed to be more similar than that of DZ twins. This suggests that shyness is a cross-situational attribute that has consistency across age. Changes in inhibition are thought to be mediated by normal child development and environmental factors.

The discontinuity of inhibition is also proposed to have a genetic influence as normal child development is in part genetically driven. The concordance of change in the behaviors of MZ twins, including shyness, is more similar than that of DZ twins. The similarity in the pattern of change between MZ twins suggests that this change is genetically driven by developmental processes. Other environmental factors such as parenting and traumatic episodes have also been observed to contribute to child inhibition.

In contrast to normal inhibition, extreme inhibition has shown a very high estimate of genetic influence. This suggests that it is a separate construct from normal shyness, possibly related to other disorders such as social phobia or obsessive–compulsive disorder. The twin literature has shown that such extreme inhibition is also a more stable trait over time. Children identified as very inhibited early in life are more likely also to be very inhibited later in life. The presence of genetic effects on extreme inhibition is quite clear. Work with twins has led researchers to study promising causes of this behavior. The serotonin transporter promoter region polymorphism gene (a gene that regulates serotonin expression) is one possible cause of inhibited behavior. This gene has both a long and a short form. The long form of this gene has been associated with shyness in children. Other genes have been proposed to relate to inhibition and anxiety-related behaviors, but less support is present. These behaviors might have a number of genes that influence behavior rather than one key gene. As findings from molecular genetic studies become clearer, so will the role that genes have on behavior.

Twin studies have also shown that physiological measures of temperament relate to inhibition. Measures of heart rate, cortisol levels, and brain activity have shown that extremely inhibited children have a physiological propensity to be behaviorally inhibited. Physiological reactions related to shyness might produce the actual feelings that account for inhibition behavior and feelings. Behavioral inhibition is thought to be linked to physiological reactions through stress-sensitive systems that govern reaction to environmental stimuli in inhibited children. Specifically, inhibited children have been shown to have higher heart rates as well as less variable heart rates in general. The role of the sympathetic and parasympathetic nervous systems have been proposed as factors in inhibition as well.

Through the use of twins, researchers have been able to study the genetic, environmental, and physiological bases of many forms of behavior. As research continues, knowledge of genetic and environmental contributions to psychological behaviors can be pinpointed. With the use of molecular genetic research, the field of twin research will move closer to understanding the impact specific genes may have on various behaviors.

Summary

Twins have always intrigued us, and they continue to fascinate psychology researchers today. Twins are interesting both in their own right as human beings growing up together, and also as a natural experiment for researchers interested in understanding genetic and environmental influences on development. Because there are two types of twins – MZ, who share 100% of their genes, and DZ, who share on average 50% of their genes – these two types can be compared to obtain estimates of the genetic and environmental influences on behaviors. There is speculation about individual characteristics of twins, such as why they seem to be more shy, more psychologically close to each other, and more likely to form special languages, but we are only beginning to examine these aspects of twins in infancy. There is still much to learn about the secrets of being a twin.

See also: Genetics and Inheritance; Language Development: Overview.

Suggested Readings

DiLalla LF (ed.) (2004) *Behavior Genetic Principles: Perspectives in Development, Personality, and Psychopathology.* Washington: APA Press.

Segal N (1999) *Entwined Lives: Twins and What They Tell Us about Human Behavior.* New York: Dutton Books.

Segal N (2005) *Indivisible by Two: Lives of Extraordinary Twins.* Boston, MA: Harvard University Press.

Thorpe K and Danby S (2006) Special section on the social worlds of children who are twins. *Twin Research and Human Genetics* 9(1): 90–174.

SUBJECT INDEX

This index is in letter-by-letter order, whereby hyphens and spaces within index headings are ignored in the alphabetization, and it is arranged in set-out style with a maximum of three levels of heading. Major discussion of a subject is indicated by a bold page range.

A

Abstract reasoning/abstraction 385
   constructions 195, 199
      holophrases, development from 193
      item-based, from 201
Academic achievement/performance
   race 439
   socioeconomic status effect 439
   twins 511–512
   See also Education; Learning; Schools/schooling
Accommodation
   definition 381
   Piaget's cognitive-developmental theory 388
Accumulator model 122
   See also Mathematical reasoning
Action
   coordination *See* Coordination
   goal-directed 370, 374
   perception and *See* Perception-action coupling
   See also Behavior; Motor development; Reflex(es)
Action system(s)
   definition 357, 369
   object concept 363
   See also Object concept
Active intermodal mapping (AIM), imitation 251
Adaptation/adaptive behavior
   accommodation 381, 388
   assessment 259
   assimilation 381, 388
   definition 256, 259
   intellectual disability 258–259
   Piaget's cognitive-developmental theory 388
Adaptive response, perception–action coupling 371
ADHD *See* Attention deficit hyperactivity disorder (ADHD)
Adjustment
   for prematurity
      Bayley Scales of Infant Development 37, 41, 44
   See also Adaptation/adaptive behavior
Adolescence
   critical periods 138
   prefrontal cortex development, behavior and 132
Adoption studies, behavioral genetics 186
Adult joking behavior, humor development as child 231–232
Adult social skills, early humor experiences 231
Advocacy, Head Start program 222
A-elements, infant learning 297
Afferent(s), definition 65
Affordance 373
   definition 369
   locomotion development 373–374
Agent, definition 456
Agent-patient relations
   agreement 197
   case 197
   definition 192
   grammar 195–196
   word order 196
Aggleton, John, habituation and novelty 213
Aggression
   genetic studies
      twin studies 515
Agreement
   agent-patient relations 197
   definition 192
Agreement-Tense Omission Model (ATOM), language development 283
Akhtar, Nameera
   semantic development 460–461
   word order 196

Allocentric reasoning *See* Object concept
Alphabetic principle, definition 301
Al-Sayyid Bedouin Sign Language (ABSL) 273
American Association of Mental Retardation (AAMR) 257
American Sign Language (ASL), acquisition, fMRI studies 130
Amnion, twins 508
Amodal information *See* Intermodal perception
Analogical reasoning *See* Reasoning
Analogy
   grammar 201
   reasoning processes 121
   See also Reasoning
Anderson, Daniel, attention 34
Angelman syndrome 184–185
A-not-B error *See under* Object concept
Anthropological theory, humor development 231
Anticipatory eye movements, perception–action coupling 379
Antisocial behavior
   heritability of traits 189
   See also Aggression
Anxiety
   8-month 468
      See also Stranger anxiety
   definition 466
   separation *See* Separation anxiety
   stranger-related *See* Stranger anxiety
Apoptosis, postnatal brain development 75
Approximate magnitude system, mathematical reasoning 316, 318, 323
Archaic reflexes *See* Primitive reflexes (PRs)
Architectonics 68, 68f
   definition 65
Argument, definition 192
Arnheim, Rudolf 14
Arousal
   attention 28
      brain areas controlling 28, 28f
      See also Attention
   habituation 209
   novelty 210
Articulation, disorders 150
Artistic development **12–26**
   divergent interpretations 22
   drawings 12
      color 16
      composition 17, 18f
      expression of feelings 17
      form 13f, 15, 16f
      motivation 17
      space 15
      tadpole figures 12, 13f
   intellectual realism 12, 14
   mentally handicapped children 20
   Piaget's theory 14
   sculpture 22
      animal figures 24, 24f
      human figures 22, 23f, 24f
   sociocultural influences 21
   synthetic incapacity 14
   talent/giftedness 19, 20f, 21f
Asperger syndrome (AS)
   heritability 189
   See also Autism spectrum disorders (ASD)
Assimilation
   definition 381
   Piaget's cognitive-developmental theory 388
Association areas
   autobiographical memory 6
   postnatal development 77

Associative learning
   conditioning *See* Conditioning
   imitation 249
Attachment/attachment theory
   critical periods 139
   disorder *See* Reactive attachment disorder (RAD)
   exploratory behavior facilitation 165–166
   secure
      curiosity facilitation 161
   separation anxiety and 471, 472
      See also Separation anxiety
   Strange Situation paradigm *See* Strange Situation paradigm
   theory of mind development 504
   twins 510
Attachment disorder *See* Reactive attachment disorder (RAD)
Attention **26–36**, 209
   arousal 28
      brain areas controlling 28, 28f
      See also Arousal
   assessment
      psychophysiological measures 29
         electrophysiological 31, 32f
         heart rate 29, 30f
   definition 26
   developmental research 27
   early childhood 27
      changes 27
   endogenous attention 29
   executive (selective) *See* Executive attention
   focused *See* Executive attention
   habituation and novelty 209
   historical aspects 209
   individual differences 35
   infancy 27
      changes 27
      recognition memory 31
   joint *See* Joint attention
   newborns 27
   orientation 28
   recognition memory, infantile 31
   selective *See* Executive attention
   semantic development and 461
   sustained *See* Sustained attention
   termination 31
   visual *See* Visual attention
Attention deficit hyperactivity disorder (ADHD) 36, 184
   clinical features
      mental developmental disabilities 148–149
   genetics
      heritability 189
   subtypes 36
   theory of mind development 505
Audiovisual perception, language development 481
Auditory perception
   pitch perception
      speech 415, 416f
      See also Speech perception
Auditory preference procedure, speech preference research 483, 484
Autism *See* Autism spectrum disorders (ASD)
Autism spectrum disorders (ASD) 151
   behavior patterns 153
   core deficits 152
      language/communication impairment 153
      restricted activities 153
      social competence 152
   definition 125
   diagnosis 152
      tools 152

519

Autism spectrum disorders (ASD) (continued)
  etiology 151
  genetic factors
    heritability 189
  imitation 255
  language
    impairment 153
    management 153
  self-knowledge development 447
  theory of mind development 505
Autistic spectrum disorders See Autism spectrum disorders (ASD)
Autobiographical memory 454
  characteristics 2
  definition 1–2
  development
    basic memory processes 7
    infantile amnesia and 9
      crossover between formation and loss 10, 10f
      rate of formation 9
      rate of loss (forgetting) 10
    language/narrative expression and 8
    neural substrates 6, 6f
      association areas 6
      hippocampus 6
      temporal cortex 7
    nonmnemonic abilities and 7
      autonoetic awareness 8
      self concept 7–8
    social context of remembering 8
  early life events 5
  language expression 8
  narrative expression 8
  parental elaboration 454, 455
  parental reminiscing 454, 455
  routine events 455
  scripts use, cognitive milestones, 24-36 months 345
  self-knowledge 454
  social construction 455
  See also Episodic memory
Autobiographical self knowledge 454
Automatic reflexes See Primitive reflexes (PRs)
Autonoetic awareness
  autobiographical memories 8
  definition 1
Autonomous language 512
Autosomal disorders 183
Auxilary, definition 192
Axon(s)
  retraction, postnatal brain development 73, 74f
  See also Synapse(s)

B

Baby Facial Action Coding System, emotional distress assessment 471
Bahrick, Lorraine, visual recognition memory paradigm 328
Baillargeon, Renee 359
Balance scale
  cognitive development 122–123
  neural net model 123, 123f
Baldwin, Dare, word learning 460
Basal rules, Bayley Scales of Infant Development 37, 40, 43
Bayley, Nancy 37–38
Bayley Scales of Infant Development (BSID) 37–48
  aims 37–38
  basal rules 37, 40, 43
  Behavior Observation Inventory 45
  Behavior Rating Scale 42
  California First-Year Mental Scale 39, 40, 42
    items 43
    task aims 39–40
  California Infant Scale of Motor Development 39, 40, 42
    items 43
    task aims 39–40
  California Preschool Mental Scale 39
  ceiling rules 37, 40, 43
  CNS injury risk groups 41, 45–46, 46f, 47f
  Cognitive Scale 45
  contemporary research use 45
  definition 37–38
  first edition (BSID-I) 39
    administration 40
    critiques 43
    early development 39
    predictive validity 43
    structure 43, 45
  Flynn effect 44
  historical background 38
  Infant Behavior Record 39, 40
  intellectual disability 261
  Mental Index 112–113
  premature birth, adjustment for 37, 41, 44
  prenatal alcohol exposure 264
  research use 45
  school readiness 437
  second edition (BSID-II) 42
    administration 45–46
    aims 42
    critiques 43
    structure 43
    standardization 37, 42
    theoretical basis 38–39, 45–46
  third edition (BSID-III) 44
    aims 44–45
    structure 45
Baysian inference framework, language acquisition 271
Beer, Jeremy, birth order 61
Behavior
  genetic factors See Behavior genetics
  means-ends, Means–end behavior/thinking
  origins, explanatory theories 348
  perceptual control See Perception-action coupling
  prediction, theory of mind 498
  structural brain development and 131–132
  See also entries beginning behavior/behavioral
Behavioral phenotype(s), definition 256
Behavioral problems, theory of mind development 505
Behavior genetics, designs and methods 185
Behaviorism/behaviorist theory
  future orientation See Future orientation
  history 349–350
  infant learning 291
  language acquisition 268
  language development 288
  nativism and 349
Behavior Observation Inventory 45
Behavior Rating Scale 42
B-elements, infant learning 297
Berkeley Growth Study 39
Bernstein, Nikolai Aleksandroich, motor programs 369–370
Between-family research, definition 58
Big five personality traits, definition 58
Bilingual first language acquisition 48
Bilingualism 48–58
  babbling in infants 53
  cognitive development 57
  early differentiation 49
    auditory preference procedure 49, 50f
    orientation latencies 49
    orientation to maternal language 50, 50f
  phonetic categories 51, 52f
    parallel phoneme systems 51
    perceptual reorganization 51
    phoneme contrasts 51, 54
  preverbal stage 49
  word learning 53
    electrophysiological measures 55
    mispronunciation 54
    morphosyntax 56
      cross-linguistic transfer 56–57
      VO-word order 56
    semantics 55
      disambiguation tasks 55–56
      lexical-referent pairings 56
      translation equivalent acquisition 56
  vocabulary size 55
  word form 54
  word segmentation (phonotactics) 53
  See also Language development
Binary relation, cognitive development 118
Binding problem
  definition 247
  imitation 249
Binet, Alfred 38, 219–220
Binet intelligence tests 14
Biological insult, mental retardation 259
Birth order 58–65
  contrasting mechanisms 61
  definition 58
  gender 64
  historical perspectives 58
  infantile amnesia 3
  intellectual development 59, 62
  personality effects 63
  research design 62
  social development 58, 62
  stereotype effects 63
  theories 60
    confluence model 60
    family niche theory 61
    parental feedback theory 60
    prenatal hypomasculinization theory 61
    resource dilution model 60
Black-White test score gap 439
Blake, Judith, birth order 60
'Blame assignment' procedure, grammar 200–201
Blindness, theory of mind development 505
Bloom, Benjamin, critical periods 143
Bloom, Lois, semantic development 458–459
Bodily awareness 447
Body development, perception-action coupling and 371
Body-environment interaction, perception-action coupling and 373
Body movements, sensitivity, perception-action coupling 372
Body schema 448
Book reading
  joint See Joint book reading
  storybooks and fantasy 244
  See also Imagination/fantasy
  See also Literacy; Reading
Bootstrapping
  definition 456
  pragmatic development See Pragmatic development
  speech perception See Speech perception
Bower experiments, object concept 361f
Bowlby, John
  critical periods 139
  See also Attachment/attachment theory
Brain
  cortex See Cerebral cortex
  development See Brain development
  functional plasticity 88, 90
    developmental See Developmental neuroplasticity
  injury/damage See Brain injury
  size 72, 126
  social 127
    development See Social brain development
'Brain architecture,' critical periods 143
Brain development 65–79
  cognitive perspective 66, 126
    language See Language acquisition
    postnatal effects 70
    regressive events and 74
  cortical layers 66, 67f
    disorders of 67
    GABAergic neurons 66–67
    neuronal migration 66–67
    preplate and temporary layers 67
    synaptogenesis 67
  cortical organization 66
  critical periods 143
    GABAergic neurons and 66–67, 71–72
    visual development 71

disorders *See* Developmental disorders
functional development/differentiation 68, **79–90**
   architectonics 68, 68f, 69
   connections/circuit formation 68f, 69
      cortical 67f, 69
      synaptogenesis 67
   face perception 83, 83f
      See also Face perception/processing
   functional specificity 68f, 69
   genetic *vs.* epigenetic influences 69
   interactive specialization theory 80, 89
   language acquisition *See* Language development
   long-term memory 86, 87f
   neocortical area definition 68, 68f
   plasticity 79, 88, 90
   protomap *vs.* protocortex hypotheses 69
   skill learning 81
   specialization 80
      theories 83f
   studies, event-related potentials 81t, 84, 89
   study methods 81t, 84
   theories 80
   topography 68–69, 68f
   working memory 85, 85f
   See also Developmental neuroplasticity
gross development 126
growth 72
gyri/sulci 126
historical aspects 66, 68, 70, 72, 73
maturation, stranger anxiety and 468
neural induction and neurulation 66–67
neuroimaging 76
   caveats 76
   functional MRI 77
   structural MRI 77
   white matter/myelination 73
overview 66
plasticity *See* Developmental neuroplasticity
postnatal *See* Postnatal brain development
Braine, Martin, theory of mental logic 429
Brain injury
   children *vs.* adults 76, 77
   neurogenesis induction 72
   neuroplasticity and *See* Neuroplasticity
   oligodendrocyte vulnerability 73
   reorganization 142
Braugh, John, imitation 255
Brazelton, Berry, imitation 249
Broad sense heritability 185
Broca aphasia, definition 65
Broca, Paul, functional cortical areas 68
Broca's area, 'pre-wiring,' 129
Brodmann, Korbinian, architectonics 68
Bronbenbrenner, Urie 218
Brown, Malcolm, habituation and novelty 213
Burack, Jake, intellectual disability 260

C

California First-Year Mental Scale *See* Bayley Scales of Infant Development
California Infant Scale of Motor Development *See* Bayley Scales of Infant Development
California Preschool Mental Scale 39
Canalization/canalized behavior 354
   definition 134, 267, 347
Candidate gene approach, quantitative trait loci 187
Candy Witch 244
Canonical babbling, bilingual infants 53
CANTAB (Cambridge neuropsychological Testing Automated Battery), prefrontal cortex development and 132
Capsula interna, maturation, stranger anxiety and 468
Cardinality, definition 102
Carlson, Stephanie, Less is More task 492
Cartesian Dualism 348–349
Case
   agent-patient relations 197
   definition 192
Case marking 197

Case, Robbie, cognitive development 117
Catalan-Spanish bilinguals
   differentiation 50
   mispronunciations 54
   phoneme contrasts 51, 53f
Catching, future oriented processes 173
Categorical coverage, reasoning 424
Categorical perception, definition 409
Categories
   definition 91, 92
   formation process *See* Categorization
   hierarchical organization 92–93
   importance of 91
   infants use of 96
      averaging (prototypes) 99
      child-basic categories 100
      problems of interpretation 97
   labels and 92
   measurement 93
      multiple habituation *See* Multiple habituation
      sequential touching 96, 96f
   object features 92
Categorization **91–102**
   as 6-12 month cognitive milestone 342
   definition 91, 92
   faces *See* Face categorization
   infants 96
      adult-defined categories and 97
      development 101
         qualitative changes over time 96–97
         timing 96
      errors 98–99, 100
      faces 93–94
      infant behavior analysis and 100–101
      new framework for 100
      problems of interpretation 97
      processes 98
         correlated attributes 99
         dynamic 100
         exampler representations 99
         prototypes 99
         summary representations 98
   measurement 93
      multiple habituation *See* Multiple habituation
      sequential touching 96, 96f, 101
   object groups 92
   referents 91
   as single *vs.* multiple process 92
   See also Concepts
Categorization errors 98–99, 100
Causality, cognitive milestones, 6-12 months 341
Ceiling rules, Bayley Scales of Infant Development 37, 40, 43
Cell death, postnatal brain development 75
Centers for Disease Control and Prevention (CDC), racial significance, school readiness 439
Central fixation procedure, speech preference research 483–484
Central nervous system (CNS)
   development *See* Neurological development
   injury
      Bayley Scales of Infant Development 41, 45–46, 46f, 47f
      See also Brain injury
   See also Brain
Cerebral cortex
   classification of areas 68
   definition 79, 125
   development *See* Brain development
   functional organization 68
      defining areas 68
      historical aspects 68
   functional specialization 80
      theories 83f
   interactive specialization 80, 89
   prenatal organization 66
      See also Brain development
   social brain areas 127
   See also entries beginning cortico-/cortical
Cerebral palsy (CP), oligodendrocyte vulnerability and 73

Chapman, Michael, cognitive development 117
Child-basic categories 100
Child-by-instruction interactions, definition 433
Child-care, school readiness and 440
Child Development Associate (CDA) Program 221
   definition 217
Child Development Group of Mississippi 220–221
Child-directed speech (CDS)
   noun use 280
   vocabulary size relationship 279
   See also Language development
Childers, Jane, noun bias 463
CHILDES database *See* Child Language Data Exchange System (CHILDES)
Child factors, school readiness 435
Childhood amnesia *See* Infantile amnesia
Child Language Data Exchange System (CHILDES) 268
   deductive reasoning studies 429
   representational mapping 111
Child obesity *See* Obesity
Child-parent relationship(s)
   mothers *See* Mother-child relationship
   temperament and, twin studies 515
   See also Family/families
Children's Defense Fund (CDF) 221
Child temperament *See* Temperament
Chomsky, Noam
   behaviorist account of language 268–269
   grammar 193
   language acquisition 291
CHRM2 gene 188
Chromosomal disorders 184
   transmission 183
Chromosome(s) 182, 183f
   abnormalities *See* Chromosomal disorders
   definition 181
Classical conditioning
   anticipatory heart-rate changes 177
   definition 290, 325
   infant capacity for 338–339
   infant learning 291
Class inclusion
   cognitive development 118–119, 118f
   concept 117
Classroom humor 236
Classroom instruction, literacy 309
Classroom-*versus*-student level dimension, literacy 310–311
Clumsiness *See* Dyspraxia (motor planning problems)
Cluttering, mental developmental disabilities 150
Cochlear implants, critical periods 141
Code-focused instruction, literacy 310
Code-*versus*-meaning-focused instruction, literacy 310
Cognition
   brain development and 66, 70, 126
      neuroimaging 76
      postnatal regressive events 74
      See also Brain development; Developmental cognitive neuroscience
   definition 114
   development of *See* Cognitive development
   heritable aspects 188
   twin studies 515
Cognitive ability, heritability 188
Cognitive appraisal, humor development 233–234
Cognitive complexity 117–118, 119
Cognitive defects/disorders
   assessment 149
   perinatal stroke and 75
   See also Cognitive development
Cognitive development **102–114**
   assessment, Bayley Scales *See* Bayley Scales of Infant Development
   behavior interpretation 107f
   child temperament influence 113
   concrete operational period 14
   context and 103
   cultural input 116
   curiosity *See* Curiosity

Cognitive development (*continued*)
　décalage 105
　emotion and 112
　environmental influences 112
　exploration *See* Exploration/exploratory behavior
　future orientation *See* Future orientation
　humor 233
　implicit *vs.* explicit cognition 119
　internal states and 112
　ladders and staircases concept of 103
　milestones *See* Cognitive milestones
　newborn skill levels 104*t*
　　numeracy 108
　　perspective taking 110
　　physical causality 106
　numeracy *See* Numeracy
　perspective taking *See* Perspective taking
　physical causality *See* Physical causality development
　physical world, understanding 122
　preoperational period 14
　reflex skill levels 104*t*
　　mapping 106, 110
　　numeracy development 108
　　perspective taking 110
　　physical causality development 107
　　single representations 107
　sensorimotor skill levels 104*t*
　　actions 105, 106, 108, 110
　　mapping 104*t*, 106, 109, 110
　　numeracy development 108
　　perspective taking 110
　　physical causality development 106
　　systems 104*t*, 106, 109, 110–111
　skill domains 103, 104*t*
　skill levels 104*t*
　　contextual effects 103
　　process of development 105
　skill testing 112–113
　stages 115
　theories of *See* Cognitive developmental theories
　theory of mind and *See* Theory of mind (ToM)
　variation 102–103
　　across children 112
　　adaptations 113
　　within children 112
　　cultural 113
　　perturbations 113
　　timing 112
　web concept of 103, 103*f*
Cognitive developmental theories **114–125**
　complexity theories 117
　infants 121
　mental states, knowledge of 119
　microgenetic analysis 120
　nativist perspective *See* Nativism
　Neo-Piagetian theories 117
　neuroscience approaches 124
　Piaget, Jean 115
　　See also Piaget's cognitive-developmental theory
　reasoning processes 121
　Vygotsky, Lev 115
　　See also Vygotsky's sociocultural theory
Cognitive domain, Head Start Impact Study 225
Cognitive dysfunction *See* Cognitive defects/disorders
Cognitive flexibility, definition 485
Cognitive function, defects *See* Cognitive defects/disorders
Cognitive growth, twin studies 516
Cognitive milestones **337–346**, 339*t*
　0-1 month 338
　　basic learning processes 338
　　recognition memory 338
　1-6 months 339
　　knowledge of objects/events 340
　　perceptual categorization 340
　　recognition memory 339
　6-12 months 340
　　causality 341
　　conceptual categorization 342
　　egocentric spatial framework 342

　　explicit memory 341
　　human agency 341
　　implicit memory 341
　　long-term memory 341
　　means-ends problem solving 342
　　object concept 341
　　planning 342
　　short-term memory 340
　　word meanings 342
　12-18 months 343
　　analogical problem solving 344
　　human agency 343
　　long-term memory 343
　　pictorial competence 344
　　pretense 344
　　word production 343
　18-24 months 344
　　desire in others 345
　　self-recognition 344
　　strategic memory 344
　　tool use 345
　24-36 months 345
　　autobiographical memory, scripts use 345
　　models as symbols 345
　　pictorial competence 345
　　pretense 346
　　sociodramatic play 346
　research challenges 346
Cognitive neuroscience
　definition 26
　of infant and child development *See* Developmental cognitive neuroscience
Cognitive Scale 45
Cognitive skills development *See* Cognitive development
Cognitive stability, twin studies 516
Cognitive stimulation, school readiness 442
Cognitive theory, play 397
Colombo, John, look duration 33–34
Color perception 487
Columbia University Mailman School of Public Health (CUMSPH) 225–226
Combination, language acquisition 272–273
Communication 400
　definition 399
　gesture use *See* Gestures/gesturing
　linguistic *See* Language development
　pragmatics *See* Pragmatic development
　speech perception *See* Speech perception
　See also Language
Communication theory, humor development 231
Communicative development inventory (CDI)
　bilingualism 55
　definition 48
Comparator model, habituation and novelty 207
Competence and intrinsic motivation theories of curiosity 157, 158, 159
Competent infant theory 107*f*, 350
Complexity theories, cognitive development 117
Complex polygenic traits 185
Comprehension skills
　definition 301
　development 278, 404
　　context dependence 279
　　definition 399
　　phonological template 279
　first words 457
　number 321
　　See also Mathematical reasoning
　pragmatic development 404
　reading 307
　strategies 308*t*
　types, discrimination between 457
Comprehensive Child Development Program (CCDP) 223
　aims 223
　school readiness 441
Concepts **91–102**
　definition 91, 93
　difficulties/controversy 93
　importance of 91

　infants use of 96
　　nature of 97
　　obtaining evidence for 93
　　problems of interpretation 97
　measurement 93
　　multiple habituation *See* Multiple habituation
　　sequential touching 96, 96*f*
　static *vs.* dynamic nature 100
　See also Categorization
Conceptual chunking 118
Concrete operational period, cognitive development 14
Concrete operational thought
　definition 381
　Piaget's cognitive-developmental theory 384, 389
Conditional probability, speech perception 418
Conditional truth-table, reasoning 428–429, 429*t*
Conditioned Head Turn procedure, speech perception research 410, 412*t*
Conditioning
　classical (Pavlovian) *See* Classical conditioning
　definition 88
　operant (instrumental) *See* Operant conditioning
Conduct disorder (CD) 189
Confluence model, birth order 60, 61
Congenital blindness, self-knowledge development 447
Conjoined twins 509
　definition 508
　incidence 509
Conjugate reinforcement 329
CONLERN process, face perception mechanisms 83–84
Connectionist accounts, language acquisition 270
Conscious thinking 486–487, 486*f*
Conservation
　cognitive development 115
　definition 102, 381, 384
　dynamic systems theory 120
　tasks, Piaget's cognitive-developmental theory 389
CONSPEC process, face perception mechanisms 83–84
Constrained invention, language acquisition 272
Constrained learning, language acquisition 270
Constraint theories, semantic development 459
Constructivist theory
　definition 157, 381
　humor development 232
　language development 282–283, 283*t*, 285–286, 288
　nativism theoretical origins 350
　Piaget's cognitive-developmental theory 350, 382
　theory of mind development 506*t*, 507
　Vygotsky's sociocultural theory *See* Vygotsky's sociocultural theory
Contagion, imitation 248
Contingent negative variation (CNV), S1-S2 paradigm 177
Contrastive evidence, definition 347, 353
Control, definition 369
Controlled attention *See* Executive attention
Control theory 117–118
　cognitive development 119
Conventional symbols, definition 399
Conversation
　future orientation processes 175
　meaningful nature 429
　metalinguistic skills 286
　pragmatics development
　　extended discourse 407
　　proto-conversation 401
　　rhetorical skills 286
　scaffolding 286
　semantic development and 461
　turn-taking 407
Cooke, Robert 218
Cooperative behavior, twins 510
Coordination 374
　crawling 372
　definition 369
　development 371
　leg movements 377

spatiotemporal 374
See also Perception-action coupling
Core systems, mathematical reasoning 315
Corpus, definition 267
Correlated attributes
  definition 91
  infants 99
Cortical development See Brain development
Cortical plate 67
Cortico-cortical connections, developmental trajectories 74–75
Cortisol, emotional distress assessment 471
Counting See Numeracy
Count noun
  definition 456
  mass noun, distinction 462
Courage, Mary, look duration 34
Crawling
  coordination 372
  object concept, search behavior 364
Creating a 21st Century Head Start 222
Criminal justice system, genetic information 191
Criptophasia 512
Critical moment, definition 134, 136
Critical (sensitive) periods **134–145**, 218
  alternative conceptions 138
  basic concepts 135
  brain development 136, 143
    GABAergic neurons and 66–67, 71–72
    visual development 71
    See also Brain development
  definition 134, 135, 136
  education and learning 144
    school transition 138
    teachable moments 144
  environmental toxins 135, 140
  events 144
  history 135
  human studies 139
    cochlear implants 141
    ethics 140
    institutionalization 140
    language development 141
    prenatal sex determination 140
  implications for early childhood 139
  imprinting 136
  negative life experiences 135
  newborn screening and 142
  possible mechanisms
    experience-expectant processes 137
    synaptic elimination 137, 138
    See also Developmental neuroplasticity
  species specificity 136–137
  stem cells 135–136
  stimulation 137
  terminology 135
  timing 141
    importance 142
    literacy development 141–142
Cross-linguistic transfer, bilingualism 56–57
Crying, emotional organization and 469
Culture
  cognitive mediation through 113
    See also Vygotsky's sociocultural theory
  infantile amnesia 3
  parenting style See Parenting styles
  pretend play differences 239–240
  theory of mind development and 505
Curiosity **157–167**
  definitions 157
  development
    facilitation 160
    importance 166
    progression 160
  developmental skills associated 162
  interrelationship with exploration 166
  manifestation 160
  theories of 158
    competence and intrinsic motivation 157, 158, 159
    drive 157, 158

incongruity 157, 158, 159
Piaget's cognitive-developmental 159
types 159, 160
See also Exploration/exploratory behavior

D

Day care See Child-care
DCD2 (doublecortin domain containing 2) gene 188
Deafness See Hearing loss
Décalage
  cognitive development 105
  definition 102
Decety, Jean, imitation 255
Declarative (explicit) memory 210
  cognitive milestones, 6-12 months 341
  definition 79, 86–87, 205, 210–211, 337
  episodic See Episodic memory
  functional brain development 87, 87f
  implicit dissociations 214
  semantic
    definition 86–87
  visual paired comparison task 87
Decoding, definition 301
Deduction See Reasoning
Deferred circular reactions, object concept 358
Deferred imitation 87–88, 250, 251–252, 252f, 333, 334f
Deictic gestures 402
  definition 399
Dejerine, Joseph Jules, functional cortical areas 68
Delay of gratification task, symbolic thought 492
Dentate gyrus, autobiographical memory 6
Denver Developmental Screening Test 148
Deoxyribonucleic acid (DNA) 182
  markers
    definition 181
    single-gene disorders 185
  See also Gene(s)
Depth perception, 'visual cliff' experiment 373, 373f
Descartes, Rene 348–349, 360–361
Desimone Robert, habituation and novelty 214
Developmental cognitive neuroscience **125–134**
  aims 89
  applications 79–80
  brain development See Brain development
  definition 79
  developmental disorders and 125
  domains 127
    frontal cortex functions 131
    language/speech development 129
    social brain development 127
  functional imaging and 125
Developmental delay 147
  humor development 230
  phenylketonuria 86
Developmental disorders
  cognitive neuroscience and 125
  fragile X syndrome 73
  language disorders See Developmental language disorders
  neocortical development
    lissencephaly 67
    periventricular heterotopia 67
  neuroimaging, white matter/myelination development 73
  white matter/myelination development
    neuroimaging 73
    periventricular leukomalacia (PVL) 73
Developmental dyscalculia (DD) 315, 322–323
Developmental dyslexia, neuronal migration and 67–68
Developmental language disorders 149
  diagnosis 150
  outcome 151
  red flags 149–150
  subtypes 150
Developmental neuroplasticity 75
  adverse effects 76
  critical (sensitive) periods 66–67, 71–72

historical aspects 75
mechanisms
  experience-dependent 70
  experience-expectant 70
  experience-independent 70
  GABAergic neurons 66–67
  sparing of function 76
  perinatal stroke and 75
  sensory perturbations and
    visual deprivation See Ocular dominance columns (ODCs)
  sensory perturbations and 75
  types 75
Developmental plasticity See Developmental neuroplasticity
Developmental reflexes See Primitive reflexes (PRs)
Developmental theories
  cognitive development See Cognitive developmental theories
  interactive specialization 75, 126–127
  maturational 126
  skill-learning hypothesis 127
  typical development 75
Developmental windows See Critical (sensitive) periods
Diagnostic and Statistical Manual (DSM), mental deficiency criteria 258
Diagnostic Classification of Mental Health and Developmental Disorders of Infancy and Early Childhood, separation anxiety assessment 474–475
Diagnostic overshadowing 260–261
  definition 256
Diamond, Adele, habituation and novelty 208–209
Dimensions of instruction, definition 433
Dimensions of parenting, definition 433
Discipline
  parental
    school readiness 442
  school readiness 442
Discordant condition, visual self recognition 452, 453f
Discourse See Conversation
Discrepancy hypothesis, habituation and novelty 208
Discrepant event concept
  separation anxiety 470
  stranger anxiety 467–468
Discrimination, definition 290
Dishabituation
  definition 91, 205
  theory of mind development 499
Disparagement humor 233
Distance vision, maturation, stranger anxiety and 467
Distress, definition 466
Distribution, definition 192
Ditransitive construction 193
Dizygotic triplets 509
Dizygotic twins (DZ) 508
  development and behavior 509
    psychological closeness 510
    school behaviors 511
    shyness 511
    social behaviors 510
  twins of opposite race 509
  twin studies
    behavioral genetics 186
    equal environments assumption 514
    monozygotic twins vs. 513
    shared vs. nonshared environments 513
DNA See Deoxyribonucleic acid (DNA)
DNMS task, explicit memory 87
Dopamine receptors
  D4 receptor *(DRD4)*
    temperament and 188–189
Dorsolateral prefrontal cortex (DLPC)
  behavioral development role 132
  definition 357
  object concept 359
  object permanence 132
Doublecortin domain containing 2 *(DCD2)* gene 188

Down syndrome 184
    cognition/cognitive functions
        humor development 229
        language acquisition 275
        learning disabilities 260
        theory of mind development 505
    education planning 263–264
    families
        stress 265
    hemispheric asymmetry 129–130
    neural substrates, 'pre-wiring'/prespecification 129
Draw-a-Man test, intelligence assessment 13–14, 20
Drawings *See* Artistic development
Drive theories, curiosity 157, 158
DSM criteria *See Diagnostic and Statistical Manual* (DSM)
Dual diagnosis, definition 257
Dual-mechanism inflectional morphology 199
Dual representation 488–489, 492–493
Dual-route model, language development 281
Duncan John, habituation and novelty 214
Dynamic systems theory 120
Dyscalculia
    acquired 323
    developmental 315, 322–323
Dyslexia, neuronal migration and 67–68
Dyspraxia (motor planning problems)
    visual-spatial disabilities 155
Dystonia, neuroplasticity and 76

E

Early care programs, critical elements 440
Early Head Start (EHS) 224
    See also Head Start
Early intervention, definition 257
'Early' memory 211
Earth, concepts of 122
Easter Bunny 244
Eccles, Jackie, school entry 138
Echolalia 153
    definition 147
Echolalic speech 153
Ecological approach to perception *See* Perceptual development
Ecological perspective, definition 433
Ecological self knowledge 446
    definition 445
    interpersonal self knowledge, coexistence 447
Economic Opportunity Act (1964) 218
Education
    critical periods 143
    twins, class separation 511
    See also Academic achievement/performance; Learning
Education for All Handicapped Children Act (EHA) (1975) 148
Effortful attention *See* Executive attention
Egocentric reasoning
    definition 357
    object concept development 358, 360
Egocentric spatial framework, cognitive milestone 342
Ekman's Facial Action Coding System, emotional distress assessment 471
Elaborative style, definition 1
Electroencephalography (EEG)
    attention 31
    brain development 81*t*, 85–86
    definition 357
    ERPs *See* Event-related potentials (ERPs)
    IQ 188
    speech perception 410–411, 412*f*, 413*t*
Elementary and Secondary Education Act (1965) 218–219
Elisabeth Dykens, intellectual disability 260
Ellipsis, definition 399
Embodied knowledge
    definition 369
    perception–action coupling 376
Emergent literacy, definition 301

Emotion(s)
    children's understandings of
        imagination/fantasy 242
    cognition
        development influence 112
        cognitive development and 112
        individual differences, twin studies 515
    organization
        crying and 469
        social smile and 468
    theory of mind development 502
    See also entries beginning emotion/emotional
Emotional distress
    assessment 471
        cortisol levels 471
        facial expression coding 471
Emotional ecology, speech perception 413
Emotional valence, infant-directed speech 414, 414*f*
Emotion-related phenotypes, twin studies 515
Empathy
    twin studies 517
    See also Prosocial behavior
Empiricism
    definition 381
    Piaget's cognitive-developmental theory 382
Emulation 248
Encoding
    definition 325
    visual-paired comparison, *vs.* 211
Endogenous attention 29
Endophenotype(s), definition 181
Entwistle, Doris, critical periods 138
Environmentality, complex traits and disorders 185
Environmental toxins, critical periods and 135
Environment/environmental factors
    behavior and
        empathy and prosocial behavior 517
        externalizing behavior 516
        internalizing behavior 517
        temperament 515
        twin studies 513
    cognition 515–516
    curiosity facilitation 161, 166
    exploratory behavior facilitation 165, 166
    postnatal brain development 70
    self–environment sensitivity
        locomotion and 373
        perception–action coupling 373, 373*f*
    See also entries beginning environmental
Epigenetic(s)
    cortical development 69
    definition 65
    See also Genomic imprinting
Episodic memory 454–455
    definition 79, 86–87, 445
    See also Autobiographical memory
Epistemology, definition 114
Equal environments assumption (EEA)
    behavioral genetics 186
    twin studies 514
Equilibration
    definition 381
    Piaget's cognitive-developmental theory 115–116, 382, 388–389
Ergative languages, definition 267
Erikson, Erik, play 396
Ernst and Angst, birth order 59
Essentialism
    definition 421
    reasoning and 424, 425
Ethnicity/race
    academic achievement/performance 439
    dizygotic twins of opposite race 509
    See also Culture
Etiology, definition 147
Event knowledge, pragmatic development 401
Event-related potentials (ERPs)
    attention 31
    brain development studies 81*t*, 84, 89
    definition 26, 125, 205
    habituation and novelty preference 214, 215*f*, 216*f*

memory 331, 332*f*
negative central (Nc) 31–32, 32*f*
prefrontal cortex development and cognition 133
social brain development
    eye-gaze 128*f*, 129
    face recognition/processing 128, 128*f*
speech perception studies 413*t*, 415, 417–418
Evidence-based programming, Head Start 225
Evoked potentials *See* Event-related potentials (ERPs)
Evolution
    mathematical reasoning 315, 316
    reflexes *See* Reflex(es)
Exampler representations, infants 99
Executive attention 29
    definition 26
Executive function (EF)
    definition 485
    symbolic thought 490
    theory of mind and 503
    See also Executive attention; Working memory
Exercise play 392
Expectation
    definition 169
    See also Future orientation
Experience-dependence
    critical periods 139
    definition 135, 347
Experience-expectant processes
    critical periods 137
    definition 135, 347
    developmental neuroplasticity 70
    language acquisition 70
    postnatal brain development 70
Experience(s), postnatal brain development and 70
Explicit memory *See* Declarative (explicit) memory
Exploration/exploratory behavior **157–167**
    age-related differences 164
    concepts/principles 162
    curiosity and 166
    definition 157, 162
    development
        facilitation 165
        influences 164
        parental modeling and reinforcement 166
        patterns 163
    developmental importance 166
    developmental skills associated 165
    exploratory play 390
    gender differences 165
    individual differences 164–165
    interrelationship with curiosity 166
    modes 163
    See also Curiosity
Exploratory play, definition 390
Expressions *See* Facial expression(s)
Expressive dysfluency disorders 150
Expressive language, definition 150, 301
Expressive style, one-word stage 458
Externalizing behavior
    twin studies 516
        class separation effects 511
        heritability 516
    See also Internalizing behavior
Eye(s)
    development 371
    information from, social brain functions 129
    movements *See* Eye movement(s)
Eye-blink paradigm, implicit memory 88
Eye-gaze
    cueing, development 129
        ERP analysis 128*f*, 129
    mutual gaze, development 129
    perception
        development 129
        perception–action coupling and 371–372
Eye-hand coordination, environmental support 112
Eye movement(s)
    anticipatory, definition 169
    object concept and 365
    perception–action coupling 371–372
        anticipatory 379

smooth visual pursuit 374
saccadic *See* Saccades (saccadic eye movements)
smooth pursuit *See* Smooth pursuit
See also Future orientation

F

Face categorization, multiple habituation tasks 93–94
Face perception/processing
    face categorization *See* Face categorization
    facial recognition *See* Face recognition
    neurobiological mechanisms
        CONLERN process 83–84
        CONSPEC process 83–84
        functional brain development 83, 83*f*
        fusiform face area 83
        fusiform gyrus 83, 83*f*
        ventral visual stream 127–128
        visuomotor pathway 127–128
    speech perception and 412–413
Face recognition
    development 127
        ERP analysis 128, 128*f*
        fMRI analysis 128
        increasing specialization of 129
    facial expressions
        See also Facial expression(s)
    spatial neglect syndromes and 127–128
    See also Face categorization
Face-to-face play 391–392
    cultural view 398
Facial Action Coding System (FACS), emotional distress assessment 471
Facial expression(s)
    coding, emotional distress assessment 471
    imitation 250
    infant self efficacy 448
Facilitation, definition 135
False-belief *See* Theory of mind (ToM)
Familial mental retardation, definition 257
Familiarization and visual paired comparison task 94, 95*f*
Familiarization, infant learning 293–294
Familiar stimulus
    negative central (Nc) 31–32, 32*f*
    recognition memory 31
Family and Child Experiences Survey (FACES) 224
    definition 217
    history 224
Family/families
    environment, theory of mind development and 504
    Head Start benefits 224
        See also Head Start
    rituals
        See also Rituals
    support
        child-care *See* Child-care
Family-focused early childhood education (ECE), school readiness 441
Family niche theory, birth order 61
Family Service Centers Project, Head Start 223
    aims 223
Fantastical beings/events 240, 243
    distinguishing from reality 384–385
    See also Imagination/fantasy
Fantasy *See* Imagination/fantasy
Fantz, Robert, habituation and novelty 205–206
Feelings
    expression in children's art 17
    See also Emotion(s)
Fetal abnormalities, *See also* Developmental disorders
Fetal development
    alcohol effects *See* Fetal alcohol spectrum disorders (FASDs)
    brain *See* Brain development
    critical periods 140
Fetus(es)
    development *See* Fetal development
    gestures 379

learning 293
    See also entries beginning feto-/fetal
Fiction, fantasy in 244
First borns 64
    achievement expectations 59
First grade schooling effects 443
First words 457
    comprehension 457
    production 458
First year play 394
Fischer, Kurt, cognitive development 117
Flexible Item Selection Task, symbolic thought 492
Fluency
    definition 301
    literacy 307
Flynn effect, Bayley Scales of Infant Development 44
Focal lesion(s)
    habituation and novelty 212
    prefrontal cortex effects 133
Forbes, James, verb learning 464
Forgetting
    differential rate 10
    individual differences 11
    rate 10, 10*f*
    See also Remembering
Formal operational thought
    definition 381
    Piaget's cognitive-developmental theory 384, 386, 389
Fragile X mental retardation syndrome *See* Fragile X syndrome (FXS)
Fragile X syndrome (FXS) 184
    neurobiology
        synaptogenesis and 73
Fraternal twins *See* Dizygotic twins (DZ)
French-English bilinguals
    object-label pairing 54–55
    phoneme contrasts 51, 52*f*, 53*f*
Frequency
    definition 290
    speech category formation 294
Freud, Sigmund
    amnesia 2, 4
    humor development 231–232
    memory regression 4
Frontal cortex
    cognitive functions 131
    postnatal development 131
        DLPC 132
        functional imaging 132–133
        neuropsychological studies 132
        object permanence and 131–132
    prefrontal *See* Prefrontal cortex (PFC)
'Full inclusion' concept, intellectual disability 263
Functional analysis, grammar 201–202
Functional imaging, cognitive neuroscience role 125
    face recognition and the social brain 127–128
    frontal cortex development 132–133
    language acquisition 130
    speech perception development 131
Functionalist theory/functionalism
    definition 381
    Piaget's cognitive-developmental theory 382, 386
Functional logic, Piaget, Jean 115
Functional magnetic resonance imaging (fMRI)
    brain development 77, 81*t*, 84, 88, 89
    definition 125
    frontal cortex, cognition and 132–133
    language acquisition 130
    speech perception 131, 412–413, 413*t*
Fusiform face area (FFA) 83, 83*f*
    face perception 83, 83*f*
    social brain and 127
Fusiform gyrus, face perception *See* Fusiform face area (FFA)
Future-directed information, perception–action coupling 374
Future orientation **169–180**
    classification taxonomy 179, 179*t*
    conversation role 175
    early social systems 174

historical roots 170
    behaviorism and 170
    law of effect 170
    locomotion system 173
    ordered sequences 175
    physiology 176
    postural system 173
    research 170
        methodological challenges 178
        oddball paradigm 177–178
        reinforcement paradigms 175
        spatial cuing paradigm 177
        S1-S2 paradigm 176–177
            contingent negative variation 177
            definition 169
        visual expectation paradigm 170–171, 171*f*, 174, 178–179
            definition 169
    saccadic eye movement system 170, 172
        definition 169
    smooth pursuit eye movement system 172
        definition 169
    temporal patterns 175
    visual-manual system 173

G

GABA/GABAergic neurons
    critical periods and 66–67, 71–72
    developmental migration 66–67
    developmental neuroplasticity 66–67
Galactosemia, critical periods 142
Gallese, Vittorio, imitation 254
Gall, Franz Joseph 349
    functional cortical areas 68
Galton, Sir Francis 349
    behavioral genetics 185–186
    birth order 59
Gelman, Rochel, information processing theory 119
Gelman, Susan 425
    infant cognitive development 122
Gender
    child
        infantile amnesia and 3
        sex-specific genetic disorders *See* Sex-linked genetic disorders
Gender differences
    exploratory behavior 165
    imaginary companion creation 245
    mathematical reasoning 323
    role play participation 245
Gene(s) 182
    definition 181
    environment interactions *See* Gene-environment (GE) interaction/correlation
    expression 182
        mechanisms 182–183
    transmission/inheritance 181
        See also Heritability
Gene-environment (GE) interaction/correlation 187
    active
        twin studies 514, 514*t*
    behavior genetics
        twin studies and 513–514, 514*t*
    definition 508
    passive
        twin studies 514, 514*t*
    reactive
        twin studies 514, 514*t*
    See also Nature *versus* nurture debate
Gene-environment (GE) relationships
    See Gene-environment (GE) interaction/correlation
Generalization 457
    definition 290
Generative grammar 193
Generic event memory, definition 445
Genetic disorders
    environmental contribution 187
    intellectual disability 260

Genetic disorders (continued)
　polygenic *See* Complex polygenic traits
　single gene (monogenic) *See* Single gene disorders (SGDs)
Genetic epistemology, cognitive developmental theories 115
Genetic factors
　behavior and *See* Behavior genetics
　cognition 515–516
　cortical development 69
　inhibition 517
　temperament 515
　See also Gene(s); Genetics; Nature *versus* nurture debate
Genetics **181–192**
　behavioral *See* Behavior genetics
　complex traits and disorders *See* Complex polygenic traits
　definition 65
　future directions 191
　influences in autism spectrum disorder *See* Autism spectrum disorders (ASD)
　monogenic disorders *See* Single gene disorders (SGDs)
　nature vs. nurture *See* Nature *versus* nurture debate
　transmission/inheritance 181
　　See also Heritability
　See also Genetic disorders; Genetic factors
Genetic transmission 181
Genomic imprinting 184
　See also Epigenetic(s)
Genotype, definition 181
Gentner, Dedre
　noun bias 463
　theory of analogical development 426
Gerken, LouAnn 298
Geschwind, Norman, hemispheric asymmetry and language 129–130
Gesell, Arnold 38
Gesell's intelligence tests 14
Gestalt perceptual theory 360–361
Gestures/gesturing
　deictic 402
　　definition 399
　language acquisition 272
　language development 401, 405
　symbolic
　　definition 400
　　pragmatic development 403
Gibson, James, perception–action loop 370
Giftedness, artistic development 19, 20f, 21f
Glial cells (glia)
　definition 65
　myelination role 72
　postnatal brain development and 72
Global learning disabilities *See* Learning disabilities
Goal-directed action 370, 374
　See also Intentionality
Goal sharing, infants 451
Go-Nogo task, symbolic thought 492
Gottlieb, Gilbert, critical periods 136–137
Grammar **192–203**
　agent-patient relations (who did what to whom) 195
　　case and agreement 197
　　combining factors (coalition and competition) 197
　　word order and 196
　construction development *See* Grammatical construction(s)
　development 280
　　morphology 280, 406
　　　definition 399
　　relational terms 426–427, 427t
　　'story,' 408
　　syntax
　　　early development 285
　　　later development 286
　　　universal 282–283
　learning processes 200
　　constraining generalization 202
　　cultural learning 200

debate 200
intention reading 200
lexical category construction 201
mechanisms 200
schematization and analogy 201
morphology *See* Morphology
phonology *See* Phonology
semantics *See* Semantics
syntax *See* Syntax
See also Abstract reasoning/abstraction
Grammatical construction(s) 193, 194t
　definition 192
　early 194t
　　abstract constructions 193, 195, 199
　　holophrases 193
　　item-based constructions 195
　　pivot schemas 195
　　word combinations 195
　external variation 274
Grapheme phoneme correspondences 305–306
Grasping
　exploration development 163
　future-oriented processes 173, 179–180
　schemes, Piaget's cognitive-developmental theory 383
　See also Reaching
Gray matter development, neuroimaging 76
Gray, Susan 218
Greenberg, Polly 220
Grennough, William, critical periods 137, 139
Groos, Karl, play 396
Groupings, Piaget, Jean 115
Gulick, Luther, play 396
Gusii 398–399
Gyri, development 126

H

Habituation 325
　arousal 209
　attention role 209
　definition 26, 91, 205, 315, 337, 338
　infant's concepts and 98
　methodologies
　　novelty paradigms *See* Habituation and novelty paradigms
　speech perception research 412t, 476, 477–478, 478–479
　See also Novelty detection
Habituation and novelty paradigms **205–217**
　attention role 209
　　memory interactions 214
　developmental trends 208
　development studies 206
　　limitations 207
　historical aspects 205–206
　memory role 210
　　attention interactions 214
　neural mechanisms involved 211
　　electrophysiological correlates 214, 215f, 216f
　　encoding vs. retrieval 211
　　hippocampus role 211
　　lesion studies 212
　　neuroimaging studies 213
　theoretical aspects 207
　　comparator model 207
　　optimal level theory/discrepancy hypothesis 208
　utility 205
Habituation-dishabituation procedure 206
　limitations 207
　VPC procedure vs. 206
Hall, Geoffrey D, semantic development 462–463
Happiness, twin studies 515
Haptic perception
　definition 369
　perception–action coupling and 372
Harris, Judith Rich, birth order 63
Harris, Paul, imitation 254
Hart, Betty, semantic development 461

Head direction parameter, language development 282–283
Head Start **217–227**
　advocacy 222
　barriers to service delivery 222
　critical periods 143
　early years 219
　evaluation 220, 223, 225
　　advisory panels 222
　　conferences role 225
　evidence-based programming 225
　funding 223
　health services 221
　intelligence, intervention effects 219
　issues 1978-89 221
　mental health services 221
　parental involvement 220, 222
　program launch 218
　school readiness 440
　social services 222
　System of Program Performance Measures 224
Head Start Act (1994) 224
Head Start Act (1998) 224–225
Head Start Bureau, definition 217
Head Start Planning Committee 218
Head Start Program Performance Standards (HSPPS) 221, 222
　definition 217
　revisions 224
Head Start-Public School Transition Projects, aims 223
Head Start Quality Research Center Consortium (2001) 224, 225
Head Start Research Scholars Program 224
Headturning, memory 327
Head-turn preference procedure, speech preference research 484
Health
　Head Start Impact Study 225
　Head Start services 221
Health Services Advisory Committee (HSAC) 221
Hearing *See* Auditory perception
Hearing loss
　communication and
　　See also Sign language
　theory of mind development 505
　See also Cochlear implants
Heart rate (HR)
　attention 29, 30f
　classical conditioning 177
　habituation 209
　speech perception studies 411–412, 411f, 413t
　stimulus orienting 29–30
Heart rate defined attention phases, definition 26
Hemispheric asymmetry, language acquisition 129–130
Heritability
　complex traits and disorders 185
　definition 181, 508
　twin studies 513
High-amplitude operant sucking procedure, definition 290
High amplitude sucking (HAS) procedure
　memory 326
　speech perception research 477–478, 480
Higher-order language syndromes 151
Hilton, Irma, birth order 60–61
Hippocampus
　definition 1
　memory role 87, 87f
　　autobiographical memory 6
　　infantile amnesia 454
　　See also Memory
　novelty preferences 211
　See also Novelty detection
Hobson, Peter, autism 255
Hodapp, Robert, intellectual disability 260, 265
Holophrases 192–193
　abstract constructions, development to 193
　combinations 195

Home learning
  literacy 309
  school readiness 442
Horn, John, birth order 61
Hubel, David, ocular dominance columns 70
Human agency *See* Intentionality
Human Genome Project 190
  ethics 190
  findings 190
  moral and legal implications 190
Human plasticity, new horizons 142
Humor **227–236**
  concept of 227
  cues 231
  definition 227
  as developmental phenomenon 228
  development of *See* Humor development
  expression 234
    individual differences 235
  fictional literacy works 227
  gender influences 230
  'relief' function 233
Humor development 228
  4-6 years 229
  6-8 years 229
  caregivers role 235
  definition 227
  fostering methods 235
  infant to 3 years 228
  relation to other developmental domains 233
  theoretical explanations 231
Humor facilitation techniques 235
  teachers role 236
Humor frame 228
  definition 227
Humorous hyperbole, definition 227
Humor-related laughter, definition 227
Huntington's disease (HD) 183–184
Huttenlocher, Janellen, verb learning 464
Hybrid models, word learning 463

I

Iacobani, Marco, imitation 255
Iambic pattern, definition 409
'I' concept 445
Iconoclastic humor 228
Identical twins *See* Monozygotic twins (MZ)
Imaginary companion(s) 240, 242, 397
  definition 390
  gender effects 245
Imaginary play 393
Imagination/fantasy **237–247**
  children's understandings 241, 243
    emotions disrupting 242
  definitions 237
    fantasy 237
    imagination 237
  developmental course 238
    individual differences 245
  fantastical beings and events 240, 243
  imaginary companions *See* Imaginary companion(s)
  mass media and 244
  Piaget's cognitive-developmental theory 388
  pretend play *See* Pretend play/pretense
  theory of mind 503–504
Imaging *See* Neuroimaging
Imitation **247–256**
  autism and 255
  comparative psychology 248
  conditions required 248
  facial expressions 250
    active intermodal mapping 251
  humans as imitative animals 247
  interdisciplinary studies 254
  learning about objects 251
    novel acts from memory 251
    peer imitation 252
  learning about people 252
    social cognition 253

social communication 252
  memory 327
  mirror neurons 254
  non-Western societies 248
  regulation of 253
    by emotions 254
    by goals and intentions 253
    by prior experience 254
  robotics 255
  social learning *vs.* 248
  theoretical aspects 249
    active intermodal mapping (AIM) 251
    associative learning 249
    binding problem and 249
    operant conditioning 249
    Piaget's theory 249, 388
  tongue protrusion 250–251
Immediate early gene (IEG) imaging, habituation and novelty 213
Implicit memory *See* Nondeclarative (implicit; procedural) memory
Imprinting
  critical periods 136
  genomic *See* Genomic imprinting
Improving the Opportunities and Achievements of the Children of the Poor 219
Incongruity humor 230
  constructivist theory 232
  definition 227
Incongruity theory
  curiosity 157, 158, 159
  stranger anxiety 467–468
Indirect effects, definition 257
Indirect physiological measures, habituation 209
Individual differences
  attention 35
  definition 237
  emotions, twin studies 515
  exploration 164–165
  forgetting 11
  humor expression 235
  imagination/fantasy
    developmental course 245
    pretend play/pretense 245
  inhibition, twin studies 515
  remembering 9
  self-regulatory processes 515
  theory of mind development 503
  traits, twin studies 515
Individual(ized) education program (IEP)
  definition 257
  elements included 263
Individual(ized) family service plans (IFSPs)
  definition 257
  intellectual disability 262
  mental developmental disabilities 148
Individualizing Student Instruction Project 312
Individuals with Disabilities Education Act (IDEA) (2004)
  intellectual disability 262
  mental developmental disabilities 148
Induction 422
  categorical coverage 424
  definition 135, 421
  See also Reasoning
Infant(s)
  behavior
    categorical, underlying representations 487
    parental responses
      maternal contingencies 449
      selectivity 449
  categorization skills *See* Categorization
  cognitive neuroscience *See* Developmental cognitive neuroscience
  health *See* Health
  language acquisition *See* Language acquisition
  movement testing 452, 453*f*
  prefrontal cortex (PFC) development 131–132
  temperament *See* Temperament
  See also entries beginning infant/infantile
Infant Behavior Record 39, 40

Infant-caregiver relationships, social contingency 450
Infant-directed speech
  definition 476
  emotional valence 414, 414*f*
  language-learning ecology 419
  prosody 413, 414, 416–417
  speech preferences 484
Infantile amnesia **1–12**
  autobiographical memory development and 9
    crossover between formation and loss 10, 10*f*
    rate of formation 9
    rate of loss (forgetting) 10
  birth order 3
  culture 3
  deficits 1
  definition 1
  gender 3
  implications 1
  neural substrates
    hippocampus 454
  phenomenon of 2
    age of earliest memory 2
    distribution of early memories 2, 2*f*
  theoretical explanations 4
    inaccessible memories 4
      cognitive lenses theory 4
      Freud's repression/screening theory 4
    lack of autobiographical memory formation 5
      conceptual changes and 5
      Piaget's cognitive deficit theory 5
  universality 3
    group differences 3, 3*t*
    individual differences 3
  See also Autobiographical memory
Infant laughter, humor development 228
Infant-parent interaction(s)
  contingent responsiveness 449
  social contingency 450
Inflec, acquisition delays 199
Inflectional morphology 198
Information processing theory, cognitive development 119
Information scaling, perception–action coupling 377
Inhibition, individual differences, twin studies 515, 517
Innate grammar 193
Inner speech, definition 485
Insight development, Piaget's cognitive-developmental theory 338
Institutional care/institutionalization, critical periods and 140
Instrumental conditioning *See* Operant conditioning
Insult jokes 231–232
Intellectual achievement, definition 58
Intellectual development, birth order 59, 62
Intellectual disability **256–266**
  adaptive behavior 259
  artistic development 20
  assessment techniques 257
  birth order effects 60
  categorization 258
  child characteristics 265
  co-morbid psychiatric condition 260–261
  definition 257, 258
  dual diagnosis 260
  education 261, 262
    etiology and planning 263
  etiology-specific approach 260
  families 264
  genetic disorders 260
  heritability 188
  identification 261
  individualized education plan 263
  intensities of needed supports 258–259
  intervention 261
  referral process 261
  severity of impairment 258–259
  specific area assessment 261
  two-group approach 259
  See also Learning disabilities

Intellectual realism, artistic development 12, 14
Intelligence
    definition 20–21
    development markers 338
    Head Start intervention effects 219
    Piaget's cognitive-developmental theory 388
    testing 38
        Bayley Scales *See* Bayley Scales of Infant Development
        Binet's 14
        Draw-a-Man test 13–14, 20
        Gesell's 14
        history 219–220
        IQ *See* Intelligence quotient (IQ)
        theoretical issues 38
Intelligence and Experience 218
Intelligence quotient (IQ)
    heritability 188
    learning disabilities 258, 259, 261
    school readiness 437
    visual-spatial disabilities 154
Intentional behavior, infants interactions with others 451
Intentionality
    cognitive milestones
        6-12 months 341
        12-18 months 343
    definition 485, 486
    self knowledge 451
    symbolic thought 487
Intentional states 497, 497t
Intention reading 200
Interactionism
    definition 347
    forms 354
Interactive social games, humor development 228
Interactive specialization theory 75, 126–127
    functional brain development 80, 89
Intermittent reinforcement, infant self-efficacy 449
Intermodal, definition 247
Intermodal perception, definition 445
Intermodal preferential looking paradigm (IPLP)
    definition 456
    syntactic bootstrapping 465
Internalizing behavior
    twin studies 517
        class separation effects 511
    See also Externalizing behavior
Internal states, cognitive development and 112
Interpersonal play 391
    cultural view 398
    definition 390
Interpersonal self-knowledge 446–447
    ecological self-knowledge coexistence 447
    infant learning 445
Interpretive diversity, definition 495
Intersensory perception *See* Intermodal perception
Intersensory redundancy *See* Intermodal perception
Intracortical connections, postnatal brain development 73
Intrinsic motivation theories of curiosity 157, 158, 159
Invisible imitation, definition 247
IQ *See* Intelligence quotient (IQ)
Irony comprehension 233–234
    symbolic thought 491
Item-based constructions 195
    abstract constructions, from 201
Izard's MAX coding system, emotional distress assessment 471

J

Jacques, Sophie, Flexible Item Selection Task 492
James, William 209
Jesting 231–232, 235
Joint attention
    definition 102, 399, 445, 456
    development 129
    pragmatic development 401

Joint book reading 442
    school readiness 442
Joint probability, definition 290
Joke telling, humor development 229–230
Joking 231–232
Joking facade, definition 227
Joseph P. Kennedy Jr. Foundation 218
Jung, Carl 350
'Junk DNA,' 190
Jusczyk, comprehension 457–458

K

Kagan, Jerome 159
Kant, Immanuel, humor 233
Keil, Frank, infant cognitive development 122
KIAA0319 188
Klahr, David, information processing theory 119
Klinefelter syndrome 184
Knowledge
    core, definition 347, 351
    forms 348
    objects/events, cognitive milestones, 1-6 months 340
    theories of 348
        nativism *See* Nativism
        neonativism *See* Neonativism
Krushinskii, Leonid 170

L

Language
    acquisition *See* Language acquisition
    bilingualism *See* Bilingualism
    development of *See* Language development
    expression, autobiographical memories 8
    literacy 304
        links between 304
    production *See* Speech
    sign language *See* Sign language
    stress-timed, definition 409
    uniqueness, question of 129
    See also Communication
Language acquisition 267–277
    cognitive accounts 269
    combination 272–273
    constrained invention 272
    constrained learning 270
    corpus analysis 271
    developmental cognitive neuroscience 129
        approaches used 129
        fMRI studies 130
        hemispherectomy effects 129–130
        language skills in very young infants 130
        language-specific phonetic sensitivity 130–131
        sign language 130
    experience-expectant development 70
    gesturing 272
    innate knowledge 269, 274
        developmental resilience 274
        external variation 274
        genetic encoding 274
        internal variation 274
        resilience mechanisms 275
    organic variation 275
    perinatal stroke and 75
    segmentation 272–273
    social accounts 269
    species-specificity question 271
    statistical learning 271, 293
    task-specificity question 271
    theoretical accounts 268
    See also Language development
Language development 277–290
    atypical 287
        See also Language disorders/impairment
    audiovisual perception 481
    behaviorist theory 288
    comprehension 279, 404

    context dependence 279
    definition 399
    phonological template 279
    constituency 287
    constructivist approach 282–283, 283t, 285–286, 288
    conversation *See* Conversation
    critical periods 141
    emotional ecology 413
    gesture use and 401, 405
    grammar *See* Grammar
    head direction parameter 282–283
    humor 234
    infancy 277
        experiments 278
        pattern skills 278
    learnability concept 287, 352–353
    mathematical reasoning, role in *See* Mathematical reasoning
    meaning assignment 279
    mechanisms 350
        Agreement-Tense Omission Model 283
        brain mechanisms 88
            hemispheric specialization 88–89
            neuroimaging 88
        dual-route model 281
        memory formation 4
    metalinguistic skills 286
    narrative *See* Narrative
    normal 149
    pragmatics *See* Pragmatic development
    production *See* Speech
    See also Language acquisition
Language disorders/impairment 287
    autism spectrum disorders 153
    developmental *See* Developmental language disorders
    Down syndrome 275
    expressive language 150
    higher-order language syndromes 151
    receptive language disorders 150
    specific language impairment (SLI) 267, 275, 287
    Williams syndrome 287
'Language instinct,' 303
Language pragmatic, definition 147
Language socialization, politeness markers 407
'Late' memory 211
Law of effect, future orientation 170
Lazarus, Moritz, play 396
Learnability concept, language acquisition 287, 352–353
Learning
    basic processes, cognitive milestones, 0-1 month 338
    Bayley Scales *See* Bayley Scales of Infant Development
    curiosity *See* Curiosity
    exploration *See* Exploration/exploratory behavior
    future orientation *See* Future orientation
    infants *See* Learning in infancy
    problems *See* Learning disabilities
Learning disabilities
    etiology
        genetic factors
            heritability 188
    literacy and 311
Learning in infancy 290–301
    current issues 298
    early work 291
    generalization 296
    historical perspectives 291
    impact on future learning 299
    laboratory considerations 299
    permanence 299
    reinforcement 292
    robustness 298
Learning to read
    learning to talk. *vs.* 303
    literacy development 305
Learning to talk
    learning to read. *vs.* 303
    See also Speech

Leg movement coordination, perception-action coupling 377
Leopold, Werner, bilingualism 49
Less is More task, symbolic thought 492
Letter-sound correspondences 306
Levin, Harry 218
Levitsky, Walter, hemispheric asymmetry and language 129–130
Lexical access, definition 301
Lexical semantics, definition 301
Lexical syntactic syndrome 151
Lexicon, definition 192, 301
'Like me framework,' 253
Linguistic rhythm, prosody perception 415–416
Lissencephaly 67
Literacy **301–313**
   brain imaging techniques 303–304
   critical periods 141–142
   definition 301
   individualizing student instruction 311
   instruction, history of 302
   language 304
      links between 304
   learning environments 307
   multiple dimensions of instruction 309, 310t
   skills 305
Local enhancement, imitation 248
Locke, John 349
   infant learning 291
Locomotion
   development *See* Locomotion development
   exploration development and 163
   future oriented processes 179–180
   self–environment interactions 373
Locomotion development
   perception-action coupling affordances 373–374
Logic, Piaget, Jean 115
Long-term memory
   cognitive milestones
      6-12 months 341
      12-18 months 343
   definition 79
   functional brain development 86, 87f
Look duration 33, 34f, 35f
Looking time methods 107f, 109, 110
   definition 102
Lorenz, Konrad, critical periods 136
Luria, Alexander, Go-Nogo task 492

M

Magnetic encephalography (MEG), brain development studies 81t
Magnetic resonance imaging (MRI)
   brain development 77, 81t
      postnatal 126
   functional *See* Functional magnetic resonance imaging (fMRI)
   speech perception studies 410–411
Maintenance, definition 135
Manual learning, object concept 365
Marginal zone 67
Markman, Ellen, constraint theories 459
Mass media
   fantasy in 244
   television *See* Television
Mass noun
   count noun, distinction 462
   definition 456
Maternal depression, childhood exploration influence 164
Maternal separation anxiety 474
Mathematical reasoning **315–325**
   abnormal 322
      dyscalculia 315, 322–323
   accumulator model 316
      definition 315
   approximate magnitude system 316, 318, 323
   core systems view 315

developmental origins 316
evolutionary continuity 315, 316
infants 340
language role 320
   learning to count 320
   number comprehension and encoding 321
   stable-order principle 320–321
object-file system 315, 317
sex differences 323
spatial imagery 324
Weak-Whorfian view of number 315, 322
Weber fraction limit 315, 316, 318
See also Numeracy
MAX coding system, emotional distress assessment 471
McClelland, J, balance scale 123–124
McGuffrey Readers 302
McGurk effect, speech perception 420, 481
McKee, Richard, memory 211
McLaughlin, Harry, cognitive development 117
Mead, Margaret, imitation 248
Meaning-focused instruction, literacy 310
Mean length of utterance (MLU), definition 456
Means-end behavior/thinking
   6-12 month cognitive milestone 342
   definition 337, 445
   self-reflective awareness 450
'Me' concept 445
Medial temporal lobe (MTL)
   definition 205
   memory role 86
      amnesia 212
      declarative memory 210, 211
Mediation (symbolic), definition 485
Meiosis 182, 183f
Meltzoff and Moore, imitation 250–251
Memory **325–336**
   age of earliest memory 2
   autobiographical *See* Autobiographical memory
   declarative *See* Declarative (explicit) memory
   deferred imitation paradigm 87–88
   development 6
      3-6 month olds 327
      6-12 month olds 333
      12-24 month olds 335
      basic memory processes 7
      language/narrative expression and 8
      newborns 326
      nonmnemonic abilities and 7
         autonoetic awareness 8
         self concept 7–8
      social context of remembering 2, 2f
         variability among children 8–9
         variability among cultures 9
         variability among families 9
   distribution of early 2, 2f
   electrophysiology 331, 331f
   encoding 4
   episodic *See* Episodic memory
   explicit *See* Declarative (explicit) memory
   formation rate 9, 10, 10f
   headturning 327
   high-amplitude sucking 326
   imitation 327
   implicit *See* Nondeclarative (implicit: procedural) memory
   inaccessible 4
   infants 7
   long-term *See* Long-term memory
   loss rate 10, 10f
   neural substrates 6, 6f
      association areas 6
      hippocampus 6
      medial temporal lobe 86
      temporal cortex 7
   nondeclarative *See* Nondeclarative (implicit: procedural) memory
   novelty preferences 210, 211
   operant conditioning 333
   parental style 9
   plasticity and 88

procedural *See* Nondeclarative (implicit: procedural) memory
rate of formation 9
rate of loss (forgetting) 10
   See also Forgetting
recognition *See* Recognition memory
retention improvements 333
   adult language cues 335, 335f
   duration 336
retrieval
   definition 325
   flexibility 336
   See also Remembering
semantic
   definition 79, 86–87
short-term
   6-12 month olds 340
strategic, cognitive milestones, 18-24 months 344
symbolic capacity 5–6
train task 333, 333f
types, distinctions between 210
visual-paired comparison interactions 214
visual preference 327
working memory
   definition 79
   functional brain development 85, 85f
Memory consolidation, sleep 299–300
Memory reconsolidation 300
Mendel, Gregor 181–182
Mendelian disorders, autosomal disorders 183
Mental developmental disabilities **147–155**
   assessment 149
   children at risk 150
   communication disorders 149
   early indicators 148
   risk factors 147–148
   See also Intellectual disability; Learning disabilities
Mental Developmental Index (MDI) 40
Mental health, services, Head Start 221
Mental representation *See* Theory of mind (ToM)
Mental retardation *See* Intellectual disability
Mesencephalic reticular activating system (MRAS), habituation 209
Mesencephalic reticular formation (MRF), habituation 209
Metalinguistics
   definition 301
   development 286
      narrative 286
      reading/writing 286–287
      See also Language development
Metarepresentational understanding *See* Theory of mind (ToM)
Middle-borns 64
Miller analogy test, reasoning 425–426
Mind-body dualism 348–349
Mind, theory of *See* Theory of mind (ToM)
Minimal consciousness 487
Mirror neurons 254, 378
   definition 369
Mirrors, infant interest 452
Mischel, Walter, delay of gratification task 492
Mismatched-negativity (MMN), speech perception 413t, 416, 417–418
Mispronunciation, bilingualism 54
Mobile conjugate reinforcement paradigm 292, 329, 329f
   implicit memory 88
   retention periods 330, 330f
Modeling (adults) **247–256**
   imitation *See* Imitation
Modularity theory 506–507, 506t
   definition 495
   See also Nativism
Modus ponens 422, 429
   definition 421
   See also Reasoning
Modus tollens 429, 430–431
   definition 421
   See also Reasoning

530 Subject Index

Monoamine oxidase A (MAO-A), antisocial behavior 189–190
Monogenic disorders *See* Single gene disorders (SGDs)
Monozygotic triplets 509
Monozygotic twins (MZ) 508
  development and behavior 509
    class separation effects 511
    psychological closeness 510
    school behaviors 511
    shyness 511
    social behaviors 510
  diamniotic 508
  dichorionic 508
  monoamniotic 508
  monochorionic 508, 509
  twins of opposite sex 509
  twin studies
    behavioral genetics 185–186
    dizygotic twins *vs.* 513
    equal environments assumption 514
    shared *vs.* nonshared environments 513
Morpheme(s) 306–307
  definition 267, 301
Morphemic access, definition 301
Morphology
  definition 192, 267, 301
  development 280, 406
    definition 399
    inflectional 198
      dual-mechanism 199
      single-mechanism 198–199
  syntax relations *See* Morphosyntax
Morphosyntax
  awareness of 305
  definition 301
  bilingualism 56
Moscovitch, Morris, memory 211
Mother(s), *See also* entries beginning maternal
Mother–child dyad, separation anxiety and 471
  See also Separation anxiety
Mother-child relationship, temperament and, twin studies 515
Mother-child synchrony, temperament and 515
Motherese
  definition 267
  See also Infant-directed speech
Motivation, school readiness 438
Motor cortex, prenatal development 69
Motor development
  humor 234
  locomotion *See* Locomotion development
  motor programs 369–370
  reflexes *See* Reflex(es)
Motor imitation *See* Imitation
Motor planning problems *See* Dyspraxia (motor planning problems)
Moving objects, catching, development 375
'Moving room' apparatus, perceptuomotor scaling 377–378, 378*f*
Mullen Scales of Early Learning, intellectual disability 261
Multimodal perception *See* Intermodal perception
Multiple gestations/births 509
  twins *See* Twins
Multiple habituation 93
  definition 91
  face categorization 93–94
  standard procedure 93, 94*f*
  variations 94
    familiarization and visual paired comparison 94, 95*f*
    object examining 95, 95*f*
Multiple intelligences, school readiness 437
Mutual exclusivity principles
  definition 48
  semantic development 460
Mutual gaze, development 129
Myelination
  defects 73
  neurological development
    postnatal 72, 126

N

Naigles, Letitia, syntactic bootstrapping 465
Narrative
  autobiographical memories 8
  definition 400
  metalinguistic skills 286
  pragmatic development, extended discourse 408
National Assessment of Educational Progress (NAEP), literacy 302, 303
National Education Goals Panel 224
National Education Longitudinal Study (NELS), school readiness 436
National Head Start Association 221, 222
National Head Start Impact Study 225
National Institutes of Health (NIH), Human Genome Project 190
National Reading Panel 307
National Reporting System (NRS) on Child Outcomes 225
  definition 217
National Research Council (NRC) 222
  Roundtable on Head Start research 223
Nativism 347–355
  definition 351, 381, 383
  evaluation 363
  innate abilities 351–352
    definitions, differences in 353
  language acquisition 269
  linguistic theories 285
  object concept 360
  phrenology and 349
  Piaget's cognitive-developmental theory 382, 388
  theoretical origins 348
    behaviorism and 349
    constructivism 350
    early philosophers 348
    innate modules 349
  theory of mind development 506–507, 506*t*
Natural kinds, definition 114, 421
Nature *versus* nurture debate 347, 348, 358
  See also Environment/environmental factors; Gene-environment (GE) interaction/correlation; Nativism
Near-infrared spectroscopy (NIRS)
  brain development studies 81*t*, 85–86, 89
  definition 125
Negative central (Nc)
  attention 31
  event-related potentials 31–32, 32*f*
  familiar stimulus 31–32, 32*f*
  memory 331
Negatively valenced traits, twin studies 515
Neisser, Ulric, self perception 446
Nelson, Charles, memory 211
Neocortex
  classification of areas 68
  development *See* Brain development
  feedback projections, development 74–75, 74*f*
  functional areas 68
    architectonics 68, 68*f*, 69
    definitions of 68
    interconnections 68*f*, 69
    properties 68, 68*f*
    specificity 69
    topography 68*f*, 69
  historical aspects 68
  laminar structure 66–67, 67*f*
Neonatal reflexes *See* Primitive reflexes (PRs)
Neonatal screening *See* Newborn screening
Neonate(s)
  assessment *See* Newborn assessment
  bodily awareness 447–448
  imitation 379
  language skills 130
  memory 326
  perceptually based self-knowledge 446
  perceptuomotor behavior 370, 371*f*
  screening *See* Newborn screening
  See also entries beginning newborn/neonatal

Neonativism 347–355
  definition 351
  theoretical origins 350
  See also Nativism
Neo-Piagetian theories, cognitive development 117
Neural net models, balance scale 123, 123*f*
Neural synchrony, definition 357
Neural systems, object concept 366
Neurogenesis
  adult 72
  historical aspects 72
  injury-induced 72
  postnatal 72
Neuroimaging
  brain development 76
    white matter/myelination 73
  functional *See* Functional imaging, cognitive neuroscience role
Neurological development
  brain development *See* Brain development
  disorders *See* Developmental disorders
  genetic *vs.* epigenetic influences 69
  plasticity *See* Developmental neuroplasticity
Neuronal migration
  neocortical laminae 66–67, 67*f*
    dyslexia and 67–68
    failure in lissencephaly 67
Neuron doctrine 72
Neuroplasticity
  definition 75
  developmental *See* Developmental neuroplasticity
Neurotransmitter(s), definition 26
Neutral sentence frame 462
Newborn(s) *See* Neonate(s)
Newborn assessment, intellectual disability 261
Newborn screening, critical periods 142
Nicaraguan Sign Language (NSL) 273
Nielsen, Mark, imitation 254
No Child Left Behind Act, literacy 302
Nondeclarative (implicit; procedural) memory 210
  6-12 month cognitive milestone 341
  definition 79, 86–87, 205, 210–211, 337
  explicit dissociations 214
  eye-blink paradigm 88
  functional brain development 88
  mobile conjugate reinforcement paradigm 88
'No negative evidence problem,' grammar 200
Nonmnemonic abilities, developments 7
Nonsense words, speech perception 412
'Nonshared (unique) environment,' 513
Nonverbal play, twin languages 512
Norm-referenced tests, definition 37
Norms
  definition 337
  function 337–338
Noun bias 463
Novelty detection
  arousal role 210
  attention role 209
    memory interactions 214
  memory types 210
    attention interactions 214
    distinctions between 211
  neural mechanisms involved 211
    electrophysiological correlates 214, 215*f*, 216*f*
    hippocampus 211
  study paradigms *See* Habituation and novelty paradigms
  See also Habituation
Novelty preference
  definition 205
  electrophysiological correlates 214, 215*f*, 216*f*
  memory types 210, 211
N170 response, brain development studies 84
Null-subject languages 267
Number comprehension 321
  See also Mathematical reasoning
Numeracy
  cognitive development 108, 109
    newborns 108
    number line 102, 108

reflex levels 108
representational levels 109
  mapping 109
  single representations 109
  representations 109
sensorimotor levels 108
  actions 108
  mapping 109
  statistically sensitive infants 109
  systems 109
definition 102
language role 320
See also Mathematical reasoning
Numerical processing *See* Numeracy

O

Obesity, heritability 190
Object categorization *See* Categorization
Object concept 357–367
  action systems 363
    definition 357
  allocentric reasoning 358, 360
    definition 357
  A-not-B error 341, 359, 359f, 379, 383
    definition 357
    prefrontal cortex role 85
  cognitive milestones, 6-12 months 341
  deferred circular reactions 358
  definition 357
  developmental mechanisms 366
  ecological approach to perception 357, 363–364
  experiments 359–360, 360f, 362f
    Bower 361f
  eye movement role 365
  manual learning 365
  nativist theory 360
  neural systems 366
  oculomotor learning 365
  origins of perception 358
  Piaget's cognitive-developmental theory 85, 358, 383
  search behavior 364
  visual preference paradigms 357, 359–360
  See also Object permanence
Object examining task 95, 95f
Object-file system, mathematical reasoning 315, 317
Object identity, definition 337, 340
Objectification 358
  definition 357, 358
  See also Object concept
Object-label pairing, bilingualism 54
Object pairing, speech perception research 412t
Object permanence
  definition 102, 337, 381, 466, 467
  EEG responses 132
  frontal cortex development and 131
  nativist perspective 351
  Piaget's work 131–132
  separation anxiety 470, 472–473
  stranger anxiety 467
    See also Stranger anxiety
  See also Object concept
Object play 391, 392
  definition 390
Objects, sensitivity to, perception–action coupling 372
Object substitution, definition 237
Observational learning
  definition 290
  infants 291, 292–293
  play 397–398
Observation–execution matching system 379
Ocular dominance columns (ODCs) 70
  experience (activity)-dependent model 70, 71f
  experience (activity)-independent model 70
  Hubel and Wiesel's discovery of 70
Oculomotor learning, object concept 365
Oddball paradigm
  future orientation 177–178
  memory 332

recognition memory 31–32
Office of Child Development (OCD) 217
Office of Economic Opportunity (OEO)
  definition 217
  Head Start launch role 217, 218
Oligodendrocytes (oligodendroglia)
  injury vulnerability 73
  migration 73
  myelination 72–73
'One-word stage' 458
Only-children 64
Onset, definition 301
Opaque imitation, definition 247
Operant conditioning
  definition 290
  imitation 249
  infant learning 291, 292
  memory 329, 333
Operational thought
  concrete
    definition 381
    Piaget's cognitive-developmental theory 384, 389
  formal
    definition 381
    Piaget's cognitive-developmental theory 384, 386, 389
Oppositional defiant disorder (ODD) 189
Optical topography (OT), speech perception studies 410–411, 412–413, 413t
Optimal level theory, habituation and novelty 208
Optimal performance, critical periods 144
Optimal period 138–139
Optokinesis *See* Eye movement(s)
Orbitofrontal cortex, social brain and 127
Ordinality, definition 102
Organic disease, mental retardation 257
Orienting 28
Orienting reflex (OR)
  definition 205
  habituation and novelty 207–208
Orofacial gestures 379
Over-generalizations
  first words 458
  grammar 202
Overhearing
  language development 404–405
  role 404–405

P

Paired-comparison procedure, definition 26
Papousek, Hanus, imitation 249
Paralinguistic cues, symbolic evaluation 490
Parasitic twins 509
Parent(s)
  child relationships *See* Child-parent relationship(s)
  discipline *See* Discipline
  infant interactions *See* Infant-parent interaction(s)
  responsivity, infant self-efficacy 449
  See also entries beginning parental; Parenting
Parental contingency levels, infant self-efficacy 450
Parental discipline *See* Discipline
Parental feedback theory, birth order 60, 61
Parental involvement, Head Start 220, 222
Parental responsivity, school readiness 442
Parentese, definition 267
Parent-focused home visiting programs, school readiness 441
Parent-infant interaction(s), contingent responsiveness 449
Parenting
  education 220
  Head Start Impact Study 225
  styles *See* Parenting styles
Parenting styles, memory formation 9
Parent reports, empathy/prosocial behavior 517
Pascalis, Olivier, visual-paired comparisons 212
Pascual-Leone, Jean, cognitive development 117
Pat-a-cake game, future orientation processes 174
Patient, definition 457

Pavlovian conditioning *See* Classical conditioning
Pavlov, Ivan, habituation and novelty 207–208
Peek-a-boo game
  future orientation processes 174
  object concept 358
  pragmatic development 401
  separation-individuation process 473
Perception-action coupling 369–381
  action understanding 378
    common coding 378
      developmental origins 379
    simulation and understanding 379
  context specificity 376
    information scaling 377, 378f
    leg movement coordination 377
    reaching in light and dark 374
  historical aspects 369–370
  mechanisms of behavior change 380
    variation and selection 380
  origins 370
    adaptive response 371
    common coding 379
    neonate perceptuomotor behavior 370, 371f
    system development 371
  planning and prospective control 374
    embodied knowledge 376
    future-directed information 374
    predictive tracking 375, 376f
    reaching 375
    smooth visual pursuit tracking 374
  principles 372
  reciprocity 372
    body movement sensitivity 372
    object/surface sensitivity 372
    self–environment sensitivity 373, 373f
  See also Coordination; Reflex(es)
Perceptual assimilation model (PAM), speech perception 482–483
Perceptual attunement, definition 409
Perceptual categorization
  cognitive milestones, 1-6 months 340
  infants 340
Perceptual development
  ecological approach
    definition 357
    object concept 357, 363–364
  face perception *See* Face perception/processing
  Gestalt theory *See* Gestalt perceptual theory
Perceptual reorganization, definition 48
Perceptuomotor behavior
  neonates 370, 371f
  See also Reflex(es)
Perceptuomotor scaling
  context specificity 377, 378f
  definition 369
Perinatal, definition 66
Perinatal stroke
  cognitive function after 75
  interaction-driven theory and 75
  neuroplasticity and 75
  sparing of function 76
Periventricular heterotopia (PH) 67
Periventricular leukomalacia (PVL) 73
Perseverative search errors 379
Person permanence
  definition 466
  separation anxiety 470, 472–473
Perspective taking
  cognitive development 109
    newborn 110
      reflex levels 110
        mappings 110
        single reflex 110
        systems 110
      representational levels 111
        mapping 111
        single representations 111
      sensorimotor levels 110
        actions 110
        mappings 110
        systems 110–111

Subject Index

Perspective taking (*continued*)
    definition 102
Pervasive developmental disorder-not otherwise specified (PDD-NOS)
    heritability 189
Phenylketonuria (PKU) 183
    critical periods 142
    developmental delay 86
Phoneme(s)
    awareness of 306
        definition 301
    categories, statistical learning 294
    contrasts, bilingualism 51, 54
    grapheme-phoneme correspondences 305–306
    language-specific sensitivity, development 130–131
    perception *See* Speech perception
Phonics
    definition 301
    literacy 306
Phonogram, definition 301
Phonological awareness 305, 306
    definition 301
Phonologic disorders 150, 151
Phonologic syntactic syndrome 151
Phonology
    awareness of 305, 306
        definition 301
    disorders 150, 151
    language comprehension 279
    speech perception 415, 417, 479
        definition 409
    word production inaccuracy 279
    word production template 279
    See also Language development
Phonotactics, bilingualism 53
Photographs, symbolic thought 489
Phrase, definition 192
Phrenology, nativism and 349
Physical causality development 106
    newborns 106
    reflex levels 106
    representations 107
        mapping 108
        single 108
    sensorimotor levels 106
        actions 106
        mapping 106
        systems 106
Physical development/growth
    humor 234
    locomotion *See* Locomotion development
    motor *See* Motor development
Physical play 392
Physical world, understanding, cognitive development 122
Piagetian A-not-B error *See under* Object concept
Piaget, Jean
    bodily awareness 448
    cognitive developmental theory *See* Piaget's cognitive-developmental theory
    deliberate symbolization 488
    equilibration 115–116
    functional logic 115
    groupings 115
    humor development 232, 233–234
    imitation 249
    infant memory 454
    logic 115
    memory 5
    object permanence 131–132
    play 394, 396
    predictive tracking of occluded objects 131–132
    psycho-logics 115
    sensorimotor development theory 370
    symbolic thought 487
Piaget's cognitive-developmental theory 115, **381–390**
    accommodation 388
    artistic development 14
    criticisms/challenges 350, 389
    curiosity development 159

empiricism 382
    See also Nativism
equilibration 382, 388–389
evaluation 359
grasping schemes 383
imitation 388
insight development 338
nativism 382, 388
object concept 85, 358, 383, 467
    See also Object concept
pushing schemes 383
themes 382
    constructivism 350, 382
    development factors 387
    functionalism 382, 386
    structuralism 382, 386
    thought levels 384, 389
Pictorial competence
    12-18 months 344
    24-36 months 345
Pictures
    formal features 490
    symbolic thought 489
Pipp agency tasks, representations 111
Pivot schemas 195
Placenta, twins 508
Planning
    cognitive milestones, 6-12 months 342
    frontal cortex development and 131
    mastery enhancement 393
    perception–action coupling 374
Planum temporale, hemispheric asymmetry and language 129–130
Plasticity
    brain function 79, 88, 90
    definition 125, 135
    human development, sensitive periods 139
    See also Critical (sensitive) periods
    neuronal *See* Neuroplasticity
Play **390–399**
    biological theory 397
    cognitive functions 392–393
    cognitive theory 397
    communication skills 393–394
    complex game initiation 391
    complexity changes 394
    culture effects 391, 394, 398
    definition 157, 165
    developmental progression 394
    exploratory behavior, relationship to 165
    expressing emotions 392
    functions 391
        related functions 395
    gender and 391, 397
    language use in child–parent play 393
    parental role 393
        father's role 396–397
        mother's role 396
    partners 391, 396
    peers' role 397
    Piaget's cognitive-developmental theory 388
    pretend *See* Imagination/fantasy
    research history 396
    siblings' role 397
    social functions 393
    social learning theory 397
    sociodramatic, cognitive milestones, 24-36 months 346
    theories of 391
    types 391
Play frame, humor development 228
Pointing, pragmatic development 402
Politeness, markers, language socialization 407
Polygenic syndromes *See* Complex polygenic traits
Polymorphism(s), single-gene disorders 185
Positively valenced traits, twin studies 515
Positive slow wave (PSW), memory 331, 332*f*
Positron emission tomography (PET)
    brain development studies 81*t*, 84, 89
    prefrontal cortex development and cognition 133

Postnatal brain development 69
    cognitive/functional perspectives 126
        frontal cortex development and 131
        interactive specialization 75, 126–127
        maturational perspective 126
        skill-learning hypothesis 127
    experience-dependent 70
    experience-expectant 70
    experience-independent 70
    frontal cortex 131
    glia and 72
    magnetic resonance imaging 126
    perception–action coupling and 371
    progressive events 72
        general growth 72
        intracortical connections 73
        myelination 72, 126
        neurogenesis 72
        synaptogenesis 73, 126
    regressive events 72, 73, 126
        axon retraction 73, 74*f*
        cell death 75
        synapse elimination 73, 74*f*
    visual cortex as model 70
        ocular dominance columns 70
    white matter maturation 73
    See also Developmental disorders; Developmental neuroplasticity
Posture
    future orientation processes 173
    perception–action coupling 370
    perceptuomotor scaling 377
Poulin-Dubois, Diane, verb learning 464
'Poverty of the stimulus,' grammar 200
Practical deception, humor development 228
Practice theory, play 396
Prader-Willi syndrome 184–185
    intellectual disability 260
Pragmatic bootstrapping 406
    definition 400
Pragmatic development **399–409**
    bootstrapping 406
        definition 400
    early infancy 400
    event knowledge 401
    extended discourse 406
        conversation 407
        narrative 408
    gesture use 401, 405
    joint attention 401
    late infancy 402
    mid-infancy 400
    multiword speech 405
    pointing 402
    proto-conversation 401
    proto-words 404, 405
        definition 400
    script knowledge 401
    social referencing 402
    still-face paradigm 401
    symbolic gestures 403
    word learning 404
    word use 404
Pragmatics 286
    definition 400, 457
    development *See* Pragmatic development
Pragmatic schema *See* Reasoning
Predicate, definition 267
Predictive tracking and reaching
    definition 369
    perception-action coupling 375, 376*f*
    Piaget's views 375
Pre-explicit memory 211
Preferential-looking
    methods/paradigms 205–206
    word order 196
Prefrontal cortex (PFC)
    cognitive functions 131
    development 131
        adolescents 132
        ERP studies 133

functional imaging 132–133
importance of 133
infants 131–132
neuropsychological assessment 132
dorsolateral (DLPC)
definition 357
object concept 359
object permanence 132
lesion effects 133
working memory 85, 85f
Prematurity, adjusted age, Bayley Scales of Infant Development 37, 41, 44
Prenatal, definition 66
Prenatal development *See* Fetal development
Prenatal hypomasculinization theory, birth order 61
Preoperational thought
definition 381
Piaget's cognitive-developmental theory 384
Preplate 67
Pre-reading phase, literacy development 305
Preschool children, memory 7
Pretend play/pretense 238, 394, 395–396
cognitive milestones
12-18 months 344
24-36 months 346
criteria 238t
cultural differences 239–240
definitions 237, 238
forms 238t
humor development 229
incidence 239
individual differences 245
parental initiation 239
role play 239, 245
scaffolding 239
sibling relationships and 239, 245
Pretense *See* Pretend play/pretense
Preterm birth *See* Prematurity
Preverbal development **409–420**
See also Speech perception
Primary circular reactions, definition 390
Primary emotions, self knowledge 451–452
Primary reflexes *See* Primitive reflexes (PRs)
Primary responses *See* Primitive reflexes (PRs)
Primary sensory cortex, prenatal development 69
Primitive reflexes (PRs), perception-action coupling 370–371, 371f
Primogeniture tradition, birth order 59
'Private langauage,' 512
Private memories 455
Private speech, symbolic thought 493
Problem solving
analogical
cognitive milestones, 12-18 months 344
definition 337
means-ends *See* Means-end behavior/thinking
symbolic thought 491
See also Reasoning
Programmed cell death (PCD)
apoptosis *See* Apoptosis
developmental
postnatal development 75
Proprioception, definition 247, 369
Prosocial behavior
twin studies 510, 517
See also Empathy
Prosody
definition 147, 409, 415, 476
grammatical information 200
infant-directed speech 413, 414, 416–417
linguistic rhythm 415–416
perception 415, 416f
Prospective control
perception–action coupling 374
See also Planning
Proto-conversation, pragmatic development 401
Protocortex hypothesis 69
Protomap hypothesis 69
Prototype 99
definition 91

Prototypic category
definition 114
formation 122
Proto-words *See* Pragmatic development
Psychiatric disorders, intellectual disability comorbidity 260–261
Psychodynamic theory, humor development 231
Psychological causality, definition 337
Psychological closeness, twins 510
Psychological development, Vygotsky's approach *See* Vygotsky's sociocultural theory
Psychological distancing
definition 485
symbolic thought 492
Psycho-logics, Piaget, Jean 115
Psychomotor Developmental Index (PDI) 40

Q

Q-SOAR theory, cognitive development 119
Quantitative trait loci (QTL), complex traits, candidate genes 187
Quaternary relation, cognitive development 118
Quine, Willard V O, semantic development 457

R

Race/racial differences *See* Ethnicity/race
Ramón y Cajal, Santiago, neuron doctrine 72
RAND report 307
Rapprochement phase, separation-individuation process 473
Rational infant theory 350
Reaching
development 375, 377
exploration development and 163
future oriented processes 173, 179–180
perception–action coupling 375
context specificity 377
reaching in light and dark 374
predictive reaching and tracking 375
variation and selection 380
See also Grasping
Reactive attachment disorder (RAD) 140–141
Reading
components of 306
comprehension 307
disabilities, new definitions 311
effective instructional practices 306
metalinguistic skills acquisition, role in 286–287
See also Book reading; Literacy
Reading-to-learn phase, literacy development 306
Reasoning **421–431**
analogical 425, 427t
assessment 428
definition 421
Miller analogy test 425–426
deduction 422, 428
conditional truth-table 428–429, 429t
definition 421
Wason task 429, 430–431
definition 422
development 422
debate associated 422
egocentric
definition 357
object concept development 358, 360
essentialism and 424, 425
formal 430
induction 422
categorical coverage 424
definition 421
inference mechanism 424
mathematical *See* Mathematical reasoning
mental models 121
modus ponens 422, 429
definition 421
modus tollens 429, 430–431

definition 421
pragmatic schema, definition 421
theories 121
See also Problem solving
Recapitulation theory, play 396
Receptive language
definition 302
disorders 150
Receptor neurons *See* Afferent(s)
Reciprocal Teaching 307
Reciprocity, perception–action coupling 372
Recognition memory 488
0-1 months of age 338
1-6 months of age 339
infancy 31
novelty preferences 31, 33
Recognitory comprehension 457
Reconstructive memories 4
Referent(s)
categorization and 91
definition 457
Referential style, one-word stage 458
Reflex(es)
classification
by development
primitive/developmental 370–371, 371f
definition 102
See also Perception-action coupling
Reflex mapping, cognitive development 104t, 106
Reflex responses *See* Primitive reflexes (PRs)
Reflex systems, cognitive development 104t, 106
Reinforcement, infant learning 292
Relational complexity matrix 118
Relational complexity theory
analogies 121
cognitive development 119
Relaxation and recreation theory, play 396
Remembering
infants (inability) *See* Infantile amnesia
social context 8
variability
among children 8–9
among cultures 9
among families 9
individual differences 9
See also Forgetting
Reminder treatment, definition 325
Repacholi, Betty, imitation 254
Repetition suppression, definition 205
Repetitive style, definition 1
Representation(s)
artistic *See* Artistic development
definition 12, 91, 93, 97, 102
exampler 99
insight development 338
mental *See* Theory of mind (ToM)
object groups *See* Concepts
objects *See* Object concept
summary 98
Representational mapping, cognitive development 104t, 107–108, 111
Representational redescription, metalinguistic skills acquisition 286
Resource dilution model, birth order 60, 61
Response to intervention (RTI), literacy 311–312
Retention, definition 325
Retinotopic organization, definition 66
Reversible transitives 196
Reynolds, Greg, look duration 34
Rhetorical skills, development 286
Rhythmic class, definition 48
Rhythmic stereotypes 392
Richards, John
familiar stimulus 31
habituation 209–210
heart rate and attention 29–30
look attention 34
Rime(s)
definition 302
phonological awareness 306
Risley, Todd, semantic development 461

Subject Index

Rituals
    Santa Claus 240–241, 243
    Tooth Fairy 240–241, 244
Rizzolatti, Giacomo, imitation 254
Robotics, imitation 255
Role play 239, 245
    definition 237
    See also Imagination/fantasy
Ronjat, Jules, bilingualism 49
Rothbart, Mary, orienting 28
Rough and tumble play 392
    humor 234
Roundtable on Head Start research, National Research Council 223
Rousseau, Jean-Jacques 349
    infant learning 291
Routine events, autobiographical memory 455
Rovee-Collier, Carolyn
    operant conditioning 329, 333
    reinforcement 292
Ruff, Holly, orienting 28

S

Saccades (saccadic eye movements)
    corrective 374
    definition 169
    development 371–372
    future orientation 170, 172
    newborn behavior 27
    perception–action coupling 371–372
        smooth visual pursuit 374
Saffran, Jenny, infant learning 295
Samuelson, Larissa, semantic development 461
Santa Claus rituals 240–241, 243
Sarcasm, symbolic thought 491
Scaffolding
    conversational skills 286
    definition 400
    pretend play 239
    Vygotsky's sociocultural theory 112
Scale errors, symbolic thought 489
Schachter, Daniel, memory 211
Schachter, Stanley, birth order 59
Schematization, grammar 201
School behaviors, twins 511
School entry 443
    birth dates 443
    core competencies 434
    language skills, stability of 443
    phonological awareness 443–444
    preparation 435
    specificity of learning 443
    See also School readiness
School readiness **433–445**
    concept 434, 434f
    definition 224
    effect/specificity of learning 443
    infant learning 433
    intervention programs 440
    language/literacy skills
        language-promoting behaviors 442
        preschool levels 437
        shared book reading 442
        stability 443
    parenting and 441
        definitions 441
        family learning environment 442
        importance of 441
        modification 441
        parental discipline 442
        parental warmth/responsivity 442
        parents beliefs about readiness 444
    preschool factors 435
        child factors 435
        cognitive skills and IQ 437
            language/literacy skills 437
            motivation 438
            self-efficacy 438
            self-regulation 438
        early childcare effects 439
        entrance age 435
        gender 436
        social-emotional skills 435
        social skills 438
        sociocultural factors 438
            race/ethnicity 439
            socioeconomic disadvantage 438
        teachers beliefs about readiness 444
    'whole child' approach 224
Schools/schooling
    school behaviors, twins 511
    special educational needs *See* Special education
    starting, readiness for *See* School readiness
    See also Academic achievement/performance; Education; Learning
School transition
    concept 434
    critical periods 138
    readiness for *See* School readiness
Script(s)
    autobiographical memory use, 24-36 months 345
    definition 337
    knowledge, pragmatic development 401
Sculpture, artistic development 22
    animal figures 24, 24f
    human figures 22, 23f, 24f
    See also Artistic development
Search behavior, object concept 364
Secondary emotions
    definition 445
    self knowledge 451–452
Second year play 395
Secret language, twins 512
Secure attachment *See* Attachment/attachment theory
Security of attachment, definition 390
    See also Attachment/attachment theory
Segmentation
    cognitive development 118
    definition 267
    language acquisition 272–273
    speech perception research 412t
    words, transitional probabilities 295
Selective attention *See* Executive attention
Selective visual attention 214
Self
    concept, autobiographical memories 7–8
    knowledge of *See* Self-knowledge
    regulation of *See* Self-regulatory processes
Self-awareness
    self-reflective 450
    See also Self-knowledge
Self-disparagement humor 233
Self-efficacy 448
    depressed mothers, children of 450
    responsiveness to mothers 449–450, 449f, 450f
    school readiness 438
Self-environment sensitivity, perception-action coupling 373, 373f
Self-fulfilling prophecy, definition 58
Self-knowledge **445–456**
    bodily awareness 447
    early biographical 446
    intentionality in self behavior 451
    intention inferences 451
    perception based 446
    self-efficacy 448
    self-reflective awareness 450
    social use of adults 451
    symbol use 451
    visual self-recognition 452
Self-recognition, cognitive milestones, 18-24 months 344
Self reflection, definition 485
Self-reflective awareness 450
    perspectives and roles of others 450
Self-regulatory processes
    individual differences 515
    school readiness and 438
    study methods
        twin studies 515
Semantic development **456–466**
    conversational settings 461
    cues 458
        combinations 462
    cultural influences 460
    definition 457
    first words 457
    memorized language 461
    noun bias 463
    socioeconomic status effects 461
    theories and mechanisms 458
        attentional mechanisms 461
        constraint theories 459
            mutual exclusivity constraint 460
            taxonomic constraint 459
            whole-object constraint 459
        hybrid models 463
        sociopragmatic theories 460
            experimental evidence 460
            parental factors 460
        syntactic and pragmatic cue combination 462
    verbs
        information sources 464
            sociopragmatic cues 464
            syntactic bootstrapping 465
        learning 464
Semantic memory, definition 79, 86–87
Semantic roles, definition 192
Semantics
    definition 147, 192, 302
    development *See* Semantic development
Sense of humor, definition 227
    See also Humor
Sensitive periods *See* Critical (sensitive) periods
Sensitivity
    object sensitivity 372
    self–environment sensitivity 373, 373f
Sensorimotor actions
    cognitive development 105, 106, 108
        numeracy 108
            actions 108
            mapping 109
            statistically sensitive infants 109
            systems 109
        perspective taking 110
            actions 110
            mappings 110
            systems 110–111
        physical causality development 106
            actions 106
            mapping 106
            systems 106
    definition 102
Sensorimotor development
    action-perception coupling *See* Perception-action coupling
    Piaget's views 370
Sensorimotor mapping, cognitive development 104t, 106, 109
Sensorimotor systems, cognitive development 104t, 106, 109
Sensory afferents *See* Afferent(s)
Sensory-based dyspraxia *See* Dyspraxia (motor planning problems)
Sensory impairment, theory of mind development 505
Sensory neurons *See* Afferent(s)
Sensory receptor neurons *See* Afferent(s)
Sentence frames, transitional probabilities 295–296
Separation anxiety **466–475**
    assessment 474–475
    attachment and 471, 472
    cognitive and social factors 470
    definition 466
    developmental significance 470, 474
    disorder of *See* Separation anxiety disorder (SAD)
    maternal 474
    mother-child dyad and 471
    normative course 469
    object permanence 470, 472–473

person permanence 470, 472–473
social referencing hypothesis 470
transitional object use 469–470
Separation anxiety disorder (SAD) 469–470, 474
    definition 466
    diagnosis 474
    etiology 475
    prevalence 474
Separation-individuation process 471, 473
    phases
        rapprochement 473
Sequential-touching 96, 96f, 101
    definition 91
Serotonin transporter gene
    promoter (5-HTTLPR)
        polymorphism, inhibition and 517
        temperament 188–189
Sex determination, critical periods 140
Sex differences See Gender differences
Sex-linked genetic disorders 184
Shape-bias 461–462
Shared book reading See Joint book reading
'Shared (common) environment,' 513
Shared play, symbol incorporation into 239
'Shared understanding, twins,' 512
Short-term memory
    6-12 month olds 340
    See also Working memory
Shyness, twins 511, 517
Siblings/sibling relationships
    play and prosocial behavior
        pretend play and 239, 245
Sign language
    acquisition, fMRI studies 130
    development 287
    manual modality 273
Simon, Tony, information processing theory 119
Simple View of Reading 305
Simulation
    action understanding and 379
    definition 369
Simulation theory 506, 506t, 507
    definition 495
Simultaneous bilingual 48
    definition 48
Simultaneous condition, visual self recognition 452, 453f
Single gene disorders (SGDs)
    autosomal traits 183
    locating genes 185
    Mendelian inheritance See Mendelian disorders
    sex-linked See Sex-linked genetic disorders
    transmission 183
Single-mechanism inflectional morphology 198–199
Single nucleotide polymorphism (SNP), single-gene disorders 185
Single reflexes, cognitive development 104t, 106
Single-route model, language development 281
Sitting, independent, exploration development 163
Skills/skill learning
    cognitive
        definition 102, 103
        development process See Cognitive development
    functional brain development 81
    skill-learning hypothesis 127
Skinner, B F, infant learning 291
Sleep
    behavioral control 28
    memory consolidation 299–300
Sloutsky, Vladimir 424–425
Slow wave component (PSW), habituation and novelty 215, 216f
Smith, Linda, semantic development 461
Smooth pursuit
    definition 169
    future orientation 172
    perception–action coupling 374
Social behaviors, twins 510, 517
Social brain development 127
    cortical areas involved 127
    eye information processing 129

ERP analysis 128f, 129
face processing See Face perception/processing
Social cognition
    definition 102, 247
    imitation 253
Social communication, imitation 252
Social competence
    autism spectrum disorders 152
    theory of mind and 504–505
    See also Shyness
Social contingency, definition 445
Social development
    birth order effects 62
    definition 58
Social ecology 413
Social–emotional development
    Head Start Impact Study 225
    humor 234
    school readiness and 435
Social facilitation, imitation 248
Social factors, twin languages 512
Social laughter
    definition 227
    toddlers 228–229
Social learning theory, play 397
Social perception, theory of mind and 498, 499t
Social phobia See Shyness
Social referencing
    attention 29
    definition 102, 400, 445
    infants 451
    pragmatic development 402
    separation anxiety 470
    theory of mind and 499
Social services, Head Start model 222
Social smile, emotional organization and 468
Social systems, future orientation 174
Society for Research in Child Development (SRCD) 225–226
Sociocultural factors
    artistic development 21
    school readiness 438
        race/ethnicity 439
        socioeconomic disadvantage 438
    See also Culture; Ethnicity/race; Socioeconomic status
Sociocultural theory, Vygotsky's See Vygotsky's sociocultural theory
Socioeconomic status
    academic achievement/performance 439
    literacy 309, 311
    school readiness 438
    semantic development 461
Sociological theory, humor development 231
Sociopragmatic cues, verb meaning 464
Sokolov, habituation and novelty 208
Somatotopic organization, definition 66
Spatial cuing paradigm, future orientation 177
Spatial framework, egocentric 342
Spatial imagery, mathematical reasoning 324
Spatial neglect
    definition 125
    face recognition and 127–128
Spatial orienting network 28
Spatiotemporal coordination 374
Special education 262
    definition 257
Special reflexes See Primitive reflexes (PRs)
Specific language impairment (SLI)
    definition 267
    language acquisition 275, 287
Speech
    articulation
        disorders 150
    multiword, pragmatic development 405
    perception See Speech perception
    registers 407
Speech category formation
    bimodal vs. unimodal stimuli distribution 294, 294f
    frequency, role of 294

investigation 297t
perceptions 297
Speech discrimination procedures 476, 477
Speech perception 476–485
    acoustic invariance 476–477
    acoustic resonance 476
    aims of study 410
    audiovisual 481
    bootstrapping 415, 418
        definition 415, 418
    coarticulation 476–477
    conditional probability 418
    contingency 476
    definition 476
    development
        fMRI studies 131
        preverbal 409–420
    emotional ecology 413
    fundamental frequency 476
    infant-directed speech See Infant-directed speech
    language-learning ecology 419
    McGurk effect 420, 481
    mismatched-negativity 413t, 416, 417–418
    morphemes 476
    non-native sounds 481
        perceptual assimilation model 482–483
    nonsense words 412
    phonemes 417, 479
        categorical 480
        definition 409, 476
        discrimination 479
        voice onset time 479
    phonology 415, 417, 479
        definition 409
    pitch 415, 416f
    preferences See Speech preferences
    prenatal 411
    pressure transducers 476
    prosody See Prosody
    research methods 477
        event-related potentials 413t, 415, 417–418
        habituation approach 412t, 476, 477–478, 478–479
        heart rate monitoring 411–412, 411f, 413t
        high amplitude sucking procedure 477–478, 480
        preverbal infants 410, 410f, 411f, 412t
        speech discrimination procedures 476, 477
        speech preference procedure 410, 410f, 411f, 412t, 483
        visually reinforced head turn procedure 478
    social ecology 413
    statistical learning 409, 418–419
    trochaic pattern 409, 415–416
Speech preference procedure 410, 410f, 411f, 412t, 483
Speech preferences 483, 484
    central fixation procedure 483–484
    head-turn preference procedure 484
    speech preference procedure 410, 410f, 411f
Speech recognition, developmental cognitive neuroscience 129
Spelke objects 351, 352
Spemann, Hans, critical periods 135–136
Spencer, Charles D, play 396
Squire, Larry, memory 211
S1-S2 paradigm 176–177
    contingent negative variation 177
    definition 169
    See also Future orientation
Stable-order principle, mathematical reasoning 320–321
Standardization, Bayley Scales of Infant Development 37, 42
Stanley, Granville, play 396
Statistical learning
    definition 290
    infants 293
    interaction with other processes 299–300
    joint probabilities 295, 295f
    language acquisition 271, 293
    phoneme categories 294
    speech perception 409, 418–419
    transitional probabilities 295

Stem cells
  critical periods 135–136, 142
  research 191
Still-face paradigm
  definition 400
  future orientation processes 174
  pragmatic development 401
Stimulation, critical periods 137
Stimulus enhancement, imitation 248
Stimulus orienting
  definition 26
  heart rate 29–30
Stimulus response associations 291
  infant learning 291
Stockard, Charles, critical periods 135–136
Storybooks, fantasy in 244
'Story' grammar, language development 408
  See also Narrative
Stranger anxiety **466–475**
  brain maturation 468
  cognitive advances underlying 467
  context 466
  definition 466
  incongruity theory 467–468
  object permanence and
    See also Object permanence
  prevalence 467
Strange Situation paradigm 472–473
Stroke, perinatal, neuroplasticity and 75
Stuttering 150
Subcortex, definition 79
Subject, definition 267
Subject verb object (SVO) order 196–197
Subplate 67
Sulci, development 126
Sulloway, Frank, birth order 59, 61, 62, 64
Summary representations, infants 98
Superior temporal sulcus (STS), social brain and 127
Suprachiasmatic nucleus (SCN),
  experience–expectant development 70
Surfaces, sensitivity, perception–action coupling 372
Surplus energy theory, play 396
Sustained attention 29
  brain areas involved 28f
  definition 26
  heart rate 29–30
  phases 31
Swedenborg, Emanuel, functional cortical areas 68
Symbolic comprehension 457
Symbolic gestures
  definition 400
  pragmatic development 403
Symbolic mediation 486
Symbolic play 395
  definition 390
Symbolic thought **485–494**
  cultural practices 491
  decoupling from referents 486–487
  definition 486
  development of 487
  facilitation 491
  intentionality and mediation without reflection 487
  mature, characteristics of 492–493
  problem solving 491
  reflection consequences 486f
  representations without stimuli 488
  symbols, treatment as symbols 488
  toys 489
Symbol-referent relations 489
  quality reflections 490
Symbols
  incorporation into shared play 239
    See also Imagination/fantasy
  models as, cognitive milestones, 24-36 months 345
  See also entries beginning symbolic
Synapse(s), definition 125
Synapse elimination 138
  critical periods and 137, 138
  learning 137

postnatal development 73, 74f
synaptogenesis and 73
  See also Developmental neuroplasticity
Synaptic pruning See Synapse elimination
Synaptogenesis
  autobiographical memory 7
  defects
    fragile X syndrome and 73
  postnatal brain development 73, 126
  prenatal brain development
    cortical layer formation 67
  synaptic elimination and 73
Synkinesis, visual-spatial disabilities 154
Syntactic bootstrapping, verb learning 465
Syntactic category-based abstraction 298t
Syntax 282, 283t, 285, 406
  definition 147, 192, 267, 400, 457
  morphology relations See Morphosyntax
  See also entries beginning syntactic
Synthetic incapacity, artistic development theory 14
System of Program Performance Measures, Head Start 224

T

Tactual perception/processing, perception–action coupling and 372
Tadpole figures, artistic development 12, 13f
Talent/giftedness, artistic development 19, 20f, 21f
Taxonomic constraint 459
Teachable moments 144
Teacher(s)
  beliefs about school readiness 444
  characteristics of effective 309
  humor facilitation techniques 236
Teacher-versus-child managed instruction, literacy 310
Teaching effect, birth order 64
  definition 58
Television, cartoons 232–233
Temperament
  cognitive development influence 113
  environmental factors 515
  genetic factors 515
  heritability 188–189
  twin studies 515
Temporal cortex (lobe)
  autobiographical memory 6
  medial See Medial temporal lobe (MTL)
  social brain and 127
Temporal cortical network
  autobiographical memory 6f, 7
  behavior changes 7
  definition 1
Texture perception, infants 487
Thalamo-cortical, definition 66
Theory of analogical development 426
Theory of mental logic, Braine's 429
Theory of mind (ToM) **495–508**
  behavior prediction 498
  definition 102, 495, 506
  development 498, 498t
    attachment and 504
    atypical 505
    cultural differences 505
    dishabituation experiments 499
    emotion and 502
    family environment and 504
    individual differences 503
    language ability and 504
    precursors 498
    social competence 504–505
    social perception 498, 499t
    social referencing 499
    theoretical explanations 506, 506t
    turn-taking 499
  executive functioning 503
  false-belief 496, 497t, 498, 501, 504
    tasks 111–112, 495
  fantasy and pretense 503–504

humor development 233–234
infants 498, 499t
interpretive abilities 502, 503t
mental representation 497
  intentional states 497, 497t
mental-state awareness 499, 500t
mental-state recursive abilities 502, 503t
metarepresentational understanding 497, 501
  definition 495
  preschoolers 502t
  older preschoolers 501, 502t
  school-age children 502, 503t
  toddlers/early preschoolers 499, 500t
Theory-theory
  definition 495
  theory of mind development 506, 506t, 507
Thorndike, Edward 170
Thought
  Piaget's theory See Piaget's cognitive-developmental theory
  representational
    See also Representation(s)
  symbolic See Symbolic thought
Three-dimensional scale, symbolic thought 489
Tired mother syndrome 61
Toddler(s)
  humor
    humor development 228
    motor element 234
    social laughter 228–229
  See also Infant(s)
'Token frequency,' grammar 201
Tomasello, Micheal
  imitation 248
  noun bias 463
  semantic development 460–461
  verb learning 464
Tongue protrusion, imitation 250–251
Tonic neck reflex, perception–action coupling 370–371
Tools/tool use, cognitive milestones, 18-24 months 345
Tooth Fairy ritual 240–241, 244
Top-down attention See Executive attention
Topography, definition 66
Toys, cultural significance 394
Train task 333, 333f
Traits
  environmental contribution 187f
  individual differences, twin studies 515
Transitional objects, separation anxiety 469–470
Transitional probabilities
  definition 267, 290
  infant learning 293
  segmenting words 295
  statistical learning 295
Transitive inference
  cognitive development 118, 118f
  definition 115
Triplets 509
Trisomy 21 See Down syndrome
Trochaic pattern, speech perception 409, 415–416
Turkish, grammar 198
Turner syndrome 184
Turn-taking
  conversational See Conversation
  future orientation processes 174
  pragmatic development 401
  theory of mind development 499
Tutor-Assisted Intensive Learning Strategies (TAILS) 312
'Twin langauage,' 512
Twins **508–518**
  birth rates 508, 509, 509f
  conjoined 508, 509
  definition 508
  development and behavior 509
    attachment and 510
    cooperative behavior 510
    language development 512
    prosocial behaviors 510

psychological closeness 510
school behaviors 511
shyness 511
See also Twin studies
dizygotic *See* Dizygotic twins (DZ)
genetic studies *See* Twin studies
maternal age and 509*f*
monozygotic *See* Monozygotic twins (MZ)
parasitic 509
'vanishing,' 509
Twin studies 185–186, 513
definition 508
environmental components 513
equal environments assumption 514
genetic influences on 513, 514, 514*t*
shared *vs.* nonshared 513
genetic influences on
See also Gene-environment (GE) interaction/correlation
heritability 513
monozygotic *vs.* dizygotic 513
normal development 515
cognition 515
empathy and prosocial behavior 517
externalizing behaviors 516
internalizing behaviors 517
temperament 515
twins reared apart 513
twins reared together 513
See also Adoption studies
Two-group approach, intellectual disability 259

U

Unary relation
cognitive development 118
definition 115
Undifferentiated mental retardation 259
definition 257
Uninversion errors 285
United States (US), Department of Energy, human genome project 190
Universal Grammar (UG) theory 269
University-Head Start Partnerships, aims 223–224
Uzgiris-Hunt test, cognitive skill testing 112–113

V

'Vanishing' twins 509
Verbal auditory agnosia 151
definition 147
Verbal dyspraxia 150
definition 147
Verbal labeling, symbolic thought 492
Verbatim repetition, symbolic thought 490–491
Verb island hypothesis 284
Verb learning 463, 464
encoding 463
Verb meaning, information sources 464
Video playback
delayed, reactions to 453
visual self recognition 452
Video, symbolic thought 489
Visual attention
development 27, 30*f*
visual fixation 33
visual-paired comparison interactions 214
'Visual cliff' paradigm, perception–action coupling 373, 373*f*

Visual cortex, postnatal development 70, 71*f*
Visual development
critical periods 69
perception–action coupling and 371–372
postnatal 70, 71*f*
Visual fixation, attention 33
Visually reinforced head turn (VRHT)procedure, speech perception research 478
Visual-paired comparison (VPC) task 206, 207*f*
attention role 209
memory interactions 214
habituation-dishabituation procedure *vs.* 206
memory role 210
attention interactions 214
explicit memory 87
neural mechanisms 211
encoding *vs.* retrieval 211
hippocampus role 211
imaging studies 213
lesion studies 212
Visual preferences
memory 327
object concept 357, 359–360
Visual recognition memory paradigm (VRM) 328, 328*f*
novelty preferences 328
retention interval, maximum 328
Visual self recognition 452
awareness of unique characteristics 453
criteria for 452
repeated limb activity 452
temporal limits 453
Visual-spatial disabilities (VSDs) 153
etiology 154
motor execution disorders 154
occupational therapy referral 154
Visual system
development, critical periods 136
maturity 27–28
Vocabulary
acquisition 279
definition 302
growth 274
bilingualism 54
size, bilingualism 55
'spurt' 458
Voice inflection, infant self-efficacy 448
Voice-onset-time (VOT) 52–53
definition 48, 409
speech perception 479
VO-word order, bilingualism 56
Voxel, definition 66
Vygotsky, Lev Semenovich 116
cognitive developmental theories 115
cultural input, cognitive development 116
language development 115–116
play 396
symbolic thought 491, 493
Vygotsky's sociocultural theory, scaffolding 112

W

Walking reflex, perception–action coupling and 377
Want, Stephen, imitation 254
War on Poverty, Head Start launch role 218
Wason task, deductive reasoning 429, 430–431
Watson, John 349–350
Watson, John B, infant learning 291

Weak-Whorfian view of number, mathematical reasoning 315, 322
Weber fraction limit, mathematical reasoning 315, 316, 318
Websters Spellers 302
'Weird word order' paradigm 196
Wernicke aphasia, definition 66
Wernicke, Carl, functional cortical areas 68
Wernicke's area, 'pre-wiring,' 129
Westinghouse Report 220
White matter
postnatal maturation 73
defects 73
imaging 73, 77
Whiten, Andrew, imitation 248
Whole-language approach, literacy instruction 303
Whole-object bias 463
Whole-object constraint 459
Whole-word method, literacy instruction 302
Wh-words, movement 199–200
Wiesel, Torsten, ocular dominance columns 70
Williams, Justin, autism 255
Williamson, Rebecca, imitation 254
Williams syndrome
education planning 263–264
intellectual disability 260
language development 287
Within-family research, definition 58
Woodward, Amanda, comprehension 458
Word combinations 195
Word learning 457
combination with gesture 405
cues 463
combining 462
first words 457
nouns 463
pragmatic development 404
verbs 464
Word meanings, cognitive milestones, 6-12 months 342
Word order 196
coalitions and competition 197
local cues 198
'Word order myth,' 197
Word pairing, speech perception research 412*t*
Word production 278
cognitive milestones, 12-18 months 343
context dependence 279
phonological inaccuracy 279
phonological template 279
Word use, pragmatic development 404
Working memory
definition 79
functional brain development 85, 85*f*
Writing, metalinguistic skills acquisition 286–287
'Wug test,' language development 281

Z

Zajonc, Robert, birth order 59, 60, 64
Zelazo, Philip David, consciousness model 486–487, 486*f*
Zigler, Edward
Head Start role 218, 221
mental retardation 259
Zone of proximal development (ZPD)s 116
definition 485
Vygotsky's sociocultural theory 112